S0-AIO-944

Sociology

Fourth Edition

David B. Brinkerhoff
Lynn K. White
University of Nebraska-Lincoln

Agnes C. Riedmann
California State University, Stanislaus

Wadsworth Publishing Company
I(T)P® *An International Thomson Publishing Company*

Belmont, CA • Albany, NY • Bonn • Boston • Cincinnati • Detroit • Johannesburg • London • Madrid Melbourne • Mexico City • New York • Paris • Singapore • Tokyo • Toronto • Washington

Editor: Denise Simon
Designer: Bill Stryker
Production Editor: Carole Balach
Cover Image: ©A. R. Lopez, Photo Network
Copy Editor: Beverly Peavler, Naples Editorial Services
Indexes and Proofreading: HTP Services, Inc.
Compositor: Parkwood Composition Services
Printer: West Publishing Company

(Photo credits follow subject index)

For more information, contact Wadsworth Publishing Company, 10 Davis Drive, Belmont, CA 94002, or electronically at http://www.thomson.com/wadsworth.html

British Library Cataloguing-in-Publication Data. A catalogue record for this book is available from the British Library.

Printed in the United States of America
04 03 02 01 00 99 98 97 8 7 6 5 4 3 2

Library of Congress Cataloging-in-Publication Data:
Brinkerhoff, David B.
Sociology / David B. Brinkerhoff, Lynn K. White, Agnes Riedmann. - - 4th ed.
p. cm.
Includes bibliographical references and index.
ISBN 0-314-02562-6 (hardcover: alk. paper)
1. Sociology. I. White, Lynn K. II. Riedmann, Agnes Czerwinski. III. Title.
HM51.B8535 1997
301--dc20

Contents in Brief

Contents

CHAPTER 18
RELIGION 508

CHAPTER 19
HEALTH AND MEDICINE 538

The most stimulating aspect of the discipline of sociology is that it directly confronts the major issues affecting our individual lives and public policy. Sociology is not an ivory tower discipline, but one that grapples with the real problems of everyday life—personal issues such as getting a job, health, and the payoff of a college education; public issues such as homelessness, immigration, and segregation. Every chapter in *Sociology,* Fourth Edition, has an "ah ha—so that's how that works!" dimension that provides readers new insights about familiar issues. For example, the student will be stimulated to consider his or her own behavior as well as considering larger issues such as immigration control and the rationing of health care.

The fourth edition of *Sociology* is a balanced and thoroughly contemporary text. It is designed to present sociology in a format that students and teachers will find enjoyable and useful. The result is an attractive and stimulating book, written in a warm personal style, that addresses issues of contemporary society in a direct way. Building from a foundation of clear, straightforward prose, *Sociology* is designed to be an effective tool for student learning.

This book covers all of the basics in the discipline and will be an excellent foundation for advanced work in the field. For those students who go on to take further courses as well as for the much larger group of non-majors, we have these goals: 1) to develop an accurate understanding of American society—for example, to understand contemporary racism and inequality; 2) to develop an awareness of the global dimension of these issues and how American society is integrated into the larger world system; and 3) to develop a sociological imagination with which to analyze the role of social structure in contemporary issues such as homelessness, alcoholism, and school failure. We hope that long after students have forgotten the distinction between mores and folkways, they will be able to apply the sociological perspective to thinking about the critical issues of their times.

The fourth edition of *Sociology* retains many of the pedagogical features that made the first three editions a success: Each chapter starts with a personal application and concludes with either a Social Application or an Application in Diversity. There is one boxed insert per chapter and clearly identified concepts, concept summaries, and chapter summaries aid students in mastering the material.

The 23 chapters of *Sociology* cover all the standard areas of discipline, plus many new and exciting theories and topics. These include topical issues such as homelessness, the war against drugs, the unique disadvantages of African American men, gun control, the environmental movement, and immigration reform. They also include exciting new sociological developments such as the debate over the "truly disadvantaged," the "new structuralism" in our discipline, and the growing body of research on the political economy of the world system. Throughout this edition, there is greater emphasis on the global dimensions of contemporary issues.

The fourth edition of *Sociology* has been revised to reflect changes in the discipline and in the world. The resulting text is contemporary, sociological, and very accessible to the undergraduate student. In addition, we believe our excellent ancillary package will make an important addition to the introductory course.

PLAN OF THE BOOK

Sociology is designed to give a comprehensive, contemporary view of the discipline in a format that students will enjoy reading and be able to master. The following features are designed to meet these goals.

MAJOR CHANGES IN THE FOURTH EDITION

Greatly Expanded International Focus

A major goal of the fourth edition of *Sociology* has been to increase students' awareness of the international dimension of the issues that we address. This has been accomplished in three important ways. First, an entire chapter has been added on international inequality. Following the basic introduction of stratification theory and issues in Chapter 9, Chapter 10 develops and contrasts the theoretical perspectives of the developmental/evolutionary and the world-system approaches to international stratification.

Because international perspectives are important to the issues raised in nearly every chapter, however, we have also added a major Global Perspective section to many chapters. For example, Chapter 12 has a Global Perspective on the women's conference in Beijing, Chapter 7 has a Global Perspective on identity work among Australian aborigines, and Chapter 17 has a Global Perspective on democratic socialism in Sweden.

The third important way through which a global perspective is enhanced is through the addition of world maps in nearly a dozen chapters. For example, maps showing the distribution of child labor (Chapter 6), women leaders (Chapter 12), and child mortality (Chapter 19) give a visual international perspective.

Broader, More Extensive Coverage of Diversity Issues

A major goal of this edition was to increase coverage of diversity issues, and this has been accomplished in many ways throughout the text. In addition to expanded treatment of issues such as cultural diversity in Native Americans in the text itself, we have used the Focus and Application boxes to address a wide-ranging set of issues related to diversity: deaf culture (Chapter 13), gay and lesbian families (Chapter 14), disability and identity work (Chapter 7), and the Hawaiian sovereignty movement (Chapter 4). Without slighting the race and ethnic issues that are the traditional focus of diversity discussions, our goal was to illuminate the wide array of groups who are outside the cultural mainstream.

Expanded Treatment of Environment

The application of the sociological imagination to environmental problems has been expanded significantly in the fourth edition. In addition to expanded treatment of values and the environment (Chapter 4), several Focus boxes highlight environmental issues including a discussion of ecofeminism (Chapter 12) and a discussion of crimes against the environment (Chapter 8).

New Technology Chapter

In addition to expanding treatment of technology and the media in many chapters of the book—for example the chapters on religion and politics—an entire new chapter has been added on Technology. Chapter 20, *Technology and Social Change*, covers major theories linking technological innovation to social change and discusses ramifications of the new electronic technologies for inequalities, social control, democracy, and productivity.

INTERNET RESOURCES

An entirely new feature of this edition is the addition of suggested Internet sites at the end of each chapter. Charles O'Connor of Bemidji State University has identified some of the most relevant and informative sites on the net for finding information relevant to the issues discussed in Sociology. For example, he directs browsers to sites that specialize in Marxism (Chapter 1), deafness (Chapter 3), gay and lesbian issues (Chapter 7), international population data (Chapter 20), and the latest on the AIDS epidemic in Africa (Chapter 19).

PROLOGUES

Each chapter begins with a short prologue that makes a direct appeal to the student's personal experience. All prologues are in a "Have You Ever . . ." format that encourages students to consider how material covered in the chapter applies to their own experiences.

APPLICATIONS

The last section of each chapter, either *Social Applications* or *Applications in Diversity,* brings the student full circle to a concern with another application, this time on the societal level. The majority of these are *Applications in Diversity,* considering, for example, the implication of the sociological perspective for understanding the effects of California's Proposition 187 on immigrant health care (Chapter 19), the governance of Indian reservations (Chapter 16), and how people with disabilities manage a "spoiled" identity (Chapter 7).

FOCUSES

One boxed insert is used in each chapter to introduce provocative and interesting issues. Because we believe that the practice of social research can be provocative and interesting, some of these cover measurement and research issues. Others add historical and cross-cultural breadth by covering such issues as a historical perspective on women of color (Chapter 11).

CHAPTER SUMMARIES

A short point-by-point summary lists the chief points made in each chapter. This will aid the beginning student in studying the text and discriminating the central from the supporting points.

CONCEPT LEARNING AIDS

Learning new concepts is vital to developing a new perspective. In *Sociology,* this learning is facilitated in three ways. When new concepts first appear in the text, they are bold-faced and complete definitions are set out clearly in the margin. Whenever a group of related concepts are introduced (for example, power, coercion, and authority), a concept summary is included in a text figure to summarize the definitions, give examples, and clarify differences. Finally, a glossary appears at the end of the book for handy reference.

SUPPLEMENTAL MATERIALS

Four kinds of supplemental materials have been developed to ease the tasks of learning and teaching from *Sociology;* a large, revised test bank, a unique instructor's manual, a student study guide, and transparency acetate packages.

TEST BANK

A revised test bank includes approximately 100 multiple choice and ten essay questions for each chapter. Many of these questions are new, reflecting both new material and new approaches to the retained material. The test bank is available in hard copy and as Westest 3.01 on microcomputer diskettes for IBM and IBM-compatible, Macintosh, and Apple computers.

INSTRUCTOR'S RESOURCE MANUAL

The instructor's manual has been revised for this edition by Tim Pippert of the University of Nebraska-Lincoln. As in previous editions, the instructor's manual provides innovative and absorbing classroom activities—for the instructor with 350 students as well as the instructor with 35. Each chapter provides at least one fully-developed class exercise. Also, new teaching tips have been added to the manual.

Several fully-developed lectures, covering such topics as social networks and educational tracking have been provided. An annotated guide to video tapes available from West Publishing, suggestions about how the "Your Research" student software may be most effectively used, and transparencies for major tables and figures for classroom use are also included.

The Instructor's Manual continues to offer instructor-oriented chapter outlines, multiple suggestions for classroom discussions and activities, and a questionnaire that may be used to collect sociological data from students. Many of the questions on this instrument are identical to those discussed in the text. We have found the comparison of class data to national data an invaluable aid for engaging student interest and for teaching about the merits and pitfalls of survey research. Suggested uses for the questionnaire are presented in the *Instructor's Resource Manual.*

STUDENT STUDY GUIDE

The Student Study Guide, written by Charles O'Connor (Bemidji State University) and Charles M. Mulford (Iowa State University), will be invaluable in helping students master the material. The study guide contains an outline of each chapter, practice questions in matching, completion, multiple-choice, and essay form.

ACETATES

There are approximately 100 transparency acetates being offered to accompany the text. Many are specific to the text, made up of figures from *Sociology*, and others will be more generic to the introductory sociology market.

ACKNOWLEDGMENTS

In the fourth as the earlier editions of *Sociology*, we have accumulated many debts.

Special thanks go to the people at West Publishing including Clyde Perlee who first prompted us to become authors and our current editor, Denise Simon, who was generous with encouragement and advice. We benefited greatly from her knowledge of what makes a college textbook usable. Our production editor, Carole Balach, played an invaluable role in turning our material into an attractive finished product. Her production skill, good sense, patience, and good-humor contributed a great deal to the quality of the final product and to the mental health of the authors. We thank Bill Stryker for once again providing an attractive design for the book. Our copyeditor, Beverly Peavler, not only saved us from technical gaffes and inconsistencies, but performed an especially valuable service in screening the manuscript for difficult or problematic examples and wording. Her questions contributed not only to clearer writing, but also to clearer thinking about sociological ideas and their implications. At all levels, the people at West have been a delight to work with—ready to make our book the best possible, but always leaving the substance and direction of the book in our hands.

Once again we wish to extend our thanks to those people who reviewed the manuscript for the first three editions of our text. Their thoughtful comments and suggestions were an enormous help.

First Edition

Paul J. Baker
Illinois State University

Carolie Coffee
Cabrillo College, California

Paul Colomy
University of Akron, Ohio

David A. Edwards
San Antonio College, Texas

William Egelman
Iona College, New York

Constance Elsberg
Northern Virginia Community College

Daniel E. Ferritor
University of Arkansas

Charles E. Garrison
East California University, North Carolina

James R. George
Kutztown State College, Pennsylvania

Rose Hall
Diablo Valley College, California

Michael G. Horton
Pensacola Junior College, Florida

Sidney J. Kaplan
University of Toledo, Ohio

James A. Kithens
North Texas State University

Mary N. Legg
Valencia Community College, Florida

Joseph J. Leon
California State Polytechnic University, Pomona

J. Robert Lilly
Northern Kentucky University

Richard L. Loper
Seminole Community College, Florida

Carol May
Illinois Central College

Rodney C. Metzger
Lane Community College, Oregon

Vera L. Milam
Northeastern Illinois University

James S. Munro
Macomb College, Michigan

Lynn D. Nelson
Virginia Commonwealth University

J. Christopher O'Brien
Northern Virginia Community College

Robert L. Petty
San Diego Mesa College, California

Will Rushton
Del Mar College, Texas

Rita P. Sakitt
Suffolk Community College, New York

Barbara Stenross
University of North Carolina

Ida Harper Simpson
Duke University, North Carolina

James B. Skellenger
Kent State University, Ohio

James Steele
James Madison University, Virginia

Steven L. Vassar
Mankato State University, Minnesota

James B. Wedemeyer
Santa Fe Community College, Florida

Thomas J. Yacovone
Los Angeles Valley College, California

David L. Zierath
University of Wisconsin

Second Edition

William C. Jenné
Oregon State University

Florence Karlstrom
Northern Arizona University

Ed Crenshaw
University of Oklahoma

Robert Benford
University of Nebraska

Mike Robinson
Elizabethtown Community College, Kentucky

Christopher Ezell
Vincennes University, Indiana

Cornelius C. Hughes
University Southern Colorado

John M. Smith, Jr.
Augusta College, Georgia

Phillip R. Kunz
Brigham Young University

Joseph Falmeier
South Dakota State University

John P. Rehn
Gustavus Adolphus College, St. Peter, Minnesota

Ruth A. Pigott
Kearney State College, Kearney, Nebraska

Martin Scheffer
Boise State University, Idaho

Third Edition

John K. Cochran
Wichita State University, Kansas

Lynda Dodgen
North Harris County College, Texas

Christopher Ezell
Vincennes University, Indiana

Charles E. Garrison
East Carolina University, North Carolina

Harold C. Guy
Prince George Community College, Maryland

William Kelley
University of Texas

Philip R. Kunz
Brigham Young University, Utah

Diane Kayongo-Malo
South Dakota State University

Adrian Rapp
North Harris County College, Texas

Ricky L. Slavings
Radford University, Virginia

Fourth Edition

Richard Biesanz
Corning Community College

Cathy Blair
Worthington Community College

Samuel Cohn
Texas A&M University

Harold E. Conway
Texas A&M University

Sue Ergle
Aiken Technical College

Harold Guy
Prince George's Community College

Michelle Hodge
Itawamba Community College

Roland H. Johnson III
Blinn College

Kathleen A. Kalab
Western Kentucky University

Jerry M. Lewis
Kent State University

John R. Mabel
Winston-Salem State University

Elizabeth E. Mustaine
University of Central Florida

Charles Norman
Indiana State University

Charles K. O'Connor
Bemidji State University

Anne R. Peterson
Columbus State Community College

James Ranger-Moore
University of Arizona

Ellen Rosengarten
Sinclair Community College

Wesley Shrum
Louisiana State University

Steve Stack
Wayne State University

Michael Stein
University of Missouri, St. Louis

Larry Stern
Collin County Community College

Robert O. Turley
Crafton Hills College

William Verkler
Harding University

George Vrhel
Sauk Valley Community College

Theodore C. Wagenaar
Miami University

John D. York
University of Houston

UNIT ONE

Introduction

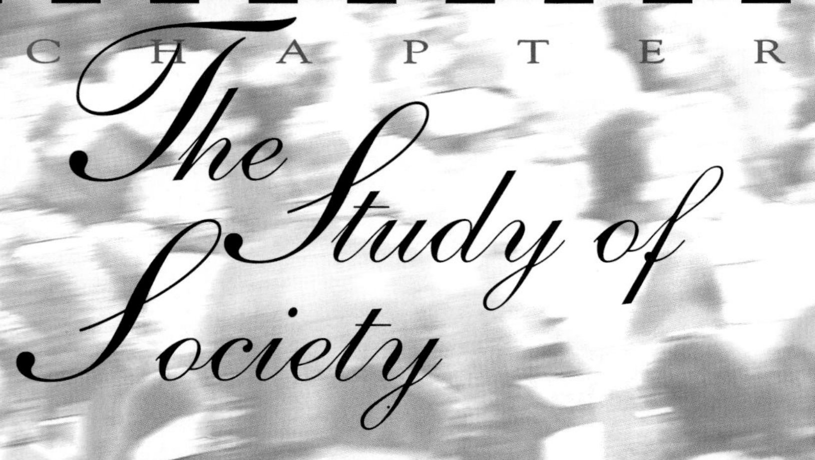

CHAPTER 1 The Study of Society

OUTLINE

PROLOGUE

Have You Ever . . . decided you can't trust the weather forecast? The storm that is forecast for tomorrow comes today, and the rain predicted to miss us, hits us with a deluge. Despite these day-to-day errors which cause so much cynicism, the weather is actually pretty predictable. It is going to be colder, much colder, this winter in Minnesota than Florida and, if you're looking for a tornado, you'll be more certain of success in Kansas than in Virginia.

People patterns are a lot like weather patterns. If we have to forecast exactly which 5 year old will grow up to be a physician and which a convenience store clerk, we'll probably make a few mistakes. On the other hand, just as surely as Minnesota is colder than Florida, women earn less than men, African Americans are more likely than whites to be murder victims, and the poor are more likely than the rich to vote Democratic. Predicting and understanding people patterns is the goal of sociology.

Meteorologists have it simple compared to sociologists. Nobody is going to say Minnesota is colder because Minnesotans like it that way or Minnesotans don't have enough ambition to become warm. Sociologists who want to explain patterns of earnings, divorce, crime, or religion have to deal more seriously with the possibility that individual choice plays a role in the patterns we observe. *Sociology* covers the gamut of human behavior—from going to church to committing crime, from getting divorced to getting a job, from race relations to urban crowding. Even if you cannot predict the weather when you're finished, our goal is that you will recognize the predictable patterns of human behavior and understand the forces that shape them.

What Is Sociology?

Each of us starts the study of society with the study of individuals. We wonder why Jason keeps getting involved with women who treat him badly, why Mike never learns to quit drinking before he gets sick, why our aunt puts up with our uncle, and why our cousin doesn't vote. We wonder why people we've known for years seem to change drastically when they get married or change jobs.

If Theresa were the only person who ever got into this predicament and if Mike were the only person who ever drank too much, then we might try to understand their behavior by peering into their personalities. We know, however, that there are thousands, maybe millions, of men and women who have disappointing romances and who drink too much. To understand Mike and Theresa, then, we must place them in a larger context and examine the forces that compel so many people to behave in a similar way.

Sociologists tend to view these common human situations as if they were plays. They might, for example, title a common human drama "Boy Meets Girl." Just as Hamlet has been performed all around the world for 400 years with different actors and different interpretations, "Boy Meets Girl" has also been performed countless times. Of course, the drama occurs a little bit differently each time, depending on the scenery, the people in the lead roles, and the century—but the essentials are the same. Thus, we can read 19th or even 16th century love stories and understand why those people did what they did. They were playing roles in a play that is still performed daily.

More formal definitions will be introduced later, but the metaphor of the theater can be used now to introduce two of the most basic concepts in sociology: role and social structure. By *role* we mean the expected performance of someone who occupies a specific position. Mothers have roles, teachers have roles, students have roles, and lovers have roles. Each position has an established script that suggests appropriate lines, gestures, and relationships with others. Discovering what each society offers as a stock set of roles is one of the major themes in sociology. Sociologists try to find the common roles that appear in society and to determine why some people play one role rather than another.

The other major sociological concept is *social structure*, which is concerned with the larger structure of the play in which the roles appear. What is the whole set of roles that appears in this play, and how are the roles interrelated? Thus, the role of mother is understood in the context of the social structure we call the family. The role of student is understood in the context of the social structure we call education. Through these two major areas, role and social structure, sociologists try to understand the human drama.

The Sociological Imagination

The **sociological imagination** is the ability to see the intimate realities of our own lives in the context of common social structures; it is the ability to see personal troubles as public issues.

The ability to see personal experience in the context of social structures has been called the **sociological imagination** (Mills 1959, 15). Sociologist C. Wright Mills suggests that the sociological imagination is developed when we can place such personal troubles as poverty, divorce, or loss of faith into a larger social context, when we can see them as common public issues. He suggests that many of the

This homeless person is obviously experiencing dire personal problems: no food, no home, no shelter, no money, no medical care. Unfortunately, there are somewhere between 300,000 and 3 million others who share the same circumstances—roughly for the same reasons. Although individual homeless people may have personal inadequacies, the extent of homelessness reflects the shortage of housing and jobs in contemporary America. Learning to see personal experiences and tragedies as part of larger patterns of social problems is a vital element of the sociological imagination.

things we experience as individuals are really beyond our control. They have to do with society as a whole, its historical development, and the way it is organized. In 1959, Mills gave us some examples of the differences between a personal trouble and a public issue:

> When, in a city of 100,000, only one man is unemployed, that is his personal trouble, and for its relief we properly look to the character of the man, his skills, and his immediate opportunities. But when in a nation of 50 million employees, 15 million men are unemployed, that is an issue, and we may not hope to find its solution within the range of opportunities open to any one individual. The very structure of opportunities has collapsed. Both the correct statement of the problem and the range of possible solutions require us to consider the economic and political institutions of the society, and not merely the personal situation and character of a scatter of individuals.
>
> Consider marriage. Inside a marriage, a man and a woman may experience personal troubles, but when the divorce rate during the first four years of marriage is 250 out of every 1,000 attempts, this is an indication of a structural issue having to do with the institutions of marriage and the family and other institutions that bear on them (Mills 1959, 9).

In everyday life, we do not define personal experiences in these terms. We frequently do not consider the impact of history and social structures on our own experiences. If a child becomes a drug addict, parents tend to blame themselves; if spouses divorce, their friends usually focus on their personality problems; if you flunk out of school, everyone will be likely to blame you personally. To develop the sociological imagination is to understand how outcomes such as these are, in part, a product of society and not fully within the control of the individual.

Some people flunk out of school, for example, not because they are stupid or lazy but because they are confused about which play they are appearing in. The roles in the "this is the best time of your life" play are very different from the roles in the "education is the key to success" play. Other people may flunk out because they come from a social class that does not give them the financial or psychological support they need. These students may be working 25 hours a week in addition to going to school. They may be going to school despite their families' indifference. In contrast, other students may find it difficult to fail: Their parents provide tuition, living expenses, a personal computer, encouragement, and moral support. As we will discuss in more detail in Chapter 9, parents' social class is one of the best predictors of who will fail and who will graduate. Success or failure is thus not entirely an individual matter; it is socially structured.

Sociological imagination, the ability to see our own lives and those of others as part of a larger social structure and a larger human drama, is central to sociology. Once we develop this imagination, we will be less likely to explain others' behavior through their personalities and will increasingly look to the roles and social structures that determine behavior. We will also recognize that the solutions to many social problems lie not only in changing individuals but in changing the social structures and roles that are available to them. Although poverty, divorce, illegitimacy, and racism are experienced as intensely personal hardships, they are unlikely to be reduced effectively through long-term personal therapy. To solve these and many other social problems, we need to change social structures; we need to rewrite the play. Sociological imagination offers a new way to look at—and a new way to search for solutions to—the common troubles and dilemmas that face individuals.

THINKING CRITICALLY

Which of your own personal troubles might reasonably be reframed as a public issue? Does such a reframing change the nature of the solutions you can see?

Sociology As A Social Science

Sociology is concerned with people and with the rules of behavior that structure the ways in which people interact. As one of the social sciences, sociology has much in common with political science, economics, psychology, and anthropology. All these fields share an interest in human social behavior and, to some extent, an interest in society. In addition, they all share an emphasis on the scientific method as the best approach to knowledge. This means they critically and systematically examine the evidence before reaching any conclusions and that they approach each research question from a position of moral neutrality—that is, they try to be objective observers. This scientific approach is what distinguishes the social sciences from journalism and other fields that comment on the human condition.

Sociology is the systematic study of human social interaction.

Sociology is a social science whose unique province is the systematic study of human social interaction. Its emphasis is on relationships and patterns of interaction—how these patterns develop, how they are maintained, and also how they change.

The Emergence of Sociology

Sociology emerged as a field of inquiry during the political, economic, and intellectual upheavals of the 18th and 19th centuries. Rationalism and science replaced tradition as methods of understanding the world, leading to changes in government, education, economic production, and even religion and family life. The clearest symbol of this turmoil is the French Revolution (1789), with its bloody uprising and rejection of the past.

Positivism is the belief that the social world can be studied with the same scientific accuracy and assurance as the natural world.

Although less dramatic, the industrial revolution had an even greater impact. Within a few generations, traditional rural societies were replaced by industrialized urban societies. The rapidity and scope of the change resulted in substantial social disorganization. It was as if society had changed the play without bothering to tell the actors, who were still trying to read from old scripts. Although a few people prospered mightily, millions struggled desperately to make the adjustment from rural peasantry to urban working class.

The picture of urban life during these years—in London, Chicago, or Hamburg—was one of disorganization, poverty, and dynamic and exciting change. This turmoil and tragedy provided the inspiration for much of the intellectual effort of the 19th century: Charles Dickens's novels, Jane Addams's reform work, Karl Marx's revolutionary theory. It also inspired the scientific study of society. These were the years in which science was a new enterprise and nothing seemed too much to hope for. After electricity, the telegraph, and the X-ray, who was to say that science could not discover how to turn stones into gold or how to eliminate poverty or war? Many hoped that the tools of science could help in understanding and controlling a rapidly changing society.

Auguste Comte, 1798–1857

The Founders: Comte, Marx, Durkheim, and Weber

Auguste Comte (1798–1857). The first major figure to be concerned with the science of society was the French philosopher Auguste Comte. He coined the term *sociology* in 1839 and is generally considered the founder of this field.

Comte was among the first to suggest that the scientific method could be applied to social events (Konig 1968). The philosophy of **positivism,** which he developed, suggests that the social world can be studied with the same scientific accuracy and assurance as the natural world. Once the laws of social behavior were learned, he believed, scientists could accurately predict and even control events. Although thoughtful people wonder whether we will ever be able to predict human behavior with the same kind of accuracy with which we can predict the behavior of molecules, the scientific method remains central to sociology.

Another of Comte's lasting contributions was his recognition that an understanding of society requires a concern for both the sources of order and continuity and the sources of change. Comte called these divisions the theory of *statics* and the theory of *dynamics*. Although sociologists no longer use his terms, Comte's basic divisions of sociology continue under the labels *social structure* (statics) and *social process* (dynamics).

Karl Marx, 1818–1883

Karl Marx (1818–1883). A philosopher, economist, and social activist, Karl Marx was born in Germany to middle-class parents. Marx received his doctorate in philosophy at the age of 23, but because of his radical views, he was unable to obtain a university appointment and spent most of his adult life in exile and poverty (Rubel 1968).

Marx was repulsed by the poverty and inequality that characterized the 19th century. Unlike other scholars of his day, he was unwilling to see poverty as either a natural or a God-given condition of the human species. Instead, he viewed poverty and inequality as two human-made conditions fostered by private property and capitalism. As a result, he devoted his intellectual efforts to understanding—and eliminating—capitalism. Many of Marx's ideas are of more interest to political scientists and economists than to sociologists, but he left two enduring legacies to sociology: the theories of *economic determinism* and the *dialectic*.

ECONOMIC DETERMINISM. Marx began his analysis of society by assuming that the most basic task of any human society is providing food and shelter to sustain itself. Marx argued that the ways in which society does this—its modes of production—provide the foundations on which all other social and political arrangements are built. Thus, he believed that family, law, and religion all develop after and adapt to the economic structure; in short, they are determined by economic relationships. This idea is called **economic determinism.**

Economic determinism means that economic relationships provide the foundation on which all other social and political arrangements are built.

A good illustration of economic determinism is the influence of economic conditions on marriage choices. In traditional agricultural societies, young people often remain economically dependent on their parents until well into adulthood because the only economic resource, land, is controlled by the older generation. In order to support themselves now and in the future, they must remain in their parents' good graces; this means they cannot marry without their parents' approval. In societies where young people can earn a living without their parents' help, however, they can marry when they please and whomever they please. Marx would argue that this shift in mate selection practices is the result of changing economic relationships. Because Marx saw all human relations as stemming ultimately from the economic system, he suggested that the major goal of a social scientist is to understand economic relationships: Who owns what, and how does this pattern of ownership affect human relationships?

THE DIALECTIC. Marx's other major contribution was a theory of social change. Many 19th-century scholars applied Darwin's theories of biological evolution to

FIGURE 1.1
THE DIALECTIC

The dialectic model of change suggests that change occurs through conflict and resolution rather than through evolution.

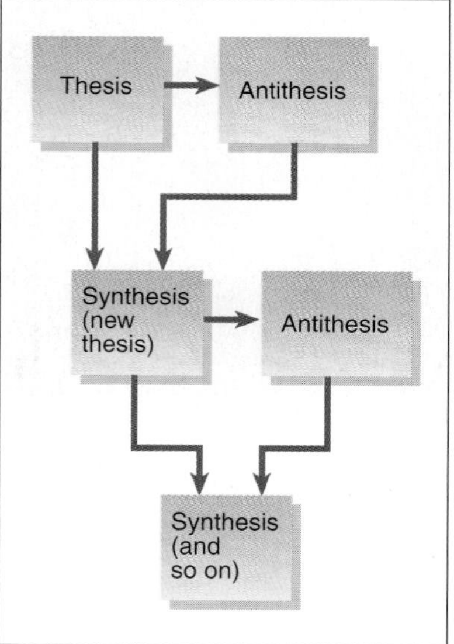

Dialectic philosophy views change as a product of contradictions and conflict between the parts of society.

Émile Durkheim, 1858–1917

society; they believed that social change was the result of a natural process of adaptation. Marx, however, argued that the basis of change was conflict, not adaptation. He argued that conflicts between opposing economic interests lead to change.

Marx's thinking on conflict was influenced by the German philosopher Georg Hegel, who suggested that for every idea (thesis), a counter-idea (antithesis) develops to challenge it. As a result of conflict between the two ideas, a new idea (synthesis) is produced. This process of change is called the **dialectic** (see Figure 1.1).

Marx's contribution was to apply this model of ideological change to change in economic and material systems. Within capitalism, Marx suggested that the capitalist class was the thesis and the working class was the antithesis. He predicted that conflicts between them would lead to a new economic system, a new synthesis that would be socialism. Indeed, in his role as social activist, Marx hoped to encourage conflict and ignite the revolution that would bring about the desired change. The workers, he declared, "have nothing to lose but their chains" (Marx and Engels [1848] 1965).

Although few sociologists are revolutionaries, many accept Marx's ideas on the importance of economic relationships and economic conflicts. Much more controversial is Marx's argument that the social scientist should also be a social activist, a person who not only tries to understand social relationships but also tries to change them.

Émile Durkheim (1858–1917). Like Marx, Durkheim was born into a middle-class family. While Marx was starving as an exile in England, however, Durkheim spent most of his career occupying a professorship at the Sorbonne, a prestigious university in Paris. Far from rejecting society, Durkheim embraced it, and much of his outstanding scholarly energy was devoted to understanding the stability of society and the importance of social participation for individual happiness. Whereas the lasting legacy of Marx is a theory that looks for the conflict-laden and changing aspects of social practices, the lasting legacy of Durkheim is a theory that examines the positive contributions of social patterns. Together they allow us to see both order and change.

Durkheim's major works are still considered essential reading in sociology. These include his studies of suicide, education, divorce, crime, and social change. Two lasting legacies are his ideas about the relationship between individuals and society and the development of a method for social science.

One of Durkheim's major concerns was the balance between social regulation and personal freedom. He argued that community standards of morality, which he called the collective conscience, not only confine our behavior but also give us a sense of belonging and integration. For example, you may have complained about shopping for a birthday or shower gift. But you probably felt a sense of satisfaction when the present was opened and the recipient appreciated it. Although we may complain about having to meet what appear to be arbitrary standards, we often feel a sense of satisfaction in meeting those standards. In Durkheim's words, "institutions may impose themselves upon us, but we cling to them; they compel us, and we love them" (Durkheim [1895] 1938, 3). This beneficial regulation, of course, must not rob the individual of all freedom of choice.

Beside pointing to the role of society, or social structure, in people's lives, Durkheim was among the first to stress the importance of using reliable statistics to examine social life. Durkheim's classic study *Suicide* ([1897] 1951) brings these two major contributions together. In *Suicide*, Durkheim used what statistics were available to show that suicide rates in Europe could not be explained without analyzing the social environment in which they occurred.

Durkheim identified three types of suicide, each of which stems from some imbalance between social regulation and personal freedom. *Altruistic* suicide occurs when society overregulates and allows too little freedom—when our behavior is so confined by social institutions that we cannot exercise our independence. As examples, Durkheim discussed devotees of religions, such as Jainism and Hinduism, who are expected to kill themselves as part of religious rituals. *Egoistic* suicide occurs when people are not regulated enough because they are not integrated sufficiently into social groups. Durkheim supported this idea with statistics showing, for example, that single people and Protestants had higher suicide rates than did married people and Catholics. The latter two groups had less personal freedom and were more integrated into their communities, Durkheim argued. Durkheim's third type, *anomic* suicide, occurs when there is too much freedom and too little regulation in the whole society. Durkheim said that this kind of suicide is most likely to occur in times of rapid social change. When established ways of doing things have lost their meaning, but no clear alternatives have developed, individuals feel lost. The high suicide rate of Native Americans (approximately twice that of Caucasian Americans) is generally attributed to the weakening of traditional social regulation.

Max Weber, 1864–1920

Each of Durkheim's works illustrates his idea of the ideal social scientist: an objective observer who only wants the facts. As sociology became an established discipline, this ideal of objective observation replaced Marx's social activism as the standard model for social science.

Max Weber (1864–1920). A German economist, historian, and philosopher, Max Weber (Veh-ber) provided the theoretical base for half a dozen areas of socio-

Baptism is a religious ritual common to most Christian faiths. We can study what baptism means in Christian theology, we can compile statistics on the percentage of the population that has been baptized, or we can follow Weber's emphasis on subjective meanings by asking what baptism means to the individuals who take part in it. The typical Presbyterian baptism in which an infant's head is sprinkled with a few drops of water during a formal service is quite different in symbolic meaning from this woman's baptism by immersion.

W. E. B. Du Bois, 1868–1963

Value-free sociology concerns itself with establishing what is, not what ought to be.

logical inquiry. He wrote on religion, bureaucracy, method, and politics. In all these areas, his work is still valuable and insightful; it is covered in detail in later chapters. Three of Weber's more general contributions were an emphasis on the subjective meanings of social actions, on social as opposed to material causes, and on the need for objectivity in studying social issues.

Weber believed that knowing the meanings people attach to behavior is more important than identifying patterns of behavior. For example, Weber would argue that it is relatively meaningless to compile statistics such as that one-half of all marriages contracted today may end in divorce compared with only 10 percent in 1890 (Martin and Bumpass 1989). More critical, he would argue, is understanding how the meaning of divorce has changed in the past hundred years. Weber's emphasis on the subjective meanings of human actions has been the foundation for scholarly work on topics as varied as religion and immigration.

Weber trained as an economist, and much of his work concerned the interplay of things material and things social. He rejected Marx's idea that economic factors are the determinants of all other social relationships. In a classic study, *The Protestant Ethic and the Spirit of Capitalism*, Weber tried to show how social and religious values may be the foundation of economic systems. This argument is developed more fully in Chapter 18, but its major thesis is that the religious values of early Protestantism (self-discipline, thrift, and individualism) were the foundation for capitalism.

One of Weber's more influential ideas was his declaration that sociology must be **value free.** Weber argued that sociology should be concerned with establishing what is and not what ought to be. Weber's dictum is at the heart of the scientific approach that is generally advocated by modern sociologists. Thus, although one may study poverty or racial inequality because of a sense of moral outrage, such feelings must be set aside to achieve an objective grasp on the facts. This position of neutrality is directly contradictory to the Marxian emphasis on social activism, and sociologists who adhere to Marxist principles generally reject the notion of value-free sociology. Most modern sociologists, however, try to be value free in their scholarly work.

Jane Addams, 1860–1935

Sociology in the United States

Sociology in the United States developed somewhat differently than in Europe. Although U.S. sociology has the same intellectual roots as European sociology, it has some distinctive characteristics. Three features that have characterized U.S. sociology from its beginning are a concern with social problems, a reforming rather than a radical approach to these problems, and an emphasis on the scientific method.

One reason that U.S. sociology and European sociology developed differently is that our social problems differ. Slavery, the Civil War, and high immigration rates, for example, made racism and racial and ethnic inequality a much more salient issue in the United States. One of the first sociologists to study these issues was W.E.B. Du Bois. Du Bois, who received his doctorate in 1895 from Harvard University, devoted his career to developing empirical data about African Americans and to using those data to combat racism.

The work of Jane Addams, an early sociologist and recipient of the 1931 Nobel Peace Prize, nicely illustrates the reformist approach of much American sociology. In 1889, Addams founded Hull House, a settlement house in Chicago. Addams and the other women who lived at Hull House used quantitative social science data to push through legislation on safer working conditions, a better juvenile justice system, better public sanitation, and services for the poor (Deegan 1987).

Recalling Du Bois and Addams illustrates the fact that U.S. sociologists are a diverse group. Although not always remembered as such, many women and many members of ethnic minorities were early sociologists (Deegan 1987). As sociology became more established, it also became more conservative. In the years between the two world wars, a new generation of sociology professors became convinced that social activism was incompatible with academic responsibility. However, by the 1950s and in the 1960s, sociologists such as C. Wright Mills, Joan Huber, Mirra Komarovsky, and others turned renewed attention to social problems and social conflict.

Today, sociologists comprise an increasingly diverse community of scholars. In 1995, about 15 percent of the members of the American Sociological Association (ASA) were of other than European descent. Men continued to outnumber women, but the gap was narrowing, with 43 percent of the members female. Members of ethnic minority groups and women are increasingly likely to run for, and to win, election to ASA offices ("1995 Report . . . ." 1995).

The first sociology course in the United States was taught at Yale University in 1876. By 1960, almost all colleges and universities had departments of sociology, and by 1990, 120 offered doctorate programs. The popularity of higher-degree sociology programs is greater in the United States than in any other country in the world. This is partly because sociology in the United States has always been oriented toward the practical as well as the theoretical. The focus has consistently been on finding solutions to social issues and problems, with the result that U.S. sociologists not only teach sociology but also work in government and industry.

Structural-functional theory focuses on the benefits that social structures provide for individuals and society. Theorists from this school argue that the regularity and routine provided by such social structures as the family and government are as necessary as the regulations governing a school crossing. These theorists often tend to focus on the advantages rather then the disadvantages of particular social structures.

FOCUS ON ANOTHER CULTURE

Sociology Around the World

"WE MAY TEND TO THINK OF SOCIOLOGY AS AN AMERICAN DISCIPLINE, BUT SOCIOLOGY IS A WORLDWIDE ENTERPRISE."

We may tend to think of sociology as an American discipline, but sociology is a worldwide enterprise. Here are some examples of the discipline's global character and membership.

- The Japan Sociological Society has a membership of more than 2,400 scholars, holds annual conferences that attract about a thousand participants, and publishes the journal *Shakaigaku Hyoron (Japanese Sociological Review)* ("On Sociology in Japan" 1994).
- A goal of the Association of Black Sociologists (ABS), begun in 1970 in the United States, is to foster research and activist links between African American scholars and African scholars here and abroad (Bonner 1991).
- The North American Chinese Sociologists' Association (NACSA) was formed in 1993 to promote scholarly exchanges among researchers on Chinese societies and populations anywhere in the world (Yu 1993). Its first conference focused on gender issues in Chinese communities.
- In 1990, two U.S. graduate students founded the Civic Education Project (CEP). Characterized by its program coordinator as a "Peace Corps for academics," the CEP organizes advanced graduate students to teach sociology undergraduate courses in Central and Eastern European countries, such as Romania, the Ukraine, and the Baltic states. The purpose of the program is to provide ongoing assistance to Central and Eastern European universities, where the social sciences suffered years of neglect under the Union of Soviet Socialist Republics (USSR), and to promote academic dialogue between East and West (Billson 1992). In 1993, CEP instructors were teaching some 2,500 students at 42 universities in nine countries (Layton 1993).
- The International Social Survey Program (ISSP) promotes international collaboration and research. The ISSP evolved in the 1980s as West German scholars began to work with scholars at the National Opinion Research Center (NORC) in Chicago. Today, the ISSP involves 10 nations, including Great Britain, Ireland, Israel, the Philippines, New Zealand, Russia, Japan, and Bulgaria. International surveys are conducted annually; topics must be relevant to all countries involved and capable of being expressed in an equivalent manner in all the necessary languages. Research themes include people's attitudes toward the role of government in their lives, family and gender roles, work, and religion, among others (Smith 1992).
- The International Institute of Sociology (IIS) was founded in Europe in 1893 to give scholars from different countries an opportunity to share ideas. The IIS is the oldest sociology association in the world. Over six hundred scholars from 32 countries attended the 31st IIS Congress, held in June 1993 at the Sorbonne in Paris. The previous congress met in Kobe, Japan; its theme was ecology, world resources, and the quality of social life.
- The International Sociological Association (ISA) is primarily an association of national and other sociology associations. The IIS is a member of the ISA, for example. The most recent meeting of the ISA was held in July 1994 in Bielefeld, Germany, with more than six thousand in attendance. The next one will be in July 1998 in Montreal, Canada.
- In 1993, the United Nations, through UNESCO, launched a program called MOST (Management of Social Transformations). MOST is meant to bring together social scientists from around the globe to research such issues as how best to manage change in multi-ethnic societies and cope locally with economic, technological, and environmental transformations (Kazancigil 1993).
- In March 1995, heads of state from all over the world convened in Copenhagen, Denmark, for the first-ever World Summit on Social Development (De Sherbinin and Kalish 1995). While not all participants were sociologists, many sociologists took part. And sociologists' research on global social issues has brought these to public attention, thereby showing reasons for having the summit.
- More and more American and international foundations and other funding agencies offer financial assistance for cross-national scholarly collaboration on such globally significant topics as the environment, the impact of international technologies, the role of women, and AIDS.

Sociology may have begun in Europe and flourished in the United States, but today it is indeed a worldwide discipline.

Sociologists around the World Who Are Members of the International Sociological Association, 1995;

Sociology is a global discipline, although the vast majority of members in the International Sociological Association are citizens of wealthy, western nations. Many of these European and American sociologists study developing regions of Asia, South America, or Africa. But increasingly, indigenous peoples bring their own experiences to analyzing their societies, especially in issues concerning population and development.

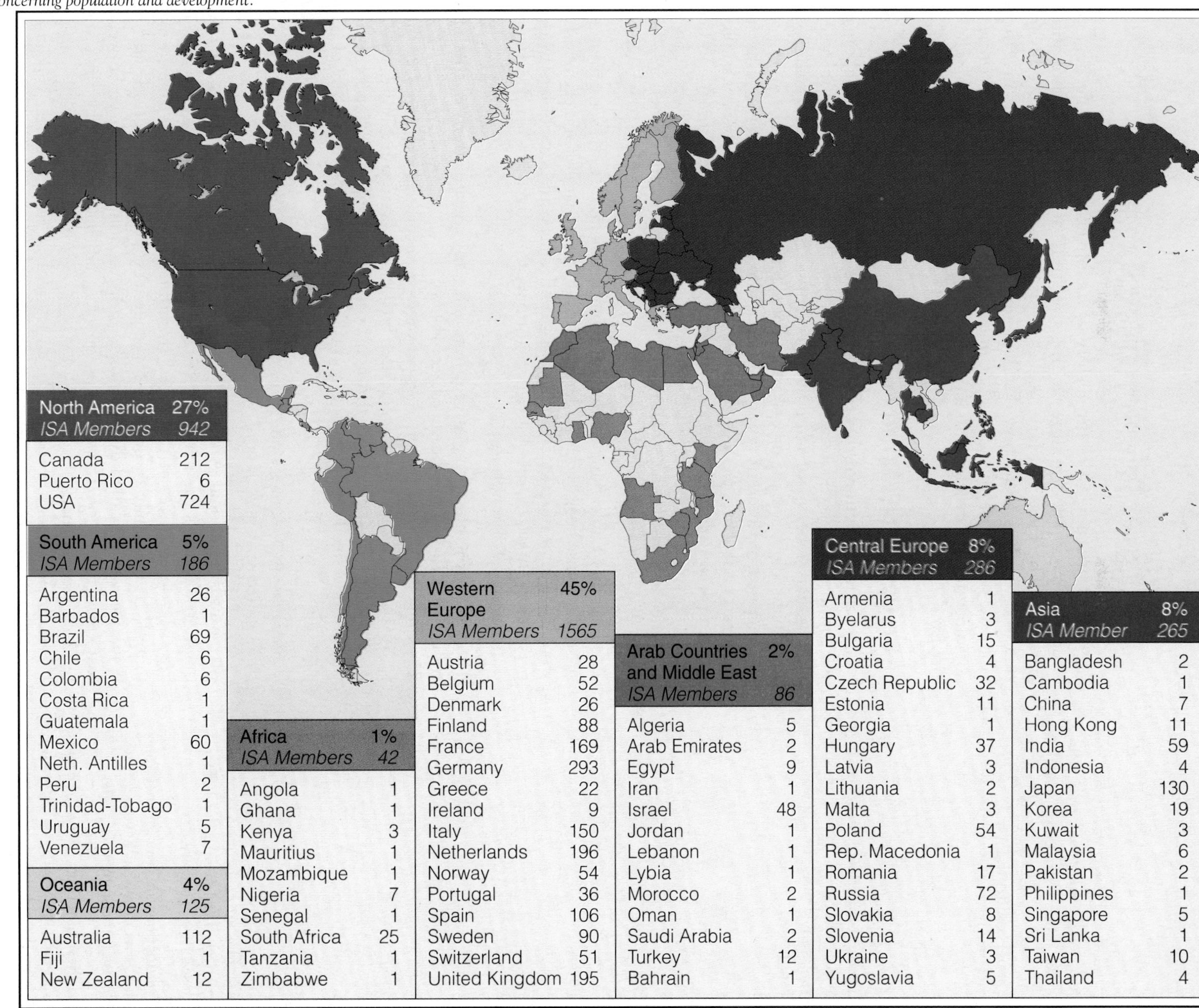

North America	27%
ISA Members	*942*
Canada	212
Puerto Rico	6
USA	724

South America	5%
ISA Members	*186*
Argentina	26
Barbados	1
Brazil	69
Chile	6
Colombia	6
Costa Rica	1
Guatemala	1
Mexico	60
Neth. Antilles	1
Peru	2
Trinidad-Tobago	1
Uruguay	5
Venezuela	7

Oceania	4%
ISA Members	*125*
Australia	112
Fiji	1
New Zealand	12

Africa	1%
ISA Members	*42*
Angola	1
Ghana	1
Kenya	3
Mauritius	1
Mozambique	1
Nigeria	7
Senegal	1
South Africa	25
Tanzania	1
Zimbabwe	1

Western Europe	45%
ISA Members	*1565*
Austria	28
Belgium	52
Denmark	26
Finland	88
France	169
Germany	293
Greece	22
Ireland	9
Italy	150
Netherlands	196
Norway	54
Portugal	36
Spain	106
Sweden	90
Switzerland	51
United Kingdom	195

Arab Countries and Middle East	2%
ISA Members	*86*
Algeria	5
Arab Emirates	2
Egypt	9
Iran	1
Israel	48
Jordan	1
Lebanon	1
Lybia	1
Morocco	2
Oman	1
Saudi Arabia	2
Turkey	12
Bahrain	1

Central Europe	8%
ISA Members	*286*
Armenia	1
Byelarus	3
Bulgaria	15
Croatia	4
Czech Republic	32
Estonia	11
Georgia	1
Hungary	37
Latvia	3
Lithuania	2
Malta	3
Poland	54
Rep. Macedonia	1
Romania	17
Russia	72
Slovakia	8
Slovenia	14
Ukraine	3
Yugoslavia	5

Asia	8%
ISA Member	*265*
Bangladesh	2
Cambodia	1
China	7
Hong Kong	11
India	59
Indonesia	4
Japan	130
Korea	19
Kuwait	3
Malaysia	6
Pakistan	2
Philippines	1
Singapore	5
Sri Lanka	1
Taiwan	10
Thailand	4

Source: Data supplied by the International Sociological Association.

THINKING CRITICALLY

Consider how a structural-functional analysis of gender roles might differ from a conflict analysis. Are men or women more likely to choose conflict theory?

CURRENT PERSPECTIVES IN SOCIOLOGY

As this brief review of the history of sociological thought has demonstrated, there are many ways of approaching the study of social structure and human behavior. The ideas of Marx, Weber, Durkheim, and others have given rise to dozens of theories about how our lives are shaped by social structure. In this section, we summarize the ideas that underlie the three dominant perspectives in sociology today: structural functionalism, conflict theory, and symbolic interactionism.

STRUCTURAL-FUNCTIONAL THEORY

Structural-functional theory addresses the question of how social organization is maintained; it is also known as *consensus theory*.

Structural-functional theory addresses the question of how social organization is maintained. This theoretical perspective has its roots in natural science and the analogy between society and a living organism. Structural functionalists stress the idea that society is made up of various parts, much as your body, a living organism, is composed of different organs. When the parts are working together properly, each part contributes to the stability of the whole. In the analysis of a living organism, the scientist's task is to identify the various parts (structures) and determine how they work (function). In the study of society, a sociologist with this perspective tries to identify the structures of society and how they function—hence the name *structural functionalism*.

Assumptions Underlying Structural Functionalism. In the sense that any study of society must begin with an identification of the parts of society and how they work, structural functionalism is basic to all perspectives. Scholars who use this perspective, however, are distinguished from other social analysts by their reliance on three major assumptions:

1. *Stability*. The chief evaluative criterion for any social pattern is whether it contributes to the maintenance of society as a whole.
2. *Harmony*. As the parts of an organism work together for the good of the whole, so the parts of society are characterized by harmony, or compatibility.
3. *Evolution*. Change occurs through evolution—the adaptation of social structures to new needs and demands and the elimination of unnecessary or outmoded structures.

Because its presumes stability and adaptation, structural functionalism is sometimes called *consensus theory*.

Functions are consequences of social structures that have positive effects on the stability of society.

Dysfunctions are consequences of social structures that have negative effects on the stability of society.

Manifest functions or dysfunctions are consequences of social structures that are intended and recognized.

Latent functions or dysfunctions are consequences of social structures that are neither intended nor recognized.

Structural-Functional Analysis. A structural-functional analysis asks two basic questions: What is the nature of this social structure (what patterns exist)? What are the consequences of this social structure (does it promote stability and harmony)? In this analysis, positive consequences are called **functions** and negative consequences are called **dysfunctions.** A distinction is also drawn between **manifest** (recognized or intended) consequences and **latent** (unrecognized and unintended) consequences.

The basic strategy of looking for structures and their manifest and latent functions and dysfunctions is common to nearly all sociological analysis. Scholars from widely different theoretical perspectives use this framework for examining society. What sets structural-functional theorists apart from others who use this language are their assumptions about harmony and stability.

Consider an example. Many states are currently discussing legislation that would allow women who have been victims of domestic violence to use the "battered women's syndrome" as a defense when they assault or kill their abusers. Such laws would explicitly recognize the right of women who assault or kill abusive partners to plead not guilty by reason of temporary insanity.

What would be the consequences of this new social structure? The manifest function (intended positive outcome) is, of course, to give legal recognition to the devastating long-term psychological consequences of domestic violence. The manifest dysfunction is that a small number of offenders might use the battered women's syndrome defense as an excuse for a malicious, premeditated assault on a significant other. A latent dysfunction might be that women acquitted of legal charges on the basis of temporary insanity might find it difficult to maintain custody of their children, given the stigma often attached to individuals diagnosed with any mental disorder.

Another latent outcome is more difficult to classify: The new policy might perpetuate the view that women are dependent on men—that is, it might perpetuate a gender bias. Is this possible outcome a function or a dysfunction? This is a difficult question to answer from a neutral point of view, and it is here that the assumptions behind structural-functional theory guide the analysis. Following the assumption that the major criterion for judging a social structure is whether or how it contributes to the maintenance of society, structural-functional analysis has tended to call structures that preserve the status quo "functions" and those that challenge the status quo "dysfunctions." Because gender bias in this law might contribute to an established pattern in which women remain in abusive family situations even when it is physically or emotionally dangerous for them to do so, the bias would be judged a latent *function* (see Table 1.1).

As this example suggests, a social pattern that contributes to the maintenance of society may benefit some groups more than others. A pattern may be functional—that is, help maintain the status quo—without being either desirable or equitable.

Evaluation of Structural Functionalism. Structural-functional theory has been criticized for tending to produce a static and conservative analysis of social systems.

TABLE 1.1

A STRUCTURAL-FUNCTIONAL ANALYSIS OF THE BATTERED WOMEN'S SYNDROME AS A LEGAL DEFENSE

Structural-functional analysis examines the intended and unintended consequences of social structures. It also assesses whether the consequences are positive (functional) or negative (dysfunctional). There is no moral dimension to the assessment that an outcome is positive; such an assessment merely means that the outcome contributes to the stability of society.

	MANIFEST	LATENT
FUNCTION	GIVES LEGAL RECOGNITION TO THE PSYCHOLOGICAL CONSEQUENCES OF DOMESTIC VIOLENCE	ENCOURAGES THE DEPENDENCE OF WOMEN ON MEN
DYSFUNCTION	MAY CONTRIBUTE TO ABUSES OF THE CRIMINAL JUSTICE SYSTEM	MAKES IT MORE DIFFICULT FOR VICTIMS OF DOMESTIC VIOLENCE TO MAINTAIN CUSTODY OF CHILDREN

Conflict theory takes a critical look at the social patterns that are part of social routine. Why, for example, are these poorly paid garment workers in Miami all women and mostly Latino? Who benefits from low wages for women and immigrants, and what social structures serve to maintain this centuries-old pattern?

A tendency toward conservatism may exist among structural-functional analysts, but conservatism is surely not a requirement. For example, enumerating the ways in which the education system contributes to the maintenance of inequality (an argument outlined in Chapter 15) is not the same thing as saying that maintaining inequality is a good thing. As another example, the sociologist Herbert Gans in 1971 listed various functions of poverty. One was to ensure that society's "dirty work" (dangerous, underpaid, or undignified labor) would get done. Gans was pointing out that there are, unfortunately, functions of poverty for the society as a whole—functions that antipoverty policies must deal with. Gans also wanted to show that structural functionalism could be employed in liberal and radical analyses (Gans 1992, 333). It's true, however, that in general structural functionalism is a more attractive perspective for those who want to preserve the status quo than for those who want to challenge it.

Conflict Theory

If structural-functional theory sees the world in terms of consensus and stability, then conflict theory sees the world in terms of conflict and change. Conflict theorists contend that a full understanding of society requires a critical examination of the competition and conflict in society, especially of the processes by which some people are winners and others losers. As a result, **conflict theory** addresses the points of stress and conflict in society and the ways in which they contribute to social change. One type of conflict theory is *feminist theory*, which focuses on conflict between females and males in society.

Conflict theory addresses the points of stress and conflict in society and the ways in which they contribute to social change.

Assumptions Underlying Conflict Theory. Conflict theory is derived from Marx's ideas. The following are three primary assumptions of modern conflict theory:

1. *Competition*. Competition over scarce resources (money, leisure, sexual partners, and so on) is at the heart of all social relationships. Competition rather than consensus is characteristic of human relationships.
2. *Structured inequality*. Inequaliies in power and reward are built into all social structures. Individuals and groups that benefit from any particular structure strive to see it maintained.
3. *Revolution*. Change occurs as a result of conflict between competing interests rather than through adaptation. It is often abrupt and revolutionary rather than evolutionary.

Conflict Analysis. Like structural functionalists, conflict theorists are interested in social structures. The two questions they ask, however, are different. Conflict theorists ask: Who benefits from these social structures? How do those who benefit maintain their advantage?

A conflict analysis of modern education, for example, notes that the highest graduation rates, the best grades, and the highest monetary returns per year of education go to students from advantaged backgrounds. The answer to the question "Who benefits?" is that educational benefits go to the children of those who are already well off. Conflict theorists go on to ask how this situation developed and how it is maintained. Their answers (developed more extensively in Chapter 15) focus on questions such as how educational resources (texts, teachers, school buildings) are allocated by neighborhood and whether the curriculum is designed for one kind of child (white middle class) rather than other kinds. They also look for ways in which this system benefits the powerful—for example, by creating a class of nongraduates who can be hired cheaply.

Evaluation of Conflict Theory. Thirty years ago, sociology was dominated by structural-functional theory, but conflict theory has grown increasingly popular. It allows us to ask many of the same questions as structural-functional theory (What is the social structure? What are its outcomes?). At the same time, it encourages us to take a more critical look at outcomes: functional for whom? Together, the two perspectives provide a balanced view, allowing us to analyze the sources of both conflict and harmony, order and change.

Conflict theory tends to produce a critical picture of society, and the emphasis on social activism and social criticism that is at the heart of conflict theory tends to attract scholars who would like to change society. In general, conflict theorists place less emphasis than other sociologists on the importance of value-free sociology.

Symbolic Interaction Theory

Both structural-functional and conflict theories focus on social structures and the relationships between them. What about the relationships between individuals and social structures? Sociologists who focus on the ways in which individuals relate to and are affected by social structures generally use symbolic interaction theory. **Symbolic interaction theory** addresses the personal, or subjective, meanings of human acts and the processes through which we come to develop and share these subjective meanings. The name of this theory comes from the fact that it studies the *symbolic* (or subjective) meaning of human *interaction*.

Symbolic interaction theory addresses the subjective meaning of human acts and the processes through which people come to develop and communicate shared meanings.

CONCEPT SUMMARY MAJOR THEORETICAL PERSPECTIVES IN SOCIOLOGY

	STRUCTURAL FUNCTIONALISM	CONFLICT THEORY	SYMBOLIC INTERACTIONISM
NATURE OF SOCIETY	Interrelated social structures that fit together to form an integrated whole	Competing interests, each seeking to secure its own ends	Interacting individuals and groups
BASIS OF INTERACTION	Consensus and shared values	Constraint, power, and competition	Shared symbolic meanings
MAJOR QUESTION(S)	What are the social structures? Do they contribute to social stability?	Who benefits? How are these benefits maintained?	How do social structures relate to individual, subjective experiences?
LEVEL OF ANALYSIS	Social structure	Social structure	Interpersonal interaction

Assumptions Underlying Symbolic Interaction Theory. When symbolic interactionists study human behavior, they begin with three major premises (Blumer 1969):

1. *Symbolic meanings are important.* Any behavior, gesture, or word can have multiple interpretations (can symbolize many things). In order to understand human behavior, we must learn what it means to the participants.
2. *Meanings grow out of relationships.* When relationships change, so do meanings.
3. *Meanings are negotiated.* We do not uncritically accept others' meanings. Each of us plays an active role in negotiating the meanings that things will have for us.

Symbolic Interaction Analysis. The premises just listed direct symbolic interactionists to the study of how individuals are shaped by relationships and social structures. For example, symbolic interactionists would be interested in how growing up in a large as opposed to a small family or in a working-class as opposed to an upper-class family affects individual attitudes and behaviors.

Symbolic interactionists are also interested in the active role of the individual in modifying and negotiating his or her way through these relationships. Why do two children raised in the same family turn out differently? The answer lies in part in the fact that each child experiences subtly different relationships and situations; the meanings the youngest child derives from the family experience may be different from those the oldest child derives.

Most generally, symbolic interaction is concerned with how individuals are shaped by relationships. This question leads first to a concern with childhood and the initial steps we take to learn and interpret our social worlds. It is also concerned with later relationships with lovers, employers, and teachers.

THINKING CRITICALLY

Can you think of situations where a change of friends, living arrangements, or jobs has caused you to have new interpretations of the events surrounding you?

Evaluation of Symbolic Interaction Theory. The value of symbolic interaction is that it focuses attention on the personal relationships and encounters that are so important in our everyday lives. By showing how the relationships dictated by the larger social structure affect our individual worlds, symbolic interactionists give us a more complete picture of these social structures.

Neither symbolic interactionism nor the conflict and structural-functional theories are complete in themselves. Symbolic interactionism focuses on individual relationships, and the other two theories focus largely on society. Together, however, they provide a valuable set of tools for understanding the relationship between the individual and society.

Interchangeable Lenses

As this brief review of major theoretical perspectives illustrates, a variety of theoretical perspectives is used in the field of sociology. These perspectives can be regarded as interchangeable lenses through which to view society. Just as a telephoto lens is not always superior to a wide-angle lens, one sociological theory is not always superior to another.

Occasionally, the same subject can be viewed through any of these perspectives. For example, one can examine prostitution through the theoretical lens of structural-functional, conflict, or symbolic interaction theory. Following are three snapshots of female prostitution using these perspectives.

The Functions of Prostitution. The functional analysis of female prostitution begins by examining its social structure. It identifies the recurrent patterns of relationships among pimps, prostitutes, and customers. Then it examines the consequences of this social structure. In 1961, Kingsley Davis listed the following outcomes of prostitution:

- It provides a sexual outlet for men who cannot compete on the marriage market—the physically or mentally handicapped and the very poor.
- It provides a sexual outlet for men who are away from home a lot, such as salesmen and sailors.
- It provides a sexual outlet for the kinky.

Provision of these services is the manifest, or intended, function of prostitution. Davis goes on to note that, by providing these services, prostitution has the latent function of protecting the institution of marriage from malcontents who, for one reason or another, have not developed a satisfactory sexual relationship in marriage. Prostitution is the safety valve that makes it possible to restrict respectable sexual relationships (and hence childbearing and child rearing) to marital relationships while still allowing for the variability of human sexual appetites.

Prostitution: Marketing a Scarce Resource. Conflict theorists analyze prostitution as part of the larger problem of unequal allocation of scarce resources. Women, they argue, have not had equal access to economic opportunity. In some societies, they are forbidden to own property; in others, they suffer substantial discrimination in opportunities to work and earn. When denied the opportunity to support themselves, women have had to rely on economic support from men. They get this support by exchanging a scarce resource: sexual availability. To a Marxist, it makes little difference whether a woman barters her sexual availability by job (prostitution) or by contract (marriage); the underlying cause is the same.

Although most analyses of prostitution focus on adult women, the conflict perspective helps explain the growing problem of prostitution among runaway and homeless boys and girls. The young people have few realistic opportunities to support themselves by regular jobs. Many are not old enough to work legally; and in any case, a minimum wage would be inadequate to enable them to support themselves. Their young bodies are their most marketable resource.

Prostitution: Learning the Trade. Symbolic interactionists who examine prostitution take an entirely different perspective. They want to know how prostitutes

Whether legal or illegal, prostitution is certainly a patterned form of behavior, occurring in nearly every culture and every epoch of history. Sociologists analyze prostitution using a variety of perspectives. Symbolic interaction would emphasize the social setting where hookers do business, the gestures and vocabulary used to communicate symbolic meanings. The conflict perspective would focus on prostitution as an economic relationship created because of differential access to legitimate rewards. A structural-functional perspective would emphasize that prostitution is a voluntary exchange that benefits both prostitutes and society.

learn the trade and how they manage their self-concept so that they continue to think positively of themselves in spite of engaging in a socially disapproved profession. One such study was done by Barbara Heyl, who intensively interviewed a middle-aged woman who had spent her career first as a prostitute and then as a madam and trainer of prostitutes. Heyl found that much of the training in the prostitute's role consists of training in business, not sex. Prostitutes learn how to hustle—how to get the maximum amount of money for the minimum amount of work. In speaking of what her training produces, the madam says she is turning out professional hustlers, not whores. She is proud of her work. She says, "They find that I am teaching them how to make money, to dress tastefully, to converse and be poised with men, to be knowledgeable about good hygiene, to have good working habits, such as punctuality, which will help them whether they stay in the rackets or not, and to have self-respect" (Heyl 1979, 105).

As these examples illustrate, many topics can be fruitfully studied with any of the three theoretical perspectives. Just as a photographer with only one lens can shoot almost any subject, the sociologist with only one perspective will not be unduly limited in what to examine. One generally gets better pictures, however, by selecting the theoretical perspective that is best suited to the particular subject. In general, structural functionalism and conflict theory are well suited to the study of social structures, or **macrosociology.** Symbolic interactionism is well suited to the study of the relationship between individual meanings and social structures, or **microsociology,** which focuses on interactions among individuals.

Macrosociology focuses on social structures and organizations and the relationships between them.

Microsociology focuses on interactions among individuals.

Sociologists: What Do They Do?

In this chapter, we have tried to give an overview of sociological perspectives so that you can get some idea of what sociology is. Another way of looking at the discipline is by looking at what sociologists do.

College and University Teaching

Nearly three-quarters of the members of the American Sociological Association teach sociology at the college or university level. They teach approximately 60,000 sociology classes every year, which works out to close to 2 million students annually. The effect that these teachers have on their students is one of the major paths through which sociology affects society.

Although teachers' goals vary, most sociology courses have two objectives: to give students a better understanding of their own society—for example, its multicultural diversity, crime rates, inequality, school systems, and population; and to help students see the degree to which individual experience is shaped by larger social structures—that is, to develop the sociological imagination.

Although one course isn't likely to change the way you view the world, studies show that social science majors do learn to view the world differently than others do. One fairly recent study asked college students and the public to rate the importance of various causes of poverty and unemployment (Guimond, Begin, and Palmer 1989). The authors found that although many students and much of the public tended to blame individuals ("poor people spend foolishly," "poor people do not try hard enough"), social science majors were much more likely to blame the system ("jobs are inadequately paid," "the economic situation is unfavorable"). Teaching students the arguments, data, and logic involved in this broader perspective is one of the most important things that sociologists do.

Research

Research (described in more detail in Chapter 2) is the other major activity of professional sociologists. It engages nearly all of the sociologists who work for government, industry, or nonprofit organizations, as well as many sociology professors. Although there are many research strategies in sociology, most sociological research relies on talking to and observing average citizens. In doing so, it has a special concern with representing the unheard and the disadvantaged. Thus, sociological research is an important mechanism through which the concerns of ordinary men and women are represented in the public arena (Gans 1989).

Much of the research in which sociologists engage is *basic sociology*, which has no immediate practical application and is motivated simply by a desire to describe or explain some aspect of human social behavior more fully. Even basic research, however, often has implications for social policy. For example, Lenore Weitzman's research on the consequences of no-fault divorce, as discussed in Chapter 14, played a key role in establishing a new federal law enforcing child-support payments ("Weitzman's Research" 1985).

In addition to the pure research motivated by scholarly curiosity, an increasing proportion of sociologists are engaged in *applied sociology*, seeking to provide immediate practical answers to problems of government, industry, or individuals. The proportion of sociologists who are engaged in applied work has more than doubled in the last two decades, from 9 percent in 1976 to more than 25 percent today. This increase is evident in government, business, and nonprofit organizations.

Working in Government. A long tradition of sociological work in government has to do with measuring and forecasting population trends. This work is vital for decisions about where to put roads and schools and when to stop building schools and start building nursing homes. In addition, sociologists have been employed to design and evaluate public policies in a wide variety of areas. In World War II, sociologists designed policies to increase the morale and fighting efficiency of the armed forces. During the so-called war on poverty in the 1960s, sociologists helped plan and evaluate programs to reduce the inheritance of poverty.

Sociologists work in nearly every branch of government. For example, sociologists are employed by the Centers for Disease Control (CDC), where they examine how social relationships are related to the transmission of AIDS, how intravenous drug users share needles, and how AIDS is transmitted along chains of sexual partners. While the physicians and biologists of CDC examine the medical aspects of AIDS, sociologists work at understanding the social aspects.

Working in Business. Sociologists are employed by General Motors and Pillsbury, as well as by advertisers and management consultants. Part of their work concerns internal affairs (bureaucratic structures and labor relations), but much of it has to do with market research. Business and industry employ sociologists so that they can use their knowledge of society to predict which way consumer demand is likely to jump. For example, the sharp increase in single-person households has important implications for life insurance companies, for food packagers, and for the construction industry. To stay profitable, companies need to be able to predict and plan for these kinds of changes. Another area of extensive involvement for sociologists is the preparation of environmental impact statements, in which they assess the impact of, say, a coal slurry operation on the social and economic fabric of a proposed site.

Working in Nonprofit Organizations. Nonprofit organizations range from hospitals and clinics to social-activist organizations and private think tanks; sociologists are employed in all of them. Sociologists at Planned Parenthood, for example, are interested in determining the causes and consequences of teenage sexual behavior, with evaluating communication strategies that can be used to prevent teenage pregnancy, and with devising effective strategies to pursue some of that organization's more controversial goals, such as the preservation of legal access to abortion on demand.

The training that sociologists receive has a strong research orientation and is very different from the therapy-oriented training received by social workers. Nevertheless, a thorough understanding of the ways in which social structures impinge on individuals can be useful in helping individuals cope with personal troubles. Consequently, some sociologists also do marriage counseling, family counseling, and rehabilitation counseling.

Sociology in the Public Service. Although most sociologists are committed to a value-free approach to their work as scholars, many are equally committed to changing society for the better. They see sociology as a "calling—work that is inseparable from the rest of one's life and driven by a sense of moral responsibility for people's welfare (Yamane 1994). As a result, sociologists have served on a wide variety of public commissions and in public offices in order to effect social change. They work for change independently, too. For example, one sociologist, Claire Gilbert, publishes an environmental newsletter, *Blazing Tattles*, that reports adverse effects of pollution (Alesci 1994).

THINKING CRITICALLY

If you were to major in sociology and become a sociologist, where might you like to work, and why?

SOCIAL APPLICATIONS

WHY ARE THERE HOMELESS PEOPLE IN THE UNITED STATES?

Every chapter in this text will end with a Social Applications section that links chapter material to an issue in today's society and encourages us to think critically about it. This Social Applications section asks us to apply a sociological imagination to the issue of homelessness.

It is nearly impossible today to live in or visit a major American city without being confronted by the homeless issue. Estimates of the number of homeless vary from 300,000 to 3 million, depending on the season of the year, the location, and who is doing the counting.

Why are so many Americans homeless? This question offers an excellent opportunity to apply the sociological imagination. Is homelessness a personal trouble? Can we lay the blame on the homeless individual's mental or physical illness, personal disorganization, lack of motivation, or other character flaws? Or, in contrast, does homelessness result from lack of affordable housing?

One sociologist, James Henslin (1994), travelled to a dozen cities in the United States and Canada, where he slept in shelters and interviewed the homeless wherever he found them—from back alleys to parks and dumpsters. The experience troubled him so much that, after he returned home, three months passed before he could sleep through the night without waking up with disturbing dreams.

As a result of his investigations, Henslin identified 12 types of homeless people. Three of these types—"Ease Addicts," "Travel Addicts," and "Excitement Addicts"—choose to be homeless. They deliberately do not work regularly, they continually travel, or they love the thrill of danger and "living on the edge." But as Henslin points out, these types represent a minority of the homeless. The majority consists of men and women of all ages, including children and the elderly, who are unemployed or minimally employed and simply cannot find affordable housing.

Even if they work regularly and spend responsibly, people who earn the minimum wage find it difficult to afford housing. According to federal poverty guidelines, a person can afford to spend 25 percent of after-tax income on housing. This means that the average full-time, full-year worker who gets paid $5.15 an hour, the Federal minimum wage at the time of this printing, can afford to pay $165 a month for rent and utilities. Do you know of any places in your community where you can get room, heat, electricity, and water for this price? In most communities, there are fewer and fewer such places as derelict and run-down housing is replaced by urban renewal projects.

Why are there homeless people in the United States? According to the sociological perspective, or sociological imagination, homelessness is not simply a personal trouble. Instead, homelessness is a socially structured public issue that results from lack of affordable housing. From this perspective, the solution is not telling homeless people to "go to work" or "be responsible" but providing more low-income housing. A sociological imagination invites us to examine both causes and solutions for social issues within a larger, societywide framework.

THINKING CRITICALLY

How might someone with a sociological imagination and someone without a sociological imagination treat a homeless person? How might the policies on homelessness proposed by a legislator who has a sociological imagination differ from those proposed by a legislator who does not have a sociological imagination? What might be the advantages of developing a sociological imagination? The disadvantages? Under what conditions would a sociological imagination be most effective, do you suppose?

Perhaps the clearest example of sociology in the public service is the award of the 1982 Nobel Peace Prize to the Swedish sociologist Alva Myrdal for her unflagging efforts to increase awareness of the dangers of nuclear armaments. Value-free scholarship does not mean value-free citizenship.

SOCIOLOGY ON THE NET

As you begin your journey on the Internet, it is important that you are aware of the norms governing Internet behavior. The University of Michigan's Electronic Library has an excellent set of selections on the topic of Internet etiquette.

http://mel.lib.mi.us/internet/INET-netiquette.html

Netiquette (Net One). Now open and read the section on the **Internet Revealed: Netiquette**. Browse through the selections and please note the ten commandments for computer ethics. Please keep these in mind as you do the exercises in this text as well as all of your other computer work.

Now that you are familiar with some of the do's and don't's of the Internet, it is time to explore some sociological sources that will give you some more insight into the life and times of Karl Marx.

http://csf.Colorado.EDU/psn/marx/index.html

Go to the section called **Bio Material** and open the first item entitled the **Marx/Engels Thumbnail Chronology.** Read the chronology and find out how Marx combined scholarship and activism in his own life. How wealthy was Marx and what kind of a life did he lead? What were the circumstances of his death? You may wish to get a more personal feel for Marx and his family by scrolling down to the **Marx and Engels Photo Gallery** and browsing through the offerings.

For further information on Marx you might continue to browse this web site or turn to another list of web sites provided by Jonathan D. Jaynes at Boise State University.

http://www.idbsu.edu/surveyrc/Staff/jaynes/marxism/websites.htm

SUMMARY

1. While its sister discipline, psychology, focuses on individual-level factors that affect human behavior, sociology focuses on how social structures affect behavior. Learning to understand how individual behavior is affected by social structures is the process of developing the sociological imagination.
2. Sociology is a social *science*. This means it relies on critical and systematic examination of the evidence before reaching any conclusions and that it approaches each research question from a position of neutrality. This is called value-free sociology.
3. The rapid social change that followed the industrial revolution was an important inspiration for the development of sociology. Problems caused by disorganization and rapid change stimulated the demand for accurate information about social processes. This social-problems orientation remains an important thread in sociology today.
4. Comte is regarded as the founder of sociology. Two Germans, Karl Marx and Max Weber, and a Frenchman, Emile Durkheim, were important early theorists. Sociology was established in the United States in the last quarter of the 19th century. U.S. sociology is distinguished from its European counterpart by its concern with social problems, its reforming rather than radical approach to these problems, and its emphasis on the scientific method.

5 There are three major theoretical perspectives for approaching the study of social structures and human behavior in sociology: structural-functional theory, conflict theory, and symbolic interaction theory. The three can be seen as alternative lenses through which to view society, each having value as a tool for understanding how social structures shape human behavior.

6 Structural functionalism has its roots in evolutionary theory. It identifies social structures and analyzes their consequences for the maintenance of society. Identification of manifest and latent functions and dysfunctions is part of its analytic framework.

7 Modern conflict theory is derived from Karl Marx's ideas. It analyzes social structures by asking who benefits and how these are benefits maintained. It assumes that competition is more important than consensus and that change occurs as a result of conflict and revolution rather than through evolution.

8 Symbolic interaction theory examines how individuals relate to and are affected by social structures. It asks how social structures affect individual, subjective experiences. While structural functionalism and conflict theory study macrosociology, symbolic interactionism is a form of microsociology.

9 Most sociologists teach and do research in academic settings. A growing minority are employed in government, business, and nonprofit organizations, where they do applied research. Regardless of the setting, sociological theory and research have implications for social policy.

SUGGESTED READINGS

The American Journal of Sociology. Chicago: University of Chicago Press. Published regularly for one hundred years, this oldest U.S. sociology journal is also one of the most accessible to non-specialists. A glance through any issue will acquaint you with the variety of issues of concern to contemporary sociologists.

BABBIE, Earl. 1994. *The Sociological Spirit*. Belmont, Calif.: Wadsworth. From a dedicated sociologist who believes that the world and national problems that concern us most have their solutions in the realm addressed by sociology; a book of essays that not only introduces the sociological imagination but also motivates the reader to develop it.

BART, Pauline, and Frankel, Linda. 1986. *The Student Sociologist's Handbook*. (4th ed.) New York: Random House. Information on sociological perspectives, research materials, and sociological writing for the beginning student.

BERGER, Peter L. 1963. *Invitation to Sociology: A Humanistic Perspective*. Garden City, N.Y.: Doubleday Anchor. Thirty years old and a classic. A delightful, well-written introduction to what sociology is and how it differs from other social sciences. Blends a serious exploration of basic sociological understandings with scenes from everyday life—encounters that are easy to relate to and that make sociology both interesting and relevant.

DEEGAN, Mary Jo, ed. 1987. *Women in Sociology: A Bio-bibliographical Sourcebook*. New York: Greenwood Press. Not only a great sourcebook but also arresting reading. A volume that tells about often-forgotten women in sociology from the early 19th century until today.

LEVIN, Jack. 1993. *Sociological Snapshots: Seeing Social Structure and Change in Everyday Life*. Thousand Oaks, Calif.: Pine Forge Press. A short, very readable collection of interesting essays on topics ranging from baby boomers to heartburn to mass murder—all helping to foster a sociological imagination.

MILLS, C. Wright. 1959. *The Sociological Imagination*. New York: Oxford University Press. A penetrating account of how the study of sociology expands understanding of common experiences.

CHAPTER 2

Doing Sociology

OUTLINE

PROLOGUE

Have You Ever . . . Heard those advertisements that start with a statement such as "Nine out of 10 doctors surveyed recommended brand X?" Most Americans have listened to so many far-fetched commercials that they are pretty cynical about such claims. Even without training in proper research techniques, many will wonder exactly how these doctors were identified and exactly what questions they were asked. Were the doctors evaluating free samples, or what?

In the case of chewing gum or brands of aspirin, the credibility of the research isn't terribly critical. We don't really care very much whether the study design is biased in favor of one brand or the other. There are many urgent contemporary issues, however, that demand our best efforts. For example, Americans generate an average of more than four pounds of household garbage each day. About 15 percent of that is recycled, but concern for our environment suggests we could do better. What programs will be most successful in encouraging more people to recycle?

Building effective programs to address problems such as waste disposal, violence, child neglect, and poverty requires reliable evidence from representative samples. We cannot afford to waste either our time or our money on programs built on a foundation of shoddy evidence. In this chapter, we cover the research strategies generally used by sociologists to provide reliable and valid data. One chapter won't prepare you to do research, but we hope it will make you a better consumer of research, more aware of its potential strengths and weaknesses.

THE SCIENTIFIC PERSPECTIVE

The things that sociologists study—for example, deviance, marital happiness, and poverty—have probably interested you for a long time. You may have developed your own opinions about why some people have good marriages and some have bad marriages or why some people use cocaine and others do not. Sociology is an academic discipline that uses the procedures of science to examine common-sense explanations of human social behavior. Science is not divorced from common sense but is an extension of it.

DEFINING SCIENCE

The ultimate aim of science is to understand the world better. Science directs us to find this understanding by observing and measuring what actually happens. This is not the only means of acquiring knowledge. Some people form their perceptions from the *Bible* or the *Koran* or the *Book of Mormon*. Others get their answers from their mothers or their husbands or their girlfriends. When you ask such people, "But how do you know that's true?" their answer is clear. They say "My mother told me" or "I read it in *Reader's Digest*."

Science is a way of knowing based on empirical evidence.

Science differs from these ways of knowing in that it requires an *objective* and *critical* approach to *empirical* evidence. What does this mean?

An *objective approach* requires that we evaluate evidence fairly and without personal bias. We must consider the evidence objectively, without regard to our race, class, or sex, without regard to how the results will affect our careers or personal profit, without regard to how well the results match our personal preferences. For example, a sociologist investigating the effects of day care programs is expected to be open to the possibility that such programs have negative effects even if his or her own children are at a day care center while the sociologist is at work.

The *critical approach* means that we take a skeptical attitude toward all new research findings. Science is slow to accept new findings, and all research results are critically examined to see if they meet technical standards. Generally, results are accepted only after they have been **replicated**—that is, only when other researchers have repeated the study and gotten the same results.

Replication is the process of repeating an empirical study with another investigator or a different sample to see if the same results are obtained.

Empirical refers to evidence that can be confirmed by the human senses. Science requires the use of evidence that we can see, hear, smell, feel, or taste. This means we cannot accept public opinion or divine revelation as a source of factual knowledge.

A simple example shows how the scientific perspective works. Suppose we undertake a scientific investigation of the saying, "An apple a day keeps the doctor away." Before we accept this statement, we need empirical evidence: We need a study that documents apple intake by a representative sample of individuals. Then we need their health records. Even if the empirical evidence shows that apple eaters go to the doctor less, we will need to be critical. Apple eating is probably part of a generally healthy lifestyle; it may be that exercise, a low-fat diet, and other aspects of a healthy lifestyle are responsible for the apple eaters' good health. If this is true, then these people would be healthier than others even if they ate no fruit at all. Finally, even if I own stock in an apple orchard, I must assess the information objectively.

The scientific perspective does not guarantee that we will arrive at the truth. It is, however, the best means that our society offers for seeking and validating new knowledge. By giving us a method for systematically evaluating evidence, science helps us gradually weed out wrong conclusions and identify correct ones. Within the field of sociology, the use of the scientific perspective allows us to examine highly charged issues—such as divorce, welfare, and drug use—and provide answers that stand up to critical evaluation by objective observers.

A Brief Primer on Sociological Research

The procedures used in sociological research are covered in classes on research methods, statistics, and theory construction. At this point, we want to introduce a few ideas that you must understand if you are to be an educated consumer of the research results you will read later in this book. We begin by looking at the general research process and then reviewing three concepts central to research: variables, operational definitions, and sampling. Then we discuss evaluating sociological research.

The Research Process

The research process has two goals: description and explanation. In sociology, we want to describe human social behavior, answering such questions as "What is the divorce rate?" and "Who are the unemployed?" After we know what is going on, we hope to be able to explain it. (What causes divorce? What causes unemployment?) There are four steps to achieving these goals.

Step One: Gathering Data. The research process begins with collecting data related to the research question. We may rely on the census to get information about people's income or unemployment or on the police to provide information about crime rates. It is important to recognize that neither of these sources provides unbiased data: People can and do give false information on census forms, and the police obviously don't have a complete and unbiased record about crime. Collecting accurate data is a difficult task that may never be complete.

Step Two: Finding Patterns. The second step in the research process is to find patterns in the data. If we study unemployment, for example, we will find that African Americans are more than twice as likely as non-Hispanic white Americans to experience unemployment (U.S. Department of Labor 1992). This generalization notes a **correlation,** an empirical relationship between two concepts—in this case, race and unemployment.

Correlation occurs when there is an empirical relationship between two variables.

In the course of daily routine, each of us provides huge quantities of data that are used for sociological research. When we marry, die, divorce, register for school or the draft, go to jail, or file taxes, we provide information that can be used to build an empirical picture of American society. In addition to the data provided on these routine occasions, every 10 years the government conducts a monumental survey research project in the form of the decennial census. Because the census includes 250 million people, it provides data on small populations—such as Native Americans and middle-aged bachelors—that are not available from sample surveys.

A **theory** is an interrelated set of assumptions that explain observed patterns.

Step Three: Generating Theories. After finding a pattern, we need to explain it. *Why* are African Americans more likely to experience unemployment? Explanations are usually embodied in a **theory,** an interrelated set of assumptions that explain observed patterns. Theory always goes beyond the facts at hand; it includes untested assumptions that explain the empirical evidence.

For example, one might theorize that the reason African Americans face more unemployment than whites is because many of today's African American adults grew up in a time when the racial difference in educational opportunity was much greater than it is now. This simple explanation goes beyond the facts at hand to include some assumptions about how education is related to race and unemployment. Although the theory rests on an empirical generalization, the theory itself is not empirical; it is . . . well, theoretical.

It should be noted that many theories may be compatible with a given empirical generalization. We have proposed that education explains the correlation between race and unemployment. An alternative theory might argue that the correlation arises because of discrimination. Because there are often many plausible explanations for any correlation, theory development is not the end of the research process. We must go on to test the assumptions of the theory by gathering new data.

Hypotheses are statements about relationships that we expect to find if our theory is correct.

Step Four: Testing Hypotheses. To test theories, we deduce **hypotheses**—statements about empirical relationships that we expect to observe if our theory is correct. From the theory linking lower African American income to educational deficits, for example, we can deduce the hypothesis that African Americans and whites of equal education will receive equal income. To test this hypothesis, we need more data, this time about education and its relationship to race and unemployment.

A recent study by Melvin Thomas (1993) tested a closely related hypothesis. Thomas asked whether educational deficits explained why African Americans earned less income than whites. He found the hypothesis was not supported: Even if educational levels were equal, the odds were that whites would earn more than African Americans.

Thomas's finding is a new correlation and can be the basis for a revised theory. This new theory will again be subject to empirical test, and the process will begin again. As this example illustrates, the process of science can be viewed as a continuously turning wheel that moves us from data to theory and from theory to data. In the language of science, the process of moving from data to theory is called **induction,** and the process of moving from theory to data is called **deduction.** These two processes and their interrelationships are illustrated in Figure 2.1.

Induction is the process of moving from data to theory by devising theories that account for empirically observed patterns.

Deduction is the process of moving from theory to data by testing hypotheses drawn from theory.

Some General Principles of Research

Research involves variables, operational definitions, and sampling. We will briefly describe each of these in this section.

Variables are measured characteristics that vary from one individual or group to the next.

Variables. Human behavior is complex. In order to narrow the scope of inquiry to a manageable size, we focus on variables rather than on people. **Variables** are measured characteristics that vary from one individual or group to the next (Babbie 1995).

For example, Thomas's study focused on three variables: race, education, and income. The individuals included in his study were, of course, complex and inter-

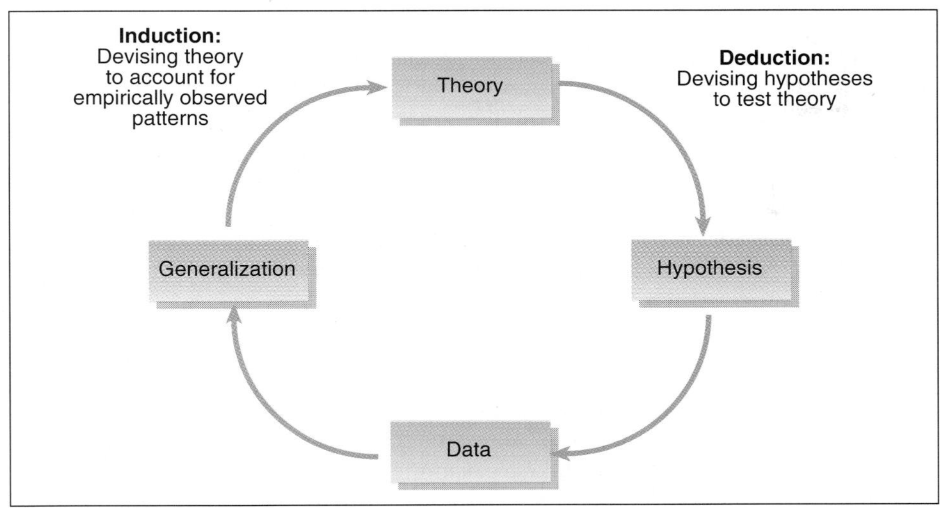

FIGURE 2.1
THE WHEEL OF SCIENCE

The process of science can be viewed as a continuously turning wheel that moves us from data to theory and back again.

SOURCE: Adapted from Wallace, Walter, 1969. *Sociological Theory*. Chicago: Aldine.

esting human beings, but Thomas was interested in their scores on these three variables. Variables, rather than individuals themselves, are the focus of sociological study.

When we hypothesize a cause-and-effect relationship between two variables, the cause is called the **independent variable** and the effect is called the **dependent variable.** In Thomas's hypothesis, for example, education was the independent variable and income the dependent variable; that is, he hypothesized that income depended on education.

The **independent variable** is the variable that does the causing in cause-and-effect relationships.

The **dependent variable** is the effect in cause-and-effect relationships. It is dependent on the actions of the independent variable.

Operational Definitions. The research process requires exact specification of how variables will be measured. How will we decide whether an individual's

What variables would you expect to assess in a study of these two people apparently performing the same task?

Operational definitions describe the exact procedures by which a variable is measured.

income is low? The exact procedures by which a variable is measured are called **operational definitions.** Reaching general agreement about these definitions often poses a problem. For example, Thomas's operational definition of income included personal income from all sources. Besides wages, he counted income from Social Security, Aid to Dependent Children, alimony, and interest-bearing investment accounts. A researcher who just used wages might get different results. Likewise, a researcher who asked people, "Do you feel that you are underpaid?" would very probably identify an entirely different set of people. Consumers of research should always check carefully to see what operational definitions are being used when they evaluate study results.

A **sample** is a systematic selection of representative cases from the larger population.

Sampling. It would be time consuming, expensive, and probably nearly impossible to get information on race, education, and income for all adults. It is also unnecessary. The process of **sampling,** taking a systematic selection of representative cases from a larger population, allows us to get accurate empirical data at a fraction of the cost that it would take to examine all possible cases.

Sampling involves two processes: getting a list of the population you want to study and then selecting a representative subset, or sample, from the list. Selecting from the list is easy: Choosing a relatively large number by a random procedure generally assures that the sample will be unbiased. The more difficult task is getting a list. A central principle of sampling is that a sample is only representative of the list from which it is drawn. If we draw a list of people from the telephone directory, then our sample can only be said to describe households listed in the directory; it will omit those with unlisted numbers, those with no telephones, and those who have moved since the directory was issued. The best surveys begin with a list of all the households or telephone numbers in the target region. Thomas's study used a national survey that drew a sample of 34,000 households from a master list of all the households in the United States. Obviously, data from such a study should be taken much more seriously than results from a study of, say, 400 people listed in the Bemidji, Minnesota, telephone directory.

Evaluation: How Good Is Sociological Research?

In the remaining 20 chapters of this book, we report the results of hundreds, even thousands, of different research studies. All of these studies appeared in professional journals, where they underwent a rigorous screening process that is designed to be both objective and critical. A brief review of this process should raise your confidence in what you are about to read.

At the conclusion of a research project, the researcher writes up the study results, being very specific about operational definitions and sampling strategy, and sends the article off to a professional journal. The journal replaces the researcher's name with a number and sends the article out for a blind review—that is, the reviewers don't know who did the research, and the researcher doesn't know who the reviewers are. This blind review reduces the likelihood that research will be accepted because the writer is somebody famous or somebody who might give the reviewer a job. At the top journals, 90 *percent of all research reports are rejected as not meeting adequate standards*. Often, they are rejected because they use small, unrepresentative samples or because their operational definitions are inadequate. As a result of this process, the research reports that do make it into the professional journals tend to be of very high quality and to meet the highest scientific standards.

This means that the results reported in this text have survived critical and objective evaluations. Nevertheless, the scientific perspective requires that all research consumers apply their own critical intelligence to evaluating the merits of claims about knowledge. As you read the results in the next 20 chapters, you should critically evaluate issues such as operational definitions and sample size.

THREE STRATEGIES FOR GATHERING DATA

The theories and findings reported in this book have used a variety of research strategies. Three of the more general strategies are outlined here: experiments, survey research, and participant observation. In this section, we review each method and illustrate its advantages and disadvantages by showing how it would approach the test of a common hypothesis, that participation in high school sports improves school attendance. In the following section, we describe three published research projects—one using each method—in order to give a more complete and realistic illustration of these data-gathering strategies.

THE EXPERIMENT

The **experiment** is a research method in which the researcher manipulates the independent variable to test theories of cause and effect. Sometimes experiments are conducted in carefully controlled conditions in laboratories, but often they take place in normal classrooms and work environments. In the classic experiment, a group that experiences the independent variable, an **experimental group,** is compared with a **control group** that does not. If the groups are equal on every other dimension, a comparison between them will show whether experience with the independent variable is associated with a unique change in the dependent variable.

The **experiment** is a method in which the researcher manipulates independent variables to test theories of cause and effect.

An **experimental group** is the group in an experiment that experiences the independent variable. Results for this group are compared with those for the control group.

A **control group** is the group in an experiment that does not experience the independent variable.

An experiment designed to assess whether sports participation affects attendance, for example, will need to compare an experimental group that takes part in sports with a control group that does not. A hypothetical experiment might begin with the researchers' observing student attendance during the first few weeks of the term (and before any students have signed up for a team) until students' normal attendance levels have been established. Then the class will be randomly divided into two groups. If the initial pool is large enough, we can assume that the two groups are probably equal on nearly every dimension. For example, we can assume that both groups probably contain an equal mix of good and poor students, of lazy and ambitious students, of students who work after school and those who do not. The control group might be requested not to participate in school sports for the remainder of the semester, and the experimental group might be requested to join a team. At the end of the semester, we will compare the attendance of the two groups. Both groups may have experienced increased attendance due to other factors—the introduction of a more interesting curriculum, for example. The existence of the control group, however, will allow us to determine whether sports participation caused an increase in attendance over and above that which occurred for other reasons.

Experiments are excellent devices for testing hypotheses about cause and effect. They have three drawbacks, however. First, experiments may be unethical if they expose subjects to the possibility of harm. It may be obvious, for example, that the hypothetical experiment described here would be unethical: Discouraging athletically gifted students from participating in high school sports might hurt their chances of getting sports scholarships to college. A more extreme example involves the question of whether people who were abused as children are more likely to abuse their own children. We could not set up an experiment in which one of two randomly assigned groups of children was beaten and the other not. Because of such ethical issues, many areas of sociological interest cannot be studied using the experimental method.

A second drawback to experiments is that subjects often behave differently when they are under scientific observation than they would in their normal environments. For example, although participation in sports might *not* normally have the effect of raising attendance, the participants in our study might find the research so interesting that their attendance actually improved. In this case, the subjects' knowledge that they are participating in an experiment affects their response to the independent variable. This response is called the **guinea-pig effect.** In sociology, it is often called the Hawthorne effect because it was first documented in a research project in the Hawthorne electric plant.

The **guinea-pig effect** occurs when subjects' knowledge that they are participating in an experiment affects their responses to the independent variable.

It may be obvious to you that not all experiments are possible in real life. In our hypothetical example, it would be unlikely that coaches, parents, or school administrators would cooperate. As a result, experiments are often done in laboratory settings. A final drawback to an experimental method is especially relevant to these laboratory experiments. When researchers try to set up social situations in laboratories, they often must omit many of the factors that would influence the same behavior in a real-life situation. The result is often a highly artificial social situation. Like the guinea-pig effect, this artificiality has the effect of reducing our confidence that the results of the experiment can be generalized to the more complex conditions of the real world.

Because of these disadvantages; relatively little sociological research uses the controlled experiment. The areas in which it has been most useful are the study of small-group interaction and the simulation of situations that seldom occur in real life.

The research method you choose will depend on your research question. If you want to know whether these pleasant-looking people go to church or vote, survey research will be entirely appropriate. They probably will be quite cooperative and reasonably honest. Even people such as this, however, cannot be depended on to give you accurate answers to questions about family violence or drug abuse. Although survey research is our best all-around strategy for gathering data, it has limitations.

THE SURVEY

In **survey research,** the investigator asks a relatively large number of people the same set of standardized questions. These questions may be asked in a personal interview, over the telephone, or in a paper-and-pencil format. This technique is the one most commonly used to gather sociological data. Because it asks the same questions of a large number of people, it is an ideal method for furnishing evidence on **incidence** (the frequency of phenomena in the population), **trends** (changes in the phenomena over time), and **differentials** (differences among population subgroups on the phenomena). For example, survey data on high school sports participation might allow us to say such things as: Thirty percent of high school seniors participate on school athletic teams (incidence); the proportion of females in sports has gone up in the last 20 years (trend); and the proportion of females on varsity athletic teams is lower than the proportion of males (differential). Because survey research can easily be used with large, national samples, it is an excellent source of descriptive data. It is also very versatile: It can be used to study attitudes, behavior, and values.

Survey research is a method that involves asking a relatively large number of people the same set of standardized questions.

Incidence is the frequency with which a phenomenon occurs.

Trends are changes in phenomena over time.

Differentials are differences in the incidence of a phenomenon across subcategories of the population.

Most surveys use what is called a **cross-sectional design;** they take a sample (or cross section) of the population at a single point in time. Thus, in our study of sports participation and attendance, we would survey a sample of students, expecting to find that some of them play on teams and some do not. We could then compare these two groups to see which has higher attendance.

A **cross-sectional design** uses a sample (or cross section) of the population at a single point in time.

If we were to do this, we might find a correlation between sports participation and attendance. The difficulty with the cross-sectional design is that we cannot reach any firm conclusions about cause and effect. We cannot tell whether, on the one hand, sports participation causes higher attendance or, on the other hand, higher attendance leads to joining a team. A more striking problem is that we cannot be sure there is a cause-and-effect relationship at all. The two categories (participants and nonparticipants) might differ on many other variables besides sports participation. For example, those in sports may have more conventional families, come from better neighborhoods, or be more religious. It could be that one of these factors is causing the higher attendance and that taking part in sports is just coincidental.

To try to rule out as many of these alternative explanations as possible, we introduce **control variables**—measures of the background factors that may be confounding the true relationship between our study variables. For example, to control for the possibility that social class is the real cause of higher attendance, we can restrict our analysis to middle-class students. Even if we were to add controls for race, sex, religion, and family life, however, we could not feel certain that the two groups were equivalent. A skeptic would still have grounds for asserting that students who participated in sports were different from those who did not.

Control variables are measures of background factors that may be confounding the true relationship between study variables.

One strategy that survey researchers use to improve the strength of their conclusions is the **panel design,** which follows a sample over a period of time. During this period of time, some sample members will experience the independent variable, and we can observe how they differ before and after this experience from those who have no contact with the independent variable. Using this design for examining the effect of sports participation on attendance would require selecting a sample of, say, 9th and 10th graders and interviewing them at several points over the next few years. This design would not alter the fact that some of them will choose to play high school sports and some will not, but it would let us look at the

The **panel design** follows a sample over a period of time.

same people before and after their decision. It would allow us to see whether students' attendance actually rose after they joined an athletic team.

One study that used a panel design examined national survey data from high school sophomores in 1984 and compared these data with data for the same students, then seniors, in 1986. The investigators found that participating in high school sports did, in fact, improve school attendance, probably because doing so led to increased feelings of popularity and greater student identification with school (Marsh 1993).

An important drawback of survey research is that respondents may misrepresent the truth. Prejudiced people may tell you that they are unprejudiced, and only a small fraction of those who abuse their children are likely to admit it. This misrepresentation is known as **social-desirability bias**—the tendency for people to color the truth so that they appear to be nicer, richer, and generally more desirable than they really are. The consequences of this bias vary in seriousness depending on the research aim and topic. Obviously, it is a greater problem for such sensitive topics as drug use and prejudice.

Social-desirability bias is the tendency of people to color the truth so that they sound nicer, richer, and more desirable than they really are.

Survey research is designed to get standard answers to standard questions. It is not the best strategy for studying deviant or undesirable behaviors or for getting at ideas and feelings that cannot easily be reduced to questionnaire form. An additional drawback of survey research is that it is a method designed to study individuals rather than contexts. Thus, it focuses on the individual smoker or nonsmoker rather than the settings and relationships in which smoking takes place. For these kinds of answers, we must turn to participant observation.

Participant Observation

Participant observation includes a variety of research strategies—participating, interviewing, observing—that examine the contexts and meanings of human behavior.

Under the label **participant observation** we classify a variety of research strategies—participating, interviewing, observing—that examine the contexts and meanings of human behavior. Instead of sending forth an army of interviewers, participant observers go out into the field to see firsthand what is going on. A recent variation on this strategy is so-called electronic participant observation (Jindra 1994), in which a "community" of computer on-line network users is tapped for ongoing discussions on a particular research topic. For example, besides attending their conventions and conducting face-to-face interviews, Michael Jindra (1994) analyzed conversations among Star Trek fans on the net.

Participant observation is used most often by sociologists interested in symbolic interaction theory—that is, researchers who want to understand subjective meanings and personal relationships. The goals of this research method are to discover patterns of interaction and to find the meaning of the patterns for the individuals involved.

The three major tasks involved in participant observation are interviewing, participating, and observing. A researcher goes to the scene of the action, where she may interview people informally in the normal course of conversation, participate in whatever they are doing, and observe the activities of other participants. Not every participant observation study includes all three dimensions equally. A participant observer studying high school sports participation, for example, would not need to play on a team. She would, however, probably conduct long, informal interviews with both athletes and nonathletes, attend team practices and games, and attempt to get a feel for how playing sports fit in with other aspects of student life.

The data produced by participant observation are often based on small numbers of individuals who have not been selected according to random-sampling techniques. The data tend to be unsystematic and the samples not very representative; however, we do know a great deal about the few individuals involved. This detail is often useful for generating ideas that can then be examined more systematically with other techniques. In this regard, participant observation may be viewed as a form of initial exploration of a research topic.

In some situations, however, participant observation is the only reasonable way to approach a subject. This is especially likely when we are examining undesirable behavior, real behavior rather than attitudes, or uncooperative populations.

In the first instance, social-desirability bias makes it difficult to get good information about undesirable behavior. Thus, what we know about running a brothel (Heyl 1979) or being homeless (Snow and Anderson 1987) rests largely on the reports of participant observers. This style of research produces fewer distortions than would have occurred if a middle-class survey researcher dropped by to ask the participants about their activities.

In the second case, participant observation is well suited to studies of behavior—what people do rather than what they say they do. Behaviors are sometimes misrepresented in surveys simply because people are unaware of their actions or don't remember them very well. For example, individuals may believe they are not prejudiced, yet observational research may demonstrate that these same people systematically choose not to sit next to persons of another race on the bus or in public places. Sometimes actions speak louder than words.

In the third case, we know that survey research works best with people who are predisposed to cooperate with authorities and who are relatively literate. Where either of these conditions is not met, survey research may not be possible. For this reason, there is little survey research on prison populations, juvenile gangs, preschoolers, or rioters. Participant observation is often the only means to gather data on these populations.

What is going on here? Survey research is not going to give you the answer. Not only is there no time to select a sample and draw up a questionnaire, this fellow doesn't appear to be a cooperative respondent. When we want to study social process or when we want to study deviant and uncooperative populations, participant research is usually our best research strategy. In this case—a confrontation between white supremacists, the police, and counter; demonstrators at the "Aryan Woodstock" festival—a researcher would need to be on the scene for as long as possible and then track down participants later to discuss their behavior and motivations.

A major disadvantage of participant observation is that the observations and generalizations rely on the interpretation of one investigator. Since researchers are not robots, it seems likely that their findings reflect some of their own world view. This is a greater problem with participant observation than with survey or experimental work, but all social science suffers to some extent from the phenomenon. The answer to this dilemma is replication—redoing the same study with another investigator to see if the same results occur.

ALTERNATIVE STRATEGIES

The bulk of sociological research uses the three strategies just described. There are, however, a dozen or more other imaginative and useful ways of doing research, many of them involving analysis of social artifacts rather than people. For example, a study of women's magazines of the 19th century illustrates changing attitudes toward spinsterhood during that period (Hickok 1981). A study of children's portraits over the centuries has shown how ideas of childhood have changed (Aries 1962). Studies of court records and government statistics have demonstrated frequencies, trends, and differentials in many areas of sociological interest. Feminist scholars have created new methods, such as writing group diaries, tracing geneologies, and analyzing unplanned personal experiences (Reinharz 1992).

EXAMPLES OF SOCIOLOGICAL RESEARCH

In this section, we present detailed descriptions of three published pieces of research that use the research strategies we have described. These case studies illus-

CONCEPT SUMMARY RESEARCH METHODS

EXPERIMENTS	
PROCEDURE	Dividing subjects into two equivalent groups, applying the independent variable to one group only, and observing the differences between the two groups on the dependent variable
ADVANTAGES	Excellent for analysis of cause-and-effect relationships; can simulate events and behaviors that do not occur outside the laboratory in any regular way
DISADVANTAGES	Based on small, nonrepresentative samples examined under highly artificial circumstances; unclear that people would behave the same way outside the laboratory; unethical to experiment in many areas
SURVEY RESEARCH	
PROCEDURE	Asking the same set of standard questions of a relatively large, systematically selected sample
ADVANTAGES	Very versatile—can study anything that we can ask about; can be done with large, random samples so that results represent many people; good for incidence, trends, and differentials
DISADVANTAGES	Shallow—does not get at depth and shades of meaning; affected by social-desirability bias; better for studying people than situations
PARTICIPANT OBSERVATION	
PROCEDURE	Observing people's behavior in its normal context; experiencing others' social settings as a participant; indepth interviewing.
ADVANTAGES	Seeing behavior in context; getting at meanings associated with behavior; seeing what people do rather than what they say they do.
DISADVANTAGES	Limited to small, nonrepresentative samples; dependent on interpretation of single investigator.

trate how research designs are actually implemented and show some of the dilemmas faced by those working within each research tradition.

The Survey: Concern for the Environment and Recycling

In 1993, Americans threw away 207 million tons of paper, aluminum, glass, plastic, and other garbage—the equivalent of over 4 pounds per person every day. That amount is up from 1980, when each American tossed out 3 1/2 pounds of trash daily (U.S. Bureau of the Census 1995, Table 380). Today, Americans recycle twice as much as they did in 1980, but the proportion of garbage that is recycled is still only about 22 percent (U.S. Bureau of the Census 1995, Table 381). With increasing concern for the environment (not to mention concern with where to put all that trash), policy makers are asking how we can be encouraged to increase recycling. A recent study bearing on this issue was carried out by Linda Derksen of the University of California, San Diego, and John Gartrell of the University of Alberta, Canada. Derksen and Gartrell (1993) wanted to better understand the circumstances under which people recycle their trash.

The authors conducted their study in the province of Alberta, Canada. They divided the province (similar to a state in the United States) into three major areas: the city of Edmonton, the city of Calgary, and the rest of the province, which is rural. Edmonton's curbside recycling program gave each household a "blue box" recycling container that could be put out weekly on the same day as regular trash. At the time of the survey, items eligible for the blue box included cans and bottles, newspapers and cardboard, household plastics (containers, food wrap), milk cartons, and motor oil. There was no cost to participate. Unlike Edmonton, neither Calgary nor rural Alberta had regular opportunities for recycling. Since Calgary was urban, however, residents did have access to neighborhood drop-off bins.

Derksen and Gartrell hypothesized that regardless of people's concern for the environment, average levels of recycling would be lower in areas that provide little

These New Hampshire residents are recycling at a collection center. Do you think they might recycle more if they could do so at their homes?

opportunity for recycling. The dependent variable in this study was recycling behavior. The researchers measured, or operationalized, recycling behavior by counting the total of the different types of items (such as cans, bottles, newspapers, and plastics) that respondents said they recycled. The two independent variables were concern for the environment and opportunity for recycling. Concern for the environment was operationalized according to respondents' answers to the question, "How concerned are you about the state of the earth's environment?" Responses were measured on a seven-point scale with 7 meaning "very concerned" and 1 meaning "not concerned at all." The authors operationalized opportunity for recycling by using area of residence—Edmonton, Calgary, or rural Alberta—as a measure of access to a recycling program.

The investigators knew that factors other than the independent variables might affect recycling. For example, even if the final results were to show a correlation between living in Edmonton and recycling, these results would not necessarily indicate a causal relationship. Two plausible rival explanations are that both recycling and living in Edmonton are influenced by respondents' age or by their social class. In order to check (or control) for these rival explanations, Derksen and Gartrell introduced age, education, and income variables as control variables.

Virtually all Alberta residents 18 years of age or older made up the study's population, or universe. The researchers drew their sample in two stages. First, they randomly selected a sample of households in each of the three areas. In Edmonton, this meant selecting from households previously enumerated during the 1989 City of Edmonton Civic Census. To select a sample of households for Calgary and rural Alberta, the researchers used random-digit telephone dialing. That is, they dialed a prefix for the area, followed by four random digits. Random-digit dialing may not be the very best way to draw a sample, because it eliminates households without telephones, and such households may be significantly different from those with telephones. For instance, in this study, if people without telephones were more inclined to recycle than those who had them, the study results would underestimate the incidence of recycling in Alberta. But cost and time constraints often prohibit finding all possible respondents in ways more thorough than random-digit dialing.

Once the Alberta households had been randomly selected, the second sampling stage began. It involved randomly selecting a member of each household over age 18 to be interviewed. This process yielded a total of 1,245 respondents: 448 respondents in Edmonton, 401 in Calgary, and 396 in the rest of the province. The researchers used a statistical test designed to measure the similarity between their sample and the population from which it was drawn, and this test showed that the sample was indeed representative.

After the sample was drawn, researchers conducted face-to-face interviews with Edmonton respondents and telephone interviews with those in Calgary and rural Alberta. We could contend that persons interviewed face-to-face might give different answers from those questioned over the telephone. However, Derksen and Gartrell asked exactly the same questions of all respondents and do not believe that any difference in answers can be attributed to this difference in interview format. Table 2.1 gives some data from this study.

What did Derksen and Gartrell find? First, Alberta residents in all three areas expressed high levels of concern for the environment. The mean average level of concern was nearly 6 out of a possible 7. Some of this finding may be due to social-desirability bias. Nevertheless, nearly half the respondents said they were "very

TABLE 2.1
FREQUENCY OF NEWSPAPER RECYCLING IN ALBERTA HOUSEHOLDS

The simplest way to present data is in a frequency, or percentage, table, which summarizes data about a single variable. (Frequencies are often converted to percentages so they will be easier to interpret.) Table 2.1 is a percentage table for recycling newspapers among all the Alberta respondents. This table presents descriptive data showing that 562 (45 percent) of the 1,245 respondents in the study did not recycle newspapers, while 683 (55 percent) respondents did.

Q: "WHAT KINDS OF THINGS DO YOU RECYCLE?" ANS: NEWSPAPERS

	NUMBER	PERCENT
NO	562	45
YES	683	55
TOTAL	1,245	100

concerned." But concern for the environment had a very low correlation with recycling. What did seem to help explain recycling behavior was having the socially structured opportunity to recycle. Edmonton residents with access to the recycling program recycled substantially more than Calgary or rural Alberta residents. For example, 72 percent of Edmonton residents recycled newspapers, compared with 54 percent of Calgary respondents, who lived in an urban area with neighborhood drop-off sites, and only 36 percent of rural Albertans. These differentials are presented in Table 2.2.

Derksen and Gartrell's study showed that the most important determinant of an individual's recycling behavior is not attitude toward the environment but access to a socially structured program that makes recycling easy and convenient. (Here you may recognize the sociological imagination, discussed in Chapter 1.) Even *unconcerned* individuals in Edmonton had high recycling levels. The researchers concluded with a statement that could be used in making social policy: If households were given boxes for recyclable items, if these boxes were picked up with the regular garbage, and if a wide variety of items were accepted for recycling, individuals would probably be more likely to recycle on a regular basis.

Because the sample in this research was limited to residents of Alberta, we can only generalize to that population. That is, we cannot be certain that these findings apply to other Canadians or to residents of the United States or other countries. Finding out is a matter for further research projects.

TABLE 2.2

FREQUENCY OF RECYCLING NEWSPAPERS AND BOTTLES AND CANS AMONG THREE TYPES OF ALBERTA HOUSEHOLDS (N = 1,245)

How to Read a Table

1. *Read the title and headings carefully. A good table will tell you something about the origin and size of the sample as well as the operational definitions used in measuring the variables. In this table, the N in the title stands for number and indicates the total sample size.*
2. *Figure out how the percentages are calculated. In this table, the n's indicate the number of respondents in each of the three areas of residence. Looking at the data for rural Alberta, we see that 143 (the number who recycle newspapers) divided by all rural Alberta residents in the sample (396) equals 36 percent. So 36 percent of the rural Albertans recycle newspapers.*
3. *This table gives differential data. Compare the percentages across categories of the independent variable. The critical information is given in the percentages across the rows. (The numbers that go across a table are rows; the vertical numbers are columns.) Reading across the rows, we see, for example, that 72 percent of the Calgary and of the Edmonton residents recycle bottles and cans, compared with 59 percent of the rural Albertans.*

	RURAL ALBERTA (n=396)		CALGARY (n=401)		EDMONTON (n=448)	
	NUMBER	PERCENT	NUMBER	PERCENT	NUMBER	PERCENT
NEWSPAPERS	143	36	217	54	323	72
BOTTLES AND CANS	234	59	289	72	323	72

FOCUS ON ANOTHER CULTURE

Survey Research in Nigeria

"How do you feel about the current government?" "Do you think men and women ought to be treated equally?" "How many televisions do you own?" Without much effort, we can imagine places in the world where questions like these—so commonplace to us—would appear foolish and would perhaps be dangerous to ask.

In the United States and much of the developed world, we are accustomed to questions about the most intimate details of our lives. It is common for bureaucratic agencies to record data pertaining to our height, weight, IQ, taxes, fertility, and credit rating. Our acceptance of intrusive questioning is based on the assumption that this information is somehow necessary to good governance and on the trust that our privacy will be protected. Because we are familiar with routine bureaucratic data gathering, it is relatively easy for survey researchers to enlist our cooperation. If called on the telephone, approximately 75 percent of persons in the United States will respond to survey researchers' inquiries on topics ranging from politics to religion.

"IN THE UNITED STATES AND MUCH OF THE DEVELOPED WORLD, WE ARE ACCUSTOMED TO QUESTIONS ABOUT THE MOST INTIMATE DETAILS OF OUR LIVES."

When survey research is conducted in Third World nations, many of these conditions do not hold. Often, people there have good reason not to trust their governments. More generally, they simply are not accustomed to opening their private lives to the probing of bureaucratic agents.

One of the most common areas in which Western survey research methods meet resistance from Third World peoples is research on fertility and family planning. Agencies such as the United Nations and the U.S. Agency for International Development wish to know how many children women in Kenya, Nigeria, and other high-fertility nations want so that they can use the discrepancy between actual and desired childbearing to develop contraceptive programs. Agnes Riedmann's (1993) analysis of a survey research project among the Yoruba of Nigeria highlights several cultural clashes that may impede such research efforts.

- In many non-Western cultures, fertility is "up to God." It would be unthinkable for individuals to put their own opinions forward. A question such as, "If you had more money, would you rather have a new car or another child?" presumes that individuals have a choice about fertility and, moreover, that dollar values can be assigned to children.
- Asking a *woman's* opinion is often considered indecent (unless her husband is present) or at best a waste of time, since women's opinions do not count.
- There is profound distrust of strangers who ask personal questions. After submitting to an ill-understood interview on fertility, for example, one Yoruban respondent asked whether the police were now coming to take her away.

In many cases, Yoruban respondents mocked, yelled at, and ran from interviewers. The persistent inquiry of strangers into their private lives seemed to some to be just one more instance of the crazy behavior of "oyinbos," or white people. Others speculated that it was a result of white people's not having enough to do! If badgered into participation, Yorubans politely told interviewers what they thought they wanted to hear and sent them on their way.

Participant Observation: Tally's Corner

One of the best participant observation studies is described in the book *Tally's Corner*, a classic study of street-corner men in an urban slum (Liebow 1967). It offers a clear example of the strengths of this methodology; it also provides insight into a world that is unfamiliar to most Americans.

In spite of urban renewal, Headstart, and open-housing laws, urban slums in the United States have become poorer and more despairing with every year. At one point in their development, they were just poor inner-city neighborhoods, but over the 45 years since World War II, they have become the source of a hereditary class of the socially dispossessed.

Little is known about the people who live in urban ghettos. Survey researchers are afraid to enter the neighborhoods, much less the tenement buildings themselves. The U.S. Census, which spends billions of dollars trying to reach each citizen, misses 20 percent of the young men in central cities. Many do not have telephones or are so transient they are hard to reach. If someone from a survey research center does reach them to ask, "How do you feel about your economic prospects: Would you say they're staying the same, getting better, or getting worse?," a large proportion will decline to participate in such a personally meaningless and possibly threatening exercise.

What we know about the people who live in ghettos comes largely from the portion of the ghetto population that is in contact with authorities. Thus, we know something about schoolchildren (their scores on standardized exams, their reading levels, their nutrition), about mothers on welfare, and about men who get picked up by the police. These people are not a representative sample of the people who live in ghettos. And overriding the question of sampling is the question of whether information given involuntarily in welfare offices and police stations is truthful and open.

Obviously, people who live in inner-city neighborhoods grow up, pair up, have children, support themselves, and belong to families and to networks of friends. They do not act randomly; their behavior is hedged around and directed by the

Frequently, sociologists are more interested in knowing about people than people are interested in being known. Refusal to cooperate is especially likely among the unsuccessful, the disadvantaged, and the alienated. Thus, what we know about such people is likely to come from coerced data collection in prisons, welfare offices, and emergency room clinics. Elliot Liebow's participant observation study of Tally's Corner *was designed to balance such coerced data with a picture of what everyday life is like for street-corner men.*

social structures of their community. A major question for social science research is what these structures are and what they mean to the individuals involved.

Elliot Liebow, author of *Tally's Corner,* wrote his doctoral dissertation as part of a larger research project that was designed to look at child-rearing practices among lower-class families. For the reasons already given, survey research with questionnaires and paper-and-pencil tests were out of the question. More important, Liebow wanted to get an insider's view, a description of lower-class people and their lives on their terms and from their viewpoints. Because something was already known about lower-class women and children, Liebow chose to concentrate on adult males.

Liebow chose a corner in Washington, D.C., and hung out there off and on for a year. He made no pretense that this was a representative corner or that the men he came to know were representative of the men in Washington's slums. What he intended to do was offer a well-rounded picture of 15 to 20 men that would enable us to see the social structure through their eyes. What did life look like in terms of their education, their economic opportunities, their environment?

Liebow was white and had many more years of schooling than the men he was studying. He presented himself at the corner wearing T-shirts and khaki pants, prepared to use bad grammar and bad language. He came, as did the real participants, just to hang out, to see "what's happening." He did not carry a tape recorder, take notes, or ask questions. He just made small talk with the regulars. After each observation period was finished, however, he returned to his office and made detailed notes on what he had observed. These field notes became his written record. When he came to write up his conclusions at the end of his year on the corner, the field notes enabled him to remember who had said what and what had actually happened.

The men on the corner knew that Liebow was there as part of his job, but since he took pains not to act, dress, or talk like a social scientist, he felt he was soon accepted by them—although always aware of his separateness from them because of his color. He was eventually invited to their homes, went out drinking with them, and was asked to come to court with them on occasion to provide support or advice when they had brushes with the law or the authorities. From this year's experience, he came to see the differences between their public performance (the kinds of stories people tell about themselves to people they meet for the first time—and to survey researchers) and their real situations.

Some of Liebow's most insightful findings cover the relationship of these men to work. Although there are excuses of health and layoffs, Liebow concludes that "getting a job, keeping a job, and doing well at it [are] clearly of low priority" (Liebow 1967, 34). Liebow tells us the life stories of several men, all of whom are failures, who know they are failures—and who cannot see that taking and keeping a job will keep them from being failures. No matter how many years of school they may have had, they are largely illiterate and unskilled. The jobs they can get (janitor, dishwasher, day laborer at construction sites) are dead-end jobs with low wages. The only people who can hold such jobs and maintain their self-esteem are students who are taking the jobs only temporarily on their way to better things. A 35-year-old man who washes dishes is a failure, in his own eyes and those of society. In short, he can get from the job neither enough money to support himself and his family nor self-esteem and self-respect. How does this affect the rest of his life?

> He carries this failure home where his family life is undergoing a parallel deterioration. His wife's adult male models also failed as husbands and fathers and she expects no less

> from him. . . . (Nevertheless, she has hoped against hope that he would be a good provider and take on a role of "man of the house.") When he fails, it enlarges his failure in both of their eyes.
>
> Increasingly he turns to the street corner where a shadowy system of values constructed out of public fictions serves to accommodate just such men as he, permitting them to be men once again provided they do not look too closely at one another's credentials (pp. 212–213).

These shadow values include the theory of manly flaws, an assertion that one is too much of a man to fulfill the expected man's role—that one's sexual urges are too strong for one to remain faithful, that one's independence is too strong for one to submit to authority on the job, and so on. In short, these men claim to have the characteristics accorded to manhood in our society in such great quantity that they are precluded from playing that social role successfully. The men do not blame the system—or they didn't in Washington, D.C., in 1962—and they are unable to acknowledge their own faults because of a need for some sense of self-worth. They create an explanation for their failure that requires neither social activism nor self-hate, a twilight world of values that parallels their twilight place in the economic structure.

The 15 to 20 men whom Liebow studied intensively may not have been representative of all poor African American men in Washington, D.C., in 1962; the street corner may not have been representative of all African American urban neighborhoods. It is sufficient, however, to know that these processes were at work among these people in this neighborhood. The study told us much that was new in a way that made it possible for many readers to grasp the subjective meaning of employment hardship for the first time. This rich and valuable information could have been provided only through participant observation. (In Chapter 10 we will consider whether things have changed in the 30-odd years since this study was completed.)

The Experiment: Does Anybody Give a Damn?

In the spring of 1962, a young woman returned from her job as manager of a bar and parked her red Fiat in a parking lot a hundred feet from the doorway of her apartment building in Queens, New York. It was after 3 A.M., and the neighborhood was quiet. As she was locking her car, she became nervously aware of a man lurking nearby, and she headed for the police call box a short distance away. Before she could get there, the man attacked and stabbed her. The woman screamed, "Oh, my God, he stabbed me! Please help me! Please help me!" One of her neighbors threw open a window and hollered down, "Let that girl alone!" This caused the assailant to move off down the street. Nobody came to help, and the woman struggled to her feet. The lights went off again in the neighboring apartments, and the woman tried to get to the door of her apartment building. The assailant returned and stabbed her again. This time she shrieked, "I'm dying! I'm dying!" Windows were thrown up and lights turned on, but no one did anything. Apparently frightened off by the lights, the assailant got in his car and drove away. The woman managed to pull herself into the doorway of her apartment building but couldn't get up the steps. She lay there for perhaps 15 to 20 minutes before her assailant returned again and stabbed her a third time, this time fatally (Rosenthal 1964).

Twenty minutes after Kitty Genovese died, the police received a call from one of her neighbors. He had waited until after the final attack and then called a friend to ask what he should do. Finally, he went to a neighboring apartment and got another

This crowd is waiting at the Soul Clinic Mission in downtown Los Angeles for the promised distribution of free Christmas trees. In the process of receiving help themselves, these passersby are nearly oblivious to the man lying along the curb. Is he drunk? Is he sick? No one makes an attempt to find out. Studies of bystanders generally suggest that when other bystanders are present, responsibility for helping becomes more diffuse, and any single bystander is less likely to offer help.

tenant to make the call to the police. He didn't want to get involved. All in all, 38 of her neighbors watched the assailant take 35 minutes to kill Kitty Genovese on the street. None of them tried to rescue her; aside from the man who shouted from his window, no one tried to interfere; none of them even lifted the telephone to call the police to come and rescue her. Several of them went back to bed.

The incident stirred the entire nation. "What are we coming to?" people asked. "Has our society become so callous that we care nothing about our fellow human beings?" Many of the initial reactions focused personally on those 38 witnesses. What was wrong with them? More careful consideration suggested that the problem did not lie with those 38 individuals. One person's refusal to act could be interpreted as a personal problem—stupidity, indecisiveness, depravity, insensitivity. For 38 persons to behave in the same way suggests that there was something about the social structure that invited noninterference. After much soul searching about apathy and insensitivity, a group of scholars finally started to investigate what is now called the bystander effect.

Under what circumstances will people intervene to help a stranger? The question is approached with experimental research rather than with participant observation or survey research. We forgo participant observation for the reason that such events, luckily, do not normally occur in any predictable way. Furthermore, a field researcher who stumbled on such a situation could not ethically stand by and examine the reactions of bystanders rather than offer help. We forgo survey research because few people would tell us that they would ignore a plea for help, that they wouldn't even make an anonymous telephone call to the police. Thus, the study is done in the laboratory, where an emergency can be simulated and where the effects of circumstances surrounding the emergency can be carefully manipulated and the likelihood of offering assistance can be gauged.

The findings reported here are drawn from the work of sociologists Shalom Schwartz and Avi Gottlieb (1980). The previous research on the bystander effect led Schwartz and Gottlieb to hypothesize that two major factors affected whether a helping response was likely to be offered:

1. *Diffusion of responsibility among potential helpers.* When bystanders are aware that other witnesses are on the scene who also ought to do something, they are less likely to feel they personally have a responsibility to help.

Hypothesis: Bystanders who know that there are other bystanders will be less likely to help than will those who believe they are alone.

2. *Fear of what others will think.* Even among strangers, we want people to think well of us. Nobody wants to be seen as the kind of clod who would fail to help somebody in trouble.

Hypothesis: Bystanders who believe their presence is unknown will be less likely to help than will bystanders aware that they are known to be on the scene.

The subjects in the experiment were 127 undergraduates who were recruited to take part in the experiment allegedly on extrasensory perception (ESP). The experiments were carried out at night in an isolated wing of the social science building. As subjects arrived separately, they were conducted past an open doorway in which they could see a man sitting at a console. Each subject was then escorted into a separate cubicle, where a video monitor showed the front view of, apparently, the same man. The subjects were told that the man was going to exchange ESP messages with a third party and that their task was to intercept the messages if possible. The experimenter said that she herself was going to leave the area so that her presence could not interfere with the transmissions but that if a subject wanted her, she could be called from the telephone in the corner of the cubicle.

After the experimenter left, each subject watched the man for 7.5 minutes. The subject then saw on the screen a large, roughly dressed man entering the transmitter's room, grabbing a calculator from the desk, throwing the other man against the wall, hitting him in the stomach, and, after he had fallen to the ground, kicking him several times. The stranger left 35 seconds after having grabbed the calculator. The research question was whether the research hypotheses would predict the subjects' responses to the crisis.

To test their hypotheses, Schwartz and Gottlieb randomly divided the student subjects into two groups. This random assignment means that other relevant factors—such as kindness, courage, and intelligence—should be equal in both groups. Then the two groups were exposed to two different sets of circumstances that roughly simulated the conditions in the hypotheses:

- **Group 1.** Students believed they were the lone bystanders and that the victim/transmitter knew of their presence. This condition was hypothesized to produce the maximum response, since each student would believe that he or she was the only one who could help and would further believe that the victim would expect this help.

- **Group 2.** Students believed there were other bystanders in the experimental area who could help and that the victim/transmitter was ignorant of their presence. This condition was hypothesized to produce the minimum response, since each student might count on someone else offering help and would further believe that the victim would not expect help.

The results showed that 89 percent of the subjects made some attempt to provide help within the first five minutes. This was true regardless of the experimental conditions. The speed with which they tried to help, however, was significantly related to experimental conditions. Results showed that people in Group 1 were nearly twice as likely as those in Group 2 (75 versus 40 percent) to provide immediate aid. Being a lone and known bystander, then, does increase the likelihood of coming to someone's aid. Further manipulations showed that either one of these conditions by itself is sufficient to encourage a helping response: Both lone bystanders and known bystanders are highly likely to come to a victim's aid. It is the situation created for Group 2, where a bystander is neither known or alone, that elicits the minimum helping response.

The results from the Schwartz and Gottlieb experiment help us understand why 38 of Kitty Genovese's neighbors watched her die without making any effort to help her. Her situation matched the condition of Group 2: Other bystanders were present, and the presence of each individual bystander was unknown to the victim and other observers. It is worth noting that the man who eventually had the police called had been caught looking out his window by another neighbor; in short, he was a known bystander. This experiment is an excellent example of how the laboratory can simulate situations that seldom occur in real life and that suffer from bias and unreliability in personal reporting.

The Ethics of Social Research

During the early 1970s, several scandalous cases of unethical medical and biological research came to public attention. One of them was a medical study designed to measure the extent to which the side effects of birth control pills are psychological rather than physical. The physicians involved in the study reasoned that if the effects were psychological, they would occur among women who thought they were taking the pill, whether they were or not. To test this hypothesis, they recruited a group of women who were interested in contraception and gave half of them real birth control pills and half of them sugar pills. All of the women thought they were taking the real pill. The results showed that the side effects were more pronounced among the group taking the real pill, thus substantiating a physical cause. Of course, one particular side effect—pregnancy—was much more pronounced among the women taking the sugar pill.

The physicians involved in this study were unconcerned about the effect an unwanted pregnancy might have on their subjects; their only concern was learning about the side effects. When asked why they didn't explain the experiment to the subjects, the physician in charge said, "If you think you could explain [this experiment] to these women, you haven't met Mrs. Gomez from the West Side" (cited in Seaman 1972).

A similar lack of concern is evident in a study sponsored by the U.S. Public Health Service between 1932 and 1972. In the so-called Tuskegee study, more than 400 African American men who had syphilis were misled about the nature of their illness and deliberately left untreated so that the doctors could observe what happened to untreated syphilis (Jones 1981). It is probably no accident that in both of these experiments the subjects were members of minority groups.

These scandalous cases of unethical research resulted in immediate demands for increased ethical training for scientists and more supervision of research ethics. The federal government instituted new requirements for all federally funded studies using human subjects; researchers conducting a study were to demonstrate that the subjects would not come to any physical, psychological, or social harm through participation in the study. Most universities and professional associations followed this pattern and established strict codes of ethics and committees designed to review research proposals that involve human subjects.

Compared with medical and biological research, sociological research raises few ethical issues. Assuming that investigators follow a few general guidelines, people who participate in sociological research—who answer questions, have their behavior observed, or participate in sociological experiments—are not likely to be harmed by the research.

Ethical Principles

The American Sociological Association is currently revising its code of ethics (Kennedy 1996). The most recent (1989) code of ethics includes the following principles for dealing with human subjects:

1. "Individuals, families, households, kin and friendship groups that are subjects of research are entitled to rights of biographical anonymity." This means that research reports should not be written in such a way that readers can identify anyone whose behaviors or attitudes are being described.
2. "Sociologists should take culturally appropriate steps to secure informed consent and to avoid invasions of privacy. Special actions may be necessary where the individuals studied are illiterate, of very low social status, and/or unfamiliar with social research." This means that subjects must understand fully the proposed research and must freely and voluntarily agree to participate.
3. "The process of conducting sociological research must not expose subjects to substantial risk of personal harm." Personal harm is interpreted broadly to include social embarrassment, possible legal penalties (for example, for admitting to drug use), job loss, and mental trauma, as well as physical harm.
4. When research subjects are promised that their behavior or replies will be anonymous or confidential, the researcher must take every possible step to make certain that all confidences are kept and that no respondent's name can be linked by others to his or her information.

Ethical Issues in Practice

To a significant extent, the ethical issues raised in sociological research depend on the type of research design used. Here we review briefly the major ethical issues associated with experiments, survey research, and participant observation.

Ethical Issues in Sociological Experiments. In spite of the fact that experimental work in other fields was the cause of the ethical furor, ethics is only a minor issue in sociological experiments. The major issue that arises in experimental research is that deception is almost always involved. Although the subjects do agree to take part, they are seldom told what the purpose is; to tell them would reduce the validity of their responses. Whether they were trying to help or confound the experimenter, they would be responding to something other than the experimental stimulus.

Experimenters are usually careful to debrief their subjects after the experiment, explaining the real purpose and answering any questions, and the deception is not usually important or challenging. Special criticism, however, has been directed at experiments such as the Schwartz and Gottlieb one reported in this chapter. Such experiments expose the subjects to a stressful situation and, for those who don't help, to painful self-knowledge. This is not what the subjects bargained for when they volunteered for an experiment on ESP.

Ethical Issues in Survey Research. Survey research raises the fewest ethical questions. If I call you on the telephone, all you have to do is decline to be interviewed. I cannot interview you without your consent. Also, any time you object to a question, you can either refuse to answer it or hang up on me. At one point, there was some concern that survey research might expose people to the risk of substantial harm by putting ideas into their heads. For example, my asking you whether you have been thinking about divorce might cause you to think about it for the first time. There is no evidence that respondents are as suggestible as this, however, and most people enjoy talking about themselves as part of survey research.

Ethical Issues in Participant Observation. Some of the most serious ethical issues in sociological research concern participant observation, which is often a disguised form of research. To avoid social-desirability bias or the guinea-pig effect, researchers often try to disguise their purpose so that people will act naturally. This means, of course, that they do not ask the subjects if they are willing to be studied.

This issue has raised serious ethical questions. A classic example of the problem is Laud Humphreys's (1970) study of homosexual encounters in public bathrooms. In this study, Humphreys presented himself in the bathrooms as a "watch queen," a person who likes to watch others' sexual encounters but doesn't want to take part. Did he violate the right to privacy of his research subjects or expose them to the risk of substantial harm?

The answers are unclear. The consensus is that people do not have a right to privacy regarding their actions in public places. People who choose to have sexual encounters in public bathrooms have given up their right to privacy. They are, however, entitled to biographical anonymity; that is, their names and any biographical details that would give their identity away must be protected. Also, when "the subjects' responses, if known, would place them at risk of criminal or civil liability or . . . when the research deals with sensitive aspects of a subject's own behavior, such as illegal behavior, drug use, sexual behavior, or use of alcohol," assurance of the researcher's ability and willingness to protect confidentiality must be given to a human-subjects review committee.

How seriously do researchers take their responsibility to protect subjects' confidentiality? In 1993, Rik Scarce, a Washington State University graduate student in sociology involved in a study of animal rights activists, spent more than two months in jail for contempt of court. He had refused to provide information about his subjects to a federal grand jury investigating break-ins at university laboratories ("Sociology Grad Student Jailed" 1993).

SOCIAL APPLICATIONS

DIVORCE, POVERTY, AND FAMILY POLICY

We have seen that objectivity is basic to scientific inquiry. This means that researchers must gather and evaluate evidence without personal bias—that is, without regard for how the results match their own values or personal preferences. The purpose of each of the research principles discussed in this chapter is to ensure the researcher's objectivity.

If we assume that absolute objectivity is humanly possible, we can conclude that anyone trained in and willing to use objective research methods can scientifically study any issue or group. White researchers can objectively conduct research on African, Asian, or Native Americans, for example. We saw in this chapter that Elliot Liebow, who studied African American men on Tally's Corner, was white. Liebow's masterpiece, a classic in understanding the meanings behind the activities of respondents, assures us that even in this kind of situation, objectivity is possible. In fact, Liebow's conclusions may have been more insightful because he was able to look at his respondents "from the outside."

But questions about who can objectively study whom remain, and taking a critical approach to research requires considering them. For one thing, bias or prejudice is often unconscious. Bias can creep into the kinds of research questions we ask and how we ask them. For example, a heterosexual sociologist studying lesbian families might be inclined to compare lesbian parenting with heterosexual parenting and unintentionally imply that straight parents are "more normal." A lesbian sociologist looking into the same topic might be more inclined to ask how becoming parents affects a same-sex couple's relationship.

Bias can also sneak into the ways that researchers operationalize their variables. For instance, activists on various issues, such as childhood hunger and sexual abuse, have been accused of operationalizing their variables so that the incidences of hunger and abuse appear larger than they might otherwise. One study counting children at risk for hunger in America used the question, "Did you ever rely on a limited number of foods to feed your children because you were running out of money to buy food for a meal?" Critics argued that many parents could answer "yes" to this question even though their children are far from undernourished (Adler 1994).

Since bias can worm its way into our research in any number of ways, we need to ask ourselves how our values and social characteristics (race, gender, age, sexual orientation) might possibly affect our work. More generally, we can consider whether sociologists should research only people like themselves. Are we more likely to make bias-based mistakes when we are studying groups different from our own, groups whose experiences we cannot truly share? For example, is a sociologist who is not Native American more likely than one who is to bring bias against using hallucinogenic drugs to the study of a Native American religious peyote ceremony? Can a heterosexual sociologist study gay male or lesbian family life without prejudice? Can a lesbian sociologist research heterosexual marriage without bias? Can a pro-choice sociologist study pro-life abortion activists objectively? Can men objectively research issues that have traditionally affected primarily women—issues such as the effect of day care on children? What do you think? Who can study whom?

THINKING CRITICALLY

Can you think of a research question in which the researcher's own background might lead to bias in the research design, findings and conclusions? Do you think that a heterosexual sociologist can effectively investigate lesbian families, for instance? Would a lesbian sociologist be less likely to be biased in this case? Why or why not? As another example, can an African American sociologist study Native American religion without bias? How might the researcher's background help to foster—or to lessen—bias? What might the researcher do to help insure against bias in these cases?

SOCIOLOGY ON THE NET

The American Sociological Association has an extensive set of guidelines governing sociological research as well as the conduct of professors towards their students.

http://www.asanet.org/ethics.htm

As you browse through this selection, answer the following questions: Why was this code of ethics established? How should sociologists go about protecting the biographical immunity of research subjects? How should sociology students be protected from exploitation? And what body within the American Sociological Association is responsible for investigating charges of ethical misconduct?

Sociological research that uses the empirical or positivist approach is not universally accepted by all sociologists. Many symbolic interactionists take an alternative approach that uses the naturalistic paradigm. An excellent comparison of these two approaches can be found at the web site of the Society for the Study of Symbolic Interactionism.

gopher://corn.cso.niu.edu:70/11/acad_dept/col_of_las/dept_soci/SSSI/faqs/si

Open and read the first three selections entitled: **What is Symbolic Interactionism?, Is Symbolic Interactionism Scientific?** and **Naturalistic Inquire—Where are its Axioms?** Keeping the debate between positivistic and naturalistic methods in mind, go back and reread the sections of the chapter that deal with Liebow's research on Talley's Corner and the research on recycling by Derkson and Gartrell. Would the same results be obtained if the naturalistic paradigm were used in both studies? Would the same results be obtained if the positivistic paradigm were used in both studies? Is one approach better than the other or can each be applied with good results depending on the research situation?

The government uses survey research to learn about such things as crime, poverty and divorce. These studies are complex and very large. This allows researchers to use highly sophisticated statistics and a wide range of control variables. Once the government has analyzed the data, it is made available to social scientists for analysis. These large surveys form the basis for much of the current research and publication by sociologists. The U.S. Bureau of the Census has a description of the SIPP or Survey of Income and Program and Participation. This survey is used to analyze the economics of households and persons in the United States.

http://www.census.gov/hhes/www/sippdesc.html

How large is the sample and how often is the survey carried out? Is this a cross sectional or a panel design? How might the data from this survey be used by the government?

SUMMARY

1 Science is not a specific set of procedures but rather a way of approaching data and theory. It is objective, critical, and empirical.

2 The four steps in the research process are gathering data, finding patterns or generalizations, forming theories, and testing hypotheses. These steps form a continuous

loop, called the wheel of science. The movement from data to theory to data is called induction, and the movement from theory through hypothesis testing is deduction.

3 Scientific research focuses on variables rather than on whole individuals. When these variables are hypothesized to have a cause-and-effect relationship, the cause is called the independent variable and the effect is called the dependent variable.

4 Operational definitions specify the precise procedures through which research concepts are measured. They seldom tap the full meaning of the words we use in our theories and hypotheses.

5 Sampling is critical to social research because there is so much variability between one research subject and the next. Systematic procedures must be used to ensure that a sample is drawn from a comprehensive list of the members of a population, chosen by random procedures, and of adequate size to provide reliable data.

6 Scientific research is subjected to rigorous evaluation before it appears in scholarly journals. The blind-review process encourages critical and objective evaluations of research findings.

7 The experiment is a method designed to test cause-and-effect hypotheses deduced from theory. Although it is the best method for this purpose, it has the disadvantage of using unrepresentative samples in highly artificial conditions. It is most often used for small-group research and for simulation of situations not often found in real life.

8 Survey research is a method that asks a large number of people a set of standard questions. It is good at describing incidence, trends, and differentials for random samples, but it is not as good at describing the contexts of human behavior.

9 Participant observation is a method in which a small number of individuals who are not randomly chosen are observed or interviewed in depth. The strength of this method is the detail it provides about the contexts of human behavior and its subjective meanings; its weaknesses include lack of generalizability and a lack of verification by independent observers.

10 Sociological research is unlikely to cause substantial harm to subjects or respondents. Nevertheless, the ethics code of sociology requires that subjects' identities be carefully guarded.

SUGGESTED READINGS

BABBIE, Earl R. 1995. *The Practice of Social Research.* (7th ed.) Belmont, Calif.: Wadsworth. A textbook for undergraduates that covers the major research techniques used in sociology. Coverage is up to date, thorough, and readable.

JONES, James H. 1981. *Bad Blood: The Tuskegee Syphilis Experiment.* New York: Free Press. Covers the long history of the Tuskegee experiment mentioned in this chapter, including lessons about ethics, experimentation, and race relations in the United States.

LIEBOW, Elliott. 1967. *Tally's Corner.* Boston: Little, Brown. A classic study that provides an excellent introduction to the richness of participant observation studies.

LOFLAND, John, and Lofland, Lyn. 1984. *Analyzing Social Settings.* (2d ed.) Belmont, Calif.: Wadsworth. In case you think participant observation is a matter of just hanging around, the Loflands' text on doing fieldwork will set you straight and give you direction.

NEUMAN, W. Lawrence. 1994. *Social Research Methods: Qualitative and Quantitative Approaches*. Boston: Allyn and Bacon. A textbook for undergraduates that covers the major research techniques in sociology.

REINHARZ, Shulamit. 1992. *Feminist Methods in Social Research*. New York: Oxford University Press. A well-written review of the relationship between feminist research methods and conventional research design. Richly illustrated with examples from feminist scholarship.

CHAPTER 3

Culture

OUTLINE

PROLOGUE

Have You Ever . . . found yourself in a place or situation that was unfamiliar and wondered what in the world was going on? Maybe you've traveled to a foreign country where the language and customs are very different from what you're used to. Often, in this kind of situation, people feel somewhat unsettled. They cannot easily ask for directions, they wonder how they'll find a restroom, and they may not know what they're eating.

One way of describing the discomfort we feel at times like this is to say we're experiencing "culture shock." We're jarred or shocked emotionally and mentally because we're encountering a different culture, one that we don't understand. Because we have taken our own culture so very much for granted, all the large and little differences of another culture startle us. We worry ourselves about things that never troubled us before: Do I pick this up to eat it or try to use one of these utensils? Do I walk on the left or right side of the walk? Is this music I'm hearing or noise? Is this a worship service or a festival? May I talk now or should I be quiet? Should I line up politely for a taxi at this corner or push my way to the front of the crowd? Are these people joking with each other or angrily fighting? Do pedestrians have the right of way here, or do I need to keep every inch of myself back from the street? Are my clothes appropriate for this occasion or not?

Culture shock is most noticeable in people traveling to a country with a language and culture completely different from their own. But people can experience culture shock in their own country, too. For example, a person from a small Nebraska town might feel culture shock upon moving to New York City—and the reverse might also be true. A person invited to the home of someone in a different social class might be faced with many of the same questions as a person visiting another country.

America's growing diversity means that, especially in our large cities, we can find ourselves among ethnically diverse people whose language and customs are different enough from our own that we feel as if we're in another country. Then too, we can find ourselves among pockets, or "subcultures," of people—for example, trekkies, punks, animal rights activists—whose language may be similar to ours but whose values are different enough from our own that we are stunned—culture-shocked.

This chapter examines culture—all those beliefs, values, norms, and behaviors, as well as physical objects, that people use to fashion a way of life.

INTRODUCTION TO CULTURE

In Chapter 1, we said that sociology is concerned with analyzing the contexts of human behavior and how these contexts affect behavior. Our neighborhood, our family, and our social class provide part of that context, but the broadest context of all is our culture. **Culture** is the total way of life shared by members of a society.

Culture resides essentially in nontangible forms such as language, values, and symbolic meanings, but it also includes technology and material objects. A common image is that culture is a "tool kit" that provides us with the equipment necessary to deal with the common problems of everyday life (Swidler 1986).

Culture is the total way of life shared by members of a society. It includes not only language, values, and symbolic meanings but also technology and material objects.

Consider how culture provides patterned responses to eating. We share a common set of tools and technologies in the form of refrigerators, ovens, toasters, microwaves, and coffeepots. And, as the advertisers suggest, we share similar feelings of psychological release and satisfaction when, after a hard day of working or playing, we take a break with a cup of coffee or a cold beer. The beverages we choose and the meanings attached to them are part of our culture.

Culture can be roughly divided into two categories: material and nonmaterial. *Nonmaterial culture* consists of language, values, rules, knowledge, and meanings shared by the members of a society. *Material culture* includes the physical objects that a society produces—tools, streets, sculptures, and toys, to name a few. These material objects depend on the nonmaterial culture for meaning. For example, a stone fragment from the demolished Berlin Wall and a rock picked up on a vacation in the mountains share many common physical features: their meanings depend on nonmaterial culture.

Theoretical Perspectives on Culture

Within sociology, there are three approaches to the study of culture. The first approach treats culture as the underlying basis of interaction. It accepts culture as a given and is more interested in how culture shapes us than in how culture itself is shaped. Scholars from this approach have concentrated on illustrating how norms, values, and language guide our behavior. The second approach focuses on culture as a social product. It asks why particular aspects of culture develop. Scholars using this approach would be interested, for example, in why the content of commercial television is so different from the content of public television. How does the economic structure of television affect its products? How does the way arts are funded in the United States affect what is accepted by the public? The third approach asks

You can find both traditional and modern medicine practiced in both Peru and Zaire, among other places. In this Peruvian scene, a traditional medicine man uses herbs and religious ritual to cure illness. In sharp contrast, the techniques of modern science are being used by a team of specialists in Zaire. Despite the obvious differences among cultures, a close look shows a great many underlying similarities. Although some rely on prayer and others on antibiotic, all cultures provide some routine set of mechanisms for dealing with illness and injury.

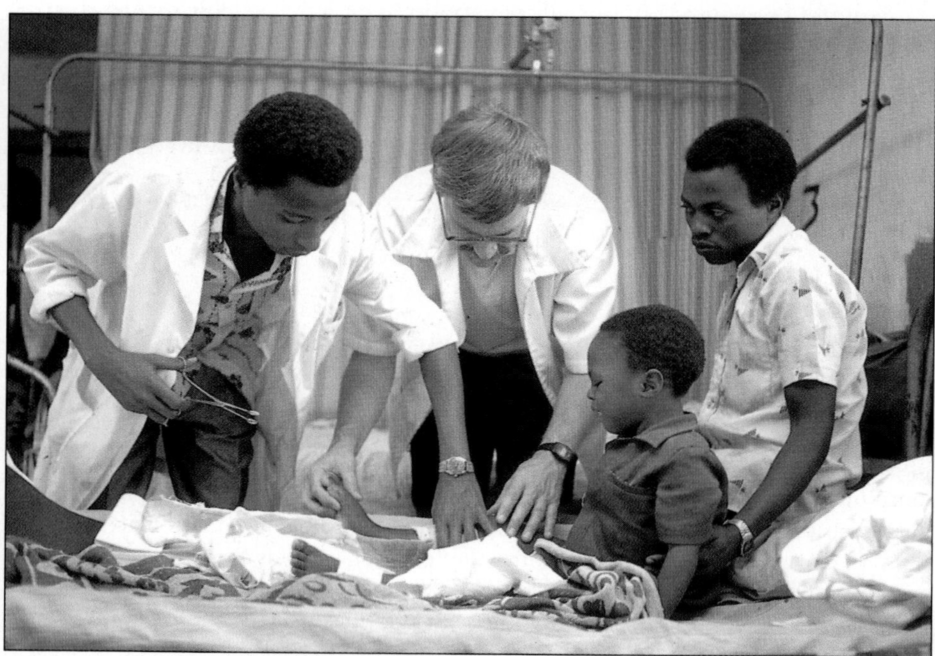

how culture is learned and communicated to newcomers. Generally, the first perspective on culture is characteristic of structural-functional theory, while conflict theorists are more interested in the determinants of culture. The third approach is characteristic of symbolic interactionism. Since not only the contents of culture but also its determinants and how it is learned are of interest to us, we will use all three perspectives.

BASES OF HUMAN BEHAVIOR: CULTURE AND BIOLOGY

Why do people behave as they do? What determines human behavior? To answer these questions, we must be able to explain both the varieties and the similarities in human behavior. Generally, we will argue that biological factors help explain what is common to humankind across societies but culture explains why people and societies differ from one another.

CULTURAL PERSPECTIVE ON BEHAVIOR

Regardless of whether they are structural functionalists or conflict theorists, sociologists share some common orientations toward culture: Culture is *problem solving*, culture is *relative*, and culture is a *social product*.

Culture Is Problem Solving. Regardless of whether people live in tropical forests or in the crowded cities of New York, London, or Tokyo, they confront some common problems. They all must eat, they all need shelter from the elements (and often each other), and they all need to raise children to take their place and continue their way of life. Although these problems are universal, the solutions are highly varied. For example, responsibility for child rearing may be assigned to the mother's brother, as is done in the Trobiand Islands; to the natural mother and father, as is done in the United States; or to communal nurseries, as is done in the Israeli kibbutz.

Whenever people face a recurrent problem, cultural patterns will have evolved to provide a ready-made answer. This does not mean that the answer provided is the best answer or the only answer or the fairest answer, merely that culture provides a standard pattern for dealing with this common dilemma. One of the issues that divides conflict and functional theorists is how these answers develop. Functionalists argue that the solutions we use today have evolved over generations of trial and error and that they have survived because they work, because they help us meet basic needs. A conflict theorist would add that these solutions work better for some people than others. Conflict theorists argue that elites manipulate culture in order to rationalize and maintain solutions that work to their advantage. Scholars from both perspectives agree that culture provides ready-made answers for most of the recurrent situations that we face in daily life; they disagree in their answer to the question "Who benefits?" from a particular solution.

Culture Is Relative. Different cultures may devise startlingly different solutions. Among the Wodaabe of Niger, for example, mothers are not allowed to speak directly to their first- or second-born children and, except for nursing, are not even allowed to touch them. The babies' grandmothers and aunts, however, lavish affection and attention on them (Beckwith 1983). The effect of this pattern of child rearing is to emphasize loyalties and affections throughout the entire kin group rather than just with respect to one's own children or spouse. This practice helps ensure that each new entrant will be loyal to the group as a whole. Is it a good or a bad practice? That is a question we can answer only by seeing how it fits in with the rest of the Wodaabe culture. Does it help the people meet recurrent problems and maintain a stable society? If so, then it works; it is functional. The idea that each cultural trait should be evaluated in the context of its own culture is called **cultural relativity.** A corollary of cultural relatively is that no practice is universally good or universally bad; goodness and badness are relative, not absolute.

Cultural relativity requires that each cultural trait be evaluated in the context of its own culture.

This type of evaluation is sometimes a difficult intellectual feat. For example, no matter how objective we try to be, most of us believe that infanticide, human sacrifice, and cannibalism are absolutely and universally wrong. Such an attitude reflects **ethnocentrism**—the tendency to use the norms and values of our own culture as standards against which to judge the practices of others.

Ethnocentrism is the tendency to view the norms and values of our own culture as standards against which to judge the practices of other cultures.

Ethnocentrism usually means that we see our way as the right way and everybody else's way as the wrong way. When American missionaries came to the South Sea Islands, they found that many things were done differently in Polynesian culture. The missionaries, however, were unable to view Polynesian ways as simply different. If they were not like American practices, then they must be wrong and were probably wicked. As a result, the missionaries taught the islanders that the only acceptable way (the American way) to have sexual intercourse was in a face-to-face position with the man on top, the now-famous "missionary position." They taught the Polynesians that women must cover their breasts, that they should have clocks and come on time to appointments, and a variety of other Americanisms that the missionaries accepted as morally correct behavior.

Ethnocentrism is often a barrier to interaction among people from different cultures, leading to much confusion and misinterpretation. This is a dysfunction of ethnocentrism. But ethnocentrism can be functional, too. In the sense that it represents pride in our own culture and confidence in our own way of life, ethnocentrism encourages social integration. In other words, we learn to follow the ways of our culture because we believe that they are the right ways; if we did not share that belief, there would be little conformity in society. Ethnocentrism, then, is a natural product of growing up in a culture. An undesirable consequence, however, is that we may simultaneously discredit or diminish the value of other ways of thinking and feeling.

Culture Is a Social Product. A final assumption sociologists make about culture is that culture is a social, not a biological, product. The immense cultural diversity that characterizes human societies is the product not of isolated gene pools but of cultural evolution.

Some aspects of culture are produced deliberately. Shakespeare picked up paper and pen to write *Hamlet;* some advertising executive worked to invent the Energizer bunny. Governments, bankers, and home owners deliberately commission the designing of homes, offices, and public buildings, and people buy publishing empires so that they can spread their own version of the truth. Other aspects of culture—such as our culture's ideas about right and wrong, its dress patterns, and its language—develop gradually out of social interaction. But all of these aspects of culture are human products; we are not born with them. People *learn* culture; and as they use it, they modify it and change it.

Culture depends on a unique human attribute: the capacity for language. Only through language can pieces of practical knowledge (such as, "don't use electricity in the bathtub") or ideas (such as, "God exists") be transmitted from one generation to the next. Inventions, discoveries, and forms of social organization are socially bestowed and intentionally passed on, so that each new generation potentially elaborates on and modifies the accumulated knowledge of the previous generations. In short, culture is cumulative only because of language.

Because of language, human beings are not limited to the slow process of genetic evolution in adapting to their circumstances; cultural evolution is a human way for a species to adapt to its environment. Whereas biological evolution may require literally hundreds of generations to adapt the organism fully to new circumstances, cultural evolution allows the changes to be made within a short period of time. In this sense, cultural evolution is an extension of biological evolution, one that speeds up the processes of change and adjustment to new circumstances in the environment (van den Berghe 1978).

Biological Perspective on Behavior

As the continued popularity of *National Geographic* attests, the wide diversity of human cultures is a continuous source of fascination. Costumes, eating habits, and living arrangements vary dramatically. It is tempting to focus on the exotic variety of human behavior and to conclude that there are no limits to what humankind can devise. A closer look, however, suggests that there are some basic similarities in cultures around the world—the universal existence of the family, religion, aggression, and warfare. When we focus on these universals, then cultural explanations are likely to be supplemented with biological explanations.

Within the past two decades, sociology has witnessed renewed interest in the role of evolution and biology in human behavior. A relatively new field, **sociobiology,** is the study of the biological basis of all forms of human behavior (E. O. Wilson 1978; Wright 1994). Sociobiology makes the assumption that humans and all other life forms developed through evolution and natural selection. According to this perspective, change in a species occurs primarily through one mechanism: Some individuals are more successful at reproduction than others. As the offspring of successful reproducers grow in number relative to those of the less successful reproducers, the species comes to be characterized by the traits that mark successful reproducers.

Sociobiology is the study of the biological basis of all forms of human behavior.

Sociobiologists define successful reproducers as those who have more children and raise more of them until they are old enough to reproduce themselves (Daly and Wilson 1983). Among the characteristics of human society that are thought to be related to these reproductive strategies are altruism and male/female differences in mating behavior, parenting, and aggression. For example, sociobiologists suggest that parents who are willing to make sacrifices for their children, occasionally even giving their lives for them, are more successful reproducers; by ensuring their children's survival, they increase the likelihood that their own genes will contribute to succeeding generations. Thus, sociobiologists argue that we have evolved biological predispositions toward altruism (an unselfish concern for others), *but only insofar as our own kin are concerned* (Troost and Filsinger 1993; Wright 1994).

Sociobiology provides an interesting theory about how the human species has evolved over 10,000 years. Most of the scholars who study the effect of biology on

In trying to uncover what may be the common nature of our species, social scientists have emphasized the search for cultural universals. They have reasoned that if the same pattern is evident in all societies, it may have a biological or genetic basis. Dominance is one such universal pattern; another is mothering. In all societies, caring for children is an important role of women.

human behavior, however, are concerned with more contemporary questions, such as, "How do hormones, genes, and chromosomes affect human behavior?" Joint work by biologists and social scientists is helping us to understand how biological and social factors work together to determine human behavior.

This approach is nicely illustrated in a recent set of studies by Udry, who asked how the biological changes that accompany puberty interact with social structures to determine adolescent sexuality. Using blood and urine analyses to determine hormone levels, Udry found that boys and girls with higher levels of testosterone reported higher levels of sexual behavior and sexual interest. He also found that strict family supervision, especially having a father in the home, could override the effect of hormonal change among girls (Udry 1988, 1994). This suggests that social *and* biological factors play a role in adolescent sexuality.

We are at the same time animals and social products. It is a false dichotomy to ask whether culture or biology determines behavior; instead, our behavior represents an intersection between the two. One leading sociologist has argued, for example, that "ignorance of biological processes may doom efforts" to create equality between women and men or to decrease the burden that child care poses for women (Rossi 1984, 11). Only by recognizing and taking into account the joint effects of culture and biology can we have the complete picture of the determinants of human behavior.

The Carriers of Culture

We turn next to three vital aspects of nonmaterial culture—language, values, and rules, or norms—and show how they shape both societies and individuals.

LANGUAGE

The essence of culture is the sharing of meanings among members of a society. The chief mechanism for this sharing is a common language. Language is the ability to communicate with symbols—orally or in writing.

What does *communicate with symbols* mean? It means that when you see the combinations of circles and lines that appear on your textbook page as the word *quiet*, you are able to understand that it means "silent, hushed, or unmoving." On a different level, it means that the noise we use to symbolize "dog" brings to your mind a four-legged domestic canine. Almost all communication is done through symbols. Even the meanings of physical gestures such as touching and pointing are learned as part of culture.

Scholars of sociolinguistics (the relationship of language to society) point out that language has three distinct relationships to culture: Language embodies culture, language is a framework for culture, and language is a symbol of culture (Fishman 1985a, 1985b).

Language Embodies Culture. Language embodies the values and meanings of a society as well as its rituals, ceremonies, stories, and prayers. Until you share the language of a culture, you cannot participate in it (Fishman 1985b).

A corollary is that loss of language may mean loss of a culture. Currently, many Native American languages have fewer than 40 speakers, most of whom are more than 50 years old. When these people die, they will take their language with them, and important aspects of those Native American cultures will be lost. This vital link between language and culture is why many Jewish parents in the United States send their children to Hebrew school on Saturdays. It is why U.S. law requires that people must be able to speak English before they can be naturalized as American citizens. To participate fully in Jewish culture requires some knowledge of Hebrew; to participate in American culture requires some knowledge of English.

Language As a Framework. Language gives us capabilities, but it also shapes and confines us. The **linguistic relativity hypothesis** associated with Whorf (1956) argues that the grammar, structure, and categories embodied in each language affect how its speakers see reality and that, therefore, reality *is* different for speakers of, say, English and Lakota (Sioux). The argument is that our thinking and perceptions are in some ways fashioned by our linguistic capacities (Fishman 1985b).

Linguistic relativity hypothesis argues that the grammar, structure, and categories embodied in a language affect how its speakers see reality.

Because language shapes how we perceive reality, one way to change perceptions is to change the words we use. For example, several years ago, a number of black leaders began to use "African American" instead of "black." This shift in language usage symbolized a distinction based on cultural heritage (African) rather than on color. It moved us away from thinking about physical differences to thinking about cultural differences. Obviously, this shift has important implications for understanding the causes of current racial inequalities and for framing policy responses. Because most of the research reported in this text is based on respondents identifying themselves by race (black or white), however, we sometimes use the racial labels in reporting research results.

Language As a Symbol. A common language is often the most obvious outward sign that people share a common culture. This is true of national cultures such as

French and Italian and subcultures such as youth. A distinctive language symbolizes a group's separation from others while it simultaneously symbolizes unity within the group of speakers (Cobarrubias 1983). For this reason, groups seeking to mobilize their members often insist on their own distinct language.

Values

Values are shared ideas about desirable goals.

After language, the most central and distinguishing aspect of culture is **values,** shared ideas about desirable goals. Values are typically couched in terms of whether a thing is good or bad, desirable or undesirable (Williams 1970, 27). For example, many Americans believe that a happy marriage is desirable. In this case and many others, values may be very general. They do not, for example, specify what a happy marriage consists of.

Some cultures value tenderness, others toughness; some value cooperation, others competition. Nevertheless, because all human populations face common dilemmas, certain values tend to be universal. For example, nearly every culture values stability and security, a strong family, and good health. There are, however, dramatic differences in the guidelines that cultures offer for pursuing these goals. In societies like ours, an individual may try to ensure security by putting money in the bank or investing in an education. In many traditional societies, security is maximized by having a large number of relatives. In societies such as that of the Kwakiutl of the Pacific Northwest, you would achieve security not by saving your wealth but by giving it away. The reasoning is that all of the people who accepted your goods would be under an obligation to you. If you ever needed help you would feel free to call on them, and they would feel obliged to help. Thus, although many cultures place a value on establishing security against uncertainty and old age, the specific guidelines for reaching this goal vary. The guidelines are called *norms*.

Values are shared sentiments about what is good and worthy. Because values rest on sentiments rather than on evidence, it is difficult to resolve conflicts between them. Value conflicts cannot be resolved by scientific evidence. When sociologists study values, they do not address issues of right or wrong but instead consider issues such as, "What effect does this value have on behavior?" and "What factors cause people to embrace this value?"

Norms

Shared rules of conduct are **norms.** They specify what people *ought* or *ought not* to do, think, or feel. The list of things we ought to do sometimes seems endless. We begin the day with, "I'm awfully tired, but I ought to get up," and many of us end the day with, "This is an awfully good show, but I ought to go to bed." In between, we ought to brush our teeth, eat our vegetables, work hard, love our neighbors, and on and on. The list is so extensive that we may occasionally feel that we have too many obligations and too few choices. Of course, some things are optional and allow us to make choices, but the whole idea of culture is that it provides a blueprint for living, a pattern to follow.

Norms are shared rules of conduct that specify how people ought to feel, think, and act.

Folkways are norms that are the customary, normal, habitual ways a group does things.

Mores are norms associated with fairly strong feelings of right and wrong; they carry a moral connotation.

Laws are rules that are enforced and sanctioned by the authority of government. They may or may not be norms.

Norms vary enormously in their importance both to individuals and to society. Some, such as fashions, are powerful while they last but are not central to society's values. Others, such as those supporting monogamy and democracy, are central to our culture. Generally, we distinguish between two kinds of norms: folkways and mores.

Folkways. The word **folkways** describes norms that are simply the customary, normal, habitual ways a group does things. This concept covers relatively permanent customs (such as fireworks on the Fourth of July) as well as short-lived fads and fashions (such as wearing your baseball cap backwards or sideways).

A key feature of all folkways is that there is no strong feeling of right or wrong attached to them. They are simply the ways people usually do things. For example, if you choose to have hamburgers for breakfast and oatmeal for dinner, you will be violating American folkways. If you sleep on the floor or dye your hair purple, you will also be deviating from the usual pattern. If you violate folkways, you may be regarded as eccentric, weird, or crazy, but you will not be regarded as immoral or criminal.

Mores. Some norms are associated with strong feelings of right and wrong. These norms are called **mores** (more-ays). Whereas eating oatmeal for dinner may only cause you to be considered crazy (or lazy), there are some things you can do that will really offend your neighbors. If you eat your dog or spend your last dollar on liquor when your child needs shoes, you will be violating a more. At this point, your friends and neighbors may decide that they have to do something about you. They may turn you in to the police or to a child protection association; they may cut off all interaction with you or even chase you out of the neighborhood. Not all violations of mores result in legal punishment, but all result in such informal reprisals as ostracism, shunning, or reprimand. These punishments, formal and informal, reduce the likelihood that people will violate mores.

This Tennessee barber shop provides explicit written instruction about appropriate language. For the most part, the norms that govern daily life are not as clear as this. Nevertheless, most of us pick up a pretty good understanding of these and other norms by observing how others behave and watching others' reactions to our behavior. Negative sanctions such as stares of surprise or consternation, grimaces of distaste, and shrugs of disdain will tell us we have crossed a sensitive line and violated a norm.

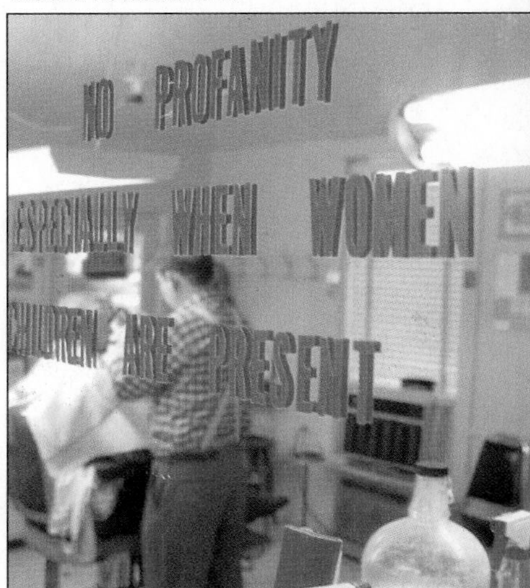

Laws. Rules that are enforced and sanctioned by the authority of government are **laws.** Very often, the important mores of society become laws and are enforced by agencies of the government. If the laws cease to be supported by norms and values, they are either stricken from the record or become dead-letter laws, no longer considered important enough to enforce. Not all laws, of course, are supported by public sentiment; in fact, many have come into existence as the result of lobbying by powerful interest groups. Laws requiring the wearing of seat belts, for example, are not a response to social norms. Similarly, laws regulating marijuana use in the United States owe their origins to lobbying by the liquor industry. In these cases, laws are trying to create norms rather than respond to them. The section, "Focus on Measurement" looks at how feminists research culture.

FOCUS ON MEASUREMENT

How Feminists Research Culture

"FEMINIST METHODS SEEK TO DOCUMENT WOMEN'S LIVES AND ACTIVITIES, TO APPRECIATE WOMEN FROM THEIR OWN PERSPECTIVES, AND TO UNDERSTAND WOMEN IN SOCIAL CONTEXT."

Feminist scholars research culture from the perspective of feminist theory. Generally, feminist theory can be considered a type of conflict theory, which sees problems in the distribution of power and scarce resources. Feminist theory views males as the more powerful and females as the less powerful in a society or group.

We can define feminist methods as those research methods that are used by feminist scholars (Reinharz 1992). Feminist methods seek to document women's lives and activities, to appreciate women from their own perspectives, and to understand women in social context.

Some feminist researchers have been critical of surveys. They see surveys as valuing surface facts over genuine understanding. From these researchers' viewpoint, it is a "male thing" to presume one knows enough about a topic to deduce hypotheses before gathering data. Feminist methods for studying culture are more likely to be qualitative and inductive. These methods purposely foster the researchers' own intuitive insights, rather than trying to minimize the part intuition and personal experience play in their work. Feminist methods include field studies, interviews, oral histories, and case studies, among others.

Feminist field studies focus on the women in the culture under investigation. Feminist field-workers maintain that while other sociologists may incorporate females into their analyses of a culture, the women often are presented as secondary characters: Their lives are not fully explored. Feminist methods seek to remedy this situation. For example, one feminist sociologist, Kristen Yount, did fieldwork among underground coal miners. Her interest was the condition of women miners, and she had noted how little research had been done about them. While living in mining communities for several months; going to parties, ball games, and company picnics; and observing work in the mines, Yount discovered a culture of sexual harassment among miners. Women miners adapted to this culture of harassment by playing one of three roles: Lady, Flirt, or Tomboy (Yount 1991).

Besides highlighting women, feminist methods often center on behaviors that have traditionally been overlooked in cultural research. For example, feminist researchers have examined mundane cultural objects such as Girl Scout manuals to study how girls learn values and norms regarding women's behavior. Nancy Henley (1985) analyzed interrupting behavior in conversations. Henley taped same-sex and mixed-sex pairs in conversation and found that an amazing proportion (96 percent) of interruptions were made by male speakers. Henley had uncovered one of many gender-related norms in our culture.

While maintaining scholarly rigor, feminist methods often challenge traditional rules. For example, feminist researchers sometimes invent words and con-

SOCIAL CONTROL

From our earliest childhood, we are taught to observe norms, first within our families and later within peer groups, at school, and in the larger society. After a period of time, following the norms becomes so habitual that we may not even be aware of them as constraints. We do not think, "I ought to brush my teeth or else my friends and family will shun me"; instead, we think, "It would be disgusting not to brush my teeth, and I'll hate myself if I don't brush them." For thousands of generations, no human considered it disgusting to go around with unbrushed teeth. For most Americans, however, brushing their teeth is so much a part of their feeling about themselves, about who and what kind of person they are, that they would disgust themselves by not observing the norm.

Through indoctrination, learning, and experience, then, many of society's norms come to seem so natural that we cannot imagine acting differently. No soci-

FOCUS ON MEASUREMENT

cepts, changing the language of social scientific analysis. Words such as *herstory*, *foresisters*, and *motherwork* are examples.

Just as they fashion new words, feminist researchers also develop new methods. For instance, Ximena Bunster (1977) and her colleagues decided that interviewing was not the best technique for understanding the culture of working-class women in Lima, Peru. Instead, they took some 3,000 Polaroid pictures of women throughout the city. These included street vendors, market women with fixed stalls, maids, and factory workers. Then, in a method they called the talking-pictures technique, Bunster and her colleagues encouraged the women to explain the pictures, telling which best depicted their culture and why. As their research progressed, these women helped choose the 120 photos that appeared in the final report.

Another new technique associated with feminist methods involves dramatic role playing. Here, people are asked to role-play their responses to a question or situation, rather than simply to register their answers on a written questionnaire.

A more common—and more inventive—way in which feminist researchers try to ascertain what is really going on in a culture involves creating group diaries. In this method, researcher and respondents meet over a period of time to discuss and write down their individual experiences in what gradually becomes a collective written volume. In one instance, a computer-based group diary was set up in a graduate sociology department (Reinharz 1992). Working anonymously and individually, female students entered their observations about being women in the department. The result was a collaborative case study on the values and norms concerning women graduate students in that department.

These new techniques illustrate another factor that typically distinguishes feminist methods: A study is a joint effort. From data gathering to finished product, the efforts tend to be collaborative between the respondents and the researchers. Collaboration further implies concern that respondents will somehow benefit from the research they take part in. To this end, feminist methods actively seek to influence public policy. Feminist scholars view their research as political as well as scientific (Reinharz 1992).

By concentrating on the women in a culture, researching behaviors that sociologists have traditionally overlooked, developing new concepts and new research techniques, and emphasizing collaboration and political activism as well as scientific rigor, feminist research methods have begun to change the ways in which sociology studies culture.

ety relies completely on this voluntary compliance, however, and all encourage conformity by the use of **sanctions**—rewards for conformity (positive sanctions) and punishments for nonconformity (negative sanctions). Some sanctions are formal, in the sense that legal codes identify specific penalties, fines, and punishments that are to be meted out to individuals found guilty of violating formal laws. Formal sanctions are also built into most large organizations to control absenteeism and productivity. Some of the most effective sanctions, however, are informal. Such positive sanctions as affection, approval, and inclusion encourage the observance of norms, whereas such negative sanctions as a cold shoulder, disapproval, and exclusion discourage norm violations.

Sanctions are rewards for conformity and punishments for nonconformity.

Despite these sanctions, norms are not always a good guide to what people actually do, and it is important to distinguish between normative behavior (what we should do) and actual behavior. For example, our own society has powerful mores

Concept Summary Values, Norms, and Laws

Concept	Definition	Example From Marriage	Relationship to Values
Values	Shared ideas about desirable goals	It is desirable that marriage include physical love between wife and husband.	
Norms	Shared rules of conduct	Have sexual intercourse regularly with each other, but not with anyone else.	Generally accepted means to achieve value
Folkways	Norms that are the customary ways a group does things	Share a bedroom and a bed; kids sleep in a different room.	Optional but usual means to achieve value
Mores	Norms associated with strong feelings of right and wrong	Thou shalt not commit adultery.	Morally required means to achieve value
Laws	Rules enforced by the authority of government	Illegal for husband to rape wife; sexual relations must be voluntary.	Legally required means; may or may not be supported by norms

supporting marital fidelity. Yet research has shown that nearly half of all married men and women in our society have committed adultery (Thompson 1983). In this instance, culture expresses expectations that differ significantly from actual behavior. This does not mean the norm is unimportant. Even norms that a large minority, or majority, fail to live up to are still important guides to behavior. The discrepancy between actual behavior and normative behavior—termed *deviance*—is a major area of sociological research and inquiry (see Chapter 8).

Dominant Cultural Themes

Cultural patterns generally contain dominant cultural themes. These themes give a distinct character and direction to a culture; they also create, in part, a closed system. New ideas, values, and inventions are usually accepted only when they fit into the existing culture or represent changes that can be absorbed without too greatly distorting existing patterns. The Native American hunter, for example, was pleased to adopt the rifle as an aid to the established tradition, or culture theme, of hunting. Western types of housing and legal customs regarding land ownership, however, were rejected because they were alien to a nomadic and communal way of life.

Weber was one of the first sociologists to stress the importance of cultural themes as a determinant of cultural variability. He suggested that cultures tend to select and reinterpret the new ideas that are meaningful to them. If they can find no point of correspondence between the new ideas and their usual ones, then the new ideas are abandoned (Gerth and Mills [1946] 1970, 63).

Society

Culture is a way of life. In some places, it cuts across national boundaries and takes in people who live in two, three, or four nations. In other places, two distinct cultures (English and French in Canada) may coexist within a single national boundary. For this reason, we distinguish between cultures and societies. A **society** is the population that shares the same territory and is bound together by economic and political ties. Often, the members share a common culture, but not always.

A **society** is a population that shares the same territory and is bound together by economic and political ties.

SUBCULTURES AND COUNTERCULTURES

Sharing a culture does not mean there is complete homogeneity. When segments of society face substantially different kinds of social environments, subcultures emerge to help them adapt to these unique problems. **Subcultures** share in the overall culture of society but also maintain a distinctive set of values, norms, lifestyles, and sometimes even language. Examples of American subcultures are ethnic and religious subcultures, regional subcultures, and youth subcultures.

Subcultures are groups that share in the overall culture of society but also maintain a distinctive set of values, norms, lifestyles, and even language.

Countercultures are groups that have values, interests, beliefs, and lifestyles that conflict with those of the larger culture. This theme of conflict can be observed for groups as varied as hippies, punks, delinquent gangs, revolutionary Marxists, and such religious sects as the Moonies, the Hare Krishnas, the Old Order Amish, and even the early Christians. Countercultures reflect radical revisions in and rejection of taken-for-granted ways of life (Berger 1981).

Countercultures are groups having values, interests, beliefs, and lifestyles that are opposed to those of the larger culture.

AN EXTENDED EXAMPLE: DEAFNESS AS CULTURE

Most of us view deafness as undesirable, even catastrophic (Dolnick 1993). At best, we see being deaf as a medical condition to be remedied. Throughout most of European history, being deaf was considered an inalterable calamity. Deaf persons, unable to participate in language, experienced profound isolation that was believed to be inevitable. The first attempts that we know of to educate deaf children came only in the 16th century. Today, we try not to exclude people who are deaf from full participation in society, but most of us still think of deafness as a disability. Indeed, many deaf persons, along with parents and teachers of deaf children, would agree.

However, some spokespersons in the deaf community maintain that deafness is not a disability but a culture (Dolnick 1993). According to this argument, deaf

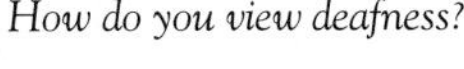
How do you view deafness?

people comprise a subculture like any other and no more need a cure for their condition than do African Americans, Hispanic Americans or Asian Americans. Spokespersons for this viewpoint capitalize the D in deaf. The uppercase D is intended to symbolize the idea that deaf people share a culture rather than merely a medical condition. The essence of deafness, they maintain, is not the inability to hear but a culture based on their shared language, American Sign Language (ASL). ASL is not just a way to "speak" English with one's hands. It is a rich and varied language of its own, different from any other language and complete with its own rules for grammar, puns, and poetry.

It is estimated that ASL is the principal language of half a million people in the United States. More than 90 percent of all deaf children in the United States today were born deaf or lost their hearing as babies before learning a spoken language. Because they have never heard words spoken, learning to read lips is very difficult for them. Many have embraced American Sign Language; they see ASL as the "natural" language of the deaf. Deaf children of deaf parents learn ASL in ways that are similar to the ways in which hearing children learn a spoken language. Where hearing babies begin jabbering nonsense syllables, for example, deaf babies of parents who sign begin "babbling" nonsense signs with their fingers (Dolnick 1993).

A shared language, as we have seen, encourages a collective cultural identity with shared values. Deaf culture values deafness and rejects the belief that medical treatment for deafness means progress. Studies show that not all deaf people would elect to hear. Asked whether she would prefer to hear, Roslyn Rosen, president of the National Association of the Deaf, answered that she doesn't want to be "fixed." From this viewpoint, being deaf is not a disability, and talk of "cures" is offensive. Indeed, deafness-as-culture activists see the use of an inner-ear operation that can reverse some children's deafness as "child abuse" or "genocide." Some see mainstreaming deaf children in the public schools as inappropriate because it results in their educational and emotional "mutilation" (Dolnick 1993, 41). Deaf people wonder why anyone would expect them to deny their roots when every other cultural group proudly celebrates its traditions and history. Why stigmatize the speakers of a particular language as disabled?

Deaf culture activists denounce "oralism," the ethnocentric attitude that values only spoken language. Oralism, activists point out, has a long history. In 1880 in Milan, Italy, an international meeting of educators affirmed "the incontestable superiority of speech over sign" and voted to banish sign language from deaf education. The ban, remembered to this day among the deaf, was effective. In 1867, every American school for the deaf taught in ASL. Ten years later, not one did.

With deaf people, as with others, shared cultural identity can be ethnocentric. For example, one young deaf man explained that if he happened to strike up a relationship with a hearing person, he's probably be negatively sanctioned by his parents: They would ask: "What's the matter? Aren't your own people good enough for you?" And they might warn that hearing people will "take advantage of you" (Dolnick 93, 40).

Partly as a result of such informal sanctioning, deaf people tend to marry each other—another step in solidifying community and culture. Interestingly, disputes have recently erupted among deaf persons about who is to be considered more authentically deaf. To be the deaf child of deaf parents has higher status within deaf culture, because this is as deaf as one can be. To be born deaf is "better" than to have gone deaf after learning to speak.

Thinking of deafness as culture illustrates many of the points made earlier in this chapter. For instance, culture is problem solving. Deaf culture embodies a way to solve the problem of human communication. As a result, deaf culture counters isolation and gives people a feeling of identity. Using American Sign Language shapes deaf people's experience, reminding them and reinforcing the fact that they are deaf and—more importantly—that they are participating in a common culture.

We have also seen that culture is relative. How deaf people communicate, along with their values regarding that communication, differ from the communication behaviors and values of hearing people. Culture is relative because it is a social product. Through interaction, deaf persons fashioned American Sign Language, then taught it to their children and others. Today, through interaction, deaf persons influence and teach each other—and the hearing as well—about their values, attitudes, and norms.

Culture and Cultural Diversity in the United States

U.S. culture is a unique blend of complex elements. It is a product of the North American environment and of the land's original inhabitants, its early and recent immigrants, its technology, and its place in history. It closely resembles the cultures of two close cousins, Australia and Canada, with which it shares vital characteristics. All three are new countries settled by diverse groups of immigrants yet dominated by English culture, all three began with uncrowded spaces and a sense of frontier, and all three now offer high levels of industrialization and wealth. Yet U.S. culture is distinguishable from the cultures of these first cousins as well as from those of more distant relatives in Europe, with which the United States shares a general Western culture.

U.S. Norms and Values

In 1970, one analyst of American values concluded that the following values were of central significance in understanding U.S. culture (Williams 1970):

- *Achievement and success:* Ours is a competitive society in which getting ahead, especially in our occupations, is assumed to be a good thing.
- *Activity and work:* The United States is a land of continuous hustle and bustle where being active (or "proactive," as the term has evolved for the 1990s) is a good thing. Work is a good thing in itself, over and above the need to work to earn a living.
- *Moral orientation:* It's not that Americans conform to some agreed-upon moral code. Rather, they *judge* behavior (their own and others') according to ethical principles.
- *Humanitarian mores:* Being kind and helpful, both personally and as a nation, as in the case of spontaneous aid in mass disasters, is a good thing.
- *Efficiency, practicality, and progress:* Americans look for better ways to get things done—ways that waste little time and promise a better future. Doing a term paper on a manual typewriter when computers are available is "backward" and not a good thing.

- *Material comfort:* Feeling no pain, being physically comfortable, taking vacations, watching movies with happy endings—in short, maximum pleasure with minimum effort—is a good thing.
- *Freedom, equality, and democracy:* Liberty and independence to develop an individual personality, equality of opportunity for all, and representative government in which the majority rules are good things.
- *External conformity:* Being individualistic in the battle for success is a good thing, but external conformity—for example, dressing, talking, and furnishing your home in much the way everyone else does—is a good thing, too.

To a significant extent, these values continue to guide Americans. However, which values are emphasized over others and how the values influence our norms and behaviors shift from generation to generation.

Changing Values. As the United States has changed to a wealthy, urban, industrialized society, some values have shifted in priority. The results of one fairly recent survey of American values are presented in Figure 3.1. They show that having a good family life is ranked number one, closely followed by having a good self-image, good health, and a feeling of accomplishment. There is a wide consensus across America that these are worthwhile goals. Old and young, women and men, Easterners and Westerners all put these values at the heads of their lists.

These survey and other indicators suggest that there have been three major shifts in American values: a reduced emphasis on work for its own sake, a growing emphasis on self-fulfillment, and a greater emphasis on consumerism.

FIGURE 3.1
AMERICAN VALUES

SOURCE: The Gallup Reports, March/April 1989, 36; see also Marks 1995.

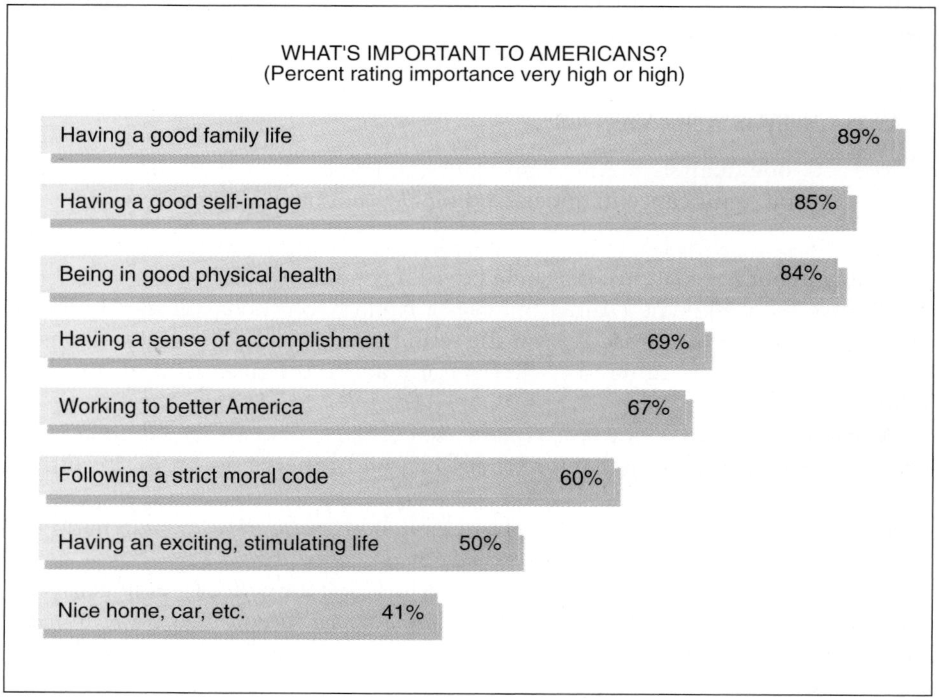

WHAT'S IMPORTANT TO AMERICANS?
(Percent rating importance very high or high)

Having a good family life 89%
Having a good self-image 85%
Being in good physical health 84%
Having a sense of accomplishment 69%
Working to better America 67%
Following a strict moral code 60%
Having an exciting, stimulating life 50%
Nice home, car, etc. 41%

REDUCED EMPHASIS ON WORK FOR ITS OWN SAKE. Valuing work for its own sake (that is, seeing work as redeeming or noble in and of itself) places emphasis on the intrinsic value of work. Americans still worry about their jobs, work long hours, and take pride in being hard-working. But there are signs of decreased emphasis on the intrinsic value of work and increased emphasis on striking a balance between work and free time. Complementing this trend is a growing emphasis on leading a self-fulfilling life through active leisure.

SELF-FULFILLMENT. Increasingly, achievement and success apply to more than work and family. More and more, it is considered desirable, even obligatory, to identify and develop one's personal potential (Glassner 1989). Evidence for this value shift is found in the explosion of the fitness industry, higher education, and self-help groups. There is concern that it might also be reflected in the high rate of divorce: Individuals are less willing to sacrifice their personal achievements for their children or family. This value is not new to American culture—it is the value that drove Daniel Boone and countless frontier explorers to abandon their families to see what was on the other side of the mountain—but it may recently have become more important to a larger share of the population.

CONSUMERISM. Material comfort is a consistent value among Americans. As a society, they have always been distinguished by the wealth of their material goods. However, many observers believe that, at least through the 1980s, acquiring material possessions grew in importance. Both the U.S. government and individual consumers are criticized for having let their debts mount and their savings slide as they pursued the goal of "more, *now*." Studies of first-year college students during that decade showed continuing declines in support of values related to social concern and helping others but sharp increases in commitment to earning a very great deal of money (Astin and Associates 1989). It remains to be seen whether we will judge the 1990s as different.

Observers from many points on the ideological spectrum have been critical of the shifts in American values (Bellah and Associates 1985). They worry that the grow-

Very high levels of consumption and waste are part of the American way of life. We buy an enormous quantity of things (gadgets, food, electronic equipment, and so on) that we don't really need; many of these purchases end up in the garbage or stuffed in the backs of closets. Although individual shoppers may be able to afford to pay for their purchases, the manufacture and disposal of these wasteful and wasted goods imposes burdens on our environment.

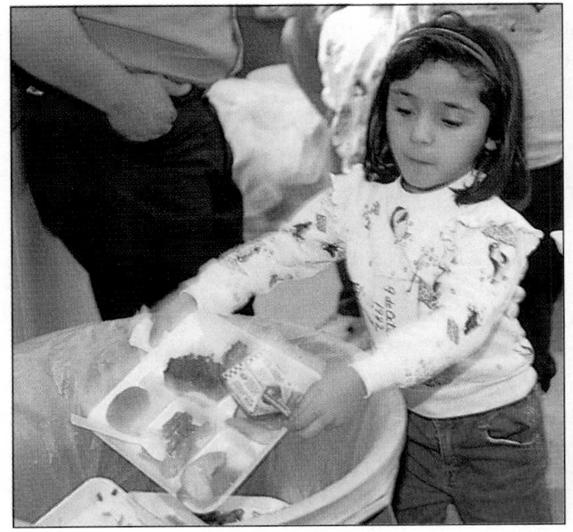

ing emphasis on consumerism and self-fulfillment may mean a reduced willingness to support families and communities and to help the less fortunate, and they suggest that changes in American values may be an important reason why the United States has fallen behind some other industrialized nations in its productivity.

Signs of Continuity. Recent decades have witnessed a sharp change in many of the norms guiding American life. Premarital sex, childless marriages, working mothers, interracial marriages—many of the things that were considered plainly wrong two decades ago are increasingly being accepted by the American public.

It would be incorrect, however, to assume that a massive change in American norms and values had taken place. American norms now allow wider variation in the means people use to achieve the value of a happy family life, but the value itself hasn't changed. Some people may court success by selling dope, others by becoming stockbrokers; some may seek self-fulfillment through drugs, others through prayer. Across America, however, there remains broad consensus that achievement, belief in God, and a strong family are good things.

Cultural Diversity

Cultural diversity refers to the social situation in which several fairly dissimilar peoples with distinct ways of life exist together in one society.

In spite of general agreement on dominant cultural values, cultural diversity is increasingly apparent in the United States. **Cultural diversity** refers to the social situation in which several fairly dissimilar peoples with distinct ways of lives exist together in one society. Even before Europeans arrived in America, the Native American culture was markedly diverse. With immigration—first from Europe, starting in the 16th century, and then from other places—diversity naturally increased.

Over the past two decades, however, U.S. culture has grown still more diverse. As an illustration, a visitor to a large U.S. city today might wander past any of the following places of worship: Jewish synagogues; Hindu, Buddhist, or Taoist temples; and churches including African Methodist Episcopal, Baha'i, Ukrainian Byzantine, Asian American Christian, Greek Orthodox, Armenian Apostolic, Lutheran Protestant, Mormon, Roman Catholic, and Metropolitan Community (for gays and lesbians). There are two principal causes for this cultural diversity: immigration and social activism.

First, recent immigration trends have resulted in greater cultural diversity. During the three decades between 1960 and 1990, 15 million people either entered the United States as legal immigrants or were granted permanent residence. During the 1980s alone, 7 million were counted. This figure approached the 8.8 million who entered the United States during the first decade of this century, when immigration to the United States was at its peak (U.S. Immigration and Naturalization Service 1994).

But numbers alone do not tell the story. In 1965, the U.S. government enacted legislation abolishing an immigration quota system that had favored European applicants. As a result, most immigrants today are from Latin America and Asia (U.S. Immigration and Naturalization Service 1994). This is in contrast with the past, when the vast majority of immigrants arrived from Europe.

Figure 3.2 shows projected changes in U.S. racial/ethnic composition and compares actual figures for 1980 with projections for 2020 and 2080. While non-Hispanic whites made up nearly 80 percent of the U.S. population in 1980, their proportion is expected to decrease to just under 65 percent by 2020 and to 50 per-

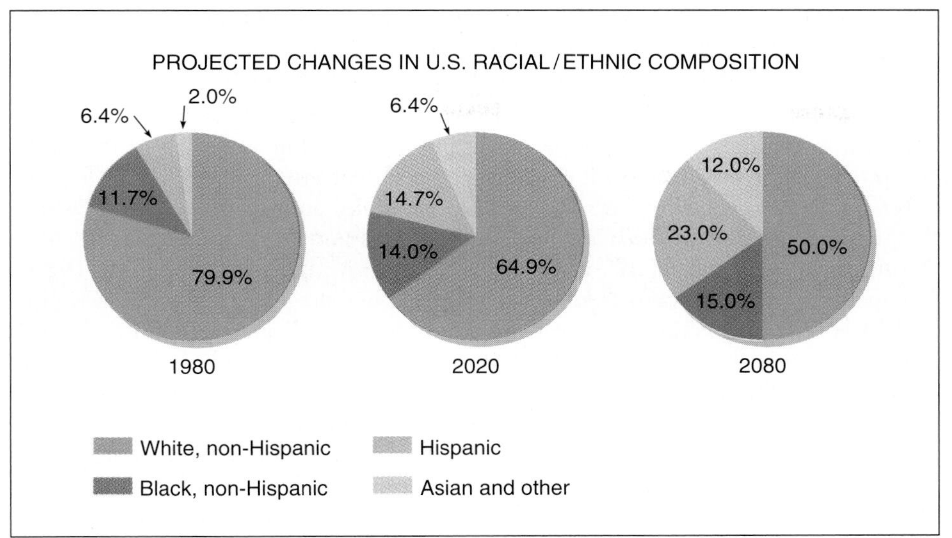

FIGURE 3.2
CHANGING COMPOSITION OF U.S. POPULATION

If annual immigration remains at 1 million and if fertility remains low, the racial and ethnic composition of the U.S. population will change substantially in the decades ahead. The most noticeable effect will be a sharp rise in the proportion who are Hispanic and a corresponding decrease in the proportion who are white non-Hispanic.

SOURCE: Bouvier and Gardner 1986; Davis, Haub, and Willette 1983, 39; O'Hare 1992.

cent by 2080. The proportion of non-Hispanic blacks will grow somewhat, while the proportion of Hispanics will climb from about 6 percent in 1980 to nearly 15 percent in 2020. The fastest growing category is composed mainly of Asians, whose percentage in the total U.S. population is expected to triple between 1980 and 2020 and to almost double again by 2080 (O'Hare 1992).

Then too, each of these diverse categories of people—non-Hispanic whites, African Americans, Hispanics, Asians, and others—is itself culturally diverse. Among the Asians, for example, are Filipinos, Koreans, Chinese, Japanese, Vietnamese, Cambodians, Laotians, Indians, and Pakistanis. From the Middle East have come Palestinians, Iraqis, Iranians, Lebanese, Syrians, Egyptians, and Israelis. Hispanics come primarily from Mexico but also from throughout Central and South America. In addition, many immigrants have recently come from Africa, Jamaica, and Haiti; and many have come from Eastern European nations since the breakup of the Union of Soviet Socialist Republics.

In addition to recent immigration patterns, social activism has made for a heightened awareness of cultural diversity. Civil rights activists for various ethnic groups have insisted that all Americans, regardless of their ethnic origins, be allowed openly to take pride in their cultural heritage while at the same time participating fully in society. Moreover, some groups in our society—for example, people with disabilities, gay males, and lesbians—have increased not in number but in visibility. Activists for these groups have challenged the dominant cultural value of external conformity and demanded the right to be seen and heard. Much of this diversity will be covered in greater detail in subsequent chapters on deviance, race and ethnicity, social class, education, religion, and so on.

Subcultures. There are hundreds and perhaps thousands of subcultures in the United States. These subcultures generally share major American values, but they are distinguished by their own vocabularies and folkways. Nearly every major occupational group can be regarded as a subculture, and there have been scholarly studies of the subcultures of coal miners, police officers, musicians, correctional officers, and physicians. Body-builders have their own subculture, as do jocks, professors, and model railroaders. In addition, of course, are subcultures built around shared religious or ethnic identity.

Among U.S. subcultures are those based on region. The stereotypes we hold about people from the Midwest, California, or the South reflect beliefs about regional subcultures. We expect people living in these different parts of the country to have some distinctive values, norms, speech patterns, and lifestyles. To some extent, these expectations are correct. For example, empirical studies show that people who live in the South *are* more likely to be frequent church attenders, have strong religious affiliations, and hold traditional attitudes (Hurlbert 1989). Compared with Americans from other regions, they are more likely to own guns and to approve of using violence to settle interpersonal quarrels (Ellison 1991). They also have distinctive speech patterns that serve to symbolize their group membership. These differences and many others reflect a unique cultural legacy that makes them, while a part of the larger American culture, distinct.

From hoedowns to bar mitzvahs, opening nights to Monday night football, the members of a subculture share rituals and ceremonies that unite them with others of their kind and separate them, if only marginally, from others. Whenever people share unique circumstances, they develop unique vocabularies and folkways to deal with them.

White supremacist groups such as the Ku Klux Klan (KKK) are examples of American countercultures. Although they usually present themselves as returning to traditional values, literally and figuratively wrapping themselves in the American flag, such groups want revolutionary changes in American society: They want to kill or deport Jews, African Americans, and communists; they want women out of politics and the labor force. Because such groups challenge the values of the larger culture, they are seen as not just different but dangerous and threatening.

American Countercultures. There are relatively few well-publicized countercultures active in the United States today. The countercultures of the past generation—the Moonies, hippies, and radical and revolutionary political factions—have largely passed from the public stage. Two exceptions are some music-related countercultures, such as punk and death metal, and white supremacists.

Punk is a form of counterculture that deliberately attempts to "offend, shock, and attack" mainstream society by dress, music, and behavior (Baron 1989; Blair 1993). Some punks are just part-timers who dye their hair purple and listen to death rock but nevertheless manage to go to school or hold a job. True punks, however, angrily reject all contact with straight society. They refuse to work or take organized charity; they live angry and sometimes hungry lives on the streets. Recent death metal culture glorifies death and violence.

Perhaps an even more dangerous counterculture consists of the white supremacists. There are several distinct organizations of white supremacists, ranging from the American Nazi Party and the Aryan Nation through small bands of armed extremists. All are characterized by extreme racism, anti-semitism, patriarchy, and patriotism. Although they typically believe that they are reestablishing traditional American values, their enthusiasm for killing all Jews, African Americans, and communists and for driving women back into the kitchen appall most Americans. As a result, most Americans see them not as a harmless variation of American culture (a subculture) but as a threat to American culture (a counterculture).

Elite Culture/Popular Culture

Social scientists always make a point of saying that culture refers to the norms and values of society as a whole, not only to elite culture, as in art, opera, and symphony. Yet culture is influenced by social class, and the norms and values of the upper classes tend to be perceived as superior to the norms and values of the lower classes (Blau 1986). If we prefer an AM station to National Public Radio, Monday night football to *Swan Lake*, Garth Brooks to Bach, we recognize that these preferences have less prestige.

Because of this variety in tastes, sociologists make a distinction between elite culture (the culture of the educated upper classes) and popular culture (what the rest of us like). Both cultures express the values and aesthetics of their distinct constituencies. Sociologists who study popular culture focus on such cultural forms as cowboy poetry (Nothof 1994), murder mysteries, gothic romances, quilts, television programming, and sports. This focus on the material and nonmaterial culture of ordinary women and men helps us to understand both the solidarities and the divisions in society (Mukerji and Schudson 1986). Popular culture may not always have high prestige, but, as Mick Jagger said, "I know it's only rock and roll, but I like it."

Sports and Popular Culture. If you are like many people, you enjoy sports in your leisure time. Many of us watch sports on TV, go to games and meets, and play tennis or golf in the time left after school or work. We may even chat about sports on the Internet. Many observers note that sports reinforce norms and values important to society, like competition and teamwork. Sports metaphors, such as "There is no I in TEAM," teach us that success is achieved by putting the group above individual glory. Slogans like "Winners never quit and quitters never win" reinforce values of competition and working hard to get ahead.

The **mass media** are the carriers of impersonal communications directed toward a very large (mass) audience.

Nevertheless, organized sports have been criticized for several things. One is that they encourage potentially harmful male aggression (Messner 1992). Another is that they direct minority students, particularly African American males, toward athletics—instead of academics—as a road to success. However, only a very small minority of high school athletes are able to support themselves through athletics (Harris 1994). In fact, according to one estimate, only one of 12,000 high school athletes will earn money as a professional athlete; among those who make it, the average professional career lasts only three years ("Career Statistics" 1990). Nevertheless, the importance of sports in teaching and reinforcing norms and values, along with the role of sports in symbolizing and integrating communities, are important reasons why nearly every nation has encouraged athletics.

The Media and Popular Culture. Another way in which you may be like many people is in watching quite a bit of TV. Television is an important component of the **mass media**—the carriers of impersonal communications directed toward a very large (mass) audience. Mass media developed along with communications technology. First newspapers and later electronic media—radio, movies, television, and videocassette recorders (VCRs)—spread information on a mass scale.

There is no question that electronic media have become a significant component in American popular culture, as well as the popular cultures of other countries. Almost every home in the United States (98 percent) now has at least one TV set. (Only 94 percent of U.S. households have telephones.) About 61 percent of U.S. households now are wired for cable TV. VCRs, found in three quarters of U.S. homes, are the fastest-selling new appliance in history (U.S. Bureau of the Census 1994, Tables 882 and 1373). The average household turns on a television for about seven hours each day. Most U.S. children watch television regularly long before they learn to read, and school children spend almost as much time in front of TVs as they do in their classroom (APA 1993).

Movies, radio, and "the tube" both reflect and influence a culture's values, norms, attitudes, and behaviors. Besides entertaining us, the electronic media report the news, identify public problems, and provide a forum for debate. As discussed in Chapter 6, television helps to teach individuals society's values and norms.

Since its emergence in the 1950s, television has generally reflected popular, as opposed to elite, culture. But today there is growing concern that how TV creates and portrays popular culture is not all that good for us. Politicians and others warn that prime-time television series and daytime talk shows convey "antifamily" and violent values, attitudes, and norms (Alter 1995; Kolbert 1995). Research studies on how TV watching affects people are inconclusive. But they increasingly suggest that TV violence influences children—and maybe adults as well—to be more violently aggressive toward their peers and others (Murr and Rodgers 1995). Noting the concern over what's on TV leads us to think about the more general question of how American culture is produced.

The Production of American Culture

In the United States, the production of popular culture is driven by market forces (Fox 1995). Commercial value and market size determine what goes on television and radio, into movie theaters, and onto store shelves. Elite culture also requires financial backing, but it is less dependent on mass appeal. Elite culture generally relies on funding from wealthy patrons and from governments. City, county, state, and federal governments subsidize galleries, museums, public television, and theaters; they also give direct grants to individual artists, writers, dancers, and playwrights.

In 1989, a major controversy arose over federal funding for the arts when a government-sponsored exhibition included a photograph entitled "Piss Christ," showing a crucifix floating in a jar of urine; another picture in the same exhibition showed children in erotic poses. Critics were outraged that tax dollars had gone to support the exhibition. They believed a large portion of the public would find the pictures blasphemous, in poor taste, offensive, and definitely not art. In response to the controversy, Congress agreed to bar federal funds from any art deemed to be obscene or to denigrate a religion, race, ethnic background, age group, or handicap (Greenfield 1995). Critics of the legislation argue that this was censorship and that the government should not be in the business of determining cultural expression. More recently, Newt Gingrich, Speaker of the House of Representatives, and some of his colleagues have proposed cutting virtually all funding to the arts and to National Public Radio as well (Gingrich 1995).

Arts funding is only the tip of the iceberg. In 1992, the combined expenditures of federal, state, and local governments were well over $2 trillion (U.S. Bureau of the Census 1994, Table 463). Whether this money was spent on education, highways, missiles, or health care affects American culture. Furthermore, what ethnic groups and other subcultures benefited (or did not benefit) from government expenditures affects cultural diversity in the United States. Similarly, laws, from tax laws to civil rights laws, affect our culture. In the Applications in Diversity section, we explore more recent governmental attempts to influence culture and cultural diversity by legislating language use.

APPLICATIONS IN DIVERSITY

SHOULD THE U.S. HAVE AN OFFICIAL LANGUAGE?

Language is the primary carrier of culture. For ethnic subcultures, it is especially important as a symbol of shared ties. This shared language is essential to maintaining such aspects of culture as religion, ceremonies, and art. Some students of language would argue that attempts to substitute the dominant group's language for the subgroup's language are equivalent to an attempt to eliminate the subgroup's culture.

In the United States, this is an especially controversial issue. The issue can be stated simply: Should we or should we not pass the English Language Amendment (ELA) to the Constitution? The amendment reads:

> The English language shall be the official language of the United States.

Some people are startled to find out that English is not already the official language of the United States. When our constitution was created in the 18th century, the writers considered and rejected an official language stipulation, believing that forced linguistic conformity was antidemocratic. Subsequently, the courts have consistently interpreted the Constitution to support people's right to speak the language of their choice, based on the First Amendment to the Constitution, which guarantees freedom of speech and freedom of religion. In recent years, the right has been given additional support by the Civil Rights Act, which states that equal protection of the law shall not be denied on the basis of race or national origin.

In the early 1980s, U.S. policy moved toward greater recognition of people's right to speak the language of their choice. It was this movement, supported by the courts, that made ELA an issue. Current rights for non–English speakers are supported by the courts in four situations (Keller 1983): the voting booth (ballots must be printed in a second language if more than 5 percent of the voters in an area speak a single non-English language and are not literate in English); the courtroom (people have the right to be tried in their own language); the classroom (if a sizable minority of students cannot get equal opportunity in education because of a language barrier, instruction must be offered in their language at least on a transitional basis, usually interpreted as the first three grades); and the radio (broadcasts must be available in an alternative language if many residents of a community are non–English speakers). In addition, many state governments, especially those of California and New Mexico, give non–English speakers further rights, such as rights to take driver's license tests and to receive other government services in their language.

The alternative language that is causing most of the concern is Spanish. The issue is not particular to Spanish or the current wave of Mexican immigrants, however. Other linguistic groups that have recently settled in large numbers in particular communities, such as Koreans in the Los Angeles area, have also felt the pressures imposed by local ELA-type enactments. The situation is similar to that in the early part of this century, when many people were concerned about floods of European immigrants whom some felt to be too slow in learning English.

Supporters of the ELA claim that it will help unify the United States and eliminate what they believe to be the false signal sent by bilingual education, that you can make it in America without learning English. Opponents argue that the ELA violates the basic rights of individuals. They propose an amendment that would recognize the right "to preserve, foster, and promote their respective historical, linguistic, and culture origins. . . .No person shall be denied the equal protection of the laws because of culture or language" (Hornblower 1995).

So far, Congress has not voted on the ELA.

THINKING CRITICALLY

Do you think that the United States should have one official language? Why or why not? Do you think that immigrants to the United States should be strongly encouraged to adopt English as their everyday language? Should they also be encouraged to retain their native language? Why or why not?

SOCIOLOGY ON THE NET

In your text, the authors discuss "deaf culture." They state that through interaction, deaf persons influence each other—and the hearing as well—about their values, attitudes and norms. One place where the deaf culture is available to all is on the Internet.

`http://deafworldweb.org`

Once you have reached the **home page**, click on the **search button**. Click in the **top box** and when the cursor appears type ***deaf and culture*** in the space provided. Activate the **search button** at the bottom of the screen. Browse through the selections. Note the selection on **guest comments** and how the Internet has helped to transmit the deaf culture to both the deaf and hearing alike. Browse a bit more and note the **DWW news** as well as the **deaf culture of the bi-week**.

If culture is problem solving, how does this site help the deaf solve their problems? As you read about cochlear implants and other deaf issues, how might the deaf culture promote ethnocentrism? How might being a member of the hearing promote ethnocentrism about these same issues and topics?

Feminist methods seek to document women's lives and activities, to appreciate women from their own perspectives and to understand women in social context. An excellent place to see feminist research in action is the Feminist Research Center.

`http://www.feminist.org/research/1_public.html`

After browsing the **web site**, open the section entitled **The Feminist Chronicles**. Scroll down to **Part II** and browse through the **events, issues** and **backlash** sections from **1953 through 1993** including the **Epilogue**. Notice how these narratives seek to document women's lives, to appreciate women from their own perspectives and to understand the women's movement in social context. What issues existed in the 1950s that gave rise to "woman's liberation"? What issues remain today from that first set of concerns? What is the backlash against and what categories of people and organizations constitute the backlash?

SUMMARY

1. Culture includes all of the material and nonmaterial products of society. It can be conceived of as a tool kit that provides us with the ideas and technology to deal with the common problems of everyday life.

2. Generally, structural functionalists take culture as a given and ask how it affects us; conflict theorists ask about the social forces that produce culture. Symbolic interactionists focus on how culture is created, then passed on, through symbols and learning.

3. Culture is problem solving, relative, and a human creation. Language is a unique human attribute that makes culture uniquely human.

4. A relatively new field, sociobiology, urges us to recognize that human behavior may be shaped by biology and evolution as well as by culture. Human behaviors

linked to successful reproduction, such as mate selection and parenting, are especially likely to be genetically encoded.

5 Language, or symbolic communication, is a central component of culture. Language embodies culture, serves as a framework for perceiving the world, and symbolizes common bonds.

6 Norms (mores and folkways) specify appropriate behavior for reaching socially valued goals. Laws may or may not be norms. Although most of us behave as expected because we accept our society's norms as right, sanctions also encourage conformity.

7 The cultures of large and complex societies are not homogeneous. U.S. culture is increasingly diverse. Subcultures with distinct lifestyles and foilkways develop to meet unique regional, class, and ethnic needs. Occasionally, countercultures develop to challenge the dominant culture.

8 Americans say that they value the family, good health, a good self-image, and a sense of accomplishment. Three shifts in American values over the last generation are more emphasis on self-fulfillment, a reduced emphasis on work for its own sake, and greater emphasis on consumerism.

9 U.S. culture is far from homogeneous; in addition to the split betwen popular culture and elite culture, there are many regional, racial and ethnic, and age subcultures. Among contemporary American coutnercultures are punks and white supremacists.

SUGGESTED READINGS

BELL, Robert W., and Bell, Nancy (eds.). 1989. *Sociobiology and the Social Sciences*. Lubbock, Tex.: Texas Tech Press. A collection of essays applying the sociobiological perspective to topics such as family violence, sexual attraction, and single parenting.

BELLAH, Robert N., and Associates. 1985. *Habits of the Heart: Individualism and Commitment in American Life*. Berkeley: University of California Press. A critical look at contemporary American values. The authors argue that an emphasis on individual fulfillment at the expense of commitment is damaging to society and to personal integration.

Journal of Popular Culture. Bowling Green, Ohio: Popular Culture Association. The official journal of the Popular Culture Association, this can be a good read. Pick up an issue and browse.

KEPHART, William M., and William W. Zellner. 1994. *Extraordinary Groups: The Sociology of Unconventional Life-Styles*. (4th ed.) New York: St. Martin's Press. A fascinating tour of some of the most interesting subcultures and countercultures in the United States, both past and present: the Amish, gypsies, Father Divine, and Jehovah's Witnesses. Painless sociology—the application of basic concepts and theory to truly extraordinary groups.

O'HARE, William P. 1992. *America's Minorities—The Demographics of Diversity. Population Bulletin* 47 (4) (December). Washington, D.C.: Population Reference Bureau.

SIMONSON, Rick, and Scott Walker. 1988. *Multi-Cultural Literacy: Opening the American Mind*. Saint Paul: Graywolf Press. An important collection of essays from prominent American authors and artists from diverse ethnic backgrounds covering what it is like to be part of a subculture in the United States. A powerful book.

Sociology of Sport Journal. A journal intended to stimulate and communicate research, critical thought, and theory development on issues pertaining to the sociology of sport. This journal is probably in your school library, and browsing through an issue or two could be interesting.

WILLIAMS, Robin W., Jr. 1970. *American Society*. (3rd ed). New York: Knopf. A classic analysis of American culture, society, and institutions, especially the dominant values operating in society after World War II.

YINGER, Milton J. 1982. *Countercultures: The Promise and the Peril of a World Turned Upside Down*. New York: Free Press. An examination of various social groups characterized by values and norms that are contradictory to the dominant values and norms of society.

CHAPTER 4

Social Structures and Institutions

OUTLINE

PROLOGUE

Have You Ever . . . gone to a party and been asked what your year is in school, what your major is, or where you work? People who meet for the first time often ask each other questions like these. They're not just being nosy; they're getting to know each other. When people ask you such questions, they are asking about the roles you play. They can use your answers as probable indicators of others things about you.

The roles that people play indicate how they spend their time and what they are likely to be interested in. If you say you play football, I can assume you might want to talk about whether the defense or the offense is more important in winning a game. If you say you work at the local pizza joint, I can hope to talk to you about who hangs out there.

In addition, knowing some roles you play means being able to bet on the rules you follow. If you say you live in an apartment, I can assume you pay your rent. If you tell me to play in a band, I can assume you show up for practice.

At work and in rock bands—even at the party where you're being asked these questions—shared rules, or norms, evolve. Sets of shared norms comprise roles. Taken together, everybody's roles and patterned ways of behaving are called social structure. In this chapter, we explore the concept of social structure and show how it helps us understand our own behavior and society.

SOCIAL STRUCTURE: THE CONCEPTUAL FRAMEWORK

Many of our daily encounters occur in patterns. Every day, we interact with the same people (our family or co-workers) or with the same kinds of people (sales clerks). These patterned relationships, these common dramas of everyday life, are called social structures. Each of these dramas has a set of actors (mother/child or buyer/seller) and a set of norms that define appropriate behavior for each actor.

Formally, **social structures** are recurrent patterns of relationships. Social structures can be found at all levels in society. Friendships, football games, families, and corporations all fall into patterns that are repeated day after day or game after game. Some of these patterns are reinforced by formal rules or laws, but many are maintained by force of custom.

A **social structure** is a recurrent pattern of relationships.

The patterns in our lives are both constraining and enabling (Giddens 1984). If you would like to be free to work on your own schedule, then you will find the nine-to-five, Monday-to-Friday work pattern a constraint. On the other hand, preset patterns provide convenient and comfortable ways to handle many of the routine aspects of daily life. They help us get through crosstown traffic, find dating partners or spouses, and raise our children.

The analysis of these patterns, or social structures, revolves around three concepts: status, role, and institution. In this section, we introduce this conceptual framework, and in the remainder of the book, we apply the framework to recurrent patterns from deviance to college graduation.

Status

A **status** is a specialized position within a group.

An **achieved status** is optional, one that a person can obtain in a lifetime.

An **ascribed status** is fixed by birth and inheritance and is unalterable in a person's lifetime.

The basic building block of society is the **status**—a specialized position in a group. Sociologists who want to study the status structure of society include two types of statuses: achieved and ascribed. An **achieved status** is an optional position that a person can obtain in a lifetime. Being a father or president of the PTA is an achieved status. An **ascribed status** is a position fixed by birth and inheritance; it is unalterable in a person's lifetime. Sex and race are examples of ascribed statuses.

The range of statuses available in a society and the distribution of people and rewards among these statuses set the stage for further relationships (Blau 1975). Sociologists who use status to analyze social structures are typically concerned with four issues (Blau 1987; Blau and Schwartz 1984).

1. *Identification*. What statuses are available in a society? Does this society, for example, have a distinct status of physician or teacher or ex-convict? What ascribed statuses—for example, what racial or ethnic categories—does this society recognize?
2. *Distribution*. What is the distribution of people among these statuses? Do 90 percent of the population hold the status "farmer"; or, as in the contemporary United States, are only 3 percent farmers? The relative size of each status shapes the opportunities open to people who occupy these statuses.
3. *Consequences*. How do rewards and resources differ among statuses? Does it matter whether one is a physician or a farmer, male or female, married or single?
4. *Combinations*. What combinations of statuses are possible? Can one be a female and a physician, or is this combination impossible or unlikely? Understanding the processes that make some combinations of statuses more likely than others is a central concern for sociology. For example, why did the physician status traditionally overlap with the statuses of white and male?

A Case Study: The Social Structure of Race. If we analyze the major achieved and ascribed statuses in our society along these four dimensions, we develop an understanding of how our lives are patterned by status membership. To illustrate this approach, we apply it to racial status and ask how holding one particular racial status—being African American—affects patterned relationships in the United States.

Identification. How many racial statuses are there in the United States? The 1990 census asked us to sort ourselves into one of five racial categories: American Indian or Alaska native, Asian or Pacific Islander, Black, White, or other (U.S. Bureau of the Census 1995, p. 4). Although the labels may change, the same question appears on many of the otπher forms you fill out, as well as on almost every social survey. The apparent consensus on which statuses are important and the nearly universal degree of concern over our racial status tell us a great deal about how race affects our relationships. It is interesting, for example, that the government is barred from asking about our religious status but appears to show almost an insatiable concern about which of these five racial statuses we occupy.

Distribution. The numerical distribution of the population among statuses may either encourage or discourage certain patterns of behavior. In 1990, for example, the census identified 2 million black residents in New York City but only 12 black residents in Worland, Wyoming. This means that in New York City, black residents may choose to restrict almost all of their associations to others of the same race: There are black neighborhoods, schools, doctors, grocery stores, and so on. In Worland, this is not possible. In New York City, there are two whites for every black; in Worland, the ratio is 742 to one. This means that a quarter of all whites in New York city *could* marry or be best friends with a black person; in Worland, it is impossible for more than a few whites to be linked closely with a black resident. To the extent that the numerical distribution of people among statuses restricts (or encourages) their interactions, we say that their behavior is socially structured. (The effect of sex ratios in schools or on army bases is another example of how the relative numbers of people in various statuses can structure interactions.)

CONSEQUENCES. On nearly every measure that we might choose, there is a substantial inequality in rewards and resources between blacks and whites in the United States. Black unemployment is twice that of whites; the percent living below the poverty level is three times higher; the infant mortality rate is twice as high; the likelihood of being murdered is six times higher. These facts demonstrate that substantial disadvantage is attached to holding the status "black" in American society. Obviously, racial status is consequential and has an enormous influence on the structure of daily experiences.

COMBINATIONS. Forty years ago, racial statuses overlapped considerably with educational and occupational statuses. Being black meant having much less education and very different kinds of jobs than whites. Today, knowing a person's racial status is not such an accurate guide to his or her other statuses. Nevertheless, 31 percent of all nurse's aides and orderlies in the United States but only 3 percent of all physicians are black (U.S. Bureau of the Census 1993a, 405–407). Understanding the processes through which this continued overlap of racial, political, and economic statuses is maintained is the focus of Chapter 11.

ROLES

The status structure of a society provides the broad outlines for interaction. These broad outlines are filled in by **roles,** sets of norms that specify the rights and obligations of each status. Roles provide the normative dimension of social structure; they define how people who occupy specific statuses *ought* to act and feel toward one another.

A **role** is a set of norms specifying the rights and obligations associated with a status.

The relationship between statuses and roles can be nicely illustrated through a theatrical metaphor: The set of statuses within a group is equivalent to the cast of characters, and roles are equivalent to the scripts that define how the characters are expected to relate to one another. Generally, there is much more variability in roles than in statuses. For example, whether we analyze kindergartens, high schools, or universities, there are two primary statuses: teachers and students. The roles attached to these statuses, however, vary dramatically from one type of school to the next.

This language from the theater helps to make a vital point about the relationships between status and role: People *occupy* statuses, but they *play* roles. This distinction is helpful when we analyze how structures work in practice—and sometimes why they don't work. A man may occupy the status of teacher, but he may play the role associated with it very poorly.

Factors Affecting Role Performance. Social structure is a concept designed to account for the patterns that appear in human behavior. Taken to extremes, it suggests a machine-like conformity in which we play the parts we are assigned. Within the general pattern, however, there are many variations. Not everyone who occupies the status "teacher" will play the role the same way. Some of these variations in role behavior are socially structured; others occur as individual actors negotiate their own roles. In this section, we cover four structural factors that affect role performance: compatibility of roles, adequacy of role definitions, existence of appropriate sanctions, and availability of resources.

COMPATIBILITY OF ROLES. Sometimes people fail to fulfill role requirements despite their best intentions. This failure is particularly likely when people are faced with incompatible demands owing to multiple or complex roles. Sociologists distinguish between two types of incompatible role demands: When incompatible role demands develop within a single status, we refer to **role strain;** when they develop because of multiple statuses, we refer to **role conflict.**

Role strain is caused by incompatible role demands within a single status. **Role conflict** is caused by incompatibility between the roles of two or more statuses held by an individual.

Some of the clearest examples of role strain, or incompatible role demands within a single status, occur in the family. For example, parents' responsibilities include supporting their children economically and emotionally, teaching them, and disciplining them. Many parents face role strains when their provider role interferes with their role of being there when their children need them. The simultaneous demand to provide loving support and discipline can also be a source of strain.

People also may find it difficult or impossible to meet all of their role expectations when role conflict—role incompatibility between the demands of two or more statuses—occurs. College students, for example, who try to combine school with work or marriage, or both, often discover that the role demands of one status interfere with the expectations of another. Not surprisingly, a spouse may expect a little attention in the evening, whereas the student role obliges one to stay at the library or lock oneself up in the bedroom to read. An employer is likely to demand

Football games offer a graphic metaphor of social structure. The 11 people on the team occupy 11 different statuses, each associated with a relatively unique role. Quarterbacks have one role to play and tight ends have another.

overtime at Christmas, which is when a student needs time off to prepare for final exams. In circumstances such as these, it becomes almost inevitable that a person will fail to meet some role obligations. Even with the best will in the world, the person is likely to be regarded as a disappointment by his or her teachers, employer, or spouse.

ADEQUACY OF ROLE DEFINITIONS. We cannot expect people to fulfill expectations that we haven't made clear. Thus, one prerequisite for good role performance is clear communication about role requirements. New college students, for example, are often confused about what is expected of them. Instructors frequently open class with the statement that no attendance will be taken and that it is entirely up to the student whether to attend class; a significant portion of each freshman class makes the mistake of thinking that this means that attendance is unimportant. In cases such as this, the likelihood of good role performance can be markedly improved by advance training and by a clear spelling out of the expectations associated with each role.

EXISTENCE OF APPROPRIATE SANCTIONS. People must be motivated to meet their role obligations by a system of sanctions. When there is little reward for proper role performance, people become more lax about meeting expectations. For example, if you have ever had a teacher who waited two months to return a major paper and then returned it, apparently unread, with an "OK" on the last page, you know how the absence of rewards can drastically reduce your motivation to put out your best effort. As students, parents, teachers, and employees, we are more likely to fulfill our role obligations if successful performance is adequately rewarded and poor performance results in unpleasant consequences.

AVAILABILITY OF RESOURCES. Adequate role performance generally requires some basic resources and opportunities. A college student cannot be successful if he or she cannot afford to buy the books, has no time to study, or cannot understand the language the professors use or the examples they give. A parent cannot meet the obligation to support his or her children if there are no jobs or if his or her skills have become outdated and are no longer in demand.

When people have no realistic opportunity to live up to their normative obligations, then they will see role expectations as irrelevant or impossible. A case study at the end of this chapter gives a detailed example of role failure among the Ojibwa Indians of Canada, a failure that can be traced directly to such a lack of opportunity. In the case of the Ojibwa and many other Native American peoples, it is no longer possible to carry out traditional roles.

The Negotiated Order. Although there is general consensus across American society on how parents ought to behave toward each other and their children, probably no two families are alike. An important reason for this is that the norms of any social structure are never complete. For example, although the norms associated with family roles provide the broad outlines for acceptable behavior, they leave many details unresolved. Being honest and standing by your family are both norms, but what do you do when telling the truth gets your brother in trouble? What do you do when something comes up that the script doesn't cover—say, when your mother wants to get a divorce and move in with you? Although social structures give us a great deal of guidance about appropriate behavior, no role is

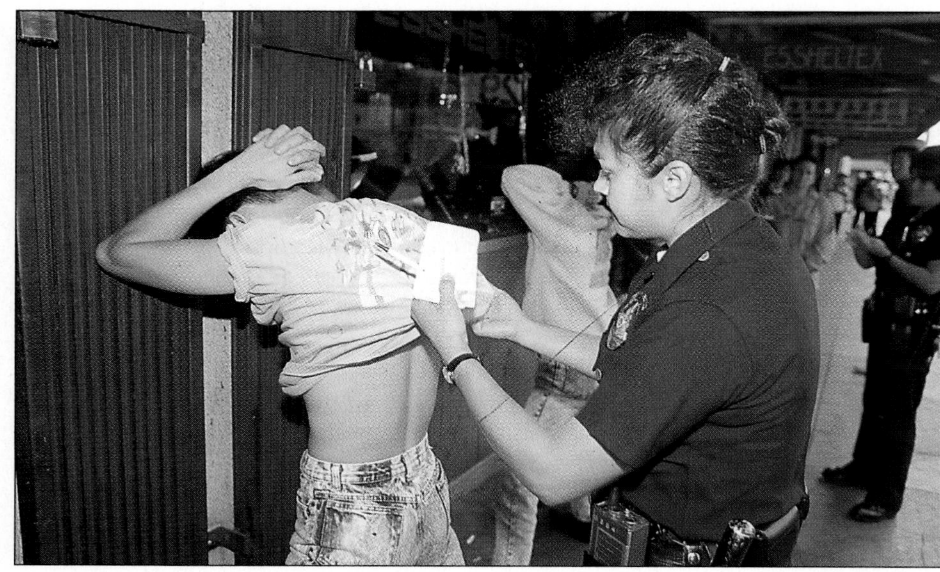

Occupational statuses are often more clearly defined than other statuses. This officer's behavior is guided by formal regulations that prescribe how she should dress, drive, speak, and act. Even in this extreme case, however, her behavior is not completely guided by formal role prescriptions. Dozens of times throughout each shift, she will face ambiguous situations that require independent decisions. Although shared social structure produces patterned regularities in the ways officers behave, there is also considerable diversity.

fully scripted. Even with the most well-defined role, there are many occasions in everyday life when we must improvise and negotiate. This means that there is variability in the ways people play their parts. This source of social heterogeneity is covered in more detail in Chapter 7.

Institutions

Social structures vary in scope and in importance. Some, such as those that pattern the Friday night poker game, have limited application. The players could change to Saturday night or up the ante, and it would not have a major effect on the lives of anyone other than members of the group. If a major corporation changed seniority or family leave policies, it would have somewhat broader consequences, not only affecting employees of that firm but setting a precedent for the way other complex organizations might come to do business. Changes in other structures, however, have the power to shape the basic fabric of our lives. We call these structures social **institutions.**

Institutions are enduring and complex social structures that meet basic human needs.

An institution is an enduring and complex social structure that meets basic human needs. Its primary features are that it endures for generations; includes a complex set of values, norms, statuses, roles, and groups; and addresses a basic human need. Embedded in the statuses and roles of the family institution, for example, are enduring patterns for dating and courtship, child bearing, and care of the elderly. Because the institution of family is composed of many separate family groups, the exact rules and behaviors surrounding dating or eldercare vary. Nevertheless, institutions provide routine patterns for dealing with predictable problems of social life. Because these problems tend to be similar across societies, we find that every society tends to have the same types of institutions. The section, "Focus on the Environment," explores how institutions affect the environment.

The Basic Institutions. Five basic institutions are found in virtually every society:

- The family, to care for dependents and rear children.
- The economy, to produce and distribute goods.
- Government, to provide community coordination and defense.
- Education, to train new generations.
- Religion, to supply answers about the unknown or unknowable.

These institutions are basic in the sense that every society provides *some* set of enduring social arrangements designed to meet these important social needs. The arrangements vary from one society to the next, sometimes dramatically. Government institutions, for example, may be monarchies or democracies or dictatorships. But all societies provide a stable social structure that has the responsibility for meeting these needs.

In simple societies, all of these important social needs—political, economic, educational, and religious—are met through one major social institution: the family or kinship group (Adams 1971). Social relationships based on kinship obligations organize production, reproduction, education, and defense.

As societies grow larger and more complex, the kinship structure is less able to furnish solutions to all the recurrent problems. As a result, some activities gradually are transferred to more specialized social structures outside the family. The economy, education, religion, and government become fully developed institutionalized structures that exist separately from the family. (The institutions of the contemporary United States are the subjects of Chapters 14 to 19.)

As the social and physical environment of a society changes and the technology for dealing with that environment expands, the problems that individuals have to face change. Thus, institutional structures are not static; new structures emerge to cope with new problems. Among the more recent social structures to be institutionalized in Western society are medicine, science, sports, the military, law, and the criminal justice system. Each of these areas can be viewed as an enduring social structure, complete with interrelated statuses and a unique set of norms and values.

In most societies, elder care is built into the family institution, and family statuses—especially that of daughter—include obligations to care for parents. Although Social Security and Medicaid have lifted the economic burden of elder support from children, most of the infirm elderly in the United States rely on their children for many direct services. Because these obligations have been institutionalized—built into statuses and roles and supported by norms and values—this help is generally forthcoming.

Institutional Interdependence. Each institution of society can be analyzed as an independent social structure, but none really stands alone. Instead, institutions are interdependent; each affects the others and is affected by them.

In a stable society, the norms and values embodied in the roles of one institution are usually compatible with those in other institutions. For example, a society that stresses male dominance and rule by seniority in the family will also stress the same norms in its religious, economic, and political system. In this case, interdependence and reinforces norms and values and adds to social stability.

Sometimes, however, interdependence is an important mechanism for social change. Because each institution affects and is affected by the others, a change in one tends to lead to changes in the others. Changes in the economy lead to changes in the family; changes in religion lead to changes in government. For example, when the number of years of school completed becomes more important than hereditary position in determining occupation, then hereditary positions will be endangered in government, the family, and religion.

Whether we are studying change or continuity, the notion of institutional interdependence leads us beyond looking at one institution at a time. To understand any single institution fully, we must understand the other institutions with which it is interdependent.

FOCUS ON THE ENVIRONMENT

Values, Institutions, and the Environment

"IF CULTURAL VALUES REGARDING THE ENVIRONMENT HAVE CHANGED, WHY HASN'T THERE BEEN A CORRESPONDING CHANGE IN SOCIAL STRUCTURES AND SOCIAL INSTITUTIONS?"

Each day, a minimum of 140 plant and animal species are condemned to extinction. Each year, about 17 million hectares of forest vanish, the equivalent of an area about half the size of Finland. The ozone layer in the heavily populated latitudes of the northern hemisphere is thinning twice as fast as scientists predicted just a few years ago (Postel 1992), and this loss is believed to explain a recent dramatic increase in the incidence of skin cancer. On Indian reservations and in minority and poor communities, exposure to toxic waste has led to a surge in the number of children born with major birth defects. How did things get this bad? What can we do about it?

Writing in 1967, a history professor, Lynn White, Jr., argued that the roots of the current ecological crisis lie in Western traditions of technology and science. White believed that a technology capable of efficiently exploiting natural resources (and other human beings, for that matter) began its unparalleled growth in medieval Europe at least partly because of the Judeo-Christian philosophy that humans are the master of nature rather than simply a part of it. White argued that the religious values of Hindus, American Indians, and traditional African cultures are quite different from Judeo-Christian values and that, at least partly for this reason, their social structures have been less ecologically destructive. The traditional Hindu and African belief that human beings are connected to all elements of nature by indissoluble spiritual and psychological bonds (Moshoeshoe 1993; Singh 1993) and the American Indian philosophy that no action should be taken without assessing its consequences for the next seven generations are simply not conducive to the wasteful lifestyles that accompanied technological and institutional developments in the West.

In U.S. culture, a belief in individualism, materialism, "progress," and growth and the idea that government should have a very limited role in controlling business complement a religious ideology that tends to emphasize humankind's dominion over all other creatures. As Weber noted, these beliefs are important cultural correlates of capitalist economic structures; as some feminists point out, they also tend to be associated with male-dominated family structures. Even though scholars debate which came first—values or technology and social institutions—and theologians question just how important Western religious values have been in destruction of the environment, research clearly shows that commitment to these dominant political and economic values is associated with lower levels of environmental concern among U.S. citizens (Dunlap and Van Liere 1984).

Despite their different histories, cultural traditions, and social structures, people living in both the industrialized West and the less developed nations of Africa and South America now show a high level of concern for environmental deterioration and widespread support for environmental protection. People in poorer countries recognize that overpopulation creates ecological problems, and residents of wealthier nations realize that technology and wasteful lifestyles have devastating consequences for the environment. Furthermore, results from an international survey indicate that a very high percentage of respondents throughout the world say they are willing to pay higher prices for goods and services if doing so will protect the environment (Dunlap, Gallup, Jr., and Gallup 1993).

If cultural values regarding the environment have changed, why hasn't there been a corresponding change in social structures and social institutions? Part of the

Institutions: Agents of Stability or Oppression? Sociologists use two major theoretical frameworks to approach the study of institutions: structural functionalism and conflict theory. The first focuses on the part that institutions play in creating social and personal stability; the second focuses on the role of institutions in legitimizing inequality (Eisenstadt 1985).

A STRUCTURAL-FUNCTIONAL VIEW OF INSTITUTIONS. Institutions provide ready-made patterns to meet most recurrent social problems. These ready-made patterns regu-

FOCUS ON THE ENVIRONMENT

answer is that current, environmentally harmful ways of doing business are profitable. Part of the answer is that the attitudes of private citizens have changed faster than business and governmental leaders realize. However, part of the answer is that even when individual values change, it is hard to change behavior if no supporting institutional structures are in place. It is difficult, for instance, to conserve energy and reduce pollution if there is no system of mass transportation in place that would allow people to get to work or school on time without relying on a private automobile. Similarly, no matter how committed one is to the principle of recycling, it is difficult to recycle if there are no groups or organizations that routinely pick up or process recyclables. Changes in cultural values or beliefs do lead to institutional change, but the process is slow, often depending on changes in one set of statuses and roles at a time.

What is the connection between a dead cormorant and rush hour traffic? High demand for oil has encouraged the development of fragile lands and has vastly multiplied the number of oil tankers plying the world's estuaries and waterways. Oil spills are thus indirectly related to our routine commuting practices. Changing values about oil consumption will not result in much changed behavior until social structures are in place for efficiently getting to work and other places without driving a car.

late human behavior and are the basis for social order. Because we share the same patterns, social life tends to be stable and predictable.

According to structural-functional theorists, institutions have "evolved" to help individuals and societies survive. This emphasis on evolution implies a neutral, natural process. Just as our natural characteristics (such as the opposable thumb and the capacity for language) are thought to have survived in our species because they aided its survival, so social characteristics are thought to have endured because they help society survive. They are a positive force. From this viewpoint,

Institutions are interdependent. Religion and politics do mix; so do religion and education, family, and economics. Generally, this means that institutions share common values and support one another. Each of the institutions represented in this picture, the church and the state, has traditionally been headed by a white man—a similarity that symbolizes the degree to which they rest on common standards. Their similarities go beyond this. Both church and state are vast bureaucracies, and features such as chains of command and copies in triplicate are common to both institutions. Church and state do not always agree, but they do have to take each other into account.

institutions are both necessary and desirable. They provide routine ways of successfully solving recurring problems.

Structural-functional theorists point out that stability and predictability are important both for societies and for individuals. The classic expression of this point of view comes from Durkheim, who argued that social institutions create a "liberating dependence." By furnishing patterned solutions to our most pressing everyday problems, they free us for more creative efforts. They save us from having to reinvent the social equivalent of the wheel each generation and thus facilitate our daily lives. Moreover, because these patterns have been sanctified by tradition, we tend to experience them as morally right. As a result, we find satisfaction and security in social institutions.

A CONFLICT VIEW OF INSTITUTIONS. By the very fact that they regulate human behavior and direct choices, institutions also constrain behavior. By producing predictability, they reduce innovation; by giving security, they reduce freedom. Some regard this as a necessary evil, the price we pay for stability.

This benign view of constraint is challenged by conflict theorists. They accept that institutions meet basic human needs, but they wonder, "Why *this* social pattern rather than another? Why *this* family system instead of another?" To explain why one social arrangement is chosen over another, conflict theorists ask, "Who benefits?"

According to conflict theorists, the development of social institutions is neither natural nor neutral. They argue that social institutions develop to maintain and reproduce a given system of inequality. They see the traditional family institution, for example, as a form of normatively supported inequality. While greater earning power and greater physical strength might enable a man to have power over a reluctant wife and children, how much easier it is for him if his wife and children have been taught that the man is the head of the household and that they *ought* to do what he says. Although the family institution is changing now, for thousands of years this power inequality was a central fact of family life. We call it patriarchy. As in this example, institutions are seen as deliberately fostering and legitimizing unequal benefits for the occupants of some statuses.

From the viewpoint of conflict theory, institutions represent a camouflaged form of inequality. Because institutions have existed for a long time, we tend to think of our familial, religious, and political systems not as merely one way of fulfilling a particular need but as the only acceptable way. Just as a 10th-century Mayan may have thought, "Of course virgins should be sacrificed if the crops are bad," so we tend to think, "Of course women's careers suffer after they have children." In both cases, the cloak of tradition obscures our vision of inequality or oppression, making inequality seem normal and even desirable. As a result, institutions stifle social change and help maintain inequality.

Institutions create order and stability; in doing so, they suppress change. In creating order, they preserve the status quo. In regulating, they constrain. In this sense, both conflict and structural-functional theories are right; they simply place a different value judgment on stability and order. The two theoretical prespectives prompt us to ask somewhat different questions about social structures. Structural-functional theory prompts us to ask how an institution contributes to order, to stability, and to meeting the needs of society and the individual. Conflict theory prompts us to ask which groups are benefiting the most from the system and how they are seeking to maintain their advantage. Both are worthwhile questions, and both will be addressed when social structures, ranging from deviance to medicine, are examined in Chapters 8 to 19.

INSTITUTIONS AND TYPES OF SOCIETIES

Institutions give a society a distinctive character. In some societies, the church has been dominant; in others, it has been the family or the economy. Whatever the circumstance, the institutional framework of a society is critical to an understanding of how it works.

The history of human societies is the story of ever-growing institutional complexity. In simple societies, we often find only one major social institution—the family or kin group. Many modern societies, however, have as many as a dozen institutions.

What causes this expansion of institutions? The triggering event appears to be economic. When changes in technology, in physical environment, or in social arrangements increase the level of economic surplus, the possibilities for institutional expansion arise. In this section, we sketch a broad outline of the institutional evolution that accompanied three revolutions in production.

HUNTING, FISHING, AND GATHERING SOCIETIES

The chief characteristic of hunting, fishing, and gathering societies is that they have subsistence economies. This means that in a good year they produce barely enough to get by; that is, they produce no surplus. In some years, of course, game and fruit are plentiful, but there are also many years in which starvation is a constant companion.

The basic units of social organization are the household and the local clan, both of which are based primarily on family bonds and kinship ties. Most of the activities of hunting and gathering are organized around these units. A clan rarely exceeds 50 people in size and tends to be nomadic or seminomadic. Because of their frequent wanderings, members of these societies accumulate few personal possessions.

The division of labor is simple, based solely on age and sex. The common pattern is for men to participate in hunting and deep-sea fishing and for women to participate in gathering, shore fishing, and preserving. Aside from inequalities based on age and sex, few structured inequalities exist in subsistence economies. Members possess little wealth; they have few, if any, hereditary privileges; and the societies are almost always too small to develop class distinctions. In fact, a major characteristic of subsistence societies is that individuals are alike. Apart from differences in age and sex, members generally have the same everyday experiences.

Horticultural Societies

The first major breakthrough from subsistence economy to economic surplus came with the development of horticulture. When people began to plant and cultivate crops, rather than simply harvest whatever nature provided, stable horticultural societies developed. The technology was often primitive—a digging stick, occasionally a rudimentary hoe—but it produced a surplus.

The regular production of more than the bare necessities revolutionized society. It meant that some people could take time off from basic production and turn to other pursuits: art, religion, writing, and frequently warfare. Of course, the people who participate in these alternative activities are not picked at random; there develops instead a class hierarchy differentiating the peasants, who must devote their full time to food production, and those who live off their surplus.

Because of relative abundance and a settled way of life, horticultural societies tend to develop complex and stable institutions outside the family. Some economic activity is carried on outside the family, a religious structure with full-time priests may develop, and a stable system of government—complete with bureaucrats, tax officers, and a hereditary ruler—often develops. Such societies are sometimes very large. The Inca empire, for example, covered an estimated population of more than 4 million.

Agricultural Societies

Approximately 5,000 to 6,000 years ago, there was a second revolution in agriculture, and the efficiency of food production was doubled and redoubled through better technology. The advances included the harnessing of animals, the development of metal tools, the use of the wheel, and improved knowledge of irrigation and fertilization. These changes dramatically altered social institutions.

The major advances in technology meant that even more people could be freed from direct production. The many people not tied directly to the land congregated in large urban centers and developed a complex division of labor. Technology, trade, reading and writing, science, and art grew rapidly as larger and larger numbers of people were able to devote full time to these pursuits. Along with greater specialization and occupational diversity came greater inequality. In place of the rather simple class structure of horticultural societies grew a complex class system of merchants, soldiers, scholars, officials, and kings—and, of course,

Even in modern industrial societies, the prosperity of society depends significantly on ability to generate agricultural surplus. In the highly mechanized agricultural industry in the United States, 2 million farmers can generate enough surplus to feed 250 million people and still leave surplus for export. In few other nations of the world, however, has agriculture taken so much advantage of industrial developments or freed so large a share of the labor force from food production. This photograph shows the much greater reliance on manual labor that characterizes agriculture in most contemporary societies.

the poor peasants on whose labor they all ultimately depended. This last group still contained the vast bulk of the society, probably at least 90 percent of the population (Sjoberg 1960).

One of the common uses to which societies put their new leisure and their new technology was warfare. With the domestication of the horse (cavalry) and the invention of the wheel (chariot warfare), military technology became more advanced and efficient. Military might was used as a means to gain even greater surplus through conquering other peoples. The Romans were so successful at this that they managed to turn the peoples of the entire Mediterranean basin into a peasant class that supported a ruling elite in Italy.

Industrial Societies

The third major revolution in production was the advent of industrialization around 200 years ago in Western Europe. The substitution of mechanical, electrical, and gasoline energy for human and animal labor caused an explosive growth in productivity, not only of goods but also of knowledge and technology. In the space of a few decades, agricultural societies were transformed. The enormous increases in energy technology, and knowledge freed the bulk of the workforce from agricultural production and, increasingly, also from industrial production. Society's political, social, and economic institutions were transformed. Old institutions such as education expanded dramatically, and new institutions such as science, medicine, and sports emerged.

When Institutions Die: The Tragedy of the Ojibwa

The story of modernization is the story of institutional change, of changes in how production, reproduction, education, and social control are socially struc-

CONCEPT SUMMARY TYPES OF SOCIETIES

HUNTING, FISHING, AND GATHERING SOCIETIES

TECHNOLOGY:	Very simple—arrows, fire, baskets
ECONOMY:	Bare subsistence, no surplus
SETTLEMENTS:	None or very small (bands of under 50 people)
SOCIAL ORGANIZATION:	All resting within family
EXAMPLES:	Plains Indians, Eskimos

HORTICULTURAL SOCIETIES

TECHNOLOGY:	Digging sticks, occasionally blade tools
ECONOMY:	Simple crop cultivation, some surplus and exchange
SETTLEMENTS:	Semipermanent—some cities, occasionally kingdoms
SOCIAL ORGANIZATION:	Military, government, religion becoming distinct institutions
EXAMPLES:	Mayans, Incas, Egyptians under the pharaohs

AGRICULTURAL SOCIETIES

TECHNOLOGY:	Irrigation, fertilization, metallurgy, animal power used to increase agricultural productivity
ECONOMY:	Largely agricultural, but much surplus; increased market exchange and substantial trade
SETTLEMENTS:	Permanent—urbanization becoming important, empires covering continents
SOCIAL ORGANIZATION:	Well-developed educational, military, religious, and political institutions
EXAMPLES:	Roman empire, feudal Europe, Chinese empire

INDUSTRIAL SOCIETIES

TECHNOLOGY:	New energy sources (coal, gas, electricity) leading to mechanization of production
ECONOMY:	Industrial—few engaged in agriculture or direct production; much surplus; fully developed market economy
SETTLEMENTS:	Permanent—urban living predominating; nation-states
SOCIAL ORGANIZATION:	Complex set of interdependent institutions
EXAMPLES:	Contemporary United States, Europe, Japan

tured. Sometimes, these institutional changes take place in harmony so that institutions continue to support one another and to provide stable patterns that meet ongoing human needs. On other occasions, however, old institutions are destroyed before new ones can evolve. When this happens, societies and the individuals within them are traumatized; societies and people fall apart.

In 1985, Anastasia Shkilnyk chronicled just such a human tragedy when she described the plight of the Ojibwa Indians of western Ontario in the book *A Poison Stronger Than Love*. Although the details are specific to the Ojibwa, her story is helpful in understanding what happened to Native Americans and other traditional societies when rapid social change altered social institutions.

In 1976, Anastasia Shkilnyk was sent by the Canadian Department of Indian Affairs to Grassy Narrows, an Ojibwa community of 520 people, to advise the band on how to alleviate economic disruption caused by mercury poisoning from a paper mill that had polluted nearby lakes and rivers. At the request of the chief and council, she stayed for two and a half years to assist the band in developing socio-economic projects and in preparing the band's case for compensation for the damages they suffered from mercury pollution and misguided government policy.

A Broken Society

Grassy Narrows in the 1970s was a community destroyed. Drunken six-year-olds roamed winter streets when the temperatures were −40°F. The death rate for both children and adults was very high compared with that in the rest of Canada. Nearly three-quarters of all deaths were linked directly to alcohol and drug abuse. A quote from Shkilnyk's journal evokes the tragedy of life in Grassy Narrows.

> Friday. My neighbor comes over to tell me that last night, just before midnight she found four-year-old Dolores wandering alone around the reserve, about two miles from her home. She called the police and they went to the house to investigate. They found Dolores's three-year-old sister, Diane, huddled in a corner crying. The house was empty, bare of food, and all of the windows were broken. The police discovered that the parents had gone to Kenora the day before and were drinking in town. Both of them were sober when they deserted their children.
>
> It's going to be a bad weekend. The police also picked up an eighteen-month-old baby abandoned in an empty house. No one seemed to know how long it had been there. . . . The milk in the house had turned sour. The baby was severely dehydrated and lying in its own vomit and accumulated excrement. Next door, the police found two people lying unconscious on the floor.

The adults in the community were not alcoholics in the sense that they had physiological reactions if they did not drink regularly. Rather, they were binge drinkers. When the wages were paid or the welfare checks came, many drank until they were unconscious and the money was gone. Shkilnyk estimated that on one occasion, when $20,000 in wages and $5,000 in social assistance was paid out on one day, within one week, $14,000 had been spent on alcohol. The children felt as much despair as their parents, and they sought similar forms of escape. Often, the children waited until their parents had drunk themselves unconscious and then drank the liquor that was left. If they could not get liquor, they sniffed glue or gasoline—and destroyed their central nervous systems so that they could not walk without falling down.

Yet 20 years before, the Ojibwa had been a thriving people. How had a society been so thoroughly destroyed?

Ojibwa Society before 1963

The Ojibwa have been in contact with whites for two centuries. In 1873, they signed the treaty that defines their relationship with the government of Canada. In the treaty, the government agreed to set aside reserves for the Indians, to give the Indians the right to pursue their traditional occupations of hunting, fishing, and trapping, and to provide schools.

Generally, this arrangement does not seem to have been disruptive to the Ojibwa way of life. Their reserve was in an area they had traditionally viewed as their own on the banks of the English River in northern Ontario. Despite the development of logging and mining in the areas around them, they had very little contact with the white community except for an annual ceremonial visit on Treaty Day.

"Time Zones" by Frank Bigbear, Jr.

The Ojibwa were a hunting and gathering people; the family was the primary social institution. A family group consisted of a husband, a wife, and their grown sons and their wives and children or of several brothers and their wives and children. The houses or tents of this family group were all clustered together, perhaps as far as half a mile from the next family group.

Economic activities were all carried out by family groups. These activities varied with the season. In the late summer and fall, families picked blueberries and harvested wild rice. In the winter, they hunted and trapped. In all of these endeavors, the entire family participated, everybody packing up and going to where the work was. The men would trap and hunt, the women would skin and prepare the meat, the old people would come along to take care of the children and teach them. They used their reserve only as a summer encampment. From late summer until late spring, the family was on the move.

Besides being the chief economic and educational unit, the family was also the major agent of social control. Family elders enforced the rules and punished those who violated them. In addition, most religious ceremonials were performed by family elders. Although a loose band of families formed the Ojibwa society, each extended family group was largely self-sufficient, interacting to exchange marriage partners and for other ceremonial activities (including, in the old days, warfare with the Sioux).

As noted, this way of life persisted in spite of the early influence of European culture. The major change was the development of boarding schools, which removed many Indian children from their homes for the winter months. When they returned, however, they were accepted back into the group and educated in Indian ways by their grandparents. The boarding schools took the children away, but they didn't disrupt the major social institutions of the society they left behind.

THE CHANGE

In 1963, the government decided that the Ojibwa should be brought into modern society and given the benefits thereof: modern plumbing, better health care, roads, and the like. To this end, they moved the entire Ojibwa community from the old reserve to a government-built new community about four miles from their traditional encampment. The new community had houses, roads, schools, and easy access to "civilization." The differences between the new and the old were sufficient to destroy the fragile interdependence of Ojibwa institutions.

First, all the houses were close together in neat rows, assigned randomly without regard for family group. As a result, the kin group ceased to exist as a physical unit. Second, the replacement of boarding schools with a community school meant that a parent (the mother) had to stay home with the child instead of going out on the trap line. As a result, the adult woman overnight became a consumer rather than a producer, shattering her traditional relationship with her husband and community. As a consequence of the women's and children's immobility, men had to go out alone on the trap line. Since they were by themselves rather than with their families, the trapping trips were reduced from six to eight weeks to a few days, and trapping ceased to be a way of life for the whole family. The productivity of the Ojibwa reached bottom with the government order in May 1970 to halt all fishing because of severe mercury contamination of the water. Then the economic contributions of men as well as women were sharply curtailed; the people became heavily dependent on the government rather than on themselves or each other.

What happened was the total destruction of the old patterns of doing things—that is, of social institutions. The relationships between husbands and wives were no longer clear. What were their rights and obligations to each other now that their joint economic productivity was at an end? What were their rights and obligations to their children when no one cared about tomorrow?

THE FUTURE

In 1985, the Ojibwa finally reached an out-of-court settlement with the federal and provincial governments and the mercury-polluting paper mill. The $8.7 million settlement was in compensation for damages to their way of life arising from government policies and mercury pollution. The band is using some of this money to develop local industries that will provide an ongoing basis for a productive and thriving society. Today, Ojibwa society has begun the process of healing and recovery.

SUMMARY

Institutions offer stable patterns for responding to stable problems. Some of these stable problems are straightforward and obvious, such as finding enough to eat. Other problems are more subtle but just as important: having something to do each day that is meaningful and having bonds of obligation and exchange with others in the community.

In the case of the Ojibwa Indians and other indigenous peoples of North America, welfare and the supermarket can take care of the first problem, but they cannot take care of the second. Stable social structures that define our roles relative to those of others in our environment, that give us assurance of the continuity of the past and the future, are an essential aspect of human society. It is often true, as conflict theorists stress, that a given institutional arrangement benefits one group over another. It is also true, as structural theorists stress, that some institutional arrangement is better than none.

SOCIAL APPLICATIONS

Why Is There a Sovereignty Movement in Hawaii?

Many of us think of Hawaii as an island paradise where the water is blue, the temperatures are warm, the beaches are beautiful, the surfing is great, and coconuts and pineapples abound for the pleasure of happy tourists and native residents alike. But Haunani-Kay Trask, director of the Center for Hawaiian Studies at the University of Hawaii, wants tourists to stay home. In her collection of essays entitled *From a Native Daughter: Colonialism and Sovereignty in Hawaii* (1993), Trask argues that Native Hawaiians (descendants of the indigenous people who inhabited Hawaii before its discovery by Captain Cook in 1778) watched in rage and desperation as conquering outsiders transfigured their social institutions.

The economy of the indigenous people depended on the collective use of the products of the land and sea. Private land ownership was unknown. There was no money. *Ohana* (extended families) inhabited and shared various regions. *Ohana* who lived near the sea traded with those who lived inland so that fresh water, fish, taro, and cultivated sweet potatoes were available to everyone.

Kinship formed not only the economic but also the political base of society. The royal Hawaiian family represented authority based on inheritance. In addition, kinship established a complex network of chiefs, who competed in terms of rank. Each chief's respect and rank depended on the number of people in his kingdom. Because ordinary people could move freely into another chief's domain, there was incentive for society's leaders to provide well for all their constituents.

Among the chiefs was a powerful priestly class, who enforced the *kapu,* or system of sacred law. The *kapu* determined everything from the time for farming and war making to correct mating behavior. Native Hawaiians believed that there were many gods and that all living things had consciousness. Together, the spiritual and the natural worlds comprised a universe of familial relations. Humans were one component of this large family. Gods had human as well as animal form, and human ancestors inhabited different physical forms after death. These religious beliefs resulted in a profound respect for sea, earth, and sky.

Outsiders introduced foreign—and unwanted—institutions into the lives of indigenous Hawaiians. Besides diseases, which reduced the indigenous population by more than 90 percent in the hundred years following Cook's arrival, outsiders brought capitalism, colonial politics, and Christianity.

Following the British explorers, more and more Americans went to Hawaii as whalers, to extract sandalwood, and as sugar growers. By 1848, they had convinced King Kamahameha III to allow private land ownership. Forty years later, outsiders owned or controlled three-fourths of the arable land on the islands. A cash economy had been introduced. Many inhabitants, forced off their communal lands, went to work alongside growing numbers of Asian and American immigrants as low-paid laborers in the booming sugar industry. By 1890, native Hawaiians made up less than half the population.

With the demise of an economic institution that had supported local chiefs, the indigenous political institution collapsed as well. These changes precipitated protests among the Native Hawaiians. In 1893, United States Marines were

SOCIAL APPLICATIONS

landed in Honolulu to "restore order." To avoid a bloody and futile battle, Queen Liliuokalani ceded her authority to the United States. Three years later, all Hawaiian-language schools were closed, and English was proclaimed the official language of the islands. In 1959, Hawaii became a state. Native Hawaiians had lost their nationality and political sovereignty.

Meanwhile, Calvinist missionaries had arrived. They taught the Judeo-Christian theme of mastery over nature and defined the mass deaths of Native Hawaiians from introduced diseases as punishment for resilient "paganism." The missionaries outlawed the hula as sinful and insisted that women wear loose dresses (mumus) rather than only grass skirts.

Today, Native Hawaiians comprise 20 percent of the resident population. Hawaii's economy is based largely on international tourism. Tourism spells humiliation for Native Hawaiians, according to Trask. For example, hotels belonging to international corporations stand on sacred burial sites. The hula, an ancient form of artistic expression with deep and complex religious meaning, has become a marketable form of exotica for tourists. Pollution is another result of tourism. Waste from Honolulu's overloaded sewer system floats near Waikiki Beach. Sugar and pineapple plantations, along with golf courses, are dusted and sprayed with pesticides and herbicides. Meanwhile, Native Hawaiians experience high unemployment, low educational attainment, and occupational segregation in the poorly paid service jobs associated with tourism.

In response, Native Hawaiians have formed a sovereignty movement, agitating for political independence from the United States and the return of traditional lands and waters. Their ultimate goal is an economy no longer dependent on tourism or the depletion of natural resources.

THINKING CRITICALLY

What kind of economic, political, family, religious, and educational institutions might Native Hawaiians fashion if they gained sovereignty? How would these institutions be like those existing now, do you think? How might they be different?

SOCIOLOGY ON THE NET

Institutions are supposed to provide enduring guidelines that last for generations. One of the most conservative and enduring institutions in this regard is the religious institution. In spite of the changes in this century, religious traditionalism remains. This institutional influence is evident in the teachings of the Catholic Church.

`http://www.christusrex.org`

Browse through the **Letter to Women** and pay special attention to **section 11**. You might also care to browse through the **Evangelium Vitae—The Gospel of Life and The Truth** and **Meaning of Human Sexuality**. In these selections, the church reaffirms its stance against women in the priesthood, against premarital sex and against abortion. These are serious and difficult issues in this time of change. Where do you stand on these issues? You may wish to examine a contrasting set of values by browsing through the web site for the **National Organization for Women**.

http://www.now.org

The Hawaiian sovereignty movement seeks to return control of the Hawaiian islands to the indigenous people of Hawaii. For insight into Hawaiian culture and how it might influence the future of Hawaii, visit the **Nation of Hawaii Home Page.**

http://www.hawaii-nation.org

Browse through this interesting site by scrolling all of the way down to the **Main Feature** area and reviewing the **Historical Information** and **Policy Statement** sections. Once you are in the **Policy Statement** section don't forget to read the section called **Malama Aina**. How would the institutions of Hawaii be structured if the sovereignty movement were to succeed? Do you believe that the United States would allow full and complete sovereignty? How would a structural-functional theorist and a conflict theorist view the issue of sovereignty?

SUMMARY

1 The analysis of social structures—recurrent patterns of relationships—revolves around three concepts: status, role, and institution.

2 Statuses are of two sorts: achieved and ascribed. The analysis of statuses is concerned with four issues: identification, distribution, consequences, and combinations.

3 Roles define how status occupants *ought* to act and feel. People may deviate from these expected role performances because of incompatible roles, inadequate role definitions, inadequate sanctions, or unavailability of resources. In addition, role performances differ because no role is fully scripted and roles must be negotiated.

4 Because societies share common human needs, they also share common institutions. The common institutions are family, economy, government, education, and religion. Each society has some enduring social structure to perform these functions for the group.

5 Institutions are interdependent; none stands alone, and a change in one results in changes in others. A detailed case study of the Ojibwa Indians of Ontario, Canada, shows how changes in economic institutions led to the disintegration of society and extraordianrily high rates of alcoholism.

6 Institutions regulate behavior and maintain the stability of social life across generations. Conflict theorists point out that these patterns often benefit one group more than others.

7 An important determinant of institutional development is the ability of a society to produce an economic surplus. Each major improvement in production has led to an expansion in social institutions.

8 There are four basic types of societies—hunting, fishing, and gathering; horticultural; agricultural; and industrial—which may be viewed as a rough evolutionary continuum. As societies move up this ladder, they are characterized by larger surpluses, more institutions, and more specialization.

SUGGESTED READINGS

LENSKI, Gerhard. 1966. *Power and Privilege: A Theory of Social Stratification*. New York: McGraw-Hill. A major work distinguishing the fundamental characteristics of different types of societies, particularly in terms of socially structured inequality.

MERTON, Robert K. 1968. *Social Theory and Social Structure*. (Enl. ed.) New York: Free Press. A work that uses structural-functional theory to draw out the basic concepts and relationships used in the analysis of social structures. Bureaucracies, deviance, religion, and politics are only a few of the illustrations used to show the application of these concepts.

NYE, F. Ivan. 1976. *Role Structure and Analysis of the Family*. Beverly Hills, Calif.: Sage. An analysis of the family using the concepts of status and roles. Because it applies the terms to a familiar social structure, it is a particularly accessible piece of sociological analysis.

O'DEA, Thomas F. 1957. *The Mormons*. Chicago: University of Chicago Press. An interesting and readable sociological account of the unique development and growth of Mormonism.

SHKILNYK, Anastasia. 1985. *A Poison Stronger Than Love: The Destruction of an Ojibwa Community*. New Haven: Yale. An ethnographic community study that focuses on the social structures of a Native American community in Canada. A powerful illustration of the extent to which individual well-being depends on stable institutions.

SMITH, Robert J., and Ella Lury Wiswell. 1982. *The Women of Suye Mura*. 1982. Chicago: University of Chicago Press. A companion volume to John Embree's now-standard Suye Mura: A Japanese Village. This book can stand alone as a unique account of the lives of rural Japanese women in the mid-1930s. It also makes an interesting contrast to the more standard focus on social organization and men's lives found in Embree's work.

SPIRO, Melford E. 1963. *Kibbutz: Venture in Utopia*. New York: Schocken Books. An anthropological analysis of basic aspects of social structure designed early in this century by young Jewish adults attempting to create a utopia. Both successes and failures are examined.

TRASK, Haunani-Kay. 1993. *From a Native Daughter: Colonialism and Sovereignty in Hawaii*. Monroe, Maine: Common Courage Press. A fiery yet factually supported description of U.S. involvement in changing all the institutions of Native Hawaiians.

CHAPTER 5

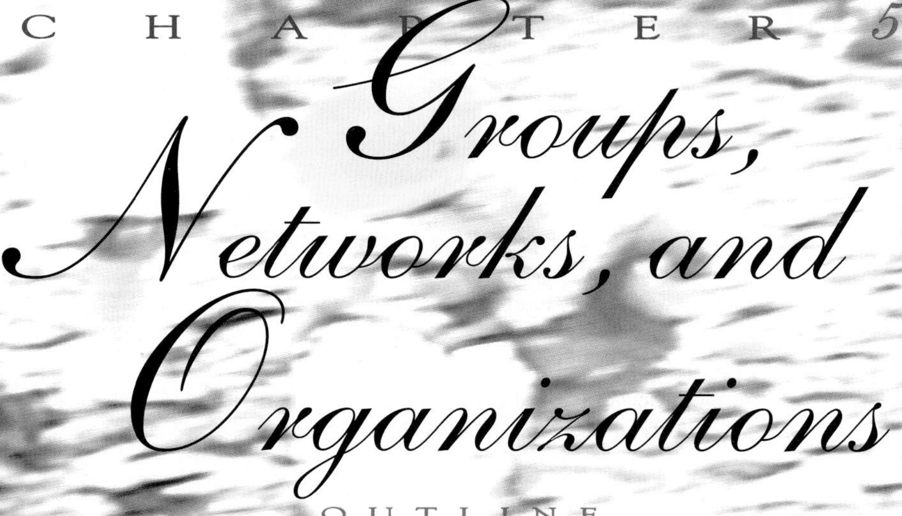

Groups, Networks, and Organizations

OUTLINE

Group Processes
Exchange
Cooperation
Competition
Conflict

Groups
How Groups Affect Individuals
Interaction in Small Groups
Types of Groups

Social Networks
Strong and Weak Ties

Focus on Measurement: Counting on Social Networks
Voluntary Associations
Community

Global Perspectives: In-Groups, Out-Groups, and Voluntary Associations in Northern Ireland

Bureaucracies
The Classic View
Organizational Culture
Criticisms of Bureaucracy

Social Applications: What Is Network Intevention, and Does It Work?

PROLOGUE

Have You Ever... met friends after a long absence and been startled by the changes in them? Perhaps they had gone off to college, been in the army, or married and moved away. Whatever the case, you may have found that they had changed so much you hardly knew them. It was not just their appearance but their values and concerns that were altered—and so were yours.

One of the most basic reasons that we change is that we start to associate with new groups of people. When we take a new job, we are often unknowingly making a commitment to a whole lifestyle and outlook. You will become a very different person if your first job after college is with IBM than if it is with the Sierra Club. Organizations mold us into their sorts of people.

In this chapter, we look at the different kinds of groups we belong to and how they influence and shape our lives. No one is an island. We are linked to others by complex ties of duty, obligation, and need. These ties have profound impacts on us. If we want to understand why people do what they do, one of our first tasks must be to identify whom they do it with—their groups, networks, and organizations.

Sociology is concerned with human behavior and how it is influenced by social structure. Although the concept of social "structure" suggests something firm and unyielding, in fact, a social structure describes ongoing, ever-changing relationships. This means that social structure has an important dynamic element; it is process as well as framework, action as much as pattern (Giddens 1984). In this chapter, we review basic group processes and also three kinds of social structures: the small group, the social network, and the complex organization.

GROUP PROCESSES

Some relationships are characterized by harmony and stability; others are made stressful by conflict and competition. We use the term **social processes** to describe the types of interaction that go on in relationships. This section looks closely at four social processes that regularly occur in human relationships: exchange, cooperation, competition, and conflict.

Social processes are the forms of interaction through which people relate to one another; they are the dynamic aspects of society.

EXCHANGE

Exchange is voluntary interaction in which the parties trade tangible or intangible benefits with the expectation that all parties will benefit. A wide variety of social relationships include elements of exchange. In friendships and marriages, exchanges usually include such intangibles as companionship, moral support, and a willingness to listen to the other's problems. In business or politics, an exchange may be more concrete; politicians, for example, openly acknowledge exchanging votes on legislative bills—I'll vote for yours if you'll vote for mine.

Exchange is voluntary interaction in which the parties trade tangible or intangible benefits with the expectation that all parties will benefit.

The **norm of reciprocity** is the expectation that people will return favors and strive to maintain a balance of obligation in social relationships.

Exchange relationships are based on the expectation that people will return favors and strive to maintain a balance of obligation in social relationships. This expectation is called the **norm of reciprocity** (Gouldner 1960). If you help your sister-in-law move, then she is obligated to you. Somehow she must pay you back. If she fails to do so, then the social relationship is likely to end, probably with bad feelings. A corollary of the norm of reciprocity is that you avoid accepting favors from people with whom you do not wish to enter into a relationship. For example, if someone you do not know very well volunteers to type your term paper, you will probably be suspicious. Your first thought is likely to be, "What is this guy trying to prove? What does he want from me?" If you do not want to owe this person a favor, you will say that you prefer to type your own paper. Nonsociologists might sum up the norm of reciprocity by concluding that there's no free lunch.

Exchange is one of the most basic processes of social interaction. Almost all voluntary relationships are entered into as situations of exchange. In traditional American families, these exchanges were clearly spelled out. He supported the family, which obligated her to keep house and look after the children; or, conversely, she bore the children and kept house, which obligated him to support her.

Exchange relationships persist only if each party to the interaction is getting something out of it. This does not mean that the rewards must be equal; in fact, rewards are frequently very unequal. You have probably seen play groups, for example, in which one child is treated badly by the other children and is permitted to play with them only if he agrees to give them his lunch or allows them to use his bicycle. If this boy has no one else to play with, however, he may find this relationship more rewarding than the alternative of playing alone. The continuation of very unequal exchange relationships usually rests on a lack of desirable alternatives (Emerson 1962).

COOPERATION

Cooperation is interaction that occurs when people work together to achieve shared goals.

Cooperation occurs when people work together to achieve shared goals. Exchange is a trade: I give you something and you give me something else in return. Cooperation is teamwork. It is characteristic of relationships where people work together to achieve goals that they cannot achieve alone. Consider, for example, a four-way stop. Although it may entail some waiting in line, in the long run we will all get through more safely and more quickly if we cooperate and take turns. This does not necessarily mean that all parties will benefit equally from cooperation. When union workers forgo a wage increase to help keep the company from going bankrupt, we say that union and management are cooperating to meet a joint goal: avoiding bankruptcy. It is the workers, however, who have made the sacrifice.

THINKING CRITICALLY

Can you think of a relationship in your own life that is governed primarily by the process of exchange? Of cooperation? Of competition? Of conflict? Which is the most satisfying for you—and why?

COMPETITION

It is not always possible for people to reach their goals by exchange or cooperation. If your goal and my goal are mutually exclusive (for example, I want to sleep and you want to play your stereo), we cannot both achieve our goals. Similarly, in situations of scarcity, there may not be enough of a desired good to go around. In these situations, social processes are likely to take the form of either competition or conflict.

A struggle over scarce resources that is regulated by shared rules is called **competition** (Friedsam 1965). The rules usually specify the conditions under which winning will be considered fair and losing will be considered tolerable. When the norms are violated, competition may erupt into conflict.

Competition is a common form of interaction in American society. Jobs, grades, athletic honors, sexual attention, marriage partners, and parental affection are only a few of the scarce resources for which individuals or groups compete. In fact, it is difficult to identify many social situations that do not entail competition. One positive consequence of competition is that it stimulates achievement and heightens people's aspirations. It also, however, often results in personal stress, reduced cooperation, and social inequalities (elaborated on in Chapters 9 to 13).

Because competition often results in change, groups that seek to maximize stability often devise elaborate rules to avoid the appearance of competition. Competition is particularly troublesome in such informal group relationships as friendships and marriages. Friends who want to stay friends will not compete for valued objects; they might compete over bowling scores, but they won't compete for the same promotion. Similarly, spouses who value their marriage will not compete for their children's affection or loyalty. To do so would be to destroy the marriage.

Competition is a struggle over scarce resources that is regulated by shared rules.

Conflict is a struggle over scarce resources that is not regulated by shared rules; it may include attempts to destroy or neutralize one's rivals.

A **group** is two or more people who interact on the basis of shared social structure and who recognize mutual dependency.

CONFLICT

When struggle over scarce resources is not regulated by shared rules, **conflict** occurs (Coser 1956, 8). Because no tactics are forbidden and anything goes, conflict may include attempts to neutralize, injure, or destroy one's rivals. Conflict creates divisiveness rather than solidarity.

When conflict takes place with outsiders, however, it may enhance the solidarity of the group. Whether we're talking about warring superpowers or warring street gangs, the us-against-them feeling that emerges from conflict with outsiders causes group members to put aside their jealousies and differences to work together. Groups from nations to schools have found that starting conflicts with outsiders is a useful device for redirecting the negative energy of their own group.

Exchange, cooperation, competition, and even conflict are important aspects of our relationships with others. Few of our relationships involve just one type of group process. Even friendships usually involve some competition as well as cooperation and exchange; similarly, relationships among competitors often involve cooperation.

We interact with people in a variety of relationships. Some of these relationships are temporary and others permanent, some are formal and others informal. In the rest of this chapter, we discuss the relationships that exist in three kinds of social structures: groups, social networks, and bureaucracies.

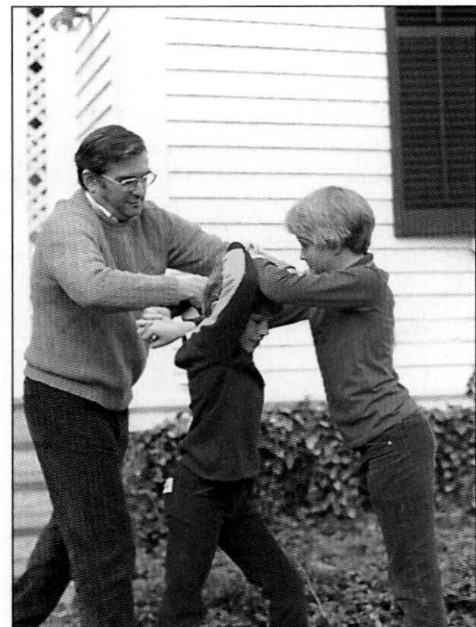

Many of the good things in life are in short supply: They are scarce resources. Some of the most serious struggles take place over intangible rewards such as respect, prestige, and honor. When the struggle is regulated by norms that specify the rules of fair play, as in a soccer game, we call it competition. When anything goes, we call the struggle conflict.

GROUPS

What is a group? A **group** is two or more people who interact and are mutually dependent. Groups may be large or small, formal or informal; they range from a pair of lovers to E-mail friends to IBM. In all of them, members share a social structure specifying statuses, roles, and norms, and they share a feeling of mutual dependency.

An **aggregate** is a collection of people who are temporarily clustered together in the same location.

A **category** is a collection of people who share a common characteristic.

The distinctive characteristics of groups stand out when we compare groups to two collections of people that do not have these characteristics. An **aggregate** is made up of people who are temporarily clustered together in the same location (for example, all the people on a city bus, those attending a movie, or shoppers in a mall). Although these people may share some norms (such as moving to the right when passing others), they are not mutually dependent. In fact, most of their shared norms have to do with procedures to maintain their independence despite their close physical proximity. The other nongroup is a **category**—a collection of people who share a common characteristic. Hispanics, welders, and students are categories of people. Most of the people who share category membership will never meet, much less interact.

The distinguishing characteristics of groups hint at the rewards of group life. Group members are the people we take into account and the people who take us into account. They are the people with whom we share norms and values. Thus, groups are a major source of solidarity and cohesion, reinforcing and strengthening our integration into society. The benefits of group life range all the way from sharing basic survival and problem-solving techniques to satisfying personal and emotional needs.

FIGURE 5.1
THE CARDS USED IN ASCH'S EXPERIMENT

In Asch's experiment, subjects were instructed to select the line on Card B that was equal in length to the line on Card A. The results showed that many people will give an obviously wrong answer in order to conform to the group.

SOURCE: From "Opinions and Social Pressure," by Solomon E. Asch. Copyright © November 1955 by Scientific American, Inc. All rights reserved.

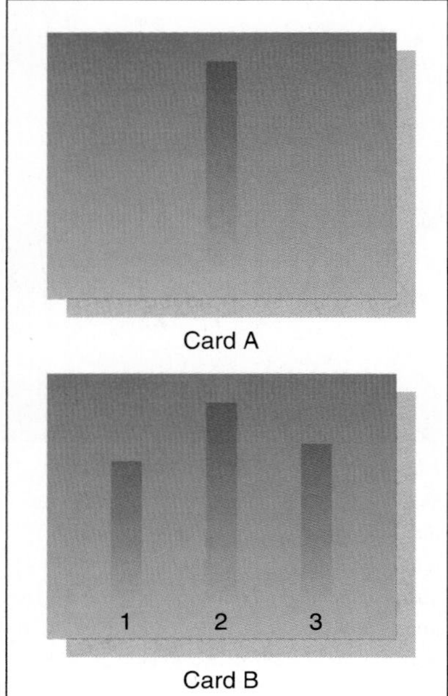

HOW GROUPS AFFECT INDIVIDUALS

When a man opens a door for a woman, do you see traditional courtesy or intolerable condescension? When you listen to acid rock, do you hear good music or mindless noise? Like taste in music, many of the things we deal with and believe in are not true or correct in any absolute sense; they are simply what our groups have agreed to accept as right.

The tremendous impact of group definitions on our own attitudes and perceptions was cleverly documented in a classic experiment by Asch (1955). In this experiment, the group consists of nine college students, all apparently unknown to each other. The experimenter explains that the task at hand is an experiment in visual judgment. The subjects are shown pairs of cards similar to those in Figure 5.1 and are asked to judge which line on Card B is most similar to the line on Card A. This is not a difficult task; unless you need glasses or have forgotten the ones you have, you can tell that Line 2 most closely matches the line on the first card.

The experimental part of this research consists of changing the conditions of group consensus under which the subjects make their judgments. Each group must make decisions on 15 pairs of cards; and in the first trials, all of the students agree. In subsequent trials, however, the first eight students all give an obviously wrong answer. They are not subjects at all but paid stooges of the experimenter. The real test comes in seeing what the last student—the real subject of the experiment—will do. Will he go along with everybody else, or will he publicly set himself apart? Photographs of the experiment show that the real subjects wrinkled their brows, squirmed in their seats, and gaped at their neighbors; in 37 percent of the trials, the naïve subject publicly agreed with the wrong answer, and 75 percent gave the wrong answer on at least one trial.

In the case of this experiment, it is clear what the right answer should be. Many of the students who agreed with the wrong answer probably were not persuaded by group opinion that their own judgment was wrong, but they decided not to make waves. When the object being judged is less objective, however—for example, whether Janet Jackson is better than Hootie and the Blowfish—then the group is

In these pictures from the Asch experiment, the subject shows the strain and consternation that comes from disagreeing with the judgments of the six other members of the group. This particular subject disagreed with the majority on all 12 trials of the experiment. He is unusual, however, as 75 percent of the experimental subjects agreed with the majority on at least one trial. Subjects who initially yielded to the majority found it increasingly difficult to make independent judgments as the experiment progressed.

likely to influence not only public responses but also private views. Whether we go along because we are really convinced or because we are avoiding the hassles of being different, we all have a strong tendency to conform to the norms and expectations of our groups. Thus, our group memberships are vital in determining our behavior, perceptions, and values.

INTERACTION IN SMALL GROUPS

We spend much of our lives in groups. We have work groups, family groups, and peer groups. In class we have discussion groups, and everywhere we have committees. This section reviews some of the more important factors that affect the kind of interaction we experience in small groups.

Size. The smallest possible group is two people. As the group grows to three, four, and more, its characteristics change.

Some of the most dramatic consequences of size occur when a group goes from two members (a dyad) to three members (a triad). In a dyad, neither person can leave the group without destroying it. When a third member joins the group, the group becomes much more stable; it can continue to exist if one person dies or just gets mad and quits. This increase in stability is purchased at the cost of decreased importance for each individual group member. Whereas a dyad dies if it allows one person to walk away in anger, a triad can afford to shrug its shoulders. This means triads have less need to compromise or to listen to unhappy members. The move from two to three also makes possible the formation of factions *within* the group (a two-against-one coalition) and the use of majority rule in decision making (Simmel [1908] 1950).

Generally, we find that as groups go from two to three to four and on up, interaction becomes more impersonal, more structured, and less personally satisfying. Consensus tends to be replaced by majority rule, and each individual has fewer opportunities to share opinions and contribute to decision making or problem solving.

Proximity. Dozens of laboratory studies demonstrate that interaction is more likely to occur among group members who are physically close to one another. This effect is not limited to the laboratory.

In a classic demonstration of the role of proximity in group formation and interaction, Festinger and his associates (1950) studied a married-student housing project. All of the residents had been strangers to one another before being arbitrarily assigned to a housing unit. The researchers wanted to know what factors influenced friendship choices within the project. The answer: physical proximity. Festinger found that people were twice as likely to choose their next-door neighbors as friends than they were to choose people who lived only two units away. In general, the greater the physical distance, the less likely friendships were to be formed. An interesting exception to this generalization was that people who lived next to the garbage cans were disproportionately likely to be chosen as friends. Why? Because many of their neighbors passed by their units daily and therefore had many chances to interact and form friendships with them.

Cohesion refers to the degree of attraction members feel to the group.

In the 1990s, we have seen the development of "electronic proximity" as people from around the globe are brought together on computer networks. Electronic proximity is not exactly the same as physical proximity, but the same principle for group interaction holds: Persons with easy access to one another are likely to form friendships.

FIGURE 5.2
PATTERNS OF COMMUNICATION

Patterns of communication can affect individual participation and influence. In each figure, the circles represent individuals, and the lines are flows of communication. The all-channel network provides the greatest opportunity for participation and is more often found in groups where status differences are not present or are minimal. The wheel, by contrast, is associated with important status differences within the group.

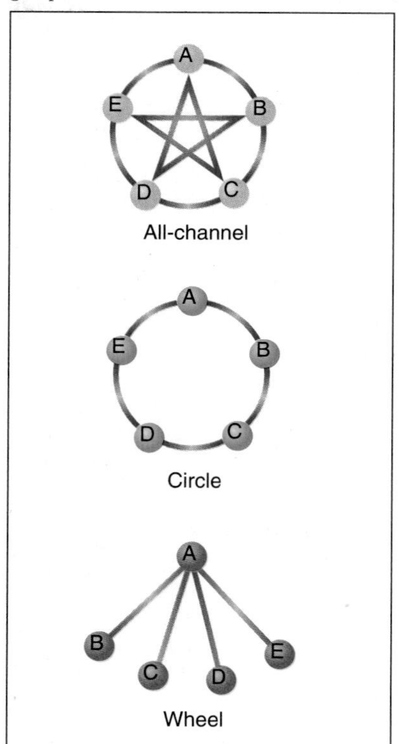

Communication Patterns. Interaction of group members can be either facilitated or retarded by patterns of communication. Figure 5.2 shows some common communication patterns for five-person groups. The communication structure allowing the greatest equality of participation is the *all-channel network*. In this pattern, each person can interact with every other person with approximately the same ease. Each participant has equal access to the others and an equal ability to become the focus of attention.

The other two common communication patterns allow for less interaction. In the *circle pattern*, people can speak only to their neighbors on either side. This pattern reduces interaction, but it does not give one person more power than others. In contrast, with the *wheel pattern*, not only is interaction reduced but also a single, pivotal individual gains greater power in the group. The wheel pattern is characteristic of the traditional classroom. Students do not interact with one another; instead, they interact directly only with the teacher, thereby giving that person the power to direct the flow of interaction.

Communication structures are often created, either accidentally or purposefully, by the physical distribution of group members. The seating of committee members at a round table tends to facilitate either an all-channel or a circle pattern, depending on the size of the table. A rectangular table, however, gives people at the ends and in the middle of the long sides an advantage. They find it easier to attract attention and are apt to be more active in interactions and more influential in group discussions. Consider the way communication is structured in the classes and groups you participate in. How do seating structures encourage or discourage communication?

Cohesion. One of the important dimensions along which groups vary is their degree of **cohesion,** or solidarity. A cohesive group is characterized by strong feelings of attachment and dependency. Because its members feel that their happiness or welfare depends on the group, the group may make extensive claims on the individual members (Hechter 1987). Cohesive adolescent friendship groups, for example, can enforce dress codes and standards of conduct on their members.

Friendship groups differ in their cohesiveness, as do marriages, churches, and other types of groups. What makes one marriage or church more cohesive than another? Among the factors that contribute to cohesion are small size, similarity of members, frequent interaction, long duration, and a clear distinction between insiders and outsiders (Homans 1950; Hechter 1987; Lawler and Yoon 1996). Although all marriages in our society have the same size (two members), a marriage in which the partners are more similar, spend more time together, and so on is generally more cohesive than one in which the partners are dissimilar and see each other for only a short time each day.

One of the most powerful mechanisms of social control is the threat of exclusion from valued groups. None of us likes to be rejected, and most of us will go to considerable lengths to avoid the threat of exclusion. This means that we conform: We dress as other group members dress, think as they think, and do as they do. This desire to please others in our intimate social circles is the most powerful pressure for conformity. Compared to this, formal sanctions such as fines and jail sentences are relatively ineffective.

Social Control. Small groups rarely have access to legal or formal sanctions, yet they exercise profound control over individuals. The basis of this control is fear—fear of not being accepted by the group (Douglas 1983). The major weapons that groups use to punish nonconformity are ridicule and contempt, but their ultimate sanction is exclusion from the group. From "you can't sit at our lunch table anymore" to "you're fired," exclusion is one of the most powerful threats we can make against others.

Zurcher (1983) gives an example of how informal social control worked in a group of men who met weekly to play poker. When somebody followed group routines, he was rewarded with a "Good play!" from fellow players. When a player violated the group norm, he was negatively sanctioned. For example, a newcomer to the group violated a group norm that required being a good loser: When he got a bad draw, he swore and threw down his cards. In this case, the dealer picked up the cards without a word, and the game went on in total silence. The group figuratively turned its back on the player by pretending he wasn't there. This form of social control is most effective in cohesive groups, but Asch's experiment shows that fear of rejection can induce conformity to group norms even in artificial lab settings.

Decision Making. One of the primary research interests in the sociology of small groups is how group characteristics (size, cohesion, and so on) affect group decision making. This research has focused on a wide variety of actual groups: flight crews, submarine crews, and juries, to name a few.

Generally, groups strive to reach consensus; they would like all their decisions to be agreeable to every member. As the size of the group grows, consensus requires lengthy and time-consuming interaction so everybody's objections can be clearly understood and incorporated. Thus, as groups grow in size, they often adopt the more expedient policy of majority rule. This policy results in quicker decisions, but often at the expense of individual satisfaction. It therefore reduces the cohesiveness of the group.

Choice Shifts. One of the most consistent findings of research is that it is seldom necessary to resort to majority rule in small groups. Both in the laboratory and in the real world, there is a strong tendency for opinions to converge. One of the classic experiments on convergence was done over 50 years ago by Sherif (1936). In this experiment, strangers were put into a totally dark room. A dot of light was flashed onto the wall, and each participant was asked to estimate how far the light moved during the experimental period. After the first session, the participants recorded their own answers and then shared them with the other participants. There was quite a bit of variation in the estimates. Then the researchers did the experiment again. This time there was less difference. After four trials, all participants agreed on an estimate that was close to the average of the initial estimates. (The dot of light was, in fact, stationary.)

The convergence effect has been demonstrated in dozens of studies since. Convergence, however, is not always to a middle position. Sometimes, the group reaches consensus on an extreme position. This is called the *risky shift* when the group converges on an adventurous option and the *tame shift* when the choice is extremely conservative. Sometimes, these choice shifts depend on persuasive arguments put forward by one or more of the members, but often they result from general norms in the group that favor conservatism over risk (Davis and Stasson 1988). For example, one might expect the PTA steering committee to choose the safest option, whereas members of a terrorist group would choose the riskiest option.

A special case of choice shift is *groupthink*. Groupthink occurs when pressures to agree are so strong that they stifle critical thinking. In such situations, people do not change; they merely hide their real opinions in order to be supportive. Irving Janis (1982) has documented the role of groupthink in a variety of 20th-century political decisions. For example, in 1962, President John F. Kennedy and his advisers rashly decided to invade Cuba. This so-called Bay of Pigs invasion ended in a disastrous rout for U.S. troops; it was poorly planned and probably foolish in any case. Afterward, nearly every member of the advisory group admitted that they had thought it was a bad idea but had hesitated to say so (Schlesinger 1965). As this example illustrates, groupthink often results in bad decisions. Research shows that better decisions usually result when a persistent minority forces the majority to consider the minority's objections (Nemeth 1985).

Summary. Whether the small group arises spontaneously among neighbors or schoolchildren or whether it is a committee appointed to solve a community problem, the operation of the group depends on the quality of interaction among the members. Research suggests that interaction is facilitated by small size, open communication networks, similarity, and physical proximity. When these circumstances align to produce high levels of interaction, then individual satisfaction, group cohesion, and social control all tend to increase.

Types of Groups

Sociologists classify groups in several ways. They call small, intimate, and lasting groups (families, for example) *primary groups;* they call large, impersonal groups (AT&T, for example) *secondary groups*. In this section, we examine these types of groups, along with *in-groups*, *out-groups*, and *reference groups*.

Primary groups are groups characterized by intimate, face-to-face interaction.

Primary Groups. **Primary groups** are characterized by intimate, face-to-face interaction (Cooley [1909] 1967). These groups represent our most complete experiences in group life. The relationships formed in primary groups are relatively permanent and constitute a basic source of identity and attachment.

The ideal primary group tends to have the following characteristics: (1) personal and intimate relationships, (2) face-to-face communication, (3) permanence, (4) a strong sense of loyalty, or we-feeling, (5) small size, (6) informality, and (7) traditional decision making (Rogers 1960). The closest approximation to an ideal primary group is probably the family, followed by adolescent peer groups and adult friendships. In addition to the family and friendship networks, coworkers and gangs may be primary groups. Groups such as these are major sources of companionship, intimacy, and belongingness, conditions that strengthen our sense of social integration into society.

Secondary Groups. By contrast, **secondary groups** are formal, large, and impersonal. Whereas the major purpose of many primary groups is simply to provide companionship, secondary groups usually form to accomplish some specific task. The perfect secondary group is entirely rational and contractual in nature; the participants interact solely to accomplish some purpose (earn credit hours, buy a pair of shoes, get a paycheck). Their interest in each other does not extend past this contract. If you have ever been in a lecture class of 300 students, you have first-hand experience of a classic secondary group. The interaction is temporary, anonymous, and formal. Rewards are based on universal criteria, not on such particularistic grounds as your effort or need. The Concept Summary shows the important differences between primary and secondary groups.

Secondary groups are groups that are formal, large, and impersonal.

Comparing Primary and Secondary Groups. Primary and secondary groups serve very different functions for individuals and societies. From the individual's point of view, the major purpose of primary groups is **expressive activity,** giving individuals social integration and emotional support. Your family, for example, usually provides an informal support group that is bound to help you, come rain or shine. You should be able to call on your family and friends to bring you some soup when you are down with the flu, to pick you up in the dead of night when your car breaks down, and to listen to your troubles when you are blue.

Expressive activities or roles provide integration and emotional support.

Because we need primary groups so much, they have tremendous power to bring us into line. From the society's point of view, this is the major function of primary groups: They are the major agents of social control. The reason most of us don't shoplift is because we would be mortified if our parents, friends, or coworkers found out. The reason most soldiers go into combat is because their buddies are going. We tend to dress, act, vote, and believe in ways that will keep the support of our primary groups. In short, we conform. The law would be relatively helpless in keeping all the millions of us in line if we weren't already restrained by the desire to stay in the good graces of our primary groups. One corollary of this, however—which Chapter 8 addresses—is that if our primary groups accept shoplifting or

Concept Summary Differences between Primary and Secondary Groups

	Primary Groups	Secondary Groups
Size	Small	Large
Relationships	Personal, intimate	Impersonal, aloof
Communication	Face to face	Indirect—memos, telephone, etc.
Duration	Permanent	Temporary
Cohesion	Strong sense of loyalty, we-feeling	Weak, based on self-interest
Decisions	Based on tradition and personal feelings	Based on rationality and rules
Social Structure	Informal	Formal—titles, officers, charters, regular meeting times, etc.

Many of the groups in which we participate combine characteristics of primary and secondary groups. The school and its classrooms are secondary groups: They are rationally designed and formally organized to meet specific instrumental goals. But they also have some of the characteristics of primary groups, including the development of personal relationships, many of which will last for 6, 12, or even 40 years.

street fighting as suitable behaviors, then our primary-group associations may lead us into deviance rather than conformity.

Instrumental activities or roles are task oriented.

The major functions of secondary groups are **instrumental activities,** the accomplishment of specific tasks. If you want to build an airplane, raise money for a community project, or teach introductory sociology to 2,000 students a year, then secondary groups are your best bet. They are responsible for building our houses, growing and shipping our vegetables, educating our children, and curing our ills. In short, we could not function without them.

The Shift to Secondary Groups. In preindustrial society, there were few secondary groups. Vegetables and houses were produced by families, not by Georgia Pacific or Del Monte. Parents taught their own children, and neighbors nursed one another's ills. Under these conditions, primary groups served both expressive and instrumental functions. As society has become more industrialized, more and more of our instrumental needs have become the obligation of some secondary group rather than of a primary group.

In addition to losing their instrumental functions to secondary groups, primary groups have suffered other threats in industrialized societies. In the United States, for example, approximately 17 percent of the population moves each year (20 percent in the western states), (U.S. Bureau of the Census 1995, Table 33).This fact alone means that our ties to friends, neighborhoods, and coworkers are seldom really permanent. People change jobs, spouses, and neighborhoods. One consequence of this breakdown of traditional primary groups is that many people rely on secondary contacts even for expressive needs; they may hire a counselor rather than call a neighbor, for example.

Thinking Critically

Can you think of a situation in your life in which the primary source of social control was a secondary rather than a primary group?

Many scholars have suggested that these inroads on the primary group represent a weakening of social control; that is, the weaker ties to neighbors and kin mean that people feel less pressure to conform. They don't have to worry about what the neighbors will say because they haven't met them; they don't have to worry about what mother will say, because she lives 2,000 miles away and what she doesn't know won't hurt her.

There is apparently some truth in this suggestion, and it may be one of the reasons that small towns with stable populations are more conventional and have lower crime rates than do big cities with more fluid populations—an issue addressed more fully in Chapter 22.

In-groups and Out-groups. There are some groups and categories to which you belong: your family, your friends, your religion, your race, your gender—any group you can refer to as "my." These groups and social categories are called **in-groups,** because you feel you belong to them. There are other groups and categories to which you do not belong—other families, cliques, religions, races, and the "other sex." These are **out-groups,** for you feel that you are outside of them. In-groups and out-groups are important because they affect behavior.

In-groups are groups or social categories to which individuals feel they belong.

Out-groups are groups or social categories to which individuals do not feel they belong.

Members of a particular group—those to whom it is an in-group—are likely to share certain values, norms, and attitudes. Nonmembers—those to whom the group is an outgroup—may share many of the same cultural values and norms, but they lack certain essentials for belonging to the group. Nevertheless, in modern society, individuals belong to so many groups that some of their in-group and out-group relationships overlap. A heterosexual may consider gay males or lesbians as belonging to an outgroup and may simultaneously participate with one or more of them on an athletic team in which they have an in-group relationship.

The fact that in-group and out-group classifications cut across many lines does not minimize their intensity. You know this if you've ever craved membership in a group that excluded you. Furthermore, exclusion from the in-group can be a physically as well as psychologically brutal process. For example, Rudolf Hess, the German Nazi who commanded the Auschwitz concentration camp, in which 700,000 Jews were put to death during World War II, characterized this slaughter as "the removal of racial-biological foreign bodies" (Hess 1960). In wartime, soldiers typically dehumanize the enemy by using names that designate an undeserving out-group. In the Vietnam war, for example, American troops thought of enemy individuals as "gooks," "slants," or "slopes"—outsiders deserving death. People who behave cruelly toward out-groups often treat their in-group associates pretty well. For instance, gang members capable of murdering outsiders typically describe their fellows as caring, protective, and "always there for you when nobody else is" (Terry 1994, 14y).

Reference Groups. Some groups are important to us as models even though we ourselves may not be a part of them. These are **reference groups,** groups or categories to which individuals refer when making evaluations or judgments about themselves. For example, your parents are a reference group for you when you use their occupational and financial circumstances as a yardstick against which you measure your own.

Reference groups are groups or categories to which individuals refer when making evaluations or judgments about themselves.

Sometimes, the in-group and the reference group are the same, as when a teenager gives more weight to the opinions of peers than to those of classroom teachers. Sometimes an out-group is a reference group: You might compare and evaluate your educational attainment against that of your instructors, even though you are not yourself an instructor (yet). An individual may have several reference groups, and these can change over time. In fact, one way to make desired changes in our lives is to work consciously at changing our reference groups.

FIGURE 5.3
NETWORK DENSITY

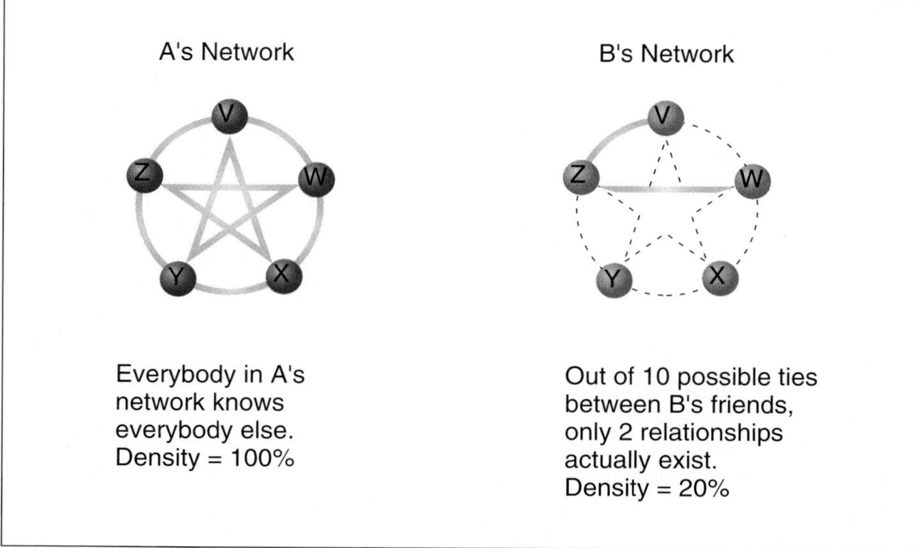

SOCIAL NETWORKS

A **social network** is an individual's total set of relationships.

Each of us has memberships in a variety of primary and secondary groups. Through these group ties, we develop **social networks**—total sets of relationships. Our social networks include our families, our insurance agents, our neighbors, our classmates and coworkers, and the people who belong to our clubs. Through our social networks, we are linked to hundreds of people in our communities and perhaps across the country. The Focus on Measurement section discusses social networks further.

STRONG AND WEAK TIES

Strong ties are relationships characterized by intimacy, emotional intensity, and sharing.

Weak ties are relationships with friends, acquaintances, and kin that are characterized by low intensity and intimacy.

Although your insurance agent and your mother are both part of your social network, there is a qualitative difference between them. We can divide our social networks into two general categories of intimacy: strong ties and weak ties. **Strong ties** are relationships characterized by intimacy, emotional intensity, and sharing. We have strong ties with the people in whom we will confide, for whom we will make sacrifices, and whom we expect to make sacrifices for us. **Weak ties** are relationships that are characterized by low intensity and intimacy (Granovetter 1973). Coworkers, neighbors, fellow club members, cousins, and in-laws generally fall in this category.

Your social network does not include everybody with whom you have ever interacted. Many interactions, such as those with some classmates and neighbors, are so superficial that they cannot truly be said to be part of a relationship at all. Unless contacts develop into personal relationships that extend beyond the simple exchange of services or a passing nod, they are not included in your social network.

Research suggests that social networks are vital for integrating an individual into society, encouraging conformity, and building a firm sense of self-identity.

FOCUS ON MEASUREMENT
Counting on Social Networks

> "... HE DETERMINED THAT THE AVERAGE PERSON HAD 12.8 PEOPLE IN HIS OR HER NETWORK."

Sociologists who study social networks are interested in finding reliable answers to three questions: How many people are in a social network? How similar are these people to one another? How many of them know each other? These questions relate to *size*, *homogeneity*, and *density*, respectively.

Network size is obviously important, but so are homogeneity and density. Consider two small networks, each with five people. In A's network, everybody is pretty much alike—all share the same gender, ethnicity, education, family status, and occupation—and they all know each other well. In B's network, members are diverse, and few of them know each other. Both kinds of networks have advantages. A's network is probably more loyal and supportive, but it also has the capacity to exercise more control over A, and it doesn't exactly open doors to new opportunities and experiences. B's network has much less control capacity (if B treats one friend badly, the others won't know it), is more likely to lead B to new experiences and opportunities, but is less warm and embracing. Whether business cliques, gangs, families, or work groups are more like A or more like B is important for understanding loyalty, social control, and diffusion of new ideas. It is precisely this focus on characteristics of relationships rather than characteristics of individual people that defines sociology as a field.

How do we measure these characteristics of social networks? If you ask people how many friends they have, most people will give reasonable answers, such as 4 or 5, but some will tell you that they have none and others will give numbers such as 200. Probably the people who say none and those who say 200 are using very different definitions of *friend*. To get around these reporting problems and improve consistency, sociologists who study social networks use more specific questions. One of the most well-known techniques is that used by Fischer (1982). Fischer asked people 10 questions, including: "Whom would you ask to water your plants or take in your mail if you were away for a few days?" "Whom would you call if you were sick?" "With whom have you recently engaged in social activities, such as dinner or the movies?" and, of course, "Whom could you borrow money from?" He counted every person listed under any question as a member of the respondent's social network. Using this technique, he determined that the average person had 12.8 people in his or her network.

After we have compiled a list of individuals in a social network, then we ask about each listed person's characteristics (age, gender, and so on), and then we ask whether each person listed knows each other person. (If there are 20 people in a social network, this means asking hundreds of questions to determine whether person 1 knows persons 2 through 20, person 2 knows persons 3 through 20, and so on.) The result can be diagrammed as in Figure 5.3. More formally, we have quantitative data on *number* of ties, *homogeneity* of ties (percent who are of the same gender, race/ethnicity, and age group as the person whose network it is), and *density* of ties (the proportion of all possible ties among the person's friends that actually exist). In this case, both networks have only 5 people, but A has a density of 100 percent and B has a density of 20 percent.

Because of their importance for the individual and society, documenting the trends in social networks has been a major focus of sociological study.

The Relationship between Ties and Groups. The distinction between strong and weak ties obviously parallels the distinction between primary and secondary groups. The difference between these two sets of concepts is that *strong* and *weak* apply to one-to-one relationships, while *primary* and *secondary* apply to the group as a whole. We can have both strong and weak ties within a primary as well as a secondary group.

For example, the family is obviously a primary group; it is relatively permanent, with strong feelings of loyalty and attachment. We are not equally intimate with

Critically important in our social networks are our strong ties—the handful of people to whom we feel intense loyalty and intimacy. For many people, family is an important source of strong ties. Although we may not be close to everyone in our families, there are usually a few family members to whom we feel very close. Women are somewhat more apt than men to choose their strong ties from among their families. Many, like these two sisters, will find that these ties provide a lifelong bond that gives a sense of continuity over the entire life course.

every family member, however. You may be very close to your mother but estranged from your brother. Similarly, although the school as a whole is classified as a secondary group, you may have developed an intimate relationship, a strong tie, with one of your schoolmates. Again, *strong* and *weak* are terms used to describe the relationship between two individuals; *primary* and *secondary* are characteristics of the group as a whole.

Strong Ties. Studies agree on the factors that affect number and composition of strong ties. The most important of these factors is education. People with more education have more strong ties, have a greater diversity of strong ties, and are less reliant on kin. The number of ties also varies by residence and age. Urban residents have more strong ties than rural residents, perhaps in part because they have a greater variety from which to choose. Older respondents consistently report the fewest strong ties. Gender does not appear to make much difference in the number of strong ties that people have, but it does affect the source: Women's ties are more likely than men's to be drawn from the kin group (Marsden 1987; Fischer 1982).

Voluntary Associations

In addition to relationships formed through family and work, many of us voluntarily choose to join other groups and associations. We may join the PTA, a bowling team, the Elks, the National Organization for Women, or the Sierra Club. These groups, called **voluntary associations,** are nonprofit organizations designed to allow individuals an opportunity to pursue their shared interests collectively. They vary considerably in size and formality. Some—for example, the Elks and the PTA—are very large and have national headquarters, elected officers, formal titles, charters, membership dues, regular meeting times, and national conventions. Others—for example, bowling teams and quilting groups—are small, informal groups that draw their membership from a local community or neighborhood.

Voluntary associations are nonprofit organizations designed to allow individuals an opportunity to pursue their shared interests collectively.

Voluntary associations are an important mechanism for enlarging our social networks. Most of the relationships we form in voluntary associations will be weak ties, but voluntary associations can also be the means of introducing us to people who will become close friends and intimates.

Voluntary associations perform an important function for individuals. Studies document that people who participate in them generally report greater satisfaction and personal happiness, longer life, greater self-esteem, more political effectiveness, and a greater sense of community (Hanks 1981; Knoke 1981; Litwak 1961; Moen, Dempster-McLain, and Williams 1989; Pollock 1982; Curtis, Grabb, and Baer 1992). The correlation between high participation and greater satisfaction does not necessarily mean that joining a voluntary association is the road to happiness. At least part of the relationship is undoubtedly due to the fact that it is precisely those happy persons who feel politically effective and attached to their communities who seek out voluntary associations. It also appears to be true, however, that greater participation can be an avenue for achievement and can lead to feelings of integration and satisfaction.

The Mediation Hypothesis. An important characteristic of voluntary associations is that they combine some of the features of primary and secondary groups—for example, the companionship of a small group and the rational efficiency of a secondary group. Some scholars have therefore suggested that voluntary associations mediate (provide a bridge) between primary and secondary groups (Pollock 1982). They allow us to pursue instrumental goals without completely sacrificing

The women Shriners in this picture are in many ways typical of the people who belong to voluntary associations: They are middle to upper-middle class, middle-aged, and urban. This picture illustrates another common feature of voluntary associations—sex segregation. As their cheerful expressions indicate, membership in such voluntary associations is generally associated with a greater feeling of integration into one's community and greater personal satisfaction.

the satisfactions that come from participation in a primary group. Through participation in voluntary associations, we meet some of our needs for intimacy and association while we achieve greater control over our immediate environment. Take, for example, the sportswoman who wishes to protect both wildlife habitat and the right to have guns. This individual can write letters to her member of Congress, but she will believe, rightly, that as an individual she is unlikely to have much clout. If this same individual joins with others in, say, the National Wildlife Federation or the National Rifle Association, she will have the enjoyment of associating with other like-minded individuals and the satisfaction of knowing that a paid lobbyist is representing her opinions in Washington. In this way, voluntary associations provide a bridge between the individual and large secondary associations

Correlates of Membership Participation. Most Americans belong to at least one voluntary association, and approximately one-fourth participate in three or more. Among those who report membership, a large proportion are passive participants—they belong in name only. They buy a membership in the PTA when pressured to do so, but they don't go to meetings. Similarly, anyone who subscribes to *Audubon* magazine is automatically enrolled in the local Audubon Club, but few subscribers become active members. Because so many of our memberships are superficial, they are also temporary. Most Americans, however, maintain continuous membership in at least one association.

Membership in voluntary associations shows much the same pattern as noted earlier for strong ties. The factors listed below tend to affect both the number and the kinds of organizations people join (Tomeh 1973):

1. *Urban/rural residence*. Urban residents are more frequently involved in voluntary associations than are rural residents. One reason may be that urban areas offer a greater variety of associations to chose from and less competition from traditional primary groups.
2. *Social class*. Most studies show that people from higher social classes are more involved in voluntary associations than are people from lower classes. Furthermore, the types of organizations joined vary by social class. Upper-class persons join historical societies and country clubs; middle-class persons, civic groups (chambers of commerce, hospital auxiliary); and working-class persons, fraternal and veteran's associations.
3. *Age*. Membership in voluntary associations tends to increase continuously through adulthood but begins to decline near retirement age. During early adulthood, the presence of young children has a depressing effect on the involvement of parents, particularly mothers. Age also affects the types of organizations joined. Young people's organizations tend to be almost exclusively expressive in nature; parents are active in youth-oriented groups such as the scouts and the PTA; middle-aged people are more active in civic groups.
4. *Gender*. We find relatively little difference in the number of associations men and women belong to but major differences in the kinds of organizations they join. In part, this reflects the fact that many voluntary associations are largely or entirely sex-segregated (for example, garden clubs, hospital auxiliaries, the Elks) (McPherson and Smith-Lovin 1986). In general, the associations that women join are smaller, less formal, and more expressive in nature.
5. *Religion*. Church membership and participation is the most widespread and intensive voluntary association in our society. People who are religious belong not

only to churches but also to church boards, study groups, sewing circles, and fund-raising committees.

COMMUNITY

In everyday life, we hear a lot of talk about the benefits of having a "sense of community" and mourn the contemporary loss of community. Such commentaries seem to regard community as a good thing, but they usually aren't very specific about what community is.

According to sociologists, a strong community is characterized by dense, cross-cutting social networks (Wellman and Berkowitz 1988). A community is strongest when everybody knows everybody else and when all members of the community are linked to one another through complex and overlapping ties. These ties need not be strong. Research shows that a network of weak ties can have important consequences for a community. As the proportion of people who know each other increases, social control and cohesion increase. Deviance and fear of crime are reduced, better control is exercised over children, and persons who are weak or disabled are more likely to be cared for (Freudenburg 1986).

A growing body of research shows the importance of voluntary associations and weak ties for community integration. Voluntary associations, especially those that cut across social class and race, create horizontal and vertical links within the community; these links increase the likelihood that community members will feel a sense of cohesion and solidarity, that they will come to one another's aid and conform to community norms (McPherson 1983).

Community cohesion is fostered by many of the same factors that create cohesion in smaller groups: high levels of interaction, stability of membership, similarity, and size. Although it is more difficult to build cohesion in a large, diverse community than in a small, homogeneous one, research shows that a high level of participation in voluntary associations can create a network of weak ties that substantially increase community cohesion (Sampson 1988).

THINKING CRITICALLY

Do you have a "sense of community" in your own life? If so, how has it affected your mental health and behavior? If not, how has the absence of a "sense of community" affected your mental health and behavior, do you think?

GLOBAL PERSPECTIVES: IN-GROUPS, OUT-GROUPS, AND VOLUNTARY ASSOCIATIONS IN NORTHERN IRELAND

In August 1994, the Irish Republican Army (IRA) announced a cease-fire in Northern Ireland. The cease-fire did not stop subsequent bombings in London (Thomas and Elliott 1966), but many believed it was a beginning toward a negotiated peace in Northern Ireland. Over the past 25 years, the IRA's bombings, drive-by shootings, and other terrorist acts had killed about half of the more than 3,000 murdered in Northern Ireland's struggle. Many of us have been hearing about the sporadic terrorism of the IRA since childhood. But just who are these people, and what exactly is their point?

The story behind the cease-fire is an often violent drama dating back four centuries, a drama in which the players are various groups and organizations. Although the antagonists in Northern Ireland's conflict are Protestants and Catholics, the struggle is not over religious doctrine. Religion is simply a convenient way for them to mark off differences between in- and out-groups.

MAP 5.1
IRELAND

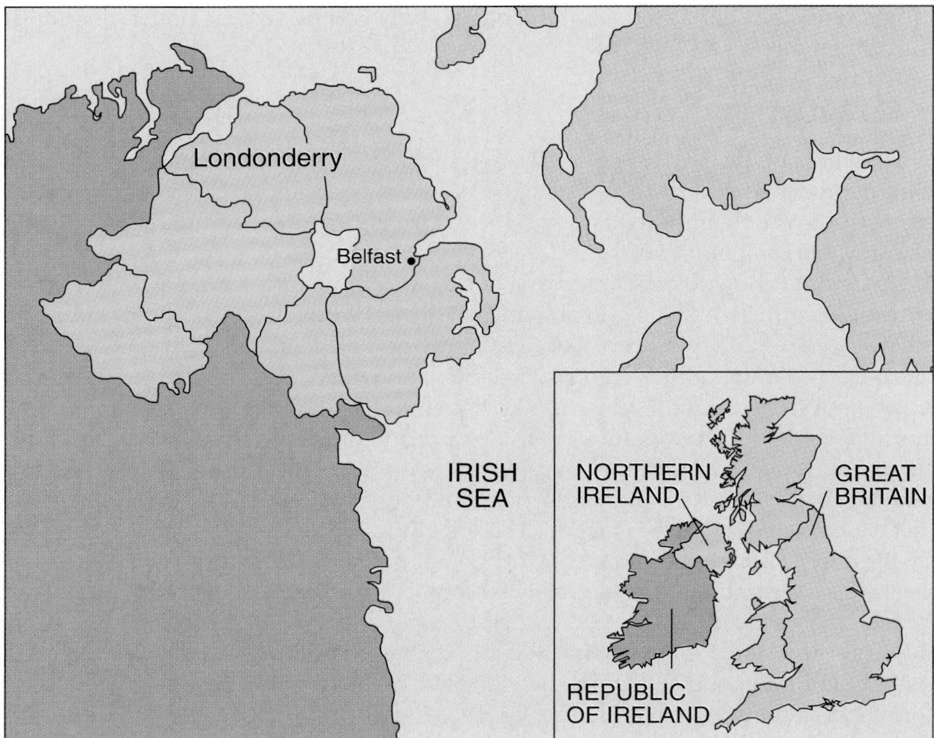

Conflict between Protestants and Catholics in Northern Ireland began in the 1600s when Protestant England colonized Catholic Ireland. In Ulster, the section of the Irish island closest to England, the British confiscated Irish land. In what is known today as the Plantation of Ulster, Scottish Presbyterians and English Anglicans settled. Whereas Catholics comprise an overwhelming majority in the rest of Ireland, in Ulster the Protestant settlers eventually outnumbered the Catholics by about three to one (Osborne and Cormack 1991). Subordinating the Irish, the Protestants took over the government and other social institutions in Ulster. Catholics were systematically denied equal rights in housing, education, and the workplace. Thus began three centuries of in-group–out-group competition and conflict between Irish Catholics and British Protestants.

Late in the 1800s, England began to consider independence for all of Ireland. The Ulster Protestants strongly resisted this, because in an independent Ireland, they would be greatly outnumbered by Catholics. Their slogan, "Home rule is Rome rule," expressed their fear of losing their identity among a Catholic out-group. The Ulster Protestants initiated efforts to stop Irish independence. A voluntary association, the Orange Order, emerged as a Protestant political and paramilitary force with the purpose of defending the status quo (Darby 1976). Today, the Orange Order remains one of the strongest organizations in Northern Ireland's political and social life.

The situation simmered until 1916, when armed Irish Catholic nationalists rebelled against British rule in the Easter Rising. To strike some compromise between the Orange Order Protestants and the nationalists, Great Britain passed the Government of Ireland Act in 1920. The act divided Ireland into North and

South. The North would remain under British protection and was named Northern Ireland. The South was granted full independence and eventually named the Republic of Ireland.

The division satisfied neither the North nor the South. The Orange Order did not want independence for any of Ireland, while the South wanted a unified and sovereign Ireland that included Ulster. Each group saw itself as an in-group with the other as the out-group. Expectedly, each of these two in-groups maintained a distinctly different set of values regarding the out-group and a unified Ireland. At this point, a terrorist Catholic voluntary association emerged to fight on for a unified, independent Ireland: the Irish Republican Army.

Despite the existence of two opposing paramilitary organizations (the Orange Order and the IRA), the period from the late 1920s until 1969 was characterized more by competition between the two factions than by conflict. Violence flared on and off during the 1930s, but World War II brought economic prosperity to Ulster's shipbuilding, aircraft, and other industries. New occupations opened to Catholics, and many gained access to higher education (McAllister 1977). Political leaders emerged among these educated Catholics. Taking African Americans as a reference group, Catholics in Northern Ireland initiated their own civil rights movement. They used protest marches and sit-ins similar to those used in America. They sang the anthem of the U.S. civil rights movement, "We Shall Overcome." Specifically, they sought to end discrimination in voting, housing, and employment. At this time, the Ulster Catholics' goal was not the eventual unification of Ulster with the Republic but more civil rights and equality for Catholics in Northern Ireland.

Unfortunately, the civil rights movement and hope for cooperation between the Catholics and Protestants in Northern Ireland failed. In 1969, rioting began in Londonderry and spread to Belfast. To restore order, the British government sent troops from England.

By 1970, the IRA was an active paramilitary force (Holland 1982). With the emergence of renewed violence, the group split into two factions, the official IRA, committed to a primarily nonviolent political course, and the provisional IRA, which favored using violent means to bring about unification with the South. Gradually, the provisional arm became the major Catholic paramilitary organization. Irish-American Catholics, seeing themselves as sharing an in-group with their Catholic Irish relatives, often sent money for arms and ammunition to the IRA.

Ulster Protestants countered the IRA with vigilante organizations of their own, such as the Ulster Volunteer Force (UVF). Paramilitary groups on both sides became the chief conflicting forces, killing each other in about equal numbers. Children grew up in families, schools, and neighborhoods where IRA or UVF terrorism was an honorable tradition to be continued. Hence, new generations, especially boys, learned to value in- and out-group violence in early primary groups and later in voluntary associations.

For nearly 25 years, little seemed to change in this basic situation. Twice as likely to be unemployed and about half as likely to be professionals (Osborne and Cormack 1991), Catholics in Northern Ireland remained economically subordinated. The British Army, though reduced in size, remained in Northern Ireland, with about 17,600 foot soldiers in 1994 (Pedersen 1994). The opposing terrorist organizations persisted in a kind of urban guerrilla warfare, intent on protecting their communities and promoting the cause of either reunification, on the one hand (the IRA), or the status quo, on the other (the UVF).

Meanwhile, however, a more moderate element in the IRA evolved: Sinn Fein, the political, not military, branch of the IRA. Sinn Fein is led by Gerry Adams (who visited the United States in February 1994 on a U.S. visa, controversially granted by President Bill Clinton). Largely because of Adams and Sinn Fein, the IRA announced "a complete cessation of military operations" in August 1994. The announced cease-fire raised hope that "the troubles" were coming to an end. Convincing the primary groups in some families and neighborhoods of Northern Ireland, where guerrilla warfare has become a valued tradition, that peace is desirable and within reach will be difficult (Pedersen and Watson 1996). Nevertheless, as John Hume, leader of Northern Ireland's moderate Catholic Party has said, "Once we start spilling our sweat together and not our blood, then the old barriers will break down" (Pedersen 1994).

BUREAUCRACIES

In addition to our involvement in small groups and voluntary associations, most of us are involved with bureaucracies. Our schools, workplaces, hospitals, military, and even churches are bureaucratic organizations.

Bureaucracies make a major contribution to the overall quality of life within society (Hall 1995). Because of their size and complexity, however, they don't supply the cohesion and personal satisfaction that smaller groups do. They may make their members feel as if they are simply cogs in the machine rather than important people in their own right.

Bureaucracy is a complex organization characterized by explicit rules and a hierarchical authority structure, all designed to maximize efficiency.

Bureaucracy is a complex organization characterized by explicit rules and a hierarchical authority structure, all designed to maximize efficiency. In popular usage, *bureaucracy* often has a negative connotation: red tape, silly rules, and unyielding rigidity. In social science, however, it is simply an organization in which the social structure has been carefully planned to maximize efficiency.

THE CLASSIC VIEW

Most large, complex organizations are bureaucratic: IBM, General Motors, U.S. Steel, the Catholic church, colleges, and hospitals. The major characteristics of bureaucracies were outlined 80 years ago by Max Weber ([1910] 1970a):

1. *Division of labor and specialization*. Bureaucratic organizations employ specialists in all positions and make them responsible for specific duties. Job titles and job descriptions specify who is responsible for each activity.

2. *Hierarchy of authority*. Positions are arranged in a hierarchy so that each position, except the one at the very top, is under the control and supervision of a higher position. Frequently referred to as chains of command, these lines of authority and responsibility are easily drawn on an organization chart, often in the shape of a pyramid.

3. *Rules and regulations*. All activities and operations of a bureaucracy are governed by abstract rules or procedures. These rules are designed to cover almost every possible situation that might arise: hiring, firing, and the everyday operations of the office. The object is to standardize all activities.

4. *Impersonal relationships*. Interactions in a bureaucracy are supposed to be guided by the rules rather than by personal feelings. Consistent application of impersonal rules is intended to eliminate favoritism and particularism.

Strong communities are built on dense networks of weak ties. When everybody knows everybody else or at least knows them through a cousin or neighbor, then community norms are reinforced, and the community is more likely to be able to work together. This is most easily accomplished in small, stable communities where the residents share much in common.

5. *Careers, tenure, and technical qualifications.* Candidates for bureaucratic positions are almost always selected on the basis of technical qualifications, such as high scores on civil service examinations, education, or experience. Once selected for a position, a person advances in the hierarchy by means of achievement and seniority.
6. *Efficiency.* Bureaucratic organizations coordinate the activities of a large number of people in the pursuit of organized goals. All activities have been designed to maximize efficiency. From the practice of hiring on the basis of credentials rather than personal contacts to the rigid specification of duties and authority, the whole system is constructed to keep individuality, whim, and particularism out of the operation of the organization.

Organizational Culture

Weber's classic theory of bureaucracy almost demands robots rather than individuals. Furthermore, a list of rules that covers every possible situation would be unwieldy and impossibly long. Not surprisingly, therefore, we find that few organizations try to be totally bureaucratic. Instead, organizations strive to create an atmosphere of goodwill and common purpose among their members so that everybody will apply their ingenuity and best efforts to meeting organizational goals (DiTomaso 1987). This goodwill is as essential to efficiency as are the rules. In most organizations, in fact, working exactly according to the rules is considered a form of sabotage. For example, unions of public employees (such as the police) that cannot legally strike engage in "working to the rule" as a form of protest: They follow every little rule and fill out every form carefully. The result is usually a sharp slowdown in work and general chaos.

Many bureaucratic organizations use the company picnic as a strategy to build a positive organizational culture. They hope that the personal ties built during such informal occasions will motivate employees to go beyond the formal rules and to give their best efforts to promoting the company's and their employer's interests. In this picture, Steve Jobs (formerly of Apple Computer and now head of Next Computers) appears at a Next company picnic barefooted. This just-one-of-the-guys informality and family atmosphere may mask the fact that such picnics are good for business.

Oligarchy is the control of a bureaucratic organization by the few at the top.

Sociologists use the term *organizational culture* to refer to the pattern of norms and values that affect how business is actually carried out in an organization. The key to a successful organizational culture is cohesion, and most organizations strive to build cohesion among their members. They do this by encouraging interaction among employees (providing lunchrooms, sponsoring after-hours sports leagues, having company picnics and newsletters, and developing unifying symbols, such as mascots, company colors, and uniforms). This is perhaps most clearly apparent in the large bureaucratic organization represented by a university, but it is also characteristic of multinational corporations.

In many organizations, the formal rules have very little to do with the day-to-day activity of the members. In situations as varied as classrooms and shop floors, people evolve their own way of doing business and may have little use for the formal rules (Ouchi and Wilkins 1985); in fact, they may not even know what the rules are. What determines whether an organization works by the rules or not?

A major factor affecting degree of bureaucratization in an organization is the degree of uncertainty in the organization's activities. When activities tend to be routine and predictable, then the organization is likely to emphasize rules, central planning, and hierarchical chains of command. When activities change rapidly in unpredictable ways, there is more emphasis on flexibility and informal decision making (Simpson 1985). This explains why, for example, classrooms tend to be less bureaucratic and ball-bearings factories more bureaucratic.

Criticisms of Bureaucracy

Bureaucracy is the standard organizational form in the modern world. Organizations from churches to governments are run along bureaucratic lines. Despite the widespread adoption of this organizational form, it has several major drawbacks. Three of the most widely acknowledged are as follows:

1. *Ritualism*. Rigid adherence to rules may mean that a rule is followed regardless of whether it helps accomplish the purpose for which it was designed. The rule becomes an end in itself rather than a means to an end. For example, individuals may interpret a rule stating that the workday ends at 5 P.M. to mean that they cannot work later even if they want to. Overemphasis on rules can stifle initiative and prevent the development of more efficient procedures (Blau and Meyer 1971).
2. *Alienation*. The stress on rules, hierarchies, and impersonal relationships can sharply reduce the cohesion of the organization. This has several drawbacks: It reduces social control, it increases turnover, and it reduces member satisfaction and commitment. All of these factors may interfere with the organization's ability to reach its goals.
3. *Structured inequality/oligarchy*. Critics charge that the modern bureaucracy with its multiple layers of authority is a profoundly antidemocratic organization. In fact, the whole purpose of the bureaucratic form is to concentrate power in one or two decision makers, whose decisions are then passed down as orders to subordinates below. Control of a bureaucratic organization by the few at the top is called **oligarchy.** The issue of oligarchy was first raised in 1911 by Robert Michels, a sociologist and friend of Max Weber. According to Michels's "iron law of oligarchy," the amassing of concentrated power in the name of efficiency and rationalism is incompatible with a truly democratic society (Michels [1911] 1949, 41). Some contemporary critics agree (Perrow 1986).

Thinking Critically

From your experience, what are some functions of bureaucracy? What are some dysfunctions? Would you classify the dysfunctions as manifest or latent? Why?

SOCIAL APPLICATIONS

What Is Network Intervention, and Does It Work?

Group membership furnishes a wide array of benefits for individuals. Furthermore, socially integrated persons are in general more likely to be conforming individuals, whose group ties keep them from violating important social norms.

The opposite of the socially integrated individual with a complex social network is the person who is socially isolated, who has few or no ties to others. Such individuals tend to require large amounts of social services and to cause a disproportionate amount of trouble—not just for themselves but also for their communities. When a large proportion of a community lacks social integration, high levels of alcoholism, drug abuse, child neglect, crime, and mental illness are likely to result.

For these reasons, many policy makers, especially at the local and state levels, encourage individuals to participate in groups. *Network interventions*, as such policy initiatives are known, take a variety of forms.

1. *Fostering neighborhood networks*. This includes facilitating such neighborhood endeavors as block parties, neighborhood watch, and block parent programs, as well as providing neighborhood centers to encourage interaction of neighbors. It also includes zoning regulations and building codes designed to encourage neighboring in housing projects and apartment buildings (Brownell and Shumacher 1984; Kalb 1996).
2. *Fostering voluntary associations*. As a matter of public policy, many agencies supply funding and support facilities for civic and recreational groups, from scouts to teen basketball teams to senior bowlers (Alter 1995b).
3. *Fostering supportive weak ties*. A wide variety of imaginative strategies have been implemented to train people in weak-tie relationships to provide more social support (Alter 1995b). One program, for example, trained hairdressers (who often receive confidences from their clients while styling hair) to offer more social support (Wiesenfeld and Weiss 1979).
4. *Fostering support groups*. A growing method of direct network intervention involves providing support groups and hot lines for individuals in special need, such as alcoholics, abused wives, dieters, teen mothers, diabetics, and so on.

But before local governments leap into the social director business, a few critical issues need to be addressed.

1. Artificially fostered support groups may not offer the same kinds of benefits as naturally occurring support groups. Nevertheless, preliminary research on support groups provided for teen mothers showed that it is precisely those young women who had the least natural social support who benefited most from support groups (Unger and Wandersman 1985).
2. Intervention strategies may put the cart before the horse. Perhaps a large part of the relationship between well-being and group membership is due to the fact that healthy, conforming individuals choose to belong to groups. If this is true, encouraging poorly adjusted individuals to join groups will not result in substantial improvements.
3. Group memberships can be a source of stress as well as support. Memberships may demand more time and energy than a person has to give and may end up being a drain rather than a support.

Group memberships and strong social networks are beneficial for individuals and the community (Gottlieb 1981; Brown 1991). However, there are obvious limitations to their effectiveness. Although social networks are helpful, they cannot be used as cheap substitutes for existing social services. Personal networks can help people deal with poverty or disability, but they cannot by themselves put food on the table or provide safe neighborhoods (Chapman and Pancoast 1985).

Thinking Critically

What kinds of network intervention have been tried or could be tried in your neighborhood? How might they be organized? Who would participate? How could they be helpful? What problems would network intervention *not* solve in your community?

SOCIOLOGY ON THE NET

A community is strongest when everybody knows everybody else and when all members are linked to one another through complex and overlapping ties. In the past we would think of neighborhoods where the residents knew each other and talked on porches and over back fences. Perhaps the community of the future will be a human community linked by computers in an "electronic village." Several American communities are electronically networked. One of the most advanced is the Blacksburg Electronic Village in Blacksburg, Virginia.

http://www.bev.net

Browse through this electronic village by starting with the sections for **newcomers**. The **Welcome Page** and **Introduction** will get you off to a good start. After you are familiar with this site visit the section called **Starting a Village**. How did this community become an electronic village? Are all segments of the community joined with links? Who is in and who is left out? Could a system like this work in your home town?

To better understand the nature and depth of the conflict in Northern Ireland let's go to the original sources and begin with the Joint Declaration on Peace.

http://www.globalgateway.com/Local/local.htm

As you browse through this document, note the constant reference to the two traditions and cultures that make up that island nation. Now take a look at one Protestant perspective.

http://www.ireland.com

Click on the section entitled **Politics** and open the section on the **Grand Orange Lodge of Ireland**. Scroll down to the menu that includes the **Qualifications of an Orangeman, The Making of the Orange Institution, Orangeism Today** and **The Traditions of Parades**. Browse through these three selections. What is an Orangeman? Why do they march? What role does religion play in the Orange culture?

Now go back to the main menu and open the section on the **Sinn Fein Party**. Browse through the site making sure to open the highlighted terms of **conflict, injustice and division in Ireland, British rule in six of Ireland's 32 counties**, and **Ard Chomhairle**. What is Sinn Fein? How does their position differ from that of the Grand Orange Lodge? What has to change so that each side will no longer see the other as the out group?

SUMMARY

1. Relationships are characterized by four basic social processes: exchange, cooperation, competition, and conflict.
2. Groups are distinguished from aggregates and categories in that members of groups take one another into account and their interaction is shaped by shared social structure.
3. Group interaction is affected by group size and the proximity and communication patterns of group members. The amount of interaction in turn affects group

cohesion, the amount of social control the group can exercise over members, and the quality of group decisions.

4 A fundamental distinction between groups is the distinction between primary and secondary groups. Primary groups are small, intimate, lasting groups that are essential to individual satisfaction and integration; they are also the primary agents of social control in society. Secondary groups are large, impersonal groups that are generally task oriented and that perform instrumental functions for societies and individuals.

5 Each person has a social network that consists of both strong and weak ties. The number of these ties is generally greater for individuals who are urban, middle-aged, and highly educated.

6 Voluntary associations may mediate between the primary and secondary group, providing a bridge that links the individual to larger groups. Voluntary associations combine some of the expressive functions of primary groups with the instrumental functions of secondary groups.

7 The centuries-long conflict in Northern Ireland between Catholics and Protestants can better be understood as paramilitary conflict between opposed in- and out-groups. Voluntary associations, such as the Orange Order and the IRA, have played central roles in "the troubles."

8 A bureaucracy is a rationally designed organization whose goal is to maximize efficiency. The chief characteristics of a bureaucracy are division of labor and specialization, a hierarchy of authority, a system of rules and regulations, impersonality in social situations, and emphasis on careers, tenure, and technical qualifications.

9 Although most contemporary organizations are built on a bureaucratic model, many are far less rational and impersonal than the classic model suggests. All effective bureaucracies rely on an organizational culture to inspire employees to give their best efforts to help meet organizational goals.

10 Bureaucracies have been criticized for promoting ritualism, alienation, and antidemocratic oligarchy.

11 The positive effects of social networks for individuals and communities are so broad that many government initiatives are designed to support and encourage the development of social networks. These network interventions have positive impacts but cannot replace direct social services.

SUGGESTED READINGS

BROWN, Leonard H. 1991. *Groups for Growth and Change*. New York: Longman. An interesting discussion of how groups, particularly reference groups, assist individuals in personal growth.

COREY, Marianne Schneider. 1992. *Groups: Process and Practice*, 4th ed. Pacific Grove, CA: Brooks/Cole. A sociology text on group definitions and processes.

CURTIS, James E., Edward G. Grabb, and Douglas Baer. 1992. "Voluntary Association Membership in Fifteen Countries: A Comparative Analysis." *American Sociological Review* 57 (2) (April): 139–152.

DOUGLAS, Tom. 1983. *Groups: Understanding People Gathered Together*. London: Tavistock. An engaging book that focuses on the similarity of group processes in teams, families, and other small groups.

FISCHER, Claude S. 1982. *To Dwell among Friends: Personal Networks in Town and City*. Chicago: University of Chicago Press. A report of Fischer's research in northern California, including an excellent overview of sociological concerns about social networks.

FISCHER, Claude S. 1992. *America Calling: A Social History of the Telephone to 1940*. Berkeley: University of California Press. Fischer's research on social networking has motivated him to investigate the social history of the telephone in the United States, a cultural artifact that facilitates networking in modern society.

HALL, Richard H. (ed.). 1995. *Complex Organizations*. Brookfield, VT: Dartmouth University Press. A collection of theoretical and research-based essays on various aspects of complex organizations in industrialized societies today.

HOMANS, George C. 1950. *The Human Group*. New York: Harcourt, Brace. A classic that deals with the dynamics of small groups in several contexts (families, work groups, gangs). The basic processes and structures of groups are examined in such a way that application to our own group memberships is made easy and straightforward.

LAWLER, Edward J., and Jeongkoo Yoon. 1996. "Commitment in Exchange Relations." *American Sociological Review 61* (1) (February): 89–108.

MARSDEN, Peter V. 1992. "Social Network Theory." Pp. 1887–1894 in Edgar F. Borgatta and Marie L. Borgatta (eds.) *Encyclopedia of Sociology*, vol. 4. New York: Macmillan.

MOR-BARAK, Michael E. 1991. *Social Networks and Health of the Frail Elderly*. New York: Garland. An examination of how social networks and their resultant sense of community positively affect health in old age.

NESTMANN, Frank, and Klaus Hurrelmann, eds. 1994. *Social Networks and Social Support in Childhood and Adolescence*. New York: Walter de Gruyter. A research-based evaluation of the way that networks and social support can be used to positively influence children and teenagers.

PERROW, Charles. 1986. *Complex Organizations: A Critical Essay*. (3rd ed.) New York: Random House. An overview of classic bureaucratic theory and the ways it operates in practice.

UNIT TWO

Conformity and Nonconformity

CHAPTER 6

The Individual and Society

OUTLINE

PROLOGUE

Have You Ever . . . wondered how you would have turned out if you had different parents? You may have considered your friends' families and wondered what you would have been like if your parents had been richer, if you had been an only child, or if your parents had been of a different race or ethnicity.

Although you may think that you would have turned out better (or worse) with different parents, we usually don't have any choice about our parents. As we get older, we have more choices about what relationships we will enter into and what roles we will take on. For example, almost everyone reading this book has made a choice to go to college and has chosen to enroll in a specific school.

The college choice reflects the complexity of the relationship between individuals and social structures. Your prior circumstances affected your college choice, and your college choice affects your present and will affect your future circumstances. Maybe you would turn out differently if your campus were richer, more prestigious, smaller, or of a different race/ethnicity mix.

As this example illustrates, it is not only in childhood that we are influenced by the social structures and relationships around us. In this chapter, we begin to examine the relationship between individuals and social structures. We are concerned with why individuals behave as they do and how their behavior is related to the social structures of which they are a part.

The previous chapters of this book have focused on macrosociology—analysis of cultures, institutions, social structures, groups, and organizations. This focus on structures should not obscure the fact that at the heart of sociology is a concern with *people*. Sociology is interesting and useful to the extent that it helps us explain why people do what they do. It should let us see ourselves, our families, and our acquaintances in a new light.

In this chapter, on socialization, and the next chapter, on the sociology of everyday life, we deal directly with individuals. These two chapters can be viewed as a pair; taken together, they help us to understand the relationship of the individual to society. This chapter looks at how individuals are molded within social structures; the next chapter examines the ways in which individuals interpret and manipulate this molding process.

THE SELF AND SELF-CONCEPT

From the newborn infant develops a complex and fascinating human being, a human being who is simultaneously much like every other human being and at the same time exactly like no other.

Each individual **self** may be thought of as a combination of unique attributes and normative responses. Within sociology, these two parts of the self are called the *I* and the *me* (Mead 1934).

The **self** is a complex whole that includes unique attributes and normative responses. In sociology, these two parts are called the *I* and the *me*.

In English grammar, *me* is used when we speak of ourselves as the object of others' actions ("She sent me to the office"); *I* is used when we speak of ourselves as the actor ("I threw spitballs"). Sociological use follows this convention. According to the sociologist George Herbert Mead, the ***I*** is the spontaneous, creative part of the self; the ***me*** is the self as social object, the part of the self that responds to others' expectations.

The ***I*** is the spontaneous, creative part of the self.

The ***me*** represents the self as social object.

As this description of the self implies, the two parts may pull us in different directions. For example, many people face a daily conflict between the *I* and the *me* when the alarm clock goes off in the morning—the *I* wants to roll over and go back to sleep, but the *me* knows it is supposed to get up and go to class. Some of these conflicts are resolved in favor of the *me* and some in favor of the *I*. Daily behavior, however, is viewed as the result of an ongoing internal dialogue between the *I* and the *me*.

The **self-concept** is the self we are aware of. It is our thoughts about our personalities and social roles.

The self is enormously complex, and we are often not fully aware of our own motives, capabilities, and characteristics. The self we are aware of is our **self-concept.** It consists of our thoughts about our personalities and social roles. For example, a young man's self-concept might include such qualities as: young, male, Methodist, good athlete, poor student, shy, awkward with girls, responsible, American. His self-concept includes all the images he has of himself in the dozens of different settings in which he interacts.

The self and self-concept are social products; they are developed through social relationships. In the following sections, we examine some of these social processes, beginning with a discussion of infancy and the necessity of nurture.

Learning To Be Human

What is human nature? Are we born with a tendency to be cooperative and sharing or with a tendency to be selfish and aggressive? The question of the basic

The family is our first experience with group living, and the quality of the experience has a lasting influence on our personalities and self-concepts. If our families shower us with warmth and acceptance, then we will learn to love and to laugh. We will also learn to conform in order to please them. Studies show that love is as important as food and shelter for a child's growth and development.

nature of humankind has been the subject of philosophical debate for thousands of years. It continues to be a topic of debate because it is so difficult (some would say impossible) to separate the part of human behavior that arises from our genetic heritage from the part that is developed after birth. The one thing we are sure of is that nature is never enough.

THE NECESSITY OF NURTURE

Each of us begins life with a set of human potentials: the potential to talk, to walk, to love, and to learn. By themselves, however, these natural capacities are not enough to enable us to join the human family. Without nurture—without love and attention and hugging—the human infant is unlikely to survive, much less prosper. The effects of neglect are sometimes fatal; and depending on its severity and length, neglect almost always results in retarded intellectual and social development.

How can we determine the importance of nurture? There are a few case studies of tragically neglected children, but luckily the instances are rare. Some of the first clinical evidence on the effects of limited social interaction on human development was provided by René Spitz's (1945) study of an orphanage where each nurse was in charge of a dozen or more infants. Although the children's physical needs were met, the nurses had little time to give individual attention to each child.

Children who spend the first years of their lives in this type of institutional environment are devastated by the experience. Because of limited personal attention, such children withdraw from the social world; they seldom cry and are indifferent to everything around them. The absence of handling, touching, and movement is the major cause of this retarded development. In time, the children become retarded intellectually and more susceptible to disease and death. Of the 88 children Spitz studied, 23 died before reaching the age of two and a half. Even if they live, Spitz found, socially deprived children are likely to become socially crippled adults.

A number of studies confirm the effects of institutionalized care described by Spitz. Provence and Lipton (1962) compared 75 physically healthy institutionalized infants with a control group of infants raised at home. The institutionalized infants received excellent food and physical care but limited social stimulation. During the first few weeks of life, there was little difference between the two groups. At about three months, however, the institutionalized infants showed increasing signs of retardation. They seldom cried or babbled, lost interest in their surroundings, and by the age of one were noticeably delayed in their language development. Because the infants were healthy to begin with, physical and genetic abnormalities cannot have caused their disabilities. Provence and Lipton concluded that the differences between the control group and the institutionalized infants clearly indicate the devastating effects of social deprivation.

Deprivation can also occur in homes where parents fail to provide adequate social and emotional stimulation. Children who have their physical needs met but are otherwise ignored by their parents have been found to exhibit many of the same symptoms as institutionalized infants. Studies of the effects of isolation and deprivation on children suggest that children need intensive interaction with others to survive and develop normally. Much of the evidence for this conclusion, however, is derived from atypical situations in which unfortunate children have been subjected to extreme and unusual circumstances. To assess the limits of these

It would be clearly unethical to examine the consequences of neglect by experimenting on human infants. And there is growing concern about using animals for this type of research. Harry Harlow, however, conducted several studies with infant monkeys some years ago. One study compared infants who had a wire-covered mother figure with infants who had a terrycloth-covered mother figure such as the one in this picture; both mother figures gave milk. This study found that infant monkeys derived much comfort from cuddling up to the terrycloth mother. Those with the cuddly mother exhibited more normal social behaviors than those with the wire-covered mother figure. Harlow's research shows that simple tactile stimulation is an important element of early experience.

findings and to examine the reversibility of deprivation effects, researchers turned to experiments with monkeys.

MONKEYING WITH ISOLATION AND DEPRIVATION

For more than 20 years, researchers have been experimenting with deprivation and isolation of infant monkeys, although studies like these are now controversial. In a classic series of experiments, Harry Harlow and his associates raised infant monkeys in total isolation. The infants lived in individual cages with mechanical mother figures, which provided milk. Although the infant monkeys' nutritional needs were met, their social needs were not. As a result, both their physical and social growth suffered. They exhibited such bizarre behavior as biting themselves and hiding in corners. As adults, these monkeys refused to mate; if artificially impregnated, the females would not nurse or care for their babies (Harlow and Harlow 1966). These experiments provide dramatic evidence of the importance of being with others; even apparently innate behaviors such as sexuality and maternal behavior must be developed through interaction. On the bright side, the monkey experiments affirm that some of the ill effects of isolation and deprivation are reversible: Young monkeys experienced almost total recovery when placed in a supportive social environment (Suomi, Harlow, and McKinney 1972).

Although it is dangerous to generalize from monkeys to humans, the evidence from the monkey experiments supports observations about human infants: Physical and social development depends on interaction with others. Even being a monkey does not come naturally. The human abilities to walk, to talk, to love, and to laugh all depend on sustained and intimate interaction with others. Clearly, our identities, even our lives, are socially bestowed and socially sustained (Berger 1963, 98) The accompanying Focus on Measurement section discusses the interplay of nature and nurture in one area. The processes through which interaction with others molds us are discussed in the next section.

SYMBOLIC INTERACTION THEORIES

Sociological theories about the development of the self are dominated by symbolic interaction theory. As noted in Chapter 1, this theoretical perspective addresses the subjective meanings of human acts and the processes through which people come to develop and communicate shared meanings.

Over the years, two distinct schools have developed within this perspective: the interaction school and the structural school (Biddle 1986; Turner 1985). The **interaction school of symbolic interaction** focuses on the active role of the individual in creating the self and self-concept. The **structural school of symbolic interaction** focuses on the self as a product of social roles. We will review each school separately and then discuss their similarities and differences.

The **interaction school of symbolic interaction** focuses on the active role of the individual in creating the self and self-concept.

The **structural school of symbolic interaction** focuses on the self as a product of social roles.

THE INTERACTION SCHOOL

The major premise of the interaction school is that people are actively involved in creating and negotiating their own roles and self-concepts. Although each of us is born into an established social structure with established expectations for our behavior, nevertheless we have opportunities to create our own selves. Three con-

FOCUS ON MEASUREMENT

Gender Differences in Mathematics

"... RESEARCHERS REASON THAT GENDER DIFFERENCES IN MATHEMATICAL ABILITY ARE AT LEAST PARTIALLY A RESULT OF BIOLOGY."

Fierce debates once raged about the relative importance of nature (inborn, biological factors) and nurture (environmental, experiential factors), but this issue no longer preoccupies most social scientists. In one area of research, however, the nature/nurture controversy remains heated—the apparent male advantage in mathematics. Studies show that boys outperform girls on standardized math tests, like the SAT; that by high school, boys substantially outnumber girls in advanced mathematics courses; and that in adulthood, women remain substantially underrepresented in occupations, like engineering, that depend heavily on a foundation in mathematics. The pattern seems so consistent that a few scholars have begun to wonder if gender differences in mathematical skills aren't biologically based, after all.

Neuroscientists are beginning to unravel the relationship between exposure to male or female hormones during pregnancy and the characteristic differences in the brain structure of adult men and women. Fetal exposure to testosterone, for instance, is associated with right brain dominance. This association may help to explain not only why more men are left-handed than women but also why they tend to have better visual–spatial skills. Conversely, the fact that language centers are typically located in the left hemisphere of the brain may account for women's tendencies to have better verbal skills.

From findings such as these, researchers reason that gender differences in mathematical ability are at least partially a result of biology. Statistically speaking, however, the differences are small. Since the differences within each sex are so much larger than the differences between sexes, critics of the biological perspective argue that hormones can explain only a very small part of overall variation in mathematical aptitude. This leaves a great deal of room for the influence of social factors. Evidence for this point of view comes from two lines of research.

First, sociologists Richard Felson and Lisa Trudeau (1991) have shown in a recent study of children in grades 5 through 12 that, contrary to results based only on the SAT, girls actually outperform boys on most tests of mathematical performance, especially those that are designed to correspond to the curriculum. Although boys are more likely to *choose* advanced mathematics courses in high school, by many other criteria girls are ahead. Girls' grades in mathematics are higher than boys'; and for required mathematics courses, girls are more likely than boys to be placed in the advanced tracks. Based on these results, Felson and Trudeau argue that males do not have a general advantage in mathematical skills but instead a very specific one—probably in the type of spatial ability usually measured by mental rotation tests.

Second, studies clearly show that the male advantage in mathematical performance has been declining over the last 20 years (Hyde et al. 1990). One possible explanation for this pattern is that boys and girls are now being socialized more similarly, thereby reducing the traditional male advantage in math. A biopsychologist, Janice Juraska, has demonstrated that female rats have fewer nerve connections than males into the hippocampus, a brain region associated with spatial relations and memory. However, when the cages of female rats are "enriched" with stimulating toys, the females develop more neural connections. As Juraska says, "Hormones do affect things—it's crazy to deny that, but there is no telling which way sex differences might go if we completely changed the environment" (quoted in Gorman 1992).

cepts—the *looking-glass self*, *role taking*, and *role making*—illustrate how this process works.

The Looking-Glass Self. Charles Horton Cooley (1864–1929) provided a classic description of how we develop our self-concepts. He proposed that we learn to view ourselves as we *think* others view us. He called the resulting self-concept the **looking-glass self** (Cooley 1902). According to Cooley, there are three steps in the formation of the looking-glass self:

The **looking-glass self** is the self-concept developed in the process of learning to view ourselves as we think others view us.

1. We imagine how we appear to others.
2. We imagine how others judge our appearance.
3. We develop feelings about and responses to these judgments.

For example, an instructor whose students openly talk to one another or doze during class and who frequently finds herself talking to a half-empty room is likely to gather that her students think she is a bad teacher. She need not, however, accept this view. The third stage in the formation of the looking-glass self suggests that the instructor may either accept the students' judgment and conclude that she is a bad teacher or reject their judgment and conclude that the students are simply not smart enough to appreciate her profound remarks. Our self-concepts are not merely mechanical reflections of the judgments of those around us; rather, they rest on our interpretations of and reactions to those judgments. We are actively engaged in defining our self-concepts, using past experiences as one aid in interpreting others' responses. A person who considers herself witty will assume that others are laughing with her, not at her; someone used to making clumsy errors, however, will interpret the laughter differently.

We also actively define our self-concepts by choosing among potential looking glasses. That is, we try to choose roles and associates supportive of our self-concepts (Gecas and Schwalbe 1983). The looking glass is thus a way of both forming and maintaining self-concept.

As Cooley's theory indicates, symbolic interaction considers subjective interpretations to be extremely important determinants of the self-concept. It is not only others' judgments of us that matter; our subjective interpretation of those judgments is equally important. This premise of symbolic interactionism is apparent in a classic statement by W. I. Thomas: If people "define situations as real, they are real in their consequences" (Thomas and Thomas 1928, 572). People interact through the medium of symbols (words, gestures) that must be subjectively interpreted. The interpretations have real consequences—even if they are *mis*interpretations.

Role taking involves imagining ourselves in the role of the other in order to determine the criteria the other will use to judge our behavior.

Role Taking. The most influential contributor to symbolic interaction theory during this century is George Herbert Mead (1863–1931). Mead argued that we learn social norms through the process of **role taking**—imagining ourselves in the role of the other in order to determine the criteria the other will use to judge our behavior. We use this information as a guide for our own behavior.

According to Mead, role taking begins in childhood, when we learn the rights and obligations associated with being children in our particular families. To understand what is expected of us as children, we must also learn our mothers' and fathers' roles. We must learn to see ourselves from our parents' perspective and to evaluate our behavior from their point of view. Only when we have learned their role perspective as well as our own will we really understand what our own obligations are.

Mead maintained that children develop their role knowledge by playing games. When children play house, they develop their ideas of how husbands, wives, and children relate to one another. As the little boy comes in saying, "I've had a hard day; I hope it's not my turn to cook dinner," or as the little girl warns her dolls not to play in the street and to wash their hands before eating, they are testing their knowledge of family role expectations.

Significant others are the role players with whom we have close personal relationships.

In the very early years, role playing and role taking are responsive to the expectations of **significant others**—those people we are very close to and whose good

Dressing up and playing mommy and daddy are almost univeral aspects of childhood. Whether they use their parents' old clothes or find some in a box at day care, little children act out their own visions of how people ought to behave. Their play is filled with little side dramas where they step out of their temporary roles and discuss what ought to happen next and what the rules of play—and life—are. Mead suggests that this role taking is an essential way in which children learn and practice acceptable behavior.

opinion is important to us. Day care teachers, siblings, and, most of all, parents are important in forming a child's self-concept. As children mature and participate beyond this close and familiar network, the process of role taking is expanded to a larger network that helps them understand what society in general expects of them. They learn what the bus driver, their schoolmates, and their employers expect. Eventually, they come to be able to judge their behavior not only from the perspective of significant others but also from the perspective of what Mead calls the **generalized other**—the composite expectations of all the other role players with whom they interact. Being aware of the expectations of the generalized other is equivalent to having learned the norms and values of the culture. One has learned how to act like an American or a Pole or a Nigerian.

Thinking Critically

Think about the student role in your own life. To what extent did you *take* it? To what extent do you *make* it?

The **generalized other** is the composite expectations of all the other role players with whom we interact; it is Mead's term for our awareness of social norms.

Role Making. Having learned the requirements, or **role prescriptions,** for the various roles we take does not mean that we all play our roles just alike. Not all teachers teach in exactly the same way, for example. Ralph Turner (1962) introduced the concept of role making to address this situation. **Role making** is the process whereby persons actively define or interpret their roles to suit their individual personalities. Initially, role making requires role taking, but a second step involves the creative adaptation of that role. For example, taking the role of dentist would require that you work on people's teeth. But as you make the role to suit your own personality, you might decide to be open during regular working hours or only on evenings and weekends. And you might be a dentist with a sense of humor or a very serious one. Turner stresses that role making is most pronounced when situations are vague and ambiguous. In this time of considerable social change regarding family structure, for instance, husbands, wives, mothers, and fathers are often engaged in role making.

Role prescriptions are the norms or requirements associated with the various roles individuals play.

Role making is the process whereby persons actively define or interpret their roles to suit their individual personalities.

In sum, the fact that everyone learns the norms and values of his or her culture does not mean that everyone behaves alike or follows the same rules. My significant others are not the same as yours. Not only do our family experiences differ by subculture, but also, as we get older, we have some freedom in choosing those whose expectations will guide our behavior. Beyond this, we fashion, or make, the roles we take to suit our individual personalities.

The Negotiated Self. Role taking and the looking-glass self are ways in which the individual can become an active agent in the construction of his or her own self-concept. The self that emerges is a *negotiated* self, a self that the individual has fashioned by selectively choosing looking glasses and significant others.

The idea of negotiation suggests that we have an end in view. What is that end? An important one is to protect and enhance our self-esteem. **Self-esteem** is the evaluative part of the self-concept; it is our judgment of our worth compared with that of others.

Self-esteem is the evaluative component of the self-concept; it is our judgment about our worth compared with that of others.

Summary. According to the interaction school of symbolic interaction, the individual takes an active role in negotiating the self and self-concept. These are not imposed by others or by the social structure; rather, they are negotiated by the individual during the process of interacting with others. An important goal in this process is the enhancement of self-esteem.

THE STRUCTURAL SCHOOL

The structural school of symbolic interaction differs from the interaction school by stressing the importance of institutionalized social structures. Unlike the interaction school, which gives the individual a great deal of freedom in negotiating a self-concept, the structural school believes that individuals are constrained and shaped in important ways by society.

Scholars from the structural school focus on institutionalized social statuses and roles such as belonging to a particular ethnic group or gender, working, parenting, and going to school. These scholars stress the profound ability of statuses and roles to shape both behavior and personality. The key concept in structural theory is **role identity,** the image we have of ourselves in specific social roles (Burke 1980, 18). For example, a women who is a professor, a mother, and an aerobics student will have a different role identity in each setting. According to structural theorists, her self-concept will be a composite of these multiple identities (Stryker 1981).

Role identity is the image one has of oneself in a specific social role.

Situated identity is the role identity used in a particular situation. It implies that a person's identity depends on the situation.

The Situated Self. Each of us has multiple role identities, one for each of our major roles. Sometimes this makes it difficult for observers—even ourselves—to decide which is the Real Me. In a sense, there is no Real Me. Instead we use one role identity at home, another at the office, and yet another one when we are out of town. We use the concept of **situated identity** to refer to the role identity used in a particular situation.

The idea of a situated self draws heavily on the analogy of life as a stage. As you move from scene to scene, you change costumes, get a new script, and come out as a different character. A young man may play the role of dutiful son at home, heavy-duty partier at the dorm, and serious scholar in the classroom. None of these images is necessarily false; but because it is difficult to carry on the roles simultaneously, the young man does not try to do so. Most of us engage in this practice with-

THINKING CRITICALLY

What role identity is most important to you now? Do you think that might change over the course of your life? Why or why not?

out even thinking about it. We adjust our vocabularies, topics of conversation, and apparent values and concerns automatically as we talk to elderly relatives, our friends, and our coworkers. In this sense, each of us is like the elephant described by the six blind men; someone trying to find the Real Me might have a hard time reconciling the different views that we present.

This man occupies many different statuses: he has a disability, he is a teacher, he is a man, he is Hispanic. Each of these statuses provides a role identity, a set of norms that defines how he ought to act. Which takes priority? In some settings, he may react primarily as a man; in others, the teacher role will take the lead. The prominence of a particular role identity can change from setting to setting, but we also have an identity hierarchy that makes some roles more important than others. Some people with disabilities are so overwhelmed by the experience that the disability becomes their dominant identity; others, such as this teacher, accord it a lower place in their identity hierarchy.

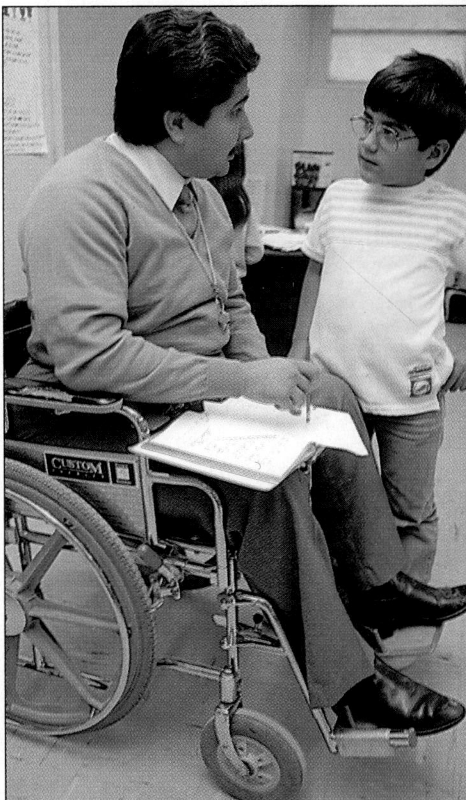

Identity Hierarchies. The concept of the situated identity implies that we play one role at a time and ignore the obligations associated with other roles. In practice, however, competing demands often develop that force us to choose between different selves. If your brother's wedding is scheduled for the weekend on which you have been offered an interview for a wonderful job, which will you attend? Which self will take priority? This is an example of role conflict, described in Chapter 4.

A related concept is status inconsistency. Each of us occupies a number of positions in the social structure, or statuses, at the same time; and some of them may seem incompatible. **Status inconsistency** results when one of a person's statuses has considerably more (or less) prestige than the others or when an individual's various statuses are socially defined as inappropriately linked. A female U.S. president might feel that those two statuses were inconsistent, for example. A househusband might experience status inconsistency between his social positions as male and homemaker. How do people respond to the conflicting feelings that status inconsistency can cause?

Some people challenge the social structure to change so that their statuses are considered consistent. The Women's Movement and the Civil Rights Movement are examples. Another mechanism for relieving the psychological effects of status inconsistency and also for making choices regarding role conflicts is to establish an **identity hierarchy,** a ranking of various role identities in order of their importance (Callero 1985). Whenever two roles come into conflict, you simply follow the role that ranks higher on your list. Research shows that in ranking role identities, we give preference to the roles that provide us with the most self-esteem. This reflects two things: the social status associated with a role and our skill in performing it.

Most women, for example, who are both professors and aerobics students will rank being a professor higher in their identity hierarchy. The relative ranking of mother and professor might present a greater problem. Undoubtedly, some women would rank the professor role higher than the mother role; such women would follow the norms of their job in cases of role conflicts. Differences in identity hierarchies help explain why two people with the same sets of roles behave differently (Serpe 1987). Some professor/mothers, for example, will go to the office on Saturday, while some will stay at home.

Social Structure and the Self. Following their assumption that individual identities are shaped by institutionalized roles, symbolic interactionists from the structural school study the processes through which people who share a social status develop into similar sorts of people. They ask whether being working class as opposed to middle class or being a physician instead of a truck driver produces different patterns of personality and self-concept.

Many studies demonstrate that people who occupy different structural positions, or statuses, tend to have different values and personalities (Ellis 1994; Grusky 1994). For example, lower-class individuals tend to be more likely to believe in living for the moment and less likely to think it is worthwhile to save for the future.

Status inconsistency results when one of an individual's statuses has considerably more (or less) prestige than the others or when an individual's various statuses are socially defined as inappropriately linked.

Identity hierarchy is a ranking of an individual's various role identities in order of their importance to him or her.

Why is this true? Some insights come from the study *Tally's Corner*, reviewed in Chapter 2. In this study, Liebow (1967) concluded that "it was inescapable that getting and keeping a job was of low priority" (p. 34) to the street-corner men he studied. Although some scholars have argued that these values are part of a subculture of poverty that is passed down from one generation to the next, structuralists take a different point of view. They argue that the reason these values reappear in one generation after another is because each generation has faced the same social structure: high unemployment, low education, discrimination. Liebow argues that similarities

> do not result from "cultural transmission" but from the fact that the son goes out and independently experiences the same failures, in the same areas, and for much the same reasons as his father. What appears as a dynamic, self-sustaining cultural process is, in part at least, a relatively simple piece of social machinery which turns out, in rather mechanical fashion, independently produced look-alikes (Liebow 1967, 222–223).

In other words, the structural school argues that people who share social statuses, who experience the same kinds of role constraints and demands in their daily lives, tend to develop similar personalities and self-concepts. Social class is one of the most important of these structured statuses, and we will return to the topic of class differences in Chapter 9.

SYNTHESIS

Despite their differences, the structural and interaction schools have much in common. Scholars from both schools are very much in the symbolic interaction tradition. They agree that meanings are embedded in relationships and that actors have some choices in the process of arriving at meanings. The two schools should not be viewed as opposites but as complements. This relationship is diagrammed in Figure 6.1. As the interaction school suggests, self-concept affects the roles we play; it is also true, as the structural school suggests, that roles affect self-concept. In studying this reciprocal relationship between roles and self-concept, we may regard the emphases of the interaction and the structural schools as a simple division of labor. Neither school would deny the legitimacy of the other's interests.

CONCEPT SUMMARY THE TWO SCHOOLS OF SYMBOLIC INTERACTION

	INTERACTION SCHOOL	STRUCTURAL SCHOOL
The self-concept is . . .	Negotiated	Determined by roles
The individual is . . .	Active in creating self-concept; has more freedom to choose self	Less active in creating self-concept; has less freedom to choose self
The self-concept is developed through . . .	Role taking (taking the role of others) and role making	Performing institutionalized roles
Roles are . . .	Negotiated	Allocated
Major concepts	Looking-glass self, role taking, and self-esteem	Role identity, role making, situated identity, and identity hierarchy

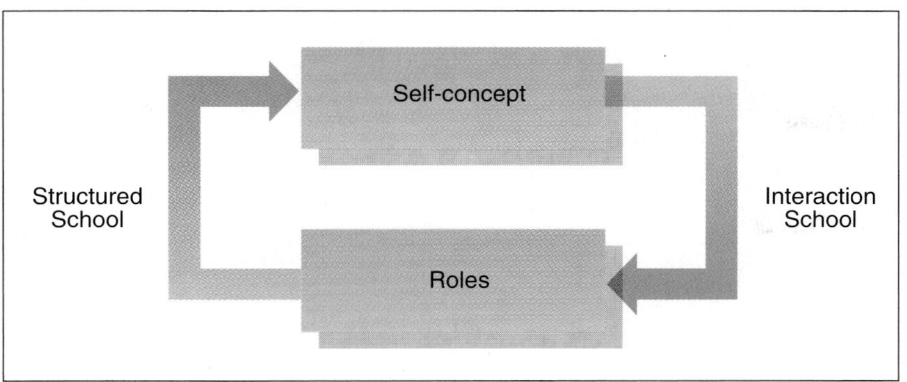

FIGURE 6.1
THE RELATIONSHIP BETWEEN THE STRUCTURAL AND THE INTERACTION SCHOOLS OF SYMBOLIC INTERACTION THEORY

The structural school of symbolic interaction theory emphasizes the effect of social structure on self-concept, while the interaction school emphasizes the active part that the individual plays in choosing and defining roles. Symbolic interactionists from both schools believe that the self-concept and social structure are interdependent: On the one hand, the roles we play and their locations in the social structure affect the self-concept we develop; on the other hand, the self is actively involved in role choices.

ROLE IDENTITY AND SELF-CONCEPT OVER THE LIFE COURSE

Our self-concepts and initial social roles are learned in childhood, but we continue to learn new roles and to renegotiate our self-concepts throughout our lives. Each time you join a new group or assume a new role, you learn new norms and redefine your identity. Sociologists are interested in two aspects of this process. One is **socialization,** the process of learning the roles necessary for participation in social institutions, and the other is how role change affects self-concept and identity. In this section, we begin by reviewing theory and research on early childhood socialization and then move on to discuss role transitions in adulthood. We conclude with a section on resocialization, the process of dramatically altering self-concept.

Socialization is the process of learning the roles, statuses, and values necessary for participation in social institutions.

EARLY CHILDHOOD

Early childhood socialization is called **primary socialization.** It is primary in two senses: It occurs first, and it is most critical for later development. During this period, children develop personality and self-concept; acquire motor abilities, reasoning, and language skills; become aware of significant others; and are exposed to a social world consisting of roles, values, and norms.

Primary socialization is personality development and role learning that occur during early childhood.

The Family. The most important agent of socialization is the family. As the tragic cases of child neglect and the monkey experiments so clearly demonstrate, the initial warmth and nurturance we receive at home are essential to normal cognitive, emotional, and physical development. In addition, our parents are our first teachers. From them we learn to tie our shoes and hold a fork, and from them we also learn the goals and aspirations that are likely to stay with us for the rest of our lives.

The activities required to meet the physical needs of a newborn provide the initial basis for social interaction. Feeding and diaper changing give opportunities for cuddling, smiling, and talking. These nurturant activites are vital to the infant's social and physical development; without them, the child's social, emotional, and physical growth will be stunted (Gardner, 1972; Lynch 1979; Provence and Lipton 1962; Spitz 1945; Werner and Smith 1992).

In addition to basic developmental tasks, the child has a staggering amount of learning to do before becoming a full member of society. Much of this early learning

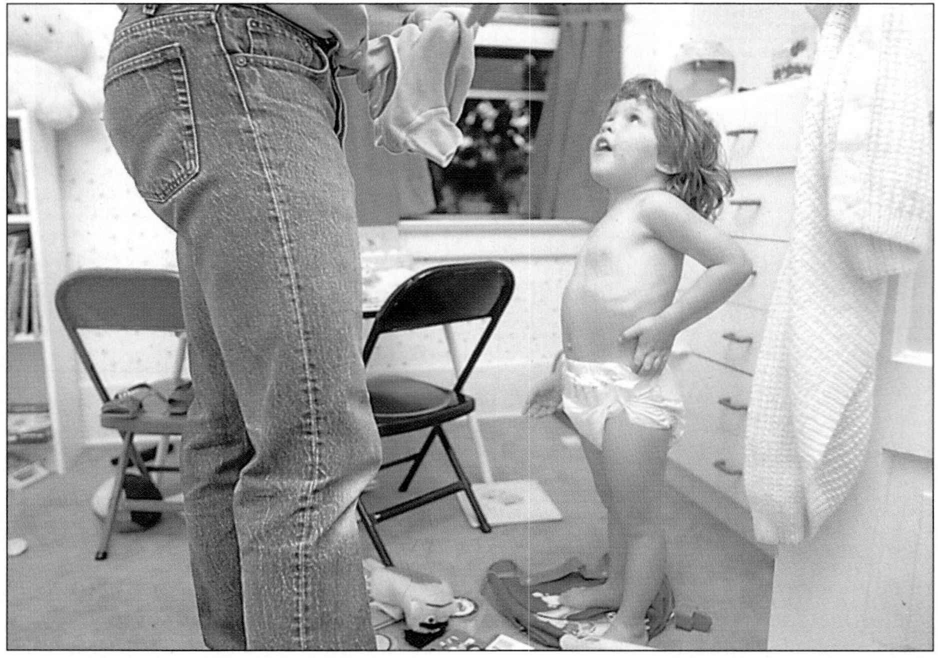

Parents have an enormous capacity to shape their children. Is Dad going to put this little girl in a frilly dress that says "Daddy's princess" on the front, or is he going to put her in overalls that declare "Big slugger"? In addition to parents' expectations, the form and stability of the family are also important. A two-parent family generally provides more income, more supervision, and more stability than a one-parent family.

occurs in the family as a result of daily interactions: The child learns to talk and communicate, to play house, and to get along with others. As the child becomes older, teaching is more direct, and parents attempt to produce conformity and obedience, impart basic skills, and prepare the child for experiences outside the family.

One reason the family is the most important agent of socialization is that the self-concept formed during childhood has lasting consequences. In later stages of development, we pursue experiences and activities that integrate and build on the foundations established in the primary years. Although the personality and self-concept are not rigidly fixed in childhood, we are strongly conditioned by childhood experiences (Bukatko 1992).

The family is also an important agent of socialization in that children acquire many characteristics from their parents. Most important, the parents' religion, social class, and ethnicity influence social roles and self-concept. They affect the expectations that others have for the child, and they determine the groups with which the child will interact outside the family. Thus, the family's ethnicity, class, and religion shape the child's experiences in the neighborhood, at school, and at work.

Thinking Critically

List some specific ways you think that a family's social class might influence the way a child is socialized. Can you think of any ways that living in the city versus living in the country might matter?

Preschools and Day Care. The increasing participation of women in the labor force has added another social structure to the experience of young children: day care. In 1994, 71 percent of married mothers of children under six years of age were employed (U.S. Bureau of the Census 1995, Table 639). About two-thirds of the children of employed mothers are cared for in their own homes by relatives, neighbors, or paid nannies (Clinton 1990). In a substantial number of cases, parents take turns caring for their children (Presser 1988). Approximately one-quarter of all preschool children with employed mothers, meanwhile, are in day care, either in a paid caregiver's home or in a day care center.

What are the consequences of day care experience for children? The answer is that it depends. As the proportion of children who attend day care has grown, so has the empirical research. Generally, research shows that enrollment in high quality day care has no apparent negative consequences and some positive effects. For example, a study of day care centers in Sweden showed that children who began their day care experiences early (before one year of age) scored better on many dimensions than children who had not attended day care or who had started later; children with early day care experience did better on tests of persistence, independence, school achievement, vocabulary, and low anxiety (Andersson 1989).

There are some important restrictions on these findings, however. For children to prosper in day care settings, the following conditions probably need to be met: stable placement, stable staff, staff training in child development, and low child-to-staff ratios (for example, one staff member for every four children) (Cole and Cole 1989, 630–632). A large number, perhaps most, day care centers in the United States do not meet these criteria. Studies show that children placed in low-quality day care centers (unstable and untrained staff, high child-to-staff ratios)

As a result of the growing number of families with both parents in the labor force, children are spending more and more time, starting from a younger age, in schools and other organized care arrangements. Studies show that these school experiences can have positive effects. Where the ratio of children to staff is low and staff placements are stable, children can build close personal relationships with teachers as well as parents.

have more difficulty attaching themselves to their parents and show fewer competent and more problem behaviors (Berk 1989, 456; Vaughn, Gove, and Egeland 1980). Low-quality day care is less costly than high-quality day care. Consequently, of those who use paid day care, children from low-income families are more likely to experience inadequate socialization. However, low-income, as well as African American and Latino, parents are less likely to use paid day care and more likely to have relatives watch their children (Otten 1990; Wilkie 1988).

Secondary socialization is personality development and role learning that occur after early childhood.

Anticipatory socialization is role learning that prepares us for roles we are likely to assume in the future.

School-Age and Adolescent Youth

Following primary socialization is **secondary socialization,** the process by which individuals learn additional attitudes, behaviors, skills, and roles that build on what they already know. As children grow older, they participate in more social institutions and develop wider social networks. Between the ages of 6 and 18, two of these social settings are particularly important: the school and the peer group. Both can play an important part in developing the child's self-concept, social and intellectual skills, and identity.

Much of this learning is what sociologists call **anticipatory socialization.** It is learning that prepares us for the roles we are likely to assume in the future. Because of this socialization, most of us are more or less prepared for the responsibilities we will face as employees, college students, parents, spouses, or employers. Identities have been established, skills acquired, and attitudes developed that prepare us to accept and even embrace adult roles. This takes place formally in the school system and informally in the peer group.

Adolescence is an awkward period in which young people are halfway between childhood and adulthood. As in this picture, they frequently are not very sure what pose to take as they negotiate their way through the dilemmas posed by growing independence. The peer group is an important arena for trying out the various selves that are available and seeing which ones work best.

Schools. In Western societies, schooling has become institutionalized as the natural habitat for children. The manifest function of schools in industrialized societies is to impart specific skills and abilities necessary for functioning in a highly technological society.

Schools do much more than teach basic skills and technical knowledge, however; they also transmit society's central cultural values and ideologies. Unlike the family, in which children are treated as special persons with unique needs and problems, schools expose children to situations in which the same rules, regulations, and authority patterns apply to everyone. In schools, children first learn that levels of achievement affect status in groups (Parsons 1964, 133). In this sense, schools are training grounds for roles in the workplace, the military, and other bureaucracies in which relationships are based on uniform criteria.

The types of learning that take place in schools and the effects of school structure on individuals are covered in more detail in Chapter 15.

Peer Groups. Both in and out of school, young people spend a lot of time with their peers. Their natural tendency to spend time with others like themselves has been increased in recent years by the growing likelihood that both parents work outside the home. This creates a vacuum that is sometimes filled through increased peer interaction.

What are the consequences of peer interaction for socialization and the development of the self-concept? Kids who hang around together tend to look and act a lot alike; they wear the same kinds of clothes, have the same kinds of grades and the same levels of deviance, like the same music, and share many attitudes. This high level of similarity has led many observers to assume that peer pressure has created conformity. The effect of peer pressure, however, has probably been substantially overestimated. Research shows that much of the similarity among group members precedes their joining the group; in other words, they hang around together *before* they share attitudes. Peer groups are often thought of as parents' enemies or competitors in terms of influence and as a source of conflict between parents and children. In fact, research shows that most adolescents are more concerned about their parents' opinions than about their friends' (Dornbusch 1989).

There are, however, three areas of a child's and adolescent's development in which peer group socialization has an important influence (Gecas, 1981). First, it has an important effect on the development and validation of the self-concept. Second, the peer group furnishes an important arena for practicing one's skills at role taking. Finally, the peer group is often a mechanism for learning social roles and values that adults don't want to teach. For example, much sexual knowledge and social deviance is learned in the peer group. (Some, but few, people learn to roll a joint at their mother's knee.)

Mass Media. Throughout our lives, we receive countless messages from radios, magazines, films, and billboards. The most important mass medium for socialization, however, is undoubtedly television. Nearly every home has one, and the average American spends many hours a week watching it.

The effect of television viewing on learning is vigorously debated, and the evidence is somewhat contradictory. The most universally accepted conclusion is that the mass media can be an important means of supporting and validating what we already know. Through a process of selective perception, we tend to give special notice to material that supports our beliefs and self-concepts and to ignore material that challenges us.

Television, however, may play a more active role than this. Studies suggest that characters seen regularly on television can become role models, whose imagined opinions become important as we develop our own roles. For example, a young child might ask, "Now how would Barney handle this?" Material on television may supplement the knowledge our own experience gives us about American roles and norms. There is also evidence that children, teens, and even adults learn techniques of aggression and violence that are modeled on television (Eron 1980; Marin 1996). These findings imply that the content of television can have an important influence.

ADULTHOOD

Adulthood spans as many as 60 years. During this time, individuals go through many role changes. Some of these changes, such as getting a job, getting married, and retiring, are voluntary; and we are more or less prepared for them by anticipatory socialization. Other role changes create more problems; we lose our jobs, become divorced, or join the army. The roles we occupy in adulthood and the changes that occur in these roles may have substantial effects on our self-concepts. We review research and theory on how one of our major adult roles—work—affects personality and self-concept. A much more detailed discussion of changes in social roles over the life course appears in Chapter 13.

The Work Role. The work role is an important one. It determines our income, our prestige in the community, what we do all day, and with whom we do it. Not surprisingly, we find that what people do for a living affects their self-concept and personality.

For example, long-term research by Kohn and his associates indicates that the *nature* of our work affects our self-concepts and behavior. The amount of autonomy, the degree of supervision and routinization, and the amount of cognitive complexity demanded by the job have important consequences. If your work demands flexibility and self-discipline, you will probably come to value these traits—at home, in government, and in religion. If your work instead requires subordination, discipline, and routine, you will come to find these traits natural and desirable (Kohn and Schooler 1983). This example of how roles affect personality and self-concept gives empirical support for the structural school of symbolic interaction.

Social standing is another aspect of work that has an important impact on self-concept and behavior. People with little power and few opportunities for upward mobility tend to reject occupation as a dominant status. Instead they base their self-concepts on such nonwork roles as runner or mother, volunteer or motorcyclist. Frequently, however, people are unable to brush aside low achievement in their work roles. As a result, those who have little opportunity or power at work may be bossier, more authoritarian, and more alienated than those whose work provides a validation of their self-worth (Kanter 1977).

Because of the salience of our work role identity, studies demonstrate that losing one's job is typically a major blow to the self-concept. Although many people who lose their jobs find ways to protect their self-esteem (for example, by blaming the economy or the government), studies show that unemployment increases depression, anxiety, physical illness, and sleeplessness (Hamilton, Broman, Hoffman, and Renner 1990). It also reduces an individual's sense that she or he is a competent actor who can negotiate what happens (Gecas 1989). Because the threat of unemployment differs substantially by social class, this is another mechanism through which social class affects self-concept.

Role Accumulation in Adulthood. Generally, adulthood can be viewed as a process of role accumulation: As individuals move from age 20 to 45, many become employees, spouses, parents, church members, members of voluntary associations, home owners, and so on. What are the consequences of this accumulation of social roles? Although multiple roles increase the opportunity for role conflict, research strongly suggests that role accumulation is generally a good thing: The more roles people have, the better off they are (Thoits 1986a). For example, women who are married and parents *and* employees show less psychological distress than women who are only married and parents (Thoits 1986a); if they add membership in a voluntary association, they are even better off (Moen, Dempster-McClain, and Williams 1989).

Why is role accumulation generally so positive? Each role gives us a role identity and the opportunity to perform that role successfully. Success in one role can balance feelings of doubt about another role. For instance, an orthopedic surgeon and mother may have a bad morning with her teenagers, who yell at her or call her names. But she can go to the operating room and do a fine job there. Her self-esteem may have been diminished by her altercation with her children, but it can be replenished by a strong performance in another role. As a result, people with multiple roles tend to have higher self-esteem and perhaps a stronger sense of purpose.

THINKING CRITICALLY

List all the roles you play. Does having several roles enhance your life, do you think? Or is the situation problematic? Why?

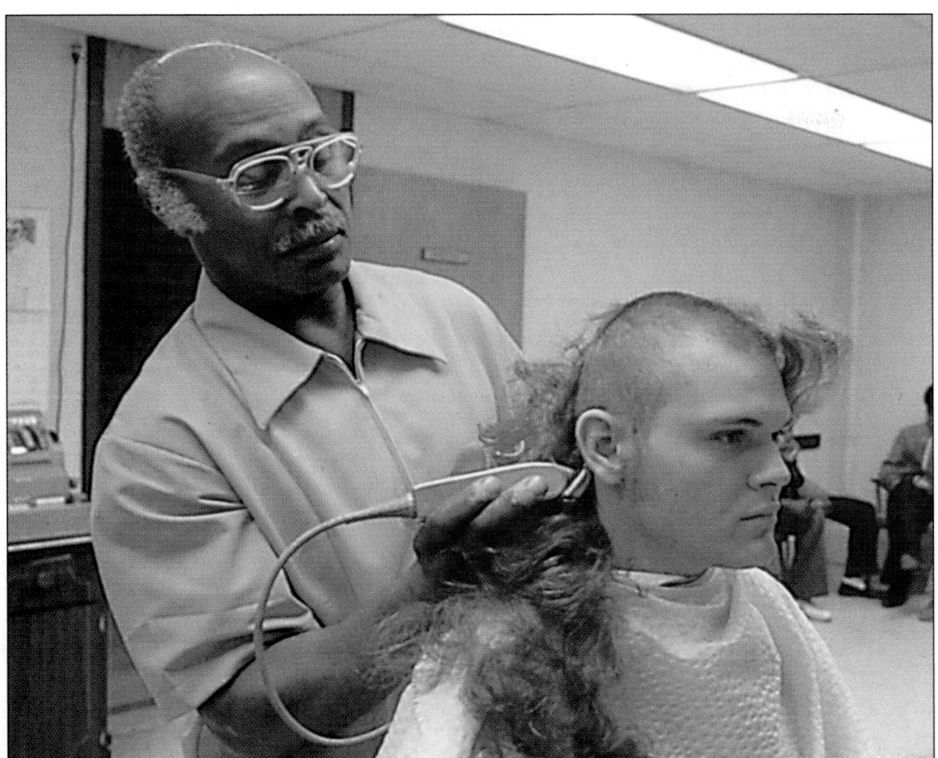

The transformation of physical appearance is a powerful symbolic way of leaving one self-concept behind and taking on another. From the traditional buzz cut that recruits receive in the armed forces to the purple spikes of the punk, physical transformation is an important part of resocialization. It signals to both self and audience that the old self has disappeared and been replaced with a new one.

RESOCIALIZATION

The development of the self-concept is usually a gradual process over the life course, and who we are at 35 is often only incrementally different from who we were at 25. Sometimes, however, there are abrupt changes in our self-concepts, and we must learn new role identities and negotiate new self-images. **Resocialization** occurs when a person abandons his or her self-concept and way of life for a radically different one. Changing the social behavior, values, and self-concept acquired over a lifetime of experience is difficult, and few people undertake the change voluntarily. In fact, usually resocialization is imposed by society.

Resocialization occurs when a person abandons his or her self-concept and way of life for a radically different one.

When an individual's behavior leads to social problems—as is the case with habitual criminals, substance abusers, and people who are mentally disturbed—society may decree that the individual must abandon the old identity and accept a more conventional one. Most of those attempting to resocialize people assume that a radical change in self-concept requires a radical change in environment. Drug counseling one night a week is not likely to alter drastically the self-concept of a teenager who spends the rest of the week among current drug users. Thus, the first step in the resocialization process is to isolate the individual from his or her past environment.

This is most efficiently done in **total institutions**—facilities in which all aspects of life are strictly controlled for the purpose of radical resocialization (Goffman 1961a). Monasteries, prisons, boot camps, and mental hospitals are good examples. Within them, past statuses are wiped away. Social roles and relationships that

Total institutions are facilities in which all aspects of life are strictly controlled for the purpose of radical resocialization.

formed the basis of the previous self-concept are systematically eliminated. New statuses are symbolized by regulation clothing, rigidly scheduled activity, and new relationships. Inmates are encouraged to engage in self-analysis and self-criticism, a process intended to reveal the inferiority of past perspectives, attachments, statuses, and roles.

In recent years, some 30 states have established prison boot camps, modeled after military boot camps and designed to resocialize first-time, nonviolent juvenile substance abusers and other offenders (Katel 1994; Souryal and MacKenzie 1994). Upon entry, the juvenile offender receives a buzz cut and is given a uniform, which is worn at all times. Absolute respect for authority is required. All verbal responses to drill sergeants' questions or orders must begin and end with "Sir," for example. The daily schedule is tightly structured. Discipline is strict, with punishments such as maintaining a sitting position without a chair for slight rule infractions. Boot camps not only cost less than traditional prisons but offer renewed hope for resocializing problem youth (Hengesh 1991). Unfortunately, however, preliminary research shows that, once released, boot-camp participants get into trouble at the same rate as juvenile offenders treated in other ways (Katel 1994; Fisher 1994).

Just as resocialization does not always occur as planned in a total institution, resocialization does not necessarily require a total institution. In fact, resocialization is a part of many religious and political conversions. For example, a Hare Krishna devotee reports, "When I first joined I was concerned most with my looks and with getting a nice car and a nice apartment. But I eventually came to realize that those material things don't really count that much. . . . Now I realize that this life and body are temporary and miserable" (Snow, Rochford, Worden and Benford 1986, 473). This woman has abandoned her old self-concept for an entirely different one. Similarly, people who drop out of school to become full-time environmental activists change their way of life, their social networks, and their self concepts.

Most of us do not experience resocialization. For most of us, change is gradual and cumulative. We get new jobs, fall in with different circles of friends, and gradually change our lifestyles as we get older. Even if we change our religion or our politics, the change is a modest one that doesn't require much rearrangement of our social relationships or our self-concepts. The Applications in Diversity section of this chapter discusses the development of a gay male or lesbian identity, a process somewhere between resocialization and making modest identity changes.

GLOBAL PERSPECTIVES: CHILDHOOD IN SOUTHEAST ASIA

The concept of childhood as different from adulthood did not emerge until about the 17th century in Europe (Aries 1962). For most of human history, childhood was not recognized as a particular status; children shared the everyday world of adults, working beside them, dressing like them, and sleeping near them. With industrialization and growing affluence, children were increasingly assigned the student role and gradually segregated from the adult world. One result is that most of us today regard children as people who need special training, guidance, and care. However, this attitude toward childhood requires a certain level of economic well-being in society. Normative standards for children are very different in our own

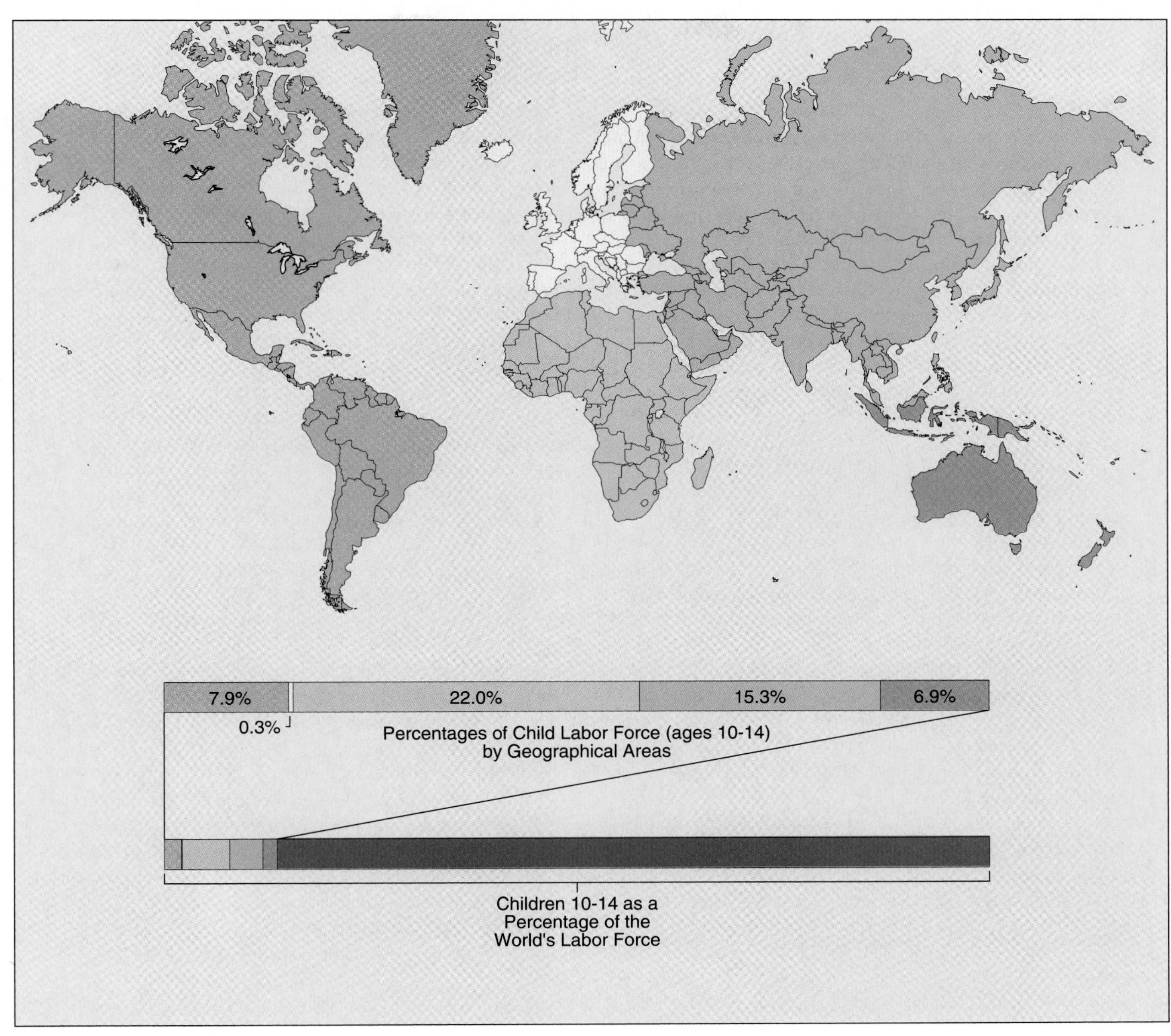

MAP 6.1

CHILDREN IN THE WORLD'S WORK FORCE, 1990

In the developed world, relatively few children 10–14 are members of the labor force. In other parts of the world, however, as many as 25% of boys and girls are working. In many cases, they are supporting not only themselves but also their families, and schooling beyond the sixth grade is a luxury they cannot afford.

SOCIAL APPLICATIONS

How Is a Gay Male or Lesbian Identity Developed?

We do not know exactly how an individual's sexual orientation—whether that individual prefers a partner of the same or opposite sex—develops. It is a matter of argument whether gay men and lesbians are born as homosexuals or choose to become so. But whether homosexuality results from nature, nurture, or a combination of both, we can examine how persons with homosexual orientations gradually develop a gay male or lesbian identity.

According to one model (Troiden 1988), the process of developing a homosexual identity occurs in four stages: sensitization, identity confusion, identity assumption (acceptance and "coming out"), and commitment to homosexuality as a way of life.

Sensitization occurs in early puberty. At this time, most children, having been socialized to accept a heterosexual generalized other, assume that they are heterosexual. But future gay men or lesbians feel sexually marginal, as if the culture's generalized other does not properly fit them. During early puberty, they have experiences that sensitize them to potentially revised definitions of themselves as lesbian or gay: "I wasn't interested in boys (girls)"; "I didn't express myself the way other girls (or boys) would."

Identity confusion occurs in later adolescence as gay males or lesbians realize that their feelings, fantasies, or behaviors could be considered homosexual. The idea that they could be homosexual goes against self-images developed during their earlier socialization. Hence, inner turmoil and uncertainty result. These adolescents typically try to deny their homosexual feelings, and some attempt to eradicate their homosexuality through therapy. They may nourish relationships with heterosexual significant others in an effort to eliminate their homosexual interests: "I thought my homosexual feelings would go away if I dated a lot and had sex with as many women as possible," or, "I thought my attraction to women was a passing fad and would go away once I started having intercourse with my boyfriend" (Troiden 1988, 48). Another response is acceptance; in such cases, behaviors, feelings, or fantasies are acknowledged as possibly homosexual, and additional information is sought.

Identity assumption, which occurs during or after late adolescence, involves developing a self-identity as homosexual. During this stage, an individual's reference group changes so that other homosexuals are increasingly viewed as acceptable human beings and companions. At this stage, a gay male or lesbian may tell a few people about being homosexual but carefully selects who will be told. This stage is highly stressful because being a gay male or lesbian ranks high on an individual's identity hierarchy, yet hiding this identity from a generally hostile society seems necessary to the individual.

The final stage, *commitment,* involves the decision to accept homosexuality as a way of life. Having "come out," even to many heterosexuals, these individuals feel satisfied about their sexual orientation but do not view their role of being homosexual as the most important in their identity hierarchy.

How is developing a gay or lesbian identity similar to developing other identities? How is it different? How does the fact that ours is a generally heterosexual society and culture affect the process of developing a homosexual identity? How might the status of gay male or lesbian cause a person to experience status inconsistency?

relatively affluent country than they are in most of the rest of the world. This section focuses on childhood for many youngsters in Southeast Asia.

Most of us in the United States believe it is appropriate for children to do such small tasks as setting the table and putting away their toys. We would be appalled, however, at the type and amount of labor required of some children in Southeast Asia (and many other parts of the world as well). The International Labor Office, a Geneva-based voluntary association, reported in 1993 that child labor is an increasing problem in Asia. Millions of Asian children as young as six are working under degrading and hazardous conditions that often involve 18-hour workdays for very low pay ("Danger: Children at Work" 1993). Many are the victims of opportunistic child snatchers, who roam impoverished or war-ravaged regions kidnapping, buying, or luring children into servitude ("Alas, Slavery Lives" 1993).

In India, some 14 million children between 6 and 14 years old are compelled to labor for as much as 16 hours a day in cramped, poorly lit factories, largely in the thriving carpet industry. These children are often undernourished and subjected to physical abuse (McDonald 1992; Ryan 1993). In Bangladesh, just east of India, child workers at Levi Strauss and Company sew jeans together (Clifford 1994). Often, these child garment workers labor at least six days per week and earn as little as $4 per month (Senser 1994). In Pakistan, just west of India, as many as 7.5 million children are working as bonded laborers in factories, on farms, and on construction projects ("Alas, Slavery Lives" 1993). Girls as young as 10 years old work full time in clothing plants (Nichols et al. 1993).

Furthermore, child prostitution is a growing concern in South and Southeast Asia. According to one report, entire villages in northern Thailand and along the Burmese border are almost without young girls aged 12 through 14 because they have been sold into prostitution, often by their impoverished parents. International tourism with the purpose of engaging in prepubescent sex has grown in recent years as thousands of Europeans, Australians, Japanese, and Americans have traveled to Southeast Asia for that purpose (Kempton 1992; Ryan 1993; Serrill 1993).

The United Nations Commission on Human Rights has called for safeguards against child labor. But freeing children from labor is a luxury that many developing or under-developed societies cannot afford. Some countries in Southeastern Asia, such as India, have national laws prohibiting child labor (McDonald 1992). However, governments often allow child labor because families depend on children's meager wages for survival. Then, too, child labor keeps wages low, thus enticing foreign investments (Hammond 1994).

We have focused on child labor in Asia. But in many other regions of the world as well—South America, Africa, and Eastern Europe, for example—the social structure and economy are such that parents can hardly afford not to work their children. Indeed, in the United States, more and more children of recent immigrants and of low-income families are engaged in child labor, some of it dangerous and much of it illegal (Dumaine 1993; Holloway 1993; Weiss 1992).

SOCIOLOGY ON THE NET

The extended childhood that most of us experienced is not available to many children throughout the world. The problem is so extensive that the United Nations, the World Bank and the World Health Organization have all addressed the issue. Let's begin with the World Bank.

`http://www.worldbank.org/html/hcovp/workp.wp_00056.html`

As you browse through this document pay close attention to the attributes of child labor and the correlates of working children. What regions of the world have the highest rate of child labor? Why do children work? What role does gender play in who works and who goes to school?

The United Nations Children's Fund or UNICEF is an advocate for the children of the world. They have a number of excellent reports that will help you learn more about the state of the children through the world.

http://www.unicef.org

Browse around the **home page** and then click on the **Information** button. Open the first highlighted item entitled **The State of the World's Children 1996**. Click on the **arrow** and check out the items on the **menu**. Pay particular attention to the selection on **regional highlights**. What region in the world presents the greatest risk to children? Click on the **Panel** selection and read a few of the reports. What is the impact of war on children? What goals have the United Nations set for the world's children in the next few years?

A unique and interesting aspect of socialization is resocialization. Resocialization occurs when a person abandons his or her self-concept and way of life for a radically different one. A good example is when a civilian joins the military and learns to adopt the military lifestyle. The United States Marine Corps is an excellent example.

http://www.usmc.mil

Open the section on **Opportunities** and browse through selections like **What you can expect of the Corps** and **Recruit Training**. Now return to the **home page** and click on the highlighted **Marines Magazine**. Skim through a few articles in the current and back issues. How would being a Marine require you to change your way of life? How would your self concept change?

SUMMARY

1. Sociologists study the ways in which social processes and relationships affect the development of the self and the self-concept.
2. The self is socially bestowed and socially sustained. Through interaction with others, we learn to be human—to walk, to love, to talk. Our innate capacities cannot develop without social interaction.
3. There is increasing evidence that nature and nurture interact to produce gender differences, such as differential math performance.
4. Symbolic interaction is the dominant theoretical framework in sociological studies of human development. It emphasizes that learning takes place through subjectively interpreted interaction and that each person has a part in constructing and maintaining his or her own self.
5. The interaction school gives the individual a very active role in constructing the self. The idea of the negotiated self suggests that we use selective interpretations to construct and maintain our self-concepts with a special eye to enhancing our self-esteem.
6. The structural school stresses the profound impact of institutionalized roles and statuses on the development of the self-concept. The concepts of role identity and situated identity suggest that our selves and self-concepts depend in important ways on the situations or roles in which we find ourselves.
7. We learn new roles and renegotiate our self-concepts throughout our lives: Primary socialization occurs in early childhood; secondary socialization occurs after early childhood; anticipatory socialization prepares us for future roles; resocialization represents an abrupt change of self-concept.

8 Among the major agents of preadult socialization are the family, day care, school, the peer group, and the media. Of these, the family is the most important. Family background and family stability have strong effects on self-concept.

9 Studies of adult role identities show that work roles affect self-concept and behavior. Characteristics demanded by one's job (for example, independence and self-discipline) come to be valued outside of work, too. Research generally shows that the more roles you have, the better off you are.

10 Resocialization is so difficult that few people seek it voluntarily. It often requires withdrawal from one's usual social relationships and entrance into a total institution that can control all aspects of one's life.

11 Childhood as a special status and role deserving education and care is a new development in human history and exists primarily in relatively affluent, industrialized societies.

12 Children in Asia and many other parts of the world labor in miserable conditions to help support their families or, worse, because they are virtual slaves to their manufacturer-owners.

13 A gay male or lesbian identity is developed through four stages: sensitization, identity confusion, identity assumption, and commitment to homosexuality as a way of life.

SUGGESTED READINGS

BENEDICT, Ruth. 1961. *Patterns of Culture*. Boston: Houghton MIfflin. Originally published in 1934. A classic that draws on several different cultures to illustrate how behavior and personality are consistent with the culture in which a person is reared. The emphasis is on the continuity of socialization.

GOFFMAN, Erving. 1961. *Asylums*. Garden City, N.Y.: Anchor/Doubleday. A penetrating account of total institutions and the significance of social structure in producing conforming behavior. Primarily an analysis of mental hospitals and mental patients, although the analysis is applicable to other total institutions.

HEUSMANN, L. Rowell, and Malamuth, Neil (eds.). 1986. Media Violence and Antisocial Behavior, *Journal of Social Issues*, special issue, vol. 42. A collection of essays that spans the range from pornography to children's cartoons. Included are several articles discussing intervening strategies and regulatory issues.

KOHN, Melvin L., Schooler, Carmi, and Associates. 1983. *Work and Personality: An Inquiry into the Impact of Social Stratification*. Norwood, N.J.: Ablex. A summary of 20 years of research on the impact of work roles on personality and the self-concept. It provides strong evidence in favor of the structural school.

ROSENBERG, Morris. 1979. *Conceiving the Self*. New York: Basic Books. A readable overview of symbolic interaction theory from the point of view of the interaction school.

TROIDEN, Richard R. 1988. *Gay and Lesbian Identity: A Sociological Analysis*. New York: General Hall, Inc. An empirical and sensitive analysis of how a gay male or lesbian identity is developed.

WILLIE, Charles Vert. 1991. *A New Look at Black Families*. 4th ed. Dix Hill, N.Y.: General Hall, Inc. A detailed discussion of class differences in African American families; provides a context for understanding the diverse socialization experiences of these families.

ZURCHER, Louis A. 1983. *Social Roles: Conformity, Conflict, and Creativity*. Beverly Hills: Sage. A provocative book that applies symbolic interactionism to issues of role choice and role negotiation.

CHAPTER 7

The Sociology of Everyday Life

OUTLINE

PROLOGUE

Have You Ever . . . been in a conversation and said all the wrong things? Stood too close to someone and received a dirty look? Gone to an event wearing the wrong clothes? Had a blemish on your face and felt reluctant to go out in public? Missed a friend's party and had to come up with an excuse? Been in a cast or wheelchair and had to figure out how to cope with people's curious glances, stares, and questions? Hoped someone would give you a compliment and fished for it?

A great deal of daily life includes the possibility of such occurrences. Although culture provides a general pattern for living, much of our day-to-day interaction can be problematic. We mix signals with others, grope to try to figure out what is appropriate and what is inappropriate, find ourselves embarrassed.

The sociology of everyday life is concerned with these processes. It focuses on how individuals negotiate their everyday routines. The sociology of everyday life also illustrates a basic sociological theme: Our self-esteem and personal identities, as we ourselves and as others define them, are to a great extent generated and reinforced by the everyday social settings in which we participate and interact.

This chapter—a companion to the previous one—examines social structures from the point of view of individual actors. Where Chapter 6 covered the development of the self-concept, this chapter looks at the self as it moves through its everyday affairs.

The **sociology of everyday life** focuses on the social processes that structure our experience in ordinary face-to-face situations. This perspective directs our attention away from the larger frameworks that structure our lives toward the processes that structure our behavior in concrete situations. For example, how do we decide what to talk about at the breakfast table? How do we respond when introduced to a stranger? These are the types of concrete situations of interest: They involve specific people in specific settings.

The **sociology of everyday life** focuses on the social processes that structure our experiences in ordinary face-to-face situations.

Concern with everyday life takes us in two rather different directions. One way shows us the ordinary routines of daily life, the patterned social regularities that govern face-to-face encounters. The other directs our attention to the management of problematic situations, where routines and norms provide ambiguous guides to conduct.

THE ROUTINE NATURE OF DAILY LIFE

Everyday life is governed by taken-for-granted routines. The most important routines we use for interaction with others are carried out through talk. We all learn dozens of these verbal routines and can usually pull out an appropriate one to suit each occasion. Small rituals such as the following will carry us through dozens of encounters every day.

"Hola! Cómo estás?"
"Yo bien, y tú?"

"Yo también!"

or

"Hi. How you doing?"
"Good. How about you?"
"Just fine."

If we supplement this ritual with half a dozen others, such as "thanks/no problem" and "excuse me/okay," we will be equipped to meet most of the repetitive situations of daily life.

To illustrate the degree to which our interaction is governed by taken-for-granted routines, let's look at the routines governing use of physical space.

THINKING CRITICALLY

Compare the norms for riding an elevator with those for using an escalator.

MANAGING PERSONAL SPACE

Careful observation of routine behavior on sidewalks, in classrooms, and in elevators shows that there are definite norms about the use of space. Like the Supreme Court judge who couldn't define obscenity but knew it when he saw it, we are able to conform to the norms and be offended by their violation even if we are not able to say exactly what these norms are.

Norms about the use of space vary substantially from culture to culture. American norms generally require more distance between people than the norms of other cultures. Each of us has an invisible circle around himself or herself that we regard as our personal space. Only selected others—by invitation only—are welcome within this space. Observation suggests that distances up to 18 inches are reserved for intimates and distances between 18 and 48 inches are reserved for personal but not intimate exchanges (Hall 1969). Most of us are very sensitive to violations of these rules. If we are waiting for an elevator or an automated teller machine, we typically stand six to eight feet away from strangers; this is not a personal relationship. When we get on a bus with only one other passenger, a stranger, we generally select a seat several rows away instead of one right next to the stranger.

When others violate the rules about the use of physical space, when they encroach on our personal space, we experience this as punishing. Suppose a coworker comes to within 12 inches of you in a conversation. You back up, he steps forward. You back up again, and he follows again. You might define this as sexual harassment. In any case, you will find such a violation of personal space unpleasant, even threatening.

Riding the Elevator. Goffman (1967) gives a detailed account of the routines we automatically follow in riding elevators. His account conveys how unknowingly rule-bound are so many of our daily encounters.

Goffman likens an elevator ride to a dance, in which the physical positioning of the riders is altered in a patterned way with each addition to and subtraction from the number of passengers. The dance is guided by two motifs: Each person faces the front, and each maintains an equal distance between himself or herself and all other passengers. A woman getting onto an empty elevator may stand wherever she chooses; when the second person gets on, she moves over so that each passenger takes up an opposite side of the elevator; when a third person gets on, all rearrange themselves so that all three are equidistant. The dance continues with every new passenger so that the principle of equal distance is maintained. When passengers start leaving the elevator, the same process is repeated in reverse: People move away from others so that equal distance is maintained as more space becomes available.

The elevator ride also illustrates the routine mechanisms we use to manage physical closeness without intimacy. On crowded elevators or buses or while waiting in ticket lines, we use a device termed *civil inattention* to discourage intimacy. Civil inattention requires a polite acknowledgment of the other's physical presence accompanied by social withdrawal: A nod or other acknowledgment is made, and then the gaze is averted and silence is maintained (Goffman 1963a). If you speak to the person against whom you are squeezed, you are likely to receive a frosty reply or more probably none at all, for you will have violated one of the rules governing social relationships.

Personal Space and Status. Norms about personal space are closely related to social status. The more important you are, the larger is your personal space. This explains several patterned regularities, such as why office size grows with status. It also explains a differential freedom to touch and be touched. Generally, we find that a superior is free to violate an inferior's personal space (Henley 1977). A coach, for example, may pat a player's bottom, but a player is not allowed to pat the coach. Although concerns about inappropriate sexual behavior have reduced the legitimacy of touching, children are touched by adults and women by men more often than the reverse.

The Importance of Routine

Routines such as those involving space are so mundane that they may appear to be a foolish topic for scholarly inquiry. Nevertheless, social life depends on the predictability of others' responses (Goffman 1983). Consider driving. Safe passage clearly requires that you and all the other drivers behave in expected ways. In a less life-threatening manner, safe passage through social encounters also depends on routine. If you had no idea what to expect of passersby on the street or sales clerks in the store, each encounter would be potentially disastrous. Because you do know what to expect, you feel relatively confident about your ability to negotiate such encounters smoothly. The routines and rituals of daily life may be very ordinary, but they are not trivial; they are vital for helping us organize and interpret our daily lives. When people do not follow the routines, we usually figure they are trying to cause trouble.

The Sociology of Everyday Life: The Assumptions

As a theoretical perspective, the sociology of everyday life is closely identified with the interaction school of symbolic interaction theory. Like that school, it stresses the role of subjective meanings assigned to symbolic communications and the active role of the individual in negotiating roles and identities. Scholars who use the everyday life (EDL) perspective, however, emphasize four additional assumptions: the problematic nature of culture, the dialectic, biography, and thick description.

The Problematic Nature of Culture

In Chapter 3, we likened culture to a design for living and to a tool kit. If you consider these two images, you will see that they offer subtly different meanings of culture. The "design for living" image suggests a set of blueprints that need only be correctly followed; the "tool kit" image, on the other hand, suggests a more dynamic approach. You do not follow a tool kit, you *use* it.

The sociology of everyday life is based on the tool kit image. It assumes that day-to-day behavior is a matter not of following clear cultural scripts but of improvising, negotiating, and adjusting to the general outline. From this point of view, culture is problematic.

Culture does furnish a great many rules and rituals, but it is not always clear which rules apply when. Being honest and standing by your friends are both norms. What do we do when telling the truth gets a friend in trouble? This predicament emphasizes that conformity to cultural norms is problematic: It requires a continual stream of choices (Oberschall and Leifer 1986).

The Dialectic

The rules that govern our behavior may contradict each other. They may also contradict our own wishes.

Scholars from the EDL perspective take seriously the *I/me* split of the self proposed by Mead (Chapter 6). They recognize that, on the sidelines of every social encounter, the *I* stands ready to assert itself—to barge in and do something impulsive and perhaps selfish. Any concrete situation can be envisioned as a negotiation between these two parts of the self.

This negotiation can be viewed as a dialectic, a process of conflict between individual freedom and social constraint (Bensman and Lilienfeld 1979). Here is a commonplace example: You are hurrying down the sidewalk, late for class, and you pass an acquaintance with a quick "Hi there, Nimrata, how are you?" Instead of replying as expected, Nimrata stops and proceeds to tell you that she is really depressed because she has just heard that her mother has cancer. So now what do you do? One aspect of your social self (the *me*) may tell you that you must pause and show interest and concern. But perhaps your *I*, the spontaneous, impulsive part of your self, wants to keep hurrying to class. After all, you hardly know Nimrata, much less her mother. In this case and in many others, your behavior represents a dialectic, a conflict between social convention and individual impulses.

A dialectic is not a simple contradiction but a process in which opposing forces engage, meet, and produce change. Viewing interaction episodes as a dialectic leads to the proposition that social interactions are never completely programmed by social structures. The outcome of a conflict is never fully predictable.

Biography

Each of us possesses a personal history, a biography, that makes us unique. Although we share many things, none of our experiences exactly duplicates the experience of another. Although all of us may face similar social constraints, as in the awkward episode of Nimrata's mother, each of us will bring a different self to the dialectic. Because of this, no two encounters are identical.

For all of us, culture is problematic, offering dozens of potentially conflicting normative prescriptions. Culture is especially problematic for those, such as these two girls, who are caught between two worlds. For all of us, however, life requires a constant stream of choices between alternative cultural imperatives. Everyday life is not just a matter of following the rules; it must be negotiated.

The uniqueness of each encounter does not mean that there is no patterned regularity in everyday life. Almost all of our daily encounters follow recognizable routines that allow us to interact without awkwardness, even with strangers. These routines explain the similarities in our encounters; biography explains why each one is just a little different from the rest.

THICK DESCRIPTION

The sociology of everyday life uses a methodological technique called *thick description*. Unlike thin description (who did what when), thick description tells us why the actors did what they did and what it meant to them. Thick description is in the tradition of Max Weber (Chapter 1), who recommended *verstehen*, or empathic understanding, as a social science method. Thick description requires that we get into the actors' conceptual world, that we understand what is going on in their heads (Geertz 1973).

The switch from thin to thick description brings about an important change in the stance that observers take toward reality. Scholars such as Durkheim and Comte assumed that there exists an objective reality and that the goal of science is to put aside all personal, or subjective, ideas so that this objective reality can be studied. Sociologists of everyday life, on the contrary, assume that there are multiple subjective realities and that the world as I see it is just as real as the world as you see it. Thick description is the attempt to understand the subjective social worlds of individual actors in specific situations (Lincoln and Guba 1985).

The sociology of everyday life is in many ways the application of the interaction school to the mundane encounters of daily life. It stands apart from other branches of sociology, however, because of its emphasis on the problematic nature of culture, the dialectic, the biography, and the reality of subjective worlds. The Focus on Yesterday section in this chapter examines everyday life for city kids in 1900.

Managing Everyday Life

As noted earlier, much of daily life is covered by routine exchanges. Nevertheless, each encounter is potentially problematic, and successful interaction requires selecting the appropriate routine and possessing the skill and motivation to carry it out (Maynard 1996).

At the beginning of any encounter, individuals must resolve two issues: (1) What is going on here—what is the nature of the action? (2) What identities will be granted—who are the actors? All action depends on our answers to these questions. Even the decision to ignore a stranger in the hallway presupposes that we have asked and answered these questions to our satisfaction. How do we do this?

Frames

A **frame** is an answer to the question, "What is going on here?" It is roughly equivalent to a *definition of the situation*.

The first step in any encounter is to develop an answer to the question, "What is going on here?" The answer forms a frame, or framework, for the encounter. A **frame,** then, is a *definition of the situation,* a set of expectations about the nature of the interaction episode that is taking place.

All face-to-face encounters are preceded by a framework of expectations—how people will act, what they will mean by their actions, and so on. Even the most simple encounter—say, approaching a salesclerk to buy a package of gum—is covered by dozens of expectations: We expect that the salesclerk will speak English, will wait on the person who gets to the counter first, will charge exactly the sum on the package and will not try to barter with us, will not comment on the fact that we are overweight or need a haircut. These expectations—the frame—give us guidance on how we should act and allow us to evaluate the encounter as normal or as deviant.

Sometimes, our initial framing of events gets us into trouble; instead of helping us, our definition of the situation only leads to greater perplexity. In such situations, we will have to revise the frame for the encounter and redefine what is going on (Goffman 1974b). Imagine, for example, a police officer coming across a group of rowdy college students. "Now kids," she says, "you'd better be getting on back to your dorms." If they respond with obscenities and thrown beer cans, she will reverse her definition of what is going on and prepare for a possibly violent encounter. Her initial frame is obviously inappropriate.

In most of our routine encounters, our frames will be shared by other actors. This is not always the case, however. We may simply be wrong in our assessment of what is going on, or other actors in the encounter may have entirely different frames. The final frame that we use to define the situation will be the result of a negotiation among the actors.

FOCUS ON EVERYDAY

Everyday Life for City Kids

"From the child's point of view, living on the streets meant freedom from adult control."

Scholars rely heavily on diaries and other personal histories to penetrate the everyday lives of people in past times (Blee and Billings 1986). These sources do not represent a random selection from the past, nor is the information contained in them necessarily objectively true. Even in diaries never intended to be shared, the authors reflect their own points of view, undoubtedly frequently mixed with accounts and disclaimers of various sorts. Nevertheless, scholars of everyday life accept such material as being a true view of life as the authors experienced it.

In *Children of the City*, David Nasaw (1985) uses this kind of material to unravel the everyday life of children in America's urban centers at the beginning of this century. Although Nasaw cites government reports and sociologists such as Jane Addams, he obviously believes that the truer picture comes from personal histories. In addition to biographies of the rich and famous, he mines a major new source of data on everyday life: oral history collections of the memories of ordinary women and men. In this way, Nasaw hopes to develop a thick description of what it meant *to the kids* to be a kid in New York or Boston in 1900.

Almost uniformly, reformers and sociologists were alarmed about children's lives in the cities. Their homes were so crowded that they virtually lived in the streets, intimate with prostitutes and bums, at constant risk of death or injury from street traffic. The kids saw it differently.

From the child's point of view, living on the streets meant freedom from adult control. A single block might have hundreds of children living on it. When they all played in the street (and there was no room for them indoors), the streets became theirs. There they organized their own lives, freely violating many of their seniors' expectations. They associated with people their parents didn't approve of, played craps and gambled for pennies, and learned things their parents would have preferred they not know. Reformers tried to help children by building playgrounds, but the children were, not surprisingly, unenthusiastic about the adult supervision that went with them.

According to these accounts, one of the best things about city living for children was the opportunity to work and earn money away from their families. These opportunities were especially great for boys: selling newspapers, running messages, selling candy or gum, or shining shoes. Although they were expected to turn all of their income over to their parents—and most boys turned most of it over—the children could easily save out a few pennies or a nickel for themselves. This could be spent in a wide variety of new establishments that courted children's custom—candy stores, hot-dog stands, cheap nickelodeons. One woman reported that when she was a girl, she often spent an entire Saturday morning spending a single nickel, walking up and down the aisles of the dime store, picking up and considering one object after another. When clerks questioned her, she just showed them her nickel and they left her alone. Having money of your own made you somebody, gave you rights.

In recollection, the children of the city around 1900 enjoyed great independence. Working was no novelty; children had always had to work. What was new was the variety of jobs to choose from, independence from their parents and often from any adult supervision whatever, personal profit from their work, and exciting places to spend their money.

Which version of children's life in the city is objectively real? The question is of more than historical interest. Children are frequently a population without a voice. People tell us about children instead of children telling us about themselves. Consider how this might affect other contemporary issues involving children—for example, the effects of television or day care.

Identity Negotiation

After we have put a frame on an encounter, we negotiate an answer to the second question: What identities will be granted? This question is far more complex than attaching names to the actors. Each of us has a repertoire of statuses and of

Despite the multitude of norms and rituals that we share, daily life is still problematic, and there are countless situations every day that puzzle us. People act in unexpected ways, messages get garbled, and dilemmas confront us. Like the man pictured here, we may have to pause a moment and ask ourselves, "What is going on here?" Negotiating our way through daily living requires real skill in analyzing social settings.

roles and identities from which to choose. Thus, we are frequently uncertain about which identity an actor is presenting *in this specific situation*.

To some extent, identities are determined by the frame being used. If a student's visit to a professor's office is framed as an academic tutorial, then the professor's academic identity is the relevant one. If the visit is framed as a social visit, then other aspects of the professor's identity (hobbies, family life, and so on) become relevant.

In many routine encounters, identities are not problematic. Although some confusion about identities is a frequent device in comedy (for example, many of Shakespeare's comedies), in real life, a few verbal exchanges are usually sufficient to resolve confusion about the actors' identities. In some cases, however, identity definitions are a matter of serious conflict. For example, I want to be considered a status equal, but you wish to treat me as an inferior.

Resolving the identity issue involves negotiations about both your own identity and the other's identity. How do we negotiate another's identity? We do so by trying to manipulate others into playing the roles we have assigned them. Mostly, we handle this through talk. For example, "Let me introduce Mary, the computer whiz," sets up a different encounter than, "Let me introduce Mary, the best party giver I know." Of course, others may reject your casting decisions. Mary may prefer to present an identity different from the one you have suggested. In that case, she will begin to try to renegotiate her identity.

Identity issues can become a major hidden agenda in interactions. Imagine an incompetent young man talking to a competent older man. If the younger man finds this situation uncomfortable, he may try to define it as an age-related encounter rather than a competence encounter. He may start with the techniques such as, "How do you, as an older man, feel about this?" To reinforce this simple device, he will probably follow up with remarks such as, "You're about to retire, and this makes me feel like my career is all ahead of me." He may interrupt the

> **THINKING CRITICALLY**
>
> Describe a time when you disagreed with someone about his or her identity. What kind of situation was it and why was identity problematic? In the end, whose definition of identity was accepted? Why do you think that was?

Although President Bill Clinton undoubtedly spends more time in a suit than in his jogging clothes, this attire symbolizes one of President Clinton's salient role identities, "jogger." All of us use clothing as a prop to support the roles we play. When we change from pumps to sneakers, from a sport coat to hip waders, we signal a change in identity. Most of us try to affect others' opinions of us by the way we dress and present ourselves.

older man by remarking on his health. Through such strategies, actors try to negotiate both their own and the other's identity.

DRAMATURGY

The management of everyday life is the focus of a sociological perspective called dramaturgy. **Dramaturgy** is a version of symbolic interaction theory that views social situations as scenes manipulated by the actors to convey the desired impression to the audience.

Dramaturgy is a version of symbolic interaction theory that views social situations as scenes manipulated by the actors to convey the desired impression to the audience.

The chief architect of the dramaturgical perspective is Erving Goffman (1959, 1963a). To Goffman, all the world is a theater. The theater has both a *front region*, the stage, where the performance is given, and a *back region*, where rehearsals take place and behavior inappropriate for the stage may appear. For example, waiters at expensive restaurants are acutely aware of being onstage and act in a dignified and formal manner. Back in the kitchen, however, they may be eating patron's leftovers.

The ultimate back region for most of us, the place where we can be our real selves, is at home. Even here, however, front-region behavior is called for when company comes. ("Oh, yes, we always keep our house this clean.") On such occasions, a married couple functions as a team in a performance designed to manage their guests' impressions. People who were screaming at each other before the doorbell rang suddenly start calling each other "dear" and "honey." The guests are the audience, and they too play a role. By seeming to believe the team's act (Goffman calls this "giving deference"), they contribute to a successful visit.

Nonverbal Cues. A successful act requires careful stage management. Not only must the script be right, but costumes and props and body gestures must support the act.

DRESS. All of us who have stood in front of our closets wondering what to wear have faced the dilemma of how to present ourselves. Although most of us have many outfits that meet the necessary criteria of covering our bodies decently and dealing with the climate, we choose among potential outfits based on the impression we would like to create. Concepts such as dressing for success are examples of this. From punk haircuts to cowboy boots, the way we dress furnishes important auxiliary information to our audience; it can either support an act or discredit it.

BODY LANGUAGE. The cues we give through facial expressions, eye contact, and posture can enhance, reinforce, or even contradict the meaning of a verbal communication. For example, when words of affection are accompanied by hugs or caresses, the verbal statements are enhanced and reinforced. When someone delivers words of encouragement and interest without looking up from the newspaper, however, the verbal statements are contradicted by actions. Whether intended or unintended, the impression given belies and discredits the verbal communication.

In other cases, gestures and posture may substitute entirely for verbal communication. Anybody who has watched a football game is familiar with the small drama wherein a receiver who has dropped an important pass falls to the ground and drums the turf with his hands. This communicates that he takes his failure seriously and is mad at himself. In effect, it says, "You don't need to bawl me out, Coach, I know I goofed, and I feel really bad about it, and I'll try my best not to do it again."

Even those who have very high self-esteem seek out ways to enhance and maintain their credit with others. Unfortunately, there are very few occasions on which we can wear all of our awards (Goffman calls them "prestige symbols") on our shirts. Most of us have to seek somewhat more subtle ways to demonstrate what wonderful people we are.

CUING STATUS. Nonverbal cues are used extensively to send out messages that would be socially awkward if expressed verbally. Sexual interest is one of these messages. Another is a message about social rank, or prestige. It is difficult to say outright, "You know that I'm more important than you, don't you?" Thus, such messages are sent through nonverbal cues.

Studies of status encounters in laboratories show that the following nonverbal strategies are used to signal dominance: looking directly into the other's eyes while listening and speaking, taking up a lot of physical space (sprawling in one's chair, putting a foot on another chair, leaning an arm across the back of another chair), choosing a seat at the end of the table, interrupting others, and being the first person to speak (Ridgeway, Berger, and Smith 1985). In these last two instances, the timing of the speech acts has an effect independent of the content. The effectiveness of these strategies is confirmed if we consider the status inferences we would make about a person who did just the opposite: who wouldn't look at us, scrunched up in the corner of the chair, chose an unassuming position at the table, and was hesitant to speak.

Although some nonverbal communication appears to have universal meaning, most nonverbal communication must be framed before it can be accurately understood. A women who takes a long glance up and down a man's body shows that she is interested in his body. Only knowledge of the context will tell you what that means. Is she a doctor looking at him with clinical interest? A tailor? A cannibal? A woman looking for a sexual encounter? An employer sizing up a laborer? As this suggests, a variety of meanings can be associated with the same behavior. The correct interpretation depends on the social context, interactions, and biographies of those involved.

WHOSE DEFINITION? EX-WIFE AT THE FUNERAL

How we act in any encounter depends in large part on the frame we have developed and the identities we and the other participants have worked out. One of the many processes of negotiation that goes on in social encounters is determining whose definition of the situation will be accepted. The person who wins this negotiation gains a powerful advantage. A paper by Riedmann (1987) on the role of the ex-wife at the funeral is an insightful illustration of this process.

In this case, Bill, a 44-year-old man, died suddenly and accidentally at the home he shared with his new wife of six months. Immediately after the accident, his 20-year-old daughter, who was staying with them, called her mother to break the news. The ex-wife was terribly upset: She had gone steady with Bill from age 16 to 22 and had been married to him for 20 years; even after the divorce and his remarriage, they had remained friends and had lunched together frequently. Although they could no longer live together, they had shared a concern for their two children and half a lifetime of memories. His parents were almost as close to her as her own; she had spent many summer afternoons with his brothers and their children.

When informed of his death, therefore, she felt bereaved. Her first response was, "What? Our dad is dead?" Her definition of the situation was that she had had a death in her family. Acting on this definition, she went to the home of her former parents-in-law. Here, she came up against a different definition. From the in-laws' position, a death had occurred in their family but not in her family. Although they did not say so, they wanted her to leave quickly before the current wife arrived.

Over the next few days, the ex-wife again and again ran into dilemmas posed by contrasting definitions of the situation. The obituary did not mention her among the relatives left behind. When she went to view the body at the mortuary, she was denied admittance on the grounds that only members of the immediate family were eligible. When the minister asked everybody but the immediate family to leave the graveyard, she was supposed to leave. Again, although the ex-wife defined Bill's death as a death in her family, it was not a definition commonly shared.

The ex-wife and the new wife formed teams, each trying to pursue its own definition of the situation. The "old family team" (made up of the ex-wife, one of her children, her relatives, and one brother-in-law) and the "new family team" competed to be recognized as the "real family team." At the funeral service itself, each team held down one corner of the lobby. When family and friends entered the lobby, they were faced with the predicament of which team to console first. Since many of Bill's old friends knew the ex-wife well and the new wife not at all, the "old family team" may be considered to have won this round.

Because of legal relationships, in the end the ex-wife was relatively powerless to impose her definition of the situation. The mortician and the priest were paid agents of the "new family team." The ex-wife was ultimately forced to reframe the situation and to recognize her powerlessness to impose her definition of the situation on others.

THE MEDIA AND IDENTITY NEGOTIATION: SEX, DRUGS, AND ROCK 'N ROLL

What kind of music do you like? People sometimes use this question to help identify what kind of person you are. If you say *alternative* or *rap* or *women's music* or *classical*, your answer may reveal things about you besides simply your taste in music. We saw in Chapter 6 that the media is an agent in socialization. The media—specifically popular music and MTV—is also a stimulus for identity negotiation.

Identity negotiation associated with music has been going on for decades, at least since the era of rock 'n roll. *Rock 'n roll* was a term applied in the 1950s to a style of music that had developed from rhythm and blues. Rock 'n roll appealed to teens, and since its beginning, many older people criticized rock 'n roll. They said it would loosen young people's sexual morals and encourage promiscuity. Some argued that rock 'n roll was the result of a plot by the Communists to weaken America's youth.

This kind of criticism has not stopped. In 1976, for instance, the Reverend Jesse Jackson tried to remove "sexy songs" from the airways because, he said, they helped cause premarital pregnancy (Weinstein 1996). Throughout the 1960s and 1970s, conservative political groups such as the John Birch Society, along with then Vice-president Spiro Agnew, attacked folk-rock as communist-inspired "drug music." Agnew particularly mentioned songs by Jefferson Airplane and the Beatles as leading young listeners into taking drugs (Weinstein 1996). More recently, parents and others have criticized rap music as too sexually provocative and unnecessarily violent. And songs such as AC/DC's "Hell Ain't a Bad Place to Be" and Ozzy Osbourne's "Suicide Solution" are cited as examples of music that encourage satanism and suicide.

Meanwhile, many young people (and others) reject this definition of the situation. They say that liking heavy metal or rap does not necessarily mean anything negative about their identity. Some point out that few who hear the music actually listen to or can understand the lyrics anyway. Sociologist Deena Weinstein (1996) argues that rock has always been a form of *symbolic rebellion* by youth. On the one hand, youth know that one day they will assume adult roles and responsibilities. On the other hand, young people's music is an expression of criticism for authority and for the world that they will inherit.

We can think of the battle over rock 'n roll and its more contemporary descendants as an example of negotiation in identity formation: Does listening to and liking such music mean you are degenerate? A Communist? Sexually promiscuous? Suicidal? Satanic? Some would answer *yes* and others, *no*.

ETHNOMETHODOLOGY

From the EDL perspective, daily life is a series of problematic encounters. Successful negotiation through this maze of predicaments requires the actor to have some fairly reliable theories about human nature and how others are likely to act (Maynard 1966).

Ethnomethodology is the study of the everyday strategies that individuals use to study and organize their worlds.

How do we arrive at these commonsense theories? The study of the everyday strategies that individuals use to understand their world is called **ethnomethodology.** Generally, *methodology* is the study of scientific and technical procedures such as sampling and statistical analysis; *ethnomethodology* studies folk methods, the procedures you and I use to analyze everyday situations.

The everyday process of understanding our own social world is similar in broad outline to the processes that sociologists use to understand social structure. We begin an interaction episode on the basis of a working hypothesis about what is going on and then watch each others' reactions. If the response is consistent with our hypothesis, we feel the hypothesis is confirmed and keep acting on this basis. If the response suggests that our hypothesis is wrong, however, we reformulate the hypothesis, test it, and watch for new clues. Every social encounter is a little bit like the wheel of science we discussed in Chapter 2, an ongoing process of discovery.

Imagine, for example, meeting your friend John after a period of a couple of months. Your working hypothesis is that nothing has changed since the last time you met. You say, "How's your wife?" John says, "We've separated." Your first hypothesis is obviously wrong, so, to test a new one, you cautiously venture, "That's too bad." "No, it's not," says John. "Our marriage was making us both miserable." Now you are starting to get enough information so that you know how to behave. In the words of Garfinkel (1967), you have "found your feet."

Ethnomethodology is closely linked to the work of Harold Garfinkel, a Harvard-trained sociologist whose central concern is determining the common understandings that individuals use in making sense out of their world. We cover just two of these here: the assumption that appearances are real and the assumption that other people know what we know, that they share our symbolic worlds.

Appearances Are Reality

A major hypothesis underlying all our daily interactions is that people are who they appear to be. Our working hypothesis in any interaction episode is that appearances can be trusted: The woman in a police uniform *is* a police officer; the man behind the counter *is* a salesclerk.

The corollary to this hypothesis is just as important: We assume that others will trust our appearances.

Some of the underlying norms that govern everyday life are not immediately obvious to us, yet we become angry when they are violated. Perhaps one of these people has failed to learn one of the basic norms that govern human relations: Don't ever criticize another person's parents or children or even agree with them when they are critical! (Another norm violation: These white, middle-class people are not expected to argue in public.)

This mutual trust is critical to social interaction. If somebody says he or she is 22 years old or Catholic, it is considered a hostile act to say, "Prove it." To appreciate the importance of accepting people at their word, you need only recall that one of the surest ways to provoke a fight on the playground is to say, "Oh yeah?" To challenge another's presentation of self is to undermine the entire basis of social interaction.

SHARED SYMBOLIC WORLDS

Another major working hypothesis that seems to be essential for social relationships is that others share our symbolic worlds. This means that we assume people know what we know and that things have the same meanings for them as they do for us.

One of the ways Garfinkel developed to bring these expectations out in the open was to disrupt normal routines by causing trouble. These deliberate attempts to cause trouble are called *breaching experiments*. Two examples show how important the assumption of shared meanings is to normal interaction (Garfinkel 1963, 221). In both cases, E, the experimenter, is one of Garfinkel's students, acting on orders, and S, the subject, is an unwitting participant.

Case 1: The subject was telling the experimenter, a member of the subject's car pool, about having had a flat tire while going to work the previous day.

S: I had a flat tire.
E: What do you mean, you had a flat tire?

The subject appeared momentarily stunned. Then she answered in a hostile way, "What do you mean, 'what do you mean?' A flat tire is a flat tire. That is what I meant. Nothing special. What a crazy question!"

Case 2: On Friday night, E and her husband were watching an old movie on television.

S: All these old movies have the same kind of old iron bedstead in them.
E: What do you mean?
S: What's the matter with you? You know what I mean.
E: I wish you would be more specific.
S: You know what I mean! Drop dead!

Both of these cases involve violations of our expectation that others know what we know. The key response in both is the subject's angry retort, "What do you mean, 'what do you mean?' " In neither case can the subject account for the lack of shared symbolic worlds except that E is crazy, sick, or hostile. The possibility that E really doesn't know what S means doesn't appear to cross S's mind. Notice that in both cases interaction breaks down completely when the assumption of shared meanings is shattered.

> **THINKING CRITICALLY**
>
> Think of a time when you tried to avoid blame. What exactly did you do? Did it work? How might your efforts at blame avoidance have worked better?

IDENTITY WORK

Most social scientists wish to go beyond simple descriptions of behavior and ask *why* people do what they do. The answer most often supplied by scholars studying everyday behavior is that people are trying to enhance their self-esteem. We assume that social approval is one of the most important rewards that human interaction has to offer and that people try to manage their identities so that this approval is maximized.

Managing identities to support and sustain our self-esteem is called identity work (Snow and Anderson 1987). It consists of two general strategies: avoiding blame and gaining credit (Tedeschi and Riess 1981).

Avoiding Blame

There are many potential sources of damage to our self-concepts. We may have lost a job or flunked a class; on a more mundane level, we may have said the most embarrassing, most stupid thing imaginable, been unintentionally rude to an older relative, or otherwise made a fool of ourselves. When we behave in ways that make us look bad, that embarrass us and make others think badly of us, then it is important to try to protect our identities.

Most of this work is done through talk. C. Wright Mills (1940, 909) noted that we learn the vocabulary for making excuses at the same time we learn the norms themselves. We learn what the rules are, and we simultaneously learn what kinds of accounts will justify violations of those rules. If we can successfully explain away our rule breaking, we can present ourselves as persons who normally obey norms and who deserve to be thought well of by ourselves and others. The three basic strategies we use to avoid blame are role distancing, accounts, and disclaimers.

Role Distancing. We occasionally find ourselves playing roles that do us no credit. Students, for example, often have low-status jobs such as working at fast-food outlets or sorting laundry at dormitories. When we have roles that do us no credit, we engage in a process of **role distancing,** explaining to anyone who will listen that this is just temporary and/or is not a reflection of who we really are. We reject this role identity.

Role distancing is believing and explaining to others that one's current role is temporary and/or not a reflection of one's "real" self.

A recent study among the homeless in Austin, Texas, investigated this identity mechanism. David Snow and Leon Anderson (1987) ate at the Salvation Army and hung out under bridges and at the plasma center. They listened to homeless people talk about themselves, trying to discover the processes that these people used to negotiate their identities and protect their self-esteem. Snow and Anderson found that role distancing was one of the most common forms of identity work among the homeless. For example, a 24-year-old man who had been on the street for only a few weeks said, "I'm not like the other guys who hang out down at the 'Sally' [Salvation Army]. If you want to know about street people, I can tell you about them; but you can't really learn about street people from studying me, because I'm different" (1987, 1349).

Accounts. Much of the rule breaking that goes on in everyday life is of a minor sort that can be explained away. We do this by giving **accounts,** explanations of unexpected or untoward behavior. Accounts are of two sorts—excuses and justifications (Scott and Lyman 1968). **Excuses** are accounts in which an individual admits that the act in question was bad, wrong, or inappropriate but claims he or she couldn't help it. **Justifications** are accounts that explain the good reasons the violator had for choosing to break the rule; often, these are appeals to some alternative rule (1968, 47).

Accounts are explanations of unexpected or untoward behavior. They are of two sorts: excuses and justifications.

Excuses are explanations in which a person admits that the act in question was wrong or inappropriate but claims he or she couldn't help it.

Justifications explain the good reasons the violator had for choosing to break the rule; often they are appeals to some alternative rule.

This photograph was taken outside of the Salvation Army in Austin, Texas, where David Snow and Leon Anderson did a participant observation study of the homeless. Their research shows that many of the people who hang out at the "Sally" manage to negotiate positive identities despite being homeless. One method for doing this is role distancing. For this man, carrying luggage and a guitar may be part of role distancing.

Disclaimers are verbal devices employed in advance to ward off doubts and negative reactions that might result from one's conduct.

> **THINKING CRITICALLY**
>
> Keep watch over your conversations for the next several days, and see if you recognize any accounts or disclaimers. How are these functional? Dysfunctional?

One of the most fertile fields for both excuses and justifications is associated with the student role. Students are expected to study and turn papers in on time. Many times, however, they don't. Kathleen Kalab, a sociology professor at Western Kentucky University, asked her students to explain in writing why they missed class. The answers she received show how students try to explain away their norm violations so that they can preserve a positive identity. For example, one student offered the following *excuse:*

> I am so sorry I missed your class, among others, Tuesday the [date]. The reason I missed is a simple yet probably unacceptable reason, I slept until 1:45 P.M. Not only did I sleep through Sociology, I also slept through these things: Geography, trash pick-up at Poland Hall, maintenance workers sawing down a tree outside my window, my alarm clock (I believe), and many other loud and interesting things. Please see your way clear of forgiving me for this horrible and strange event. (Kalab 1987, 79)

Other students *justified* sacrificing student performance in order to be good sons or employees. For example,

> Sorry I wasn't here but Friday my parents called and our entire herd of cattle broke out and were all over the county and then I got to castrate two 500-lb. bull calves. So needless to say I was extremely busy. (Kalab 1987, 75)

Or

> I am really sorry for missing your class Friday. The reason being I was part of my Reserve unit's advance party to Fort Knox. I didn't know this until late Thursday night. So please excuse me for not being there. (Kalab 1987, 76)

Accounts such as these are verbal efforts to resolve the discrepancy between what has happened and what can legitimately have been expected. If they are accepted, self-identity is preserved and interaction can proceed normally.

Disclaimers. A person who recognizes that he or she is likely to violate expectations may preface that action with a **disclaimer,** a verbal device used, in advance, to ward off doubts and negative reactions that might result from conduct (Hewitt and Stokes 1975, 3). Students commonly begin queries with "I know this is a stupid question, but. . . ." The disclaimer lets the hearer know that the speaker knows the rules, even though he or she doesn't know the answer.

Disclaimers occur before the act; accounts occur after the act. Nevertheless, both are verbal devices we use to try to maintain a good image of ourselves, both in our own eyes and in the eyes of others. They help us in trying to avoid self-blame for deviant behavior and to reduce the blame that others might attribute to us. If we are successful in this identity work, we can retain fairly good reputations despite a few failures in meeting our social responsibilities.

GAINING CREDIT

Just as there are a variety of ways to avoid blame, there are many ways to claim credit. One way is to link yourself spatially or verbally to situations or individuals that have high prestige. This can be done through methods that range from making a $1,000 donation to a political fund-raiser so that you can have a photograph of yourself with the president, to wearing T-shirts that announce exotic places you've been, to aligning yourself verbally with "our" team (when it is winning).

Claiming credit is a strategy that requires considerable tact. Bragging is generally considered inappropriate, and if you pat yourself too hard on the back, you are likely to find that others will refuse to follow suit. The trick is to find the delicate balance wherein others are subtly reminded of your admirable qualities without your having actually to ask for or demand praise.

Again, the classroom and the negotiation of the student identity are good sources of examples about how we go about doing positive identitics work. In an imaginative study, Daniel and Cheryl Albas (1988) at the University of Manitoba did a systematic analysis of how their students managed their identities when papers were returned. We focus here on how the "aces," the students who have done very well on examinations, manage to claim credit successfully. The aces want to claim all the credit they can but must somehow avoid the appearance of bragging or being condescending toward the "bombers," their classmates who have done poorly.

The Albases note that the aces differ in the sophistication with which they claim credit. Almost all aces leave their examinations open on their desks with the grades prominently displayed; some go so far as to tap their exams noisily on the desks and otherwise try to draw attention to their scores. In general, however, the aces want more than notice; they want praise. This means that they have to induce others to talk to them about their grades. A crude tactic is simply to walk up to another student and say, "I got 95 percent. What did you get?" Such tactics are not very effective. Unless the other student has done as well as or better than the ace, he or she will be annoyed, may refuse to answer, and will certainly withhold the desired praise. After an exam or two, aces who use this tactic will find that people are avoiding them. Experienced aces use a variety of more subtle tactics. They start with, "Boy, that was a hard exam. I didn't do as well as I thought. How did you do?" This expression of sympathy is likely to elicit both the other student's score and a question about how the ace did. This strategy protects the ace from the criticism of having bragged; the ace gives his or her own score only in response to a question from another.

Being a gracious winner is sometimes harder than being a gracious loser, and it is difficult for an ace to interact with a bomber in a way that protects the bomber's identity. One strategy that is used is to blame both success and failure on luck. When talking to a bomber, an ace may argue that "it was only luck that I studied the stuff that was on the exam." Through strategies such as this, the ace gets double credit: for being a good student and for being a nice person.

We can refer here to a point made in Chapter 2: Research findings can be generalized only to the population from which the sample was drawn. The findings in this study, done at the University of Manitoba, cannot necessarily be applied to all college students. For example, in some subcultures, the aces would have no claim to credit and might even risk ostracism. In such instances, the aces would more likely try to avoid blame by role distancing or offering excuses and justifications.

GLOBAL PERSPECTIVES: A CASE STUDY OF IDENTITY WORK AMONG AUSTRALIAN ABORIGINALS

"I want to owe you five dollars," one Australian Aboriginal forthrightly says to another, requesting a loan of that amount. According to Nicolas Peterson, an Australian National University anthropologist, "bumming" like this is expected among Aboriginals. Peterson (1993) studied the everyday life of indigenous, or native, Aboriginals in northeastern Australia, particularly those who lived near

Cape York. Spending several months with them in the bush, he used the research strategy of participant observation described in Chapter 2. For the details reported here, he also reviewed the published thick descriptions of other anthropologists who had done fieldwork among the Aboriginals.

Unlike the Native American Indians, the Australian Aboriginals today retain sufficient control over enough land that some of them can continue to be nomadic hunters and gatherers, especially in northeastern and central Australia. As compensation for lands they were forced to relinquish to British colonizers, the Aboriginals also receive regular pension checks from the Australian government. Primarily hunters and gatherers (as described in Chapter 4), the Australian Aboriginals have virtually no surplus or storage.

Hunters and gatherers typically share food and other objects. Because food is found (or not found) on a day-to-day basis, the everyday life of hunters and gatherers entails uncertainty. Sharing makes good sense and is a principal component of the Aboriginals' cultural tool kit. But this sharing is not necessarily unsolicited or automatic. Except in special situations, such as funeral distributions, very little spontaneous giving takes place outside the household. In fact, it is rude to offer something that was not asked for, because this situation puts people in a position in which it is difficult to refuse—and refusing is even ruder. Instead, sharing is continually negotiated. Typically, Aboriginals exchange food and other things because someone demands it of them. Peterson called this practice *demand sharing*.

Demands for food and other items are common among the Aboriginals and do not always take spoken form. Simply presenting yourself when food is being prepared and eaten means you have to be included. (We in the United States have this norm, too.) Adults usually present themselves for something to eat only when large amounts of food have been brought into camp by one household. Children commonly "bum" food, however. When children overhear anybody talking about food, they often go to have a look. This behavior has given rise to the mild rebuke, "Your ears have fingers."

A particularly interesting practice is known as *wamarrkane*. At a public event, A may give B a compliment, such as, "You are a fine dancer." A then has the right to make a substantial demand on B. Even a casual everyday remark, such as, "Oh, what a beautiful baby!" allows the speaker to demand something from the person complimented.

Demand sharing makes accumulation difficult but not impossible. A person can manage to save money or artifacts by declaring that they are being accumulated for a specific and commonly valued purpose, such as buying a car. The declaration protects the property from demands—although use of the car may be demanded once it has been acquired.

Sharing is expected, but so is having enough for yourself. What do you do when you don't want to share? While making demands is normative, there are everyday routines to halt excessive demanding. For instance, you can stop a man in the middle of a demand simply by saying his mother-in-law's name. By carving sacred designs on their pipes, old men render them taboo and hence keep others from demanding them.

Once a demand is made, it should not be directly refused. Nevertheless, meeting a demand can be avoided by culturally normative strategies, such as trickery, lying, and hiding things that might be demanded. For example, adult men frequently demand spears and other weapons from each other. Peterson found that the men use trickery to avoid having to meet these demands. In one strategy, valued spears or guns are given to elderly women by their sons or other male relatives, although the women never use the weapons. Or a woman may purchase these weapons with her pension check and allow them to be used by particular males. These practices function in two ways. First, it ensures that the elderly women receive adequate food, because the owner of the weapon used in a kill has a right in the distribution of the meat. Second, the practice allows the man who customarily uses the weapon, and who normally keeps it in his possession, to refuse demands for it. He can justify his refusal by explaining that the weapons are not his to give.

Hiding things is also an everyday routine. (If ears have fingers, so do eyes.) In one report, a man hid cooked meat in a flour drum on hearing of the arrival of his close relatives from a nearby community. When the relatives got there, one of them asked whether the man had any meat. He told them he was empty-handed. In light of the evidence of cooking strewn about, his relatives did not believe him. The relatives were not the least bit angry, however, because they were engaging in a mutually understood, negotiated, everyday ritual. The relatives simply proceeded to open all the flour drums lying around until they found the meat. The reluctant host was not angry that his relatives were ransacking his home, for this too was an expected part of the negotiating routine. Once discovered, the game was shared.

Not only potential givers hide resources. Demanders do, too, so that they can appear needy enough to ask for more. One day in the field, an Aboriginal asked Peterson for a cigarette. Peterson refused. (Maybe Peterson was conducting a breaching experiment.) The Aboriginal did not take offense at the refusal. Instead, he instructed Peterson on how to hide a pack of cigarettes in his socks so that he could tell people he had none. Then he gave Peterson a pack of cigarettes and told him that he had several more buried near his camp.

Aboriginals alternately demand, relinquish, and conceal—all as part of the routine rituals of everyday life. An individual's prestige depends largely on being able and willing to engage in this exchange process. Moreover, demand sharing is a complex behavior that is not based simply on need. A demander may be testing—or even reinforcing—her or his relationship with the potential giver. Demanding can also be a self-affirming activity undertaken to make others recognize the demander's rights. When we think about it this way, the complicated give and take of demand sharing comprises everyday identity work among Australian Aboriginals. By demanding, receiving, sharing, and skillfully avoiding the demands of others, Australian Aboriginals reinforce their self-esteem.

Where This Leaves Us

In the 1950s, structural-functional theory dominated sociology, and there was a great deal of emphasis on the power of institutionalized norms to *determine* behavior. Durkheim, with his views on positivism and constraint, was a favorite classic theorist. Similarly, during this period, the structural school of symbolic interaction theory clearly dominated the interaction school, and theorists stressed the power of institutionalized roles to influence behavior and personality.

Beginning in the 1960s, sociologists grew increasingly concerned that this view of human behavior reflected an "oversocialized view" of people (Wrong 1961). In 1967, Garfinkel signaled rebellion against this perspective when he argued that the deterministic model presented people as "judgmental dopes" who couldn't do their own thinking.

In the last two decades, sociological thinkers have increasingly tended to view social behavior as more negotiable and less rule-bound. This change is most obvious in the sociology of everyday life, but it is also evident in most other areas of sociology. Studies of mental hospitals, businesses, and complex organizations now suggest that the behavior of actors may be best understood as a game in which each player chooses a strategy to maximize her or his self-interest (Crozier and Friedberg 1980). Even bureaucracies are not seen as wholly deterministic. Employees stress some rules, ignore others, and reinterpret the rest (Fine 1984).

This does *not* mean that social structure does not constrain and influence behavior. Of course it does, as we have seen in the last six chapters. Indeed, the rules make a great deal of difference, and there are obvious limits to the extent to which we can negotiate given situations. As W. I. Thomas noted in 1923, "The child is always born into a group of people among whom all the general types of situation which may arise have already been defined and corresponding rules of conduct developed, and where he has not the slightest chance of making his definitions and following his wishes without interference" (cited in Shalin 1986).

The perspective of life as problematic and negotiable is a useful balance to the role of social structure in determining behavior. Our behavior is neither entirely negotiable nor entirely determined.

APPLICATIONS IN DIVERSITY

How Do People with Disabilities Manage a "Spoiled" Identity?

An illustration of identity work can be seen in individuals who have what Erving Goffman (1963b) calls *spoiled identities*—identities that stigmatize them as repulsive and rejected by society. Examples include the noticeably disabled, traitors, and, in some communities, people with AIDS. Stigmatized people often experience invasions of privacy, as when strangers stare or ask intrusive questions. When the stigmatized interact with others (Goffman calls them "normals"), the stigmatized are likely to feel "on"—self-conscious and wary about the impression they are making (Goffman 1963b). How do individuals with spoiled identities sustain their self-esteem?

In a *Newsweek* essay titled, "Hush: It's Epilepsy," Shirl Rapport (1994), a 59-year-old businesswoman, described how she manages her "spoiled" identity. Goffman (1963b) argued that stigmatized people use four strategies for protecting their self-esteem: (1) physically *withdrawing* from others; (2) *passing* as members of the nonstigmatized group; (3) *covering*, or trying to minimize the stigma when passing is impossible; and (4) explaining the stigma to normals by using culturally acceptable "disclosure etiquette."

When Shirl Rapport realized that she had epilepsy at age 22, she read everything she could about the disease but insisted on keeping it a secret from almost everyone: "If no one spoke about epilepsy, and some books referred to it as a sign of the Devil, why should I advertise it?" Rapport was protecting her self-esteem by passing.

Eventually, however, it became impossible to pass. At one unforgettable dinner party, she looked up from the table to find people staring at her. Her hand was squeezing the roast beef and mashed potatoes on her plate, and she had wet her pants. Mortified, she looked at the people who were waiting for an explanation and disclosed the truth. She had just had an epileptic seizure.

As her seizures got worse, Shirl often fell, breaking ribs, a shoulder, and her nose. Her neurologist ordered her to get something to protect her head and ribs. A police friend gave her a bulletproof vest, and she now wears a professional football helmet. "You can't imagine what it's like," she wrote, "to walk into a library, supermarket or business meeting wearing the sports equipment I have to put on every day. But it was that or break body parts."

An insurance representative, Rapport explains to people that she wears her "costume" for seizures she can't control and because it keeps her independent. By referring to her gear as a "costume," she minimizes, or "covers," her condition. By accenting her desire to remain independent, she refers to central American values, such as achievement, activity, and work, discussed in Chapter 3. Doing so is probably part of our society's disclosure etiquette, one that Rapport has discovered through personal experience.

Rapport ended her essay by writing that she is grateful to her employer, "who doesn't care what I wear on my head," and to her husband, "who always walks beside me, regardless of stares." Here Rapport illustrates what society defines as a "good adjustment." She cheerfully accepts herself as essentially the same as normals, while not pressing her luck, testing the limits of the acceptance shown her, or making further demands. According to Goffman, expecting a "good adjustment" from those with disabilities means expecting them never to demonstrate to normals all the unfairness and pain of being stigmatized; nor will normals have to admit how limited their tolerance is (Goffman 1963b, 121).

Thinking Critically

What do you think? Do you know anyone (including yourself) who is physically challenged? If so, do you think that person is stigmatized by "normals"? If yes, in what way or ways? If no, why not? Do you agree that a "good adjustment" on the part of an individual with a spoiled identity protects normals from facing their own intolerance? If not, why not? If so, how, exactly? What might be some other kinds of stigma in our society? Are people expected to deal with these other kinds of stigma in similar ways?

SOCIOLOGY ON THE NET

In managing everyday life, we constantly engage in framing our encounters and identity negotiation. The frame defines the situation and in identity negotiation, we negotiate our own identity as well as the identity of others. These activities are carried out by individuals and groups alike. The case of homosexuality is an excellent example. America is a homophobic nation with a strong hatred and dislike of homosexuals. This is especially the case in the religious institution.

`http://www2.bitstream.net/~thebible/FBNS1.html`

You have reached the Fundamentalist Baptist News Service. Scroll down through the sections on **recent and past articles** and select out several articles on homosexuality. What kind of a frame is being used here? How is this organization trying to negotiate the identities of homosexuals? What identity do they negotiate for themselves? You might also look for articles dealing with contemporary music.

Certainly, most gay and lesbians do not want to accept the identities negotiated for them by most religious organizations. In response to the identities being thrust upon them, a number of gays and lesbians have formed their own church.

`http://www.ufmcc.com`

This web site is maintained by the Universal Fellowship of Metropolitan Community Churches. Click on the **Enter Our World** highlight. A good place to begin your browsing is in the section entitled **Who the UFMCC Is... What Do We Do?** Now go to the section on **Homosexuality and the Bible** and continue with the discussion of **Homosexuality: Not a Sin...Not a Sickness**. You may wish to follow this discussion of the bible by following the links at the end of the discussion. How do these discussions constitute identity negotiation? What kind of an identity is being negotiated? How does your faith look at this issue?

1. The sociology of everyday life is a perspective that analyzes the patterns of human social behavior in concrete encounters in daily life.
2. Social life depends on routines. Because we share expectations, we can coordinate our behavior with others. Thus, we find that even very mundane aspects of our social relationships, including how we ride on elevators and greet people in the hall, are covered by routine expectations.
3. Four assumptions guide theory and research in this approach to studying human interaction: Culture is problematic; individuals experience a dialectic between freedom and social constraint; each individual is unique, possessing a biography unlike that of any other individual; and understanding everyday life can be accomplished best through thick descriptions.
4. Deciding how to act in a given encounter requires answering two questions: What is going on here? What identities will be granted? These issues of framing and identity resolution may involve competition and negotiation between actors or teams of actors.
5. Dramaturgy is a perspective pioneered by Erving Goffman. It views the self as a strategist choosing roles and setting scenes to maximize self-interest.

6 Ethnomethodology is a perspective linked with Harold Garfinkel. It is concerned with the commonsense assumptions that individuals make about human nature and society in going about their everyday affairs. Two of these assumptions are that appearances are reality and that others share our symbolic worlds.

7 The desire for approval is an important factor guiding human behavior. To maximize this approval, people engage in active identity work to sustain and support their self-esteem. This work takes two forms: avoiding blame and gaining credit.

8 Three methods for avoiding blame are role distancing, giving accounts (excuses and justifications), and offering disclaimers.

9 The Australian Aboriginals have developed a complicated system of demand sharing in which negotiating individuals alternately demand, relinquish, and conceal their goods as part of the routine everyday life.

10 The old image of people as "judgmental dopes" whose actions are determined by culture has been replaced by an image of people as active agents in interpreting culture. This change is reflected in the development of the sociology of everyday life and also in increased emphasis on the negotiated order in bureaucracies and social institutions.

11 Stigmas are "spoiled identities" that must be managed and negotiated. According to Erving Goffman, individuals do this in one or more of four ways: physically withdrawing from others, passing as nonstigmatized, covering, and disclosing the stigma according to accepted disclosure etiquette.

Suggested Readings

BARNES, J. A. 1994. *A Pack of Lies: Toward a Sociology of Lying*. New York: Cambridge University Press. An interesting book on lying in everyday life. Barnes would argue that almost all of us lie once in a while, especially in socially "ambiguous domains." Barnes also looks at lying among politicians, bureaucrats, and medical practitioners.

GOFFMAN, Erving. 1959. *The Presentation of Self in Everyday Life*. New York: Doubleday. The book in which Goffman lays out the basic ideas behind dramaturgy. Each of Goffman's books is enjoyable reading and easily accessible to the undergraduate.

GOFFMAN, Erving. 1963. *Stigma: Notes on the Management of a Spoiled Identity*. Englewood Cliffs, N.J.: Prentice-Hall. A fascinating and readable book on identity management in everyday life with implications for and applications to various aspects of discrimination, prejudice, and diversity.

GOFFMAN, Erving. 1967. *Interaction Ritual: Essays in Face-to-Face Behavior*. New York: Doubleday-Anchor. A collection of essays dealing with identity work in a variety of familiar as well as unfamiliar settings.

NASAW, David. 1985. *Children of the City: At Work and at Play*. New York: Oxford. An everyday-life perspective on the lives of urban children at the turn of the last century.

WEIGERT, Andrew J. 1981. *Sociology of Everyday Life*. New York: Longman. An introductory sociology book written entirely from the EDL perspective.

CHAPTER 8

Deviance, Crime, and Social Control

OUTLINE

PROLOGUE

Have You Ever . . . seen the heavy smog in Los Angeles? Or thought about the fact that people and things in Los Angeles—and in the United States in general—travel mostly on highways designed for gas-powered vehicles, even though the technology for cheaper and environmentally cleaner forms of transportation is available?

You may have heard that Los Angeles residents simply choose to drive cars because of the freedom and mobility associated with car travel. But there's more to the story than that. Fifty years ago, 3,000 pollution-free electric trains transported 80 million people annually throughout the Los Angeles metropolis. Today, this railway system no longer exists. Beginning in 1940, a group of businesses led by General Motors and including the Greyhound Bus, Firestone Tire, and Mack Truck companies acquired and scrapped the city's rail lines with the aim of converting the electric system to one using GM motorbuses. In fact, by 1949, GM and its partners had destroyed more than a hundred electric systems in over 45 cities, including New York, Philadelphia, Baltimore, St. Louis, Oakland, Salt Lake City, Los Angeles, and San Francisco.

The collusion of these companies violated U.S. antitrust law, and they were convicted of criminally conspiring to replace electric transportation with gas-powered buses and to monopolize bus sales throughout the country. Each company was fined $5,000, and no one went to jail (Mokhiber 1982, 221–227).

If asked to name a crime, most of us might mention burglary, drug dealing, or murder—"crimes in the streets." But it's quite likely that "crimes in the suites," such as the GM conspiracy, have a greater impact on most of us than do street crimes. This chapter examines various aspects of crime, deviance, and social control.

CONFORMITY, NONCONFORMITY, AND DEVIANCE

In providing a blueprint for living, our culture, along with its various subcultures and even countercultures (Chapter 3), supplies sets of norms and values that structure our behavior. These norms and values tell us what we ought to believe in and what we ought to do. Because we are brought up to accept them, for the most part we do what we ought to do and think as we ought to think. Only for the most part, however, since none of us follows all the rules all the time.

Previous chapters concentrated on how norms and values structure our lives and how we learn them through socialization. This chapter considers some of the ways people break out of these patterns—from relatively unimportant eccentric behaviors to serious violations of others' rights.

SOCIAL CONTROL

An understanding of deviance and nonconformity requires that we first consider what brings about conformity. As discussed in Chapter 3, the forces and processes that encourage conformity are known as **social control.** Social control takes place at three levels:

Social control consists of the forces and processes that encourage conformity, including self-control, informal control, and formal control.

1. Through self-control, we police ourselves.
2. Through informal controls, our friends and intimates reward us with positive sanctions for conformity and punish us with negative sanctions for nonconformity.
3. Through formal controls, the state or other authorities discourage nonconformity.

Internalization occurs when individuals accept the norms and values of their group and make conformity to these norms part of their self-concept.

Informal social control is self-restraint exercised because of fear of what others will think.

Formal social controls are administrative sanctions such as fines, expulsion, and imprisonment.

Deviance refers to norm violations that exceed the tolerance level of the community and result in negative sanctions.

Self-control occurs when individuals **internalize** the norms and values of their group. They make conformity to these norms part of their self-concepts. Thus, the reason that most of us do not murder, rape, or rob is not simply that we are afraid the police would catch us but that it never occurs to us to do these things; they would violate our self-concepts. A powerful support to self-control is **informal social control,** self-restraint exercised because of fear of what others will think. Thus, even if your own values did not prevent you from cheating on a test, you might be deterred by the thought of how embarrassing it would be to get caught. Your friends might sneer at you or drop you altogether; your family would be disappointed in you; your professor might publicly embarrass you by denouncing you to the class. If none of these considerations is a deterrent, you might be scared into conformity by the thought of **formal social controls,** administrative sanctions such as fines, expulsion, or imprisonment. Cheaters, for example, face formal sanctions such as failing grades and dismissal from school.

Whether we are talking about cheating on examinations or murdering people, social control rests largely on self-control and informal social controls. Few formal agencies can force compliance to rules that are not supported by individual or group values (Scheff 1988). Sex is a good example. In some states, sex between unmarried persons is illegal, and you can be fined or imprisoned for it. Even if the police devoted a substantial part of their energies to stamping out illegal sex, however, they would probably not succeed. In contemporary America, a substantial proportion of unmarried people are not embarrassed about having sexual relations; they do not care if their friends know about it. In such conditions, formal sanctions cannot enforce conformity. Prostitution, marijuana use, seat-belt laws—all are examples of areas in which laws unsupported by public consensus have failed to produce conformity.

Getting a tattoo isn't against the law. Tattooing is an example of behavior that steps out of conventional rules without necessarily crossing over into deviance, depending on the subculture. It is an example of nonconformity, but it does not violate any major norms or arouse organized public disapproval.

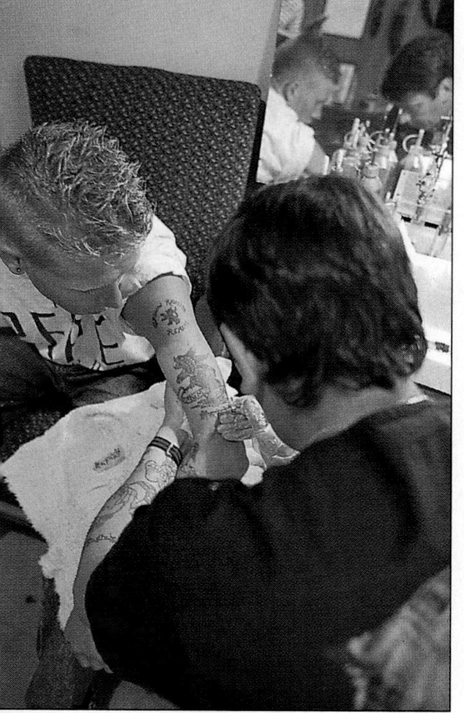

Deviance versus Nonconformity

People may break out of cultural patterns for a variety of reasons and in a variety of ways. Whether nonconformity is regarded as deviant or merely eccentric depends on the seriousness of the rule that is violated. A person who wears bib overalls to church or carries a potted palm everywhere is challenging the rules of conventional behavior. Probably nobody will care too much, however; these are minor kinds of nonconformity. **Deviance** exists when norm violations exceed the tolerance level of the community and result in negative sanctions. Deviance is behavior of which others disapprove to the extent that they believe something ought to be done about it (Archer 1985).

Defining deviance as behavior of which others disapprove has an interesting implication: It is not the act that is most important. Few acts are intrinsically deviant. Even taking another's life may be acceptable in war, police work, or self-defense. Whether an act is regarded as deviant may depend on the time, the place, the person performing the act and that person's status, and the audience. For this reason, sociologists stress that *deviance is relative*. Some examples: Alcohol use is deviant for adolescents but not for adults; having two wives is deviant in the United States but not in Nigeria; wearing a skirt is deviant for an American male but not for an American female (or a Scottish male). Sleeping on a park bench may be defined as deviant and illegal loitering when an apparently homeless person does it but as relaxing during the lunch hour when an apparently middle-class executive does it.

The sociology of deviance has two concerns: why people break the rules of their time and place and how the rules are established. In the following sections, we review several major sociological theories of deviance before looking at one form of deviance—crime—in the United States.

THEORIES ABOUT DEVIANCE

There are a dozen or more theories about deviant behavior. For the sake of order, we present the major ones used by sociologists today in three groups, according to our familiar theoretical framework: structural-functional theory, symbolic interaction theory, and conflict theory.

STRUCTURAL-FUNCTIONAL THEORY

In Chapter 1, we said that the basic premise of structural-functional theory is that the parts of society work together like the parts of an organism. From this point of view, deviance is alien to society, an indication that the parts are not working right.

This perspective was first applied to the explanation of deviance by Durkheim in his classic study of suicide ([1897]1951). Durkheim was trying to explain why people in industrialized societies are more likely to commit suicide than are people in other societies. He suggested that in traditional societies, the rules tend to be well known and widely supported. As a society grows larger, becomes more heterogeneous, and experiences rapid social change, the norms of society may be unclear or no longer applicable to current conditions. Durkheim called this situation **anomie;** he believed that it was a major cause of suicide in industrializing nations.

Anomie is a situation in which the norms of society are unclear or no longer applicable to current conditions.

The anomie idea was broadened to apply to all sorts of deviant behavior in Robert Merton's (1957) **strain theory.** Strain theory suggests that deviance results when culturally approved goals cannot be reached by culturally approved means. This is most likely in the case of our strong cultural emphasis on economic success and achievement. The goals of educational and economic achievement are widely shared. The means to live up to these goals, however, are not equally accessible. In particular, Merton argued, people from the lower social classes have less opportunity to become successful. They find that the norms about achievement are not applicable to their situation.

Strain theory suggests that deviance occurs when culturally approved goals cannot be reached by culturally approved means.

Of course, not all people who find society's norms inapplicable to their situation turn to a life of crime. Merton identified four ways in which people adapt to situations of anomie (see the Concept Summary): *innovation*, *ritualism*, *retreatism*, and *rebellion*. The mode of adaptation depends on whether an individual accepts or rejects society's cultural goals and does or does not have access to appropriate ways of achieving them.

People who accept both society's goals and society's norms about how to reach them are conformists. Most of us conform most of the time. When people cannot successfully reach society's goals using society's rules, however, deviance may result. One form deviance may take is innovation. *Innovators* accept society's goals but

CONCEPT SUMMARY TYPES OF STRAIN DEVIANCE

Merton's strain theory of deviance suggests that deviance results whenever there is a disparity between institutionalized goals and the means available to reach them. Individuals caught in this dilemma may reject the goals or the means or both. This theory defines deviance as a social problem rather than a personal trouble.

MODES OF ADAPTATION	CULTURAL GOALS	INSTITUTIONAL MEANS
CONFORMITY	Accepted	Accepted
DEVIANCE		
INNOVATION	Accepted	Rejected
RITUALISM	Rejected	Accepted
RETREATISM	Rejected	Rejected
REBELLION	Rejected/replaced	Rejected/replaced

SOURCE: Adapted from Merton 1957, 140.

develop alternative means of reaching them. For example, they may pursue academic achievement through cheating, athletic achievement through steroids, or economic success through prostitution or selling drugs. In these instances, deviance rests on using illegitimate means to accomplish socially desirable goals.

Other people who are blocked from achieving socially desired goals respond by rejecting the goals themselves. *Ritualists* slavishly go through the motions prescribed by society, but their goal is security, not success. Their major hope is that they will not be noticed. Thus, they do their work carefully, even compulsively. Although ritualists may appear to be over-conformers, Merton says they are deviant because they have rejected our society's values on achievement and upward mobility. They have turned their backs on normative goals but are clinging desperately to procedure. *Retreatists*, by contrast, adapt by rejecting both procedures and goals. They are society's dropouts: the vagabonds, drifters, and street people. The final mode of adaptation is rebellion. *Rebels* reject society's goals and means and adopt alternatives that challenge society's usual patterns. These are the people who start communes or revolutions to create an alternative society. Unlike retreatists, they are committed to working toward a different society.

The basic idea of Merton's theory is that, in complex and rapidly changing societies, there are structural contradictions, or inconsistencies, between ends and means that encourage individuals to commit acts that are defined as deviant (Douglas and Waksler 1982). This theory explicitly defines deviance as a social problem rather than a personal trouble; it is a property of the social structure, not of the individual. As a consequence, the solution to deviance lies not in reforming the individual deviant but in reducing the mismatch between structured goals and structured means.

SYMBOLIC INTERACTION THEORIES

Symbolic interaction theories of deviance suggest that deviance is learned through interaction with others and involves the development of a deviant self-concept. Deviance is believed to be a direct product not of the social structure but of specific face-to-face interactions. There are three forms of this argument: differential association theory, deterrence theories, and labeling theory.

Differential Association Theory. In the late 1940s, Edwin Sutherland developed a theory to explain the common observation that kids who grow up in neighborhoods where there are many delinquents are more likely to be delinquent themselves. **Differential association theory** argues that people learn to be deviant when more of their associates favor deviance than favor conformity.

Differential association theory argues that people learn to be deviant when more of their associates favor deviance over conformity.

How does differential association encourage deviance? There are three primary mechanisms. First, if we interact mostly with deviants, we may develop a biased image of the generalized other. We may learn that, of course, everybody pays bribes or steals or, of course, being able to beat other people up is the most important criterion for judging a person. The norms that we internalize may be very different from those of conventional society. Second, in master-apprentice type relationships, individuals learn the skills necessary for the particular form of deviance in which they become involved. In the 1970s, for example, executives at Ford Motor Company taught other employees how to avoid complying with the 1970 Clean Air Act by keeping two separate computer files, one for federal inspection and the other for only company use (Mokhiber 1988, 210). The third mechanism has to do with reinforcements. Even if we learn conventional norms, a deviant subculture will not reward us for following them. In fact, a deviant subculture may reward us for violating the norms. Through these three mechanisms, then, we can learn that deviance is acceptable and rewarded.

> **THINKING CRITICALLY**
>
> Can differential association theory explain why some boys/girls who grow up in bad neighborhoods do not become delinquents? Can you?

Differential association theory stems largely from the structural school of symbolic interaction. People develop a deviant identity because they belong to a deviant subculture. The situation determines the identity.

Deterrence Theories. Many contemporary scholars use some form of deterrence theory to explain deviance. **Deterrence theories** suggest that deviance results when social sanctions, formal and informal, provide insufficient rewards for conformity. Deterrence theories combine elements of structural-functional and symbolic interaction theories. Although they place the primary blame for deviance on an inadequate (dysfunctional) sanctioning system, they also assign the individual an active role in choosing whether to deviate or conform. These theories assume that the actor assesses the relative balance of positive and negative sanctions and makes a cost/benefit decision about whether to conform or be deviant (Pilavin et al. 1986; Paternoster 1989). When social structures do not provide adequate rewards for conformity, a larger portion of the population will choose deviance.

Deterrence theories suggest that deviance results when social sanctions, formal and informal, provide insufficient rewards for conformity.

Empirical studies show that three kinds of rewards are especially important in deterring deviance: instrumental rewards, family ties, and self-esteem.

INSTRUMENTAL REWARDS. Unemployment and low wages are among the very best predictors of crime rates at any age (Devine, Shaley, and Smith 1988; Crutchfield 1989). People with no jobs or with dead-end jobs have little to lose and perhaps much to gain from deviance. People who have or can look forward to good jobs, on the other hand, are likely to conclude that they have too much to lose by being deviant.

FAMILY TIES. Consistent evidence shows that young people with strong bonds to their parents are more likely to conform (Hirschi 1969; Messner and Krohn 1990).

Posters such as this one were widely distributed in the 1930s in the successful attempt to criminalize marijuana use. Who sponsored this campaign? The answer is on the bottom line of the poster: The Consolidated Brewers Association of America. It doesn't take a financial genius to figure out why the breweries opposed marijuana use. This is an obvious example of the extent to which what is legal and what is illegal depends on politics and economics rather than on unambiguous moral codes.

Labeling theory is concerned with the processes by which labels such as *deviant* come to be attached to specific people and specific behaviors.

Parents are in a very strong position to exert informal sanctions that encourage conformity, and young people who are close to their parents are vulnerable to these informal sanctions. Because divorce frequently results in reduced ties to noncustodial parents, this theory helps explain why youths from broken homes are more likely to be delinquent (Matsueda and Heimer 1987; Sampson and Groves 1989).

SELF-ESTEEM. On a more symbolic level, deterrence theory suggests that people chose deviance or conformity depending on which will do the most to enhance their self-esteem (Kaplan, Martin, and Johnson 1986). For most of us, self-esteem is enhanced by conformity; we are rewarded for following the rules. People whose efforts are not rewarded, however, may find deviance an attractive alternative in their search for positive feedback. Especially among lower-class boys, delinquency has been found to be a means of improving self-esteem (Rosenberg, Schooler, and Schoenbach 1989).

According to deterrence theorists, positive sanctions give individuals a "stake in conformity"—something to lose, whether it's a job, parental approval, or self-esteem. When social structures fail to reward conformity, individuals have less to lose by choosing deviance.

Labeling Theory. A third theory of deviance, which combines symbolic interaction and conflict theories, is labeling theory. **Labeling theory** is concerned with the processes by which the label *deviant* comes to be attached to specific people and specific behaviors. This theory takes to heart the maxim that deviance is relative. As the chief proponent of labeling theory puts it, "Deviant behavior is behavior that people so label" (Becker 1963, 90).

The process through which a person becomes labeled as deviant depends on the reactions of others toward the nonconforming behavior. The first time a child acts up in class, it may be owing to high spirits or a bad mood. This impulsive act is *primary deviance*. What happens in the future depends on how others interpret the act. If teachers, counselors, and other children label the child a troublemaker *and* if she accepts this definition as part of her self-concept, then she may take on the role of troublemaker. Continued rule violation stemming from a deviant self-concept is called *secondary deviance*.

This explanation of deviance fits in neatly with the structural school of symbolic interactionism. Deviance becomes yet another role identity that is integrated into the self-concept.

POWER AND LABELING. A crucial question for labeling theorists is the process by which an individual comes to be labeled deviant. Many labeling theorists take a conflict perspective when answering this question. They assume that one of the strategies groups use in competing with one another is to get the other group's behavior labeled as deviant while protecting its own behavior. Naturally, the more power a group has, the more likely it is to be able to brand its competitors deviant. This, labeling theorists allege, explains why lower-class deviance is more likely to be subject to criminal sanctions than is upper-class deviance.

In a classic study, Becker (1963) describes how this competition between interest groups caused marijuana users in the United States to be labeled deviant. Before 1937, marijuana use was not illegal in the United States. In 1937, however, a powerful vested-interest group, the Federal Bureau of Narcotics, campaigned to have it declared illegal. (Since Prohibition had ended, the bureau either had to find a new enemy or go out of business.) In conjunction with another vested-interest group, the Consolidated Brewers, the FBN launched a major media campaign to stigmatize marijuana use by associating marijuana with violence and other criminal behaviors. As a result of its successful campaign, it created a new group of deviants. Becker refers to those who are in a position to create and enforce new definitions of morality as **moral entrepreneurs.**

Moral entrepreneurs are people who are in a position to create and enforce new definitions of morality.

FROM SIN TO SICKNESS. Labeling theory's emphasis on subjective meanings gives us a framework for understanding the changing definitions of deviance. In recent years, there has been an increasing tendency for behaviors that used to be labeled deviant to be labeled illnesses instead. For example, many now consider alcoholism to be a disease. When a form of deviance comes to be viewed as illness, social reaction changes. It is no longer appropriate to put people in jail for being public drunks; instead they are put in hospitals. Physicians and counselors, rather than judges and sheriffs, treat them. Other forms of deviance, such as child abuse, gambling, murder, and rape, also may be regarded as forms of mental illness that are better treated by physicians than sheriffs (Link 1987; Rosecrance 1985). At present, we have reached few firm decisions on these issues. The public seems to believe that although some murderers, rapists, and so on are mentally ill and should be treated by physicians, others are just bad and should be put in jail.

Individuals who acquire *sick* rather than *bad* labels are entitled to treatment rather than punishment and are allowed to absolve themselves from blame for their behavior (Conrad and Schneider 1980). As you might expect, people in positions of power are more apt to be successful in claiming the *sick* label. For example, the upper-class woman who shoplifts is likely to be labeled neurotic, whereas the lower-class woman who steals the same items is likely to be labeled a shoplifter. The middle-class boy who acts up in school may be defined as hyperactive, the lower-class boy as a troublemaker.

Labeling theory, as mentioned, combines elements of symbolic interaction and conflict theory. The deviant label becomes part of the self-concept, affecting further interaction. But this deviant label is imposed by powerful others rather than being self-selected.

CONFLICT THEORY

Conflict theory proposes that competition and class conflict within society create deviance. Class conflict affects deviance in two ways (Archer 1985): (1) Class interests determine which acts are criminalized and how heavily they are punished. (2) Economic pressures lead to offenses, particularly property offenses, among the poor.

Defining Crime. The conflict perspective on defining crime has already been described in the section on labeling theory. Marxists argue that often the law and police are weapons used by the ruling class to maintain the status quo (Liska, Chamlin, and Reed 1985). This interpretation fits with the Marxist principle that social institutions, including law, rationalize and support the current distribution of economic resources.

Supporters of this position note that we spend more money deterring muggers than embezzlers. We give more severe sentences for street crimes than corporate crimes. We are more likely to arrest those who assault members of the ruling class (well-off white males) than we are to arrest those who assault the powerless (non-whites, women, and the poor) (Smith 1987). Finally, even when people from the upper and lower classes commit similar crimes, those from the lower class are more likely to be arrested, prosecuted, and sentenced (Williams and Drake 1980). The system clearly seems to benefit the upper classes.

Conflict theorists point to documented statistics showing that corporate and other upper-class crime costs American more money and lives than does lower-class crime (Messner and Rosenfeld 1994, 31–33). For instance, the annual cost to taxpayers and consumers of crime by corporate executives is about $200 billion a year—20 times the yearly loss due to street crime (Coleman 1989; Kappeler et al. 1993). Moreover, each year in the United States, deaths and injuries due to upper-class criminal behavior (for example, disregarding antipollution laws, failing to provide safe workplaces, and selling unsafe or defective merchandise) outnumber deaths and injuries from homicides and assaults (Kappeler et al. 1993, 104). Because of their control of the labeling apparatus—the state, the schools, the courts, the media—the upper class has been able to avoid deviant labels, to focus our attention on "crime in the streets" and hence divert our attention from "crime in the suites."

Concept Summary **Theories of Deviance**

	Major Question	Major Assumption	Cause of Deviance	Most Useful For Explaining Deviance Of
STRUCTURAL FUNCTIONAL THEORY				
Strain theory	Why do people break rules?	Deviance is a structurally induced characteristic of society.	A disparity exists between the goals of society and the means to achieve them.	The working and lower classes who cannot achieve desired goals by prescribed means
SYMBOLIC INTERACTION THEORIES				
Differential association theory	Why is deviance more characteristic of some groups than others?	Deviance is learned like other social behavior.	Subcultural values differ in complex societies; some subcultures hold values that favor deviance. These are learned through socialization.	Delinquent gangs and those integrated into deviant subcultures and neighborhoods
Deterrence theories	When is conformity not the best choice?	Deviance is a choice based on cost/benefit assessments.	Due to a failure of the sanctioning system, the benefits of deviance exceed the costs.	All groups, but especially those lacking a "stake in conformity"
Labeling theory	How do acts and people become labeled *deviant?*	Deviance is relative and depends on how others label acts and actors.	People whose acts are labeled deviant and who accept that label become career deviants.	The powerless, who are labeled deviant by powerful individuals; the label becomes part of the self-concept
CONFLICT THEORY	How does unequal access to scarce resoures lead to deviance?	Deviance is a normal response to competition and conflict over scarce resources.	Class conflict and economic competition lead to deviance.	All classes: Lower class is driven to deviance to meet basic needs

Lower-Class Crime. Although the preceding view of the way crime is defined would be accepted by all Marxists, some believe that the lower class really is more likely to commit criminal acts. One Marxist criminologist has declared that crime is a rational response for the lower class (Quinney 1980). These criminologists generally seem to agree with Merton's strain theory, which holds that a means-versus-ends discrepancy is particularly acute among the poor and that it may lead to crime (Greenberg 1985). They believe, however, that this is a natural condition of an unequal society rather than an unnatural condition.

SUMMARY OF DEVIANCE THEORIES

There are many theories of deviance in the field of sociology. These theories reflect differences in basic theoretical assumptions as well as differences in the kinds of deviance they try to explain (see the Concept Summary). All, however, are sociological, not psychological or biological, theories: They place the reasons for deviance within the social structure rather than within the individual. In the following sections, we apply these theories as we review major differentials in U.S. crime rates.

CRIME

Most of the behavior that is regarded as deviant or nonconforming is subject only to informal social controls. **Crimes** are acts that are subject to legal penalties. Most, though not all, crimes violate social norms and are subject to informal as well as legal sanctions. In this section, we briefly define the different types of crimes, look at rates for some types of crimes in the United States, and examine the findings about who is most likely to commit these crimes.

Crimes are acts that are subject to legal penalties.

INDEX CRIMES: MAJOR "STREET" CRIMES INVOLVING VIOLENCE OR PROPERTY

Each year, the federal government publishes the *Uniform Crime Report* (UCR), which summarizes crimes known to the police for eight major index crimes "in the streets" (U.S. Department of Justice 1993a):

- *Murder and nonnegligent manslaughter.* Overall, murder is a rare crime, yet some segments of society are touched by it much more than others (MacKellar and Yanagishita 1995); more than 50 percent of all murder victims in 1993 were African American and 77 percent were male (U.S. Bureau of the Census 1995, Table 313).
- *Rape*. Rape accounts for about 6 percent of all violent crimes, and reported rapes have more than doubled in the last two decades. About 105,000 women were raped in 1993 (U.S. Bureau of the Census, 1995, Table 308).
- *Robbery*. Robbery is defined as taking or attempting to take anything of value from another person by force, threat of force, or violence, or by putting the victim in fear. Unlike simple theft, or larceny, robbery involves a personal confrontation between the victim and the robber and is thus a crime of violence.
- *Assault*. Aggravated assault is an unlawful attack for the purpose of inflicting severe bodily injury. Kicking and hitting are included in assault; but increasingly,

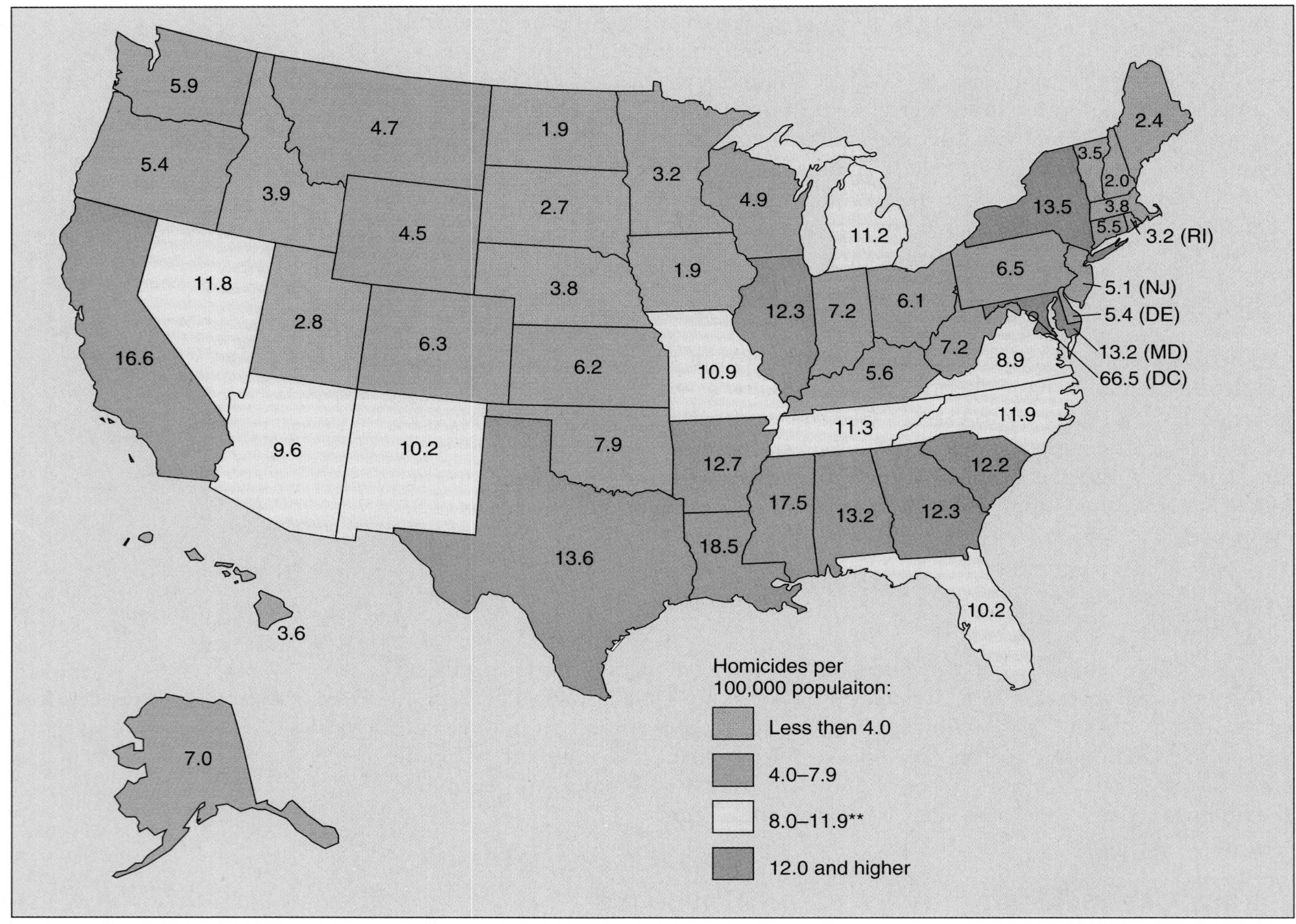

MAP 8.1
HOMICIDE RATES BY STATE, 1994

SOURCE: MacKellar and Yanagishita 1995, p. 20.

assault involves a weapon. Aggravated assault is currently the fastest-growing category of crime included in the UCR.

- *Burglary, larceny-theft, motor-vehicle theft,* and *arson* are the four property crimes included in the UCR. (Arson has only been added recently and is not covered in the trend data in Figure 8.1.) Property crimes are much more common than crimes of violence and account for 86 percent of the crimes covered in the UCR.

It is a common public perception that crime rates are much higher than they used to be. The accuracy of this perception depends on the time frame one uses and the specific crime. Figures 8.1 and 8.2 depict trends in seven index crimes over the last 20 years. They show that crime rates are indeed higher than they were in 1973—in the case of rape and assault, twice as high. After a general slump in crime rates during the first years of the 1980s, all the UCR index crimes except burglary began to rise. Then, for the first time since 1984, the overall UCR crime index declined in 1992 and again in 1993. All crimes were down, except rape and assault (U.S. Bureau of the Census 1995, Table 308).

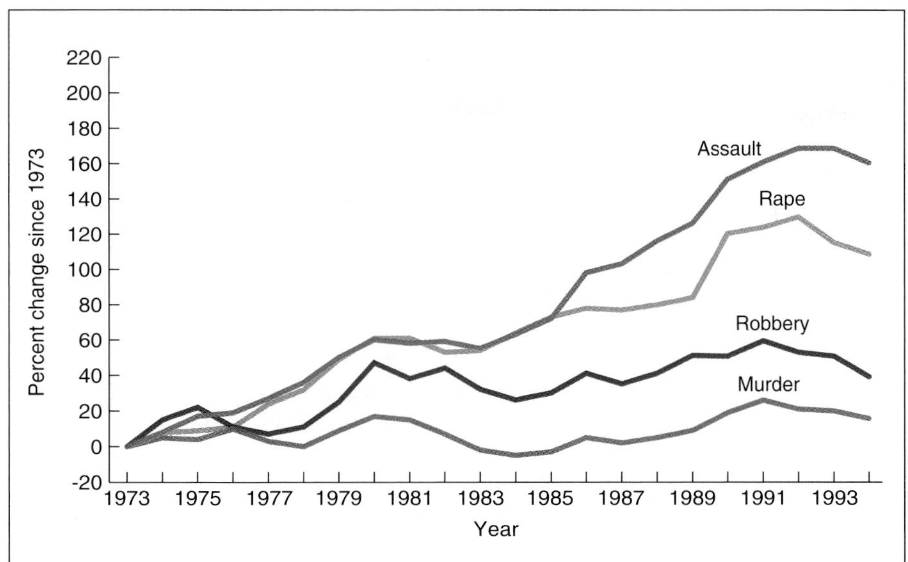

FIGURE 8.1
CHANGES IN VIOLENT CRIME RATES, 1973–1994

Violent crime rose during the 1970s. After a dramatic slump in the early 1980s, violent crime rates are again on the upswing. Assault and rape rates are at their highest recorded levels.

SOURCE: U.S. Department of Justice 1995a.

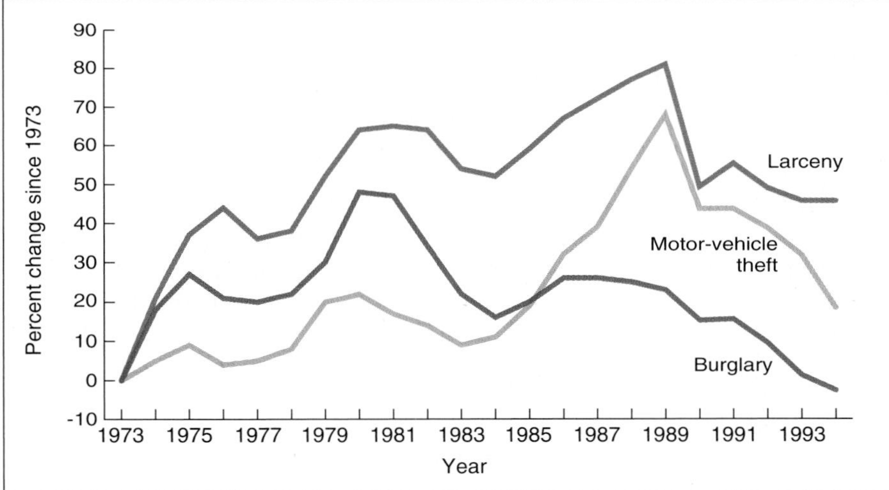

FIGURE 8.2
CHANGES IN PROPERTY CRIMES, 1973–1994

Property crime increased throughout the 1970s. Although all property crime rates dropped in the early 1980s, larceny-theft and motor-vehicle theft rates have returned to or exceeded their previous high levels. Burglary rates remain substantially lower than they were 10 years ago.

SOURCE: U.S. Department of Justice 1995a.

THINKING CRITICALLY

Why do you think most Americans view street crime as more serious than corporate crime? What would a conflict theorist say? A structural functionalist?

VICTIMLESS CRIMES

The so-called **victimless crimes**—such as drug use, prostitution, gambling, and pornography—are voluntary exchanges between persons who desire goods or services from one another (Schur 1979). They are called victimless crimes because participants in the exchanges typically do not see themselves as being victimized or as suffering from the transaction: There are no complaining victims.

Victimless crimes such as drug use, prostitution, gambling, and pornography are voluntary exchanges between persons who desire goods or services from each other.

There is substantial debate about whether these crimes are truly victimless. Many argue that prostitutes, drug abusers, and pornography models *are* victims: Even though there is an element of choice in the decision to engage in these behaviors, individuals are usually forced or manipulated into such decisions by their disadvantaged class position. Others believe that such activities are legitimate areas of free enterprise and free choice and that the only reason these acts are considered illegal is because of some self-righteous busybodies (Jenness 1990).

Because there are no complaining victims, these crimes are difficult to control. The drug user is generally not going to complain about the drug pusher, and the illegal gambler is unlikely to bring charges against a bookie. In the absence of a complaining victim, the police must find not only the criminal but also the crime. Efforts to do so are costly and divert attention from other criminal acts. As a result, laws involving victimless crimes are irregularly and inconsistently enforced, most often in the form of periodic crackdowns and routine harassment.

Hate Crimes

Hate crimes are motivated by bigotry based on race, religion, national origin, or sexual orientation.

Hate crimes are crimes motivated by bigotry based on race, religion, national origin, or sexual orientation. Typically, hate crimes involve vandalism, arson, brutal beatings, and murder. Some activists are seeking to have rape reclassified as a hate crime based on gender (Leo 1993).

Hate-motivated atrocities have a long history throughout the world and in the United States. Since Europeans entered the Americas, Native Americans have suffered countless brutalities at the hands of whites. Between 1889 and 1919, when many whites resented the end of slavery, 3,200 African Americans were killed by lynchings, burnings, beatings, and other means. Throughout the second half of the 19th century, Chinese, Irish, Jewish, Mormon, and Italian Americans were criminally harassed, stoned, beaten, lynched, and otherwise murdered (Browning and Gerassi 1980, 263–275). During World War II, many Japanese Americans suffered similar fates.

Hate crimes have persisted to the present. In 1956, an African American Chicago teenager named Emmet Till was accused of whistling at a white woman while visiting his uncle in Mississippi. Whites took him from his uncle's house, beat him brutally, shot him in the head, then threw him into the Tallahatchie River with a cotton gin motor tied around his neck (Dyson 1993, 194–198). During the U.S. war with Iraq in 1991, Arab Americans were the targets of various hate crimes ("The War at Home," 1991). The Skinheads, a white supremacist gang with about 3,500 U.S. members, are blamed for many grisly murders, such as the 1993 stomping death of a Vietnamese immigrant in Houston (Van Biema and Jackson 1993). Recently, someone who hated the Amish set Amish people's barns on fire near Williamsport, Pennsylvania ("Man Gets 10 Years" 1994).

The 1988 Hate Crimes Statistics Act requires the U.S. Justice Department to collect and publish data on the incidence of hate crimes. With 4,558 hate crimes reported to the FBI in 1992 and more than 7,000 in 1993, current data indicate that hate crimes have increased over the past several years (Filipowski 1992; "U.S. Had More" 1994). According to the Department of Justice, the most frequent victims today are African Americans, Latinos, Southeast Asians, Jews, and lesbians and gay men. Homosexuals are probably the most frequent victims (Singer and Deschamps 1994; Jenness 1995). About 50 percent of hate crimes are committed by youths under age 21 (Comstock 1991; Jacobs 1993).

In response to this apparent increase, at least 25 states have enacted stricter sentencing penalties for hate crimes. Unanimously upheld by the U.S. Supreme Court, the stricter sentencing laws remain controversial. Opponents argue that imposing stiffer sentences, based on establishing hateful intent, violates the First Amendment guarantee of free speech: "A free society cannot afford to police its members' thoughts" (Dority 1994; Hentoff 1993). Proponents argue that the sentences punish conduct, not speech (Strossen 1993).

WHITE-COLLAR CRIMES

Crime committed by respectable people of high social status in the course of their occupation is called **white-collar crime** (Sutherland 1961, 1983). White-collar crime occurs at several levels. It is committed, for example, by employees against companies, by companies against employees, by companies against customers, and by companies against the public (for example, by dumping toxic wastes into the air, land, or water). Sometimes, corporate crime more closely parallels racketeering and organized crime than anything else. In the wake of a bailout that will cost taxpayers hundreds of billions of dollars, investigators now believe that many failed savings and loan institutions were created for the sole purpose of generating personal profit from illegal activity. The only thing distinguishing this type of corporate crime from organized crime is that the savings-and-loan embezzlers wore Brooks Brothers suits and white collars while "racketeers," at least in popular mythology, often wear black shirts and white ties (Calavita and Pontell 1993).

White-collar crime is committed by respectable people of high status in the course of their occupations.

Because most white-collar crime goes unreported, its total economic cost is difficult to assess. However, as we have seen, many scholars and law enforcement officials believe that the dollar loss from corporate crime dwarfs that from street crime. And in addition to the economic cost, there are social costs. Exposure to repeated tales of corruption tends to breed distrust and cynicism and, ultimately, to undermine the integration of social institutions. If you think that all members of Congress are crooks, then you may quit voting. If you think that every police officer can be bought, then you may cease to respect the law. Thus, the costs of such crime go beyond the actual dollars involved in the crime itself.

> **THINKING CRITICALLY**
> Devise a strategy for deterring white collar or corporate crime.

The reasons for white-collar crime tend to be about the same as those for street crimes: People want more than they can legitimately get, and the benefits of crime outweigh its potential costs (Coleman 1988). Differential association also plays a role. In some corporations, organizational culture winks at or actively encourages illegal behavior. Speaking of the insider trading scandals that rocked Wall Street a few years ago, one observer notes:

> You gotta do it. . . . Everybody else is. [It] is part of the business. . . . You work at a deli, you take home pastrami every night for free. It's the same thing as information on Wall Street. . . . I know you want to help your mother and provide for your family. This is the way to do it. Don't be a schmuck. Nobody gets hurt. (Cited in Reichman 1989)

The magnitude of white-collar crime in our society makes a mockery of the idea that crime is predominantly a lower-class phenomenon. The Focus section addresses the impact of corporate crime on the environment. Instead, it appears that people of different statuses simply have different opportunities to commit crime. Those in lower statuses are in a position to engage only in high-risk, low-yield crimes such as robbery and larceny. In contrast, higher-status individuals are in a position to engage in such activities as price fixing, stock manipulation, and tax evasion: low-risk, high-yield crimes (Schur 1979).

Because of the complexity of the transactions involved, white-collar crime is difficult to detect. Even if detected, white-collar offenders usually receive more lenient treatment than street criminals. For example, a recent study found that health care professionals guilty of Medicaid fraud were much less likely to be incarcerated than

FOCUS ON THE ENVIRONMENT

When Accidents Are Criminal: Oil Companies and Oil Spills

"ANOTHER CATEGORY IN WHICH GREAT DAMAGE IS DONE IS ENVIRONNMENTAL CRIME."

As we said earlier, many people think of street crime when crime is mentioned. We have already seen that white-collar crime, though often overlooked in crime statistics, takes an enormous toll on society. Another category in which great damage is done is environmental crime. Here, we look at some examples of the extent of this damage.

The Exxon Corporation caused the nation's most disastrous oil spill in March 1989, when its tanker the Exxon *Valdez* went off course and struck a reef in Prince William Sound, off the coast of Alaska in one of the world's richest wildlife areas. More than 11 million gallons of crude oil spilled over a 1,600-square-mile area, contaminating more than 800 miles of shoreline (Clinard 1990, 44–53). Two rich fisheries—pink salmon and herring—were devastated. Half a million birds in 90 species died, including more than 150 bald eagles. About 4,500 sea otters, up to 30 percent of the local population, died. So did at least 300 harbor seals. Marine bird and mammal populations are far from recovery; the thick crude oil that sank through the sand and gravel still oozes to the surface (Kay 1994).

Exxon had been criminally negligent in shipping the oil. The Exxon employee who captained the tanker had a known history of alcoholism that included several arrests for drunken driving. Nine hours following the incident, testing revealed an unacceptable level of alcohol in his blood. In difficult waters, he had turned the ship over to an uncertified third mate. Moreover, the tanker was not properly equipped with the double bottom required by law, which would have made it safer.

In a 1991 settlement, Exxon agreed to pay $900 million, the largest payment ever to settle an environmental damage case. The money is to purchase new wildlife habitats and to restore fisheries, seabird colonies, and marine mammal populations (Kay 1994). In 1994, a federal jury in Anchorage awarded another $286.8 million to commercial fishers in compensation for damage the spill caused to fishing ("Awarded" 1994, 45).

Critical observers, however, have questioned the extent to which Exxon executives were truly punished for their crime. For instance, although offending corporations are required by law to clean up oil spills, Exxon received (or was allowed to take back) $40 million of the $900 million settlement in payment for its cleanup efforts. And Exxon received this money even before the bulk of restoration projects was underway or paid for (Kay 1994).

Furthermore, although it is the world's largest company, Exxon responded late and ineffectively to this very serious incident. Even with huge profits accruing from Alaskan oil, Exxon had prepared no real contingency plan to deal with potentially large spills that might devastate Alaskan waters, and the Coast Guard termed the plans that Exxon did make on government orders after the accident "very thin" (Clinard 1990, 46).

The Exxon *Valdez* oil spill is not an isolated case. The oil industry's cleanups have improved with the tightening of federal pollution laws, but still their compliance record has not been good (Clinard 1990, 47). Oil spills are just one instance of *environmental crime*—crimes that damage the environment. Other examples include illegally cutting forests and dumping toxic wastes, along with disobeying clean-air laws.

persons charged with grand theft, despite the fact that the dollar losses from the Medicaid crimes, on the average, were much greater (Tillman and Pontell 1992).

Critics argue that the absence of white-collar crime statistics from the UCR and the relative absence of white-collar criminals from our prisons reflect the fundamental class bias in our criminal justice system (Braithwaite 1985). Since the UCR indexes only "street crimes," we tend to think of crime only in these terms and to label only those who commit these particular crimes as "real" criminals.

Correlates of Crime: Age, Sex, Race, and Class

Only 21 percent of the crimes reported in the UCR are cleared by an arrest. This means that the people arrested for criminal acts represent only a sample of those who commit reported crimes; they are undoubtedly not a random sample. The low levels of arrests coupled with the low levels of crime reporting warn us to be cautious in applying generalizations about arrestees to the larger population of criminals. With this caution in mind, we note that the persons arrested for criminal acts are disproportionately male, young, and from minority groups. Figure 8.3 shows the pattern of arrest rates in 1992 by sex and age. As you can see, crime rates, especially for men, peak sharply during ages 15–24; during these peak crime years, young men are about four times more likely to be arrested than women of the same age. Minority data are not available by age and sex, but the overall rates show that African Americans and Hispanics are more than three times more likely than whites to be arrested (U.S. Bureau of the Census 1995, Table 322).

It is important to point out that these differentials apply to crimes indexed in the Uniform Crime Report (that is, street crimes) and not to white-collar crimes, which are primarily committed by whites. Moreover, in the vast majority of street crimes, the victim is of the same race or ethnicity as the offender. Bearing all this in mind, what accounts for the differentials in arrests? Can the theories reviewed earlier help explain these patterns?

Age Differences. The age differences in arrest rates noted in Figure 8.3 are characteristic of nearly every nation in the world that gathers crime statistics (Hirschi and Gottfredson 1983). A great deal of controversy exists over the reasons for the very high arrest rates of young adults, but deterrence theories have the most promise for explaining this age pattern.

In many ways, adolescents and young adults have less to lose than older people. They don't have a "stake in conformity"—a career, a mortgage, a credit rating (Steffensmeier et al. 1989). When young people do have jobs, and especially when they have good jobs, their chances of getting into trouble are much smaller (Allan and Steffensmeier 1989).

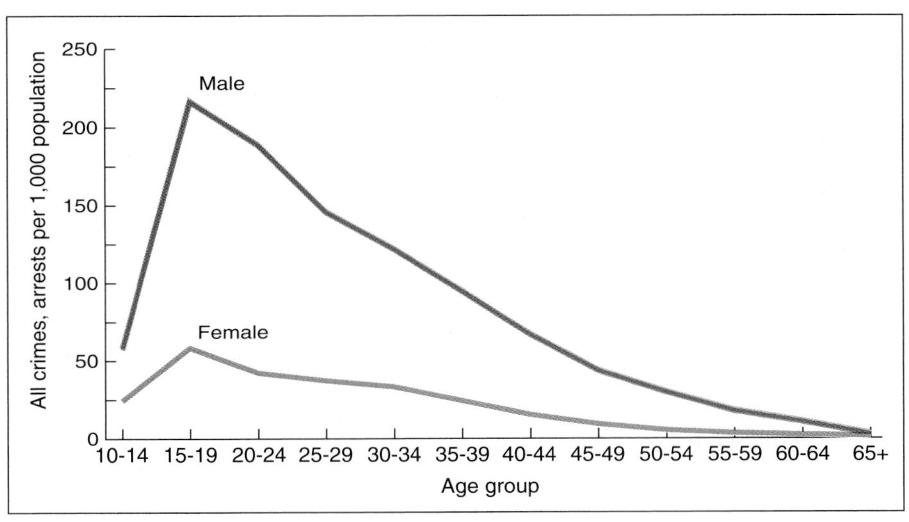

Figure 8.3
Arrest Rates by Age and Sex, 1994

Arrest rates in the United States and most other nations show strong and consistent age and sex patterns. Arrest rates peak sharply for young people aged 15–24; at all ages, men are about four times more likely than women to be arrested.

Source: Arrest rate data are from Uniform Crime Reports, Ts 40–41; population base data come from U.S. Statistical Abstract 1995, T. 21.

Delinquency is basically a leisure-time activity. It is strongly associated with spending large blocks of unsupervised time with peers (Agnew and Petersen 1989; Osgood and Wilson 1989). When there is "nothing better to do," a substantial portion will get in trouble. Conversely, deviance is deterred by spending a lot of time with one's parents or with conforming peers (Gardner and Shoemaker 1989).

Sex Differences. The sex differential in arrest rates has both social and biological roots. Women's smaller size and lesser strength make them less likely to use violence or personal confrontation; they have learned that, for them, these are ineffective strategies. Evidence linking male hormones to aggressiveness indicates that biology also may be a factor in women's lower inclination to engage in violent behavior.

Among social theories of deviance, deterrence theory seems to be the most effective in explaining sex differences. Generally, girls are supervised more closely than boys, and they are subject to more social control; this is especially true in the lower class (Hagan, Gillis, and Simpson 1985; Heidensohn 1985; Thompson 1989). Whereas parents may let their boys wander about at night unsupervised, they are much more likely to insist on knowing where their daughters will be and with whom they will be associating. The greater supervision that girls receive increases their bonds to parents and other conventional institutions; it also reduces their opportunity to join gangs or other deviant groups.

These explanations raise questions about whether changing roles for women will affect women's participation in crime. Will increased equality in education, labor-force participation, smoking, and drinking also show up in greater equality of criminal behavior? The evidence shows little tendency for this to happen. It is true that the crime rate for women has increased faster than the crime rate for men in a few areas (vagrancy, disorderly conduct, property crimes), but there has been no increase in women's participation in violent crime. Furthermore, female arrest rates may actually be lower now than they were in the mid-1800s (Boritch and Hagan 1990).

Differences by Social Class. The effect of social class on crime rates is complex. Although sociologists have historically held that social class is an important correlate of criminality (Braithwaite 1981; Elliott and Ageton 1980; Thornberry and Farnworth 1982), some studies have found that the relationship is not very strong and in some cases is nonexistent (Hirschi 1969; Johnson 1980; Krohn et al. 1980; Tittle, Villemez, and Smith 1978). Much of the inconsistency appears to center on difficulties in measuring both social class and crime.

Braithwaite's (1981) review of more than a hundred studies leads to the conclusion that lower-class people commit more of the direct interpersonal types of crime normally handled by the police than do people from the middle class. These are the types of crime reported in the UCR. Middle-class people commit more of the crimes that involve the use of power, particularly in the context of their occupational roles: fraud, embezzlement, price fixing, and other forms of white-collar crime. There is also evidence that the social class differential may be greater for adult crime than for juvenile delinquency (Thornberry and Farnworth 1982).

Nearly all the deviance theories we reviewed offer some explanation of the social class differential. Strain theorists and some Marxists suggest that the lower class is more likely to engage in crime because of blocked avenues to achievement. Deterrence theorists attribute greater crime among the lower class to the fact that these people may be receiving fewer rewards from conventional institutions such as school and the labor market.

All of these theories accept and seek to explain the social class pattern found in the UCR—where, indeed, the lower class is overrepresented. Labeling and Marxist theories, on the other hand, argue that this overrepresentation is not a reflection of underlying social class patterns of deviance but of bias in the law and within social control agencies (Williams and Drake 1980). It also reflects the particular mix of crimes included in the UCR; if embezzlement, price fixing, and stock manipulations were included in the UCR, we would see a very different social class distribution of criminals.

Differences by Race. Although African Americans comprise only 12.6 percent of the population, they comprise 58 percent of those arrested for murder, 41 percent of those arrested for rape, and 40 percent of those arrested for assault. Hispanics make up about 10 percent of the total population but about 15 percent of those arrested for violent crimes (U.S. Bureau of the Census 1995, Tables 13 and 322). These strong differences in arrest rates are explained in part by social class differences between minority and white populations. Even after this effect is taken into account, however, African Americans and Hispanic Americans are still much more likely to be arrested for committing crimes.

The explanation for this is complex. As we will document in Chapter 11, race continues to represent a fundamental cleavage in American society. The continued and even growing correlation of race with unemployment, inner-city residence, and female-headed households reinforces the barriers between African Americans and whites in American society. An international study confirms that the larger the number of overlapping dimensions of inequality, the higher the "pent-up aggression which manifests itself in diffuse hostility and violence" (Messner 1989). The root cause of higher minority crime rates, from this perspective, is the low quality of minority employment—a factor that leads directly to unstable families and neighborhoods (Sampson 1987; Sampson and Groves 1989).

Poverty and segregation combine to put a disproportionate number of African American children in the worst neighborhoods in the country, neighborhoods where getting into trouble is a way of life and where conventional achievement is remote (Matsueda and Heimer 1987). Differential association theory thus explains a great deal of the racial difference in arrest rates. Deterrence theory is also important. African American children are much more likely to live in fatherless homes and thus lack an important social bond that might deter deviant behavior. In addition to these factors that may increase the propensity to deviance among minorities, there is also evidence that whether we are talking about troublemaking in school, stealing cars, or petty theft, minority-group members are more likely than others to be labeled deviant and, if apprehended by the police, more apt to be cited, prosecuted, and convicted (Peterson 1988; Unnever, Frazier, and Henretta 1980).

THE SOCIOLOGY OF LAW

We have reviewed theories about deviance and examined current findings about crime and criminals. In the last sections of this chapter, we look at the formal mechanisms of social control. Among the questions of interest are these: Why punish? What is a just punishment? How does the criminal justice system work? Can we reduce crime? We begin by taking a broad theoretical overview of the sociology of law.

THEORIES OF LAW

The cornerstone of the formal control system is the law. Generally, law is seen as serving three major functions: It provides formal sanctions to encourage conformity and discourage deviance, it helps settle disputes, and it can be an instrument for social change (Vago 1989). Beyond this simple summary, there is substantial discussion among scholars about how the law operates.

Most citizens, and probably even most sociologists, take a general structural-functional approach to law (Rich 1977). By clearly spelling out expected behaviors and punishing violators, the law helps maintain society. Although some may benefit more than others from particular laws and laws may be unequally enforced, law itself is a good thing, often a reflection of shared-cultural values, a benefit to society.

Conflict theorists take a different position: They argue that the legal apparatus was designed to maintain and reproduce a system of inequality. Law, in this view, is a tool used by elites to dominate and control the lower classes (Chambliss 1978).

Both perspectives have obvious merit. Although law does serve the general interest by maintaining order, it serves some interests better than others. The relationship between law and inequality is a central concern of sociologists of law. One of the more influential and controversial theories of law is that of Donald Black (1976). Among his propositions are the following:

1. *Quantity of law.* The greater the inequality in society, the more law there will be. A society of equals needs fewer laws than a society with great inequality.
2. *Quality of law.* The law works differently when the victim and offender are status unequals than when they are status equals. When the victim and offender are of equal rank, then the law usually tries to mediate between them rather than punish. For example, in many domestic violence cases, counseling and probation are the preferred strategies. When the victim and the offender are status unequals, then the law takes a more punitive approach. A high-status offender, such as a white-collar criminal, is more likely to be punished with a fine, however, while a low-status offender, typically a "street criminal," will be punished by imprisonment.

WHAT IS JUSTICE?

Justice is an enormously difficult concept to define. Some argue that justice is served when everyone is treated equally—for example, when everyone who commits first-degree murder gets 30 years, no exceptions and no parole. Others believe that justice should be more flexible. They believe that circumstances should make a difference.

In this, as in many other fields, Max Weber's contributions are insightful. Weber ([1914] 1954) distinguished between two types of legal procedures: rational and substantive. *Rational law* is based on strict application of the rules, regardless of fairness in specific cases. *Substantive law,* in contrast, takes into account the unique circumstances of the individual case. For example, although the penalty for motor-vehicle homicide might be three years, substantive law might levy a lower penalty on a grief-stricken father who has killed his child than on someone who has killed a stranger.

Studies of actual sentencing outcomes suggest that law tends to be much more substantive than rational. If law were rational, one would expect that sentences would be highly correlated with the nature of the crime; they are not. If law were a tool of the elite, one would expect sentences to be affected by the race and class of the offender and the victim. There is evidence that death penalty decisions *are* affected by the race of the victim; convicted murderers, for example, are less likely to get the death penalty if the victim was African American (Radelet 1989). The most general conclusion, however, is that sentencing has only a rough association with the crime or the characteristics of the victim or offender. Decisions seem to depend more on the individual judge, who usually is allowed some leeway in sentencing, than on any characteristic of a particular case.

There is a great deal of discretion in police work. In most situations, the police officer is away from supervision and direction, must make snap decisions about whether to pursue violations or let them go. Because we recognize that there are not enough police officers to pursue every violation, we hope officers will use good judgment about what kinds of violations and violators are worth pursuing and will not let prejudice or bias affect their decisions.

THE CRIMINAL JUSTICE SYSTEM

The formal mechanisms of social control mentioned at the beginning of the chapter are administered through the criminal justice system. In the United States, this system consists of a vast network of agencies set up to deal with persons who deviate from the law: police departments, probation and parole agencies, rehabilitation agencies, criminal courts, jails, and prisons.

THE POLICE

Police officers occupy a unique and powerful position in the criminal justice system because they are empowered to make arrests in contexts of low visibility: Often there are no witnesses to police encounters with suspected offenders. Although they are supposed to enforce the law fully and uniformly, this is neither practical nor possible. In 1992, there were 2.8 full-time law enforcement officers for every 1,000 persons in the nation (U.S. Department of Justice 1993). This means that the police ordinarily must give greater attention to more serious crimes. Minor offenses and ambiguous situations are likely to be ignored.

Police officers have a considerable amount of discretionary power in determining the extent to which the policy of full enforcement is carried out. Should a drunk and disorderly person be charged or sent home? Should a juvenile offender be charged or reported to a parent? Should a strong odor of marijuana in an otherwise orderly group be overlooked or investigated?

The decisions the police make in the initial stages of an investigation are called **street-level justice.** Unlike the justice meted out in courts, street-level justice is relatively invisible and thus hard to evaluate (Smith and Visher 1981). The majority of street-level decisions made by the police present no problems. Recently, however, we have seen instances in which, by chance, street-level justice has been visible and has revealed a continuing problem of police brutality, an obvious abuse of discretionary power. This was the case, for example, when an onlooker with a video camera filmed the 1991 beating of Rodney King by Los Angeles police.

Street-level justice consists of the decisions the police make in the initial stages of an investigation.

THE COURTS

Once arrested, an individual starts a complex trip through the criminal justice system. This trip can best be thought of as a series of decision stages. There is considerable attrition as defendants pass from arrest to prosecution to sentencing and punishment. Even in felony cases, as many as 40 to 50 percent of those arrested will not be prosecuted, because of problems with evidence or witnesses (Brossi 1979). At the same time, approximately 90 percent of all convictions are the result of pretrial negotiations (Figueira-McDonough 1985). This means that only about 10 percent of criminal convictions are processed through public trials. Thus, the pretrial phases of prosecution are often more crucial to arriving at judicial decisions of guilt or innocence than are court trials themselves. Like the police, prosecutors have considerable discretion in deciding whom to prosecute and on what charges.

Throughout the entire process, the prosecution, the defense, and the judges participate in negotiated plea bargaining. The accused is encouraged to plead guilty in the interest of getting a lighter sentence, a reduced charge, or, in the case of multiple offenses, the dropping of some charges. In return, the prosecution is saved the trouble of assembling evidence sufficient for a jury trial.

Getting Tough on Crime: How and Why?

Until they fell slightly in 1992 and 1993, crime rates had gone up over the previous 20 years, especially those crimes of violence that are highly publicized by the media and that people fear most. Recent surveys demonstrate that 44 percent of Americans are afraid to walk at night in their own neighborhoods (Gallup Report 1992). As a result of this fear, the topic of crime evokes a gut-level response in most Americans, and there is strong public demand to "get tough on crime." In this section, we start by examining theories of punishment and then review current penal practices in the United States.

Punishment Rationales. Any assessment of prisons and punishment must come to grips with the issue: Why are we doing this? Before we can assess the adequacy of punishment, we need to be clear about its purpose. Traditionally, there have been five major rationales for punishment (Conrad 1983):

1. *Retribution*. Society punishes offenders to avenge the victim and society as a whole; this is a form of revenge and retaliation.
2. *Reformation*. Offenders are not punished but rather are corrected and reformed so that they will become conforming members of the community.
3. *Specific deterrence*. Punishment is intended to scare offenders so they will think twice about violating the law again.
4. *General deterrence*. By making an example of offenders, society scares the rest of us into following the rules.
5. *Prevention*. By incapacitating offenders, society keeps them from committing further crimes.

Today, social control agencies in the United States represent a mixture of these different philosophies and practices. However, as a result of crowded court dockets and prisons, in the 1980s and 1990s, some scholars argue that the goal of prisons and community corrections has shifted from the punishment or rehabilitation of individual criminals to the identification and management of unruly "high-risk" groups (Feeley and Simon 1992).

Prisons. For many people, getting tough on crime means locking criminals up and throwing away the key. In response to public demand, the rate of imprison-

Prisons are total institutions where inmates are assigned numbers, wear identical uniforms, live in identical cells, and follow the same routines. They are also environments full of anger, hatred, violence, boredom, and insecurity. In this totally negative environment, prisons become warehouses for the deviant and the violent. They are unlikely environments for rehabilitation.

ment has risen in the last 15 years (see Figure 8.4). In 1991, there were more than twice as many prison commitments per 1,000 index crimes as there were in 1970 (U.S. Department of Justice 1993b, 608; Snell 1995).

As a result, prison populations are soaring. In 1993, there were 909,000 people in state and federal prisons—two and one-half times the number in 1980. The number of prisoners rose by almost 7 percent in 1993, the equivalent of 58,000 inmates (Snell 1995, 2). About 94 percent of all prisoners are men. Disproportionately, these prisoners are young men who are uneducated, unskilled, poor, and African American. Recent figures show that 22 percent are under age 25; nearly two-thirds are African American, Asian, Native American, or Hispanic;

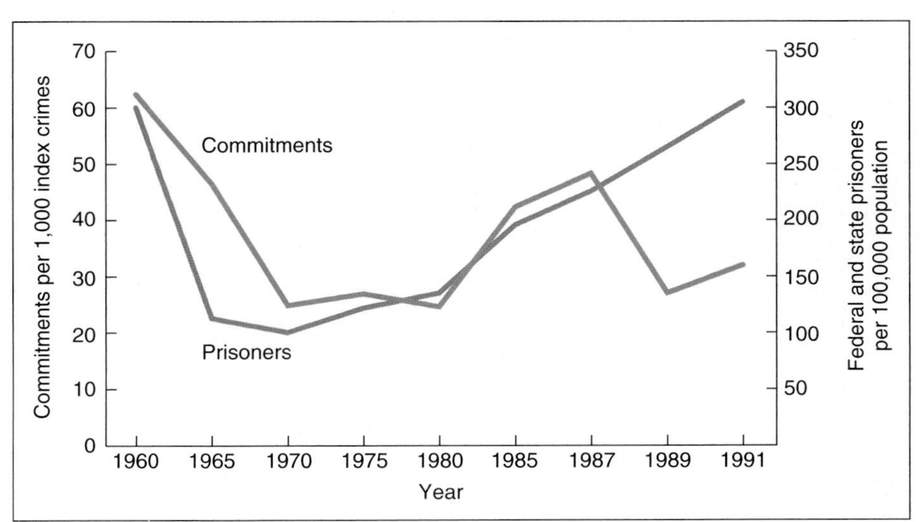

FIGURE 8.4
RATES OF IMPRISONMENT PER 1,000 INDEX CRIMES AND PER 100,000 POPULATION

Since 1970, there has been a sharp upturn in the use of prison sentences to control crime in the United States. Both the number of prisoners per crime and the number of prisoners per 100,000 population have more than doubled since 1970. The consequence is a "crisis in penalty." The economic and social costs of imprisonment may be so high that we must consider alternative strategies.

SOURCE: U.S. Department of Justice 1989b, 6; U.S. Bureau of the Census 1989a, 183; U.S. Department of Justice 1993b, 608; Snell 1995.

and slightly less than half have graduated from high school (Bureau of Justice Statistics, 1995). More than four in five have been in prison before. (U.S. Bureau of the Census 1993a, 210–211; Snell 1995).

The sharp increase in the use of prison to control crime has resulted in a crisis in prison conditions. Many facilities are housing twice as many inmates as they were designed to hold. These overcrowded conditions have been shown to be the chief determinant of violence in prisons (Siegel 1995, 574). As a result, court orders in more than 30 states have required prisons to reduce crowding and improve prison conditions. This is an enormously expensive undertaking. The costs are so huge that one observer has called this a "crisis of penalty" (Young, cited in Currie 1989). Most observers agree that "a total commitment to the incarceration of all adult felons . . . cannot be sustained in practice" (Mushane et al. 1989, 137). Do we really want to spend billions and billions of dollars to build more prisons to warehouse a growing proportion of those convicted of crime? Do we need to?

Empirical studies have demonstrated that the certainty of getting caught has more deterrent effect on crime than the length of the sentence (Klepper and Nagin 1989). These findings suggest that we are pursuing the wrong strategy. Rather than building more prisons to warehouse criminals for longer periods of time, we need to put more money into law enforcement. Today, many experts

Not everyone who commits a UCR-indexed crime comes from a bad neighborhood or suffers economic disadvantage. Delinquency, in fact, seems to show relatively little correlation with social class. Nevertheless, economic disadvantage can mean that adolescent delinquency turns from an occasional leisure-time activity into a permanent way of life. One strategy for reducing crime is to provide opportunities for better school performance, better jobs, and economic advancement.

believe that increasing the certainty that criminals will be caught will reduce crime more than will increasing penalties for the few that we do catch.

Community-Based Corrections. Another approach to solving the prison crisis is to change the way we punish convicted criminals. Only one quarter of the convicted offenders under the jurisdiction of social control agencies are actually in jail or prison. The other three quarters are on probation or parole. The public has been generally negative about probation and parole, believing—often rightly—that probation has meant giving criminals a "slap on the wrist" and parole has meant letting criminals out without effective supervision.

As the cost of imprisoning larger numbers of people balloons to crisis proportions, there has been increased interest in effective community-based corrections. New intensive supervision probation (ISP) programs are being used across the country. They include curfews, mandatory drug testing, supervised halfway houses, mandatory community service, frequent reporting and unannounced home visits, restitution, electronic surveillance, and split sentences (incarceration followed by supervised probation) (Lurigio 1990). These programs are alleged to cost only half as much as imprisonment and to be more likely to result in rehabilitation. Such claims are still being evaluated (Petersilia 1992; Siegel 1995, pp. 560–561).

COMBATING CRIME THROUGH SOCIAL CHANGE

The politically conservative approach to confronting crime has generally been to define crime as only the street crimes indexed in the Uniform Crime Report and to increase penalties for convicted street criminals. This **punitive approach** dominated the 1970s and 1980s and is one reason why prison populations have soared. The punitive approach is also significant in the $30 billion 1994 federal crime law, which allocated federal funds to help state and local governments pay for 100,000 new police officers, authorized thousands of new prison cells, and created more than 50 new death penalties, including those for drive-by shootings and assassinating a member of Congress (Gibbs 1993; "Senate Delivers on Crime" 1994). Other examples of the punitive approach are various states' "Three-Strikes-and-You're-Out" laws. For example, according to legislation passed in California in 1994, someone with a record of two serious or violent felonies would serve 25 years to life if convicted of a third felony (Peyser 1994b).

The **punitive approach** to confronting crime involves increasing penalties for convicted criminals, especially street criminals.

Criminologists and other informed critics have argued that the punitive approach will not work. For one thing, the criminal justice system actually convicts someone for only about 5 percent of all the serious crimes committed. More police and jail cells can hardly take care of the 95 percent gap (Anderson 1994). Moreover, our nation has increased its efforts toward punitive social control over the course of a quarter century to almost no avail. We have much more control today, but just as much—indeed, more—crime than twenty years ago (Gordon 1990).

An alternative way to confront street crimes is the **preventive approach**—addressing the social problems that give rise to them. A limited preventive approach, evident in the 1994 federal crime law, is the prohibition of assault-type weapons and the creation of neighborhood programs that involve teens and young adults in positive activities. One recent major study concluded that a dollar's worth of drug treatment is worth seven spent on the most successful law enforcement efforts to curb cocaine use (Treaster 1994).

The **preventive approach** to confronting crime involves addressing the social problems that give rise to it.

On a broader scale, a leading criminologist advocates four major strategies for reducing crime in the streets (Currie 1989):

1. Reduce inequality and social impoverishment.
2. Replace unstable, low-wage, dead-end jobs with decent jobs.
3. Enact a supportive national family policy.
4. Increase the economic and social stability of communities.

These strategies would require a massive commitment of energy and money.

So far, we have been talking mainly about street crimes. For confronting hate crimes, spokespersons advise not only stiffer law enforcement but also the preventive policy of recognizing and challenging the various forms of prejudice in our culture and doing everything possible, through education and otherwise, to eradicate these forms of hatred (Herek 1990).

To confront hate crimes committed against citizens by police in abuses of street-level justice, cities have attempted to integrate their police forces and offer training programs in diversity issues. The proportion of African American and Hispanic police officers still does not match the proportion of those ethnic groups in the major populations of our nation's 10 major cities, however (Kilborn 1994).

To confront white-collar crimes, one criminologist, Marshall Clinard (1990), proposes the following combination of punitive and preventive measures:

1. Urge stronger enforcement of present legislation, including detection, investigation, and prosecution.
2. Give stiffer corporate penalties so that corporations and executives truly suffer from fines levied for illegal activities.
3. Convict and imprison top corporate executives who have broken the law.
4. Create a comprehensive, industrywide code of ethics that is strongly enforced by business leaders.
5. Urge the faculties at business schools to place stronger emphasis on business ethics.
6. Pass laws that guarantee protection from being fired or harassed to whistle-blowers (employees who report wrongdoing to authorities).
7. Publicize corporate wrongdoing as diligently as street crimes are now publicized.
8. Increase the consumer role in punishing corporate offenders. For example, when the immensity of the Alaskan oil spill became evident, some consumers boycotted Exxon products.
9. Because giant corporations are more difficult to patrol, legally regulate corporate size.
10. Because many offending corporations are multinational, stretching beyond the boundaries of one nation, devise an international code of corporate ethics to be enforced under the direction of the United Nations.

THINKING CRITICALLY

Think of an example of the punitive approach to street crime. Now think of an example of the preventive approach. Which would be more effective, in your estimation?

Observers from all sociological perspectives and all political parties recognize that social control is necessary. They recognize that crime is a serious problem that must be addressed. The issue is how. The sociological perspective suggests that crime can be addressed most effectively by examining social institutions rather than individual criminals.

APPLICATIONS IN DIVERSITY

Is Capital Punishment Racist?

In 1972, in the case of *Furman v. Georgia,* three black defendants appealed their death sentences to the U.S. Supreme Court on the grounds that capital punishment, at least in cases of rape and murder, constituted cruel and unusual punishment. Their argument was that other defendants, many of whom were white, committed equally serious or more serious crimes and were not sentenced to death.

There was, in fact, good statistical support for their claim that capital punishment is racist. Between 1930 and 1967, 54 percent of all civil executions involved nonwhite offenders. Eighty-nine percent of those executed for rape during this time period were black (Radelet 1981). These figures are clearly much higher than the percentage of nonwhites in the general population and also much higher than the percentage of nonwhites among convicted rapists. Between 1945 and 1965, 13 percent of the blacks convicted of rape were sentenced to death whereas only 2 percent of the convicted whites received a similar sentence (Wolfgang and Reidel 1973). In a 5 to 4 decision, the Supreme Court agreed with the defendants, holding that the uncontrolled discretion of judges and juries in capital cases denied defendants constitutionally guaranteed rights to due process (Bell 1992).

The *Furman* decision put a temporary stop to capital punishment, but states attempted to solve the problem of disparity in sentencing by passing capital punishment statutes that gave judges and juries less discretion. Have the new, less discretionary, laws eliminated earlier racial discrepancies in the administration of the death penalty?

Studies conducted in the post-Furman era continue to show that, even where legal factors are similar, race is a strong determinant of who is sentenced to death. Fifty-six percent of those executed between 1977 and 1990 were white, 39 percent were black, and 5 percent were Hispanic (Culver 1992). Research also shows, however, that the race of the victim is at least as important as the race of the defendant. In a rigorous study of sentencing patterns in Georgia, Baldus and his associates found that after statistically controlling for 39 nonracial variables, defendants charged with killing white victims were 4.3 times more likely to receive a death sentence than those charged with killing a black (Baldus, Pulaski, and Woodworth 1986; Radelet 1989).

On the basis of evidence such as this, Warren McCleskey, a black man convicted and sentenced to death for the 1978 murder of a white police officer, appealed to the U.S. Supreme Court, arguing that his sentence was a product of racial discrimination. Speaking for the majority, Supreme Court Justice Powell found that statistical evidence of racial disparity in sentencing was insufficient to "demonstrate a constitutionally significant risk of racial bias." While the Court admitted that there was "some risk of racial prejudice influencing a jury's decision in a criminal case," the level of risk documented by social science research was not "unacceptable." The Court reasoned that the criminal justice system would be immobilized by the "impossible" task of making itself even-handed, if the only test of constitutionality was statistical evidence of arbitrary sentencing. Significantly, the Court never disputed the results of the Baldus study and never denied the influence of racial prejudice on capital sentencing in Georgia. Instead, it seemed to accept discrimination as an unfortunate cost of doing law enforcement's business (Bell 1992, 332–337).

Thinking Critically

Why would the race of the victim be as important as the race of the defendant in predicting whether a convicted killer would be sentenced to death? What does this research finding tell us about how our society values ethnic and cultural diversity? About how our society values whites, relative to others? If racial discrimination exists in sentences to capital punishment, is that a good reason to stop capital punishment altogether? Why or why not?

SOCIOLOGY ON THE NET

We are bombarded every day with crime statistics and news reports of criminal behavior. It seems that we are surrounded by crime and it seems to be getting worse. For a real look at what is happening let's abandon the tabloid atmosphere of the mass media for the United States Justice Department for a clearer look at the statistics.

`http://www.usdoj.gov`

Scroll down the page and open the **Topical Index** section. Browse through the different topics being sure to read the **Press Releases, Statistics and the Violence Against Women Home Page**. What kinds of crime does the government seek to eliminate? What crimes are the most common and which are relatively uncommon? What is the government doing to combat violence against women?

Now let's take a good look at the bad guys and gals by returning to the **Topical Index** and opening the section on **Fugitives—Wanted**. Who are the bad guys? Why aren't there more women on these lists?

There are many ways for society to label deviance and crime. One way is to label criminal behavior as illness. The hospital and the treatment center replace the jail and treatment replaces punishment. Drunks used to be tossed into jail. Now they are taken to a detoxification center. This change is referred to as the medicalization of deviance. Today, the treatment of chemical dependency is big business. One of the older and more respected treatment facilities is Hazelden.

`http://www.hazelden.com`

Begin your tour of this web site by clicking on the **Visit Us** section. Next, return to the **home page** and open the section entitled **Resource Center** and browse through the topics. You might even try your luck at the **Quiz**. What is the Hazelden mission? How does Hazelden refer to the people who come for treatment and successfully complete the program? What kinds of deviance are treated at Hazelden? What is the difference between this approach and the one taken at a prison?

SUMMARY

1. Most of us conform most of the time. We are constrained to conform through three types of social control: (1) self-restraint through the internalization of norms and values, (2) informal social controls, and (3) formal social controls.
2. Nonconformity occurs when people violate expected norms of behavior. Acts that go beyond eccentricity and challenge important norms are called deviance. Crimes are a specific kind of deviance for which there are formal sanctions.
3. Deviance is relative. Whether an act is regarded as deviant may depend on the time, the place, the person performing the act and that person's status, and the audience.
4. All three major theoretical perspectives in sociology have explanations of deviance. Structural functionalists use strain theory to blame deviance on social disorganization; symbolic interactionists propose differential association, deter-

rence, and labeling theories, which lay the blame on interaction patterns that encourage a deviant self-concept; Marxists and other conflict theorists find the cause of deviance in inequality and class conflict.

5 Most index crimes are property crimes rather than crimes of violence. In 1992, all index crimes except rape and assault decreased for the first time in almost a decade.

6 Many arrests are for victimless crimes—acts for which there is no complaining victim. Such crimes are the most difficult and costly to control.

7 Hate crimes—crimes motivated by bigotry based on race, religion, national origin, or sexual orientation, have occurred throughout our history and appear to be on the increase.

8 The high incidence of white-collar crimes, those committed by respectable people of high status in the course of their occupations, indicates that crime is not merely a lower-class behavior. White-collar crimes cost Americans more in dollars, injuries, and lost lives than do street crimes.

9 Males, minority-group members, lower-class people, and young people are disproportionately likely to be arrested for crimes. Some of this differential is due to their greater likelihood of committing a crime, but it is also explained partly by their differential treatment within the criminal justice system.

10 The sociology of law is concerned with how law is established and how it works in practice. While structural-functional theory emphasizes that law serves the general interest of society, conflict theory points out that it best serves the interests of the elite. In practice, legal decisions are highly variable rather than determined by formal rules.

11 The criminal justice system includes the police, the courts, and the correctional system. Considerable discretion in the execution of justice is available to authorities at each of these levels.

12 The United States faces a "crisis of penalty," as our "get-tough" approach to crime is populating prisons far beyond capacity. Evidence suggests that imposing longer sentences is less effective in reducing crime than increasing the certainty of being caught. Alternatives to imprisonment include community-based corrections and social change to reduce the causes of crime.

14 Despite evidence that capital punishment is racist, the practice continues.

SUGGESTED READINGS

BEN-YEHUDA, Nachman. 1985. *Deviance and Moral Boundaries*. Chicago: University of Chicago Press. A wide-ranging coverage of deviance from witchcraft and the occult to cheating in science. A nice balance to the usual emphasis on criminal deviance.

CHAMBLIS, William J., and Seidman, Robert B. 1982. *Law, Order, and Power*. Reading, Mass.: Addison-Wesley. A major text from the conflict perspective.

CLINARD, Marshall B. 1990. *Corporate Corruption: The Abuse of Power*. New York: Praeger. Clinard is a renowned criminologist who focuses in this book on white-collar crime within the prestigious Fortune 500 companies.

COHEN, Stanley. 1985. *Visions of Social Control: Crime, Punishment, and Classification*. Cambridge, England: Polity Press. A thoughtful book that considers the rationales that we use to justify punishment and the evidence supporting them. Cohen draws a provocative distinction between doing justice and doing good.

ELLIOTT, Delbert, Huizinga, David, and Ageton, Suzanne. 1985. *Explaining Delinquency and Drug Use*. Beverly Hills: Sage. A research report on this familiar form of deviance. It includes a good introductory coverage of symbolic interactionist theories of deviance.

MACKELLAR, F. Landis, and Machiko Yanagishita. 1995. "Homicide in the United States: Who's at Risk?" Washington, D.C.: Population Reference Bureau. An interesting pamphlet on the growing problem of homicide in the U.S. today, including the roles of firearms, gender, race, and poverty, among others.

SUTHERLAND, Edwin H. 1983. *White Collar Crime: The Uncut Version*. New Haven: Yale University Press. An up-to-date analysis of various forms of white-collar crime in the United States by the theorist who first named them.

VAGO, Steven. 1989. *Law and Society*. (2nd ed.) Englewood Cliffs, N.J.: Prentice-Hall. This book covers the sociology of law, including a historical treatment of theories of the law, as well as contemporary issues.

UNIT THREE

Differentiation and Inequality

C H A P T E R 9

Stratification

OUTLINE

PROLOGUE

Have You Ever . . . considered where the kids you went to high school with are now? Some may have gone to Harvard, some to major state universities, some to community colleges, and some to vocational-technical schools. Some may be working on assembly lines, and some may be selling shoes; some may be on welfare.

What determines which path people will take? Are the people who go to Harvard really that much smarter than those who are selling shoes? Or are they harder working, or maybe luckier? Or do their parents have more money? Consider what the future holds for those who go to major universities compared with those who are selling shoes or working on assembly lines. Their lives are bound to be very different; they already are very different.

This chapter considers how occupations are assigned and what the consequences are for individuals and societies. It also considers the issue of fairness and how Americans deal with the significant inequalities that exist all around them. How did the kids who drove their parents' old Ford station wagons cope with the knowledge that some kids got new Camaros for their 16th birthdays? And what about the kids who had no car to drive at all? As you read this chapter, you might consider how well it explains the origins and destinations of your high school senior class and how its explanations compare with those that you yourself have offered.

STRUCTURES OF INEQUALITY

Inequality exists all around us. Maybe your mother loves your sister more than you, or your brother received a larger allowance than you did. This kind of inequality is personal. Sociologists study a particular kind of inequality called stratification. **Stratification** is an institutionalized pattern of inequality in which social statuses are ranked on the basis of their access to scarce resources.

Stratification is an institutionalized pattern of inequality in which social statuses are ranked on the basis of their access to scarce resources.

If your parents gave your brother more money because they decided he was nicer than you, this inequality is not stratification. Inequality becomes stratification when two conditions exist:

1. The inequality is *institutionalized*, backed up by long-standing social norms about what ought to be.
2. The inequality is based on occupancy of a position in the social structure, or a status (such as oldest son, blue-collar worker, female, Hispanic, disabled, or over age 65), rather than on personal attributes.

The scarce resources we focus on are generally of three types: material wealth, prestige, and power. When inequality in one of these dimensions is supported by widely accepted and long-standing social norms and when it is based on status occupancy, then we speak of stratification.

TYPES OF STRATIFICATION STRUCTURES

Stratification is present in every society that we know. All societies have norms specifying that some categories of people ought to get more wealth, power, or prestige than others. There is, however, wide variety in the ways in which inequality is structured. The Focus section of this chapter asks the question whether a community without inequality is possible.

A key difference among structures of inequality is whether the categories used to distribute unequal rewards are based on ascribed or achieved statuses. As noted in Chapter 4, *ascribed statuses* are those that are fixed by birth and inheritance and are unalterable during a person's lifetime. *Achieved statuses* are optional ones that a person can obtain in a lifetime. Being African American or female, for example, is an ascribed status; being an ex-convict or a physician is an achieved status.

Every society uses some ascribed and some achieved statuses in distributing scarce resources, but the balance between them varies greatly. Stratification structures that rely largely on ascribed statuses as the basis for distributing scarce resources are called **caste systems;** structures that rely largely on achieved statuses are called **class systems.**

Caste systems rely on ascribed statuses as the basis for distributing scarce resources.

Class systems rely largely on achieved statuses as the basis for distributing scarce resources.

Caste Systems. In a caste system, whether you are rich or poor, powerful or powerless, depends entirely on who your parents are. Whether you are lazy and stupid or hardworking and clever makes little difference. Your parents' position determines your own.

This system of structured inequality reached its extreme form in 19th-century India. The level of inequality in India was not very different from that in many European nations at the time, but the system for distributing rewards was markedly different. The Indian population was divided into castes, roughly comparable to occupation groups, that differed substantially in the amount of prestige, power, and wealth they received. In India, the top caste was the Brahmans, whose sole responsibility was to study, while the bottom caste was the Untouchables, who could not even approach a village unless no one in a higher caste was there. The distinctive feature of the caste system was that caste membership was unalterable; people had to remain in the caste to which they were born. Moreover, one's caste marked one's children and one's children's children. The inheritance of position was ensured by rules specifying that all persons should (1) follow the same occupation as their parents, (2) marry within their own caste, and (3) have no social relationships with members of other castes (Weber [1910] 1970b). In the United States before the Civil War, slavery was a caste system.

Class Systems. In a class system, achieved statuses are the major basis of unequal resource distribution. Occupation remains the major determinant of rewards, but it is not fixed at birth. Instead, you can achieve an occupation better or worse than that of your parents. Theoretically, the amount of rewards you receive is influenced by your own talent and ambition or their lack.

The primary difference between caste and class systems is not the level of inequality but the opportunity for achievement. The distinctive characteristic of a class system is that it permits **social mobility**—a change in social class. Technically, mobility that occurs from one generation to the next is **intergenerational mobility.** Change in occupation and social class during an individual's own career is **intragenerational mobility.** Both kinds of mobility may be downward as well as upward.

Social mobility is the process of changing one's social class.

Intergenerational mobility is change in social class from one generation to the next.

Intragenerational mobility is change in social class within an individual's own career.

Semi-caste Systems and Life Chances. Even in a class system, ascribed characteristics have an influence. Whether you are male or female, Hispanic or non-Hispanic,

Jewish or Protestant is likely to influence which doors are thrown open and which barriers have to be surmounted. The realization that ascribed statuses do indeed affect the likelihood of social mobility has led some sociologists to define societies such as that of the United States as a **semicaste,** or **castelike system:** a class system with some caste-system characteristics. (Chapter 11 discusses the semicaste model in detail.)

A **semicaste,** or **castelike, system** is a class system with some caste-system characteristics.

Nevertheless, ascribed statuses are much less important in a class society than in a caste society. Because class systems predominate in the modern world, the rest of this chapter is devoted to them. The following three chapters then address structured inequality based on race and ethnicity, sex, and age and show how these ascribed characteristics interact with class to determine **life chances**—the probability that throughout the life course one will have (or not have) a wide range of opportunities, experiences, and achievements, from surviving as an infant, to having good health and a place to live, to developing one's talents through schooling, to enjoying travel and leisure throughout adulthood and old age.

Life chances describe the probability that throughout the life course one will have (or not have) a wide range of opportunities, experiences, and achievements.

CLASSES—HOW ARE THEY DIVIDED?

A class system is an ordered set of statuses. Which statuses are included, and how are they divided? Two theoretical answers to these questions are presented here.

Marx. Karl Marx (1818–1883), who was writing during the early phase of industrialization, concluded that industrialized society would become polarized into two classes. We might call them the haves and the have-nots; Marx called them the bourgeoisie (boor-zhwah-zee) and the proletariat. The **bourgeoisie** is the class whose members own the tools and materials necessary for work—capital, or the means of production. Some members of the bourgeoisie, who make up the **petit bourgeoisie,** own only modest capital, which they use to establish small enterprises in which they and their families provide primary labor (Bechhofer and Elliott 1985). Others—factory owners, for example—own a great deal of capital. Members of the **proletariat** own no capital at all and must therefore support themselves by selling their labor to those who do, such as the factory owners. In Marx's view, **class** is determined entirely by one's relationship to the means of production.

The **bourgeoisie** is the class whose members own the tools and materials for their work—the means of production.

The **petit bourgeoisie** includes those members of the bourgeoisie who use their modest capital to establish small enterprises in which they and their families provide primary labor.

The **proletariat** is the class whose members do not own the means of production. Members of this class must support themselves by selling their labor to those who own the means of production.

Relationship to the means of production obviously has something to do with occupation, but it is not the same thing. According to this analysis, your college instructor, the manager of the Sears store, and the janitor are all proletarians, because they work for someone else. The person who manages an apartment complex is probably also a proletarian who sells her labor to an employer; if the manager owns the apartment building, however, then she is a member of the (petit) bourgeoisie. The key factor is not income or occupation, then, but whether individuals control their own tools or means of production, their own work, and hence their own life chances.

Class, in Marx's Theory, refers to a person's relationship to the means of production.

But Marx was not blind to the fact that in the eyes of the world, college instructors are usually regarded as more successful than janitors. College teachers may indeed think of themselves as being superior to janitors. This is **false consciousness**—a lack of awareness of one's real position in the class structure. Marx, a social activist as well as a social theorist, hoped that college instructors, managers, and janitors could learn to see themselves as part of the same oppressed class. If they developed **class consciousness**—an awareness of their true identity—a revolutionary movement to eliminate class differences would be likely to occur, Marx believed.

False consciousness is a lack of awareness of one's real position in the class structure.

Class consciousness occurs when one is aware of one's relationship to the means of production and recognizes one's true class identity.

Weber: Class, Status, and Power. Marx's prediction about the polarization of society has not come about. Instead, a whole new middle class of managers and university-trained professionals developed. Max Weber, who wrote 50 years later than Marx, thus believed that we needed a more complex system for analyzing classes. Instead of Marx's one-dimensional ranking system, which provided only two classes, Weber proposed three independent dimensions on which people could be ranked in a stratification system (see Figure 9.1). One of them, as Marx suggested, is class. The second is **status,** social honor or prestige, expressed in lifestyle. (Note that Weber did not use the term *status* as we have been using it throughout this book—to mean a position in the social structure. Instead, Weber used *status* as a synonym for social honor or prestige.) Unlike people united by a common class, people united by a common lifestyle form a community. They invite one another to dinner, marry one another, engage in the same kinds of recreation, and generally do the same things in the same places. The third dimension is **power,** the ability to get others to act against their wishes, the ability to overcome resistance. Power is fully explored in Chapter 16.

In Weber's model of social class, **status** means social honor or prestige, expressed in lifestyle, and is one component of social class.

Power is the ability to direct others' behavior, even against their wishes.

Weber argued that although status and power often follow economic position, they may also stand on their own and have independent effects on social inequality. In particular, Weber noted that prestige often stands in opposition to economic power, depressing the pretensions of those who "just" have money. Thus, for example, a member of the Mafia may have a lot of money, may in fact own the means of production (a brothel, a cocaine manufacturing plant, a casino)—but this person does not have social honor.

Especially in the United States, most sociologists use some version of Weber's framework to guide their examination of stratification systems. Rather than speaking of class (the Marxian dichotomy), we speak of *social* class. A **social class** is a category of people who share roughly the same class, status, and power and who have a sense of identification with one another. When we speak of the upper class or of the working class, we are speaking of social class in this sense.

A **social class** is a category of people who share roughly the same class, status, and power and who have a sense of identification with each other.

FIGURE 9.1
WEBER'S MODEL OF SOCIAL CLASS

Weber identified three independent dimensions of stratification. This multidimensional concept is called social class.

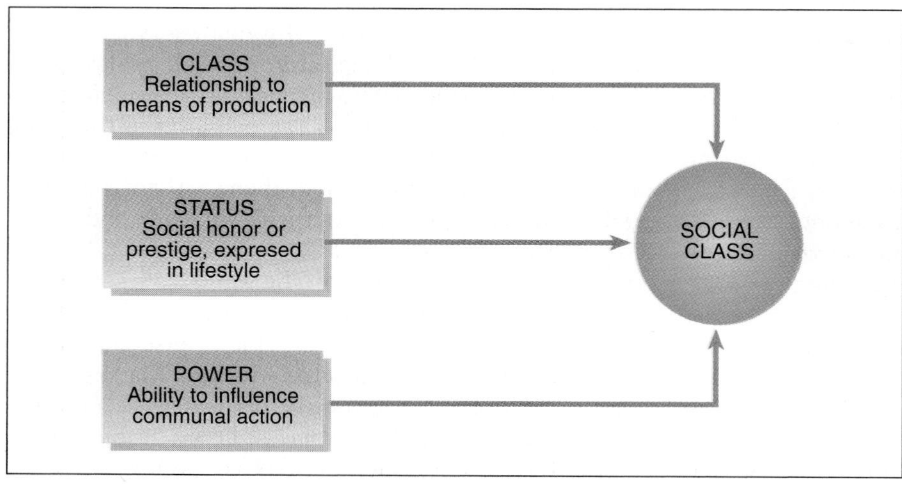

Social class differs from *class* in two ways. First, it recognizes the importance of status and power as well as class. Second, it includes the element of self-awareness. Although people may be ignorant of their class situation, they are usually well aware of their social class position, often using it as an important means to map the social world and their own place in it. People recognize that they are similar to others of their own social class but different in important ways from those in other social classes. The manager of the Sears store and the janitor, for example, are likely to be aware that they are members of the middle and working class, respectively.

Inequality in the United States

Stratification exists in all societies. In Britain, India, and Russia alike, social structures ensure that some social classes routinely get more rewards than do others. This section considers how the system works in the United States.

Measuring Social Class

If you had to rank all the people in your classroom by social class, how would you do it? There are many different strategies you could use: their incomes, their parents' incomes, the size of their savings accounts, or the way they dress and the cars they drive. Some students would score high no matter how you ranked them, but others' scores might be very sensitive to your measurement procedure. The same thing is true when we try to rank people in the United States; the picture of inequality we get depends on our measurement procedure.

Self-Identification. A direct way of measuring social class is simply to ask people what social class they belong to. This is called the *subjective* method of measuring social class. Given that a social class is a self-aware group, people should be able to tell you which social class they are in. Sure enough, when we ask Americans, "Which of the following social classes would you say you belong to?" fewer than 1 percent say they don't know, and even fewer tell you that we don't have social classes in the United States. The concept of social class is meaningful to most Americans, and they have an opinion about where they fit in the hierarchy. Nevertheless, results of a 1986 survey (Davis and Smith 1986) show that only a small minority of Americans see themselves as belonging to the upper and lower classes—7 percent and 3 percent, respectively. The bulk of the population sees itself as middle-class (Kelley and Evans 1995).

Socioeconomic Status (SES). An alternative way to measure social class is by **socioeconomic status (SES),** which ranks individuals on income, education, occupation, or some combination of these. SES measures do not produce self-aware social class groupings but result in a ranking of the population from high to low on criteria such as years of school completed, family income, or occupation. This is an *objective* method of measuring social class.

Socioeconomic status (SES) is a measure of social class that ranks individuals on income, education, occupation, or some combination.

Many scholars use occupation alone as their indicator of social class position. The device most often used to rank occupations is the Occupational Prestige Scale. The scale is based on survey research in which large random samples are given lists of occupations and asked "to pick out the statement that best gives your own personal opinion of the general standing that such a job has: excellent, good, average, somewhat below average, or poor." The prestige of an occupation rests on the overall evaluation that sample respondents give to the occupation. Repeated tests have shown that this procedure yields consistent results; the same ordering of occupations has been demonstrated in American samples since 1927, as well as in other Westernized societies, from urban Nigeria to Great Britain (Hodge, Siegel, and Rossi 1964; Hodge, Treiman, and Rossi 1966). And in spite of the fact that the question is specifically about *men* who hold these occupations, occupations are ranked the same way for women (Bose and Rossi 1983). Thus, we can be confident that the scale produces a reliable ordering of occupations (see Table 9.1 for a partial list of ranked occupations).

Economic Inequality

In this section we use income as a general index to social class, although you'll recall that income is not necessarily the only element of social class. All contemporary class systems have high levels of inequality. In the United States, income inequality is higher than in many other industrialized societies (Menard 1986; Kerbo 1991; 37), and this inequality has been substantial since the beginning of the republic. Despite wars on poverty, large-scale increases in educational attainment, and a fourfold increase in the number of two-earner households, inequality in the distribution of household income has changed little over the past two centuries. In fact, recent data indicate that inequality has increased since 1973 (Kerbo 1991; Thomas 1994). In 1992, the poorest 20 percent received only 4 percent of all personal income, whereas the richest 20 percent received 47 percent—almost 12 times more (see Figure 9.2).

Income includes payments that people receive periodically from an occupation or investments.

Wealth includes all accumulated assets, such as savings, investments, homes, land, cars, and other possessions.

The inequality documented by income distribution is actually an underestimate of the inequality that actually exists. **Income** is made up of payments that people receive periodically from an occupation or investments. **Wealth** includes all assets that the person and the person's family have accumulated over the years, such as savings, investments, homes, land, cars, and other possessions. We have seen that *income* is unevenly distributed, but *wealth* is allocated even more unequally. The richest 20 percent of households hold between 75 and 80 percent of all wealth.

The Consequences of Social Class

The following chapters point out the influence of social class in a number of areas—among them religious affiliation and participation, divorce, prejudice and discrimination, and work satisfaction. Here, it suffices to say that almost every experience and attitude we have is related to our social class. Can you afford a vacation in Europe? What kind of movies do you like (they call them films in the upper class)? Have your teeth been straightened by an orthodontist? These choices and nearly all the others we make are influenced by our social class. Knowledge of a person's social class often tells us more about that person than any other single piece of information. This is why "What do you do for a living?" almost always follows "Glad to meet you."

TABLE 9.1
OCCUPATIONAL PRESTIGE RATINGS

OCCUPATION	SCORE	OCCUPATION	SCORE	OCCUPATION	SCORE
PHYSICIAN	82	SOCIAL WORKER	52	BARBER	38
COLLEGE PROFESSOR	78	FUNERAL DIRECTOR	52	JEWELER	37
JUDGE	76	COMPUTER SPECIALIST	51	WATCHMAKER	37
LAWYER	76	STOCK BROKER	51	BRICKLAYER	36
PHYSICIST	74	REPORTER	51	AIRLINE STEWARDESS	36
DENTIST	74	OFFICE MANAGER	50	METER READER	36
BANKER	72	BANK TELLER	50	MECHANIC	35
AERONAUTICAL ENGINEER	71	ELECTRICIAN	49	BAKER	34
ARCHITECT	71	MACHINIST	48	SHOE REPAIRMAN	33
PSYCHOLOGIST	71	POLICE OFFICER	48	BULLDOZER OPERATOR	33
AIRLINE PILOT	70	INSURANCE AGENT	47	BUS DRIVER	32
CHEMIST	69	MUSICIAN	46	TRUCK DRIVER	32
MINISTER	69	SECRETARY	46	CASHIER	31
CIVIL ENGINEER	68	FOREMAN	45	SALES CLERK	29
BIOLOGIST	68	REAL ESTATE AGENT	44	MEAT CUTTER	28
GEOLOGIST	67	FIREMAN	44	HOUSEKEEPER	25
SOCIOLOGIST	66	POSTAL CLERK	43	LONGSHOREMAN	24
POLITICAL SCIENTIST	66	ADVERTISING AGENT	42	GAS STATION ATTENDANT	22
MATHEMATICIAN	65	MAIL CARRIER	42	CAB DRIVER	22
SECONDARY SCHOOL TEACHER	63	RAILROAD CONDUCTOR	41	ELEVATOR OPERATOR	21
REGISTERED NURSE	62	TYPIST	41	BARTENDER	20
PHARMACIST	61	PLUMBER	41	WAITER	20
VETERINARIAN	60	FARMER	41	FARM LABORER	18
ELEMENTARY SCHOOL TEACHER	60	TELEPHONE OPERATOR	40	MAID/SERVANT	18
ACCOUNTANT	57	CARPENTER	40	GARBAGE COLLECTOR	17
LIBRARIAN	55	WELDER	40	JANITOR	17
STATISTICIAN	55	DANCER	38	SHOE SHINER	9

SOURCE: James A. Davis and Tom W. Smith, National Data Program for the Social Sciences: General Social Survey, Cumulative File, 1972–1982 (Ann Arbor, Mich.: Inter-University Consortium for Political and Social Research, 1983), Appendix F. Reprinted with the permission of the Inter-University Consortium for Political and Social Research.

FIGURE 9.2
INCOME INEQUALITY IN THE UNITED STATES, 1992

Distributions of income in the United States have shown little change in income inequality since World War II. In 1992, 47 percent of the total income in the United States went to the richest 20 percent of the population, whereas the poorest 20 percent of the population received only 4 percent.

SOURCE: U.S. Bureau of the Census 1993b.

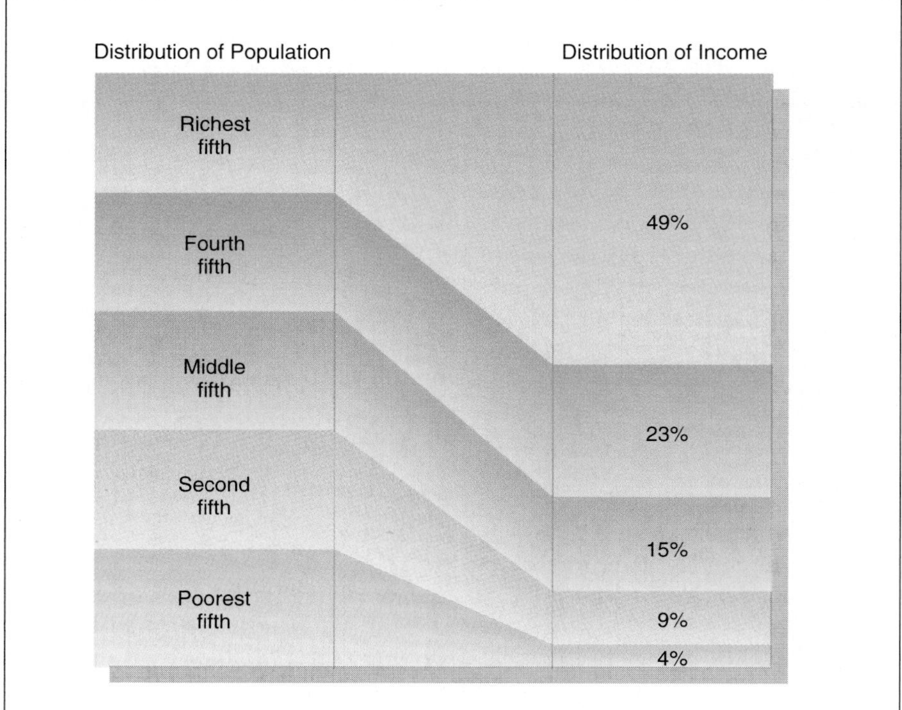

Can Money Buy Happiness? Some social class differences are merely subcultural differences in tastes and lifestyles. If you prefer all-star wrestling to the symphony, there is no objective way to say that your tastes are worse than the tastes of those who subscribe to elite culture; they are just different. On many dimensions, however, social class differences are far more meaningful. Consider the following:

- People with incomes below $10,000 a year have nearly three times as many disability days as those with incomes of $35,000 or more (U.S. Bureau of the Census 1995, Table 204).
- People with incomes of less than $7,500 a year are more than three times as likely to have been victims of violent crime as those with incomes over $50,000 (U.S. Department of Justice 1993b).
- Infants whose mothers fail to graduate from high school are twice as likely to die before their first birthday as infants born to mothers with college degrees (Bertoli et al. 1984).
- People who fail to graduate from high school are twice as likely to get divorced within the first five years of marriage as those who complete at least one year of college (Martin and Bumpass 1989).

On these and many other indicators, the better off are not just different, they are also healthier and happier. For instance, the proportion of women who have professional breast examinations to screen for cancer increases steadily with income (Figure 9.3). The same pattern applies to mammograms. In fact, among women earning at least $50,000 annually, the proportion who get periodic mammograms is

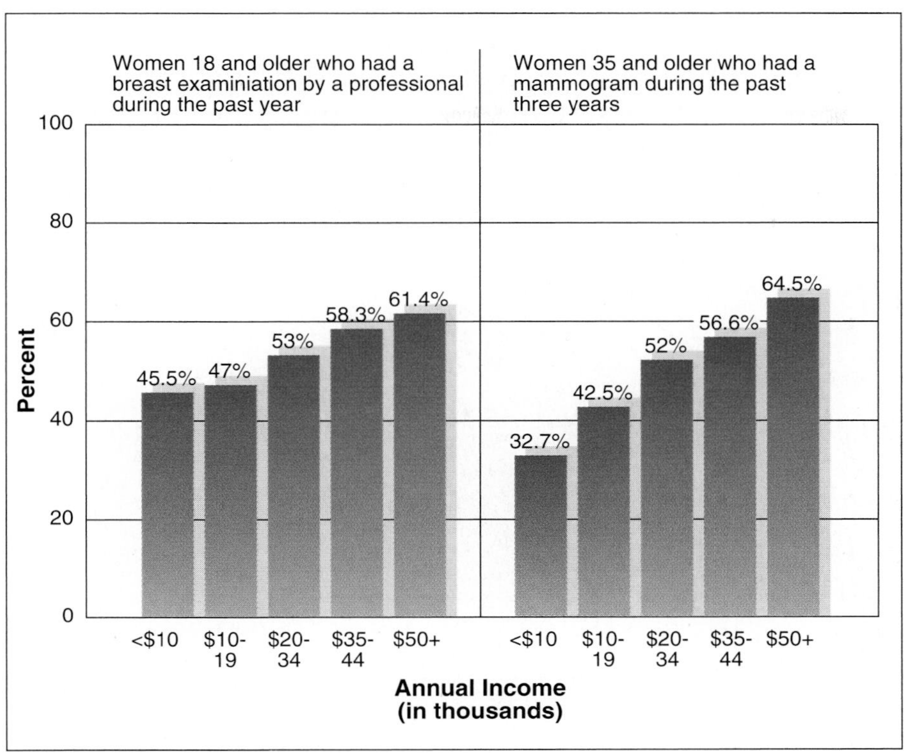

FIGURE 9.3
PREVENTATIVE BREAST CANCER MEASURES UNDERTAKEN BY U.S. WOMEN, 1990, BY INCOME

The differences in life chances due to social class make for fundamental differences in the quality of people's lives. As one example, women who earn more are more likely to have had a professional breast exam in the past year. In the figure, 45.5 percent of those earning less than $10,000 had done so, compared with 61.4 percent of those earning $50,000 or more. For mammograms, the differences are even more pronounced. Fewer than one-third (32.7 percent) of women who earned under $10,000 had had a mammogram in the past three years; almost twice that proportion—64.5 percent—of those earning $50,000 or more had done so. For both mammograms and professional breast exams, proportions increase directly with income.

SOURCE: U.S. Bureau of the Census. 1994 Statistical Abstract of the United States, Table 214.

nearly twice that among women earning less than $10,000 (U.S. Bureau of the Census 1993a, Table 212). The differences in life chances between social classes make for fundamental differences in the quality of people's lives.

Change and Continuity in the Consequences of Social Class. Differences in wealth have been remarkably constant over the past 185 years; and as noted, income inequality has actually increased somewhat over the last two decades. Meanwhile, there have been some striking changes in the consequences of divergent wealth, income and education levels. We can examine these changes in two ways: We can compare the experiences of the working class with those of the middle class (Rubin 1992) and we can compare the life chances of the wealthy with those of the poor.

Comparing the working class with the middle class, we can see clear evidence of change in two studies of Middletown (Muncie, Indiana), the first done in 1924–1925. After the original investigation, the researchers concluded that social class "is the most significant single cultural factor tending to influence what one does all day long throughout one's life" (cited in Caplow and Chadwick 1979). In 1972, another team of investigators went back to see how Middletown had changed in the ensuing 50 years. The second study found a dramatic decline in social class differences (see Table 9.2). There was a marked convergence on all measures except a directly economic one—percentage unemployed.

Comparing the life chances of the wealthy with those of the poor shows a different picture: Class differences are marked and dramatic. As the differentials we

TABLE 9.2

CHANGES IN LIFE-STYLES BY SOCIAL CLASS IN MIDDLETOWN BETWEEN 1924 AND 1972

Differences in social class declined sharply in Middletown between 1924 and 1972. With the exception of unemployment, the lifestyles of working-class families and business-class families were much more similar in 1972 than they were in 1924. (Business class here is synonymous with middle class.)

	1924	1972
PERCENTAGE OF FAMILIES RISING BEFORE 6 A.M. ON WORKDAYS		
BUSINESS CLASS	15%	31%
WORKING CLASS	93	38
PERCENTAGE OF FAMILIES WHERE HUSBAND UNEMPLOYED IN LAST YEAR		
BUSINESS CLASS	1	4
WORKING CLASS	28	25
PERCENTAGE OF FAMILIES WITH A WORKING WIFE		
BUSINESS CLASS	3	42
WORKING CLASS	44	48
PERCENTAGE OF MOTHERS WANTING THEIR CHILDREN TO GO TO COLLEGE		
BUSINESS CLASS	93	90
WORKING CLASS	23	83
PERCENTAGE OF PARENTS STRESSING INDEPENDENCE IN CHILDREN		
BUSINESS CLASS	46	82
WORKING CLASS	17	68

SOURCE: Caplow and Chadwick, 1979. "Inequality and Life-Styles in Middletown, 1920–1978." *Social Science Quarterly* 60 (3). Reprinted with permission of The University of Texas Press and authors.

reported earlier on disability days, infant mortality, victimization, and divorce demonstrate, social class still does make a big difference. Nevertheless, the difference is less than it was 70 years ago. To some extent, this is a result of the fact that major increases in real income (that is, income adjusted for inflation) have been experienced in this country since 1924. The increases have been particularly important for those who were barely keeping their heads above water. Although the cars, televisions, and homes of the working class are not of the same quality as those of the middle class, the working class does have them. An additional factor in reducing some of the major differences in life chances is the extension of public services. Public schools, the GI Bill, and veterans' benefits have helped reduce some of the more severe consequences of lower social class.

These explanations assume that the working class has become more like the middle class. In contrast, some scholars have suggested that—over the past 25 years, in any case—a stagnant economy has caused the middle class to become more like the working class (Kerbo 1991). For instance, the white, middle-class Americans who reached adulthood during the 1980s were the first for whom upward intergenerational mobility could not be routinely expected. And as some newer white-collar jobs require routine and mundane activities in the office—not unlike the routine and mundane activities on the assembly line—more and more white-collar jobs mean lack of independence and boredom. As we will discuss in Chapter 17, the jobs that have provided relative affluence for the unionized working class and for much of the middle class are declining. In their place are minimum-wage service jobs that push a growing segment of the working class, along with young-adult offspring of the middle class, to the poverty level. Then too, as we will document later in this chapter, truly disadvantaged people exist in this country. Over the past two decades, the truly disadvantaged have been growing both in number and as a proportion of the population.

Conclusion. Social class is important in American society. It affects our attitudes, behaviors, values, health, and opportunities. Although some social class differences have been reduced through federal programs and through mass culture, many important differences—including very substantial income inequality—remain. Next we look at the factors that explain this continuing inequality.

EXPLANATIONS OF INEQUALITY

Steven Spielberg earned over $300 million in 1993, Troy Aikman earned over $10 million, Bill Clinton earned $200,000, and the average police officer and teacher earned about $30,000; some 10 percent of American families earned annual incomes of less than $10,000. How can we account for such vast differences in income? Why isn't somebody doing anything about it?

We begin our answers to these questions by examining the social structure of stratification—that is, instead of asking about Steven and Troy and Bill, we ask why some *statuses* routinely get more scarce resources than others. After we review these general theories of stratification, we will turn to explanations about how individuals are sorted into various statuses.

STRUCTURAL-FUNCTIONAL THEORY

The structural-functional theory of stratification begins (as do all structural-functional theories) with the question: "How does this social structure contribute to the maintenance of society?" This theoretical position is represented by the work of Davis and Moore (1945), who assume that stratification is necessary because it contributes to the maintenance of society. To explain how stratification is functional, Davis and Moore begin with the premise that each society has essential tasks (functional prerequisites) that must be performed if it is to survive. The tasks associated with shelter, food, and reproduction are some of the most obvious examples. They argue that we may need to offer high rewards as an incentive to make sure that people are willing to do these tasks. The size of the rewards must be proportional to three factors:

1. *The importance of the task.* When a task is very important, very high rewards may be necessary to guarantee that it is done.
2. *The pleasantness of the task.* When the task is relatively enjoyable, there will be no shortage of volunteers, and high rewards need not be offered.

3. *The scarcity of the talent and ability necessary to perform the task.* When relatively few have the ability to perform an important task, high rewards are necessary to motivate this small minority to perform the necessary task.

Let us apply this reasoning to two tasks, health care and reproduction. The tasks of the physician require quite a bit of skill, intelligence beyond the average, long years of training, and long hours of work in sometimes unpleasant and stressful circumstances. To motivate people who have this relatively scarce talent to undertake such a demanding and important task, Davis and Moore would argue that we must hold out the incentive of very high rewards in prestige and income. Society is likely to determine, however, that little reward is necessary to motivate women to fill the even more vital task of reproducing and raising a new generation. Although the function is essential, the potential to fill the position is widespread (most women between 15 and 40 can do it), and the job has sufficient noncash attractions that no shortage of volunteers has arisen.

In many ways, this is a supply-and-demand argument that views inequality as a rational response to a social problem. This theoretical position is sometimes called consensus theory because it suggests that inequality is the result of societal agreement about the importance of social positions and the need to pay to have them filled.

Criticisms. This theory has generated a great deal of controversy. Among the major criticisms are these: (1) High demand (scarcity) can be artificially created by limiting access to good jobs. For example, keeping medical schools small and making admissions criteria unnecessarily stiff reduce supply and increase demand for physicians. (2) Social class background, sex, and race or ethnicity probably have more to do with who gets highly rewarded statuses than do scarce talents and ability. (3) Many highly rewarded statuses (rock stars and professional athletes, as well as plastic surgeons and speech writers) are hardly necessary to the maintenance of society.

The Conflict Perspective

A clear alternative to the Davis and Moore theory is given by scholars who adhere to conflict theory. They explain inequality as the result of class conflict rather than as a result of consensus about how to meet social needs. We review traditional Marxist thought first and then describe more recent applications of conflict theory to the study of inequality.

Marxist Theory. Marx argued that inequality was rooted in private ownership of the means of production. Those who own the means of production seek to maximize their own profit by minimizing the amount of return they must give to the proletarians, who have no choice but to sell their labor to the highest bidder. In this view, inequality is an outcome of private property, where the goods of society are owned by some and not by others. In Marxist theory, stratification is neither necessary nor justifiable. Inequality does not benefit society; it benefits only the rich.

Although Marx did not see inequality as either necessary or justifiable, he did see that it might be nearly inevitable. The reason lies in the division of labor. Almost any complex task, from teaching school to building automobiles, requires some task specialization: Some people build fuel pumps and others install them,

FOCUS ON YESTERDAY

A Community Without Inequality?

In 1920, a group of 90 young Jewish pioneers from Poland set up a commune in Palestine that attempted to eliminate inequality. Their successes and failures, described in a 1956 book by Melford Spiro, *Kibbutz: Venture in Utopia*, illuminate how difficult it is to eliminate inequality.

"Did it work? Partially."

The Goals

The settlers of Kiryat Yeddidum were Marxists. They hoped that by abolishing private property and investing ownership and control of the means of production in the entire community, they could eliminate all inequality—inequality of status and power as well as inequality in wealth, inequality between women and men as well as inequality between classes. They took the following steps.

1. *All property belonged to the community.* Even the clothes they wore were not their own. Each week, each of them checked out a different suit of clothing from the community laundry. In the beginning, they went so far toward equality that everybody got the same size!
2. *The emphasis was on community rather than on individuals.* Each couple or single person had a sparsely and identically furnished room for sleeping, but all activity beyond sleeping was expected to be communal: communal toilets, showers, dining rooms. It was regarded as selfish to want to be by yourself.
3. *Jobs were rotated.* Not all jobs are equally prestigious. People who manage have more power than those who milk cows; people whose work produces substantial profit have more prestige than those who do the laundry. In order to equalize these elements of inequality, job assignments were temporary and were rotated annually. Thus, one might manage one year, scrub toilets the next, and drive a tractor the third.

The Outcome

Did it work? Partially. The settlers established equality in material wealth, but not in prestige. The major difficulty was job rotation. Not everyone had the skills to do accounting. More important, in an agricultural community with a low level of mechanization, much of the work was so physically demanding that sex and age made a difference in how effective a worker was. Because the commune was living on the edge of subsistence, it could not afford to be less than totally efficient in allocating labor. Thus, strong men worked in the fields, where they made an immediate contribution to the community's livelihood, and women and old men worked in the laundry or the kitchen or scrubbed toilets. Out of economic necessity, these assignments, with their obvious inequalities in prestige, existed year after year rather than being rotated. These inequalities were bitterly resented.

Assessment

What lessons about the possibility of establishing equality can we draw from this attempt? First, the experience of Kiryat Yeddidum tells us that equality in material rewards is easier to establish than equality in prestige. Second, inequality in prestige *is* important; those with low status will find it galling. Third, equality in status and prestige probably does rest on effective job rotation.

Effective job rotation is very difficult to implement, however. Recognizing this difficulty, most groups and societies striving for equality have concentrated on equalizing differences in material wealth. Most have also been content to try to eliminate class inequality without tackling the more difficult issues of gender and age inequalities. These issues are addressed in more detail in Chapters 11 and 12.

some teach algebra and others teach poetry. To make such a division of labor work effectively, somebody has to coordinate the efforts of all the specialists. Individuals who do this coordination are in a unique position to pursue their own self-interest—to hire their own children in preference to others', to give themselves more rewards than they give others, and generally to increase the gap between themselves and those they coordinate. Marx's patron and coauthor, Friedrich Engels, explained it this way:

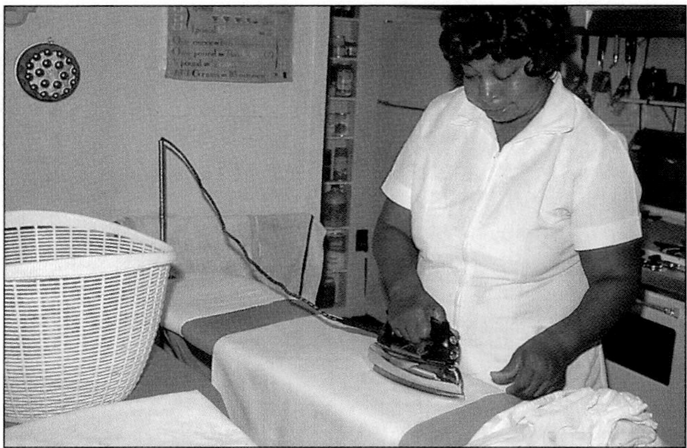

Which job is the hardest? Which one pays the most? Ironically, people who work the hardest often earn the least; they earn the least income and the least honor. A more critical problem for structural-functional theory is the issue of how these two jobs are assigned. Would you feel safe in concluding that the woman who irons for a living has less talent and ability than the white-collar worker? Critics point out that social class background and race are often more important than ability in determining who gets the good jobs and who gets the bad jobs.

> It is therefore the law of the division of labor that lies at the basis of the division into classes. But this does not prevent the division into classes from being carried out by means of violence, and robbery, trickery and fraud. It does not prevent the ruling class, once having the upper hand, from consolidating its power at the expense of the working class, from turning its social leadership into an intensified exploitation of the masses (Engels [1880] 1965, 79).

Modern Conflict Theory. During the early days of industrialization when Marx was writing, ownership and control were inseparable: Those who owned the factories also managed them. In modern capitalism, however, ownership may be divided among dozens or even thousands of stockholders, while management control is concentrated among a handful of expert managers. Thus, in the modern economy, control may exist independent of ownership (Wright 1985).

Modern conflict theory goes beyond Marx's emphasis on ownership to consider how control may affect the struggle over scarce resources (Grimes 1989). It shares with earlier Marxist theory the idea that those in control are able to oppress those who work for them by claiming the profits from their labor (Wright 1985). Conflicts of interest and manipulation of the less powerful by the more powerful are still the bases of inequality.

Criticisms. There seems to be little doubt that people who have control (through ownership or management) systematically use their power to extend and enhance their own advantage. Critics, however, question the conclusion that this means that inequality is necessarily undesirable and unfair. First, some people *are* harder working, smarter, and more talented than others. Unless forcibly held back, these people will pull ahead of the others—even without force, fraud, and trickery. Second, coordination and authority *are* functional.

A Contemporary Synthesis

Structural-functional theory and conflict theory address important issues in the explanation of inequality; each also has a blind side. Structural-functional theory disregards how power may be used to create and enhance inequality; conflict theory generally ignores the functions of inequality.

In 1989, Beegley provided a general theory of contemporary stratification that pulls together some ideas from structural-functional and conflict theory. His synthesis rests on three major points:

1. *Power is the major determinant of the distribution of scarce resources*. People who have power, whether because of ownership or because of control, will use that power to enhance, protect, and extend their resources. For example, they will try to shape the labor market in ways that benefit themselves.
2. *The distribution of power (and hence of scarce resources) is socially structured*. The level of poverty in a society, the salaries of rock stars, and the opportunities to get ahead depend on public and private policies. For example, if professional schools require annual tuitions of $20,000 and more a year, then it is almost automatic that most of the professionals of the next generation will come from today's advantaged families. One implication of this idea is that, if we wanted to, we could change this policy and increase access to professional statuses.
3. *Individuals can make a difference*. As we saw when we looked at the development of the self-concept, individual behavior is not wholly determined by social structures. Individual characteristics such as talent and ambition play a role. Thus, scarce talents and abilities may allow some to rise to the top despite a disadvantaged position in the social structure.

The first two of Beegley's points are drawn from modern conflict theory, the third from structural functionalism. Although his theory does allow a role for scarce talents and abilities, it focuses on the social structure of power as the major determinant of inequality.

Concept Summary A Comparison of Three Models of Stratification

Basis of Comparison	Structural-Functional Theory	Conflict Theory	Beegley's Synthesis
1. Society can best be understood as . . .	Groups *cooperating* to meet common needs	Groups *competing* for scarce resources	Groups competing for scarce resources
2. Social structures . . .	Solve problems and help society adapt	Maintain current patterns of inequality	Determine opportunities and their allocation
3. Causes of stratification	Importance of vital tasks, unequal ability, pleasantness of tasks	Unequal control of means of production maintained by force, fraud, and trickery	Inequalities of power
4. Conclusion about stratification	Necessary and desirable	Difficult to eliminate, but unnecessary and undesirable	Inevitably built into social structure; no value judgment
5. Strengths	Consideration of unequal skills and talents and necessity of motivating people to work	Consideration of conflict of interests and how those with control use the system to their advantage	Value free; recognizes that structure is more important than individual talents
6. Weaknesses	Ignores importance of power and inheritance in allocation of rewards; functional importance overstated	Ignores the functions of inequality and importance of individual differences	Applies only to modern capitalist societies

Conclusion. So why *do* Steven Spielberg and Troy Aikman make so much money? Neither appears to be engaged in force, fraud, or trickery or to be using his authority to exploit others. Beegley's theory suggests an explanation for their earnings. First, of course, Spielberg and Aikman are very good at what they do (see Beegley's third point). At least as important, however, is the fact that entertainment is a huge industry in the United States, which supports Beegley's second point. Finally, and this is Beegley's first point, the people who *control* the entertainment industry (as opposed to those who merely work in it) have incomes that dwarf Spielberg's and Aikman's. One of the reasons, in fact, that Spielberg makes more than Aikman is that, over the years, he has acquired control of his own production; Aikman still works for the owner of the Cowboys. Although it takes a stretch of the imagination to see Aikman as exploited, the professional football strike of the 1988 season illustrates the conflict of interest between management and labor even at this level. The fact that the players lost and the owners won also illustrates Beegley's first point: Those in control have the resources to protect and maintain their advantage.

The Determinants of Social Class Position

With each generation, the social statuses in a given society must be allocated anew. Some people will get the good positions, and some will get the bad ones; some will receive many scarce resources, and some will not. In a class system, this allocation process depends on two things: the characteristics of the individuals (their education, aspirations, skills, and so on) and the characteristics of the labor market. We refer to these, respectively, as micro- and macro-level factors that affect achievement.

Microstructure: Status Attainment

If *Sports Illustrated* gave you the job of predicting the top 20 college football teams in the country next year, you could go to the trouble of finding out the average height, weight, and experience level of each team's members, the dollars allocated to the athletic department, the years of coaching experience, and the attendance at games. From this information, you could devise some complex system of predicting the winners. You would probably do a better job with a lot less trouble, however, if you predicted that last year's winners will be this year's winners. The same thing is true in predicting winners and losers in the race for class, status, and power. The simplest and most accurate guess is based on social continuity.

American culture values achievement rather than ascription, and occupations are not directly inherited. Yet people tend to have occupations in a social class similar to that of their parents. How does this come about? The best way to describe the system is as an **indirect inheritance model.** Parents' occupations do not directly cause children's occupations, but a family's social class and income determine children's aspirations and opportunities (Blau 1994).

The **indirect inheritance model** argues that children have occupations in a social class similar to that of their parents because family's social class and income determine children's aspirations and opportunities.

Inherited Characteristics: Help and Aspirations. The best predictor of your eventual social class is your education—and the best predictor of your education is your parents' education. A small part of this effect is directly financial. Better-educated parents are more often able to afford their children's college expenses. Most of the impact of parents' education, however, is less direct. If your parents graduated from

Despite the fact that social class is not directly inherited in the United States, there is a remarkable degree of similarity in a family's social class across the generations. The same families that were middle and upper-middle class in one generation tend to be middle and upper-middle class two and three generations later. Each generation passes its attitudes and aspirations on to its children; more concretely, the family largely determines the opportunities that children have.

college or have middle-class jobs, then you have probably always assumed that you, too, would go to college. You automatically signed up for algebra and chemistry in high school. If your parents didn't graduate from high school and tend to think that education is a necessary evil, then you probably bypassed algebra for a shop or sewing class.

The atmosphere of the home and a parent's support and encouragement may have important effects on a child's success. Bright and ambitious lower-class children may find it hard to do well in school if they have to study at a noisy kitchen table amidst a group of people who think that their studies are a waste of time; middle-class children with even modest ambitions and intelligence may find it hard to fail within their very supportive environment.

The Wild Cards: Achievement Motivation and Intelligence. The social class environment in which a child grows up is the major determinant of educational attainment. There are, however, two wild cards that keep education from being directly inherited: achievement motivation and intelligence. Neither of these factors is strongly related to parents' social class, and both act as filters that allow people to rise above or fall below their parents' social class (Duncan, Featherman, and Duncan 1972).

Achievement motivation is the continual drive to match oneself against standards of excellence. Students who have this motivation are always striving for A's, are never satisfied with taking easy courses, and have a real need to compete. Not surprisingly, students with high achievement motivation do better than others in school.

Achievement motivation is the continual drive to match oneself against standards of excellence.

High achievement motivation appears to be the major reason for the remarkable social mobility of many recent Asian American immigrant groups in the United States. For example, Vietnamese Americans are twice as likely to be enrolled in college as the average American (Gardner, Robey, and Smith 1985).

Asian American families and culture value and strongly encourage high achievement. With high achievement motivation, some individuals from disadvantaged backgrounds can make it.

Intelligence is another important factor in determining educational and occupational success (Duncan, Featherman, and Duncan 1972). Because intelligent people are born into all social classes, intelligence is a factor that allows for both upward and downward intergenerational mobility. (Chapter 15 looks at the issue of social class and intelligence in greater detail.)

Summary. The indirect inheritance model summarizes the processes of individual status attainment. It shows how some people come to be well prepared to step into good jobs, while others lack the necessary skills or credentials. By themselves, however, skills and credentials do not necessarily lead to class, status, or power. The other variable in the equation is the labor market.

Macrostructure: The Labor Market

If there is a major economic depression, you will not likely be able to get a good job no matter what your education, achievement motivation, or aspirations. The character of the labor market and the structure of occupations it provides have a significant effect on individual achievements.

Within the last 90 years, the occupational structure of the United States has changed rapidly. As Figure 9.4 shows, the proportion of positions at the top has expanded dramatically during this century, providing opportunities for upward mobility. Despite this general improvement, the labor market is not equally open to all workers. Women and minorities especially have been virtually shut out of some high-earning occupations. No matter what their talents and credentials, they have found the labor market inhospitable. As an example of the effect that the structure of the labor market can have, consider that between 1960 and 1980, the racial composition of the National Basketball Association shifted from 80 percent white Americans to 80 percent African Americans. This shift did not occur

FIGURE 9.4
THE CHANGING OCCUPATIONAL STRUCTURE, 1900–1990

Since the turn of the century, the occupational structure of the United States has shifted away from farm labor. Today, there are many more white-collar, professional, and managerial jobs.

SOURCE: U.S. Bureau of the Census, 1975, 139; U.S. Department of Labor 1990, 30.

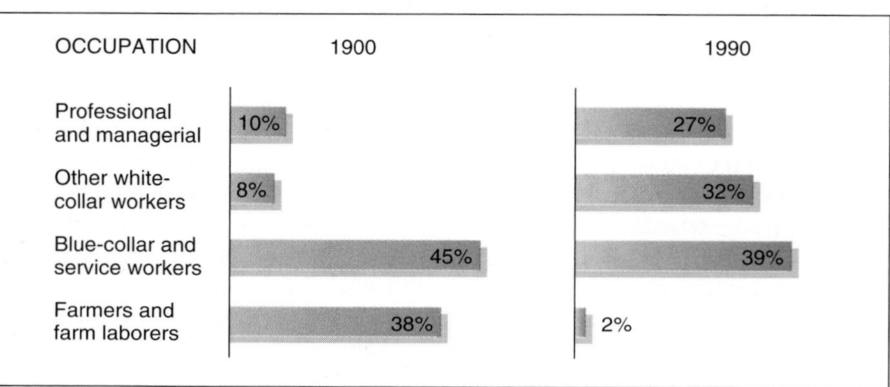

because African American basketball players suddenly got better; it was a function of the changed structure of the labor market. Employers were finally willing to hire African American players.

Labor market theorists suggest that the United States has a **segmented labor market:** one labor market for good jobs (usually in the big companies) and one labor market for not-so-good jobs (usually in small companies). Good jobs offer relatively high salaries, good benefits, and opportunities for career advancement; not-so-good jobs pay only the minimum wage or slightly more, have few or no benefits, and are usually "dead end" positions without chances for advancement. A management trainee in a large investment firm is an example of the former. Examples of the latter are a bartender and a restaurant waiter.

The **segmented labor market** parallels the dual economy. There is one labor market for good jobs and another labor market for not-so-good jobs.

The labor market is not just segmented according to the kinds of jobs offered but also according to the social characteristics of the workers themselves. Women and minorities are disproportionately directed into companies with low wages, low benefits, low security, and short career ladders. (The contemporary economic structure is discussed in more detail in Chapter 17.)

Summary. The stratification structure of any society depends on both macro- and micro-level processes. Some aspects of inequality are best explained on the macro level. For example, if we want to know what percent have good jobs or why some groups have poor jobs despite their credentials, then we look at the structure of the labor market and how it is changing. If we want to know which individuals are prepared to take the good jobs, then we need to look at micro-level processes that determine individual characteristics (Blau 1994).

The American Dream: Ideology and Reality

A system of stratification is an organized way of ensuring that some categories of individuals get more social rewards than others. As we have seen, often this means a great disparity not only in income but also in health, honor, and happiness. Yet, in most highly stratified systems, there are few successful revolutionary movements. For the most part, inequality is accepted as natural, even as God-given.

This acceptance of inequality indicates the role of the normative structure in reinforcing and justifying a system of stratification. Each system furnishes an **ideology**—a set of norms and values that rationalizes the existing social structure (Mannheim 1929). The ideology is built into the dominant cultural values of the society—often into its religious values. For example, the Hindu religion maintains that a low caste in this life is a punishment for poor performance in a previous life. If you live well in this life, however, you can expect to be promoted to a higher caste in the next life. Thus, the Hindu religion offers mobility (extragenerational mobility, we might call it) and also an incentive to accept one's lot in life. To attack the caste system would be equivalent to saying that the gods are unfair or the religion is stupid (Sharma 1995).

An **ideology** is a set of norms and values that rationalizes the existing social structure.

In the United States, the major ideology that justifies inequality is the *American Dream,* which suggests that equality of opportunity exists in the United States and that your position in the class structure is a fair reflection of what you deserve. That is, if you are worthy and if you work hard, you can succeed. Since your position comes entirely from your own efforts, no one but you can be blamed for your failure. The upper class is the most likely to believe that America is a land of opportunity and that everybody gets a fair shake, but most others believe this, too.

The preparation that you receive for the labor market—your education, training, and aspirations—have an enormous impact on whether you get a good or bad job. Nevertheless, your fate ultimately depends on the job market. If the aerospace industry is in a slump, even aeronautical engineers may be unemployable. Even in a booming economy, many labor markets implicitly discriminate against people on the basis of their age, sex, race, or ethnicity. These market factors are critical for understanding why some groups consistently have worse jobs and lower earnings than others.

There are critics, to be sure, especially among minority groups, such as the disenchanted person who stated, "The rich stole, beat, and took. The poor didn't start stealing in time, and what they stole, it didn't value nothing, and they were caught with that!" (Huber and Form 1973).

The critics, however, are few, and most of them are less interested in changing the rules of the game than in being dealt into it (Hochschild 1995). Americans believe in "fair shares" rather than in "equal shares" (Ryan 1981). They believe that people who work harder and people who are smarter deserve to get ahead. A typical attitude toward the wealthy is represented by the comments of one unemployed laborer: "If a person keeps his mind to it, and works and works, and he's banking it, hey, good luck to him!" (cited in Hochschild 1981, 116).

Variations on a Theme: The Rich, the Working Class, and the Poor

The United States is a middle-class nation. If given only three categories for self-identification, more than two-thirds of the population identifies itself as middle class. American norms and values are the norms and values of the middle class. Everybody else becomes a subculture. This section briefly reviews the special conditions of the nonmiddle classes in America.

The Upper Class

In 1992, it required a family income of "only" $145,244 a year to put one in the richest 5 percent. Thus, a variety of more-or-less ordinary salespersons, doctors, lawyers, and managers in towns across the nation qualify as being very rich compared with the majority. Although their incomes are nothing to sneeze at, most of this upper 5 percent is still in the middle class, albeit the upper-middle class. Like members of the working class, they would have a hard time making their mortgage payments if they lost their jobs.

The true upper class is the top 5 percent of the top 5 percent. There are nearly half a million millionaires in the United States—people whose assets total over $1 million. At the very top of the heap are the nearly 5,000 whose *earnings* in a single year top $1 million.

Every year, *Forbes* magazine provides a glimpse at the very rich by publishing profiles of the richest 400 people in the United States. (A review of the top 10 for 1995 appears in Table 9.3.) The average person who made it into the Forbes 400 was a 63-year-old white male with a degree from an Ivy League school. He made his fortune in manufacturing, the stock market, or media. Forty percent inherited their way to the top. Of the 214 who were self-made, few went from rags to riches; most got an excellent start: They had at least middle-class parents with business experience who sent their children to excellent schools. For example, William Henry Gates III dropped out of college at 19 to found Microsoft, a company that produces extremely popular software. At 39, he had a net worth of $15 billion. Gates, who got a perfect 800 on the math portion of the SAT, is obviously very smart in addition to being extraordinarily hardworking. He did not make it on grit and talent alone, however. He had the right background: His father is a prominent attorney in Seattle; his mother is on the University of Washington Board of Regents; and the college he dropped out of was Harvard ("The Forbes" 1995, 108–109).

TABLE 9.3
THE TEN RICHEST PEOPLE IN THE UNITED STATES, 1995

Each year, Forbes magazine publishes a list of the 400 richest people in the United States. About 40 percent of these fabulously wealthy individuals inherited their fortunes; two-thirds are largely individually responsible for generating their vast wealth. Their major avenues to riches were the stock market, manufacturing, and the media.

NAME, AGE	COLLEGE	ESTIMATED NET WORTH	MAJOR WEALTH SOURCE
WILLIAM HENRY GATES III, 39	Harvard (dropout)	$15 billion	Microsoft; self-made, son of prominent Seattle lawyers
WARREN BUFFETT, 65	Columbia	$12 billion	Stock market; self-made, with help of $100,000 family investment fund
JOHN KLUGE, 81	Columbia	$6.7 billion	Metromedia; self-made; began with a radio station in Washington D.C.
PAUL G. ALLEN, 42	Harvard	$6.1 billion	Microsoft stock shares, America On-line, and other investments
SUMNER REDSTONE, 72	Harvard	$4.8 billion	Viacom (movie and cable television); took over father's small chain of drive-in theaters
RICHARD DE VOS, 69 AND JAY VAN ANDEL, 71	None given	$4.3 billion each	Partners and founders of Amway; self-made; sons of electrician and car dealer, respectively; began Amway after several business failures
SAMUEL I. NEWHOUSE, 67 DONALD NEWHOUSE, 66	None given None given	$4.3 billion each	Advance Publications; inherited from father but greatly expanded
HELEN WALTON, 76 S. ROBSON WALTON, 51 JOHN T. WALTON, 49 JIM C. WALTON, 47 ALICE L. WALTON, 46	Oklahoma Columbia None given None given Trinity	$21.5 billion, shared	Walmart; inherited from father
RONALD PERELMAN, 52	Wharton	$4.2 billion	Finance (leveraged buyouts); self-made, but as child sat in on father's business deals
LAWRENCE J. ELLISON, 51	U. of Illinois (dropout)	$4.2 billion	Helped develop first IBM compatible main frame; self-made

SOURCE: "The Forbes Four Hundred" 1995, 108–113.

The very rich not only have many more choices in their lives than do those whose next mortgage payment depends on their keeping their job but they also have the capacity to affect large numbers of others through their choices. By controlling media resources, contributing money to political campaigns, building museums, and deciding to open or close manufacturing plants, they have the power to affect the lives of millions of ordinary citizens. Yet we know relatively little about the lives of the very rich. Although occasionally their stories and pictures appear in the news, they are hardly available to social researchers.

The one aspect of the rich that has been extensively studied is their attitudes toward inequality. A social scientist who has made a career of studying elites concludes that the people at the top "share a consensus about the fundamental values

When was the last time you wore a mink coat to a football game? Even if you had one, you probably wouldn't wear it for fear of getting beer and popcorn on it. Such fears are irrelevant for these wealthy patrons of the Dallas Cowboys. Much more important than their luxurious lifestyle, however, is the ability of the wealthy to affect the lives and incomes of the rest of us. The ability to create or terminate jobs, affect elections, and subsidize education and the arts is the real focus of sociological study of the wealthy.

of private enterprise, limited government, and due process of law. . . . [They] believe in equality of opportunity rather than absolute equality" (Dye 1983, 273). As conflict theory would suggest, they are interested in maintaining a system that has been good to them.

The Working Class

Who are the members of the working class? The answer is determined partly by occupation, partly by education, and partly by self-definition. Generally, the working class includes those who work in blue-collar industries and their families. They are the men and women who work in chemical, automobile, and other manufacturing plants; they load warehouses, drive trucks, and build houses. Although they sometimes receive excellent wages and benefits, it is the working class that suffers 10–15 percent unemployment during economic recessions and slumps.

To find out what life was like for the working class, the sociologist David Halle (1984) spent seven years studying the blue-collar employees of a New Jersey chemical plant. His participant observation study involved hanging around in the plant itself and going to taverns, football games, and Christmas parties. Because of his own sex, Halle found it easier to observe working-class men than women, so his conclusions focus primarily on men. His work suggests that the following dimensions make working-class life distinct from that of the middle class: education, economic prospects, leisure, and gender differences.

Education. The working class is more highly educated than it used to be. A majority are probably high school graduates. Still, an eleventh-grade education is more common than a year of college. More importantly, many did not do well in school. Finding school alienating and its curriculum irrelevant to their future job prospects, many young people in this study did not absorb the school's middle-class values.

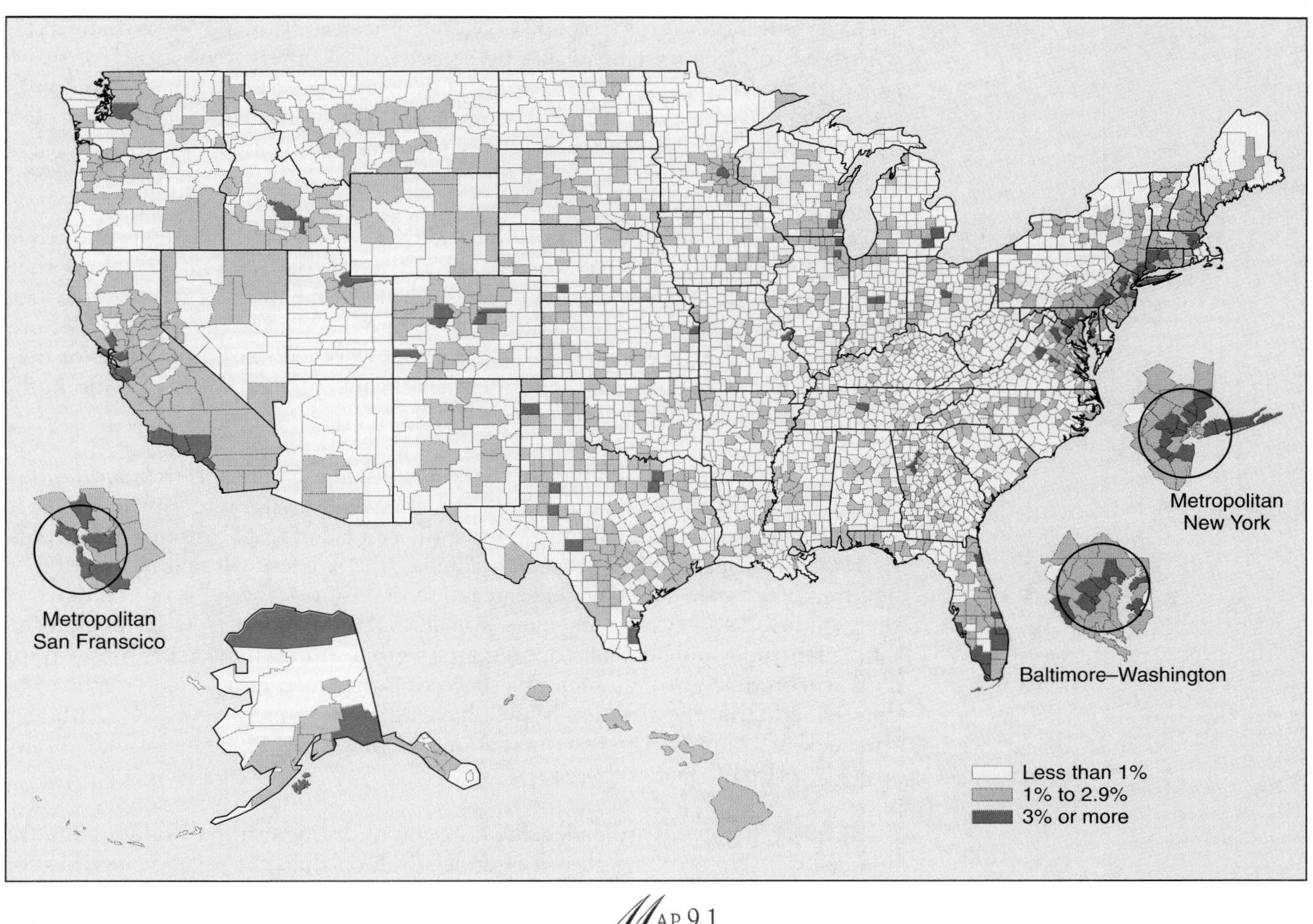

MAP 9.1
WHERE THE AFFLUENT LIVE

SOURCE: *Atlas of Contemporary America* ©1994, p. 124.

> What was school like? It was horrible, horrible! . . . They [the teachers] were cuckoos. They gave you *Romeo and Juliet* to read, and I looked at it and I said, "What is this! What has this got to do with me?" I looked at the flyleaf. . . . And I saw Joe Smith's name from three years ago. I knew he was digging ditches now, so I said to myself, "This book didn't do anything for him. What's it going to do for me?" (Halle 1984, 49).

Economic Prospects. Quite a few members of the working class have incomes as good as or better than those of the lower-middle class. Some make as much as or more than public school teachers and people in retail sales. As a result, they live in the same neighborhoods as these members of the lower-middle class. Their economic prospects differ from those of their white-collar neighbors, however, in two ways. First, they have little or no chance of promotion. The barrier between manual labor and management is virtually impassable. The height of one's earning power may be reached at age 25. Second, layoffs and plant closings expose them to more economic uncertainty.

As a result of low prospects and economic uncertainty, members of the working class tend to place a higher value on security than others. One aspect of this is home ownership. Nearly three quarters of the working class own their own homes. For most, it is their major financial asset and their only effective savings plan. Their resulting interest in property taxes, property values, and neighborhood maintenance drives much of their political activity.

Leisure. While middle-class workers may have a hard time separating their leisure time from their work time (going to the office on Saturdays, taking their work home with them, or having business dinners), members of the working class have no difficulty separating work from leisure—and they much prefer leisure. According to Halle, working-class men do their work without joy and live for their leisure. When they dream of the future, they dream of a new boat or a cabin in the mountains, not of a better job.

Gender Differences. Scholars of working-class life emphasize the sharp differences between the worlds of men and women. Men's leisure interests lie largely in sex-segregated activities: watching football, going hunting, drinking in taverns. Even when social activity is based on couples, the women will talk in the kitchen and the men in the den. Gender segregation of leisure activities is not confined to the working class, but working-class women and men appear to have less in common than their middle-class counterparts. Perhaps more important, the working class is more likely to follow norms suggesting that men and women ought to be different and that they "naturally" will have different interests and roles. Although this lack of common interests may damage some marriages, social class is not strongly related to marital happiness.

Summary. Income is an inadequate criterion to distinguish the working from the middle class. The working class is often less well off than the middle class, but the primary distinctions are in occupation, education, and lifestyle rather than income.

The Poor in America

Each year, the U.S. government fixes a poverty level that is calculated to be the amount of money a family would need to meet the minimum requirements of a decent standard of living. The poverty level is adjusted for family size, and in 1993, the poverty level for a nonfarm family of four was $14,763 (U.S. Bureau of the Census 1995, Table 746). Under this definition, 39.3 million people, 15 percent of the population, were classified as poor in 1993 (U.S. Bureau of the Census 1995, Table 747).

Who Are the Poor? Poverty cuts across several dimensions of society. It is found among white Americans as well as nonwhites, in rural areas as much as in urban centers, in families as well as in single households. As Table 9.4 indicates, more than half (51 percent) of the poor in 1992 were too old or too young to work. Of those in the working ages, a substantial proportion could not earn a wage that would lift them out of poverty.

A significant portion of the women and children who live in poverty do so simply because they have no husband or father in their house. Granted that having a

TABLE 9.4
THE POPULATION BELOW THE POVERTY LEVEL IN 1992

Many of the people below the poverty level in 1992 were unable to work. Many of those who were able to work could not have earned a wage that would put them above the poverty level.

	MILLIONS OF PEOPLE	PERCENTAGE OF POVERTY POPULATION	PERCENTAGE OF GROUP IN POVERTY
TOTAL	39.3	100%	15.1%
RACE AND HISPANIC ORIGIN			
WHITE	26.2	66	12.2
BLACK	10.9	29	33.1
HISPANIC ORIGIN[a]	8.1	18	30.6
RESIDENCE			
CENTRAL CITIES	15.6	42	20
OTHER URBAN	11.7	32	10
NONMETROPOLITAN	9.5	26	17
LIVING IN FAMILIES			
MALE HEADED	12.8	35	8
FEMALE HEADED	14.6	37	38.7
LIVING ALONE			
MALE	3.3	8	18.1
FEMALE	5.1	13	25.7
CHILDREN UNDER 18	14.9	40	22.7
PEOPLE OVER 65	3.8	11	12.2

SOURCE: U.S. Bureau of the Census 1993c, 1995.
[a]Hispanics may be of any race. Because almost all Hispanics are also included in counts of the white or black population, total numbers add to more than 100 percent.

man in the house is no guarantee of being out of poverty (12.8 million male-headed families are below the poverty level), it does significantly decrease the likelihood of being in poverty: Eight percent of all male-headed families are below the poverty level, whereas 39 percent of all female-headed families are below that level.

Although some categories of people, such as minorities and those in female-headed households, top the poverty charts year after year, one study shows that there is less continuity than one might suppose in the individual experience of poverty. A study of a large sample of Americans between 1969 and 1978 found that one quarter of all Americans were poor at least one year between 1969 and 1978, but only one third of those who were poor in 1978 had been poor for eight or more of those 10 years. The persistently poor fell into one of two categories: They were elderly, or they lived in households headed by a black woman (Duncan 1984).

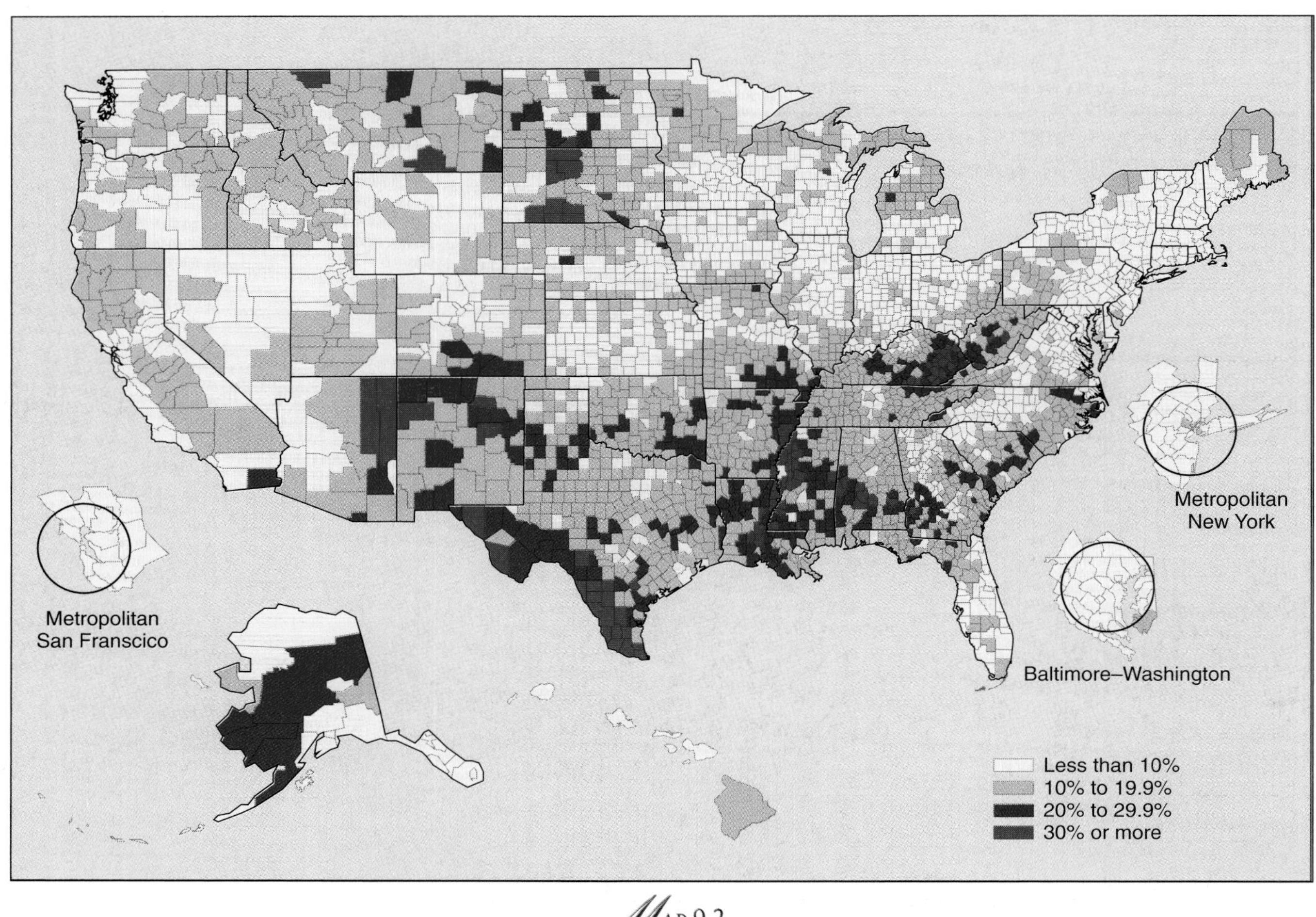

MAP 9.2
WHERE THE POOR LIVE

SOURCE: *Atlas of Contemporary America* ©1994, p. 120.

Absolute poverty is the inability to provide the minimum requirements of life.

Relative poverty is the inability to maintain what your society regards as a decent standard of living.

The **underclass** is the group whose members are unemployed and unemployable, a substratum that is alienated from American institutions.

How Poor Are the Poor? An important issue that arises in discussing American poverty is how poor the poor actually are. Two concepts are important here: absolute poverty and relative poverty. **Absolute poverty** means the inability to provide the minimum requirements of life. **Relative poverty** means the inability to maintain what your society regards as a decent standard of living.

The poor in America come in both forms. Those who live at or close to the poverty level have a roof over their heads and food to eat. On the other hand, their car is broken down and so is the television, the landlord is threatening to evict them, they are eating too much macaroni, and they cannot afford to take their children to the doctor or the dentist. Although they may not be absolutely poor, they are deprived in terms of what Americans regard as a decent standard of living. There are also Americans who are absolutely poor, the truly disadvantaged: These include the underclass and the homeless.

At the bottom of the social class hierarchy is a group that has been called the **underclass,** a group whose members are unemployed and unemployable, a substratum that is alienated from American institutions (Myrdal 1962). Although two-thirds of those in poverty are white, and there is indeed a white underclass (Whitman and Friedman 1994), the underclass in America is disproportionately black. It is a group characterized by high nonmarital birthrates, high drug use, high murder rates, and high unemployment rates (Wilson 1987). Children born in this environment start at the bottom and will almost undoubtedly stay there. When a researcher asked some young Italian-American boys from the underclass what they expected to be doing in 20 years, he got the following replies (MacLeod 1987, 61):

> STONEY: Hard to say. I could be dead tomorrow. Around here, you gotta take life day by day.
>
> FRANKIE: I don't f—— know. Twenty years. I may be f——— dead. I live a day at a time. I'll probably be in the f—— pen.
>
> SHORTY: Twenty years? I'm going to be in jail.

Most college students feel poor. Their money runs out before the end of the month, they buy gas $5 worth at a time, and they are always in debt and overcharged on their Visa. This poverty is generally only temporary and very relative, however. There are many Americans who are truly poor. They are not only without income but are alienated from American society. They may be illiterate or nearly so, cut off completely from the major currents of American life, and living one day at a time. The indirect inheritance process makes it extremely unlikely that these children will break out of their parents' social class.

None of these young men mentioned work as part of their future. All of them use drugs heavily; all are just barely literate; few will graduate from high school. Their futures seem very likely to be as bleak as they predict.

Not ordinarily considered a part of the underclass, the **homeless** are also truly disadvantaged. There are probably 500,000 homeless people in the United States. Many of them are single adults; but perhaps one quarter of the homeless are families with children. Not only do they lack a roof over their heads but many also eat one meal a day or less. They are homeless, hungry, and often ill. By any standards, they are absolutely poor. As discussed earlier (Chapter 1), some of these people are mentally ill or have substance abuse problems; many are simply unable to match their low earning ability with high rents.

Causes of Poverty. Earlier in this chapter, we said that both micro- and macro-level processes are at work in determining social class position. The causes of poverty are simply a special case of these larger processes. At the micro level, poverty is explained by the hypothesis that there is a "culture of poverty"; at the macro level, poverty is explained by the lack of an adequate structure of opportunity.

THE CULTURE OF POVERTY: BLAMING THE VICTIM? The indirect inheritance model suggests that people born into poverty are likely to stay there: They have poorer preparation for school, lower aspirations, and less help at every step of the way.

The **culture of poverty** is a set of values that emphasizes living for the moment rather than thrift, investment in the future, or hard work.

An additional mechanism that has been proposed to explain the inheritance of poverty is what Oscar Lewis (1969), an anthropologist, called the **culture of poverty.** Lewis argued that in rich societies, people who are poor develop a set of values that protects their self-esteem and maximizes their ability to extract enjoyment from dismal circumstances. This set of values—the "culture of poverty"—emphasizes living for the moment rather than thrift, investment in the future, or hard work. Recognizing that success is not within their reach, that no matter how hard they work or how thrifty they are, they will not make it, the poor come to value living for the moment. Like Stoney and Frankie, they live one day at a time.

The culture-of-poverty hypothesis fits neatly into American ideology, and a substantial majority of Americans agree that the poor are poor because of their values. In one survey, the two reasons most often endorsed as causes of poverty were that the poor "are not motivated because of welfare" and "lack . . . drive and perseverance" (Smith and Stone 1989). Blaming failure—or success—on personal characteristics, however, overlooks the role of social structure in shaping both values and opportunities.

THE STRUCTURE OF OPPORTUNITY. The culture-of-poverty hypothesis implicitly blames the poor for perpetuating their condition. Critics of this hypothesis suggest that we cannot explain poverty by looking only at micro-level processes. To understand poverty, they argue, we need to look at the structures of opportunity. If there are no jobs available, then we don't need to psychoanalyze people in order to figure out why they are poor.

Two structural issues are particularly critical for understanding contemporary poverty: the changing labor market and the growing link between education and wages. As we documented in Figure 9.4, the shift from an agricultural to an industrial society produced major structural pressure for upward mobility earlier in this century. Now, at the end of the century, the de-industrialization of America is squeezing the lower middle of the American occupational structure and creating structural pressure for downward mobility among the traditional working class: Good jobs have virtually disappeared for the high school graduate who has no advanced training. Instead of the good union jobs that their parents held, today's high school graduates often find themselves working at dead-end jobs for the minimum wage. A little arithmetic shows that the minimum wage means poverty.

This macrostructural approach to poverty suggests that a major cause of poverty is the absence of good jobs. The issue is a critical one, and we will look at the changing occupational structure in more detail in Chapter 17.

The Future of Inequality: Social Policy in the United States

If the competition is fair, inequality is acceptable to most Americans. The question is how to ensure that no one has an unfair advantage. Social policy has taken three different approaches to this: taxing inheritances, outlawing discrimination, and creating special educational programs.

Estate Taxes

The policy regarding estate, or inheritance, taxes is designed to reduce the direct inheritance of social position, to create greater equality at the start of the race. There is substantial consensus that although it is acceptable for ambitious, lucky, or clever persons to amass large fortunes, it is not fair that their children should start their race with such a large advantage. Thus, since 1931, the United States has had a progressive estate tax. The maximum tax has varied over the years from 50 to 90 percent of the estate.

In fact, however, inheritance taxes have not significantly reduced unequal advantage. If wealthy individuals die at 70, their children are already middle aged. The $90,000 the parents spent to give them the best private education money could buy, the new homes they bought for the children when they married, the businesses they set them up in, the trusts they set up for their grandchildren—none of these are part of the estate. By the time the parents die, the children have already been established as rich themselves (Lebergott 1975). Unless we ban private schools, transfers of money to one's children, and giving one's children good jobs, this inheritance is outside the scope of public policy.

Outlawing Discrimination

Antidiscrimination and affirmative-action laws are not aimed at reducing the inequalities that one starts the race with; rather, they attempt to ensure that no unfair obstacles are thrown in the way during the race. Antidiscrimination laws have had some effect. Able people have been and still are held back unfairly. If the race itself is not rigged, however, those who work very hard and are very able can overcome the handicaps they begin with. Because people start out with unequal backgrounds, however, they do not have an equal chance of success just by virtue of running the same course.

EDUCATION

Education is widely believed to be the key to reducing unfair disadvantages associated with poverty. Prekindergarten classes designed to provide intellectual stimulation for children from deprived backgrounds, special courses for those who don't speak standard English, and loan and grant programs to enable the poor to go to school as long as their ability permits them to do so—all these are designed to increase the chances that students from lower-class backgrounds will get an education.

The programs have had some success. Certainly, colleges and universities see many more students from disadvantaged backgrounds than they used to. Because students spend only about 35 hours a week at school, however, and over 130 hours a week with their families and neighbors, the school cannot reasonably overcome the entire deficit that exists for disadvantaged children. A study entitled the Beginning School Study documents the fact that poor children and better-off children perform at almost the same level in first- and second-grade mathematics while school is in session. For children in poverty, however, every summer means a loss in learning, whereas every summer means a gain for those not in poverty (Entwisle and Alexander 1992). The home environments of less-advantaged children do not include trips to the library and other activities that encourage them to use and remember their schoolwork. Consequently, for every step they take at school, they slide back half a step at home during the summer.

CONCLUSION

This review of programs designed to reduce unfair advantages or disadvantages leads to several conclusions. First, the family is at the root of the inheritance of both advantage and disadvantage. As long as some people are born in tenements or shacks, as long as their parents are uneducated and have bad grammar and small

Headstart programs and other educational programs alone cannot reasonably be expected to yield equality of opportunity. If the children in these two pictures went to the same school, their achievements would probably be very different. Equality of opportunity can only be achieved where there is already substantial equality in background. When children come to school from very unequal backgrounds, their achievements in school are likely to repeat the patterns of their parents.

vocabularies, and as long as they have no encyclopedias or intellectual stimulation—while others are born to educated parents with standard speech patterns who flood them with intellectual stimulation and opportunity—there can never be true equality of opportunity. To some extent, the pursuit of equal opportunity will come at the expense of the family: Any attempt to reduce inheritance of status requires weakening the influence of parents on their children.

In any culture, individuals espouse values that conflict with one another and values that are so idealistic that few attempt to live by them. America's ambivalent feelings about inequality are no exception. Do we want equal opportunity enough to pay the costs, or will it remain, like premarital chastity and marital stability, an ideal but not a reality?

APPLICATIONS IN DIVERSITY

SUBSIDIES, INCENTIVES, AND WELFARE—WHO BENEFITS?

The U.S. budget deficit has soared to over one trillion dollars; and despite campaign promises, neither Reagan, Bush, nor Clinton has managed substantially to reduce it. Middle-class families complain bitterly about their increasing tax burden and point their finger at the cost of antipoverty programs such as Medicaid and the former federal Aid to Families with Dependent Children and Food Stamp programs. But if lawmakers want to get control over the budget, they will need to carefully consider the issue of who gets what.

Can you answer the following questions about "welfare" benefits?

1. Does the government spend more on: (a) job training for the poor; (b) Headstart for low-income children, (c) Women, Infants, and Children nutrition subsidies, or (d) health care for the richest 10 percent of elderly Medicare beneficiaries?
2. Government housing subsidies end up going: (a) ten times as much to the poor as the middle class, (b) five times as much to the poor, (c) more to the middle class than the poor, or (d) about equally to both groups?
3. Taking spending programs and tax subsidies together, on the average, which of the following gets the most money in federal benefits: (a) a person with income less than $10,000, (b) a person with income from $10,000 to $40,000, (c) a person with income from $40,000 to $100,000, or (d) a person with income of more than $100,000? (Adapted from Waldman 1992, 56)

The correct answer to Question 1 is d; in 1989, the government spent more for medical care for well-off seniors than it did for all of the other programs combined. The answer to Question 2 is c; taking tax credits for mortgage interest and other home ownership tax breaks into account, the federal government spends four times as much to support the housing of middle- and upper-income families as it does to house the poor. Finally, the answer to Question 3 is d; if the entire range of subsidies, incentives, and welfare programs is considered, an average upper-income individual gets considerably more than a typical poor person, even though it is middle- and upper-middle-class individuals who are most likely to complain that the government is ignoring them.

According to a study by one conservative taxpayers' group, the average person with an income over $100,000 receives direct cash benefits—like social security—that are slightly higher than those received by persons with income of less than $10,000. If tax breaks such as mortgage interest deductions, health care reimbursement accounts, and IRAs are also considered, the poor receive substantially less than families with incomes ranging from $30,000 to $100,000 a year. The average benefit for the wealthiest group, $9,283, is highest of all.

Nevertheless, in Oregon, angry taxpayers have insisted that welfare mothers be required to work for their assistance. In Nebraska, legislators are currently considering a maximum two-year period of eligibility for welfare benefits.

APPLICATIONS IN DIVERSITY

Meanwhile, Senator Hank Brown from Colorado was defeated on a proposal in the early 1990s that would have cut government payments to a farm family for holding land out of production if the family's income exceeded $120,000.

U.S. census figures show that the portion of the benefit pie that goes to the poor has been shrinking for the past 25 years, while the portion going to the rest of the country has grown. As we grapple with the federal budget deficit, it would be wise to consider again the question, "Just who are those welfare 'kings and queens'?"

SOURCE: Steve Waldman, 1992, "Benefits 'R' Us," *Newsweek* (August 10), 56–58; Michael Wines, 1994, "Taxpayers Are Angry. They're Expensive Too," *New York Times*, November 20, E5.

THINKING CRITICALLY

What do you think? Should the federal government limit medical care for well-off seniors in order to begin to reduce the budget deficit? Why don't people think of Medicare for well-off seniors as "welfare"? Why don't people think of home ownership tax breaks as "welfare"? Now that legislation has been enacted to limit welfare for the poor, what federal policies or legislation might be enacted to limit welfare for the middle class? For the wealthy? Which social class most needs welfare?

SOCIOLOGY ON THE NET

It is always fun to find out who is the richest of the rich so let's go to the "List of Lists"!

`http://hoovweb.hoovers.com`

Once you are on the Hoover home page, open the selection called **Who's On Top?** and then click on the **List of Lists**. Take your pick, but be certain that you read the **Forbes 400 Richest Americans**. How many of these names do you recognize? Do you shop at their stores? Do you buy their gasoline? Do you root for any of their professional sports teams? If you were on this list how would your life be changed? What would remain the same and what would you do differently?

We can dream about wealth, but the probability of ever being on this list is very slim. In fact there are far more people living in poverty than there are millionaires. Poverty is defined as a relative inability to subsist. What is the so-called "poverty level" and how does it vary with family size?

`http://aspe.os.dhhs.gov/poverty/poverty.htm`

We have reached the United States Department of Health and Human Services. Browse around and check out the various offerings. When you have scrolled down near the bottom of the menu, click on **The 1996 HHS Poverty Guidelines**. Read this brief summary. Exactly what is a poverty guideline? Why are there different guidelines for Alaska and Hawaii. How would you live if your family fell within these parameters? How do people that live in poverty differ from those on the Forbes 400 Richest Americans list? Who do you think lives longer and has better health?

In the past decade there has been a significant shift in the distribution of wealth in the United States.

http://www.census.gov/population/pop-profile/toc.html

We have reached a very rich source of data and information. It is the United States Census Bureau Population Profiles. You may wish to **bookmark** this address because we will return to it many times throughout these exercises. Scroll down to the section entitled **Money Income**. Open this document and read it thoroughly. Pay particular attention to the colored graph showing the changes in household income by quintile. What has been the trend in income since 1989 for the lowest 20%? For the middle 60%? For the top 20%? And for the top 5%? Who are the winners and the losers? (Hint: Calculate who had the largest percentage increase and who had the largest percentage decrease in income from 1989 through 1993.) Do you support a tax break for the rich?

SUMMARY

1 Stratification is distinguished from simple inequality in that (1) it is based on social roles or membership in social statuses rather than on personal characteristics and (2) it is supported by norms and values that justify unequal rewards.

2 Marx believed that there was only one important dimension of stratification: class. Weber added two further dimensions. Most sociologists now rely on Weber's three-dimensional view of stratification, which embraces class, status, and power.

3 Inequality in income and wealth is substantial in the United States and has changed little over the generations. This inequality has widespread consequences and affects every aspect of our lives. Although the negative consequences of being in the working class or lower class are less than they were 70 years ago, members of the lower class and working class continue to be disadvantaged in terms of health, happiness, and lifestyle.

4 Structural-functional theorists use a supply-and-demand argument to suggest that inequality is a functional way of sorting people into positions; inequality is necessary and justifiable. Conflict theorists believe that inequality arises from conflict over scarce resources; those with the most power manipulate the system to enhance and maintain their advantage.

5 Beegley provides a contemporary synthesis of conflict and structural-functional theories. His theory argues that power and social structure are critical factors, but it allows some role for individual characteristics.

6 Allocation of people into statuses includes macro and micro processes. At the macro level, the labor market sets the stage by creating demands for certain statuses. At the micro level, the status attainment process is largely governed by indirect inheritance.

7 There is a great deal of continuity in social class over the generations. In the United States, this inheritance of social class is indirect and works largely through education. Achievement motivation and intelligence, however, are factors that allow for upward and downward mobility.

8 In spite of high levels of inequality, most people in any society accept the structure of inequality as natural or just. This shared ideology is essential for stability. In the United States, this ideology is the American Dream, which suggests that success or failure is the individual's choice.

9 Approximately 15 percent of the American population is below the poverty level. Many of the poor are children or elderly people. Although some part of poverty

may be due to micro-level processes (the culture of poverty and indirect inheritance), the structure of opportunity determines how extensive poverty is in a society.

10 Because families pass their social class on to their children, any attempt to reduce inequality must take aim at the intergenerational bond between parents and children and must reduce the ability of parents to pass on their wealth and values.

11 The portion of federal monies going to the poor has been shrinking over the last quarter century, while the portion going to the rest of the country has grown.

SUGGESTED READINGS

BARLETT, Peggy F. 1993. *Rural Realities: Family Farms in Crisis*, Chapel Hill: University of North Carolina Press. A study of poverty in the Midwestern Corn Belt that reminds us that stratification and poverty are not peculiar to urban America.

ELLIS, Lee (ed.) 1994. *Social Stratification and Socioeconomic Inequality*. Westport, Conn.: Praeger. An up-to-date edited collection of empirical and theoretical writings on social stratification, primarily in the United States.

GRUSKY, David B. (ed.) 1994. *Social Stratification: Class, Race, and Gender in Sociological Perspective*. Boulder, CO: Westview Press. A collection of readings on the intersection of race, gender, and social class in the U.S. stratification system today.

HURST, Charles E. 1992. *Social Inequality: Forms, Causes, and Consequences*. Boston: Allyn and Bacon. A sociology textbook on social stratification.

HOCHSCHILD, Jennifer L. 1995. *Facing up to the American Dream: Race, Class, and the Soul of the Nation*. Princeton, NJ: Princeton University Press. A book that examines the extent to which the American Dream is inaccessible to many Americans and addresses the issue of why there is so little support for redistribution among America's poor.

LENSKI, Gerhard. 1966. *Power and Privilege: A Theory of Social Stratification*. New York: McGraw-Hill. A classic, this major work distinguishes the fundamental characteristics found in different types of societies, particularly in terms of socially structured inequality.

MCFATE, Katherine, Roger Lawson, and William Julius Wilson. 1995. *Poverty, Inequality, and the Future of Social Policy: Western States in the New World Order*. New York, NY: Russell Sage Foundation. A contemporary discussion of the incidences of poverty and inequality throughout the world, with emphasis on policy decisions that will affect the future.

PATTERSON, James T. 1994. *America's Struggle against Poverty, 1900–1994*. Cambridge, Mass.: Harvard University Press. A history of poverty, poor people, and poverty legislation in the United States during this century.

RUBIN, Lillian B. 1992. *Worlds of Pain: Life in the Working-Class Family*. New York: Basic Books. A second edition (with a new introduction) of Rubin's 1972 qualitative study of 50 white, working-class couples compared with 25 white professional middle-class couples. The book explores all facets of their lives: gender roles, childrearing, and leisure activities, among others.

SHARMA, K.L. (ed.). 1995. *Social Inequality in India: Profiles of Caste, Class, Power, and Social Mobility*. Jaipur: Rawat Publications. A collection of theoretical, historical, and empirical essays on the topics of caste and class in India.

WILSON, William Julius. 1987. *The Truly Disadvantaged: The Inner City, the Underclass, and Public Policy*. Chicago: University of Chicago Press. A strong statement about the growing American underclass by one of the nations' most prominent experts. Wilson argues convincingly for new government programs to put a floor under all citizens.

CHAPTER 10

International Inequalities

OUTLINE

THREE WORLDS

THE HUMAN SUFFERING INDEX

INEQUALITY AND DEVELOPMENT—TWO THEORIES
Modernization Theory
World System Theory

GLOBAL PERSPECTIVE: CASE STUDY: **Russia as a Second-World Nation**

FOCUS ON THE ENVIRONMENT: **Economic Development, the Environment and the Second World**

THIRD WORLD DEPENDENCY
Forms of Economic Dependency
The Consequences of Dependency

COMPETITION, CHANGE, AND INTERNATIONAL RELATIONSHIPS
Third World Challenges to the Status Quo
First World Responses

TWO CASE STUDIES: HAITI AND THE UNITED STATES
The Third World: Haiti
The First World: The United States

THE CONFLICT PERSPECTIVE ON INTERNATIONAL INEQUALITY: THE THIRD WORLD AS A MARKET

APPLICATIONS IN DIVERSITY: **What Roles Do Third World Women Play in Development?**

PROLOGUE

Have You Ever . . . visited another country and been struck by the poverty there? Heard about beggars in some other countries and how tourists can try to avoid them? Read about crime in some foreign countries and how international travelers need to watch out?

James Yuenger (1994) of the *Chicago Tribune* went to Nigeria, then wrote about it in his paper. "Hello, sucker," his article began, "and welcome to the Lagos airport, a gigantic system organized to pry into your pockets." Yuenger wrote that five different government agencies were working at the airport—immigration, state security, airport police, local police, and customs—and all were "equally and unreservedly venal."

While examining his passport, immigration officers demanded $200 not to report him as a spy. Picking up his luggage, Yuenger found the lock broken and the contents rifled. To get through customs, he had to give the official $60, which she put into her pocket. After leaving the airport, Yuenger was stopped by a uniformed man who hopped into his taxi and demanded his passport, then broadly smiled, asking, "Do you have something for me?" Yuenger concluded that at the Lagos airport, extortion is "business as usual."

Why? A sociological imagination prompts us to look beyond the individual personalities of the Nigerian officials. With a sociological perspective, we would ask how social structure bears on what happened to Yuenger. On average, Nigerians earn just $320 a year; they are much less well off than American tourists. Might such economic disparity have had something to do with Yuenger's misfortune?

This chapter examines international inequalities. Social science could not have advised Yuenger on what exactly to do about his plight. But it can help to explain it.

Vast inequality is a central fact in today's world. In 1993, the average U.S. citizen produced $24,750 worth of goods and services; the average citizen of Mozambique produced only $80 worth. The average American will live to age 76 compared with age 46 for the average person living in Mozambique (Population Reference Bureau 1995). The massive disparities that exist not only in wealth and health but also in security and justice are the driving mechanism of current international relationships. This chapter focuses on the inequalities of our international system.

THREE WORLDS

In discussing international inequality, we use a common typology that classifies countries on the basis of their economic position in the world. As we saw in Chapter 9, we can think of three general social classes in the U.S. stratification system—upper, middle, and lower. Similarly, the world is stratified into roughly three levels. In everyday language, these levels are the First World, the Second World, and the Third World.

The **First World** consists of those rich nations that have relatively high degrees of economic and political autonomy: the United States, the Western European nations, Japan, Canada, Australia, and New Zealand. Taken together, these nations make up roughly 16 percent of the world's population, produce between 55

The **First World** consists of those rich nations that have relatively high degrees of economic and political autonomy: the United States, Western Europe, Japan, Canada, Australia, and New Zealand.

and 60 percent of the gross world product, and consume approximately 54 percent of the world's energy (Chirot 1986). Politically, economically, scientifically, and technologically, they dominate the globe.

The **Second World,** mainly Russia and the former Communist bloc nations in Eastern Europe, comprises countries that hold an intermediate position in the international stratification system.

The **Second World** comprises countries that hold an intermediate position in the international stratification system. These countries are richer than those of the Third World but have far lower standards of living than those of the First World. Russia and the former Communist bloc nations in Eastern Europe make up the vast majority of these countries. (Some scholars also include countries such as Portugal and Argentina.) The crumbling of the Iron Curtain set the stage for outbreaks of ethnic rivalries such as those in Bosnia; and these may currently be the most compelling characteristics of Second World nations. In 1990, Second World nations represented roughly 9 percent of the world's population, produced between 22 and 25 percent of the gross world product, and consumed nearly one-fourth of its energy.

The **Third World** consists of the less developed nations that share a peripheral or marginal status in the world capitalist system.

The remaining 75 percent of the world's population lives in the **Third World**—the less developed nations that are characterized by poverty and political weakness. Although these nations vary in their populations, political ideologies, and resources, they are all considerably behind the First and Second World in every measure of development. They produce only 20 percent of the world's gross product and consume approximately 20 percent of the world's energy (see Figure 10.1).

The First, Second, and Third Worlds, as mentioned, are familiar terms to describe international stratification. A second, more scientific way to understand international stratification is through the human suffering index.

THE HUMAN SUFFERING INDEX

The differences among the world's nations are obvious: First World countries are more politically stable and their people are healthier, more educated, and

FIGURE 10.1

COMPARISON OF POPULATION, PRODUCTION, AND ENERGY CONSUMPTION IN FIRST, SECOND, AND THIRD WORLD COUNTRIES

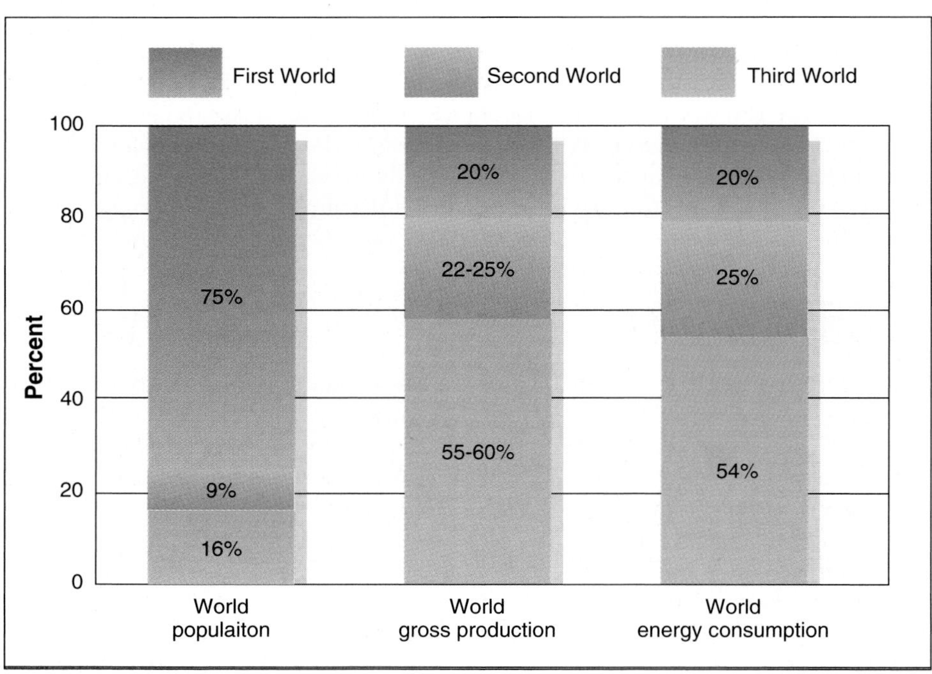

richer. How important are these differences? How do they affect the average person's day-to-day quality of life and hope for the future?

One approach to answering questions like these is to select variables that have been measured for each nation and compare the differences: illiteracy, unemployment, children in the work force, and physicians per capita, for example. Analysts who use this approach are often restricted in the choice of variables. The variables used must meet at least three essential criteria. Comparable information must exist for all nations, the measures selected must be quantified in a similar way so that comparisons are valid, and the measures for each nation must be judged to be reliable and accurate. These standards mean that some comparisons simply cannot be made.

Analysts on the Population Crisis Committee have combined 10 measures that meet these criteria into a human suffering index (HSI) (Camp and Barberis 1992). The 10 criteria used to assess human suffering on a global basis are life expectancy, daily calorie supply, access to clean drinking water, infant immunization, secondary school enrollment, gross national product (GNP) per capita, rate of inflation, communications technology, political freedom, and civil rights. Each nation is ranked from 0 to 10 on each indicator. For example, Japan, with an average life expectancy of 79 years, gets a 0 on this indicator. Afghanistan, with an average life expectancy of just 41 years, gets a 10. The values on all 10 measures are added, yielding a single figure, ranging from 0 to 100, for each country. This figure is the human suffering index.

Scores on this index range from a low of 1 for Denmark to highs of 92 for Somalia and 93 for Mozambique. The United States has a score of 5. According to this index, nearly three-fourths of the world's population live in countries with extreme or high measures of human suffering (Table 10.1). These countries are disproportionately located in Africa, Asia, and Latin America—Third World countries. By contrast, except for Japan, Australia, and New Zealand, the nations with the lowest human suffering are in either Western Europe or North America.

TABLE 10.1
DISTRIBUTION OF WORLD POPULATION ON THE HUMAN SUFFERING INDEX, 1992

Nearly three-fourths of the world's population—all of Africa and large portions of Asia and South America—are classified as being high in human suffering. These people are increasingly aware of their disadvantaged conditions, and pressures for immediate change are growing. These pressures may destabilize political and economic patterns in the world system.

SCORE	HUMAN SUFFERING CATEGORY	PERCENTAGE OF WORLD POPULATION
0–24	MINIMAL	15%
25–49	MODERATE	12
50–74	HIGH	65
75–100	EXTREME	8

SOURCE: Camp and Barberis 1992.

The human suffering index can be criticized on a number of technical and conceptual grounds (Ahlburg 1988). An obvious problem is that it treats each of the 10 measures as equally important. For example, it treats communications technology as if it were as important as life expectancy. Most of us, however, would agree that life expectancy is a far more important indicator; if a nation can achieve a long life expectancy without high-tech communication systems, this is fine.

Despite criticism, the HSI gives us a rough but generally accurate picture of where suffering occurs across the world. As Map 10.1 graphically demonstrates, this suffering is concentrated in the Southern Hemisphere, in Africa, Asia, and South America.

INEQUALITY AND DEVELOPMENT—TWO THEORIES

Many of the differences between nations are matters of culture. There is general consensus, however, that having enough to eat is better than going hungry, health is better than sickness, and security is better than insecurity.

Clearly, no nation wants to be a Third World nation. And most better-off nations also would prefer to reduce international inequality—not only for humanitarian reasons but also because massive inequality leads to political instability. The most accepted way to attempt to reduce international inequality is through development—that is, through raising the standard of living of the less developed nations.

What is development? First development is *not* the same as Westernization. It does not necessarily entail monogamy, three-piece suits, or any other cultural practices associated with the Western world. **Development** refers to the process of increasing the productivity and raising the standard of living of a society, leading to longer life expectancies, better diets, more education, better housing, and more consumer goods.

Development refers to the process of increasing the productivity and standard of living of a society—longer life expectancies, more adequate diets, better education, better housing, and more consumer goods.

Here, we examine two general theories of development—modernization and world system theory. These theories address the causes of current inequalities and the prospects for their relief.

MODERNIZATION THEORY

Modernization theory sees development as the natural unfolding of an evolutionary process in which societies go from simple to complex institutional structures.

Modernization theory sees development as the natural unfolding of an evolutionary process in which societies go from simple to complex institutional structures. This is a structural-functional theory based on the premise that adaptation is the chief determinant of social structures. According to this perspective, more developed countries (MDCs) are merely ahead of lesser developed countries (LDCs) in a natural evolutionary process. Given time, the developing nations will catch up.

Modernization theory was very popular in the 1950s and 1960s. It implied that developing nations would follow pretty much the same path as the developed nations. Greater productivity through industrialization would lead to greater surpluses, which could be used to improve health and education and technology. Initial expansion of industrialization would lead to a spiral of ever-increasing productivity and a high standard of living. Modernization theorists believed this process would occur more rapidly in the Third World than it had in Europe because of the direct introduction of Western-style education, health care, and technology (Chodak 1973).

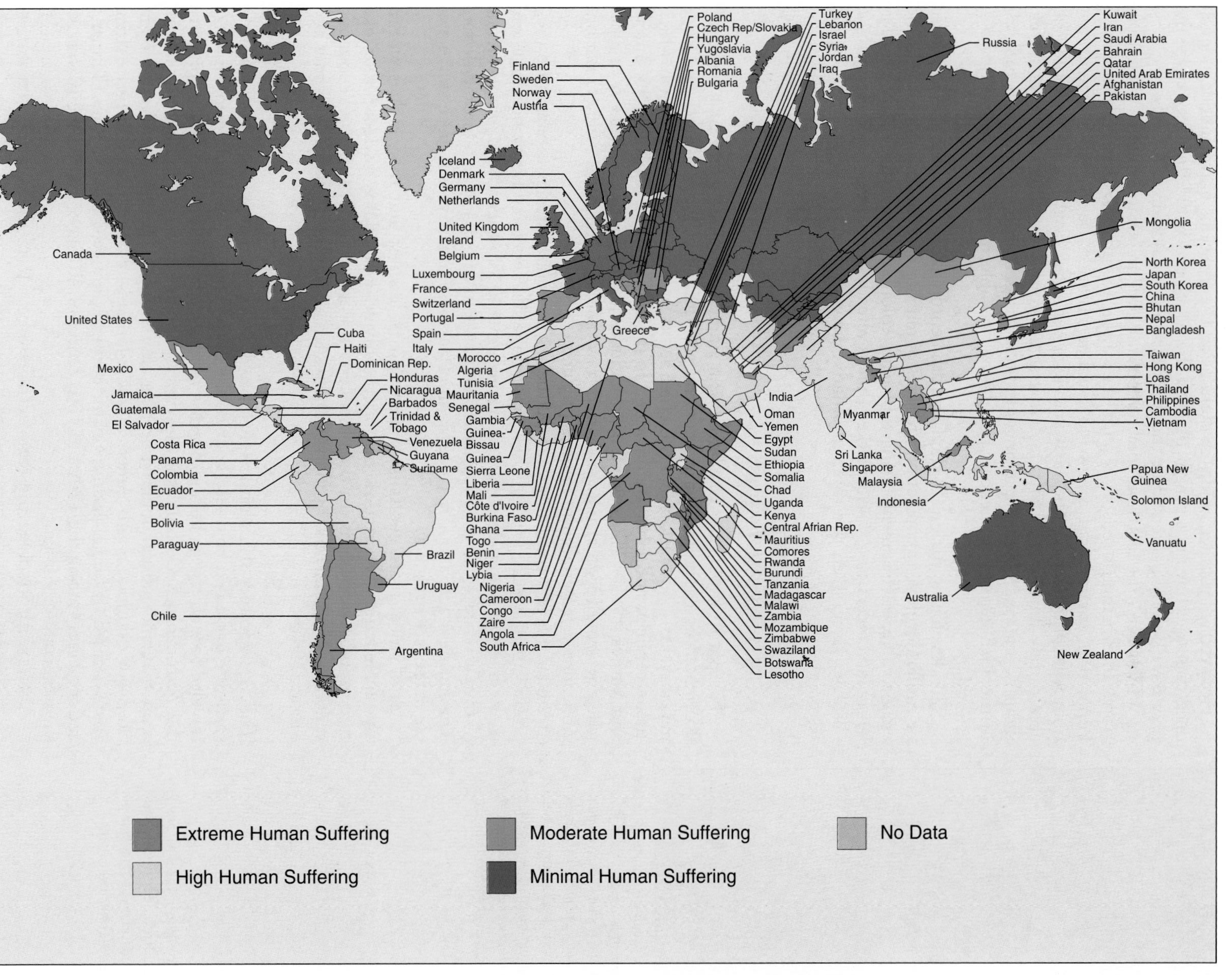

MAP 10.1
HUMAN SUFFERING AROUND THE WORLD

SOURCE: (to come)

Despite the rapidity with which new ideas and new technologies can be diffused throughout the world, a very large share of the world's population does not share in the increased standard of living that development makes possible. Throughout much of the world, rickshaws, bicycles, mules, and walking are more common modes of transportation than are automobiles.

From today's vantage point, modernization theory seems naïve. The less developed countries have not caught up with the developed world. In many cases, the poor have become poorer, while the rich have become richer.

Why haven't the less developed nations followed in our footsteps to modernization? The primary reason is that they face an entirely different context: Population, environment, and world social organization are all vastly different now from what they were in the 17th and 18th centuries. England, for example, was able to rely on raw materials freely extracted from her colonies in order to fuel industrialization. When improving conditions caused an overpopulation problem in the 19th century, the excess population was able to migrate to America and Australia.

The developing nations of the late 20th century face many obstacles not faced by earlier developers: population pressures of much greater magnitude and with no escape valve, environments ravaged by early colonialists, plus the disadvantage of being latecomers to a world market that is already carved up. These formidable obstacles have given rise to an alternative view of world modernization—world system theory.

World System Theory

The entire world may be viewed as a single economic system that has been dominated by capitalism for at least the past 200 years. Nation-states and large multinational corporations are the chief actors in a free market system in which goods, services, and labor are organized to maximize profits (Chirot 1986; Turner and Musick 1985). This organization includes an international division of labor whereby some (poorer) nations extract raw materials and other (richer) nations fabricate raw materials into finished products.

Under this system, nations can pursue a variety of strategies to maximize their profits on the world market. They can capture markets forcibly through invasion, they can try to manipulate markets through treaties or other special arrangements, or they can simply do the international equivalent of building a better mousetrap. The Japanese auto industry (indeed, all of Japanese industry) is a successful example of the latter strategy.

On a global basis, capitalism operates with less restraint than it does within any single nation. There is no organized equivalent of welfare or Medicaid to take care of indigent nations. In the absence of a world political structure, economic activity is regulated only by market forces such as supply and demand (Turner and Musick 1985).

Colonialism involves a foreign power's maintaining political, economic, and cultural domination over another people for an extended period of time.

The Background of Colonialism. The origin of a single economic system that spans the globe can be traced back to the 15th century, when European explorers traveled around the globe and began a period of colonialism that lasted well into the 20th century. **Colonialism** involves a foreign power's maintaining political, economic, and cultural domination over another people for an extended period of time. For example, South America was colonized by Spain and Portugal; Africa was colonized by Great Britain, Spain, Portugal, France, Belgium, Italy, Germany and Holland. During the 17th and 18th centuries, Russia colonized the islands off the west coast of Alaska.

Colonialism involved the removal of resources from the colonized territories. From the Americas, the Spanish and Portuguese took tons of gold, silver, rubber, and precious woods, for example. European powers extracted gold, diamonds, precious metals, jewels, and palm oil from Africa. The Russians took thousands of beaver, seal, and other furs from their island colonies. Raw materials were shipped to the colonizing country to be manufactured into goods. Some of these goods were then exported back to the colonized peoples, who became new consumers.

Along with extracting natural resources, colonizers introduced the concept of land ownership and purchased or simply claimed what had been considered communal property. Assuming land ownership, colonizers introduced *cash crops*—that is, crops that are grown for profit and export rather than to feed the local population. Giant sugar, coffee, cocoa, banana, rubber, and palm oil plantations were established, and these cash crops displaced native food crops. The colonized peoples, having been displaced from their lands and local food supplies, were subsequently hired to work on the plantations but paid extremely low wages. Moreover, having been brought into an international money economy, the colonized now found themselves purchasing their food and other supplies.

The colonial system collapsed after World War II, but the heritage of colonialism persists: Countries that were colonized are at a marked disadvantage today. Currently, we use the term **neocolonialism** to indicate the continued economic domination of less developed and weaker nations by more developed and more powerful nations.

Neocolonialism is the current economic domination of less developed and weaker nations by more developed and more powerful nations.

World System Theory. World system theory is a conflict analysis of the economic relationships between developed and developing countries. It looks at this economic system with a distinctly Marxist eye. Developed countries are the bourgeoisie of the world capitalist system, and underdeveloped and developing countries are the proletariat. The division of labor between them is supported by a prevailing ideology (capitalism) and kept in place by an exploitive ruling class (rich countries and multinational corporations), which seeks to maximize its benefits at the expense of the working class (underdeveloped and developing countries).

World system theory is a conflict perspective of the economic relationships between developed and developing countries, the core and peripheral societies.

This combine in the American Midwest will help reap a bountiful harvest of wheat. This bounty may not do anybody much good, though. Because the people who need it most cannot afford to pay for it, the farmers will make little money, and people will go hungry. The world economic system is capitalistic: Goods and services are distributed on a for-profit basis.

Core societies are rich, powerful nations that are economically diversified and relatively free of outside control.

Peripheral societies are poor and weak, with highly specialized economies over which they have relatively little control.

Semiperipheral societies are neither as wealthy and powerful as core nations nor as destitute and weak as peripheral countries.

World system theory distinguishes three classes of nations: core societies, semiperipheral societies, and peripheral societies. **Core societies** are rich, powerful nations that are economically diversified and relatively free of outside control. They arrive at their position of dominance, in large part, through exploiting the periphery.

Peripheral societies, by contrast, are poor and weak, with highly specialized economies over which they have relatively little control (Chirot 1977). Peripheral societies are vulnerable to change and little able to control their environment. In the aftermath of colonialism, some of the poorest countries rely heavily on a single cash crop for their export revenue. For example, 90 percent of Chad's export earnings come from raw cotton; coffee accounts for 96 percent of Uganda's total exports; and in Cambodia, one of the poorest countries in the world, rubber and timber together provide 90 percent of the export revenue (Europa Yearbook 1994).

The economies of these and many other developing nations are vulnerable to conditions beyond their control: world demand, crop damage from infestation, flooding, drought, and so on. For instance, many African nations south of the Sahara Desert are among the world's poorest. After making some developmental progress in the 1970s, their governments went broke in the 1990s, partly because their economies—largely dependent on exporting single commodities like coffee, cocoa, and copper—fell apart when markets for these goods crashed in the worldwide recession of the 1980s (Darnton 1994a, Y5). As another example, in many Caribbean nations, colonizers introduced sugar as a cash crop for export. Today, sugar is the bedrock of the Caribbean economy. But First World countries have begun to produce and export their own sugar, and farmers in the Caribbean have lost their markets (Elliott 1994).

Somewhere in between the peripheral nations and the core nations are the **semiperipheral societies.** Semiperipheral societies are neither as wealthy and powerful as core nations nor as destitute and weak as peripheral countries. An example is Russia.

GLOBAL PERSPECTIVE: CASE STUDY: RUSSIA AS A SECOND-WORLD NATION

In 1917, the Russian Empire was an authoritarian state badly weakened by massive losses from World War I. Disgruntled civilians and soldiers joined forces to topple the monarchy of Czar Nicholas II. After a period of political uncertainty and civil war, the Bolshevik wing of the Communist party gained control of the government, and the Soviet Union became the first nation to decide to follow Marx's revolutionary path to socialism and economic development.

Throughout a long post–World War II era, during which the Soviets and the United States engaged in a Cold War that lasted until the late 1980s, the Soviets invested in defense, heavy industry, and foreign military aid at the expense of consumer goods. By the mid-1980s, the Soviets were spending between 15 and 17 percent of their total GNP on defense (compared with between 5 and 7 percent for the United States) (Treverton 1990). In addition, the Soviets spent another 2.5 percent for foreign aid to subsidize Eastern European allies and other dependent countries, such as Cuba and Vietnam.

Except for arms sales, the Soviet Union was not a serious economic competitor in the world capitalist system. In a free market, neither its buying power nor its products made it a major force. The Soviet commitment to a strong military, however, enabled it to control the economies of nearly 20 percent of the world's population and to have a powerful influence on world political events (Black 1986, Chirot 1986).

The cost of the Soviet strategy was enormous. By the end of the 1980s, the Soviet Union had decided to admit the failure of its previous policies of central planning, domestic authoritarianism, and international militarism. The Cold War fizzled largely because the Soviet Union couldn't afford it anymore (Bundy 1990). The nation's deepening economic crisis caused it to cast off the ideal of making the world Communist and to cut its defense budget. In 1991, the Soviet Union was dissolved.

Before the Soviet Union's dissolution, its dynamic leader, Mikhail Gorbachev, embarked on a plan to restructure the Soviet economy, and many hoped that Russia and other Eastern Bloc nations would soon enjoy a standard of living close to that of the First World. Such has not been the case, however, as agricultural and industrial production have plummeted (Nagorski 1995) and inflation has "turned fistfuls of rubles into worthless tissue" (Specter 1994, 31). Today, Russia has a score of 31 on the human suffering index. Although this score is not terribly high, the country lags far behind the First World in productivity and standard of living.

A key element of world system theory is the connectedness between First World prosperity and Third World poverty. The message is clear: *First World prosperity is Third World poverty*. In other words, in order for people in the First World to have inexpensive shoes, transistors, bananas, and other such goods, people in Third World nations must get low wages. Were their wages to rise, prices would rise and the standard of living in the First World would drop. Testing the implications of this situation requires examination of the actual forms of Third World dependency.

CONCEPT SUMMARY MAJOR ANALYTICAL FRAMEWORKS FOR INTERNATIONAL INEQUALITIES

	Everyday Language	Human Suffering Index	Modernization Theory	World System Theory	Examples
Richest nations	First World	Minimal human suffering—score of 0–24	More developed countries (MDCs)	Core	Denmark Canada United States Japan New Zealand
Intermediate nations	Second World	Moderate human suffering—score of 25–49		Semiperiphery	Portugal Russia Hungary Poland Argentina
Poorest nations	Third World	High and extreme human suffering—score of 50–100	Less developed countries (LDCs)	Periphery	Colombia Haiti Afghanistan Niger Mozambique

FOCUS ON THE ENVIRONMENT

Economic Development, the Environment, and the Second World

"In the Chinese capital of Beijing, two-thirds of all families currently own a fridge."

Development means raising the standard of living and improving the quality of life of a society. In theory, development programs should be as concerned with improving access to education and health care and with ensuring the rights of all citizens—regardless of age, gender, race, or ethnicity—as with increasing labor productivity. In practice, however, aid to Third World nations has focused almost exclusively on fostering economic development, and its success is most often measured simply in terms of increases in gross national product or access to consumer goods. Under this model of development, First World lifestyles become the goal that Third World nations aspire to reach.

Interestingly, even in Europe and the United States, the experience of mass consumption has occurred only recently. In the late 1940s, for instance, only one British household in 25 had a washing machine and only one in 50 had a refrigerator. However, by the mid-1980s in Kuala Lumpur, Malaysia, 13 percent of the very poorest households and 50 percent of those in the next poorest group owned a refrigerator. In the Chinese capital of Beijing, two-thirds of all families currently own a fridge. Given these trends in consumption and an estimated world population of 10 billion people by the year 2050, it is estimated that at that time there will be only enough aluminum to last another 20 years, enough copper and oil to last another 4.5 years, and enough coal to last another 51 years (State of World Population 1992).

Paradoxically, threats to the so-called "renewable" resources may be even more severe. Water and trees, for example, are renewable resources. With wise use, they are self-replenishing. Overuse, however, can destroy such resources within a generation. In the late 1980s, 11 nations—primarily in the Middle East—were already using water at a rate much faster than it can be replaced. In addition, although only 6 African nations faced water stress or scarcity in 1982, it is estimated that by the year 2025, 21 countries will be affected. These nations will be home to 1,100 million people, or approximately two-thirds of the population of the African continent.

Irrigation for agriculture consumes most of the water used by people—nearly 70 percent worldwide. Industry accounts for about 23 percent of worldwide water use; and households use only about 8 percent. Although irrigation and industry have improved nutrition and access to goods in the short run, in the long term both may have serious detrimental consequences. Agriculture is the least efficient user. It is not uncommon for 70 to 80 percent of the water diverted to irrigation systems to be lost before it ever reaches the fields (Falkenmark and Widstrand 1992). This runoff leaches important nutrients from the soil and contributes to increased soil salinity. In the long run, then, irrigation may reduce agricultural productivity. Industry is the second largest user of water. Moreover, the kinds of industry often held up as models for Third World development—food processing, petroleum refining, and pulp and paper refineries—are particularly water intensive. Thus, in many Third World countries, eco-

THIRD WORLD DEPENDENCY

Many contemporary scholars use some form of world system theory to understand development. Although they might reject the Marxist implications of the theory, there is fairly general agreement that international inequality is the result of conflict and competition within an international capitalist economic framework.

FOCUS ON THE ENVIRONMENT

nomic development is likely to place extraordinary demands on already fragile water supplies. Water is used by factories for cooling, for generating steam to run equipment, and as a method of transport. It is also used as a dumping ground for industrial waste. Industrial contamination of rivers and lakes has reached such epidemic proportions in Eastern Europe and the former Soviet Union that it is estimated that 50 to 80 percent of the drinking water in many of these nations is unfit to drink (French 1991).

Indeed, Eastern Europe and the former Soviet Union are good examples of what can happen to the environment when industrialization and economic growth and development are pursued at any cost.

- According to a 1979 report by the local Communist youth league, a lake near one Soviet chemical plant was so polluted that citizens of the town disposed of stray dogs by throwing them into the water. The report added that the lake was so contaminated by phenols that the carcasses dissolved within days.
- The Vistula River, which runs through Poland, is so laden with poisons and corrosive chemicals that it is considered unusable, even for factory coolant systems (Jensen 1990).
- Near the industrial center of the eastern part of Germany, life expectancy is six years less than in other parts of the region, and four out of five children in the region will develop chronic bronchitis or heart problems by the age of seven (Painton 1990).
- When 300 children attending two kindergartens in Estonia began to lose their hair, residents were horrified. Eventually, the former director of a local factory revealed that his company had dumped radioactive waste where the schools were later built (French 1991).

A report prepared by the Russian Environmental Ministry for the 1992 Earth Summit in Rio de Janeiro blamed the ecological woes of the nation on the "growth-at-any-cost" mentality that drove Soviet economic development beginning approximately in the late 1920s. Coupled with concerns about national security and the rapid rise of a huge military-industrial complex, Soviet bloc emphasis on production over efficiency created both a badly outdated industrial sector and environmental hazards of unparalleled magnitude (Stanglin 1992).

Of course, this creates a real quandary: How can the countries of Eastern Europe and the former Soviet Union revitalize their economies *and* clean up the environment when the costs of repairing the ecological damage alone are estimated at $100 billion each, just for Poland and the former Czechoslovakia (Marshall 1991)? If affluence means more environmental destruction, it seems that these nations—and others—are caught on the horns of a dilemma. Is eliminating poverty more or less important than preserving the environment?

THINKING CRITICALLY

If affluence means more environmental destruction, it seems like we're caught on the horns of a dilemma. Is eliminating poverty more or less important than preserving the environment?

FORMS OF ECONOMIC DEPENDENCY

The primary characteristic of the periphery is that these nations have relatively little control over their economies: They are dependent. In many cases, these dependent relationships represent a triple alliance among three actors: multinational corporations (generally based in the First World), the governments of the peripheral societies, and local elites. Scholars who study the world system identify three types of dependency (Bradshaw 1988): classic "banana republic" dependency, industrial dependency, and foreign-capital dependency.

The "Banana Republic." The classic case of dependency occurs in a Third World nation whose economy is dependent on the export of raw materials—fruit, for example, or minerals. African nations, the Indian subcontinent, and Latin American countries have all fallen into this situation; many of the world's peripheral nations are still in it.

Colombia's economy provides an excellent example of a nation that still operates under the "banana republic" form of dependency. Table 10.2 provides a breakdown of the imports and exports of Colombia. This table illustrates the classic case of Third World dependency: Colombia exports raw materials and imports manufactured goods. (Of course, the table omits one of Colombia's most profitable raw-material exports: cocaine.)

Colombia today exports more than it imports, so the nation has a positive net balance of trade. However, since bananas are cheaper than cars and printing presses, Colombia must try to produce more and more export crops. This emphasis on production of export crops such as coffee and sugar reduces the nation's ability to feed itself and retards the development of economic diversity.

Industrial Dependency. Increasingly, multinational corporations are making use of one of the other major assets of less developed countries: cheap labor. Most of the work done in Third World countries is labor intensive, and multinational corporations are setting up industrial assembly plants throughout the Third World. Third World assembly reduces labor costs dramatically (say, from $10 an hour to $3 a day).

For example, Southeast Asia's semiconductor factories, owned by U.S. corporations like Texas Instruments and Motorola, are part of a "global assembly line" that stretches around the world. Silicon wafers made in New Jersey are shipped to Southeast Asian countries where, through intricate and tedious labor requiring great dexterity, workers cut the wafers into tiny chips, then bond them to circuit boards. The average hourly wage paid in the semiconductor industry in the United States in 1982 was $5.92; in Hong Kong it was $1.15; in Singapore, $.79; in Malaysia and the Philippines, $.48; and in Indonesia, $.19 (Clinard 1990, 153). As a result, it is more cost effective to ship this work halfway around the world and back again than to complete it in the United States.

Many observers have hoped that investment in Third World industrial plants would provide jobs, spur development of indigenous auxiliary industries, and generally stimulate local economies. This was one argument made by proponents of the North American Free Trade Agreement (NAFTA) and of the General Agreement on Tariffs and Trade (GATT) that took effect in 1994. While we don't yet know the full impact of NAFTA or GATT, empirical data gathered before 1994 demonstrate that better jobs and higher wages in the Third World seldom result from First World investment because such investment depends on low-paying jobs.

Consider that assembly plants in Third World countries do provide jobs and are thus attractive to local labor pools. Moreover, local materials and labor are used to build the factories. Then, too, factory monies are funneled through local banks. All this makes assembly plants in the Third World appear to be plums worth having, and many nations are competing for them. This puts the First World manufac-

TABLE 10.2
COLOMBIA'S INTERNATIONAL TRADE

Colombia's international trade situation demonstrates the classic "banana republic" form of Third World dependency. Instead of gradually developing a modern economy, Colombia remains dependent on imports for industrial products.

GOODS	VALUE (IN MILLIONS OF U.S. DOLLARS)
IMPORTS	
MECHANICAL AND ELECTRICAL EQUIPMENT	$1,260
CHEMICAL PRODUCTS	1,053
TRANSPORT EQUIPMENT	380
MINERAL PRODUCTS	342
PLASTIC AND RUBBER GOODS	294
PAPER AND PAPER PRODUCTS	217
VEGETABLES AND VEGETABLE PRODUCTS	193
TEXTILES	159
METALS	157
FOOD AND DRINK	87
TOTAL (INCLUDING OTHER MISCELLANEOUS)	$4,967
EXPORTS	
MINERALS OTHER THAN COAL	$1,516
RAW COFFEE	1,336
COTTON	817
COAL	630
BANANAS	405
FLOWERS	280
FOOD AND RAW TOBACCO	277
BASIC METALS	253
CHEMICALS	189
PAPER	176
TOTAL (INCLUDING OTHER MISCELLANEOUS)	$7,269
NET BALANCE OF TRADE	$2,296

SOURCE: Adapted from Europa World Yearbook 1993, Vol. 1, p. 2157.

turing company in a position to bargain, and it is thus able to impose a variety of conditions on the government. These conditions usually include government guarantees on two points:

1. *No unionization.* The government must agree to outlaw unionization in general or otherwise to stop union movements in foreign plants. For example, in 1982, Philippine President Ferdinand Marcos outlawed all strikes in the semiconductor industry. Results of bans on unionization include persistently low wages as well as absence of health and retirement benefits and often appalling working conditions. Employees may, for example, work 12-hour days amid toxic fumes or dangerous liquids without protective gear (Clinard 1990, 154).
2. *No tax on corporate profits.* The multinational company that invests in a Third World country wants to take the profits back to the First World and distribute them among its stockholders. Thus, corporations try to negotiate sweetheart deals that will either excuse them from all tax on profits or provide them with a more favorable rate than that imposed on local companies. What government would negotiate this kind of deal? The answer, of course, is only the poorest and most desperate. Nations with strong states and better local economies are able to negotiate much better deals.

Foreign-Capital Dependency. Third World dependency may also take the form of dependency on loans and investment. In this case, the firms are owned and operated by locals, rather than by foreign corporations. International banking organizations controlled by core nations, such as the International Monetary Fund (IMF) and the World Bank, lend money or guarantee loans to semiperipheral and peripheral countries. In theory, this should encourage development by providing additional capital.

Instead, the extension of loans to Third World nations has resulted in a dramatic debt crisis and further dependency. Because of high inflation and worldwide recession in the early 1980s, many Third World countries suffered the double blow of spiraling interest rates and sharply reduced demand for their products. The result has been budget deficits that we can hardly imagine. For instance, the 1991

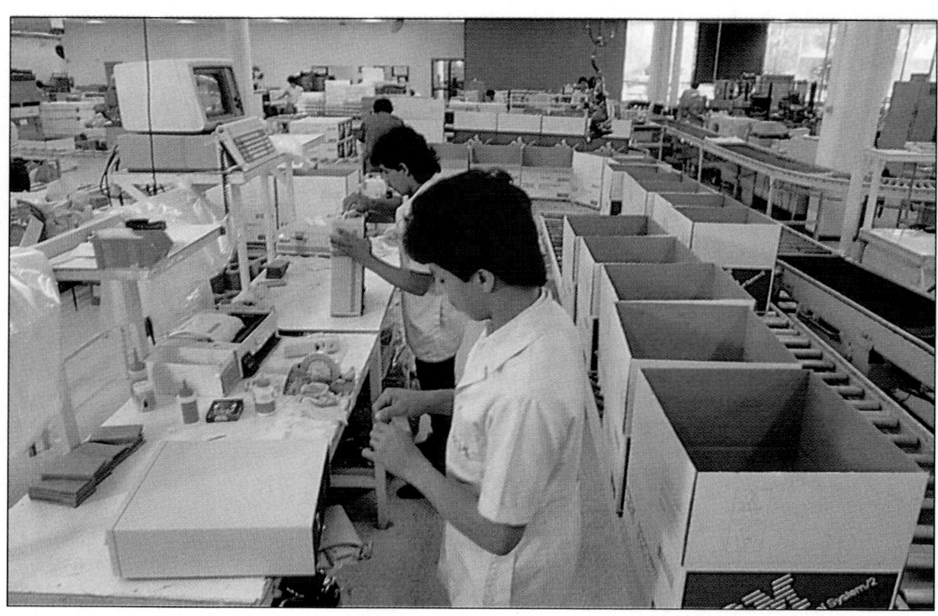

These workers in Guadalajara, Mexico, are assembling IBM computers for the giant U.S. firm. By locating assembly plants in Third World nations, multinational firms realize huge savings in labor costs, and U.S. consumers get cheaper products. Among the undesirable side effects, however, are loss of jobs for U.S. workers and the growth of inequality in Third World nations.

international debt, or budget deficit, of Mozambique was more than 426 percent of its gross national product (Darnton 1994b, A6). Compare this figure with 2.5 percent for the United States (Craig 1995).

In order to meet or renegotiate their payments, debtor nations are typically required to follow the prescriptions of a "structural adjustment program" designed by the IMF or the World Bank (Darnton 1994b). These international banking organizations can end up controlling a broad range of issues—even political matters, such as the calling of multiparty elections—that affect the lives of the people. Debtor nations have at times been required to devalue their local currencies, lay off civil employees, and cut social services, thus reducing investment in their own economies and squeezing their own people even harder (Wimberly 1990).

THE CONSEQUENCES OF DEPENDENCY

By definition, dependency is a bad thing. It means that you do not have control—over your economy and perhaps over your government. Although ties to richer, stronger economies may theoretically be expected to benefit less developed nations, research has not borne out these expectations. Here, we explore the consequences of dependency for both First and Third World nations. We begin by examining the extent of international inequalities.

The Extent of International Inequalities. As we saw in Chapter 9, not everyone in rich nations is rich. Similarly, not everyone in poor nations is poor. But in general the richer a nation is, the better the quality of life for its people. Table 10.3 compares several quality-of-life indicators for six nations. Two of these nations, Japan and the United States, are First World, or core, countries. Poland can be

TABLE 10.3
THE EXTENT OF INTERNATIONAL INEQUALITY: COMPARING SIX COUNTRIES

	JAPAN	UNITED STATES	POLAND	NICARAGUA	HAITI	MOZAMBIQUE
PER CAPITA GROSS NATIONAL PRODUCT (GNP), U.S. DOLLARS	31,450	24,750	2,270	360	380	80
LIFE EXPECTANCY AT BIRTH (IN YEARS)	79	76	72	65	57	46
INFANT MORTALITY RATE (ANNUAL NUMBER OF DEATHS OF INFANTS YOUNGER THAN 1 YEAR PER 1,000 LIVE BIRTHS)	4.3	8.0	13.7	49	74	148
DAILY CALORIE SUPPLY (PERCENT OF DAILY REQUIREMENT, PER CAPITA)	125	138	132	119	94	76
PERCENT OF POPULATION WITH ACCESS TO CLEAN DRINKING WATER	>95	>95	UNKNOWN	54	41	24
MOTOR VEHICLES PER 1,000 POPULATION	408	728	137	23	10	8
HUMAN SUFFERING INDEX SCORE	7	5	33	66	89	93

SOURCES: Population Reference Bureau 1994, 1995; Camp and Barberis 1992; Population Reference Bureau 1991.

considered a Second World nation. Nicaragua, Haiti, and Mozambique are Third World, peripheral nations.

In general, the more productive a nation is, the better the quality of life for its people. Japan has the highest per capita gross national product in the world today—$31,450 in 1995. Correspondingly, Japanese citizens enjoy a long life expectancy (79 years), have more than enough to eat, and experience one of the lowest infant mortality rates in the world: Each year, for every 1,000 live births, 4.3 infants who have not yet reached their first birthday die.

Similarly, on average, residents of the United States have more than enough to eat, live relatively long lives, and experience fairly low infant mortality—although high infant mortality rates among the poor in the United States make this figure higher than it otherwise would be. One striking thing about life in the United States is our relatively easy access to owning automobiles.

Poland, a Second World country, has a GNP much lower than that of Japan or the United States. Nevertheless, it produces more per capita than Third World countries.

As mentioned earlier, the poorest nation in the world today, Mozambique, has an annual GNP of just $80. Correspondingly, life expectancy there is but 46 years at birth; and of every 1,000 babies born annually, 148 die before reaching their first birthday. On average, people in Mozambique do not have enough to eat, and only about one quarter of them have access to clean drinking water. Most Haitians do not have enough to eat, either, while more than 7 percent (74 per 1,000) of their babies die before age one. Only 41 percent of Haitians have access to clean drinking water.

As you can see when comparing Japan with the United States, not all First World nations are just alike. Nor are all Second or Third World countries exactly the same. Nicaragua, for example, has a higher GNP than does either Haiti or Mozambique. Along with that goes a longer life expectancy (65 years) and an infant mortality rate of 49—much less than half that of Mozambique but almost 6 times that in the United States.

Speaking more generally, one-fifth of the people in less developed countries go hungry every day. In contrast, those born in more developed countries not only have enough to eat but also tend to be overweight owing to fat-rich diets. Over 1.5 billion people in the world today lack access to safe water; in more developed countries, the percentage of people with access to clean drinking water exceeds 95 percent (Camp and Barberis 1992). International inequality is indeed dramatic.

Consequences for First World People. As mentioned in Chapter 1, Herbert Gans, a sociologist, wrote an essay in 1971 on the functions of poverty. While Gans did not take a specifically global view, some of this work can be applied to the issue of international inequalities. Gans (1992) argued that poverty is functional—albeit mainly for the rich—in a number of ways, including the following five:

1. Poverty ensures that society's "dirty work"—dangerous, dead-end, underpaid, and undignified jobs—will get done. International inequality results in a low-wage labor pool that is willing—"or rather, unable to be unwilling" (Gans 1992, 329)—to do the dirty work. Handling the world's household garbage and hazardous waste is an example. The United States and other core countries export tons of waste to peripheral nations in Africa, Asia, and Central and South America (Bright 1990).

2. Working for low wages, the poor subsidize many commodities and services that benefit the affluent. People in the United States can readily buy imported beef, coffee, tropical fruit, flowers, compact disk players, Levi jeans, Rockport shoes, Bell telephones, and Spalding "official NBA" basketballs—all at lower cost because these commodities, and countless others, are produced using cheap Third World labor (Clinard 1990, 153). In a startling example, a private hospital in London paid Turkish peasants 2,000 pounds apiece to be flown to England, where each donated a kidney for transplant to a British patient (MacKinnon and Kelsey 1989).

3. The poor buy goods that others do not want and thus prolong the economic usefulness of such goods. An example is tobacco. Partly because of declining sales at home, U.S. cigarette manufacturers have embarked on aggressive and highly successful advertising campaigns in Third World countries (as well as Japan). Other examples include various drugs and pesticides manufactured in the First World but considered unsafe for use here and hence exported to the Third World for use there (Clinard 1990, 150–157).

4. The poor, being powerless, can be made to absorb the costs of change and growth in richer societies. For example, environmental protection laws in First World countries have motivated multinational companies, such as Union Carbide, Monsanto, Dow, and Chevron, to set up factories in the Third World, where state-of-the-art chemicals can be manufactured with few environmental controls (Clinard 1990, 146–147). As a second example, the Mexican government and residents buy used buses and cars from the United States, replaced here when they become too old for First World standards.

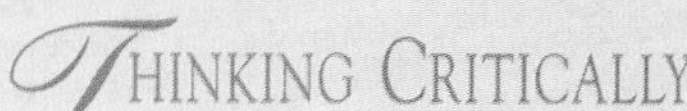

Consider how the major themes of U.S. stratification covered in Chapter 9 apply to international inequality. *You* are a hundred times better off than the average person in Mozambique. Is this a necessary and just reflection of your greater contribution to society? Is it surprising that so many Third World peoples ascribe to a conflict theory of international inequality?

Life is and will continue to be markedly different for these two children. This little girl can expect to live about 15 years longer than this little boy. And hers will probably be a comfortable life; together, her parents most likely earn almost $50,000 a year. The little boy lives where the average per capita yearly income is $950. The little girl doesn't know it; but in part, her "good life" depends on the poverty of Third World people like this little boy. For example, her clothing may have been made in the Third World with low wages, making them affordable novelties.

5. Poverty creates jobs for a number of people in occupations that serve the poor or protect the rest of society from them. An example of employment opportunities in service to the Third World poor is the organization United States Aid in Development (USAID), which employs hundreds of U.S. citizens around the globe.

Gans's exploration of the functions of poverty may sound a bit cynical. As we shall see later in this chapter, First World responses to international inequality include considerably more than blindly enjoying any benefits of the disparities. Many individuals and governments in core nations are determined to reduce these inequalities. Nevertheless, Gan's analysis does identify some consequences of peripheral dependency for members of core nations. What about those in the Third World?

Consequences for Third World People. Scholars have documented four primary consequences of foreign-capital penetration for people in peripheral nations (Bradshaw 1988; Stokes and Anderson 1990; Wimberly 1990).

1. *Sectoral inequality.* The effort to develop the industrial infrastructure in order to attract foreign capital usually results in excessive investment in industrial and urban sectors and undesirably low investment in agricultural and rural sectors. Because the majority of the nation's population is likely to live in rural areas, this means that the many are ignored for the benefit of the few. Long-term consequences include reduced per-capita food production, increased investment in urban roads and airports at the expense of human welfare programs, and the growth of elephantine cities resulting from people's flight from the land. This is one reason for high rates of international migration, such as that from Mexico to the United States.

2. *Income inequality.* It is not surprising to learn that income inequality is one outcome of foreign-capital penetration: Low wages are what attract foreign capital in the first place. Agreements to keep wages low and prevent unionization maintain and aggravate this condition. Low industrial wages, in turn, depress agricultural wages. (If urban wages were high, agricultural workers would need to be paid more to stay on the farm.)

Urban elites are people native to peripheral countries who grow wealthy by collaborating with foreign investment and capital.

There *are*, however, people who benefit from foreign-capital penetration. Generally, these are **urban elites** and the small urban middle class. These are the people who make the deals and manage the workers. Because these people are making more money while the workers are not, inequality grows. As a result, income disparity in peripheral countries is typically much higher than that in core nations. For example, the top 20 percent of Brazil's population earns 26 times as much as the bottom 20 percent; in the United States, the disparity is 9 to 1 (Michaels 1993).

3. *Growing authoritarianism.* As noted, in order to entice foreign investors, governments are frequently forced to agree to keep wages low. This means that they must prevent unionization and many efforts at democratic reform. Certainly this may be done with the best of intentions, but it usually results in an antidemocratic regime that cooperates in the oppression of its own people. In Rio de Janeiro and Sau Paulo, Brazil, for instance, hundreds of *meninos de rua* (street kids) run in packs because they are homeless and without families or work. They may be as young as seven years old. Because these children threaten the social order, business owners hire off-duty police to locate and murder them (Michaels 1993).

4. *Conflict increases*. The end result of foreign-capital penetration is that a small local elite and the state ally themselves with foreign capital against their own people. Both the local elites and the foreigners are likely to invest their profits in American or European banks rather than in indigenous industries. Thus, investment in the nation may actually decrease. Certainly, anger and inequality grow. As a result, multinational penetration has been shown to increase the risk of political violence (London and Robinson 1989).

Taken together, these four consequences point to the fact that in the Third World (as well as in the First and Second Worlds), the economy is strongly bound to government politics. For this reason, scholars often use the term *political economy* when discussing the conditions in First, Second, and Third World nations. That concept is further discussed in Chapter 17.

To sum up, a substantial amount of research documents the undesirable consequences of foreign-capital penetration of Third World economies. (The implications of the word *penetrate* alone hint at these consequences.) Not only does it not bring prosperity but it often exacerbates poverty, inequality, and political instability.

Competition, Change, and International Relationships

As we saw in Chapter 9, serious income and wealth inequalities can make for class conflict. Just as there is evidence of class conflict *within* core nations, there is international class conflict among nations. This section discusses Third World challenges to the status quo and First World responses.

Third World Challenges to the Status Quo

Throughout the past four decades, the world has witnessed a high and increasing level of political violence in poor nations. We have seen nationalist revolutions or violent class struggles in Vietnam, Angola, Cuba, Chile, Algeria, Ethiopia, Nicaragua, El Salvador, Zimbabwe, and Afghanistan, to name just some (Kerbo 1991, 512). Now that the Cold War between the Soviet Union and the United States seems to be over, some observers believe that the Third World may be a more real source of peril. Nearly half a dozen peripheral and semiperipheral nations—Argentina, Brazil, India, Iraq, Pakistan, and South Africa—now have nuclear capacities.

Persistent and growing inequality within some peripheral nations, and between peripheral and core nations, is a primary cause for uncertainty and unrest. Other reasons contribute as well. For one thing, Second and Third World peoples have more and more contact—either by television or in person (with travelers, for example)—with relatively rich First World people. This situation creates a greater awareness of deprivation and increases expectations, potentially resulting in anger and frustration. When this relative deprivation leads to organized nationalist movements, it can result in violent, revolutionary challenges to the status quo (Kerbo 1991, 513).

Revolutionary movements are mainly made up of people from the lower classes. But they tend to be led and maintained by persons who are more educated.

> **THINKING CRITICALLY**
>
> One reason nations use coercion to force their will on others is that there is no authority to compel them to get along. Consider how relations among U.S. states might differ if federal power was as weak as the United Nations is in international affairs.

Historically, such potential revolutionary leaders were unwittingly created by colonial and neo-colonial systems established by core nations. To help manage colonial regimes in colonized regions, the core helped to educate administrators from the indigenous populations. Today, core nations invite international students, many of them from the Third World, to attend colleges and universities in the First World. Increasingly, these better-educated people have led Third World revolutionary movements. An example is Fidel Castro, who attended Harvard University before returning to Cuba and leading its socialist revolution.

FIRST WORLD RESPONSES

First World responses to Third World challenges to the status quo can be placed in two broad categories: military and humanitarian.

Military Responses. The principal First World response to possible revolutionary challenges from peripheral nations has been military action to quiet unrest. Such military action can be *overt* (open and observable) or *covert* (secret and concealed). The use of military force around the world—U.S. actions in such places as Vietnam, Korea, the Dominican Republic, and Panama, for example—illustrates overt intervention. Covert actions include propaganda campaigns, bribes to core-friendly elites, rigged elections, and help in staging coups. In the 1960s, the U.S. Central Intelligence Agency (CIA) considered giving Fidel Castro LSD before a major speech in order to damage his public image in Cuba (Kerbo 1991, 517).

Humanitarian Responses. There is evidence that the United States has begun to use its military for primarily humanitarian interventions. The 1992–1993 food

One consequence of international inequality is that members of core nations volunteer to try to relieve suffering in peripheral nations. In this photo, First World volunteers are helping to treat a suffering Rwandan refugee.

relief effort in Somalia (a Third World nation) and the more recent efforts at keeping peace in Bosnia (a Second World country) are examples.

In March 1995, representatives of the United States went to Copenhagen to participate in the first World Summit on Social Development, organized by the United Nations. The summit sought to find ways to increase the share of the world's resources devoted to social development in lesser developed countries, ultimately assuring universal access to education and basic health services around the globe (De Sherbinin and Kalish 1995).

Meanwhile, citizens in core nations provide both tax dollars and private donations to aid people in the Second and Third Worlds. As to tax dollars, recent statistics show that in 1990, First World nations gave a total of $68.4 billion (in U.S. dollars) to developing countries (U.S. Bureau of the Census 1994, Table 1407). While U.S. expenditures have declined since 1985, the United States still spends about 1.1 percent of its annual budget (about $20 billion) in foreign aid to Second and Third World nations such as Israel, Turkey, and El Salvador (Walte and Hasson 1995, 4A). Measured in dollars donated per citizen (per capita), the Scandinavian nations spend the most (more than $200 per capita in Denmark, Norway, and Sweden), followed by the United Kingdom, with the United States next at about $45 per citizen (U.S. Bureau of the Census 1994, Table 1407).

In addition to spending tax dollars, individuals in core countries give private and voluntary aid to less developed nations. In 1991, residents of the United States voluntarily gave what amounted to $11 per capita in private and voluntary aid (by comparison, Australians gave $6 and Norwegians gave $30) (U.S. Bureau of the Census 1994, Table 1408). Then, too, more Americans are investing in and spending money with corporations that are concerned about international exploitation (Kindel 1995). Finally, many American individuals volunteer in agencies such as the Peace Corps to make conditions better in less fortunate parts of the world.

TWO CASE STUDIES: HAITI AND THE UNITED STATES

To conclude this chapter and to illustrate many of the points we've made, we present two case studies: Haiti and the United States. The first is a Third World, or peripheral, nation in the Caribbean; the second, of course, is a First World, or core, nation.

THE THIRD WORLD: HAITI

Haiti, a Third World nation in the Caribbean, has a predominantly agricultural economy. Approximately 63 percent of the labor force is involved in agriculture, mostly on small family plots worn away by severe soil erosion. Coffee and sugar are the major cash crops, but light manufacturing—cosmetics, textiles, toys, and baseballs—provides the major source of export revenues (Europa Yearbook 1994). With a population of about 7 million people and an annual growth rate of 2.3 percent, Haiti is one of the fastest growing and poorest countries in the Western Hemisphere. Per capita productivity is $380 per person. Yet even this figure does not accurately reflect Haitian poverty, given the wide earnings gap between local elites and the remaining population, who make on average less than $100 a year

(Nelan 1993). Almost 80 percent of all Haitians are illiterate (Cobb 1987). Life expectancy is only 46 years, and the infant mortality rate is over 12 times higher than it is in North America.

Background. From the beginning, Haiti's role in the world system has been unique. Originally a French colony, the Haitian Republic gained its independence in 1804 as the result of a slave uprising. As the first black republic in a world system still dominated by slavery, Haiti was diplomatically isolated for more than three decades by both the United States and European powers, who feared that the Haitian revolution would set a dangerous example for blacks in their own countries and colonies (Plummer 1985). This concern did not, however, stop foreign companies from trading with Haiti, and Haitian migrant labor played a major role in the Cuban and Dominican Republican sugar economies.

Because political unrest threatened U.S. economic interests and because the United States wanted to use Haiti as a base to protect its routes to the Panama Canal, the U.S. Marines occupied Haiti from 1915 to 1934. Working with local elites, the marines helped found the modern Haitian military and ran the customs and banking business of the country (Wilentz 1993). Overt racism also played a role in the U.S. decision to occupy Haiti. U.S. Assistant Secretary of State William Phillips explained at the time: "These facts all point to the failure of an inferior people to maintain the degree of civilization left them by the French, or to develop any capacity of self-government entitling them to international respect and confidence" (Schmidt 1971, p. 63).

The Duvalier Dictatorship. Between 1957 and 1986, Haiti was governed by the Duvalier family. In cooperation with foreign investors, the Duvaliers and a small economic and military elite amassed fortunes. The Duvaliers robbed the country of many millions of dollars before a popular uprising led to their ouster. Although the United States issued strong verbal protests about human rights violations during the Duvaliers' reign, U.S. foreign policy provided tacit support for the dictators and even helped François Duvalier (Papa Doc) stay in power in exchange for supporting sanctions against Cuba, which was perceived to pose a communist threat.

Aristide and Modern Haiti. In December 1990, the Haitian people elected the socialist Jean-Bertrand Aristide as president by a 67 percent majority, in the first free and fair election since the Duvaliers took power. In February 1991, Aristide was sworn in, but in September he was overthrown by the military, in a coup led by two U.S.–trained Haitian generals. Although the United States had previously expressed some concern about Aristide's economic agenda, it played a key role in negotiating and militarily enforcing his return to power, perhaps in hope that his return would stem the tide of Haitians seeking refuge in the United States. Ironically, the international embargo spearheaded by the United States in the period preceding the reinstatement of Aristide had little impact on the Haitian elite; it did, however, substantially increase the suffering of Haiti's poor (Post 1993).

Future Prospects. Haiti remains very much a Third World country, one that may in fact be more vulnerable and more dependent than most. Haiti has no valuable natural resources; the land has been all but stripped bare of its once rich forests, and its soil is damaged, almost beyond repair. Although Haiti can offer cheap labor (the average worker earns the equivalent of 14 cents an hour to assemble toys, electronics, and clothes) (Wilentz 1993), better educated labor in Mexico and the newly developing nations of Southeast Asia make Haitian labor less attractive. Finally, with the end of the Cold War, the United States no longer needs Haiti even as a strategic foothold against communism. In short, Haiti has virtually nothing to trade on the world market. If it is to survive as a nation, let alone develop, Haiti will need resources from abroad. Research suggests, however, that those resources must take the form of foreign aid (gifts) if they are to help Haiti on the road to development (Wimberly 1990). Foreign investment and loans are only likely to help a very determined elite to maintain its power.

The First World: The United States

The United States is a leading economic power with the highest domestic productivity in the world (U.S. Bureau of the Census 1994, Table 1368). It has an extremely diversified economy and is in most respects self-sufficient, with the result that it has a great deal of economic independence. Although not the wealthiest nation in the world (that honor goes to Switzerland), the United States is very close to the top in every indicator of development. Productivity, life expectancy, education, and standard of living are all high.

Background. The United States developed in a unique social and physical environment. Rich natural resources and a sparse population encouraged replacement of human labor with innovative technology. Commitment to mass education, the absence of military invasion, and exploitation of resources in undeveloped parts of the world are additional reasons for the emergence of the United States as a dominant economic force.

Still, it was not until the decade following World War II that the United States experienced great prosperity. Industrial rearmament during the war provided jobs, fueled the economy, and boosted the nation out of its worst depression ever. While the industries of Europe and Asia were demolished during the war, the industrial sector in the United States remained intact and in full swing. By the late 1940s, 60 percent of the world's total manufacturing output came from the United States (Chirot 1986).

Threats to Preeminence. In the aftermath of the war, American assistance to countries in Western Europe and Asia (especially Japan) was instrumental in rebuilding cities and industries destroyed by the war. Foreign aid and credits were made available under the Marshall Plan in 1947; and in 1957, many of the core countries of Europe consolidated under the European Economic Community (EEC), also known as the Common Market. Both reconstruction and consolidation proved effective, causing the United States to lose some of its competitive advantage to other core countries in the world system.

Since World War II, the economy of the United States has shifted toward increased foreign investment and trade. Rather than invest profits in new equipment and technology in the United States, many U.S. corporations diversified into international markets for short-term profits. As a result, the productive capacities of U.S. factories and plants lost ground to those of core nations committed to maximizing long-term profit and modernizing their facilities. Since the 1960s, investments in secondary production (manufactured goods) have given way to a growing service economy (Chapter 17), which is based on consumption rather than production. The overall effect of these changes is that America's share of manufactured products for world export has shrunk.

Future Prospects. Although it is one of the most economically independent of all nations (unlike Japan and Germany, it does not depend heavily on imported energy), the prosperity and security of the United States are very much bound up in the international economy. Many of the goods used in everyday life in the United States have been made possible by the cheap labor of people in less developed countries.

The United States faces four challenges in the world economy. First, it imports more than it exports. Many U.S. goods are not competitive on the international market. Second, the Third World debt crisis has resulted in many bad debts for U.S. banks. This particular form of multinational capital penetration makes U.S. and other First World bankers very interested parties to foreign policy decisions. Third, the United States must decide how generous to be. After World War II, the Marshall Plan was essential in the redevelopment of Western Europe and Japan. There are now requests for a similar sort of investment in Eastern Europe. If this occurs, the Third World might lose out once again as U.S. and European nations look east rather than south. Finally, the United States must decide whether to intervene militarily in order to maintain access to international markets and resources on which the U.S. economy depends.

THE CONFLICT PERSPECTIVE ON INTERNATIONAL INEQUALITY: THE THIRD WORLD AS A MARKET

Why do First and Second World nations interfere in Third World countries? Why have countries such as Nicaragua and Cuba become battlegrounds for more developed nations? Why, as in the 1991 war with Iraq, do First and Second World nations find themselves at war with the Third World nations they have armed? Although ideology plays a part, the importance of the Third World as a market provides a more compelling answer.

Nearly one-third of all world trade is with Third World nations. These nations are both an important market for manufactured goods and an important source of cheap labor and raw materials. Any closure of Third World trade would strike a major blow to international trade and world capitalism. Although the avowed aim of U.S. foreign policy has been to ensure each nation's right to self-determination, in practice U.S. policy has been more concerned with keeping nations open to capitalist interests than with protecting political liberty. In an effort to keep Third World markets open to American-owned multinationals, the United States has provided economic and military support to repressive right-wing, totalitarian regimes in nations such as South Korea, Vietnam, Chile, Nicaragua, and Iran. Despite evidence of continuing human rights violations, the Clinton administration has renewed China's most favored nation trade status, presumably because a market for U.S. goods that consists of 1 billion people is simply too lucrative to

THINKING CRITICALLY

One reason nations use coercion to force their will on others is that there is no authority to compel them not to do so. Consider how relations among U.S. states might differ if federal power to control these relations were as weak as the power of the United Nations to control international affairs.

penalize or ignore. Likewise, it is hard to assess the extent to which the recent presence of European and U.S. peacekeeping forces in Somalia was a result of humanitarian concerns and the extent to which it was a result of pressure from the European and U.S. petroleum firms that hold large oil exploration contracts in the country.

In the Cold War era, as a matter of official policy, Second World nations espoused the right of Third World peoples to employ force as a means to liberation. In Soviet foreign policy, however, liberation frequently meant liberation from capitalism and an alliance against Western capitalist states; it did not mean independence for Third World nations (McFarlane 1985). Pressured by a stagnating domestic economy and by heavy military expenses in nations such as Afghanistan, Soviet foreign policy under Mikhail Gorbachev became much less ideological; under Boris Yeltsin, Russian diplomacy is increasingly driven by its own need for foreign currency and by the need to ensure a supply of raw materials and a market for its manufactured goods. In that respect, it is like U.S. policy.

Nowhere are the political and economic interdependencies of First, Second, and Third World nations more clear than in the Iraqi conflict. Although the Middle East has a long history of religious and ethnic strife, the conflicts have changed dramatically over the last two decades. Ever since oil prices quadrupled in 1973, First and Second World nations have exchanged arms for oil, with little attention to either their own diplomatic objectives or those of their client states. The United States, one of the world's largest arms exporters, enamored with cheap energy and unwilling to pay a higher price for oil and gasoline, faced the irony of

Now that the Cold War has virtually ended, arms manufacturers in Russia, China, Western Europe, and the United States increasingly rely on foreign markets for their products. Saddam Hussein bought Mirage fighters and Exocet missiles from the French, mines from Italy, radar from Brazil, and tanks and artillery from China and the Soviet Union. German companies sold munitions and communications equipment to Iraq and helped to build its bunkers and chemical weapons plants. British and U.S. firms provided weapons parts and apparently some of the equipment necessary for the manufacture of nuclear weapons. Ironically, Kuwait and Saudi Arabia provided much of the financing for the arms that Saddam Hussein would later turn against them. At present, there is little to prevent a massive military rearmament in the region.

waging the Desert Storm campaign against an Iraqi army equipped with weapons provided by U.S., British, French, German, and Italian arms suppliers. As diplomats continue to struggle with the political consequences of the most recent war in the Middle East, defense industries in the First and Second World have already

APPLICATIONS IN DIVERSITY

What Roles Do Third World Women Play in Development?

The Fourth World Conference on Women, held in Beijing, China, during the summer of 1995, pointed to a fact already well known by the participants: Third World women are important. In fact, in many parts of the Third World, women are the main producers of food crops. Where women do not actually cultivate crops, they are almost always the main cooks and food processors. In several parts of sub-Saharan Africa, for instance, women are responsible for at least 70 percent of the total production, processing, and marketing of food. In addition to providing food and being almost exclusively responsible for the rearing of children, women also have the burden of collecting fuelwood and water; in areas where there are severe fuelwood deficits—Burkina, Faso, Haiti, and Nepal, for example—women spend 5 to 10 hours a week seeking wood for their cooking fires (United Nations Population Fund 1991). Although women and girls form only half of the world's population, their labor appears to account for at least two-thirds of the total work hours expended on any given day or in any given year. Yet they receive only a small portion of the world's income in return and own little of the world's property. Despite the economic contributions of women to both their families and their nations, at least until the mid-1970s, development agencies routinely directed educational programs about the advantages of using new types of seed, fertilizer, and cropping systems almost exclusively to male audiences. No wonder these programs failed to increase agricultural productivity, when the people doing the actual farming were female!

Most specialists now recognize that sustainable development will only become possible when women are full partners in the process. Research clearly shows that overall economic growth has been fastest in those areas of the world where women have higher status and slowest where they face the greatest disadvantage (State of World Population 1992). Where women attain higher levels of education, their productivity in both the paid and unpaid labor market is enhanced. Furthermore, because women appear to be more likely than men to invest new resources in the nutrition, medical care, and education of their children (Schultz 1993), investments in women's education may be particularly crucial to development efforts.

As a result of the growing awareness of the critical role that women play in societal as well as domestic economies, new development strategies are more often aimed at women. These include programs designed to improve women's literacy, programs to help women market handicrafts and agricultural produce, changes in legal systems so that women can own and manage their own property, and access to contraceptive knowledge and technology for women so that they can control their reproduction. Such programs cannot take the place of broader programs designed to reduce massive international and national disparities, but including women in development programs will help to ensure that their benefits reach down to the household level (Walsh 1995).

Thinking Critically

What do you think? Why might development agencies have directed their efforts toward men until about 20 years ago? What conditions or events may have changed this? Why might development strategies aimed toward women be more successful? Should development agencies be concerned about the roles of men in today's less developed countries? Why, or why not?

begun to rearm the region. Whatever the resolution, the issue reminds us of a lesson we learned in Chapter 9: Power is the most important determinant of the distribution of scarce resources, internationally as well as locally.

SOCIOLOGY ON THE NET

The wealth and riches of America can blind us to the extent of international inequality throughout the world and even in our own hemisphere. One of the more impoverished nations is Haiti.

`http://www.odci.gov/cia`

Surprise, you are now at the Central Intelligence Agency Home Page! Click on the **Publications** section. Now open the **1995 World Fact Book**. Scroll down the table of contents to Haiti. Open the section on **Haiti** and carefully review this information. Some of the more telling statistics are the infant mortality rate, life expectancy and the literacy rate. Return to the table of contents and open the document on the **United States**. How does the U.S. compare to Haiti? Try a few more countries like Japan, India and Germany. These statistics tell us that inequality refers to not only the quality of life, but also to the length of life. Now try to come up with a picture of everyday life in Haiti. How would you be living if you were born there? There are other nations around the world that are poorer than Haiti. Can you find some of them?

The United Nations has a great deal of information on international inequality. One of the more dramatic indicators is the World Poverty Clock.

`http://www.undp.org`

Click on the highlighted phrase entitled **Poverty Clock**. Think back to the previous chapter and remember the definitions of absolute poverty and relative poverty. What kind of poverty is the United Nations measuring? How does the United Nations definition of poverty differ from the one used by the United States government? How many people in the world are currently living on less than a dollar day?

UMMARY

1. Analysis of the world political economy often divides the world's nations into three categories. The First World consists of the rich, diversified, independent nations of the capitalist core. The Second World consists mainly of Russia and the former Communist bloc countries. The Third World refers to those economically disadvantaged nations that have a peripheral status in the world economic system.
2. The human suffering index uses 10 criteria to assess human suffering on a global basis: life expectancy, daily calorie supply, access to clean drinking water, infant immunization, secondary school enrollment, GNP per capita, rate of inflation, communications technology, political freedom, and civil rights.
3. Inequality is the key fact in the international political economy. Reduction of this disparity through development of less developed countries is a common

international goal. Development is not the same as Westernization; it means increasing productivity and raising the standard of living.

4 Modernization theory, a functionalist perspective on social change, rests on the assumption that less developed countries will evolve toward industrialization by adopting the technologies and social institutions used by the developed countries.

5 World system theory, a conflict perspective, views the world as a single economic system in which the already industrialized countries control world resources and wealth at the expense of the less developed countries. The processes of economic exchange favor the developed countries so that the gap between rich and poor countries is increasing.

6 Third World dependency can take one of three forms: "banana republic" dependency on the export of raw materials; industrial dependency on assembly projects for First World firms; and dependency on international capital. All entail a triple alliance among multinational (First World) firms, local elites, and the local state.

7 The extent of international inequality is dramatic. Herbert Gans identified several favorable consequences for the First World: poor people to do the "dirty work"; cheap consumer items; markets for goods no longer useful in the core; a cushion to absorb the cost of technological changes in the core; and jobs for core citizens involved in serving or policing the periphery.

8 Empirical studies document that multinational penetration has four types of negative consequences for Third World nations: It increases sectoral inequality, income inequality, authoritarianism, and conflict.

9 As the international political economy undergoes competition, change, and conflict, there are often Third World challenges to the international status quo. First World responses can be broadly categorized as military or humanitarian.

10 Haiti is an example of a Third world, or peripheral nation. Originally colonized by France, Haiti was occupied by United States Marines from 1915 to 1934 in order to protect American economic interests there. The 1994 humanitarian military intervention in Haiti seems mainly to have been for the purpose of stopping the flood of refugees to U.S. shores.

11 The U.S. exemplifies a core nation. Its own economy is productive, diverse, and independent, and its multinational corporations have been very active in turning the cheap goods and cheap labor of the Third World to their economic advantage.

12 In many parts of the Third World, women are the principal food producers, but until at least the mid-1970s, they were largely ignored by development programs. New development strategies are more often aimed at women.

SUGGESTED READINGS

CHIROT, Daniel. 1986. *Social Change in the Modern Era.* New York: Harcourt Brace Jovanovich. A historical and comparative approach to understanding social changes in the world. Excellent introduction to a complex area.

ECKSTEIN, Susan (ed.). 1988. *Power and Popular Protest Latin American Social Movements.* Berkeley, Calif.: University of California Press. A collection of essays outlining the causes and consequences of Latin American protest and resistance movements. Factors unique to the Latin American experience are discussed, and features common to all protest movements are identified.

GEORGE, Susan. 1984. *Ill Fares the Land: Essays on Food, Hunger, and Power.* Great Britain: Writers and Readers Publ. A very readable collection of essays by a well-known science and policy writer who employs a conflict and world system perspective in her analysis of international inequalities.

GEORGE, Susan. 1988. *A Fate Worse Than Debt.* New York: Grove Press. A readable analysis of the results of international debt in peripheral nations by a well-known and respected world system analyst.

GRADOLPH, Rebecca Sue. 1994. *Social Stratification in Soviet Russia, 1991: Inequality of Opportunity and Outcome.* A contemporary study of social inequality in Russia after the demise of the Communist regime there in 1989.

KURTZ, Lester, with Dillard, John, and Benford, Robert. 1988. *The Nuclear Cage: A Sociology of the Arms Race.* Englewood Cliffs, N.J.: Prentice-Hall. A primer on the nuclear arms race and a recipe for its resolution. This explicitly sociological account gives special attention to the symbolic meanings that fuel conflict and impede resolution.

ROBINSON, Kathryn. 1986. *Stepchildren of Progress: The Political Economy of Development in an Indonesian Mining Town.* Albany: SUNY Press. A monograph based on two years of fieldwork in an Indonesian village that is an indictment of multinational investment. It is an enormously readable book, more like a horror story than a scholarly compendium.

CHAPTER 11

Racial and Ethnic Inequalities

OUTLINE

PROLOGUE

Have You Ever . . . been the victim of a racist or ethnic joke? Felt the sting of bigotry in some other way? If not, have you ever thought about how being the target of ethnic intolerance might feel?

A few years ago, a university sociology student wrote about his experiences with racism. A Chinese American, he had immigrated to the United States from Taiwan as a seven year old. He knew just three words in English—*dog, cat,* and *fish.* But he learned the Pledge of Allegiance, and the first day of school he stood to recite it "so proudly that I shook with excitement the whole way through." He recalled looking around and thinking that he was equal with any one of his class–mates; but that changed before the day was over.

When he tried to pick a seat in the lunchroom, the kids already at the table told him to leave. He recalls their chanting, "Hey, Ching Chong!" A little later, a few children approached and offered to show him how to eat his lunch. Not understanding, he said OK. The kids mixed together everything on his plate, then poured milk all over it. They said the mess looked more like Chinese food that way.

A fight broke out, and his parents were called to school. The principal suggested that he was emotionally disturbed and antisocial. After all, he had made no attempts to talk to anyone. "However," the student wrote, "the principal made no attempt to talk to me while I sat for an hour in his office waiting for my parents to arrive. If he did, maybe he would have realized that I spoke no English."

Although there are obvious signs of progress, most minority Americans must cope daily with the disadvantage of minority status. The culture of prejudice is alive: In overt as well as covert ways, people discriminate—even those who say they do not. Can you think of examples in your school?

Race remains an important source of intergroup tension and hostility in the United States, as the aftermath of the O. J. Simpson murder trial verdict dramatically showed. None of us is immune to this tension. In this chapter, we consider how class and race have interacted to produce this tension, and we examine prospects for the future.

RACE, ETHNICITY, AND INEQUALITY

In Chapter 9, we reviewed the general picture of inequality in the United States and examined theories of inequality based on achieved characteristics. We also, however, need to consider differences in rewards and life chances that are associated with ascribed characteristics. In Chapters 11, 12, and 13, we examine three such ascribed characteristics: race and ethnicity, sex, and age. In each case, we deal with the differences in life chances that exist by virtue of ascribed characteristics and consider whether these differences can be explained by the usual processes of social class or whether some other processes are at work. In short, we ask whether the greater poverty of African Americans, Hispanics, and Native Americans can be explained by color-blind forces of educational and occupational attainment or whether it is in some way a direct product of being African American, Hispanic, or

Native American. To the extent that the latter is true, we need to introduce some new ideas to explain how ascribed statuses work in a class system.

Race and Ethnicity

A **race** is a category of people treated as distinct on account of physical characteristics to which *social* importance has been assigned.

An **ethnic group** is a category whose members are thought to share a common origin and to share important elements of a common culture.

A **race** is a category of people treated as distinct on account of physical characteristics to which *social* importance has been assigned. An **ethnic group** is a category whose members are thought to share a common origin and to share important elements of a common culture—for example, a common language or religion (*Marger* 1994). Both race and ethnicity are handed down to us from our parents, but the first refers to the genetic transmission of physical characteristics whereas the second refers to socialization into cultural characteristics.

Although race is based loosely on physiological characteristics, such as skin color, both race and ethnicity are socially constructed categories. Both individual self-identity, and institutional forces play a role in the creation and maintenance of racial and ethnic statuses. For example, in 1930, the U.S. Bureau of the Census declared that those with Mexican background should be classified as nonwhite. The Mexican government complained, and the bureau reversed itself. Now the census bureau defines Hispanic Americans as an ethnic group, declaring that Hispanics can be of any race (U.S. Bureau of the Census 1994, 4). The 1980 census revealed that there were 6.7 million people who claimed Native American (American Indian) as their ethnic group, but only 1.4 million who claimed it as their race (Lieberson and Waters 1988). More recently, the shift from "black" to "African American" is an example of changing from a racial to an ethnic group identification. Then, too, the growing number of multiracial births in the United States helps to blur the very concept of race (Kalish 1995; Morganthau 1995). As these examples illustrate, racial and ethnic statuses are not fixed. Over time, individuals may change their racial and ethnic identification, and society, too, may change the statuses it recognizes and uses.

Race and ethnicity *could* be of primary importance to sociologists as the basis of subcultures. Sociologists could (and some do) focus on racial and ethnic differences in musical preferences, language use, and values. Overshadowing these subcultural differences among racial and ethnic groups, however, is the issue of inequality. In the United States today, African Americans, Hispanics, and Native Americans do not simply comprise subcultures, they comprise *disadvantaged* subcultures. In the rest of this chapter, we analyze the types and degree of disadvantage involved.

Caste and Class: Racism As a Special Case of Stratification

How do we explain the development and persistence of racial and ethnic inequalities? Most contemporary scholars use some form of conflict theory. In the conflict over scarce resources, this theory suggests, historical circumstances (such as slavery, technological advantage, and so on) gave some groups an edge over others. The advantaged groups developed a **dominant culture**—the culture seen as "best," the standard against which other cultures or subcultures are compared. (Chapter 3 discussed dominant cultural values in the United States.) In order to maintain and enhance their advantage, the advantaged groups also created social institutions that perpetuated and rationalized the status quo.

A **dominant culture** is the culture seen as "best," the standard against which other cultures or subcultures are compared.

As we saw in Chapter 9, the indirect inheritance model built into our family and educational institutions is one way to maintain advantage. In the United States, another way to maintain advantage involves the ideology of the American Dream: Equality of opportunity is assumed to exist, and your position in the class structure is believed to be a fair reflection of what you deserve. In addition, however, racial advantages have been maintained through racism, an ideology that justifies and rationalizes racial differences. **Racism** is a belief that inherited physical characteristics determine the presence or absence of socially relevant abilities and characteristics and that such differences provide a legitimate basis for unequal treatment.

Racism is a belief that inherited physical characteristics determine the presence or absence of socially relevant abilities and characteristics and that such differences provide a legitimate basis for unequal treatment.

A major question for scholars of racial and ethnic inequality today is how important a part racism plays in the maintenance of contemporary racial disadvantages.

The Semicaste Model. Early theorists of stratification confidently expected that industrialization would be followed by the virtual elimination of castelike ascribed statuses in favor of achieved status. Clearly, however, ascribed characteristics such as race and sex continue to be important in allocating scarce resources in our society. Many scholars of race relationships in the United States believe that in our country there are two stratification systems, class and caste. This *semicaste structure* is a hierarchical ordering of social classes within racial categories that are also hierarchically ordered (see Figure 11.1).

As in a full caste system, race represents an unchangeable status associated with unequal evaluation of worth. The analogy extends to the mechanisms for maintaining separation between the categories. The barriers between races are maintained in the same ways as in the Indian caste system described in Chapter 9: All children are assigned the racial category of their parents (or, in the case of mixed parentage, of their nonwhite parent), intermarriage between races is frowned on (was in fact illegal in many states in the United States until the 1967 Supreme Court decision *Loving vs. Virginia*), and residential segregation has discouraged contact between the races. These mechanisms ensure the maintenance of inherited castelike status from one generation to the next.

Unlike the Indian system, however, the semicaste structure includes social class groupings within each race. Data from 1993 (Table 11.1) show that, although the median income of white families is nearly double that of black families ($39,300 versus $21,542), the races display very similar patterns of internal inequality. In both the white and black populations, the wealthiest 20 percent of families get about half of all income. We can also see another implication of the semicaste

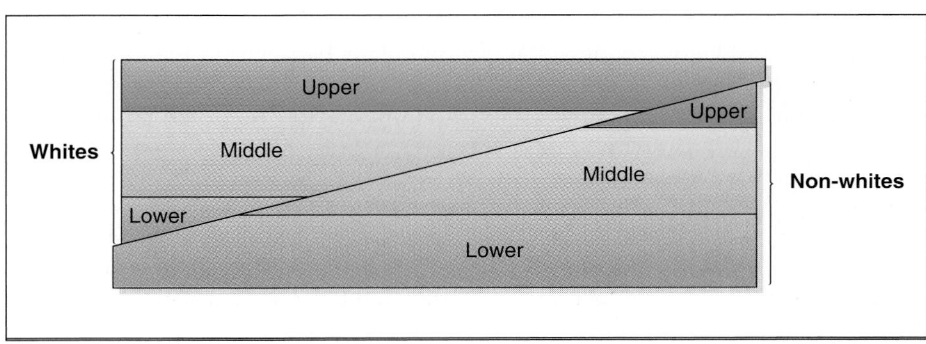

FIGURE 11.1
THE SEMICASTE MODEL

Race and ethnicity are factors in the stratification system of the United States. There is a social class hierarchy within each race, but there is also a castelike barrier between races. Upper-class nonwhites are not as upper class as upper-class whites, and the lowest positions in the social class hierarchy are reserved for nonwhites.

TABLE 11.1
INCOME AND WEALTH DISTRIBUTIONS AMONG FAMILIES BY RACE AND ETHNICITY, 1993

United States income data support the semicaste model. The wealthiest 20 percent of black and Hispanic families receive 51 and 49 percent of all family income, a figure very comparable to the 48 percent received by the wealthiest 20 percent of white families. Nevertheless, wealthy white families are much better off than wealthy black and Hispanic families and poor black and Hispanic families have only a small fraction as much wealth as poor white families do.

	PERCENTAGE OF INCOME RECEIVED			MEDIAN NET WORTH		
	BLACK	HISPANIC	WHITE	BLACK	HISPANIC	WHITE
POOREST FIFTH	3%	4%	4%	$ 250	$ 499	$10,743
SECOND FIFTH	8	9	9	3,406	2,900	27,057
THIRD FIFTH	14	15	15	8,480	6,313	36,341
FOURTH FIFTH	24	23	23	20,745	20,100	54,040
RICHEST FIFTH	51	49	48	45,023	55,923	123,298
MEDIAN NET WORTH				$ 4,418	$ 4,656	$ 45,740

SOURCE: U.S. Bureau of the Census, 1996a and http://www.census.gov/hhes/wealth/wlth93.

model in this table; wealthy blacks have less money than wealthy whites, and poor blacks are much poorer than poor whites.

American scholars have hotly debated whether race (caste) or class is most important for understanding the structure of inequality in the United States. The operation of the general processes of stratification noted in Chapter 9 is surely important, but the condition of minorities cannot be understood in terms of social class alone. Rather, as the semicaste model suggests, both race and class are important (Thomas 1993). We will return to this issue in the final section of this chapter.

SEPARATE AND UNEQUAL: THE MAINTENANCE OF INEQUALITY

How is it possible for groups to interact on a daily basis within the same society and yet remain separate and unequal? In this section, we introduce sociological concepts that help explain how societies maintain and reinforce group differences.

A **majority group** is a group that is culturally, economically, and politically dominant.

A **minority group** is a group that is culturally, economically, and politically subordinate.

MAJORITY AND MINORITY GROUPS

Rather than speaking of white and black or Jew and Arab, sociological theories of intergroup relations usually refer to majority and minority groups. A **majority group** is a group that is culturally, economically, and politically dominant. A **minority group** is a group that is culturally, economically, and politically subordinate. Although minority groups are often smaller than majority groups, this is not always the case. In the Union of South Africa, for example, whites have been the majority group, although they make up only 15 percent of the population; until May 1994, when newly elected President Nelson Mandela and his African National Congress assumed power, whites had long controlled all of South Africa's major political, economic, and social institutions. Relations between majority and minority groups may take one of four general forms: conflict, accommodation, acculturation, or assimilation.

Conflict. Following the definition in Chapter 5, **conflict** is a struggle over scarce resources that is not regulated by shared rules; it may include attempts to neutralize, injure, or destroy one's rivals. In European contact with the native populations of North America, the scarce resource was land, and open conflict was the means used to acquire it. In other instances, racial conflict is less violently expressed through laws requiring segregation or forbidding social, political, or economic participation by the minority group.

Conflict is a struggle over scarce resources that is not regulated by shared rules; it may include attempts to destroy or neutralize one's rivals.

Accommodation. When the two groups coexist as separate cultures in the same society, we speak of **accommodation.** The groups are essentially parallel cultures, each with its own institutions. Canada's French and English provinces and Switzerland's German, Italian, and French cantons are examples of this type of relationship. Although the two cultures are seldom equal, the relationship between them is not based on direct subordination. The idea of parallel cultures is sometimes referred to as *pluralism*. Such systems are often difficult to maintain.

Accommodation occurs when two groups coexist as separate cultures in the same society.

Acculturation. Another possible outcome of intergroup contact is for the minority group to adopt the culture of the majority group. This process is called **acculturation.** It includes learning the language, history, and manners of the majority group; it may even include accepting its loyalties and values as one's own. As middle-class African Americans in the United States have learned, however, acculturation does not necessarily lead to acceptance. They may find, for example, that their colleagues at work choose not to be their friends outside the workplace.

Acculturation occurs when the minority group adopts the culture of the majority group.

Assimilation. When the minority group is fully integrated into the institutions of society and ceases to be a subordinate group, we speak of **assimilation**. This usually includes going to the same schools, living in the same neighborhoods, belonging to the same social groups, and being willing to marry one another. Under conditions of full assimilation, members of a minority group cease to be defined as a distinct group. Put another way, assimilation—and, to a lesser degree, acculturation—require that minority group members give up some (or most) of their own heritage and culture.

Assimilation is the full integration of the minority group into the institutions of society and the end of its identity as a subordinate group.

Racial and ethnic relations in the United States have shown aspects of all these patterns. We're well aware of conflict. As discussed in Chapter 3, ours is a culturally diverse society—one composed of fairly dissimilar peoples with distinct subcultures. Cultural diversity incorporates aspects of both accommodation and acculturation. To varying degrees, our dominant and minority cultures accommodate one another, as many ethnic subcultures maintain their own separate institutions (schools, community associations, language, newspapers). At the same time, through acculturation, ethnic minorities learn the language and manners of the

In 1991, an onlooker videotaped the beating by police of Rodney King, an African American. In the police officers' subsequent trial, prosecutors presented evidence that the incident was racially motivated. After a jury acquitted the officers, rioting African American youths pulled Reginald Denny, a white truck driver, from his rig at a Los Angeles intersection and beat him. The rage displayed in both incidents shows that serious racial tension exists in the United States. Nevertheless, it is equally important to note that both Rodney King and Reginald Denny later went on national television to beg for interracial harmony and forgiveness. Rodney King's plea, "Can we all get along?" became something of a one-line national poem.

Thinking Critically

In recent years, racial and ethnic conflict on college and university campuses (as well as in high schools) has concerned students, parents, school officials, and policy makers. Campus racism and inter-ethnic conflict are especially discouraging after decades of hope for improvement through integration. Can you think of specific examples of prejudice or discrimination on your campus? What do you think are the causes of campus racism and ethnic conflict today? How have these issues been addressed in your school?

dominant culture. Except for a few white immigrant groups such as 19th-century Germans, full assimilation (the so-called melting pot) has rarely been achieved in the United States.

In fact, full assimilation is a relatively rare form of intergroup contact. Whether we look at Nigeria, Russia, Belgium, or the United States, we see that groups remain separate and often unequal after generations of living in the same society. This separatism is achieved through processes that promote what sociologists call **social distance.** Social distance is operationally defined by questions such as "Would you be willing to have members of this group as good friends?" It is a measure of the degree of intimacy and equality in the relationship between two groups.

Two processes that encourage social distance even when physical distance is absent are prejudice and discrimination. Most societies also use segregation, or physical distance, as an aid to maintaining social distance.

Social distance is the degree of intimacy in relationships between two groups.

Prejudice

The foundation of prejudice is **stereotyping,** a belief that people who belong to the same category share common characteristics—for example, that athletes are dumb or that African Americans are naturally good dancers. **Prejudice,** like stereotyping, is irrational, but prejudice moves beyond stereotyping in that it always involves a negative image. It exists in spite of the facts rather than because of them. A person who believes that all Italian Americans are associated with the Mafia will ignore or explain away all instances of law-abiding behavior of Italian Americans. If confronted with an exceptionally honest man of Italian descent, the bigot will rationalize him as the exception that proves the rule.

Stereotyping is a belief that people who belong to the same category share common characteristics.

Prejudice is irrationally based negative attitudes toward categories of people.

A startling example of the irrationality of prejudice is the decision by the United States to intern its West Coast Japanese American citizens during World

Despite major changes in race relations over the past 30 years, racism is still apparent in the United States. These people were photographed as they watched the announcement of the not-guilty verdict in the O. J. Simpson criminal trial. Their faces reflect the response throughout the nation: Many whites were dismayed; many African Americans were delighted. In one Newsweek *poll, 85 percent of African Americans agreed with the jury's verdict of not guilty, and 80 percent thought the jury was fair and impartial. Among whites, just 32 percent agreed with the verdict, and only half thought the jury was fair and impartial (Whitaker 1995a). Once again, Americans became aware of how racially divided our experiences can be.*

War II. The decision was made to go ahead with the internment in spite of the lack of any evidence that this was necessary. Said General John DeWitt (1943): "The very fact that no sabotage has taken place to date is a disturbing and confirming indication that such action will be taken."

Prejudice is a powerful obstacle to the kinds of interaction that might reduce intergroup barriers. It ensures that when people from different groups interact, they see not each other but only their conception of what the other is like. What causes prejudice? We review three factors: cultural norms, institutional patterns, and personal factors.

Cultural Norms. We learn to hate and fear through the same socialization processes by which we learn to love and admire. While they may be obvious, these processes are often subtle. For instance, in the popular Disney movie "Beauty and the Beast," the beauty is white with Anglo features. So is the beast, once he turns into a human being. Both these characters are to be admired. In contrast, the evil men in the movie, whom we are expected to fear and hate, have darker complexions and Arabic features.

Prejudice is a shared meaning that we develop through our interactions with others. Most prejudiced people learn prejudice when very young as they are internalizing other social norms. This prejudice may then grow or diminish, depending on whether groups and institutions encountered during adulthood reinforce these early learnings (Marger 1994).

Institutional Patterns. Prejudice also arises from and is reinforced by institutionalized patterns of inequality. In a stratified society, we tend to rate ourselves and others in terms of economic worth. If we observe that no one pays highly for a group's labor, we are likely to conclude that the members of the group are not

These children are taking part in a Ku Klux Klan rally in Stephensville, Texas. Their participation is an example of how racism is learned through the process of socialization, described in Chapter 6.

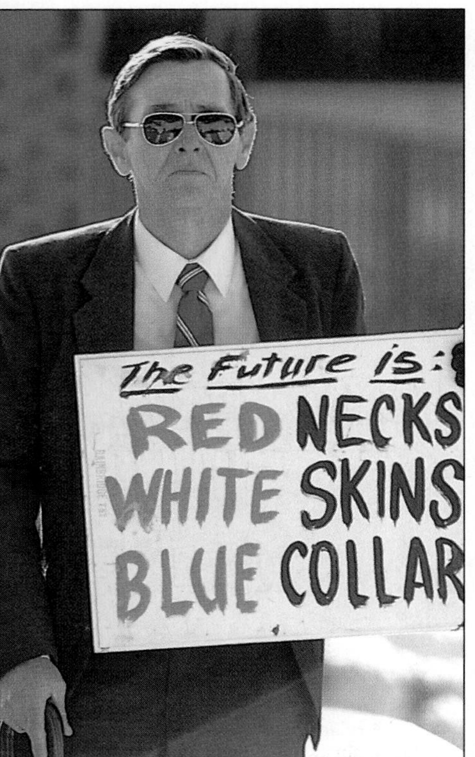

Prejudice is a negative and irrational attitude toward others. Because it is based on feelings and values rather than facts or experiences, prejudice is often difficult to eliminate. This man almost certainly learned racial hatred before he learned his ABCs. Instead of trying to change people's beliefs, most public policy is designed to prevent acts of discrimination and to eliminate public demonstrations of racism such as burning African American churches or painting swastikas on synagogues.

Authoritarianism is a tendency to be submissive to those in authority coupled with an aggressive and negative attitude toward those lower in status.

Scapegoating occurs when people or groups who are blocked in their own goal attainment blame others for their failure.

The **self-fulfilling prophecy** occurs when acting on the belief that a situation exists causes it to become real.

worth much. Through this learning process, members of the minority as well as the majority group learn to devalue the minority group (J. Q. Wilson 1992).

Prejudice is also powerfully reinforced by patterns of segregation and discrimination. A child growing up in a society where racial separation is well established in housing, schooling, and work is very likely to learn to devalue members of the minority group—especially if this separatism is accompanied by differential social class rankings.

Personal Factors. Personality factors alone cannot explain widespread prejudice (Stone 1985). Nevertheless, some people are more prone to prejudice than others. Three factors that dispose such people to prejudice are authoritarianism, frustration, and beliefs about stratification.

Authoritarianism is a tendency to be submissive to those in authority and aggressive and negative toward those lower in status (Allport 1979). Regardless of their own race or ethnic group, authoritarians in the United States tend to be strongly anti-black and anti-Semitic.

Frustration is another characteristic associated with prejudice. People or groups who are blocked in their own goal attainment are likely to blame others for their problems. This practice, called **scapegoating**, has appeared time and again. From anti-Chinese riots in 19th-century California to anti-Jewish atrocities in Nazi Germany, setbacks for majority group members often result in attacks against the minority group. As a current example, illegal immigrants in California are blamed for economic problems in the state, although there are significant other causes, such as a lowered tax base and increased unemployment.

Finally, prejudice is more likely among individuals who believe strongly in the American Dream. People who subscribe to the view that we can all get ahead if we work hard and that poor people have only themselves to blame are substantially more likely to attribute poverty or disadvantage to personal deficiencies. In the case of disadvantaged minorities, these people believe that the disadvantage is the fault of undesirable traits within the minority group (NORC 1993; Marger 1994).

The Self-Fulfilling Prophecy

An important mechanism for maintaining prejudice is the **self-fulfilling prophecy**, which occurs when acting on the belief that a situation exists causes it to become real. A classic example is the situation of women in feudal Japan. Because women were considered to be inferior and capable of only a narrow range of social roles, they were given limited education and barred from participation in the institutions of the larger society. The fact that they subsequently knew nothing of science, government, or economics was then taken as proof that they were indeed inferior and suited only for a role at home. And, in fact, most women were unsuited for any other role. Having been treated as inferiors had made most of them ignorant and unworldly.

The same process reinforces boundaries between racial and ethnic groups. The prediction of whites that their neighborhood will soon become "all black" or "all Hispanic," for example, after a few African American or Hispanic families move in, can lead them to sell their homes—mostly to African Americans or Hispanics.

DISCRIMINATION

Treating people unequally because of the categories they belong to is **discrimination.** Prejudice is an attitude; discrimination is behavior. Often, discrimination follows from prejudice, but it need not. Figure 11.2 shows the possible combinations of prejudice and discrimination. Most individuals fit into the two consistent cells: They are prejudiced, so they discriminate (bigots); or they aren't prejudiced, so they don't discriminate (friends). Some people, however, are inconsistent, usually because their own values are different from those of the dominant culture. Fair-weather friends do not personally believe in racial or ethnic stereotypes; nevertheless, they discriminate because of what they think their customers, neighbors, or parents would say. They do not wish to rock the boat by acting out values not shared by others. The fourth category, the timid bigots, have the opposite characteristics: Although they themselves are prejudiced, they hesitate to act on their feelings for fear of breaking the law or of what others would think (Merton 1949).

Public policy directed at racism is aimed almost entirely at reducing discrimination—allowing fair-weather friends to act on their fraternal impulses and putting some timidity into the bigot. As Martin Luther King, Jr., remarked, "The law may not make a man love me, but it can restrain him from lynching me, and I think that's pretty important" (cited in Rose 1981, 90).

THINKING CRITICALLY

In thinking about the relationship between prejudice and discrimination, we generally assume that prejudice is the cause of discrimination. Can you think of a time or a situation when the reverse might be true—that is, when prejudice might follow from discrimination?

Discrimination is the unequal treatment of individuals on the basis of their membership in certain categories.

SEGREGATION

The mechanisms of prejudice and discrimination may be carried out between groups in close, even intimate, contact; they create social distance between groups. Differences between groups are easier to maintain, however, if social distance is accompanied by **segregation**—the physical separation of minority and majority group members. Thus, most societies with strong divisions between majority and minority groups have ghettos, barrios, Chinatowns, or Little Italies, where, by law or custom, members of the minority group live apart.

Historical studies suggest that high levels of residential segregation of Hispanic, Asian, and African Americans are not new; they have existed since at least 1940 and have changed relatively little. Such segregation is not established by law, but neither is it a historical accident. It occurs partially as a result of social class segregation of neighborhoods, but it also occurs because whites have exerted economic and political pressure, including violence and intimidation, to keep minorities "in their place" (Saltman 1991). An example of economic pressure to maintain residential segregation is *redlining*—designating certain areas within which real estate loans will not be made. Redlining is further discussed in Chapter 22.

Reasons for segregation differ by group. Among white Hispanics and Asian Americans, income and occupation are important predictors of segregation. Once new immigrants improve their socioeconomic status, they are able to move into integrated neighborhoods. The same is less true for African Americans. Even if they have the same status characteristics as their white neighbors, African Americans are much more likely to remain segregated. The authors of one study concluded that "blacks experience a consistent, powerful, and highly significant penalty in the process of spatial assimilation" (Massey and Denton, 1988, 621).

Segregation refers to the physical separation of minority and majority group members.

FIGURE 11.2
THE RELATIONSHIPS BETWEEN PREJUDICE AND DISCRIMINATION

Prejudice is an attitude; discrimination is behavior. They do not always go hand in hand. Some people act on their attitudes, whereas others curb their behavior to conform to community standards. Fair-weather friends are unprejudiced people who will discriminate anyway; timid bigots are prejudiced people who are deterred from discrimination by community standards.

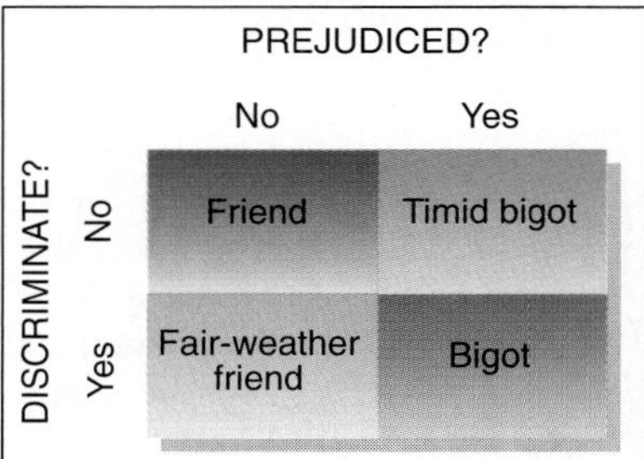

FOCUS ON YESTERDAY

America's Concentration Camps

"IN FEAR, THEY BURNED OR DESTROYED ALL THEIR TIES TO JAPAN— BOOKS, LETTERS, BIBLES, AND CLOTHING."

One of the darkest blots on the U.S. conscience is the relocation of 123,000 Japanese Americans during World War II. Although not as extreme as the enslavement of African Americans or the extermination of Native Americans, the relocation startles and shames because it occurred only 50 years ago. It brings home the reality that racism in a virulent form was alive and well very recently; it is not something our nation left behind with the last century.

Anti-Japanese racism was strong on the West Coast almost from the beginning of Japanese settlement. The relative economic success of the Japanese immigrants only strengthened the resentment. Thus, when Japan bombed Pearl Harbor in December 1941, there were immediate demands to do something about the Japanese in the United States—two-thirds of whom were U.S. citizens. During this period, Japanese Americans huddled in front of their radios, eager to hear the news but afraid to go out into the streets, to school, or to work. In fear, they burned or destroyed all their ties to Japan—books, letters, Bibles, and clothing (Sone 1953).

There were relatively few hostile incidents, but the fears turned out to be justified. In February 1942, President Roosevelt signed Proclamation 9066, the document that gave the army the right to do what it thought necessary to protect national security. The army's solution was the relocation of the West Coast Japanese Americans.

The people were given less than two months to sell all their belongings or to find a trusted white American to care for their property. Dealers in second-hand goods roamed like vultures through Japanese neighborhoods, trying to buy cheaply from people who had no time to look for a decent price. One woman remembers her mother breaking every piece of a treasured set of china rather than sell it for $15 (Houston and Houston 1973). Long-term land leases were voided, and many lost their homes and businesses. Things left behind were vandalized or stolen.

The army had as little time to prepare as did the Japanese Americans, and initially the internees were confined on fairgrounds, housed in exhibition halls and barns. Within six months, however, large relocation camps had been thrown up in isolated regions of the Western United States—Tule Lake, Manzanar, Minedoka. The inmates themselves provided all the labor in the camps; they were cooks, nurses, and even internal security forces. The weather was awful, and the conditions were Spartan at best.

Almost immediately, some Americans began to try to undo the damage. Through the American Friend's Service Committee (a Quaker organization), Japanese college students were sent to the East Coast to resume their studies. Efforts were made to find jobs and relocate families in the Midwest and the East. As a result, the camps were entirely empty before the war itself ended. And although it did not come close to covering actual losses, the U.S. government paid out $37 million in property damages to the internees.

One of the tactics the government used to defuse anti-Japanese sentiment and to integrate the Japanese Americans into American society was to encourage their enlistment in the armed forces. It is hard to imagine how a recruiter could enter an internment camp and urge young men to serve their country. Nevertheless, young men did volunteer and did serve with distinction in Europe and the Pacific, even in the army of occupation. For its size, the all-Nisei (American-born Japanese) 100th Battalion and 442nd Regimental Combat Team was the most decorated combat team in the war. Memorial services for dead soldiers were held in

FOCUS ON YESTERDAY

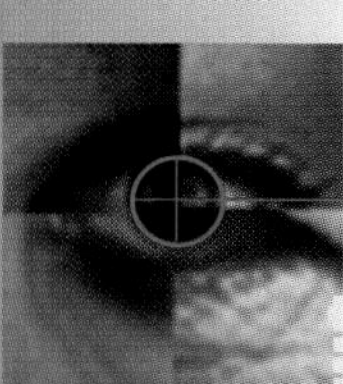

internment camps as well as at Arlington National Cemetery.

The deed of relocating Japanese Americans was shameful. Not a single act of sabotage or espionage was ever uncovered to justify the incarceration of a single individual, much less the entire West Coast Japanese American population (Girdner and Loftis 1969). Although wartime fear was a factor, so was racism; there was no move to imprison German Americans or Italian Americans. Racism plus fear resulted in the violation of the constitutional rights of more than 100,000 U.S. citizens.

In evaluating U.S. acts and principles, it is useful to remember that the United States was not the only nation evacuating people of Japanese ancestry. Canada and Mexico also evacuated West Coast Japanese. In the case of Canada, it was done far less humanely than in the United States. For example, the Canadian government confiscated all the goods of Japanese Canadian citizens, sold them at sacrifice prices, and gave the people back the money minus a sales commission. It broke up families by putting the men into work crews and sending the women, children, and elderly to fend for themselves in abandoned ghost towns (Kogamawa 1981). Having company in a disgraceful act does not reduce the burden, but it does make it clear that racism is not a particularly American character fault.

After decades of wrangling about whether or not the U.S. government was at fault in interning Japanese Americans, in September 1987 the U.S. Congress finally approved the extension of formal apologies to Japanese Americans interned during World War II. The bill also authorized $20,000 in reparation to each person of Japanese ancestry who was "relocated, confined, held in custody, or otherwise deprived of liberty or property.

Maximum population and dates of operation

Poston, AZ (17,814)
5/8/42–11/28/45
Tule Lake, CA (18,789)
5/27/42–3/20/46
Manzanar, CA (10,046)
6/1/42–11/21/45
Gila River, AZ (13,348)
7/20/42–11/11/45
Minidoka, ID (9,397)
8/10/42–10/28/45
Heart Mountain, WY
8/12/42–11/10/45
Granada, CO (Amache) (7,318)
8/27/42–10/15/45
Topaz, UT (8,350)
9/11/42–10/31/45
Rohwer, AR (9,475)
9/18/42–11/30/45
Jerome, AR (8,497)
10/6/42–6/30/44

Minidoka
Heart Mountain
Tule Lake
Topaz
Manzanar
Amache
Poston
Rohwer
Jerome
Gila River

MAP 11.1
WORLD WAR II "RELOCATION" CAMPS

SOURCE: U.S. Department of Justice.

INSTITUTIONAL RACISM

Institutional racism occurs when the normal operation of apparently neutral processes systematically produces unequal results for majority and minority groups.

Once well established, disadvantage can be perpetuated without explicit reference to race or ethnicity. The persistence of racial disadvantage through apparently neutral social processes is called **institutional racism.** Where this type of racism operates, apparently color-blind forces such as educational attainment and majority rule produce systematically unequal results for members of majority and minority groups. Institutionalized racism works in two primary ways:

1. *The indirect inheritance model.* The normal operation of the status attainment process described in Chapter 9 ensures that patterns of inequality established in past generations persist: Poorly educated parents tend to have poorly educated children. When a group starts out far behind the majority in terms of social class, the indirect inheritance process makes it enormously difficult to catch up.
2. *Majority rule.* In the United States, racial and ethnic minority groups are, in fact, numerical minorities. This means that their voting power is often insufficient to allow them to be heard. Political structures further weaken their vote. For example, when city council or school board members are elected on a citywide basis, it is difficult for numerically small groups to elect representatives. When elections are held by district, however, residentially concentrated minorities are more likely to be represented.

These two processes—indirect inheritance and majority rule—work together in the United States. As a result, racism, even if unintended, pervades U.S. social institutions. The following are some examples:

- As we have seen, there continue to be income differences between whites and blacks today, but the greatest disparity is in overall wealth. In 1991, the median net wealth of white households ($44,408) was almost 10 times that of black households ($4,604) (U.S. Bureau of the Census 1995, Table 742). This difference is mainly due to differences in home ownership. Home equity allows people to borrow for their children's educations or for future capital investments, among other things. But through three decades, starting in 1939, blacks were routinely denied affordable Federal Housing Authority (FHA) home loans (Duster 1995).
- Because of the types of questions included, IQ testing favors middle-class children, especially the white middle class. Nevertheless, IQ tests continue to be used as an indicator of intelligence and sometimes as a justification for structured inequality. Charles Murray's controversial 1994 book, *The Bell Curve,* is an example of, among other things, using IQ test scores as evidence of real differences in mental capacity among groups (Morganthau 1994).
- The criminal justice system, from the police officer to the judge and jury (particularly the judge), is dominated by whites (more precisely, white males) who have not experienced minority or ghetto life. The Social Applications section of Chapter 8 discussed capital punishment as institutionalized racism.
- From primary schools to universities, minority students are faced with subject matter and curricula that they find either irrelevant or racially insensitive or both.
- Minority students whose first language is not English face an often unappreciated hurdle when competing for grades.
- Minority citizens who speak little English find it difficult to vote when ballots are not available in their native languages. They also find it difficult to read such documents as driver's manuals and pass required written tests.

- Minorities can face obstacles in adhering to their religions when these depart from the dominant culture. The struggle of Native Americans to use peyote or eagle feathers in sacred rituals is an example.
- A growing body of research points to the existence of *environmental racism*. That is, members of minority groups are exposed to a disproportionately large number of health and environmental risks in their neighborhoods and on their jobs. Nationally, three of the five largest commercial hazardous-waste landfills are located in areas where African Americans and Hispanics make up the majority of the population (Bullard 1990). Farmworkers (the vast majority of whom are persons of color) and their children are poisoned by pesticides sprayed on crops. Indian reservations are increasingly asked to serve as high-level radioactive waste disposal sites for public utilities that are running out of space to store used nuclear fuel rods.

For much of American history, institutionalized racism was overshadowed by the more simple racism of individuals. Today, however, this more subtle form of racism is the major cause of continuing race and ethnic inequalities.

> **THINKING CRITICALLY**
>
> Some scholars contend that the major causes of racial/ethnic inequality in the United States today come from institutionalized, not individual, racism. What recommendations would you offer to policy makers interested in reducing racial or ethnic differences in quality of life?

EXTRAORDINARY SOLUTIONS

Prejudice, discrimination, and segregation are what might be called ordinary solutions that societies use to maintain boundaries between majority and minority groups (Marger 1994). If they fail, however, or if the minority group is seen as particularly threatening, extraordinary solutions may be invoked: apartheid, concentration camps, expulsion, or extermination. All too often, the history of intergroup relations is the study of extraordinary solutions.

RACIAL AND ETHNIC GROUPS IN THE UNITED STATES

The United States and, indeed, the entire Western Hemisphere comprise an ideal location for the study of racial and ethnic relations. For 400 years, Americans from diverse backgrounds have jostled one another—assimilating, accommodating, and conflicting. Some have come to escape persecution, some have come to strike it rich, some were dragged here, and some were here in the first place. In this section, we give a snapshot of each of the major racial and ethnic groups in the United States.

WHITE ETHNIC AMERICANS

The earliest immigrants to North America were English, Dutch, French, and Spanish. By 1700, however, English culture was dominant on the entire Eastern seaboard. The English became the majority group, and everybody else, regardless of degree or number, became a minority group in North America.

The Melting Pot. The extent of interaction and assimilation among white ethnic groups led some idealistic observers to hope that a new race would emerge in North America, where "individuals of all nations are melted into a great race" (Crèvecouer [1782] 1974).

Many white Americans still claim some ethnic identity; they say they are Polish, or Norwegian, or German. Over the past three decades, white ethnic Americans have demonstrated a resurgence in ethnic pride. Meanwhile, high rates of intermarriage mean that an increasing proportion of the white population have such complex ethnic heritages that they give up trying to figure it out and just call themselves Americans.

Anglo Conformity. In fact, careful observers suggest that the melting pot never existed. Instead of a blending of all cultures, what has occurred is a specific form of acculturation—**Anglo conformity**, the adoption of English customs and English language. To gain admission into U.S. society, to be eligible for social mobility, one has to learn to speak correct English, become restrained in public behavior, work on Saturday and worship on Sunday, and, in general, act like the American version of English people. Put another way, one has to learn and practice the dominant culture.

The bulk of white ethnic immigrants arrived in the United States during the last half of the 19th century and the first two decades of the 20th century, and they were often met with serious prejudice and discrimination. Their various languages (for example, Gaelic, Polish, and Italian) were not allowed in the public schools. Many immigrants were Catholic and faced both informal and formal anti-Catholic attitudes and policies (Schaefer 1990, 115). Partly as a result, their children emphasized Anglo conformity as a means of assimilation into American society. Some changed their names; the majority were proud to have given up their parents' old-country ways. But despite two or more generations of acculturation and assimilation, many white Americans still identify with their ethnic heritage.

Anglo conformity is the process of acculturation in which new immigrant groups adopt the English language and English customs.

The Third-Generation Principle. Marcus Hansen (1987), a historian, first proposed the *principle of third-generation interest* in 1937. His thesis was that grandchildren of the original immigrants would find renewed interest and pride in their ethnicity. What the child wishes to forget, the grandchild wishes to remember, Hansen wrote. Various empirical studies support Hansen's hypothesis (Schaefer 1990, 142).

Over the past three decades, white ethnics have demonstrated a resurgence in ethnic pride. Interestingly, this resurgence began at about the time when African Americans, Hispanic Americans, and Native Americans were beginning to assert pride in their own ethnic cultures (Fishman 1985b). Scholars have debated how much of the resurgence in white ethnic pride is due to the principle of third-generation interest and how much to feelings of increased competition from groups of color (Schaefer 1990, 143). But attributing ethnic pride simply to feelings of increased competition is an oversimplification of how people think and feel in our diverse society.

The Future of White Ethnicity. Whatever the answer, it is also true that high rates of intermarriage are blurring ethnic identities. As a result of intermarriage, a growing segment of the population cannot identify themselves with a single ethnic group (Lieberson and Waters 1993).

To a significant extent, ethnicity has ceased to be a basis for stratification among white, Gentile, non-Hispanic Americans. Although ethnic differences do exist and assimilation is not complete for white ethnics, these differences are not related to structured inequality. The integration of 80 percent of the population from diverse sets of backgrounds and conditions is a remarkable achievement. Yet it leaves out a significant portion of Americans. Next we consider the other 20 percent, nonwhites and Hispanics. We also consider Jews, a predominantly white group that has suffered discrimination.

African Americans

African Americans are the largest racial minority in the United States, representing one-ninth (or 12 percent) of the entire population. Their importance goes beyond their numbers. Next to Native Americans, African Americans have been the greatest challenge to the United States' view of itself as a moral and principled nation.

Like that of Native Americans, the history of African Americans has two essential elements that distinguish it from the history of other ethnic groups. First, blacks did not voluntarily come to the United States as hopeful immigrants. Second, African Americans are almost uniformly descendants of people who have been here since the founding of the nation, having roots in this country deeper than those of the Swedish, Norwegian, Italian, Irish, and German settlers who followed them.

At the beginning of the 19th century, more than 90 percent of the blacks in the United States were slaves, mostly in the rural South. Occasionally, they knew a skilled trade; more often, they were laborers. The limited evidence available suggests that slave families were usually stable two-parent families and had health and life expectancies similar to those of lower-class white Americans (Sowell 1981).

As the Civil War approached, southern society became more defensive about its "peculiar institution" and increasingly afraid of slave uprisings. For the first time, education of blacks was banned, and it appears that conditions affecting health and life expectancy deteriorated in this period (Eblen 1974). The Civil War and emancipation did little to change these conditions. Rather, 4 million illiterate slaves were freed to go out and support themselves in a land ravaged by war. They began their careers in freedom as a poor, rural, and southern people; they remained poor, rural, and southern until World War II.

In many ways, World War II was a benchmark for African Americans. A move from the rural South to the industrial North and Midwest, which had begun during World War I, was greatly accelerated. The defense effort sharply increased the demand for labor and made possible some real gains in income for blacks relative to whites. In addition, the Nazi slaughter of 6 million Jews in the name of racial purity deeply shocked the Western world, causing a renewed soul searching about racism in the United States.

Compared with the century before, the years following World War II have seen rapid social change: segregation banned in the armed forces (1948), school segregation outlawed (1954), the Civil Rights Act passed (1964), affirmative-action laws passed (1968). For the first time, African Americans appeared on television, on baseball diamonds, in ballet companies, and on the Supreme Court. In the following sections, we review some evidence about the differences in life chances for black and white Americans. In many cases, comparisons over time show that these differences have been significantly reduced.

Political Change. African Americans have been entitled to vote and hold office since the passage of the Fourteenth Amendment immediately after the Civil War. It took the Civil Rights Act of 1964, subsequent voter registration laws, and the civil rights activism of the late 1960s to make these political rights effective, however. The results have been dramatic, and African American voters are now an active and influential political force, especially in the Democratic Party. African

African Americans have had the right to vote since 1864 (a right, incidentally, not granted to Native Americans until 1924). Until the civil rights movement of the 1960s, however, many were too intimidated to use their voting rights. Martin Luther King Jr. played an important role in the effort to secure African American voting rights by presenting black and white Americans with a vision of racial equality and a sense that justice could be achieved.

American political leadership is also growing. The number of African Americans holding elected position increased by more than 500 percent between 1970 and 1991 (Joint Center for Political Studies 1991); cities with and without African American majorities have elected African American mayors (Atlanta, Seattle, Memphis, New York, and Los Angeles, for example), and 1989 saw the election of the first African American governor (L. Douglas Wilder in Virginia). Nevertheless, African Americans remain significantly underrepresented at all levels of government. In 1995, for instance, there were 40 African Americans in the U.S. House of Representatives, which has a total of 435 members. In the Senate, with 100 members, there was one African American (U.S. Bureau of the Census 1995, Table 444).

Education. African Americans have made significant progress in education, too. In 1940, young white adults were nearly three times more likely to have graduated from high school than blacks of the same age (39 versus 11 percent). By 1994, the racial difference in high school education was down to 9 percentage points (82 and 73 percent, respectively). Unfortunately, the educational gap remains wide at higher levels. Among young adults, blacks are only about half as likely as whites to have graduated from college (U.S. Bureau of the Census 1995, Table 238). Despite considerable improvement, then, significant educational differences remain between white and black Americans.

Economic Disadvantage. As we have seen, black income continues to lag behind white income. In 1964, the median income for black families was only 54 percent of that for white families. By 1993, this figure had increased only to 55 percent. This striking economic disadvantage is due to two factors: Black families are less likely to have two earners, and black workers earn less than white workers.

FEMALE-HEADED FAMILIES. About half of the gap between the incomes of black and white families is due to the fact that African American families are less likely to include an adult male. Because women earn less than men and because a one-earner family is obviously disadvantaged relative to a two-earner family, these female-headed households have incomes far below those of husband-wife families. The fact that so many more black than white families are headed by females—46 percent compared with 13 percent—has led some commentators to conclude that poverty is the result of bad decisions by African American men and women. This type of argument is an example of "blaming the victim," and empirical evidence suggests that it simply isn't true. Female headship is not the ultimate cause of poverty. Rather, research indicates that it is itself a result of the severe lack of well-paying jobs for African American males (Lichter, LeClere, and McLaughlin 1991).

LOW EARNINGS. One of the reasons individual blacks earn less than whites is that they are more than twice as likely to be unemployed. In 1994, black unemployment was 11.5 percent compared with 5.3 percent for whites; among those under 25, the figures were 29 and 12 percent (U.S. Bureau of the Census 1993a, 1995). Even when employed, however, black workers earn less than white workers.

Blacks are less well educated than whites (this is especially true of older blacks), and a relatively high proportion live in the South, where wages are low; the average black worker is also somewhat less experienced than the average white worker. However, these differences account for only part of the earnings gap between black and white Americans (Brooks 1994). The other part is the result of a pervasive pattern of discrimination that produces a very different occupational distribution, a very different pattern of mobility, and a very different earnings picture for black and white Americans.

Thanks largely to government employment opportunities, there is a growing African American middle class (Hout 1986). However, even among African American professionals, there is evidence of considerable inequality. For instance, many African American executives and managers have been assigned to corporate positions that were created explicitly to deal with African American demands for civil rights. The existence of these jobs depends, then, on the continuing sensitivity of employers to racial pressures (Collins 1993). The positions, often in public relations or personnel, are in full public view. Yet the people who hold these positions usually remain outside the true corporate power structure. Thus, even though the African American middle class has become highly visible, it remains economically vulnerable. In fact, some studies show that racial disparities in earnings are more pronounced at these higher occupational and educational levels than among the working class or the lower class (Thomas 1993).

Some 92 percent of African Americans and 84 percent of whites say that U.S. race relations are only fair or poor (Whitaker 1995b). During the unprecedented 1995 "Million Man March" to Washington, hundreds of thousands of African Americans gathered in the Capitol Mall to pray, sing, and resolve to make things better when they got back home. The march was controversial: Some observers disapproved that women were left out. Other critics argued that any benefit of the march was overshadowed by previous racist and anti-Semitic remarks by its principal organizer, Louis Farrakhan. Nevertheless, the march showed that African Americans are an important force in the United States and that they are deeply concerned about their lives, their children and their communities.

Continued Concerns. Between 1940 and 1970, there were major improvements in nearly every arena for African Americans: Civil rights, income, and education all improved. During the 1980s, however, little progress was made, and a large black-white gap persisted virtually unchanged (McFate 1995). In fact, today, being black is a better predictor of poverty and unemployment than it was 25 years ago. Among the symptoms of concern:

- *Health*. Black infants are more than twice as likely as white infants to die before their first birthdays (Universal Almanac 1996, 221).
- *Crime*. One in four black men aged 15 to 24 is in jail or under correctional supervision. Homicide has become a leading cause of death for young men, and black men stand a 1-in-10 chance of dying from homicide (MacKellar and Yanagishita 1995).
- *Family Structure*. Nearly half of all black families are headed by women, and 68 percent of black children are born to unmarried women (U.S. Bureau of the Census 1995, Tables 70 and 94).
- *Unemployment*. Black unemployment rates are twice as high as white unemployment rates; and this is true even when we compare those with one to three years of college (U.S. Bureau of the Census 1995, Table 662).
- *Education*. Rates of college enrollment have declined for black males. Although some black Americans are able to use the educational system to pursue the American dream, an important segment continues to be alienated from the economic benefits of American society.

These multiple responses to poverty and lack of opportunity create a vicious circle that may perpetuate or even increase the disadvantage of blacks. We return to these issues, and public policy responses to them, later in this chapter.

How do we reconcile this troubling picture with the general improvements noted earlier? Many perceive a fissure in the African American population: On the one hand, a working- and middle-class population that is increasingly integrated into American society; on the other, an underclass that has not been included in the overall improvement. In fact, for members of this underclass, the situation has deteriorated. The black underclass has been left behind by the more prosperous of all races (Benjamin 1991; W. J. Wilson 1978).

There have been real improvements for African Americans in the last 20 years; income, education, and political power have increased. Nevertheless, there is a substratum of black society that has not participated in these improvements, a group that experiences extraordinarily high rates of illegitimacy, female headship, and poverty.

Hispanic Americans

Hispanics, or Latinos, are an ethnic group rather than a racial category, and a Hispanic may be white or black. This ethnic group includes immigrants and their descendants from Puerto Rico, Mexico, Cuba, and other Central American and South American countries. Hispanics constitute about 9 percent of the U.S. population. The largest group of Hispanics is of Mexican origin (63 percent), with 11 percent from Puerto Rico and the remaining 26 percent from Cuba and elsewhere. These various Hispanic groups live in different parts of the country and have different cultural backgrounds and levels of social and economic integration.

As with other ethnic categories, it is very misleading to treat all Hispanics as if they were the same. Because this chapter is too short to go into detail about all the various Hispanic groups, we focus mainly on the largest—Mexican Americans.

Mexican Americans. Mexican Americans trace their ancestry back to the merging of Spanish colonialists with the Mayan and Aztec Indians of Middle America. Despite this commonality, the U.S. Mexican American population itself is diverse. Many Mexican Americans are not immigrants. In fact, their ancestors were here as far back as the 16th century, long before the United States became a recognized nation. These people, called *Hispanos*, first became Mexican Americans with the conclusion of the Mexican-American War. The Treaty of Guadalupe Hidalgo, signed in 1848, allowed for the annexation of Texas, California, Arizona, and New Mexico to the United States from Mexico. In exchange, the United States granted citizenship to the Hispanos living there and officially guaranteed them religious freedom, property rights, and the right to continue to use the Spanish language. The proposed English Language Amendment to the U.S. Constitution, discussed in the Applications section of Chapter 3, would violate this treaty. However, the language right and guarantee written into the treaty are all but forgotten today.

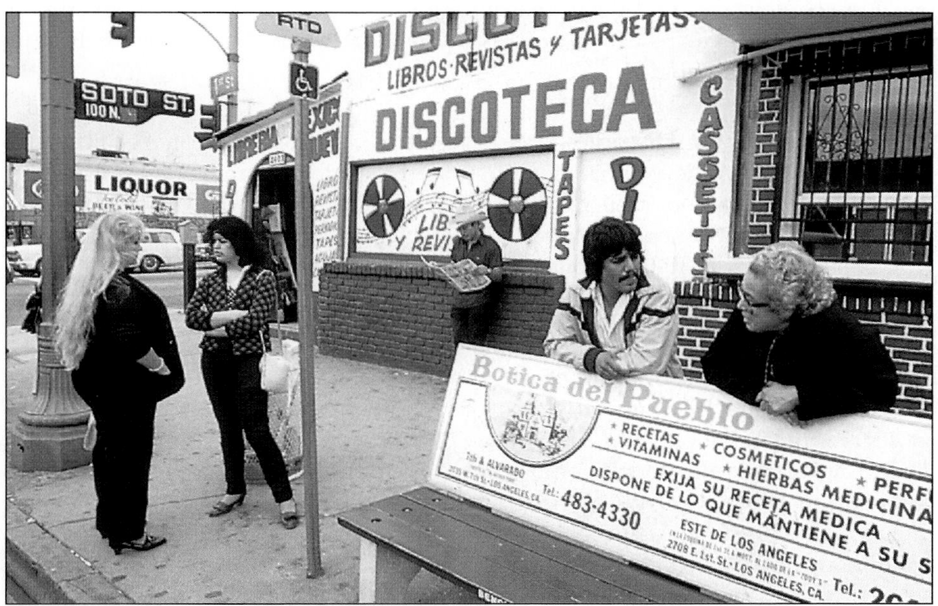

Hispanics, or Latinos, comprise an ethnic group rather than a racial category. The largest group of Hispanics is Mexican; the second largest group is Puerto Rican. Since 1898, residents of Puerto Rico have been U.S. citizens, free to move back and forth between Puerto Rico and the mainland. Many have moved to New York City, where they live in communities such as this one in Spanish Harlem. Like many recent Cuban immigrants, some Puerto Ricans face the double jeopardy of being Hispanic and black. With 36 percent of Puerto Rican families living below the poverty line, they are perhaps the poorest racial or ethnic group in the United States.

Moreover, as the newly annexed regions were gradually settled by Anglos and others, Hispanos lost much of their land (Schaefer 1990, 299–300).

Following annexation, there have been three waves of immigrants. The first wave, between 1900 and 1930, was caused by civil unrest in Mexico and labor demand in the United States. The second wave, between 1942 and 1950, brought thousands to the United States under the *bracero* (contract labor) program to fill jobs opened by absent servicemen and the relocation of Japanese Americans. The third wave, from 1960 to the present, is due to the substantial wage differences between Mexico and the United States. Following the first two waves of immigration, massive deportations took place—1 million in 1951 alone. Despite the fact that the third, and current, wave of immigration is largely illegal, there has been little effective control of it. Deportation is relatively rare, and the U.S. border patrol has been helpless to stem the rising tide of job-seeking immigrants. (Recent political responses to illegal immigration are discussed in the Applications in Diversity section of this chapter.)

Socioeconomic Status. It is misleading to describe the socioeconomic status of Hispanics as if they comprised a single group. Their experiences in the United States have been and continue to be very different. Evidence suggests that their economic and political experiences have been growing more divergent rather than becoming more similar. For example, although Cubans are becoming increasingly assimilated, as signaled by a very high rate of American citizenship, much of the Mexican American population is not.

Figure 11.3 compares the various Hispanic groups to one another and to the overall white and black populations on three measures: education, poverty, and family structure. (Because race and Hispanic origin are overlapping categories, Hispanics are included twice in this table—once under their ethnic group and again under their racial identification.) On two of these measures, a Hispanic group comes out at the very bottom; Mexican Americans are the poorest educated racial or ethnic group, and Puerto Ricans are the most likely to live in poverty. In addition, Puerto Ricans are almost as likely as African Americans to live in female-headed households.

Special Concerns for Hispanics. As a result of continuous streams of Hispanic immigrants, mostly from Mexico but also from the Caribbean and Central America, the Hispanic population is the fastest-growing ethnic group in the United States. If current growth continues, Hispanics are expected to constitute 18 percent of the U.S. population by 2030 (U.S. Bureau of the Census 1995, Table 19).

This rapid growth raises four concerns:

1. Because most of the new immigrants are young and poorly educated by U.S. standards, the socioeconomic position of the Hispanic population is falling. Between 1975 and 1993, poverty rates for Hispanics grew considerably faster than those for African Americans (U.S. Bureau of the Census 1995, Table 744).

2. A growing Hispanic population has raised concerns among non-Hispanics about competition over jobs, thus spurring greater prejudice, discrimination, and conflict. Some—although assuredly not all—of this conflict is between Hispanic Americans and African Americans, as the two largest minority groups in the United States vie for their fair share in the American Dream (Boyce 1991; Chavira 1991).

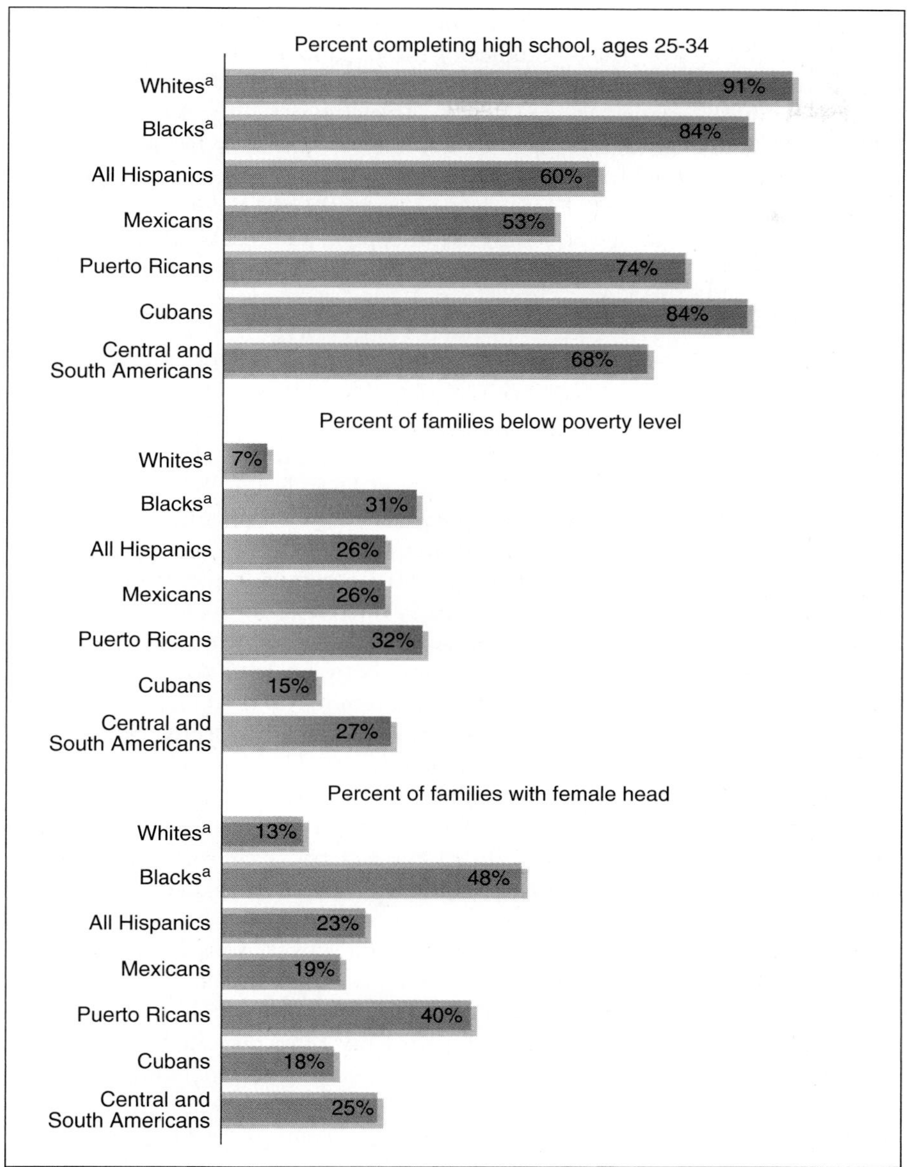

FIGURE 11.3
EDUCATION, POVERTY, AND FAMILY STRUCTURE BY RACE AND HISPANIC ORIGIN, 1992

On two out of three measures of disadvantage, a Hispanic ethnic group comes out at the bottom. A significant portion of this disadvantage, however, can be traced to recent immigration and poor English-language skills.

SOURCE: U.S. Bureau of the Census 1993, a, b, and d.
[a]Each racial category includes people of all ethnic backgrounds, including Hispanics.

3. Like the white ethnic newcomers of the last century, today's Hispanic immigrants bring with them a language and way of life different from those of the dominant culture. Because native-born Americans have internalized and value their culture and institutions, possible changes provoke concern. As the United States becomes more pluralistic, perhaps on its way to becoming a bilingual society, the nation may have to redefine itself.
4. Rapid growth is associated with increasing residential segregation (Massey and Denton 1988). Segregation, in turn, may retard the rate at which new immigrants integrate themselves into American society.

Despite these concerns, the problems of white Hispanic Americans are substantially less than those of blacks. Studies of the assimilation process show that the castelike barrier separating races operates much less dramatically in the case of ethnicity. For white Hispanics, the problem is largely one of class. As a result, by the second and third generation, Hispanics are able to translate education into occupational prestige and are able to leave segregated barrios. The exception is the 7 percent of Hispanics (mostly Puerto Ricans and other Caribbean islanders) who suffer the triple disadvantage of being Hispanic, poor, and black (Marger 1994).

Jewish Americans

Anti-Semitism (hatred of Jews) dates as far back as written history but was heightened by the emergence of Christianity and the blaming of Jews for the death of Jesus. The most tragic example of anti-Semitism was Adolf Hitler's Third Reich and "final solution" to Germany's problems, which led to the Holocaust—the calculated extermination of 6 million scapegoated Jews during World War II. Two-thirds of Europe's Jewish people were killed; in Poland, Germany, and Austria, 90 percent were murdered (Adler 1995; Schaefer 1990, 422–423).

Today, the United States has the largest Jewish population in the world, larger than Israel's. The first Jews arrived in North America from Spain and Portugal in 1654. Expelled from Europe, they came seeking refuge. By the late 19th century, many Jews of German origin had joined them. Between 1880 and 1920, outbreaks of violent anti-Semitism in Russia and Poland resulted in the emigration of three-quarters of the Jewish population of Eastern Europe to the United States. By the 1930s, sensing the impending horror of Hitler's Third Reich, German and Austrian Jews fled Europe in large numbers, many of them coming to the United States (Adler 1995). Today, Jewish Americans live mostly in the big cities of the Northeast.

Compared with the brutalities in Europe, the United States does not have a history of severe anti-Semitism. Nevertheless, anti-Semitism has been apparent since Jews first arrived here. In 1654, Peter Stuyvesant, governor of New Amsterdam, made a failed attempt to expel them from the city that would later be named New York. Henry Ford, founder of the automobile company, widely published many anti-Semitic statements. Groups like the Ku Klux Klan preached of Jewish (and Catholic) conspiracies to take over all world governments, including that of the United States.

Meanwhile, early Jewish immigrants, valuing education, sticking together, and working hard in businesses such as the emergent garment industry, experienced a rate of upward mobility twice as high as that of other white ethnic immigrant groups (Peterson 1978). By 1950, Jews far exceeded other Americans in education and income; in that year, 25 percent of all Jewish men had a college degree, compared with 10 percent of all men in the United States. Today, Jews, on average, enjoy high incomes and are relatively wealthy, although certainly not all Jews have high incomes, and some are poor.

Most scholars agree that U.S. anti-Semitism has declined since World War II. But it still exists. Swastikas, symbols of the Third Reich, are sometimes found painted on synagogues. In the past decade, Jews have been murdered simply because they were Jewish.

Despite an increased level of intermarriage and what may seem the perfect example of the American economic success story, Jews have remained a minority group. Until the last decade, Jews were commonly excluded from clubs and colleges across the country. Jewish Americans remain conspicuously absent from the boards of banks, utilities, insurance companies, and many major corporations (Schaefer 1990, 429).

Jewish ethnic identity involves maintaining Jewish culture and traditions in a society that values Christian Anglo conformity. Jewish ethnic identity also means telling the story of (and grieving about) the Holocaust, coupled with vigilance against the possibility of its ever happening again. The recently erected Museum of the Holocaust in Washington, D.C., and Steven Spielberg's movie "Schindler's List" are examples.

ASIAN AMERICANS

The Asian population of the United States (including Japanese, Chinese, Filipino, Korean, Laotian, and Vietnamese Americans) almost doubled between 1980 and 1990, yet it still constitutes only 2.9 percent of the total population. The Asian population can be broken into three segments: the 19th century immigrants (Chinese and Japanese), the post–World War II immigrants (Filipinos, Asian Indians, and Koreans), and the recent refugees from Southeast Asia (Kampucheans, Laotians, and Vietnamese).

A century ago, Asian immigrants were met with sharp and occasionally violent racism. Racism directed at Chinese and Japanese immigrants in the early years of this century was virulent. Many states passed laws forbidding Japanese immigrants from owning land; from 1906 to 1947, federal laws singled out Japanese immigrants and said that they could never become United States citizens (Jiobu 1988). The Focus on Yesterday earlier in this chapter recounts a particularly striking example of discrimination against Japanese Americans.

Today, incidents of racial violence directed at Vietnamese and other Asians continue to make headlines. Despite these handicaps, Asian Americans have experienced high levels of social mobility. Americans of Japanese and Chinese descent have surpassed the educational attainment of white Americans, and it appears that many of the more recent streams of Asian immigrants will follow the same path. For example, although many of the Southeast Asian refugees who came to the United States between 1975 and 1984 began their American lives on welfare, almost twice as many Vietnamese youth aged 20–24 are enrolled in school as white youth of the same age.

This high level of education is a major step in opening doors to high-status occupations; the 1990 census showed that Asian American families had the highest average incomes of any major racial or ethnic group in the United States. As a result, Asian Americans are sometimes viewed as a "model minority," whose success validates the ideology of the American Dream.

Yet discrimination is not all in the past. Asian American applicants are less likely to be accepted at elite colleges and universities than white Americans with the same credentials (Takagi 1990). Recent studies have concluded that highly educated, native-born Asian males earn substantially less than similarly qualified white men (Suzuki 1989, 16) and that they are promoted more slowly (Tang 1993). Discrimination can be even more direct. In 1982, two unemployed autoworkers beat a Vietnamese man to death because they thought he was Japanese and they blamed the Japanese for the loss of their jobs. The judge found their stress understandable and sentenced them to only three years of probation (Saigo 1989).

Asian Americans experience a great deal of frustration about being held up as a "model minority," whose successes are used to illustrate and justify American structures of opportunity. Many Asians point out that they succeeded despite terrible obstacles and that they still suffer discrimination in employment opportunities as well as outright violence and abuse.

Native Americans

Between 25,000 and 40,000 years ago, Asians crossed over into North America on a land bridge that joined the two continents near what is now Alaska. These are the ancestors of Native Americans (American Indians). Hundreds of cultures evolved, including the complex societies of the Mayas, Incas, and Aztecs, as well as of the Anasazi and Pueblo "cliff dwellers."

The arrival of Columbus to the Western Hemisphere in 1492 marked the beginning of a new period in Native Americans' history. Columbus wrote the following in his diary: "The [Native American] people are ingenious and would be good servants. . . . These people are very unskilled in arms . . . . with fifty men they could all be subjected to do all that one wishes" (quoted in Schaefer 1990, 168). It took far more than 50 men, and Native Americans were never convinced to do all that European conquerors wished; but over the next 400 years, American Indians were indeed subjected. North of the Rio Grande, they numbered 12 to 15 million in 1500; by 1850, there were just 250,000. What killed them? Invading settlers introduced new and fatal diseases, such as measles and smallpox, and robbed the Native Americans of their lands, resources, and traditional livelihoods (Schaefer 1990, 168).

Today, Native Americans are one of the smallest minority groups in the United States (about 0.8 percent of the population). Partly due to the 1830 Indian Removal Act, which forced the relocation of all Eastern tribes to west of the Mississippi River, nearly half of today's American Indians live in just four states: Oklahoma, Arizona, California, and New Mexico. Native Americans are widely regarded as the nation's most disadvantaged minority group. Incomes of husband–wife families are lower for American Indians than for African Americans, and the former tend to live in more crowded conditions (U.S. Department of Commerce 1994). Native Americans suffer the highest rates of alcoholism and premature death of any U.S. racial or ethnic group. This situation exists despite hopeful new signs of economic vitality on some Indian reservations over the past 15 years—for example, development of mineral reserves on the Navajo reservation in the Southwest (Schaefer 1990, 199–200) and (to a lesser degree) the advent of gambling casinos on other reservations (Johnson 1994).

Within a general picture of low social and economic status, there is enormous variability. Native Americans represent more than 200 tribal groupings, with different cultures and languages. Some have been successful: fish farmers in the Northwest, ranchers in Wyoming, bridge builders in Maine. In urban areas, Native Americans experience less racial segregation than do other nonwhite groups (Bohland 1982) and have entered the professions and other occupations of modern industrial society.

More than any other minority, meanwhile, Native Americans have remained both unacculturated and unassimilated. Perhaps more than any other minority group in the United States, the culture of Native Americans clashes with the dominant culture. American Indians cherish a culture that values the land and animals as worthwhile in themselves, that disregards schedules and clocks, that honors tradition as much as the future. Those who cling to earlier values face a severe case of anomie, since the traditional means to achieve the old goals are gone forever. The story of the Ojibwa described in Chapter 4 represents an extreme case of what has happened to Native American culture. In addition, discrimination, prejudice, and insensitivity persist. An example is the conflict several years ago over names of sports teams, such as the "Washington Redskins." (Imagine naming a team the "Boston Blackskins!")

Many Native Americans play roles in modern U.S. industrial society. And like the white ethnics pictured earlier, many don traditional dress and dance at festivals. Unlike white ethnics, however, Native Americans do not so easily assimilate into the dominant culture when they take off their ceremonial attire. It may be difficult, for example, to be a proud U.S. soldier when the U.S. army once nearly destroyed your people.

EQUALITY: PROSPECTS AND CHALLENGES

With the important exceptions of Native and African Americans, the United States is a land of voluntary immigrants. Diverse peoples came here from all over the world in pursuit of the American Dream: They wanted better lives than they were experiencing at home. We have discussed the current situations of several of these groups. Now let's consider the broader picture. In this final section, we examine the ethnic and racial fabric of the United States. What have been and continue to be some of the pressures toward ethnic equality in our society? What are the prospects for the future?

PRESSURES TOWARD EQUALITY

Structural–Functionalism: White Ethnic Americans. White ethnic immigrants of the late 19th and early 20th centuries were welcomed with discrimination, anti-immigrant demonstrations, riots, and other outbursts of ethnic conflict that exploded throughout the country. But for the most part, the children of white ethnics conformed and assimilated to the dominant culture. Partly they were able to do so because they were white: Having changed their names, replaced their old-world clothing, and lost their accents, they were no longer so visibly "different." Then, too, they arrived at a time in history when even unskilled labor was sorely needed. Many Irish immigrants were met with signs saying, "NINA," or "No Irish Need Apply." But there were jobs elsewhere, and white ethnics were able to find them and go to work. Moreover, many white immigrants arrived when land was still available. The open frontier provided another avenue toward equality. Because of these social structural conditions, the assimilation of white ethnics seems to support the structural-functional theory of social change, presented in Chapter 1. Through gradual adaptation, social structures responded to new situations and demands. This has not been the case for other American ethnic groups, however.

African Americans. We have already mentioned the black civil rights movement of the 1960s and the 1964 Civil Rights Act. As a direct result of these events, we have seen important political and educational advances. There is an increasingly strong African American middle class that wields more economic and political power than ever before (Benjamin 1991). But there are continued concerns—both about persistent racism, even against middle-class African Americans, and about the economic and structural plight of many impoverished African Americans.

This leads to the obvious question, Why are so many African Americans still so substantially disadvantaged? The answers are complex and not at all clear. One important reason is that the historical circumstances of African Americans were very different from those of white immigrants. For one thing, blacks did not choose to come here; they were transported here to be slaves. Trying to assimilate to a culture that has treated your ancestors so badly can precipitate ambivalence and anger. Second, African Americans are visibly physically different. No matter how well they speak "standard" English or how they dress, African Americans cannot slip into the mainstream of American culture as easily as white ethnics did. Although, as noted, there have been real gains for many African Americans in the last 40 years, there is growing consensus that the condition of the African American *poor* has been substantially deteriorating. Whether this poorest third of the African American population is called the ghetto underclass or the inner-city poor, the point is the same: Joblessness is up, the number of female-headed households is up, crime and homicide rates are up, drug use is up, and so on. The physical concentration of so many social problems has created explosive levels of social disorganization in poor, African American neighborhoods. Twenty years ago the people in these neighborhoods were poor; now they are poor and hopeless.

Why the change? Although racism remains a factor that limits African American progress in the United States, reasons also lie in America's changing economy and its differential effect on the African American middle and lower class. A key factor is the de-industrialization of America, which has hurt all classes and races that depended on jobs in the manufacturing sector. Many of the good factory jobs that drew African Americans to cities such as Detroit, Chicago, and Buffalo after World War II have disappeared forever. A second factor is the shift of economic activity from the central city to the suburbs. Ironically, a third factor contributing to the disintegration of inner-city African American communities is the existence of more opportunities for middle-class African Americans (Benjamin 1991; Billingsley 1989; Wilson 1988). As better-off African Americans have moved to the suburbs, they have taken with them much of the stability and civic energy that previously held their communities together despite relatively high levels of poverty. With their departure, the innner city has become virtually isolated from major social institutions. Children may grow up without having known *anybody* who holds a regular job; consequently, they don't know how to get a job or how to keep one (Wilson 1988, 60–61).

For a variety of reasons, both practical and moral, the problem posed by the ghetto underclass must be addressed by public policy. It is, however, a problem so complicated that it seems to defy solution. To put it in its bleakest form: How much good can a Headstart program do for a youngster whose father is in jail, whose mother is a drug addict?

William Julius Wilson (1987), one of the most prominent African American scholars in America, argues that the solution is a national job policy directed toward creating full employment and better jobs for *all* Americans. His vision includes a substantially higher minimum wage, universal health care, retraining programs, relocation assistance, and public child care.

Wilson's agenda is obviously controversial. It is far more liberal than even most Democrats are likely to endorse. Nor is there universal scholarly agreement that jobs are the solution. Conservatives believe the jobs are there but that the blocked opportunities created by past racism have established a "culture of poverty" that makes the underclass unemployable. Radicals believe that the only way to achieve the goal of good jobs for all is to dismantle capitalist institutions. Currently, *none* of these agendas is being pursued with any vigor. Indeed, like the Reagan and Bush administrations before it, the Republican-majority Congress of the mid-1990s recommended cutting social programs for the poor as an avenue to balancing the federal budget—a policy that would disproportionately affect African Americans.

Conflict theory sees competition for scarce resources at the core of social relations. Changes toward equality result from open conflict between majority and minority groups rather than through gradual adaptation. During the Los Angeles riots of 1992, conflict was dramatically evident. However, much of it was directed by African Americans against other minority groups, such as Korean merchants, rather than directly against members of the dominant culture.

Conflict Theory: Hispanic Americans and Native Americans. If structural-functionalism best explains white ethnic assimilation, conflict theory better applies not only to the African American experience but also to the experiences of Hispanic and Native Americans. Recall from Chapter 1 that conflict theory sees competition for scarce resources at the core of social relations. In this view, changes toward equality result from open conflict between competing groups rather than through gradual adaptation. The social protest that characterized the black civil rights movement in the 1960s was mirrored in Hispanic and American Indian communities.

Hispanics forged the Chicano movement, sometimes called *Chicanismo*. Chicanismo stressed a positive self-image and challenged the dominant culture's belief that orderly assimilation was the avenue to equality. The best known Chicano leader is César Chavez, who organized the United Farm Workers Union (UFW) for migrant workers in southern California. Chavez's first success was the national 1965 grape boycott, which attacked inhumane wages and working conditions. While still miserable by many other American workers' standards, conditions improved somewhat because of UFW efforts. Since the 1960s, various Hispanic political organizations have emerged, all bent on improving conditions (Schaefer 1990, 305–313). Recently, Hispanic organizations have protested and taken political action against state propositions (such as California's Proposition 187, passed in 1994) that limit health care and schooling for illegal immigrants. The Applications in Diversity section of this chapter discusses recent immigrants to the United States.

Like Hispanics, Native Americans began to protest their conditions during the 1960s. In 1964, Indians in Washington state organized *fish-ins*: They defiantly fished waters that had been declared off-limits by the government. The protesters argued that they were fishing in accordance with the 1854 Treaty of Medicine Creek. After the U.S. Supreme Court upheld their treaty rights in 1968, other protests followed. A year later, for example, Native Americans occupied Alcatraz Island in the San Francisco Bay. Once a federal prison, Alcatraz had been abandoned, and the Indians claimed land rights to it. The protest was unsuccessful, however; the island is now a national park.

Meanwhile, the American Indian Movement (AIM) was founded in 1968 by Clyde Bellecourt and Dennis Banks. AIM's initial purpose was to document and protest police brutality. In 1973, AIM leaders led a highly publicized 70-day occupation of Wounded Knee, South Dakota, the site of an 1890 massacre of some 300 Lakota women and children by the cavalry. Since the 1960s, AIM's activities have been less dramatic. Today, Native Americans are more likely to go through the courts to demand, for instance, that conditions of 18th- and 19th-century treaties be legally honored.

Symbolic Interactionism: Jewish and Asian Americans. Symbolic interactionism assumes that important symbolic meanings are actively negotiated by various individuals or groups in a society. For instance, people's surnames and physical appearances do not inherently have a symbolic meaning. Instead, what surnames and appearances symbolize is socially constructed by interaction among ethnic groups. Understanding this process, Jews and Asian Americans (among others) have striven to renegotiate what being of Jewish or Asian descent symbolizes in American culture.

For Jews, this has largely meant informing the public about Jewish identity and history, as well as challenging anti-Semitic stereotypes. The Anti-Defamation League of the Jewish international organization B'nai B'rith and the Jewish Defense League are organizations dedicated to this purpose.

Asian Americans also strive to negotiate a more accurate portrayal, or symbolic meaning, for themselves. For instance, David Mura (1988), a third-generation Japanese American author, points out that the images he grew up with in school and in the media were all white. The books he read, beginning with Dick and Jane, were about whites and later about European civilization. Furthermore, the way the dominant culture defines beauty means that "slanted eyes, flat noses, and round faces just don't make it" (p. 137). Wanting to be nice, his white friends sometimes say they think of him as a white person. Mura wonders why they can't simply think of him as an equal—*and* a Japanese American.

Resistance in the Dominant Culture: Efforts to Dismantle Affirmative Action

As we have seen, the three major theoretical perspectives in sociology help explain various groups' assimilation, protests, and struggles—pressures toward equality. Conflict theory further helps explain resistance to these pressures in the dominant culture. According to conflict theory, individuals and groups that benefit from any particular social structure will strive to see it maintained. We can find many historical and current examples of this. Today, one of the most important involves attacks on affirmative action.

Affirmative action refers to active efforts to recruit minority group members or women for jobs, promotions, and educational opportunities. Generally, affirmative action programs set minimum standards for employment or school admission, and no one who does not meet those standards need be hired or admitted. At the same time, the highest-scoring applicants need not be selected when selecting them would continue white (male) dominance in the workplace or school.

Affirmative action refers to active efforts to recruit minority group members or women for jobs, promotions, and educational opportunities.

The phrase "affirmative action" originally appeared in a 1963 executive order issued by President John F. Kennedy. The order required businesses and contractors hired by the government to "take affirmative action to ensure that applicants are employed, and that employees are treated during employment, without regard to their race, creed, color, or national origin" (Schaefer 1990, 103). The order was later amended to prohibit discrimination on the basis of sex as well. Employers were cautioned against doing anything that might be in any way discriminatory, such as asking questions during an employment interview that might tend to eliminate certain groups. In a 1975 policy statement, the U.S. Commission on Civil Rights decreed that the lack of minority (black, Asian, American Indian, and Hispanic) or female employees in a company could in itself be evidence of unlawful exclusion (Schaefer 1990, 104). By the 1980s, affirmative action programs had been extended to colleges and universities; entrance policies were aimed at creating a student body and faculty that fairly represented minority groups.

From its beginning, affirmative action sparked legal debates. One of the best known is the 1978 case *Regents of the University of California v. Bakke*. The U.S. Supreme Court ordered the University of California–Davis medical school to admit Allan Bakke, a white engineer who had scored very high on the entrance requirements but had been denied admission. The Court ruled that the university had violated Bakke's civil rights by establishing a fixed quota system for minority students. However, in a confusing statement, the Court added that it was constitutional for universities to use race as a factor in making decisions. Indeed, a problem with affirmative action from the beginning has been that the policy is vaguely defined.

Defenders of affirmative action argue that past and current institutionalized discrimination results in continuing disadvantage for women and ethnic minorities. They say that affirmative action programs work and are still needed to counter continuing institutionalized discrimination (Jones 1995). Furthermore, while they may feel threatened, white males still hold the overwhelming majority of prestigious and high-paying jobs (Galen 1994).

Meanwhile, surveys beginning in the 1980s have repeatedly shown that few non-Hispanic white Americans are in favor of affirmative action. Many see the program as "reverse discrimination," unfairly victimizing white males (Fineman 1995; Thomas and Cohn 1995). Furthermore, opponents argue that African Americans suffer when affirmative action policies place their real achievements under a cloud of suspicion (Custred and Wood 1995). Ironically, Asian Americans (intended as a "protected" minority group under affirmative action) have begun to say the programs discriminate against them: Their high scores on college entrance exams do not necessarily translate into admission. It seems clear that the battle over affirmative action will continue at least throughout the 1990s.

Living in Diversity

Only 30 years ago, African Americans were subjected to violence for registering to vote, using "white" drinking fountains, or attending "white" colleges. Only 55 years ago, all the Japanese Americans on the West Coast were rounded up and placed into detention camps. The last major massacre of Native Americans occurred only a little over 100 years ago. Viewed from this perspective, the changes in the last 30 years have been enormous. Racial and ethnic discrimination is illegal, prejudicial attitudes are mostly no longer normatively supported, and there are signs of progress in most social and economic areas.

Moreover, focusing on racial and ethnic inequalities in the United States can cloud our awareness that such tensions exist throughout the world. The family of the student whose essay is described in this chapter's prologue left Taiwan to escape discrimination there against mainland Chinese. In the Mideast, Jews are terrorized by Muslims (Reiss and Katel 1994). In Russia, plans for a new Muslim mosque sparked protest (Gallagher 1994). Bosnia's "ethnic cleansing" would eliminate all Serbs (Barnes 1993). In Germany, neo-Nazis attack immigrant Turks (Kinzer 1993). In Africa, ethnic rivalries result in massacres such as that in Rwanda in 1994 (Hammer 1994). In Central and South America, native Indians struggle with descendants of the Spanish and Indians. Australia's aboriginal peoples contend with oppression by the descendants of British and Irish settlers.

Nevertheless, even against this global backdrop, racial and ethnic inequalities and injustices remain important in the United States. It cannot be ignored that prejudice, discrimination, and disadvantage persist for most American minority groups. Being African American is particularly critical. Traditional racism has decreased; few people believe that blacks earn less money than whites because of innate inferiority, and few believe that people should be discriminated against on account of their race and ethnicity. Nevertheless, subtle forms of racism persist. Widespread belief in the ideology of the American Dream means that many people continue to blame the poor for their poverty; the predominant white explanation for poverty stresses the lack of motivation. As a result of such beliefs, some whites are reluctant to support governmental policies designed to promote economic equality between blacks and whites (Bobo and Kluegel 1993).

Meanwhile, as discussed in Chapter 3, the United States is becoming more and more diverse. This new diversity rests on tradition. Throughout its history, the United States has been largely a nation of immigrants of many colors and cultures, most of whom arrived in search of greater justice and equality. The challenge today is for Americans first to envision and then to realize pluralistic tolerance and equality. Maybe one day, Americans will boast of genuine appreciation for one another in an increasingly multicultural society. We conclude this chapter with an Applications in Diversity section on recent immigrants to the United States.

Thinking Critically

An exhibit mounted by the Smithsonian Institution showed the horrors that resulted from the United States' dropping the atom bomb that destroyed Hiroshima and led to the end of World War II. The exhibit angered some American veterans, who said the display gave an undue amount of attention to Japanese suffering and portrayed the United States as an unfeeling aggressor (Sidey 1994). How can a multicultural society like the United States deal with such issues? What would you have done if you had been in charge of the display? Why?

APPLICATIONS IN DIVERSITY

THE NEW IMMIGRANTS—ALIENS OR AMIGOS?

Beginning with the Chinese Exclusion Act of 1882, much of U.S. immigration policy has been frankly racist and ethnically discriminatory. Since 1965, however, immigration policies have ceased to give preference to people from Northern and Western Europe; as a result, the U.S. population is changing.

CONCERNS ABOUT IMMIGRATION

It is a myth that America is being overrun with immigrants. As of 1990, foreign-born people made up 8 percent of the U.S. population, compared with about 15 percent from 1870 to 1920 (Cole 1994). Estimates are that about 600,000 immigrants take up permanent residence in the United States each year (Morganthau 1993). About half of these are illegal aliens, 90 percent of whom come from Mexico or other Latin American countries. Immigrants' presence raises concern for two primary reasons, one cultural and one economic.

Cultural

Almost all recent immigrants are from Asia, Mexico, or Central America. A rough estimate suggests that nearly two-thirds are from Central America or Mexico, 25 percent are from Asia, and fewer than 10 percent are from the rest of the world. If this mix continues and if immigration continues at its current rate, the racial and ethnic composition of the United States will change substantially (see Figure 3.2). Some fear that the expected changes in the ethnic mix signal major changes in U.S. culture and institutions. Pat Buchanan, a presidential candidate in both 1992 and 1996, has argued that current immigration patterns will result in the slow erosion of the English-speaking culture we call "American" (Morganthau 1993, 22). But studies show that immigrants do learn English. Repeating the pattern of 19th-century Europeans, the grandchildren of Asian and Mexican immigrants speak English fluently (Moore 1990, 59). (Whether the United States should adopt English as its official language was discussed in the Applications in Diversity section of Chapter 3.)

Economic

Little consensus exists about the economic consequences of legal or illegal immigration. There seem, however, to be three well-supported generalizations: (1) Immigrants are not taking jobs away from American citizens, but (2) the availability of low-wage illegals helps to keep wages low in some sectors of the economy, and (3) the citizens hardest hit by this are Hispanic Americans and other minorities (Bouvier and Gardner 1986; Morganthau 1993). Some scholars offer evidence that immigrants actually *create* jobs by starting new businesses and buying goods and services (Cole 1994; Moore 1990).

Are Illegal Immigrants Scapegoats?

In 1986, Congress passed the Immigration Reform and Control Act (IRCA), designed to control illegal immigration to the United States. The act granted amnesty to illegals who were in the United States before 1982, forbade employers from hiring new illegals, and increased border patrols. It is generally conceded that IRCA did not work (Donato, Durand, and Massey 1992).

Nearly 10 years later, concern about illegal immigration is again mounting. It is unrealistic to think that the United States can totally eliminate illegal immigration. The bottom line is that it is a very rich nation sharing a border with a poor one. But some states, such as California and Texas, have begun to tackle the problems they see. In November 1994, California voters passed Proposition 187, also known as the Save Our State (or S.O.S.) Initiative. Now being

THINKING CRITICALLY

How much concern about negative effects of illegal immigrants is justified by evidence, do you think? What does it mean to say that illegal immigrants are scapegoats? Can you think of examples in which this might be true? How does what you know about international inequalities (discussed in Chapter 10) help explain this issue? What can and should be done about illegal immigration to the United States? What about legal immigration? How are the issues different? How are they the same? Should we view the diversity that immigration helps to foster as an asset or a problem?

APPLICATIONS IN DIVERSITY

challenged in the courts, the proposition would deny social, educational, and all but emergency health care services to illegals. The reasoning is that this policy will discourage future illegal immigration and motivate illegals now in the United States to go home.

However, opponents of Proposition 187 argue that it unfairly scapegoats illegal immigrants. They point out that there are far more serious causes for California's present economic woes. Chang-Lin Tien, chancellor of the University of California at Berkeley and himself an immigrant, states: "Immigrants are not the cause of America's major problems." Tien advises that it's time to stop blaming immigrants and face up to the difficult reality of a world in transition (1994).

SOCIOLOGY ON THE NET

The dynamics of racial change can be seen throughout contemporary America. As the racial numbers change, so will the political landscape on which the racial wars of the past have been won and lost. The United States Census Bureau keeps close tabs on these changing figures.

`http://www.census.gov/population/pop-profile/toc.html`

We are back to the current Population Profile that we first discovered in Chapter 9. This time, let's look at the characteristics of the different minority groups in the U.S. Begin by browsing through the selections on **The Black Population, The Hispanic Population, The Asian and Pacific Islander Population** and **The American Indian, Eskimo and Aleut Population**. Can you figure out one or two unique findings from each of these reports?

Now open and read the sections entitled **National Population Trends** and **National Population Projections**. What is the overall trend of our population growth? What is meant by the term "natural increase"? What are the differences in the rate of natural increase for the various racial categories? How will the relative proportions of the minority populations change by the year 2050? How will this changing racial composition touch you as you grow older?

Statistics tell one story of possible change. If we are to understand how minorities have experienced America, we must heed Weber and exercise some *verstehen* and try to understand what is happening from the standpoint of the participants. Let's take a look at the American Indian Movement.

`http://www.netgate.net/~jsd/McCloud.html`

You have just entered a network of Native American internet home pages. Browse around. Pay special attention to **Leonard Peltier's Pre-Sentencing Statement** and Russel Means' speech, **"For America to Live, Europe Must Die."** How do you react to these statement? Does your status as a minority or majority group member influence you as you consider what is being said? Can you identify with the situation of the Native Americans now that you have come in contact with some of their views?

For a further look into one of the more infamous Indian massacres, click on the **Wounded Knee Home Page**.

SUMMARY

1. Both race and ethnicity are passed on from parent to child, but race refers to the genetic transmission of physical characteristics, and ethnicity refers to socialization into distinct cultural patterns.
2. Race and ethnicity interact with social class to determine an individual's position in the hierarchy of life chances. Prejudice, discrimination, and segregation aimed at a group tend to decrease as the group improves its educational and economic position.
3. Four basic patterns of contact between majority and minority groups are conflict, assimilation, accommodation, and acculturation.
4. Prejudice is an attitude; discrimination is a behavior. Prejudice is difficult to change because it is irrational; thus, most social policy is aimed at reducing discrimination.
5. Although prejudice and discrimination are more typical of some kinds of individuals than others, these pervasive social patterns cannot be explained by individual characteristics. Instead, institutionalized patterns of segregation, racism, and inequality help perpetuate disadvantage from one generation to the next.
6. Despite significant progress, African Americans continue to experience serious disadvantage on indicators such as health, crime, unemployment, and family structure. The African American underclass has been left behind by the more prosperous of all races.
7. On indicators of poverty, educational attainment, and female-headed families, some Hispanic groups are at great disadvantage. Hispanic disadvantage appears to stem largely from recent immigration and poor facility with the English language.
8. Asian Americans have shown remarkable social mobility through education but still earn less than white Americans with the same credentials. Native Americans are one of our most disadvantaged minority groups.
9. While structural-functional theory may best explain the assimilation of white ethnic immigrants, conflict theory better describes the situation of African, Hispanic, and Native Americans. Symbolic interaction theory helps explain issues raised by Jewish and Asian Americans.
10. William J. Wilson argues that the situation for the African American underclass has deteriorated substantially. His agenda for the future, from the social class perspective, consists of a national job policy.
11. Resistance to change is evidenced in efforts to dismantle affirmative action programs. Affirmative action programs first appeared in the 1960s; their goal is to combat the persistent effects of past and ongoing institutionalized discrimination.
12. Concerns about current immigration patterns and the "new immigrants" in the United States are both cultural and economic. Illegal immigrants are generally seen as harming the U.S. culture and economy, but some spokespersons argue that illegal immigrants are scapegoats for larger problems.

SUGGESTED READINGS

HAIZLIP, Shirlee Taylor. 1994. *The Sweeter the Juice: A Family Memoir in Black and White*. New York: Simon & Schuster/Touchstone. A wonderfully readable personal story of the African American author's search to find her mother's sister and other relatives, who had left her when she was a child because they passed for whites. The book illustrates that racial categories are not accurate—and that our own racial genes may not be exactly what we think they are.

HOROWITZ, Ruth. 1983. *Honor and the American Dream: Culture and Identity in a Chicago Community*. New Brunswick, N.J.: Rutgers University Press. An absorbing account of a Mexican American community in Chicago.

LIEBOW, Elliot. 1967. *Tally's Corner*. Boston: Little, Brown. This classic study provides an insightful look at how poverty and lack of opportunity affect family and personal life in urban slums.

MARGER, Martin N. 1994. *Race and Ethnic Relations*, 3rd ed. Belmont, Calif.: Wadsworth. A current textbook that covers theoretical issues and includes a separate chapter on each major race and ethnic group in the United States.

MILLS, Nicholaus, ed. 1994. *Arguing Immigration: Are New Immigrants a Wealth of Diversity . . . or a Crushing Burden?* New York: Simon & Schuster/Touchstone. A collection of reprinted essays from policy makers on both sides of this issue.

MILLS, Nicolaus, ed. 1994. *Debating Affirmative Action: Race, Gender, Ethnicity and the Politics of Inclusion*. New York: Delta. A collection of essays on both sides of the affirmative action issue.

TERKEL, Studs. 1992. *Race: How Blacks and Whites Think and Feel about the American Obsession*. New York: Doubleday/Anchor Books. Honest interviews in the style and tradition of Terkel's classic book *Working*, this collection offers insights into America's race conflict as interviewees from both races "tell it like it is."

WILSON, William J. 1987. *The Truly Disadvantaged: The Inner City, the Underclass, and Public Policy*. Chicago: University of Chicago Press. A controversial book by one of America's leading African American scholars.

CHAPTER 12

Sex and Gender

OUTLINE

PROLOGUE

Have You Ever . . . heard of Charley Parkhurst? Charley was a tobacco-chewing, cigar-smoking stage driver, known as one of the best "whips" in the West. Born in 1812 in New Hampshire, Parkhurst moved to California in the early 1850s and soon became known as a fearless stagecoach driver. Once the team suddenly veered off the road and threw Charley from the coach. Hanging tight to the reins, Parkhurst was dragged along but eventually managed to turn the runaway team into some bushes. The passengers were so appreciative that they gave their driver a $20 tip.

There were two things Parkhurst enjoyed discussing—horses and every citizen's obligation to vote. On November 3, 1868—52 years before the 19th Amendment made it legal—Charley became the first woman to vote in a U.S. national election.

Yes, Charley was a woman! Born Charlotte Parkhurst, she was placed in an orphanage as a young girl. At age 15, she disguised herself as a boy in order to escape. Evidently she found life less difficult for males than for females: She decided to masquerade as a man for the rest of her life. Her secret wasn't discovered until her body was being prepared for burial in 1879 (Seagraves 1990, 117–121).

Parkhurst's story says a lot about sex and gender. First, Charley's story shows that the sex a person is born with doesn't necessarily dictate the roles she or he plays in society. Second, Charley's saga points up the limited opportunities for women over the course of history. Third, the story illustrates women's persistence (and creativity) in challenging those limits.

This chapter is about all these topics. The roles of women and men have been changing in recent decades. Nevertheless, enough of the old stereotypes about males and females remain that most people are surprised when they find out that Charley was a woman. In this chapter, we use the sociological perspective to examine some of the roles played by women and men today.

SEXUAL DIFFERENTIATION

Men and wom;en are different. Biology differentiates their physical structures, and cultural norms in every society differentiate their roles. In this chapter, we describe some of the major differences in men's and women's lives as they are socially structured in the United States. We will be particularly interested in the extent to which the ascribed characteristic of sex has been the basis for structured inequality.

SEX VERSUS GENDER

Sex is a biological characteristic, male or female.

Gender, or **gender role,** refers to the expected dispositions and behaviors, along with the rights and duties, that cultures assign to each sex.

In understanding the social roles of men and women, it is helpful to make a distinction between gender and sex. **Sex** refers to the two biologically differentiated categories, male and female. It also refers to the sexual act that is closely related to this biological differentiation. **Gender,** or **gender role,** on the other hand, refers to the expected dispositions and behaviors, along with the rights and duties, that cultures assign to each sex.

Although biology provides two distinct and universal sexes, cultures provide almost infinitely varied gender roles. Each man is pretty much like every other man in terms of sex—whether he is upper class or lower class, black or white, Chinese or Apache. Gender, however, is a different matter. The rights and obligations, the dispositions and activities, of the male gender are very different for a Chinese man than for an Apache man. Even within a given culture, gender roles vary by class, race, and subculture. In addition, of course, individuals differ in the way they act out their expected roles. Some males play an exaggerated version of the "manly man," whereas others display few of the expected characteristics.

Men and women *are* different. Their biological differences—in average size and strength and in childbearing capability, to name a few—have consequences for social behavior. Just how much of the difference between men and women in a particular culture is normative and how much is biological is a question of considerable interest to social scientists (Udry 1994). For the most part, however, social scientists are more interested in gender than in sex. They want to know about the variety of roles that have been assigned to women and men and, more particularly, about what accounts for the variation. Under what circumstances do women have more or less power, prestige, and income? What accounts for the recent changes that have occurred in gender roles in our society?

Cross-Cultural Evidence

A glance through *National Geographic* confirms that there is wide variability in gender roles across cultures. The behaviors we normally associate with being female and male are by no means universal. Despite the wide variety across human cultures, there are two important universals: In all cultures, child care is primarily a female responsibility, and in all cultures that we know about, women have less power than men.

In spite of the fact that women do substantial amounts of work in all societies, often supplying more than half of the food as well as taking care of stock, children, and households, women universally have less power and less value. A simple piece of evidence is parents' almost universal preference for male children (Sohoni 1994). This preference can be life threatening to girls. Demographers have determined that worldwide there are 100 million fewer women than there would be if boys and girls were equally valued. A 1992 Bombay study found that of 8,000 abortions performed after parents had used amniocentesis to determine the sex of the fetus, only one aborted fetus was male. Beyond selective abortion and female infanticide (killing of infant girls), boys often receive preferential treatment—for example, more food and medical care—while girls are more likely to be neglected. The preference for boys is less strong in modern industrial nations, but parents in the United States prefer their first child to be a boy by a 2-to-1 margin (Holloway 1994; Pebley and Westoff 1982; Sohoni 1994).

Determinants of Women's Power. There are no known societies in which women have more power than men, but important variations exist from society to society in the amount of power and prestige women have. In some societies, women's power is very low, whereas in others it approaches equality with men's. Four key factors determine women's power in any society: (1) the degree to which women are tied to the home by bearing, nursing, and rearing children; (2) the degree to which economic activities in a society are compatible with staying close to home and caring for children; (3) the degree of physical strength necessary to carry on the subsistence activities of the society; and (4) the degree to which the society is militaristic, valuing waging war and weapons.

Until the sharp fertility declines of the last 200 years, the first factor showed relatively little variability: Most women in most societies were more or less continually tied close to home by pregnancy and subsequent responsibility for nursing and rearing children. The degree to which women could participate in the economic life of their society and contribute to subsistence depended substantially on the second and third conditions. When economic activities required little physical strength and could be carried on while caring for children, women made major contributions to providing subsistence for their families and communities (Chafetz 1984).

As a result of these factors, women have the highest power and prestige in gathering and simple horticultural societies (Quinn 1977). In these societies, the major subsistence activities (gathering and simple hoe agriculture) are compatible with women's child-related roles, and women may be responsible for 60–80 percent of a society's subsistence (Blumberg 1978). Moreover, their economic activities make them an active part of their community and increase the likelihood of their being involved in community and group decisions. Partly because war traditionally required physical strength, the power of women in warring societies tends to be lower.

These four factors help explain most of the important differences in women's power across societies, and they allow us to understand why women's power was low during industrialization but now shows signs of rising. Industrialization moved work away from home and made it difficult for women to be economically productive while bearing and rearing children. Reduced fertility, however, has allowed women to leave the household and increase their participation in society's economic and public life. As a result, the status of women is improving. Nevertheless, men remain substantially advantaged in prestige and power. A recent study sponsored by the United Nations concludes that, at the current rate of change, women will not be equal to men economically until the year 2490 (Wright 1995).

One result of female power disadvantage is widespread violence toward women. "Domestic violence is a leading cause of female injury in almost every country in the world," concluded an international study by the Human Rights Watch organization in 1995 (Wright 1995). For example:

- In the United States, in 1992, over half a million women were murdered, raped, assaulted, or robbed by an intimate (spouse, ex-spouse, or boyfriend). That number is more than 10 times the number of male victims of intimate violence for the same year, 49,000 (U.S. Department of Justice 1994, 3). Violence between intimates, or domestic violence, is further discussed in Chapter 14.
- In Peru, the beating of women by their husbands makes up 70 percent of all reported crime, according to a United Nations study (Wright 1995).
- In Russia, where an estimated 15,000 women were killed by their mates in 1994, there are no laws that effectively protect women from domestic violence, although a man beating his wife can be charged with the minor offense of hooliganism (Edwards 1995).
- An estimated 110 million women, mostly in African countries but also in Asia, South America, and Europe, have undergone the ritual of genital mutilation—

removal of some or all of the clitoris and surrounding genitalia in order to control sexual desire and behavior (Daly 1991; Holloway, 1994; Woods and Clouse 1994).

- In India, since 1990, more than 20,000 brides have been murdered in "dowry deaths," the consequence of a new wife's bringing an inadequate dowry (sum of money and goods) to her husband's family (Wright 1995).

Violence against women is not caused by men's attitudes and actions only. Throughout the world, women are often full or partial participants, whether by aborting a female fetus, arranging for a daughter's genital mutilation, or murdering a daughter-in-law in a dowry death. The point is, "Violence against women derives essentially from the lower status accorded to women in the family," according to a U.N. report (Wright 1995). Meanwhile, in growing numbers, women around the world are demanding equal rights. The next section gives an example.

Global Perspectives: The World Conference on Women in Beijing, China

In 1995, 45,000 government delegates from 189 countries focused on human rights for women at the Fourth World Conference on Women, sponsored by the United Nations and held in Beijing, China. It was the largest conference on women ever held. Near Beijing, in the town of Huairou, another 40,000 women took part in an accompanying international conference for members of women's nongovernmental organizations (NGOs), such as family planning and health organizations and anti-violence organizations (Chen 1995). In some places, such as San Francisco, people kept in touch with conference goings-on by Internet (Abate 1995).

After negotiating for more than two weeks, delegates to the official United Nations conference adopted a 149-page "Platform for Action" that designated international priorities for women into the next century. Endorsing a range of advances that the United Nations has vowed to pursue and member countries have promised to implement, the platform calls on countries to bolster education and health care for women and girls, to fight violence against women, and to empower them economically and legally. The platform also urges developed nations to help poor ones implement the program (Burdman 1995).

Controversy surrounded the conference and threatened to draw attention from the real issues being discussed. Some criticized the selection of China to host the conference, given that country's generally poor record on human rights. NGO participants protested that their meetings had been scheduled away from the official conference and in very uncomfortable quarters (Bogert and Chubbuck 1995).

There was also conflict within the official conference itself, mainly over the "sexual rights" clause in the platform. According to the controversial paragraph, sexual rights "include the individual's right to have control over and decide freely on matters related to her or his sexuality, free of coercion, discrimination and violence." Representatives from the United States and other countries that support the wording saw the clause as a way of protecting women against rape, unwanted pregnancy, coercive contraception, and violence. Opponents included delegates from Iran, Sudan, and the Vatican, as well as religious and political conservatives—both men and women—from the United States and elsewhere. They argued that the clause gives both women and men excessive sexual license and hence potentially undermines the family (Burdman 1995).

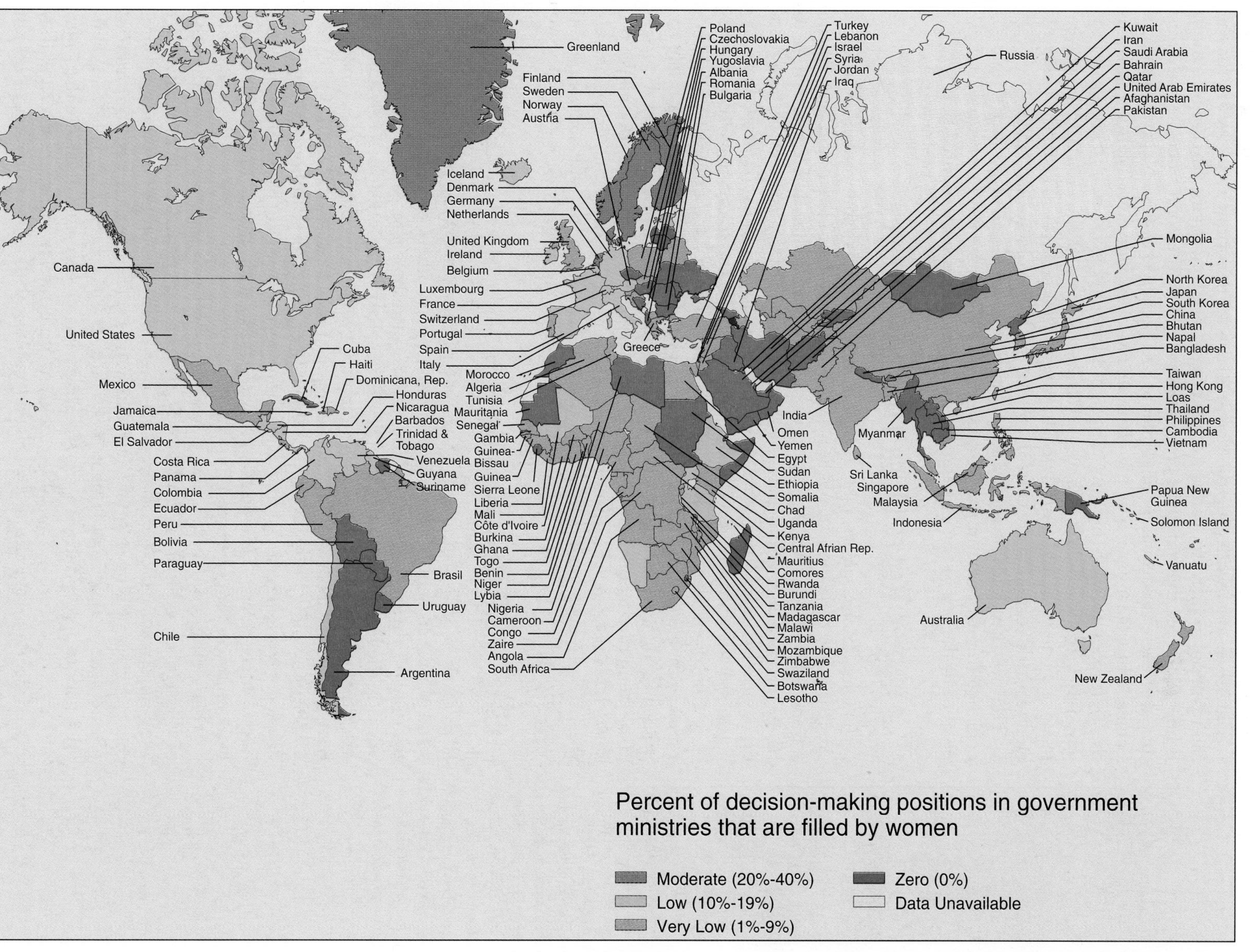

MAP 12.1
WOMEN IN PUBLIC LIFE, 1994

SOURCE: United Nations. 1995. The World's Women 1995: Trends and Statistics. Social Statistics and Indicators, Series K, No. 12. New York: United Nations.

Despite many changes in American gender roles, boys and girls still tend to experience large doses of traditional gender role socialization. Boys are more likely to want to race motocross and girls are more likely to want to play with dolls. Some of these differences may be due to our genetic heritage, but studies show that parents' and teachers' expectations have a tremendous influence on the degree to which children ascribe to and act out traditional roles. Dad and mom, after all, provided the motorcycle or doll, not nature.

Feminists, meanwhile, see the document as an important step forward for the international women's movement. An all-important concern for developing nations is how to pay for the ambitious programs espoused by the conference, and whether they will ever be adequately implemented remains to be seen. Nevertheless, as a Bangladeshi woman from a family-planning NGO explained, the platform "gives us the legitimacy to walk into a government office and say, 'Look, these were your promises'" (in Bogert 1995, 52). "There's a sense here of the enormous empowerment of women," noted Betty Friedan, whose 1963 book *The Feminine Mystique* is credited with beginning the current wave in the U.S. women's movement.

The need to hold a worldwide conference on the state of women's rights is evidence that throughout the world women's rights have not been equal to those of men. In the rest of this chapter, we focus on gender in the United States.

Gender Roles Over the Life Course

In some things, such as table manners, we expect men and women to be alike. A great many characteristics, however, are *gendered*—considered more appropriate for one sex than another. We expect women and men to like different activities, to have different personalities and skills, and to perform different tasks. Many of these differences are normative—that is, we think men and women *ought* to think and act in specific, different ways. People who violate these norms may receive sanctions from friends and family. More important, if they have internalized society's norms, individuals who violate gender norms will feel guilty and uncomfortable.

Gender differences begin with pink and blue blankets in the hospital nursery and extend throughout life. In this section, we provide an overview of some of the basic differences in American gender roles over the life course. Later, we address the issue of male/female inequalities in scarce resources and offer some explanations for them.

Developing a Gendered Identity

Early Childhood Socialization. Chapter 6 pointed out that we begin to develop a sense of our self-identity by seeing ourselves through others' eyes—the looking-glass self. One of the first elements youngsters distinguish as part of their looking-glass selves is their gender identity. By the age of 24 to 30 months, they can correctly identify themselves and those with whom they come into contact by sex, and they have some ideas about what this means for appropriate behavior (Cahill 1983).

Because young children are not capable of complex thinking, they tend to develop very rigid ideas of what it means to be a boy or girl. These ideas are often highly stereotyped: "Boys don't play with dolls (or lipstick)!" and "Ladies don't work on trucks (or computers)!"

Young children develop strong stereotypes for two reasons. One is that the world they see is highly divided by sex: In their experience, women usually don't work on trucks, and boys usually don't dress dolls. The other important determinant of stereotyping is how they themselves have been treated. Substantial research shows that parents treat boys and girls differently. They give their children gender-appropriate toys, they respond negatively when their children play with cross-gender toys, they allow their boys to be active and aggressive, and they encourage their daughters to play quietly and visit with adults (Orenstein 1994). If parents do not exhibit gender-stereotypic behavior and if they do not punish their children for cross-gender behavior, the children will be less rigid in their gender stereotypes (Berk 1989).

As a result of this learning process, boys and girls develop fairly strong ideas about what is appropriate for girls and what is appropriate for boys. Because males and male behaviors have higher status than female behaviors, boys are punished more than girls for exhibiting cross-gender behavior. Thus, little boys are especially rigid in their ideas of what girls and boys ought to do. Girls are freer to engage in cross-gender behavior, and by the time they enter school, many girls are experimenting with boyish behaviors.

Differences in Aptitudes and Personality. If you ask young children what they are like, boys will often tell you that they are independent, aggressive, and adventurous; girls will often tell you that they are gentle, cooperative, and quiet. They are responding to gender stereotypes. Considering how strongly children hold these stereotypes and how much pressure there is from others to encourage gendered behavior, it is surprising that the actual differences in boys and girls are quite small.

A review of thousands of studies over the last several decades points to the following differences between boys and girls (Berk 1989; Hedges and Nowell 1995; Hyde, Fennema, and Lamon 1990).

- On average, boys have better spatial abilities, are more active and aggressive, and perform better in mathematics (but only after junior high).
- On average, girls have better verbal skills, are more fearful and anxious, are more compliant and dependent, and are less likely to have developmental or behavioral problems.

The most impressive thing about these sex differences in personality and cognitive ability is that they are so small. Most of the differences have declined over time, and today sex is a very poor predictor of either math scores or personality among children (Hyde, Fennema, and Lamon 1990).

There are few differences in level of education between women and men. Women are as likely as men to graduate from high school and college and just as likely to get postgraduate degrees. The primary sex difference is in type of education. If you had to guess which of these students was in electrical engineering and which in English, you would do well to take sex into consideration. Although women students are majoring into engineering and computer sciences in greater proportions than before, the traditional sex differences in college majors persist.

EDUCATION

As of the early 1990s, women and men were equally represented among high school graduates and among those receiving bachelor's and master's degrees. At the level of the Ph.D. or advanced professional degrees (law and medicine), however, women were disadvantaged in quantity of education.

Probably more important than the differences in level of education are the differences in types of education. From about the fifth grade on, sex differences emerge in academic aptitudes and interests (Orenstein 1994). As a result of these early differences, women college graduates are overrepresented in the fields of education and the humanities, and men are overrepresented in the fields of physical sciences, engineering, and law. Table 12.1 shows the proportion of bachelor's degrees earned by women in various fields of study in 1971 and in 1992, the latest statistics available. You can see from the table that there were changes over this period. Women were far more likely in 1992 than in 1971 to major in pre-law. Furthermore, women and men graduates in 1992 were about equally likely to have majored in business or management—a significant change since 1971, when only 9.1 percent of such graduates were women. Women and men were also about equally divided in 1992 in the fields of mathematics and social sciences.

TABLE 12.1
BACHELOR'S DEGREES EARNED, BY FIELD, 1971 AND 1991

Between 1971 and 1992, there was a substantial narrowing of the sex gap in educational focus. Nevertheless, engineering continues to be largely a male preserve, while education attracts a disproportionate number of women undergraduates. Since engineers earn roughly three times what teachers earn, this difference in educational direction is one reason why, on average, women earn less than men.

	PERCENT FEMALE	
FIELD OF STUDY	1971	1991
BUSINESS AND MANAGEMENT	9.1	47.2
COMPUTER AND INFORMATION SCIENCES	13.6	28.7
EDUCATION	74.5	79.0
ENGINEERING	0.8	14.0
HEALTH SCIENCES	77.1	83.5
HOME ECONOMICS	97.3	88.7
LIBRARY AND ARCHIVAL SCIENCES	92.0	91.8
PRE-LAW	5.0	67.3
MATHEMATICS	37.9	46.6
SOCIAL SCIENCES	36.8	45.5

SOURCE: U.S. Bureau of the Census, 1995, Table 300.

The most striking differences between men and women were in the fields of education, home economics, library sciences, and engineering. In 1992, only 14 percent of graduates in engineering were women. Meanwhile, 79 percent of graduates in education, 89 percent in home economics, 84 percent in the health sciences, and 92 percent in library sciences were women (U.S. Bureau of the Census 1995, Table 300). Since engineers make a great deal more money than teachers, librarians, and most health science workers, these differences in educational aspirations have implications for future economic well-being. This situation is an example of institutionalized discrimination against women—a persistence of disadvantage through presumably neutral social processes, such as educational attainment, that produces systematically unequal results for members of a designated group or category. (Recall that Chapter 11 discussed institutionalized discrimination in the form of racism.)

PARTICIPATION IN THE LABOR FORCE

In 1994, 93 percent of men compared with 75 percent of women aged 25–54 were in the labor force (U.S. Department of Labor 1995). This gap is far smaller than it used to be (see Figure 12.1) but is probably larger than it will be in the future. Studies show no sex differences in the proportion of male and female col-

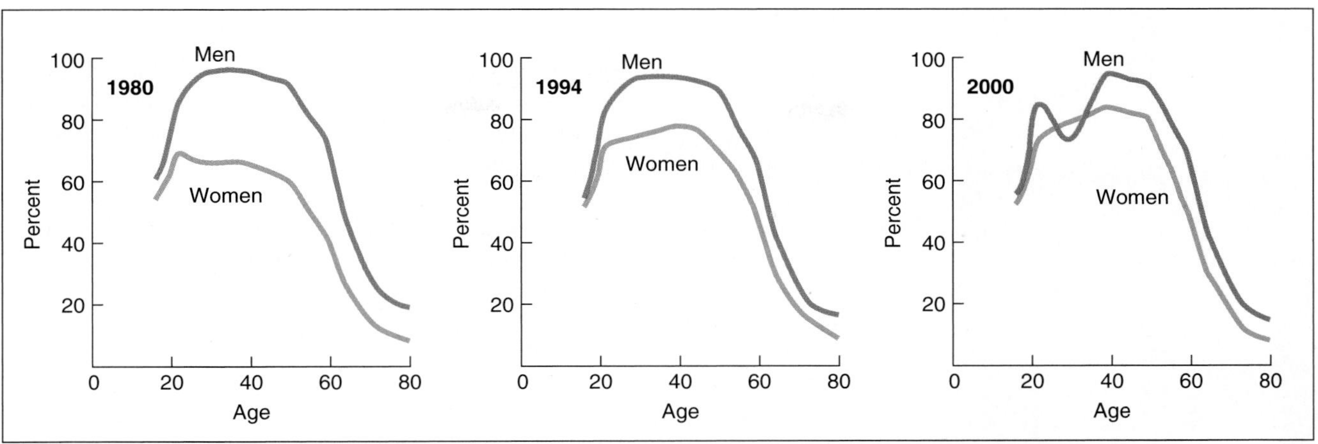

FIGURE 12.1
LABOR-FORCE PARTICIPATION RATES OF MEN AND WOMEN AGED 16 AND OVER, 1980 TO 2000 (EST.)

In the 20 years between 1980 and 2000, two major changes occur in labor-force participation: Men's and women's rates become very similar, and fewer of either sex work past age 60.

SOURCE: U.S. Bureau of the Census 1995, Table 627; U.S. Department of Labor.

lege students who expect to be employed at age 25 or age 50 (Affleck, Morgan, and Hayes 1989). Although most young women expect to be mothers, they also expect to be full-time, permanent members of the labor force.

Although women and men are nearing equality in the proportion employed, U.S. norms still send out very different messages about the importance of employment. There is little ambiguity about a man's role: His major adult role continues to be provider. Although his wife may work, the moral responsibility for supporting the family falls on his shoulders. Women, however, receive mixed messages about the importance of work and family. Just 25 years ago, the majority of the American public considered it wrong for women with children to work; now only a minority feel this way. Labor-force participation is still more an option than an obligation for women, however, and women are far less likely than men to be sanctioned by their friends and neighbors for their inability to support their families. They will, however, be sanctioned if their employment results in neglect of their children's or husband's needs. American norms make it clear that, although employment is an acceptable option, their families should be women's primary obligation.

At the same time, these different cultural messages about the importance of employment and family responsibilities also restrict men. They may be encouraged, for instance, to go into majors and, later, jobs (such as engineering) that pay well but are not what they really want to do (such as teaching, perhaps). Indeed, differences in norms about the importance of work and about the types of work appropriate for women and men have dramatic consequences for the types of work both men and women actually do and for their earnings (Bielby and Bielby 1989). These differences will be the topic of later sections in this chapter.

Contemporary gender roles ask fathers to do much more for their children than just support them economically and play catch on Saturday afternoons. Today, we expect dads to change diapers, cook dinners, and listen to their children's troubles—many of the tasks that were left primarily to mothers only a generation ago. Unfortunately, nearly 40 percent of America's children live apart from their fathers. As a result, the overall picture may be one of less rather than more fathering.

Family Roles

Although society has changed dramatically in the last half century, the great majority of Americans continue to marry, become parents, and take on family roles. These family roles are sharply gendered: husband and wife, mother and father, have different obligations and different rights.

Parenting. Because of modern contraceptives, childbearing is a choice for most women rather than a biological imperative. This "choice" is not made in a vacuum, however. In fact, enjoyment of small children and the wish to be a mother are both normative expectations for women. Until very recently, women who did not want families were regarded as unnatural, unwomanly. There is now greater tolerance for the choice not to have children, but the vast majority of American women nevertheless expect to have children. The decision to have children has enormous economic, social, and emotional consequences.

If children are to be born, then women, of course, must be the ones to bear them. Despite science fiction stories to the contrary, today's culture cannot redistribute this role. Subsequent care of the child is not so clearly a biological imperative. Nevertheless, all societies, including U.S. society, have viewed this as primarily a female responsibility. The last few years have seen increased emphasis on fathers' involvement with their children, and some modest shifts in child-care responsibility have occurred. The increase in the proportion of fathers changing diapers, however, has been overshadowed by the increase in the number of children being raised by single mothers. The major responsibility for child care in most American households rests on the mother.

Household Production. In addition to child care, home and family involve a substantial amount of domestic work. Clothes must be purchased and washed; meals must be purchased, prepared, and cleaned up after; houses must be taken care of and lawns mowed. In addition, family relationships require work: Somebody has to plan holiday dinners, buy wedding presents for nieces and cousins, and generally keep the family together. Almost all of this work is women's work in U.S. society. (Thompson and Walker 1989). There have been some changes in attitude but relatively few changes in behavior (Shelton 1992).

Caring for Aging Parents. Today's middle-aged parents have been called the "sandwich generation" because some of them are pressed from two sides—by their children's demands and those of their aging parents. The term *sandwich generation* sounds gender neutral, but in fact it is most often women who are spread thin. The vast majority of informal care of the elderly is provided by female relatives, usually daughters and (less often) daughters-in-law (Dwyer and Seccombe 1991).

Conclusion

Marriage and parenthood do not dominate women's lives in the way that they did a generation ago (McLaughlin and Associates 1988). Women are marrying later and having children later; growing (though still small) proportions will never marry or have children. More important, marriage and parenthood no longer signal withdrawal from other spheres of activity. For the most part, both girls and boys expect to spend a large portion of their adult life in the labor force, and they expect significant equality in social relationships. Nevertheless, family roles remain sharply gendered, and getting married and especially becoming a parent continue to be powerful forces for differentiating male and female experience. This situation is one reason why very substantial differences remain in men's and women's access to such scarce resources as income and power. We address these inequalities in the next section.

WHO BENEFITS? SOCIAL INEQUALITIES BETWEEN WOMEN AND MEN

In the United States today, almost twice as many women as men live in poverty. This section examines some of the structured social inequalities that exist between women and men.

ECONOMIC INEQUALITIES

Despite the growing equality in labor-force involvement, major inequalities in the rewards of paid employment persist. In 1991, women who were full-time, full-year workers earned 70 percent as much as men, down from an all-time high of 72 percent reached in 1990. Younger women (aged 25 through 34) are doing better, earning about 83 percent of what their male counterparts do (U.S. Bureau of Labor Statistics 1994, Table A). But the overall percentage has not changed much since 1950. Why do women earn less than men? The answers fall into two categories: workplace segregation and different earnings.

Workplace Segregation. Women and men tend to be employed in different jobs, as shown in Figure 12.2, and the jobs women hold pay less than the jobs men hold. Figure 12.2 shows that women dominate clerical jobs, whereas men dominate blue-collar jobs. The clerical and sales jobs occupied by nearly one-half of the female labor force are generally nonunion and poorly paid, with low benefits and few promotional opportunities. Although the blue-collar jobs dominated by male workers also have few promotional opportunities, many are unionized and have high hourly wages and good benefit packages. The proportion of men and women in professional and managerial jobs is nearly equal. Generally, though, doctors in the United States are still more likely to be men, and nurses, women. Generally, men are more likely to manage steel plants; and women, dry-cleaning outlets.

Studies of sex segregation in the workplace show that there has been only marginal improvement in the last 30 years (Wellington 1994: Steiger and Wardell 1995). There are three primary reasons why women and men have different jobs: gendered jobs, different qualifications, and discrimination.

> **THINKING CRITICALLY**
>
> Chapter 11 discussed institutionalized discrimination. Can you think of some specific examples of how institutionalized discrimination works against women in the workplace? Against men? How specifically might affirmative action programs (also discussed in Chapter 11) help to alleviate this discrimination?

GENDERED JOBS. Because of historical circumstances, many jobs in today's labor market are regarded as either "women's work" or "men's work." Construction work, warehousing, and much manual labor are almost exclusively men's work; nursing, library work, medical technology, and keyboarding are largely women's work. These occupations are so sex segregated, or gendered, that many men or women would feel uncomfortable working in one of them if they were the "wrong" sex for the job. Women in male-dominated occupations have reported being made to feel uncomfortable by such subtle forms of discrimination as exclusion from informal

FIGURE 12.2 DIFFERENCES IN OCCUPATION BY SEX, 1994

Men and women continue to be employed in different occupations in the United States. The most striking differences are in technical, sales, and clerical work, where women predominate, and in various blue-collar jobs, held primarily by men. Within categories, men typically hold higher-status positions than women.

SOURCE: U.S. Bureau of the Census. 1995, Table 649.

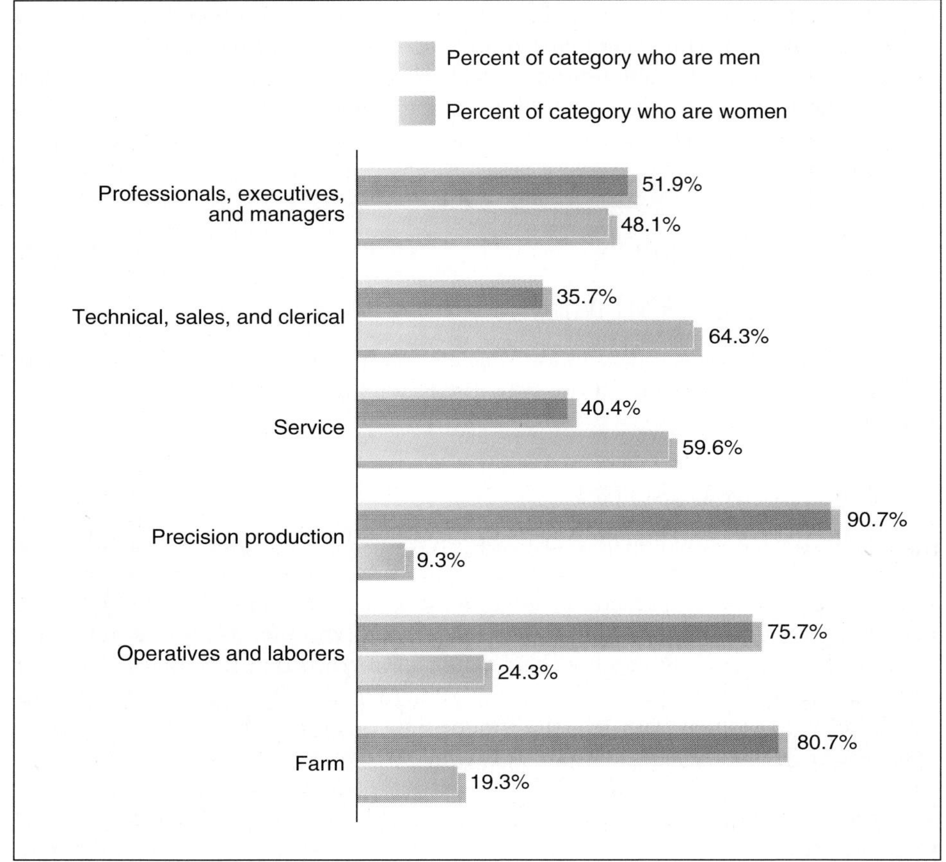

leadership and decision-making networks, sexual harassment, and other forms of hostility from male co-workers (Jacobs 1989). These forms of informal discrimination serve as *glass ceilings*—invisible barriers to women's promotions in traditionally male careers (Freeman 1990). In contrast, men working in female-identified occupations report that negative stereotypes about men who do "women's work" are the major barrier to more men entering these occupations, such as nurse, elementary school teacher, librarian, and social worker. However, when men do work in non-traditional fields, they are likely to encounter "glass escalators"—rapid promotions "up" to more masculine administrative positions (Williams 1992).

Although there has been virtually no change in the number of men employed in female-dominated occupations, a growing number of jobs that used to be reserved for men—such as insurance adjuster, police officer, and bus driver—have opened up to women in the last decade. Research shows, however, that this is not because of women's increased access to good jobs. Rather, women are moving into jobs that men are abandoning because of deteriorating wages and working conditions (Reskin 1989).

DIFFERENT QUALIFICATIONS. We have already seen that, although the differences are smaller than they used to be, women tend to major in fields that prepare them to work in relatively low-paying jobs, such as education, while men are more likely to choose more lucrative fields. More important than these differences in educational qualifications, however, are disparities in experience and on-the-job training. Because many women have taken time out of the labor force for child rearing, they have less job experience than men their own age (Marini 1989). Furthermore, perceiving that women are more likely to be short-term employees than men, employers have invested less in training women. As a result, women employees have lower qualifications than men. All of these factors mean that women are less likely to be promoted into management positions—another example of institutionalized discrimination.

DISCRIMINATION. Although occupational preparations are somewhat different for men and women, many of the occupational differences between them are due to discrimination by employers. Employers reserve some jobs for men and some for women on the basis of their own stereotypes. This covers not only major occupational differences (men drive forklifts and women perform data entry) but also minor distinctions in job titles. Within the same objective task, men and women will be given different titles—women will be executive assistants and men doing the same tasks will be assistant executives, often at much higher pay.

Why do employers discriminate? An important reason is that they believe in gender stereotypes. They believe that men are competent and analytical and that women are emotional and timid. It is not surprising, then, that they prefer to hire men for managerial or other responsible positions.

Several studies document that another important reason that men and women have different jobs is that women are less likely to be promoted (Wellington 1994). One study of women engineers, for example, found that 5 to 10 years after finishing school, women were already significantly behind their male peers, even though they were identical in terms of education and experience (Robinson and McIlwee 1989).

SEXUAL HARASSMENT. A special form of discrimination that is especially problematic for female workers, military personnel, and students is **sexual harassment**—unwelcome sexual advances, requests for sexual favors, and other unwanted verbal or physical conduct of a sexual nature. Harassment may be just an annoyance. It may, however, turn into real discrimination. The courts use the following guidelines to determine when unwelcome sexual advances constitute unlawful discrimination (Schapiro 1994).

Sexual harassment consists of unwelcome sexual advances, requests for sexual favors, or other verbal or physical conduct of a sexual nature.

- *Quid pro quo harassment*. This occurs "when an employee's submission to unwelcome sexual conduct becomes an explicit or implicit condition of employment, or when personnel actions such as promotion, transfer, compensation, or discipline are determined on the basis of an employee's response to such conduct."
- *Hostile environment*. A hostile environment develops when there is "unwelcome sexual conduct which unreasonably interferes with an individual's job performance or creates an intimidating, hostile, or offensive work environment."

Sexual harassment ranges from subtle hints about the rewards of being more friendly with the boss or teacher to rape. In the less severe instances (and sometimes even in the more severe instances), the subordinate may be reluctant to make, literally, a federal case of it. This pattern of reluctance to report the matter became an issue several years ago when Anita Hill, a law professor, accused the

Supreme Court nominee Clarence Thomas of sexual harassment that allegedly had occurred years earlier.

Same Job, Different Earnings. Not all jobs are substantially sex segregated. Some, such as flight attendant and research analyst, contain considerable proportions of both men and women. Generally, however, men earn substantially more than women even within the same occupation (see Table 12.2), and these same-occupation wage differences are a major source of sex inequities (Steiger and Wardell 1995).

Within integrated occupations, such as hotel management and law, men tend to be in high-paying firms and women tend to be in low-paying firms. Men tend to be in large firms and women in small. These differences in type of firm reflect the segmented labor market: *Where* you work may be as important as what you do in determining your income and opportunity.

Another important reason that women are paid less well than men within the same occupation is that women's ability to maximize their careers is sharply curtailed by their family responsibilities. More often than men, women choose jobs close to home so that it is easy to drop the children off at day care or take them to the doctor during the lunch hour. Similarly, women are much less likely than men to be able to uproot their families and move to advance their careers.

Recognizing these family claims on women employees, employers are less likely to hire them for jobs requiring long career tracks or geographical moves. As we have seen, they are also less likely to invest in training for them and less likely to promote them. This pattern affects all women, even those who intend to work for 40 years or who are the sole support for themselves or their families (Marini 1989). However, studies show that discrimination is strongest against women who are married and have children. Partly as a result of the greater opportunities that are open to them, women with fewer family ties earn more than women with husbands and children (Shellenbarger 1992).

In the contemporary labor force, few jobs require sex-specific abilities, such as being able to lift 100 pounds. As a result, there are a growing number of jobs that include women and men. Just having the same job, however, does not produce equal earnings. Even among full time, full-year employees with the same occupational title, women earn substantially less than men. As women's employment becomes a life-long role and fewer women take sustained periods off for child rearing, some of this earnings gap may be reduced.

TABLE 12.2
SEX DIFFERENCES IN EARNINGS FROM THE SAME OCCUPATION

Even when women have the same occupation as men, they tend to earn substantially less money. In part because of their family responsibilities, women tend to be employed in smaller and lower-paying firms. They also experience substantial discrimination in both employment and promotional opportunities.

Occupation	Median Earnings Males	Median Earnings Females	Male/Female Ratio
Accountants	$40,469	$27,750	1.46
Engineers	46,512	40,341	1.15
Natural scientists and mathematicians	42,308	34,208	1.24
Computer equipment operators	29,131	21,595	1.35
Lawyers and judges	71,530	50,296	1.42

SOURCE: U.S. Bureau of the Census 1992a, pp. 153, 156.

POWER INEQUALITIES

As Max Weber pointed out, differences in prestige and power are as important as differences in economic reward. When we turn to these rewards, we again find that women are systematically disadvantaged. Whether we are talking about the family, business, or church, we find that women are less likely to be given positions of authority.

Unequal Power in Social Institutions. Women's subordinate position is built into most social institutions. From the church to the family, we find that norms specify that women's roles are subordinate to men's. The Bible's New Testament, for example, urges, "Wives, submit yourselves unto your own husbands" (Ephesians 5:22); the traditional marriage vows require women to promise to obey their husbands; until 1919, women were not allowed to vote in the United States.

In politics, prejudice against women leaders is declining—but it is still quite strong. Whereas women comprise 53 percent of the voters, they represent only 21 percent of all state legislators and only 11 percent of the U.S. Congress. In every institution, traditional norms have specified that men should be the leaders and women the followers. Social scientists call this situation patriarchy.

Unequal Power in Interaction. As we noted in Chapter 7, even the informal exchanges of everyday life are governed by norms. That is, they are patterned regularities, occurring in similar ways again and again. Careful attention to the roles men and women play in these informal interactions shows some rather clear differences—all of them associated with women's lower prestige and power in U.S. society.

An easy-to-see example is that women smile more (Goffman 1974a). They smile to offer social support to others, and they smile to express humility. Studies of informal conversations also show that men regularly dominate women in verbal interaction. Men take up more of the speaking time, they interrupt women more often, and most important, they are more often successful interrupters. Finally, women are more placating and less assertive in conversation than men, and they are more likely to state their opinions as questions ("Don't you think the red one is nicer than the blue one?" (Tannen 1990). This pattern is also apparent in committee and business meetings—one reason women employees are less likely than men to get credit for their ideas (Tannen 1994).

Laboratory and other studies show that this male/female conversational division of labor is largely a result of differential status (Kollock, Blumstein, and Schwartz 1985; Tannen 1990; Wagner, Ford, and Ford 1986). When clear-cut situational factors, such as a student/teacher situation, give women more status in a conversation, they cease to exhibit low status interaction styles. Nevertheless, a study of conversations between physicians and patients showed that patients are much more likely to interrupt when the doctor is a woman (West 1984). It would appear that the lower status accorded to women in U.S. society cannot be overturned merely by changes in occupational or political roles.

THE OTHER SIDE: MALE DISADVANTAGE

Women are at a substantial disadvantage in most areas of conventional achievement; and in informal as well as formal interactions, they have less power than men. They pay for their disadvantage in higher levels of mental illness and poverty (see Chapter 10). Men, too, face some disadvantages from their traditional gender roles.

Girls' play is generally less competitive than boys' play, and it is less likely to be governed by formal rules, such as those that govern sport. In part through their play, girls develop skills in cooperation and negotiation that follow them into adult life. Studies of informal interaction between women and men show that women are more apt than men to smile and to give signals of verbal support.

Mortality. Perhaps the most important difference in life chances involves life itself. In 1992, men in the United States could expect to live 72.3 years and women 79.1 years. (Kochanek and Hudson 1995, 3). On the average, then, women live seven years longer than men. Although part of this difference is probably biological (Waldron 1983), the social contribution to differential life expectancy begins at a very early age and continues through the life course. At high school and college ages, males are nearly three times more likely than females to die. To a significant extent, this difference has to do with the more dangerous lifestyle (particularly drinking and driving) associated with masculinity in our culture.

The sex differential in life expectancy is more complex than the greater risk taking of young men, however. Even at the earlier ages just mentioned, men are more likely than women to die of cancer or heart disease. Consider men's disadvantage in heart disease, for example. Evidence suggests that men have this disadvantage not because they experience more stress than women but because, under the same levels of stress, they are more vulnerable to heart disease than women. Current thinking attributes men's greater risk of heart disease at least partly to the male gender role's low emphasis on nurturance and emotional relationships. Where women's personalities and relationship characteristics seem to protect them from this consequence of stress, lack of social support appears to leave men especially vulnerable to stress-related diseases (Nardi 1992). This suggests that, despite increasing female participation in politics and the labor force, women's life expectancy will continue to remain substantially higher than men's. The sex differential in mortality is likely to decline only when differences in personality and dispositions are reduced.

Social Integration. The low emphasis on nurturance and expressiveness in the male role appears to reduce men's interest in and ability to form close relationships with their children, other kin, and friends. Maintaining family relationships is usually viewed as women's work, and when men end up without women to do this work for them (never married, divorced, or widowed), they also frequently end up alone (Kessler and McLeod 1984; Stroebe and Stroebe 1983; Wallerstein and Kelly 1980). Ultimately, this leaves them substantially disadvantaged in health.

Higher Stress. In addition, the focus of the male gender role on achievement and success can prove stressful. Even men who are successful by any reasonable standard may feel pressured by the constant striving, and those who fail often compensate by excessive aggressiveness in other spheres. Then, too, some men today experience anxiety and stress over losing some of their higher prestige and power in the workplace (Galen 1994) and at home. This stress may be reflected in higher rates of heart disease, a suicide rate that is three times higher than women's, and an alcoholism rate that is five times higher (U.S. Bureau of the Census 1989a).

> **THINKING CRITICALLY**
>
> If men are the more powerful gender, why is it that they die earlier and have higher rates of heart disease, suicide, and alcoholism? As women gain power, should we expect them to have similar health problems? Why or why not?

SUMMARY

Although there are individual exceptions, men as a category have more prestige, more income, and more power than women. One consequence of this is that five times more female-headed than male-headed households are living in poverty. Men pay a price, however, in terms of foregone intimacy and higher mortality. Many changes have occurred in the last decades, and most of them have reduced the differences between women and men. However, in two areas—life expectancy and earnings—the gap between men and women is as large as or larger than it was 20 years ago. We will see in the next section that the mass media help to reinforce this gap.

MASS MEDIA AND GENDER INEQUALITIES

Chapter 3 explored the mass media as a prominent component in popular culture, and Chapter 6 noted the media's role in socialization. Here, focusing on television, we explore how the media promote gender stereotypes and inequalities.

Children's television programming more often depicts boys than girls in active, problem-solving, or dominant roles. In some instances, this has been due to a deliberate marketing decision by the major networks, based on research showing that girls will watch shows with either male or female lead characters but boys will watch only shows with male leads (Carter 1991).

On music video programs, such as those on MTV, females are likely to be shown trying to get a man's attention. Furthermore, a considerable number of music videos broadcast violent messages toward women.

The proportion of lead characters on prime-time television who are working women has increased since about 1985. However, men continue to outnumber women as leads, especially in adventure shows. Meanwhile, most shows featuring a female professional focus on family, not work (Atkin, Moorman, and Lin 1991). Increasingly, TV shows, such as "Melrose Place," depict successful career women as manipulative and vindictive.

In TV commercials, males predominate by about nine to one as the authoritative narrators or voice-overs, even when the products are aimed at women. Daytime commercials, targeted for women, portray men in family or dominant roles; weekend ads, aimed more toward men, emphasize male escape from home and family (Craig 1992; Kilbourne 1994). There are exceptions; but overall, TV reinforces, rather than challenges, the assumptions that women, more than men, are family-oriented and that men, more than women, are otherwise effective (Zillman 1994).

PERSPECTIVES ON SEX STRATIFICATION

The fact that women bear all the children is due to physical differences between men and women. Most of the differences in life chances, however, are socially structured. How do these differences arise? What explains women's lower power? Different sociological theories have offered different answers to these questions.

STRUCTURAL-FUNCTIONAL THEORY: DIVISION OF LABOR

The structural-functional theory of sex stratification is based on the premise that a division of labor is often the most efficient way to get the job done. In the traditional sex-based division of labor, the man does the work outside the family and the woman does the work inside the family. Functionalists have argued that this division of labor is functional because specialization will (a) increase the expertise of each sex in its own tasks; (b) prevent competition between men and women, which might damage the family; and (c) strengthen family bonds by making men dependent on women and vice versa.

As Marx and Engels noted, any division of labor includes the seeds of control and domination. In this case, the division of labor has a built-in disadvantage for women: Because women's specialty is the family, they have fewer contacts, less information, and fewer independent resources. Because this division of labor contributes to family continuity, however, structural functionalists have seen it as necessary and desirable.

Structural-functional theories of sex stratification are still popular among conservative factions of the population, especially religious fundamentalists. Certainly not all, or even most, structural-functional sociologists oppose the Equal Rights Amendment (ERA). But groups that do oppose it have argued from a structural-functional perspective. They believe that it is best if women and men have different roles.

CONFLICT THEORY: SEGMENTED LABOR MARKETS

According to conflict theorists, women's disadvantage is not a historical accident. It is designed to benefit men. In addition, contemporary sex differences are designed to benefit the capitalist class.

It is relatively easy to see how women's lower status can benefit men, but how can it benefit capitalists? The answer lies in the segmented labor market (discussed in Chapter 9 and Chapter 17). The segmented labor market is two-tiered and sharply gendered. It creates one set of jobs for women and another, better set of jobs for men. In this way, capitalists divide the working class and coax working-class men into a coalition against working-class women. Further, the female labor force can be used to provide a cushion against economic cycles: Women can be laid off during slack times and hired back when employment demands are up (Bonacich 1972; England and Dunn 1988).

One of the most important mechanisms for keeping women in their place is **sexism**—the belief that women and men have biologically different capacities and that these differences form a legitimate basis for unequal treatment. Conflict theorists explain sexism as an ideology that is part of the general strategy of stratification. Whenever any group has access to class, status, or power, its first step is to try to exclude others from it. If it can exclude others categorically (that is, on the basis of membership in a category such as sex or race), the need to compete individually is reduced. Sexism, then, is a means of restricting access to scarce resources.

Sexism is a belief that men and women have biologically different capacities and that these form a legitimate basis for unequal treatment.

Symbolic Interaction Theory: Learned Expectations

If two strangers are thrown together in an airplane or a waiting room, they will not start their relationship with a blank slate. Rather, they will find cues in each other's dress, manner, age, race, and sex to frame their interaction. Although subsequent conversations may cause them to change this framework, it is likely that their presuppositions will color the course of the relationship.

Expectation states theory argues that status characteristics (race, sex, class) create expectations in others about probable abilities and social status. When people act on the basis of these expectations, the expectations are confirmed (Berger, Rosenholtz, and Zelditch 1980). For example, if there are no other cues about status, a man and a woman set in an interactive situation are likely to assume that the other possesses characteristics stereotypically associated with their sex. This means she will assume that he is competent and aggressive, and he that she is nurturant and sensitive. It also means he will assume that he has higher status than she, and the whole style of their interaction will follow from these assumptions. As a result, he will likely dominate her and she will probably defer, and any observer would conclude that he does in fact have higher status.

Expectation states theory argues that status characteristics create expectation states in others about probable abilities and social status. When people act on the basis of these expectations, the expectations are confirmed.

Expectation states theory is an extension of earlier ideas about the self-fulfilling prophecy. It has been developed to explain the findings, noted previously, that men usually dominate women in daily interaction. Although laboratory studies demonstrate that this dominance pattern can be reversed when women's higher status is clearly established (Wagner, Ford, and Ford 1986), such clear status cues are usually missing in real-life encounters. Where cues about actual competence are absent or ambiguous, expectation states give men the edge.

These expectation states have a powerful influence in day-to-day interaction, affecting exchanges with salesclerks, friends, colleagues, and supervisors. They affect the likelihood that women will be hired as managers as well as the likelihood that they will be touched, called by their first name, or interrupted. An implication of this research is that when women move away from the kitchen and

Thinking Critically

Think of a conversation or encounter you've had recently with a member of the other sex. How can expectation states theory help to explain what was going on? How might you integrate expectation states theory with either structural-functional or conflict theory to further explain the conversation or encounter?

the data entry pool, they will have to demonstrate superiority clearly in order to be treated as equals.

Feminist Theories

Generally, all feminist theories share the view that gender inequalities are socially rather than biologically constructed and that they should be eliminated (Sapiro 1986). Within this general framework, however, there are many varieties of feminism. Some feminists fit comfortably into conventional political positions, while others take extremely radical positions. Here we outline three general classes of feminist theory: liberal feminism, socialist feminism, and radical feminism. The accompanying Focus on the Environment describes a fourth category, ecofeminism.

Liberal feminism argues that *all* people are created equal. Liberal feminists do not want to change society drastically; they just want to extend basic rights to women. Although their proposals occasionally give rise to real conflict with those who oppose the extension of these rights, liberal feminism is not a radical program.

Socialist feminism uses a Marxist framework (as does conflict theory) to explain differences between the status of men and that of women. Women are the proletarians in the sexual division of labor, men the bourgeois (Engels [1884] 1972). This perspective suggests that men control the means of production. Capitalist institutions are set up to preserve power differentials between men and women.

Socialist feminists, then, believe that women's inequality is rooted in the institutions of private property and the means of production. As a result, private property, including the individual ownership of and responsibility for children, must be eliminated to create equality for women. Socialist feminism is obviously a more radical approach than liberal feminism. It suggests that the problem is not the access of women to conventional institutions but the institutions themselves.

The most extreme of all feminist theories is radical feminism. Those who adopt this perspective argue that men, not institutions, are the problem. They see all of history as a more or less successful domination of men and men's ideas over women and women's ideas. Since they define men as the problem, they do not believe that changing social institutions will help. The solution they advocate is separation of women from men—severing all heterosexual relationships and creating a separate women's culture. They believe such a culture will be characterized by specifically female virtues—nurturance, sharing, and intuition (Sapiro 1986).

Summary

Each of the four bodies of theory just discussed gives a different view of sex stratification. Structural functionalism stresses how society benefits from a gendered division of labor, while the remaining three perspectives usually assume that sex stratification should be minimized. Symbolic interactionism focuses on how women and men structure inequality in personal relations. Conflict theory and feminist theories emphasize that gender inequality is socially structured or culturally condoned and highlight methods for change.

FOCUS ON THE ENVIRONMENT

Ecofeminism

"... MANY ECOFEMINISTS HAVE BEEN INSPIRED BY ANCIENT GODDESS MYTHS."

In 1962, Rachel Carson published a book called *Silent Spring*. It changed the world. Raising an emotional yet scientific voice of protest against pollution, Carson predicted, among other things, that many bird species would soon become extinct because of unrestricted pesticide use. One outcome of the book was a ban on the use of the pesticide DDT in the United States. Today, we can thank Carson for the return of the bald eagle, which is no longer an endangered species ("Averting a Death Foretold" 1994). Carson's voice was certainly not alone, but her book helped propel an environmental movement that celebrated the first national Earth Day in 1970.

Carson was not an avowed feminist. But because she was a woman, by the late 1970s, the idea that women must be central to protecting the environment had emerged among feminists.

Ecofeminism is a term describing not only the wide range of women's efforts to save Earth (with a capital E and thought of as female) but also changes in feminism that have emerged through a new vision of women in nature. The feminist movement has always asserted that women should participate equally in creating social institutions and culture. In the 1970s, some feminists began to see *higher* value in *women's* ways of thinking and doing things. They came to view the dominant culture's neglect of Mother Earth as a product of masculine ways of thinking and behaving.

In addition, ecofeminism has a spiritual component. Hoping to fashion new cultures that could live *with* Earth rather than master her, many ecofeminists have been inspired by ancient goddess myths. In these myths, the creator is female, and Earth is revered as sacred. Other ecofeminists have been drawn to the philosophy and rituals of Native Americans, because American Indian cultures take seriously the effects of their decisions on future generations.

Three different, although related, themes are present in ecofeminism:

1. The Earth is sacred in and of itself (not because of the uses to which humans can put her). All of Earth's forests, rivers, and creatures have intrinsic value; the individual life of any one of Earth's creatures is valuable simply because the creature is living.
2. Because human life is dependent on Mother Earth, her fate and ours are intertwined. Humans must care for Earth; our survival is directly linked to hers. Social justice cannot be achieved apart from respecting Earth.
3. While Earth and all creatures have intrinsic value, it is also true that humans must use some of Earth's resources in order to survive. Thus, we must learn and appreciate the many and varied ways in which we can walk the fine line between using Earth as a resource and respecting her own needs, cycles, and ecosystems.

Today, ecofeminism embraces a diverse array of innovative communities and co-ops, dedicated to such things as tree planting, alternative healing, organic food, performance art, benevolent witchcraft, and new forms of political activism based on ancient myths. A common thread is the belief that the degradation of nature is culturally and politically related to the patriarchal exploitation of women (Adams 1994; Diamond and Orenstein 1990).

CONCLUSION

An understanding of women's status can gain much from an analogy to race relations. Women can be viewed as a minority group and men as the majority (dominant) group. The same mechanisms that help maintain boundaries between racial groups also maintain boundaries between the sexes: prejudice, discrimination, self-fulfilling prophecies, segregation, and physical violence. The analogy

The feminist movement today is very diverse. On the one hand, many business and professional women fight for equal rights in legislatures and courtrooms. On the other hand, radical feminists want to dismantle the entire set of institutions, which they see as embodying principles of male domination. One issue that unites nearly all feminists is defense of legal abortion, a woman's right to choose.

extends to the use of labels to keep minority groups in their place. Just as African American men were called boys to remind them of their inferior status, middle-aged women continue to be called girls. Is this just a friendly term that doesn't have any political meaning, or is it a subtle suggestion that women are not full grown-ups with responsibilities equal to men's? Although people who use the term *girls* usually deny any negative intent, the fact that this usage is most common toward women in lower-status occupations (for example, keyboard operators and housewives) suggests that it is a mechanism for reinforcing status.

Sojourner Truth

Gender roles have changed over the past 30 years. With fewer exceptions, those changes have affected us deeply. Changing gender roles have brought stress to many people—to men who have had to give up rights and power and also to women.

It would be a mistake, however, to think that the past has been swept away. In many respects, continuity with the past is much more important than change. This is especially true at home. Although childbearing itself is a biologically determined capacity, many aspects of childbearing are socially determined. How many children to have, when to have them, and who will care for them are issues that are determined by social structure rather than biology. In our society, the house, children, and elderly parents are still largely her responsibility; breadwinning remains primarily his. The lack of responsiveness of family roles to other changes is a source of conflict in many American marriages, and the family is increasingly being identified as the most critical frontier for women's equality

APPLICATIONS IN DIVERSITY

"AND AIN'T I A WOMAN?" WHAT ARE THE SPECIAL CONCERNS OF WOMEN OF COLOR?

During the first half of the 19th century in the United States, many civic-minded northern women were active in the movement to abolish slavery. The discrimination they experienced in trying to speak out against slavery radicalized many of these women, who soon realized that they couldn't free anyone else while they were not free themselves. As a result, in the 1840s, some women split away from the abolitionist movement to promote women's rights. Many who stayed within the ranks of the abolitionist movement thought that once rights were extended to black men, they would surely be extended to white and other women.

Of course, many activists continued to work hard both for the end of slavery and for women's rights. One of the most eloquent speakers on the women's rights circuit was a former slave who took the name Sojourner Truth. In response to male hecklers who claimed that women were weak and needed the protection of a dependent position, she responded:

> The man over there says women need to be helped into carriages and lifted over ditches, and to have the best place everywhere. Nobody ever helps me into carriages or over puddles, or gives me the best place—and ain't I a woman?
>
> Look at my arm. I have ploughed and planted and gathered into barns, and no man could head me—and ain't I a woman? I could work as much and eat as much as a man—when I could get it—and bear the lash as well! And ain't I a woman? I have born thirteen children, and seen most of 'em sold into slavery, and when I cried out with my mother's grief, none but Jesus heard me—and ain't I a woman? (Cited in Flexner 1972, 90–91).

Despite Sojourner Truth's effective advocacy of women's rights, many women of color have found the struggle for women's rights and that for minority rights to be an uneasy combination.

Women of color face a dilemma. On the one hand, they have not benefited from the sheltered position of traditional women's roles. As Truth so eloquently illustrated, nobody held doors for them or protected them from heavy work. Women of color have always worked hard outside the home: At the turn of the century, married African American women were six times more likely than married white women to be employed (Golden 1977). At the same time, they faced the economic and civic penalties of being women. Thus, they have had less to lose and more to gain from abandoning traditional gender roles. On the other hand, women of color face a potential conflict of interest: Is racism or sexism their chief oppressor? Should they work for an end to racism or an end to sexism? If they choose to work for women's rights, they may be seen as working against men of their own racial and ethnic group.

Current income figures indicate that sex is more important than race in determining women's *earnings:* The difference between Hispanic, black, and non-Hispanic white women is relatively small compared with the difference between women and men. This suggests that fighting sex discrimination should be more important than fighting racial discrimination. But this conclusion overlooks the fact that the total *income* of women and their children depends to a significant extent on the earnings of their husbands and fathers. For example, black women and children are three times more likely than white women and children to live

THINKING CRITICALLY

What specific issues separate white non-Hispanic women from women of color? What specific issues unite them? Do you think that the problems and dilemmas faced by African American women are mainly the same as or different from those faced by Hispanic American women? Why? What about the issues faced by Asian American women? Does it make sense to talk about "women" as one single minority group? Why, or why not?

APPLICATIONS IN DIVERSITY

below the poverty level. The reason, of course, is the low earnings and employment of black men. From this perspective, women of color could advance their cause most effectively by fighting racial and ethnic discrimination.

The dilemma remains a real one. The women's rights movement is seen as a middle-class white social movement; racial and ethnic movements have been seen as men's movements. Nevertheless, minority women have a long history of resistance to both forms of discrimination: racism and sexism. Increasingly, women of color strive for gender equality within traditional racial and ethnic organizations (Collins 1991).

SOCIOLOGY ON THE NET

America has experienced a civil rights movement that has improved the status of women and minorities. While true equality is still a hope and not a reality, much of the rest of the world still lags far behind the U.S. To more fully grasp the worldwide status of women, let's turn to the organization called Human Rights Watch.

`gopher://gopher.humanrights.org:5000/11/int/hrw`

Feel free to browse through the various reports starting with **"About Human Rights Watch."** Then click on the **Human Rights Watch Women's Rights Project**. Scroll down to the **Global Report On Women**. How many kinds of rights violations can you find listed in this report? What are the goals set forth by Human Rights Watch for the women of the world? How would you rate the U.S. by these standards?

Westerners are particularly offended by the practice of female genital mutilation. We are offended by the acts as well as repulsed by the pain and suffering that these women and children must endure. Feminists see the practice as one more form of male domination over women. The practice is so widespread that the World Health Organization and the United Nations have both condemned it.

`http://www.hollyfeld.org/fgm`

This is the FGM home page. It is an excellent source for information on genital mutilation and circumcision. Browse through the extensive set of topics and make certain to read the first three selections entitled **What is FGM?**, **What Population Groups Practice FGM** and **How Widely Practiced is FGM?** What exactly is female genital mutilation and where in the world is it practiced? What kinds of beliefs sustain this practice? Why would Americans and others from the industrialized nations not engage in this behavior? For a more detailed look at the subject scroll down to and open the **WWW FGM Resources**. You might care to look at the statement by the World Health Organization listed as **For the Elimination of FGM (WHO)**.

Given the fact that this happens to young women, the United Nations Children's Fund has taken a strong position against the practice.

http://oneworld.org/unicef/first_sept/fgm.html

The United Nations UNDP Human Development Report outlines the economic status of women throughout the world.

http://www.undp.org/undp/index.html

Go the **main menu** and click on the section dealing with **UNDP Publications and Videos**. Now open the **Human Development Report** and click on the appropriate **language** button. Now click on **Women's Invisible Contribution to Global Economy** and read the highlights. What percent of women's work goes unrecognized in the world? Who does more unpaid work, men or women? How is work treated in your family?

SUMMARY

1 Although there is a universal biological base for gender roles, a great deal of variability exists in the roles and personalities assigned to men and women across societies. Universally, however, women have had less power than men.

2 From earliest childhood, females and males integrate ideas about sex-appropriate behavior into their self-identities. Nevertheless, differences in aptitudes and personality are surprisingly small and are declining.

3 Women and men are growing more similar in their educational aspirations and attainments and in the percentage of their lives that they will spend in the work force. Family roles remain sharply gendered. Parenting and household production remain largely female responsibilities.

4 Women who are full-time, full-year workers earn 70 percent as much as men. This is because they have different (poorer-paying) jobs and because they earn less when they hold the same jobs. Causes include different aspirations and educational preparation, discrimination, and women's greater family obligations.

5 Women's subordinate position is built into family, religious, and political institutions. Although some of this has changed, men disproportionately occupy leadership positions in social institutions. They also dominate women in conversation.

6 Men also face disadvantages due to their gender roles. These include higher mortality, fewer intimate relationships, and higher stress.

7 Structural-functional theorists argue that a division of labor between the sexes builds a stronger family and reduces competition. Conflict theorists stress that men and capitalists benefit from a segmented labor market that relegates women to lower-status positions.

8 Sex stratification is maintained through socialization and learned expectations and by the same types of mechanisms used to maintain boundaries between racial groups: prejudice, discrimination, and sexism.

9 Feminist theories come in several forms: liberal, socialist, and radical. All types of feminists share a belief that gender inequalities are socially constructed and should be eliminated.

10 Violence against women is an important element of the disadvantage that women face, and many aspects of our culture encourage this violence.

11 Women of color are affected by both sexism and racism; they are economically disadvantaged by their own low earnings as well as by the low earnings of their husbands. To combat this double economic jeopardy, women of color increasingly pursue gender equality within traditional minority organizations.

Suggested Readings

BLY, Robert. 1990. *Iron John: A Book about Men*. Reading, Mass.: Addison-Wesley. The much publicized classic "bible" of one branch in the 1990s men's movement.

DIAMOND, Irene, and Orenstein, Gloria, (eds.). 1990. *Reweaving the World: The Emergence of Ecofeminism*. San Francisco: Sierra Club Books. A collection of readings on various topics on the general subject of ecofeminism.

FREEMAN, Jo (ed.). 1995. *Women: A Feminist Perspective*, 5th ed. Mountain View, Calif.: Mayfield. A textbook collection of essays by and about feminists and feminism.

GILMORE, David D. 1990. *Manhood in the Making: Cultural Concepts of Masculinity*. New Haven, Conn.: Yale University Press. A cross-cultural analysis of what it means to be a "real man" in various cultures around the world.

KIMMEL, Michael. 1995. *Manhood in America: A Cultural History*. New York: Free Press. An authoritative, entertaining, and wide-ranging history of men in America by a respected social scientist in the field of men, manhood, and masculinity.

ORENSTEIN, Peggy. 1994. *School Girls: Young Women, Self-Esteem, and the Confidence Gap*. New York: Doubleday. A very good book, written in association with the American Association of University Women, on young women in today's middle schools. Based on participant observation in two California schools.

RUTH, Sheila. 1995. *Issues in Feminism*, 3rd ed. Mountain View, Calif.: Mayfield. A textbook collection of essays by and about feminists and feminism.

SAPIRO, Virginia. 1994. *Women in American Society*, 3rd ed. Mountain View, Calif.: Mayfield. A textbook in women's studies designed for undergraduates. A thorough review of American gender inequalities.

TUCKER, Judith E. 1993. *Arab Women: Old Boundaries, New Frontiers*. Bloomington: Indiana University Press. A collection of essays addressing women's issues in traditional and changing Islamic thought and culture.

WELLINGTON, Alison J. 1994. "Accounting for the Male/Female Wage Gap Among Whites: 1976 and 1985." *American Sociological Review*, 56(6) (December): 839–849.

ZAVELLA, Patricia. 1987. *Women's Work and Chicano Families*. Ithaca, N.Y.: Cornell University Press. An ethnographic account of the Chicanas who work in northern California's fruit and vegetable canneries. Zavella documents the linkages between Chicano family life and gender inequality in the labor market, concluding that the rigidity of work in the canneries tends to reinforce traditional family roles.

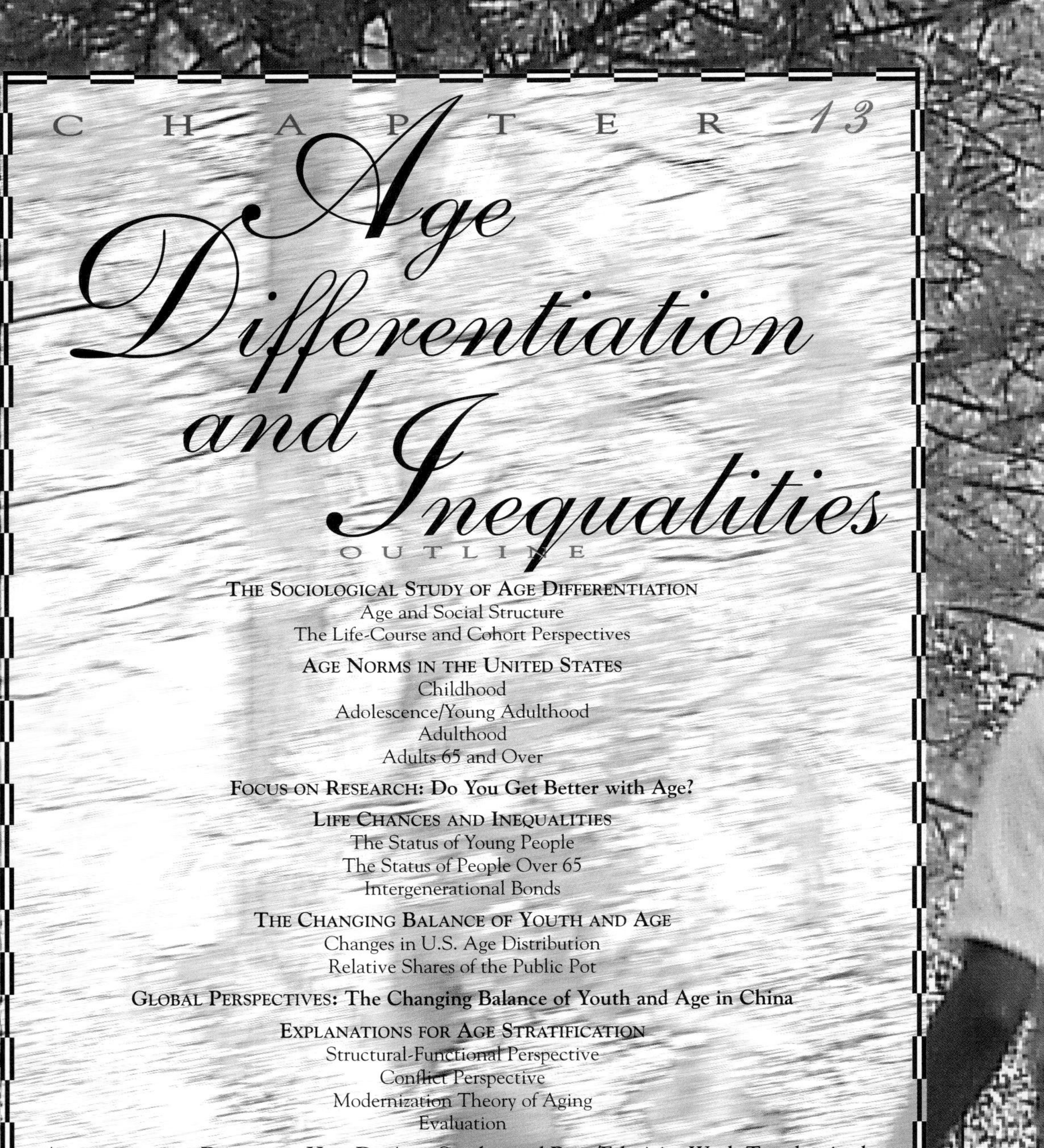

CHAPTER 13

Age Differentiation and Inequalities

OUTLINE

PROLOGUE

Have You Ever . . . experienced age discrimination? Of course you have. When you were in high school, you were turned away from R-rated movies because you weren't old enough and didn't bring your mother; you were told that you weren't old enough to buy liquor or cigarettes or rent a car; you weren't old enough to work in some establishments or on some shifts.

Many of those reading this book still aren't legally entitled to drink, smoke, or rent a car. You can go to jail and join the army and pay taxes, but you do not have a full set of rights. Others reading this text may wonder whether they'll be "too old" to get a better job once they've finished their education. You can go to college and even rock music festivals if you want, but you may increasingly feel that you "don't get no respect."

Age discrimination is pervasive in our society, but it has seldom created much public outcry. This is especially true when age discrimination targets youth. Most young people have enough on their plates already without starting a social movement to improve their legal rights. All they have to do, after all, is wait a few years.

In this chapter, we consider how age is socially structured in our society. In addition to considering norms for age-appropriate behavior, we will also consider structured inequalities between age groups. How are they created and maintained?

Unless we die, we all move from childhood through adolescence into adulthood and finally into old age. Each of these age categories is a status, or position, within society. Recall from Chapter 4 that there are achieved and ascribed statuses. Achieved statuses are optional; they can be obtained, or not. Ascribed statuses are fixed at birth and unalterable. Age categories have characteristics of both achieved and ascribed statuses. We attain a certain age, moving through age categories sequentially, casting off one and going on to the next. But there isn't anything we can do about our age at any given time. For this reason, sociologists consider age an ascribed status. Like race, ethnicity, and sex (also ascribed statuses), age categories form a basis of differentiation in society. Because some behaviors and attitudes are considered appropriate for one age category and not for another, we change our roles as we age. This chapter is about the social transitions that accompany physical aging and the differences in roles and life chances that are associated with membership in an age category.

THE SOCIOLOGICAL STUDY OF AGE DIFFERENTIATION

In all cultures, people have been assigned different roles according to age. At a minimum, all societies distinguish among young, adult, and elderly. Some role differentiation by age is inevitable, especially at the two extremes. Children cannot perform as well as adults; elderly people experience declining strength and endurance as they age.

But what is young? What is elderly? We can measure age in many ways. We can measure simple chronological age—whether a person has reached the 20th or 50th birthday. There is a certain merit to this measurement, since people of the same chronological age share many experiences. For example, virtually everybody who is now 65 shares a remembrance of World War II and of a childhood without television. Nevertheless, it is important to recognize that just because people are the same age does not mean they have reached the same place, have traveled a similar way to get there, or are going in the same direction (Thorson 1995). In addition, chronological age may be a poor indicator of physical condition or emotional and intellectual maturity. Some 70-year-olds are in wheelchairs, but some are on the tennis courts. And some 25-year-olds are independent, whereas others are still bringing their laundry home to mother.

The physical and psychological changes associated with aging are not of primary interest to sociologists. Rather, we are concerned with social norms and roles that structure the behavior of people in different age categories. In short, we want to know what is implied when we tell someone to "act your age." That is, what norms govern age-related behavior, and what roles are considered appropriate for particular age groups? We also want to consider whether the rights and privileges associated with age roles represent a pattern of structured inequality. Is there a consistent pattern of unequal reward by age that is justified by age norms?

Age and Social Structure

Aging and age expectations are, in large part, products of social structure. In our own society, critical points in the age distribution are 6, 16, 18, 21, and 65. These ages represent points at which social structures treat you differently or declare that you have different rights or responsibilities. You must go to school, you may drive, you must register for the draft, you may vote, you may drink, or you may draw retirement benefits. These significant ages are products of culture, not biology. Because these culturally designated points vary from one society to the next, so does the experience of growing up and aging.

Modern bureaucracies are giving the aging experience more and more formal structure. Especially during the first 21 years, there are a great many explicit formal expectations of what we should be doing and not doing at each age (Saraceno 1984). At 10, for example, one should be in fifth grade—not the fourth or the sixth, but exactly in the fifth grade. Although they do not disappear, these age-graded expectations become far less rigid after high school graduation. Nevertheless, at the other end of the life course, institutionalized social structures affecting pension benefits create age norms about retirement.

Because age requirements have been built into modern bureaucracies, age norms have become institutionalized. The experience of being 16 or 35 or 65 depends not only on your own physical and mental vigor but also on the social structures in which you participate. This point is an application of the sociological imagination concept, described in Chapter 1. The aging process and all of the transitions involved in growing up and growing old differ across societies, and within societies, by class, race, and sex.

Thinking Critically

Do age norms affect what people wear? The music people like? The kinds of foods people eat? Are these decisions based on individual taste only, or can you apply your sociological imagination to even these seemingly personal preferences?

The Life-Course and Cohort Perspectives

Life course refers to age-related transitions that are socially created, socially recognized, and shared.

A key concept in the sociological approach to age is the **life course,** "the age-related transitions that are socially created, socially recognized, and shared" (Hagestad and Neugarten 1985, 35). The life-course perspective implies no necessary or universal experience with aging; rather, it is concerned with how aging is socially structured.

This approach to aging takes explicit account of the fact that the experience of aging is somewhat different for each generation. The life choices available to your grandparents are no longer available to you, and those of your children will be different again. For this reason, sociological studies of aging focus on unique experiences of a **cohort,** a category of individuals who share a particular experience at the same point in time. For example, we might study the birth cohort of 1930 or the marriage cohort of 1990. Application of the cohort perspective to experience with the Great Depression has shown that the experience was very different for those who were young children in 1930 than for those who were teenagers (Elder 1974). For the youngest children, poverty and uncertainty were the conditions they were born into, and post-World War II prosperity seemed to them to represent progress and security. Those who were older at the time of the depression, however, saw a cyclical pattern in which prosperity was erased and then returned. Even 60 years later, these people may still be saving their old socks in case hard times return. Thus, these cohorts experience old age differently because of the different paths they took to get there.

A **cohort** is a category of individuals who share a particular experience at the same point in time—for example, all of those who were born in 1930 or who married in 1990.

Age Norms in the United States

Age norms are made up of the behaviors and attitudes expected of us when we "act our age." These age norms are much less specific than those associated with sex, and generally few sanctions are associated with violating them (Marini 1984). Nevertheless, these norms guide the behaviors of the majority of individuals so that those who are out of step feel set apart from their age-mates. In this section, we describe the general norms for age roles in the United States. These norms are the roadmap that social structures use to guide our journey from childhood to old age.

Childhood

For most of human history, there was no such thing as childhood as we know it. (This remains true in much of the Third World today. From a very early age, children work alongside adults.) The concept of childhood as different from adulthood did not emerge until about the 17th century in Europe (Aries 1962).

Today, in the United States and other industrialized countries, the norms of childhood establish a rather clear set of rights and responsibilities for children. Legal rights include health care, freedom from physical abuse, freedom from labor, and access to state-provided education. We also believe that young children, at least, should be shielded from offensive language, sexuality, worry, and danger. The obligations of the contemporary child are to play and to accomplish certain developmental tasks, such as learning independence and self-control, as well as mastery of the school curriculum.

At least in the dominant culture, children are not expected to do much work and, in fact, are legally barred from employment. Contemporary norms specify that parents give to children, not vice versa.

Nevertheless, childhood is seldom the oasis that our ideal norms specify. A sizable fraction of children are physically or emotionally abused by their parents; estimates suggest that one out of four girls experiences sexual abuse during childhood

Normative standards for today's child in affluent Western society are very different from standards in most of the world. But early in this century children were expected to work as long as 12 hours a day in jobs like sorting coal where pay was low and conditions were grim. Today's child, however, is more likely expected to do small tasks such as helping mom make tortillas.

(Finkelhor 1986). Nearly one-fourth of U.S. children will grow up in poverty, and evidence suggests that the gap between rich and poor children is growing (Lichter and Eggebeen 1993; "Income Gap . . ." 1996).

An important change in the social structure of the child's world is the sharp increase in the proportion of children who grow up in single-parent households: 30 percent are born to single mothers (Ventura et al. 1995) and it is estimated that at least 70 percent of all children born in the 1980s will spend some time in a single-parent household before they are 18 (Popenoe 1993, 531). This rapid and extensive change in the primary social structure of childhood is likely in many cases to reduce the protection from harsh reality that our ideal norms specify.

Adolescence/Young Adulthood

Like childhood, adolescence is not simply a biological condition but a social invention, or construction. That is, adolescence is a stage created by industrialization—a social phenomenon. Because industrialized societies require highly trained workers, an individual's education and other preparation for adult roles continues beyond the onset of biological maturity. As a result, an "in-between" stage develops when a person is neither child nor adult. This is not the case in nonindustrialized societies, where biological maturity marks the onset of fully adult roles.

In U.S. society, adolescence is often a period of irresponsibility. Because our industrialized society has relatively little need for the contributions of youth, it encourages a concern among young people for trivialities—such as concern over personal appearance and the latest music. Yet because adolescence is a temporary state, the adolescent is under persistent pressure. Questions such as "What are you going to do when you finish school?" "What are you going to major in?" and "How serious are you about that girl [or boy]?" have an urgent reality that creates strain.

What are the rights and obligations of adolescence? Basically, in the dominant U.S. culture, there appear to be four (Campbell 1969):

Because industrialized societies have little need for the contributions of youth, adolescence is often seen as a period of irresponsibility. Among other rights and obligations of adolescence, teenagers are supposed to have fun. One problem teens face, however, is the fact that our society allocates few places in which they can do so.

1. Adolescents are supposed to become independent of their parents. The change from family to peer groups as a source of esteem is the first step in this process.
2. They are supposed to experiment with new roles and behaviors, to test their values and the worth of social roles. Throughout childhood, they have taken their parents' word for what is valuable and normative. During adolescence, they either make these values their own or discard them.
3. They are supposed to acquire adult skills. These include social skills (how to work in committees and how to meet and impress new people, for example) and technical skills (how to make change, use a computer, and differentiate equations, for example).
4. Last, but not least, they are supposed to have fun. If they do not (if they stay home every single weekend, if they are always serious and never silly), they will be violating a norm and may be sanctioned by their peers. Their parents will probably begin to worry about them, and they may even find themselves seeing a psychologist.

Thus, in spite of the fact that society does not appear to expect much of adolescents, they are under a great deal of role strain. Indeed, adolescence is one of the most stressful stages in the life course. This may be even more true now than it was 15 years ago. Today, a stagnant economy increases teens' concern about what they will do as adults (Gaines 1991).

ADULTHOOD

The role of adult in our society carries with it more rights and responsibilities than any other age role. Within each institution—family, education, religion, politics, economy—adults are expected to carry the load. They also reap many of the benefits. In addition to having greater rights and responsibilities within each

Rites of passage mark the end of one status and the beginning of another. In U.S. society, rituals such as graduations and weddings continue to have symbolic significance, but the transitions they mark are less clear than they used to be. When as many as half of all couples cohabit before their weddings, when many people receive advanced academic degrees years after they have married and borne children, the transition to adulthood becomes somewhat fuzzy.

Rites of passage are formal rituals that mark the end of one age status and the beginning of another.

Thinking Critically

Describe rites of passage experienced by you and your friends. How might these rites of passage be functional in U.S. society? How might they be dysfunctional? How would conflict theory analyze these rites of passage, do you think? How about the symbolic interaction perspective?

institution, adults are involved in more institutions than other age categories. It is a stage of maximum engagement in social structures.

As we saw in Chapter 12, adult roles differ substantially by sex. Although this is less true today than it was 50 or even 20 years ago, the experience of moving across the age span differs for women and men. Women marry earlier and have children earlier than men; they also retire earlier. The meaning of various adult roles also differs for women and men. The decision to become a parent, for example, is much more significant for women's roles than for men's. Entering and leaving the labor force, too, generally means different things for men and women.

The Transition to Adulthood. Some societies have **rites of passage,** formal rituals that mark the end of one age status and the beginning of another. In U.S. society, however, there is no clear point at which we can say that a person has become an adult.

In psychology, adulthood may be defined by responsibility and maturity. The sociological concept of adulthood, however, focuses on social roles. Although expectations vary by sex, adulthood means that a person adopts at least some of the following roles: being employed and supporting oneself and one's dependents, being out of school, marrying, having children, voting, and being a church member. Some of these social roles are voluntary; and people may be considered adults if they never marry, never vote, never join a church, or, in the case of women, never hold a paid job (Hogan and Astone 1986). Nevertheless, the majority of people follow the conventional route to adulthood: They make the transition to adulthood by finishing school, getting a job, marrying, and raising a family.

Much of the research on the transition of adulthood focuses on the sequencing of these four transitions. The normative and most common transition sequence is to finish school and then to get a job, a spouse, and children—in that order. Three major changes have occurred in this sequence in the last two decades. First, the four transitions occur much closer together than they used to. Men born in 1907 had an average of 18 years between the first and last of these transitions; the span was only 8 years for men born in 1947 (Hogan 1981). Second, the order of these transitions is much more variable than it used to be. Increasing numbers of men and women marry and have children (even grandchildren) before they finish school; some have children before they marry. Third, on the average, these transitions are occurring at later ages. Age at marriage is up, age at finishing education is up, and age at leaving home is up (see Table 13.1).

Middle Age. The busiest part of most adult lives is between the ages of 20 and 45. There are often children in the home and marriages and careers to be established. This period of life is frequently marked by role strain and role conflict, simply because so much is going on at one time. Middle age, that period roughly between 45 and 65, has been by contrast a quieter and often more prosperous period. Studies show that both men and women tend to greet the empty nest (if they get one) and then retirement with relief rather than regret (Goudy et al. 1980; White and Edwards 1990).

The norms of U.S. society suggest that people will have achieved many of their life goals by the time they reach middle age. Thus, middle age is a period of assessment (Neugarten 1968; Thorson 1995). It is a time for evaluating one's own situation—family, career, standard of living, physical appearance—relative to the norms of society. For a few people, this evaluation results in what is called the

TABLE 13.1
THE CHANGING TRANSITION TO ADULTHOOD

In the last generation, the transition to adulthood has been postponed by two to three years. As a result of growing educational demands and a changing economy, young people are less quick to marry and are spending more years in school and with their parents.

	1970	1988–1992
Median age at first marriage (women)	20.6	24.5
Percent aged 18–21 in school	39.8	43.8
Percent aged 18–24 still living with parents	47.3	54

SOURCE: U.S. Bureau of the Census 1989a, 49, 62, 86, 128; U.S. Bureau of the Census 1989e, 63; U.S. Bureau of the Census 1993; Tables 72, 143.

midlife crisis—an awareness that goals not yet reached are probably forever beyond reach. More positively, people recognize that youthful norms are no longer as applicable as they used to be, and they reorganize life's priorities (Tamir 1982).

ADULTS 65 AND OVER

Older adults, those 65 and over, are extremely diverse, defying easy categorization. For the most part, they are retired, although 17 percent of the men and 9 percent of the women are in the labor force (U.S. Bureau of the Census 1995, Table 627). Social norms are more explicit about what older adults are not supposed to do than about what they are supposed to do. This has led some commentators to suggest that being elderly is a roleless role—an absence of both rights and duties. The socially appropriate role for older people is to be nonproductive, nonaggressive, and noncompetitive but also independent and out of their children's hair—and homes, except when invited.

Some observers suggest that the comparative rolelessness of older adults reduces life satisfaction. Nevertheless, one of the most consistent findings in research—such as the research described in the accompanying Focus feature—is that retirement is generally a positive stage in the life course (Thorson 1995). Although some women and men may require a little adjustment, almost all believe that their new leisure is legitimate (that is, normatively approved); they do not feel bad about not having more demanding social roles. As long as they stay healthy, older adults report high levels of life satisfaction. The best predictors of satisfaction among the elderly are the same factors that predict satisfaction at every other stage of the life course: good health, adequate income, and a satisfying family life (Brubaker 1991; Larson 1978).

LIFE CHANCES AND INEQUALITIES

Society is run mainly by adults between the ages of 30 and 65. These adults control jobs, industry, education, and wealth. The various benefits of this control are reflected in age-related suicide rates (see Figure 13.2). Among white males, suicide rates have increased since 1970 for those aged 15 through 44 and 75 and

FOCUS ON RESEARCH

Do You Get Better with Age?

"IN FACT, GETTING OLDER SEEMS TO BE ASSOCIATED WITH GETTING BETTER—WITH BEING A NICER AND MORE CAPABLE PERSON."

DO YOU GET BETTER WITH AGE?

As we move from age 20 to 40 to 60, our lives change in more or less predictable ways. We leave home, form families, work, and retire. In early adulthood, the process is largely one of role acquisition; in middle and old age, it is a process of role loss. According to some symbolic interactionists, the addition of roles in adulthood should improve self-concept, whereas the loss of roles in later life should decrease it. Others suggest that adulthood is a period of growth and maturation, so that older individuals become more, not less, satisfied with themselves and their roles.

A study by Walter Gove, Suzanne Ortega, and Carolyn Style (1989) addressed this issue. They asked a national random sample to read a list of adjectives and check the ones that described them. The adjectives measured four dimensions of self-concept:

- *Competent:* hardworking, well-organized, self-confident, strong, logical, and intelligent
- *Supportive:* helpful, flexible, considerate, content
- *Calm:* not emotional, not nervous, not frustrated
- *Cooperative:* not lazy, not disorganized, not stubborn.

Because the researchers reasoned that these characteristics might be affected by social class, race, and sex, they adjusted for these factors. The adjusted results, presented in Figure 13.1, show clearly that the older people surveyed felt better about themselves than the younger people. Young people rated themselves as relatively uncooperative, incompetent, uncalm, and unsupportive. In contrast, the older respondents felt very positive about their identities.

These results suggest that, despite the high esteem in which youth is held in U.S. society, youth is not all wonderful, and growing old is not altogether a bad thing. In fact, getting older seems to be associated with getting better—with being a nicer and more capable person. These results led Gove, Ortega, and Style to conclude that maturation is more important than role loss in affecting self-concept.

In interpreting these data, however, the authors ran into a serious problem. These are *cross-sectional data*. That means that the respondents who were 65 to 74 and those who were 18 to 24 were of entirely different generations. This raises the very realistic possibility that the older people did not become more cooperative, competent, and so forth with age but that their generation was always more competent and cooperative.

Whenever we look at age differences from a cross-sectional sample, we face two possibilities: that the differences result from *age effects* or that they result from *cohort effects*. The age effect takes the data at face value and hypothesizes that, as today's young people age, they will become more competent, cooperative, supportive, and calm. The cohort effect suggests that these are permanent generational differences and will not change with age—that even at 65, today's young people will feel uncooperative, unsupportive, uncalm, and incompetent.

Gove, Ortega, and Style chose to believe that their results showed an age effect. They concluded that

older; suicide rates have declined for white men between 45 and 75 years old. One worrisome trend is the dramatic increase in teen suicides: The rate more than doubled (from 9.4 to 19.3 per 1,000) between 1970 and 1990. Moreover, the rate for white males in their early 20s is higher than for the middle-aged. The very high rates for elderly white males in part reflect the fact that they are less well integrated into society than either younger men or women, a point discussed in Chapter 12. A general conclusion from Figure 13.2 is that today the young and the old have relatively high suicide rates compared with the middle-aged. In the following sections, we examine the extent to which young and elderly persons can be considered structurally disadvantaged relative to this middle-aged group.

FOCUS ON RESEARCH

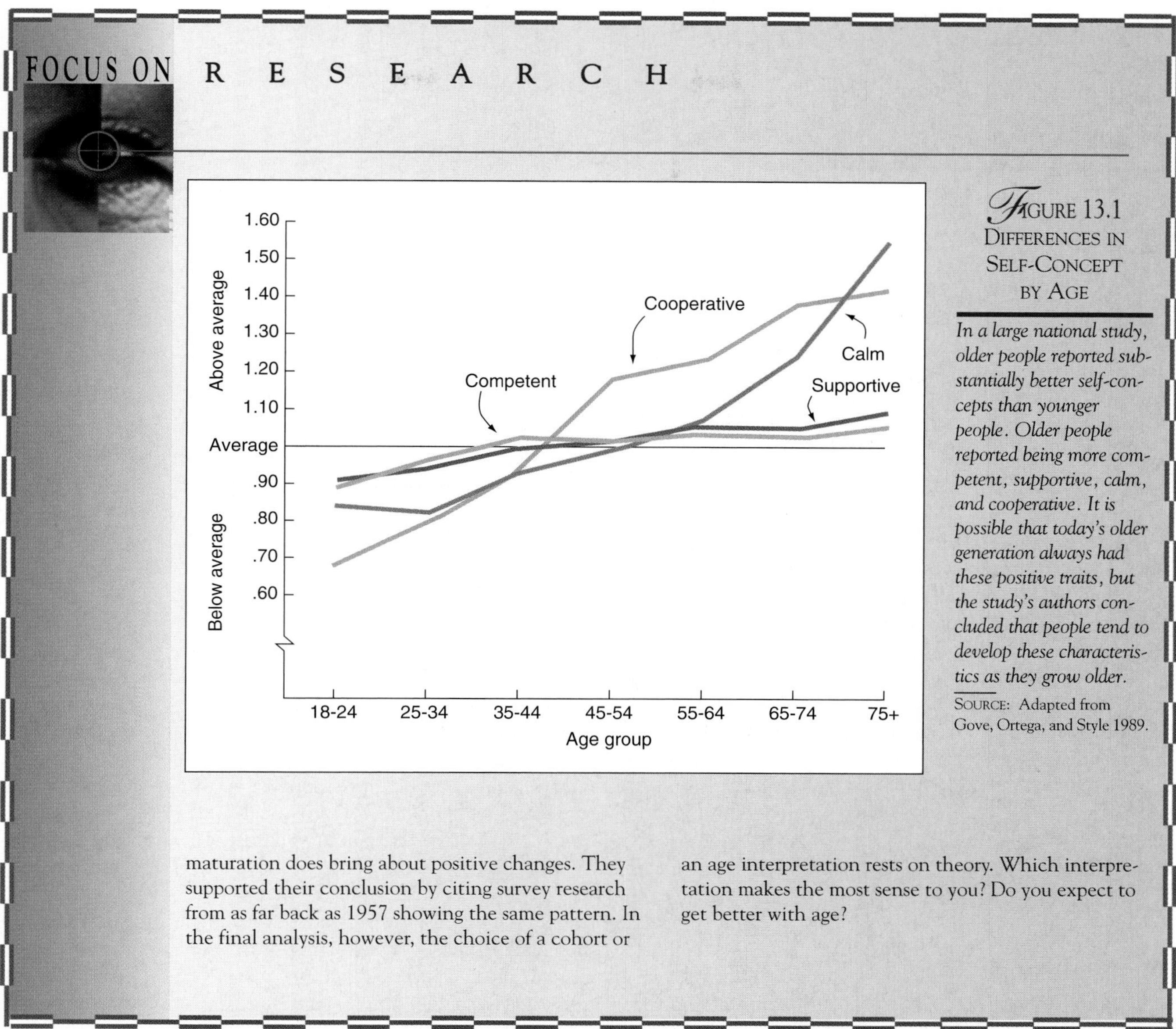

FIGURE 13.1
DIFFERENCES IN SELF-CONCEPT BY AGE

In a large national study, older people reported substantially better self-concepts than younger people. Older people reported being more competent, supportive, calm, and cooperative. It is possible that today's older generation always had these positive traits, but the study's authors concluded that people tend to develop these characteristics as they grow older.

SOURCE: Adapted from Gove, Ortega, and Style 1989.

maturation does bring about positive changes. They supported their conclusion by citing survey research from as far back as 1957 showing the same pattern. In the final analysis, however, the choice of a cohort or an age interpretation rests on theory. Which interpretation makes the most sense to you? Do you expect to get better with age?

THE STATUS OF YOUNG PEOPLE

Legal Restrictions. In law, people under 18 are called infants (Sloan 1981). They are not responsible for their contracts (thus, they usually are not allowed to make any), and they are considered less responsible than adults for their bad deeds. Just as legal statutes once declared women and minority members incapable of self-government, the law still declares the young to be incapable. As you may be painfully aware from personal experience, young people have few legal rights. Their rights to drink, drive, work, own property, and marry are abridged. In some cities, curfew laws require them to be off the streets at night. They have to pay

FIGURE 13.2
SUICIDE RATES (NUMBER OF SUICIDES PER 1,000 INDIVIDUALS) OF WHITE MALES FOR SELECTED AGE GROUPS, 1970 AND 1990

SOURCE: U.S. Bureau of the Census 1993, Table 137.

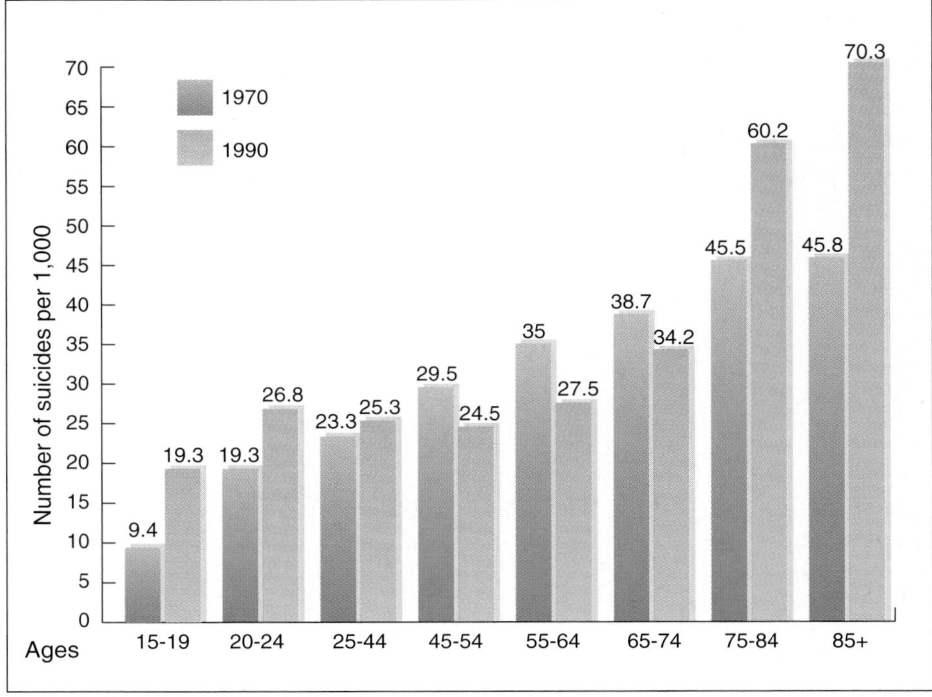

THINKING CRITICALLY

The Focus on Research section introduces the question whether changes over time are due to age effects or cohort effects. Think of some age effects that might explain age-related suicide rates. Think of some cohort effects that could help explain changes in age-related suicide rates between 1970 and 1990.

THINKING CRITICALLY

Should U.S. society treat all people, regardless of age, as individuals? Do age requirements for voting, driving, and so on assume that, for example, *all* 18-year-olds are more responsible and better-informed citizens than any 17-year-old? Isn't this stereotyping? If so, is there some justification for it?

adult prices but cannot see adult movies. In church, school, and industry, they find they must pass age barriers before they are allowed full participation. Unlike the case of women and minorities, there is no movement to reduce inequality for teenagers. The voting age was reduced from 21 to 18 in 1970, but the drinking age has been raised to 21. Once again, we face the irony of staffing our armed forces with young people we will not trust with a beer. Although raising the drinking age springs from the praiseworthy objective of reducing deaths from drinking and driving, it is nevertheless a reminder that many people believe the young cannot make responsible decisions and need to be protected.

For the most part, these age-related rules reflect society's belief that age is a reasonable indicator of competency; moreover, it is one that can be administered easily and efficiently. Thus, instead of devising some test of maturity that one must pass before obtaining voting privileges, society uses a simple rule of thumb: Persons under 18 are not mature, but persons 18 and over are mature enough for this purpose.

Although there is growing sentiment that neither ethnicity nor sex is a good guide to competency, no such change of sentiment has occurred about the utility of age for making relevant judgments about youth. In fact, discrimination against the young may be the last bastion of approved inequality before the law. The Supreme Court, in siding with parents who wished to prohibit a teenage daughter's abortion, concluded that "the rights of children cannot be equated with those of adults" (Justice Powell in *Bellotti* v. *Baird* [1979], cited in Eglit 1985, 532). These age rules receive very high consensus approval from society; and little, if any, pressure exists to repeal them.

Economic Status. Owing to underdeveloped work skills, limited experience, and desire for part-time or flexible schedules, and also owing to simple discrimination, a very large share of young people in the United States earn the minimum wage. In 1996, the minimum wage was raised to $5.15 per hour. Despite much fanfare this wage is still relatively low. Furthermore, the law provides for a subminimum training wage; this training wage was targeted largely at young people. Finally, young people's rate of unemployment is very high: In 1994, when 6 percent of the civilian labor force was unemployed, unemployment was 18 percent for those aged 16–19 and 10 percent for those 20–24 (U.S. Bureau of the Census 1995, Table 661). For African Americans, these figures were 37 and 17 percent, respectively. As a consequence, families headed by people under 25 are three times more likely to be in poverty than the average family.

Young people are frequently disadvantaged in the labor market. Although young men can sometimes get good jobs working in construction, young people often have to settle for the minimum wage working in supermarkets and fast food franchises. Although these wages might be acceptable to those who are still living at home and just working for pocket money, low wages and high unemployment pose a hardship for young people who must support themselves or their families.

Crime. Failure to integrate young people—especially those in minority groups—fully into major social structures is reflected in several indices of social disorganization. Although young people are underrepresented among voters and workers, they are overrepresented in accident and crime statistics. In 1992, people between the ages of 10 and 24 represented only 22 percent of the population, but they accounted for 43 percent of the rape arrests, 39 percent of the arrests for aggravated assault, 55 percent of murder arrests, and 74 percent of arrests for motor vehicle thefts (U.S. Department of Justice 1993a).

Research shows that these youthful crime rates are strongly related to the availability of employment for juveniles and the quality of work (wages) for young adults (Allan and Steffensmeier 1989). Although some observers downplay the importance of youthful unemployment and low wages, assuming that the problem will solve itself as individuals age, the clear message is that failure to include young people in the labor market has severe consequences for society as well as for the young people themselves.

School. Nearly all Americans under age 16 are enrolled in school full time; at ages 20–21, one-third are still enrolled in school. Thus, educational roles play an enormous part in structuring the experience of young people. Not only does education provide a daily routine (when to get up, where to go, when to come home, and what to do with most of one's waking hours) but school roles are also critical for identity. The best predictor of adolescent self-esteem is performance at school: Students who do well in school feel competent and confident, whereas poor students feel less competent (Orenstein 1994). Moreover, young men who get low rewards at school have been found to be more likely to pursue delinquent careers; those who are rewarded at school, on the other hand, are more likely to stay out of trouble (Rosenberg, Schooler, and Schoenbach 1989). Unfortunately, perceived low prospects for future good jobs can demoralize young people so that they don't try for rewards in school (Gaines 1991).

Youth Subculture. In Chapter 3, we said that culture is a set of patterned responses for dealing with the common problems that a society faces. Similarly, a subculture may be distinguished as a set of patterned responses to problems that are unique to a particular group within society. Young people comprise such a group.

The primary characteristics of youth subculture are an emphasis on passive escape types of entertainment (music, home videos, television, movies) and an emphasis on style. Style, as embodied in the youth subculture, has been described as having three major elements: (1) image—appearance created by costume, accessories such as hairstyle, and jewelry; (2) demeanor—made up of expression, gait,

Adolescence is a period in which children grow more independent of their parents. Although parental support and approval remain very important, the peer group also becomes an important source of self-esteem. In the peer group, young people experiment with behavior and language that their parents would probably disapprove of. Although some children model smoking, drinking, and swearing directly on their parents' behavior, many learn these behaviors independently in the peer group.

and posture (how the image is delivered); and (3) argot—special vocabulary and how it is delivered (Brake 1985, 12). Although youth itself is an ascribed status, the style of youth must be achieved. Mastery of this style can be an important basis of self-esteem that partially compensates for youths' disadvantaged position in society's economic and political institutions.

There is some debate about the origins and merits of youth subculture. Some Marxist analysts see youth subculture as a synthetic creation, a mass-marketing strategy beamed out to millions of bored young people on the airwaves of MTV, created to exploit them for the profit of a few. In this view, youth subculture is indeed false consciousness, a sense of belongingness and control that is entirely at odds with the economic and social reality. Others see elements of authenticity in youth subculture, noting that rock and roll and music videos and other elements of style give young people a chance to express themselves and their interests.

Summary. Young people are systematically excluded from participation in many of U.S. society's institutions. In some cases, they are excluded by formal rules, such as restrictions on drinking, driving, or renting a car. In other cases, they are excluded because there is no room for them, as in the labor force. In terms of class, status, and power, young people rank significantly behind older adults. For most of us, this lower status has been, or will be, temporary: We eventually get jobs, get married, finish school, have children, and generally become plugged into society. For those who never become integrated into society's economic and social structure, the lower class, status, and power of youth become permanent.

THE STATUS OF PEOPLE OVER 65

Although they may have less prestige than they used to, older people in U.S. society do not seem to be particularly disadvantaged—as long as they keep their health. The following sections review some of the basic findings about older people in the United States.

Health, Life Expectancy, and Changing Definitions of "Old." Perhaps the most important change in the social structure of the population over 65 is that being over 65 is now a common stage in life—and often a long one. The average person, on reaching 65, can now expect to live 18 more years—19 more if a white woman and 16 more if a white man; for African Americans, the figures are 17 and 14 years, respectively (U.S. Bureau of the Census 1995, Table 116). Because more and more Americans are living into their 80s and beyond, demographers now tend to divide the over-65 population into two categories: the "old old" (age 75 and above) and the relatively "young old" (ages 65–74) (Treas 1995).

For the majority of us, most of the "young old" and even many of the "old old" years will be healthy years. Certainly most people at 65 or 70 experience some loss of energy and physical stamina, and most older people report having at least one chronic health problem, such as arthritis, hypertension, or hearing loss (Treas 1995, 32–35). But a remarkably large proportion experience no major health limitations. Demographers estimate that three-fourths of the years of life remaining after age 70 will be spent in good enough health to permit independent living in the community (Crimmins, Hayward, and Saito 1994).

THINKING CRITICALLY

Society has greater tolerance for the inequalities of the young than for those of the old. We more often think that the disadvantages of old age are "unfair." Why do you suppose society is so tolerant of the disadvantages of young people?

Income. The economic condition of older people has improved sharply over the last 35 years. In 1959, 35 percent of the population over 65 had incomes below the

As more Americans live into old age—and actively!—you can expect to see a few more runners and surfers like these "old old" athletes.

poverty level; in 1993, this figure was 12 percent (U.S. Bureau of the Census 1995, Table 748). This improvement is directly related to increases in Social Security, expanded coverage by private pension plans, and a more comprehensive system of benefits (Treas 1995, 26). As a result of this system, the proportion of older people below the poverty level is no greater than the proportion of the entire population that is poor. (See Chapter 9 for a review of poverty data.)

Retirement. The growing adequacy of Social Security and pension coverage has meant substantial reductions in labor-force activity of older workers. Between 1970 and 1994, the percent of men over 65 who were still in the labor force dropped from 27 to 17 percent; at ages 55–64, labor force participation dropped from 83 to 66 percent. Older women's labor force participation rates, however, have remained relatively constant over this period at about 45 percent (U.S. Bureau of the Census 1995, Table 627).

Studies show that the primary predictors of early retirement are poor health, a physically demanding job, and a mentally unrewarding job. Not surprisingly, people whose jobs require hard physical labor and provide little mental stimulation quit as soon as they can afford to; those who have mentally challenging jobs are more likely to stay at work (Hayward et. al 1989).

The jobs that encourage early retirement are disproportionately working-class jobs. Since members of the working class are less likely to have the savings necessary to cushion retirement, many find that they cannot really afford to be out of the labor force. As a result, an increasing number of retired workers are reentering the labor market. The average person now retires 1.3 times rather than simply once. Reentry jobs are usually much less demanding, and they pay a substantially lower salary than preretirement jobs (Hayward, Grady, and McLaughlin 1988).

Postretirement Incomes. Although only 12 percent of the population over 65 have incomes below the poverty level, the other 86 percent are not all that wealthy. The average person experiences only a minor income loss in the years immediately following retirement, but there are dark spots in this picture. First, over a quarter of the population experiences an income drop of over 50 percent following retirement. Those people who were living close to the economic margin during middle age—who accumulated no assets, who didn't pay off a home mortgage, and who

Most older people "age in place"—that is, they remain in the same neighborhood and the same house in which they have lived for 40 years. Nevertheless, a number of elderly people, particularly non-Hispanic whites, have taken advantage of their new prosperity, earlier retirement, and longer life expectancy to move to Arizona and other retirement meccas of the Sunbelt. "Snowbirds," such as these women, have created rapid growth for communities such as Sun City, Arizona—a community where three-quarters of the population are over 65 and where some neighborhoods have zoning ordinances specifying that no one under 50 can buy a house!

contributed relatively little to either Social Security or a pension fund—find that retirement brings poverty or near poverty. These people are disproportionately women and minorities, people whose work-life earnings are low. Second, because of increased property taxes, even those who have fully paid for their homes may find it hard to afford to live there. Third, widowhood produces a severe economic blow for most older women, many of whom find that a substantial portion of their retirement income dies along with their husbands (Treas 1995).

Thinking Critically

Affirmative action legislation, explained in Chapter 11, applies not only to racial and ethnic minorities but also to women—and to all men and women over 40 years old. Why do you think this last point is often neglected in current discussions about the pros and cons of affirmative action?

Discrimination. In the past, mandatory retirement regulations forced some people out of the labor force regardless of their physical ability, economic need, or desire to work. In 1986, however, federal legislation outlawed mandatory retirement except in a few cases (such as police officers) where age-related abilities are considered essential to the job.

A far more important problem than mandatory retirement is age discrimination that begins during middle age, when women and men over 40 are often considered too old to learn new skills or take new jobs. One study examined what happened to men who were laid off after plant closings. The results showed that workers over 55 had to wait twice as long to find a new job as workers under 45 and that the new jobs of older workers were substantially worse than the new jobs of younger workers (Love and Torrence 1989). Affirmative-action legislation uses age 40 to define when age discrimination begins.

Political Power. Age and even illness or infirmity in no way abridge one's legal rights. Older people are more likely to vote than people in other age groups. Seventy percent of people 65 years and over reported voting in the 1992 national elections, compared with 61 percent of the total population and only 43 percent of American citizens aged 18–20 ("Voting Registration" 1993). Their relatively high voting rate makes older Americans a potentially powerful group. There is no evidence that the entire older population acts together as a cohesive voting bloc. Cleavages of race, class, and sex work against such unity. Nevertheless, recent turmoil over possible cuts to Medicare (national health insurance for the elderly) makes it clear that the 33-million-member American Association of Retired Persons (AARP), a political lobbying association, is taken seriously by elected officials (Rosenstiel 1995).

Honor and Esteem. Societal rewards distributed by stratification systems go beyond income and power. They also include prestige, esteem, and social honor. It is in this regard that the status of older people has been most seriously at issue. Our idealized version of the past holds that elderly people used to be highly regarded and respected. Careful examinations of cross-cultural and historical data, however, suggest that older people seldom have as much prestige as younger adults (Stearn 1976) and that, historically, our attitude toward them has been ambivalent at best (Achenbaum 1985). Hags, crones, dirty old men, and other negative stereotypes of older people crowd our literature. Whether scheming hags or dear old things, older people are seldom regarded with complete respect or admiration (Cool and McCabe 1983; Levin 1988).

Ageism is the belief that chronological age determines the presence or absence of socially relevant characteristics and that age therefore legitimates unequal treatment.

Stereotypes about older people—as inflexible or less competent, for example—form the basis of **ageism**—the belief that chronological age determines the presence or absence of socially relevant characteristics and that age therefore legitimizes unequal treatment. In U.S. society, many circumstances work to reduce the esteem in which we hold older people. Age is associated with reductions in vigor and physical beauty, both of which are highly prized in U.S. society (Thorson

In the contemporary United States, retirement is a generally satisfactory stage in the life course. Blessed with good health, adequate incomes, and leisure time, many people between 65 and 75 find that life is very enjoyable. Although few have the physical stamina they had 20 or 30 years ago, increases in health and income have dramatically improved the quality of life for the population over 65.

1995). Moreover, because of rapid expansion of the educational system within the last several decades, older people are substantially less well educated than younger adults. In 1993, only 48 percent of those over 75 had completed high school, compared with 80 percent of all Americans over age 25 (U.S. Bureau of the Census 1994, Table 234). In a society where knowledge and education are taken as indications of intelligence and worth, older people are considered less worthy than others. Then, too, the life experience of older people is considered less valuable in a society that is changing rapidly, as U.S. society is today. Finally, because people over 65 (or 70) are generally outside the mainstream of economic competition, they seldom receive the prestige of active earners (Thorson 1995). Together, these factors mean that, although individual older people may have good educations, incomes, and health and be politically active, they often find themselves being patronized and condescended to by younger individuals.

Social Integration. We have defined adulthood as a period of maximum integration into social institutions. This involvement is gradually reduced during old age. Active parenting is the first role to drop off, followed by the work role. Many, especially women, also experience the loss of the marital role through the death of their spouses. The world of church, family and friends, and community, however, often remains active, at least until the advent of old, old age, when health limitations may restrict activities.

Studies of older people demonstrate that one of the most important predictors of life satisfaction is relationships with close friends. These are usually age peers and often, at the end of the life course, brothers and sisters. Interestingly, close ties with their children are not a uniform blessing. Especially when age starts to become a serious handicap, ties with children become tinged with dependency and ambivalence (Thorson 1995). Because ties with age peers usually lack this element, they tend to be more gratifying.

Summary. An assessment of the status of older people over the last 35 years would show substantial economic improvements. With this improvement in economic circumstances has come increased independence from their families, better health, and greater community involvement. Nevertheless, among the "old old," a substantial group are "ill fed, ill housed, ill clothed, and just plain ill" (Hess 1985, 329). This group is disproportionately female and minority.

Intergenerational Bonds

Relations between age groups, like relations between the sexes, are qualitatively different from relations between races or classes. Generations are intimately tied to one another through family. As more of us live longer, three- and even four-generation families will become more and more common (Thorson 1995). Some people have worried that geographical mobility and the increased role of the state in providing support for dependents might weaken these intergenerational ties. In this respect, as in many others, the rumor of the death of the family has been much exaggerated.

Young People and Parents: The Generation Gap. The relationship between teens and their parents is not as bad as is often suggested. Although many families go through a prolonged period of conflict, both parents and children being relieved when they are able to live apart, they maintain a strong bond and many common values (Dornbush 1989). Dozens of studies of college students demonstrate that apparent differences are more often in style than in substance and that young people and parents agree about basic values. As Mark Twain is alleged to have said, "When I was a boy of 14, my father was so ignorant I could hardly stand to have the old man around. But when I got to be 21, I was astonished at how much the old man had learned in seven years." Nevertheless, pollsters do find a generation gap on some political issues. Younger adults are more likely to choose protecting the environment over economic growth, for example, while older Americans are less likely to do so (The Gallup Organization 1995).

Family ties are important at all stages of the life course. In addition to ties of obligation and affection, we often find our parents and children to be good companions because they tend to share our values and lifestyles. As we get older, we find that they also share our memories. Together, this older man and his middle-aged son can laugh over shared adventures and shake their heads over family disasters of 50 years ago.

Adults and Their Parents. At the other end of the age scale, sociological concern has focused on the nature of the relationship between older people and their children and grandchildren. Empirical studies document a reassuring level of family commitment and involvement across the generations. One study confirmed that 60 percent of those over 65 had seen at least one of their children the previous week, and fully 53 percent of those over 85 had seen a child the previous day (U.S. Bureau of the Census 1989a, 37).

The nature of intergenerational relationships between adult children and their older parents depends very substantially on the ages of the generations. Members of the older generation who fall into the "young old" category are, on the average, still providing more help for their children than the children are for their parents (Neugarten and Neugarten 1986). They are helping with down payments and grandchildren's college educations or providing temporary living space for children who have divorced or lost their jobs.

As the senior generation moves into the "old old" category, however, relationships must be renegotiated (Mutran and Reitzes 1984). Even in the "old old" category, most people continue to be largely self-sufficient; but eventually, most need help of some kind—shopping, home repairs, or social support. A critical difficulty is that many of the children to whom they would turn for this kind of help are themselves no longer young. This gives rise to what has been called the generation squeeze, where the middle generation is caught between demands for support, social or financial, from both their children and their parents. Mostly women but sometimes men, the members of this "sandwich generation" (also discussed in Chapter 12) may suffer substantial role strain (Kinsella and Taeuber 1993, 61).

Summary. Family ties across the generations make inequality between age strata qualitatively different from class inequality. Because of intimate ties across the age span, age stratification has not resulted and is not likely to result in polarized political groups that seek their own goals at the expense of other age groups. Nevertheless, there is competition among age groups. The competition between youth and age for shares of the public purse is described in the next section.

The Changing Balance of Youth and Age

Changes in U.S. Age Distribution

The United States has historically been a society with a youthful population. As indicated in Figure 13.3, in 1820 fully 58 percent of America's population was

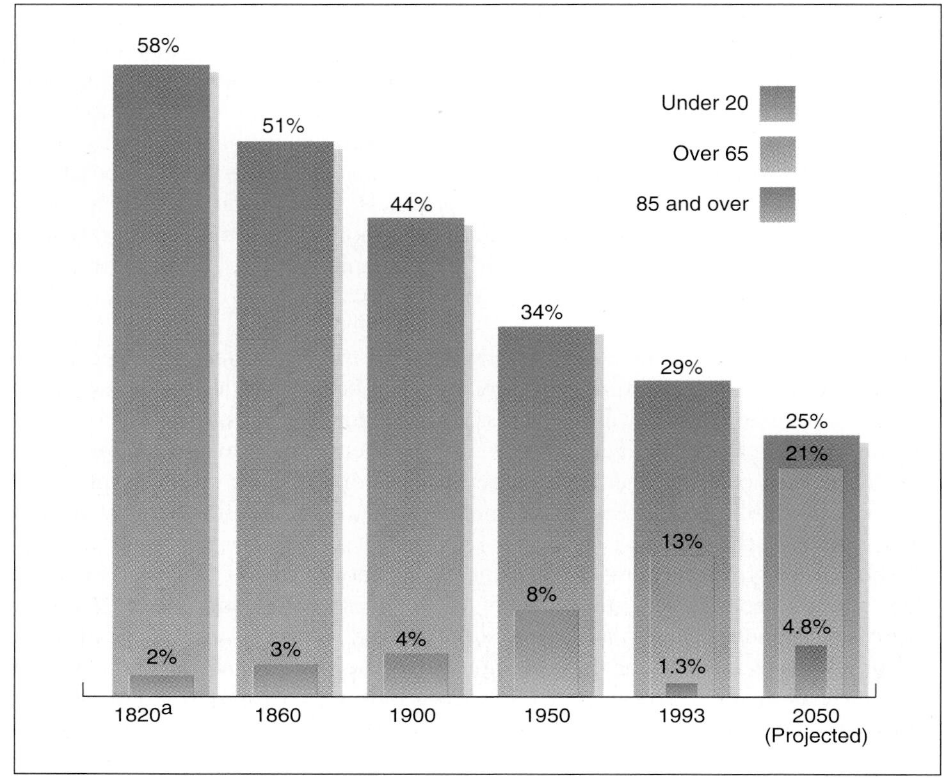

FIGURE 13.3
CHANGING U.S. AGE DISTRIBUTION, 1820–1993

In 1820, there were 29 children for every person over age 65. In 1993, there were approximately two children for every older person. The Census Bureau projects that by 2050, the proportion of older persons will nearly equal the proportion of children in the U.S. population. Partly as a result of this shift, investment in children consumes a much smaller part of society's resources today.

[a]Data for 1820 are based on the white population only.

SOURCE: U.S. Bureau of the Census 1988, 1975; U.S. Bureau of the Census 1993, Table 17; "How We're Changing" 1994, Figure 1.

under 20. Now, this proportion is down to 29 percent. At the other end of the age spectrum, the proportion of the population over 65 has increased more than sixfold since 1820, from 2 to 13 percent ("How We're Changing " 1994).

The increased proportion of the population that is over 65 is due not to decreased mortality but to decreased fertility. In a high-fertility population, the proportion of the elderly is always small. This is roughly the situation that prevailed in 1820, when on average American women bore 6.7 children. When fertility is relatively low, however, the result is that an increasing proportion of the population is elderly and a decreasing proportion consists of children.

Although fertility change is the major determinant of our changing age structure, increased life expectancy does play a part. The last decade has witnessed an unprecedented and largely unanticipated increase in life expectancy among older people.

RELATIVE SHARES OF THE PUBLIC POT

The ratio of children to old people was 29 to 1 in 1820; in 1993, it was only 2.2 to 1. In numerical terms, then, the relative power of young people has declined substantially. If numbers were the only criterion, we would still expect youth to retain advantages over age. In point of fact, however, older people vote and children do not. Children have various representatives to act in their interests (parents, social workers, and so on), but they are basically disenfranchised. One result is that, increasingly, children lose out in the battle for scarce public resources (Leach 1994; Rosenstiel 1995).

Federal expenditure on child-related programs (the former Aid to Families with Dependent Children, Head Start, food stamps, child nutrition, child health, and aid to education) is only one quarter the size of federal expenditures on programs for elderly people. When figured on a per-capita basis, the federal government spends 9 percent as much on the average child as it does on the average person over 65. This situation has been gradually worsening. The major programs hit by recent federal cutbacks on social expenditures have been child-related programs (Leach 1994). In 1996, the federal government ended its 61-year-old Aid to Dependent Children program which guaranteed financial assistance to low income single mothers and their children (O'Rourke 1996). Cutting programs for older people, especially Social Security, has become too politically risky, and they have remained largely immune to major decreases in social spending.

A consequence of these changes is that the condition of children in the United States has deteriorated, whereas the condition of older people has improved. A 1995 report by the Carnegie Council on Adolescent Development, the result of a nine-year study, warned that as a nation the United States is seriously neglecting its youth (Wulf 1995). Figure 13.4 compares changes in poverty rates between 1970 and 1994. These data show that poverty has increased among children and decreased among older people. Within about 20 years, the United States went from a society in which older people were much *more likely* than children to be poor to a society in which they are much *less likely* to be poor. These trends are similar for African Americans, non-Hispanic whites, and Hispanics.

Why have children become less advantaged than older people? Several explanations have been suggested. An obvious one is that, although everybody has parents, not everybody has children. Some childless people have little sympathy with the problems of providing for children. Expecting someday to be 65 (or already 65), they are more likely to support government programs that help older people

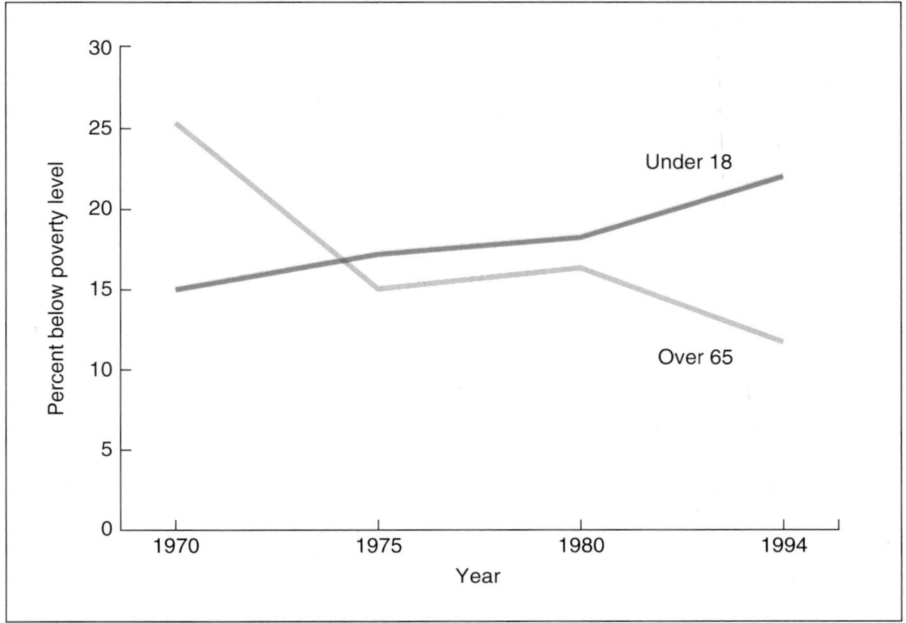

FIGURE 13.4
CHANGING LEVELS OF POVERTY AMONG CHILDREN AND OLDER AMERICANS, 1970–1994

Over the last two decades, the poverty rate for older people has declined sharply but the poverty rate for children has increased. As a result, children are now substantially more likely than older people to live in poverty.

SOURCES: Data from 1970, 1975, and 1980 are from U.S. Bureau of the Census 1982, 11. Data for 1992 are from U.S. Bureau of the Census, 1996, Tables 728 and 731.

than to support programs that help children. (This issue is further explored in Chapter 16.) A related explanation involves family norms: In the United States, we generally believe that parents are obligated to support their children but that children are not obligated to support their parents. We have given the government the responsibility for allocating resources to older people, and it does so relatively evenhandedly. Distribution of resources to children, however, still rests largely with their parents and varies widely, depending on the earnings of the parents and whether the children live with one or two parents. Some observers have also wondered if the decreasing benefits to children might not reflect the fact that 24 percent of the population under 15 is Hispanic or African American, double the percentage in the entire population (Kozol 1991; Leach 1994).

The United States is not the only nation experiencing a change in relations between younger and older people. In the next section, we look at the changing balance of youth and age in China.

Global Perspectives: The Changing Balance of Youth and Age in China

If we describe world regions by the proportion of their population 65 and older, Europe is the oldest, followed by North America. Africa is the youngest. Asia (of which China is a part) is in between but aging the fastest (Kinsella and Taeuber 1993).

In China, an ever-larger part of the population is growing old. People 60 and older made up 9 percent of the population in 1990, but that figure is expected to grow to 19 percent by 2025. Newspaper columnists in China have called this trend the "raging silver wave" (Mufson 1995).

Populations age when people start living longer and also have fewer children (Kinsella and Taeuber 1993). China's life expectancy has gradually increased to 70 years (69 for men and 72 for women) (Population Reference Bureau 1994). Meanwhile, Chinese parents are not having enough children to replace themselves (fewer than two per couple) (Population Reference Bureau 1994).

The rising ratio of senior citizens to young people has an interesting history in China. In the 1950s, the country's leaders believed large families were necessary so that China could be strong. In that atmosphere, many couples had four or five children. By 2025, these children will be senior citizens or close to it. In the 1970s, however, China's leaders began to advise birth control because the population was growing so rapidly. By 1980, China had instituted its "one child only" policy, whereby couples were pressured to have only one child. An obvious result is that the *parent support ratio (PSR)*—the number of children available to care for elderly parents—is about to decline drastically (Kinsella and Taeuber 1993).

Traditionally, Chinese parents wanted a lot of boys—and they prefer a boy to a girl today—because sons are responsible for taking care of their parents in old age. The cultural value of *filial piety,* involving a system of children's obligations to their parents, has governed Chinese intergenerational relationships for centuries. Children, and especially sons, are expected to provide their parents with devotion and reverence, economic aid, and affection and companionship throughout the parents' lifetime. In addition, children are expected to bring glory and prestige to their parents by doing well in school and at work (Lin and Liu 1993).

This value system could disintegrate, however. China's only children may find it impossible to be occupationally successful while providing for two aging parents and grandparents as well. A recent article in a Chinese newspaper warned that "many families will become breathless and crumble under the impact of this burden." There is some evidence to support this prediction. According to government surveys, elderly people in some Chinese cities comprise a disproportionately large number of the homeless (Mufson, 1995).

With 1.2 billion persons, China has one-fifth of the world's people. There are 110 million persons 60 or older in China; by 2025, there will be nearly 400 million. Furthermore, when we look at the world population of people over the age of 80, we find that Chinese people make up 16 percent of this population—a higher proportion than any other nationality (Kinsella and Taeuber 1993). In a country with no old-age or nursing homes and very little in the way of pension funds or social security insurance (Mufson 1995), the changing balance of youth and age will strain families, companies, and the government.

Explanations For Age Stratification

In everyday usage, most people rely on a physiological explanation of age stratification. The young and the old have less status because they are less competent and less productive. To some extent, this explanation is correct. It does not, however, explain cross-cultural or historical variations in the status of age groups. Conflict and structural-functional perspectives, as well as modernization theory, furnish insightful explanations about why age stratification exists and varies across societies.

Structural-Functional Perspective

The structural-functional perspective focuses on the ways in which age stratification helps fulfill societal functions. From this perspective, the restricted status of youth is beneficial because it frees young people from responsibility for their own support and gives them time to learn the complex skills necessary for operating in society.

At the other end of the age scale, the functionalist perspective is the basis for **disengagement theory.** The central argument of this theory is that older people voluntarily disengage themselves from active social participation, gradually dropping roles in production, family, church, and community even before actual disability connected with age requires it. This disengagement is functional for society because it allows younger people, with new ideas and skills appropriate to a fast-changing society, to take their places. Disengagement also makes possible an orderly transition from one generation to the next, avoiding the dislocation caused by people dropping dead in their tracks or dragging down the entire organization by decreased performance. It is functional for the individual because it reduces the shame of declining ability and provides a rest for the weary. Disengagement theory is a perfect example of why functional theory is sometimes called consensus theory: The lack of participation of older people is agreed on by older people and others and benefits all (Hendricks and Hendricks 1981).

Disengagement theory, a functionalist theory of aging, argues that older people voluntarily disengage themselves from active social participation.

Conflict Perspective

The conflict view of age stratification produces a picture of disengagement that is far less benign—a picture of simple rejection and discrimination springing from

Young adults are in an ambiguous position in society. Although youth may be the time of their lives, it is also a time generally characterized by low earnings, galling dependence on parents, and relatively high rates of deviance and suicide. The structural-functional perspective suggests that the low status of young people is part of a natural evolution from childhood to maturity, a necessary step on the road to adult status. Conflict theorists, in contrast, suggest that the low status of young adults has been built into social institutions so that their elders may benefit.

competition over scarce resources. These resources are primarily jobs but also include power within the family. Conflict theorists suggest that barring young and older people from the labor market is a means of categorically eliminating some groups from competition and improving the prospects of workers between 25 and 65.

There is empirical evidence to support this view. Early in American history, few people retired. Not only could they not afford to, but their labor was still needed. As immigration provided cheap and plentiful labor, the need for the elderly worker decreased. In addition, as unions established seniority as a criterion for higher wages, older workers became more expensive than younger ones. In response to these trends, management instituted compulsory retirement to get rid of older workers. The mandatory retirement rules occurred long before Social Security, in an era when few employees had regular pension plans. Thus, compulsory retirement usually meant poverty for the older worker (Atchley 1982).

It was not until 1965 that social structures such as Social Security and private pensions began to make retirement a desirable personal alternative. Between 1959 and 1992, the proportion of older people who were poor declined dramatically, from 35 percent to about 13 percent. At present, retirement suits both the aging worker and the economic system. As the growing elderly population becomes an increasing burden on a shrinking working-age population, however, conflict may once again emerge between the generations over economic interests.

In the United States, the problem is expected to be most severe around 2030. At that time, the more frail "old old," who spend considerable tax dollars in Medicare, will make up more than half of the elderly population (Treas 1995, 6). At the same time, the huge baby-boom generation will be over 65, and the proportion of the total population 65 and older will climax at 18 percent. The biggest baby-boom crop will be wanting to retire and live off the Social Security taxes of younger workers. Because of the low birth rates in the 1970s and 1980s, however, there won't be very many of these younger workers. As Figure 13.5 demonstrates, in 1960 there were over five workers per Social Security recipient; by 2030, the

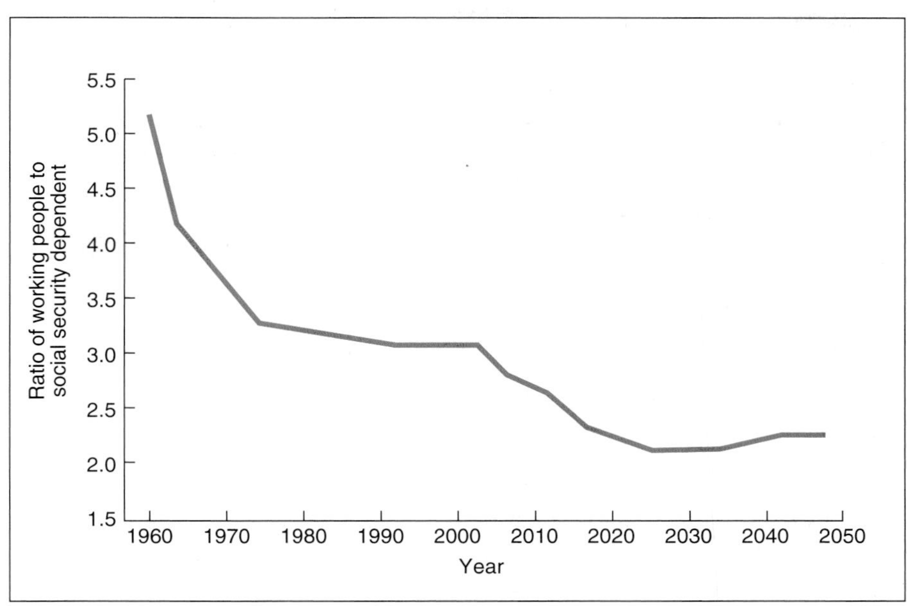

FIGURE 13.5
RATIO OF EMPLOYEES PER SOCIAL SECURITY DEPENDENT, 1960–2050

In 1960, there were five people working for every person over 65 who was drawing a Social Security check. By 2030, there will be only two earners for every person over 65. The result is sharply higher payroll taxes and a burgeoning pension industry.

SOURCE: Treas 1995, Figure 2.

ratio of workers to recipients will be down to two. This changing age structure will impose a heavy burden on the working-age population, and it raises questions about the viability of the current Social Security system. Recognizing the fiscal dilemma posed by the changing age structure, Congress tried, in 1983, to head off the coming crisis by passing new laws. It sharply raised payroll taxes—so that baby boomers could pay ahead of time for their own retirement—and it raised the age at which workers could draw full retirement benefits from 65 to 67 beginning in 2017 (Treas 1995).

The burden posed by the changing age structure goes beyond the fiscal issue. Even if baby boomers save for their retirement, who will produce the goods and services that they will be able to afford to buy? A change from five workers per retiree to two workers per retiree implies the need for immense increases in productivity if this diminishing pool of workers is to keep up with demand.

As a result of these dilemmas, many observers are concluding that the current Social Security system is unworkable. One solution is to encourage longer work lives by raising further the age at which full benefits can be drawn. This would keep more people in the productive work force and reduce the number drawing benefits. However, this "solution" would also mean fewer well-paying jobs available to younger Americans, particularly youth under about age 25. From a conflict perspective, the good health and relative prosperity of some of the "young old" population may cause the entire older population to be viewed as a new leisure class, whose motor homes and trips to Florida or Arizona are being paid for by an overburdened working generation (Bengston et al. 1985); Rosenbaum and Button 1993).

MODERNIZATION THEORY OF AGING

The **modernization theory of aging** argues that older people have low status in modern societies because the value of their traditional resources has eroded.

According to the **modernization theory of aging,** older people have low status in modern societies because the value of their traditional resources has eroded. This is due to three simultaneous events: the decline in importance of land (disproportionately owned by older people) as a means of production, the increasing productivity of society, and a more rapid rate of social change (Cowgill 1974). Next, we look at each of these in turn.

First, when land is the most vital means of production, those who own it have high status and power. In many traditional societies, land ownership is passed from father to son. This gives fathers a great deal of power even if they live to an age when they are physically much less able than their sons. This explanation, of course, applies only in a society where wealth resides in transferable property, either land or animals.

Second, in societies with low levels of productivity, it is not feasible to exclude either young or elderly persons from productive activity. Everyone's labor is needed. In industrial societies, however, productivity is so high that many people can be freed from direct production. They can study, they can do research, they can write novels, or they can do nothing at all. In such a society, the labor of young and elderly persons becomes expendable: Society doesn't need it anymore.

Third, technological knowledge has grown at an every-accelerating pace. Since most of us learn the bulk of our technological skills when we are young, this rapid change produces an increasing disadvantage for older workers. Their technical skills become outdated. Thus, rapid social change works to the disadvantage of older people (Thorson 1995).

> **Thinking Critically**
>
> Chapter 3 discussed basic values in America's dominant culture (for example, achievement, efficiency, progress, and individual freedom). Based on what you know about modernization theory, how might these basic values affect the prestige of older people in U.S. culture and society?

Evaluation

Although both young people and old people have lower status than adults in midlife, their experiences are rather different. Thus, theories that explain the status of young people may not be as effective in explaining the status of older people (see the Concept Summary).

Concept Summary A Comparison of Three Explanations of Age Stratification

A Comparison of Three Explanations of Age Stratification

	Major Assumptions	Conclusions about Youth	Conclusions about Old Age	Overall Evaluation
Structural-Functional Theory	Age groups cooperate for common good	Young people's exclusion from full social participation is for good of self and society	Older people disengage voluntarily; good for self and society	Currently adequate to explain status of older people but not compelling to explain status of young people
Conflict Theory	Age groups compete for scarce resources	Young people are excluded so that others may benefit	Older people are excluded so that senior positions open up for younger adults	Useful to explain status of young people but not to explain today's older people
Modernization Theory	Changes in institutions alter the value of special resources that age groups hold (land, labor, and knowledge)	Unspecified; by implication, status goes down because labor not necessary	Status of older people has decreased because traditional bases of power have eroded	Useful to explain low social honor of older people and young people

Overall, it would appear that all three theories can contribute to understanding the status of the young. Certainly, as functional theorists suggest, when people are protected from full responsibilities while very young, both the young people and society benefit. Nevertheless, the continued disadvantage of young adults and their subsequent poverty, lack of social integration, and deviance are hardly functional for them or society. In this case, it seems appropriate to attribute their low status to the systematic disadvantages they face in competing for scarce resources controlled by an older generation. Part of this disadvantage stems, as modernization theory suggests, from devaluation of their traditional resource: the capacity for low-skill, physically demanding work.

The status of older people is harder to account for. Modernization theory is not really applicable to their rising economic status, though it may explain their low social honor. Nor does conflict theory seem entirely adequate to explain the economic status of older people: Rather, at this point in history, the disengagement of the older worker seems mutually attractive to younger and older people.

The improved economic status of older people and the expansion of government programs to provide health care and other services to this group appear to rest on a consensus across the entire age span that this is appropriate. Such a consensus is based on the ability of a productive society to be generous without being hurt too much by this generosity. The grounds for such a consensus may not always exist.

The Applications in Diversity section of this chapter examines how age, gender, and race/ethnicity work together in the U.S. stratification system.

Double or triple jeopardy means having low status on two or three different dimensions of stratification.

APPLICATIONS IN DIVERSITY

How Do Age, Gender, and Race/Ethnicity Work Together in the U.S. Stratification System?

We began the major section on stratification by examining inequalities in life chances. So far we have dealt with unequal life chances related to social class, race/ethnicity, sex, and age. On each of these dimensions, we have been able to demonstrate that there is a hierarchy of access to the good things in life and that some groups are substantially disadvantaged.

When a person has lower status on more than one dimension, that person experiences **double or triple jeopardy.** This means that disadvantage snowballs. Black teenagers are twice as likely as white teenagers to be unemployed; old women are more likely than old men to be poor. In this section, we review briefly the special problems of old age as affected by gender and race/ethnicity.

The quality of life one experiences in old age probably has less to do with age than with social class, sex, and race/ethnicity. Those who are most disadvantaged in old age are those who were close to the poverty line during their earning years. Even among relatively affluent retirees, widowhood often means sharp reductions in income.

Aging and Gender

Aging poses special problems for women. First is the problem of the double standard of aging: The signs of age—wrinkles, loose skin, gray hair—are considered more damaging for women than for men. Thus, age is associated with greater decreases in prestige and esteem for women than for men.

The life expectancy gap between men and women also makes the experience of old age very different for women than for men. On average, women live about seven years longer than men. Taken together with the fact that women are usually two years or so younger than their husbands, this works out to a nine-year gap between when a woman's husband dies and when she dies. This mortality difference has enormous consequences for the quality of life. First, it means that most men will spend their old age married, have the care of a spouse during illness, and be able to spend their last years at home being cared for by a spouse. The average woman, on the other hand, will spend the last years of her life unmarried, will spend most of these years living along with no one to care for her, and is more likely to be cared for in a nursing home during her last illness.

Sex differences in mortality mean that old age is disproportionately a society of women. Above age 75, there are nearly twice as many women as men. The decreasing availability of men in older age groups has consequences for social roles. It means that, as people get older, heterosexual contacts, whether through marriage or in bridge groups, are less important for structuring social life. It also means that fewer of the elderly

APPLICATIONS IN DIVERSITY

are married and more of them live alone (U.S. Bureau of the Census 1994, Table 63). The feminization of old age is an increasing component of the poverty of old age. Female-headed households are poorer than male-headed households at all ages, and older people are no exception. As the elderly population rose out of poverty over the last three decades, female-headed households were disproportionately left behind.

Aging Among Minority Groups

Ethnic minorities earn substantially less during their peak years than do non-Hispanic whites, and this means they are less likely to have accumulated assets such as home ownership to cushion income loss during retirement. Further, there is evidence that the economic status of racial/ethnic minorities becomes worse, relative to that of non-Hispanic whites, in old age (Taeuber 1992). That is, the disparity in wealth and income between non-Hispanic whites and others increases from adulthood into old age.

But the most significant link between minority status and aging is that minorities are less likely to live to experience old age! Whereas 75 percent of white males can expect to survive until they are 65, only 58 percent of black males will live until retirement age. For women, the figures are 85 and 75 percent, respectively.

An issue that applies to minority aging in today's increasingly diverse society concerns how elderly immigrants experience U.S. culture. Many immigrants, such as those from Asian or Latino countries, have internalized their native culture's belief that an old person deserves respect and prestige simply because she or he has lived a long time. However, U.S. culture places high value on activity, productivity, and individual achievement—values that are inconsistent with high prestige for old people. The assimilation of elderly immigrants and their children and grandchildren requires mutual adjustments in age roles and expectations (Lin and Liu 1993; Paz 1993).

Thinking Critically

Can you think of an example of double or triple jeopardy in your own life or in the life of someone you know? Outline what you think might be the process or processes that result in double or triple jeopardy.

How do you respond to old people whom you meet on the sidewalk or at the grocery store? How about on the freeway? What do you think when you see an old person? Do your thoughts differ depending on whether the old person is a man or a woman? Depending on whether the old person belongs to a racial/ ethnic minority group? What do your responses tell you about how your culture values older people?

Sociology on the Net

One of the most important changes in America is the aging of our population. This has recently led to political fights over Social Security, medical care for the elderly and has even fostered attacks on organizations that represent the interests of the elderly. Let us return once more to the Census Bureau's Population Profiles.

`http://www.census.gov/population/pop-profile/toc.html`

Return to the selection on **National Population Projections** and reread the part called "The U.S. population will be older than it is now." In what year will the median age peak? Who are the "Baby Boomers" and why are they an important part of the aging population? When were they born?

Now go back to the **main menu** and open the selection entitled **The Elderly Population**. How has the age structure of America changed in the last 90 years? What is the fastest growing segment of the aging population? What kinds of problems might this create?

A lot of the controversy centers on the future of the social security program. What does the Social Security Administration have to say about this? Go to:

`http://www.ssa.gov/coss_speech.html`

Browse through the commissioners speech on social security. What is social security and why do some people feel that it is in trouble? What impact will the "Baby Boomers" have on the social security system?

Older people get out and vote in much larger proportion than any other age group. This makes them a formidable voting block. One of the strongest organizations representing the elderly is the American Association of Retired Persons.

`http://www.aarp.org`

This is the home page of the AARP. Start your browsing by clicking on the section called **Who We Are**. Take a look around and then open the section on **Advocating For Our Members**. When you have read to the end of this selection, open the section entitled **Where We Stand**. Click on the highlighted phrase **Where We Stand** in this section. What issues are listed here that are currently hot topics in Congress? How do the interests of this group coincide with your own interests? On what issue do you differ? If the AARP achieves all of these goals, who will pay for them?

SUMMARY

1. Age roles are less highly structured than many others. Although there are accepted criteria for "acting your age," there are few sanctions for violating these norms.
2. The meaning of age depends on social structure and thus varies across time and societies. The institutionalization of age-linked criteria in bureaucracies such as school and Social Security systems has increased the uniformity of experience by age.
3. Two perspectives are important to the sociological study of age: the life-course perspective and the cohort perspective. They alert us to focus on the changing relationships of individuals to social structures as they age and the ways this process can differ from one cohort to the next.
4. Childhood, adolescence, and old age are almost roleless roles. We expect very little from people in these age groups and specify few obligations for them. The ages from 20 to 65, however, are crowded with obligations, and role strain may result.
5. Young people suffer many structured inequalities and are not well integrated into society's institutions. Among the consequences of this are a high crime rate and the development of a youth subculture that emphasizes style and passive escape.
6. The population over 65 is perhaps better off now than it has ever been. Although the older population still suffers from low honor, improvements in health and in economic circumstances have sharply decreased the disadvantages

associated with age. The disadvantages of aging are more pronounced for women and those who were living on the economic margin during their working years.

7 There have been major changes in the U.S. age distribution. Owing to reduced fertility and, to a lesser extent, increased life expectancy, the proportion of the population over 65 is growing rapidly and the proportion under 20 is declining.

8 As indexed by the poverty rate, children are more disadvantaged than older people. This is due to two factors: the greater willingness to support older people out of the public purse and the increasing proportion of children whose fathers do not help support them.

9 Structural-functional theory (disengagement theory), conflict theory, and modernization theory provide competing explanations of why young and old people tend to have lower status in U.S. society. Right now, conflict theory seems more appropriate to explain the disadvantages of young people and structural-functional theory more appropriate to explain the improved status of older people.

10 Of the world's regions, Europe is the oldest (with the highest proportion of people over age 65), followed by North America, then Asia. Africa is the youngest.

11 Double or triple jeopardy means having low status on two or three different dimensions of stratification. These dimensions, each examined in a chapter in this major section on stratification, are age, gender, and race/ethnicity.

SUGGESTED READINGS

ARIES, Phillipe. 1962. *Centuries of Childhood.* New York: Knopf. A classic social history of childhood. Aries argues that childhood is a social construction, or invention, that did not develop (at least in the West) until about the 17th century.

BENGSTON, Vern L., and W. Andrew Achenbaum. (Eds.) 1993. *The Changing Contract Across Generations.* New York: Aldine de Gruyter. Using an intergenerational perspective, this book integrates information from the areas of the family and politics to assess the effect of the changing age distribution in the United States in regard to the social contract that exists between the generations and age groups.

FRIEDAN, Betty. 1993. *The Fountain of Age.* New York: Simon and Schuster. Most known for her book, the *Feminine Mystique,* published in 1963, Friedan now has tackled the issue of aging in our society, particularly as aging affects women in the United States.

KERTZER, David, and Schaie, K. Warner (Eds.). 1989. *Age Structuring in Comparative Perspective.* Hillside, N.J.: Erlbaum. A collection of articles showing how the experience of age from childhood to old age is socially structured around the world.

HAVEMAN, Robert H., and Barbara Wolfe. 1994. *Succeeding Generations: On the Effects of Investments in Children.* New York: Russell Sage Foundation. A policy book that argues that we need to invest in America's children in order to assure the future of the United States.

LEACH, Penelope. 1994. *Children First.* New York: Knopf. A policy book by an author who has become a television personality. The book argues that the industrialized world is forgetting its children and that we need to put children first in our family and national political decisions.

MODELL, John. 1989. *Into One's Own: From Youth to Adulthood in the United States, 1920–1975*. Berkeley: University of California Press. A social history of the transition to adulthood. Modell draws from a variety of sources—from *True Confessions* to census data—to describe and explain how growing up has changed.

THORSON, James A. 1995. *Aging in a Changing Society*. Belmont, Calif.: Wadsworth. A textbook on aging designed for undergraduates.

TREAS, Judith. 1995. Older Americans in the 1990s and Beyond. *Population Bulletin* 50 (2) (May). Washington, D.C.: Population Reference Bureau, Inc. Short, readable booklet with up-to-date information on many issues regarding the over-65 population in the United States today.

UNIT FOUR

Social Institutions

CHAPTER 14

The Family

OUTLINE

PROLOGUE

Have You Ever . . . stopped to consider how many of the people in your family you would choose as friends? If you are like the average person, there are some people in your family whom you really like, people you would seek out whether you were obliged to or not. You might, however, be able to identify one or two family members whom you really don't like very well, people you would not choose as your friends. Probably, ties of family loyalty bind you to these people so that you would come to their aid if they needed help, you would feel sorry if they had troubles, and you would expect them to help you if you had problems. But you wouldn't shed any tears if you did not see them for the next 10 years.

The family is a remarkable arrangement for binding people together with ties of obligation. Your obligations to your parents, brothers, sisters, and children will bind you to them long after you have ceased to live together in the same household—and, to a significant extent, regardless of the affection between you. You may be able to divorce a spouse or end a friendship, but there is no such thing as an ex-child or an ex-brother. These relatives are with you forever.

The poet Robert Frost once said that "home is the place where, when you have to go there, they have to take you in." As we grow up and achieve economic independence, most of us choose not to live with our parents, brothers, and sisters. In times of unemployment, bereavement, divorce, and trouble, however, family members can usually be counted on to provide a sanctuary. Although we hope we will not need them, it is nice to know they are out there.

This chapter begins a six-chapter section on social institutions. We cover the five basic institutions—family, education, government, economy, and religion—and one relatively new institution, medicine. *Institutions* are enduring and complex social structures that provide ready-made arrangements to meet human problems (see Chapter 4). The chief characteristic of institutions is their stability. Their major function is to produce continuity in social organization from one generation to the next. Yet institutions are also responsive. Old ones adapt, evolve, and change; new ones emerge to meet new needs.

The paradox of change and continuity is perhaps nowhere as clear as in our first institution—the family. In many ways, the American family of 1997 is similar to the family of 1897, yet there have been dramatic changes. These changes in family life have been felt, either directly or indirectly, by all of us and they have sparked heated public debate over "family values." Is the family a dying institution, or is it simply a changing one? In this chapter, we examine the question from the perspective of sociology. We begin with a broad description of the family as a basic social institution.

Marriage, Family, and Kinship: Basic Institutions of Society

Universal Family Functions

In every culture, the family has been assigned major responsibilities, typically including (Murdock 1949; Pitts 1964):

1. Replacement through reproduction
2. Regulation of sexual behavior
3. Economic responsibilities for dependents—children, persons who are elderly or ill, and persons with disabilities
4. Socialization of the young
5. Ascription of status
6. Provision of intimacy, a sense of belonging, and emotional support

Because these activities are important for individual development and the continuity of society, every society provides some institutional pattern for meeting them. No society leaves them to individual initiative. Although it is possible to imagine a society in which these responsibilities are handled by religious or educational institutions, most societies have found it convenient to assign them to the family.

The importance of these tasks varies across societies. Status ascription is a greater responsibility in societies where social position is largely inherited; regulation of sexual behavior is more important in cultures without contraception. In U.S. society, we have seen the priorities assigned to these family responsibilities change substantially over time. In colonial America, the family's primary responsibilities were care of dependent children and replacement through reproduction; the provision of emotional support was a secondary consideration. More recently, however, much of the responsibility for socializing the young has been transferred to schools and day-care, or child-care, centers; financial responsibility for dependent elderly persons has been shifted to the government. At the same time, intimacy has taken on increased importance as a dimension of marital relationships.

The **family** is a relatively permanent group of persons, linked by ties of mutual consent, blood, marriage, or adoption, who live together and cooperate economically and in the rearing of children.

Unlike most social structures, the **family** is a biological as well as a social group—a relatively permanent group of persons, linked by ties of mutual consent, blood, marriage, or adoption, who live together and cooperate economically and in the rearing of children. This definition includes both the single- and the two-parent family. The important criteria for families are that their members are bound together—if not by blood, then usually by some cultural ceremony such as marriage or adoption that ties them to each other relatively permanently—and that they assume responsibility for each other.

A **kin group** is a set of relatives who interact on the basis of shared social structure.

The family is a subset of a larger set of relatives—the kin group. A **kin group** is a set of relatives who interact on the basis of a shared social structure. The kin group need not include all of a person's blood relatives. In the Trobriand Islands, social relationships are organized around mother's kin rather than father's, so that only the relatives (both male and female) on her side of the family fall into a person's socially defined kin group; among the Zulu, kinship is organized around male siblings. In U.S. society, the group we call kin covers both our mother's and father's side of the family but seldom extends beyond first cousins. In addition to blood relatives, most Americans include their in-laws as part of their kin groups.

Marriage is an institutionalized social structure that provides an enduring framework for regulating sexual behavior and childbearing. Many cultures tolerate other kinds of sexual encounters—premarital, extramarital, or homosexual—but all cultures discourage childbearing outside marriage. In some cultures, the sanctions are severe, and almost all sexual relationships are confined to marriage; in others, marriage is an ideal that can be bypassed with relatively little punishment.

Marriage is an institutionalized social structure that provides an enduring framework for regulating sexual behavior and childbearing.

Marriage is important for child rearing because it imposes socially sanctioned roles on parents and the kin group. When a child is born, parents, grandparents, and aunts and uncles are automatically assigned certain normative obligations to the child.

This network represents a ready-made social structure designed to organize and stabilize the responsibility for children. Children born outside marriage, by contrast, are more vulnerable. The number of people normatively responsible for their care is smaller; and even in the case of the mother, the norms are less well enforced. One consequence is higher infant mortality for illegitimate children in almost all societies, including U.S. society.

Marriage, family, and kinship are among the most basic and enduring patterns of social relationships. Although blood ties are important, the family is best understood as a social structure defined and enforced by cultural norms.

Cross-Cultural Variations

Families universally are expected to regulate sexual behavior, care for dependents, and offer emotional and financial security. That is where the universals end, however. Hundreds of different family forms can fill these roles. Children can be raised by their grandmothers or their aunts; wives can have one husband or three; children can be cared for at home or sent to boarding school; older people can be put out in the cold to die or put on Social Security. This section reviews some of the most important variations in the ways cultures have fulfilled family functions. (The Focus at the end of this section describes in some detail the unique family system of a 19th-century utopian community.)

Around the world, the family is a central social institution. Although the tasks of families may differ among cultures, in all cultures family members are charged with the responsibility for taking care of one another. Parents must take care of children and wives and husbands of each other. As this photograph of a family in Ecuador shows, the family is also often a primary source of personal warmth and satisfaction.

A **nuclear family** consists of a husband, a wife, and their dependent children.

An **extended family** exists when the wife-husband pair and their children live with other kin and share economic and child-rearing responsibilities with them.

Family Patterns. The basic unit of the family is the wife-husband pair and their children. When the couple and their children form an independent household living apart from other kin, we call them a **nuclear family.** When they live with other kin, such as the wife's or husband's parents or siblings, we refer to them as an **extended family.**

Extended families are found in all types of societies, although they are defined as the ideal family form only in some premodern, nonindustrialized societies. Where extended families occur in the United States, they are often the result of financial hardship.

Neolocal residence occurs when norms of residence require that a newly married couple take up residence away from their relatives.

Matrilocal residence occurs when norms of residence require that a newly married couple take up residence with the wife's kin.

Patrilocal residence occurs when norms of residence require that a newly married couple take up residence with the husband's kin.

Residence Patterns. Whether a society favors nuclear or extended families has a great deal of influence on where a newly married couple will live. By definition, the nuclear family lives by itself; this is called **neolocal residence.** Extended families, however, may exhibit a wide variety of residence patterns. They may live with the wife's relatives (**matrilocal residence**), with the husband's relatives (**patrilocal residence**), or in some unique combination. Like the extended family itself, complex residence patterns are gradually being displaced by the neolocal pattern of the nuclear family. There are still hundreds of small societies that prescribe complex residence patterns, but the great majority of the world's population now lives in societies practicing neolocal residence.

Courtship Patterns. As it does for all recurring behaviors, culture furnishes a set of standards for how and when to select a mate. It also specifies the extent to which parents and kin are involved (Goode 1959; see Figure 14.1).

Whenever marriage has as strong an impact on families or communities as it does on the couples themselves, it is unlikely that mate selection will be left up to individuals. When dowries or bride prices are exchanged, when the new spouse will move in with relatives, or when prestige is strongly related to family ties, then the activities leading to marriage are likely to be controlled by parents and kin. Under these circumstances, mate selection is based on the interests of the kin group rather than on any emotional bond between the young people. Love between a couple is regarded as a lucky accident and more likely follows than precedes marriage.

In the extreme case, this may mean that the family arranges a marriage between young people who have never met each other. In less extreme cases, chaperoning

FIGURE 14.1
TYPES OF COURTSHIP SYSTEMS AND THEIR DETERMINANTS

Parental control over courtship is more direct when the child's mate selection directly affects the parents.

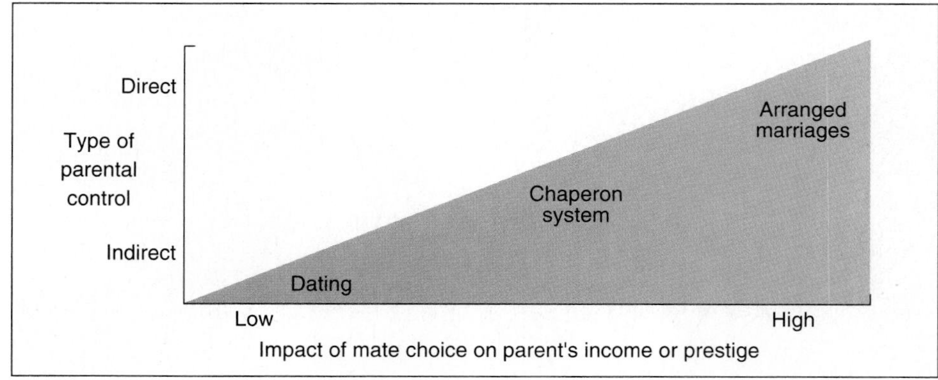

Where the choice of marriage partners affects the economic welfare of the parents or the community, courtship practices are likely to be closely supervised. Among the Old Order Amish, one form of supervision is the requirement that the buggies used by courting couples be open so that others can supervise their behavior. Only after a couple is married are they entitled to the privacy afforded by a covered buggy.

and careful supervision, especially of girls, gives some scope for individual choice while ensuring that young people will meet only those who are socially and economically acceptable to their parents. In extended family systems, family control of mate selection is important because marriage affects the economic interests of kin groups. Where the young people will live by themselves, however, and where the kin group's economic interests are not affected by the young people's choices, there is a corresponding decrease in the family's involvement in choosing children's mates (Lee and Stone 1980).

In U.S. society, dating and courtship are relatively free of direct parental control. We have considerable freedom of choice and need not consider the wishes of others, including our parents, in choosing dating partners or spouses. Parental influence is still important, however, in both indirect and direct ways. Where our parents live, where they send us to school, where they vacation, and what activities they engage in all influence the types of people we meet. Such arrangements increase the likelihood that the partners we choose will be acceptable to our parents in terms of race, religion, and social class.

Marriage Patterns. In the United States and much of the Western world, a marriage form called **monogamy** is practiced; each man may have only one wife (at a time), and each woman may have only one husband. Many cultures, however, practice some form of **polygamy**—marriage in which a person may have more than one spouse at a time. The most frequent pattern, that practiced by the 19th-century Mormons, is to allow a man to have more than one wife at a time **(polygyny)**. Less frequently, the form is **polyandry,** in which a woman may have more than one husband at a time.

Monogamy is marriage in which there is only one wife and one husband.

Polygamy is any form of marriage in which a person may have more than one spouse at a time.

Polygyny is a form of marriage in which one man may have more than one wife at a time.

Polyandry is a form of marriage in which one woman may have more than one husband at a time.

Viewed cross-culturally, polygyny has been the most popular marriage pattern. In a study of 250 cultures, Murdock (1949, 1957) found that 75 percent prefer polygyny as a marriage pattern, 24 percent prefer monogamy, and only 1 percent prefer polyandry. In the contemporary world, polygyny is most common in African societies. Approximately 24 percent of married African men have more than one wife (Ingoldsby and Smith 1995; Welch and Glick 1981). The practice of polygyny is, of course, restricted by the nearly equal number of men and women in a society; if some men have more than one wife, other men have to go without. Thus, even in societies where polygyny is the preferred marriage pattern, the majority of men have only one wife—and even though a clear majority of cultures favor polygyny, the great majority of the population of the world lives in cultures that practice monogamy.

Polygyny is by definition an extended family system. It tends to be best adapted to preindustrial societies in which both geographic and social mobility are limited. It is also characteristic of societies in which wealth depends on kinship ties. In some cultures, polygyny enhances a man's wealth by bringing in more dowries, providing more women and children for labor, and producing more heirs (Reiss 1980). In other cultures, husbands pay a bride price for their wives; hence, polygyny is costly, and only wealthy men have more than one wife. Everywhere polygyny is practiced, it tends to become an important symbol of the prestige and status of the wealthy. Monogamy tends to flourish where there are other means to demonstrate wealth and status and where the costs of children exceed their economic benefits.

Patriarchal authority is normatively approved male dominance.

Matriarchal authority is normatively approved female dominance.

Egalitarianism emphasizes equality in decision making, control of family resources, and child rearing.

Authority Patterns. Both in and out of the family, human societies have been characterized by **patriarchal authority;** the oldest male of the family typically controls economic resources, makes decisions, and has the final say in all matters related to the family. Although the influence or authority of wives varies from one society to another, there are no societies in which the cultural norms specify **matriarchal authority** and few in which the norms specify equality of authority. Increasingly, however, contemporary Western societies are coming to accept a new norm of **egalitarianism,** in which spouses jointly share in decision making, control of family resources, and child rearing. Even in the societies where equality is most highly developed, however, husbands continue to have more power than wives and are less involved in child rearing.

The American Family in Perspective. The American or, more generally, the Western European family is nuclear and neolocal; it is characterized by independence in mate selection; and marriages are monogamous. These basic outlines of the American family have remained relatively constant. In 1797 as well as in 1997, these characteristics distinguished our family form from that of Hindus or Kenyans or Chinese. In the remainder of this chapter, we will talk about some of the rather dramatic changes in the American family that have occurred within this basic framework.

THE AMERICAN FAMILY OVER THE LIFE COURSE

On nearly every dimension of American family life, there have been remarkable changes in attitude and behavior in recent decades. A few statistics set the stage:

- *Staying Single*. In 1994, approximately 9 percent of the population aged 40 to 45 had never married (U.S. Bureau of the Census 1995, Table 59); most of these people will never marry. Some of them would have married if their health or choices had been better, but perhaps half *chose* the independence of remaining single (Austrom and Hanel 1985).
- *Divorce*. Recent estimates suggest that 50 percent of all first marriages will end in divorce (Bumpass, Raley, and Sweet 1995).

- *Nonmarital Births*. Nearly a third (30 percent) of U.S. babies are born to unmarried mothers. The majority of those infants (59 percent) are born to white mothers. However, 23 percent of white births are outside marriage, compared with 69 percent of African American births (U.S. Bureau of the Census 1995, Table 94).
- *Parenting*. Approximately two-thirds of American children will spend at least some part of their childhood in a single-parent home (Bumpass 1984). At any given time, more than a quarter (27 percent) of American children are living with just one parent; another 4 percent live with neither parent (U.S. Bureau of the Census 1995, Table 79).
- *Working Mothers*. Almost two-thirds (64 percent) of married mothers are back in the labor force before their child's first birthday (U.S. Bureau of the Census 1995, Table 639).

These changes in family life have been felt, either directly or indirectly, by all of us. Is the family a dying institution, or is it simply a changing one? In the following sections, we use a life-course framework to examine some of the major family roles, how they are changing, and what these changes mean for societal and individual well-being.

Dating and Mate Selection

We do not have many matchmakers or formally arranged marriages in U.S. society; and at first glance, it may appear that everyone is on his or her own in the search for a suitable spouse. On further reflection, however, we see that parents, schools, and churches are all engaged in the process of helping young people pair up with suitable partners. Schools and churches hold dances and other social events designed to encourage heterosexual relationships; parents and friends introduce somebody "we'd like you to meet." Although going out with someone or dating may be fun, it is also an obligatory form of social behavior—it is normative.

Recent Trends. In the 1950s, teenagers dated in order to find a spouse. Many found one very quickly, and over 50 percent of American women were married before their 21st birthday. Times have changed. Teenagers no longer date with the expectation of settling down early, and dating is no longer an activity restricted to the teenage years. Nearly one-third of women and one-half of men aged 25–29 are unmarried. Although not all of these people are looking for a spouse, most are looking for at least a temporary partner.

Two trends have been responsible for the changes in dating patterns. First, people are making first marriages later in life. In the short span between 1970 and 1993, the average age at first marriage rose from 20.6 to 24.5 for women and from 22.5 to 26.5 for men (Ahlberg and De Vita 1992; U.S. Bureau of the Census 1994b, Table B). Second, high divorce rates mean that more people are marrying a second and even a third time. Today, only about 50 percent of all weddings are first marriages for both the bride and groom. As a result of these two trends, courtship and dating are often activities of 28- or 35-year-olds as well as 16-year-olds.

Narrowing Down the Field. Over the course of one's single life, one probably meets thousands of potential marriage partners. How do we narrow down the field?

FOCUS ON YESTERDAY

Group Marriage in the 19th Century

"THE ONEIDA COMMUNITY WAS ONE OF THE MOST SUCCESSFUL AND MOST DARINGLY DIFFERENT OF THESE 19TH-CENTURY GROUPS."

The United States in the late 19th century was remarkably tolerant in some respects. The moral code of the dominant culture stressed premarital chastity and monogamy. Nevertheless, dozens of sectarian groups with very different ideas of sexual and familial morality emerged and briefly prospered. The Mormons are the only one of them to have survived to the present day; and one of the conditions of their survival was the adoption of the family structure of the dominant culture.

The Oneida community was one of the most successful and most daringly different of these 19th-century groups. Oneida was founded in 1847 by a Yale-trained theologian named John Humprey Noyes. It began as a group of 20 to 30 in Oneida, New York, and grew to 300 children and adults before it disbanded in 1879.

Noyes's community was based on the principles of Christian communism. (Acts 2:32–35 offers biblical support for Christian communism.) In the Oneida community, there was no private property, and monogamy, the exclusive ownership of a spouse, was not allowed. Noyes recognized that the early Christians applied the communistic principle only to material goods.

> Yet we affirm that there is no intrinsic difference between property in persons and property in things. . . . The new command is, that we love one another, and that, not by pairs, as in the world, but *en masse*. We are required to love one another fervently. The fashion of the world forbids a man and woman who are otherwise appropriated to love one another fervently. But if they obey Christ they must do this (Noyes [1869] 1961, 625–627).

In the Oneida community, the practice of group marriage meant that all men were considered married to all women. Oneida, however, was hardly the place to go if one was looking for sex without commitment. Entrance into the community required signing over all of one's worldly goods to the community as well as embracing a life of considerable physical toil, and group marriage was not simply a matter of sleeping around. Rather, the selection of sexual partners was done through a committee. At Oneida, all members lived together in a big mansionlike house. Each woman had a private bedroom, whereas all the men slept together in a dormitory. When a man wished to sleep with a particular woman, he submitted a written request to the committee, which then referred it to the woman. The request could be denied by the woman on personal grounds or by the committee on the grounds that too much particularism was developing in this relationship and that the brother did not show himself willing to love all his sisters.

During the first two decades of the community's existence, the Oneidans avoided having children. They wished to establish both their economy and their family structure before adding the burden of children. During these 20 years, they practiced a form of contraception called *coitus reservatas*, in which the man does not ejaculate. Since this technique takes a great deal of willpower and some practice, it is reported that young men were required to sleep only with women past childbearing age until they had perfected the technique. (In a parallel practice, younger women were encouraged to sleep with older men. In this case, greater spiritual growth was given as the reason.) The teaching method must have worked reasonably well, as only two children were born during this period.

Between 1869 and 1879, the Oneidans produced 59 children. The women and men who became parents were "scientifically" matched by a committee. The selection process was designed to produce children with superior mental and physical abilities. The children were nurtured by their mothers for the first 12 months

Propinquity is spatial nearness.

Factors important in determining original attraction include propinquity, homogamy, and physical attractiveness. Despite "cyberspace" romance, you are simply less likely to meet or marry someone who lives far away than someone who is nearby. **Propinquity,** or spatial nearness, can also operate in subtle ways by increasing the opportunity for continual interaction. It is no accident that so many

FOCUS ON YESTERDAY

This photograph of the Oneida community depicts the women and men of the community on a free afternoon in front of the Mansion House. Note that the women wore pantaloons under their short skirts and bobbed their hair, styles unconventional for the time. Oneida was obviously economically successful as a community, a major factor that contributed to group marriage lasting as long as it did.

and then raised in a communal nursery. As with spouses, there was to be no exclusive attachment; adults were supposed to love all children equally. The children of Oneida apparently got exceptional care; their infant mortality rate was very low, and their educational training was excellent.

In 1879, the Oneida community disbanded. A major cause for the breakup was the erratic leadership provided by Noyes. Additional problems included the management of an increasingly large household and diversified economic enterprises. The problems were internal rather than external; the community never received a great deal of harassment from outsiders. It even advertised for visitors and sold Sunday lunches to day-trippers from New York who came to satisfy their curiosity about these strange people. The community's hard work and economic success, as well as a strategic willingness to buy locally and help neighbors, meant that its members were generally well regarded in upstate New York in spite of their odd family system.

When the community disbanded, many members stayed on in Oneida, most of them legally marrying one of the other members. The financial enterprises of Oneida were incorporated and divided among the members. One of these enterprises, the Oneida Silver Manufacturing Company, is still a successful corporation supplying tableware for millions. If you look, you may find Oneida silverware in your own kitchen.

SOURCE: Whitworth 1975.

people end up marrying coworkers or fellow students. The more you interact with others, the more likely you are to develop positive attitudes toward them—attitudes that may ripen into love (Homans 1950).

Spacial closeness is also often a sign of similarity. Research demonstrates that people tend to be drawn to others like themselves—people of the same class, race,

Romantic love is the ideal against which Americans judge their dating relationships. Although love and physical attraction can cross many barriers, most people fall in love with people who are similar to themselves in terms of education and social class background. As this picture of college students suggests, we also tend to fall in love with people we see regularly—people we work with and people we go to school with.

religion, age, and interests. Of course, there are exceptions, but faced with a wide range of choices, most people choose a mate similar to themselves (Rawlings 1978). This tendency is called **homogamy.**

Homogamy is the tendency to choose a mate similar to oneself.

Physical attractiveness may not be as important as advertisers have made it out to be, but studies do show that appearance is important in gaining initial attention (Elder 1969; Saks and Krupat 1988; Walster et al. 1966). Its importance normally recedes after the first meeting.

Dating is likely to progress toward a serious consideration of marriage if the couple discover similar interests, aspirations, anxieties, and values (Reiss and Lee 1988). When dating starts to get serious, couples begin sharing information about marriage expectations. Do they both want children? How do they feel about traditional marriage roles for men and women? If he expects her to do all the housework and she thinks that idea went out with the hula hoop, then they will probably back away from marriage.

Thinking Critically

Analyze the mate selection process that you (or someone close to you) have undergone. Show how propinquity, homogamy, and appearance were or were not involved. What role did parents or friends play?

This description of the courtship process is diagrammed in Figure 14.2 as a set of filters that gradually narrow down the field of eligibles (Kerckhoff and Davis 1962). At each stage in the courtship process, the screens become a little finer, and the pool of eligibles is finally reduced to one person. Is mate selection really all that sensible? Probably not. Some people do follow this sensible set of steps from top to bottom, but others jump to the final choice without passing through all the filters. Some get married in the fever of love at first sight, and some are caught by unexpected pregnancies.

Dating can be viewed as a shopping trip in which each person is evaluating the available goods and searching for the best bargain. Each is trying to get the most in return for personal assets (looks, talents, money). If this sounds too crass, consider the times you have heard someone say, "I know he can do better than that" or "She's throwing herself away on him." These statements basically imply that the shopper has bought overpriced merchandise and should have done a little more shopping around. A commitment to marriage is likely to occur when the individual decides that a particular person is the best buy in the market (Adams 1979).

The Sexual Side of Courtship. Some of the more important norms surrounding dating behavior are concerned with the amount of acceptable sexual contact. In the United States, we have seen two revolutions in premarital sexual norms and behavior. The first occurred in the 1920s, when there was a major increase in the proportion of both women and men who engaged in premarital sexual intercourse (Kinsey 1948, 1953) although a *double standard,* according to which men were granted more sexual freedom than women, persisted. The second began in the late 1960s. Studies of adolescents and college students indicate that this second revolution had two components: an increase in permissiveness and a decline of the double standard.

All major surveys have found increases in permissiveness in recent years; more people engage in sex before marriage, and fewer see anything wrong with it. Increasingly, both men and women believe that a strong commitment is unnecessary for a sexual relationship to be acceptable. Moreover, these changes in the last decade have been more pronounced for women than for men, with the result that men and women are now much more alike in both attitudes and levels of experience (Laumann et al. 1994).

One-quarter of 15-year-old women and one-half of 17-year-old women were sexually active in 1988, according to a major national survey (Ahlberg and De Vita 1992, 19). These figures suggest that for the majority—though not all—of Americans, dating involves sex. Although American norms have changed to the point where few see anything wrong about this, it nevertheless raises two potential problems: pregnancy and sexually transmitted diseases.

PREGNANCY. Study after study demonstrates that unmarried people and especially young unmarried people take great risks with sex (Frost and Forrest 1995; Santelli et al. 1995). Less than half of all unmarried couples use contraception at first intercourse, regardless of how old they are (Pratt 1984), and many wait a year or more to begin using effective birth control. There is evidence that teen contraceptive use has risen slightly over the past 15 years (Ahlberg and De Vita 1992). Nevertheless, very high rates of unwanted pregnancy exist today (Small and Luster 1994). Between one-third and one-half of American women become pregnant at least once between the ages of 15 and 19. The vast majority of these pregnancies are unwanted, and 40 percent end in induced abortion. For women aged 20 to 24, nearly one-third of all pregnancies end in abortion (U.S. Bureau of the Census 1995, Table 106).

SEXUALLY TRANSMITTED DISEASES. Over the past 25 years or so, U.S. society has undergone a change whereby people are engaging in sexual activity earlier and spending more years single before marriage and between marriages. The result is more years of nonmarital sexual activity. Usually this means more partners, and this in turn makes sexually transmitted diseases more likely. Of most concern is exposure to AIDS (acquired immunodeficiency syndrome). It is possible that widespread concern over AIDS may lead to a third sexual revolution in which people again become more conservative in their sexual behavior. It is too early to have empirical evidence of such a trend, but the necessity of a more prudent approach to the selection of sexual partners is so widely discussed that it seems likely to have

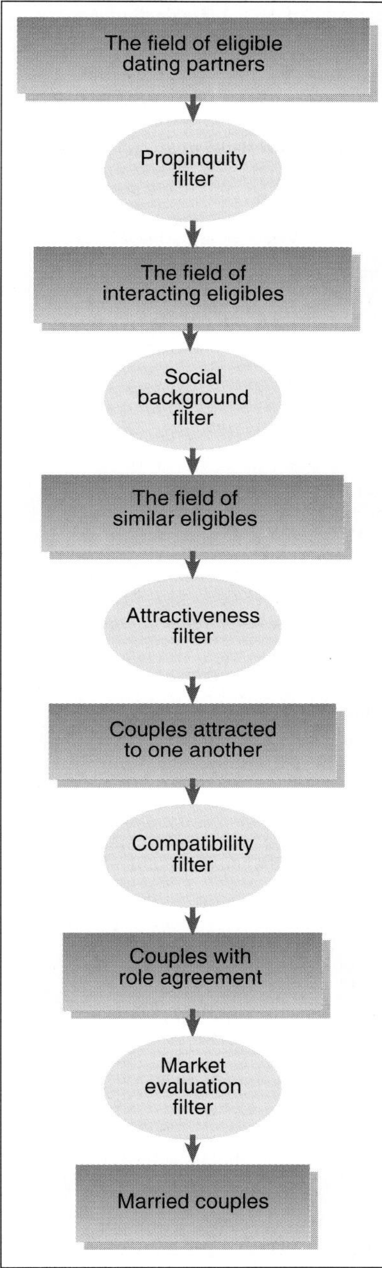

FIGURE 14.2
PROCESS OF SELECTING A MATE

Mate selection can be viewed as a series of filters that help us narrow the field of eligibles to one or two people who share our interests and expectations—and who seem to be good bargains.

SOURCE: Kerckhoff and Davis 1962.

some effect on sexual behavior and sexual standards. (AIDS is discussed at length in Chapter 19.)

Cohabitation is living together without legal marriage.

Cohabitation. Another major change in the mate selection process is the significant rise in **cohabitation—**living together without legal marriage. In 1994, approximately 3.6 million couples in the United States were cohabiting (U.S. Bureau of the Census 1995, Table 60). The chances that an individual will *ever* live in a cohabiting relationship have increased more than 400 percent for men and 1,200 percent for women within the last 30 years (Bumpass and Sweet 1995). Changes in the incidence of cohabiting are displayed in Table 14.1.

Cohabitation is an increasingly common stage of the courtship process, and approximately half of all recently married couples cohabited before they were married (Bumpass and Sweet 1989, 1995). Interestingly, the evidence suggests that the trial-marriage aspect of cohabitation is not very effective: Divorce rates are significantly *higher* for couples who cohabited before marriage (Booth and Johnson 1988; Thomson and Colella 1992). Generally, observers attribute this to the fact that the kind of people who flout convention by cohabiting are the same kind of people who are likely to get a divorce.

Marriage and Marital Relations

Despite the seeming disorganization of the dating process, about 90 percent of Americans end up having been married at least once by the time they reach 45. A sizable proportion also get divorced at least once, but most of the people who divorce eventually remarry. As a result, the majority of Americans spend the bulk of their adult years in the married state. What is it like?

Gender Roles in Marriage. Marriage is a sharply gendered relationship. Both normatively and in actual practice, husbands and wives, mothers and fathers have different responsibilities. Although many things have changed, American norms specify that the husband *ought* to work; it is still considered his responsibility to provide for his family. Similarly, norms specify that the responsibility for housework falls on the wife, not the husband. Although attitude surveys indicate this

Table 14.1
The Increasing Number of Cohabitors, 1970–1994

	1970	1994
Total	523,000	3,661,000
Age Under 25 Years Old	55,000	772,000
25–44 Years Old	103,000	2,169,000
45–64 Years Old	186,000	537,000
65 Years Old and Older	178,000	183,000

Source: U.S. Bureau of the Census 1995, Table 60.

norm is changing, the actual division of labor remains virtually unchanged whether the wife works or not (Ferree 1991; Potuchek 1992). As a result, wives who work, and especially mothers who work, often end up with a severe case of role overload, or role strain. One adaptation families make to this overload is to lower their standards for cleanliness, meals, and other domestic services. They eat at McDonald's and let the iron gather dust.

In addition to these important continuities in marital gender roles, there have also been some important changes. American norms now specify an egalitarian authority pattern. Only a minority of husbands still expect to "wear the pants" in the family, and most wives expect to be considered equals in the marital relationship. This equality is probably seldom achieved in practice. In many marriages, husbands still have more power than wives to decide where the family will live; how much housework, meal preparation, and child care the husband will do; and how much he can spend on himself. Nevertheless, egalitarianism is the standard against which a growing number of wives and husbands compare their marriages.

Sexual Roles in Marriage: A Changing Script. In few areas of our lives are we free to improvise. Instead, we learn social scripts that direct us toward appropriate behaviors and away from inappropriate ones. Sex is no exception. Unfortunately, we know relatively little about the sexual script for marriage partners and how it has changed. Most of the attention in the sexual revolution has gone to young people. Did the revolution pass married folks by, or have sexual roles changed within marriage as well as outside it?

The serious studies that have been done find that frequency of sexual activity seems to have changed very little among married people in the last 6 years (Call, Sprecher, and Schwartz 1995; Laumann et al. 1994). There have, however, been two notable trends. One is an increase in oral sex, a practice that was limited largely to unmarried sexual partners and the highly educated in earlier decades. The second is that women have reached parity with men in their probability of having an affair. The double standard has disappeared in adultery, and recent studies suggest that up to 50 percent of both men and women have had an extramarital sexual relationship (Laumann et al. 1995; Thompson 1983).

One of the most consistent findings about sexuality in marriage is that the frequency of intercourse declines steadily with the length of the marriage (see Table 14.2). The decline appears to be nearly universal and to occur regardless of the couple's age, education, or situation. After the first year, almost everything that happens—children, jobs, commuting, housework, finances—reduces the frequency of marital intercourse (Call, Sprecher, and Schwartz 1995).

> Oh, it's getting worse all the time. Maybe it's three or four times a month now instead of three or four times a week. But I guess it's natural—it's like "I'm tired, you're tired, let's forget it" (cited in Greenblat 1983, 296).
>
> Sex has become less important now—in the beginning there was a feeling that newlyweds screw a lot; therefore, we ought to. It was great and I loved it, but now I think that other things have become more important as we found other things that are satisfying to do besides sex (cited in Greenblat 1983, 297).

The overall conclusion drawn from research is that, after the first year of marriage, sex is of decreasing importance to most people. Nevertheless, satisfaction with both the quantity and the quality of one's sex life is essential to a good marriage (Blumstein and Schwartz 1983; Laumann et al. 1994).

TABLE 14.2
FREQUENCY OF SEXUAL INTERCOURSE PER MONTH IN THE EARLY YEARS OF MARRIAGE

The frequency with which married couples engage in sexual intercourse steadily declines after the first year of marriage for most couples. Couples attribute this decline to such things as work, child rearing, fatigue, and familiarity.

YEAR OF MARRIAGE	AVERAGE (PER MONTH)	RANGE (PER MONTH)
FIRST	14.8	4–45
SECOND	12.2	3–20
THIRD	11.9	2–18
FOURTH	9.0	4–23
FIFTH	9.7	5–18
SIXTH	6.3	2–15

What Makes It Good? A lasting marriage and a good marriage are not necessarily identical. Today's couples expect more emotional intimacy as a requisite to a "good" marriage than couples of a few decades ago. This change is one reason for our high divorce rate today.

If we ask people a simple question—"Overall, how satisfied are you with your marriage: very satisfied, pretty satisfied, or not too satisfied?"—about two-thirds will tell us that they are very satisfied with their marriages. This suggests that marriage is a pretty satisfactory arrangement for most people. Paradoxically, one reason for these high levels of reported marital happiness is our high divorce rate. In the contemporary United States, people who are unhappy in their marriages often get a divorce. The people who stay married are thus a select group who probably have good marriages.

Studies of marital happiness reveal two consistent determinants of marital satisfaction: years married and gender-role agreement (Glenn 1990). You may know of exceptions, but studies have consistently demonstrated that marital happiness is pretty much a downhill slope. Whether they have children or stay childless, most couples experience a decline in satisfaction, particularly within the first years of marriage. Another important determinant of marital happiness is agreement on gender roles. Disagreement over gender roles can take place in several arenas: Do both partners agree on the importance of the wife's career? Do they agree on who should do the housework and take care of the children? Failure to agree on these fundamental aspects of marriage gives rise to dissatisfaction (Perry-Jenkins and Folk 1994; Pina and Bengston 1993).

PARENTING

In the past, most couples entered marriage with the expectation of becoming parents—often immediately. This link between marriage and parenthood is being broken in two ways: nonmarital births and delayed childbearing.

Although most studies show that marital happiness peaks during the honeymoon and takes a downhill course after that, the majority of middle-aged people report that their marriages are very satisfactory. Agreement on gender roles is more important than high income in creating a happy marriage, and couples who share the same values and lifestyle have an easier task in creating a happy as well as a lasting marriage. Many people, both youthful and middle-aged, list their spouses as their best friends—the people in whom they are most comfortable confiding and who give them the most emotional support.

Nonmarital Births. Nearly one third (30 percent) of all births in the United States are to unmarried women. Most of these births (about two-thirds) are to women 20 years of age and older. However, the rate of unmarried childbearing among teenagers has risen sharply; in just 20 years, the rate has increased by over 80 percent. Since teenage mothers are less likely to complete either high school or college, they are also likely to suffer economic hardship (Wu 1996). Consequently, many view the rise in childbearing among U.S. teenagers with alarm (Musick 1993). Interestingly, increased rates of teen births have also been observed in Europe and Japan over the past decade, but the levels of teen births are much lower than in the United States. Studies indicate that teen childbearing is more frequent in the United States than in other industrialized countries in large part because information about sexuality and contraception is less readily available to teenagers in the United States than in Europe. As a result, fewer American women use any form of contraception, and fewer still use the most effective forms (Ahlberg and De Vita 1992).

Delayed Childbearing. Many married women are choosing to postpone childbearing until 5 or even 10 years after their first marriages. Today, 26 percent of American women aged 30 to 34 are childless (U.S. Bureau of the Census 1993e; 1995, Table 102). Although most still intend to have children eventually, childbearing is no longer seen as an inevitable consequence of marriage.

Currently, the average number of children born to American women is approximately two. This small family size is due largely to changes in the role of women and changes in the security of family roles. Although the average woman does not yet place career roles over family roles, women today desire economic security and more personal freedom, both of which are reduced by taking time out to have children (McLaughlin and Associates 1988). If the divorce rate remains high and if women's labor-force participation rises—both of which appear likely—then having children will grow even less attractive.

Thinking Critically

How many children do you plan to have, if any? Why? What do you think the advantages and disadvantages will be? If you do plan to have children, how do you think you and your significant other will decide whose child-care responsibilities are whose?

The Decision to Have a Child: A Leap of Faith. The decision to become a parent is a momentous one. Children are extremely costly, both financially and in terms of emotional wear and tear. Recent estimates suggest that it may cost as much as $133,000 to raise a middle-class child to adulthood (Kalish 1994). Parenthood, however, is one of life's biggest adventures. Few other undertakings require such a large commitment of time and money on so uncertain a return. The list of disadvantages is long and certain: It costs a lot of money, takes an enormous amount of time, disrupts usual activities, and causes at least occasional stress and worry. And once you've started, there is no backing out; it is a lifetime commitment. What are the returns? You hope for love and a sense of family, but you know all around you are parents whose children cause them heartaches and headaches. Parenthood is really the biggest gamble most people will ever take. In spite of this, or maybe because of it, the majority of people want and have children.

Who's Watching the Baby? A central question for the American family today is child care. Relatively high rates of divorce, nonmarital births, and mothers' labor-force participation have threatened previous child-rearing structures. Obviously, we need to reconsider the question, "Who's watching the baby?"

In the traditional American family, there was little question about who was watching the baby: Mom. To a significant extent, this is still true today (Atkinson and Blackwelder 1993). Nevertheless, over two-thirds of married mothers are now in the labor force, and 64 percent of mothers return to the labor force before their children's first birthday. This means that families must come up with alternative child-care arrangements. For most families, this does *not* mean day care. Only about 16 percent of children under five are in day-care centers while their mothers are at work. Approximately one half of all preschoolers are cared for by relatives while their mother is at work; about one out of five children of employed married mothers is cared for by his or her father; and nearly one out of ten is cared for by

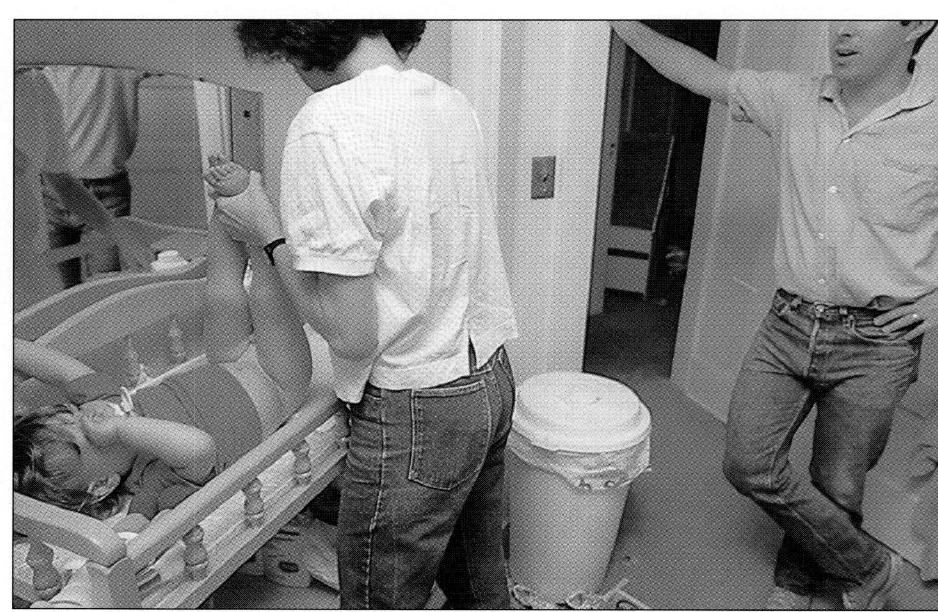

Traditionally, parenting has been a sharply gendered behavior, and the roles of mothers and fathers were very different. Mothers spent much more time with children than did fathers. Today, approximately 64 percent of American mothers are back in the labor force before their children's first birthday, and children of married parents are likely to spend nearly equal time with dad and mom. Nevertheless, many child-care activities remain disproportionately mothers' responsibility.

the mother herself, either working at home or away from home (U.S. Bureau of the Census 1995, Table 615). Frequently this arrangement involves not day care but *night* care. Nearly a quarter of all two-earner couples with children work alternate shifts so that one of them can be home with the children. (Day care is also discussed in Chapter 6.)

There is growing emphasis on the father's role in child care. Both women and men expect that fathers will do more than play catch with their children on Saturday afternoons and provide economic support for them. They expect fathers to change diapers and take part in the day-to-day responsibility for child care. Studies show that attitudes have changed faster than actual behavior (Ahlberg and De Vita 1992, 27), but there is little doubt that the parenting responsibilities of married parents are less sharply divided by sex than before (LaRossa 1988).

Of course, fewer than 60 percent of American children live with both of their biological parents. Figure 14.3 shows living arrangements of U.S. children. More than a quarter live with a single parent, most often the mother, and another 15 percent are being raised in a stepfamily situation. How does parenting work in these families?

Single Parents. As addressed earlier in this chapter, lower marriage rates have increased the number of unmarried women at the same time that changes in sexual behavior have increased their risk of pregnancy. As a result, an increasing proportion of U.S. babies are born to unmarried women: Thirty percent of the next generation will start life in a fatherless home. This is a major change in fertility patterns and family structure. Partly as a result, before they reach the age of 18, an estimated two thirds of all U.S. children born in the 1980s and 1990s will spend some time living with a single parent. Of those whose parents divorce and remarry, nearly half will experience the breakup of the second marriage, too.

Most single parenting is done by mothers: Nearly seven out of eight single-parent families in the United States are headed by women. There has been a slight

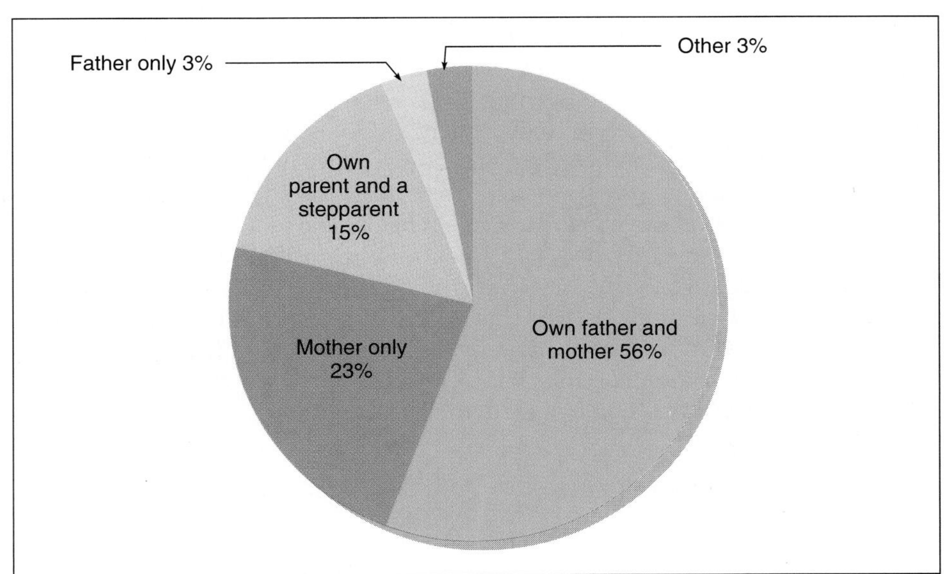

FIGURE 14.3
LIVING ARRANGEMENTS OF CHILDREN UNDER 18 IN THE UNITED STATES, 1992

Current rates of births outside marriage and divorce have substantially reduced the likelihood that a child will grow up with both parents. These figures from 1992 show that only a little over half of all American children under the age of 18 live with both of their biological parents.

SOURCE: Adapted from U.S. Bureau of the Census 1993, Tables 78, 80; 1995, Tables 72 and 76.

increase in fathers having custody after divorce, especially when the children are older or are boys. This has been more than offset, however, by the formation of single-mother families through nonmarital births.

These changes in family experience have had a negative impact on children. In more than 25 percent of cases, the noncustodial parent disappears entirely from the child's life—no child support and no visits. In many other cases, both contact and child support are sporadic. As a result, the child's economic and social welfare often depends on a single adult.

Perhaps because single parents cannot provide as much money or time as two parents, studies show that, on the average, children raised in single-parent families have lower self-esteem and academic performance and poorer-quality social relations (Amato and Keith 1991a; McLanahan and Booth 1989). It is important to note, however, that children of divorce do no worse on most of these measures than children raised in conflict-ridden families (Amato and Keith 1991b).

Stepparenting. It is estimated that 60 percent of Americans will live in stepfamilies at some point over their life course (Bumpass, Raley, and Sweet 1995). Children in stepfamilies are most frequently being raised by their mother and a stepfather.

If parenting is difficult, stepparenting is more so. In addition to the problems all parents face, stepparents often have to contend with an ex-husband or an ex-wife, plus the trials of giving equal love and attention to his children, her children, and their children. As a result, both stepparents and stepchildren indicate they experience more conflict and stress in stepfamilies than in original families (Peterson 1996). One way stepfamilies relieve this stress is by encouraging teenage stepchildren to leave home as soon as possible; the other "solution" is a divorce rate that is nearly double the divorce rate for families without stepchildren (White and Booth 1985).

The Empty Nest: Crisis or Release? For the first 18 years or so of their lives, children usually live under the same roof as at least one of their parents. More years of schooling and the postponement of marriage have extended the period during which young adults stay with their parents: In 1992, 60 percent of all men aged 18 to 24 were still living at home, up from 43 percent in 1970.

The reason adult children are staying at home longer has more to do with economics than it does with lack of independence (Goldscheider and Goldscheider 1994). Studies show that children are more eager to leave home than parents are to have them go. Traditional parents are especially likely to expect that their children will stay at home until they get married (Goldscheider and Goldscheider 1989).

Nevertheless, the majority of parents look forward to their children's eventual departure. That doesn't mean they want their children to disappear from their lives—far from it. One study showed that parents respond positively to the empty nest only if they retain frequent contact with their children (White and Edwards 1990). Parenthood is an important lifelong role, and most parents want and have frequent contact with their children all of their lives.

Across the Generations

Despite all the publicity accorded to very real trends such as divorce and nonmarital births, family ties remain very important to Americans. Over two-thirds of

American adults talk to their parents at least once a week; one-fifth talk to a parent every day (Gallup Report 1989c). In addition, siblings keep in touch with each other, and grandchildren keep in touch with their grandparents. The parent-child bond is the strongest family relationship, and it stays strong until very old age.

The nature of intergenerational relationships between adult children and their older parents depends very substantially on the ages of the generations. When the older generation falls into the "young old" category, the older generation is, on the average, still providing more help for their children than the children are for their parents (Hogan, Eggebeen, and Clogg 1993). They are helping with down payments and grandchildren's college educations or providing temporary living space for children who have divorced or lost their jobs.

As the senior generation moves into the "old old" category, however, relationships must be renegotiated (Mutran and Reitzes 1984). Even in the "old old" category, most people continue to be largely self-sufficient, but eventually most need help of some kind—shopping, home repairs, and social support. Although these services are available from community agencies, most older people rely heavily on their families, especially their daughters.

It has been said that one of the most important roles that women play in American families is that of *kinkeepers*. They send the birthday cards, organize family parties, and generally keep the family in touch with one another. One result of this gender-based division of labor is that women are usually closer to their relatives than men are and that female relatives are closer to each other than are male relatives. The mother-daughter and sister-sister bonds are substantially closer than the father-son and brother-brother bonds (Gallup Report 1989c).

THINKING CRITICALLY

Do you know anyone who is taking care of an elderly parent or grandparent? Why do you think that person, rather than some other family member, has assumed that responsibility? What personal characteristics and what social characteristics are involved?

MINORITY FAMILIES

Most of what we have said about the American family is true of all types of families, regardless of race or ethnicity. There are, however, two ways in which African American and Hispanic families are distinct: higher rates of female headship and higher reliance on an extended kin network.

Historically, disadvantaged minority groups (African Americans, Hispanics, Asians) have compensated for economic marginality through an extensive kin-based support network. They have been more likely to live in extended families, to live close to their relatives, and to exchange significant economic and social support with kin (Ruggles 1994). The strong extended family reflects subcultural norms about family roles and responsibilities as well as a "resilient response to socioeconomic conditions of poverty and unemployment" (Taylor 1986, 67).

In the relatively recent past, the stronger extended family system among minority Americans more or less made up for higher rates of female headship. In contemporary America, however, the rates of female headship are much higher, and there is consensus that the old safety net of extended family doesn't work as well (Billingsley 1989). This is a special problem for African American families. Black women have higher rates of nonmarital births (69 percent of black infants are born to unmarried women), lower marriage rates, and higher divorce rates. The result is that 48 percent of all black families are female headed compared with 25 percent of all Hispanic families and 14 percent of all white families (see Figure 14.4).

The chief cause of high rates of female headship is the weak position of minority males in the labor force (Gerson 1993; Schoen and Kluegel 1988; Tucker and Taylor 1989). The breadwinner role continues to be the central male role in the

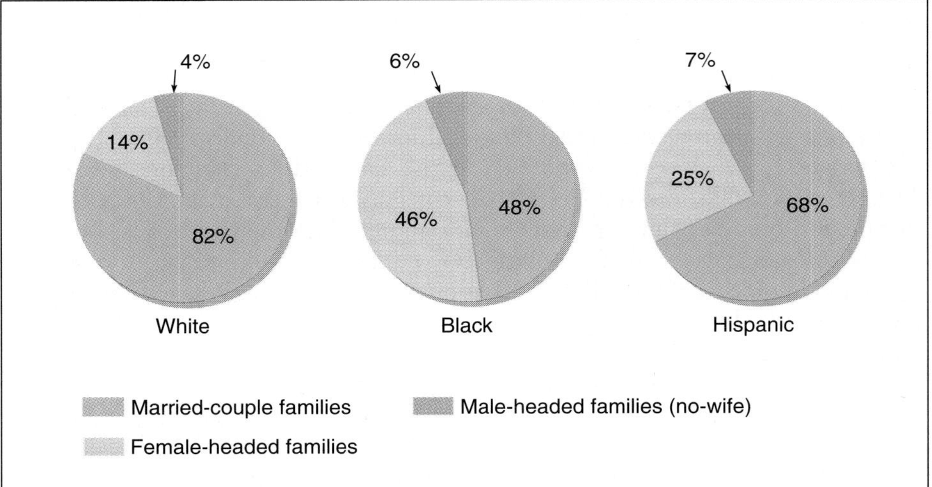

FIGURE 14.4
FAMILY TYPES BY RACE AND HISPANIC ORIGIN, 1994

Minority families, especially African American families, have high rates of female headship. The primary underlying cause of these high rates is the disadvantaged position of the minority male in the labor market.

SOURCE: U.S. Bureau of the Census 1995, Table 70.

family: If he isn't working regularly, isn't bringing in a steady paycheck, then he has only a marginal place in the family. When male unemployment rates are high, marriage rates go down, and divorce rates go up. Thus, the key to strengthening minority families lies in changing the structure of economic opportunity.

We turn now to a discussion of problems in the American family.

PROBLEMS IN THE AMERICAN FAMILY

There are couples who swear that they never have an argument and never disagree. These people must certainly be in the minority, however; most intimate relations involve some stress and strain. We become concerned when these stresses and strains affect the mental and physical health of the individuals and when they affect the stability of society. In this section, we cover two problems in the American family: violence and divorce.

TABLE 14.3
VIOLENCE IN THE AMERICAN FAMILY

Nobody likes to admit that he or she has behaved violently and tried to hurt family members. As a result of strong social desirability bias, these figures probably seriously underestimate the amount of violence that actually occurs in American families.

	PERCENT REPORTING SEVERE VIOLENCE
PARENT TO CHILD	10.7%
WIFE TO HUSBAND	4.4
HUSBAND TO WIFE	3.0

SOURCE: Adapted from Straus and Gelles, 1988.

VIOLENCE IN FAMILIES

Child abuse is nothing new, nor is wife battering. These forms of family violence, however, didn't receive much attention until recent years. In a celebrated court case in 1871, a social worker had to invoke laws against cruelty to animals in order to remove a child from a violent home. There were laws specifying how to treat animals, but no restrictions on how wives and children were to be treated. In recent years, however, we have become much more aware of and less tolerant of abuse and violence.

The incidence of abuse is hard to measure. The social desirability bias on this question is enormously high (that is, survey respondents are highly likely to answer according to what is socially acceptable). Nevertheless, a series of studies by scholars at Rhode Island University provides a relatively reliable set of figures on abuse. Table 14.3 shows the percent of the population reporting severe violence in the year prior to being interviewed. The operational definition of "severe violence" is a report of one or more of the following: kicked, bit, or hit with fist; hit or tried to hit with some object; beat up; threatened with a gun or a knife; used a gun or a knife. Using this definition, 10.7 percent reported severe violence from a parent to a child, 4.4 percent reported severe violence from a wife to a husband, and 3 percent reported severe violence from a husband to a wife (Straus and Gelles 1986).

These data show that when "severe violence" is defined as the Rhode Island University scholars operationalized it (for example, including *trying* to hit someone with an object or *threatening* someone with a knife or gun), the victim is more likely to be the husband than the wife. Some men's activist groups have argued that this fact goes largely ignored and that battered husbands need shelters and other help as much as battered wives (Cose 1994). Nevertheless, the fact is that wives, as well as girlfriends and ex-wives, are far more likely to be seriously injured by their male partners than vice-versa (Dobash and Dobash 1992). For one thing, a blow from a woman is much less likely to cause physical damage than is a blow from a man. According to the National Crime Victimization Survey of the U.S. Justice Department, in over 90 percent of violent crimes between intimates, the victim is female. In 1992, 70 percent of victims murdered by intimates were female (U.S. Department of Justice 1994).

THINKING CRITICALLY

How would you test this hypothesis: "Although husband abuse is slightly more frequent than wife abuse, it is less serious"? What ethical issues would your research design raise? How might society respond adequately to *both* wife and husband abuse?

Family violence is not restricted to any class or race. It occurs in the homes of lawyers as well as the homes of welfare mothers. Studies suggest that violence is most typical in families with multiple problems: unemployment, alcohol and drug abuse, money worries, stepchildren, physically or mentally handicapped members, or members who were abused themselves as children (Gelles and Straus 1988). Although these problems can occur in any social class, it is also true that lower-class families are more likely to experience unemployment and money worries that add to the difficulty of coping with normal family stresses.

Solutions to family violence are complex. The first step, however, is to make it clear that violence is inappropriate and illegal. New laws against spousal rape and other forms of family violence may clarify what used to be rather fuzzy norms about whether family violence was appropriate (Straus and Gelles 1986).

DIVORCE

In the United States, more than two million adults and approximately one million children are affected annually by divorce. The **divorce rate,** calculated as the number of divorces each year per 1000 married women, rose steadily since World War II, then began to level off in the past few years (National Center for Health Statistics 1996). In 1993, it stood at 20.5—that is, 20.5 out of 1000, or about 2 percent, of all married women in the United States divorce annually. Another way of looking at divorce is to calculate the probability that a marriage will *ever* end in divorce—the **lifetime divorce probability.** Of marriages begun in 1890, for example, the proportion eventually ending in divorce was approximately 10 percent (Cherlin 1981). Experts estimate that half of first marriages contracted in the last decade will end in divorce (see Figure 14.5) (Bumpass, Raley, and Sweet 1995).

The **divorce rate** is calculated as the number of divorces each year per 1,000 married women.

Lifetime divorce probability is the estimated probability that a marriage will ever end in divorce.

Which Marriages End in Divorce? Half of recent first marriages are expected to eventually end in divorce, but half will last. For second marriages, the odds of failure are higher. What are the factors that make a marriage more likely to fail? Table 14.4 displays some of the predictors of marital failure within the first five years of

FIGURE 14.5
CHANGING PROBABILITY OF DIVORCE, 1870–1995

There has been a dramatic increase in the likelihood that marriages will end in divorce. Half of recent first marriages are expected to end in divorce.

SOURCE: Adapted from Cherlin 1981 (reprinted by permission, Harvard University Press); Martin and Bumpass 1989; and Bumpass, Raley, and Sweet 1995.

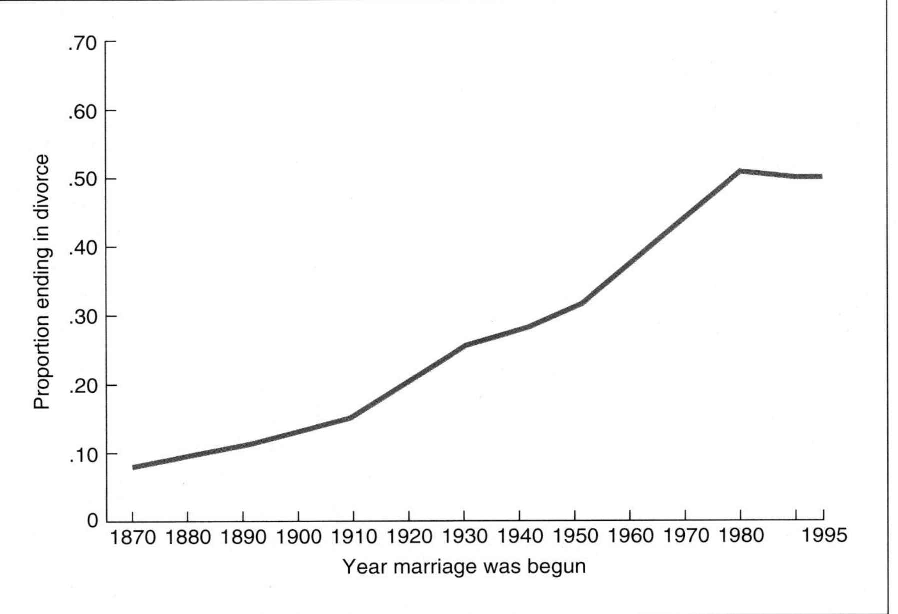

marriage. A review of empirical results over the last decades suggests that six factors are especially important (White 1990):

- *Age at marriage*. Probably the best predictor of divorce is a youthful age at marriage. Marrying as a teenager or even in one's early 20s *doubles* one's divorce probability relative to those who marry later. Not surprisingly, if you are already on a second marriage before your 20th birthday, your chances of failure are very high. (See Table 14.4.)
- *Parental divorce*. People who were raised in single-parent families because their parents divorced are more likely to divorce.
- *Premarital childbearing*. Having a child before marriage reduces the stability of subsequent marriages. Premarital conception followed by a postmarital birth, however, does not seem to increase the likelihood of divorce.
- *Education*. The higher one's education, the less likely one's marriage is to end in divorce. In part, this is because people with higher educations are likely to come from two-parent families, avoid premarital childbearing, and marry later. Independent of these other factors, however, higher education does reduce the chances of divorce.
- *Race*. African Americans are substantially more likely than white Americans (Hispanic or non-Hispanic) to end their marriages in divorce. Even if we restrict the comparison to women who marry late, go to college, and have no premarital births, African American women are twice as likely as white women to divorce (Martin and Bumpass 1989).
- *Bad behavior*. As you might expect, alcohol and drug abuse, adultery, and abusive behavior are all predictors of divorce. Surveys that ask newly divorced people what happened in their marriages find that these bad behaviors crop up frequently. One woman said, "He was running around and the first time we had sex after the baby's birth, he gave me VD." Another ex-spouse described the former mate as "a

TABLE 14.4
PROBABILITY OF MARITAL BREAKING UP WITHIN THE FIRST FIVE YEARS

The probability that a first marriage will ever end in divorce is about 50 percent. If we limit our focus to the first five years of marriage, about 23 percent of all first marriages and 27 percent of second marriages end in this period. Divorce is more likely for those who marry young, those with low levels of educational attainment, African Americans, and those who had a child before the marriage.

	FIRST MARRIAGES	SECOND MARRIAGES
TOTAL	23%	27%
AGE AT MARRIAGE		
14–19	31	40
20–22	26	26
23–29	15	27
30+	14	14
EDUCATION		
LESS THAN 12 YEARS	33	36
12 YEARS	26	26
13 YEARS OR MORE	16	22
CHILDREN BEFORE MARRIAGE		
NO	21	24
YES	36	28
RACE		
WHITE	22	26
BLACK	36	43
HISPANIC	24	28

SOURCE: Martin and Bumpass 1989.

liar and a cheater and a gambler" (Booth et al. 1984). Although many people just drift apart, citing irreconcilable differences, nearly one-third of the people who seek divorce have a specific and important grievance.

Societal Factors. Age at marriage, premarital childbearing, education, and bad behavior affect whether a particular marriage succeeds or fails. These personal characteristics, however, cannot account for why an estimated 50 percent of recent first marriages will fail. The shift from a lifetime divorce probability of 10 to 50 percent within the last century is a social problem, not a personal trouble, and to explain it we need to look at social structure.

The change in marital relationships is probably most clearly associated with changes in economic institutions. Rising divorce rates are not unique to the United

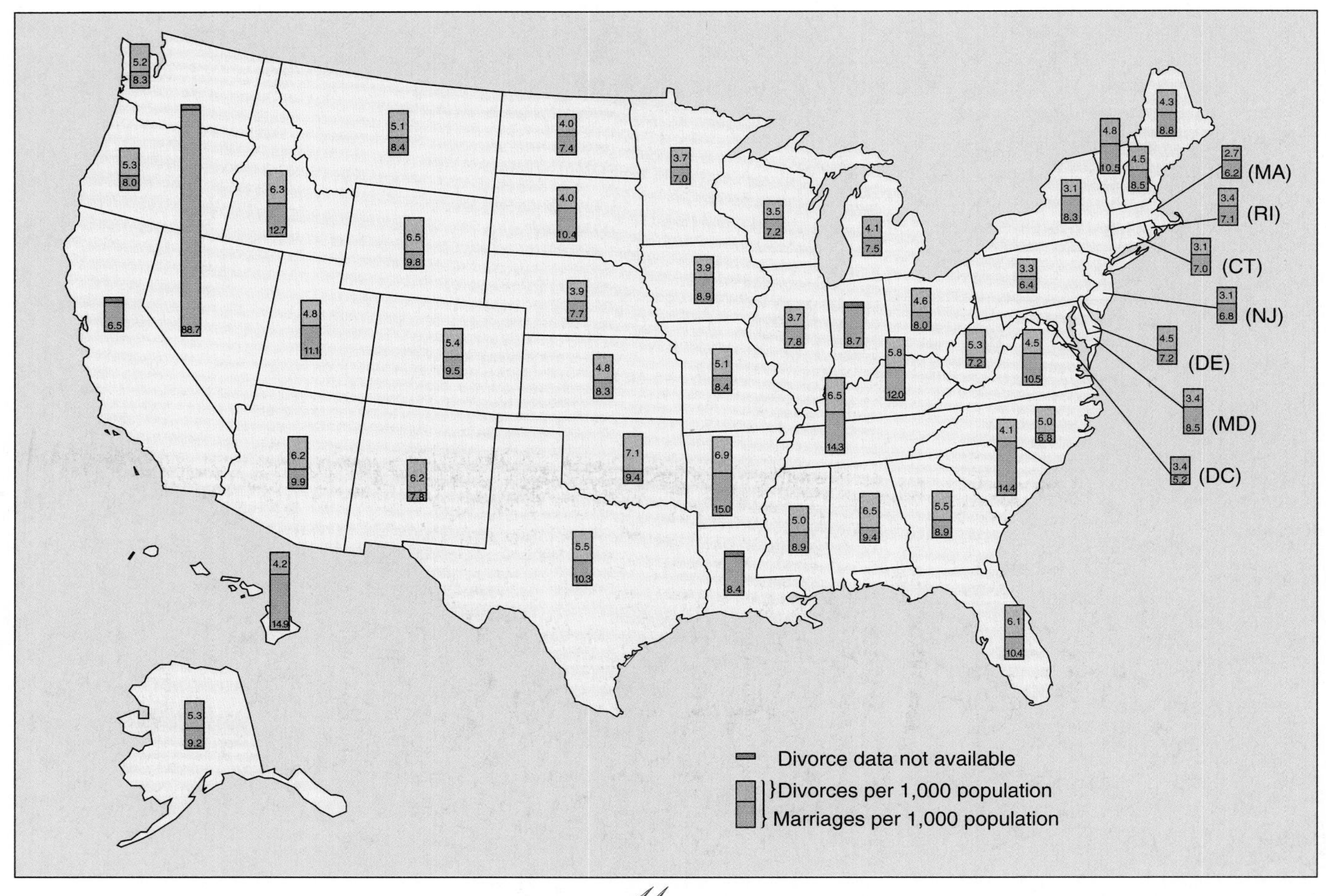

MAP 14.1
DIVORCE RATE BY STATE, 1993
(PER 1,000 POPULATION)

SOURCE: U.S. Bureau of the Census 1995, Table 149.

States (see Table 14.5). Although divorce has always been more prevalent in the United States than elsewhere, most industrialized nations have experienced substantial increases in divorce. In Sweden and Germany, for instance, the divorce rate doubled between 1960 and 1988 (Ahlberg and De Vita 1992). In these countries and in the United States, the shift from an industrial and agricultural to a service economy, a change detailed in Chapter 9, has revolutionized the technologies and relationships essential to production. One result of this revolution is that an earner's chief economic assets are education and experience. You can walk away from a marriage and take these assets along; the same is not true with land, which is often tied up in family relationships. Another result is the increased opportunity for women to support themselves outside marriage. Thus, women and men are less and less impelled to marry or to stay married by economic necessity. Since no incentive

TABLE 14.5
DIVORCE RATES FOR SELECTED COUNTRIES, 1960–1992

	DIVORCES PER 1,000 MARRIED WOMEN				
COUNTRY	1960	1970	1980	1990	1992
UNITED STATES	9	15	23	21	21
CANADA	2	6	11	11	11
FRANCE	3	3	6	8	9
GERMANY*	4	5	6	8	7
JAPAN	4	4	5	5	6
SWEDEN	5	7	11	12	12
UNITED KINGDOM	2	5	12	13	12

* Prior to 1991, data are for former West Germany.

SOURCE: U.S. Bureau of the Census 1995, Table 1366.

for marriage more effective than economic need has arisen to replace this factor, marriages have less institutional support than before (Fine and Fine 1994).

Divorce and Poverty. Empirical data in the United States reveal a substantial link between divorce and poverty. There are three reasons. First, poor families are more likely to divorce than well-off families.

Second, divorce reduces family income—especially for women and children. A simple example shows how this can happen. Say that a couple has one child and a total family income of $42,000 (the husband earns $25,000, and the wife earns $17,000). Each family member has an income of $14,000. After the divorce, the mother will usually get custody of the child, and the father will be ordered to pay 17 percent ($4,250) of his gross income in child support (Beller and Graham 1986). After the breakup, the husband will have an income of $20,750, and the wife and child will have incomes of $10,625 each. In short, his per capita income will go up substantially, while his ex-wife and child will each experience an income drop of nearly one-third (Smock 1993).

A third factor linking divorce to poverty is that many noncustodial parents fail to pay child support regularly (U.S. Bureau of the Census 1995, Table 609). When this occurs, the economic damage of divorce is often even greater (Peters 1993; Seltzer 1994).

Despite the fact that never-married motherhood has significantly increased, rising divorce rates are still the primary cause of rising rates of female headship, particularly among whites (U.S. Bureau of the Census 1994b, xii). In addition to the important factor of low wages, rising rates of female headship are a primary cause of rising rates of poverty among women and children. In 1993, nearly one out of four children was living below the poverty line, compared with one in seven 25 years earlier (U.S. Bureau of the Census 1995, Table 745). Because childhood poverty has been shown to have significant negative effects on nearly every dimension of life, from educational attainment to mental health (Acock and Kiecolt 1989), increasing childhood poverty is perceived to be a serious problem.

MAKING DADS PAY. Public policy has been directed primarily at the third link in the chain between divorce and poverty: making dads pay. In 1988, federal legislation was passed to increase noncustodial parents' support of their children. This legislation sets higher minimum child support awards and, more important, sets new enforcement procedures. Beginning in 1994, every parent required to pay child support has the amount automatically deducted from his or her paycheck. The easy passage of this legislation reflects the strong consensus about "a father's first responsibility: He must support his children, even if he no longer lives with them and even if he marries again" (Cherlin 1990, 2).

This new legislation has helped somewhat (Teachman 1991). But mostly it represents a moral victory rather than a solution. Because many of the fathers whose children are in poverty are unemployed or have low earnings, their contributions do not help much. One study estimated that full enforcement would reduce the number of children receiving welfare by only 25 percent (Mclanahan, Garfinkel, and Watson 1986). More recent research supports that finding (Braver, Fitzpatrick, and Bay 1991).

THE DEEPER ISSUE: GENDER AND THE FAMILY. A primary reason that divorce increases childhood poverty is that children normally live with the lower-earning parent (the mother) after divorce. In the example given here, for instance, per capita income would have been unchanged—with everybody still getting approximately $14,000—if the child had lived with the father after divorce and the mother had paid 17 percent of her income in support.

This raises several deeper issues about gender and the family. Although we could "solve" the poverty problem by giving custody of a child to the higher-paid parent, this overlooks a critical linkage between family and the labor market: Women are paid less *because* they have parented more (see Chapter 12). Getting custody and earning less both reflect the fact that, on the average, women devote more time to their families and less time to their careers than do men. The root cause of women's and children's poverty is the gender-based division of labor in the family (Scanzoni 1989). An intact marriage disguises women's and children's dependence on their husbands and fathers under the cloak of a division of labor. Divorce brings this dependence out in the open.

HOW SERIOUS ARE PROBLEMS IN THE AMERICAN FAMILY? A THEORETICAL APPROACH

In Chapter 4, we noted that some people view institutions as constraints that force people into uncomfortable and perhaps oppressive relationships; others see institutions as providing the stability and comfort frequently associated with old shoes. This conflict of views is nowhere more present than in the case of the family.

Theoretical viewpoints sharply influence perceptions of the health of the modern family (Adams 1985). If the family is an oppressive institution, then divorce is a form of liberation; if the family is the source of individual and community strength, then divorce undermines society. In this section, we briefly review some of the major criticisms of the contemporary family and conclude with a perspective on the future.

Loss of Commitment. Critics argue that a major problem with the American family, and some would argue with American culture, is an accent on individual growth at the expense of commitment. This criticism is most likely to come from structural functionalists, who traditionally stress the subordination of individual to community needs, but it also comes from symbolic interactionists concerned with stable personal identity.

The most prominent symptom of the alleged emphasis on individual happiness and growth at the expense of long-term commitment is the rapid rise in the number of women who are raising children on their own. Because men don't want to be tied down by wives and children and because wives don't want to be tied down by husbands, fathers have walked away and mothers have let them, even encouraged them, according to this perspective. The result is that the basic family unit, in the sense of long-term commitment to sharing and support, is the mother-child pair. Husband-wife and father-child relationships are increasingly seen to be temporary and even optional. For many critics, this increasingly voluntary nature of family ties is dysfunctional, reducing the stability of the family and reducing its ability to perform one of its major tasks: caring for children. Among the ill consequences these critics note are the increasing proportion of women and children in poverty.

Thinking Critically

Should U.S. laws and courts make divorces more difficult to obtain? Why, or why not?

Welfare Changes and Family Commitment. Recent federal and state government efforts to change welfare are motivated both by the high federal deficit and by some policy makers' desire to renew Americans' commitment to two-parent families. A primary issue involves the federal government's ending Aid to Families with Dependent Children (AFDC or ADC) as of July 1997. Established in 1935 under the Social Security Act, AFDC was created primarily to help widows raise their children. The program increasingly served the never-married and divorced. In 1992, enrollment reached nearly 14 million recipients—almost 5 percent of the American population (U.S. Bureau of the Census 1995, Tables 589 and 591). The proportion of whites, blacks, and Hispanics receiving AFDC were 3 percent, 16 percent, and 10 percent, respectively (U.S. Bureau of the Census 1995, Table 591). Even with these disparate percentages, however, in terms of absolute numbers, more whites than blacks have received AFDC.

Legislators have proposed denying benefits to mothers under age 18 and denying additional benefits to any mother who has an additional child while receiving federal or state benefits. Proposals also require recipients to become employed after two years on welfare benefits and to name the child's father before receiving benefits. A major goal of these proposals is to reduce births outside marriage, with particular focus on teen unwed births. Monies saved by denying welfare benefits to unwed teen mothers would go to fund programs to reduce out-of-wedlock pregnancies and promote adoption (Gillespie and Schellhas 1994; "What the States Are Doing" 1995).

More generally, the goal of these changes is to renew commitment to marriage and to raising children in two-parent families. Not everyone agrees with these changes, as you might suspect. Some opponents predict that this kind of welfare "reform" will result in more children living in poverty. Other opponents wonder whether strengthening the nuclear family as we know it is necessarily a good thing (Stacey 1993; Risman and Ferree 1995).

Oppression. Critics from a conflict perspective are more apt to criticize the family for its oppression of women and children. They point to the lower power of

The contemporary American family is experiencing many problems—high levels of divorce, illegitimacy, and child abuse, among others. The publicity accorded to these problems has led some commentators to conclude that the American family is dying. Despite very real problems, however, family relationships continue to be a major source of satisfaction for most Americans across the entire life course. The importance of the tasks families perform suggests that they need to be moved closer to the top of the national agenda.

women and children relative to men, to working women's inability to get help with the housework, and to the number of women and children who suffer abuse in the family. From this perspective, the family is not particularly changed for the worse: It has traditionally been an oppressive institution maintained by force and fraud. These critics do note the development of greater egalitarianism in the contemporary family but generally find these changes too slow.

The major developing problem from this perspective is that women's and children's independence from husbands and fathers in the family is coming before their independence in the marketplace. The solution they recommend is equal opportunity and equal pay for women and state support for children in the form of family allowances.

Perspectives on the Future. Some of the functions performed by the traditional family, such as care of the dependent, are not as often performed just by families today as in the past. Nevertheless, the family continues to perform vital functions for society and individuals.

The family is the central socializing agent, the arena in which we develop our self-concepts, learn to interact with others, and internalize society's norms. Without the strong bonds of love and affection that characterize family ties, completing these developmental tasks is difficult, if not impossible. Thus, the family is essential for the production of socialized members, people who can fit in and play a productive part in society.

The family and the larger kin group are important for individuals not just in childhood but throughout the life course. To cite just a few examples, people with close ties to their kin report greater satisfaction with their lives, their marriages, and their health; they are less likely to abuse their children or get divorced; and they are more likely to be able to ride out personal and family crises (LaVee, McCubbin, and Patterson 1985; McGhee 1985; Rosenthal 1985).

Given these benefits to both the individual and society, it would seem to be a reasonable goal to keep and support the family while simultaneously reducing some of its more oppressive features. This goal is not impossible. Despite current rates of divorce, illegitimacy, and domestic abuse, there are signs of health in the family: the durability of the mother-child bond, the frequency of remarriage, the frequency with which stepfathers are willing to step in and support other men's children, the frequency with which elderly persons rely on *and get* help from their children.

There is no doubt that the family is changing. When you ask young people what their fathers did when they were growing up, you are increasingly likely to hear, "What father?" or "Which father?" These recent changes must be viewed as at least potentially troublesome. At present, we have no institutionalized mechanisms comparable to the family for giving individuals social support or caring for children. The importance of these tasks suggests that the family and especially children need to be moved closer to the top of the national agenda.

SOCIOLOGY ON THE NET

The changing American family is cause for a great deal of concern and hope. Many are uneasy about changing what they see as a good situation, while others see the changes as bringing new freedoms and fairness to the family. Let's see how the family has changed in recent years by returning to our old friend, the U.S. Census Bureau.

`http://www.census.gov/population/pop-profile/toc.html`

Start by reading the selection on **Households and Families**. What is a family and how does the government define the term "family"? Who is included and who is left out? What percent of families include children? What percent of families are headed by single parents and how do blacks and whites differ?

Go back to the **table of contents** and open the selection entitled **Marital Status and Living Arrangements**. What is happening to the median age at first marriage? Why has it changed? What do you feel is a good age for young people to marry? Why do you feel that way?

With both parents working, finding decent childcare has become an important part of family life. Return to the **table of contents** and click on **Child Care**

APPLICATIONS IN DIVERSITY

Is the Gay Family a Contradiction in Terms?

Analysis of the family institution often focuses exclusively on heterosexuals. A little reflection, however, will show that most of the issues discussed in this chapter—mate selection, intergenerational ties, and even child rearing—are relevant to the millions of Americans who are largely or entirely homosexual in their sexual preference. Almost all have traditional family ties: They are close to their parents and perhaps brothers and sisters; many have long-term partners despite the lack of normative support for their unions. A substantial minority have children, many from previous marriages. Some states make it difficult for gay males or lesbians to gain custody of their biological children from prior heterosexual unions. However, several states have recently opened the doors for legal adoption of children by homosexuals, reasoning that unconventional homes are preferable to institutionalized care. Estimates suggest that there are between 6 and 14 million gay and lesbian biological or custodial parents in the United States (Bozett 1987; Singer and Deschamps 1994). There have been no large, national studies of how these parents and their children fare. Available evidence, however, suggests that they face the same dilemmas of other single-parent families and stepfamilies plus the added problems of coping with neighborhood and playground prejudice and discrimination aimed at the parents' lifestyles.

In a landmark 1986 decision upholding a Georgia law criminalizing same-sex sexual activity, Supreme Court Justice Byron White argued that laws granting privacy rights to families did not apply to homosexuals. There was, he said, "No connection between family, marriage, or procreation on the one hand and homosexual activity on the other" (cited in Weston, 1991, 208). Is Justice White right: Are heterosexuals the only ones with families?

Because lesbians and gay men have parents, siblings, and cousins, the definition of *family* at issue in this decision is obviously a narrow one that centers around marriage and children. On the question of marriage, the Justice is correct by definition in suggesting that lesbians and gay men do not have families. In a few jurisdictions, gay or lesbian partners may gain some legal protection by registering their union as a "domestic partnership," but no state allows them to marry. Same-sex lovers obviously cannot produce children from their union, but they can have children in a variety of other ways. As mentioned, many lesbians and gay men can (and do) have children from previous heterosexual relationships; in some states, they can adopt children; and lesbian women can have children through artificial insemination. As a result, somewhere between 6 and 14 million children have homosexual parents (Bozett 1987; Singer and Deschamps 1994).

SOCIOLOGY ON THE NET (Continued)

Arrangements. Who provides childcare in most families? How are these statistics changing? What are the reasons for the changes?

There are many different segments of our society that see the changing family as an important social issue. Many conservative religious organizations stress what they call "family values." One such organization is the American Family Association.

`http://www.afa.net/`

Browse through this home page. Read the section on **Who is AFA?** Note their **Current Boycott Information**. Scroll down to the section entitled **AFA Resources**. Open the **AFA Journal** and check out the topics. What kind of family values are stressed? What actions are being taken by this organization to realize their goals? Have you encountered other organizations that share these goals? Hint – remember the Internet exercises from Chapter 7?

As families change, there is mounting pressure to change the older definitions to accommodate the diverse family arrangements that are now becoming more evi-

APPLICATIONS IN DIVERSITY

The issue of gay families has become a public issue in both gay and straight communities (Editors, *Harvard Law Review*, 1989). Should gays be allowed to adopt children? Should being gay be sufficient by itself to make a parent unfit for child custody or visitation rights? Should lesbians be able to use artificial insemination? Should gay and lesbian partners be allowed to legally marry, so that their health insurance and Social Security benefits can be shared by their partners?

These are questions that go to the heart of the family. The traditional view is that homosexual unions are both unnatural and sinful. Others define the family by long-term commitment, and they are willing to tolerate and encourage a variety of family forms—including gay and lesbian families—as long as they contribute to stable and nurturing environments for adults and children. A 1996 poll found that only 28 percent of Americans favor the legalization of gay marriages, while 67 percent are against it (Saad 1996).

It is not only heterosexuals who question the desirability of a gay family (Weston 1991). Many gay men and lesbians reject the idea of family as an oppressive straitjacket of conformity and patriarchy. They argue that family is an oppressive institution that traps women and men into rigid gender roles and ties us forever to people we don't like. One of the good things about the gay community, they contend, is that people can form "chosen families" based on shared interests and affection.

Others within the gay community find that family is a good thing, and they would like to stretch the legal as well as the functional bonds of family to include same-sex marriage, adoptions, and protection for child custody. Contrary to Justice White's opinion, gay men and lesbians obviously do have families. The question society must address is whether such families should receive the same legal recognition and protection (through access to legal marriage, for example) as other families.

THINKING CRITICALLY

How do *you* define *family?* Using your definition, is a gay male or lesbian family a "real" family? If gay males or lesbians are raising children, should they be afforded the respect and support that society gives to heterosexual parents? Why do we tend to define families as heterosexual, do you think?

dent. One segment of the population that supports broadening definitions of the family are gays and lesbians who want the same legal benefits of marriage that others enjoy.

`http://www.eskimo.com/~demian/index.html`

You have reached the home page of the Partners Task force for Gay and Lesbian Couples. Begin your browsing by opening the **Table of Contents**. Click on the topic box under the heading of **Legal Marriage Essays**. Scroll down to and read the selection called **Everything Possible**. Now go back and read the **Most Compelling Reasons for Legal Marriage**. Finally, let's check out what two politicians have to say about a recent bill in Congress. Return to the table of contents and click on **A Mean Bill** and **I Have Anguished**. (Note: the bill under discussion passed the House of Representative with an overwhelming majority.) What marriage benefits do gays and lesbians seek? What harm could come to society from allowing gay and lesbian marriages? Where do you stand?

SUMMARY

1 Marriage, family, and kinship are the most basic institutions in society. In all societies, these institutions meet such universal needs as regulation of sexual behavior, replacement through reproduction, child care, and socialization.

2 Cross-cultural comparisons demonstrate that the structure and function of the family vary considerably. Preindustrial economies tend to place greater emphasis on extended families, on family participation in mate selection, and on male dominance. In industrial societies, norms prescribe a nuclear family, individual choice in mate selection, and more egalitarian authority patterns.

3 Major changes in the U.S. family include the increased probability of divorce, increased illegitimacy, increased single parenting, and increased labor-force participation by wives and mothers.

4 Because of postponement of marriage and high divorce rates, dating is no longer just a teenage activity. Sexual relations are a common aspect of contemporary courtship, producing high rates of unwanted pregnancy and an increased risk of sexually transmitted diseases. Cohabitation is a common courtship stage.

5 Marriage and family roles continue to be sharply gendered, and agreement on gender roles is crucial for marital satisfaction. Men's breadwinning role and women's child-care and housekeeping roles are changing slowly, and there has been an increase in wives' and mothers' labor-force participation and increased normative support for egalitarian authority patterns.

6 Parenting has changed substantially. Divorce and nonmarital births mean many children do not live with both of their parents. It is also likely that their mother is employed. As a result of dilemmas about child care, American women are choosing to have relatively few children.

7 Family roles are important to most Americans. Although few parents and children want to live together after the children grow up, the ties remain important. Family members tend to keep in close contact and provide substantial support to one another.

8 Minority families have historically been distinct from majority families on two dimensions: higher rates of female headship (this is especially true for African American families) and stronger extended kin networks. Poor economic prospects for minority males are the major cause of higher rates of female headship.

9 Family violence is relatively commonplace in American homes. It is more characteristic of parent-child relationships than of husband-wife relationships. It is strongly related to multiple family problems.

10 It is estimated that 50 percent of first marriages will end in divorce. Factors associated with divorce include age at marriage, parental divorce, premarital childbearing, education, race, and bad behavior. Reduced economic dependence on marriage underlies many of these trends.

11 Divorce is the primary cause of rising rates of poverty for women and children. Public policy has tackled this issue by raising child support awards and enforcing them more strictly. At a deeper level, the poverty of women and children is an outgrowth of the gender-based division of labor in the family.

12 Perceptions of the health of the family depend on the theoretical orientation of the viewer. Two problems are loss of commitment and inequality within the family.

13 Lesbians' and gay men's families exist today amid controversy both outside and within the gay community about whether the gay or lesbian family should receive the same legal recognition and protection—for example, through access to legal marriage—as other families.

SUGGESTED READINGS

CHERLIN, Andrew (ed.). 1988. *The Changing American Family and Public Policy*. Washington, D.C.: Urban Institute Press. A collection of six essays that contain a rich mixture of factual information and recipes for public policy. Topics such as divorce, fatherhood, day care, and gender-role change are addressed.

CLINTON, Hillary Rodham. 1996. New York: Simon and Schuster. *It Takes a Village*. A call for commitment and policy that supports America's children.

FINEMAN, Martha A., and Mykitiuk, Roxanne (eds.). 1994. *The Public Nature of Private Violence*. New York: Routledge. A collection covering all forms of domestic violence with essays and research articles by well-known researchers and writers in the field.

FURSTENBERG, Frank F., and Cherlin, Andrew J. 1991. *Divided Families: What Happens to Children When Parents Part*. Cambridge, Mass.: Harvard University Press. An argument for directing public policy toward helping custodial parents function better and shielding children from parental conflict after divorce.

GARBARINO, James. 1992. *Toward a Sustainable Society: An Economic, Social and Environmental Agenda for Our Children's Future*. Chicago: Noble Press. A realistic but positive and hopeful appraisal of the challenges families and society face today, along with visions and policies for solutions.

GERSON, Kathleen. 1993. *No Man's Land: Men's Changing Commitments to Family and Work*. New York: HarperCollins, Basic Books. Readable and convincing analysis of the changing options and expectations for men in today's constricting economy, along with the various choices men make as a result.

PARKMAN, Allen M. 1992. *No-Fault Divorce: What Went Wrong?* Boulder, Colo.: Westview Press. An analysis of the aftermath of no-fault divorce laws in the United States.

RUBIN, Lillian B. 1994. *Families on the Fault Line: America's Working Class Speaks about the Family, the Economy, Race, and Ethnicity*. New York: HarperCollins. A book based on interviews conducted with 162 working-class and lower-middle-class families of various ethnic and racial backgrounds during a period in which the economy had contracted and shifted. The author examines the impact of this change on family life and the stress it caused.

STAPLES, Robert (ed.). 1995. *The Black Family: Essays and Studies*. 5th ed. Belmont, Calif.: Wadsworth. A collection of very current readings, compiled by a leading authority on African American families. The readings explore trends and issues surrounding the African American family today.

TAYLOR, Ronald E. 1994. *Minority Families in the United States*. Englewood Cliffs, N.J.: Prentice Hall. A volume containing a chapter on each of the major racial minorities in the United States. Leading scholars discuss the historical and socioeconomic factors that have influenced minority family structure and processes. Attention is given to the diversity within ethnic communities as well as between them.

THORNE, Barrie, and Yalom, Marilyn (eds.). 1992. *Rethinking the Family: Some Feminist Questions*. Rev. ed. Boston: Northeastern University Press. A book that raises and addresses thorny questions, such as why women in industrialized societies will continue to choose to have children when their parenting is seldom or meagerly supported by advanced capitalistic societies.

WESTON, Kath. 1991. *Families We Choose: Lesbians, Gays, Kinship*. New York: Columbia University Press. A book based on the premise that we create our own families; families are those persons whom we actively choose to include as members. This theme is specifically applied to lesbians and gay men as they create families through involved decision making.

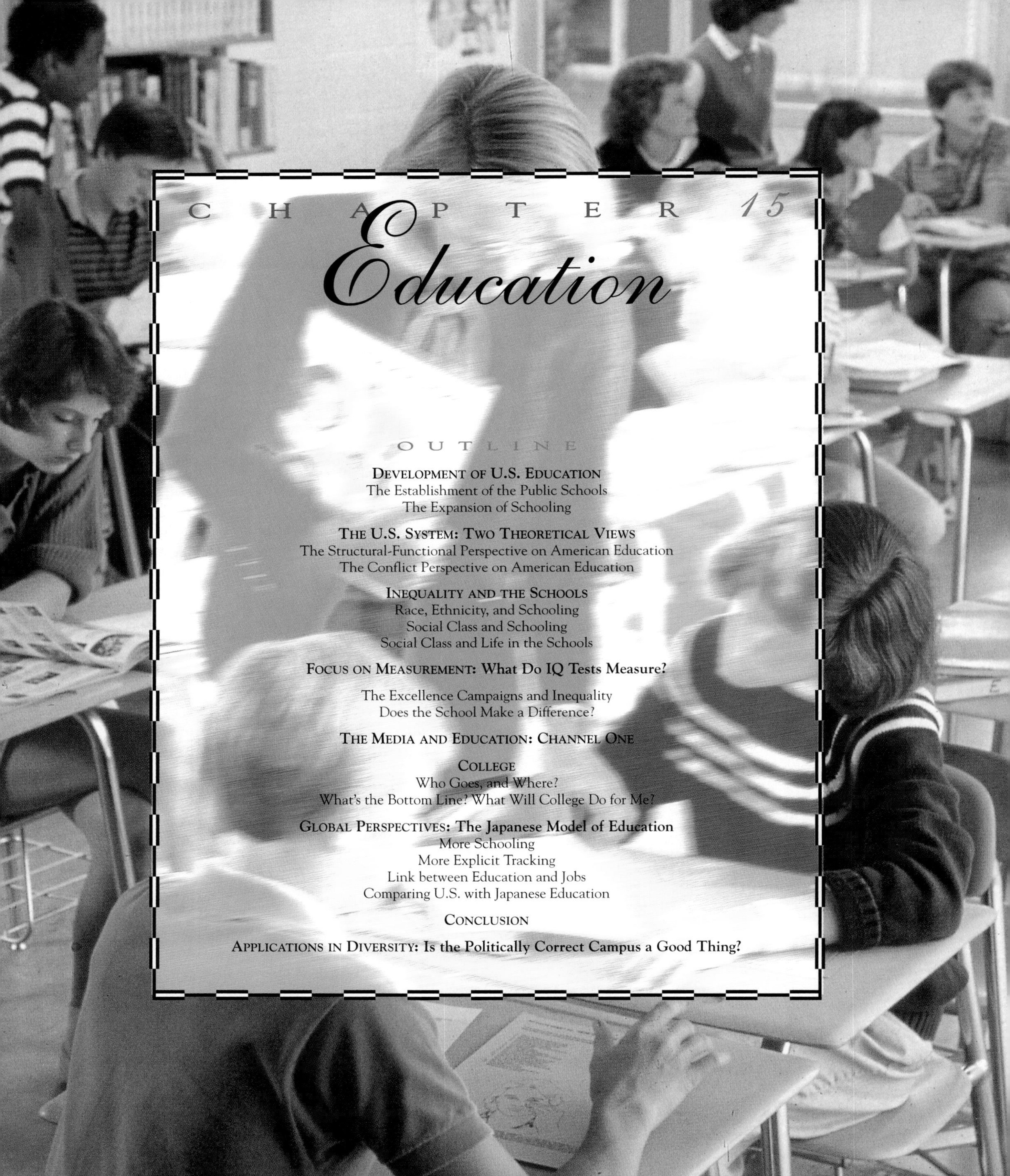

Chapter 15

Education

Outline

PROLOGUE

Have You Ever . . . had doubts about whether college was worth it? Going to school is hard work, it is expensive, and it is stressful. For most of us, going to school means nearly constant pressure. Even on Saturdays and Sundays, we really ought to be starting that term paper or studying. There are no legitimate days off when you're a college student. If you go ahead and take two or three days off, you'll probably have to pay for it with an all-nighter at exam time.

For the majority of college students, going to school also means a temporary sacrifice of income. Although there are a growing number of students who work part-time and even full-time, the majority of college students earn much less than they would if they were able to devote full effort to earning.

Given the work, the stress, and the poverty, why are you and 15 million others going to school? Most of us go to school because we expect to receive an economic payoff. We expect to earn more money and have more satisfying and respected jobs if we graduate from college. These are realistic expectations. If you get a college degree, you will have substantially increased your earning power.

Despite these inducements, only about one-third of young high school graduates are enrolled in college. Those who are not enrolled are most likely to be from the lower or working class. Thus, the pattern of college enrollments virtually guarantees that the social class structure of the next generation will be like that of this generation. The role of education in reproducing inequality is at the heart of the sociological study of education.

The **educational institution** is the social structure concerned with the transmission of knowledge, particularly to society's newcomers, children, and immigrants. Education is one of our most enduring and familiar institutions. In hunting and gathering as well as early agricultural societies, education was embedded in the family and kinship group. Children learned the ways of the culture simply by living with their elders and imitating their skills and customs. Gradually, with modernization, education became more formal and specialized: schools, teachers, homework assignments, and grades emerged.

The **educational institution** is the social structure concerned with the transmission of knowledge, particularly to society's newcomers, children and immigrants.

Today, nearly 3 of every 10 Americans are involved in education on a daily basis as students or staff. As former students, parents, or taxpayers, all of us are involved in education in one way or another. In this chapter, we describe education in the United States and how that institution affects our personal lives and life chances. Why is such a large part of our lives (and our dollars) devoted to education? What purposes are being achieved? Who benefits?

DEVELOPMENT OF U.S. EDUCATION

During the earliest years of this nation, there was little consensus on the form that education should take. Charity schools for paupers and immigrants, private schools, military academies, and church schools existed alongside free public schools. Although most people managed to pick up enough education to achieve basic literacy, there was no coherent, formal system. During the 19th century, however, education changed dramatically. Consensus developed on the desirability of free public schools, and schooling expanded rapidly.

The Establishment of the Public Schools

At the beginning of the American republic, most jobs did not require literacy. Education was enjoyed more often by the children of the elite than by the average child. During the 19th century, however, education came to be viewed by all classes as such a critical necessity that attendance became compulsory. There were three major forces driving the growth of the public schools during the 19th century: parental demand, labor demand, and social control demands.

Parental Demand. From very early in American history, the ability to read and write was seen as essential for reading the Scriptures and being an informed citizen. As a result, rural parents established schools almost as soon as they established churches. The curriculum in these schools focused on basic intellectual skills such as reading, writing, and arithmetic rather than on vocational training. They were public institutions that reflected the dominant cultural and social values of the communities that established and supported them.

Labor Demand. As industrialization developed during the 19th century, so did organized labor. As the working class became more self-conscious about its disadvantaged position, organized labor became a strong advocate for the public schools as a way to provide upward mobility for its children. The labor-versus-capitalist battle also affected the curriculum. Where the capitalists wanted vocational training to prepare working-class children for working-class jobs, organized labor wanted an academic curriculum that would enable children to leave the working class.

Social Control Demands. Rapid urbanization and very high rates of immigration in the late 19th century raised many concerns about social control. Compulsory schooling was seen as a way to get children off the streets and out of trouble. New York, for example, established reform schools for delinquent children in 1823, several years before they considered establishing public schools for nondelinquent children (Katz 1987). The schools were also considered a way to ensure the rapid Americanization of immigrants. The demand for schools as a form of social control came from elites rather than from the average citizen.

Almost from the beginning, people from different social classes and different political perspectives have wanted different things from education. The content of education has been and continues to be "contested terrain" (Edwards 1979). Whether we want excellence for a few, opportunity for all, or social control is an issue still being debated (Dow 1991; Sommer 1995).

The Expansion of Schooling

By the turn of the century, compulsory school attendance was established by law everywhere but the South (Richardson 1980). These laws were not always well enforced, but schooling through the eighth grade was well entrenched across

The expansion of education has been accompanied by increasing standardization. From our first achievement test in elementary school through the SAT and then graduate school exams, the mark-sense form and the number 2 pencil are a familiar part of life in the schools. Because standardized tests scores determine college entrance, there is increasing pressure on school districts to teach the standard curriculum that will prepare their students for these examinations.

most of America by 1900. High schools, however, were substantially behind. In 1910, fewer than 10 percent of America's 18-year-olds had a high school diploma, and it was not until the 1930s that high school education became common (Parelius and Parelius 1987). Even in 1950, only half of America's young adults had graduated from high school. If your grandparents graduated from high school, they were part of a minority. Today, however, nearly 90 percent of young adults have a high school diploma.

The expansion of secondary and college education is largely a phenomenon of the post–World War II years (see Figure 15.1). Numerous social conditions contributed to this expansion. The GI Bill sent millions of veterans of World War II, the Korean War, and the Vietnam War to college. In the 1960s, expanded federal loan programs and the development of the community college system also helped bring a college education within reach of more Americans. Structural-functional and conflict theories offer two different views of education in the United States.

The U.S. System: Two Theoretical Views

If education is now available to more Americans than in the past, what are its effects? Many Americans believe that the goal of formal education is to offer everybody an equal chance for economic success. Does the U.S. system actually accomplish this goal? In this section, we review structural-functional and conflict perspectives on American education. In doing so, we examine both the accomplishments and the weaknesses of the U.S. educational system and put them into a larger theoretical perspective.

FIGURE 15.1
EDUCATIONAL ACHIEVEMENT OF PERSONS 25 AND OLDER BY RACE AND ETHNICITY, 1940–1994

Among whites, the proportion of adults graduating from high school has more than tripled in the last 55 years; among blacks, the increase in education is even more dramatic. Nevertheless, blacks and Hispanics continue to be disadvantaged in terms of quantity of education.

SOURCE: U.S. Bureau of the Census 1975, 380; U.S. Bureau of the Census 1995, Table 238.

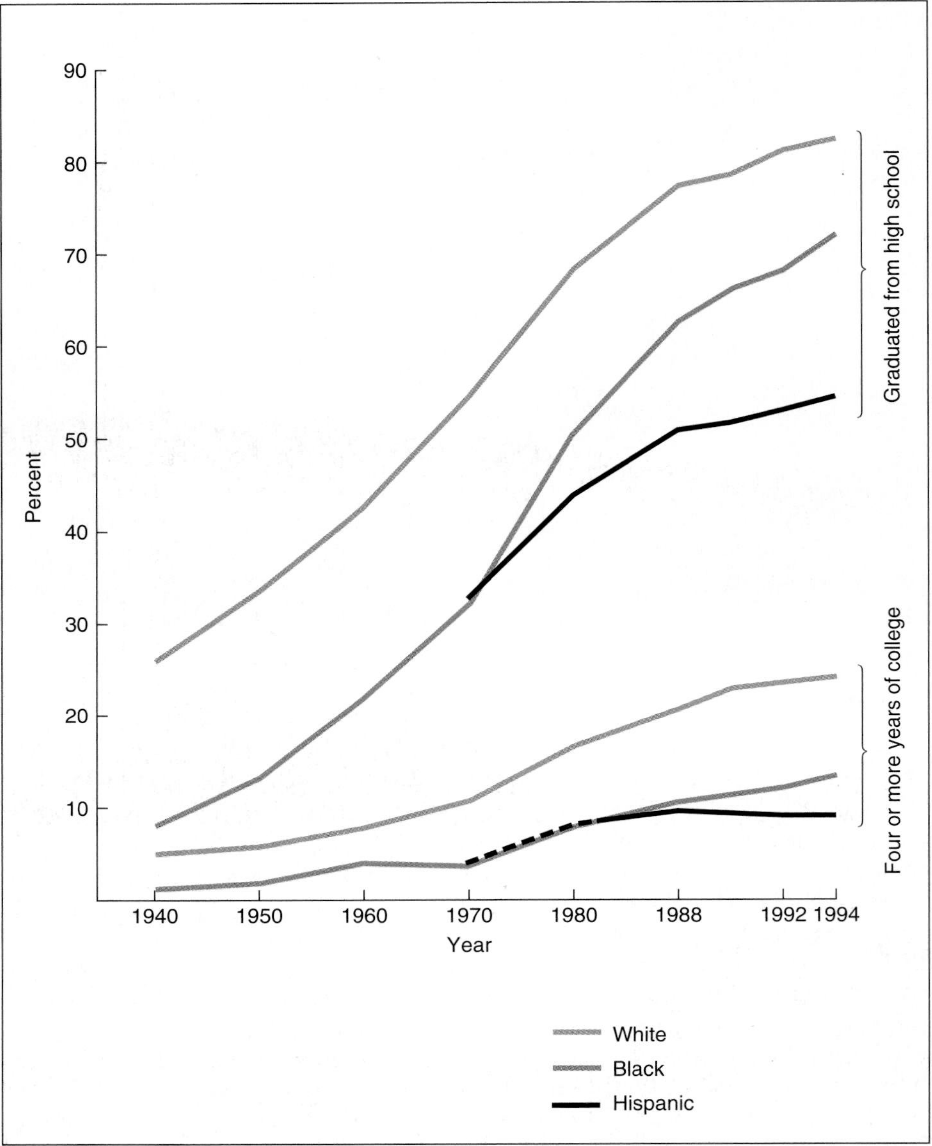

THE STRUCTURAL-FUNCTIONAL PERSPECTIVE ON AMERICAN EDUCATION

The structural-functional analysis of education is concerned with the consequences of educational institutions for the maintenance of society. It points out both how education contributes to the maintenance of society and how educational systems can be forces for change and conflict.

The Manifest Functions of Education. The educational system has been designed to meet multiple needs. Major manifest (intended) functions of education include the following.

- *Cultural Reproduction*. Schools transmit society's culture from one generation to the next by teaching the ideas, customs, and standards of the culture. We learn to read and write our language, we learn the Pledge of Allegiance, and we learn history. In this sense, education builds on the past and conserves traditions.
- *Social Control*. Second only to the family, schools are responsible for socializing the young into patterns of conformity. By emphasizing a common culture and instilling habits of discipline and obedience, the schools are an important agent for encouraging conformity.
- *Assimilation*. Schools function to assimilate persons from diverse backgrounds. By exposing students from all ethnic backgrounds, all regions of the country, and all social backgrounds to a common curriculum, they help create and maintain a common cultural base.
- *Training and Development*. Schools teach specific skills—not only technical skills such as reading, writing, and arithmetic but also habits of cooperation, punctuality, and obedience.
- *Selection and Allocation*. Schools are like gardeners; they sift, weed, sort, and cultivate their products, determining which students will be allowed to go on and which will not. Standards of achievement are used as criteria to channel students into different programs on the basis of their measured abilities. Ideally, an important function of the school system is to ensure the best use of the best minds. The public school system is a vital element of our commitment to equal opportunity.
- *Promotion of Change*. Schools also act as change agents. Although we do not stop learning after we leave school, the transmission of new knowledge and technology is usually aimed at schoolchildren rather than at the adult population. In addition, the schools promote change by encouraging the development of critical and analytic skills and skepticism. Schools, particularly colleges and universities, are also expected to produce new knowledge.

Latent Functions and Dysfunctions. In addition to its many manifest functions, a system as large and all-encompassing as education is bound to have unintended, or latent, consequences. These may be either functional or dysfunctional, depending on one's point of view. Latent functions and dysfunctions include the following.

- *Generation Gap*. As schools impart new knowledge, they may drive a wedge between generations. Courses in sociology, English, history, and even biology expose students to ideas different from those of their parents. What students learn in school about evolution, cultural relativity, or the merits of socialism may contradict the values held by their parents or their religion.
- *Custodial Care*. Compulsory education has transformed schools into settings where children are cooped up seven to eight hours a day, five days a week, for nine months of the year (Bowles 1972). Young people are kept off the streets, out of the labor force, and, presumably, out of trouble in small groups dispersed throughout communities in special buildings designed for close supervision. This enables their elders to command higher wages in the labor market and relieves their parents of the responsibility for supervising them.
- *Youth Culture*. By isolating young people from the larger society and confining them to the company of others their own age, educational institutions have contributed to the development of a unique youth culture. This youth culture is fractured into half a dozen subcultures, some of which stress athletics, some popularity, some grades, and some partying. Youth culture does not arise spontaneously; to a

In all societies, education is an important means to reproduce culture. Children not only learn neutral skills such as reading and writing but they also learn about their heritage. In America, this means learning about George Washington and the American Revolution (although not necessarily about Chief Red Cloud or Sojourner Truth). In Japan, it means learning about the devastation caused when the United States dropped the atom bomb on Hiroshima (although not necessarily about Pearl Harbor) (Gordon 1993).

very significant extent, it is fostered and created by the school structure. Grades, tracking, formal athletic programs, sponsored social activities—all help to divide the student body into the same types of cliques from one generation to the next.

- *Rationalization of Inequality.* One of the chief consequences of life in the schools is that young people learn to expect unequal rewards on the basis of differential achievement. Schools prepare young people for inequality. Some consider this preparation undesirable in that it leads young people to believe that all inequality is earned and that it is a fair response to unequal abilities.
- *Perpetuation of Inequality.* Abundant evidence exists that ascriptive characteristics of students (race, sex, and social class) affect how students are treated in school. The evidence supports the conclusion that schools prepetuate inequality and function to maintain and reinforce the existing social class hierarchy. From the functionalist point of view, this is a latent dysfunction of the schools—an unfortunate and unintended consequence that should be rectified.

A structural-functional analysis begins with the premise that any ongoing institution of society is contributing to the maintenance of society. The enumeration of the functions of education clarifies what some of these contributions are. Although there are unanticipated side effects, both positive and negative, functionalists tend to concentrate on how education benefits society and individuals.

The Conflict Perspective on American Education

Conflict theories of education look much like structural-functional theories, except in their value judgments on the final product. Conflict theorists are less likely to see opportunities for upward mobility in education. These theorists agree that education reproduces culture, socializes young people into patterns of conformity, sifts and sorts, and rationalizes inequality. Since conflict theories see the social structure as a system of inequality designed to benefit the rich at the expense of the rest, however, naturally they criticize any institution that reproduces this culture. (Davies 1995). Three of the major conflict arguments are summarized here.

Education As a Capitalist Tool. Some conflict theorists argue that mass education developed because it benefited the interests of the capitalist class. Capitalists demanded educated workers not only because literacy made workers more effective but also because educated workers had been taught obedience, punctuality, and loyalty to the economic and political system (Bowles and Gintis 1976; Spring 1995). The schools, they argued, were developed to meet this demand.

The **hidden curriculum** of schools socializes young people into obedience and conformity.

To support this argument, theorists point to the schools' **hidden curriculum,** which socializes young people into obedience and conformity. This curriculum—learning to wait your turn, follow the rules, be punctual, and show respect—prepares young people for life in the industrial working class (Dale 1977; Dow 1991).

It may occur to you that the hidden curriculum may be viewed, by some, as a latent function of education. So it may be no surprise that there is a great deal of controversy over this point. Certainly, capitalists and industry have tried to affect the content of schooling in ways that support their interests. Most recently, this has taken the form of demanding more basic skills—better reading, writing, and arithmetic skills—rather than more obedience. Nevertheless, the school system does prepare young people to accept inequality and hierarchy, and this does make it easier for their employers to control them.

Credentialism. One supposed outcome of free public education is that merit will triumph over origins, that hard work and ability will be allowed to rise to the top. Conflict theorists, however, argue that the shift to educational credentials as the mechanism for allocating high-status positions has had little impact on equalizing economic opportunity. Instead, a subtle shift has taken place. Instead of inquiring who your parents are, the prospective employer asks what kind of education you have and where you got it. Because these educational credentials are highly correlated with social class background, they serve to keep undesirables out. Conflict theorists argue that educational credentials are mere window dressing; apparently based on merit and achievement, credentials are often a surrogate for social class background. The use of educational credentials to measure social origins and social status is called **credentialism.**

As the level of education in society increases, educational requirements also must rise to maintain the status quo. This credential inflation can be seen in nursing, in public school teaching, and in government. Jobs that used to require a high school diploma now require a bachelor's degree; jobs that used to require a bachelor's degree now require a master's degree. Because the elite increases its pursuit of higher degrees as quickly as the lower class increases its pursuit of a high school diploma, no real change occurs. Credentialism, it is argued, is a way of manipulating the educational system for the benefit of the well-off (Collins 1979; Powers 1984).

Thinking Critically

Have you seen credentialism at work in your own life? How? If you compare your own educational attainment and job with the educations and jobs of your parents, do you see evidence of credential inflation? What, if any, are some positive effects of credential inflation? What, if any, are some negative ones?

Credentialism is the use of educational credentials to measure social origins and social status.

Reproduction of Inequality. Both the "capitalist tool" and "credentialist" arguments imply that the elite is scheming to keep down the masses. Conflict theory, however, has a much broader application that does not require the assumption of a manipulative elite. The heart of the conflict perspective on education—as of the conflict perspective on any institution—is the idea that those who benefit from the system (society's elite) seek to perpetuate it (Davies 1995).

In the modern world, the elite cannot directly ensure that their children will stay members of the elite. To pass their status attainments on to their children, they must provide their children with appropriate educational credentials (Robinson 1984). To an impressive extent, they are able to do so: Students' educational achievements are very closely related to their parents' social status, as well as to race/ethnicity (Davies 1995).

How does this happen? Do schools discriminate? Or, in a fair and open competition, do students with the most resources win? To answer these questions, we need to look at the processes that take place within the schools.

Inequality and the Schools

The central concern of the sociology of education in the last 40 years or so has been the link between education and stratification (Davies 1995). This concern exists on both micro and macro levels. On the micro level, we want to know what happens to individual children—how the school experiences of working-class and middle-class children differ. On a macro level, we want to understand whether the structure of the schools to which we send our children affects their learning.

Race, Ethnicity, and Schooling

The expansion of education in the United States, described earlier in the chapter, occurred unevenly. Working- and lower-class whites, African Americans,

Native Americans, and Hispanics have experienced a great deal of difficulty participating in this expansion. These groups have generally been offered less education, worse education, segregated education, and more oppressive education.

Before 1954, when the Supreme Court's decision against the Topeka, Kansas, Board of Education outlawed the purposeful and legalized racial segregation of schools (*de jure* segregation), many minority Americans attended poorly funded, segregated schools. While *de jure* segregation is a thing of the past, many minority children continue to attend schools that are, in fact, segregated (*de facto* segregation). This is because most public schools are neighborhood schools that reflect the ethnic makeup of the area of attendance. This remains true despite several decades of organized efforts to change the situation, such as through busing (Kunen 1996).

Hispanics and Native Americans have faced added hurdles of mandatory deculturation. Native American children were educated at boarding schools that sought to Americanize them. In part of the Southwest, laws that made it illegal to teach in any language but English effectively disenfranchised Mexican American children (San Miguel 1987). Minority children studied from textbooks that either omitted or maligned their people, their culture, and their history. Partly as a result of these factors only 50 to 60 percent of today's African American, Hispanic, and Native American adults over age 25 have completed high school. Including these disadvantaged segments of society in the expansion of the public school system is an unfinished project.

In all societies, education is an important means of reproducing culture. In addition to neutral skills such as reading and writing, children learn many of the dominant cultural values. (The Focus section in this chapter explores how dominant cultural values affect I.Q. tests.)

Thus the cultural heritage children learn at home may not be consistent with the values and history they learn at school. For example, Native American children, taught by their parents never to embarrass a peer, are suddenly expected to publicly correct one another in the classroom. Until recently, U.S. history texts often described violence between whites and Indians without examining the factors that provoked Native American nations to warfare; they also often failed to mention such things as the waves of anti-Chinese violence in the United States towards the turn of the 20th century, the removal of Japanese Americans to relocation camps during World War II, and the rich cultural and economic presence of Hispanics who lived in the Southwest long before settlers from the United States arrived. Likewise, the contributions of African civilizations to modern science, mathematics, and engineering have been ignored.

Not surprisingly, minority students and parents increasingly ask the question "Education for whom?" In response, more and more school districts and universities are adopting multicultural education programs. Educators hope that such programs will provide a potential solution to the joint problems of racism and the disproportionately high dropout rates characteristic of U.S. minority students. The Applications in Diversity section at the end of this chapter addresses multicultural education on college and university campuses.

Social Class and Schooling

Children from larger families (Downey 1995) and from disadvantaged backgrounds are likely to experience economic hardships that work against them in all their daily experiences in school. They are likely to lack a set of encyclopedias and a home computer. Furthermore, it is likely that their parents will be too caught up in the struggles of day-to-day living to have the time or energy to help them with their studies. Paying the bills may be more important than trying to improve their children's SAT scores.

The differences are far more subtle than simple economics. For example—while it may not be true of American Jewish or Asian parents (Fejgin 1995)—poorly educated parents in general are likely to give more attention to conformity than to independent thinking when socializing their preschoolers. (Alexander et al. 1987). Further, they are less likely to attend parent/teacher conferences, are less comfortable talking to their children's teachers, and are less able and often less willing to help their children with their schoolwork. The way this adds to the disadvantage of their children is illustrated in the comments of one working-class mother.

> My job is here at home. My job is to raise him, to teach him manners, get him dressed and get him to school, to make sure that he is happy. Now her [the teacher's] part, the school's part, is to teach him to learn. Hopefully, someday he'll be able to use all of that. That is what I think is their part, to teach him to read, the writing, any kind of schooling. (Lareau 1987, 79).

This mother's remarks reveal several attitudes that are more common among lower- and working-class parents than among middle-class parents. First, the mother sees a division of labor between home and school; she does not think it is her responsibility to review homework or reinforce school-taught skills. Reading and writing are things you do at school, not at home. Second, she *hopes* the boy can use the skills. Obviously she isn't very sure that school will do him any good, and this uncertainty is likely to affect the boy's enthusiasm for learning. Third, this mother's emphasis on manners illustrates the repeated social science finding, mentioned earlier, that working-class parents give more attention to being quiet and

Children enter school with very unequal backgrounds. Some have been taken to the library and read to, while others have been abandoned to the company of the television; some have been playing learning-readiness games on their computers while others have been playing in dirty stairwells. These inequalities pose an almost impossible obstacle to equality in educational opportunity. As a result, studies show that the benefits of education go disproportionately to those who originally had the advantages.

polite and less attention to independent thinking than do middle-class parents (Alexander et al. 1987).

Cultural capital refers to social assets, such as familiarity and identification with elite culture.

In addition, children of the middle and upper-middle classes have more of what has been called **cultural capital**—social assets, such as familiarity and identification with the elite culture (Bourdieu 1973). They are more likely to have been introduced to art, music, and books at home and to define themselves as cultured people. This doesn't mean that they all prefer Beethoven to Pearl Jam, but it does mean that they accept books and reading as a natural and important part of life. This cultural capital will help them to do well in school (DiMaggio and Mohr 1985; Farkas et al. 1990; Teachman 1987), and it may influence how effectively they are able to translate their educations into occupational success.

Social Class and Life in the Schools

To understand how social class background translates into educational experiences, we need to look at two processes in the schools: cognitive development and tracking. Each is critical to eventual educational attainment, and each has been shown to be affected by social class background.

Cognitive Development. One of the major processes that takes place in schools, of course, is that students learn. When they graduate from high school, many can use a computer, write essays with three-part theses, and differentiate equations. In addition to learning specific skills, they also undergo a process of cognitive development wherein their mental skills grow and expand. They learn to think critically, to weigh evidence, to develop independent judgment. The extend to which this development takes place is related to both school and home environments.

An impressive set of studies demonstrates that cognitive development during the school years is enhanced by complex and demanding work without close supervision and by high teacher expectations. Teachers and curricula that furnish this setting produce students who have greater intellectual flexibility and higher achievement test scores. They are also more open to new ideas, less authoritarian, and less prone to blind conformity (Cose 1995; Leslie 1995; Miller, Kohn, and Schooler 1985, 1986).

Unfortunately, the availability of these ideal learning conditions varies by students' social class. Studies show that teachers are most demanding when they are of the same social class as their students. The greater the difference between their own social class and that of their pupils, the more rigidly they structure their classrooms and the fewer demands they place on their students (Alexander, Entwisle, and Thompson 1987; Leslie 1995). As a result, students learn less when they come from a social class lower than that of their teacher. The social class gap tends to be largest when youngsters are the most disadvantaged, and this process helps to keep them disadvantaged.

Tracking (or homogenous grouping) is the practice of assigning students to instructional groups on the basis of ability or past achievement.

Tracking. **Tracking** (or homogenous grouping) is the practice of assigning students to instructional groups on the basis of ability or past achievement. Ideally, tracking is supposed to benefit both gifted and slow learners. By having classes geared to their levels, both groups should learn faster, and both should benefit from increased teacher attention. Instead, one of the most consistent findings from education research is that assignment to a high-ability group has positive effects whereas assignment to a low-ability group has negative effects. Tracking apparently has little or no effect on middle-ability students (Hallinan 1994).

When students enter first grade, they are sorted into reading groups on the basis of ability. This is just the beginning of a pervasive pattern of stratification in the schools. By the time they are out of elementary school, some students will be directed into college preparatory tracks, others into general education (sometimes called vocational education), and still others into remedial classes.

An important reason students assigned to low-ability groups learn less is that they are taught less. In an example of the self-fulfilling prophecy (whereby acting on the belief that a situation exists causes it to become real), students who are defined as having less ability are exposed to less material, asked to do less homework, and, in general, not given the same opportunities to learn (Oaks 1994). One study found that, on average, students in high-track English classes were asked to do 42 minutes of homework a night; in low-track English classes, the average was 13 minutes (Oaks 1985).

In addition to these concerns about tracking, researchers have pointed to the following latent dysfunctions (Hallinan 1994).

1. Tracking tends to segregate students by race/ethnicity or socioeconomic status.
2. Tracking leads to a social hierarchy in the school, with lower-track students receiving less respect from their peers and the staff.
3. Tracking results in numerous classroom interruptions in the lower tracks owing to disciplinary problems.

Other processes also operate in tracking. Students who are assigned to high-ability groups, for instance, receive strong affirmation of their academic identity; they find school rewarding, have better attendance records, cooperate better with teachers and develop higher aspirations. The opposite occurs with students placed in low-ability tracks. They get fewer rewards for their efforts, their parents and teachers have low expectations for them, and they have little incentive to work hard. Many will cut their losses and look for self-esteem through avenues such as athletics or delinquency (Rosenberg, Schooler, and Schoenbach 1989). As Figure 15.3 shows, the result is a downward spiral of academic performance (Vanfossen, Jones, and Spade 1987).

Recent studies show, however, that the effects of tracking vary across schools (Hallinan 1994). Between-track inequality is less pronounced, for instance, in Catholic schools and schools that permit more mobility between tracks. Where teachers are more optimistic about the possibility of remediation and schools continue to place academic demands on students in noncollege tracks, evidence suggests that between-track differences in academic performance are reduced. Importantly, the narrowing of the gap seems to occur because low-track students are brought up and not because high-track students are held down (Gamoran 1992).

The manifest goal of tracking is not to discriminate by social class. Yet tracking produces systematic disadvantage for children from lower socioeconomic backgrounds. Because they received less preschool stimulation, children from disadvantaged backgrounds start the first grade already behind, and many of them never catch up: Their scores on standardized tests start low and stay low. Because their parents did not attend college, the children are less likely to aspire to go to college themselves. Finally, the combination of low achievement and low aspiration tends to alienate children from the school, and they generally have more behavior problems. As a result, social class is a powerful predictor of track assignment.

FOCUS ON MEASUREMENT

What Do IQ Tests Measure?

- How many legs does a Kaffir have?
- Who wrote *Great Expectations?*
- Which word is out of place?
sanctuary–nave–altar–attic–apse
- If you throw the dice and 7 is showing on top, what is facing down? 7–snake eyes–boxcars–little joes–11

If you answered two, Dickens, attic, and 7, then you get the highest possible score on this test. What does that mean? Does it mean that you have genetically superior mental ability, that you read a lot, that you shoot craps? What could you safely conclude about a person who got only two questions right?

"THE STANDARDIZED TEST IS ONE OF THE MOST FAMILIAR ASPECTS OF LIFE IN THE SCHOOLS."

The standardized test is one of the most familiar aspects of life in the schools. Whether by the California or the Iowa Achievement Test, the SAT or the ACT, students are constantly being evaluated. Most of these tests are truly achievement tests; they measure what has been learned and make no pretense of measuring the capacity to learn. IQ tests, however, are supposed to measure the innate capacity to learn—mental ability. On these tests, African American, Hispanic, and Native American students consistently score below non-Hispanic white students, and working-class students score substantially below middle-class students. The obvious question is whether these tests are fair measures (Jacoby and Glaubeiman 1995). Are African American, Hispanic, Native American, and working-class youths lower in mental ability than middle-class or non-Hispanic white youths? This question has been hotly debated, on and off, for decades; the 1994 publication of the book *The Bell Curve* (Herrnstein and Murray 1994) brought the question into the public forum once again.

Before we can answer the question whether IQ tests accurately measure intelligence, we must first ask another: What is mental ability? Most scholars recognize that it is a combination of genetic potential and prior social experiences. It is an aspect of personality, "the capacity of the individual to act purposefully, to think rationally and to deal effectively with his environment" (Wechsler 1958, 7).

Do questions such as those that opened this section measure any of these things? No. We can all imagine people who act purposefully, think rationally, and deal effectively with the environment but do not know who wrote *Great Expectations* and are ignorant about dice and church architecture. These people may be foreigners, they may have lacked the opportunity to go to school, or they may have come from a subculture where dice, churches, and 19th century English literature are not important.

For this reason, good IQ tests try to measure reasoning ability as well as knowledge. Nonverbal IQ tests are supposed to measure the ability to think and reason independently of formal education. Examples of items from such a nonverbal test are reproduced in Figure 15.2. Do these nonverbal tests achieve their intention? Do they measure the ability to reason independently of years in school, subcultural background, or language difficulties? Again, the answer seems to be no.

There are two ways in which these tests are not culture-free. The first is that they reflect not only reasoning and knowledge but also competitiveness, familiarity with and acceptance of timed tests, rapport with the examiner, and achievement aspiration. Students who lack these characteristics may do poorly even though their ability to reason is well developed (Fraser 1995).

A more serious fault with such nonverbal tests is their underlying assumption. Reasoning ability is not independent of learning opportunities. How we reason, as well as what we know, depends on our prior experiences. Deprivation studies of infant monkeys and hospitalized orphans (described in Chapter 6) demonstrate that mental and social retardation occur as a result of sensory deprivation. Just as the body does not develop fully without exercise, neither does the mind. Thus, reasoning capacity is not culture-free; it is determined by the opportunities to develop it. For this reason, there will probably never be an IQ test that does not reflect the prior cultural experiences of the test taker.

FOCUS ON MEASUREMENT

1. From the array of four, choose that form that is identical to the target form.

(a) (b)

Target form

(c) (d)

2. From the array of four, choose that form which is a rotation of the target form.

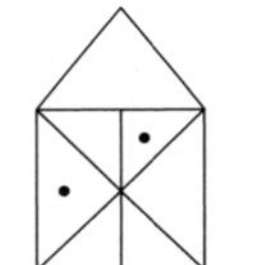

(a) (b)

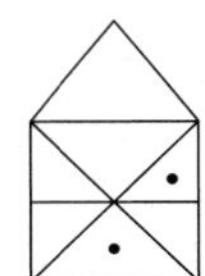

Target form

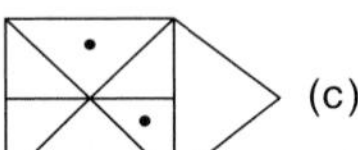

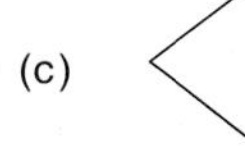

(c) (d)

3. (For a, b, c,) indicate whether the second form in each pair is a rotation of the first or is a different form.

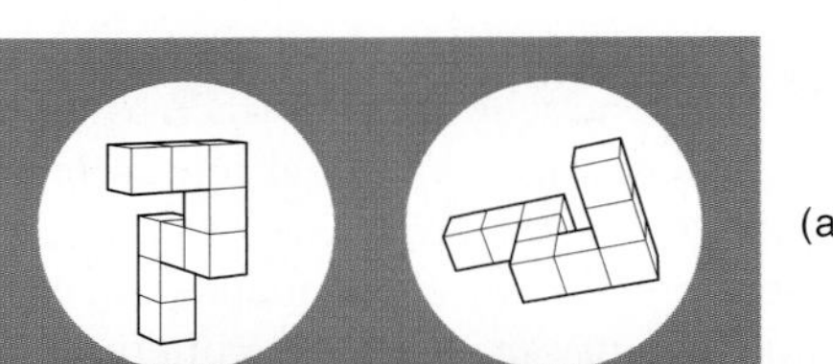

(a)

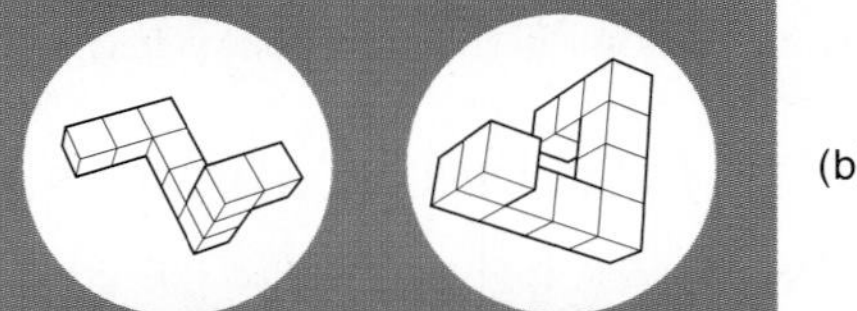

(b)

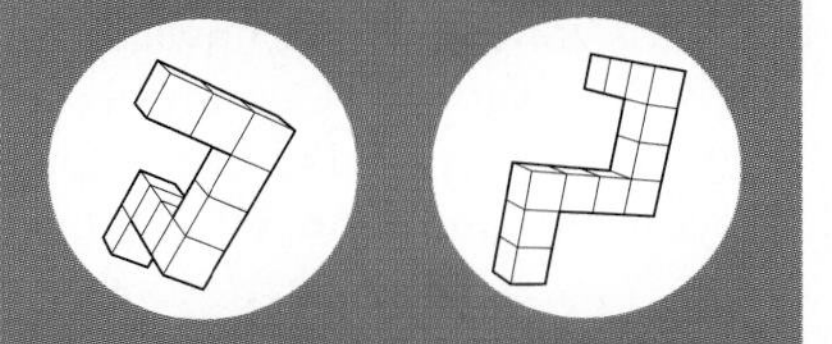

(c)

FIGURE 15.2 CULTURE-FREE INTELLIGENCE TESTS?

What can we conclude about your intelligence from your score on this simple test? Does a high score mean that you are naturally intelligent, or have some of your experiences in life and in school prepared you for these kinds of problems? Increasingly, scholars believe that it is impossible to make an intelligence test that is free of cultural influences.

SOURCE: From *Frames of Mind: The Theory of Multiple Intelligences* by Howard Gardner © 1983 by Howard Gardner. Reprinted by permission of Basic Books, Inc., Publishers.

FIGURE 15.3
THE TRACKING PROCESS

The tracking system has a feedback loop that produces an upward spiral of advantage for middle-class children and a downward spiral of disadvantage for lower-class children.

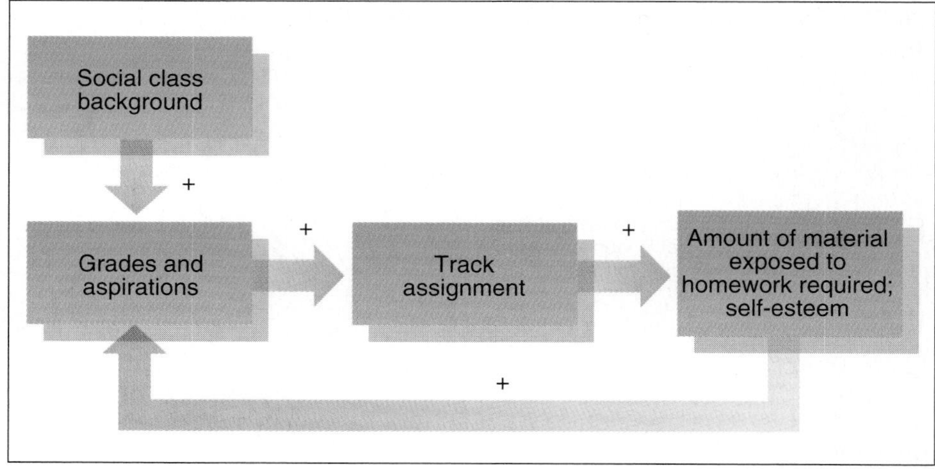

There are, however, two important factors that work to dilute the effect of social class (Gamoran and Mare 1989). First, African Americans are more likely than white Americans from the same social class background to aspire to go to college. This means that schools are likely to place African American children in college tracks to a greater degree than their test scores alone would warrant. As a result, the tracking process has been found to *reduce* the inheritance of disadvantage by race. Second, being in the top third of one's class is probably more important than one's absolute score on standardized tests. For administrative convenience, nearly every school divides its students into ability groupings. If your scores are only average but your classmates' scores are even worse, you are likely to get into the high-ability track of your school (Gamoran and Mare 1989). Because schools tend to be segregated by social class, this structured factor ensures that some working-class children get college preparatory training.

In summary, there is no doubt that tracking benefits those in the high-ability groups and systematically lowers the achievement of those in low-ability groups, nor is there any doubt that track assignment is related to social class. The result is that tracking plays a critical role in reproducing social class. If this is true, why do we keep doing it? The answer from a conflict perspective is obvious: It perpetuates the current system of inequality. (Oaks 1994). From a structural-functional viewpoint, the answer is that it facilitates administration (Hallinan 1994). A first-grade teacher cannot teach reading to 35 students simultaneously, so she must divide them into groups; homogeneous ability groups are easier to work with. Tracking (stratification) is thus necessary and justifiable, according to this view.

THINKING CRITICALLY

Given the same levels of funding now available for public education, how would you organize elementary and secondary classrooms to best meet the needs of all students? What would be the manifest functions of your system? What might be the latent functions? The dysfunctions?

THE EXCELLENCE CAMPAIGNS AND INEQUALITY

While sociologists criticize the educational institution for its failure to equalize opportunity for all social classes, the general public is most likely to criticize this institution for its lack of quality. Excellence rather than equity is the major public concern. This concern is not unwarranted.

In 1983, the National Commission on Excellence in Education issued a report that was extremely critical of U.S. education. The report indicated that 13 percent of all 17-year-olds and as many as 40 percent of minority youths were functionally illiterate. In a comparison of U.S. students with students from 21 other nations, Americans had the lowest scores on 7 of 19 achievement tests and never came in either first or second. The commission argued that the problem was caused not by factors beyond our control but simply by lack of insight and will. The solutions recommended included (1) a more demanding sequence of basic courses, (2) longer school days and school years, and (3) higher standards for school achievement.

Will more basics, more time, and higher standards improve the quality of education? The answer is, "on the average, yes." As with almost everything else in the school system, however, the greatest benefits seem to go to those who already are achieving.

The implementation of higher standards, especially the implementation of standard competency tests for graduation or promotion, may have disproportionate effects on disadvantaged students: The already high dropout rate (14 percent) could soar. The result could be to tighten rather than loosen the strong chain of interconnected problems that reproduce poverty and disadvantage.

Recent research suggests several strategies for increasing the scores and achievement of all of students without losing half along the way. First, raise teacher expectations. This has been found to raise attendance and performance levels of both good and poor students. This change should especially benefit poor students, many of whose teachers have such low expectations for them that they are given passing grades for attending class or for not causing trouble. Second, reduce the size of schools. In smaller schools, teachers have greater ability to influence students; and perhaps as important, students have greater ability to influence the schools. They have more opportunities for extracurricular activities that will enhance their attachment to school. Third, build some flexibility into the system so that young people who work, marry, or bear children can participate. Fourth, use grants and loans to encourage college students from disadvantaged backgrounds to enter the teaching profession.

> **THINKING CRITICALLY**
>
> Given growing concern about guns, violence, and gangs in schools, do you think the strategies listed here would help alleviate the situation of guns, violence, and gangs in schools? Why or why not? If not, what would?

DOES THE SCHOOL MAKE A DIFFERENCE?

Arkansas, one of the poorest states in the nation, spends about $3,000 per pupil annually on public education; New Jersey spends about $7,000 annually per pupil. The same variation appears within states and metropolitan areas, since local schools depend in part on local taxes, and taxpayers in well-off areas produce higher tax revenues. Some schools, mostly in the inner city, may run out of toilet paper before the end of the year, while other schools, mostly in suburban areas, invest in the latest computer equipment (Kozol 1991; Traub 1994).

A question is, how much difference does expenditure make? The answer seems to be that the amount a school district spends does not, by itself, make much difference. Rather, the social class characteristics of the students largely determine the average achievement at a school; having the best-equipped libraries and laboratories does not add very much (Hallinan 1988), although it may help somewhat (Arum 1966).

If expenditures don't appear to make very much difference, what is it about schools that might affect the quality of education? Educators and policy makers have examined several questions in this regard: (1) whether private schools are better than public schools, (2) whether racially integrated schools are better than segregated ones, (3) whether sex-segregated schools are better, and (4) what makes schools effective.

Are Private Schools Better? In the 1980s, a major controversy developed over a two-volume study that concluded that Catholic schools do a better job than public schools. (Coleman and Hoffer 1987; Coleman, Hoffer, and Kilgore 1982). Public school administrators and staff were disheartened by this finding. The reason Catholic school students do better is fourfold:

- *Curriculum.* Catholic schools teach more basics, especially math.
- *Higher expectations.* They demand more homework, emphasize study habits, have higher expectations, and have better discipline.
- *Selective enrollment.* Catholic schools (and other private schools) do not have to take or keep any student. They weed out those who aren't interested or who are chronic discipline problems.
- *Parental involvement.* Parents of Catholic school students attend more PTA meetings, are more active in school governance, and work more closely with their children's teachers.

There appears to be little doubt that Catholic schoolchildren do perform better. It is likely that similar findings would apply to students in other types of private schools as well. The critical difference is probably parental involvement; not necessarily the quality of the school itself. Sending one's children to a private school takes extra thought and money. Hence, only parents who care about their children's education—and are in a social class that can afford it—send their children to private schools.

Are Racially Integrated Schools Better? In 1954, the U.S. Supreme Court, in *Brown v. Board of Education of Topeka,* ruled that racial segregation in public education is unlawful and said that "the doctrine of 'separate but equal' has no place" in public schools. In 1966, a controversial but influential report concluded that black students learned substantially better in integrated schools and white students learned no worse (Coleman 1966). That study was part of the social science arsenal that was used to promote busing. During the ensuing decade, however, there has been little real progress in school desegregation. While some schools have become less racially segregated because of busing, other schools have become *more* segregated as a result of changing patterns of residential segregation.

Because of widely different property tax bases and revenues, some school districts in the United States are relatively poor while others have the latest equipment and more highly paid teachers. Research shows that such differences do not directly affect children's achievement. Going to a poorly equipped, poorly maintained, and perhaps even dirty school can affect achievement, partly because it is generally demoralizing to both children and their parents, as well as their teachers.

Recent evidence continues to support the conclusion that students who attend schools with a large African American majority learn less and drop out more. The problem is social class more than race: Such schools include a disproportionate share of youngsters from disadvantaged family backgrounds.

In opposition to the *Brown v. Board of Education* decision, a few African American parents and educators have begun to argue that school integration is not absolutely necessary for high-quality education. As one African American father put it, "It's insulting to be told the quality of my child's education depends on the number of white children in the room" ('"Separate but Equal' Again?" 1994). Some African American leaders have suggested that all-black "academies," which have been instituted or proposed in several major cities, can do a better job than integrated schools. With special cultural programs and events, for instance, segregated schools can foster ethnic pride and positive attitudes in minority children. Meanwhile, others argue that integration is a valuable goal and that ceasing to press toward integrated schools is "a gesture of despair" (Traub 1994, 37).

Are Sex-Segregated Schools Better? Just as some minority parents and educators want racially separate schools, other parents and educators are exploring whether sex-segregated classrooms are better. Their main concern is with math and science. The gender gap in math and science may be closing (Hyde, Fennema, and Lamon 1990), but a slew of studies still show that after middle school, girls lag behind boys in these subjects, especially in higher-level math and science skills that lead to careers in these fields (American Association of University Women 1992; Catsambis 1994).

Why is this the case? Many researchers agree that the situation results from divergent expectations and opportunities, not genetic differences (Canada and Pringle 1995; Maracek 1995). By the eighth grade, fewer girls than boys enjoy math, feel confident about their abilities in math or science, or want careers in these fields (Catsambis 1994). As Chapter 12 pointed out, there are causes for this in the general culture (Entwisle, Alexander, and Olson 1994). But researchers (American Association of University Women 1992; Catsambis 1994; Orenstein 1994) found several causes specifically associated with the classroom:

1. Boys receive more attention from teachers and generally dominate the classroom.
2. Math and science books and teachers use male-focused examples and illustrations.
3. Teachers expect boys to do better than girls in math and science.
4. Teachers and counselors give boys more advice in math and science and more often encourage boys to take advanced courses in these subjects.
5. Math teachers tend to use a male instructional model (competition, not relational skills) to motivate students.
6. Girls have fewer females teacher role models in math and science.

Would sex-segregated classrooms help? One recent study (Lee, Marks, and Byrd 1994) compared how young women and men were taught in 60 private, non-Catholic all-girl, all-boy, and coeducational high schools across the country. The researchers not only observed in classrooms but also analyzed school records and SAT scores, as well as survey questionnaires from and interviews with students, teachers, and school administrators.

Their findings were interesting.

- *All-male schools*. On the positive side, all-male schools more often encouraged students to explain and defend their views. But on the negative side, teachers in all-male schools were more likely to make or allow negative remarks about women. Only rarely did either of these things happen in all-female or coed classrooms.

- *All-female schools*. On the positive side, all-female schools did not evidence overt sexism in the classroom and provided girls with more same-sex role models. On the negative side, teachers tended to talk down to students and assume that the girls would have trouble learning, especially in math and science. Nor did all-female schools encourage aggressive intellectual dialogues in class.
- *Coeducational schools*. Teachers in coed classes were unlikely to make or allow negative remarks about females or talk down to them. Male students did dominate classroom activities, but only in the physical sciences, especially chemistry.

The researchers concluded that sex-segregated classes are not necessarily better. Instead, they recommended strong school policies that require the equitable treatment of males and females in enrollment, facility hiring, and classroom materials and activities.

> **THINKING CRITICALLY**
>
> How, specifically, would the recommendations of these researchers address the six causes for females' lower achievement in math and science listed above? What, if any, problems might be associated with these recommendations?

The "Effective School." Despite the almost overwhelming odds that many inner-city schools face, some of them have excellent records. A recent body of research asks about the characteristics of these "effective schools." The answers appear to be that these schools have the following characteristics (Bryk 1988):

- A strong, required basic core.
- Discipline and order.
- Smaller size.
- Committed teachers.
- Positive climate.

Each of these points is critical. Teaching math for 90 minutes a day and putting a police officer in the corridor will not create an effective school. A positive climate, where students are motivated to learn and where both teachers and students feel that discipline is fair and in their best interests, is essential. Punitive law-and-order reforms are not likely by themselves to create effective schools.

Summary. In the United States, we like to believe that our public elementary and secondary schools offer equal opportunity and give children of every social class, race, and gender a good start in life. In fact, as we have seen, this is not the case. The evidence on tracking suggests that schools may even increase the degree of inequality among students. Voices for racially segregated or sex-segregated classrooms have proposed one way to reduce inequality. Opponents of separate schools focus on ways to alleviate the problems within an integrated public school system.

In a later section of this chapter, we will ask what happens when we move to the college level, a level at which school is voluntary and explicitly depends on aspirations and ability to pay tuition. Right now, though, we will take a short detour to look briefly at the relationship between the media and education.

THE MEDIA AND EDUCATION: CHANNEL ONE

Did you watch Channel One in high school? Not if you went to school in New York, because that's one state that doesn't allow it. But since its beginning in 1989, Channel One has found its way into the classrooms of some 12,000 secondary schools. What does the school get in return for using Channel One in its classrooms? For one thing, a free teaching assistant. For another, video or television equipment to show the programs.

With content designed specifically for secondary students, Channel One gives news and views on current events from election campaigns to what's happening in Bosnia. You might think of Channel One as a kind of public television service with commercials. But the commercials have caused controversy. The issue is whether public school students should be exposed to advertising in their classrooms. Indeed, the ads must work. Commercials on Channel One cost $200,000 for 30 seconds. That's because they reach over 8 million teenagers at a time.

On the one hand, opponents argue that students in public school classrooms should not be made captive audiences for TV ads selling cosmetics, junk food, sneakers, and sodas. The Parent-Teacher Association (PTA) and the National Education Association (NEA) are against Channel One for this reason. Another group, called UNPLUG, has produced a video called "Schools for Sale"; the title makes the group's point. As one member of UNPLUG explained, exposing a student to two minutes' worth of commercials daily throughout the school year (180 days) means donating two full days of a student's time to watching ads. There is also the problem that some students (wrongly) assume that the school endorses the products advertised.

On the other hand, proponents argue that students will watch commercials anyway and that Channel One provides a way for schools suffering from budget cuts to fund needed new equipment. They also argue that students can be encouraged to watch with a critical eye, so that the commercials can provide material for lessons in critical thinking (Brown 1996).

A related issue, however, is whether encouraging television watching is good for students generally, even if they are not exposed to commercials. In this regard, one study found that television watching reduces people's interest in reading newspapers, with an overall negative effect on vocabulary development (Glenn 1994).

Whether or not you watched Channel One in high school, you may soon be watching it in college. The company is developing a college channel.

COLLEGE

WHO GOES, AND WHERE?

As Figure 15.1 at the beginning of the chapter shows, all segments of the population have been affected by the expansion in education, but significant differences still remain. Since the data reported in Figure 15.1 are for the population over 25, they reflect not only the experiences of today's young people but also those of people who went to school 20, 40, and even 60 years ago. Has the educational gap been eliminated among the current generation? The answer is no.

Today, approximately 43 percent of all high school graduates between the ages of 18 and 21 are enrolled in colleges or universities (U.S. Bureau of the Census 1995, Table 269). This means that 57 percent are not enrolled. Twenty percent of high school graduates aged 25 to 29 have graduated from college; this means that 80 percent have not. Thus, although you and many of the people you know have gone to college, you are in the minority.

Until just a few years ago, non-Hispanic white males were the group most likely to be enrolled in college, but this has changed (see Figure 15.4). Today

We tend to speak of "going to college" as if it were a homogeneous experience. In fact, there is wide diversity in the extent to which colleges offer access to traditional collegiate life. This community college in Austin, Texas, is obviously designed for the highly motivated. There is no beautiful campus, no football team, and no frills. It is not surprising that studies show that intelligence and achievement motivation are more important determinants of success at community colleges than four-year schools.

non-Hispanic white females are the group most likely to be in college. Except for professional and doctoral degrees, which still go mainly to white men, white female collegiates are also the most likely to graduate (U.S. Bureau of the Census 1995, Table 298). At least among women, racial/ethnic differences in college attendance are smaller today than they used to be (see Figure 15.4). Nevertheless, non-Hispanic whites—both women and men—are far more likely to attend and to graduate from college than are African Americans or Hispanics (U.S. Bureau of the Census 1995, Table 303). The percentages of non-Hispanic whites and Asian Americans who earn degrees just about match these groups' proportions in the total U.S. population. This is not the case for African Americans and Hispanics. For these two groups, the percentages earning degrees are considerably smaller than their proportions in the population (U.S. Bureau of the Census 1995, Table 303).

Partly, this racial/ethnic divergence in the proportions of college graduates results from factors discussed earlier in this chapter: Textbooks do not necessarily address issues relevant to African Americans' or Hispanics' history or experience; faculty members have lower expectations for these minority students; the students have fewer role models. Then, too, college educations are expensive—as you no doubt know. A resident student in a four-year public college pays about $9,000 a year. A private college costs a whopping $18,000 a year (U.S. Bureau of the Census 1995, Table 288). Scholarships and student loans help, but it still ends up costing a chunk of money to get a higher education. Because they have lower average incomes and are more likely to be poor (see Chapter 9), African Americans and Hispanics are less able to afford college than are non-Hispanics whites and Asian Americans. Furthermore as Table 15.1 shows, African American and Hispanic students are less likely to have other resources—home computers, for example—that facilitate college success.

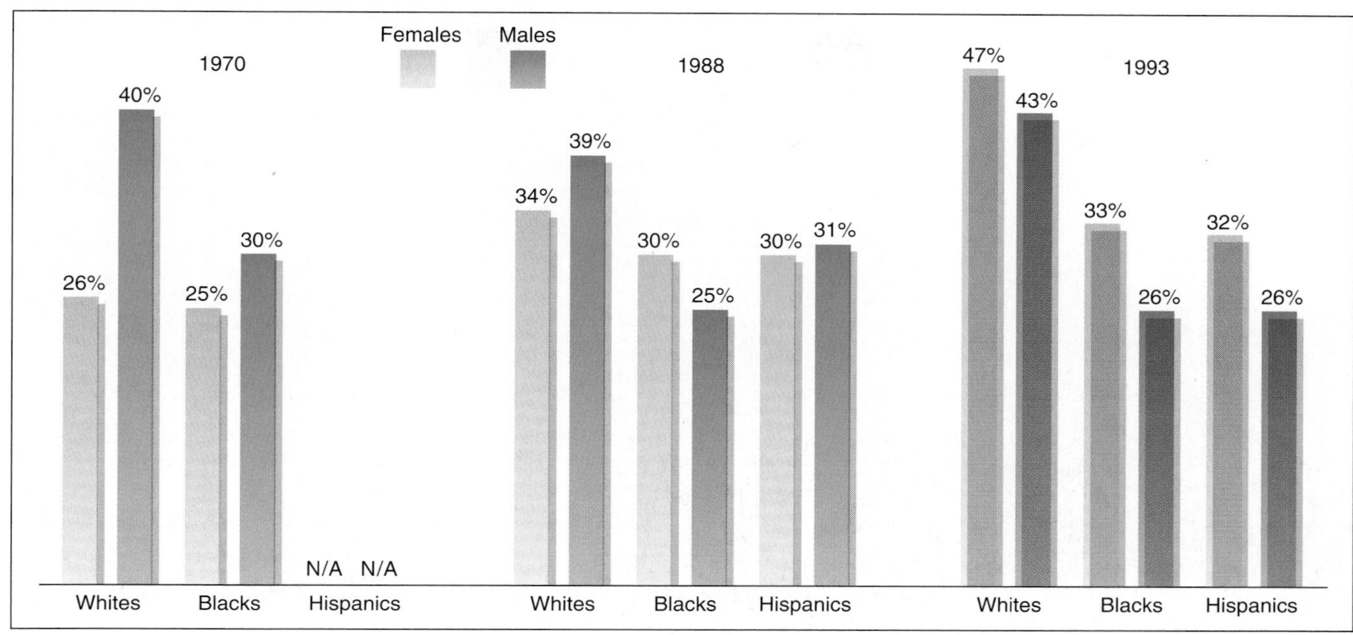

FIGURE 15.4
PERCENTAGE OF HIGH SCHOOL GRADUATES AGES 18 TO 24 ENROLLED IN COLLEGE, BY RACE, ETHNICITY, AND SEX, 1970 AND 1988

Comparisons by sex, race, and ethnicity show increasing similarity in the likelihood that high school graduates from each category will attend college. The declining enrollment rates for black males are a cause for concern.

SOURCE: American Council on Education 1990; U.S. Bureau of the Census 1995, Table 269NA: Data for Hispanics not available in 1970.

WHAT'S THE BOTTOM LINE? WHAT WILL COLLEGE DO FOR ME?

For many people, the chief objective of getting a college education is to get a good job and earn more. This objective has been and continues to be realistic. In 1993, the average college graduate, male or female, earned about 50 percent more *annually* than the average high school graduate (U.S. Bureau of the Census 1995, Table 742). Some of this additional income is related to background characteristics rather than years in school. That is, people who complete college generally have higher high school test scores and higher-status parents. These factors would have raised their incomes even if they had not completed college. Nevertheless, college continues to pay a handsome profit.

As Table 15.2 shows, this profit does vary by sex. At every educational level, males' earnings exceed those of females.

Nevertheless, people who graduate from college not only have higher incomes than those with less education but also get better jobs and experience lower unemployment, as Table 15.3 shows. Economically, then, your investment in a college education will pay off.

It can pay off in other ways too. It is a value judgment to say that a college education will make you a better person, but it is value judgment that the majority of

TABLE 15.1
PERCENT OF STUDENTS WITH COMPUTERS AT HOME TO USE FOR SCHOOLWORK, 1993

Even if they are sitting side by side in the same college classroom and had exactly the same ACT or SAT scores, a non-Hispanic white student and an African American or Hispanic student may not have the same resources that translate into chances for college success. Non-Hispanic white college students are more than twice as likely to have home computers, for example.

	TOTAL	GRADES 1–8	GRADES 9–12	1ST TO 4TH YEAR OF COLLEGE
NON-HISPANIC WHITE	18	14	27	26
AFRICAN-AMERICAN	6	4	7	12
HISPANIC	6	3	7	16

SOURCE: U.S. Bureau of the Census 1995, Table 260.

college graduates are willing to make. Surveys show that people feel positively about their college education, believing that it has made them better and more tolerant people.

Whether it makes you a better person or not, a college education is likely to have a lasting effect on your knowledge and values. If you finish college, you will have sat through 30 to 45 different courses. Even the least dedicated students are

TABLE 15.2
ECONOMIC RETURNS OF ADDITIONAL EDUCATION, 1994

For both men and women, there is a substantial economic payoff for educational attainment after high school. Full-time, full-year workers who completed college annual earn 55 percent more than college graduate and a Master's degree adds another 23-24 percent. Although women earn far less than men, men and women receive nearly identical percentage returns from their educational investments.

	FEMALE	MALE
MEDIAN TOTAL MONEY INCOME FOR FULL-TIME, FULL YEAR WORKERS 25 AND OVER WITH:		
4 YEARS OF HIGH SCHOOL	$20,373	$28,037
4 YEARS OF COLLEGE	31,741	43,663
MASTER'S DEGREE	38,457	53,500
PERCENTAGE INCREASE IN INCOME FOR GOING FROM:		
4 YEARS OF HIGH SCHOOL TO 4 YEARS OF COLLEGE	56%	56%
4 YEARS OF COLLEGE TO A MASTER'S DEGREE	23%	24%

SOURCE: U.S. Bureau of the Census, 1996.

TABLE 15.3
SOCIOECONOMIC CONSEQUENCES OF EDUCATION, 1991–1992

Education pays off in terms of good jobs and good income. The differences shown in this table, however, are not all directly related to additional years of schooling. People who graduated from college have, on the average, higher high school grades and more background advantages than those who graduated from high school only. These circumstances may have as much to do with their achievements as do their additional years of schooling.

EDUCATION	PERCENTAGE WITH MANAGERIAL OR PROFEESIONAL OCCUPATION	PERCENTAGE UNEMPLOYED	MEDIAN INCOME OF FULL-TIME, FULL-YEAR WORKERS (MALE)
LESS THAN 4 YEARS OF HIGH SCHOOL	5%	11%	$19,432
EXACTLY 4 YEARS OF HIGH SCHOOL	12	7	26,218
1–3 YEARS OF COLLEGE	25	6	31,034
4 OR MORE YEARS OF COLLEGE	67	3	42,367

SOURCE: U.S. Bureau of the Census 1993a; U.S. Bureau of the Census 1992a.

bound to learn something from these courses. In addition, students learn informally. Whether you go to college in your hometown or across the country, college will introduce you to a greater diversity of people than you're likely to have experienced before. This diversity will challenge your mind and broaden your horizons. As a result of formal and informal learning, college graduates are more knowledgeable about the world around them, more tolerant and less prejudiced, more active in public and community affairs, less traditional in their religious and gender-role beliefs, and more open to new ideas than those who don't have a college degree (Funk and Willits 1987; Weil 1985).

GLOBAL PERSPECTIVES: THE JAPANESE MODEL OF EDUCATION

In the last decade or so, the U.S. public school system has received a great deal of bad press. Standardized scores for America's children are down compared with their own earlier scores, and they compare very unfavorably with those of children in the rest of the world. American employers and college professors complain that high school graduates lack basic skills. In addition to being accused of being too soft, the schools are also accused of being unfair. Before assessing the American educational system, let us put it in perspective by taking a look at an educational system that is sometimes held up as a model.

The Japanese educational system looks much like ours on the surface. Over 90 percent of children age 15 to 17 are enrolled in high school, and substantial proportions go on to college. Nevertheless, the system differs from ours in three fundamental ways: more schooling, more explicit tracking, and a stronger link between school performance and jobs.

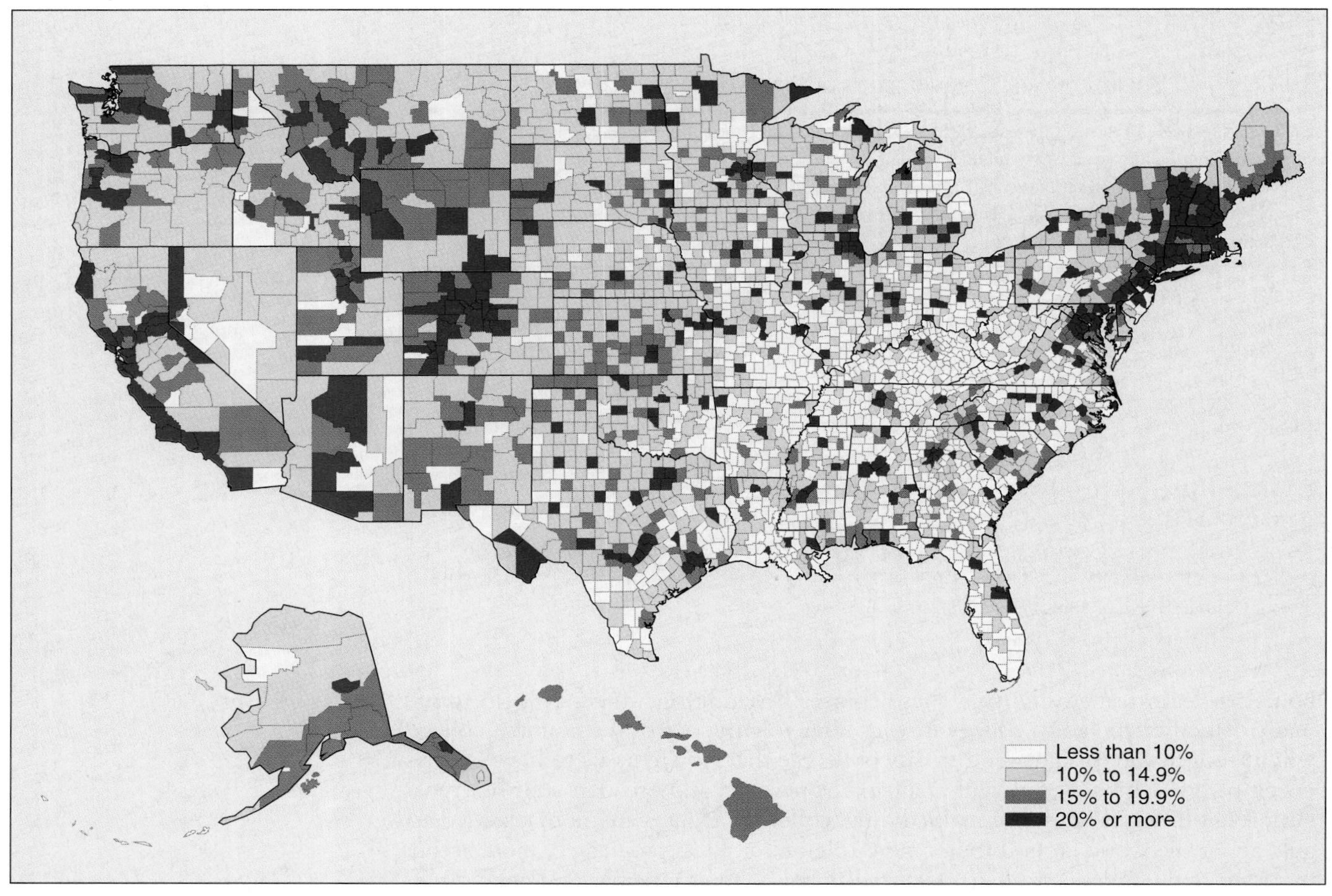

MAP 15.1
PERCENT OF PEOPLE 25 AND OVER WITH BACHELOR DEGREES, 1990

SOURCE: *Atlas of Contemporary America: Portrait of a Nation*, Text © 1994 by Rodger Doyle; Illustrations © 1994 by Facts on File.

MORE SCHOOLING

In Japan, children begin school at age three (Unks 1992), and the school year is 240 days long, compared with 180 days in the United States. Since students spend so much more time in school, it is not surprising that they learn more. In the first and second grades, Japanese students probably receive less academic instruction than U.S. students; their primary task in these early grades is to learn appropriate attitudes about learning and cooperation. (Peach 1994). Once they start their academic curriculum in the third grade, however, they get a very heavy dose of the basics. Their homework demands are much heavier than those of American students.

> **THINKING CRITICALLY**
>
> How might the United States incorporate what is good about the Japanese model of education without reproducing the negative aspects—or is this possible, given the two different cultures?

MORE EXPLICIT TRACKING

In Japan, public high schools are formally differentiated by purposes and status: There are top-notch college preparatory high schools, average college preparatory high schools, vocational schools, and general education schools. You cannot get into a top-notch university unless you go to a top-notch high school. (Rosenbaum and Kariya 1989).

High school assignment is based on an examination taken at age 15. Your score on this examination affects which high school you go to, which will in turn determine which—if any—college you go to and ultimately what job you get. As a result of the overwhelming importance of this single test, Japanese students study very hard for it. Most parents who aspire to a college education for their children make major financial sacrifices to send their children to special "cramming" schools called *jukos*. These cramming schools may run until 10 o'clock at night up to six days a week (Pettersen 1993). If you want to go to college, you have to decide early enough to study hard for your examination. You cannot decide at 18 that you really want to go to college after all.

Although the U.S. and Japanese educational systems are superficially similar, Japanese children have a very different experience in the schools. In the early grades, Japanese schools place less emphasis on academic basics and more emphasis on learning cooperation and positive attitudes. The uniforms that Japanese schoolchildren wear symbolize commitment to group identification and loyalty, values that apply both in kindergarten and industry.

LINK BETWEEN EDUCATION AND JOBS

Unlike the American student, the Japanese student doesn't need to write up a résumé and start knocking on doors when he or she is ready to start working. At both the college and the vocational high school level, schools have contracts with employers (Rosenbaum and Kariya 1989). These agreements specify, for example, that Ido Vocational High School will send 45 students to Sony for work on its video recorder assembly line or that Ido Community College will send the company 10 computer technicians. This link between school and labor market covers the best jobs available—the jobs with big companies, better wages, more security, and higher benefits. School performance and teacher recommendations cast a long shadow over one's life. Again, there is relatively little forgiveness in the system. Unless you were well behaved and hardworking in school, you are likely to find yourself at a substantial disadvantage in the labor market.

COMPARING U.S. WITH JAPANESE EDUCATION

Japan has the highest literacy rate in the world (Concar 1993). Surely this is an accomplishment to be proud of! Nevertheless, the Japanese model of education has been criticized on four fronts.

First, some observers argue that the excellence of Japan's public school system is a myth. In fact, students do well because they invest the money and time to attend private cramming schools, the *jukos* (Goya 1993). Private *jukos*, not Japan's public school system, are responsible for high achievement.

Second, going to the *jukos* requires money, and consequently—as in the United States—those in the higher social classes are most likely to benefit. Hence, the wealthier Japanese get into the best universities and, later, get the best jobs (Stevenson and Baker 1992). This is a Japanese illustration of the reproduction of inequality, discussed earlier in this chapter.

A third criticism is that high school competition in Japan places undue stress on students. For example, parents who can afford it even send their toddlers to cram preschools, or "escalator schools" (Rosario 1992). Doing so helps youngsters get places in the better elementary and secondary schools and eventually in the best universities (Whitburn 1994). Relentless stress is thought to be responsible for the high suicide rate among Japan's adolescents (Concar 1993). Recognizing this, in 1992, Japanese public schools began giving students one Saturday off each month (Shiomi 1993).

Finally, critics argue that the high literacy rate and competence with numbers of the Japanese people result mainly from rote memorization and that Japanese students are actually discouraged from creative thinking (Concar 1993; Young 1993).

Compared with Japan's, the U.S. educational system is less demanding, more flexible, and more forgiving. We try to keep students' options open as long as we can. Our colleges welcome nontraditional students who decide at age 25 or 35 or 45 that they would like to go to college. The link between school and labor market is also much looser; students who cut up in school can become serious and get a good job. To many Americans, these traits appear to be advantages of our system. They appeal to our desire to give everybody an equal chance and a second and even a third chance.

CONCLUSION

Most contemporary sociological analyses of schooling focus on the role of the school in reproducing social class advantage and disadvantage. These analyses illuminate how a lower social class background puts children at a disadvantage that is magnified rather than eliminated by school processes.

The people who benefit from today's educational system are the middle-and upper-middle-class parents whose children get good public educations that allow them access to colleges and universities and ultimately to good jobs. These parents are not scheming to put down the masses, but they are trying to protect their children and their schools.

U.S. educational institutions have many critics. These critics are chiefly concerned with two issues: equity and quality. Those more concerned about equity argue that the schools do too little to create equality of opportunity and are actually a chief agent in reproducing social and economic inequality. Those concerned primary about quality tend to focus on average outcomes, such as SAT scores. The former are likely to support affirmative action programs and multicultural curricula in colleges and universities. The latter are inclined to favor college admissions and faculty hiring based strictly on merit as determined by objective criteria, such as SAT scores, and to prefer a traditional curriculum based on the classics.

Schools are a vitally important institution. In 1993, the United States spent $438 *billion* on education; over 62 million children and young adults were enrolled. Over 3 million people are employed by the schools. Perhaps more important, the schools play a vital role in determining the character of future generations. They provide new citizens, new workers, new parents.

For all of these reasons, we must care about how well the schools are doing their job. From many points of view, the answer appears to be "poorly," especially with regard to poor, female, African American, and Hispanic students. (Oakes and Quartz 1995). In the Applications in Diversity section that closes this chapter, we examine how colleges have addressed diversity issues.

APPLICATIONS IN DIVERSITY

IS THE POLITICALLY CORRECT CAMPUS A GOOD THING?

Just 40 years ago, the vast majority of college students and their teachers were white and male. They followed a curriculum based mostly on the works and ideas of white men of European or North American heritage. They could say anything they wanted on campus without worrying whether their attitudes and remarks were belittling or degrading to minority ethnic groups or females.

As you know, things are changing. The majority of college faculty are still white males, but more ethnic minorities and women attend and teach in colleges today than in the past. Especially in humanities and social science courses, they are likely to study works by and about women and people of color. Many colleges and universities now have speech codes prohibiting public language that is offensive to certain ethnic groups or women.

Change began in the 1960s and continued throughout the 1970s and 1980s as colleges and universities increasingly focused on diversifying their student bodies and faculties. As classrooms grew more diverse, it became clear that many students were studying curricula that failed to address their history, literature, or personal experience. For the most part, students still read the works of white European males and not those of women, African Americans, Hispanics, Asians, or Native Americans. Students heard about the European Renaissance but not the Harlem Renaissance. In response to this situation, colleges and universities began to diversify their curricula.

Meanwhile, ethnic and gender diversity on campus gave occasion for some students to provoke race- or gender-related uneasiness—by publicly making pejorative remarks or posting signs demeaning to certain minorities, for example. In response, many administrators instituted policies against "hate speech" on campus.

By the 1990s, some observers were questioning whether multiculturalism had gone too far. Critics dubbed the movement "politically correct," or "PC"; and they used these terms derogatorily to designate a climate in which the concerns of women and minorities had higher priority than those of white males. Today, there is considerable debate over whether multicultural education and the politically correct campus are good things. The controversy centers on four questions: Who will be taught? Who will teach? What will be taught? In what atmosphere will students learn?

Who Will Be Taught?

Aiming to create a student body with ethnic proportions that mirror those in the U.S. population as a whole, the University of California at Berkeley refused admission to an immigrant Vietnamese boat person who had higher SAT scores and high school grades than did many African American and Hispanic students who were admitted (D'Souza 1991). The situation not only angered Asian American organizations but also has encouraged critics to question affirmative action policies and practices more generally. As a result, the University of California system may scrap its affirmative action policy (Fineman 1995c).

We have seen that education sifts and sorts students, determining who will be allowed to go on, graduate, and hence be qualified for the better jobs. Ideally, education functions to ensure the best use of the best minds. But we have also seen that IQ tests and tracking in elementary and high schools discriminate against lower-class students and many minority students. As a result, education has the latent dysfunction of perpetuating inequality. A question emerges whether admission to higher education should be based solely on merit without regard for the resulting ethnic and gendered student mix. Or is it preferable to actively pursue the goal of student diversity, even when this means admitting students with lower scores and grades than some nonadmitted students?

Who Will Teach?

Over the past 15 years, college administrations have tried to create a more ethnically diverse faculty of both men and women. To do so, many have given preference to qualified women and minorities. Some schools have created new faculty positions specifically designated for minority professors. The goals of these practices are twofold: (1) to give opportunities to faculty who might otherwise not have been hired owing to discrimination and (2) to create a faculty that is more hospitable to female and minority students, providing them with role models to whom they can better relate. But the National Association of Scholars (1992), a faculty organization opposed to this practice, argues that "two-track hiring" should be stopped because it threatens to produce a divided faculty rather than a genuinely integrated one.

APPLICATIONS IN DIVERSITY

What Will Be Taught?

An introductory political science course at Johns Hopkins University has replaced some classics with Spike Lee's movie *Do the Right Thing* ("Minor Curriculum Adjustment" 1992). From the structural-functional perspective, an important purpose of education is to assimilate persons from diverse backgrounds by exposing them to a common curriculum, thereby promoting a common cultural base. Opponents of the politically correct campus contend that to replace classics with multicultural requirements not only dilutes academic rigor but also threatens American culture and derails assimilation. Meanwhile, proponents of a multicultural curriculum argue that teaching only the classics is inappropriate because there *is* no common cultural base or historical experience for all Americans (Stimpson 1992, 44). The cultures and histories of Native Americans and African Americans, for example, are not the cultures and histories of Irish, Italian, or Jewish Americans.

In What Atmosphere Will Students Learn?

A freshman at the University of Pennsylvania successfully challenged the school's speech code concerning racist language when he admitted calling some African American women on campus "water buffaloes" but said he did not mean anything racist ("University of Pennsylvania" 1993). Proponents of speech codes argue that minority and female students need to feel safe on campus. Hostile language, demonstrations, and other activities deny minority students truly equal access to education and threaten the academic atmosphere (Painter 1994). Opponents maintain that the codes violate free speech rights and discourage intellectual debate because they intimidate students of the dominant culture and thereby stifle free-flowing classroom discussion (Sidorsky 1993).

Conclusion

Those in favor of multiculturalism on campus tend to proceed from the conflict perspective on education: They view the institution as it has existed until recently as a tool of the elite. It comes as no surprise, in this view, that those who benefit from the system seek to perpetuate it. Proponents argue that the opposition exaggerates the relatively few instances of abuse and has created a propaganda campaign aimed at preserving a threatened status quo (Bader 1992).

Opponents counter that, while traditional education may have some drawbacks, political correctness is wrong for several reasons: It results in discrimination against white men; is intolerant of dissent (Kimball 1993); has divided U.S. society into discordant, complaining groups (Hughes 1993); and aims at social transformation rather than truth (Kimball 1993; Mirsky 1993; Searle 1993). At least one writer has argued that both the multicultural movement and its opponents have at times gone too far (Thelin 1992).

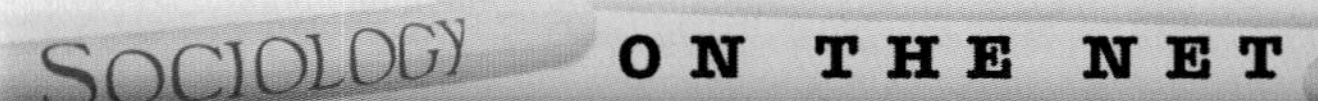

Education, like the family, is a hot topic. American students often compare poorly to students from other nations on standardized tests. Teachers' unions are criticized and dropout rates are far too high. Our inner city schools are crumbling. How well is America educating its young?

http://aft.org/index.htm

The American Federation of Teachers is one of the largest and most influential teacher unions in the country. Browse around the **home page** and note the services for members and the issues of importance to the members. Click on the highlighted title **The Research Department;** now, click on the **Publications, Reports and Surveys** section. Scroll down to the **International** section and at long last click on the highlighted title **How and How Much the United States Spends on K-12 etc.** Browse through this extensive document paying special attention to the charts, summary statements and the conclusion section. Why is how we spend our money as important a question as how much we spend? How does the U.S. spend its money differently than other nations? What alternatives do we see when we look to other nations?

Listening to the critics may lead to inaccurate conclusions. Once more the Census Bureau has some important facts for us to consider.

`http://www.census.gov/population/pop-profile/toc.html`

Let's begin our education by reading the selections entitled **School Enrollment** and **Educational Attainment**. How well are our schools doing from a statistical standpoint? How is the graduation rate and who is going on to college? What are some of the problems that still confront our educational system? How do these measures compare to the statements from the previous report? Now return to the **table of contents** and click on the report dealing with **Postsecondary School Financing**. What kind of school are you currently attending? Do you receive any financial aid? How much do you have to pay for your education? How does this compare to the figures provided in the report?

The issue of political correctness has permeated nearly all aspects of higher education. As noted in the text, this can be a very divisive issue on college campuses. According to the Hegelian Dialectic, social change occurs through the steps called *thesis*, *antithesis* and *thesis*. If political correctness is the thesis, then the backlash is the antithesis. The National Association of Scholars is an organization opposed to much of what is called political correctness.

`http://www.nas.org/home.htm`

Once you have reached the **home page**, click on the **NAS Statements**, now open the selection entitled **Is The Curriculum Biased?** How do you rate the curriculum at your school? Is it politically correct? Is it eurocentric and patriarchal? Or, does it fall somewhere in between? Return to the home page and click on the **Press Releases** section. Now open the selection entitled **The Dissolution of General Education 1914 - 1993**. Browse through this extensive document paying attention to the introduction, findings and especially the conclusion. How do you view your general education requirements? Do they provide a rigorous foundation for your education or are they simply one more hoop to jump through in order to graduate? Think ahead to about twenty-five years from now. How well will your general education classes serve you then?

1 During the 19th century, a consensus developed that public education was so desirable that it should be compulsory. Contributing factors were parental demand, labor demand, and demands for social control.

2 Elementary education was universal by 1900, but high school education didn't become commonplace until the 1930s. College education expanded dramatically after World War II,. African Americans, Hispanics, and Native Americans have not been full participants in the expansion of education.

3 The sociology of education is largely concerned with the link between educational and stratification.

4 Structural-functional theories of education argue that education performs many functions (cultural reproduction, social control, assimilation, teaching of specific skills, selection of students for future adult roles, and promotion of change); failure to equalize opportunity for the disadvantaged is one latent dysfunction.

5 Conflict theory suggests that education helps maintain inequality in three ways: hidden curriculum, credentialism, and the reproduction of inequality. Most contemporary analyses of education focus on the role of education in reproducing advantage and disadvantage.

6 Social class affects preparation for school, attitudes toward school, and thus school performance and deportment. Students from lower-class backgrounds are more likely to end up tracked into low-ability groups; this process builds on previous disadvantage so that disadvantage snowballs.

7 Attempts to improve the quality of America's schools by stiffening requirements could backfire if they simultaneously increased the already high dropout rate. Strategies that might raise achievements levels without encouraging disadvantaged students to drop out are to raise teacher expectations; to reduce school size; to maintain flexible curricula and schedules for youths who marry, work, or bear children; and to use grants and loans to encourage disadvantaged students to become teachers.

8 Compared with social class effects, school effects are relatively weak. Greater Catholic school success is probably due to more caring parents rather than to characteristics of the schools. Schools with a majority of students from disadvantaged backgrounds (regardless of racial composition) retard student achievement. Effective schools are characterized by a positive attitude, not by get-tough policies.

9 About 43 percent of U.S. high school graduates between 18 and 21 are enrolled in college. Minority enrollment is rising but still does not equal that for non-Hispanic whites.

10 College pays off in terms of more income, better jobs, and less unemployment.

11 Japanese education differs from American education in three ways: more schooling, more explicit tracking, and a stronger link between school performance and jobs.

12 In the 1990s, public debate erupted over the "politically correct," multicultural college campus. Concerns focused on who would or should be admitted, who would be hired as faculty, whether curricula should be multicultural or emphasize the classics, and whether campus administrators should initiate speech codes.

SUGGESTED READINGS

ARTHUR, Richard. 1992. *Gangs and Schools*. Holmes Beach, Fla.: Learning Publications, Inc. A book written by an educator who spent over 25 years working with gangs as a teacher, a principal, and a neighborhood counselor. The book provides insights about what must be done by educators and their communities to turn around inner city schools and neighborhoods.

AUFDERHEIDE, Patricia (ed.). 1992. *Beyond PC: Toward a Politics of Understanding*. St. Paul: Graywolf. A collection of essays on both sides of the issue of political correctness in universities.

COLEMAN, James, and Hoffer, Thomas. 1987. *Public and Private High Schools: The Impact of Communities*. New York: Basic Books. The latest "Coleman report." (The first "Coleman report" is considered responsible for busing.) In this work, —which, like the first report, ignited major public debate—Coleman and Hoffer argue that Catholic schools are better.

FRASER, Steven (ed.). 1995. *The Bell Curve Wars: Race, Intelligence, and the Future of America*. New York: Basic Books. Essays on both sides of the controversial issue of whether IQ tests accurately measure intelligence and whether African Americans' average scores are lower than those of non-Hispanic whites because of innate abilities or sociocultural factors.

JACOBY, Russel, and Glaubeiman, Naomi (eds.). 1995. *The Bell Curve Debate: History, Documents, Opinions*. New York: Random House/Times Books. Similar to Fraser's book, described above, but with more explanation of the history of this issue along with excerpts from Richard Herrnstein and Charles Murray's book *The Bell Curve*.

KOZOL, Jonathan, 1991. *Savage Inequalities: Children in America's Schools*. New York: Crown. A comparison with detailed examples of schools and school districts across the United States that illustrates serious inequalities, with minority children generally attending America's most crowded and least well-equipped schools.

OAKES, Jeannie. 1992. *Educational Matchmaking: Academic and Vocational Tracking in Comprehensive High Schools*. Santa Monica, Calif.: Rand. An argument that the tracking process in schools seriously reduces the ability to provide equal education and social opportunities to disadvantaged youngsters.

OAKES, Jeannie, and Quartz, Karen Hunter (eds.). 1995. *Creating New Educational Communities*. Chicago: University of Chicago Press. A collection of essays and research reports by respected sociologists of education that give concrete suggestions for improving the U.S. educational system.

ORENSTEIN, Peggy. 1994. *School Girls: Young Women, Self-Esteem, and the Confidence Gap*. New York: Doubleday. A book, written in association with the American Association of University Women, that describes young women in three California middle schools. The book illustrates the socially structured processes by which these young women lower their academic and career expectations.

SAN MIGUEL, Guadalupe. 1987. *Let Them All Take Heed*. Austin: University of Texas Press. A historical and impassioned study of the processes by which Hispanic students were kept out of education for a century after the United States annexed Texas.

WHITE, Merry. 1987. *The Japanese Educational Challenge*. New York: Free Press. A (most admiring) look at education in Japan, with challenges to American readers to emulate Japan's commitment to educational achievement.

CHAPTER 16

Political Institutions

OUTLINE

PROLOGUE

Have You Ever . . . wondered what would happen if they held an election and nobody came? Voters in the United States are pretty apathetic. The 1992 presidential election was good news as far as voter turnout goes. For the first time in over 20 years, the proportion of Americans who voted increased. But still, fewer than two-thirds (61.3 percent) cast a ballot. Compared with those in other democracies, U.S. citizens don't appear to care very much. This apparent apathy makes a startling contrast against, for example, the 96 percent of Australians who vote because they are required to by law ("Different Votes" 1994) or the two-thirds of Peruvians who voted in an election in the 1980s in the face of threats by Shining Path guerrillas that they would cut off the right hand of anybody seen voting?

It is possible that you *do* vote. You may even have donated to a political cause, participated in a demonstration, or written to your Congressional representative. But it's more likely that you haven't done any of these things. Only about two-fifths of people under 25 voted in the last presidential election (U.S. Bureau of the Census 1995, Table 459). And few students can identify their own state's U.S. senators. (Poll your class and see.)

Why are Americans apathetic? There are two reasons. First, they don't think that their vote counts—that anybody cares what they think. Second, they don't see much difference between the candidates or the parties. Who cares who wins?

In this chapter, we examine the basis for these opinions. We identify major political actors and ask who makes the decisions. We also look at rates of individual participation and see whether participation makes a difference. In the course of the chapter, we may confirm some of your reasons for not voting, but we also provide some ideas that may increase your ability to affect political decisions.

POWER AND POLITICAL INSTITUTIONS

The concept *power* is essential to understanding political institutions. This section examines that connection between power and politics.

POWER

Lisa wants to watch *Batman* while John wants to watch *Sesame Street;* Christian fundamentalists want prayer in the schools, and the American Civil Liberties Union wants it out. Pro-choice activists want abortion to stay legal and pro-life activists don't. Senior citizens want Social Security and Medicare benefits to stay pretty much as they are; others want to lower benefits to help balance the budget. Who decides?

Whether the decision maker is mom, dad, grandma, or the Supreme Court, decision makers who are able to make and enforce decisions have power. **Power** is the ability to direct others' behavior, even against their wishes. To the extent that grandma's decision determines what Lisa and John do, she has power; if the

Power is the ability to direct others' behavior, even against their wishes.

Supreme Court's decision affects prayer in the school, then it has power. As these examples illustrate, power occurs in all kinds of social groups, from families to societies.

Although both grandmothers and courts have power, there are obvious differences in the basis of their power, the breadth of their jurisdiction, and the means they have to compel obedience. The social structure most centrally involved with the exercise of power is the state, and that is the focus of this chapter. Before we begin, however, we give a broad overview of two kinds of power, coercion and authority, as well as a closely related phenomenon—influence.

Coercion is the exercise of power through force or the threat of force.

Coercion. The exercise of power through force or the threat of force is **coercion.** The threat may involve physical, financial, or social injury. The key is that we do as we have been told only because we are afraid not to. We may be afraid that we will be injured, but we may also be afraid of a fine or of rejection.

Power through coercion may or may not be legitimated by social norms and values. If you see a state patrol officer stop someone for driving recklessly and know that the driver will have to pay a fine, you generally accept this as legitimate; the activities of the mugger who takes the same amount of money are not legitimate. Similarly, although it has been generally acceptable to threaten your children ("Clean your room or you cannot go out") and even to spank them, it is considered unacceptable to threaten your spouse.

Authority is power supported by norms and values that legitimate its use.

Authority. Threats are sometimes quite effective in making people follow orders. They tend to create conflict and animosity, however, and it would be much easier if people would just agree that they were supposed to do whatever it was they were told. This is not as rare as you might suppose. This commonplace kind of power is called **authority** and refers to power that is supported by norms and values that legitimate its use. When you have authority, your subordinates agree that, in this matter at least, you have the right to make decisions and they have a duty to obey. For example, most students agree that their instructor has the right to make up and grade tests.

In a classic analysis of power, Weber distinguished three bases on which this agreement is likely to rest: tradition, extraordinary personal qualities (charisma), and legal rules.

Traditional authority is a right to make decisions for others that is based on the sanctity of time-honored routines.

TRADITIONAL AUTHORITY. A right to make decisions that is based on the sanctity of time-honored routines is **traditional authority** (Weber [1910] 1970e, 296). Monarchies and patriarchies are classic examples of this type of authority. For example, only 40 years ago, the majority of women and men in our society believed that husbands ought to make all the major decisions in the family; husbands had authority. Today, much of that authority has disappeared. Traditional authority, according to Weber, is not based on reason; it is based on a reverence for the past.

Charismatic authority is a right to make decisions that is based on perceived extraordinary personal characteristics.

CHARISMATIC AUTHORITY. Individuals who are given the right to make decisions because of perceived extraordinary personal characteristics have **charismatic authority** (Weber [1910] 1970e, 295). These characteristics (often including an assumed direct link to God) put the bearer of charisma on a different level from subordinates. Gandhi's authority was of this form. He held neither political office nor hereditary position, yet he was able to mold national policy in India. John F.

Power is an important part of all institutions and most social relationships. Teachers have power over their students, parents have power over their children, and coaches have power over their players. Teacher/student power inequalities are built into institutionalized statuses and supported by widely shared norms. In most cases, students agree that professors have the right to set the syllabus and the course requirements. In addition to this institutionalized authority, many good teachers also influence their students outside of the classroom.

Kennedy, Malcolm X, and the Reverend Martin Luther King were also leaders with charismatic authority.

Charismatic authority may be very powerful, gaining followers' loyalty as well as obedience. By nature, however, it is unstable; it resides in an individual and is therefore mortal. If efforts are made to pass on charisma—if, for example, it is argued that charisma is a property of the son as well as the father—then charismatic authority may evolve into traditional authority.

RATIONAL-LEGAL AUTHORITY. When decision-making rights are allocated on the basis of rationally established rules, as through a constitution, we speak of **rational-legal authority.** An essential element of rational-legal authority is that it is impersonal. You do not need to like or admire or even agree with the person in authority; you simply follow the rules.

Rational-legal authority is a right to make decisions that is based on rationally established rules.

Rational-legal authority is the kind on which U.S. government is based. When we want to know whether the president or the Congress has a right to make certain decisions, we simply check our rule book: the Constitution. As long as they follow the rules, most of us agree that they have the right to make decisions and we have a duty to obey.

SUMMARY. Analytically, we can make clear distinctions among these three types of authority. In practice, the successful exercise of authority often combines two or more. An elected official who adds charisma to the rational-legal authority stipulated by the law will have more power; the successful charismatic leader will soon establish a bureaucratic system of rational-legal authority to help manage and direct followers.

All types of authority, however, rest on the agreement of subordinates that someone has the right to make a decision about them and that they have a duty to obey it. This does not mean that the decision will always be obeyed or even that each and every subordinate will agree that the distribution of power is legitimate. Rather, it means that society's norms and values legitimate the inequality in power. For example, if a parent tells her teenagers to be in at midnight, they may come in later. They may even argue that she has no right to run their lives. Nevertheless, most people, including children, would agree that the parent does have the right—even the obligation—to supervise her children.

Because authority is supported by shared norms and values, it can usually be exercised without conflict. Ultimately, however, authority rests on the ability to back up commands with coercion. Parents may back up their authority over teenagers with threats to lock them out of the house or take the car away. Churches back up their authority with threats to excommunicate. Teachers back up their authority with threats to flunk, suspend, or expel students. Employers can fire or demote workers. Authority rests on a legitimation of coercion (Wrong 1979).

Influence is the ability to affect others' decisions through persuasion and personal appeals.

Influence. A concept closely related to power is **influence.** The wielder of influence has no right to make the decision and no way to compel obedience; instead, the person must rely on persuasion and personal appeals. Charismatic leaders, discussed above, wield influence. When you try to persuade people to change their opinion, party, or creed (or when you try to sell them a vacuum cleaner), you are attempting to use influence.

Influence is not institutionalized; it rests on an individual appeal based on personal or ideological grounds rather than on social structure. It is typically the strategy of groups that are structurally powerless. But even people who have a great deal of power must often use influence if they want to affect actions outside the scope of their authority. The president of the United States, for example, has no authority to compel Congress to support his legislative proposals. To get congressional approval, he must try to exercise influence. He calls individual senators on the telephone, invites them to dinner, and generally courts their favor, using personal appeals and persuasive arguments to move them to his position.

As this example suggests, influence and power often exist side by side. For example, many parents first try to influence their children to do what they want and use authority and then coercion as last resorts. In bureaucracies, there are patterns of influence as well as authority. Thus, who eats lunch with whom may be more important than the formal lines of authority in determining decision making.

Political Institutions

Power inequalities are built into almost all social institutions. In institutions as varied as the school and the family, roles associated with status pairs such as student/teacher and parent/child specify unequal power relationships as the normal and desirable standard.

Political institutions are institutions concerned with the social structure of power; the most prominent political institution is the state.

In a very general sense, **political institutions** are all those institutions concerned with the social structure of power. This general definition includes many of the institutions of society. The family, the workplace, the school, and even organized religions have structured social inequality in decision making. The most prominent political institution, however, is the state, or government—that is, in the United States, the federal government and the governments of the individual states, as well as county and city governments. The Focus section of this chapter explores the states' power regarding the environment.

Concept Summary Power

Concept	Definition	Example from Family
Power	Ability to get others to act as one wishes in spite of their resistance; includes coercion and authority	"I know you don't want to mow the lawn, but you have to do it anyway."
Coercion	Exercise of power through force or threat of force	"Do it or else . . ."
Authority	Power supported by norms and values	"It is your duty to mow the lawn."
Traditional authority	Authority based on sanctity of time-honored routines	"I'm your father, and I told you to mow the law."
Charismatic authority	Authority based on extraordinary personal characteristics of leader	
Rational-legal authority	Authority based on submission to a set of rationally established rules	"It is your turn to mow the lawn, I did it last week."
Influence	Not power but ability to persuade others to change their decisions	"I don't feel very well today; would you help me mow the lawn?"

The State

The State As the Dominant Political Institution

The **state** is the social structure that successfully claims a monopoly on the legitimate use of coercion and physical force within a territory. It is usually distinguished from other political institutions by two characteristics: (1) Its jurisdiction for legitimate decision making is broader than that of other institutions, and (2) it controls the use of coercion in society.

The **state** is the social structure that successfully claims a monopoly on the legitimate use of coercion and physical force within a territory.

Jurisdiction. Whereas the other political institutions of society have rather narrow jurisdictions (over church members or over family members, for example), the state exercises power over the society as a whole.

Generally, the state has been considered to be responsible for gathering resources (taxes, draftees, and so on) to meet collective goals, arbitrating relationships among the parts of society, and maintaining relationships with other societies (Williams 1970). As societies have become larger and more complex, the state's responsibilities have grown. A recent poll (see Figure 16.1) indicates that the majority of Americans think the government should also do such things as provide day care and reduce income differences between rich and poor.

Coercion. The state claims a monopoly on the legitimate use of coercion. To the extent that other institutions use coercion (for example, the family or the school), they do so with the approval of the state. In recent years, the state has withdrawn approval of physical coercion between husband and wife, has sharply restricted the amount of physical punishment that parents can legitimately administer to children, and has generally declared physical punishment illegitimate within the school system. As a result, the state is increasingly unique as a legitimate user of coercion.

Thinking Critically

The family and the classroom are more often authoritarian than democratic. Try to explain this in sociological terms.

FOCUS ON THE ENVIRONMENT

Government and Our Environment

"In contemporary nations, the state is the guardian of the environment."

Who owns the water and the air, the wolf and the whooping crane? The answer is everybody—and that is part of the problem. In a classic article titled "The Tragedy of the Commons," Garrett Hardin (1968) pointed out that a resource held in common is very likely to be abused. Each person's share is so small and diffuse that it doesn't seem worthwhile defending it. Your share of the national forests, for example, is .000000004 (1 divided by 260 million). If a timber company comes in and clear-cuts a forest, you are unlikely to hire a lawyer to defend your tiny share. If a specific tree was your individual property, however, you might camp out there to defend it. And you can bet that if a private individual held the patent or copyright on a species, it wouldn't be disappearing. But because resources are owned in common, no specific individual has a vested interest in taking care of them.

In contemporary nations, the state is the guardian of the environment. In almost all nations, however, the state has been a slum landlord rather than a careful investor and so far has not done much to protect and preserve its property. Instead, the public guardian has allowed people and corporations to pollute the environment and eliminate habitats without asking for payment for the damages.

One strategy to reduce the environmental problem is to make individual polluters pay the state the full cost of their environmental damage. For example, the state might put a $2-per-gallon tax on gasoline to pay for the costs of cleaning up dirty air. Another example is charging $10 for a single polystyrene cup. The manufacture of polystyrene releases pollutants into the air; and because it may take more than 100 years to decompose, its disposal contributes to filling up landfills. Faced with the full cost of lifestyle or production choices, many of us probably would make different choices.

A different strategy is to rely on the coercive power of government to legislate the care of its (our) property—the environment. Such laws might regulate industrial pollution, restrict the kinds of product packaging we can use, limit the size or use of our cars, and make recycling mandatory. Some laws of this kind are being passed. Such laws will change our lives by imposing far more regulation—but will perhaps also provide cleaner water and air, along with more animals and birds.

The jobs these political protesters are so cavalier about are not their own jobs but somebody else's. Protecting the environment is not a simple case of good versus evil; it is a complex problem that involves competition among regions and social classes.

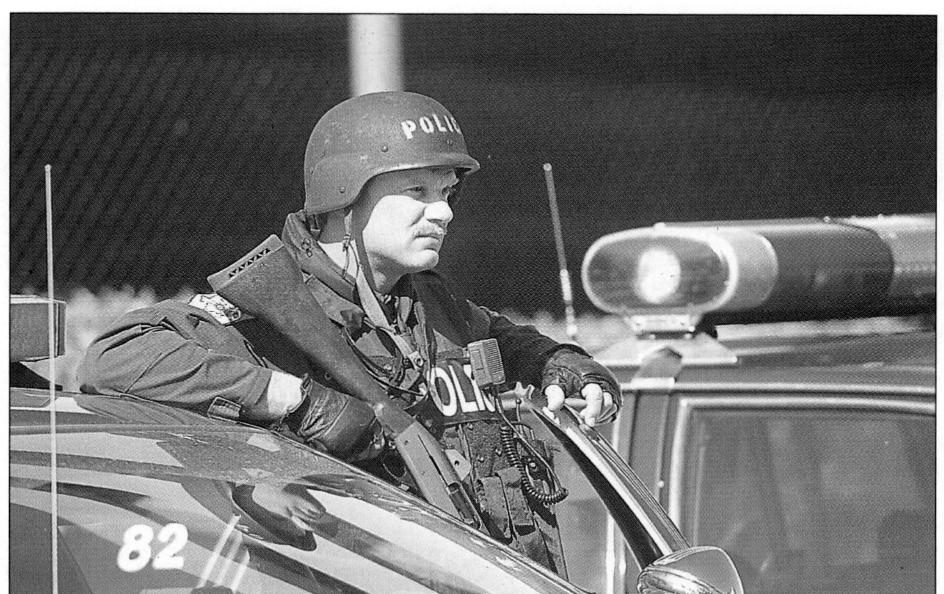

The dominant political institution is the state. Although fathers have power and biology teachers have power, only the state can legitimately arm its authority figures with M-16s. Sometimes the state goes too far, however. In 1995, the U.S. government agreed to pay $3.1 million to Randall Weaver and his three surviving children for the wrongful shooting death of Weaver's wife Vicki, by the FBI in 1992. Coercion and threats of coercion are important weapons used by the state in backing up its authority. Although most of us pay our taxes and obey the laws without any direct threat, we are all aware of the state's ability to fine or imprison should we stray from the rules.

The state uses three primary types of coercion. First, the state uses its political power to claim a monopoly on the legitimate use of physical force. It is empowered to imprison people and even impose the death penalty. This claim to a monopoly on legitimate physical coercion has been strengthened in recent years by the declining legitimacy of coercion in other institutions, such as the home and the school. Second, the state uses taxation, a form of legitimated confiscation. Finally, the state is the only unit in society that can legally maintain an armed force and that is empowered to deal with foreign powers.

Thinking Critically

What factors do you think decide whether the state acts as a slum landlord or a protective guardian over the environment? What might Garrett Hardin say about the state as guardian of the environment?

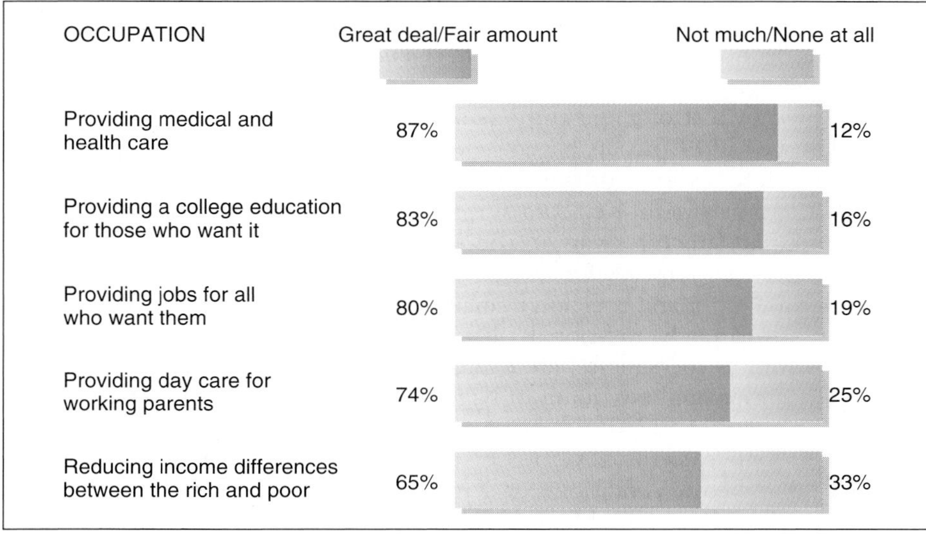

Figure 16.1
Question: How Much Responsibility Should the Government Take for . . .

Source: Gallup Poll 1993.

Democracy is a political system that provides regular, constitutional opportunities for a change in leadership according to the will of the majority.

An **authoritarian system** is a political system in which the leadership is not selected by the people and legally cannot be changed by them.

Democratic versus Authoritarian Systems

A variety of social structures can be devised to fulfill the functions of the state. Here we review two basic political forms: democracy and authoritarian systems.

You can think of democratic and authoritarian systems as political forms that occupy opposite ends, or poles, on a continuum, or imaginary line between the two poles. Countries can be authoritarian, such as the Republic of China, or democratic, such as the United States. Most countries combine at least some elements of both systems; they may be more democratic than authoritarian, or vice versa. For example, Mexico is a democracy with aspects of authoritarianism. Saudi Arabia is an authoritarian government with some aspects of democracy.

Democracy. There are several forms of **democracy,** many of them rather different from that of the United States. All democracies, however, share two characteristics: There are regular, constitutional procedures for changing leaders, and these leadership changes reflect the will of the majority—or, at least, a majority of those who actually vote.

In a democracy, there exists two basic groups: the group in power and one or more opposition groups that are trying to get into power. The rules of the game call for good conduct on both sides. The losers have to accept their loss and wait until the next constitutional opportunity to try again, and the winners have to refrain from eliminating or punishing the losers. Finally, there has to be public participation in choosing among the competing groups.

Authoritarian Systems. In the course of human history, democratic governments have been quite rare. After the period when humans were mainly hunter-gatherers, most people in most times have lived under **authoritarian systems.** Authoritarian governments go by many other names: dictatorships, military juntas, despotism, monarchies, theocracies, and totalitarian regimes. What they have in common is that the leadership is not selected by the people and legally cannot be changed by them.

The former Soviet Union, when it was governed by Communist Party officials, was an example. A current example is Saudi Arabia, ruled by the Saudi monarchy, the world's largest royal family ("Saudi Arabia" 1996). Over the past 40 years, Nigeria has fluctuated between being more democratic than authoritarian and being more authoritarian than democratic. Today, Nigeria can only be classified as authoritarian. Ruled by a strong and ruthless military dictatorship since General Sani Abacha's successful 1993 coup, Nigeria's government has assassinated at least nine of the country's leading human rights activists and environmental crusaders, including the well-known playwright Ken Saro-Wiwa (Hammer 1995a; "Nigeria" 1996).

Authoritarian structures vary in the extent to which they attempt to control people's lives, the purposes for which they exercise control, and the extent to which they use terror and coercion to maintain power. Some authoritarian governments govern through traditional authority. Monarchies such as that in Saudi Arabia, as well as theocracies, are examples. Other authoritarian governments, such as the current military junta in Nigeria, rest their powers almost exclusively on coercion.

Why are some societies governed by democracies and others by authoritarian systems? What are the conditions for democracy? The answer appears to have less to do with virtue than with economics.

Conditions for Democracy

Democracy is found almost exclusively in the wealthier nations of the world. The key factor, however, is not the overall wealth of the nation but the way the wealth is distributed; democracy generally is found in nations that do not have extremes of income inequality (Simpson 1990). A large and relatively affluent middle class is especially important. Members of the middle class usually have sufficient social and economic resources to organize effectively. Their economic power and organization enable them to hold the government accountable.

Democracy also flourishes only in societies with many competing groups, each of which comprises less than a majority (Williams 1970, 271). In such a situation, no single group can win a majority of votes without negotiating with other groups. Since each group is a minority, safeguarding minority political groups protects everybody.

Although democratic stability depends on competing interest groups, two additional conditions must be met. First, if minority political groups are so divided or ineffective that there is little chance they can win an election, the public may become disillusioned with the democratic process (Weil 1989). Second, competing interest groups must share the same basic values. If they do not, they are not likely to be able to abide by the rules of the game. For example, fundamental differences between the values of Israelis who want peace with the Palestinians and the values of Israelis who do not, together with different values among different factions of Palestinians, make it difficult for democracy to thrive in the West Bank and Gaza strip.

Global Perspectives: Government in Mexico

The border we share with Mexico is one of the longest borders in the world between a rich and a relatively poor nation. The 1994 North American Free Trade Agreement (NAFTA), which opened the door for more trade between the United States and Mexico, and the issue of illegal immigration into the United States from across the Mexican border keep U.S.–Mexico relations in the news. What kind of government does Mexico have?

Before the Spanish arrived in what is now Mexico, the area was populated by the vast priest-ruled empires of the Mayas in the Yucatan peninsula and the Aztecs near what is now Mexico City. In 1517, the Spanish began to explore the region. Thirty years later the conquest of the Aztec Empire was complete, and the area became known as "New Spain."

After nearly 300 years of colonial rule, Mexico revolted against Spain in 1810. An 11-year struggle ended in Spain's recognizing Mexican independence with the Treaty of Cordoba in 1821. The ensuing 1824 constitution, modeled on the U.S. constitution, created Mexico as a federal republic.

In 1910, a second revolution broke out, resulting in the somewhat revised constitution of 1917. According to the 1917 constitution, Mexico is a "federal, democratic, representative Republic" and "all public power originates in the people and is instituted for their behalf." The constitution states that democracy is to be considered "not only as a legal structure and a political regimen, but as a system of life founded on a constant economic, social, and cultural betterment of the people."

The 1917 constitution provides for executive, legislative, and judicial branches of government. In theory, Congress and the judiciary are independent of the executive branch, and the constitution guarantees the autonomy of the country's 31 states as well as many individual and social rights. Elections are held every six years for the presidency, the Senate, the state governorships and every three years for the Chamber of Deputies (analogous to the U.S. House of Representatives) and municipal posts. All parties are given free time on television for their political messages, and the government spends heavily on public service advertising urging the electorate to vote.

All this sounds very democratic; but in fact, Mexico is not fully democratic. For one thing, while there are as many as nine political parties in Mexico, the country has essentially a one-party government. The Institutional Revolutionary Party (PRI) has governed in Mexico since 1929. The PRI, funded mainly by a few wealthy families, has won every election for president, senator, and state governor since its formation in 1929 and has frequently resorted to fraud and even murder to avoid defeat (Sallot and Fraser 1994).

Then, too, the president is more powerful than Congress or the judiciary and controls both, as well as the 31 state governors, the PRI, and the huge national bureaucracy (Riding 1985). The Supreme Court has never overturned any key government decision, and the PRI's huge majority guarantees the obedience of Congress. Moreover, although the president is allowed to serve only one term, he (or, theoretically, she, although there has not yet been a woman president in Mexico) in effect chooses his successor by selecting who will run on the PRI ticket. The president also chooses other PRI candidates for key posts. And finally, the press is not always free, as journalists sometimes hesitate to anger government officials for fear of reprisals (Morrison 1994). All this has led some observers to characterize Mexico as an essentially authoritarian regime with a democratic mechanism for elections (Kerr 1994; Riding 1985).

There are several roadblocks to full democracy in Mexico. One is the existence of topographic barriers, such as high mountains. Some Mexicans, such as the Chiapas of southern Mexico, remain separated by the hills into isolated communities and have not been assimilated into the dominant Mexican culture. Another barrier is a history of (nondemocratic) empires followed by long colonial rule. For the vast majority of Mexicans at the outbreak of the 1810 revolution, democracy was an alien practice. Mexico had been denied the opportunity to evolve the skills and understanding of political democracy by three centuries of Spanish rule. An economic barrier also works against full democracy, as the gap between rich and poor is much higher in Mexico than in the United States.

January 1995 brought hope for further moves toward genuine democracy as the newly elected president, Ernesto Zedillo, promised to reform the PRI and to put at least one non-PRI member in his Cabinet (Smith 1994). Zedillo also called for reform in the justice system (Golden 1994). With new voter identification cards issued during the summer of 1994, moves had already been made to help eliminate election fraud. Most observers argue that greater concern for the poor in Mexico is necessary for establishing real democracy in the future.

Political Parties in the United States

Sustained democracy requires an effective opposition but the absence of fundamental cleavages. Generally, this means that democracy rests on an effective system of political parties. A **political party** is an association specifically organized to win elections and to secure power over the personnel and policies of the state.

The Two-Party System

In democratic systems, political parties are voluntary associations with open recruitment—membership is by self-designation. In many democratic societies, there are four or five or even a dozen political parties competing for votes and legislative seats. Such a proliferation of splinter groups often makes it hard for any one group to win firm control of the government, and thus they must govern through coalitions. The United States is virtually unique in having a relatively stable two-party system, each party representing a loose coalition of competing interest groups.

Although the two-party system is relatively stable in the United States, third parties have developed occasionally throughout U.S. history. One reason a higher proportion of Americans voted in the 1992 presidential election was that their interest was piqued by the third-party candidacy of H. Ross Perot (Schmidt, Shelley, and Bardes 1995, 376). Although Perot did not win the White House (and probably never expected to), he brought the idea of an alternative third party to life. Later, in 1995, Perot announced that he was establishing the Independence Party, which would hold a "cyber-convention" in the spring of 1996: Thousands of voters would be linked by satellite and computers to adopt a party platform and choose their presidential candidate (Fineman 1995; Goodgame 1995).

A **political party** is an association specifically organized to win elections and secure power over the personnel and policies of the state.

Obviously, the two-party system is not mandated by the Constitution, which indeed does not mention parties at all. Rather, the character of American political parties can be seen as an outgrowth of our formal system of government and the heterogeneity of our population.

Formal Structure and the Winner-Take-All Rule. An important characteristic virtually unique to the American brand of democracy is the winner-take-all rule. In most European democracies, legislative seats are apportioned according to the popular vote. A party getting 10 percent of the vote gets 10 percent of the legislative seats. In the United States, a group that got only 10 percent of the vote would come out with nothing. Thus, to gain any representation at all in our system, the small group must ally itself with others in a coalition that may ultimately appeal to a majority of the voters. The winner-take-all rule has prevented radical or special-interest groups from gaining political power or even having an effective voice. This situation is one reason that the two major parties in the United States can sound very much alike. As one observer remarked, these groups have run up against the "50 percent wall" (Przeworski 1985).

Heterogeneity. In a homogenous nation, broad national appeal might be attained with a very specific, even extreme, program of action. In a heterogeneous society, however, majority backing can be gained only by a program that combines and balances the interests of many smaller groups—farmers, labor, Hispanics, big cities, conservationists, heavy industry, and so on. The strength and stability of American political parties is thus partly attributable to the diversity of the American population and its many cross-cutting interest groups.

In order to win a presidential election in the United States, a candidate must appeal to the majority of the population. In a nation as diverse as the United States, this means that he or she must appeal to a broad spectrum of potential voters. For a while, Americans seemed excited by the prospect that General Colin Powell would be a candidate in the 1996 presidential election. Powell had become a familiar and trusted face as he regularly briefed the American public by television during the Gulf War. He would have been the first African American to run for president. However, shortly after Israeli Prime Minister Yitzhak Rabin was assassinated in November 1995, Powell announced that he would not run. Many speculated that his family's desire to protect him from potential physical danger was at least partly the reason.

PARTY AFFILIATION

In the 1994 state and national elections, the Republican Party won majorities in the U.S. Senate, in the U.S. House of Representatives, and in more state legislatures than Republicans had controlled since 1954 ("GOP SweepStates" 1995). Representative Newt Gingrich became Speaker of the U.S. House of Representatives and immediately began to lead the Republican Party to the more conservative right. Gingrich's "Contract with America" stressed moving regulatory powers and administrative services from the federal government to the states and balancing the federal budget by lowering government spending on social programs such as Medicare and welfare for the poor (Burleigh 1995; Rosenstiel 1995b). Meanwhile, Robert Dole, Republican leader of the Senate, worked to keep the party in a more centrist position.

Both the major political parties in the United States have been centrist throughout the nation's history. There are philosophical distinctions between the two parties, however. Traditionally, the Democratic Party has been more likely to support the interests of the poor and the working class, and the Republican Party has been more likely to support policies favoring an unrestricted free market economy (discussed in Chapter 17) and big business. Because of these characteristics, Republicans tend to attract business-oriented people with higher incomes, and Democrats tend to attract minority and lower-income voters as well as labor union leaders and some highly educated liberals (see Table 16.1).

Currently, a growing proportion of voters align themselves with neither party. These independents are not themselves a political party but have declared an intent to vote on the basis of the issues rather than party loyalty. When the one third of voters who call themselves independents (U.S. Bureau of the Census 1995 Table 458) go to the polls, however, they usually have to choose between a Democratic and a Republican candidate.

WHY DOESN'T THE UNITED STATES HAVE A STRONG WORKERS' PARTY?

The Socialist Labor Party, begun in 1877, and the Socialist Party, begun by Eugene Debs in 1901, are two very minor parties in the United States. Many of you may never have heard of them! The United States is almost alone among Western democracies in not having a strong party that explicitly supports the interests of the working class. As a direct result, it is almost alone among Western democracies in not having national health insurance, family allowances, and a comprehensive system of unemployment benefits (Quadagno 1990). Working-class interests have been diluted and compromised in Democratic Party platforms, and there has been no clear political voice for the working and lower classes. There have been few congressional representatives whose reelection depended on whether they supported a working-class agenda; certainly there have been no presidents who felt that the workers were their unique political constituency. As a result, no one has spoken very loudly or very often for labor. In nearly every other democratic society, there is a major labor or socialist party that stands for the redistribution of society's wealth, greater equality, and social welfare programs for the working and lower classes. Why is the United States an exception?

Four answers are usually given. First, the proportion of U.S. workers who belong to labor unions is relatively small and has declined in recent decades. Second, U.S.

TABLE 16.1
PARTY IDENTIFICATION

Although American parties are not closely tied to social class, the better-off tend to be Republicans, and the poor and nonwhite tend to be Democrats. The growing proportion who identify themselves as independent tend to be young, well educated, non-Hispanic whites.

"In general, would you call yourself a Democrat, a Republican, or what?"

	DEMOCRAT	REPUBLICAN	INDEPENDENT
RACE/ETHNICITY:			
NON-HISPANIC WHITE	34%	32%	34%
BLACK	71	9	20
HISPANIC	52	23	25
EDUCATION:			
LESS THAN 12 YEARS	50	21	29
HIGH SCHOOL GRADUATE	38	28	34
SOME COLLEGE	34	33	33
COLLEGE GRADUATE	32	36	32
INCOME:			
UNDER $15,000	51	23	26
$15,000–24,999	41	26	33
$25,000–39,999	34	32	34
$40,000–AND OVER	32	35	33

SOURCE: The Gallup Report 1992b.

labor unions have organized around specific occupations and have had little success in creating superunions that would represent the interests of labor as a whole (Quadagno 1990). One reason for this is that U.S. labor law has given unions the right to negotiate only over wage and wage-related issues (McCammon 1993). A result is that unionized workers earn four times more than those working at the minimum wage. Coupled with cross-cutting loyalties based on race and ethnicity, religion, and geographic region, the union focus on wages and the inequality in working-class income that it produces means that American workers seldom recognize or vote for a common economic and political agenda (Form 1985; Western 1993).

Third, despite significant income disparities, the American standard of living is luxurious by almost any comparison. Describing the failure of American workers to sustain a socialist movement, one 19th-century socialist noted: "On the reefs of roast beef and apple pie, socialist utopias of every sort are sent to their doom" (Sombart [1906] 1974, 87).

Finally, of course, there is the American Dream (see Chapter 9). The American worker has not been interested in absolute equality but rather in equality of opportunity. Because workers believe they can make it within the current system, they have not wanted to reduce the privileges associated with success.

Very early in this century, labor unions often aligned themselves with radical platforms favoring redistribution of wealth; at mid-century, they were less radical but solidly Democratic. In the early 1990s, only about one-half of union members were members of the Democratic Party. This collapse of working-class liberalism has led some observers to speculate that any future pressure for redistribution will come from the minimum-wage service sector and from the unemployed, groups that so far have shown little political muscle (Form 1985).

Who Governs? Models of American Democracy

Political Actors: Publics and PACs

The political process involves many actors. These can be viewed roughly as a pyramid (see Figure 16.2). As we move from the top to the bottom of the pyramid, actors increase in number but decrease in political effectiveness (Lehman 1988). The state occupies the top of the pyramid, and legislators and political parties occupy the next level. Below these two major actors are two additional levels: publics and interest groups.

A **public** is a category of citizens who are thought to share a common political agenda.

Publics. A **public** is a category of citizens who are thought to share a common political agenda. For example, Hispanics make up a public, as do women, farmers, and small business owners.

The distinctive feature of a public is that it is not organized. It is a *category*, not a *group*. This means that it is a relatively ineffective political actor. Although individual members of a public may affect political decisions through their votes, their donations to political causes, and even their answers to public opinion polls, lack of organization reduces their impact. For example, public opinion polls consistently show that the majority of Americans favor gun control. Yet the strong gun lobby, specifically the National Rifle Association (NRA), has made effective gun

FIGURE 16.2
THE U.S. POLITICAL PROCESS

The political process occurs at several levels. As we move from unorganized publics to organized interest groups to political parties to the state, the number of actors becomes smaller and their capacity to act effectively in pursuing their self-interest grows.

SOURCE: Adapted from Lehman 1988.

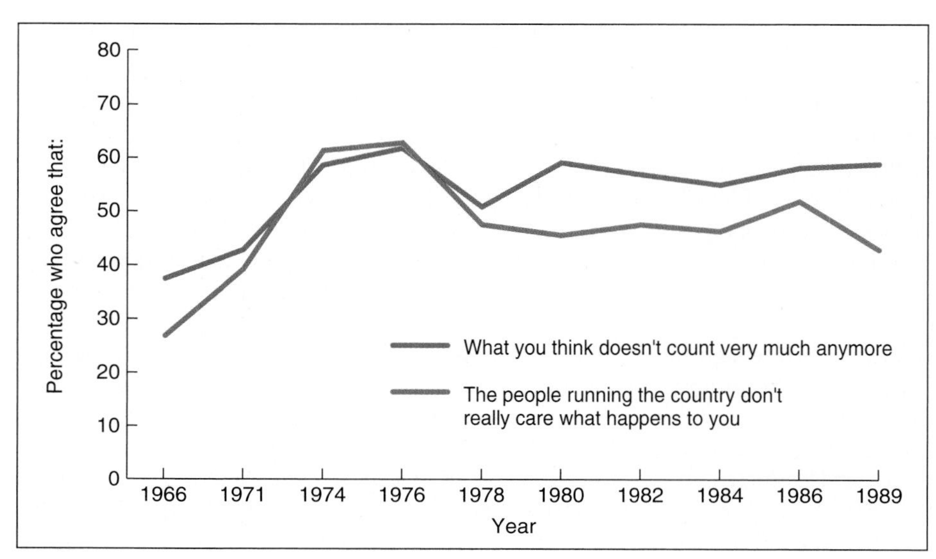

control legislation difficult to enact. Power requires organization; it requires that a public become a self-conscious interest group that can speak for all members.

Interest Groups and Political Action Committees (PACs). A group or organization that seeks to influence political decisions is called an **interest group** (Welch et al. 1990). (Recall our discussion of the concept *influence* earlier in this chapter.) There are thousands of interest groups in the United States, from the PTA to the Tobacco Growers of America. Some of these interest groups, such as the PTA, are multipurpose organizations; affecting government policy is only one part of their purpose. Other interest groups, such as the National Rifle Association, exist largely in order to affect political decisions.

An **interest group** is a group or organization that seeks to influence political decisions.

Interest groups use two strategies to affect political decisions: lobbying and financial contributions. Lobbyists try to "educate" legislators or officials about the need to protect their groups' interests. Some interest groups can afford to hire permanent lobbyists who work year-round in their behalf. As just one example, the Aerospace Industry Association (AIA) is a permanent lobby in Washington dedicated to promoting U.S. weapons sales around the world. (Mesler 1995). Other interest groups rely on volunteer letter writers to bring their position to legislators' attention. In each case, lobbyists are able to say that they are speaking not just for themselves but also for the thousands or millions of people who belong to their organization.

Another way for interest groups to affect political decisions is to provide financial help for political candidates who agree with their point of view. Because of widespread concern that candidates were being "bought" by big donors, however, federal election reforms have limited the amount of money that individual donors could give to campaigns. For example, an individual cannot donate more than $1,000 to any single U.S. Senate election and no more than $17,500 to all Senate races in a single year (Welch et al. 1990).

To circumvent this law, interest groups have formed political action committees (PACs). Beginning in 1974, the federal government has allowed corporations, labor unions, and other special interest groups to set up PACs to raise money for candidates. The number of PACs has grown astronomically, as has the amount they spend on elections. There were about 1,000 PACs in 1976; by 1992, there were more than four times that many.

For a PAC to be legitimate, the money must be raised from at least 50 volunteer donors. PACs can contribute up to $5,000 to each candidate in an election. Although PACs, like individuals, are limited in the amount they can *directly* give to specific candidates, the U.S. Supreme Court has ruled that they can spend unlimited amounts working *on behalf of* candidates or issues.

Interest groups see a PAC contribution as an investment in a relationship with a member of Congress, whoever that member may be. Consequently, PACs give to both Democrats and Republicans—another reason that the two parties can seem so much alike. The two PACs that gave the most money in the 1992 national elections were the National Association of Realtors, which spent over $3 million, and the American Medical Association, which spent $2.6 million. Both these PACs divided their contributions about evenly between Democrats and Republicans (Schmidt, Shelley, and Bardes 1995, 272–274).

The PAC is a powerful vehicle for giving an interest group political clout. The richer the PAC, the more likely it is to get its candidates elected. Also, the richer the PAC, the more likely it is that a candidate may be persuaded to favor the

PAC's position in exchange for financial support. The PAC has proven to be such an effective instrument that no interest group can afford to be without one. There is a FishPAC, a BeefPAC, a cigar PAC, a PAC for the National Organization for Women, and even a PAC for the alcohol industry, called—you guessed it—the SixPAC (Welch et al. 1996).

Four Models

Students of the U.S. political process agree that the process involves a variety of political actors, each pursing a different agenda. Some of these actors are bigger, better funded, and better organized than others. Which ones are spinning their wheels, and which ones are effective in getting their way? Put another way, who governs? To answer this question, we turn to four models of the democratic process.

The Pluralist Model. The pluralist model of American government focuses on the processes of coalition and competition that take place in state and federal governments. For example, two brief federal government shutdowns in 1995 resulted from competition between President Bill Clinton, a Democrat, and Congressional Republicans over how to balance the federal budget. A vital part of the pluralist model is the hypothesis of shifting allegiances. According to pluralist theorists, different coalitions of interest groups arise for each decision. For example, hospitals and medical workers will ally themselves with older people to fight Medicare cuts; when it comes to the rising costs of a hospital stay, however, these two groups will oppose each other. This pattern of shifting allegiances keeps any interest groups from consistently being on the winning side and keeps political alliances fluid and temporary rather than allowing them to harden into permanent and unified cliques (Dahl 1961, 1971). As a result of these processes, pluralists see the decision-making process as relatively inefficient but also relatively free of conflict, a process in which competition among interest groups keeps any single group from gaining significant advantage.

Critics believe that the pluralist model is naïve at best. They argue that, although all of these interest groups may be skirmishing in Congress, the real decisions are being made in higher circles. At worst, critics argue, the pluralist model "obscures and shelters the citadels of domination" by refusing to recognize the controlling hand of the ruling class (Bowles and Gintis 1986).

The Power-Elite Model. Theorists associated with the power-elite model wave aside competing organized interest groups as the middle levels of power. Power-elite theorists contend that there is a higher level of decision making where an elite makes all the major decisions—in its own interests (Parenti 1993). In his classic work *The Power Elite*, C. Wright Mills (1956) defined the **power elite** as the people who occupy the top positions in three bureaucracies: the military, industry, and the executive branch of government. From these "command posts of power" and through a complex set of overlapping cliques, these people share decisions having at least national consequences (Mills 1956, 18).

The **power elite** consists of the people who occupy the top positions in three bureaucracies—the military, industry, and the executive branch of government—and who are thought to act together to run the United States in their own interests.

The power-elite theory is a positional theory of power. It argues that individuals have power by virtue of the positions they hold in key institutions. If the interests of these individuals and institutions were in competition with one another, this model would not be significantly different from the pluralist model. The key factor in the elite theory is that these elites share a common world view and act together to promote their own interests (Domhoff 1983; Orum 1987).

The suggestion that individuals occupying the top positions represent a unified elite is supported by evidence of a strong similarity in background among the top members of the three bureaucracies. They have gone to the same colleges and prep schools, summered at the same resorts, skied at the same lodges, and joined the same clubs. One study used a generous definition of "top position" to identify 5,800 individuals as the power elite. The majority of the elite are white men who had graduated from 12 prestigious private universities; fewer than 5 percent of the elite were women, only 20 individuals on the list were African American, and only 25 percent had graduated from a public university (Dye 1986).

That an upper class exists in America and that this upper class is highly overrepresented in the power elite seems unarguable (Dye and Ziegler 1993). The critical question is whether there is any evidence that these top position holders act together to promote the interests of the upper class.

The Conflict/Dialectic Model. A Marxist version of class conflict is at the root of the conflict/dialectic model. Like the power-elite model, the conflict/dialectic model features an elite that runs the show. The Marxist elite differs from the power elite in two ways. First, the Marxist elite is made up of a much smaller category of people—the people who actually own the means of production. Managers, bureaucrats, and generals are not considered to be members of the Marxist elite; they are rather tools of the elite. Second, Marxists do not require a unified elite tied together by social custom and tradition. Instead, they recognize that there are factions within the elite with competing economic interests. For example, financiers like high interest rates; automobile manufacturers do not. The Marxist elite includes more of what one political scientist (Dye 1986) calls cowboys: They are aggressive about making and keeping their money, and they don't care much for fancy manners and old school ties. As a result, the Marxist elite includes built-in competition that may ultimately weaken it and lead to change.

Another difference between the conflict/dialectic and power-elite models is the tension they see between the elite and nonelites. Marxists argue that the working class has its own resources for power: class consciousness and the possibility of class action. The power of the subordinate class can be likened to that of a sleeping rattlesnake; the snake is not hurting you now, but you want to be certain not to awaken it. Thus, the conflict/dialectic model sees underlying tensions between the elite (dominant class) and nonelites that are largely missing from the power-elite model.

A further element of this model is its emphasis on the dialectic as the process of social change. As noted in earlier chapters, the dialectic suggests that social change will emerge as a result of contradictions and conflicts within and between social institutions. Marxists believe that

> social institutions, economic systems, and political institutions contain inherent contradictions. These produce conflicts and strains that eventually lead to the transformation of those institutions and systems. *Contradictions* are thus engines of social change and their analysis is central also to understanding the dynamics of political power (Whitt 1979, 84).

In terms of the American political structure, the dialectic suggests that the elite has to be constantly on its toes to ward off the potential consciousness and power

The pluralist model of American politics stresses the importance of Congress and the state legislatures as arenas for making decisions. Floor debates are seen as occasions when competing interest groups vie for votes and power. According to this model of the American political process, no side consistently wins, and there is a shifting balance of power.

of the subordinate class in a climate of shifting economic and political conditions. Change rather than stability is the key to the conflict model. Whereas the power-elite model sees the elite striving to maintain privilege, the conflict model envisions a more rough-and-tumble battle in which both sides strive to structure change for their benefit. This conflict occurs within as well as between classes.

The State Autonomy Model. A growing number of scholars argue that the government bureaucracy is a powerful independent actor in political decisions. The federal government employs 3 million people directly. In addition, its policies determine the employment of tens of millions more people who work for national military contractors, state and local governments, schools, and social welfare agencies. In 1995, the federal government collected over $1.3 trillion in revenue and spent over $1.5 trillion! It seems only common sense to suppose that the state is in a position to get what it wants. The state autonomy model suggests that the state (meaning the federal bureaucracy) is a powerful independent actor that pursues its own agenda. This agenda is not class linked (as in the power-elite model) but is linked to the maintenance and extension of bureaucratic power.

A good example of this approach is Hooks's (1990) analysis of the profound effect that Pentagon and Defense Department policies have had on the development of the microelectronics and aeronautics industries. Hooks's findings show that the competitiveness of U.S. high-technology firms has been seriously jeopardized by defense policy. Because the Pentagon's goals have been strategic rather than commercial, the state has pursued its own interests at the expense of the capitalist class.

THINKING CRITICALLY

Which of these four models do *you* think best describes politics in the United States, and why?

SUMMARY AND EVALUATION: WHO DOES GOVERN?

These four models differ on several points. Is the elite divided? Are there shifting coalitions? Does an elite make all the decisions? Research in the United States

CONCEPT SUMMARY COMPARISON OF FOUR MODELS OF AMERIAN POLITICAL DECISION MAKING

	PLURALIST	POWER-ELITE	CONFLICT DIALECTIC	STATE AUTONOMY
BASIC UNITS OF ANALYSIS	Interest groups	Institutional elite	Classes	Government bureaucracy
SOURCE OF POWER	Situational; depends on issue	Positional; top positions in bureaucracies	Class based; ownership of means of production	Control of personnel and budget of government
DISTRIBUTION OF POWER	Dispersed among competing diverse groups	Concentrated in relatively homogeneous elite	Held by dominant class, potentially available to lower class	Held by bureaucrats
LIMITS OF POWER	Limited by shifting and cross-cutting loyalties	No identifiable limits to elite domination	Limited by class conflict and contradiction among social institutions	Limited if elite is unified and nonelites are unorganized
ROLE OF THE STATE	Arena where interest groups compete	One of several sources of power	Captured by the ruling class	A major source of power

supports two conclusions. First, there is a little evidence for the pluralist expectation of shifting allegiances. Instead, research indicates that business interests are relatively unified. Studies of PAC contributions show that these interests are unified by shared conservatism: They act together as a class to support probusiness candidates (Burris and Salt 1990; Clawson and Su 1990). Second, there are only a few issues on which other interest groups in the United States have the unity or resources to challenge the power of business effectively (Korpi 1989). In the United States, redistributive programs—such as civil rights and Social Security—have been passed under two conditions: A sense of crisis caused the elite to favor the change, or the elite disagreed among themselves (Jenkins and Brent 1989). There is little evidence that any other interest group—either the state or the working class—has the resources or the unity to challenge a unified business class.

A final point is important. Although there are some important differences among the four major models of decision making in the United States, a notable feature of all four is that organized entities—businesses, unions, PACs, government agencies—rather than individuals are the key actors. (See the Concept Summary.) Individuals play a very small role unless they represent or are represented by one of these organizations (Laumann, Knoke, and Kim 1985). The next section examines the role of the media in political campaigns.

THE MEDIA AND POLITICAL CAMPAIGNS

All forms of media—television, newspapers, radio, and magazines—have tremendous political influence on American society, but the media's impact is perhaps most obvious during political campaigns. Because television is the main news source for most Americans (Moore 1995), candidates find ways to use television to their benefit. Campaign strategists use three types of TV coverage: paid political announcements, news coverage management, and campaign debates.

Paid Political Announcements

Paid political announcements are media messages about a political candidate that are paid for by the candidate's campaign committee.

Paid political announcements are media messages about a political candidate that are paid for by the candidate's campaign committee. They are commercials promoting the candidate as the best product. Research shows that many voters get most of their information from and form their opinions based on paid political announcements. In the last 30 years, paid political announcements have become increasingly negative as candidates have produced more and more "attack" ads against their opponents. The public claims not to like negative advertising, but as one consultant put it, "negative advertising works" (Schmidt, Shelley, and Bardes 1995).

Using paid political announcements is very expensive. More than $230 million was spent on television advertising in the 1992 campaign (Schmidt, Shelley, and Bardes 1995, 381). Consequently, the practice limits those who can run for office to the wealthy (for example, Ross Perot in the 1992 presidential campaign) and to those who can raise monies from lobbyists and interest groups.

News Coverage Management

News coverage management involves ensuring that a candidate receives favorable media coverage.

While paid political announcements are costly, news coverage is free. **News coverage management** involves ensuring that a candidate receives favorable media coverage. Taking advantage of the media's interest in campaign politics, the campaign staff works to influence how much and what kind of coverage the campaign receives. The staff plans political events that will be especially photogenic and will take place at times when the press will be most likely to show up. Candidates also grant interviews with members of the media. Sometimes campaign managers actually create newsworthy events for journalists to cover. During an election year, for instance, the president of the United States is likely to call the media into the Oval Office of the White House to televise the signing of a piece of legislation. A related goal is to convince reporters that a particular interpretation of an event is correct. This is called putting a *spin* on a story. A **spin** is an interpretation of events that is favorable to the candidate. Campaign advisers who try to convince journalists of the truth of a particular interpretation of events are called **spin doctors.**

A **spin** is an interpretation of events that is favorable to the candidate. Campaign advisers who try to convince the media of a particular interpretation of events are called **spin doctors.**

Televised Debates

How a candidate performs in a televised debate against one or more opponents may be as important to the campaign's success as paid political announcements. The first televised debates in a presidential campaign occurred in 1960 between John Kennedy, then a young senator from Massachusetts, and U.S. Vice President Richard Nixon. The 1992 presidential debates included President George Bush, the Republican incumbent, Democratic candidate Bill Clinton, and independent candidate H. Ross Perot.

The public may want information about issues from televised debates. However, the candidates are more interested in pointing out their opponents' weaknesses and projecting a favorable image (Schmidt, Shelley, and Bardes 1995). Kennedy's fresh appearance in 1960 gave him the advantage over Nixon, who—without TV makeup—looked tired and haggard. The second debate in the 1992 presidential campaign allowed the candidates to answer questions from members of the studio audience. Most at home with this format, Bill Clinton ultimately was elected.

Thinking Critically

Have you ever watched a news event or political debate and then later heard a journalist's spin on it that differed from your own opinion? Who was more likely to be right, do you think, and why? Under what circumstances might spin doctors be functional for American politics? Dysfunctional? Explain your answer.

ARE THE MEDIA BIASED?

Many Americans believe that the media are biased, and many studies have been done to test this hypothesis. Most studies conclude that, when taken as a whole, the media do not favor Democrats or Republicans. In fact, journalists and networks are likely to be more interested in furthering their careers and profits than in championing any cause. The media's goal is producing news that will attract many viewers without seriously threatening the American way of life (Exoo 1994). Therefore, the media are not biased toward Democrats or Republicans but are biased toward our democratic and capitalist system.

FUNCTIONS AND DYSFUNCTIONS OF THE MEDIA'S ROLE IN POLITICAL CAMPAIGNS

The media play both functional and dysfunctional roles in political campaigns. Newspaper, radio, and television are functional inasmuch as they bring candidates and concerns before the public and even help to set the agenda for debate on some issues. Cable television networks such as C-SPAN allow viewers to see the day-to-day workings of the government. Television programs such as *Nightline* and *Meet the Press* and radio journalism such as that on National Public Radio (NPR) influence what is debated and talked about. For instance, videotaped footage of the massacres associated with "ethnic cleansing" in Bosnia helped bring these atrocities before the American public and policy makers. As a second example, an animal-rights group infiltrated a tuna fishing crew and videotaped the deaths of many dolphins accidentally caught in the fishing nets. TV broadcasts of their films led to public outrage, congressional investigations of the tuna industry, and consequent changes in the way much of the tuna we eat is caught.

At the same time, the media can be dysfunctional. Because access to the media costs so much, a latent dysfunction is that less wealthy candidates have little ability to successfully run for office. Furthermore, paid political announcements are necessarily short; 30-second commercials may be catchy, but they fail to explain and discourage debate on complicated issues.

In the view of Thomas Patterson (1993), a political scientist, the media actually increase voter cynicism. After studying the 1992 election, Patterson concluded that the media mostly dwelled on bad news and thereby cast doubt on all the candidates. This situation arises because the most important goal for the media is to find an exciting story every day that will capture people's attention. Since studies show that the public's attention is more often captured by negative than by positive stories, the media focus on bad news. Scandals and candidates' mistakes, rather than serious political issues, take center stage. Patterson suggests that one way this situation could be remedied is to have a shorter campaign period so that journalists would not be hard pressed for so many months to come up with attention-getting stories.

> **THINKING CRITICALLY**
>
> In your opinion, are the media more functional or dysfunctional for American politics? What are some ways in which we could make the media more functional, do you think?

INDIVIDUAL PARTICIPATION IN AMERICAN GOVERNMENT

Democracy is a political system that explicitly includes a large proportion of adults as political actors. Yet it is easy to overlook the role of individual citizens while concentrating on leaders and organized interests. This section describes the American political structure and process from the viewpoint of the individual citizen.

WHO PARTICIPATES?

The average citizen is not politically oriented. A significant proportion of the voting-age population (about 32 percent in 1992) do not even register to vote; of these people who do register, many do not vote. In recent presidential elections, 40 to 50 percent of the voting-age population have not bothered to go to the polls. Electoral participation declines markedly as one gets closer to the local level, and often only 20 to 25 percent vote in local elections.

Voting is in many ways the easiest and most superficial means of participating in politics. If we think of letter writing, returning congressional questionnaires, and making campaign contributions as elements of political activity, we have to conclude that less than 20 percent of U.S. citizens take an active part in politics. And, of course, only a very small proportion take part to the extent of running for or occupying elective office.

The studies demonstrating low levels of political participation and involvement pose a crucial question about the structure of power in American democracy. Who participates? If participants are not a random sample of citizens then some groups probably have more influence than others. In fact, studies do show that voters differ from nonvoters on social class and age.

Social Class. Ross Perot has proposed that we hold national elections on Saturday and Sunday, as opposed to Tuesday, so that more working people can vote (Ostrowidzki 1995). One of the firmest findings in social science is that political participation (indeed, participation of any sort) is strongly related to social class. Whether we define participation as voting or letter writing, people with more education, more income, and more prestigious jobs are more likely to be politically active. They know more about the issues, have stronger opinions on a wider variety of issues, and are much more likely to try to influence the nature of political decisions. This conclusion is supported by data on voting patterns from the 1992 election (see Table 16.2). The higher the level of education, the greater the likelihood of voting; those who have graduated from college are twice as likely to vote as those who have not completed high school.

It should be stressed that lower voting participation by underprivileged groups is not a characteristic of all democratic systems. Rather, the low participation of the poor and the working class in the United States can be attributed to the absence of a political party that directly represents their interests (Zipp, Landerman, and Luebke 1982). In European political systems with pro-worker parties, this class differential in political participation is largely absent. In the United States, however, there is no exclusive political vehicle for the working class or the poor. If U.S. political parties were not so centrist and hence so much alike, it is possible that voter interest would be higher.

Age. Another significant determinant of political participation is age. There is a steady increase in political interest, knowledge, opinion, and participation with age. Nearly half of all voters in the 1992 election were 45 or older. Even in the turbulent years of the Vietnam War, when young antiwar demonstrators were so visi-

TABLE 16–2
PARTICIPATION IN THE 1992 ELECTION

Political participation is greater among people who are older, better educated, and non-Hispanic

	PERCENTAGE REGISTERED	PERCENTAGE REPORTING THEY ACTUALLY VOTED
TOTAL	68	61
EDUCATION		
8 YEARS OR LESS	44	35
9–11 YEARS	50	41
12 YEARS	65	58
13–15 YEARS (COLLEGE)	75	69
16 OR MORE YEARS (COLLEGE GRADUATE)	85	81
RACE/ETHNICITY		
NON-HISPANIC WHITE	70	64
BLACK	64	54
HISPANIC[a]	35	29
AGE		
18–24	53	43
25–34	61	53
35–44	69	64
45–64	75	70
65+	78	70

[a] Underestimates participation among eligible voters; 32 percent of Hispanics are ineligible to register because they are not citizens.

SOURCE: U.S. Bureau of the Census 1993a.

ble, young adults were significantly less likely to vote than were middle-aged people. In that period, young adults engaged in other forms of political participation that did, in fact, influence political decisions. In most time periods, however, the low participation of younger people at the polls is a fair measure of their overall participation.

Race and Ethnicity. Political participation is no longer strongly related to race. In fact, after social class has been taken into consideration, it seems likely that being African American increases political participation. African Americans are more apt than whites to want changes made in the system, and they turn to political participation as a means to effect these changes (Guterbock and London 1983, 440).

THINKING CRITICALLY

How might voting outcomes change if voting patterns changed significantly by social class? By age? By race/ethnicity?

Hispanics, however, are less likely to vote than other Americans (see Table 16.2). Their low participation is traceable partly to low socioeconomic status. Much of the apparent low participation of Hispanics is an artifact of the measurement procedure, however: One-third of the voting-age population of Hispanics consists of aliens (legal as well as illegal), and these people are not eligible to register or to vote.

The data on voting patterns demonstrate that established people are more likely than others to try to influence political decisions. These people are middle aged, are middle to upper class, are well educated, and have vested economic interests. They are the people who have the highest stake in preserving the status quo. Thus, differential patterns of participation give added weight to conservative positions and reduce the voice of the dissatisfied.

Differentials in Office Holding. By law, almost all native-born Americans over the age of 35 are eligible to hold any office. In practice, elected officials tend to be white men from the professional classes. Thus, for the most part, the political activities of other groups (women, minorities, nonelites) have been directed at choosing which white elite males will represent them. This practice has been changing; African Americans, Hispanics, and women (though not nonelites) are increasingly holding elected office, especially at local levels. Still, only about 6 percent of all state legislators are African American, and only 21 percent are female (U.S. Bureau of the Census 1995, Table 451). The proportions in the U.S. Congress are much smaller: In 1995, only 11 percent of U.S. Representatives and just 8 percent of Senators were women. Also in 1995, 9 percent of U.S. Representatives were African American, and just 4 percent, Hispanic. In 1995, there were no Hispanic Senators and only 1 (of 100) was black (U.S. Bureau of the Census 1995, Table 444).

WHY PARTICIPATE?

Social choice theory (or exchange theory) argues that individual decisions are based on cost/benefit calculations.

Scholars of voting behavior suggest that calculation of personal costs and benefits is an important factor in determining whether we vote and whom we vote for. This is part of a general perspective called **social choice theory** (or sometimes exchange theory), which argues that individual decisions on matters ranging from voting to marriage are based on cost/benefit calculations.

Voting. The costs of voting in the contemporary United States are not high: Polling places are usually conveniently located, and they are open at times during which most people can go. Many states, however, require a preliminary procedure of registering to vote that may demand a visit to a government office between 8 A.M. and 5 P.M. Of course, there is also the bother of reading the paper and watching the news and figuring out what the issues are. Any trouble is too much trouble when you cannot see that it matters much who wins.

An important factor reducing incentive to vote is the centrist nature of American political parties. Their platforms often seem so similar that it is unlikely that one party's victory will mean personal prosperity and the other disaster. As mentioned earlier, this lack of effective choice helps to explain why political participation is so much lower in the United States than in many European democracies and why, in contrast to the situations in these other nations, the American working class is less likely to vote than the middle class (Bollen and Jackman 1985; Davis 1986).

Political Alienation. As social choice theory suggests, an important determinant of whether citizens participate in political decision making is their judgment of the usefulness of the exercise. Citizens who believe they can influence outcomes through their participation are apt to be active. Those who suffer from **political alienation**—who believe that voting is a useless exercise and that individual citizens have no influence on decision making—are not going to be active. Alienated voters are likely to think that their votes do not count, that no one cares what they think, and that the system is run for the benefit of the few (Elshtain 1995). Opinion poll results show that alienation has increased substantially among voters since the mid 1960s (see Figure 16.3), and it has contributed to low voter participation.

Political alienation is a belief that voting is a useless exercise and individual citizens have no influence on decision making.

Consequences of Low Participation

Elite theorists see popular elections as little more than games designed to delude the masses. Since no real decisions are made in Congress, much less by the governor or the mayor, the level of participation is irrelevant. These theorists point out that opinion polls show a drop in political alienation immediately after elections

In the United States, all citizens over the age of 18 have the right to vote. A surprisingly large proportion of the population choose not to exercise this right. The pattern of political decisions reflects the fact that the people who are most apt to vote are middle-aged, better off, and well-educated. If less advantaged segments of the population would increase their political participation, the nature of U.S. political decisions might change.

FIGURE 16.3
POLITICAL ALIENATION IN THE UNITED STATES, 1966–1995

An increasing number of Americans are politically alienated. A majority now feel helpless to affect the course of government.

SOURCE: Harris Survey 1989b, January 1996.

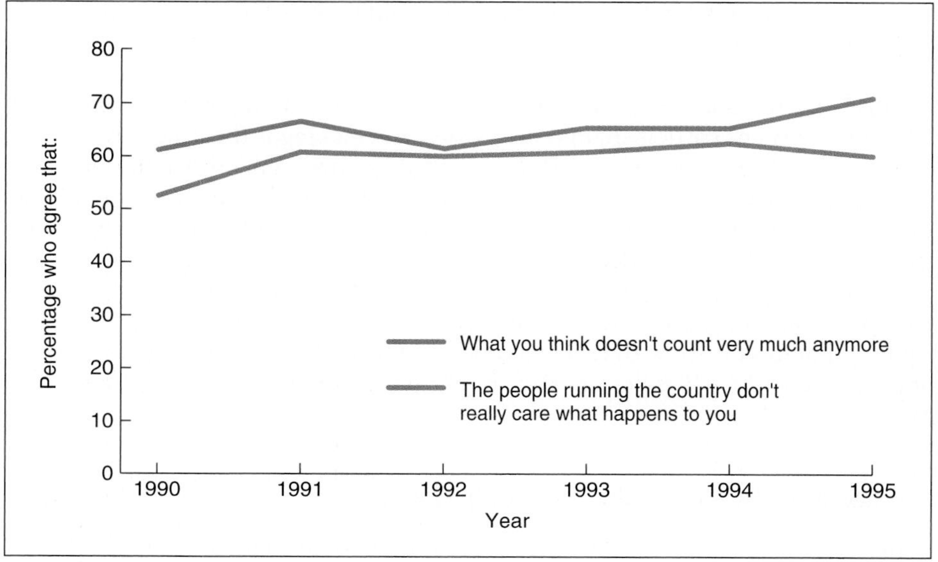

(Ginsberg and Weissburg 1978), and they interpret elections as a ritualized form of participation that serves to confirm the legitimacy of the system.

This is probably unduly cynical. Participation in democracy *does* matter. Studies of Western Europe demonstrate that the existence of a unified workers' party is one of the most powerful predictors of the generosity of a nation's social welfare programs (Korpi 1989). Similarly, the size of the old-age pensions has been shown to be directly related to the size of the voting bloc comprising older people (Pampel and Williamson 1985).

People who want to have an effective voice in shaping government policy need to do more than vote: They need to *organize*. Nevertheless, simply going to the polls makes you hard to ignore. The strong correlation between participation and social class means that the government is unrepresentative of the whole and, in particular, that it underrepresents the poor and the poorly educated.

CAN WE REVITALIZE CITIZENSHIP?

In the past several years, many political scientists and other observers have alerted us to a crisis in American politics. The crisis involves voter apathy coupled with citizens' self-interest and divisiveness. The 1995 book *Democracy on Trial*, by Jean Elshtain, is one such warning. A second is Newt Gingrich's book *To Renew America* (1995). Elshtain, a professor of social and political ethics at the University of Chicago, worries that Americans no longer listen to each other so they can have real debates about serious moral issues. Instead, Elshtain argues, Americans simply repeat their preconceived opinions. Gingrich tells Americans to stop whining and *do* something—such as vote or volunteer in their communities.

There are cases in which ordinary citizens have made tremendous improvements in their communities by becoming politically active (Selznick 1995). For example, Chattanooga, Tennessee, was once labeled the dirtiest city in the country. Today, it is one of the cleanest, because more than 1,700 Chattanoogans decided to do something about it. They attended public meetings, where they came up with 40 community goals, and then they worked out a plan for meeting those goals. One element in their plan was supporting local candidates who also believed in their efforts (J. D. Wilson 1995).

Here are some key rules for improving things in a community, according to one writer (J. D. Wilson 1995):

1. Work together with others you don't know, don't like, or don't agree with.
2. Focus on problems in common, not issues dividing you.
3. Be inclusive; invite people from all ages, social classes, and racial/ethnic groups.
4. Set ground rules (no verbal personal attacks, for instance).
5. Set specific, attainable goals.
6. Celebrate victories.
7. Use the local media to get the word out.
8. Be patient and persistent.

Besides doing volunteer work for better communities, Americans can become more active politically—that is, read about the issues and vote. One columnist suggests that people need to stop labeling each other "conservative" or "liberal," "left" or "right," "far left" or "far right" and pay more attention to each issue separately (Greenfield 1995b). Americans may also need to focus on what works a little more, rather than only on what doesn't.

APPLICATIONS IN DIVERSITY

HOW ARE AMERICAN INDIAN RESERVATIONS GOVERNED?

Native Americans living on reservations occupy a special legal status in the United States, one that has gradually developed through history and reflects American Indians' status as indigenous, or native, peoples. During the early years of the United States and throughout much of the 19th century, Indian tribes were viewed as separate nations to be dealt with by treaties negotiated with the U.S. federal government. Reflecting the government's conflict with Native Americans over land and resources, federal relations with the American Indians were the responsibility of the Secretary of War. Fittingly, when the Bureau of Indian Affairs (BIA) was created in 1824 to coordinate federal relations with the Native American tribes, it was placed in the War Department.

By the late 1800s, however, the majority of Native Americans had been moved to or had found their ways to federally established reservations, where they were promised refuge from European settlers, along with food and clothing—necessary commodities because of the Indians' loss of lands and other economic resources, such as the buffalo. By this time, the U.S. military had virtually defeated the Native Americans; consequently, the government abandoned its policy of treating Indian tribes as separate nations. As one indication of this change in federal policy, the BIA was transferred from the War Department to the Department of the Interior.

The period that began in the late 19th century and lasted until the 1930s has been called the Assimilation Era. Along with defeating the Native American tribes militarily, the federal government passed laws that limited the authority and functions of tribal leaders. If tribal governments were weakened, it was reasoned, Native Americans would be more rapidly assimilated. The government's intent to merge the Native Americans into the dominant culture and society was particularly evident in the 1887 Dawes Act, also called the General Allotment Act.

The General Allotment Act ignored tribal organization and leadership and proposed to make individual landowners of tribal members. Reservations were broken up, and individual Native Americans were given title to acreages. The government assumed that with privately owned land, Indians would become European-like homesteaders and farmers.

The effect of the Allotment Act on Native Americans was disastrous. Because it was hoped that the Indians would become homesteaders, they were not allowed to sell their land for 25 years. Yet no effort was made to teach them agricultural skills. Moreover, through fraud and lease agreements, much of the land initially deeded to Native Americans eventually came into the possession of Europeans. By 1934, Native Americans had lost approximately 90 million of the 138 million acres in their possession prior to passage of the Allotment Act (Schaefer 1990, 172).

The assumptions behind the Allotment Act were that assimilation was best for Native Americans and that they were best considered as individuals apart from their tribal identity. Slowly, however, the U.S. government began to question these assumptions. The Indian Reorganization Act of 1934, also known as the Wheeler-Howard Act, was meant to support rather than diminish tribal identity. Revoking the Allotment Act, the Reorganization Act allowed tribes to adopt written constitutions and elect tribal councils with chairpersons. Furthermore, for the first time, the Wheeler-Howard Act recognized the right of Native Americans to approve of some federal actions taken on their behalf. The act maintained substantial non-Indian control over the reservations, however. For instance, the tribal governments owed their existence (and consequently, perhaps, at least partial allegiance) to the BIA.

More recent policies have focused on increasing political self-determination, or *tribal sovereignty*, for Native Americans. The special U.S. government services that Native Americans receive (such as medical care provided by

APPLICATIONS IN DIVERSITY

In 1988, the federal government passed the Indian Gaming Regulatory Act. It states that Native Americans can promote gambling, such as bingo halls or casinos, such as this elaborate one in Ledyard, Connecticut, on Indian lands—provided that the specific gaming activity is not prohibited by federal law or by the laws of the state in which the Indian lands are located. Although Indian-sponsored gaming accounts for just 4 percent of total U.S. gambling profits, opposition from state governments and non-Indian gambling interests threaten gaming activities on reservations (Wilkins and Ritter 1994). The gaming issue points to the larger question of Native American sovereignty: Is the Indian reservation a sovereign nation within a nation, or not?

the U.S. Public Health Service and university scholarships) fulfill various treaty obligations. Legal cases over the past several decades have concluded that tribes are separate governments, that states have no jurisdiction over the reservations, that the federal government has a responsibility to the tribes, and that Indians have a substantial right to the resources on their land, including profits from gambling (Wilkins and Ritter 1994).

Nevertheless, more than any other segment of the population except the military, reservation Indians find their lives determined by the federal government. From the conditions of the roads to the level of fire protection to the quality of the schools, reservation life is effectively controlled by the U.S. government through such federal agencies as the Bureau of Indian Affairs and the Public Health Service. Indian tribes and their leaders are now consulted more than in the past, but the ultimate decisions rest with the states in some cases and in Washington (Schaefer 1990; Wilkins and Ritter 1994).

THINKING CRITICALLY

What might be some manifest functions of federal control over Native Americans on reservations? Some latent functions? Some dysfunctions? How would conflict theory explain the present status of governance of Native Americans on reservations? How would symbolic interaction theory approach this question, do you think?

SOCIOLOGY ON THE NET

Over the past few decades politics have changed. Organized political parties have lost a great deal of power and political action committees (PACs) had emerged as a central player in the political world. The Federal Election Commission keeps track of all PAC contributions.

http://www.fec.gov/

Once you have arrived at the Federal Election commission **home page,** open the section on **Financial Information About Candidates, Parties and PACs.** Scroll down to the section dealing with PACs and click on **View a Graph.** What type of PAC is most prevalent? How have the number of PACs changed since 1977? Return to the section on PACs and click on the other selection called **PAC Summary Financial Information.** Browse through the selections. What organizations seem to be the biggest contributors? Who gets more money from PACs, incumbents or challengers? Why would these organizations be interested in influencing politics?

Return to the section on **Financial Information About Candidates, Parties and PACs** and click on the highlighted phrase **U.S. House Candidates**. Go to your home state and find your local representative. How much money does that person have? For more detailed information on any candidate you might wish to try Campaign Central.

http://www.clark.net/central

While America has maintained a stable democratic government, Mexico has struggled with the democratic process. Today, the Chiapas rebels stand in opposition to the current policies of the Mexican government. Thanks to the Internet, we can view the struggle from their perspective.

http://www.peak.org/~justin/ezln/ezln.html

Begin your browsing by scrolling down to the background section and clicking on **EZLN FAQ**. When you have acquainted yourself with the EZLN, return to the background section and open the highlighted section entitled **The Southeast in Two Winds** by Subcomandante Marcos. What is the EZLN? What is the history of this struggle? How does conflict theory help you understand the rebel position? You may wish to find a few shorter statements under the heading of **Communicados**.

SUMMARY

1. Power may be exercised through coercion or through authority. Authority may be traditional, charismatic, or rational-legal. Influence is less effective than power, since it does not allow one person to compel another's obedience.
2. Any ongoing social structure with institutionalized power relationships can be referred to as a political institution. This definition includes the family, the school, and the church, but the most prominent political institution is the state.
3. The state is distinguished from other political institutions because it claims a monopoly on the legitimate use of coercion and it has power over a broader array of issues.

❹ Democracy requires a supportive institutional environment. Such an environment is characterized by the absence of extreme income inequality, the existence of competing interest groups, and absence of fundamental cleavages.

❺ Mexico has a government that can be characterized as an essentially authoritarian regime with a democratic mechanism for elections.

❻ The stable two-party system in the United States is a product of our heterogeneous population and of the formal structure of U.S. government.

❼ Although Democrats tend to attract working-class and minority voters and Republicans tend to attract better-off voters, both U.S. political parties are necessarily centrist. Unlike many other democracies, the United States has no strong working-class party.

❽ Political effectiveness depends on organization. Interest groups, especially those with political action committees (PACs), have far more influence on policy than do members of unorganized publics.

❾ Four major models describe the American political process: the pluralist model, the power-elite model, the conflict/dialectic model, and the state autonomy model. None of them suggests that the average voter has much power to influence events.

❿ Political participation is rather low in America; fewer than half of the people of voting age vote in most national elections, and fewer yet take an active role in politics. Political participation is greater among those with high social status and among middle-aged and older people—categories that are more likely to support the status quo.

⓫ All forms of media have tremendous political influence on American society, but television is the most influential, from the way TV handles paid political announcements, news coverage, and campaign debates.

⓬ Political participation is based on individual calculation of costs and benefits. When costs of participating are low and benefits are relatively high, people will vote.

⓭ American Indian reservations are governed by tribal councils that derive their authority from the federal Bureau of Indian Affairs. More than those of any other civilian segment of the population, reservation Indians' daily lives are directly influenced by the U.S. federal government.

SUGGESTED READINGS

BIRNBAUM, Jeffrey. 1993. *The Lobbyists*. New York: Times Books/Random House. An excellent account of lobbyists in Washington, D.C., written by a journalist.

DOMHOFF, G. Williams. 1993. *Who Rules America?* Englewood Cliffs, N.J.: Prentice Hall. A classic by a scholar who spent 20 years chronicling the antics of the power elite.

DONOVAN, Robert, and Scherer, Ray. 1991. *Unsilent Revolution: Television News and American Public Life, 1948–1991*. New York: Cambridge University Press. An exploration of the effect television has had on the institution of government in the United States, as well as on current events and public opinion over the last 50 years.

ELSHTAIN, Jean Bethke. 1995. *Democracy on Trial*. New York: Basic Books. A work in which the author, a professor of social and political ethics at the University of Chicago, argues that Americans have become too self-absorbed and politically alienated and that as a result American democracy is in serious crisis.

EXOO, Calvin F. 1994. *The Politics of the Mass Media*. St. Paul: West. An extended critique of the mass media, which discusses not only what the mass media are presenting to the public but why they support the system and present the views of the dominant culture.

GILLESPIE, J. David. 1993. *Politics at the Periphery*. Columbia: University of South Carolina Press. A historical review of the roles played by third parties in American politics and a look at the impact of a third-party candidate, H. Ross Perot, on voting patterns in the 1992 presidential election.

MILLS, C. Wright. 1956. *The Power Elite*. New York: Oxford University Press. One of the most important discussions of the relationship among three areas of power in America: government, business, and the military. Mills, a conflict theorist, argues that the members of a small elite make the decisions that control American society.

ROSENTHAL, Alan. 1993. *The Third House: Lobbyists and Lobbying in the United States*. Washington, D.C.: Congressional Quarterly Press. A study that uses interviews with lobbyists and state government officials, as well as other data, to examine interest groups and lobbying at the state level.

ROSENTIEL, Tom. 1993. *Strange Bedfellows: How Television and the Presidential Candidates Changed American Politics, 1992*. New York: Hyperion Press. An analysis of the 1992 presidential election, in which the author, a correspondent for the *Los Angeles Times*, criticizes the press for treating the campaign as a horse race and for searching for gossip rather than news.

SCHMIDT, Steffin W., Shelly, Mack C., II, and Bardes, Barbara A. 1995. *American Government and Politics Today*, 1995–1996 Edition. St. Paul: West. An up-to-date and very readable textbook on politics and government in the contemporary United States.

CHAPTER 17

Economic Institutions

OUTLINE

PROLOGUE

Have You Ever. . . seriously tried to imagine what it might have been like to live in the United States 200 years ago? You would probably have lived on an isolated farm. If you were average, you would have had eight children, two to three sets of clothes, a one-room house, and a life expectancy of 35 years. Life would probably have been hard and short.

In the 1990s, the situation is very different. You are much more likely to work in a crowded office or store than on an isolated farm. You have far more clothes than you have children (a situation for which you are probably thankful). This transition from rural to urban, from poor to relatively well off can be traced directly to the transformation of our economy.

What does the future hold? Will you work in a crowded office, or at home with your modem? Will your employer be in the United States or in some distant part of the globe? Will you even *have* an employer, or will you be self-employed?

Will you be better off than your parents' generation? Will you be able to buy a house before you are 35? Retire before you are 65? Some students borrow up to $75,000 to finance their educations; they are betting that the future economy will be at least as good as today's. Whether this is a good bet depends to a large extent on the productivity of our own—and the world's—economy. How successfully will American workers compete with those in Central and South America, Asia, and other parts of the globe? More than any other institution, the economy will determine our future prosperity and lifestyles.

Economic institutions are social structures concerned with the production and distribution of goods and services. Such issues as whether there will be scarcity or abundance, whether resources will be used to produce guns or butter, and whether goods will be produced through craftwork or by assembly lines are all part of the production side of economic institutions. Issues of distribution include what proportion goes to the worker versus the manager, who is responsible for supporting nonworkers, and how much of society's production is distributed on the basis of need rather than effort or ability. The distribution aspect of economic institutions intimately touches the family, stratification systems, education, and government.

Economic institutions are social structures concerned with the production and distribution of goods and services.

Sociology is not concerned with the intricate workings of economic systems. Such issues as monetary policy, inflation, and the national debt are all left to the discipline of economics. Some understanding of such issues is required, of course. For example, do high interest rates lead to an increase or a decrease in income inequality? Sociologists, however, focus on the enduring pattern of norms, roles, and statuses that make up the economic system.

THINKING CRITICALLY

Think of some ways in which the economy affects the family. How does the family affect the economy?

In this chapter, we look at the economic system from two points of view. At the macroeconomic level, we examine the social structures of economic institutions and their relationships to other social institutions. Then we turn to an examination of the microeconomic level, looking at the economic system from the point of view of the individual. In the case of economic institutions, this means jobs and the organization of work. We close the chapter with a detailed examination of the often uneasy relationship between labor and technology in our increasingly globalized workplace.

TYPES OF ECONOMIC INSTITUTIONS

All societies must deal with the problems of producing and distributing goods. At a minimum, each must produce food, clothing, and shelter and must institutionalize some set of rules for distributing them. From a historical and cross-cultural point of view, we distinguish three major types of economic institutions: preindustrial, industrial, and postindustrial. They differ from one another in the typical organization of work as well as in the kind and amount of goods produced.

PREINDUSTRIAL ECONOMIC STRUCTURES

Preindustrial/economic structures include hunting, fishing, and gathering societies; horticultural societies; and agricultural societies—all discussed in Chapter 4. In these societies, most goods are produced by the clan or family unit. There may be limited barter or trade, but most of the goods consumed by a family are also produced by it. The family also serves as the distribution system. Family ties obligate the more productive to share with the less productive; thus, children, older people, and sick people are provided for by ties of family responsibility.

Preindustrial economic structures were characteristic of Europe until about 200 years ago and are still typical of many societies. Although the economies vary in complexity, their dominant characteristics are as follows:

1. Production units are small, and settlements are small and widely dispersed.
2. The major sources of energy are human and animal power, occasionally supplemented by primitive waterwheels.
3. The vast majority of the labor force is engaged in **primary production,** extracting raw materials from the environment. Prominent among primary production

Primary production consists of extracting raw materials from the environment.

Primary production involves direct contact with natural resources—as in fishing, hunting, farming, and forestry. Until a few hundred years ago, the vast majority of human beings were engaged in extracting these raw materials. Because primary production is almost necessarily rural production, it usually entails small, kin-based communities and a close association between work and other aspects of life.

activities are farming, herding, fishing, logging, hunting, and mining. As late as 1900, 36 percent of the U.S. labor force was engaged in primary production.

Because of limited energy resources, preindustrial economies do not produce much more than they need. Some have produced enough surplus to support giant cities such as Rome, Cairo, and Tenochtitlán, as well as artistic and scholarly elites, but this standard of living for the few required great inequality. It also required that the great majority of the population continue to give constant attention to primary production.

For the average person, a preindustrial economy means a close integration of work with all other aspects of life. Work takes place at or near home in family or neighborhood units. Some observers who deplore modern industrial work organization (assembly lines, time clocks, and so on) have romanticized preindustrial work organization as a situation in which people set their own pace, organize their own work, and have the satisfaction of seeing the results of their own labor. In fact, the average person in preindustrial societies probably works very hard; and if the impetus to go to work is the amount of work to be done, there is little individual choice about working. Getting to organize one's work is probably limited to deciding which end of the field to weed first, and the products of one's labor are undoubtedly too few to give rise to a great deal of satisfaction. Nevertheless, a preindustrial style of work organization does offer flexibility and variety. Its content and tempo change with the seasons; the hectic pace of the harvest is followed by the relative relaxation of harness mending and stock tending in the winter. All too often, it is also followed by malnutrition in the early spring, as last season's small surplus dwindles (Lenski, Lenski, and Nolan 1991).

Industrial Economic Structures

Industrialization means a change in both the organization and the content of production. Its major characteristics are:

1. Large and bureaucratically organized work units.
2. Reliance on sources of energy (gasoline, electricity, coal, steam) other than muscle power.
3. A shift to **secondary production,** the processing of raw materials.

Secondary production consists of the processing of raw materials.

For example, ore, cotton, and wood are processed by the steel, textile, and lumber industries; other secondary industries will turn these materials into automobiles, clothing, and furniture. Obviously some part of the labor force must still produce ore, cotton, and timber, but the proportion in primary production drops steadily as greater use of nonmuscle energy decreases the labor requirements for primary production. For example, one American farm family, thanks largely to machinery produced in the secondary sector, can today grow enough to feed over 30 nonfarm families.

The shift from primary to secondary production is characterized by growing surpluses. Even with substantial inequalities in distribution, this abundance generally leads to better education, better health, and a higher standard of living for the entire population. Other changes, however, are not so desirable: population growth, the assault on the environment, and the growth of cities. (Many of these problematic aspects of industrialization are covered in Unit 5, which deals with change.) In spite of its drawbacks, industrialization has been eagerly sought by most societies. As a means of increasing productivity and the standard of living, at least, its short-run advantages have been unquestioned.

Postindustrial Economic Structures

Tertiary production consists of the production of services.

Postindustrial development rests on a third stage of production, **tertiary production**—the production of services. The tertiary sector includes a wide variety of occupations: physicians, schoolteachers, hotel maids, short-order cooks, and police officers. It includes everyone who works for hospitals, governments, airlines, banks, hotels, schools, and grocery stores. None of these organizations produces tangible goods; they all provide services to others. They count their production not in barrels or tons but in numbers of satisfied customers.

The tertiary sector has grown very rapidly in the last half-century and is expected to grow still more. As Figure 17.1 illustrates, only 19 percent of the U.S. labor force was involved in tertiary production in 1920; by 1956, the figure had grown to 49 percent. The latest available statistics, for 1991, show 73 percent of U.S. workers in the tertiary sector, and by 2000 that sector is expected to include over three-quarters—76 percent—of the labor force. Simultaneously, the portion of the labor force employed in primary production has been reduced to almost nil (3 percent in 1991), and the proportion employed in secondary production (24 percent in 1991) has also fallen considerably (U.S. Bureau of the Census 1995, Table 1389).

Figure 17.1
Changing Labor Force in the United States

The labor force in the United States has changed drastically. The proportion of workers engaged in primary production has declined sharply while the proportion engaged in service work has expanded greatly.

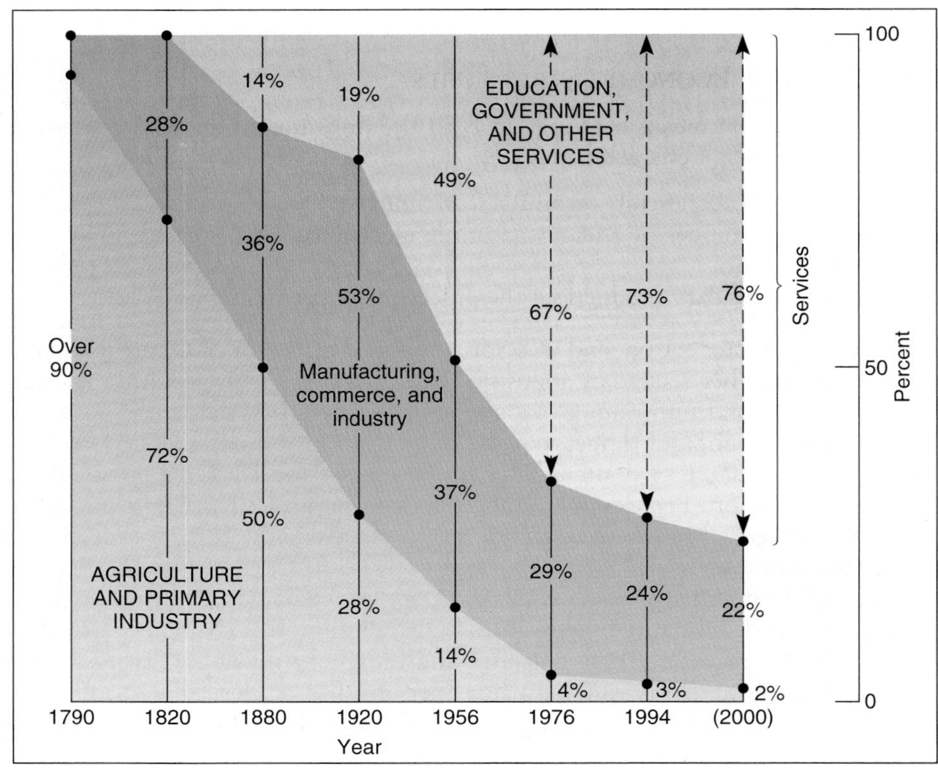

Other industrialized nations, such as Western European countries, Japan, and Australia, show the same general trend (U.S. Bureau of the Census 1995, Table 1389). These shifts do not mean that primary and secondary production are no longer important. A large service sector depends on primary and secondary sectors that are so efficiently productive that large numbers of people are freed from the necessity of direct production.

The expansion of the tertiary sector is largely a post–World War II phenomenon, and the consequences of this change for societies and individuals are not yet fully understood. Some of these changes are addressed later in this chapter when we discuss the changing nature of work in the United States.

CAPITALISM AND SOCIALISM

In the modern world, there are two basic types of economic systems: capitalism and socialism. Just as with democratic and authoritarian political systems, discussed in Chapter 16, you can think of capitalism and socialism as two social forms that occupy opposite ends on a continuum. Because economic systems must adapt to different political and natural environments, we find few instances of pure capitalism or pure socialism. Most modern economic systems represent some variation on the two and often combine elements of both.

CAPITALISM

Capitalism is an economic system in which most wealth (land, labor, equipment, money) is private property; both the production and the distribution of goods are carried out on a for-profit basis. Ideally, such an economic system harnesses individual self-interest to the broader goal of increasing overall productivity and efficiency. For example, Josiah Wedgwood devised a better way to make pottery. He invested his own capital in a factory, where with his new system (a precursor to today's assembly line) he produced pottery faster and better than his competitors. In order to avoid bankruptcy, his competitors also began to use the more efficient technique.

Capitalism is an economic system in which most wealth (land, capital, and labor) is private property, to be used by its owners to maximize their own gain; this economic system is based on competition.

In a capitalist economy, everyone attempts to get the most return on what they have to offer in the marketplace. For most of us, what we have to offer is our labor. We try to maximize our rewards (wages, benefits, satisfaction) by making our labor more valuable (getting more training, working harder). The money we get in exchange for our labor will enable us to buy food, shelter, and clothing. The harder we work and the more we have invested in our own training, the more money we'll have, or so the story goes. Because self-interest is a powerful spur, such economies can be very productive.

Even when it is very productive, a capitalist economy has two drawbacks. First, it neglects the aspect of distribution. The capitalist system at its most ideal represents a competitive bargain between the owner of capital and the supplier of labor, each of whom controls a necessary resource. What happens, however, to those who have neither? With nothing to exchange, they are outside the market. Although the family may continue to care for members who cannot sell their labor (children, older people, people with disabilities), what happens when whole families—indeed, whole communities—have no one who is willing to buy their labor? In theory, it is assumed that labor, like capital, will move to a new area of demand. An unemployed steelworker in Youngstown, Ohio, however, cannot easily transform himself into a computer technician or a frogman for an off-shore oil rig (Thurow 1980). Second, pure capitalism does not provide for public goods: streets, sewers, defense. These goods must be produced, even if they offer profit to no one. Thus, capitalist systems must have some means of distribution other than the market.

SOCIALISM

If capitalism is an economic system that maximizes production at the expense of distribution, socialism is a system that stresses distribution at the expense of production. As an ideal, **socialism** is an economic system in which productive tools are owned and managed by the workers and used for the collective good.

Socialism is an economic system in which productive tools (land, labor, and capital) are owned and managed by the workers and used for the collective good.

In theory, socialism has several major advantages over capitalism. First, societal resources can be used for the benefit of society as a whole rather than for the benefit of individuals. This advantage is most apparent in regard to common, or shared, goods such as the environment. A related advantage is that of central planning. Because resources are controlled by the group, they can be deployed to help reach group goals. This may mean diverting them from profitable industries (say, those making bicycles, televisions, and compact discs) to industries that are viewed as more likely to benefit society in the long run, such as education, agriculture, and steel production. The major advantage claimed for socialism, however, is that it produces equitable (though not necessarily equal) distribution.

The creed of pure socialism is "from each according to ability, to each according to need." An explicit goal of socialism is to eliminate unequal reward as the major incentive to labor. The Cuban revolutionary Che Guevara argued that "one of the fundamental objectives of Marxism is to remove interest, the factor of individual interest and gain from men's psychological motivations" (cited in Hollander 1982). Workers are expected to be motivated by loyalty to their community and their comrades. Unfortunately, the childless woman is not likely to be motivated to do her best when the incompetent worker next to her takes home a larger paycheck simply because she has several children and thus a greater need. Nor is the farmer as likely to make the extra effort to save the harvest from rain or drought if his rewards are unrelated to either effort or productivity. Because of this factor, production is usually lower in socialist economies than in capitalist economies.

MIXED ECONOMIES

Most Western societies in the late 20th century represent a mixture of capitalist and socialist economic structures. In many nations, services such as the mail and the railroads and key industries such as steel and energy have been socialized. These moves to socialism are rarely the result of pure idealism. Rather, public ownership is often seen as the only way to ensure continuation of vital services that are not profitable enough to attract private enterprise. Other services—for example, health care—have been partially socialized because societies have judged it unethical for these services to be available only to those who can afford to pay for them. Education is a socialized service, but it went public so long ago that few recognize the public schools as one of the first socialized industries.

In the case of many socialized services, general availability and progressive tax rates have gone far toward realizing the maxim "from each according to ability, to

The primary goal of socialist economies is equitable distribution, not high productivity. Many socialist nations have achieved this equality at rather low levels of productivity. In order to improve productivity, the Chinese government has experimented with free markets where farmers can sell surplus goods for profit. The markets have been enormously successful, boosting farm productivity and income and improving food availability.

each according to need." There are still inequalities in education and health care, but many fewer than there would be if these services were available strictly on a cash basis. The United States has done the least among major Western powers toward creating a mixed economy, and its future direction is unclear. Although the direction in the United States since the 1930s has been toward greater socializing of services, some of this commitment was reduced during the Reagan/Bush years. A conservative Republican-controlled Congress elected in 1994 promises to further reduce the socializing of services, particularly to the poor. The future mix of socialist and capitalist principles in the United States will reflect political rather than strictly economic conditions.

The Political Economy

Although all institutions are interdependent, the link between economic and political institutions is particularly strong. In fact, earlier generations often referred to the two as a single institution—the political economy—and a growing number of scholars today follow this practice as well. Marxist scholars, of course, focus on the extent to which governments serve economic elites. Of equal interest is the question we address in this chapter: To what extent can contemporary socialist and capitalist economies be regarded as *political* economies—economies in service of political goals or political elites?

The Political Economy of Socialism. By definition, socialism is a political economy. The state rather than private enterprise owns and controls production and distribution. It makes an enormous difference, however, whether the state is democratic or authoritarian. Democratic socialism, such as that practiced in Sweden, has been achieved with the support of the people. The economy is in many ways controlled by the voters. Communism is socialism grafted onto an authoritarian political system. It is a socialist economy guided by a political elite and enforced by

FIGURE 17.2
FOUR TYPES OF POLITICAL ECONOMIES

Economic institutions are not the same as political institutions, but the link between economic and political institutions is strong. The two types of political institutions can be related to the two types of economic institutions. Combining authoritarian politics with a socialist economic system, for example, results in a communist political economy, such as those in the former Soviet Union and contemporary China. Combining democratic politics with a socialist economy, results in a democratic socialist political economy, such as that in Sweden. Similarly, a capitalist economy can be combined with either authoritarian or democratic politics. The United States is a democratic capitalist political economy.

SOURCE: Graph adapted from Graham T. T. Molitor. 1981. The Futurist. With permission from Public Policy Forecasting, 9208 Wooden Bridge Road, Potomac, Maryland 20854; 1994 figures are from U.S. Bureau of the Census 1995, Table 653.

TYPES OF ECONOMIC INSTITUTIONS	TYPES OF POLITICAL INSTITUTIONS: Authoritarian	Democratic
Capitalist	Authoritarian capitalist political economies **Examples** • Saudi Arabia • Nigeria	Democratic capitalist political economies **Examples** • United States • Japan
Socialist	Communist political economies **Examples** • Former Soviet Union • China	Democratic socialist political economies **Example** • Sweden

a military elite (Ebenstein 1980). The goals of socialism (equality, efficiency) are still there, but the political form is authoritarian rather than democratic. Many contemporary Marxists bitterly reject the former Soviet and the Chinese brand of communism as an "antidemocratic perversion of socialism" (Stephens 1980), run at the expense of the workers instead of for their benefit (Oppenheimer 1985). These critics allege that the inefficiencies and inequalities rampant in communism have everything to do with authoritarianism and excessive bureaucratization and nothing to do with socialism as an economic system.

In Poland, Romania, Russia, and other countries throughout the former communist bloc, the last few years have revealed widespread agreement that these critics have a point. Some economic decision making is being transferred from the state to the market in these nations. The goal of such restructuring is not to abandon socialism altogether but to shift production decisions from political to economic units—to reduce the political domination of the economy. Factory managers are expected to respond to the market instead of to directives from central planners. The goal, or manifest function, of these reforms is to make production more efficient. The latent function, however, will be to shift power from government bureaucrats to those people who run factories and agricultural collectives (Nee 1989).

The U.S. Political Economy. It is not only under state socialism that the government intervenes in the economy. On the one hand, pro-business critics argue that the U.S. economy has been captured by government and that excessive regulation and interference reduce the ability of capitalism to respond to market forces. On the other hand, critics from the left argue that government has been captured by economic elites and that it pursues pro-business interests to the detriment of other citizens' interests.

The relative merits of the arguments depend largely on two factors. The first factor is the segment of the economy we examine. In the industrial core, there are often cozy relationships between business and government that work for the benefit of business. The so-called military/industrial complex is one such relationship. On the periphery, small businesses are much more likely to be hemmed in by unwanted government interference than they are to have any influence over government. The second factor is the level of government we examine. At the federal level, government has considerable power over business, large and small (although this is changing owing to the emergence of transnationals, discussed below). The situation has been very different at the local level. Major corporations dwarf many cities in their assets and power, and local governments are often in a subservient position with regard to these businesses, having to offer special tax packages, zoning exceptions, and environmental quality concessions to gain or retain jobs that improve the health of the local economy.

Transnationals. Corporate size and the link between political and economic interests are of particular concern when the economic actors enter the international arena as transnationals. Japan controls 149 of the world's 500 largest corporations, and they have almost 4 trillion U.S. dollars in combined revenues. The highest number of the world's largest 500 corporations (151) are headquartered in the United States; together they have total revenues of nearly $3 trillion (U.S. Bureau of the Census 1995, Table 1393). These international companies, such as International Telephone and Telegraph, IBM, General Motors, and Ford, are so large that they dwarf many national governments in size and wealth. Their ability to move capital, jobs, and prosperity from one nation to another gives them power that transcends the law of any particular country (Michalowski and Kramer 1987).

Transnationals are large corporations that operate internationally and have power that transcends the laws of any particular nation-state.

There is considerable debate about the possible effects, good and ill, of such international economic enterprises. A few observers hope that ties of international finance will create a more interdependent (and peaceful) world (Tannenbaum [1968] 1979). Others are concerned that transnationals are exercising a thinly veiled imperialism. They allege that having labor-intensive work done in the Third World exposes workers in those countries to dangers that are banned by law in most Western nations (Michalowski and Kramer 1987); this practice works to the disadvantage of U.S. workers at the same time that it helps to perpetuate economic dependence in less developed countries (Barnet and Muller 1974). Yet another concern about transnationals is their influence on U.S. foreign policy. In the 1920s, U.S. fruit, copper, and oil companies dominated the economic life of Latin America. These companies used bribes, guns, and cannons to affect national and international policy (Patterson, Clifford, and Hagan 1983). Occasionally, they even brought in the U.S. Marines; during the 1920s, the United States invaded 12 Latin American countries, including Nicaragua and El Salvador.

GLOBAL PERSPECTIVES: Democratic Socialism in Sweden

What would it be like to live and work in Sweden? You would have a guaranteed job and income (or pension, if you were retired or disabled), guaranteed access to comfortable housing, free education through college, and free medical care. After you or your partner gave birth to or adopted a baby, you would be entitled to a full year of paid parental leave (Haas 1990). Once you went back to work, you could use a state-funded or cooperative day-care center. And you would give more than half your paycheck to the government in taxes. Some Swedish politicians want to expand social benefits—and raise taxes to as much as 70 percent of everyone's income (Helco and Madsen 1987).

Sweden is a democratic socialist society. Sometimes called *market socialism*, Sweden's economy is a mix of corporate capitalism with significant welfare benefits for workers and nonworkers alike. According to the nation's democratic constitution, the majority of Swedes have voted to receive these benefits and to pay high taxes for them. But Sweden's economy wasn't always arranged this way.

Sweden owes its economic organization to the rise of a strong labor movement, beginning simultaneously with industrialization in the 1870s (Koblik 1975). By 1889, labor union members had founded the Social Democratic Party, a political party dedicated to equitable wages, job security, and welfare programs for the entire society. While communists in Russia were fighting and winning the Russian Revolution in 1914–1917, members of Sweden's Socialist Democratic Party were politicking for seats in parliament. After holding power on and off during the 1920s, the Socialist Democratic Party won an important election in 1932 and then retained political power for over 40 years. Nonsocialist parties, or "bourgeois" parties, as they are referred to in Sweden, held power between 1976 and 1982, when the Socialist Democrats took over again and retained control until 1991 (Olsen 1992). Today, the government is controlled by more conservative politicians, but the welfare state that emerged during 40 years of socialist majority government remains in place.

One reason the Swedish labor movement has been so successful in getting workers' benefits is that Swedes have an unusually high degree of humanitarianism, grounded in "voluntariness, sympathy, and Christian help" (Sanuelsson 1975, 336). Then, too, the ideas of development and progress, coupled with faith in the inherent goodness of all individuals, have led the majority of Swedes to believe that virtually all future problems can be resolved and all wants supplied (Nilsson 1975).

Not everyone in Sweden is a member of the Socialist Democratic Party, of course. Conservative groups favor a freer market economy. Furthermore, Socialist Democrats today are worried about whether Sweden's welfare society can survive the international economic downturn of the 1970s, along with increasing globalization of the economy and workforce (Olsen 1996). For one thing, controlling Sweden's transnational corporations so that they do not export jobs and so that they continue to pay high taxes at home may prove more and more difficult. Some economists are beginning to point out that Sweden's market socialism is based on an inherent irony: Strong and profitable capitalist businesses and corporations are necessary so that workers can be employed and taxes collected to provide socialist welfare benefits. But insisting on generous worker benefits and full employment eats into capitalist profits (Olsen 1992, 1996).

THINKING CRITICALLY

As an employee, what would you like about working in Sweden? What would you dislike? As an employer, what would you like about doing business in Sweden? What would you dislike? How can Sweden's democratic socialist government continue to resolve these differences, do you think?

THE DUAL ECONOMY IN THE UNITED STATES

A **dual economy** consists of the complex giants of the industrial core and the small, competitive organizations that form the periphery.

The U.S. economic system can be viewed as a **dual economy.** Its two parts are the complex giants of the industrial core and the small, competitive organizations that form the periphery. These two parts are distinguished from each other on two dimensions: the complexity of their organizational forms and the degree to which they dominate their economic environments (Baron and Bielby 1984).

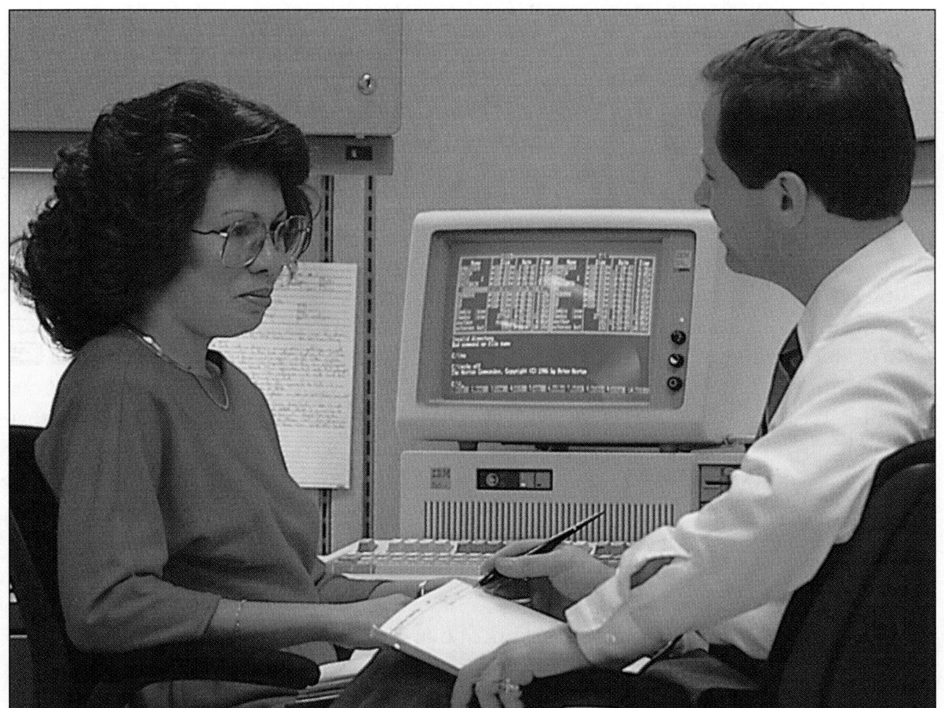

The majority of American workers are employed in the service sector (tertiary production). We don't grow anything, harvest anything, or make anything. Like these bank auditors, growing numbers of us work in financial, health, education, or government institutions. We move money, ideas, paper, and people around, but we do not produce tangible products. This vast superstructure of tertiary workers, however, rests on a highly productive agricultural and industrial labor force that can supply us with all the food, computers, and other tangible goods that we need.

The Industrial Core: Corporate Capitalism

In classic capitalism, the market is peopled with a large number of small producers who are competing among themselves for labor, customers, and capital. This competition is what makes the market efficient. To a very significant extent, however, this competition is absent in today's industrial core. In place of small, independent producers, we have a tightly knit group of industrial giants, many of them transnationals (Stearns and Allan 1996). The increase in size and interdependence has significantly changed the way capitalism operates. Meanwhile, the new high tech companies such as Microsoft, for example, seem to be an exception where competition is fierce.

Size of Units. There are more than 15 million businesses in the United States (U.S. Bureau of the Census 1995, Table 846), but most of the nation's capital and labor are tied up in a few corporate giants that form the industrial core. The largest U.S. companies—such as General Motors, Exxon, Ford, and IBM—control billions of dollars of assets and employ hundreds of thousands of individuals around the world. These giants loom large on both the national and international scene: They exceed many nations of the world in wealth and population.

Interdependence and Ties to Government. At the local level, we have mentioned that a region's one major employer can successfully bargain with city and county government for tax advantages and favorable zoning regulations in exchange for increasing or retaining jobs. Research strongly suggests that the growing size and interdependence of firms in the industrial core are causing this scene to be reenacted at the federal level.

Wealthy capitalists are linked to each other by shared ownership of large firms; large firms are linked to one another by having common members on their boards of directors and through their dealings with the same financial institutions. As a result of this interdependence, relations among large firms have become more cooperative than competitive. In strictly economic terms, decreased competition reduces productivity and efficiency. At the same time, decreased competition means that large firms and the capitalist class become a more potent political force (Mizruchi 1989). There is good evidence that large firms generally support the same political candidates and seldom engage in direct political opposition (Mizruchi 1990). Furthermore, one study showed that as the proportion of the nation's assets held by the top 100 firms increased, the effective rate of corporate taxation underwent a corresponding decrease (Jacobs 1988). The fact that individual income tax rates have increased over the last 40 years while corporate income tax rates have actually declined reflects both the increasing wealth and power of the capitalist elite and the erosion of organized labor as a significant political force (Campbell and Allen 1994).

THE COMPETITIVE SECTOR: SMALL BUSINESS

The competitive, or "small business," sector of the U.S. economy is made up largely of small businesses that are family owned or operated by a small group of partners. There are over 5.5 million businesses with fewer than 20 employees in the United States; in 1992, they had a total annual payroll of more than $500 billion (U.S. Bureau of the Census 1995, Table 859). Small businesses are characterized by having relatively few employees, economic uncertainty, and relatively little bureaucratization of management and authority. The chief examples of these kinds of businesses are farming, small banks and retail stores, and restaurant and repair services. Some small manufacturing companies continue to meet these criteria as well. Marx called people in this segment of the competitive sector the petit (pronounced petty) bourgeois. The **petit bourgeois** are those who use their own modest capital to establish small enterprises in which they and their families provide the primary labor (Bechhofer and Elliott 1985).

The **petit bourgeois** are those who use their own modest capital to establish small enterprises in which they and their families provide the primary labor.

About 150 years ago, Marx predicted that the economy would become polarized into wealthy capitalists and impoverished workers. The disappearance of the small business class would be "the last act of the tragedy" (cited in Steinmetz and Wright 1989, 982). Yet this class has not disappeared. After steadily declining for over 100 years, it has recently reestablished itself at a solid one quarter of the labor force (U.S. Bureau of the Census 1995, Table 857).

Small business has offered an especially important avenue of opportunity for minority Americans. Koreans, Hispanics, and African Americans who doubt their ability to be hired by or make a successful career with a major corporation may nevertheless achieve moderate prosperity by operating neighborhood grocery stores, laundries, and restaurants. Women of all ethnicities have increasingly been starting their own businesses, particularly in services.

Who are the petit bourgeois? Some are professionals (doctors, lawyers, consultants), but many are blue-collar workers who own their own trucks, do independent contracting, own hamburger franchises, or have their own beauty salons. Many of those who own their own businesses live on the edge of economic disaster; failure is just around the corner, and they may soon be working for someone else. Nevertheless, owning one's own business is enormously attractive to many Americans. There is a real possibility of economic success; but more important, there is an opportunity for independence. Furthermore, the economic pitfalls that face the self-employed are not significantly greater than those facing the average blue-collar worker, for whom layoffs and unemployment are common experiences. Although many of the smallest businesses fail, the competitive sector contains many secure and profitable small businesses.

The Informal Economy. An important sector of the periphery is the underground economy, or **informal economy.** This is that part of the economy that escapes the record keeping and regulation of the state. It includes illegal activities such as prostitution, selling drugs, and running numbers, but it also includes a large variety of legal but unofficial enterprises, such as home repairs, housecleaning, and garment subcontracting. Often referred to disparagingly as "fly-by-night" businesses, enterprises in the informal sector are nevertheless an important source of employment. This is especially true for those segments of the population that would like to avoid federal record keeping: illegal aliens, aliens whose visas do not permit them to work, senior citizens and welfare recipients who don't want their earnings to reduce their benefit levels, adolescents too young to meet work requirements, and many others (Portes and Sassen-Koob 1987). While the informal economy is important in the United States, it is far more significant in the economies of Third World nations.

The **informal economy** is that part of the economy that escapes the record keeping and regulation of the state.

The **segmented labor market** is a dual labor market in which hiring, advancement, and benefits vary systematically between the industrial core and the periphery.

The Segmented Labor Market

Parallel to the dual economy is a dual labor market, generally referred to as a **segmented labor market,** in which hiring, advancement, and benefits vary systematically between the industrial core and the periphery.

In the industrial core, firms generally rely on what are called internal labor markets. Almost all hiring is done at the entry level, and upper-level positions are filled from below. At all levels, credentials are critical for hiring and promotion. Within core firms, there are predictable career paths for both blue- and white-collar workers. Employment is generally secure, and benefits are relatively good. Wages and benefits are best in the very largest firms (Hodson and Sullivan 1995).

In the competitive sector, credentials are less important, career paths are short and unpredictable, security is minimal, and benefits are relatively low. However, bureaucratization and red tape are less pervasive in the competitive sector, and both workers and managers have more freedom in their work.

The competitive sector offers a haven of employment for those who do not meet the demands of the industrial core—for example those who do not have the required credentials, who have spotty work records, or who want to work part time. As a result, a disproportionate number of minorities and women work in the competitive sector. Because keeping a job and getting a promotion are governed almost exclusively by personal factors rather than by seniority or even ability, however, this sector is less likely to promote minorities or women; there is no affirmative action officer in Joe's Café. The predominance of women and minorities in the competitive sector is an important reason for the relatively small gains shown by affirmative action programs. The programs have been effective within the industrial core, but many of the people to whom the programs are directed are not in that sector.

The garment industry is part of the competitive sector of the economy, and it offers a classic example of the segmented labor market. The garment industry historically has relied on poorly paid immigrant and female labor. Employees are usually paid a piece rate, and they have no job security, no health insurance, no retirement benefits, and no career ladder.

TABLE 17.1
UNEMPLOYMENT RATES, 1996

Overall unemployment rates fell from close to 11 percent in 1983 to 5.5 percent in 1996. Nevertheless, some pockets of the population, especially racial and ethnic minorities, continue to face very high unemployment. Not counted in these figures are all of the people who are working part time because they cannot find a full-time job.

PERCENTAGE OF THE CIVILIAN LABOR FORCE OVER 16 UNEMPLOYED, BY RACE/ETHNICITY	
WHITE	4.7%
BLACK	10.0
HISPANIC[a]	8.8
TOTAL	5.4

[a] Hispanics may be of any race.

SOURCE: U.S. Bureau of Labor Statistics, http://stats/bls:gov:80/datahome.htm.

WORK IN THE UNITED STATES

From the individual's point of view, economic institutions mean jobs. For some, jobs are just jobs; for others, they are careers. Either way, spending 40 years in the world of work makes this world central to most people's lives.

EMPLOYMENT AND UNEMPLOYMENT

In the contemporary United States, approximately two-thirds of all adults are in the labor force at any given time. Labor force participation is higher for men than for women, but the gap is closing rapidly.

The labor force includes the unemployed as well as those actually working. Over the last 40 years, unemployment has averaged about 5 percent of the labor force. Unemployment hit a postwar peak in 1983 with close to 11 percent unemployed; in 1994, unemployment was 5.5 percent. As noted in Table 17.1, minorities are much more likely than whites to experience unemployment: Blacks experience more than twice as much unemployment as whites, and Hispanics fall about halfway between black and white Americans.

Employment is a critical necessity for most people. It determines their status in their families and communities, it provides their income, and it structures their lives. Unemployment, then, is a critical problem, and dozens of studies show that involuntary unemployment has negative effects on mental and physical health. It is associated with depression, alcoholism, and family violence. (Gelles, 1994).

Unemployment depends on two sets of factors: individual factors (education, race, skill) and structural factors (such as whether one works in the construction or the health care industry, the competitive sector or the industrial core). In recent years, the press has focused on layoffs among middle-class and white-collar workers. Nevertheless, those most vulnerable to unemployment are minorities and blue-collar workers (Hodson and Sullivan 1995). The degree of vulnerability to unemployment varies by economic sector. Unemployment due to involuntary layoffs is much higher in the industrial core than in the periphery. The degree of bureaucratization in the core seems to ensure that a last-hired, first-fired principle operates, and hence there is little evidence of direct and purposeful racial discrimination in this sector's unemployment. It is also true, however, that a last-hired, first-fired principle is typically a factor in institutional racism, a concept explored in Chapter 11.

THE STRUCTURE OF WORK: OCCUPATIONS

Aside from the simplest consequences of working (earning income and filling up 40 hours or more of time each week), what you do at work is probably as important as whether you work. Your income, status, security, and work satisfaction will be very different if you are a retail sales clerk working at the minimum wage than if you are a teacher, for example.

A **profession** is an occupation that demands specialized skills and creative freedom.

Professions. Occupations that demand specialized skills and creative freedom are **professions.** Their distinctive characteristics include (1) the production of an unstandardized product, (2) a high degree of personality involvement, (3) a wide knowledge of a specialized technique, (4) a sense of obligation to the profession, (5) a sense of group identity, and (6) a significant service to society (Hodson and Sullivan 1995, 287–314). The definition of *profession* was originally developed for the so-called learned professions (law, medicine, college teaching). It applies equally well, however, to artists, dancers, and potters.

There is a great deal of variability in the rewards that professionals achieve. Some, such as physicians and lawyers, receive very high incomes, dancers and potters may earn very little. The major reward that all professionals have shared, however, is substantial freedom from supervision. Because their work is nonroutine and requires personal judgments, professionals have been able to demand—and get—the right to work their own hours, do things their own way, and arrange their own work lives.

Freedom from supervision remains the most outstanding reward of professional work, but it is a reward that is being eroded. Increasingly, people in the professions work for others within bureaucratic structures that constrain many of the characteristic aspects of professionalism. Rather than being self-employed, for example, more and more physicians work for HMOs.

White-collar workers appear across nearly the entire spectrum of occupational prestige. They range from the top executives of major firms down to minimum-wage clerks in government offices. This commodities broker with Charles Schwab is typical of the upper end of the white-collar spectrum. His job demands a college education, ability to think independently, and excellent communication skills. Although it is a high-stress job, it also is a very well-paid job that provides intrinsic as well as extrinsic rewards.

What Color Is Your Collar? Fifty years ago, the color of your collar was a pretty good indication of the status of your job. People who worked with their hands wore blue (or brown or flannel) collars; managers and others who worked in clean offices wore white collars. Those days are past. The labor force is far more diversified, and some of the old guidelines no longer work. The bagger at Safeway wears a white shirt and tie; the librarian may wear blue jeans and sandals. Yet the librarian is a white-collar worker and the bagger is not.

Traditional white-collar workers are managers, professionals, typists, salespeople—those who work in offices and are expected to be able to think independently. Blue-collar workers are people in primary and secondary industry who work with their hands; they farm, assemble telephones, build houses, and weld joints. Although some blue-collar workers earn more than some white-collar workers, their jobs in general are characterized by lower incomes, lower status, lower security, closer supervision, and more routine.

Fifty years ago, this simple, two-part division of the labor force included most workers. These days, it leaves out a growing category of low-skilled, low-status workers who fry hamburgers, stock K-Mart shelves, and collect money at the "U-Serv" gas station. An important characteristic of the jobs these workers hold is that they have a short career ladder or none at all and they earn the minimum wage or close to it. When these workers are women, they are sometimes called pink-collar workers.

Occupational Outlook

As the graph in Figure 17.1 indicated, the outlook for the future includes greater expansion of the tertiary sector and even more reductions in employment in secondary and primary production. What will this mean for the kinds of jobs that are available in the future? Some projected changes are illustrated in Table 17.2.

Some traditional occupational categories are expected to suffer major declines. The occupations with the largest projected decreases include both blue- and white-collar jobs: Typists and teachers will have a harder time finding jobs, as will sewing machine operators and farmers. The declining opportunities in these occupations

TABLE 17.2
THE SHIFTING JOB MARKET: PROJECTED CHANGES BETWEEN 1994 AND 2005

The demand for labor is expected to grow betwen 1994 and 2005, but opinion differs over the kinds of jobs that will be available for future workers. Although some observers note with satisfaction the growth of high-skill positions, others point with concern to the fact that many of the fastest growing jobs are low-skill and low-wage.

	CHANGES 1994–2005	
	PERCENTAGE INCREASE	NUMBER OF NEW JOBS
THE FIVE FASTEST-GROWING JOBS RELATIVE TO THEIR SIZE IN 1994		
HOMEMAKER-HOME HEALTH AIDES	107%	640,000
COMPUTER SCIENTISTS & SYSTEMS ANALYSTS	91	755,000
PHYSICAL THERAPY ASSISTANTS & AIDES	83	64,000
OCCUPATIONAL THERAPY ASSISTANTS & AIDES	82	13,000
PHYSICAL THERAPISTS	80	81,000
THE FIVE FASTEST-GROWING JOBS IN ABSOLUTE NUMBER		
COMPUTER SCIENTISTS AND SYSTEMS ANALYSTS	91	755,000
HOMEMAKER-HOME HEALTH AIDES	107	640,000
SCHOOL TEACHERS (K-12)	22	634,000
RETAIL SALES WORKERS	14	584,000
JANITORS, CLEANERS, & CLEANING SUPERVISORS	18	582,000

SOURCE: U.S. Bureau of Labor Statistics, news release 7/3/96, http://stats.bls.gov/pub/news.release/ecopro1.

reflect a variety of factors: changing age structure, loss of American jobs due to migration of industry overseas, and new technology.

The most controversial issue is what kinds of new jobs the economy will offer. Optimistic observers point to the fact that executive and professional jobs are growing faster than average and point to the high quality and good pay of these new jobs as indicators of what awaits today's college graduates. Others focus on the rapid increase in "McJobs." Although not all entail selling hamburgers, many are low-status jobs with low wages and no benefits: health aides, waiters and waitresses, custodians and maids. Table 17.2 shows the five jobs that are expected to grow the most in absolute number and the five jobs that will grow the most in percentage terms (that is, in relation to their size in 1992). This list suggests that there will be growth at all educational and status levels. Big growth is expected for computer engineers and scientists and for some highly trained support personnel, such as nurses. Unfortunately, the list also suggests that some of the fastest growing occupations are at the low-paying end of the service sector: home health aides, retail salespersons, and cashiers. Between 1992 and 2005 nearly three-quarters of the new jobs in the rapidly growing service sector will be in food service, health service, and cleaning and building service (U.S. Bureau of the Census 1995, Tables 650 and 651). Increasingly, these jobs are part time and/or temporary (Pearson 1994).

Both the optimists and the critics are correct in their expectations for the future: There is growth in good jobs for college graduates and those with technical training, but there is also rapid growth in bad jobs. Where there is no growth—where there may even be decline—is in good jobs for those who lack technical training or college degrees. The losers in the transformation of the labor market are likely to be the traditional working-class men and women who did skilled manual labor.

THE MEANING OF WORK

For most people, work is essential as the means to earn a livelihood. As noted in Chapter 9, one's work is often the most important determinant of one's position in the stratification structure and, consequently, of one's health, happiness, and lifestyle.

Work is more than this, however. It is also the major means by which most of us structure our lives. It largely determines what time we get up, what we do all day, whom we do it with, how much time and energy we have left for leisure, how we feel about ourselves, and who we tell people we are. Thus, the nature of our work and our attitude toward it can have a tremendous impact on whether we view our lives as fulfilling or painful. If we are good at our work, if it gives us a chance to demonstrate competence, and if it is meaningful and socially valued, then it can be a major contributor to life satisfaction.

Work Satisfaction. American surveys consistently find that the majority of workers report satisfaction with their work. Although such a report may represent

The fastest-growing jobs today in the United States are in the service sector. Many of these are what have been called "McJobs." They are minimum-wage jobs offering few benefits and very limited career ladders. The U.S. job market appears to be splitting in two very different directions: high-technology jobs that require advanced education and low-skill jobs. The decline of well-paid working-class jobs is a major concern.

The kind of work that we do determines what we do all day, who we do it with, and, not least, how much income and prestige we have. For these reasons, our jobs are one of our most critical roles, and our jobs spill over to affect what we do at home and in our communities. Studies show that people who have flexibility and independence at work are also flexible and independent at home. On the other hand, people whose work requires rigid authority may be more authoritarian at home.

Intrinsic rewards are rewards that arise from the process of work; they include enjoying the people you work with and taking pride in your creativity and accomplishments.

Extrinsic rewards are tangible benefits such as income and security.

Alienation occurs when workers have no control over the work process or the product of their labor; they are estranged from their work.

an acceptance of one's lot rather than real enthusiasm, it is remarkable that so few report dissatisfaction.

Studies of job satisfaction distinguish between two kinds of rewards that are available from work. **Intrinsic rewards** arise from the process of work; you experience them when you enjoy the people you work with and feel pride in your creativity and accomplishments. **Extrinsic rewards** are more tangible benefits, such as income and security; if you hate your job but love your paycheck, you are experiencing extrinsic rewards.

Ideally, work would be most satisfying if it provided high levels of both intrinsic and extrinsic rewards. A review of dozens of studies shows that the most satisfying jobs are those that offer (1) autonomy and freedom from close supervision, (2) good pay and benefits, (3) job security, (4) opportunity for promotions, (5) use of valued skills and abilities, (6) variety, (7) interesting work, and (8) occupational prestige (Hodson and Sullivan 1995). Jobs vary a great deal in the extent to which they supply these attributes. Some jobs score high on all of them, and some score low on nearly all of them.

Generally, the most satisfied workers are those in the learned professions, people such as lawyers, doctors, and professors. These people have considerable freedom to plan their own work, to express their talents and creativity, and to work with others; furthermore, their extrinsic rewards are substantial. The least satisfied workers are those who work on assembly lines. Although their extrinsic rewards are moderately high, their work is almost completely without intrinsic reward; they have no control over the pace or content of the work and are generally unable to interact with coworkers. In between these extremes, professionals and skilled workers generally demonstrate the greatest satisfaction; semiskilled, unskilled, and clerical workers indicate lower levels of satisfaction.

Alienation. Another dimension of the quality of work life, alienation, relates to Marxist theory. **Alienation** occurs when workers have no control over their labor. Workers are alienated when they have no control over *how* they work, when they do work that they think is meaningless (push papers or brooms) or immoral (build bombs), or when their work takes their physical and emotional energies without giving any intrinsic rewards in return (Davis and Milbank 1992).

The factory system of the mid 19th century was the ultimate in alienation. In 1863, a mother gave the following testimony to a committee investigating child labor:

> When he was seven years old I used to carry him [to work] on my back to and fro through the snow, and he used to work 16 hours a day. . . . I have often knelt down to feed him, as he stood by the machine, for he could not leave it or stop. (Cited in Hochschild 1985, 3.)

This child was truly an instrument of labor. He was being used, just as a hammer or a shovel is, to create a product that would belong to someone else. The Focus section in this chapter describes worker alienation in the 17th and 18th centuries.

Although few of us work on assembly lines any more, modern work can also be alienating. Telephone customer service personnel are often strictly monitored, for example. Service work, in fact, has its own forms of alienation. In occupations from nursing to teaching to working as a flight attendant, not merely our bodies but also our emotions become instruments of labor. To turn out satisfied customers, we must smile and be cheerful in the face of ill humor, rudeness, or actual abuse.

Studies of individuals in these occupations show that many have trouble with this emotional work. After smiling for eight hours a day for pay, they feel that their smiles have no meaning at home. They lose touch with their emotions and feel alienated from themselves (Appelbaum and Batt 1994; Hochschild 1985).

Alienation is not the same as job dissatisfaction. Alienation occurs when workers lack control. It is perfectly possible that workers with no control but with high wages and a pleasant work environment will express high job satisfaction. Marxist scholars believe that job satisfaction in such circumstances is a sign of false consciousness.

Self-Direction at Work. A key aspect of work that relates to both job satisfaction and alienation is self-direction (Davis and Milbank 1992). A 20-year program of studies by Kohn and his associates shows that the degree of self-direction in work affects satisfaction, alienation, and personality.

Self-direction has three components: job complexity, degree of supervision, and degree of routinization. Low-routine, low-supervision, high-complexity jobs provide the greatest satisfaction and give the greatest opportunity for self-expression. Such work includes not only that of college professors but also that of blue-collar workers with flexible jobs requiring active decision making, such as plumbing, carpentry, and some other forms of construction work. In contrast, high-routine, high-supervision, low-complexity jobs such as working on an assembly line or running groceries over a scanning machine give the least satisfaction and the most alienation.

These job characteristics, as noted, also affect personality. In studies in the United States and Japan, Kohn and his associates have consistently demonstrated that people who have more self-direction at work have greater mental flexibility, more trust, and greater receptivity to change; they also have lower levels of authoritarianism, conservatism, fatalism, self-depreciation, and conformity (Kohn and Schooler 1983; Naoi and Schooler 1986).

Technology, Globalization, and the Future of Work

The productivity of workers and the quality of their work experiences are often tied directly to the tools they work with. Some work technologies such as the assembly line, increase alienation while they increase productivity. Others, such as the photocopier, appear to be unmixed blessings. The rapid introduction of computerization and automation has had far-reaching effects on the nature of work. Rapidly developing technology, communication systems, and transportation systems have globalized our world economy. This situation will cause still more changes in the future of work.

The Effects of Technology

Many people argue that new technology is inescapably antilabor. These critics point out three negative effects of technology on labor: de-skilling, displacement of workers, and greater supervision.

1. *De-skilling.* Many observers believe that increased mechanization has reduced the skill level needed for many jobs to the point where it is difficult to take pride in craft or a job well done. The process of automating a job so that it takes much less skill than it used to is called *de-skilling*. For example, in the days before word processors, photocopiers, and self-correcting typewriters, good typists could take pride in their work. With the new technologies, almost anyone can turn out decent-looking copy.

An important element of the de-skilling process is that it reduces the scope for individual judgment. In hundreds of jobs across the occupational spectrum, computers make decisions for us. In the sawmill industry, for example, a computer now assesses the shape of a log and decides how it should be cut to yield the most board feet of lumber. An important element of skill and judgment honed from years of experience is now made worthless. According to the chief proponent of this argument, the central process in de-skilling is the separation of mind and hand (Braverman 1975; see also Beamish 1992).

> **THINKING CRITICALLY**
>
> What traits will you need to cultivate and demonstrate in order to get a job in a postindustrial economy? To keep a job?

2. *Displacement of the labor force*. One of the most critical complaints about automation is that it replaces people with machines. A few examples should suffice. Computerization in grocery stores has resulted in sharp reductions in employment by eliminating inventory clerks and pricing/repricing personnel, as well as reducing the skill level in cashiering. In the automobile industry, it is estimated that one robot can replace 1.5 human workers per shift—and the robot can work three shifts a day (U.S. Department of Labor 1985, 1986b).

In industry after industry, more sophisticated technology has made sharp inroads into the number of hours of labor necessary to produce goods and services. Many have concluded that fear of job loss is one of the reasons why employees seldom complain about the de-skilling aspects of their jobs. If they still have jobs, they are happy (Vallas and Yarrow 1987).

3. *Greater supervision*. Computerization and automation give management more control over production. More aspects of the production process are determined by management through computerized instructions and less is determined by employ-

This photograph shows robotic assembly in action. Studies show that, on the average, a robotic welder can do the work of 1.5 men per shift—and the robot can work three shifts per day. The replacement of human labor with robots and other computerized tools saves money, reduces human error, and frees people from dangerous and unpleasant work. All too often, however, it frees them from any work at all. Displacement of human labor with machines raises serious questions about the future of the industrial working class.

FOCUS ON YESTERDAY

The Luddites: Down with Machines

"NOW, EVERY YEAR MANY NEW TECHNOLOGIES ARE DEVELOPED THAT CAN REDUCE EVEN FURTHER THE DEPENDENCE OF INDUSTRY ON HUMAN LABOR."

Since the dawn of the industrial era, there has been tension between labor and technology. In 1675, weavers rioted against the introduction of looms that could allegedly do the work of 20 people; and in 1768, sawyers in London destroyed a mechanized sawmill. The most widely known revolt of labor against machinery, however, was the Luddite uprising in England between 1811 and 1816.

Wool was a major part of the English economy in the early 19th century. It was largely a home industry; and in Lancashire, nearly every home was engaged in wool production. The work was tedious and difficult. Particularly difficult was the last stage, in which a worker wielding 50-pond shears finished the fabric by cutting off all the nubs. Being able to handle these shears for 88 hours a week (the standard work week) required great strength and skill. It was an esteemed occupation.

In 1811, finishing machines were introduced to do this work. Each machine replaced six men. Not only were the men out of a job, but also the skills developed over a lifetime were made worthless. As use of the machines spread, large numbers of men were thrown out of work, and their families starved. On the horizon were more machines to take over other phases of wool production. Added to this, England was engaged in the Napoleonic Wars, and associated trade embargoes made the price of food high. The classic ingredients for insurrection were in place. The focus of the workers' anger was the machines, and their response was to destroy them.

In 1811, a young man named Ned Ludd, or Lud, or maybe Ludlam is alleged to have broken up his father's hosiery loom because he resented a rebuke. The incident, which may have been imaginary, coincided with the eruption of machine-breaking demonstrations, and the labor movement came to be called the Luddites.

In the early 19th century, any organization of labor was illegal. Nevertheless, laborers met secretly at taverns and later in the woods to plan well-organized attacks. A body of men with blackened faces would break into a shop and destroy all of the machinery. As the movement progressed, it became less disciplined, and owners too were assaulted and their homes looted. It was, said one observer, collective bargaining by riot.

The government was uncertain how to respond. There were a few liberals who were sympathetic with labor. Lord Byron, for example, wrote that "however much we may rejoice in any improvement in ye arts which may be beneficial to mankind; we must not allow mankind to be sacrificed to improvements in Mechanism" (cited in Reid 1986). The hard-liners won, however, and troops were sent in to restore order. Leaders and alleged leaders of the Luddites were hanged or deported to the far corners of the empire.

The Luddite movement caused hardly a pause in the increasing use of machines to replace workers. Now, every year many new technologies are developed that can reduce even further the dependence of industry on human labor. Although we have unemployment insurance, early retirement schemes, and welfare to cushion the blows, the process still causes human misery as valuable skills are debased and employment is lost. If we use the term *Luddite* to include all of those who "resist mechanization, automation, and the like, and who are the supposed enemies of 'progress' where the adoption of labour-saving devices is concerned" (Thomis 1970, 12), there are probably plenty of people who remain Luddites in spirit.

ees. Computers also keep more complex and thorough records on employees. For example, the scanner machines used in grocery stores do more than keep inventory records and add up grocery bills. They also keep tabs on checkers by producing statistics such as number of corrections made per hour, number of items run through per hour, and average length of time per customer. It is not surprising, therefore, that studies show that computers have increased work alienation among the cashiers and typists who use them (Vallas and Yarrow, 1987).

Whether new technologies are an enemy of labor may depend on which laborer we ask. From the standpoint of professionals in the knowledge industries (education, communications), new technology is a boon. Computers have expanded their job opportunities and enhanced their lives. Those whose work is being replaced rather than aided by computers, however, are less likely to see anything wonderful about them. Those most adversely affected are women and less-skilled workers (Hodson and Sullivan 1995).

One scholar has argued that technology itself is a neutral force: It can aid management, or it can aid workers (Davies 1986). Which technologies are implemented and how they are implemented reflect a struggle between labor and management, and this struggle, not the technology itself, will determine the outcome.

> **THINKING CRITICALLY**
>
> How has technology affected your schoolwork in the last 5 years? Has it given you new tools or robbed you of old skills? Has it given your instructors an excuse to demand more of you?

PROTECTING AMERICAN JOBS

The consequences of "de-laborization"—loss of jobs—are substantial. Not only individual workers but entire communities are impoverished as new technologies facilitate corporate decisions to move factories to other parts of the world where labor is much cheaper. In fact, the national economy is undergoing a process of reverse development: Like a Third World country, we export raw materials such as logs and wheat and import manufactured products such as VCRs and automobiles. People in Mexico and Japan and Korea have jobs manufacturing products for the U.S. market while American workers are making hamburgers.

What can public policy do to protect America's jobs? There are three general policy options: the conservative free-market option, new industrial policies, and the social welfare option (Hooks 1984).

The Conservative Free Market Approach Generally, business leaders and conservatives argue that the way to keep jobs in the United States is to reduce wages and benefits. If labor is cheap, they argue, business will have less incentive to automate or to move assembly plants to Mexico or Indonesia.

By default, this policy has been implemented. In communities across the nation, managements have used threats of plant closings to force wage concessions and reduce benefits. Labor unions are reduced to negotiating benefit protection in the face of wage reductions; in many cases, they have even failed to do this. Because so many workers have been afraid of losing their jobs, organized labor's power has been sharply reduced. Thus, one result of "de-laborization" is the reduced economic circumstances of workers who still have jobs.

New Industrial Policies Liberals argue that private profit should not be the only goal of economic activity and that the state should see to it that economic decisions protect communities' and workers' interests (Genovese 1989). Among the specific policies recommended are: (a) federal trade policies that make American-made goods more competitive in international markets and that reduce the advantage that foreign-made products have in the United States, (b) vigorous state investment in industries that will provide the largest number of decent jobs, (c) government oversight of mergers and plant closings to make sure plants behave responsibly, and (d) state support for worker efforts to buy and manage their own industries.

Social Welfare Policies New industrial policies are designed to keep people working; social welfare policies are aimed at protecting those who are thrown out of work. Among the policies recommended are (Blakely and Shapira 1984): (a) six-month notification of plant closings, (b) paid leave for soon-to-be displaced employees to look for jobs, (c) retraining programs for displaced workers, (d) relocation assistance for displaced workers, and (e) substantially more generous unemployment benefits. Of course, such suggestions are open to the same concerns that Sweden is now experiencing in regard to its welfare economy.

THINKING CRITICALLY

How will a postindustrial economy affect *your* working and economic future, do you think? In what ways is a postindustrialized economy a global economy? Which of the three general policy options outlined here do you think the United States will follow, and why? Which, in your opinion, would be the best one to follow, and why?

CONCLUSION

As you sit in the classroom in order to prepare yourself for a good position in the labor force, the economy itself is changing. Indeed, it is changing so fast that you may need to retool several times before your work life is complete. Increasingly, rapid developments in technology have dramatically changed the workplace from what it was 20 or even 10 years ago. The globalization of the economy has further changed the job situation for Americans. While the specter of unemployment still haunts ethnic minorities and blue-collar workers the most, the middle class is also experiencing the pangs of job insecurity and alienation. More and more workers are choosing to work for themselves, perhaps as consultants, in the tertiary sector of the economy. One political approach to the changing job situation involves conservative views that advocate the free market approach. A differing view advocates social welfare policies, similar in some ways to those in Sweden, that would provide greater security to workers. That the United States will expand its welfare policies in this time of a budget deficit and expressed need for a balanced budget seems a bad bet. It is more likely that American workers will increasingly need to learn new skills and be creative in finding and keeping jobs.

SOCIOLOGY ON THE NET

As we all know, work and the economic situation are very serious business. Will there be a decent job when graduation day rolls around? What are the prospects for job security in a given occupation? What are the employment and unemployment statistics? A look at the Census Bureau might provide some insights.

http://www.census.gov/population/pop-profile/toc.html

Scroll through the **Contents** and open the report on **Labor Force and Occupation**. Browse around this brief document and note the different historical patterns of female and male employment. What has the trend been since 1950? Why has the pattern developed the way that it has? (Hint: see Chapter 12.) Where has much of the current unemployment been happening? What does this mean for future college graduates? What occupations enjoy the highest numbers of employed workers? What does your text tell you about these kinds of jobs?

Labor unions have always been concerned about the working conditions and wages of the working people. Let's take a look at some labor unions.

http://www.aflcio.org/unionand.htm

Scroll down the list of unions. This is only a list of unions affiliated with the AFL-CIO. At the bottom of the page click on the **AFL-CIO Home Page**. Click on and open each of the following sections: **Policy Statements, Press Releases** and **Issue Papers**. What is the union view? Is there more here than simply wages and

SOCIAL APPLICATIONS

NANNIES AND THE PROFESSIONALS WHO HIRE THEM

Talking about "the American economy" or "American workers" may tempt us to forget the great diversity that exists within our labor force. Professionals and other middle- and upper-middle-class workers may be revising their résumés and looking forward to becoming self-employed consultants in today's changing economy (Bridges 1994; Pearson 1994). Meanwhile, the maids and nannies who are likely to work for them have qualitatively different work experiences.

Nannies are important to a growing number of two-career, professional families. As one public relations executive and mother of a preschooler said of her nanny, "I'm completely dependent on her. She's in my home more than I am. We could not earn a living without her" (Rimer 1988).

Yet for all their importance, many nannies and maids complain bitterly about how they are treated. Doing "just domestic work" means low pay and long hours. Federal law requires nannies and maids to be paid at least the minimum wage. If the domestic worker lives in, the law allows employers to deduct something for room and board. But some families earning as much as $200,000 annually pay their nannies as little as room, board, and $50 a week.

Moreover, "it's long hours," explains a live-in caregiver who works in Aspen, Colorado. "When you travel with them, it's 24 hours. Sometimes it's two or three weeks before you get time off. There's no overtime" (Rimer 1988). One nannie did keep track of her overtime until she figured her boss owed her $800. But when she asked for it, her employer balked and paid about half. "There's nobody here on our side," the woman explained. "The only thing you can do is to report them [to labor officials], but then you'd be out of a job. It's a no-win situation" (Lipman 1993).

Employers often boast that they treat their nannies "as one of the family" (Romero 1992). But nannies point out that they are essentially paid employees; being treated "like family" does not make up for long hours, low pay, and other forms of exploitation.

Some efforts are underway to introduce standards. The International Nanny Association now seeks better pay and working conditions for in-home caregivers (Rimer 1988). However, abuses can be great, because nannies are vulnerable. Many are illegal aliens, who are grateful to be paid "off the books" and who risk deportation or homelessness if they complain. Furthermore, employers can exploit illegal immigrant employees if they sponsor them for permanent residency. Currently, the waiting period for green cards (cards that permit noncitizens legally to reside and work in the United States) for nannies, considered unskilled workers by the Immigration and Naturalization Service, is over five years. If she leaves her job, a nanny loses her place in line and must begin her waiting period all over again after finding a new employer. "They're stuck, like indentured servants," according to a Manhattan immigration lawyer (Lipman 1993). The reports of nannies' exploitation remind us that "the American worker" is a term that embodies people diverse in gender, race/ethnicity, social class, education, and job skills.

THINKING CRITICALLY

How does this section illustrate the globalization of the institution of economics? How would the working conditions of nannies change, do you think, if they were to become unionized? In many instances, it is professional women who employ (and perhaps exploit) nannies, who are also typically female. What does this say about the concept of gender inequality, discussed in Chapter 12? How does this section illustrate the relationship between the institution of economics and that of the family? The relationship between economics and politics?

working conditions? Why are they opposed to things like child labor and the English Language Amendment? Can you find information about other unions on the web?

Work can be dangerous and life threatening. Let's see what the Bureau of Labor Statistics has to say about workplace safety and dangerous occupations.

http://stats.bls.gov/oshhome.htm

Open the selection entitled **Census of Fatal Occupational Injuries**. On **Table 3**, click on the highlighted **(txt)**. This appears to be a long and complex chart, but in reality it is very simple. Read across the top of the chart and you can see the different categories for fatal injuries. Pick out a category and simply scroll down it stopping at particularly high or low figures. Look to the left side of the screen to see the occupation that produces that type of fatality. What occupations have very high fatality rates? Do you work in one of these? What category of work produces high numbers of fatalities from homicides? How about fires and explosions? Are there any surprises here? Before you become too frightened, look at the top left of the chart and note the total number of fatalities. Remember, the population of the U.S. is over 265 million! Feel free to look at other charts and note the differences by race, class and gender.

For a tongue-in-cheek look at the anti-machine movement, look up the Luddites and click on the **Luddites On-Line Beta Test**.

http://www.luddites.com/index.html

SUMMARY

1. The economic institution has a profound effect on other institutional structures, particularly government, stratification systems, education, and the family. Changes from preindustrial to industrial to postindustrial economies have thus had profound effects on social organization.

2. The tertiary sector of the economy has expanded rapidly and is expected to employ over three-quarters of the labor force by 2000. The tertiary sector includes highly paid professional occupations as well as custodians and retail sales clerks.

3. Capitalist economies are based on competition, socialist economies on cooperation. Capitalist economies are designed to maximize productivity, and socialist economies emphasize equality of distribution. Many modern societies are mixed; they try to balance productivity and equality.

4. The operation of an economic system depends on the political structure in which it operates. Socialism in combination with an authoritarian government is called communism. The former communist bloc is now trying to unlink socialism from authoritarianism.

5. In the United States critics allege that the political/economic link presents problems for two reasons: the politically powerful use the economic system to maintain their advantage, and the economic system has too much power over government, nationally and internationally.

6. Sweden's political economy is characterized as democratic socialism: The majority of Sweden's electorate has voted to maintain a socialist economy with copious welfare benefits and high taxes.

7. The United States has a dual economy containing two distinct parts: the industrial core and the competitive sector at the periphery. These are paralleled by a segmented labor market.

8. Economic projections show substantial changes in occupations over the next several years. The largest number of new jobs will be in highly trained professions or in

low-status, low-wage service positions. The major losers will be those who have occupied traditional blue-collar jobs.

9 Scholars look at the individual meaning of work from two perspectives: work satisfaction and alienation. Although most U.S. workers report satisfaction with their work, Marxists often argue that they are nevertheless alienated because they are estranged from the products of their labor.

10 Critics argue that automation and computerization have had three ill effects on labor: de-skilling jobs, reducing the number of jobs, and increasing control of workers. Nevertheless, some occupations have grown or been made easier through new technology.

11 The United States is losing many of the good jobs that kept the working class afloat. Three major approaches to relieving this problem are: the conservative free-market option, new industrial policies, and the social welfare option. Although it has negative effects for the working class, the United States seems to be pursuing the free-market option.

Suggested Readings

Applebaum, Eileen, and Rosemary Batt. 1994. *The New American Workplace*. Ithaca, N.Y.: ILR Press. A book that describes the contemporary U.S. workplace and jobs in a society that is changing rapidly because of technology and globalization.

Dix, Keith. 1988. *What's a Coal Miner to Do? The Mechanization of Coal Mining*. Pittsburgh: Pittsburgh University Press. An analysis of one of the industries hardest hit by de-industrialization. Keith takes a historical look at the development of new equipment throughout the 20th century and how it has affected the miners and communities that have depended on work in the mines.

Gamst, Frederocl C. (ed.). 1995. *Meanings of Work: Considerations for the Twenty-first Century*. Albany, N.Y.: State University of New York Press. An up-to-date analysis of what it means to work today, given all the changes in the workplace and workforce over the past several decades.

Halle, David. 1984. *America's Working Man: Work, Home, and Politics among Blue-Collar Property Owners*. Chicago: University of Chicago Press. An ethnography of the blue-collar workers in a single plant in New Jersey, using the workers' own words to illuminate issues such as alienation, de-skilling, and class consciousness.

Hochschild, Arlie R. 1985. *The Managed Heart: The Commercialization of Human Feelings*. Berkeley: University of California Press. A study of alienation in service occupations, with detailed examination of how flight attendants handle emotional work. This book is becoming a classic.

Hodson, Randy, and Sullivan, Teresa A. 1995. *The Social Organization of Work*, 2nd ed. Belmont, Calif.: Wadsworth. A readable textbook on the social institution of the economy and work in the United States today.

Pearson, John. 1994. "Special Report: Rethinking Work." *Business Week*. October 17: 74–93. A well-written and thoughtful account by a collection of journalists on how work is changing and how workers will need to change in order to keep up.

ROMERO, Mary. 1992. *Maid in the U.S.A.* New York: Routledge. Research monograph, written mainly from a conflict, or critical, perspective, on the occupation of domestic workers in the United States today.

RUBIN, Beth A. 1996. *Shifts in the Social Contract: Understanding Change in American Society*. Thousand Oaks, Calif.: Pine Forge Press. A thoughtful analysis of how changes in the American and world economies have resulted in changes in politics, in the institution of family, and in the way we can expect to live our everyday lives.

CHAPTER 18

Religion

OUTLINE

PROLOGUE

Have You Ever . . . seriously considered what the concept *God-given rights* means? Most people who use this phrase appear to imply that God was the real author of the U.S. Bill of Rights. Many seem to believe that the right to bear arms, the right to freedom of speech, and the right to assemble were handed down to our founding fathers much as God handed Moses the Ten Commandments on Mount Sinai. (Is it just a coincidence that there are ten of each?)

The Declaration of Independence claims that "all men are created equal, that they are endowed by their Creator with certain unalienable Rights, that among these are Life, Liberty, and the pursuit of Happiness." The rights spoken of are not religious rights, such as forgiveness or salvation; they are political, economic, and civil rights.

The issue of God's role in economic and political affairs has been controversial for 4,000 years, and it continues to be a vital contemporary issue. All around the globe, revolutions and civil wars are fought in the name of religion: Sikhs fight Hindus in India, Moslems fight Jews in Palestine, Christians fight Moslems in Lebanon, Protestants fight Catholics in Northern Ireland, and Christians fight Moslems in the former Yugoslavia. Most of these struggles are more about economic and political rights than about religion, but each side uses religion as a means of building internal unity and of rationalizing domination or rebellion.

We need not go halfway around the world to find evidence that religion is involved in the turmoil of public life. Current U.S. battles about abortion, prayer in the schools, state funding for parochial schools, and public support for Christmas displays are examples of the many areas in which religion and politics overlap. In this chapter, we introduce the basic concepts of the sociology of religion and consider their implications for American society.

As one of the five basic social institutions, religion is an important part of social life. Each of the world's major religions—Hinduism, Buddhism, Judaism, Christianity, and Islam—is intertwined with culture and politics and intimately concerned with integration and conflict. The Focus section of this chapter describes the Islamic religion. On a macrosociological level, sociologists examine how society affects religion and how religion affects society. Of particular interest is the contribution of religion to social order and social change. At the microsociological level, sociologists examine the consequences of religious belief and involvement for the lives of ordinary people like you and me.

THE SOCIOLOGICAL STUDY OF RELIGION

The first step in studying religion is to agree on what it is. How can we define religion so that our definition includes the contemplative meditation of a Buddhist monk, the speaking in tongues of a modern Pentecostal Christian, the worship of nature in Native American cultures, and the formal ceremonies of the Catholic church? Sociologists define **religion** as a system of beliefs and practices related to sacred things that unites believers into a moral community (Durkheim [1915] 1961, 62). This emphasis on the sacred allows us to include belief systems that invoke supernatural forces as explanations of earthly struggles (Hamilton 1995), as

Religion is a system of beliefs and practices related to sacred things that unites believers into a moral community.

> **THINKING CRITICALLY**
>
> Although sociologists are not concerned about whether religious beliefs are true or false, a latent function (or dysfunction) of their research is often to cast doubt on the beliefs of many religions. Do you think that an individual can believe strongly in a religion and also study it objectively? Why or why not?

well as cosmic religions that give personal qualities to the forces of nature. It does not include, however, belief systems much as Marxism or science that do not emphasize the sacred.

Sociologists who study religion treat it as a set of beliefs. As with beliefs about the desirability of monogamy or democracy, our concern is not whether the beliefs are true or false. The scientific study of religion does not ask whether God exists, whether salvation is really possible, or which is the true religion. Rather, it examines the ways in which culture, society, and class relationships affect religion and the ways in which religion affects individuals and social structure.

WHY RELIGION? SOME THEORETICAL ANSWERS

With a few exceptions, such as China and the former Soviet Union, religion is a fundamental feature of all societies. Whether simple or complex, each society has forms of religious activity and expressions of religious behavior. Why? The answer appears to lie in the fact that every individual and every society must struggle to transcend death (Monroe 1995) and to find explanations of events and experiences that go beyond personal experience. The poor man looks around him and wonders, "Why me?" The woman whose child dies in its sleep wonders, "Why mine?" The community struck by flood or tornado wonders, "Why us?" Beyond these personal dilemmas, people may wonder why the sun comes up every morning, why there is a rainbow in the sky, and what happens after death. Individuals and societies struggle with questions like these, searching for meanings and explanations. The answers vary widely from culture to culture, but each culture furnishes answers that help individuals understand their place in the universe. Many of these answers are given by religion.

Religion helps us interpret and cope with events that are beyond our control and understanding: our own mortality as well as tornadoes, droughts, and plagues become meaningful when they are attributed to the workings of some greater force (Hamilton 1995). Beliefs and rituals develop as a way to explain, control, or appease this greater force, and eventually they become patterned responses to the unknown. Rain dances may not bring rain, and prayers may not lead to good harvests; but both provide a familiar and comforting context in which people can confront otherwise mysterious and inexplicable events. Regardless of whether they are right or wrong, religious beliefs and rituals help people cope with the extraordinary events they experience.

Within this general sociological approach to religion, there are two distinct theoretical perspectives. One school, associated with Durkheim, sees religion as a thinly disguised worship of society, serving to create and maintain social solidarity (Durkheim, in O'Dea 1966, 12). The second school, associated with Weber, views religion as an intellectual force that may challenge society as well as support it. Let us briefly examine both of these schools.

DURKHEIM: RELIGION AS THE WORSHIP OF SOCIETY

Durkheim's approach to the study of religion is structural-functional. He assumed that if religion is universal, then it must meet basic needs of society; it must serve important functions. Durkheim began his analysis of religion by trying to identify what was common to all religions.

Although religion is common to all cultures, the forms that religious activity can take vary widely. This monk, spends much of his day in meditation, silence, and fasting. A very different application of religious belief is required of the Holy Ghost People, who include the unusual practice of handling live poisonous snakes as part of their religious rituals. This particular practice is a demonstration of their faith that God will protect them and they will not be harmed.

Durkheim ([1915] 1961) compared religions from all over the world and concluded that all share three elements, which he called the elementary forms of religion: (1) a distinction between the sacred and the profane, (2) a set of beliefs, and (3) a set of rituals.

The Sacred and the Profane. A central component of all religions is the division of human experience into the sacred and the profane. The **profane** represents all that is routine and taken for granted in the everyday world, things that are known and familiar and that we can control, understand, and manipulate. The

The **profane** represents all that is routine and taken for granted in the everyday world, things that are known and familiar and that we can control, understand, and manipulate.

The **sacred** consists of events and things that we hold in awe and reverence—that we can neither understand nor control.

sacred, by contrast, consists of the events and things that we hold in awe and reverence—that we can neither understand nor control.

In premodern societies, a large proportion of the world is viewed as sacred. Many events are beyond control and manipulation. As advances in human knowledge increase a society's ability to explain and even control what was previously mysterious, Durkheim argued, fewer and fewer events require supernatural explanations; less is held sacred. When an event can be explained without reference to supernatural forces, then it is no longer sacred. This process of transferring things, ideas, or events from the sacred to the profane is called **secularization.** Science and technology have been major contributors to secularization. They have given us explanations for lightning, rainbows, and death that rely on physical rather than supernatural forces.

Secularization is the process of transferring things, ideas, or events from the sacred realm to the profane.

Beliefs, Myths, and Creeds. A second common dimension of all religions is a set of beliefs about the supernatural. Religious beliefs center around uncertainties associated with birth, death, creation, success, failure, and crisis. They become part of the world view constructed by culture as a rationale for the human condition and the recurrent problems experienced. As beliefs become organized into an interrelated set of assumptions about the supernatural, they form the basis for official religious doctrines, which find expression in rituals.

Rituals. Religion is a practice as well as a belief system. It brings people together to express through ritual the things they hold sacred. In contemporary Christianity, rituals are used to mark such events as births, deaths, weddings, and Christ's birth and resurrection. In an earlier era, when most people lived off the land and life was more uncertain, planting and harvest were occasions for important rituals in the Christian church; they are still important ritual occasions in many religions.

Weber: Religion As an Independent Force

Durkheim looked at the forms of religion and asked about the kinds of functions they perform: the consequences of religion for individuals and society. Weber shared this interest, but he was also concerned with the processes through which religious answers are developed and how their content affects society.

For most people, religion is a matter of following tradition; people worship as their parents did before them. To Weber, however, the essence of religion is the search for knowledge about the unknown. In this sense, religion is similar to science; it is a way of coming to understand the world around us. And as with science, the answers provided may be uncomfortable; they may challenge the status quo as well as support it.

Where do the answers to questions of ultimate meaning come from? Often, they come from a charismatic religious leader. **Charisma,** you will recall from Chapter 16, refers to extraordinary personal qualities that set the individual apart from ordinary mortals. Because these extraordinary characteristics are often thought to be supernatural in origin, charismatic leaders can frequently be the agents of dramatic change in individuals and society. Charismatic leaders include Christ, Muhammad, and, more recently, John Humphrey Noyes (Oneida community) and Joseph Smith (Mormonism). Such individuals often give answers that disagree with traditional answers. Thus, Weber saw religious inquiry as a potential source of instability and change in society.

Charisma refers to extraordinary personal qualities that set the individual apart from ordinary mortals.

Ritual is an important part of all religions. Ritual occasions such as Passover Seders and Easter masses bring people together as a community of believers and reaffirm their shared values. Even people who are not particularly devout in their beliefs may find the traditional ritual comforting. For many of us, as for these Jews, our religion is also part of our ethnic heritage; participating in religious rituals is an important means of tying us to our cultural heritage.

In viewing religion as a process, Weber gave it a much more active role than did Durkheim: Weber argued that religion could change other social institutions, not simply reflect them. This is most apparent in Weber's analysis of the Protestant Reformation. In a classic analysis of the influence of religious ideals on other social institutions, Weber ([1904–1905] 1958) argued that the Reformation paved the way for bourgeois capitalism.

Three ideas found in early Protestantism were critical: an emphasis on hard work and doing one's earthly duty, a stress on individualism, and a belief in rationalism. These elements were most developed among the Puritans. They rejected hymn singing and religious ritual as an emotional rather than a rational approach to understanding God. For them, religion was not a matter of making a joyful noise but a serious business that emphasized hard work and rational rather than emotional assessment of the Scriptures. Their serious approach to life and religion led to an emphasis on plain living and a rejection of earthly pleasures and vanities.

The result was what Weber called the Protestant ethic, a belief that work, rationalism, and plain living are moral virtues, while idleness and luxury are sinful. Although this ethic was developed for religious reasons, one of its latent functions was the tendency for those who lived by it to get rich. In the Protestant ethic, wealth was an unintended consequence of behavior directed by religious motives. According to Weber, however, it was not long before wealth became an end in itself. At this point, the moral values underlying early Protestantism became the moral values underlying early capitalism: (1) work is moral and everybody should work hard; (2) profits should be reinvested rather than spent on luxuries.

In the more than 90 years since Weber's analysis, other scholars have explored the same issues, and many have come to somewhat different conclusions. Some argue that the spirit of capitalism arose from class antagonisms set in motion by the decline of feudalism and that the Protestant Reformation was a part, not a cause, of the rise of capitalism. Nevertheless, such scholarship has not changed Weber's major contribution to the sociology of religion: the idea that religion is not merely a passive supporter of the status quo but can be an important element in social change.

Marx: Religion As Opiate

Like Durkheim, Marx saw religion as a supporter of tradition. This support ranges from relatively mild injunctions that the poor and oppressed should endure rather than revolt (blessed be the poor, blessed be the meek, and so on) and that everyone should pay taxes (give unto Caesar) all the way to the extreme endorsement of inequality implied by a belief in the divine right of kings.

Marx differed from Durkheim by interpreting the support for tradition in a negative light. Marx, an atheist, saw religion as an "opiate of the people": a delusion deliberately fostered by the elite—a sort of shell game designed to keep the eyes of the downtrodden on the hereafter so they would not notice their earthly oppression. This position is hardly value free, and much more obviously than either Weber's or Durkheim's, it does make a statement about the truth or falsity of religious doctrine.

Functions and Dysfunctions of Religion

Durkheim saw religion as functional while Marx saw it as dysfunctional, at least for the working class. More recently, sociologists (Hamilton 1995, 120–121; O'Dea 1966) have specified several functions of religion, along with corresponding dysfunctions. You will see that these functions and dysfunctions are derived from the theories of Durkheim, Weber, and Marx.

The Functions of Religion. Religion can be functional on both the macrosociological and the microsociological level. On the societal level, religion gives tradition a moral imperative. This means that most of the central values and norms of any culture are taught and reinforced through its religion. These values and norms cease to be merely the usual way of doing things and become the only moral way of doing them. They became sacred. Some religions provide otherworldly rewards and punishments (heaven and hell) for obeying or disobeying social norms. For example, religions teach that theft, murder, and adultery are sins to be punished not only in this life but after death as well.

When a tradition or norm is sacred, it is continually affirmed through ritual and practice and is largely immune to change. At the same time, however, religion sometimes can provide sacred standards that become a basis for social protest or criticism of existing social patterns. This is called religion's **prophetic function.**

The **prophetic function** of religion involves its ability to provide sacred standards that become a basis for social protest or criticism of existing social patterns.

For individuals, the beliefs and rituals of religion can offer support, consolation, and reconciliation in times of need. Religion can also help people during life's transitions, such as marriage or the birth of a child. On ordinary occasions, many people find satisfaction, security, and feelings of identity and belongingness in religious participation. This feeling of belongingness is provided by the moral community, or community of believers, that is part of the definition of religion.

The Dysfunctions of Religion. By making existing social beliefs, values, and norms sacred, religion may legitimate superstition and thereby thwart progress in science or other fields of knowledge. Because of its conservatism, religion can prevent necessary adaptation to changing social circumstances. Moreover, as Marx pointed out, religion may inhibit protest against injustice by reconciling the oppressed. Conversely, religion's prophetic function can lead to utopianism and unrealistic hopes for change and, consequently, inhibit practical action to this end. Finally, religion can be dysfunctional for society by promoting harmful ethnocentrism, which can result in hatred for anyone outside the community of believers, conflict, and wars.

Religion can be dysfunctional for individuals by fostering psychological and emotional dependence on religious institutions or leaders, thereby stifling personal reflection and maturity. Furthermore, some individuals find religion anything but consoling or supportive. For them, talk of judgment and punishment, insiders and outsiders, promotes feelings of *not* belonging and alienation.

THINKING CRITICALLY

Given the various functions and dysfunctions of religion, do you see religion as generally a good thing for society, or not? How about for individuals? For *you*? Why?

TENSION BETWEEN RELIGION AND SOCIETY

A society's religion is a part of its culture, its traditional ways of doing things. The Muslim religion is an integral part of Middle Eastern culture, just as Judeo-Christianity is an important part of Western culture. Despite this overlap between culture and religion, there is a universal tension between them.

Each religion is confronted with two contradictory yet complementary tendencies: the tendency to reject the world and the tendency to compromise with the world (Troeltsch 1931). When a religion denounces adultery and fornication, does the church categorically exclude adulterers and fornicators, or does it adjust its expectations to take common frailties into account? If "it is easier for a camel to go through the eye of a needle than for a rich man to enter the kingdom of God," must the church require that *all* members forsake their worldly belongings?

How religions resolve these dilemmas is central to their eventual form and character. Scholars distinguish two general types of religious organizations: church and sect. The *church* represents the successful compromisers, and the *sect* represents the outsiders. The categories of church and sect are what Weber referred to as *ideal types*. The distinguishing characteristics of each type are summarized in the Concept Summary later in this section. Although it may be that no church or sect has all of these characteristics, the ideal types serve as useful benchmarks against which to examine actual religious organizations.

CHURCHES

Churches are religious organizations that have become institutionalized. They have endured for generations, are supported by society's norms and values, and have become an active part of society. Their involvement in society does not necessarily mean that they have compromised essential values. They still retain the ability to protest injustice and immorality. From the abolition movement of the 1850s to the sanctuary movement for Central American refugees and the antinuclear movements of the 1980s, church members have been in the forefront of social protest. Nevertheless, churches are generally committed to working with society. They may wish to improve it, but they have no wish to abandon it.

Churches are religious organizations that have become institutionalized. They have endured for generations, are supported by society's norms and values, and have become an active part of society.

Churches are typically large formal bureaucratic structures with hierarchical positions, specializations, and official creeds specifying religious beliefs. Leadership is provided by a professional staff of ministers, rabbis, or priests, who have received formal training at specialized schools. Religious services almost always prescribe formal and detailed ritual, repeated in much the same way from generation to generation.

Generally, people are born into churchlike religions rather than being converted to them. People who change churches, who become Methodists instead of Lutherans, Catholics instead of Presbyterians, usually do so for practical reasons. They marry somebody of the other faith, the other church is nearer, or their friends go to the other church (Roof 1989). Individual commitment is based more on tradition or intellectual commitment than on the emotional experience of conversion (Hamilton 1995).

Within the general category of churches are two major types: the ecclesia and the denomination.

An **ecclesia** is a religious organization that automatically includes every member of a society.

The Ecclesia. The most institutionalized of all religious structures is an **ecclesia**—a religious organization that automatically includes every member of a society. People do not join ecclesiae; membership comes with citizenship (Becker, in Yinger 1957, 149). The Roman Catholic church in Europe was an ecclesia during the Middle Ages; Ireland and Iran have many of the characteristics of a modern ecclesia. The fate of the church and the fate of the nation are wrapped up in each other, and the church is vitally involved in supporting the dominant institutions of society.

Denominations are religious organizations that are separate from the larger society or state but have accommodated to society and to other religions.

The Denomination. Religious organizations that are separate from the larger society or state but have accommodated to society and to other religions are **denominations.** Most of the largest religious organizations in the United States fit this definition: Catholic, Jewish, Lutheran, Methodist, and Episcopalian. Their clergy meet together in ecumenical councils, their members pray together at commencements, and they generally adopt a live-and-let-live policy toward one another. They support and are supported by the other institutional structures. This endorsement of the broad and basic fabric of the social order often convinces the mostly middle-class members that the ways of both their religion and their society are moral and just. As part of their accommodation to the larger society, U.S. denominations generally allow the Scriptures to be interpreted in ways that are relevant to modern culture. Because of all these characteristics, denominations are frequently referred to as *mainline churches*, a term denoting their centrality in society.

SECTS

Sects are religious organizations that reject the social environment in which they exist.

Sects are religious organizations that reject the social environment in which they exist (Johnson 1957). Religions that reject sexual relations (Shakerism), automobiles (Amish), or monogamy (19th-century Mormonism) are examples of sects that differ so much from society's norms that their relationships with the larger society are often strained. They reject major elements of the larger culture and are in turn rejected by it. The hundreds of sects in the United States exhibit varying degrees of tension with society, but all are opposed to some basic societal institutions. Not surprisingly, these organizations tend to be particularly attractive to people who are left out of or estranged from society's basic institutions—people who are poor, underprivileged, disabled, or alienated. For this reason, sects have been called "the church of the disinherited" (Niebuhr [1929] 1957).

Sect membership is often the result of conversion or emotional experience. Members are reborn, or born again. Not all of the people converted to sectlike religions are poor or oppressed. Many are middle-class people who are spiritually rather than materially deprived. They are individuals who find established churches too bureaucratic. They seek a moral community that will offer them a feeling of belongingness and emotional commitment, and they support their communities enthusiastically (Iannaccone 1994).

Religious services are more informal for sects than for churches. Leadership remains largely unspecialized, and there is little, if any, professional training for the calling. Sects share many of the characteristics of primary groups: small size, informality, and loyalty. They are relatively closely knit groups that emphasize conformity and maintain significant control over their members. Members may be required to observe specific norms related to patterns of dress (Amish, Oneida), speech (Quaker), shunning of modern technology (Amish), and so on. These requirements are symbolic reminders to community members of their religious identity. They function to foster cohesion and reinforce group identity.

Many, if not all, of the churches in the world today started out as sects. Over the centuries, they grew and became part of the institutional structures of society. Not all sects, of course, adjust and become assimilated in this way. In fact, we can differentiate among sects by their degree of assimilation into the larger society.

The institution of religion in modern societies has traditionally been male-dominated, even sexist, although this is changing. Unlike many cosmic religions of simple societies, today's religions have almost universally perceived God as male. Even though most U.S. congregations have more female than male members, men more often hold ministerial and other positions of authority. In the Roman Catholic Church, for example, women are officially denied access to the priesthood. As a result of such male dominance, some feminists refuse to take part in any religion. Others fashion new forms of spirituality, such as eco-feminism (discussed in Chapter 12). Meanwhile, there are feminist Catholics and Muslims, among others, who advocate change from within their churches and mosques.

Cults. Exhibiting the greatest tension with society are **cults,** religious organizations that are independent of and often in conflict with the religious traditions of society (Hamilton 1995). Christianity began as a cult. Because they do not support the religious heritage of society, cults challenge the moral community of established religions and are often the objects of strong social disapproval.

Examples of cults in the United States today are Scientology, founded by a science fiction writer, L. Ron Hubbard, in California in 1959; the Unification Church, or "Moonies," brought to the United States by Sun Myung Moon, a Korean charismatic preacher, in the 1960s; and the Hare Krishna, which began in the United States in the 1960s when a guru from India began recruiting young people in California and Oregon (Monroe 1995, 393–394).

As you might surmise from these examples, cults tend to arise in times of social stress and change, when established religions do not seem adequate to explain the upheavals that individuals are experiencing. They often urge their members to alter their lives drastically and to withdraw from society altogether. Because of the radical changes they demand, cults generally remain small; many survive only a few years.

Established Sects. In contrast with a cult, an **established sect** has adapted to its institutional environment to some degree, although not as thoroughly as a church. Unlike a church, an established sect often retains the belief that it is absolutely the one true faith, but it is less antagonistic to other religions than are cults. Whereas cults often withdraw from the world to preserve their spiritual purity, established sects are active participants. Frequently, the motivation for this participation in the world is to spread their message, to make converts, and to change social institutions. To effect social change, they must have lobbying groups and participate in political, economic, and educational institutions.

The Mormons are a classic example of an established sect. In the last 160 years, they have increased their accommodation to the larger society: They have for the most part abandoned plural marriage, left the seclusion of a virtual ecclesia in Utah, and spread throughout the world seeking converts. Mormons nevertheless

A **cult** is a sect that is independent of and often in conflict with the religious traditions of society.

An **established sect** is a sect that has adapted to its institutional environment, but not to the same degree as a church.

Concept Summary: Distinctions between Churches and Sects

Church and sect are ideal types against which we can assess actual religious organizations. Many religious organizations combine some characteristics of both.

	Churches	Sects
Degree of tension with society	Low	High
Attitude toward other institutions and religions	Tolerant	Intolerant, rejecting
Type of authority	Traditional	Charismatic
Organization	Bureaucratic	Informal
Membership	Establishment	Alienated
Examples	Catholic, Lutheran	Jehovah's Witnesses, Old Order Amish

retain many characteristics of sects, including lack of a paid clergy and an emphasis on conversion.

Within the general category of sects, those that occupy a middle position between cults and established sects are simply called sects. They reject the social world in which they live, but they do embrace the religious heritage of society. The Amish are an excellent example: They base their lives on a strict reading of the Bible and remain aloof from the contemporary world.

Case Study: The Old Order Amish Sect

The Old Order Amish sect developed from the Protestant reform movement in Switzerland in 1520 and migrated to Lancaster County, Pennsylvania, in 1727. Now living in communities scattered throughout New York, Ohio, Iowa, Pennsylvania, and other states, members of this sect believe in the Scriptures as the literal word of God, in adult rather than infant baptism, and in strict separation from the ways of the world (Hostetler 1963).

The Amish pride themselves on being a "peculiar" people who follow the Bible rather than the ways of the world. As a result, they differ sharply from other Americans in dress and behavior. The Amish use Bible verses to support a clothing style that is modest, shows a distinction between the sexes, and does not appeal to vanity. All women dress alike in dark-colored skirts, blouses, matching aprons, and homemade bonnets (following a biblical injunction that women who pray with their heads uncovered are dishonored), and none wears jewelry. Men too must all dress alike, in jackets that have no lapels, no outside pockets, and no buttons. Zippers are forbidden except in utilitarian work clothes. These distinctive dress patterns serve a vital function; they constantly remind members of the group that they are outside the ways of the world. Neither the Amish nor their neighbors are likely to forget that they are a peculiar people.

The Amish reject almost all modern conveniences. They are not allowed to have rugs, electricity, telephones, or any modern appliances except sewing machines. Most important, they are not allowed to use automobiles. Instead, both farm equipment and pleasure vehicles are horse drawn. The Amish are forbidden

The Old Order Amish pride themselves on being a "peculiar" people. They have managed to successfully withdraw from the ways of the modern world that surrounds them by adopting a lifestyle based on self-sufficiency. They reject modern conveniences, make almost all of their goods by hand, and are excellent farmers. This photograph of a large family saying grace before their meal shows the typical dress worn by members of the Amish community.

to dance, to go to movies, to live in cities or towns, to serve in the military, to go to court, to join any association other than the church, or to go to public school.

Both boys and girls attend Amish schools for eight years. They learn reading, writing, and arithmetic from teachers who have had the same eighth-grade education. The purpose of education is to allow the Amish to read the Bible and to manage farm accounts. Any further learning is considered not only unnecessary (for the Bible is the source of all knowledge) but actually wrong, as it will expose young people to the ways of the world and make them unhappy with Amish society. The Amish have no established clergy; the leadership positions in the church are established by lot. Thus, every man in the community is expected to be familiar with the Bible and with church doctrine.

The Amish have managed to escape from secularization almost completely for more than 400 years. They have withdrawn physically—in the 18th century moving all the way from Germany to America—to escape the influence of the world. They seek neither converts nor worldly influence; they wish only to be left alone.

Whether the Amish can continue to ward off the world is questionable. Busy highways and the increasing price of land and consequent high property taxes are challenging the Amish way of life. More direct challenges are offered by the draft, taxes, and education. For example, the Amish refuse to pay Social Security taxes, believing that such a plan indicates distrust of God's care. After much legal skirmishing, Congress exempted the Amish from the taxes and benefits of Social Security. More troubling is education. In Pennsylvania, officials have long since worked out an accommodation to allow the Amish to have their own schools without state-certified teachers and to have their children stop at the eighth grade. Population pressure (the Amish often have eight children), however, is pushing the Amish and their way of life into other states, which are unwilling to make this accommodation. The governments of Iowa and Nebraska have levied heavy fines on Amish families who refuse to send their children to public schools.

As a result of these changes, the Amish are finding it increasingly difficult to remain aloof from the world. (In fact, this situation poses a dilemma for all sects.) Amish young people inevitably see some of the pleasures available in American society, and many are reluctant to turn their backs completely on dancing, driving, and other amusements. As a result, many Amish communities now allow their young people a year in the larger world, hoping that they will get their curiosity out of their systems and be willing to return to the Amish way of life.

Liberation Theology and Social Justice

Churches tend to be part of the world, while sects tend to withdraw from the world. Ironically, this gives churches much more incentive for radical political activism. A fairly recent survey of U.S. Christian leaders asked them to indicate whether the primary goal of the church should be to "bring people to Jesus" or to "help the poor." Among leaders who called themselves fundamentalists, 95 percent said that their primary mission was bringing people to Jesus; only half of the Catholic and mainline Protestant leaders chose this option (Lerner, Rothman, and Lichter 1989). For the other half, social justice, sometimes called the *social gospel*, was more important than or as important as bringing people to Jesus.

In 1980, Archbishop Oscar Romero, an outspoken critic of army repression and death squads, was assassinated in El Salvador while saying mass. His assassination is widely attributed to top officials of the right-wing government. Romero, one of the most potent symbols of liberation theology, is widely regarded as a hero and saint by the people of Central America. Each year, the anniversary of his assassination is marked by demonstrations and processions.

The link between religious activism and political and economic activism is most marked in *liberation theology*, a religious movement associated with Latin American Catholicism. Liberation theology aims at the establishment of a democratic Christian socialism that eliminates poverty, inequality, and political oppression.

The harnessing of a moral community to politics creates a powerful team. One South American organizer notes:

> People do not come to [meetings] when there is no praying and singing. They come four or five times to organize practical things., but nothing further will come of it. When, however, people pray and sing, when they feel themselves together, when the gospel is read and, *on this basis*, concrete actions are organized and the national situation is analyzed, then the group remains united. (Emphasis added; cited in Neuhauser 1989, 239).

The priests who are active in liberation theology may spend more time picketing than praying, more time organizing than saving souls. This radical activity has caused controversy in the church; and in 1987, the Pope ordered Catholic priests and nuns to stay out of politics. Many have disregarded the order, facing the perils of excommunication as well as the perils of political activism under violent circumstances. Every year in Central America, there are new incidents in which religious workers (Episcopalians and Mennonites as well as Catholics) are killed by right-wing guerrillas. In November 1989, six Catholic priests and their household staff were killed in El Salvador by government agents trying to stop their organizing among the poor. Two of these priests were also sociologists. One of them, Dr. Segundo Montes, wrote shortly before his death: "I consider it a duty to work for human rights; it is the duty of every human being who has the sensibility and sensitivity to the suffering of people. As a Christian who follows the God of Life and who is against the idols of death, . . . I want to live with the people who suffer and deserve more." Of the conflict in Central America, he wrote that "the establishment of a real democracy, together with economic development for the majority, are both indispensable for the achievement of an authentic and durable peace" (cited in "Observing" 1990).

The dilemmas of social justice may not be so acute in the United States; and today, the church in the United States has more visibility as a conservative than as a radical political actor. It is worth remembering, however, that the civil rights movement of the 1960s was based largely in the African American church and that the Southern Christian Leadership Conference took the lead in securing African American political and economic rights. And some U.S. religions, such as the Unitarian Universalist religion, which was founded in New England in the first half of the 19th century, see the social gospel as a principal purpose for their existence (Monroe 1995, 361–367).

An analysis of the role of religion in the world suggests that both Marx and Durkheim overestimated the conservative force of religion. Religion does much more than simply support the status quo; it can be an active agent for change, as Weber noted. Time and again, its moral community has been the foundation for political organization; its ideals can be the basis of political and economic ideals.

RELIGION IN THE UNITED STATES

When asked what religion they belong to, only 5 percent of the people in the United States say they have no religion (Gallup Poll 1994). Most people identify themselves not only as religious but also as affiliated with some particular religious organization. Most (59 percent) call themselves Protestants, but 27 percent are Catholics and 2 percent are Jews (see Figure 18.1). Within the category of Protestants and among the 6 percent of the population who belong to other religious faiths, there is a great deal of variety. The *Yearbook of American and Canadian Churches* lists more than 200 religious organizations, and researchers have identified more than 500 cult movements and more than 400 sects in the United States.

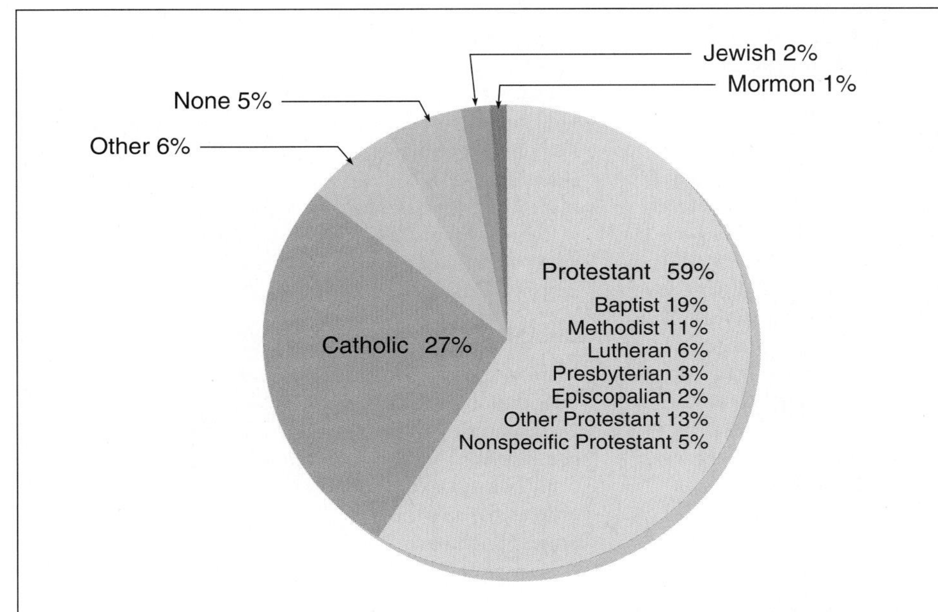

FIGURE 18.1
RELIGIOUS AFFILIATION IN THE UNITED STATES

Although nearly 90 percent of Americans call themselves Protestant, Catholic, or Jewish, there are more than 200 religious organizations in the United States and as many as 1,000 cults and sects.

SOURCE: Gallup Poll 1994.

FOCUS ON ANOTHER CULTURE

Islam

"IN SOME NATIONS, ISLAM MORE CLOSELY RESEMBLES A CHURCH, AND IN OTHERS IT MORE CLOSELY RESEMBLES A SECT."

Islam has roots in Judaism and in Christianity: Moses and Jesus are seen as prophets. Islam was founded in the seventh century A.D. by an Arab prophet named Muhammad, near Mecca, in what is now Saudi Arabia. It is estimated to be the fastest-growing religion in the world, encompassing one-fifth of the world's population in all parts of the world.

No matter where they are found, believers in Islam share a set of common beliefs. Muslims believe in a single all-powerful Creator whose word is revealed to the faithful in the Koran, a book similar to the Christian Bible and the Jewish Torah. All Muslims must follow the Five Pillars of Islam. They must: (1) profess faith in one almighty God, Allah, and Muhammad, his prophet; (2) pray five times daily; (3) give alms to the Muslim community and the poor; (4) fast during daylight hours during the month of Ramadan, the time when the Koran was revealed to Muhammad; and (5) if possible, make at least one pilgrimage to Mecca. Prayer usually takes place in a mosque (an Islamic house of worship) and is led by an Imam (a religious scholar) (Monroe 1995). There is no formal central authority.

Apart from this basic doctrine, there is considerable variation across countries in the relationship between Islamic clergy and the government and in the interactions between followers of the faith and members of the larger community. In some nations, Islam more closely resembles a church, and in others it more closely resembles a sect.

Islam in Iran and Egypt

Iran, with its Islamic government, is a good example of a modern-day ecclesia. Church and state are intertwined, with every citizen being bound by religious law. For instance, all Iranian women, regardless of religion or nationality, must cover their hair and all skin, save the hands and face. Failure to comply with this rule is punishable by up to 80 lashes. Since the Islamic clergy came to political power in Iran on the tide of a popular revolution, there is generally little tension revealed between religion and the larger society.

In contrast, Egypt has a secular government, even though 90 percent of its population belong to the Islamic church. Although there has been a recent upsurge in antigovernment violence by radical fundamentalist sects, Islam in Egypt is still more like a denomination than a sect. Christians and Muslims share the streets and businesses in relative peace. The government tacitly allows more moderate Islamic groups, like the Islamic Brotherhood, to exist in spite of official bans. Recently, the Egyptian government has also increased public discussion of moderate Islamic values and promised to improve services to the less fortunate, suggesting a willingness of church and state to work together in supportive roles (Murphy 1994).

Islamic Fundamentalism

Recent years have seen a worldwide increase in Islamic fundamentalism. Like fundamentalist churches in the United States, fundamentalist sects within Islam have been particularly appealing to individuals who lack economic and political power. Islamic fundamentalists have called for a rejection of the excesses and corruption of modern, secular culture and a return to "true" religious principles. Only the most radical Islamic fundamentalist sects have advocated violence as a means of restoring religious values and law. Most Muslims, in fact, say the concept of the *jihad*—the holy war—"refers not to battlefield wars, but to the inner spiritual struggle of Muslims for self-control in order to do good" (Sudo 1993, 5). Islamic fundamentalism does not uniformly endorse violence nor is it a single unified movement or sect (Monroe 1995). It varies from country to country and includes both religious and political elements; acts of violence do not derive from core Islamic fundamentalist beliefs but from the behavior of a limited number of individuals, sects, and political regimes (Gordon 1993). Nor is fundamentalism characteristic of all Islam. One Islamic theologian in Iran's University of Tehran, for instance, argues for religious freedom, along with finding ways to reconcile Islam with modernism (Wright 1995b).

Islam in the United States

Islam in the United States can be traced back to the importation of African Muslim slaves in the 18th and 19th centuries. In the late 1800s, new Muslim immigrants arrived and began to settle in the Midwest, especially North Dakota and Iowa. Today, there are an estimated 4 to 6 million Muslims living in the United States (Buchsbaum 1993). Some are recent Arabian or African immigrants, who live sectlike lives as they try

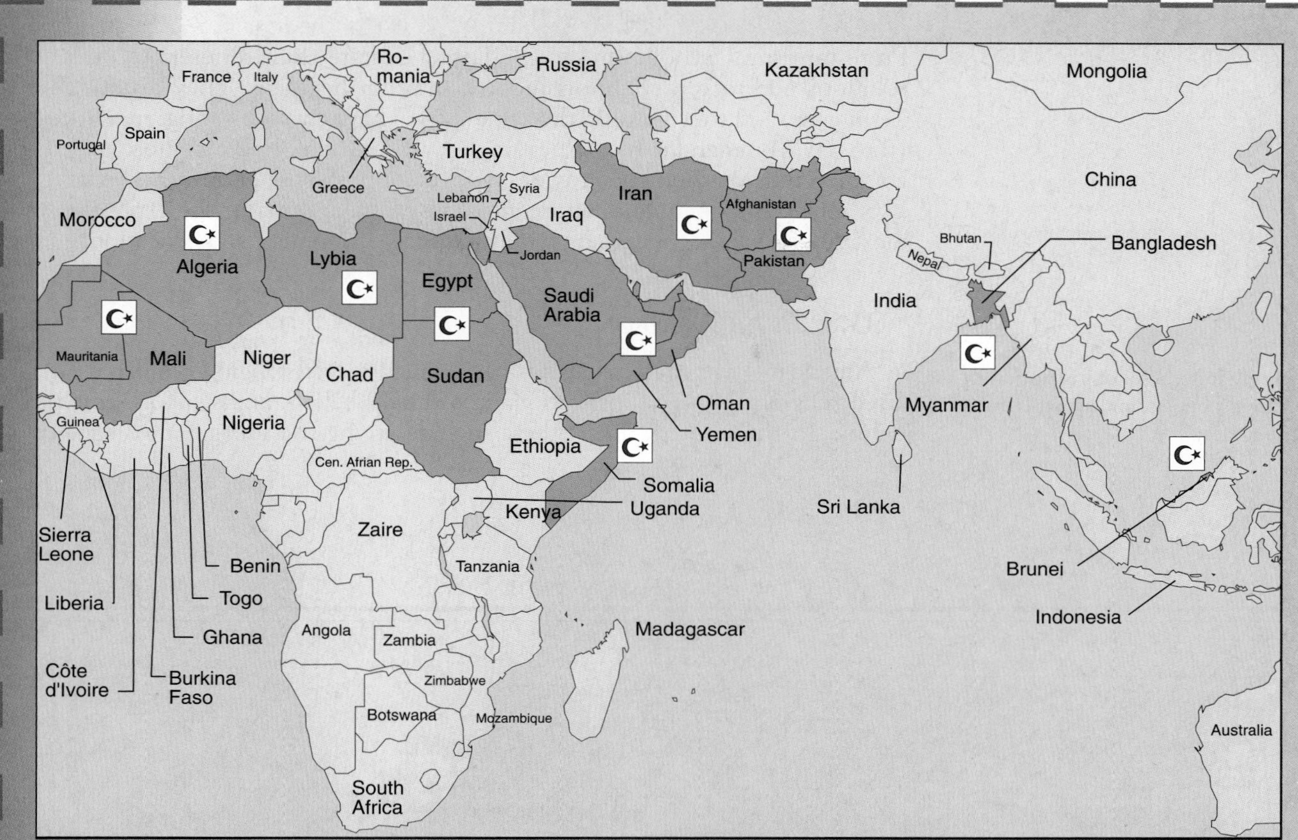

MAP 18.1
WHERE THE ISLAMIC RELIGION SERVES AS THE BASIS FOR LAW

to insulate themselves and their children from what they see as the unsavory influences of Western society (Asimov 1995). But assuredly the vast majority of U.S. Muslims are not fundamentalists (or terrorists), as the U.S. media has sometimes incorrectly portrayed them (Said 1981).

A substantial and growing proportion of U.S. Muslims (about one-third) are African American (Buchsbaum 1993). Some of these people see Christianity as the religion of their oppressors and Islam as more compatible with their African heritage. Furthermore, because Islam rejects visual depictions of the Creator, African American Muslims can pray to a formless Allah instead of to a Caucasian-looking Jesus. And Islam's emphasis on dignity and self-discipline appeals to many African American men (Power 1995). Membership is growing most rapidly among poor and disenfranchised inner-city residents, for whom Islam provides a sense of hope and community. The Muslim emphasis on community activism—antidrug campaigns and economic development—and on discipline and modest dress supplies the sense of order and belonging commonly provided by sects.

Of the many different Islamic sects in the United States, the most well publicized is the Nation of Islam, headed by Louis Farrakhan, who organized the 1995 Million Man March to Washington, D.C. With just 20,000 members, however, the Nation of Islam hardly represents the majority of African American Muslims. In fact, many Muslims do not think the Nation is actually Islamic. Orthodox Muslims of all races believe Allah created all human beings and preach racial harmony; the Nation of Islam advocates racial separation (Power 1995).

There are, then, many, many religions in the United States—including Hinduism and Buddhism, for example—but the three major U.S. religions are Protestantism, Catholicism, and Judaism. Despite their differences, these three religions embrace a common Judeo-Christian heritage. They accept the Old Testament, and they worship the same God. They rely on a similar moral tradition (the Ten Commandments, for example), which reinforces common values. This common religious heritage provides an overarching sense of unity and character to U.S. society—a dominant culture, providing a framework for the expression of our most crucial values concerning family, politics, economics, and education.

U.S. Civil Religion

Civil religion is a set of institutionalized rituals, beliefs, and symbols sacred to the nation.

Americans also share what has been called a civil religion (Bellah 1974, 29). **Civil religion** is a set of institutionalized rituals, beliefs, and symbols sacred to the nation. In the United States, these include giving the Pledge of Allegiance and

MAP 18.2
CHRISTIAN DENOMINATIONS IN THE U.S.

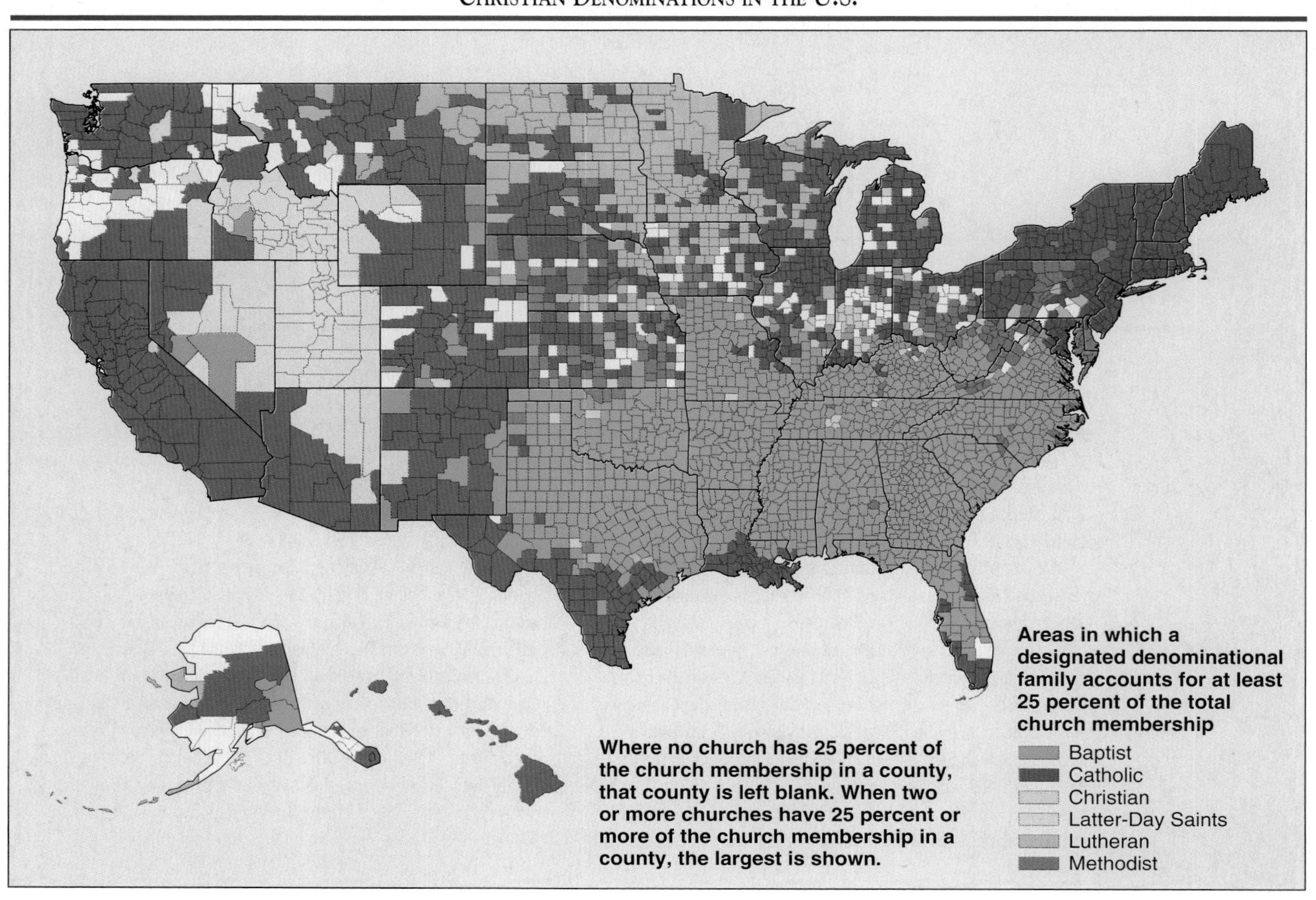

singing the national anthem, as well as folding and displaying the flag in ways that protect it from desecration. In many American homes, the flag is displayed along with a crucifix or a picture of the Last Supper. And in many American churches, the U.S. flag stands near the altar.

Civil religion has the same functions as religion in general: It is a source of unity and integration, providing a sacred context for understanding the nation's history and current responsibilities (Wald 1987). To a significant extent, we have made liberty, justice, and freedom sacred principles; as a result, the American way of life—our economic and political system—has become not merely the usual way of doing things but also the only moral way of doing them, a way of life that is blessed by God. Thanksgiving has become virtually a religious holiday.

A great deal of the sacredness of American civil religion depends on the tie that many people believe exists between God and America. The motto on U.S. currency, the pledge of allegiance, and the national anthem all bear testimony to the belief that God has blessed the nation and that America operates "under God" with God's direct blessing. This is clearly ethnocentric; but for many Americans, civil religion and regular religion are virtually inseparable.

Not surprisingly, many African Americans, Native Americans, and disadvantaged minorities have been less than enthusiastic about endorsing American civil religion (Woodrum and Bell 1989). The recent elevation of Martin Luther King, Jr., to secular sainthood, as evidenced by state and federal holidays honoring his birth, is a step toward making civil religion more inclusive of all Americans.

Trends and Differentials in Religiosity

Many scholars have argued that there has been a long-term trend in modern society toward secularization, a decline of religious influence in social life. On the macro level, secularization involves the increasing accommodation of churches to

We associate the concept civil religion *with the dominant culture, but subcultures can develop civil religions as well. The recent popularization of the African American celebration Kwanzaa is an example. Derived from African tradition and celebrated at the end of December, Kwanzaa is rapidly winning a place on the nation's holiday calendar alongside Chanukah and Christmas. An estimated 10 million African Americans now celebrate Kwanzaa as a ritual of family, roots, and community (Woodward and Johnson 1995).*

changing social values—for example, tolerance of gay male and lesbian unions, nonmarital sex, birth control, abortion, and divorce. On a micro level, secularization means the reduced importance of religion for individuals (Hamilton 1995).

The evidence on secularization is mixed, and the picture one gets depends on the historical era one chooses for comparison. In 1776, it is estimated that only 10 to 12 percent of the U.S. population belonged to a church (Sark and Finke 1988). In 1993, approximately 71 percent of all Americans belonged to a church or synagogue. So based on church membership, U.S. society was more religious in 1993 than in 1776. Since the 1950s, however, there has been some decline in individual religiosity (see Table 18.1). Church attendance has changed little. However, some studies suggest church attendance may actually be 50 percent lower than opinion polls indicate (Hadeway, Marler, and Chaves 1993). Furthermore, there has been a substantial drop in the proportion of persons who say that religion is very important in their lives and in the proportion who believe that the Bible is the actual word of God.

Although almost everybody believes in God, some people place more emphasis on religion than others (see Table 18.2). The most striking differences in religiosity are related to age and sex. Older people and women report greater attachment to religion than do younger people and men.

One interesting question is the relationship between socioeconomic status and religiosity. To many scholars, it has seemed logical that religion should appeal disproportionately to the poor, who may be in greater need of hope and help in dealing with the world. As the data in Table 18.2 indicate, however, people with a college education are as likely to attend religious services as people with no college. Nevertheless, they are significantly less likely to say that religion is very important to them. Higher-status people also belong to somewhat different religious organizations. They are more often members of churchlike religions, whereas lower-class individuals are more often members of sects.

TABLE 18.1
CHANGING RELIGIOUS COMMITMENT, 1947 TO 1993

Over the last 40 or 50 years, there has been little decline in outward religious observance. There has, however, been a substantial drop in the proportion who say that religion is very important to their lives, and there has been a sharp decrease in the proportion who think that the Bible is the actual word of God.

	1947–1952	1993
Belong to a church or synagogue	76%	71%
Attended church last week	46	45
Have no religion	6	6
Religion is very important to their own lives	75	59
Believe Bible is actual word of God, to be taken literally word for word[a]	65	35

[a]The first measure on this variable was taken in 1963.

SOURCE: Gallup Report 1987, 1993.

TABLE 18.2
RELIGIOUS PARTICIPATION AND ATTITUDES, 1995

There are some pronounced patterns in U.S. religiosity. For example, men are less religious than women, and young people are less religious than their elders. The well educated go to church, but they are not otherwise as religious as the less well educated.

	PERCENTAGE OF ADULTS WHO	
	ATTEND CHURCH OR SYNAGOGUE WEEKLY	SAY RELIGION IS VERY IMPORTANT
NATIONAL	30%	60%
REGION:		
MIDWEST	29	55
SOUTH	38	70
EAST	27	56
WEST	22	54
AGE:		
BELOW 30	23	48
30–49	26	58
50 AND OLDER	39	70
SEX:		
MALE	26	50
FEMALE	33	68
EDUCATION:		
NO COLLEGE	32	69
COLLEGE INCOMPLETE	26	56
COLLEGE GRADUATE	31	45
POSTGRADUATE	29	39
RACE:		
WHITE	29	56
BLACK	35	82

SOURCE: THE Gallup Poll: Public Opinion 1995. 1996. Wilmington: Scholarly Resources.

Why does religion appeal to some groups more than others? After examining several competing explanations, Roof and Hoge (1980) concluded that religious involvement for adults is strongly associated with community attachment and conventional values. People who are involved in their communities—who belong to voluntary associations and civic groups and are integrated into their neighborhoods—tend to extend that involvement to religious participation. Liberal attitudes toward sexual morality, gender roles, civil liberties, and drug use, however, tend to be inconsistent with church involvement. These factors help explain why well-educated people participate in church despite their lack of enthusiasm for it and why young people are less likely to participate or believe.

THINKING CRITICALLY

Drawing on the experiences of your own family or someone close to you, would you say Americans are becoming less religious? Can you foresee a time in your own life when at least some aspects of religion might be more important or less important than they now are? Why do you say so?

Are American Catholics secularized? Pope John Paul II is afraid so. That's why he visited New York's Giant Stadium in 1995, where he stood in the rain while the throng greeted him with the wave. Whether U.S. Catholics are secularized depends on how you define the term. The U.S. Roman Catholic Church has gained about 25 percent in membership over the past 40 years (Monroe 1995, 383), but these Catholics aren't as likely to attend Sunday Mass as Catholics used to be. And they don't follow their leader the way they once did. The Pope sees artificial birth control as sinful, but 82 percent of U.S. Catholics disagree; 64 percent disagree that abortion is always wrong. Just one-third agree that only males should be priests. Nevertheless, 86 percent say they approve of their Pope (Sheler 1995)—a sign that in the American Catholic church, members take what they like and leave the rest.

Fundamentalism and the Christian Right

During the 1800's, the Western world increasingly embraced science and reason rather than dependence on God as avenues to well-being. By about 1900, American Protestantism had become seriously divided over issues regarding science and religion. Mainline churches accommodating scientific theories, such as human evolution, were labeled anti-Christian, pro-atheistic, and heretical by conservatives, who favored a literal (or *fundamental*) interpretation of the Bible. By 1909, these conservatives had become known as "the fundamentalists" (Monroe 1995, 384).

Many observers, including Marx, have thought that religion ought to appeal disproportionately to the poor and the disadvantaged because it should serve as a painkiller for their poverty and oppression. Although the poor and disadvantaged are more likely than others to be fervent in their beliefs, studies show that churchgoing is correlated more strongly with being conventional than with being disadvantaged. It is characteristic of people who are involved in their communities, belong to other voluntary associations, and hold traditional values.

The Growth of Fundamentalism. One of the most striking changes in modern American religion has been the vitality and growth of fundamentalist churches compared with mainline denominations. Since about 1950, mainline denominations have lost as much as 10 percent of their membership per decade, while conservative Protestant churches have increased their membership as much as 100 percent (Monroe 1995, 383).

Fundamentalists can be found in all religions; there are fundamentalist Catholics, Baptists, Jews, Muslims, and Lutherans. Their common aim is to reverse the accommodation of the church to the secular world and to bring the church back to its tension with society. The split between the fundamentalists and the modernists is one of the most significant religious cleavages in the United States. On many social and political issues, it is much more important than whether one is Catholic or Protestant. For example, consider the issue of creationism in the schools. Fundamentalists generally favor a requirement that the Genesis story be taught in the schools along with, or even instead of, evolutionary theory. They believe that the two theories are incompatible, and they wish to make certain that students are exposed to Judeo-Christian theory. Leaders of established churches are generally not in favor of creationism in the schools. They have interpreted the Genesis story as a parable rather than as literal truth, and they see no contradiction between scientific evolution and religion. One Catholic authority, for example, notes: "We're more concerned with God as the creator of the world than with how he created. . . . So long as whatever is taught in the schools allows room for that interpretation, there's no problem" (Rev. Thomas Gallagher, Secretary for Education, U.S. Catholic Conference, cited in Bollier 1982, 196). In an extreme example of civil religion, fundamentalists tend to believe that God will take away America's freedom as punishment for the failure to keep the nation Christian (Alexander 1994).

The Christian Right. Fundamentalists are not all alike, and we wrongly stereotype them if we assume that all of them support the Christian Right (Hadden and Shupe 1988). The new Christian Right is a loose coalition of fundamentalists who believe that the U.S. Constitution's strict separation of church and state is essentially heretical and that American government and social institutions must be made to operate according to Christian principles. They believe the United States is God's chosen instrument to fight evil and that it is a Christian obligation to be politically active in making the United States a Christian nation. Two quotes give a flavor of this mixture of Christianity and political activism:

> The idea that religion and politics don't mix was invented by the Devil to keep Christians from running their own country. (Jerry Falwell, cited in Bollier 1982, 54)

> Not voting is a sin against God. . . . Perverts, radicals, leftists, Communists, liberals, and humanists have taken over the country because Christians didn't want to dirty their hands in politics. (Pat Robertson, cited in Bollier 1982, 70)

The Christian Right is best understood as a political rather than a religious movement. It uses normal political processes—lobbying, making campaign contributions, running candidates for offices, and getting out the vote—as means of influencing public policy. It works locally as well as nationally—by trying to gain control of local school boards, for example. In doing all this, it is attempting to build on the existing foundations of civil religion.

Despite this link to established values and despite the growth in fundamentalist religions, the movement may have had more publicity than power. Fundamentalists differ among themselves on matters of religious conviction; they are also divided on political issues such as abortion, gun control, military defense, and pornography (Isikoff 1995; Moore and Whitt 1986; Shupe and Stacy 1982). This divisiveness, plus the centrist nature of American political parties (noted in Chapter 16), has kept the actual political power of the Christian Right in check. Nevertheless, nonfundamentalists are concerned. In the words of a historian and religious scholar, Charles Monroe:

> If the fundamentalist churches should gain control of the United States, and they did their best to do so when Ronald Reagan was elected president in 1980 [and again with the 1994 Congressional elections], they would place the Bible ahead of the Constitution. (Monroe 1995, 385)

Issues such as creationism pit two groups against one another. The broader issues of state support for religion arises when we look at *which* religions the state supports.

Thinking Critically

The historian Charles Monroe warns that the result of fundamentalists' controlling the government and placing the Bible ahead of the Constitution could be a society in which feminist movements would be regarded as subversive and public funds now supporting social and welfare programs would be used to support a strong military program. Do you agree with this forecast? Why or why not? Do you think such changes would be good for the United States, or not? Explain your answer.

Which Religions Are Protected by Government?

In a 1944 case, the Supreme Court concluded that it was illegal to ban the Jehovah's Witnesses from going from door to door to distribute religious material and raise money. In reaching this decision, Justice Robert Jackson argued that citizens have the right "to believe anything they want, however bizarre those beliefs may appear to others" (Richardson 1988). Justice Jackson went further and argued that the "mental and spiritual poison" that "false prophets" disseminate is beyond the reach of the law (Robbins 1986). In other words, church and state are separate. Not everyone agrees that religion is beyond the law, however; and it is not surprising to find that the more bizarre your beliefs, the less likely you are to have your religious rights supported by courts of law. We briefly discuss five areas related to this issue.

1. Parents' Rights. The right to free religious expression means that one has the right to speak on street corners or distribute booklets about one's faith; certainly it has meant that one has the right to raise one's children in one's own faith. Is there a limit to this right? Say you believe in human sacrifice. Do you have a right to raise your children in this religion? To demand their sacrifice? Most people would probably say that you do not have this right. But how do we draw the line between the rights of people who practice this religion and the rights of Presbyterians?

A recent court case involved a divorced mother who was raising her children in an extreme fundamentalist commune that emphasized corporal punishment as a means of exorcising the devil. The children's father and maternal grandparents sued for custody of the children—and received it. The judge allowed the mother visitation rights but ordered her not to make "any comments to the minor children with regard to her religious beliefs, whatsoever, under the penalties of contempt." He argued that the mother's church, the Good Life Pentecostal Church, had "adopted systems of corporal punishment and fear to force obedience and submission of her children to the doctrine of her church. . . . When [religious] beliefs threaten the health and well-being of children, then the courts have a duty to act to remove children from such abuse" ("York Woman" 1990). In a somewhat similar vein, when children of Christian Scientists need medical help, parents are often obligated by court order to get it.

2. Racism and Religion. In 1982, the U.S. Supreme Court ruled that Bob Jones University did not qualify as a religious organization for tax purposes because it publicly espoused racism. The U.S. Internal Revenue Service reasoned, and the Supreme Court agreed, that a religious organization must be a charitable organization and a charitable organization must support public policy. Since racism is a contradiction of U.S. public policy, it followed that Bob Jones University was not a religious organization! Although many people probably were pleased to see Bob Jones University get into trouble for its racist practices, this decision raises a troubling issue: Will only those religious organizations that do not create tension between religion and society be regarded as "real" religions (Richardson 1988)?

3. Forcible Deprogramming. If your child falls under the "undue influence" of a charismatic leader and becomes a member of the Moonies or the Hare Krishna, what can you as a parent do about it? Some parents have hired deprogrammers to kidnap their children and forcibly deprogram them. Should this be legal?

Proponents argue that the right to "free religious expression" doesn't apply to religious movements that use brainwashing techniques; they believe that children who have joined these movements have not made an informed, free choice. Legal scholars who support deprogramming argue that the First Amendment does not cover "coerced" cultist beliefs (Delgado 1984). Opponents, however, wonder how the courts can decide whether someone's religious beliefs are based on informed choice (Shepard 1985). Does a child raised as a Jew make an informed choice not to believe in Christ? Does a Catholic child make an informed decision to do so?

As American culture becomes increasingly diverse, so does the institution of religion. This apartment has been converted for religious service of an Eastern religion by its tenant. Whether such houses of worship deserve tax-exempt status relates to a broader question: What religions are protected by the U.S. government?

4. Campus Publications. In 1995, the U.S. Supreme Court ruled 5 to 4 that a Christian student organization at the University of Virginia should be allotted university money to help publish its magazine, *Wide Awake*. The Court reasoned that to refuse money for a Christian publication while giving funds to a wide range of other clubs violates Christian students' right to free speech. "We're finally beginning to move away from government hostility to religion, and going in the direction of neutrality," said the student who sued the university (Mauro 1995). But opponents see the decision as a breach in the Constitution's separation of church and state. And the decision raises the question of whether funds must be provided for student publications of other religions, such as Muslim and Hindu.

5. Native American Religions. In 1978, Congress sought to reverse its long history of oppressing Native American tribal religious practices by passing the American Indian Religious Freedom Act. However, subsequent Supreme Court decisions denied some Native Americans the right to use peyote, a traditional sacrament, in their religious ceremonies. As a result, American Indians are seeking passage of a more effective act, the Native American Free Exercise of Religion Act. The act would do the following: (1) protect Native American, Alaskan, and Hawaiian sacred sites from development and scientific investigation; (2) guarantee Indians' right to religious use of peyote; (3) protect the religious rights of Native American prisoners to the same extent as those of prisoners of other faiths; and (4) permit the use of eagle feathers in religious ceremonies, even though bald eagles have been a protected species since 1990 (Association on American Indian Affairs 1994). That the rights of Native American religions are being discussed in Congress and the Supreme Court suggests that the United States has recognized their right to be protected.

Conclusion. Despite America's deeply rooted value and norm prescribing separation of church and state, many laws and court decisions provide (or deny) state support for religions. Issues about just *which* religion the state supports emerge. Which religions' prayers are we considering for use in the schools? Which religions are granted legitimacy by the Internal Revenue Service? The answers suggest that underlying current controversies about eagle feathers, school prayer, and abortion is a high level of consensus in the United States about which religions are appropriate (Judeo-Christian) and which are not (all the rest).

THINKING CRITICALLY

Which religions do *you* think should be protected by the U.S. government? Why? Can you devise a definition for *religion* that includes all those—but *only* those—religions protected by the U.S. government?

THE MEDIA AND RELIGION: TELEVANGELISM

Along with a growing world audience, Americans can take part in religion's *electronic church* with the touch of a dial. Programs from radio and television ministries are aired virtually 24 hours a day every day on network and cable stations and channels. People who tune in to these religious broadcasts are similar to those who watch the most TV generally (Bruce 1990) and also to those who attend churches: They are older, mostly female, Protestant, and disproportionately from rural areas and the southern and midwestern regions of the country. They also tend to have less education and lower socioeconomic status (Alexander 1994).

Evangelist means literally one who spreads the gospel, and televangelists spread the gospel on television. The U.S. electronic church is overwhelmingly a Christian church. American Jews, for instance, have never had a national religious broadcast, because they do not actively seek converts (Abrams 1990). There are moderate television ministers (Robert Schuller is an example), but for the most part televangelism is Christian fundamentalism.

Televangelism has been the target of several major criticisms, which have come almost entirely from nonviewers. First, some have criticized it for failing to fulfill one of the major functions of traditional religion: bringing people together into a moral community. Since most people who listen to televangelists also attend church, however, this criticism has relatively little merit. And one researcher (Alexander 1994) argues that viewers, who often feel maligned or misunderstood by mainstream society, may not find face-to-face community but do find safety and a *consciousness of kind*, or sense of similarity to others, in televangelism.

More important than the first are two other criticisms of televangelism. Michael Horton, an Episcopal minister, argues that the "prosperity evangelists" of the airwaves preach an erroneous and harmful gospel that promises freedom from sickness and poverty to people who just ask, are obedient to the New Testament Scriptures, and claim their earthly rewards in faith. For example, a televangelist told his audience: "You are suffering . . . because you have refused your place in Christ" (Horton 1990, 126). Jewish scholars worry that this kind of statement fosters anti-Semitism (Abrams 1990). On a microsociological level, prosperity evangelism can be dysfunctional as well: For those whose prayers go unanswered, the emotional pain of religious confusion is added to previous suffering.

> **THINKING CRITICALLY**
>
> Explain prosperity evangelism in terms of Karl Marx's view of religion.

A related criticism is that televangelists use their persuasive powers to bilk a naive audience. For instance, failure to "seed" one's faith by sending money to the ministry is often interpreted as disobedience of the Scriptures. Hence, one's failure to receive what one requires can be charged to one's disobedience in withholding the appropriate contribution (Horton 1990). Oral Roberts first popularized the "seed faith" concept, but many have copied his scheme. One calculation shows that televangelists spend an average 21 percent of airtime soliciting funds; direct mail is used as well. As a result, the major televangelists pull in $150 million or more every year (Abelman 1990; Hoover 1990).

Nonetheless, Stewart Hoover (1990), a Temple University communications professor, argues that it is a myth that televangelists rob the poor. According to the well-known sociologist and Catholic priest Andrew Greeley, "It ought not to be assumed implicitly that all electronic preachers are corrupt, money-grubbing hypocrites" (in Abelman and Hoover 1990, 157). Research indicates that the average contribution is about $32 per month, and most of that money comes from middle-income viewers. Some ministries, such as Pat Robertson's 700 Club, raise most of their funds from a small group of wealthy supporters, who may even be regular viewers (Hoover 1990).

Defenders further argue that the electronic church makes religion available to those who otherwise would be shut off from participation: older people, people with physical disabilities, and other isolated individuals. Furthermore, the high costs of air time make televangelism enormously expensive, and the electronic church could not exist without devoting considerable time to soliciting contributions (Alexander 1994). Finally, if we assume that televangelists survive by manipulation, we reduce the electronic flock to passive, nonthinking sheep.

In the late 1980s, the televangelist industry was rocked by scandals involving sex and financial fraud: Jimmy Swaggart and Jim and Tammi Bakker fell from grace (Mertz 1987). Far from alienating televangelists' chief audiences, however, the scandals had strong negative effects only on those who already had negative opinions (Gallup Reports 1989d). And these scandals were only a temporary embarrassment to televangelism. The electronic church has actually grown since (Alexander 1994) and continues to be an important means by which to reach a religious audience.

CONSEQUENCES OF RELIGIOSITY

Because religion teaches and reinforces values, it has consequences for attitudes and behaviors. People who are more religious tend to hold more conservative attitudes on sexuality and personal honesty; they are also likely to hold more conservative attitudes about family life, being more likely, for instance, to support the use of corporal punishment in disciplining children (Alwin 1986; Ellison and Sherkat 1993; Hoge and Zulueta 1985). They also tend to be happier and more satisfied with their lives (Ellison 1991) and their marriages (Thomas and Cornwall 1990) and to be friendlier, more cooperative people (Ellison 1992).

Although data such as these generally support the view that religious training teaches and reinforces conventional behavior, religion and the church can be forces that promote social change. As mentioned, in the United States, African American churches and clergy played a significant role in the civil rights movement of the 1950s and 1960s. Religion also played a supportive role in the struggle of Appalachian coal miners to unionize in the 1920s and 1930s (Billings 1990). In Latin America, liberation theology aims at the establishment of democratic Christian socialism and the elimination of poverty, inequality, and political oppression.

If you are a practicing member of any church, probably you are already convinced that religion can do something positive for you. Religion can help people feel wanted within a community of like-minded folks, and it offers answers to hard questions, from why you slept through an important exam to why your loved one had to die. There is evidence that religion can help keep you from committing suicide (Stack and Wasserman 1995), as Durkheim argued in the last century (see Chapter 2).

At the same time, it appears that religion can harm you. It may inflict emotional pain, especially if you don't adhere to the beliefs or follow the rules of the religion that nevertheless holds some influence over you. Also, religion can encourage you to be ethnocentric—less accepting of others and their beliefs in this increasingly diverse society.

Speaking of religion as a whole seems to assume that American religions are alike. They are not. The Unitarian Universalists, for example, stress open-mindedness and tolerance. Fundamentalist Christian religions tend to do just the opposite, although even fundamentalists are not all alike. Mainline religions fall somewhere in between. The Applications in Diversity section that follows explores one religion in the United States that attempts to pull us all together.

APPLICATIONS IN DIVERSITY

WHAT IS THE BAHA'I FAITH?

Have you ever met anyone who is a member of the Baha'i Faith? Maybe you yourself are a Baha'i. The odds are slim, however, since there are relatively few in the United States. The Baha'i Faith began in the 19th century in what is now Iran. Since its beginning, it has spread to over 300 countries. The World Center for the Baha'i Faith is Haifa, Israel.

The word *Baha'i* comes from the names of the religion's founder, Bahaullah—a name that means "the Glory of God." *Baha'i* means a follower of Bahaullah. Baha'is see all the major religious prophets—not only Bahaullah but also Buddha, Jesus, Muhammad, and others—as equally important spiritual messengers. The basic message of Bahaullah is the oneness of humankind—races, classes, nations, and religions—in a spirit of understanding under the guidance of One God, in whom everyone believes. The cultural differences between people should be cherished, not ignored, however. Bahaullah saw unity in diversity as the remedy for all the world's ills.

As a means of bringing all peoples together, Bahaullah emphasized overcoming prejudice, working to eliminate the extremes of poverty and wealth, giving women opportunities equal to those of men, providing all children with an education, and protecting the natural environment. In addition, Baha'is believe that nations must choose an international language to be used along with their mother tongues as an avenue to overcoming misunderstanding and mistrust. Baha'is believe that eventually there will be a world government that will make sure all countries are treated fairly and the planet survives in a healthy state.

You cannot become a member of the Baha'i Faith by birth or because your parents are Baha'is. You must actively seek it for yourself. There is no priesthood in the Baha'i Faith. Each individual is responsible for her or his own spiritual progress. Baha'is believe that heaven and hell are not places but states of being. Heaven is nearness to God; hell is separation from God. You can be in heaven while still on earth if you have done something virtuous; you can be in hell on earth if you have done something evil.

Baha'is meet together regularly to pray, discuss, and enjoy each other's company. This is called a "feast." Where there are only a few Baha'is, feasts are held in someone's home. In a few places, there are large Baha'i houses of worship. One Baha'i house of worship in the United States is in Wilmette, Illinois; another is near Washington, D.C.

Along with meditation, daily work is considered prayer in the Baha'i Faith as long as it is done to the best of one's ability. Work done as service to humans is the finest kind of prayer. Baha'i devotions involve no elaborate rituals or sermons but consist of prayers and readings from the holy writings of all the great religions. Baha'is observe 9 holy days a year and fast from sunrise to sunset for a period of 19 days in March. The use of alcohol is always forbidden, as is the use of any other habit-forming drug.

Baha'is advocate that people take a more spiritual, less selfish attitude toward the earth and live in harmony with their environment ("Baha'i Faith" n.d.). Above all, Baha'is do everything they can to encourage world peace—by joining and supporting other groups and by putting forward their own ideas for an international peace conference (Hainsworth 1986).

THINKING CRITICALLY

From what you know of the Baha'i Faith, would you call it a church or sect in the United States? How might Christian fundamentalists differ with Baha'is in their beliefs? Islamic fundamentalists? What functions, if any, might you expect the Baha'i Faith to perform for society? For individuals? What dysfunctions, if any, might result from adherence to the Baha'i Faith?

SOCIOLOGY ON THE NET

One indication of the extent to which America has become a multicultural nation is to examine the diverse religious landscape. A good place to start is the Nation of Islam Home Page.

`http://www.noi.org/main.html`

For insight into the formation of the Nation of Islam, click on the **Brief History of The Nation of Islam**. Who is the honorable Elijah Muhammad? Have you seen Minister Louis Farrakhan on the news? Click on the **flag** at the bottom of the screen. You are now back at the home page. Scroll down to the bottom and click on **The Final Call**. Browse around for a while and then click on the **Analysis & Perspectives** section. Read a few of the articles. Why might this religion prove to be popular with African Americans? Have you heard of any African Americans who have adopted this religion? How well does this perspective fit with the major churches and denominations in America?

As you might have noticed from this exercise and others in the text, religion can be a contentious subject that brings out strong feelings. Religious tolerance can on occasion be hard to come by. Let's see what The Ontario Centre For Religious Tolerance has to say on the topic.

`http.//www.religioustolerance.org/ocrt_hp.htm`

You will find this a very useful home page if you have a personal interest in religion or if you are writing a term paper on religion. Click on the highlighted **index of topics**. Scroll through the list of religions until you come to the **Spiritual Topics Menu**. Click on the section entitled **What is Religious Tolerance?** Read through this section and go back to the next selection on the **Spiritual Topics Menu** entitled **Test Your Religious Tolerance**. Do you agree with this definition of tolerance? Are you a tolerant person by the standards of this test?

Return to the **Main Menu** and click on **Religiously Hot Topics**. Browse through some of the topics. Have any of these topics come up in discussions with your friends or family? How do your own religious views inform you about how to approach these topics? Before you leave this excellent web site, you might wish to browse around and satisfy your own curiosity about a particular religion or religious group. You may wish to visit the **Glossary of Confusing Religious Terms** that can be found under the **Spiritual Topics Menu**. And don't forget to take the time to browse through the list of **35 Religious and Ethical Systems**.

SUMMARY

1. The sociological study of religion concerns itself with the consequences of religious affiliation for individuals and with the interrelationships of religion and other social institutions. It is not concerned with evaluating the truth of particular religious beliefs.
2. There are two distinct viewpoints about the role of religion in society. One, associated with Durkheim, suggests that religion provides support for the traditional practices of a society and a force for continuity and stability. The other, associated with

Weber, suggests that religion generates new ideas and challenges the institutions of society.

3 All religions are confronted with a dilemma: Should the religion reject the secular world, or should it compromise with the world? The way a religion resolves this question determines its form and character. Those that make adaptations to the world are called churches, whereas those that reject the world are called sects.

4 The primary distinction between a cult and an established sect is that a cult is outside a society's traditional religious heritage whereas an established sect is more assimilated to society.

5 Because churches participate more in the world, they are more likely to be involved in political affairs. Liberation theology aims to establish democratic Christian socialism that eliminates poverty, inequality, and oppression. The church's moral community has often been the foundation for political organization.

6 The great majority of Americans consider themselves religious. Age and sex are the best predictors of religiosity. College-educated people attend religious services as often as others but are less likely to say religion is very important in their lives.

7 Civil religion is an important source of unity for the American people. This "religion" holds the nation sacred: It is composed of a set of beliefs (for example, that God guides the country), symbols (the flag), and rituals (the pledge of allegiance) that many Americans of all faiths hold sacred.

8 There is mixed evidence on the progress of secularization. Compared with religion in the 1950s, religion today does appear to have less influence on social life.

9 Fundamentalist churches that stress a return to basic religious principles have grown in influence. The political arm of the fundamentalist churches, the Christian Right, seeks to bring religion into government, education, and all social institutions.

10 Most church/state issues pit two establishment groups against one another. Deeper issues of religious freedom arise when we consider unpopular or bizarre religions that do not enjoy public support.

11 Despite scandals, televangelism remains a strong form of religious ministry. For the most part, televangelism reaches an audience already heavily involved in the church. Viewers are older, mostly female, Protestant, lower in socioeconomic status, and from the South or Midwest.

12 The Baha'i Faith began in the 19th century in what is now Iran and has a relatively small following in the United States. Baha'is believe in working toward the unity of all human beings while valuing cultural diversity.

SUGGESTED READINGS

ALEXANDER, Bobby C. 1994. *Televangelism Reconsidered: Ritual in Search for Human Community*. Atlanta: Scholars Press. A thoughtful research study and analysis of televangelism and its current function in viewers' lives after the 1987 Bakker and Swaggart scandals.

HADDEN, Jeffrey K., and Shupe, Anson. 1988. *Televangelism: Power and Politics on God's Frontier*. New York: Henry Holt & Co. A favorable and generally supportive sociological analysis of fundamentalists and televangelism in the United States today. Hadden is a sociology professor at the University of Virginia, and Shupe chairs the sociology and anthropology department at Indiana University–Purdue, Fort Wayne.

HAMILTON, Malcolm B. 1995. *The Sociology of Religion*. London and New York: Routledge. A basic and current text in the sociology of religion. It covers much that is addressed in this chapter but in greater detail.

HORTON, Michael (ed.). 1990. *Agony of Deceit: What Some TV Preachers Are Really Teaching*. Chicago: Moody Press. A collection of essays by various mainline ministers that analyze and critique the Christian gospel as it is preached on television.

KEPHART, William M., and Zellner, William. 1994. *Extraordinary Groups: An Examination of Unconventional Lifestyles*, 5th ed. New York: St. Martin's Press. A very good overview of specific utopian groups and religious sects in America. The book includes coverage of modern communes and gypsies, as well as religious sects: the Amish, Jehovah's Witnesses, and the Father Divine movement.

MONROE, Charles R. 1995. *World Religions: An Introduction*. Amherst, N.Y.: Prometheus. A well-written and interesting introduction to the world's major religions by a historian. In addition to presenting basic tenets and rituals, the book describes the historical dynamics surrounding the emergence of the religion and discusses current religio-political controversies.

POPE, Liston. 1942. *Millhands and Preachers*. New Haven, Conn.: Yale University Press. A classic study of the confrontation between economic and religious forces in a textile mill strike in the South in 1929. The narrative illuminates the very real tension between religion and society.

WEBER, Max. 1959. *The Protestant Ethic and the Spirit of Capitalism*. New York: Scribner's. An influential essay on the relationship between religion and economics. Weber argues that early Protestantism became the basis for economic capitalism. (Originally published 1904–1905.)

CHAPTER 19

Health and Medicine

OUTLINE

The Social Construction of Health and Illness

Health and Social Structure

Focus on Measurement: Epidemiological Research Beginnings

Health Care Professions

The High Cost of Medical Care: Who Pays?

Strategies for Improving America's Health

Global Perspectives: Improving Third World Health

AIDS: A Case Study in the Sociology of Medicine

Applications in Diversity: How Will California's Proposition 187 Affect Public Health?

PROLOGUE

Have You Ever . . . thought about purposefully vomiting up your dinner in order to lose weight? If you have, you are probably either a wrestler or a young woman. Wrestlers go through all sorts of tortures to make weight limits: They sweat, they vomit, they dehydrate themselves. Young women who are fanatic about the quest for slimness may develop eating disorders such as anorexia (simply not eating) or bulimia (eating and then purging). Ironically, staying slim is the number one reason that young women give for smoking cigarettes.

Wrestlers and anorexics are taking chances with their health in order to meet socially prescribed standards. Many of the rest of us also take chances with our health in meeting norms for our age, sex, class, and social roles: We may drive too fast, drink too much, have unsafe sex, subject ourselves to too much stress, use too many drugs, sleep irregularly, eat the wrong foods, or abuse steroids. Then, too, sometimes the "chances" we take with our health are not our choices at all but come from our social environment. We may be uninsured or underinsured, for instance, through no fault of our own but because we truly cannot afford adequate health insurance.

The sociology of health is really the sociology of life. To understand why some people are healthy and others are not, we need to understand age and gender roles, family and work roles, social class, racial and ethnic inequalities, and cultural values. Although some of your health comes from your genes and some of it comes from the medical system, most of health comes from daily living. It reflects how you sleep, work, play, and eat. It is a *social product,* which reflects your social class and social roles.

Medical sociology is the largest single specialty within sociology and nearly one out of every 10 sociologists claims medical sociology as a primary interest. The reason is that life and health are basic prerequisites to participation in society. The study of health is relevant to almost all branches of sociology. It is of interest to those who study inequalities by class, race, and sex and to those who study the elderly. It is of interest to those concerned with the family and to those concerned with professions, as well as to those who study socialization and self-identity.

In this chapter, we address the social structuring of health and medicine. We begin at the micro level, by taking a symbolic interaction approach to understanding the meaning of health and illness. Then we move toward the macro level by examining how health and health care are affected by class, gender, and race and how American health care is organized and paid for. For the most part, we focus on physical rather than mental health.

THE SOCIAL CONSTRUCTION OF HEALTH AND SICKNESS

Mental and physical health can be viewed as achieved, even socially constructed, statuses. Rather than having them simply bestowed on us by social structure, we work toward them. We negotiate them, just as we negotiate the rest of our social identities. In this section, we use the symbolic interaction perspective to examine how individuals negotiate the health aspects of their self-concepts.

Conceiving the Physical Self

In the dramaturgical perspective developed by Goffman (1959), all the world is a stage, and each of us chooses props and scripts to support the roles we choose to play. One of the most central of these accessories is the physical body, and health can have an important effect on the kinds of roles we can play successfully.

Obviously, a crippling condition such as paralysis or cerebral palsy places physical limitations on the roles we can play successfully. More important than purely physical limitations, however, are the symbolic meanings that we (and others) attach to physical conditions. Losing a breast to cancer, losing the use of one's legs, or developing arthritis or AIDS can be the signal to redefine oneself as ugly, sickly, infirm, or old (Goffman 1963b). Yet others with the same conditions can sustain a very positive self-image (Olesen et al. 1990). The symbolic meanings attached to physical conditions depend on the relationships and social structures in which an individual finds himself or herself.

Most of us, of course, do not have to negotiate our self-identities around such dramatic incidents of ill health. Instead, we must cope with more mundane concerns about our physical selves: being too short, being overweight and out of shape, and growing older. For all of us, however, our feelings about our bodies and our health have consequences for how we interact with the social world—whether we embrace new roles or hide from them.

Taking the Sick Role

Under normal conditions, self-esteem is enhanced by negotiating the healthiest self-concept possible. Under some conditions, however, people want to negotiate a sick identity.

One sociologist, Peggy Thoits, has illustrated the reasons why this occurs in the case of mental illness. Thoits points out that the majority of people who seek treatment for mental illness have voluntarily adopted the label "mentally ill"; they are self-labeled (1986b). Why would they do this? They adopt this label, Thoits argues, as a way to negotiate a positive self-image. These are people who keep getting into trouble of some sort or other—they cannot hold a job, keep friends, or stay sober. In order to explain their failures to others and themselves, they adopt the label "mentally ill." A similar logic explains why some people embrace the role of being physically sick. Their bad back or mononucleosis is used to excuse or explain failures to meet society's expectations. If others agree that a person is indeed sick, then self-esteem may be protected.

In 1951, Talcott Parsons suggested that we could conceive of sickness as a role, a role that brings both responsibilities and rights. According to Parsons, the rights and responsibilities of the **sick role** are:

The **sick role** consists of the rights and obligations that accompany the social label sick.

1. *Sick people are exempt from normal social roles*. They can stay home from school and from work and not clean their homes, all without incurring censure from others. The sick are excused from fulfilling normal obligations.

2. *Sick people are not responsible for their condition*. When people are granted the sick role, they are absolved from any blame for their condition. We agree that it is not their fault that they are sick, and we do not believe that they could get well if they only wanted to.

3. *Sick people should try to get well.* Although it is not their fault that they are sick, it is their obligation to follow instructions and to wish to be well.

4. *Sick people should seek technically competent help and cooperate with physicians.* Not only should they abstain from behaviors that will extend the sickness but they should also actively seek to get better.

In order to keep the rights of the sick role, then, the sick individual must follow instructions, seek competent help, and wish to be well.

Whether people are granted the sick role depends on many factors. The visibility of the problem and the degree to which the patient is thought to have brought it on himself or herself are two important factors. For example, if a student claims the rights of one sick role as an excuse for not taking a midterm, the claim is more likely to be honored if the student has a broken leg (a visibly apparent condition) rather than a headache, or has the flu instead of a hangover, and has been to the medical center. Even the broken leg may not be excused if it resulted from some deliberately risky behavior.

Labeling Theory

The concept of the sick role emphasizes the individual actor's participation in negotiating a sickly or a healthy identity. This negotiation is not entirely an individual process, however, and society also plays a role in deciding who will be considered sick. Labeling theory (which was applied to deviance in Chapter 8) is used to explain how individual characteristics (such as sex, age, and social class) and socio-historical circumstances affect how the label "sick" is applied.

Labeling theory is particularly helpful in understanding current debates about whether some forms of deviance may actually be better understood as diseases. Alcoholism is a prime example. In the 1970s, efforts were made to relabel alcoholism from "deviance" to "sickness." As a result of this *medicalization of deviance*, alcoholics are now granted the sick role: Their condition is judged to be beyond their control; it is not their fault. Instead of being thrown in jail, alcoholics are put in hospitals; physicians and counselors rather than sheriffs and wardens take care of them. Some alcoholics stay sober on prescribed "sobriety pills," which shield the brain from alcohol's pleasurable effects (Cowley 1995).

> **Thinking Critically**
>
> Can you think of some examples of the medicalization of deviance besides the ones mentioned here? What, if any, might be some problems associated with the medicalization of deviance?

Many other forms of behavior that were formerly considered deviance are now being considered forms of mental illness. For example, schoolchildren who would have been defined simply as behavior problems in the past are often diagnosed today as having "attention deficit disorder" and treated with a drug, Ritalin. As another example, although many murderers and rapists are still judged to be deviants who should go to jail, others are labeled sick and sent to mental hospitals. There is no clear agreement on this issue among experts or the public, and this labeling process is still very much in flux (Conrad 1992).

A classic example of how both deviance and illness are socially constructed is our society's attitude toward homosexuality. For many decades, homosexuality was regarded as both deviant (actually criminal) and a form of mental illness. In 1976, however, the American Psychological Association took homosexuality off its list of mental illnesses. By simply taking a vote, they "de-medicalized" homosexuality. Although many Americans continue to regard homosexuality as deviant, there is also a growing movement to de-criminalize it.

A symbolic interactionist approach to health helps us recognize the relative quality of illness. What is regarded as illness in one time or place may not be regarded as illness in another; what is regarded as an illness for one age group may not be regarded as an illness in another. Obviously, however, there is more to health than symbolic meanings. Regardless of how positive a meaning you assign it, a malignant tumor threatens your life. The balance of this chapter examines differentials in physical health and reviews research on the health care system.

HEALTH AND SOCIAL STRUCTURE

Good health is not simply a matter of taking care of yourself and having good genes. Although both elements play important parts in health, we also find that good health is related to such social statuses as gender, social class, and race or ethnicity. The study of how social statuses relate to the distribution of illness and mortality in a population is called **social epidemiology** (Rockett 1994). In this section, we review social epidemiology in the United States, and then look at the social structuring of healthy lifestyles. The Focus on Measurement section of this chapter describes the historic beginnings of epidemiological research.

Social epidemiology is the study of how social statuses relate to the distribution of illness and mortality.

SOCIAL EPIDEMIOLOGY

In the United States, the average newborn can look forward to 75.5 years of life (U.S. Bureau of the Census 1995, Table 114). Although some will die young, the average American now lives to be a senior citizen (see Table 19.1). This is a remarkable achievement given that life expectancy was less than 50 years at the

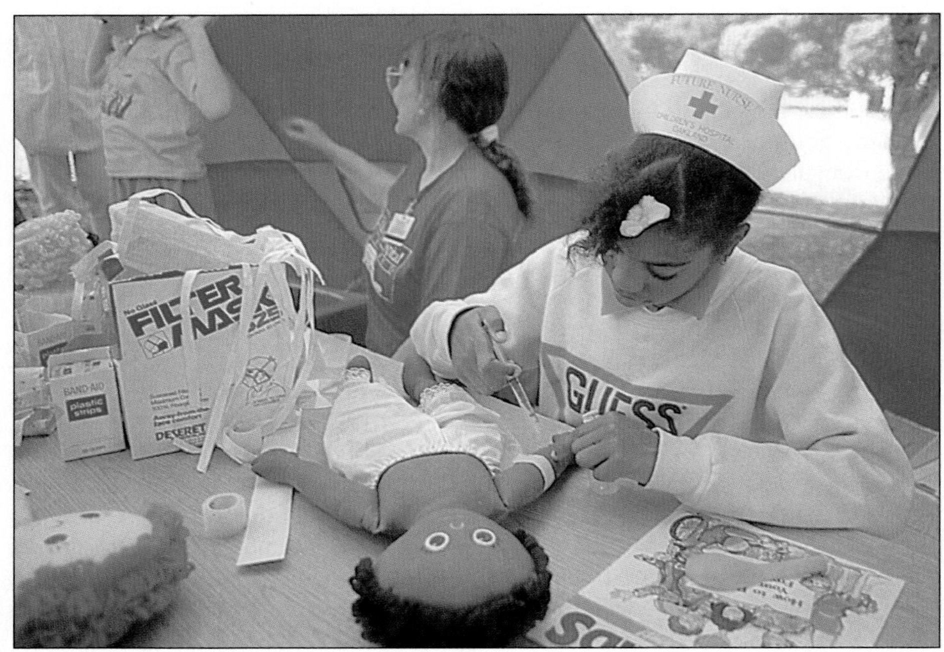

Medicine is one of our most familiar institutions. Nearly all children have enough experience with the medical institution to add playing doctor and playing nurse to their role-playing repertoires. Although playing doctor has some comical overtones, the popularity of doctor and nurse play sets and the large numbers of children who aspire to medical professions are indicators of how important medicine is to contemporary society.

TABLE 19.1
HEALTH AND LIFE EXPECTANCY BY SEX, RACE, AND FAMILY INCOME, UNITED STATES, 1992–1993

Generally, people of higher status report better health: Men report better health than women, white Americans report better health than black Americans, and those with higher incomes report better health than those with lower incomes. For the most part, differentials in life expectancy parallel these differentials in health. The exception is sex: Despite their better health, men have lower life expectancy than women.

	LIFE EXPECTANCY AT BIRTH, 1993	PERCENTAGE REPORTING EXCELLENT HEALTH
TOTAL	75.5	38%
SEX		
MALE	72.1	41
FEMALE	78.9	35
RACE		
WHITE	76.3	39
BLACK	69.3	30
FAMILY INCOME		
UNDER $10,000	NA	25
$10,000–$19,000	NA	29
$20,000–$34,999	NA	36
$35,000 AND OVER	NA	49

SOURCE: U.S. Bureau of the Census 1993a; U.S. Bureau of the Census 1995, Table 114; U.S. National Center for Health Statistics 1994.

beginning of this century. Not everyone benefited equally, however, and men and African Americans are significantly disadvantaged in terms of years of life, as are people of lower socioeconomic status.

There is a great deal more to health, of course, than just avoiding death. The incidence of nonfatal conditions is at least as important as the distribution of mortality in evaluating a population's overall well-being (Verbrugge 1989a). Although only one out of every 100 people dies each year in the United States, well over half experience some sort of long-term or serious illness that affects the quality of their lives and their ability to hold jobs or maintain social relationships. In the following sections, we consider why gender, social class, and race are related to ill health and mortality.

Gender. On the average, U.S. women live almost seven years longer than U.S. men (Table 19.1). Some of this difference appears to be the result of a lifelong biological advantage: From conception to old age, females experience lower death rates than males. Ironically, however, women report significantly worse health than men: more high blood pressure, arthritis, asthma, diabetes, cataracts, corns, and hemorrhoids (U.S. Bureau of the Census 1995, Table 215).

Why do men have higher mortality rates despite apparently better health? Some of the answer may lie in biology, but social factors also play a very important and perhaps dominant role. Two aspects of the male gender role in America appear to put men at a disadvantage in terms of mortality.

First, contemporary gender roles encourage males—particularly young males—to be rowdy, aggressive, and risk-taking. There is *normative* approval for higher rates of drinking, fighting, fast driving, and dangerous behavior for males. As a result, young men are two and one-half times as likely to die in motor vehicle accidents and six times more likely to be homicide victims (see Table 19.2). Even into their 40s, men are more than twice as likely as women to die from motor vehicle accidents (U.S. Bureau of the Census 1995, Table 127).

Second, men appear to cope less well with stress than women do. Generally, studies find that men report lower levels of stress than women (Thoits 1987; Ulbrich, Warheit, and Zimmerman 1989) and that men are less likely than women to have high blood pressure. Nevertheless, men are more likely than women to die of stress-related diseases such as heart attack and stroke. Why is stress more deadly for men than women? Although there may be a biological difference in vulnerability to stress, different gender-role socialization plays an important part (Verbrugge 1989b). On the average, men do not take care of themselves as well as women do—men are less likely to go to the doctor when ill, to follow doctors' recommendations, and to watch their diets. In addition, men are less likely to have a network of intimates in whom they can confide and from whom they can seek support (Nathanson 1984). Thus, men's stress is more likely than women's stress to develop into life-threatening proportions.

Social Class. The higher one's social class, the longer one's life expectancy and the better one's health (see Table 19.1). The effects of social class are complex. They are partially attributable to the fact that poorer people cannot afford expensive medical care. For example, one study found that uninsured infants taken to hospitals got significantly fewer health services than newborns covered by some

TABLE 19.2

LEADING CAUSES OF DEATH AMONG 15- TO 24-YEAR-OLDS, BY SEX, 1992

	NUMBER OF DEATHS			DEATH RATE PER 100,000 POPULATION		
	TOTAL	MALE	FEMALE	TOTAL	MALE	FEMALE
ALL ACCIDENTS	13,662	10,253	3,409	37.8	55.5	19.3
MOTOR VEHICLE ACCIDENTS	10,305	7,438	2,867	28.5	40.3	16.2
HOMICIDE	8,019	6,891	1,128	22.2	37.3	6.4
SUICIDE	4,693	4,044	649	13.0	21.9	3.7
CANCER	1,809	1,084	725	5.0	5.9	4.1
HEART DISEASE	968	626	342	2.7	3.4	1.9
AIDS	578	419	159	1.6	2.3	0.9

SOURCE: U.S. Bureau of the Census 1995, Table 127.

health plan (Waldholz 1991). But the causes go far beyond simple access to health care (Ross and Wu 1995; Rutter and Quine 1990). Figure 19.1 diagrams the paths through which low socioeconomic status affects health.

1. *Standard of living.* The lower your income, the more likely you are to live in unhealthy environmental conditions, such as near an air-polluting factory or a toxic waste dump, have substandard housing, eat a poor diet, and receive inadequate health care. These purely economic consequences of low income have a direct effect on health.

2. *Stress.* Low-income people have less control over the world around them than do those who are better off. Among the kinds of stresses they encounter are inability to pay their bills, evictions, unsatisfactory and demeaning jobs, and low self-esteem. High levels of stress directly affect health by increasing the incidence of high blood pressure, ulcers, and heart conditions. They also have an indirect effect on health by encouraging poor coping strategies—such as drinking, smoking, and risky behaviors.

3. *Low education.* The highly educated consult their doctors and get health care information on the Internet (Rubin 1995). Poorly educated people generally have

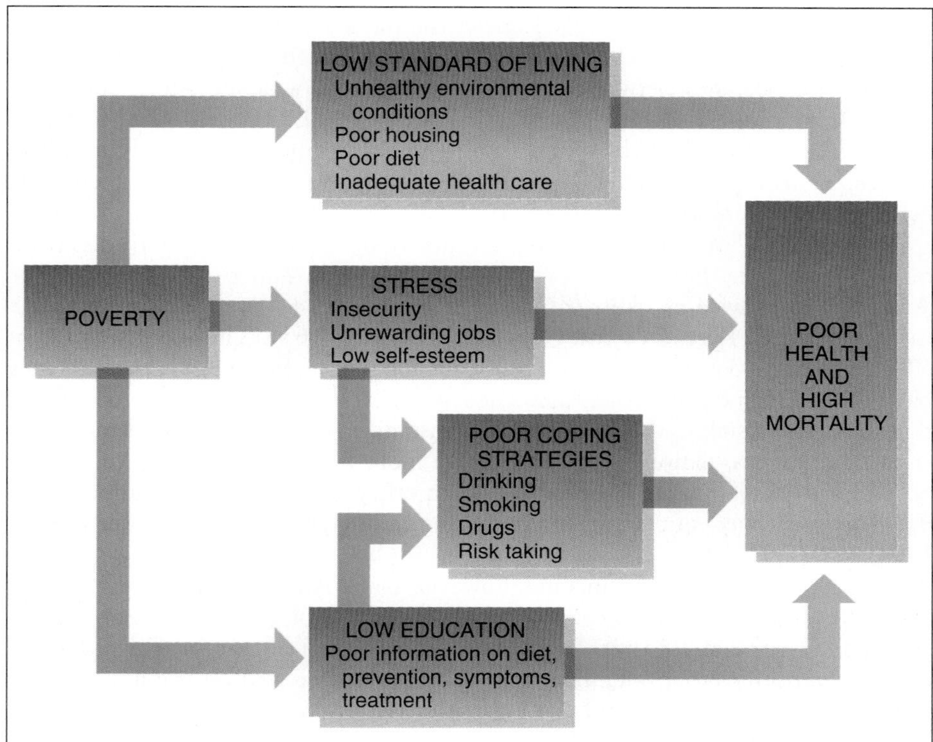

FIGURE 19.1
HOW POVERTY AND DISADVANTAGE CREATE ILL HEALTH

The relationship between poverty and poor health is complex. Not only do poor people have less access to health care but they are also more apt to get sick in the first place. Equalizing access to health care will not produce equal health as long as standards of living, stress, and education are unequally distributed.

SOURCE: Adapted from Rutter and Quine 1990.

less access to accurate information about health and health care. They are less likely to be well informed about the need to vaccinate their children against measles, for example, or about proper eating habits or appropriate responses to symptoms; and they are less likely to seek appropriate treatment. Watching one's cholesterol levels, joining a health club, and eating fiber are as closely related to education as is watching *Masterpiece Theater*.

As long as social class differences in stress, education, and standard of living increase the likelihood that those with lower socioeconomic status will become sick in the first place, free medical care will not eliminate social class differences in health.

Race. Because a higher proportion of African Americans, Hispanics, and Native Americans than non-Hispanic whites are poor, the impacts of low socioeconomic status on health disproportionately affect these minorities. In addition, racial and ethnic minorities face obstacles to good health *because they are minorities*. For instance, a language barrier often separates Hispanic patients from health care professionals (Vega and Amero 1994).

African Americans are disadvantaged compared with all whites, including Hispanics on most indicators. In the United States today, black infants are more than twice as likely as white infants to die in their first year of life (U.S. Bureau of the Census 1995, Table 120). At every age after that, black Americans' mortality rates are substantially higher than those of white Americans. At ages 55 to 64, for example, black men are 50 percent more likely to die of cancer than are white men (U.S. Department of Health and Human Services 1995). As a result of this lifelong disparity in mortality rates, the average white male can expect to live seven years longer than the average black male; the difference is four years for females. Although this difference is far less than it was at the beginning of the century, the gap in life expectancy between white and black males widened during the 1980s (U.S. Department of Health and Human Services 1995). When asked to report about their current health, black Americans are only half as likely as white Americans to report excellent health (see Table 19.1). What social factors lie behind these differentials?

Lower average income is obviously an important factor in the health disadvantage of minorities. Because of lower incomes, African Americans and Hispanic Americans are twice as likely as non-Hispanic whites to be without any health insurance (U.S. Bureau of the Census 1994, Table 165). The most significant effects of low income, however, are those diagrammed in Figure 19.1: Because they have lower incomes, minority Americans are more likely to live in circumstances that make them sick in the first place. For instance, research shows that racial and ethnic minorities, mainly because they are more likely to be poor (Austin and Schill 1994), are 47 percent more likely than others to live near a hazardous waste facility, which may emit toxins into the surrounding ground, air, or water (Ember 1994).

Even after we control for income, however, black Americans have higher mortality rates than white Americans. Many observers attribute this noneconomic disadvantage to the stress that accompanies minority-group status. Regardless of income, minority group members experience prejudice and discrimination that raise their risk of physical and psychological stress (Cooper et al. 1981; Ulbrich, Warheit, and Zimmerman 1989).

This pervasive pattern of disadvantage raises heart disease and cancer levels among older members of minority groups, and it also encourages risk-taking behaviors among young adults. Although most of the black/white differential in mortality is due to higher rates of heart attack, stroke, and cancer, it is notable that the cause of death demonstrating the single largest racial differential is homicide and legal intervention (deaths occurring during arrests and legal executions). Black Americans are six times more likely than white Americans to die from this cause, with the result that homicide is the fourth leading cause of death for black males—and the first leading cause of death for black men between ages 15 and 34 (U.S. Bureau of the Census 1995, Table 126).

Healthy Lifestyles and Social Structure

In the United States today, there is a great deal of emphasis on the relationship between health and lifestyle. Magazine and newspaper articles seem to proclaim it your moral duty to take care of your health.

What is a healthy lifestyle? A long-term federal study uses seven personal health practices, stated in terms of risk factors, to assess healthy lifestyle. The risk factors include never eating breakfast, getting less than six hours of sleep per night, being less physically active than one's contemporaries, smoking, being overweight, and having five or more alcoholic drinks in any one day (U.S. Bureau of the Census 1995, Table 221). This study makes the very good point that good health is more likely to result from good daily habits than from a miracle drug.

A central point made by medical sociologists, meanwhile, is that lifestyle choices cannot fully explain the gender, race, and social class differences we observe in mortality and illness. The trouble is that this list of health practices is very narrow. For example, the list omits living near a pollution-spewing factory or toxic garbage dump. One recent sociological study of the media and health bemoaned the fact that the media focus on individual behaviors, while neglecting social factors, that affect Americans' health (Signorielli 1993).

From a sociological perspective, a healthy lifestyle is one that includes satisfying social roles, some control over one's social environment, and integration into one's community (Williams and Collins 1995). These aspects of a healthy lifestyle are closely correlated with social class and race (Williams and Collins 1995). Although it couldn't hurt, one cannot overcome a lifetime of disadvantage by eating one's vegetables.

Even if we are lucky, clean living, and well off, most of us get sick occasionally. At this point, our return to health may depend significantly on the health care system and our access to it. We turn now to a detailed examination of health care professions and the medical/industrial complex.

Health Care Professions

Medicine may be regarded as a social institution. It has a complex and enduring status network, and the relationships among actors are guided by shared norms or roles. Most of us occupy the status of patient in this institution. There are, however, dozens of other statuses. Approximately 10 million Americans are employed in health institutions. They include phlebotomists and X-ray technicians, aides, pharmacists, and hospital administrators. We focus here on just two of these statuses: physician and nurse.

FOCUS ON MEASUREMENT

Epidemiological Research Beginnings

"EPIDEMIOLOGY TODAY MAKES USE OF SOCIAL RESEARCH SIMILAR TO THAT PIONEERED BY JOHN SNOW."

Today, we hear about amazing new technologies used to combat disease and improve our health. We read about complicated laser surgery, for instance, and gene therapy that can find and fix specific genes that cause certain inherited illnesses (Watson 1994). In 1996, a San Francisco man who was dying with AIDS was injected with baboon cells in the hope that the procedure would stop his disease (Gorman 1996). But much of today's very important research on the causes and control of mortality and diseases is sociological, or epidemiological, and does not make use of high-tech treatments, test tubes, or petri dishes.

Epidemiology, the study of how diseases are socially distributed, derives its name from the word *epidemic*, along with the Greek root *logos*, which means "to study." The study of how social statuses or conditions relate to the distribution of illness and mortality originated in writings ascribed to the Greek physician Hippocrates, who lived in the fifth century B.C. In his book *On Airs, Waters, and Places*, Hippocrates showed his ahead-of-the-times awareness of the impact of environment and behavior on personal well-being. However, Hippocrates overlooked the importance of research measurement, which today we consider absolutely necessary for assessing the nature and severity of health problems as well as for understanding their causes. For example, our knowledge of AIDS, discussed elsewhere in this chapter, is largely derived from rigorous research measurement in epidemiology.

John Snow (1813–1858), an English physician, is considered one of the founders of modern epidemiology because he showed how social scientific research can lend insight into the causes and treatment of diseases. Here's what happened.

From the late 1840s to the mid 1850s, London was besieged by an epidemic of cholera. Cholera causes violent diarrhea and vomiting and is often fatal. Europe had been plagued by periodic cholera epidemics since at least the 16th century. During the mid-19th century, most physicians attributed the disease to *miasma*—"bad air" believed to be formed from decaying organic matter. John Snow held a different view. He suspected that the actual cause was drinking water that had been contaminated by fecal waste in sewage.

In 1854, Snow determined by means of systematic observation that the cholera deaths in a recent London outbreak clustered around a particular source of drinking water, the pump on Broad Street. After Snow shared his data with local authorities, along with his hypothesis about cholera's cause, city officials removed the pump's handle. This move effectively shut down the suspected disease source. And indeed, shortly thereafter, the Broad Street cholera outbreak subsided. Because cholera fatalities were already declining in London, however, Snow was unable to attribute the end of the outbreak directly to the closing of the pump. Put another way, the removal of the pump handle followed some scientific principles for research experimental designs, but there was no way to control for factors other than the water source, such as the already evident decline in cholera cases.

The cholera–pump water connection remained in doubt only until 1855, however, when Snow published the results of a carefully controlled test of the hypothesis that sewage in drinking water causes cholera. For this research, Snow obtained information on cholera mortality occurring among 300,000 residents of a specified area of London whose water suppliers could be identified. By walking door to door, Snow found out the names of the specific water companies servicing the houses where cholera fatalities had occurred—an approach to data collection that scientists now call "shoe-leather epidemiology." Snow's research demonstrated that the cholera fatality rate in households receiving contaminated water was higher than the rate in households getting cleaner water. This finding confirmed Snow's hypothesis. It was later revealed that one specific water company had negligently marketed and supplied the unfiltered water through which cholera bacteria had been transmitted (Rockett 1994).

Epidemiology today makes use of social research similar to that pioneered by John Snow. Measurement and analytical techniques are assuredly more sophisticated now, but the overall approach remains the same.

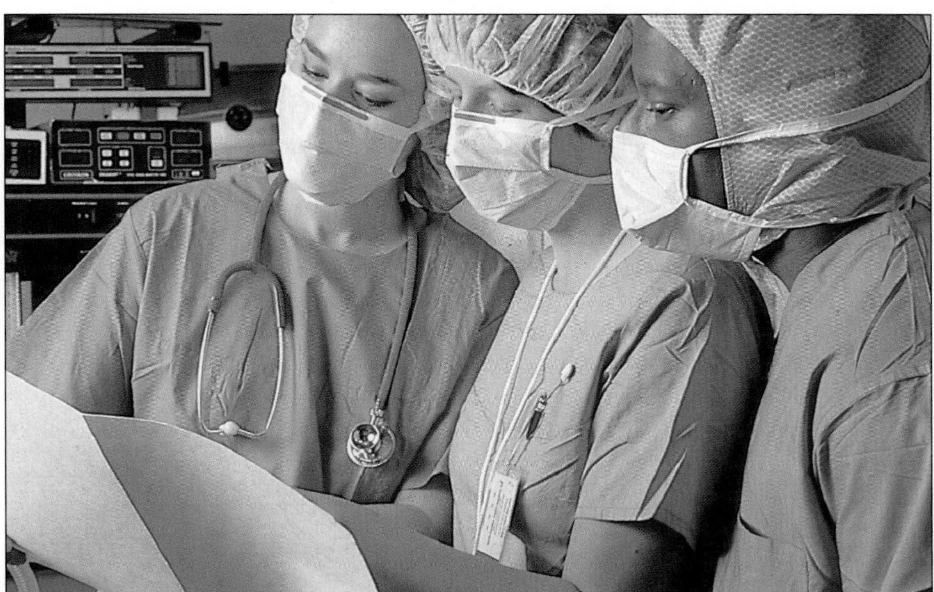

One of the most striking changes in American medicine is the growth in number of women physicians. More than one-third of medical school graduates in 1992 were women (U.S. Bureau of the Census 1995, Table 302), and it seems likely that sex will no longer be a good guide to which green-suited specialists are nurses and which are physicians.

PHYSICIANS

Less than 5 percent of the medical workforce consists of physicians. Yet they are central to understanding the medical institution. Physicians are responsible both for defining ill health and for treating it. They define what is appropriate for those with the status of patient, and they play a crucial role in setting hospital standards and in directing the behavior of the nurses, technicians, and auxiliary personnel who provide direct care.

Physicians As Professionals. As we saw in Chapter 17, a profession is a special kind of occupation, one that demands specialized skills and creative freedom. No occupation fits this definition better than that of physician. Until about 100 years ago, however, almost anybody could claim the title of doctor; training and procedures were highly variable and mostly bad (Starr 1982). About the only professional characteristic of these early practitioners was that the product was highly unstandard! With the establishment of the American Medical Association in 1848, the process of professionalization began; the process was virtually complete by 1910, at which point strict medical training and licensing standards were adopted.

Learning the Physician Role. Most people who enter the medical profession have high ideals about helping people. Studies of the medical school experience, however, suggest that the strenuous training schedule of student physicians deals a temporary blow to these ideals and makes daily endurance the chief objective. On crowded days, patients become defined as enemies who create unnecessary work. Thus, interns and residents learn to GROP (get rid of patients) by referring patients elsewhere, giving them the minimum amount of time, and discharging them as soon as possible (Mizrahi 1986). After school, the biggest rewards in medicine go to those who have the most technical and least personalized types of practices. Although many physicians renew their commitment to helping people once they survive the rigors of medical school, nowhere in the medical profession does the structure of rewards encourage personal care (Bloom 1988).

Understanding Physicians' Income and Prestige. The medical profession provides a controversial case study of stratification theories. Why have physicians been predominantly male and nurses predominantly female? Why are physicians among the highest-paid and highest-status professionals in the United States? In 1990, the average physician earned $164,500 after paying for deductible professional expenses. The lowest average was $102,700, for pediatricians, and the highest average was $236,400, for neurosurgeons (U.S. Bureau of the Census 1993a).

The structural-functional explanation of the status of physicians directly follows the Davis and Moore theory outlined in Chapter 9: There is a short supply of persons who have the talent and ability to become physicians and an even shorter supply of persons who can be neurosurgeons. Moreover, physicians must undergo long and arduous training. Consequently, high rewards must be offered to motivate the few who can do this work to devote themselves to it. The conflict perspective, on the other hand, argues that the high income and prestige accorded physicians have more to do with how physicians use power to promote their self-interest than with what is best for society.

Central to the debate on whether physicians' privileges are deserved or are the result of calculated pursuit of self-interest is the American Medical Association (AMA). The AMA sets the standards for admitting physicians to practice, punishes physicians who violate AMA standards, and lobbies to protect physicians' interests in policy decisions. Although only about half of all physicians belong to the AMA, it has enormous power. One of the major objectives of the AMA has been to ensure the continuance of the capitalist model of medical care, where the

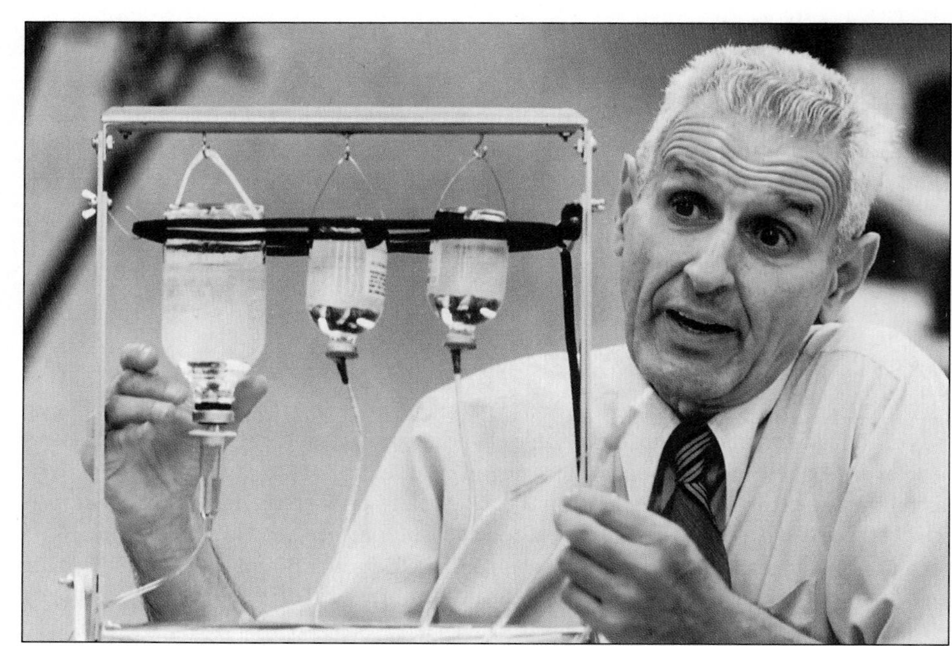

Pictured here with his "suicide machine" is Jack Kevorkian, a Detroit physician. Kevorkian has been called Dr. Death by the media since 1990, when the first of the suicides with which he assisted became public. On trial in Michigan for refusing to obey the state's assisted-suicide law, Kevorkian argued that a higher authority guides him to help relieve suffering in those who find their lives intolerable because of incurable disease or pain. Kevorkian said that many of his fellow physicians agree with his position, and an Oregon survey of physicians found that 60 percent supported legalizing doctor-assisted suicide ("Surveys Find" 1996). From a sociological standpoint, the controversy sparked by Kevorkian is essentially about defining—or redefining—the doctor's role in health care. Do you think assisting suicides should be part of the physician's role? Why or why not?

physician remains an independent provider of medical care on a fee-for-service basis. In pursuit of this objective, the AMA has consistently opposed all legislation designed to create national health insurance, including Medicare and Medicaid. It has also tried to ban or control a variety of alternative medical practices, such as midwifery, osteopathy, and acupuncture. In 1987, the U.S. Supreme Court found that the American Medical Association was unfairly restraining trade by trying to drive osteopaths out of business. As a result of these apparent attempts to protect physicians' profits and independence rather than improve the nation's health care, the AMA has lost credibility among the public.

The Changing Status of Physicians. A few decades ago, the physician was an independent provider who had substantial freedom to determine the conditions of work and who was looked on as a nearly godlike source of knowledge and help by patients. Much of this has changed. Among the many signs of change are the following (Light 1988):

1. A growing proportion of physicians work in incorporated group practices, where fees, procedures, and working hours are determined by others. As a result, physicians have lost a significant amount of independence. These bureaucratized structures are also more likely to have profit rather than service as a dominant goal.
2. The public has grown increasingly critical of physicians. Getting a second opinion is now general practice, and malpractice suits are about as common as unquestioning admiration. Patients are critical consumers of health care rather than passive recipients.
3. Fees and treatments are increasingly regulated by insurance companies and the government. The fact that private and government insurance agencies pay the bills for a vast number of patients allows these agencies to determine what treatments will be given at what fee.

Being a physician is still a very good job, associated with high income and high prestige. It is also part of an increasingly regulated industry that is receiving more critical scrutiny than ever before.

Nurses

Of the nearly 10 million people employed in health care, the largest category includes the 1.8 million who are registered nurses. Nurses play a critical role in health care, but they have relatively little independence. Although the nurse usually has much more contact with the patient than the physician, the nurse has no authority over patient care. Nurses are subordinate to physicians both in their day-to-day work and in their training. Physicians determine the training standards that nurses must meet, and they enforce these standards through licensing boards. On the job, physicians give instructions and supervise. Since the majority of physicians are male and the majority of nurses are female, the income and power differences between doctors and nurses parallel the gender differences in other institutions (see Table 19.3). This makes the hospital a major arena in the battle for gender equality.

In part, women have fought the battle by "joining them" rather than "beating them." Many women who would previously have become nurses are now aspiring to become physicians: Between 1975 and 1986, for example, the number of female physicians increased twice as fast as the number of male physicians. Although

Thinking Critically

Nurses earn less than physicians, but they earn more than people in many other jobs with similar training requirements. Why do so few males enter nursing? What could change this gender gap?

TABLE 19.3

PHYSICIANS AND REGISTERED NURSES: INCOME, SEX, AND RACE, 1992

Nurses earn less than a quarter as much as physicians. Critics wonder whether this reflects real differences in training and responsibility or whether it is another instance of traditional women's jobs being evaluated as less worthy than traditional men's jobs.

	PHYSICIANS	REGISTERED NURSES
MEAN INCOME	$164,500	$33,488
PERCENTAGE FEMALE	20%	94%
PERCENTAGE BLACK	3%	9%

SOURCE: U.S. Bureau of the Census 1993a, 120, 121, 405.

women constitute only 20 percent of practicing physicians, they comprise over one-third of current medical school graduates.

Meanwhile, training standards for nurses have risen and so have salaries. A decade or so ago, the standard credential in the field was the RN (registered nurse), which represented three years of classroom and practicum experience in a hospital training program. As nurses have attempted to raise their status in medical care, two new positions have developed. At the top of the nursing hierarchy is a relatively new status, the nurse practitioner, who may provide direct patient care (for example, prescribing birth-control pills) with only very general supervision from a physician. Below this position are nurses with a BSN (bachelor of science in nursing) degree, who have the training of an RN plus a full bachelor of science college degree. The BSN is becoming the new standard in nursing, and greater education is a lever nurses are using to demand higher wages and a greater role in health care management.

HOSPITALS

The hospital was once idealized as the "temple of healing." Today, it is more often part of a complex bureaucracy whose major concern is the bottom line—that is, money. There are three types of hospitals in the United States: the for-profit proprietary hospital, the nonprofit community or church hospital, and the state (government, or public) hospital. While only proprietary hospitals exist specifically to *make* money, nonprofit hospitals are expected to break even, and public hospitals, designed to treat those who cannot afford a private hospital, are expected to minimize their drain on the taxpayers' pockets. Because costs have been rising and tax dollars don't go as far as they once did, some public hospitals are cutting services or closing down entirely (Sack 1995). None of the three types of hospitals, then, can afford to neglect the dollars-and-cents aspect of medical care.

THE HIGH COST OF MEDICAL CARE: WHO PAYS?

Although the rate of increase has declined somewhat in the last few years, medical care is the fastest-rising part of the cost of living. The overall inflation rate between 1983 and 1992 was 40 percent, but the inflation rate for medical care was 90 percent. Americans spent $361 billion dollars—the equivalent of $1,490 each—for health care in 1983. By 1993, Americans' health care bill was $884 billion, or $3,299 each. Back in 1960, health care expenditures comprised 5 percent of the nation's gross domestic product; in 1993, that figure was 14 percent (U.S. Bureau of the Census 1995, Table 150).

The most dramatic cost increase in medicine has been in hospitalization. In 1970, the cost for a day in the hospital averaged $74; by 1975, that amount had nearly doubled to $134. In 1993, Americans paid an average of $881 for just one day's stay in the hospital. A patient's average cost *per stay* is a whopping $6,132 (U.S. Bureau of the Census 1995, Table 186).

Why are medical costs spiraling? With some risk of oversimplification, the reasons appear to be four: expensive new technologies, competition among providers, high consumer demand, and defensive medicine.

Expensive New Technologies

Computerized axial tomography (CAT) and magnetic resonance imaging (MRI), both of which provide a sort of three-dimensional X ray that illuminates soft tissue as well as bone, are just two of the many new technologies that have been developed in the health care industry in the last two decades. Used for diagnosing tumors, heart murmurs, and a variety of other conditions, these machines are incredibly expensive. The minimum installation fee is $1 million.

Competition among Providers

The original plan was the CAT and MRI machines, as well as other advanced and expensive technologies such as those used in organ transplants, kidney dialysis, and some cancer treatments, would be available only selectively in major research and public hospitals. But interhospital rivalries soon put an end to that idea. In the late 1970s and early 1980s, many American hospitals expanded; some remodeled, some built entirely new and larger facilities. Because too many did so, an unanticipated effect was that many hospitals found their patient censuses dwindling. In 1972, for instance, hospitals had an average occupancy rate (the ratio of average daily census to every 100 beds) of 78. By 1985, the occupancy rate had fallen to 69.5. Today, it is 67.6 percent (U.S. Bureau of the Census 1995, Table 183). With dwindling patient censuses, some hospitals failed; in 1988, a record number of 106 closed their doors (U.S. Bureau of the Census 1995, Table 183). One way that hospital administrators saw to counter this trend was to beat the competition by advertising, acquiring the latest equipment, and passing the cost to the consumer.

High Consumer Demand

Another factor in rising health care costs is higher consumer demand. It is one of the laws of economics that whenever demand is higher than supply, costs go up. In the case of demand for medical services, there is apparently no upper limit. When consumers buy insurance or a computer, they engage in a cost/benefit analysis to see whether the expected gains are worth the cost. Such an analysis seems to be considered immoral in the case of medical care. Many members of the public

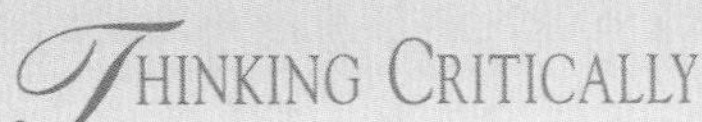

How would you explain the high cost of medical care from a structural-functional perspective? From a conflict perspective?

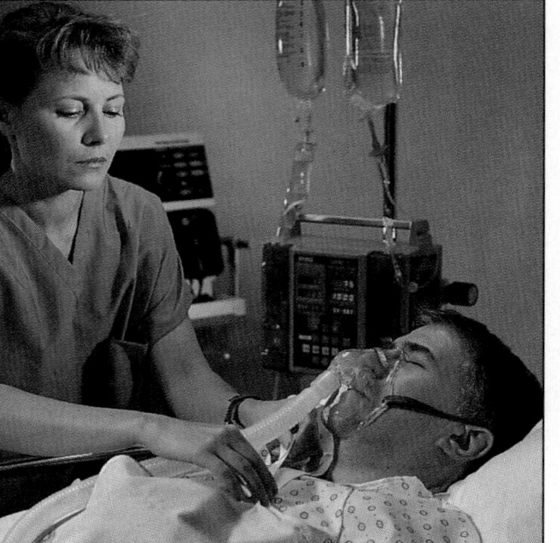

The practice of modern medicine is increasingly technical. Engineering and computer skills may be as valuable as a good bedside manner. Although this technology has increased our capacity to diagnose and cure illnesses, it has sharply increased the cost of medical care. The practice of defensive medicine—avoiding a malpractice suit by prescribing every possible test—has also played an important role in increasing costs.

believe that no cost is too great to save themselves or their loved ones, especially when the cost will be borne by their insurance company or the government.

DEFENSIVE MEDICINE

A sharp increase in malpractice suits has also played a part in rising health care costs. If 1,000 decisions to skip a CAT scan or MRI result in even one lawsuit over a tumor that could have been treated if detected earlier, the million-dollar lawsuit will cancel the savings from the 999 unnecessary tests. From physicians' point of view, there is no contest: They pay for the malpractice insurance (or the damages); an insurance company or the government pays for the tests. Rational physicians cover themselves by ordering every possible test. This "defensive medicine" raises the cost of medical treatment substantially.

WHO PAYS THE BILLS?

Underlying many analyses of health care is one question: "Who pays?" There are three primary modes of financing health care in the United States: private payments, insurance, and government. The cost of health care is so high that only the very rich can rely on private payments. The bulk of the population must rely on private insurance or government programs. Table 19.4 shows the proportions of Americans covered by private or government insurance in 1993.

TABLE 19.4

AMERICANS' HEALTH INSURANCE COVERAGE, 1993

	PERCENT COVERED BY		PERCENT NOT COVERED BY ANY INSURANCE
	PRIVATE INSURANCE	GOVERNMENT INSURANCE	
TOTAL SEX	70.2	14.5	15.3
MALE	70.4	12.5	17.1
FEMALE	70.0	16.4	13.6
RACE/ETHNICITY			
NON-HISPANIC WHITE	73.7	12.1	14.2
AFRICAN AMERICAN	50.2	29.3	20.5
HISPANIC	45.1	23.3	31.6
AGE			
UNDER 18	67.4	18.9	13.7
18–24	61.5	11.7	26.8
25–34	68.3	10.1	21.6
35–44	75.7	7.5	16.8
45–54	79.0	7.1	13.9
55–64	76.9	9.7	13.4
65+	66.0	32.8	1.2

SOURCE: U.S. Bureau of the Census 1995a, Table 169.

Private Insurance. In 1987, 76 percent of Americans were covered by a private health insurance plan. As shown in Table 19.4, by 1993, the proportion had dropped to about 70 percent (U.S. Bureau of the Census 1995, Table 169). Almost all private insurance programs are available through place of employment, and insurance coverage tends to be limited to employed adults (and their families) who have jobs in the corporate core. While those who have private insurance may be considered fortunate, they are not as advantaged as in prior decades. Insurance costs have risen dramatically, and despite high profits, insurance companies are increasingly sparing with benefits. Many companies refuse to cover a new customer's previously existing health conditions for a specified period of time, a situation that has helped create concern about the underinsured—Americans who have private health insurance but who may nevertheless have to pay substantial amounts for health care.

Senior citizens are the only group in the United States covered by a national health insurance plan. The introduction of Medicare in 1965 has guaranteed that virtually all citizens over the age of 65 have medical insurance. However, because this insurance leaves many costs of nursing homes and catastrophic health problems uncovered—and because some federal legislators have proposed limiting the growth in Medicare expenditures—senior citizens remain concerned about health care costs.

Government Programs. The government has several programs that support medical care. The federal government provides some health care through its Veteran's Administration hospitals, but its two largest programs are Medicaid and Medicare. In addition, local governments provide medical care through public health agencies and public hospitals.

Medicare is a government-sponsored health insurance policy for citizens over 65. Premiums are based on ability to pay and deducted from Social Security checks. Since many elderly persons have health problems that would make private insurance coverage impossible or prohibitively expensive, the government-sponsored program is an essential means of providing insurance coverage for the elderly. (See Table 19.4.) The enactment of this program in 1965 did a great deal to improve the quality of health care for the elderly. The program is not cheap, however. In 1993, the government paid over $154 billion in Medicare benefits—two and one half times what it had spent just 10 years before (U.S. Bureau of the Census 1995, Table 150). Much of the increase is due to the skyrocketing expense of medical procedures such as catheterization, bypass surgery, and angioplasty (Fineman 1995d).

Medicaid is a federal cost-sharing program that provides federal matching funds to states that provide medical services to the poor. Although the program was originally limited to people who were on welfare, in many states it is now available for poor children and pregnant women who have low incomes but are not actually on welfare. The eligibility of individuals and the services available are determined by states. As a result, some states offer much more generous medical care than others. In Oregon, legislators have made an explicit attempt to control costs by prioritizing the types of services that will be available to Medicaid recipients (Ginzberg 1994).

The Uninsured. A significant portion of the American population—over 15 percent—have no medical coverage at all. As Figure 19.2 and Table 19.4 show, those who fall through the cracks are low-income Americans, most often young adults between the ages of 18 and 24, African Americans and Hispanics who are unemployed or the working poor. Many jobs in the periphery and most minimum-wage jobs do not include insurance benefits. Less than one-third of jobs in retail sales or food services (the fastest-growing sector of the economy) are covered by health insurance.

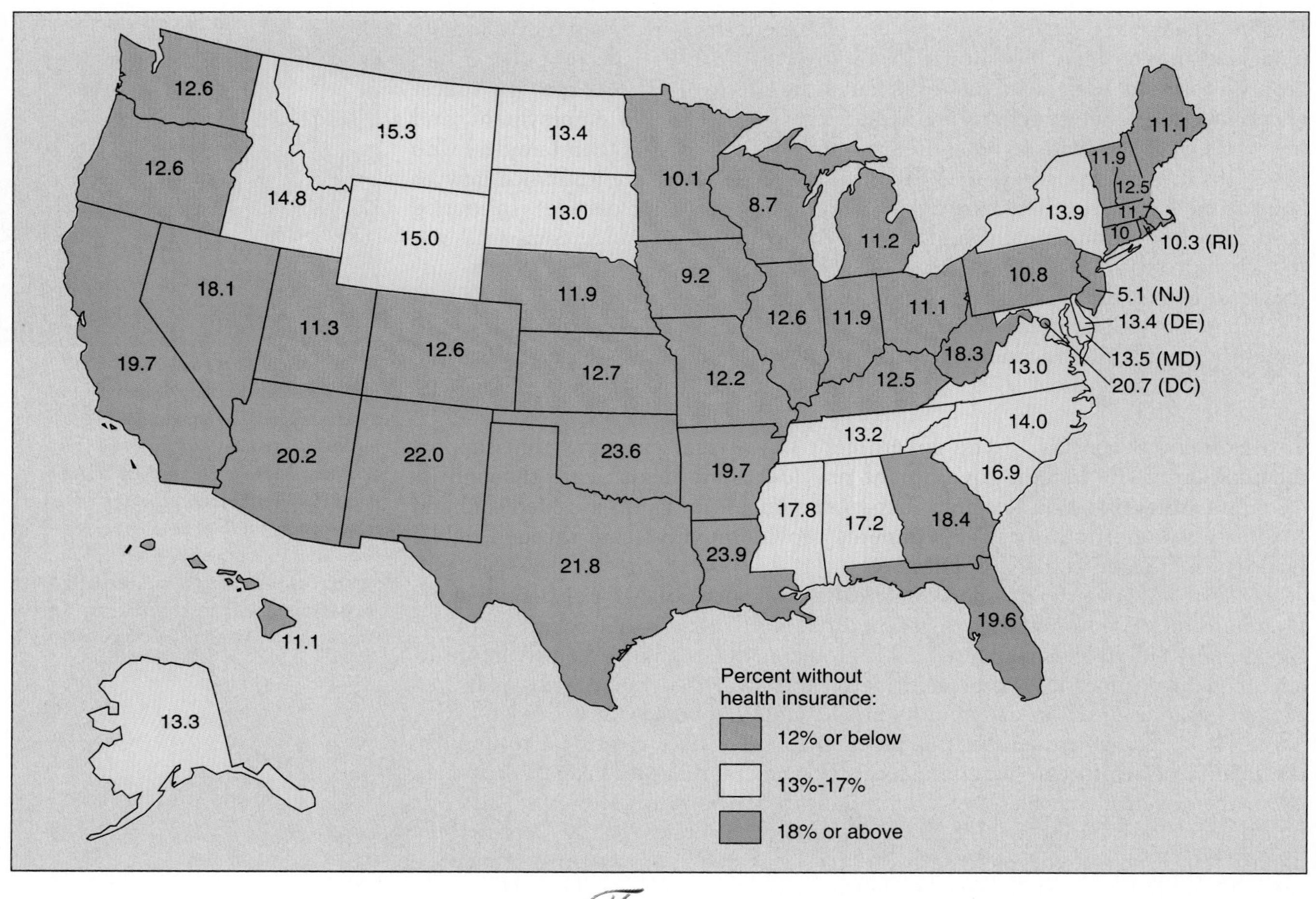

FIGURE 19.2
PERCENT OF PERSONS WITHOUT HEALTH-CARE COVERAGE, 1993

Approximately 15 percent of the U.S. population has no health insurance. These people, generally the unemployed and the working poor, are concentrated among those who are under 65 and have family incomes of less than $20,000. Interestingly, those without health insurance have worse health than those with insurance.

SOURCE: U.S. Bureau of the Census, 1995, Table 170.

The uninsured are not entirely without health care. Every county in the United States makes some provision for the so-called medically indigent. The care provided for these people is largely emergency treatment—and may be limited to that necessary to save a person's life—rather than prevention and diagnosis. Care is provided at public hospitals, clinics, and emergency wards, where patients are often treated as unworthy, kept standing in long lines, and sometimes given second-rate treatment by overworked and underpaid staff. According to one physician who regularly treats indigent patients, "The public hospitals provide to the poor a level of treatment the rest of us would find absolutely unacceptable" (Hilfiker, in Jones, Jr., 1994).

Why Doesn't the United States Have National Health Insurance?

Health care in the United States is available on a fee-for-service basis. As with dry cleaning, you get what you can afford. If you cannot afford health care, you might not get any. This situation makes the United States unique among industrialized nations. In the rest of the industrialized world, medical care, like education, is regarded as a good that should be available to all regardless of ability to pay (Ginzberg 1994). Thus all industrialized nations except the United States provide health care to their citizens through provision of national health insurance, which is funded by the government and paid for by taxes.

The advantages alleged for a national health insurance program are that it equalizes care to rich and poor and that it balances the costs and benefits of providing health care. In the United States, the current combination of private insurance for the employed (healthier) and public insurance for the unemployed (less healthy) means that private companies get the profitable cases and government the expensive ones. National health insurance is seen as a way to benefit the taxpayer by letting government use the profits from insuring its healthy citizens to balance the costs of insuring its sick citizens. Critics of national health insurance argue that government programs are less efficient and cost effective than private programs and that we need more diversity in health care options than might be available under a single monolithic program.

Why is the United States alone among industrialized nations in having no national health insurance? Certainly the AMA has strongly opposed national health insurance, but that cannot be the whole reason. Nor is public opposition the reason. Polls show that a large majority of the American public believe that adequate medical care is a right to which a person is entitled as a citizen rather than a privilege that must be earned, and over half are willing to pay somewhat higher taxes to provide adequate health care to all who need it (Gallup Poll 1993). The reason that the United States has no national health insurance is suggested by research showing that the quality of national health insurance across countries and the rapidity with which it was implemented vary directly with the political strength of the working class (Navarro 1992, 1994). If this is true, then the absence of national health insurance is linked directly to the absence of a working-class or socialist party in the United States (see Chapter 16 and 17).

America's Fleeting Effort to Reform Health Care

During 1993 and 1994, Americans were inundated with news, public service announcements, and paid advertisements concerning President Bill Clinton's health care reform initiative. His plan was two-pronged: (1) slow the soaring growth of health care costs and (2) assure that all Americans have uninterrupted health insurance coverage, regardless of employment status, the existence of disabilities or chronic conditions, early retirement from work, or self-employment. While maintaining current programs such as Medicare, the administration's proposal would have required all employers to provide, and all employees to purchase, medical insurance. Government subsidies would help offset insurance costs for small businesses, early retirees, and others for whom the cost of insurance was prohibitive. Some analysts predicted that President Clinton's presidency would

Americans receive continuous messages about how to lead a healthy life: less salt, less fat, fewer calories, more roughage, and lots of exercise. Although more of us are paying attention to these messages, research shows that they are most likely to be picked up by well-educated and well-off people. Almost anybody can go for walks or do sit-ups at home, but the people who are most likely to exercise are those who can afford memberships at health clubs.

succeed or fail on the basis of his health care reform initiative; but by 1995, the plan was dead, and few were discussing health care reform at all. The private health insurance industry, along with the AMA, was mainly responsible for squelching the plan. Insurance companies lobbied in Congress against the reforms and spent millions of dollars on advertisements that frightened people about the proposed changes (Lacayo 1994; Waldman 1994).

STRATEGIES FOR IMPROVING AMERICA'S HEALTH

Like other people's education, other people's health affects each one of us. Sick people may spread contagious diseases, for instance, and poor health costs Americans money in lowered economic productivity resulting from missed work.

Good health depends on social roles and economic conditions, on genetic background, on biological agents such as hostile bacteria and viruses, on preventive health care and a healthy lifestyle, and on good medical care after illness develops. Efforts to improve the health of the population thus have to take a many-pronged approach. Generally, there are three strategies for improving America's health: encouraging healthy lifestyles, extending health care service, and reducing inequality. Each has its own political and economic price tag.

ENCOURAGING HEALTHY LIFESTYLES

The first policy alternative, encouraging people to adopt healthy lifestyles and educating them about the risks associated with lifestyle choices, is inexpensive and politically safe. It assumes that the cause of poor health lies in individual bad habits and that the cure also lies in individual hands. Aspects of this plan include seat-belt legislation, anti-smoking campaigns, fitness programs, and the like (Becker 1993).

Conflict theorists generally see the emphasis on wellness and healthy lifestyles as yet another instance of blaming the victim (Navarro 1993, 1994). They argue that the cause of disadvantage in health is the fundamental inequalities in our social structure, inequalities that cannot be alleviated by lectures about "just say no," "eat your vegetables," and "get plenty of exercise."

PROVIDING MORE EQUITABLE HEALTH CARE

A second policy alternative, in line with that proposed by President Clinton in 1993, is to extend health care services to all citizens, rich and poor. Such a policy would provide better prenatal care, more vaccinations and inoculations, more screening and diagnostic tests, and more equitable distribution of treatment. Although the United States remains alone among industrialized countries in not having a comprehensive health insurance plan, Medicaid and Medicare have gone far to address some of the worst inequalities in our system.

More universal availability of health care would decrease infant mortality and raise general life expectancy. A system of free, comprehensive health care, however, would not equalize mortality differences by social class. Studies in Britain demonstrate that although overall mortality dropped after socialized medicine was instituted, class differences in mortality remained. Equal availability of treatment

> **THINKING CRITICALLY**
>
> What would *you* do, if you were President of the United States, to provide more equitable health care to U.S. citizens?

cannot erase the results of a lifetime of living under very different circumstances: worse neighborhoods, more dangerous jobs, less self-esteem and happiness, more unemployment, less control over one's life in general (Marmot, Kogevinas, and Elston 1987).

Reducing Class and Race Disadvantage

The most radical health care policy would be to equalize life chances by reducing poverty, racism, unemployment, and other disadvantages that damage health and encourage poor health habits. Such a program would reduce the differentials in illness as well as the differentials in health care for people who have become ill.

Because the racial differential in life expectancy is so embarrassingly large, the government has appointed several task forces to make recommendations about minority and low-income health problems. However, Americans' current unwillingness to spend money to work toward this goal makes it seem very unlikely that any substantial progress will be made on the health deficit suffered by either minorities or the poor.

Summary

Sociological analysis suggests that health and illness are socially structured. To paraphrase C. Wright Mills again, when one person dies too young from stress or bad habits or inadequate health care, that is a personal trouble, and for its remedy we properly look to the character of the individual. When whole classes, races, or sexes consistently suffer significant disadvantage in health and health care, then this is a social problem. The correct statement of the problem and the search for solutions require us to look beyond individuals to consider how social structures and institutions have fostered these patterns. The sociological imagination suggests that significant improvements in the nation's health will require changes in social institutions. Many of these changes will need to take place outside of the medical institution itself.

Global Perspectives: Improving Third World Health

Nearly every nation in the world has a policy objective of providing its citizens with longer, healthier lives. Many industrialized nations have already gone far toward meeting this goal, and the average citizen can expect to live to his or her mid 70s. Among the 41 poorest nations in the world, however, life expectancies are closer to 45, and more than one in 10 infants dies before its first birthday (Camp and Barberis 1992). How can the world's poor countries, many with a GNP per capita of less than $300, improve their people's health?

Obviously, they cannot rely on the same kinds of health care institutions that exist in industrialized nations. In nations where 90 percent of the people live in poverty and in rural villages, many people will never see a physician. Instead, two general strategies are being pursued: reducing risk of infection and providing primary health care.

Reducing Risk of Infection

In the less developed world, the majority of people who die are not dying from stress or from drinking too much or from old age; they are dying of infectious disease. Many infants die of diarrhea associated with parasitic infection (Goliber 1989). Relatively inexpensive strategies to reduce infectious disease include immunizing and vaccinating children, providing safe drinking water, providing for sewage disposal, and keeping down flies and mosquitoes.

On a somewhat more expensive level, the risk of infection can be reduced by even modest improvements in standard of living—in particular, by better diets and better personal cleanliness. Cleanliness, of course, requires water—a commodity often in short supply. Better diets are also difficult to implement among impoverished peoples. One of the easiest and most effective ways to reduce infant vulnerability to infection is to encourage mothers to breast-feed their children for a longer period.

Providing Primary Health Care

Primary health care programs emphasize accessible caregivers over well-trained caregivers; they aim to get the largest amount of basic care to the most people. The best example of the primary health care approach is China's "barefoot doctor" program. In the Chinese system, each neighborhood elects three individuals who will have part-time responsibility for health care: the barefoot doctor, the health aide, and the midwife. The barefoot doctor, who is given a three-month training course, is charged with basic health education and illness prevention, treatment of minor illnesses, vaccinations, and contraception. Since the barefoot doctor is responsible for only 100 to 200 people, he or she is expected to know them intimately and to be able to provide them with suggestions that will led to a healthier life. The

This health care worker confirms studies that show that a modest investment in training and vaccine can make a big dent in mortality in poor countries. Wide dispersion of primary health care workers is probably more effective at reducing Third World mortality than building high-tech hospitals.

health aide's primary responsibility is sanitation—making sure that water and food supplies are clean. The midwife delivers babies. Only in larger communities are physicians with Western-style training available, and even these physicians have much shorter training periods than do U.S. physicians.

The quality of care provided by this system is not as high as what would be offered if Western-style physicians were available for everyone. A difficult birth is more likely to result in the death of either infant or mother; more time is likely to pass before cancer is diagnosed. Nevertheless, this system allowed China, a nation whose 1990 GNP per capita was still only $330, to increase its life expectancy to 68 years and lower its infant mortality to 4 percent (Population Reference Bureau 1990).

SUMMARY

Most people in the poorest, least developed nations have little access to modern health care (Goliber 1989). Happily, substantial increases in life expectancy can be realized even with few physicians, nurses, and hospitals. Aggressive use of infection reduction and primary care strategies may increase life expectancy to age 60 or 65 even without substantial increases in standard of living. According to the United Nations, however, closing the remaining gap in life expectancy will depend on "the promotion of social justice, social mobility, and social development, and a more equitable distribution of income, land, social services, and amenities" (United Nations 1984, 45).

AIDS: A CASE STUDY IN THE SOCIOLOGY OF MEDICINE

In the fewer than 20 years since AIDS was first recognized, virtually no American has escaped being touched by it. Many of us have family members, friends, or acquaintances with AIDS, and all of us help foot the nation's bill for AIDS research and treatment. Although only a small portion of the population is currently infected by AIDS, the disease already represents a severe burden on our health care system and threatens to become a modern-day plague. We use the AIDS epidemic as a case study to illustrate the varieties of concern in the field of medical sociology.

AIDS: WHAT IS IT?

AIDS (acquired immunodeficiency syndrome) was first recognized in 1981, when 185 cases were reported in the United States. At present, it is assumed to have virtually a 100 percent fatality rate. By 1995, 513,485 cases of AIDS had been reported to the U.S. Centers for Disease Control, and 319,849 of these people had already died (U.S. Centers for Disease Control 1995). AIDS is now the leading cause of death among American men aged 25 to 44 ("The AIDS Front" 1995).

AIDS begins with exposure to a virus, HIV (human immunodeficiency virus). Present estimates suggest that somewhere between 800,000 and 1 million Americans carry HIV (Centers for Disease Control 1994). Estimates suggest that 30 percent of HIV carriers will develop AIDS within nine years of becoming infected. Whether all those infected will eventually develop AIDS is simply not known.

THE SOCIAL EPIDEMIOLOGY OF AIDS

The social epidemiology of AIDS varies around the world. It can be spread by exchange of blood, but it is primarily a sexually transmitted disease (STD). Like all STDs, it is most characteristic of people who have multiple sexual partners.

Table 19.5 gives a breakdown of AIDS cases diagnosed in the United States according to sex, age, and risk factors. In the United States, the primary risk factor leading to AIDS has been homosexual contact: Seventy-three percent of diagnosed cases are homosexual or bisexual males (51 percent without and 7 percent with intravenous drug use). The next largest category consists of intravenous (IV) drug users (25 percent). The fastest-growing categories of victims, however, are heterosexuals and children. Most of the children who have AIDS contracted it from their infected mothers during gestation. The rapidity with which AIDS may spread to the heterosexual population is indicated by a survey of blood donors in New York who were found to be HIV positive. Seventy percent of the homosexual males said they had had sexual intercourse with a woman in the last six months; nearly all of the intravenous drug users had had heterosexual relations.

TABLE 19.5

REPORTED AIDS CASES BY AGE, SEX, AND RISK FACTOR, UNITED STATES, 1995

The single largest category of AIDS victims consists of adult homosexual or bisexual males. The fastest-growing categories, however, are heterosexual intravenous drug users and their partners and children. Because taking precautions against AIDS is related to social class, it is expected that AIDS will become disproportionately a disease of the disadvantaged.

TOTAL	100%
SEX, ADULTS	
MALE	86
FEMALE	14
AGE	
ADULT	99
CHILDREN	1
ADULTS, BY RISK FACTOR	
HOMOSEXUAL/BISEXUAL MALE	51
HOMOSEXUAL/BISEXUAL MALE AND INTRAVENOUS DRUG USER	7
INTRAVENOUS DRUG USER ONLY	25
TRANSFUSION	2
HETEROSEXUAL CONTACT WITH ONE OF ABOVE	8
OTHER/UNDETERMINED	7
CHILDREN, BY RISK FACTOR	
PARENT WITH HIV OR AT RISK OF HIV	90%
TRANSFUSION	9
OTHER/UNDETERMINED	1

SOURCE: United States Centers for Disease Control 1996, http://www.cdc.gov/nchstp/hiv_aids/dhap_hi.htm.

AIDS is not spread through casual contact. If you don't use drugs intravenously (or share needles when you do), if you are sexually inactive or your sexual activity is restricted to a single, faithful partner who is not infected, and if you don't admit unscreened blood into your system, you are not likely to get AIDS (Bolton 1994). For those who have multiple sexual partners, using a condom during intercourse reduces (but does not eliminate) the chances of contracting AIDS. Who takes all of these precautions? The answer is the same kinds of people who watch their cholesterol and exercise regularly.

Greater awareness of the risks of AIDS has reduced the number of AIDS cases among homosexual men—a group that spans the entire social class distribution of society. Intravenous drug users, however, are disproportionately drawn from lower social classes. They comprise a group that, by definition, is not particularly health conscious. As a result, it is expected that AIDS will become increasingly a disease of the poor and the disadvantaged. The Centers for Disease Control estimates that up to 20 percent of the nation's homeless carry HIV (Dahl 1991). African Americans and Hispanics are two to five times more likely to contract AIDS than non-Hispanic whites with the same risk factors. Twenty-nine percent of children with AIDS are African American, and another 16 percent are Hispanic (Centers for Disease Control 1992).

AIDS AND THE NEGOTIATION OF IDENTITY

When AIDS was first identified in the United States, it was a disease associated with groups that were already stigmatized as deviant: gay men and IV drug users (Hassin 1994). The combination of a mysterious, fatal disease and stigmatized subgroups made AIDS doubly feared. Schools rejected children with AIDS, homes of

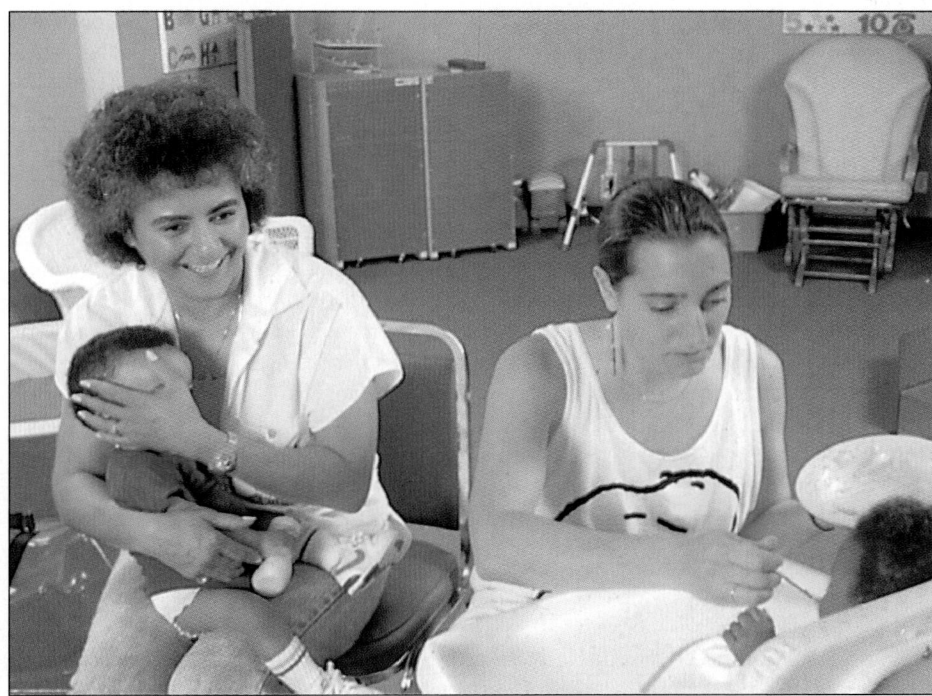

The largest group of AIDS victims is made up of gay or bisexual men, and this group continues to be disproportionately at risk of contracting AIDS. Nevertheless, the fastest-growing group of AIDS victims is made up of infants and children. These children's futures are short and their presents bleak. Because their parents also have AIDS, many are being reared in institutions. Here, volunteers help care for AIDS babies at the Birk Childcare Center in New York.

AIDS victims were burned, and AIDS victims were discriminated against in transportation, housing, and employment.

Because AIDS is associated with lifestyle choices, AIDS victims were largely denied the sick role. The disease was thought to be their fault, something they could have avoided. The spread of AIDS into the heterosexual population and the growing number of children with AIDS have reduced the tendency to divide the victims into the innocent and the guilty and have increased the likelihood that AIDS victims will be granted the sick role. Increasingly, AIDS victims and HIV carriers are offered the same legal protection and health care available to people with other infectious diseases (Fee and Fox 1992).

All of us enter into a difficult negotiation when we face dying, a new role for which we are generally not well prepared (Lofland 1978). Whom do we tell? How should we act? Dying of AIDS is even more difficult than dying of some other terminal condition. Some people dying of AIDS must deal with the first public acknowledgment of their homosexuality, bisexuality, or drug use. Nearly all AIDS victims find that some members of their communities respond to their condition with fear and hostility rather than sympathy. The stigma that AIDS patients face makes their maintenance of a positive identity especially difficult, and AIDS patients often experience great distress in dealing with the social as well as the physical consequences of AIDS.

AIDS and the Health Care System

In 1993, it was estimated that the United States spent more than $2 billion on the diagnosis and treatment of HIV and AIDS (Krieger 1995). As more HIV-positive individuals come down with full-blown AIDS, the disease may swamp our medical facilities and our capacities to pay for treatment. Already, in some central African nations, one out of every four hospital beds is occupied by an AIDS patient, and a similar situation is developing in Asia, where AIDS is now spreading rapidly (Cowley 1994). How are we to meet the demand?

The potential cost of AIDS treatment threatens to overwhelm current mechanisms of paying for health care. To focus on only one indicator of this cost, consider drug regimens involving azidothymidine (AZT) and protease inhibitors, drugs that can temporarily control, but not cure, AIDS. Such a drug regimen can cost $18,000 annually for one person (King 1996). The cost of drugs is only a small part of the total cost of AIDS treatment from the patient's diagnosis to his or her death. Because AIDS is more and more a disease of the disadvantaged and because private insurance companies are finding ways to avoid covering AIDS-related costs, fewer AIDS patients will be covered by private health insurance, and the burden on federal, state, and local health agencies threatens to be enormous.

Furthermore, how will health care workers cope with the risk of contracting AIDS? Doctors, nurses, and dentists deal with blood on a daily basis, which means that they are at risk if their patients have HIV. If HIV-infected blood touches an open sore on their hands or if they nick themselves with a needle just used on an AIDS patient, they risk getting the disease themselves. The risk is enough to have driven some people out of the medical field.

What Can Be Done?

Public policy on AIDS must advance on several fronts. First, we need to continue to invest research efforts into learning how to keep HIV from turning into

AIDS and how to cure AIDS. Second, we need to reduce the transmission of HIV to uninfected populations. We have already virtually eliminated blood transfusions as a source of AIDS infection (Yankauer 1988); we need to move decisively on the other risk factors.

One such risk factor is intravenous drug use. Although one would not expect IV drug users to be especially health conscious, programs encouraging needle sterilization have been effective (Becker and Joseph 1988). More generally, we need strong programs to prevent and treat intravenous drug abuse, which is a public health menace in itself (Ball et al. 1988).

Another risk factor concerns sexual activity. We need to continue to encourage safer sex practices, primarily use of latex condoms (they *must* be latex) and monogamy. Because sexual transmission plays such a major role in the disease, education about safe sex is a critical step. Studies in San Francisco show that the threat of AIDS *can* scare people into using safer sex practices and can actually reduce the rate at which new HIV cases are added to the population (Rogers 1994). In areas where AIDS is less widespread, however, the attitude may resemble that of one Phoenix resident who decided not to use safer sex practices because "there's only nine people in Arizona who have it and four of them are dead and two of them live in Tucson. So what are your chances?" (Weitz 1989, 273). The man subsequently got AIDS.

Concern with AIDS ultimately brings us back to the same policy options that we confronted earlier in this chapter: promoting more healthful lifestyle choices, offering better health care, and reducing the social and economic inequities that damage health and encourage poor health practices. Educating people about their individual responsibility for their own health is important; but so, too, is changing the social structures that make some groups more vulnerable than others.

SOCIOLOGY ON THE NET

Social forces play a very important role in the health of an individual. One's health can be especially influenced by something as basic as health insurance.

`http://www.census.gov/population/pop-profile/toc.html`

The Census Bureau even keeps statistics on the health of Americans. Click on the report on **Health Insurance**. What percent of Americans were covered by health insurance? What are the characteristics of those who are not covered by health insurance? How do age, race and education influence who is covered? Are you covered by health insurance?

One of the more frightening aspects of our world is the AIDS epidemic. It is a controversial disease whose victims are often blamed for their own affliction. What is happening in the U.S. and throughout the world with regards to AIDS?

`gopher://odie.niaid.nih.gov:70/11/aids/cdcds`

We have reached the Center For Disease Control's AIDS Daily Summary. Browse through some of these files. What kind of information do they provide? How is the AIDS battle going? Now let's shift to the world scene by visiting the United Nations and the World Health Organization.

`http://www.unaids.org.`

APPLICATIONS IN DIVERSITY

How Will California's Proposition 187 Affect Public Health?

In November 1994, citizens of California passed Proposition 187, which denies schooling and nonemergency medical services to the state's 1.7 million undocumented immigrants, most of whom are from Mexico and Central America. In passing Proposition 187, voters also required health workers to report any "illegal" who might show up seeking care.

Proposition 187 is meant to deter the influx of illegal immigrants to California, enabling the state to cut spending on them and hence to improve health services for legal citizens. But the measure could backfire. For one thing, the proposition may cost the state money by eliminating less expensive, basic health care for illegal immigrants while preserving emergency services. Fighting off a strep infection, for example, can be done with a prescription for antibiotics, which might cost about $50. But allowing the infection to worsen and then treating it in a hospital emergency room could cost the state as much as $20,000.

Moreover, the medical impact of Proposition 187 will not necessarily be confined to illegal immigrants or their children. As illegal immigrants begin to avoid clinics and hospitals, their untreated diseases are expected to threaten the larger population. For instance, the Community Health Foundation of East Los Angeles normally immunizes about 400 children every two weeks. However, in the first two weeks after the passage of Proposition 187, the number dropped to 83.

As another example, surveys of California's Asian and Central American immigrants have found that as many as 70 percent arrive carrying the germ that causes tuberculosis (TB). Though most carriers remain healthy and noncontagious, they are always at risk of developing the disease and transmitting it to others. Treatment requires consistent drug therapy for as long as two years, during which the patient regularly sees the appropriate health care practitioner. The incidence of TB in California was rising before Proposition 187 passed, and officials are concerned that rates will increase faster now. Governor Pete Wilson, who generally favors Proposition 187, vowed to preserve medical services that "protect the general public," including screening and treatment for TB. But if doctors become de facto immigration agents, it will be difficult to persuade people without papers to seek any kind of nonemergency health care. As Dr. Shirley Gannin, director of disease control programs for Los Angeles County, explained, "It's hard to educate [illegal immigrants] to the need for prevention when there's a threat attached" (in Cowley and Murr 1994, p. 33).

Proposition 187 could also undermine the health of children born on U.S. soil to illegal immigrant mothers. By virtue of being born in the United States, these children are U.S. citizens. If illegal immigrants could demonstrate financial need, they qualified for free prenatal care under pre-Proposition 187 conditions. But Proposition 187 denies pregnant women who are illegal immigrants any treatment unless they appear at a public hospital in labor. The goal is to encourage these women to go back to their home countries. But there is no reason to assume that this will happen. If it does not happen, health experts predict that more mothers and infants will die and more U.S. citizens will be born in need of chronic and expensive medical care.

Legal battles over Proposition 187 could go on for years. Almost immediately after it was passed, opponents challenged its constitutionality in the courts. Pending these various court challenges, a federal judge in Los Angeles stayed the law (put enforcement of the law on hold). Until Proposition 187 clears the courts, public hospitals in California will not check patients' immigration status. In the meantime, California officials are working to translate the somewhat vague language of Proposition 187 into specific regulations. Some doctors and other health practitioners say that they will defy the new law before they will help to enforce it (Cowley and Murr 1994).

Thinking Critically

What do you think? How might states like California control the costs of state services to illegal immigrants without jeopardizing public health? Is it moral to deny health care to anyone who requests it? What kind of health care should be provided to illegal immigrants who are pregnant? Does the United States have any moral obligation to protect the health of its neighbors in Mexico? If so, what?

Click on the **Research Documents** section, and under the title **Epidemiology** open **The HIV/AIDS Situation**. How many people are currently infected with AIDS and how many have died from this disease throughout the world? What are the projections for next year? How do children contract this disease and in what parts of the world are children at the greatest risk?

The American Medical Association is a very powerful organization that speaks for the majority of physicians in the U.S. Let's go to the AMA home page.

`http:www.ama-assn.org`

Browse around the **home page** and then open the section entitled **About the American Medical Association**. Pay particular attention to the Mission Statement. What does the American Medical Association seek to promote? Who does this organization claim to represent? Now scroll down to the bottom of the page and click on the **Advocacy and Communications** button. Open the section on **Grassroots Political Action** and open the highlighted report **About Grassroots Political Action**. What is POLEGRA? What is AMPAC? Now it is time to shift gears and return to the Federal Election Commission which keeps track of organizations like AMPAC.

`http://www.fec.gov/finance/finmenu.htm`

We are back at the section that deals with PACs and candidates. Scroll down to the section on **PACs** and click on **PAC Summary Financial Information**. Scroll down to and open the **Top 50 PACs—Contributions to Candidates**. Can you find the American Medical Association Political Action Committee? Return to the previous **menu**, only this time open the **Top 50 PACs—Cash on Hand**. Where is AMPAC? You might also check out the **Top 50 PACs—Disbursements**. Does it appear that the AMA is politically active? What conclusions can you draw based upon these findings? Please note that donating money to politicians does not necessarily guarantee success for your position, but it certainly guarantees that you will be heard.

SUMMARY

1. Health and illness are negotiated statuses. If we can negotiate a sick role, we are excused from our normal obligations as long as we follow instructions and seek to get well. Whether a condition is labeled as sick, deviant, or perfectly normal is relative.
2. Three statuses are especially relevant to the social epidemiology of health in the United States: gender, social class, and race/ethnicity. Men, racial and ethnic minorities, and those with lower socioeconomic status have higher mortality rates.
3. The health disadvantage associated with lower socioeconomic status goes beyond a simple inability to afford health care. Lower social class is associated with lower standards of living, more stress, lower education, and poorer coping strategies, all of which increase the likelihood that individuals will need health care.
4. From a sociological point of view, a healthy lifestyle is one that includes satisfying social roles, some control over one's social environment, and integration into one's community. Much more than smoking, drinking, and eating one's vegetables, these aspects of healthy lifestyle are related to class and race.
5. Physicians are professionals; they have a high degree of control not only over their own work but also over all others in the medical institution. Structural

functionalists argue that physicians earn so much because of scarce talents and abilities, but conflict theorists argue that high salaries are due to physicians' use of power, in part through the AMA. Physicians' independence is lower now than it used to be.

6 Nurses comprise the largest single occupation in the health care industry. Nurses earn much less than physicians, have less prestige, take orders instead of give them, and are predominantly female. The hospital is a major arena in the battle for gender equality.

7 There are three kinds of hospitals: proprietary, nonprofit, and state hospitals. Hospital costs are driven up by expensive new technologies, competition among providers, high consumer demand, and the practice of defensive medicine.

8 Most Americans (about 70 percent) are covered by private insurance. Medicare helps cover senior citizens, but the poor are seriously underinsured. About 15 percent of Americans have no insurance. The uninsured are less healthy than the insured.

9 The United States does not have national health insurance because it does not have a strong workers' party. It is one of the few nations in the Western world that does not make medical care available regardless of the patient's ability to pay.

10 There are three strategies for improving America's health: encouraging healthy lifestyles, extending healthcare service, and reducing inequality. The first is cheapest but may lead to blaming the victim. Better health care is important but does not address the fact that the poor and disadvantaged are more likely to have serious illnesses in the first place.

11 In the less developed world, people are more likely to die from infectious diseases than from old age. Reducing infection risk in peripheral nations involves relatively inexpensive strategies such as vaccinating children as well as providing primary health care.

12 The two largest categories of AIDS victims are homosexual or bisexual men and intravenous drug users. Heterosexuals and children are the fastest-growing categories of victims. AIDS is likely to swamp the U.S. health care system. Public policy must address its prevention and cure.

13 California's Proposition 187, passed in 1994, is an example of attempts to keep the costs of health care down. But it may backfire, since denying all but emergency medical care to illegal immigrants could be costly both in money and in terms of the public health.

Suggested Readings

AUERBACK, Judith D., Wypijewska, Christina, and Brodie, H. Keith (eds.). 1994. *AIDS and Behavior: An Integrated Approach*. Washington, D.C.: National Academy Press. A collection of writings that discuss the epidemiology of HIV/AIDS, along with ways to address the epidemic.

BLANK, Robert H., and Bonnicksen, Andrea (eds.). 1994. *Medicine Unbound: The Human Body and the Limits of Medical Intervention*. New York: Columbia University Press. Essays and research reports on the fascinating technological advances in medicine in recent years, along with warnings that technology cannot solve all our health challenges.

CHAPMAN, Audrey R. (ed.). 1994. *Health Care Reform: A Human Rights Approach*. Washington, D.C.: Georgetown University Press. Research reports and essays that argue for health care reform of various types and point out ways to achieve it.

COCKERHAM, William. 1995. *Medical Sociology*, 6th ed. Englewood Cliffs, N.J.: Prentice-Hall. A textbook on medical sociology by an active researcher in the field. The volume provides a balanced presentation of theoretical views along with a detailed analysis of how medical institutions and professions operate.

HILFIKER, David, M.D. 1994. *Not All of Us Are Saints*. New York: Hill and Wang. A physician's personal account of how he left his successful medical practice in rural Minnesota and moved with his family to inner-city Washington, D.C., to work with the poor.

MOSLEY, W. Henry, and Cowley, Peter. 1991. *The Challenge of World Health*. *Population Bulletin* 46 (4). December. Washington, D.C.: Population Reference Bureau. A readable and informative pamphlet on the health status of people around the world and what can be done to improve humans' health.

NAVARRO, Vincente. 1993. *Dangerous to Your Health: Capitalism in Health Care*. New York: Monthly Review Press. A conflict analysis of how inequalities in medical care and in health are produced by an unequal society, which, in turn, is produced by capitalism.

SCHOUB, B. D. 1994. *AIDS and HIV in Perspective: A Guide to Understanding the Virus and Its Consequences*. New York: Cambridge University Press. Less sociological than medical, this book gives the facts about the virus and its effects on the human body.

SIGNORIELLI, Nancy. 1993. *Mass Media Images and Impact on Health*. *Westport*, Conn.: Greenwood Press. A study of how the media present health issues in the areas of physical disabilities, AIDS, smoking, alcoholism, nutrition, and environmental risks, among others. The overall conclusion is that the media tend to focus on individual behaviors rather than social structure.

UNIT FIVE

Change

CHAPTER 20

Technology and Social Change

OUTLINE

PROLOGUE

Have You Ever . . . wandered through an antique shop and wondered what some of the things you saw there were for? Unpacked a new computer and questioned how you would ever connect all those cables? Both these situations point to the rapid technological changes characteristic of our society. It's possible that some of those antiques you marveled at were little more than 25 years old!

Ours is a particularly swiftly changing society. For one thing, the individualism characteristic of U.S. culture is highly compatible with change. For another thing, through government funding, the United States has institutionalized scientific research, which encourages innovation and change.

Two decades ago, a scholar hit the best-seller list with a popular book that questioned people's ability to direct or adjust to the hurtling pace of social change. Alvin Toffler (1970) gave the name *future shock* to the personal and social problems people might experience as a result of rapid social change. He maintained that a growing number of people would be baffled and disoriented by social change so brisk that many previously learned attitudes and skills would no longer work.

Toffler expected future shock to grow more widespread and severe and was not optimistic about the ability to relieve it. His pessimism may have been short-sighted, however. Young people especially—and even many grandparents—seem to have readily adapted to modems, faxes, CD-ROMs, and color copy machines. Nevertheless, fast-moving technology means grappling with many unprecedented—and sometimes profoundly serious—issues of social change. This chapter explores today's changing technology and its impact on social change.

It's a pretty safe bet that you have made use of technology from the minute your alarm clock woke you this morning. You may have made coffee in your electric coffeemaker or grabbed a sandwich from a vending machine. Maybe you used a modem to read your E-mail or listened to your favorite music on a new CD. It's possible that you walked into your neighborhood drugstore and checked your blood pressure. The pervasive influence of technology in our daily lives today is obvious. Moreover, our tools are far more powerful—and potentially more dangerous—than ever before. As a result, it is vitally important that we understand the impact of technology on our society and search for ways to limit its negative effects as well as maximize its positive ones. This chapter explores technology and its relation to social change.

We define **technology** as the human application of knowledge to the making of tools and hence to humans' use of natural resources. It is important to note that the term *technology* refers not only to the tools themselves (aspects of material culture) but also to our beliefs, values, and attitudes regarding those tools (aspects of nonmaterial culture). Moreover, while we may be inclined to think of technology in terms of today's "high-tech" advances, such as computers and lasers, technology has been a component of culture from the beginnings of human life. Clay vessels and woven baskets are examples.

Technology involves the human application of knowledge to the making of tools and hence to humans' use of natural resources.

Technology and social change are closely related concepts. **Social change** is any significant modification or transformation of social structures or institutions over

Social change is any significant modification or transformation of social structures and sociocultural processes over time.

time. Technology is one important cause of social change. Chapter 4 describes how technology (the hoe, subsequent irrigation systems, and eventually coal and electricity) helped transform human communities from hunting, fishing, and gathering societies to horticultural, then agricultural, and then industrial societies.

Because technology defines the limits of what a society can do, technological innovation is a major impetus to social change. Meanwhile, new technologies are propelled by new needs created by a changing culture and society. The result is a never-ending cycle in which social change both causes and results from new technology. This point becomes more apparent as we examine the nature of technology.

The Nature of Technology

A **discovery** is the finding or uncovering of something that existed before but had remained unnoticed.

An **invention** is a new use of or a new combination of existing knowledge or technologies.

Technology is inseparable from human behavior. From their earliest beginnings, human beings have been uniquely innovative. They used their intellects to make **discoveries** by finding things that already existed but had gone unnoticed, such as bacteria and blood circulation. They also created **inventions** by combining existing components of their environment (a round log and a pole, for example) to come up with new ideas and tools (a wheel and axle). In making discoveries and inventions, humans have continuously created, improved, and used tools to facilitate their necessary adaptation to their surroundings.

Tooling for Survival

Technology arose as an ongoing type of human activity because, first of all, humans have the necessary intelligence to apply knowledge to problems—that is, to fashion technologies. As human beings, our ability to invent and use tools sets us apart from other creatures. It's true that beavers build dams and otters use rocks to open shellfish. But humans are indeed exceptional both in their capacity to make tools and in their reliance on them.

A second reason why technology has always been integral to human life is that the human condition requires creating tools. As a species, human beings lack many of the innate abilities that characterize other animals. Humans do not run as fast as cheetahs, for example, or see as sharply as eagles. Unaided by tools, human

Why are the Inuits of Alaska different from the Australian Aboriginals? One apparent reason involves differences in their physical environments. The physical and natural environment of an area sets the stage for the technological and other cultural adaptations of a society. Hot or cold climates, fertile or sandy soils, dense or sparse vegetation, the presence of animals, rainfall, and fuels—all are environmental conditions to which people must adapt. Because different societies face different physical challenges, they develop an array of different technologies.

beings' physical abilities are seriously limited. For instance, humans do not have weather-resistant pelts to protect them from the cold and rain—hence the need to fashion clothing. Not equipped with sharp claws or teeth for hunting, humans had to fashion tools, such as the bow and arrow, to acquire animal protein for food. The additional power gained through the use of technology has enabled human beings to survive.

The original purpose of technology may have been basic human survival, but its purpose was broadened over thousands of years of human existence. Gradually, technologies were developed so that people could be more comfortable or do things more quickly and with less effort. Humans could have continued to live in caves, but they designed alternative housing, which they saw as an improvement. In short, humans develop and apply technology in order to do things not otherwise possible or to do them more easily. Put another way, the purpose of technology has always been and continues to be to expand the realm of human possibility.

Technology Is Cumulative

The development of technology is an inherently dynamic and cumulative process. It is dynamic, or ongoing, because humans seldom see a tool as absolutely perfect; there almost always seems to be room for improvement. An arrowhead can be honed more finely and sharply. A computer disk can be made to hold more information on a smaller surface. Technology is cumulative inasmuch as every innovation paves the way for yet another. The transistor, developed in the late 1940s, helped pave the way for the personal computers we use today. The lessons learned in working with an existing technology very often provide materials, tools, and, most importantly, a knowledge base for the next stage of development. The Focus section of this chapter describes one example of technology as cumulative—biotechnology.

Without thinking about the social consequences of technology for now, we can say that the process of change in a particular technology or tool is almost always characterized by improvement. Once invented, the internal combustion engine was made more powerful and efficient; computer circuits pack more and more components on a single chip. When judged only on the basis of what can be done and how efficiently, technology exemplifies continuing advancement. But we need to ask whether, to what extent, and under what conditions technological advances constitute "progress" in a more general sense. Before answering this question, we first explore how technology causes social change.

How Technology Causes Social Change

Besides technological advances, other things can prompt social change—although usually these are connected with technological advances. For instance, population growth prompts social change: U.S. society is not as uncrowded as it used to be, and the apartment house and condominium are replacing the single-family home on its quarter-acre lot. Sometimes, random, unpredictable events affect the course of social change. The 1995 bombing of an Oklahoma City federal office building prompted changes in federal building security systems, along with other changes such as increased concern about gun control and heightened awareness of U.S. paramilitary groups. Our emphasis in this chapter, however, is on how technological advances cause social change. We begin with a principal factor in social change: technological diffusion.

The Diffusion of Technology

Diffusion is the process by which cultural traits spread from group to group when one culture or subculture comes into contact with another.

Even the most creative society discovers or invents only a small portion of all its innovations. Much of the content of U.S. culture and most cultures has come from diffusion. **Diffusion** is the process by which cultural traits spread from group to group when one culture (or subculture) comes into contact with another. The concept does not apply only to technology. For example, the idea that humans could control the number of children they would conceive originated in and was slowly diffused throughout Western Europe (Chapter 21). In this chapter, however, we focus on technological diffusion.

Figure 20.1 shows the diffusion of Internet and E-mail technology around the globe. The information revolution began in the United States and is rapidly spreading over the world (Watson 1995). One way this happens is that computer hardware that has become outdated in the United States is bought by interna-

Figure 20.1
Diffusion of Internet and E-Mail Technology

Source: Russell Watson, "When Words Are the Best Weapon," *Newsweek*, February 27, 1995, 39.

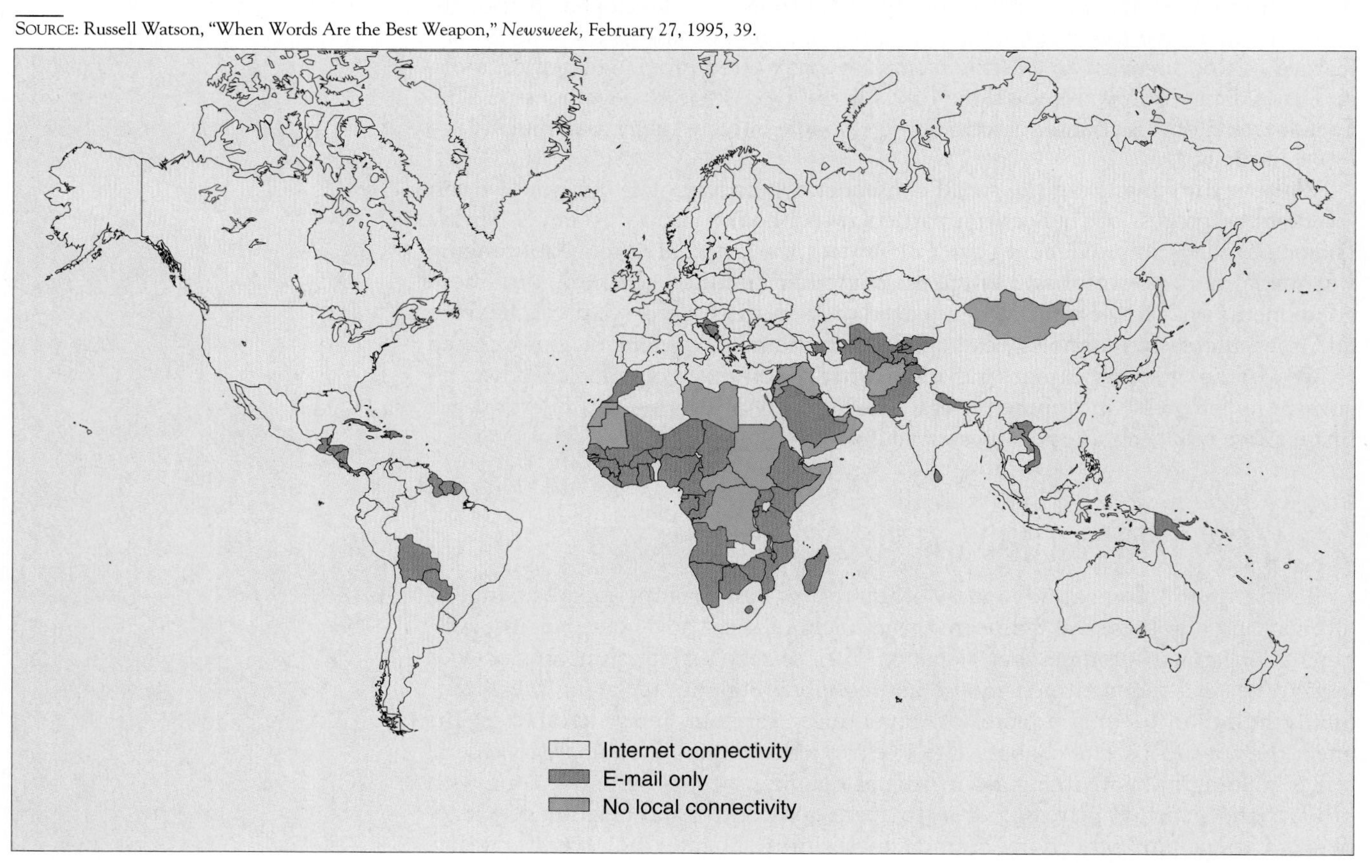

tional recyclers, who sell or donate it to countries such as Russia and Ethiopia (Bryant 1994).

Modern technology not only is diffused itself but also enables cultural diffusion to take place much more rapidly than before. Ideas can sweep the world within days and be introduced into the remotest villages within weeks and months. A fervor of democracy, for example, swept the world in 1989. The year began with pro-democracy student protests in Tienanmen Square in Beijing, China, and ended with the fall of the Berlin Wall and the toppling of communist governments in Eastern Europe. Many of those seeking freedom and democracy relied on the ideals and symbols of the French and American revolutions of 200 years ago; the Statue of Liberty lent her symbolic support to the demonstrations at Tienanmen Square.

The speed of contemporary diffusion means more rapid change in all areas of life, and it also means growing international similarity. In Moscow, Beijing, Nairobi, and Boston, business leaders are wearing the same kinds of suits, and young people are listening to the same kinds of music. An article published in a Soviet sociology journal not long before the dissolution of the U.S.S.R., for example, analyzed the ill effects of "khard-roka and khevi-metallu" on Soviet youth (Sarkitov 1987). On a more serious level, the speed of diffusion means that nuclear weapons and terrorist technologies are also widespread.

THINKING CRITICALLY

Max Weber argued that no single factor can explain social change. Besides a new technology, an idea or a charismatic leader can transform a culture. Can you think of an idea that has caused U.S. society to change? A charismatic leader?

The "Goddess of Liberty," which symbolized the pro-democracy demonstrations in Tienanmen Square in Beijing in 1989, bears a marked resemblance to the U.S. Statue of Liberty. The ideals of democracy, its symbols, and even the constitutional forms that have been developed to embody it have been diffused throughout the world. The rapidity of global diffusion means that ideas, fashions, and technologies are spread rapidly. Nevertheless, economic and political realities may distort or repulse ideas that do not fit with established patterns.

In a striking image of technological diffusion, a Samburu warrior in a remote region of northern Kenya makes a call on his cellular telephone. This photo also illustrates the fact that diffusion is typically a selective process: A group accepts some technologies from outside (the cellular phone) while rejecting others (the navy blue business suit).

CHANGING VALUES AND INSTITUTIONS

Once a new technology is invented or diffused, how, specifically, does it cause social change? Technological advances prompt transformations in values and social institutions according to the following process.

First, new tools and techniques for using those tools create fresh opportunities for individuals. The telephone was patented by Alexander Graham Bell in 1876 and commercialized in the 1880s, and long-distance lines were developed in the 1890s. Together, these developments gave people the novel option of talking with friends and relatives back home even after they had moved away. In another example, technologies meant to counter infertility, such as artificial insemination, *in vitro* fertilization, and embryo transfers, make it possible for otherwise infertile couples—as well as lesbian and postmenopausal women—to bear children.

Second, because they expand our options and possibilities, the new opportunities alter our values and preferences (Mesthene 1993). For example, because they are now able to conceive and bear children, more and more lesbian couples today value pregnancy and biological parenthood.

Third, the new possibilities and altered values prompt changes in the social structure as people take advantage of a new technology. As the highly publicized 1987 "Baby M" case illustrated, surrogate motherhood creates the possibility that an infant can have both a gestational (surrogate) mother and a social (child-raising) mother. In such a situation, our taken-for-granted definition of motherhood comes into question. As a second example, the increasing popularity of biological parenthood among lesbian couples has helped propel their efforts to redefine the family as not necessarily heterosexual (see the Social Applications section of Chapter 4).

Finally, the alteration in social structure means that at least some previously existing functions of institutions are transformed. If marriage and the family should be redefined as not necessarily heterosexual, one previously taken-for-granted function of that institution—to provide children with both a (female) mother and a (male) father—will change.

Any innovation disrupts existing institutions to some extent. As the example in this section suggests, not everyone will appreciate the social changes that a technology makes possible. Put another way, technological advances and the social changes that follow are not always or solely a good thing. Is it desirable for women over 50 to become pregnant and bear children? If so, under what circumstances? Not all of us agree. In the following section, we examine the two faces of technological change.

TECHNOLOGY'S TWO FACES

Technology is neither an unallayed blessing nor an unmitigated curse. Rather, technology has "two faces" (Mesthene 1993). That is, technological change creates both benefits and costs. "Technological optimists" stress the former while "technological pessimists" focus on the latter.

THE "TECHNOLOGICAL OPTIMISTS"

"Through technology," writes an engineer, Samuel Florman, a bit whimsically, "we get better dishwashers, permanent-press blouses, and rust-proof law furniture"

(Florman 1993, 112). More seriously, technological advances, as we saw earlier in this chapter, have been fundamental to human beings' very survival as a species. Moreover, most of us would have to agree that, at least in some of its forms, technology has been a positive force in our lives. Technology has brought us longer life expectancies through better sanitation, antibiotics to combat bacteria, advanced surgical techniques, and organ transplants. Technology has given us painkillers, better hearing and eyesight, and longer-lasting teeth. For some of us, technology has meant thicker hair or thinner thighs. Technological advances have resulted in increased agricultural productivity: Crops yield larger harvests, cows give more milk, chickens produce more eggs. And refrigeration allows us to keep foods longer without their spoiling. These are but a few examples of how technology can be considered to have improved our lives. No doubt you can think of more.

Some technological optimists have argued that in addition to giving us longer lives, better health, and easier living, technology can be applied to thorny social problems. Alvin M. Weinberg, a physicist, introduced the term *technological fix* in a classic article, first published in 1966, entitled, "Can Technology Replace Social Engineering?" Weinberg wrote that social problems are much more complex and difficult to solve than technological problems. Solutions to social problems are hard for people to agree on and put into practice. Virtually all Americans may see the U.S. budget deficit as a social problem, for example, but just how to fix it is a matter for debate. Furthermore, solving a social problem by somehow convincing people to change their behavior is extremely difficult in a diverse and democratic society.

By comparison, technological engineering is simple. Rockets and robots are expensive and difficult to develop, of course. But once we understand the basic scientific principles on which they are based, their manufacture is relatively straightforward. In view of all this, Weinberg proposed that we might circumvent social problems or at least make them less formidable by reducing them to technological problems and then applying technology as a solution. He argued, for instance, that widespread poverty in the 19th century was "fixed" to a great extent by new industrial technologies. In this case, technology expanded productive capacity enough so that, even though the distribution of wealth remained unequal, there were "more than enough material goods to go around." Weinberg proposed contemporary technological fixes, such as the desalination of ocean water to circumvent shortages of fresh water (rather than the more difficult job of convincing people not to waste the resource). Another technological fix would involve developing new energy sources rather than learning to use less energy.

It is important to note that Weinberg did not believe technology could in itself solve all social problems completely. His argument was that technology would allow us to "buy time" and that many social problems could be partially resolved by technological solutions. Eventually human behavior would have to change (Weinberg 1993).

Meanwhile, less optimistic observers stress that virtually no technological change occurs without social costs and that a technological solution to one social problem may well result in the emergence of new and unforeseen problems. Uncontrolled desalination of ocean waters, for example, might result in unanticipated environmental costs—or in ethnic or class wars over access to the new supplies of clean water.

THINKING CRITICALLY

Samuel Weinberg proposed a "really fanciful" technological fix in which air conditioners and free electricity to operate them would be given to central-city African American families "on the assumption that race riots are correlated with hot, humid weather" (1993, 37). To what extent do you think this policy would help relieve racial tensions, if at all? What are some reasons for your answer?

TECHNOLOGY'S DARK FACE: UNANTICIPATED COSTS

It has become a cliché, notes Emmanuel Mesthene, a philosophy and management professor, that a particular technology is in itself "neutral" and can be used for either good or evil purposes. A daughter uses an airplane to transverse an ocean or a continent so that she can visit aging parents while a smuggler uses an airplane to transport illegal drugs. But there is less appreciation for a more subtle point: Seldom, if ever, does technology yield benefits without exacting a cost (Mesthene 1993). As one example, the account of the devastated Ojibwa society in Chapter 4 illustrates the adverse effects of advancing technology and the social changes that followed. A less dramatic example of technologically induced social costs is provided by the Skolt Lapp people.

The Skolt Lapp people of northern Finland traditionally used reindeer sleds to get around. After the snowmobile was diffused into Skolt Lapp society in the 1960s, it quickly replaced the reindeer sled. Its benefits were predictable. It substantially cut the time required to go between the Lapp settlements and their main trading post across the border in Norway. Furthermore, snowmobile transportation offered improved access to better health care, more varied diets, and recreational activities. However, the snowmobile also brought a number of unforeseen—and costly—social changes.

Older Skolt men, drivers of reindeer sleds, had been respected teachers, instructing younger men on how to care for and use the animals. But the older men did not have the strength or dexterity to drive snowmobiles over rough terrain. And their accumulated reindeer knowledge was no longer essential for the education of the young. Consequently, they quickly lost their traditional source of prestige. Moreover, the Skolts' relatively egalitarian and self-sufficient subsistence economy became an increasingly stratified cash economy dependent on the outside world to provide such things as fuel and spare parts. Then, too, the reindeer herds, which had provided ample food and clothing, were disturbed by the noise of the snowmobiles, and consequently the number of calves born substantially declined. Many Skolts were distressed and expressed dismay over the social changes wrought by the snowmobile (Pelto 1973).

As this example illustrates, new technology creates new opportunities, but it simultaneously generates new problems. Technological change "is often a subversive force" that results in the modification or destruction of established social roles, relationships, and values (Mesthene 1993).

In sum, technology has both positive and negative effects. Sociologists have long been interested in examining and explaining these effects. In the next section, we explore the two major sociological theories concerning technologically induced social change.

TWO THEORIES OF TECHNOLOGICALLY INDUCED SOCIAL CHANGE

Social change is a central topic in sociology. As discussed in Chapter 1, the early sociologists were bent on understanding the consequences of the Industrial Revolution, an event that triggered dramatic social change. Auguste Comte, the founder of sociology, argued that any understanding of society required not only an understanding of the sources of order (statics) but also of the process of change (dynamics). Throughout this text, we examine many important aspects of social change, such as population growth (Chapter 21), urbanization (Chapter 22), and increasing cultural diversity in America, to name but a few. This section explores how the three dominant perspectives in sociological theory explain social change. As you might expect, all confront the topic differently.

STRUCTURAL-FUNCTIONAL THEORY: SOCIAL CHANGE AS EVOLUTIONARY

While structural-functional theory primarily asks how social organization is maintained in an orderly way, the theory does not ignore the fact that societies and cultures change. As pointed out in Chapter 1, according to the structural-functional perspective, change occurs through evolution: Social structures adapt to new needs and demands in an orderly way while outdated patterns, ideas, and values gradually disappear. Often, the new needs and demands that prompt this evolution are technological advances. This evolutionary approach owes much to the influence of Charles Darwin's 19th-century work in biological evolution. According to Darwin, there has been a continuing progression of life forms from simple (such as the amoeba) to very complex (such as human beings). Sociologists used an analogy to create evolutionary social theory, which views societies as moving from simple to more complex as well. Talcott Parsons (1966), a major 20th-century American structural-functional theorist, argued that social evolution is a continuous process of differentiation as societies move from simple to more complex. Society may change, but it remains stable through new forms of integration. For instance, in place of the strong kinship ties that once provided social control and cohesion, there develop laws and judicial processes, along with new values and belief systems.

To the idea of evolutionary change, the sociologist William T. Ogburn (1922) added the concept of cultural lag. Since the components of a society are interrelated, Ogburn reasoned, changes in one aspect of the culture invariably affect other aspects. The society will adapt, but only after some time has passed. This time interval between the arrival of a change and the completion of the adaptations it prompts is called **cultural lag.** As an illustration, Ogburn noted that by 1870, large numbers of U.S. industrial workers were being injured in factory accidents; but workers' compensation laws were not passed until the 1920s—a cultural lag of about 50 years. Ogburn pointed out that a society can hardly adapt to a new technology before it is introduced. Hence, cultural lag is a temporary period of maladjustment during which the social structure adapts to new technologies.

Cultural lag is the time interval between the arrival of a change in society and the completion of the adaptations that this change prompts.

Were they to analyze the introduction of the snowmobile into Skolt Lapp society, described earlier, structural functionalists would see the Lapp culture as evolving from a simpler one that used only the reindeer sled to a more complex one. Not only would Lapp technology be more complex, but also Lapp social structure would become more complex. For instance, snowmobile mechanics would emerge, a social change that would call for greater differentiation in jobs, skills, and necessary education. Structural functionalists would see the ability to get around more quickly as a manifest function of the snowmobile. Against a backdrop of gradual and generally orderly change, these theorists might recognize that the snowmobile was also associated with latent dysfunctions. That the reindeer bore fewer calves is an example. Structural functionalists would see the distress experienced by the older Skolt men at the loss of their former prestige and status as temporary, a cultural lag after which the Skolt society and culture would eventually adjust and adapt.

Evolutionary theories of social change make intuitive sense to many of us, and there is empirical evidence to support them. However, a major problem of evolutionary theories of social change is that they do not posit a clear mechanism that explains just how a society or culture adapts to an innovation. The process of social change is more complicated than can be explained by evolutionary theories alone. Some critics note that we need to introduce the concepts of power and conflict if we are to comprehend processes of social change properly.

Conflict Theory: Power and Social Change

While structural functionalism sees social change as orderly and generally consensual, conflict theorists contend that change results from conflict between competing interests. Furthermore, conflict theorists assert that those with greater power actually direct social change to their own advantage. In a process characterized by conflict and disruption, social structure changes (or does not change) as powerful groups act either to alter or to maintain the status quo.

Vested interests are stakes in either maintaining or transforming the status quo.

According to Thorstein Veblen (1919), those for whom the status quo is profitable are said to have a vested interest in maintaining it. **Vested interests** represent stakes in either maintaining or transforming the status quo; people or groups who would suffer from social change have a vested interest in maintaining the status quo, while those who would profit from social change have a vested interest in transforming it. We can think of many examples of people or groups with a vested interest in maintaining the status quo. Communities with a military post have a vested interest in retaining it because the inflow of government money and jobs is good for local business. Many university students have a vested interest in the U.S. government's retaining federally guaranteed loans. The American Medical Association has strongly opposed national health insurance because physicians fear it would limit their autonomy or income (Starr 1982).

We can also think of instances in which a vested interest in maintaining the status quo involves efforts to halt technological innovations. For example, automobile and oil companies have blocked widespread production and marketing of the electrically powered car, even though this technology has been available for a long time. As another example, movie theater operators did their best to impede cable television. While a group may advocate technological advance in general, it seldom does so in specific instances in which its vested interests are threatened.

Meanwhile, other groups in a society have a vested interest in changing things. Those who would benefit from an innovation have a vested interest in working to see that it is introduced and typically appear as its promoters. In the early decades of the 20th century, the American Medical Association worked hard to officially and legally replace midwives with licensed physicians (Starr 1982). In a current example, Bill Gates, the Microsoft mogul, has a vested interest in promoting future software and Internet innovations, along with the ongoing diffusion of computers throughout the world.

Thinking Critically

How might you analyze the current debate over affirmative action policies and programs in terms of various groups' vested interests?

Just as the benefits of a particular social innovation are unevenly distributed, so also are the costs. Benefits go to the more powerful, while costs tend to go to the less powerful. As one observer has pointed out, corporate managers and others who put new technologies into place usually do not take into account what economists like to call "external costs"—costs that will not be paid by the corporation itself.

FOCUS ON THE ENVIRONMENT

Biotechnology's Power, Promise, and Peril

"How society will weave its way among the two faces of biotechnology remains to be seen."

Plants glow like fireflies, and goats give milk containing human medicine. This may sound like science fiction, but it's not. These innovations and others like them exist today because of *biotechnology*—scientists' purposeful and direct manipulation of genetic material in animals and plants. Sometimes a gene is simply altered through biotechnology. To invent the "Flavr Savr" tomato, first marketed in 1994, scientists identified the tomato gene that promotes softening and changed it. The engineered, or "designer," tomatoes can stay on the vine longer, ripening and gaining flavor without getting too mushy to ship (Shapiro 1994). Other times, a gene from one organism is introduced into another; this process creates a different, or "transgenic," plant or animal that never existed before. Scientists invented plants that glow by inserting firefly genes into the plants' genetic materials.

Originating with pioneering work in the 1960s, biotechnology is a powerful new tool that promises dramatic improvements in human beings' lives. Through biotechnology, we can create longer-lasting foods; plants that yield more food; new plants that can be grown specifically for fuel; animals that secrete medicines, such as insulin for diabetes and TPA for blood clots; and laboratory animals that allow scientists to better study and perhaps find cures for diseases like AIDS, cancer, and sickle-cell anemia.

While acknowledging the promised benefits of biotechnology, environmentalists point out serious risks. Most scientists dismiss the fear sometimes voiced in the popular culture that they will inadvertently create monsters. There are concerns more real, immediate, and pressing, however. Some risks remain unknown because it is still too early even to imagine all the possible consequences of biotechnology. There are knowable risks to our health and ecosystem as well. For instance, scientists can now design crops with pesticides in their genes. These plants would kill damaging insects "automatically." However, eating the food from such crops would require ingesting the pesticide, a situation possibly hazardous to health. Beside pesticides, the expanded use of herbicides causes concern.

Biotechnology can now create plants that are genetically resistant to weed killers. Farmers growing such plants as crops can more effectively spray herbidices over their fields without damaging the crop itself. Meanwhile, environmentalists point out that herbicide-resistant crops run directly counter to the goal of reduced dependence on agricultural chemicals that pollute land and ground water.

More direct risks to our ecosystem involve potential catastrophes that could result if transgenic organisms are introduced into the environment. Nonnative animals introduced into a new environment (for example, rabbits taken into Australia from Britain) have often caused havoc in their new environment. Similar to nonnative species inasmuch as they have traits novel to the ecosystem, engineered species pose similar serious risks. As an example, scientists are now creating engineered fish, such as a carp with an "antifreeze" gene that can live in very cold water. If introduced into an ecosystem, the carp might expand its feeding range and thereby displace or destroy some or all of the native fish species.

In addition to these issues, animal rights activists have raised concerns that biotechnology sometimes causes cruel treatment of animals (Varner 1994). About 10 years ago, for instance, scientists genetically implanted pigs with a growth hormone to increase meat production and reduce fat. The pigs experienced serious and very likely painful health complications that precluded their immediate commercial use. In a second example, laboratory mice are genetically engineered to be born with human-like diseases such as cancer and cystic fibrosis. Producing such mice allows scientists to research new, effective ways to treat such diseases. But the mice suffer in this role, a morally objectionable situation in the view of animal rights activists.

How society will weave its way among the two faces of biotechnology remains to be seen. There is currently evidence of cultural lag. In the opinion of many scientists, neither federal law nor the Food and Drug Administration (FDA), the federal agency responsible for regulating engineered organisms, is yet equipped to handle all the possible issues or situations that could emerge. Is biotechnology potentially more dangerous than helpful? No, most scientists say, but the new technology must be understood, debated, monitored, and effectively regulated (Donnelley, McCarthy, and Singleton, Jr., 1994; Mellon 1993).

This situation can be seriously problematic—and unfair—because society at large then pays the external costs (Mesthene 1993, 79). The costs to the environment caused by the gasoline-powered engine, for instance, are not directly paid by motor or petroleum companies. Instead, these costs are paid by us all in the form of air pollution. This chapter's Focus on the Environment further explores the relation between technology and the environment.

Conflict theorists looking at the introduction of the snowmobile into Skolt Lapp society would note conflicting vested interests: the vested interests of the older males, who would have preferred to maintain the status quo (reindeer sleds only), versus the vested interests of younger men, whose strength and dexterity allowed them to maneuver the faster machines. Reflecting the world system perspective (Chapter 10), conflict theorists might also examine exactly how (and why) the snowmobile was introduced into Skolt Lapp society in the first place. Was the machine purposely marketed to the Lapps by an international manufacturer, for example, who stood to profit from its global diffusion? If so, a conflict theorist would be quick to point out that it was very probably the more powerful manufacturer who benefitted most from this social change and who bore the least cost. The Skolt Lapp society and culture, by virtue of its subsequent disorganization and apparent dismay, paid the "external" costs.

Like evolutionary theories, the conflict perspective on social change makes intuitive sense to many, and there is empirical evidence to support it. However, a general assumption of the conflict perspective—which dates back to its founder, Karl Marx—is that those with a disproportionate share of society's wealth, status, and power have a vested interest in preserving the status quo. In today's rapidly changing society, this may no longer be the case, as powerful factions may be just as likely to find reason to push for more and more technological innovations. Furthermore, some scholars have argued that technology is virtually "autonomous." That is, once the necessary supporting knowledge is developed, a particular invention will be created by someone, even if this invention is terribly costly to nearly everyone in the society, including many of the powerful. In other words, technological changes may be caused by social forces beyond our effective control. We return to this issue near the end of this chapter. At this point, we look at some ways in which today's information technology affects our society.

People in the academic community—students and teachers—have been prime beneficiaries of developments in information technology. Our ability to access and process information has been expanded enormously over the past 20 years. Because today's hardware and software are both much better and much cheaper than those of even 10 years ago, a very large portion of all college students have access to personal computers and sophisticated word processing programs.

INFORMATION TECHNOLOGY: HOW WILL IT CHANGE SOCIETY?

Consider the student in 1967 who is assigned the task of writing a term paper on the consequences of parental divorce. She goes to the library and walks through the periodicals section until she stumbles on the *Journal of Marriage and the Family*, in which she eventually finds five articles—the number her professor requires—on her topic. She takes notes on three-by-five-inch cards (there are no photocopying machines) and goes home to draft her paper on her new electric typewriter. She cuts and tapes her draft copy until it looks good, checks words of dubious spelling in her dictionary, and then retypes a final copy. She uses a carbon paper so she will have a copy for herself. When she makes a mistake, she erases it carefully and tries to type the correction in the original space.

Now consider the student in 1997. This student starts her paper by logging onto SOCIOFILE©, an electronic bibliography of more than 100,000 sociology articles on a single CD-ROM disk. When she enters the keywords *divorce* and *parental,* the program prints out full citations and a summary for 41 articles. After identifying and photocopying the 5 articles she wants, she drafts a report on her word processor, edits it to her satisfaction, runs it through her spelling checker, and adjusts the vocabulary a bit by using the built-in thesaurus. She also runs the report through her new grammar checker, which will catch errors in punctuation, capitalization, and so forth. Finally, she sends the whole thing to her mother (who lives 2,000 miles away) by electronic mail and asks her to read it for logic and organization. She receives the edited version from her mother in an hour, prints two copies, and hands in the report. If she is taking an off-campus course, she may send the paper to her instructor via electronic mail, or she may fax it.

Joel Schatz travels all over the world in the course of his job. To keep in touch with his office, he simply hooks his portable computer up to any telephone and dials an electronic mailbox to check for messages.

Information technology comprises computers and telecommunication tools for storing, using, and sending information.

Information technology—computers and telecommunication tools for storing, using, and sending information—has changed many aspects of our daily lives. Over the past few decades, the United States has become an "information society." More and more workers are employed in information acquisition, processing, and communication (Beninger 1993). More important in its social implications has been the convergence of various information technologies—mass media, telecommunications, and computing—to form a unified system. Aside from enabling us to write term papers more easily, how will information technology change our lives? Will it reduce or increase social class inequality? Make life safer and better? Or make life more stressful and isolated?

The answer is likely to be some of each. In addition to the many blessings associated with information technology, there are new worries. For example, advances in information technology have introduced new forms of crime (hacking and electronic theft), new defense worries (breaches of defense data systems and faulty software programs that may inadvertently launch World War III), and new inefficiencies ("I'm sorry, the system is down"). In this section, we focus on four social implications of information technology: social integration, social control, work, and politics.

On-Line to the Whole World

If you had moved from Ohio to Oregon in 1850, chances are your contacts with your family would have been limited to one or two letters a year. It might have taken months for news of a major world event to reach you. However, today's information technology provides all of us with access to far more information than ever before, faster than ever before. As a result of information technology, we are all linked to the rest of the world; we are linked to distant family and friends, to doctors and medical information, to libraries and data banks, and to world events. Within hours of Iraq's takeover of Kuwait in 1990, gasoline prices went up at stations in almost every rural hamlet across America. In 1995, the news media carried a story describing how a young woman refugee from Bosnia had found asylum in the United States; she had located a sponsor in California through the Internet. Linked in "cyberspace," some of us find support networks, "cyberpals," and even marriage partners in distant parts of the country or world.

Improved communication has many ramifications for social institutions. Any new cultural invention—from fashion to software—will be introduced around the world very quickly, with the probable effect of reducing regional and international cultural differences. Such information sharing *may* help reduce social isolation, encourage world peace and understanding, and help people make better decisions.

TABLE 20.1
USE OF COMPUTERS AND THE WORLD WIDE WEB, UNITED STATES, 1996

Computer users are disproportionately young, well-educated, and well off. Using the computer to access the world wide web is even more likely to be restricted to younger, more affluent individuals. This Harris poll found that over half of those using the web to access political information had incomes over $50,000 and more than two-thirds were college graduates. Because polls are aimed at adults, these poll data on computer and web users omit one of the biggest user groups: those 12–18.

	USE A COMPUTER AT HOME AND/OR WORK	ACCESS THE WORLD WIDE WEB
TOTAL	51%	9%
SEX		
MALE	NA	13
FEMALE	NA	6
RACE/ETHNICITY		
WHITE	NA	10
BLACK	NA	3
HISPANIC	NA	8
AGE		
18–24	55	18
25–29	69	14
30–39	62	10
40–49	68	10
50–64	45	3
65 PLUS	13	
EDUCATION		
LESS THAN HIGH SCHOOL	25	
HIGH SCHOOL GRADUATE	37	5
SOME COLLEGE	63	9
COLLEGE GRADUATE	76	24
POST GRADUATE	82	
INCOME		
$7,500 OR LESS	27	
7,500–15,000	32	4
15,001–25,000	41	6
25,001–35,000	52	6
35,001–50,000	63	11
50,001 AND OVER	79	18

SOURCE: The Harris Poll, 1996:11 (February) and 1996:27 (May).

Of course, information technology may also be used for less admirable purposes, such as allowing terrorists to monitor and sabotage air travel or economic markets. Information technology is vastly increasing the number of people to whom we are linked, but the content of our relationships with those people is still determined by social institutions. Just how our institutions will change as a result of all this information sharing remains a matter for conjecture and debate.

For many of us, information technology simply provides convenience and speed. For people with disabilities, new technologies can mean the difference between social isolation and social participation, between silence and communication. If this man has a computer and modem, he may be on-line to doctors, support groups, discussion groups, and lobbyists for his favorite political causes.

Big Brother Is Watching: Social Control

One of the most important consequences of information technology is an increased ability to monitor and control (Beninger 1993). This includes the control of guided missiles, grocery store inventories, and the stock market (through, for example, programmed trading). It also includes a greater ability to monitor and control people—such as students, taxpayers, drivers, and employees.

How many bushels of storage are available at the elevator? How many trucks are available for transport? Information technology is useful in helping farmers monitor their crops and their markets.

When a police officer pulls you over, your license plate number and your driver's license number are entered into a computer. If the car you're driving has been stolen, if there are warrants out for your arrest, or if you have unpaid citations from another state, the record will be there. Increasingly, your life will be an open book—available for bureaucratic surveillance at every step. Just over the horizon is the probability that your Social Security number will be encoded in a bar code on a plastic card; you will present it whenever you make a transaction covered by government regulations—for example, when you buy or sell a car, get married, register a birth, get a traffic ticket, receive income, or pay taxes.

This increased monitoring arouses concerns about potential invasions of privacy and loss of personal control (Rule and Attewell 1989). Even people who have nothing to hide may not want their age, credit rating, marital history, and so forth available for public scrutiny. There are two issues here. First, can adequate safeguards be built into huge, interlinked data banks to ensure that no unauthorized persons can use the information? Second, how will the authorities use the information? Will law enforcement agencies cross-check marriage and divorce records to identify bigamous marriages? Will authorities check marriage records to verify whether children were really born after a marriage rather than before it? Will local, state, and federal tax officials use these records? The legal ramifications for controlling personal data banks is still evolving.

WORK: THE ELECTRONIC COTTAGE

Some futurists have suggested that computer and telecommunications will allow us to return to a preindustrial social organization in which people can live in small communities and carry out income-generating work at home. The so-called "electronic cottage" will allow people to live in, say, Dalton, Georgia, and work for a firm in New York City. Employees will receive and send work via electronic mail, keeping in touch daily, even hourly, with others (who may be scattered across the country and even the world).

This scenario has many attractive features. It would enable people to live in smaller communities if they wanted to; it would reduce the time and costs associated with commuting; it would eliminate the need for—and expense of—"dressing for success"; it would enable workers to have more flexible working hours so that they could spend more time with their families. Is this glowing scenario likely?

It appears that it probably is not. The reasons have more to do with people than with technology. Many people find electronic mail an inadequate substitute for coffee breaks with fellow employees (Forester 1989). In addition, most people cannot work effectively with children underfoot. Working at home generally works well only for people who are single or childless or those whose children and spouse leave home for the day. Far from integrating the worker with family, working at home may create family stress. Another obstacle to so-called telecommuting is that working at home requires a great deal more self-motivation and willpower than going to the office. Many people find that they get more work done, enjoy their work more, and experience more self-esteem working at the office than working at home.

For the upper-level white-collar worker who wants the freedom to work at home occasionally or who wants to be able to write books while living in a cabin in the mountains, the electronic cottage is a clear blessing. As with many blessings, however, there may be a social class difference in its availability. Many observers believe that working at home will be another means to oppress women, especially lower-level clerical workers. People who do routine clerical tasks such as data entry at home are usually paid on a piecework—rather than salaried—basis. This means that they rather than their employers must buy and maintain the equipment; they receive few or no benefits (such as sick leave, vacation, or health insurance). Labor unions are strongly opposed to this sort of work, seeing it as a way to isolate workers and prevent solidarity. Many feminists oppose it because they see it as a tool to restrict women's lives to home and children. The Applications in Diversity section at the end of this chapter further explores the impact of information technology on women. The more general impact of changing technology on the labor force is discussed in Chapter 17.

From Town Hall to Cyberdemocracy

New information technologies cause us to reconsider what we mean by participatory democracy. We associate the New England town meetings that occurred before the first U.S. Constitution was written with the ideal democratic society, because each citizen had a direct voice in decisions. As the country grew, however, this ideal became infeasible; we consequently elect representatives to vote our opinions. But soon, as suggested by Ross Perot, a 1992 presidential candidate, it could be possible for citizens to vote directly through electronic mail or interactive television.

Already, politics is being changed by new information technologies, such as fax machines and electronic mail. The Democratic and Republican National Committees are on-line. Both houses of Congress and many state and local governments have Internet addresses where voters can check out position papers and legislative records. Individual politicians are logging onto bulletin boards and electronic discussion groups to debate voters and measure public opinion (Kantrowitz and Rosenberg 1994). Speaker of the House Newt Gingrich has proposed extending federal hearings into cyberspace. He envisions, for instance, a House committee holding "a hearing in five cities by television" while the actual committee sits in Washington and monitors citizens' faxed and E-mailed responses (Wright 1995, 15).

Will cyberpolitics mean more and better democracy? Some critics say probably not, for at least three reasons. First, "instant" opinions quickly keyed into cyberspace may be less well considered; simplistic slogans may replace concerned debate. Second, hired opinion makers using computerized mass mailing, faxes, and E-mail can now orchestrate thousands of citizens' opinions on a particular issue overnight. This changes what constitutes a truly grass-roots response. Politicians already have a name for this phenomenon; they call it "Astroturf." Third, not everyone has a modem; more importantly, E-mail technology is not distributed throughout the population in any representative way. In 1995, about one-third of U.S. homes had computers, and only about 5 percent of Americans were on-line—hardly a majority. Furthermore, on-line service users tend to be young (more than half are under 30), male (95 percent), middle class, and white ("Netwatch" 1994). What happens in cyberpolitics to the voices of older, female, and poorer Americans, as well as members of ethnic minorities?

New and emerging information technologies challenge us to clarify what we mean by democracy (Mesthene 1993). Is democracy the will of an undifferentiated majority, the considered judgment of the people's elected representatives, the result of "instant" and transient coalitions of various interest groups, or some happy combination of all three?

How likely is it that this person will log on to the Internet to voice her opinion about, say, public housing or environmental pollution? It's true she may never have voted in the past, but the rapid spread of information technology threatens to cut her off even further from participating in today's information society.

> **Thinking Critically**
>
> If you were to run for office, how might you use E-mail in your campaign? Which of your constituents would you be more likely to hear from via the Internet? How would you know whether they were actually American citizens with the legal right to vote—and would it matter? How might you make sure that other voices, those without modems, were heard as well?

Summary

The effect of information technology on society will depend as much on social institutions as it does on the technological capacities of computers and telecommunications. Information technology offers us more freedom of residence, and more input into local and federal legislative bodies; but we simultaneously lose some privacy and autonomy. Whether the blessings or costs will be predominant will depend on how these technologies are implemented in schools, workplaces, and government bureaucracies. To the extent that they affect relationships among work, class, neighborhood, and family, the new technologies are of vital interest to those concerned with social institutions.

Does Technology Mean Progress?

The capacity of humans to employ technologies sets us apart from other creatures. Without the capacity to invent and use a great variety of technologies, human beings would never have been able to establish themselves in virtually every part of the world. Both in its material and nonmaterial aspects, technology is a pervasive system whose effects are manifest in virtually every aspect of our lives. Our past as well as our future as a species is linked to our capacity to shape our existence through the invention and application of tools that allow us to transcend our physical constraints.

Progress is change in a desirable direction.

Until just a few decades ago, almost all Americans assumed that technological advances and the social changes they cause spell progress. Increasingly, however, we have recognized an important distinction between change and progress. The latter term carries a value judgment: **progress** means change in a desirable direction. Are faster modems, domed sports arenas, and easier and safer abortions necessarily desirable? What about nuclear energy? The answers depend on whom you are asking.

The **technocratic idea of progress** is a belief in the sufficiency of scientific and technological innovation as the basis for general progress.

Americans' equating of technological advances with social progress dates to the founding of the republic. From its beginnings, American culture embraced the evolutionary theory of social change, which held that society was inevitably moving toward higher and better states. Advancing technology promised to improve all of life's conditions—material, political, moral, and intellectual. New technologies would mean new freedoms for ordinary people from economic, political, and intellectual domination. During the 19th century, however, Americans gradually began to change their understanding of technology's purpose. No longer did they believe that the primary aim of technology was to benefit the common good by means of social and political liberation. Over time, new machine power in and of itself became the primary symbol of progress, quite apart from its broader social or political significance. This emergent **technocratic idea of progress** saw scientific and technological innovation as synonymous with general progress. This view assumes that if society can continue to advance technologically, the rest will take care of itself. For instance, there will be "technological fixes" for social and environmental problems.

Fewer Americans hold this view today than in the past. For example, Wendell Berry (1993), a Kentucky farmer and writer, gives the following opinion in an essay entitled "Why I Am Not Going to Buy a Computer": "I do not see that computers are bringing us one step nearer to anything that does matter to me: peace, economic justice, ecological health, political honesty, family and community stability, good work" (67). Like Berry, a growing minority have developed skeptical and negative opinions about technological innovations. They may remind us of the Luddites in 19th-century England (described in Chapter 17), who vandalized machines to protest loss of jobs. Indeed, today we use the term *Luddite* (or *neo-Luddite)* to include those who resist mechanization, automation, and technological advances.

Whether Luddite or not, environmentalists and others are increasingly pointing out that the technocratic view of progress relegates what were once considered primary values (justice, for example) to secondary importance (Marx 1987). They remind us that, although technology can make things easier and better for people, it is not necessarily the motor of all progress. Nor can technology be expected to solve social problems. Only with planning might technology be a source of greater economic prosperity and might it help to further liberate individuals. One authority states:

> Does improved technology mean progress? Yes, it certainly *could* mean just that. But only if we are willing and able to answer the next question: progress toward what? What is it that we want our new technologies to accomplish? What do we want beyond such immediate, limited goals as achieving efficiencies, decreasing financial costs, and eliminating the troubling human element from our workplaces? In the absence of answers to these questions, technological improvements may very well turn out to be incompatible with genuine, that is to say *social*, progress. (Marx 1987, 41)

Making the best use of advancing technology and helping assure that advances prompt desirable social changes, requires social planning—the conscious and deliberate process of investigating, discussing, and coming to some agreement regarding desirable action based on common values.

SOCIOLOGY ON THE NET

As you have browsed the web, you must have stumbled across a number of unique and unexpected web sites from around the world. Certainly this is making the world much smaller by allowing for the diffusion of ideas. As more cultural content is shared we may gain a greater understanding of cultures unlike our own. This is especially the case for children who have access to a computer in school or at home.

`http://www.visualpenpals.org/main.html`

We have reached the web site of Visual Pen Pals. This organization connects classrooms around the world so that students can exchange their art work. Read the various statements of support on this home page. Think back to your grade school days. What kind of art did you and your classmates create? To what extent did it contain cultural images? What kind of art would you expect from children in Bosnia and neighboring countries? How might it differ from the work of American children? What kind of art work would be created by South African children? How would the sharing of this material enhance cross-cultural understanding? Why might this work better with children than with their parents?

Technology can serve many masters. One use of technology can be to unite people who have something in common. This can include right-wing militia groups, environmentalists, or minority group members.

SOCIAL APPLICATIONS

How Is Technology an Equity Issue?

"Technology is an equity issue," writes Corlann Bush of Montana State University. It has "everything to do with who benefits and who suffers, whose opportunities increase and whose decrease, who creates and who accommodates" (Bush 1993, 206). To a significant extent, who benefits and who suffers depends on the social conditions in place when technological innovations appear (McGinn 1991). We can examine a few ways in which technology has affected African Americans and women in our society. In some cases, technology has apparently benefitted African Americans or women, while in other cases it assuredly has not.

Technology and African Americans

- Eli Whitney's 1793 invention of the cotton gin made large-scale plantations profitable and created the need for a large supply of cheap labor—a problem solved by importing many more African slaves (McGinn 1991, 118).
- Automobiles made it easier for people to live in neighborhoods distant from their workplaces, but the resultant suburbs have been primarily white, with blacks concentrated in central cities (Chapter 22). New expressways destroyed cohesive city neighborhoods and parks, further alienating racial minorities (Johnson 1993).
- In the 1950s and 1960s, television gave impetus to the civil rights movement as millions of Americans watched Dr. Martin Luther King's demands for racial justice and also saw police dogs and fire hoses unleashed on demonstrators (McGinn 1991, 120). Yet, contemporary television tends to depict African Americans either relatively infrequently or in negatively stereotyped or lesser roles (Johnson 1993, 272).
- Good jobs in today's information society are disproportionately unlikely to go to African Americans, who are less inclined to show interest in computer skills (Wessells 1990). Largely because of economic disparities, African American children are less likely to attend computer camps or to have computers at home (McGinn 1991).
- Current biomedical technologies concern some African American observers, who worry, for instance, that "dead or dying Black bodies" will be seen as little more than resources for human organs going to whites (Johnson 1993, 280).

Technology and Women

- Beginning with the development of the factory during the Industrial Revolution, women have increasingly engaged in paid employment—a situation that gradually liberated them from sole reliance on family roles as their only means of economic support.
- A proliferation in recent decades of new technical jobs in many sectors from dentistry to machine maintenance has meant expanding job options for women. According to some research findings, working-class women see new work technologies as generally improving their circumstances (Walshok 1993).
- Nevertheless, the debilitating physical condition RSI (repetitive motion syndrome), which can result from keyboarding on word processors, has increasingly afflicted women; many have difficulty getting compensation from their employers (Elmer-Dewitt 1994).
- Despite electronic "labor-saving" devices, women spend just about as much time today in domestic work as they did 50 years ago (Walshok 1993). Partly, this situation is due to more rigorous cultural standards for cleanliness. Also, technology helped change housekeeping tasks like clothes washing from communal or neighborhood activities to individual, isolated ones (Cowan 1993).
- Software development and programming as well as other high-paying computer jobs are currently less available to women than to (white) men. Reasons include a lack of female role models in computer programming and an emphasis in video games and computer-based learning programs on activities of interest primarily to boys (Rosenberg 1994; Wessells 1990).
- Many women find much discussion on the Internet rude and insensitive (Rosenberg 1994). Furthermore, snuff porn (depicting women being mutilated, raped, and murdered) has infiltrated this technology (Elmer-Dewitt 1995)—a situation of dire concern to many feminists and others.

Because technology has two faces and social institutions ultimately shape just how technology affects social change, women and African American spokespersons alike warn that we must all become knowledgeable about technology today and participate in forming technology-related social policies (Bush 1993; Johnson 1993).

http://www.afrinet.net/main

Welcome to Afrinet. Click on **Information** and feel free to browse around the **Afrinet Information Center.** Now open and enter the **AfriNET Background Information** section. What is Afrinet? Scroll down to the bottom of the page and click on **Community.** What is the Afrinet community and how does it work? How can technology foster a consciousness of kind? How can technology like this help to bring economic strength to a minority group?

SUMMARY

1 Technology is the human application of knowledge to the making of tools and hence to humans' use of natural resources. The term refers not only to the tools themselves (aspects of material culture) but also to people's beliefs, values, and attitudes regarding those tools (aspects of nonmaterial culture).

2 Social change is any significant modification or transformation of social structures or institutions over time. Technology and social change are closely related concepts; technology is one important cause of social change.

3 Technology is inseparable from human behavior. From their beginnings, humans have made discoveries by finding things that already existed but had gone unnoticed and have created inventions by combining existing components of their environment to come up with new ideas and tools.

4 Technology's original goal was human survival, but gradually its purpose broadened to making humans more comfortable and allowing them to do things more quickly and with less effort. The development of technology is an inherently dynamic and cumulative process.

5 Diffusion is the process by which cultural traits spread from group to group when one culture (or subculture) comes into contact with another. Much of the content of most culture has been diffused from others. Modern technology not only is diffused itself but also enables cultural diffusion to take place much more rapidly than before.

6 Technological advances prompt transformation in values and social institutions. First, new technologies create new opportunities. Then, the new opportunities transform our values and preferences. The new possibilities and changed values prompt changes in the social structure. Finally, the alteration in social structure means that some previously existing functions of institutions are transformed.

7 Technology has "two faces"; that is, technological change creates both benefits and costs. "Technological optimists" stress the former while "technological pessimists" stress the latter. Some technological optimists have argued that in addition to giving us longer lives, better health, and easier living, technology can be applied to thorny social problems. This controversial concept is called the "technological fix."

8 Structural-functional theory primarily asks how social organization is maintained in an orderly way and sees social change as occurring through gradual evolution. Cultural lag is the time interval between the arrival of a change in society and the completion of the adaptations that this change prompts.

9 While structural functionalism sees social change as orderly and generally consensual, conflict theorists contend that change results from conflict between competing interests. Furthermore, conflict theorists assert that those with greater power actually direct social change to their own advantage. People or groups who would

either suffer or profit from social change have vested interests—stakes in either maintaining or transforming the status quo.

10 Information technology—computers and telecommunication tools for storing, using, and sending information—has changed many aspects of our daily lives. Four social implications of information technology involve social integration, social control, work, and politics.

11 Until just a few decades ago, almost all Americans held the "technocratic idea of progress." That is, they believed that technical advances and the social changes they cause spell progress. But there is an important distinction between change and progress. Progress means change in a desirable direction. To help ensure that advancing technology does mean progress, our society needs to engage in social planning: The deliberate process of coming to some agreement regarding desirable action based on common values.

12 Because technology has two faces and social institutions ultimately shape how technology affects social change, technology has sometimes benefitted and sometimes proven costly to African Americans and women.

SUGGESTED READINGS

MCGINN, Robert E. 1991. *Science, Technology, and Society*. Englewood Cliffs, N.J.: Prentice-Hall. A fairly concise and readable textbook in which the author, a Stanford University professor, explores the impacts of scientific and technological innovations on society.

TEICH, Albert H. 1993. *Technology and the Future*, 6th ed. New York: St. Martin's Press. A collection of essays by recognized authors from many fields addressing the impact of technology on social change. Topics include biomedical technology, environmental and energy issues, and technology and women.

TOFFLER, Alvin. 1970. *Future Shock*. New York: Random House. A classic exploration of how society responds to rapid social change.

Union of Concerned Scientists. 1993. *Nucleus*. *Nucleus* is a quarterly publication of the Union of Concerned Scientists devoted to environmental and other social issues resulting from scientific and technological research and innovation. (The address is 26 Church Street, Cambridge, MA 02238.)

WESSELLS, Michael G. 1990. *Computer, Self, and Society*. Englewood Cliffs, N.J.: Prentice Hall. A survey of computer applications in diverse fields such as business, medicine, and education and an exploration of how society is being changed by advancing computing technologies.

WRISTON, Walter. 1993. *The Twilight of Sovereignty: How the Information Revolution Is Transforming Our World*. New York: Scribner's. An argument that the microchip and satellite technologies have created a world community, with political and economic ramifications far beyond our imagination. The author believes that the new technology fosters democracy and can be used to improve economic conditions throughout the world.

Chapter 21

Population

Outline

The Demographic Transition
The Current Situation
Population in Preindustrial Times
The Transition in the West

Focus on Yesterday: The Calamitous Century
The Transition in the Non-West

Fertility, Mortality, and Social Structure
The Effects of Social Structure on Fertility
The Effects of Social Structure on Mortality
The Effects of Fertility on Social Structure
The Effects of Mortality on Social Structure

Global Perspectives: Population and Social Structure—Three Examples
Kenya: The Six-Child Family
Europe: Is Fertility Too Low?
China: Mandatory Low Fertility

Population Growth, Food Supplies, the Environment, and Poverty
Population Growth and Food Supplies
Environmental Devastation: A Population Problem?
Third World Poverty
Programs to Reduce Fertility
Sustainable Development
Outlook: Good News/Bad News

Population in the United States
Population Growth
Fertility
Mortality
Migration
The Future of U.S. Population

Applications in Diversity: What Do We Know about International Migration?

PROLOGUE

Have You Ever . . . considered having a child? If you have given it any thought at all, you have probably come up with a list of pros and cons. For most people, the list of cons is a long one: Children are expensive, they tie you down, they interfere with school or work, and they give you a frightening level of responsibility. Yet, every year, about 70 out of every 1,000 American women aged 15 to 44 have babies. Of course, some bumble into it by accident, and some do it unthinkingly as part of the normal adult role, but others look over the list of pros and cons, gulp, and take the plunge. The amazing thing about fertility is that in spite of the diversity of motives on the individual level, the result on the societal level is very similar year after year.

Whether you have children and how many you have are likely to depend on your other goals. If you are committed to a career or to getting a graduate degree, the likelihood is that, male or female, you will postpone having children or even decide not to have any. Your decision will have ramifications far beyond your own life. For example, the age structure of the population is largely determined by fertility. If you and others of your generation look at the list of disadvantages and decide that child-rearing isn't for you, the proportion of children in our population will go down. This will mean relatively fewer jobs in elementary education and relatively more jobs in social services for the elderly. In 40 years, your decision will translate into relatively few middle-aged people to support you in your old age! Having a child is one of the most intimate and private of experiences, yet perhaps nothing else we do has so much public impact.

In 1995, the world population was 5.7 billion, give or take a few hundred million. And it is growing—rapidly! Every hour, 10,000 persons are added to the globe (U.S. Bureau of the Census 1994c). The world's population is expected to reach 6 billion by the turn of the century—in just a few years (Ashford 1995). This chapter explores the interrelationships of population and social structures. It takes a historical and cross-cultural perspective to illustrate how births and deaths relate to the social institutions that we examined in earlier chapters of this text. Although studies of population are often highly technical and statistical, this chapter focuses on how population processes relate to social issues such as gender roles, family, poverty, and the environment.

THE DEMOGRAPHIC TRANSITION

By the time current college students reach retirement age, the world population is likely to be 10 billion. This tremendous growth is totally alien to most human experience. Most societies before the industrial revolution grew either slowly or not at all (see Figure 21.1).

The world today has more than twice as many people in it as it did as recently as in 1950. In part because of this growth, millions are poor, underfed, and undereducated. In part because of this growth, the world's water supply is in serious

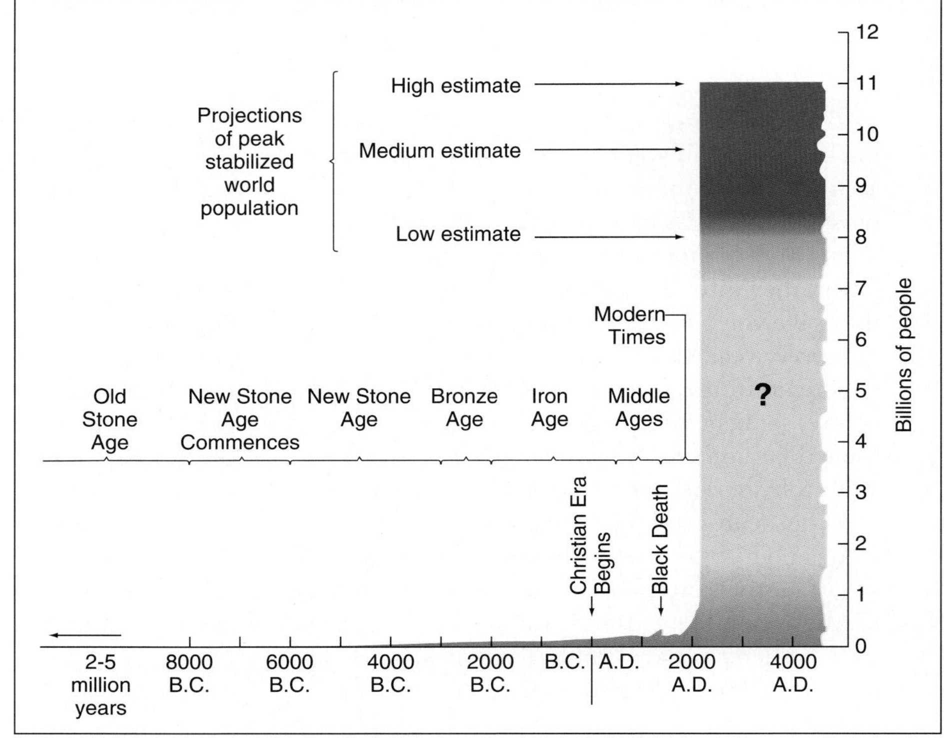

FIGURE 21.1
THE GROWTH OF WORLD POPULATION

Until the last 100 years or so, world population grew very slowly or not at all. The population bomb is as much a child of the 20th century as is the atom bomb.

SOURCE: Van der Tak, Haub, and Murphy 1979.

jeopardy (Falkenmark and Widstrand 1992). In part because of this growth, the world economic system is in danger of bankruptcy. Perhaps no other issue is so vitally connected to so many of our era's crises. This section first describes the current world population and then the process by which it was reached.

THE CURRENT SITUATION

Although population is concerned with such intimate human experiences as birth and death, the big picture of population growth and change can be understood only if we use statistical summaries of human experience. Four measures are especially important: the crude birthrate, the crude death rate, the crude natural growth rate, and the doubling time.

$$\text{Crude birthrate (CBR)} = \frac{\text{Number of births in a year}}{\text{Estimated midyear population}} \times 1{,}000$$

$$\text{Crude death rate (CDR)} = \frac{\text{Number of deaths in a year}}{\text{Estimated midyear population}} \times 1{,}000$$

$$\text{Crude natural growth rate} = \frac{\text{CBR} - \text{CDR}}{10}$$

$$\text{Doubling time (in years)} = \frac{70}{\text{Crude natural growth rate}}$$

Table 21.1 shows these rates in 1995. For the world as a whole, the crude birthrate in 1995 was 24 births per 1,000 population; the crude death rate was a

TABLE 21.1
THE WORLD POPULATION PICTURE, 1995

In 1995, the world population was 5.7 billion and growing at a rate of 1.5 percent per year. Growth was uneven, however the less developed areas of the world were growing much more rapidly than the more developed areas. As a result, most of the additions to the world's population were in poor nations.

AREA	CRUDE BIRTH-RATE	CRUDE DEATH RATE	CRUDE NATURAL GROWTH RATE	TOTAL POPULATION (IN MILLIONS)	DOUBLING TIME (IN YEARS)
WORLD	24	9	1.5%	5,702	45
AFRICA	41	13	2.8	720	24
ASIA	24	8	1.7	3,451	42
LATIN AMERICA	26	7	1.9	481	36
NORTH AMERICA	15	9	0.7	293	105
EUROPE	11	12	−0.1	729	—[a]

SOURCE: Population Reference Bureau 1995.

[a]Since Europe's crude death rate now exceeds its crude birth rate, its natural growth rate is negative, and the concept of doubling time is no longer applicable.

much lower 9 per 1,000. Because the number of births exceeded the number of deaths by 15 per 1,000, the crude natural growth rate of the world's population was 1.5 percent. If your savings were growing at the rate of 1.5 percent per year, you would undoubtedly think that the growth rate was very low. A growth rate of 1.5 percent in population, however, translates into a doubling time of 45 years. This means that *if* this growth rate continues, the population will double to over 11 billion in just 45 years.

The frightening prospect of welcoming another 45 billion people in our lifetime is complicated by the fact that the growth is uneven. As Table 21.1 shows, growth rates are startlingly different across the areas of the world. Africa is the world's fastest-growing continent. At a growth rate of 2.8 percent per year, it will double its population size in only 24 years. In Europe, by contrast, deaths now exceed births, and the natural growth rate is negative.

These differentials in growth are of tremendous importance. As you can see from Figure 21.2, almost all the additions to world population in the next several decades will take place in the less developed nations. As a result, the world is likely to be proportionately poorer in 2030 than it is now. How did we get into this fix?

POPULATION IN PREINDUSTRIAL TIMES

For most of human history, **fertility** (the incidence of childbearing) was barely able to keep up with **mortality** (the incidence of death), and the population grew little or not at all. Historical demographers estimate that in the long period before population growth exploded, both the birthrate and the death rate hovered around 40 to 50 per 1,000.

Fertility is the incidence of childbearing.

Mortality is the incidence of death.

FIGURE 21.2
WORLD POPULATION GROWTH, 1750–2150

SOURCE: Ashford 1995, 4.

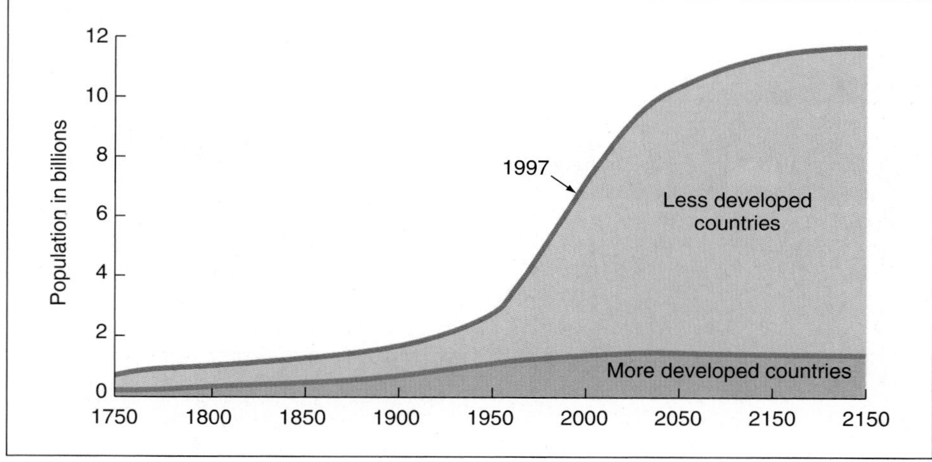

Translated into human terms, a birthrate of 40 to 50 means that the average woman spends most of the years between ages 20 and 45 pregnant or nursing. If both she and her husband survive until they are 45, she will produce an average of 6 to 10 children. Estimates drawn from the first U.S. census in 1790 suggest that the average woman over 40 had borne eight children. Such high levels of childbearing have a powerful effect on the role of women. They virtually preclude any participation in social structures outside the home. Women are tied close to home and excluded from participation in political, community, or economic affairs beyond the household. If women fail to keep up this level of childbearing, however, the death rate exceeds the birthrate, and the population begins to dwindle.

Life expectancy is the average number of years that a group of infants can expect to live.

On a personal level, a crude death rate of 40 to 50 per 1,000 translates into a life expectancy of 25 to 30 years. **Life expectancy** is the average number of years a group of infants can expect to live. A simple example will show how high childhood mortality can bring down this average. Let us take a hypothetical group of 10 infants: Three die in infancy and therefore live zero years; two die at the age of 10; the other five live to 70. The total number of years lived by these 10 infants is 370:

3 × 0 years =	0
2 × 10 years =	20
5 × 70 years =	350
Total	370

The average number of years lived by this group of 10 infants—their life expectancy—is 37 (370 divided by 10). The example illustrates why preindustrial societies had such very low life expectancy: Although those who escaped the perils of childhood might manage to live to be elderly, as many as one-third of the population died before their first birthday.

When mortality is this high, death is a frequent visitor to most households. In the United States in 1900, life expectancy was approximately 45 to 50 years (Omram 1977). At this level of mortality, it is estimated that 62 percent of all parents experienced the childhood death of one of their children, and a quarter of all children experienced the death of a parent before they reached age 15 (Uhlenberg 1980).

The Transition in the West

The industrial revolution set in motion a whole series of events that revolutionized population in the West. First, mortality dropped; then, after a period of population growth, fertility declines followed. Because statistical studies of population are called **demography,** this process is called the **demographic transition.**

Demography is the study of population—its size, growth, and composition.

The **demographic transition** is the process of moving from the traditional balance of high birthrates, and death rates to a new balance of low birthrates and death rates.

Decline in Mortality. General malnutrition was a major factor supporting high levels of mortality. Though few died of outright starvation, poor nutrition increased the susceptibility of the population to disease. Improvements in nutrition were the first major cause of the decline in mortality that accompanied industrialization. New crop varieties from America (corn and potatoes especially), new agricultural methods and equipment, and increased communication all helped improve nutrition. Productivity increased, and greater trade reduced the consequences of localized crop failure. A second major reason mortality began to decline was a general increase in the standard of living: better shelter and clothing—and soap. Changes in hygiene were vital in reducing communicable diseases, especially those affecting young children, such as typhoid fever and diarrhea (Razzell 1974). Because of these factors, the death rate gradually declined between 1600 and 1850. Nevertheless, the life expectancy for women in the United States was only 40 years at the time of the Civil War. The Focus section of this chapter describes the disastrous mortality that hit Europe in the 14th century.

In the late 19th century, public health engineering led to further reductions in communicable disease by providing clean drinking water and adequate sewage systems. Medical science did not have an appreciable effect on life expectancy until the 20th century, but during the 20th century its contributions have sparked a remarkable and continuing increase in life expectancy. During this century, the life expectancy of U.S. women has increased from 49 to 78 years. Thus, although mortality began a steady decline in about 1600, the fastest decreases have occurred in the 20th century. This decline reflects the almost total elimination of deaths from infectious disease and steady progress in eliminating deaths caused by poor nutrition and an inadequate standard of living (McKeown and Record 1962; McKeown, Record, and Turner 1975).

Decline in Fertility. The industrial revolution also affected fertility, though much later and less directly. The reduction in fertility was not a response to the drop in mortality or even a direct response to industrialization itself. Rather, it appears to have been a response to changed values and aspirations triggered by the transformation of society (Coale 1973).

Industrialization meant increasing urbanization, greater education, the real possibility of getting ahead in an expanding economy, and, most important, a break with tradition—an awareness of the possibility of doing things differently than they had been done by previous generations. The idea of controlling family size to satisfy individual goals spread even to areas that had not experienced industrialization, and by the end of the 19th century, the idea of limiting family size had gained widespread currency (van de Walle and Knodel 1980). In England and Wales, the average number of children per family fell from 6.2 to 2.8 between 1860 and 1910, the space of just two generations (Wrigley 1969).

FOCUS ON YESTERDAY

The Calamitous Century

"THE PLAGUE CAME BACK AGAIN AND AGAIN THROUGHOUT THE CENTURY UNTIL THE POPULATION OF EUROPE WAS REDUCED TO HALF OF WHAT IT HAD BEEN."

In the fifth decade of the 14th century, one-third of the world population died. An international epidemic of the bubonic plague struck first in China, then followed the caravan routes to the Mediterranean and traveled by ship to Western Europe. In 1351, a ghost ship with a cargo of wool and a dead crew ran aground in Norway, and the disease spread to Scandinavia and Russia. In its first assault, perhaps one-third of the population of Europe and Asia died. The plague came back again and again throughout the century until the population of Europe was reduced to half of what it had been.

Among those who caught the plague, death was both certain and quick. Stories were recorded of people who caught the plague in their sleep and died before they awoke. The death rate was enormous; people died faster than they could be buried. Bodies piled up in the streets, and shallow mass graves were filled as fast as they could be dug.

The disaster was too large to comprehend in ordinary terms, and many believed that it meant the end of the world. This belief, plus the very realistic expectation of sudden death, meant that normal social relationships stopped. Crops went unharvested and fields unplowed; cathedrals being built were abandoned, never to be completed; livestock went untended and died almost as fast as their masters.

Overwhelming fear did not encourage human kindness. People were afraid to go near one another, and the usual social ties were torn. Parents abandoned children, and wives left husbands.

In yet a darker spirit, people looked for a scapegoat to blame for their misfortune. The answer in the 14th century, as it was in the 20th, was the Jews. Despite a papal statement that it was unreasonable to think that Jews were poisoning the wells they too used, a flame of anti-Semitism swept Europe: Jews were burned to death in Maintz (Germany) on August 24, 1349; in Worms, York, Antwerp, and Brussels, entire Jewish communities were exterminated. The survivors moved eastward to Poland and Russia, and by 1350 there were few Jews left in Germany or the Low Countries.

In the long run, the 50 percent reduction in population had significant economic impact and may have hastened the end of feudalism. Europe in the 14th century was a preindustrial agricultural society. Since there were no mechanical aids, the productivity of the soil was directly proportional to the amount of labor put into it. The plague cut the amount of labor by half. The immediate consequence was an enormous fall in productivity. The very foundations of feudalism were shaken. Labor's bargaining power rose sharply, and wages for craftsmen and laborers doubled. Tenant farmers no longer had to stay with exploitive masters but could choose among manors competing for their services. Rents tumbled, and many tenant farms went empty; fields returned to the wild. Attempts were made to arrest this rapid change in economic relationships by legally restricting wage increases to 35 percent and by binding tenants to their land. In the face of severe competition for labor, however, these laws were ineffective, and labor gained significant advantage.

A change in the supply and demand of labor did not revolutionize society. The people of the Middle Ages, both landlords and tenants, were still bound to one another by ties of custom. Nevertheless, the loss of half the population and the subsequent economic response deeply affected medieval society.

SOURCES: Hatcher 1977; McNeil 1976; and Tuchman 1978.

This decline in fertility took place without benefit of modern contraceptives. Toward the end of the decline, diaphragms and condoms were important, but much of the fertility decline in Europe was achieved through the ancient method of withdrawal—coitus interruptus.

The Transition to Low Growth. In the West, mortality began to decline nearly 150 years before fertility started to drop. As a result, Europe and North America experienced a long period of unprecedented population growth (see Figure 21.3).

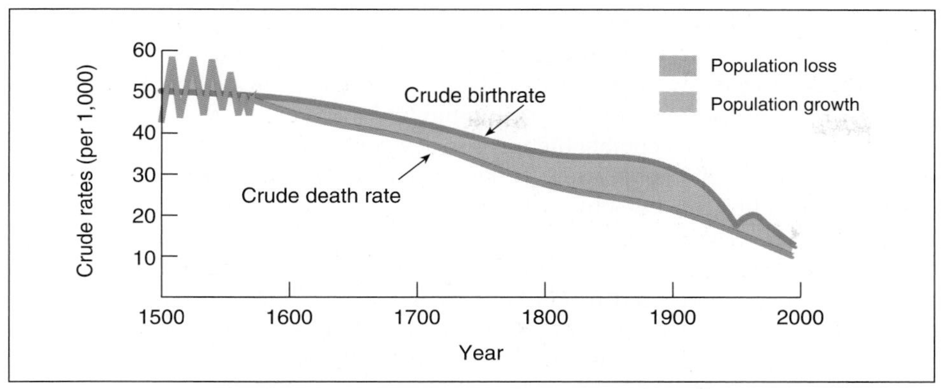

FIGURE 21.3
THE DEMOGRAPHIC TRANSITION IN THE WEST

Preindustrial populations were characterized by fluctuating death rates and relatively stable birthrates. Mortality rates gradually stabilized and fell below the fertility rate. Because the decline in mortality was slow and because many of the excess people moved to North America or Australia, this growth did not cause dramatic problems for Europe.

Three factors reduced the problems associated with this century-long population boom: (1) Technology grew even more rapidly than population, so that the standard of living grew much faster than the population; (2) the population boom coincided with the colonization of North America and Australia, so that the extra population simply moved overseas; and (3) growth rates were relatively modest because the decline in death rates was so slow.

At the end of the 20th century, the demographic transition is nearly complete in the West. Fertility and mortality rates are once again close to equal, and the population has virtually ceased to grow. This new equilibrium is being reached with current birthrates and death rates of 11to 15 instead of 40 to 50 per 1,000.

THE TRANSITION IN THE NON-WEST

In the non-West, the demographic transition is taking a very different course. Both birthrates and death rates remained at roughly preindustrial levels until World War II. Since then, mortality has fallen sharply, while fertility declines are just getting under way. In 1995, the birthrate in the Third World exceeded the death rate by 19 per 1,000, implying a growth rate of 1.9 percent per year and a doubling time of 36 years. The result is rapid population growth (see Figure 21.4).

In the developing world today, life expectancy stands at about 64 years. This is a remarkable achievement in a short time. Much of the improvement in life expectancy has been the result of imported technology from the developed world:

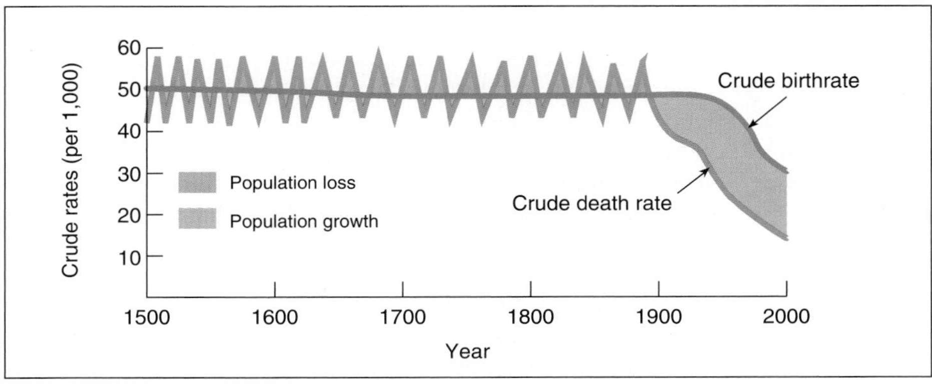

FIGURE 21.4
THE DEMOGRAPHIC TRANSITION IN THE THIRD WORLD

In the less developed regions of the world, mortality rates fell suddenly while fertility rates continued to be very high. The result was dramatic growth in the population. Fertility rates have begun to decline but are still far higher than mortality rates.

The importation of modern medicine from the West has reduced mortality significantly throughout the Third World. Vaccinations and basic education about nutrition and sanitation have reduced infant mortality to 6 percent in Papua–New Guinea. Nevertheless, life expectancy is only 57 years—below the average of 64 years for all less-developed countries.

vaccinations and inoculations, insecticides to control malaria, and public health engineering to provide clean water in cities. This fall in mortality is unlike the mortality decline in the West in two ways: (1) It has been far more rapid, and (2) it has not been accompanied by rising standards of living.

Mortality is still unacceptably high in less-developed regions of the world: Nearly one in 15 children die before their first birthdays. Although substantial improvements in mortality can be achieved through inexpensive preventative strategies (see Chapter 19), major improvements in mortality await increases in standard of living: better diets, cleaner water, better housing, better domestic sanitation.

Drops in fertility also depend on better standards of living. Experience tells us that fertility goes down when preindustrial social institutions—family, gender roles, and agricultural economies—are changed. In the following sections, we explore more deeply the link between social structures and fertility and mortality, and then we return to the question of how to bring both fertility and mortality rates down to acceptable levels.

Fertility, Mortality, and Social Structure

The relations of social structure, fertility, and mortality are broad and complex. Not only does social structure affect both fertility and mortality, but fertility and mortality affect social structure.

The Effects of Social Structure on Fertility

In Kenya, the average woman has five or six children; in Italy, the average woman has only one or two (Population Reference Bureau 1995). These differences are not the result of biological differences; they are the product of values, roles, and statuses in very different societies. The average woman in Kenya wants five or six children, and the average woman in Italy wants only one or two.

The level of fertility in a society is strongly related to the roles of women. Generally, fertility is higher where women marry at younger ages, where they have less access to education, and where their roles outside the household are limited. Fertility also reflects the development of society's institutions. When the family is considered the source of security, income, social interaction, and even salvation, fertility is high.

The Effects of Social Structure on Mortality

The single most important social factor affecting mortality is the standard of living—access to good nutrition, safe drinking water, protective housing, and decent medical care. Differences in living standards almost entirely account for the fact that the average American can expect to be healthier and to live 20 years longer than the average Nigerian and that the average white in the United States can expect to live almost 7 years longer than the average black; differences in living standards and access to health care also explain findings from Britain (Marmot, Kogevinas, and Elson 1987) and the United States that show death rates are higher and health is poorer among members of the lower social classes.

More subtly, social structure affects mortality through its structuring of social roles and lifestyle. Race, socioeconomic status, and gender all affect exposure to unhealthy

Thinking Critically

Because African Americans are more likely to be poor than white Americans, their lower life expectancy is not surprising. Women are more likely to be poor than men, yet their life expectancy is higher. Is the reason biology or social structure?

or dangerous lifestyles. People with less education, for example, get less physical exercise and are more likely to smoke than those with more education (Chapter 19).

THE EFFECTS OF FERTILITY ON SOCIAL STRUCTURE

Fertility has powerful effects on the roles of women. The greater the number of children a woman has and the older she is at the time of the last birth, the less likely she is to have any involvement in social structures outside the family.

In the United States in 1995, the average woman has 2.0 children, the first born when the woman is 26 and the second shortly thereafter. This means that she has plenty of time to finish her education and establish herself in a career before she starts childbearing. Both of her children will be in school before she is 35, and she still has 45 years of life expectancy to look forward to. Active childbearing and child rearing take only 6 to 8 years of her life instead of 30 to 40. The difference has vast implications for women's social, economic, and political roles.

In addition to affecting women's roles, fertility has a major impact on the age structure of the population: The higher the fertility, the younger the population. This is graphically shown in the population pyramids in Figure 21.5, which com-

FIGURE 21.5
A COMPARISON OF AGE STRUCTURES IN LOW- AND HIGH-FERTILITY SOCIETIES

When fertility is high, the number of children tends to be much larger than the number of parents. When this pattern is repeated for generations, the result is a pyramidal age structure. When fertility is low, however, generations are similar in size and a boxier age structure results.

SOURCE: Ashford 1995, 13.

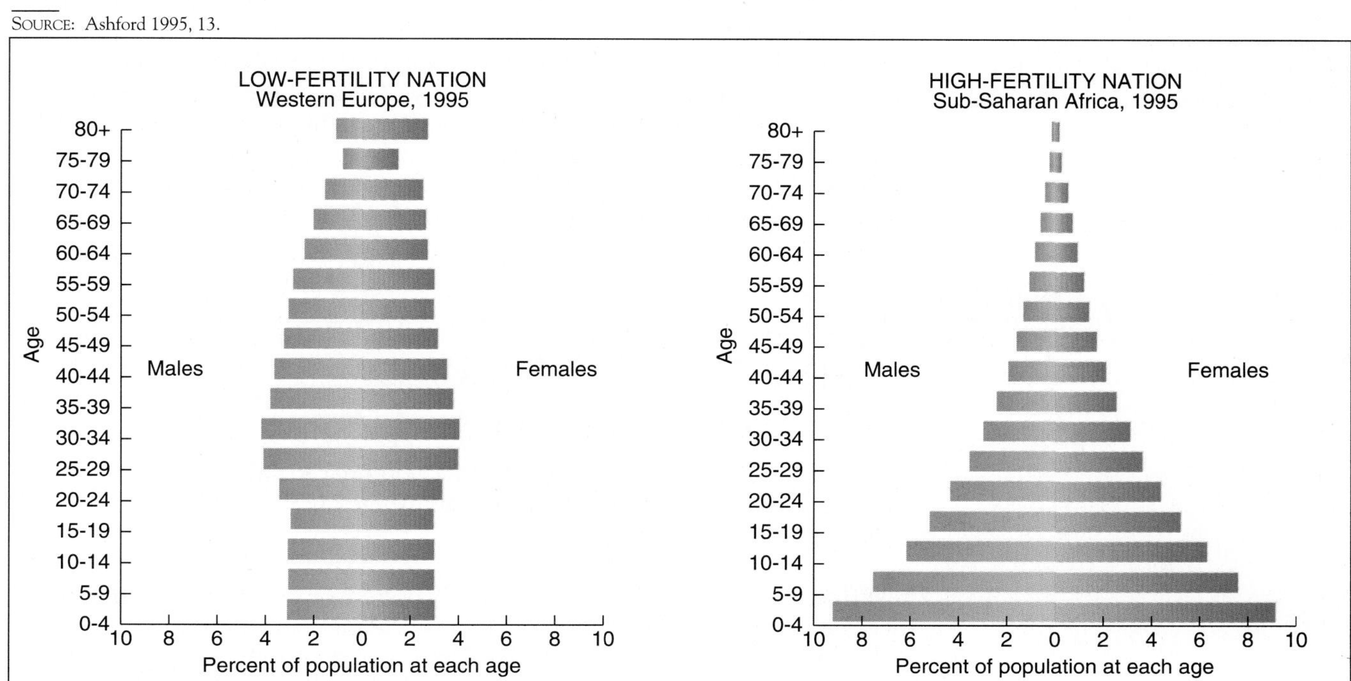

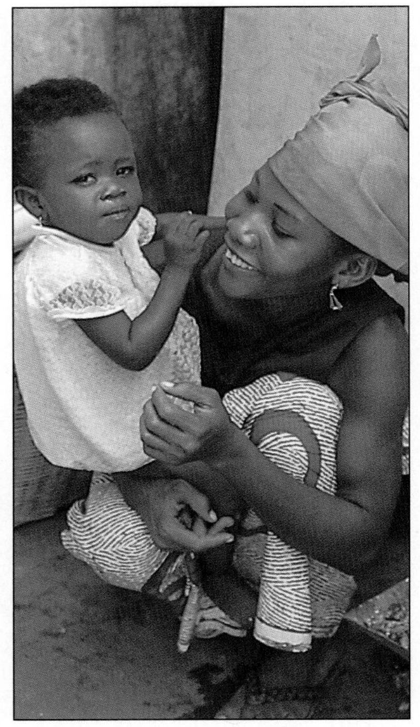

Although children impose burdens on parents, they also bring joy and fulfillment. Moreover, children are one of the few sources of joy and reward equally available to rich and poor. As this photograph indicates, women and men with few economic rewards may still find pleasure in their children. Thus, poverty and children are not incompatible, and poor people find it rational to have children.

The **dependency ratio** is the number of people under 15 and over 65 divided by the number of people aged 15 to 65.

pare the age structure of Western Europe with that of sub-Saharan Africa. When fertility is low, the number of children is about the same as the number of adults; when fertility is high, there are many more children than adults, and the age structure takes on a pyramidal shape. This pyramidal age structure has long-term consequences for population growth. In fact, it translates into the potential for explosive population growth. In sub-Saharan Africa, the number of girls aged 0 to 4 is twice the number of women aged 20 to 24. This means that in the next generation, there will be twice as many mothers as there are today.

One measure of a society's age structure is the **dependency ratio**—the number of people under 15 and over 65 divided by the number of people aged 15 to 65. This ratio is a rough measure of the number of dependents per productive adult. On a worldwide basis, it varies from 0.92 in Africa to 0.49 in Europe. This means that in Africa there is nearly one dependent for every producer and in the West there is one dependent for every two producers (see Figure 21.6). On an individual level, this is the difference between a family in which one parent supports one child and a family in which two parents support one child. Obviously, the two-parent family is better off. Not only is it better off now, but it is more likely to be able to set aside some savings for the future, with the result that in the long run it will be even better off.

The Effects of Mortality on Social Structure

Like fertility, mortality has particularly strong effects on the family. A popular myth about the preindustrial family is that it was a multiple-generation household—what we call an extended family. But reconstructions tell us that only a small percentage of all families could have been three-generational. A little reflection will demonstrate how unlikely it is that many children lived with their grandparents when fertility was seven to eight children per woman. Even if the grandparents survived into old age, they could live with only one of their surviving children, leaving the other households without a grandparent. And quite often, if the children lived with their grandparents, it was because their parents were dead. In short, the three-generation household was impossible for many and affordable for few (Wrigley 1969). The households of a high-mortality society were probably as fractured, as full of stepmothers, half-sisters, and stepbrothers, as are the current households of the high-divorce society.

Global Perspectives: Population and Social Structure—Three Examples

Kenya: The Six-Child Family

Kenya is an example of a society where traditional social structures encourage high fertility. It is also an example of a society where high fertility may ensure continuing traditionalism—and poverty.

The Effects of Social Roles on Fertility. Like many nations in sub-Saharan Africa, Kenya still has a high birthrate: 45 per 1,000 population. Mortality, however, is down to 12 per 1,000. This means that the population of Kenya is growing at 3.3 percent per year. If that rate continues, the population will double in just 21

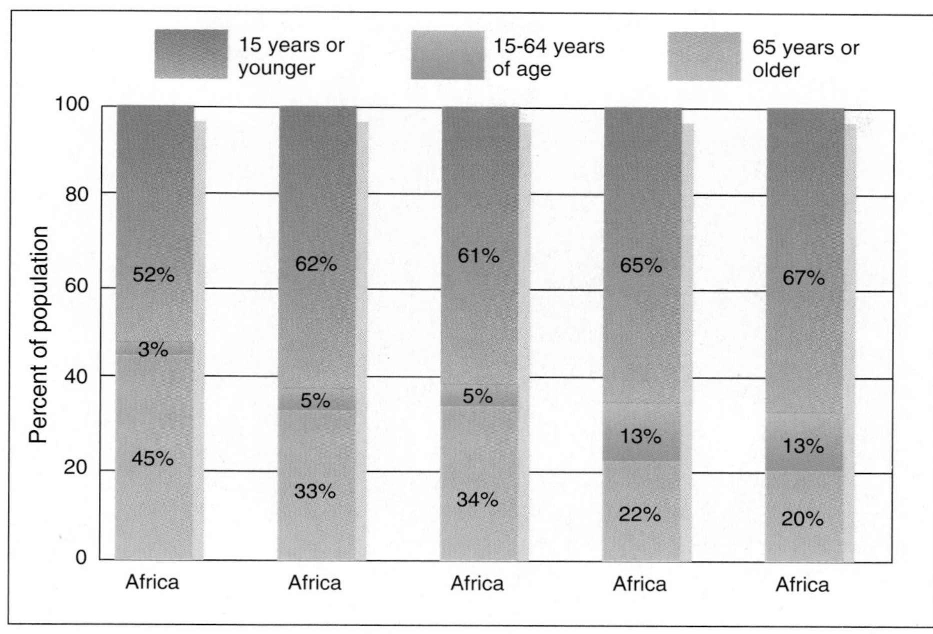

FIGURE 21.6
AGE COMPOSITION AND DEPENDENCY

In the less-developed nations of the world, high fertility means that children make up a large proportion of the population. Much of current production has to go to feed new mouths.

SOURCE: Population Reference Bureau, 1995.

years (Population Reference Bureau 1995). An aggressive family-planning program is unlikely to reduce this growth: The average woman in Kenya wants five or six children.

The high value placed on fertility in Kenyan society is a reflection of several **pronatalist** (profertility) pressures. Among the pressures are tribal loyalties, women's roles, and the need for economic security (Mott and Mott 1980).

Pronatalism refers to the social forces that encourage childbearing.

TRIBAL LOYALTIES Kenya is a diverse nation in which there is jealous competition among tribal groups. Because the size of each tribe's population is an important factor in political power, large families are seen as politically advantageous. This is a common pronatalist pressure in any diverse society.

WOMEN'S NEED FOR CHILDREN Regardless of the needs of their tribe or nation, most women give first consideration to how another child will affect them and their family. For the 80 percent of Kenyan women who are responsible for family farms, children are an asset. A substantial minority of Kenyan men work away from the family farm; even when they are there, their role is largely supervisory. Women bear the chief responsibility for planting, plowing, and harvesting and have full responsibility for cooking, drawing water, and finding firewood. As a result, three-quarters of Kenyan women list "help with work" as a reason for having children. In addition to helping with the work, children are an important, perhaps the only, source of esteem and power open to women. This is especially true of the 30 percent of Kenyan women who live in polygamous unions. The number of children, especially the number of sons, is an important determinant of a woman's position relative to that of other wives.

ECONOMIC SECURITY Children add to their parents' economic security in a number of ways. They are the only form of old-age insurance available. When they grow up

In Kenya, the family continues to be the center of economic and social relationships. Women and men find that having many children enhances their prestige, helps with their work, and provides them with economic security for their later years. Because there are few costs associated with having children, the average woman in Kenya desires six and has seven children.

and marry, they may also add to the family's economic and political security by their marriages. The greater the number of children, the greater the number of in-laws. A family that can bind itself to many other families has greater political power and more security.

In short, a family's income, status, and long-term security are all enhanced by its having many children. There are comparatively few rewards for having a small family. Children are virtually cost free—no expensive medical treatment is available, what schooling there is has no direct cost for the parents, and children's desires do not run to designer jeans and $150 tennis shoes. With a cost/benefit ratio of this sort, it is not surprising that Kenyans desire many children.

The Effects of Population Growth on Society. Although high fertility may appear to be in the best interests of individual women, it has negative consequences for the society. At current rates of fertility and mortality, Kenya's population is doubling every 21 years. As a result, development goals are shooting at a moving target. To double the proportion of children getting an elementary school education (from 45 to 90 percent), the government had to raise the dollars spent on education fourfold because the total number of children needing schooling doubled. Simply to maintain that level over the next 21 years, the Kenyan government would have to double again the dollars spent on education. Unfortunately, there are other demands on the budget—for defense, for highways, for development, for agriculture. All these areas face the same problem of escalating demand (Straus 1996).

Thus, a decision that is rational on the individual level turns out to be irrational on the societal level. Occasionally, people in the West make remarks of this sort:

"Can't they figure out they would be better off if they had fewer children?" Unfortunately for the argument, nations don't have children; women do. High fertility continues to be a rational choice for individual Kenyans.

Policy Responses. Two related policy responses help to lower birth rates in lesser-developed countries: raising the status of women and instituting family planning programs.

WOMEN'S STATUS AND POPULATION GROWTH "Whether and when the world's population stabilizes will depend in large measure on changes in the status of women around the world" (Ashford 1995, 17). Elevating their status gives women alternatives to motherhood. It also increases a wife's decision-making authority relative to her husband and in-laws, thereby enabling her effectively to choose to bear fewer children.

Education is the primary way to raise women's status, and research consistently shows that more educated women have fewer children (Ashford 1995). Education lowers fertility by providing employment opportunities. Furthermore, educated women tend to marry later, delaying childbearing and hence having fewer children over the course of their lives. In Kenya, as in many Third World countries, women with a secondary education have about half as many children as those with no education (Figure 21.7).

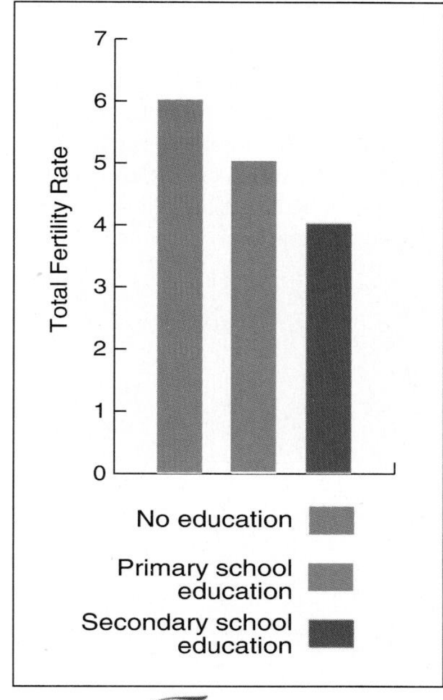

FIGURE 21.7
WOMEN'S EDUCATION AND FAMILY SIZE IN KENYA, 1993

SOURCE: Ashford 1995, 20.

FAMILY PLANNING PROGRAMS Kenya was the first sub-Saharan African nation to establish an official family-planning program. The program has had some notable successes, and Kenya has now relinquished the title of having the highest fertility rate in the world to another sub-Saharan African country, Niger. Over the past 20 years, the total fertility rate in Kenya has fallen from 8.4 to 5.7 children per woman, and the percentage of married women using contraception has more than doubled, to about 33 percent ("Kenya" 1989). Still, only 33 percent of married women use contraception (United Nations 1994). One reason for low contraceptive use is the desire for large families. When women *want* five to six children, contraceptives aren't very relevant. For many women in Kenya and throughout the developing world, however, there is another element: Contraceptives are hard to use. They are available only at distant sites, they are expensive, and they are culturally alien and frightening.

So far, fertility declines and contraceptive improvements have been documented largely in urban areas among the minority of women who have some secondary education. These are the women who have experienced some change in social institutions *and* who find contraception more accessible and familiar. For the mass of the population that lives in rural areas, the pronatalism built into basic social institutions cannot be quickly eliminated just because the official policy is **antinatalist.**

Antinatalism refers to social forces that discourage childbearing.

EUROPE: IS FERTILITY TOO LOW?

In a world reeling from the impact of doubling populations in less-developed countries, it is ironic that many developed countries, such as Japan (Yanagashita 1993) and nations in Europe, are worried that fertility is too low.

With modern levels of mortality, fertility must average 2.1 children per woman if the population is to replace itself: two children so that the woman and her partner

Replacement-level fertility is the level of fertility at which each woman bears approximately two children, one to replace herself and one to replace her partner. When this occurs, the next generation will be the same size as the current generation of parents.

are replaced and a little extra to cover unavoidable childhood mortality. This is called **replacement-level fertility.** If fertility is less than this, the next generation will be smaller than the current one.

The average fertility in Europe is 1.5 children per woman. This means that Europe as a whole will begin losing population over the next few generations. The problem is more severe in some nations than others (Table 21.2). In Spain and Italy, the average is 1.2 children per woman. This means that the next generation will be only two-thirds the size of the current one. Since the collapse of the former Soviet Union and the resulting economic uncertainty, the fertility rates of countries in Eastern Europe have sharply declined. For instance, in 1988, before the fall of the Iron Curtain, Russia had a total fertility rate of 2.12 (Haub 1994a). As you can see in Table 21.2, Russia's total fertility rate had plummeted to 1.4 by 1995. Similarly, Russia's crude birthrate fell from 14 in 1990 to 9 in 1995—a drop of more than one-third and the lowest birthrate recorded in any nation since World War II (Population Reference Bureau 1995). Public opinion polls taken in Russia point to insufficient income, inadequate housing, and lack of improvement in living standard as factors discouraging childbearing (Haub 1994b, 13). If this situation continues for several generations, the populations of these countries will be sharply reduced.

Why Is Low Fertility a Problem? Given the serious worldwide dilemmas posed by population growth and the very high density of many European nations, why should this be a problem? There are three broad areas of concern:

TABLE 21.2

FERTILITY AND POPULATION GROWTH IN EUROPE, 1995

Births and deaths are nearly equal in Europe as a whole, but several nations are already experiencing substantial population decline.

COUNTRY	CRUDE BIRTH-RATE	CRUDE DEATH RATE	CRUDE NATURAL GROWTH RATE	AVERAGE NUMBER OF CHILDREN PER WOMAN
EUROPE, TOTAL	11	12	−0.1	1.5
AUSTRIA	12	10	+0.1	1.4
DENMARK	13	12	+0.1	1.8
GERMANY	10	11	−0.1	1.3
HUNGARY	12	14	−0.3	1.7
ITALY	9	10	0	1.2
ROMANIA	11	12	−0.1	1.4
RUSSIA	9	15	−0.6	1.4
SPAIN	10	9	+0.1	1.2
UNITED KINGDOM	13	11	+0.2	1.8

SOURCE: Population Reference Bureau 1996.

1. *Population suicide*. In 1984, French Prime Minister Jacques Chirac said, "[the prospect] is terrifying. In demographic terms, Europe is vanishing. Twenty years or so from now, our countries will be empty, and no matter what our technological strength, we shall be incapable of putting it to use" (Teitelbaum 1987).
2. *Too many old people*. A society with very low fertility takes on an age structure that looks like an inverted pyramid. Because each generation is smaller than the preceding one, the older generation is larger than the younger generations on which it relies for support. This age structure will cause a major dilemma for the old-age portions of many nations' social welfare programs—including that of the United States.
3. *Labor-force shortages*. The decline in fertility has already caused labor-force shortages in many European nations. These shortages have been felt in industry and in the armed forces. The industrial shortages have, until recently, been made up by importation of workers from the Middle East and the Mediterranean. No nation, however, wants to staff its army with outsiders. In any case, concern for cultural dilution has caused many European nations to reduce the importation of workers and to urge their guest workers to return home.

Thinking Critically

One alternative to the problems posed by population aging is for the current 20-something generation to have more children. Another is to postpone retirement until 70 or so. Would you rather have more children or work longer? Which problems of population aging will longer-lasting careers not solve?

Policy Response. In response to these concerns, many European nations have established incentives to encourage fertility. Among them are paid maternity leave, cash bonuses for extra children, longer vacations for mothers, and graduated family allowances. In some countries, new mothers are eligible for six months of paid maternity leave, and many benefits (family allowances, housing subsidies, and even a lower retirement age) are graded according to number of children. Low-interest loans for buying and furnishing homes are available to newly married couples; and with each additional child, an increasing proportion of the loan is written off.

Studies suggest that these incentive plans have had modest effects. In some countries, birthrates jumped after the incentives were introduced, but subsequent analysis suggests that this was because some couples had their children earlier than they intended; the incentives did not prompt very many people to have third or fourth children (David 1982). The difficulty is that children are an expensive, intensive 20-year project. The incentives being offered—for example, Quebec offered a one-time payment of $3,000 for a third child ("Quebec" 1988)—are simply not enough to tempt a sensible person to have another child. Quebec's payment works out to 50 cents a day for the child's first 18 years. Since current estimates suggest that it costs as much as $100,000 to raise a middle-class child, any serious attempt to defray child-rearing costs would be prohibitively expensive (Keyfitz 1987). As long as women and men have attractive alternatives outside the home, it is unlikely that governments can afford to bribe them into voluntarily taking on more than one or two children (Oppenheimer 1994).

China: Mandatory Low Fertility

Half the people in the world live in just six countries: China, India, the United States, Indonesia, Brazil, and Russia (U.S. Bureau of the Census 1994c). Over one-fifth of the world's people—more than 1.2 billion in 1995—live in China. In 1982, China conducted its first modern census. The results confirmed a population of slightly more than 1 billion. One billion is a lot of people to feed, educate, build roads for, and employ. It seems an especially daunting task in a nation with a per capita GNP of $490. In order to meet its people's needs and to implement ambitious plans for economic development, China concluded that it needed to keep its population below 1.2 billion.

Policy Response. In 1949, when the communists first came to power in China, they claimed that China had no population problem. "Of all things in the world, people are the most precious. Under the leadership of the Communist Party, as long as there are people, every kind of miracle can be performed" (Mao Zedong, September 1949, cited in Aird 1972). After 20 years of poor harvests and near famine, however, this naive approach was finally abandoned. During the 1970s, China experimented with a variety of policy options to reduce fertility, including exhortations to marry late and have few children and voluntary family-planning programs.

These programs had modest effects, but the population still grew alarmingly. In a last-ditch effort to try to contain the Chinese population to 1.2 billion by the end of this century, China launched its famous one-child policy in 1982. Incentives for a one-child family include supplementary food and housing, free health care, preferential treatment in schooling and jobs, larger farm allotments in rural areas, and higher pensions. Contraceptives and abortion are widely available, and sterilization is encouraged.

In many nations, family size is considered personal business. In China, fertility is everybody's business. At the height of the one-child program, whole communities were punished if more than 5 percent of their new babies were second or higher births. Women who had a second pregnancy were under intense community pressure to get an abortion, a policy strongly criticized as a violation of women's rights at the 1994 International Conference on Population and Development in Cairo (Ashford 1995). A third birth might cause the woman and her husband to lose their jobs and their home, be shunned by their families, be left out of community affairs, and be denied basic privileges.

Second Thoughts. China's dramatic birth-control program was aided by the transformation of social institutions through the Communist revolution. Nevertheless, China remains a very poor, largely rural country, where many people still depend on their families for labor and security.

Officially, China's birthrate dropped from 33 per 1,000 in 1971 to 18 per 1,000 in 1995, and its growth rate went from 1.8 to 1.1 percent. The average number of children per woman fell dramatically, but the one-child family program has proved nearly impossible to enforce. The average number of children per woman is 2, not 1. The policy has made lawbreakers out of the hundreds of millions of rural couples who still depend on their children for farm labor and their sons for old-age security (Greenhalgh, Chuzhu, and Nan 1994). Policy makers have now admitted that insistence on a one-child policy would impose tremendous hardships on their people and would, in any case, be impossible to enforce. Currently, rural couples whose first child is a girl are allowed to have a second child.

China has had the most aggressive family-planning program in the world. This level of effort, coupled with dramatic changes in social institutions, has allowed China's birthrate to tumble despite continuing poverty. Even though China has not held its population to under 1.2 billion, the country's family-planning efforts have slowed population growth markedly, and China is trying to reach an $800 per capita income by the turn of the century (Post 1994). Without a police officer in

THINKING CRITICALLY

Some people speculate that the most serious drain on world resources in the next decades will not be due to simple population growth but rather to the growing affluence of the Chinese—who can now afford more food, cars, and material goods. Consider both the advantages and disadvantages of growing Chinese affluence for Americans.

Even if you cannot read Chinese, the message on this billboard is unmistakable: One child is enough, even if that child is a girl. Although Chinese officials continue to press for a one-child family, they have relaxed their sanctions against people who have two children—especially when the first child is a girl. Strict enforcement of the one-child policy has been abandoned because of concerns about the age structure and because of widespread recognition that children continue to be valuable to rural families.

every household, however, it is doubtful that China can really achieve even a 1.5-child family until it has realized greater economic development.

Moreover, China's family-planning policy has recently come under attack over three disturbing ethical issues. First, using ultrasound, doctors and parents can discern the sex of a fetus and then use abortion as a sex-selection method. Without any medical intervention, the natural birth ratio is 105 boys born for every 100 girls. The practice of selectively aborting female fetuses in China, however, has resulted in a ratio of 114 boy babies born for every 100 girls (Post 1994). Second, it has recently come to world attention that babies and children in Chinese orphanages are often neglected to the point of death or even killed outright as part of the country's goal of controlling its population ("Report: Chinese" 1996). Third, in 1995, in an effort to weed out "inferior births," China banned marriages between those "with certain genetic diseases of a serious nature" unless they agreed to sterilization or long-term contraception (Post 1994). All three of these concerns point to a question: When, if ever, do individual rights supersede society's need to control its population?

Population Growth, Food Supplies, the Environment, and Poverty

Mention the world *population* and many people immediately think of *population problems*. Certainly the fact that the population is likely to grow to between 10 and 11 billion in their lifetimes seems like a problem to most people. There are, however, many population problems: high mortality, illegal migration, low fertility in Europe, starvation, environmental devastation, and Third World poverty. In this section, we address three of these concerns—food supplies, the environment, and poverty—and analyze the role of population growth in creating and resolving these problems.

Population Growth and Food Supplies

Two hundred years ago, the English economist Thomas Robert Malthus warned that rapid population growth would have dreadful effects on society. In his classic *An Essay on the Principle of Population* (1982 [1798]), Malthus predicted terrible disasters resulting from "the problem between the natural increase of population and food." Malthus argued that population grows geometrically (from 3 to 6 to 12 to 24, for example) but the food supply increases only arithmetically (from 1 to 2 to 3 to 4 and so on). This means that a rapidly growing population will outstrip its food supply.

Whether Malthus was right is a matter of debate. Those who insist that he was right, the "neo-Malthusians," point to rapidly decreasing periods of population-doubling time, together with evidence of starvation in much of the world today. Meanwhile, the "anti-Malthusians" (Simon 1981, 1986) believe that Malthus was wrong. Anti-Malthusians insist that *people* are the world's ultimate resource and that enhanced technology, along with more equal distribution of wealth and resources, can indeed fill our growing world population's dietary and other human needs.

Perhaps half a billion people in the world are seriously malnourished, and some, such as this starving child, face permanent physical and intellectual damage or even death. Few such cases are directly related to overpopulation. Instead, they are due to war, drought, and poverty—and a capitalist world economic system in which rich countries have storehouses of grain and poor nations starve. When the world population reaches over 10 billion in 40 to 50 years, however, there could actually be too little food to go around, even with equal distribution.

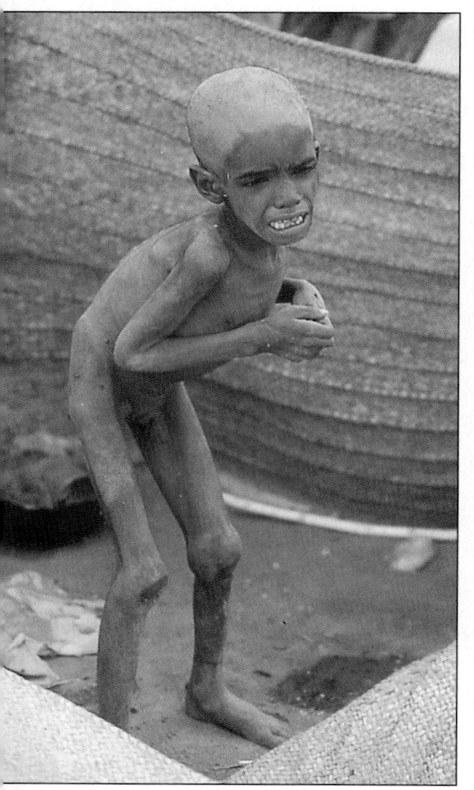

Demographers disagree about the maximum number of people the earth can support. In 1982, the United Nations estimated that under optimal conditions the world could support as many as 33 billion people—almost six times the number we have now. However, a realistic number is probably much lower because most countries would be unable to achieve the highly efficient food production levels assumed in the U.N. estimate. A more likely estimate is that sufficient food could be produced to support 10 to 15 billion people over the 21st century (Lutz 1994). Related to the question of efficient and optimal food production is the issue of maintaining the earth's environment.

Environmental Devastation: A Population Problem?

All around the world, there are signs of enormous environmental destruction. In the developed world, we have acid rain and oil spills; in South America, there is the destruction of the Amazon forest; in Africa, there is the rapid spread of desert environments through deforestation and overgrazing. Although all of these pose serious threats to the natural order, only the last one is truly a population problem.

It is estimated that the United States, which contains only 5 percent of the world's population, consumes one-quarter of the world's resources and produces nearly three-quarters of the world's hazardous waste (Ashford 1995). Our affluent, throwaway lifestyle requires large amounts of petroleum and other natural resources. This unceasing demand for more lies behind oil exploration of fragile lands and subsequent events such as the Exxon oil spill in Price William Sound, Alaska, in 1989. Our unwillingness to pay the price for emission controls lies behind the acid rain and smog that are killing forests and polluting lakes and rivers. Although these problems would be less severe if there were half as many of us (and hence half as many cars, factories, and styrofoam cups), they are not really population problems. They stem from our way of life rather than our numbers.

The destruction of the Amazon forest is also not a population problem. It is a poverty problem (Durning 1989). Brazil needs export dollars to pay its foreign debt and to establish an industrial economy. To get these dollars, it sells what it has most of: trees. In addition, Brazil has encouraged settlement of the Amazon in order to postpone the demand for land redistribution among the landless poor. Reducing the number of Brazilians would not make a serious dent in problems of internal or international poverty.

In sub-Saharan Africa and on the Indian subcontinent, however, population pressure is a major culprit in environmental destruction. The typical scenario runs like this: Population pressure forces farmers to try to plow marginal land and to plant high-yielding crops in quick succession without soil-enhancing rotations or fallow periods. The marginal lands and the overworked soils produce less and less food, forcing farmers to push the land even harder. They cut down forests and windbreaks to free more land for agricultural production. Soon, water and wind erosion become so pervasive that the topsoil is borne off entirely, and the tillable land is replaced by desert or barren rock.

In Haiti, once lush forests of mahogany and tropical oak have been nearly obliterated. The people have cleared land in order to plant quick-growing crops, and the few remaining trees are rapidly being felled to make charcoal, the country's primary fuel. As a result of deforestation, nearly a quarter of the nation's soil is rapidly eroding, and rivers now flow in torrents, decreasing their effectiveness for irrigation. Without a minor miracle, Haiti's few remaining forests will disappear by the middle of the next century (Cobb 1987).

This cycle of environmental destruction—which destroys forests, topsoil, and the plant and animal species that depend on them—is characteristic of high population growth *in combination with poverty*. These people are between a rock and a hard place. When one's children are starving, it is hard to make long-term decisions that will protect the environment for future generations.

Reducing population growth would reduce future pressure on natural resources, but it is no solution to the present problem. Immediate solutions include better management of existing resources, better crop varieties, better storage and less waste, and more scientifically managed crop rotation. Implementing these changes will require diverting investment dollars from cities to rural areas (Repetto 1987). This is a risky political strategy, however, since most governments depend for their support on urban settlements, not rural hinterlands. If these governments raise rural incomes and the price of food, urban riots are possible.

In summary, the world's environment is being destroyed at an alarming rate. Population growth has contributed to some of this problem, and sharply reduced population growth can keep the problems from accelerating. Unless we are willing to countenance mass mortality, however, population control cannot be the only or the most immediate solution. The solution rests in an international moral and financial commitment to reducing rural poverty, improving farming practices, reducing Third World debt, and reducing our own wasteful and destructive practices.

Third World Poverty

Three-quarters of the human race live in less-developed nations, where the GNP per capita is 1/20 that in the developed world. At least 500 million are seriously undernourished, and each year outbreaks of famine and starvation occur in Africa and Asia; a billion more are poorly nourished, poorly educated, and poorly sheltered. These people live in the nations that have high population growth.

There are some observers who blame Third World poverty on high fertility, thus neatly laying the entire fault at the victim's door. It is clear, however, that high fertility is not the only or even the primary cause of Third World poverty. The causes lie in the system of international stratification (described in detail in Chapter 10).

Although fertility does not directly cause poverty, the two do go hand in hand. Poverty is synonymous with lack of development; it means that people lack education and that there is no system of old-age pensions, welfare, or insurance other than the family. Thus, fertility remains at its traditional high levels. Before fertility

The level of fertility in any society is closely related to the roles women play. These women attending an open market near Nairobi (Kenya) are either choosing their family's groceries or marketing their farm's produce, tasks for which women are largely responsible. Neither activity is hampered by having many children. As long as women's roles remain centered around household activities, there is little incentive to have smaller families in societies like Kenya's.

will fall, there must be some social or economic development that encourages people to change traditional ways of life.

Third World poverty and starvation, then, do not result solely from high fertility. Nevertheless, rapid population growth does provide a hurdle for developing nations. Short doubling times make it difficult to make any substantial progress in protecting the environment, increasing education, or raising the standard of living.

Programs to Reduce Fertility

High fertility, as noted, is not the primary cause of most of the problems that are often linked to population growth. Nor will reducing fertility by itself solve most of these problems. Nevertheless, fertility reduction programs are widely seen as desirable and even necessary. Lower growth rates will make it easier for governments to meet environmental and economic goals, will free parents to take better care of the children they have, and will prevent the birth of additional children into impoverished circumstances. Programs to reduce fertility are of two general types: family-planning programs and economic development programs.

1. *Family-planning programs*. Family-planning programs attempt to make modern contraceptives and sterilization available inexpensively and conveniently. The programs are designed to help people plan their families; they do not attempt to alter the number of children individuals desire. There is a great need for these kinds of programs. For example, a 1989 survey in Haiti found that 41 percent of the Haitian women who were not using contraception desired to do so (Barberis 1994).

Easily available contraception will help women avoid unwanted births and, if it is easy enough to use, may even change their ideas about how many children they want. Between 1973 and 1987, an aggressive family-planning program doubled contraceptive use in Mexico and moved sterilization to the most popular form of birth control. The result was that the average number of children per woman dropped from 6.3 to 3.8 in just 15 years ("Survey Report" 1990). Between 1975 and 1991, an aggressive family-planning program increased contraceptive use in Bangladesh by 500 percent and decreased the average number of children per woman from 7.0 to 4.9 in just 16 years (Kalish 1994a). Mexico's and Bangladesh's success may be difficult to repeat in areas such as Kenya, however, where income, education, and access to medical clinics are so much lower.

2. *Economic development*. Experience all over the world shows that a rise in education and other indices of development reduces fertility. For example, South Korea's fertility has plummeted from 6.0 children per woman in 1960 to only 1.6 in the wake of its dramatic economic development (Haub 1991). Since development is highly desired in its own right, this is an attractive policy for reducing fertility.

The most successful programs to reduce fertility have combined an aggressive family-planning program with a push toward economic development (Poston and Gu 1987). Nations such as Indonesia, Mexico, and Colombia have reduced their fertility sharply within a matter of decades by use of such programs. Both family planning and development can have some effect on fertility by themselves, but the combination of easy access to contraception *and* a changed way of life is much more effective than either alone.

Sustainable Development

With a population of 5.7 billion and growing, it is clear that planet Earth simply cannot sustain the kind of energy-hungry, wasteful, pollution-riddled development that has driven the economies of First and Second World nations. In 1987, the Brundtland Commission defined **sustainable development** as "development that meets the needs of the present without compromising the ability of future generations to meet their own needs." There is broad agreement within the international community that two major changes will be necessary to achieve this type of development.

Sustainable development meets the needs of the present without compromising the ability of future generations to meet their own needs.

First and foremost, sustainable development will require the elimination of absolute poverty so that the 1.1 billion poorest of the world's people can produce or buy the food, clothing, and housing necessary to ensure health and self-respect (State of World Population 1992). Ending absolute poverty will depend, then, on improving access to education, health care, clean water, and sanitation. It will depend, too, on increasing the status of women and reducing the buildup of military arms that already costs Third World nations an enormous share of their scarce resources (Sen and Grown 1987). Ending poverty is a goal in itself, but since poverty and rapid population growth are often found together, it will also enhance development by limiting population size.

In addition to eliminating destitution, sustainable development will require meeting the legitimate aspirations of the 3.6 billion people who are neither very poor nor rich. In today's world, the most affluent 1 billion satisfy their aspirations with little regard for sustainability, but the world will not be able to satisfy the aspirations of billions more people in this way. Consequently, in order to meet the needs of the middle third of the world's population, the economic inequalities that exist within and between countries will have to be reduced and the benefits of development more fairly distributed.

Second, sustainable development will require slower population growth. Smaller increases in world population, coupled with an evolution to lower-consumption lifestyles and more efficient production, will reduce the environmental impact of development and help to ensure equal access to "the good life" across generations (State of World Population 1992).

Outlook: Good News/Bad News

Analysis of world population puts us in a good-news/bad-news situation. The good news is that fertility is declining. The decline is uneven, but it is visible in almost all corners of the world (see Table 21.3). Worldwide, fertility declined by 32 percent between the late 1960s and the mid-1990s.

The bad news is that the population of the world will double within 40 to 50 years anyway. The reason for this gloomy prediction lies in the current age structure. The next generation of mothers is already born—and there are a lot of them. As the pyramidal shape of sub-Saharan Africa's age structure in Figure 21.5 demonstrates, high-fertility nations have a population of children (future parents) that is much larger than the current generation of parents. This force for population growth is called *momentum*, and it is roughly measured by the ratio of girls aged 0 to 4 to the number of women aged 25 to 29. In sub-Saharan Africa, the ratio is 2 to 1. As we have already seen, this means that the next generation will have twice as many mothers as (and hence more babies than) this generation.

TABLE 21.3
CHANGES IN AVERAGE FAMILY SIZE

In the last several decades, the average number of children being born per woman has decreased 36 percent worldwide. Although African fertility decline has just started, this decrease has been noticeable in all parts of the world. Because mortality has fallen too, however, and because of the momentum of the age structure, population is still growing rapidly.

AREA	AVERAGE NUMBER OF CHILDREN PER WOMAN 1968–1972	1996	PERCENTAGE CHANGE
WORLD	4.7	3.0	−36%
AFRICA	6.4	5.7	−11
ASIA	5.4	2.9	−46
LATIN AMERICA	5.5	3.1	−44
EUROPE AND NORTH AMERICA	2.8	1.6	−43

SOURCE: Data for early years from Freyka 1973, T.4–1; 1995 data from Population Reference Bureau 1995

Zero population growth (ZPG) means that the number of births is the same as the number of deaths, so the population does not grow.

Demographers often posit zero population growth as a demographic goal. **Zero population growth (ZPG)** means that the number of births is the same as the number of deaths; no growth occurs. This goal is almost impossible when the age structure is pyramidal. When the population bearing children is much larger than the elderly population, it is likely that there will be many more births than deaths even when fertility is relatively low.

Zero population growth, then, is not on the immediate horizon. There are only two possible ways to stop population growth *now:* massive mortality or forced sterilization and abortion programs that would restrict each woman to no more than one child. Since these solutions are widely regarded as worse than the problem, we must continue to plan for a world that will soon hold 10 to 11 billion people.

POPULATION IN THE UNITED STATES

The United States does not have a population problem in the same way that less-developed countries do, but population issues can still cause heated debate. The conflict usually centers on the changing composition of the U.S. population rather than its overall growth rate. In this section, we examine fertility, mortality, immigration, and growth issues in the United States.

POPULATION GROWTH

In 1994, the United States had a total resident population of 260 million persons. The U.S. Census Bureau projects that by 2000, the population will have increased to 276 million, and it will continue to grow until it reaches about 392 million in 2050 (U.S. Bureau of the Census 1995, Tables 2 and 3). Figure 21.8

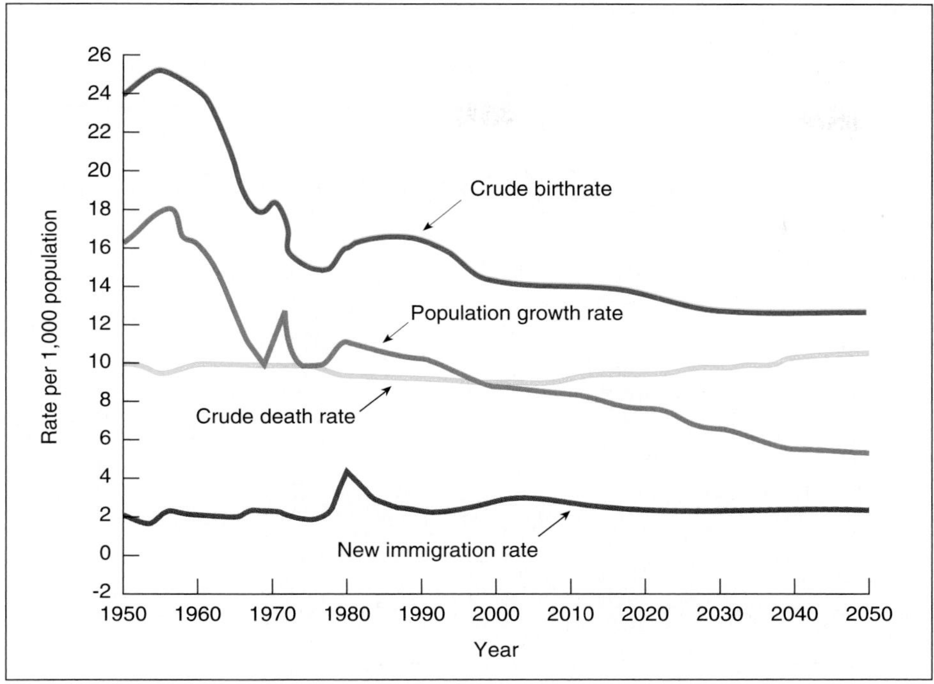

FIGURE 21.8
THE FUTURE OF U.S. POPULATION GROWTH

By 2030, the natural population growth rate of the U.S. is predicted to dip below zero. Because of immigration, however, it does not seem likely that the U.S. population will actually decline.

shows the components of U.S. population growth: birthrate, death rate, and net immigration rate (the number who permanently enter the United States minus those who leave).

FERTILITY

For nearly 25 years now, the number of children per woman in the United States has stood at 1.8 to 2.0. The Census Bureau projects that by 2010, the total fertility rate of American women will be slightly more than the 2.1 necessary to replace the population (U.S. Bureau of the Census 1995, Table 92).

Table 21.4 shows birthrates, death rates, net immigration rates, and population growth rates for various racial/ethnic groups in the United States. As you can see from that table, Hispanics have the highest birthrate, followed by non-Hispanic blacks. Non-Hispanic whites have the lowest birthrate. As recently as 1988, Census Bureau statisticians assumed that fertility rates would gradually converge among racial and ethnic groups. The bureau has since abandoned that assumption (Pear 1992). While all birthrates are projected to fall somewhat by 2000, minority women are expected to continue having more children than non-Hispanic whites. The total fertility rate for white women is about 2.0. As a result, the U.S. white population, like the populations of Europe and Japan, had a negative rate of natural increase (−2.5 percent) in 1992, the last year for which this figure is available. Meanwhile, the 2.4 total fertility rate among racial and ethnic minorities is projected to remain about that through 2010, giving racial and ethnic minority populations an annual natural increase of 7.5 percent (U.S. Bureau of the Census 1995, Tables 91 and 92).

TABLE 21.4
COMPONENTS OF U.S. POPULATION CHANGE

	PROJECTIONS			
	BIRTHRATE	DEATH RATE	NET IMMIGRATION RATE	POPULATION GROWTH RATE
NON-HISPANIC WHITE				
1995	13.1	9.3	1.0	4.8
2000	11.9	9.5	1.0	3.4
NON-HISPANIC BLACK				
1995	20.5	8.8	1.9	13.7
2000	19.4	9.1	1.8	12.1
HISPANICS				
1995	23.8	3.7	12.0	32.1
2000	22.1	4.0	10.3	28.5
ASIANS AND PACIFIC ISLANDERS				
1995	17.5	2.7	32.5	47.2
2000	16.9	2.9	26.1	40.1
NATIVE AMERICANS				
1995	17.9	4.4	0.1	13.7
2000	17.7	4.6	0.1	13.2

SOURCE: U.S. Bureau of the Census 1995, Table 20.

MORTALITY

The average age at death is now in the 70s or early 80s. Men who survive to 65 can expect to live another 15 years; women another 19 years. In the last 25 years, we have added almost five years to life expectancy and also reduced racial and social class differentials in mortality, although they still exist (U.S. Bureau of the Census 1995, Tables 114 and 115). At the time of World War II, black women lived a full 12 years less than white women; by 1992, the gap was down to just over 5 years. As we saw in Chapter 13, a declining death rate, coupled with a low fertility rate, results in an aging population. The average age of the U.S. population, now 34, is projected to be 39 by 2050 (U.S. Bureau of the Census 1995, Table 13). As you can see in Figure 21.8, the death rate will continue to fall until about 2000, after which it will rise slightly. The projected rise after 2000 will occur because the overall population will be older, not because individuals will cease to live as long as they do now.

MIGRATION

Demographers are interested in the study of migration patterns for two reasons: First, migration is one of the major determinants of population size. Although it can safely be ignored as a factor in world population growth, migration often has dramatic effects on the growth of individual nations. The United States is one of the nations where immigration, the permanent movement of people into another country, has had an important impact. Second, patterns of internal migration have enormous consequences for most of our social institutions. In the United States, the processes of urbanization, suburbanization, and migration from Rustbelt to Sunbelt have created a unique set of problems and have dramatically changed our political landscape.

An estimated 1 million people enter the United States each year. Almost all of the recent immigrants come from Latin America or Asia. Perhaps as many as half are illegal immigrants, most of whom are from Mexico or Central America. The causes of immigration are primarily economic; immigrants, legal and illegal, are pushed from their native lands by poor local economies and are pulled by an unmet demand in the United States for low-skilled, low-paid labor. The consequences of current immigration trends are likely to be both economic and cultural. From the standpoint of economics, three generalizations seem to be supported: (1) Immigrants are not taking jobs away from American citizens; but (2) the availability of low-wage illegals does depress wages in some economic sectors; and (3) Hispanics and other minorities are the ones hardest hit by this.

The Future of U.S. Population

Figure 21.9 shows the racial and ethnic composition of America in 1993 and gives two alternative projections for the U.S. population in 2050. One projection involves no further immigration at all and shows moderate population growth to about 320 million persons in 2050. This growth would be due entirely to *natural*

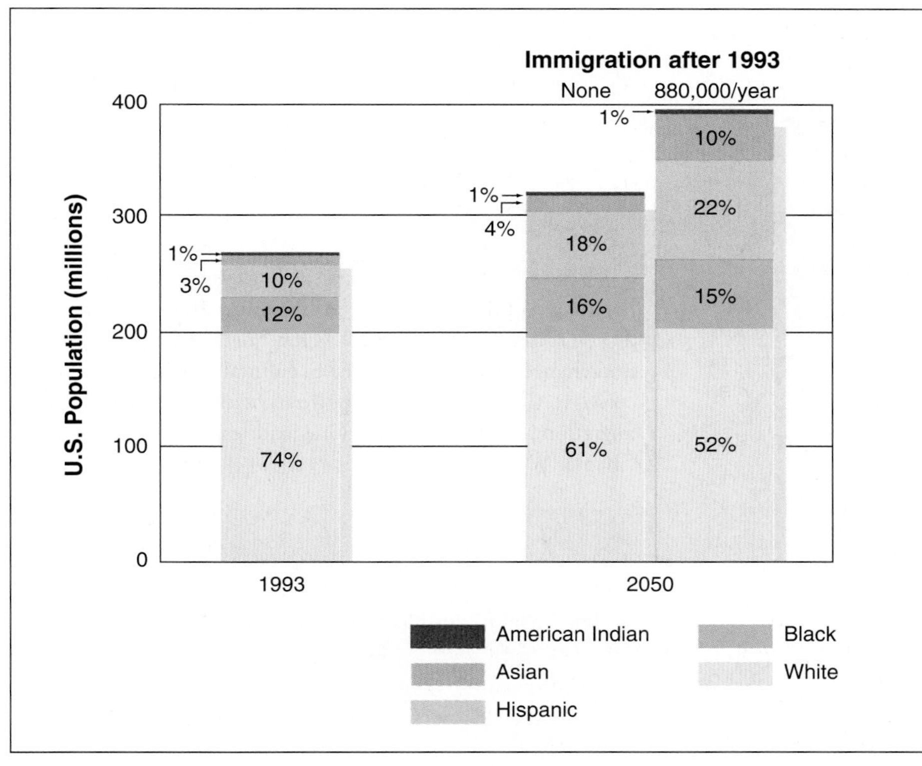

FIGURE 21.9
U.S. POPULATION IN 1993 AND 2050 BY RACE/ETHNICITY, WITH AND WITHOUT IMMIGRATION AFTER 1993

[a] *American Indians make up 1 percent of the population in each bar.*

SOURCE: Martin and Midgley 1994, 9.

APPLICATIONS IN DIVERSITY

WHAT DO WE KNOW ABOUT INTERNATIONAL MIGRATION?

Some are pushed out of their homeland by violence and drought, while others are pulled by new opportunities. Perhaps as many as 40 percent have left their homes involuntarily. These 40 percent of international migrants are refugees, or "forced migrants"—individuals for whom ethnic conflict or changes in national boundaries have produced refugee-like situations. Although the United States has long grappled with the question of how many immigrants and refugees its educational and economic institutions can successfully absorb, what do we know about international migration?

Estimates are that in the mid-1980s, 100 million people were "living outside of their countries of birth or citizenship." Of these, a high proportion were refugees, approximately two-thirds of whom had moved to other developing countries. Demographers believe that the political turmoil and violence in Eastern Europe, Southeast Asia, and sub-Saharan Africa have substantially increased the numbers of involuntary migrants living in other Third World nations. The result, of course, is that enormous strain is placed on the already limited capacities of host countries to sustain their own growing populations.

Although push factors such as war and famine account for much of the movement between developing countries, some migrants are also pulled by the economic growth and employment opportunities in newly industrializing nations, such as South Korea, Singapore, and Malaysia. Pull factors also account for much of the immigration from less to more developed countries. Strong European economies provide increasing numbers of jobs to a growing non-Western labor force. Migrants traditionally have been young men, but women and girls now make up 40 to 60 percent of the international migrant stream; many of these are mothers who, in growing numbers, seek employment opportunities in more affluent neighboring countries in order to send money to the family, friends, or neighbors who are raising their children.

The money sent back home by migrants—both men and women—is a large and growing source of revenue for many nations. In 1990, payments amounted to $71 billion, a sum second in value globally only to trade in crude oil. In the late 1980s, remittances to developing countries alone ($37 billion) amounted to almost two-thirds the value of official development assistance. It is not yet clear, however, who profits most from the international migrant stream. Although countries such as Germany, France, and Italy do face new challenges stemming from an ethnically diverse population, workers from developing nations are, in fact, helping to sustain the continued expansion of the European economy. Low birthrates have led to smaller labor forces and aging populations in much of Europe. Thus, migrants from countries such as Turkey and Pakistan fill the demand for more workers, particularly those at the low end of the labor hierarchy. Whether the money that migrants send home will significantly improve the quality of life in Third World nations remains an open question.

SOURCE: Kalish 1994b.

THINKING CRITICALLY

How will international migration patterns affect the population of the United States in the next 20 to 50 years, do you think? (See Figure 21.9.) How might these population changes affect dominant U.S. cultural values, discussed in Chapter 3? How do patterns of international migration reflect international inequalities, described in Chapter 10?

APPLICATIONS IN DIVERSITY

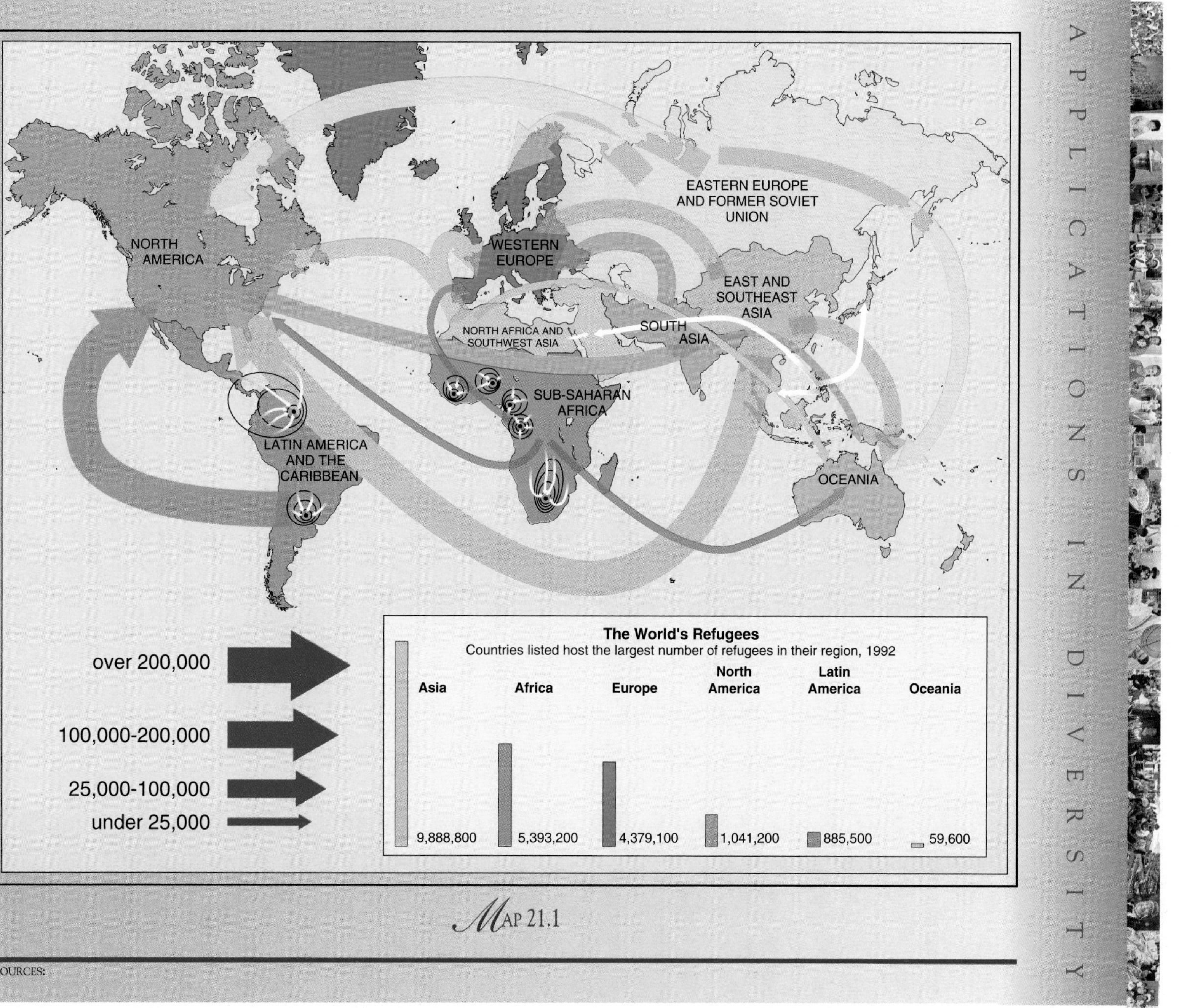

MAP 21.1

SOURCES:

increase—that is, to the birthrate's being slightly higher than the death rate. As the figure shows, even without further immigration, ethnic diversity in the United States will increase, because of differential fertility rates. The non-Hispanic white population, with a negative rate of natural increase, will decline in relation to total population to 61 percent in 2050, while the black, Hispanic, and Asian populations will increase to 17, 18, and 4 percent, respectively.

At present, immigration accounts for about one-third of U.S. population growth. The projection on the right in Figure 21.9 assumes an annual immigration rate of 880,000. Immigration at this level would yield a grand total of nearly 400 million Americans by 2050 and further enhance the nation's ethnic mix. From the standpoint of culture, the United States would become a far more pluralistic society, perhaps one that is multilingual and has no majority population.

In 1970, there were 57.5 Americans per square mile in the United States; by 1995, there were 75. If U.S. population increases to 400 million by 2050, there will be about 113 persons per square mile. This is hardly crowded by some standards. For instance, Bangladesh has a population of 2,478 persons per square mile (U.S. Bureau of the Census 1995, Tables 28 and 1361). Whether a population with as many as 400 million will feel too crowded to Americans, as well as whether increasing ethnic diversity is desirable, are matters of individual values, not necessarily questions for scientific or demographic investigation.

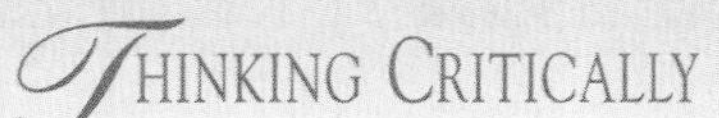

Do you think the United States should encourage or limit further immigration? Explain your answer.

SOCIOLOGY ON THE NET

The world's population is rapidly changing in ways that will influence the lives of each and every one of us. There are many organizations throughout the world that are carefully monitoring these changes and their impact on our lives. One of these organizations is the Population Reference Bureau.

`http://www.igc.apc.org/prb`

Let's begin our tour by playing population jeopardy. Click on **Play population jeopardy!** How well did you do? Now go back to the **home page** and browse around for a bit. What is the Population Reference Bureau and what do they do? Scroll down to **Read *Population Today*** and open this section. Scroll down and open the **April 1996** issue. Find the earth day feature article entitled Population, Consumption, and the Earth's Future. What resources do the top fifth of the world's population consume? What is the environmental impact caused by a birth in the U.S. versus a birth in India or sub-Saharan Africa? What does the future hold in terms of natural resources and population?

`http://www.undp.org`

Welcome to the United Nations Development Programme on sustainable development. Click on the button entitled **About UNDP**. Now click on the button for the **UNDP Statement of Purpose**. What is sustainable development and how does it differ from the development of past decades? How does the U.N. seek to promote sustainable development? Return to the **UNDP Information page** and open the **UNDP Programme Activities** section. Open and briefly skim through the sections on **UNDP and the Communications Revolution** and the **SDNP – Sustainable Development Networking Programme**. How can technology be used to help foster sustainable development?

The International Institute for Sustainable Development is a private non-profit organization concerned with sustainable development.

`http://iisd1.iisd.ca/about`

Open the selection on **Our Signature Design**. What is the symbolism of the design and how does it reflect the central concerns of sustainable development? Return to the previous page and click on the **You are @iisdnet bar**. This opens the home page. Click on the **Contents** bar. Open and read the brief summaries entitled **What is SD?**, **Chronology and Principles**. Where did the notion of sustainable development originate? What are the principles of sustainable development? Why haven't we heard much more about sustainable development on the news? What barriers keep us from achieving sustainable development? What price are you willing to pay for sustainable development?

SUMMARY

1. For most of human history, fertility was about equal to mortality, and the population grew slowly or not at all. Childbearing was a lifelong task for most women, and death was a frequent visitor to most households, claiming as many as one-third of all infants in the first year of life.
2. The demographic transition in the West began with a decline in mortality. Major causes of the decreased mortality, in order of occurrence, were improved nutrition, improved standard of living and hygiene, improved public sanitation, and modern medicine.
3. The decline of fertility in the West is attributable to the entire transformation of the social fabric that occurred as a result of industrialization, especially the changing roles of women and the family and a break with traditional values.
4. In the non-West, mortality declined very rapidly after World War II, while fertility remained relatively unchanged. The result has been rapid population growth, with a doubling time of about 36 years. Future declines in fertility and mortality will depend on economic development and improved standards of living.
5. Social structure, fertility, and mortality are interdependent; changes in one affect the others. Among the most important consequences of high fertility are restricted roles for women and a high dependency ratio.
6. The level of fertility in a society has much to do with the balance of costs and rewards associated with childbearing. In traditional societies, such as that of Kenya, most social structures (the economy, religion, and the family, for example) support high fertility. In many modern societies, such as those of Europe and the United States, social structure imposes many costs on parents.
7. Population growth is not the only or even the primary cause of environmental devastation or Third World poverty, nor is limiting it the primary solution. Continued population growth does contribute to these problems, however, and reducing growth will make it easier to seek solutions.
8. Sustainable development is the ability to meet the needs of the present without compromising the ability of future generations to meet their own needs. Sustainable development will require (1) the elimination of absolute poverty and the reduction of inequality within and between nations, and (2) a reduction in population growth, coupled with more efficient production and less wasteful lifestyles.

9 Fertility levels are declining all over the world. Nevertheless, the population of the world will reach 10 to 11 billion in the next 40 to 50 years. The age structure of the current population provides momentum toward growth, and zero population will not be achieved any time soon.

10 U.S. women are reproducing at about replacement levels. Differentials in fertility by race and ethnicity mean that gradually the United States will become more ethnically diverse owing to different rates of natural increase.

11 Approximately 1 million immigrants, legal and illegal, enter the United States each year. Concerns include changes in the ethnic/cultural mix of the population and the effect on citizens' economic prospects.

12 International migrants leave their homelands because of push and/or pull factors. About 40 percent of international migrants are refugees—"forced migrants" for whom ethnic conflict or changes in national boundaries produce refugee-like situations.

SUGGESTED READINGS

ASHFORD, Lori S. 1995. "New Perspectives on Population: Lessons from Cairo." *Population Bulletin* 50 (1) (March). Washington, D.C.: Population Reference Bureau. A pamphlet that discusses current population growth and its implications and explains events and controversies at the 1994 International Conference on Population and Development (ICPD) in Cairo.

FALKENMARK, Malin, and Widstrand, Carl. 1992. "Population and Water Resources: A Delicate Balance." *Population Bulletin* 47 (3) (November). Washington, D.C.: Population Reference Bureau. A pamphlet that explores one aspect of the impact of population growth on the environment by examining in detail the world's water supply and how population growth affects this absolutely necessary resource.

HAUB, Carl. 1994. "Population Change in the Former Soviet Republics." *Population Bulletin* 49 (4) (December). Washington, D.C.: Population Reference Bureau. A pamphlet describing changing social conditions in countries of the former Soviet Union and the dramatic impact of these changes on population measures such as birthrates, death rates, and consequent rates of natural increase.

LUTZ, Wolfgang. 1994. "The Future of World Population." *Population Bulletin* 49 (1) (June). Washington, D.C.: Population Reference Bureau. A pamphlet explaining how demographers project population for the world and various regions and describing in detail some of those projections, along with their implications. Basic concepts, such as demographic transition, are also discussed.

MALTHUS, Thomas Robert. 1982. *Essay on the Principle of Population*. New York: Penguin Classics. A reprint of Malthus's classic 1798 essay in which he argued that population growth would have dire consequences for the world, mainly because arithmetically increasing food supplies could not possibly keep up with the geometrically burgeoning demand.

MARTIN, Philip, and Midgley, Elizabeth. 1994. "Immigration to the United States: Journey to an Uncertain Destination." *Population Bulletin* 49 (2) (September). Washington, D.C.: Population Reference Bureau. An interesting pamphlet describing migration around the world.

MCFALLS, Joseph A., Jr. 1991. "Population: A Lively Introduction." *Population Bulletin* 46 (2). Washington, D.C.: Population Reference Bureau. A pamphlet summarizing contemporary issues and trends in world and U.S. population while defining basic demographic terms.

Population Today. Washington, D.C.: Population Reference Bureau. This monthly publication is a digest of important population news intended for an educated audience of nonprofessionals. It covers U.S. foreign policy and domestic population news and includes information about specific nations around the world.

SIMON, Julian L. 1981. *The Ultimate Resource*. Princeton, N.J.: Princeton University Press. An "anti-Malthusian" answer to Malthus and "neo-Malthusians" which argues that people are the world's ultimate resource and that enhanced technology, along with more equal distribution of wealth and resources, can indeed fill our growing world population's dietary and other human needs.

VISARIA, Leela, and Visaria, Pravin. 1995. "India's Population in Transition." *Population Bulletin* 50 (3) (October). Washington, D.C.: Population Reference Bureau. A pamphlet describing the demographic transition as it applies to contemporary India. Many of the concepts and issues addressed in this chapter are discussed in the context of India.

CHAPTER 22

Metropolitan Living and Patterns of Settlement

OUTLINE

URBAN GROWTH AND CHANGE

GLOBAL PERSPECTIVES: THIRD WORLD CITIES

URBAN LIFE IN THE UNITED STATES

THE POLITICAL ECONOMY OF SPATIAL DISTRIBUTION

URBAN REVITALIZATION

FOCUS ON ANOTHER CULTURE: Copenhagen—Why Does It Work?

SOCIAL APPLICATIONS: Why Are Metropolitan Areas Racially Segregated?

PROLOGUE

Have You Ever... thought about whether you prefer living in the central city, in the suburbs, or in the country? Do you like the cultural diversity characteristic of cities? The variety of activities, restaurants, concerts, and other events available in large cities? Or do you prefer the relative spaciousness, quiet, fresh air, and ethnic homogeneity associated with country living? Maybe you prefer suburban life, with its fairly easy access to a large central city and yet more room and less traffic.

Today it has become common in some circles to disparage city living. Some critics view America's inner cities as not worth saving. Urbanization has definitely been associated with social problems: crowding, traffic congestion, poverty, crime rates, and environmental concerns, to name but a few. And this seems to be the case worldwide. Some people describe inner cities as looking like bombed-out war zones. Some sections of some cities do!

On the other hand, there are those who enjoy city life—and not just to visit. Urban residents, sometimes called *metropolites*, appreciate the cultural and ethnic diversity, the varied shops, the cafes, the musical variety, the museums, the international foods. And some urban dwellers point out that many of them do indeed care and show concern for their metropolitan neighbors.

In this chapter, we consider the factors that shape the residential distribution of the population, both globally and in the United States. And we look at the consequences of residential choices for individuals and society.

For most people in the contemporary United States, to speak of social life is to speak of metropolitan (urban or suburban) life. More than 75 percent of this generation's college students were born and raised in metropolitan areas. This chapter takes a look at the residential settings of contemporary social activity. Among the questions it considers are the consequences of residential patterns for human social behavior, the changing balance among urban, suburban, and rural life, and the political economy of spatial distribution.

URBAN GROWTH AND CHANGE

Urban growth and change is largely a story of the last century. It has been estimated that as late as 1850, only 2 percent of the world's population lived in cities of 100,000 or more (Davis 1973). Today, nearly a quarter of the world's population and more than two-thirds of the U.S. population live in cities larger than 100,000. Paralleling this increasing urbanization of the world is an evolution in the character of the city. The modern city is very different from the city that developed in the 2nd century—or even the 19th.

THE PREINDUSTRIAL CITY

The preindustrial economy is dominated by primary production. Whether it is farming, herding, mining, or forestry, economic activity is essentially rural activity.

This street scene in Morocco is typical of many of the ancient cities that grew up in preindustrial times. The narrow streets are built for pedestrians, not for automobiles. Many of the shops also include living quarters, and there is much less separation of residential and business areas.

The cities that emerge under these conditions are largely trading and administrative centers.

The preindustrial city was a much smaller affair than the modern city, and it was also very differently organized. Most people got from place to place by walking. Because transportation was difficult, people lived and worked in the same building. Children, cooking odors, and laundry pervaded all parts of the city.

Then, as now, the city was a major force in the development of art, culture, and technology. It was also a crowded, filthy, and dangerous place. Human and animal waste turned streets and canals into open sewers, and the birthrate in cities could not keep up with the death rate. The only way cities could maintain their populations was by constantly drawing new recruits from the countryside.

This description probably fit most of the world's cities until at least 1800. Like Damascus or Cairo, early U.S. cities lacked sewers and safe drinking supplies. And far from offering bright lights, cities closed down at nightfall, since there were no streetlights.

The Industrial City

With the advent of the industrial revolution, production moved from the countryside to the urban factory, and industrial cities were born. These cities were mill towns, steel towns, shipbuilding towns, and later, automobile-building towns. They were the products of new technologies, new forms of transportation, and vastly increased agricultural productivity that freed most workers from the land.

The new industrial cities grew rapidly during the 19th century. In the United States, the urban population grew from 2 to 22 million in the half century between 1840 and 1890. In 1860, New York became the first U.S. city to reach 1 million. The industrial base that provided the impetus for city growth also gave the industrial city its character: tremendous density, a central business district, and a concentric zone pattern of land use (Knox 1995).

Density. A critical factor in explaining the character of the industrial city as it developed in the 19th century is that most people still walked to work—and everywhere else, for that matter. The result was dense crowding of working-class housing around manufacturing plants. Even in 1910, the average New Yorker commuted only two blocks to work. Thus, the industrial city saw much more crowding than either the preindustrial or postindustrial city. Entire families shared a single room; and in major cities such as New York and London, dozens of people crowded into a single cellar or attic. The crowded conditions, accompanied by a lack of sewage treatment and clean water, fostered tuberculosis, epidemic diseases, and generally high mortality.

Central Business District (CBD). The lack of transportation and communication facilities also contributed to another characteristic of the industrial city, the central business district (CBD). The CBD is a dense concentration of retail trade, banking and finance, and government offices, all clustered close together so messengers could run between offices and people could walk to meet one another. By 1880, most major cities had electric streetcars or railway systems to take traffic into and out of the city. Because most transit routes offered services only into and out of the CBD rather than providing crosstown routes, the earliest improvements over walking enhanced rather than decreased the importance of the CBD as the hub of the city.

Concentric Zone Pattern. Spatial analysis of early industrial cities suggests that they often approximated a series of rings, or concentric zones (see Figure 22.1). Zone 1, the CBD, was characterized by dense building; land values were so high that only the most profitable commercial operations could afford to locate there. Residential use and large commercial operations were pushed to the periphery of the city. Meanwhile, high land values encouraged vertical growth, and eventually skyscrapers came to dominate the landscape of the CBD.

Zones 2 and 3 included the manufacturing plants and the families who worked in them. The working class was still largely dependent on walking to work; thus, most workers lived close to the plants. Noise, smoke, and pollution reduced the attractiveness of Zone 3 for residential use, thereby bringing housing prices into the reach of the working class. For the most part, Zone 3 housing consisted of tenements, apartment blocks, and row houses.

In the industrial city, everyone who could afford to live away from the noise and smoke and smell did so. The upper class occupied the periphery of the city, Zone 5. The middle class occupied the intermediate area, Zone 4. Again, because of transportation problems—most residents did not have access to automobiles until around 1920—all areas of the industrial city were densely packed (Knox 1995). Even middle-class families more often lived in duplex and row houses than in single-family homes; as drives through older neighborhoods still indicate, single-family homes occupied small lots, with the houses almost touching each other.

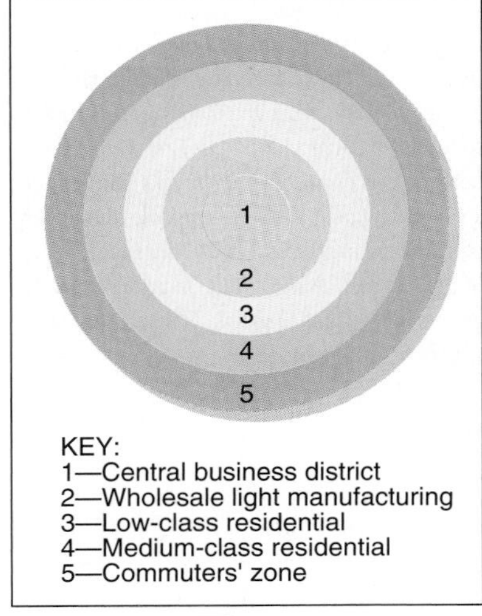

FIGURE 22.1
CONCENTRIC ZONE MODEL OF URBAN SPATIAL PATTERNS

The early industrial city developed a characteristic circular pattern. Because transportation was limited, business activity and working-class housing were densely concentrated toward the center. Only the more affluent could afford to live on the edges, away from the noise and pollution.

SOURCE: Harris and Ullman 1945.

THE POSTINDUSTRIAL CITY

The industrial city was a product of a manufacturing economy plus a relatively immobile labor force. Beginning about 1950, these conditions changed, and a new type of city began to grow. Among the factors prominent in shaping the character of the post industrial city are the change from secondary to tertiary production and greater ease of communication and transportation. These closely related changes have led to a much diminished role for the central business districts; a dispersion of retail, manufacturing, and residential areas; and a much lower urban density.

Change from Secondary to Tertiary Production. As we noted in Chapter 17, the manufacturing plants that shaped the industrial city are disappearing. Many of those that remain have moved to the suburbs, where land is cheaper, taking working-class jobs, housing, and trade with them.

Instead of manufacturing, the contemporary central city is dominated by services or tertiary production: medical and educational complexes, information-processing industries, convention and entertainment centers, and administrative offices. These are the growth industries. They are also white-collar industries. These same industries, plus retail trade, also dominate the suburban economy.

Easier Communication and Transportation. The central business district of the industrial city was held together by the need for physical proximity. Development of telecommunications and good highways greatly reduced this need. Once that happened, high land values and commuting costs led more and more businesses to locate on the periphery, where land was cheaper and housing more desirable. Many corporate headquarters moved from the northeast industrial cities to Arizona or Texas.

A key factor in increasing individual mobility was the automobile. Without the automobile, workers and businesses could not have moved to the city periphery,

During the 19th and early 20th centuries, many cities grew up around manufacturing plants. These industrial cities are characterized by high density. Since the working class walked to work (and everywhere else), working-class housing was crowded in the blocks immediately surrounding the plants. The middle and upper classes lived in the city's outer rings and, later, in the suburbs. Although the plants are largely gone, this residential social-class pattern persists to a significant extent.

and space-gobbling single-family homes would not have been built. In this sense, the automobile has been the chief architect of U.S. cities since 1950. It has given them a freedom of form that older cities could not have (Goddard 1994).

Urban Sprawl. The new cities are much larger in geographical area than the industrial cities were. (See Figure 22.2.) The average city in 1940 was probably less than 15 miles across; now many metropolitan areas are 50 to 75 miles across, giving rise to the term *urban sprawl*. No longer are the majority of people bound by subway and railway lines that only go back and forth to downtown. Retail trade is dominated by huge, climate-controlled, pedestrian-safe suburban malls. A great proportion of the retail and service labor force has also moved out to suburban centers, and many of the people who live in the suburbs also work in them (Adler 1995b; Knox 1995).

Multiple Nuclei. Spatial analysis of new cities suggests that they are no longer divided into concentric zones and are far less dominated by the central business district. The vertical growth so apparent earlier has been partially replaced by horizontal growth in the form of urban sprawl. The general configuration of modern cities often conforms to a multiple nuclei pattern (see Figure 22.3). In cities that grew up before 1950, the development of multiple nuclei in the periphery has caused real problems, as the once-vital central business districts are increasingly abandoned by business and shoppers, leaving behind empty buildings, unprofitable businesses, and a declining tax base (Teaford 1993).

Urbanization in the United States

More than half—although surely not all!—of the U.S. population live in metropolitan areas with more than 1 million population. This section reviews some of the major patterns in American metropolitan spatial distribution.

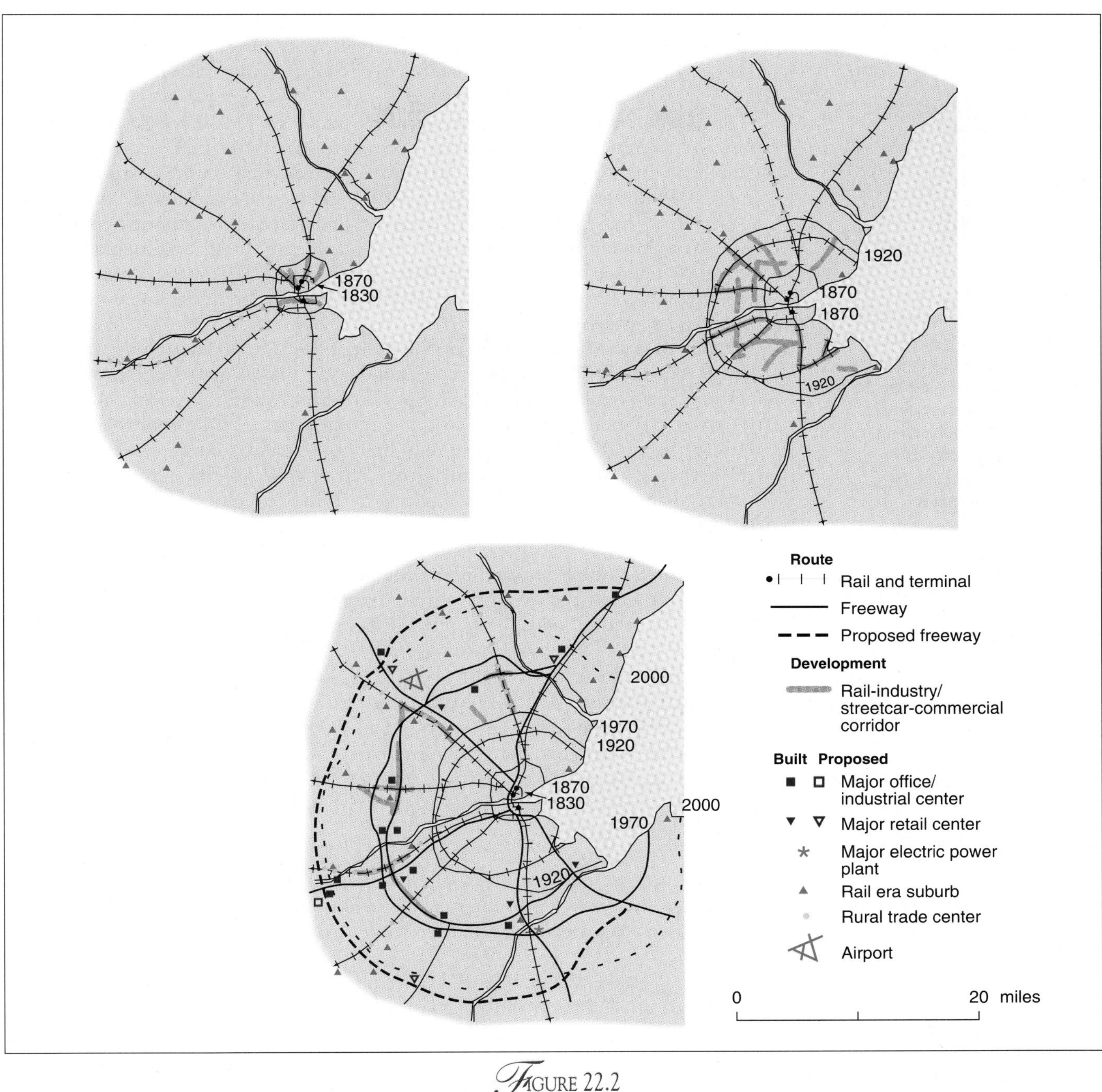

FIGURE 22.2
URBAN SPRAWL, 1830–2000

With automobiles, freeways, and more freeways, cities have spread out over increasingly larger geographical areas. Industrial and retail centers are no longer confined to the CBD and are often near freeway interchanges.

SOURCE: Knox 1995, 29.

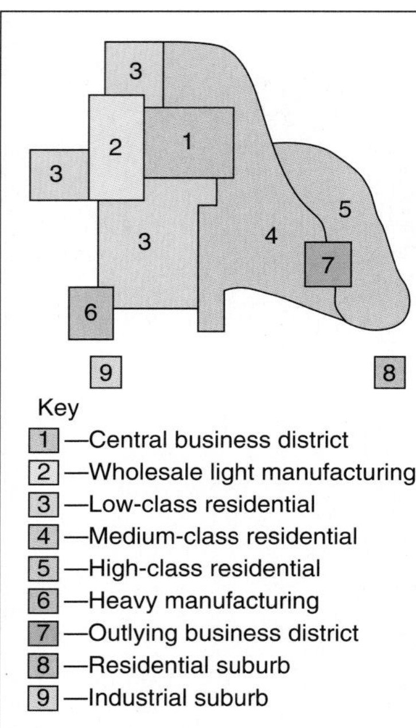

FIGURE 22.3
THE MULTIPLE NUCLEI MODEL OF URBAN SPATIAL PATTERNS

The automobile has given the post industrial city a freedom of form that its predecessors did not have. Commercial and residential areas are spread throughout the city and the suburbs. The city center has declined in importance, and many smaller centers have developed.

SOURCE: Harris and Ullman 1945.

A **metropolitan area** is a county that has a city of 50,000 or more in it plus any neighboring counties that are significantly linked, economically or socially, with the core county.

A **nonmetropolitan area** is a county that has no major city in it and is not closely tied to a county that does have such a city.

Urbanization is the process of population concentration in metropolitan areas.

What Is Metropolitan? What is considered urban in one century or nation is often rural in another. To impose some consistency in usage, the U.S. Bureau of the Census has replaced the common words *urban* and *rural* with two technical terms: *metropolitan* and *nonmetropolitan*.

A **metropolitan area** is a county that has a city of 50,000 people or more in it plus any neighboring counties that are significantly linked, economically or socially, with the core county. The Census Bureau refers to these units as MSAs (metropolitan statistical areas). Some MSAs include only one county; others, such as New York, San Francisco, and Detroit, include several neighboring counties. In each case, the metropolitan area goes beyond the city limits and includes what is frequently referred to as, for example, the Greater New York area. A **nonmetropolitan area** is a county that has no major city in it and is not closely tied to a county that does have such a city.

Figure 22.4 shows the current distribution of the U.S. population by type of residence. A total of 77.5 percent of the population live in metropolitan areas. This metropolitan population is divided into those who live in the central city (within the actual city limits) and those who live in the balance of the county or counties, the suburban and rural ring. More than half of the metropolitan population live in the suburbs (and some even on farms) rather than in the central city itself. Although they are judged to have access to a metropolitan way of life, they may live as far as 30 or even 50 miles from the city center.

The nonmetropolitan population of the United States has shrunk to 22.5 percent. Although there are nonmetropolitan counties in every state of the union except New Jersey, the majority of the nonmetropolitan population live in either the Midwest or the South. Only a small proportion of these people live on farms; many live in small towns and cities of 10,000 to 30,000.

Changing Patterns. Until 1970, the story of the U.S. population was one of progressive **urbanization,** the process of population concentration. For most of our history, urban areas grew faster than rural areas, with the largest urban areas growing the most. Over the last 25 years, however, there have been three major variations on this pattern: Sunbelt growth; shrinking central cities, and nonmetropolitan growth.

SUNBELT GROWTH. Almost all of the metropolitan growth in the last two decades has been in the Sunbelt—southern and western states. All of the 50 fastest-growing metropolitan areas are in the South or West.

SHRINKING CENTRAL CITIES. Central cities have grown much less rapidly than their suburban rings, and many of the largest central cities have actually lost population. As the 1990 census showed, even Atlanta, whose metropolitan area grew by 28 percent between 1980 and 1988, lost population in its central city. The losses are greatest in midwestern and northern cities such as Detroit and Pittsburgh but are notable even in the Sunbelt. You can see from Figure 22.4 that more Americans now live in suburbs than in central cities or nonmetropolitan areas.

Nonmetropolitan Resurgence. Since 1970, nonmetropolitan areas have stopped shrinking and have even begun to experience modest growth (Johnson 1989). Fewer people are moving away, and some areas are receiving in-migration. Although not growing as rapidly as metropolitan areas, small town and rural

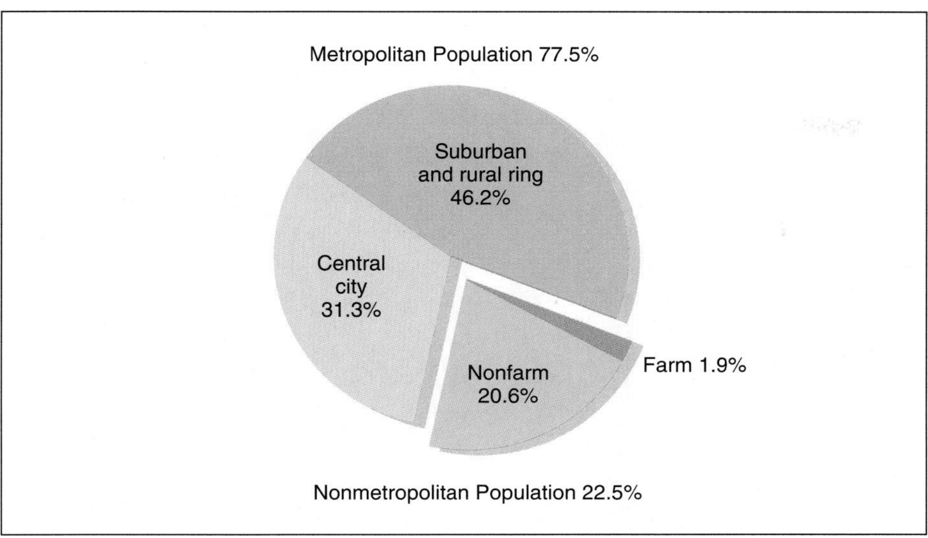

FIGURE 22.4
THE URBANIZATION OF THE U.S. POPULATION, 1990

More than three-quarters of the U.S. population live in metropolitan areas, and more than half live in areas with more than 1 million people. Nevertheless, only about a third actually live in central cities.

SOURCE: U.S. Bureau of the Census 1990.

America are not disappearing either. Most of this growth reflects lifestyle choices: The people moving to nonmetropolitan areas are willing to give up urban amenities for outdoor recreation, lower taxes, and a slower pace of life. Most of the nonmetropolitan growth is in the South or the West, often in areas that are within a few hours' driving distance of a big city.

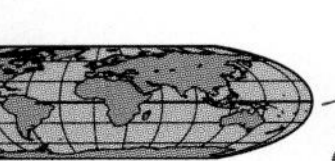

GLOBAL PERSPECTIVES: THIRD WORLD CITIES

Whereas the West has been predominantly urbanized since at least 1950, the world as a whole—and Africa and Asia in particular—are still predominantly rural. This is changing within our lifetime, however, on a scale that is difficult to grasp. Within the next 30 years, nearly two-thirds of the world's population will live in urban areas, as will the majority of people on all the earth's continents (see Figure 22.5).

Table 22.1 shows the 1994 populations of the world's 15 largest urban areas; 11 of those cities are in developing countries. If the growth of large cities and an urban way of life has occurred everywhere fairly recently, in the Third World it is happening almost overnight. São Paulo, Mexico City, Seoul, Calcutta—these and many other Third World cities are growing at 5 to 8 percent per year. This means that their populations will double in approximately a decade.

"MEGA-CITIES"—URBAN AGGLOMERATIONS

By the end of this century, there will be up to 20 million people living in greater Shanghai, and seven other Chinese cities will have populations of more than 5 million (Wehrfritz 1995). In as few as 30 years, Bombay will have nearly 30 million residents—more than one-tenth of the U.S. population (United Nations 1994b)! This dramatic urban growth results in what some demographers call "mega-cities," or *urban agglomerations*, in peripheral nations. In 1950, Shanghai was the only city in a less-developed country with over 5 million inhabitants. The United Nations

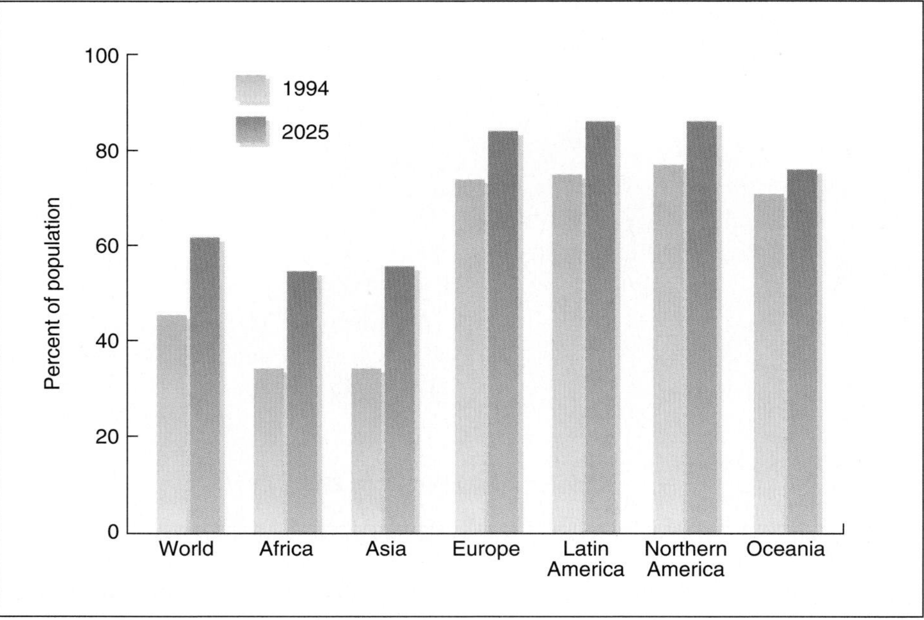

FIGURE 22.5
URBANIZATION TRENDS IN THE DEVELOPED AND LESS DEVELOPED WORLD, 1994 AND 2025

Although the world is still more rural than urban, this is changing within our lifetimes. Urbanization is growing particularly quickly in the less-developed world. In 1960, only three of the world's ten largest cities were in developing countries: Shanghai, Buenos Aires, and Calcutta. In 1990, all except three (Tokyo, New York, and Los Angeles) were in the developing world. By 2025, three-quarters of the world's urban population will live in less-developed countries.

SOURCE: Haub 1993; United Nations 1995.

predicts that by 2000, there will be more than 21 cities with 10 million or more; 17 of them will be in peripheral nations (Ashford 1995).

CAUSES FOR THIRD WORLD URBANIZATION

Urban growth occurs from high fertility rates and the consequent natural increase of the urban population (as described in Chapter 21) and also from rural-to-urban migration. Most of the urban growth in Latin America during the 1990s stems from natural increase. In Africa, however, urban growth is mainly the result of rural-to-urban migration (Ashford 1995).

Why do so many people want to move to the city? For one thing, they hope to find opportunity there. In rural areas, the only means to wealth is land, and that means is static—its quantity never changes, and its ownership is seldom transferred. Thus, the possibility for self-improvement lies almost entirely in urban areas. Furthermore, environmental degradation has led to a serious shortage of arable land in many parts of the less-developed world. A shortage of basic services, such as schools and medical care, also prompts peasants to move to the city (Ashford 1995), often in search of what they hope will be a better life for their children. Then, too, there is the seductive promise of cities. As a social scientist in China explained, "Each time a migrant worker visits home in city clothes and jewelry, everyone asks that same question: 'How can I go too?' " (in Wehrfritz 1995, 107). But city life is often not better.

CONSEQUENCES OF RAPID URBAN GROWTH IN THE THIRD WORLD

Third World cities have been overwhelmed by rapid urbanization. The roads, schools, and sewers that used to be enough no longer are; neighborhoods triple their populations and change their character from year to year. These problems are

TABLE 22.1
THE WORLD'S LARGEST URBAN AGGLOMERATIONS, 1994

RANK	AGGLOMERATION	COUNTRY	POPULATION (MILLIONS)
1	TOKYO	JAPAN	26.5
2	NEW YORK	UNITED STATES	16.2
3	SÃO PAULO	BRAZIL	16.1
4	MEXICO CITY	MEXICO	15.5
5	SHANGHAI	CHINA	14.7
6	BOMBAY	INDIA	14.5
7	LOS ANGELES	UNITED STATES	12.2
8	BEIJING	CHINA	12.1
9	CALCUTTA	INDIA	11.5
10	SEOUL	KOREA	11.5
11	JAKARTA	INDONESIA	11.0
12	BUENOS AIRES	ARGENTINA	10.9
13	OSAKA	JAPAN	10.6
14	TIANJIN	CHINA	10.4
15	RIO DE JANEIRO	BRAZIL	9.8

SOURCE: United Nations 1994b.

similar to the problems that plagued Western societies at the onset of the industrial revolution, but they are on a much larger scale.

Unemployment and Rising Crime Rates. Third World urbanization differs from that of the developed world (Flanagan 1993). For one thing, as noted, cities in less-developed countries have grown much faster than their counterparts in the industrialized world. It took London 130 years to increase from 1 to 8 million; Mexico City grew that much in the 30 years between 1940 and 1970 (Ashford 1995). Furthermore, many of the urban agglomerations in the periphery have never been industrial cities. They have grown from government, trade, and administrative centers. These cities offer few working-class jobs, and the jobs that do exist pay little. The growing unskilled populations become part of a shadow labor force of the self-employed—artisans, peddlers, bicycle renters, laundry workers, beggars, and thieves. Public officials worry over the soaring number of unemployed urban youth, particularly males, who contribute to rising rates of crime and violence (Ashford 1995).

Shanty Towns and Disease. Having trekked to the city with few possessions and virtually no money, newcomers make do in sprawling shanty towns made of tin or cardboard. These squatter settlements often spring up along waterways, and their

This shanty town (or favela) in Rio de Janeiro is considered to be Rio's best. Such shanty towns abound in Third World cities. They have no streets, water, electricity, or garbage service, but they are the only homes available to the rural migrants who surge into the cities looking for employment opportunities—which, for the most part, are nonexistent.

wastes spill directly into the urban water source. Many municipal governments have avoided improving the services to shanty towns, either because they cannot afford it or they don't want to encourage these settlements. As a result, the number of Third World urbanites without access to clean water grew by 31 million during the 1980s, while those without sanitation grew by 85 million. It goes without saying that such living conditions foster disease. In greater Lima, Peru, upstream pollution not only increased water treatment costs by 30 percent but also caused a serious cholera epidemic in 1991 (Falkenmark and Widstrand 1992).

Some Third World governments have tried to alleviate these problems by launching rural development programs and encouraging migrants to return to rural areas. But urbanization is not *necessarily* negative. Problems mount when there aren't enough jobs in the city and urbanization is so rapid that housing, schools, sanitation, public safety, and other fundamental services are inadequate (Ashford 1995).

URBAN LIFE IN THE UNITED STATES

Those who study urbanization are concerned with the extent of urban growth and the forces that encourage the development of urban living. Although this is an important area of study, sociologists are mainly interested in **urbanism**—a distinctively urban mode of life that is developed in the city though not confined there (Wirth 1938). They are concerned with the extent to which social relations and the norms that govern them differ between rural and urban settlements, (Orum 1995).

Urbanism is a distinctively urban mode of life that is developed in the cities but not confined there.

THEORETICAL VIEWS

The Western world as a whole has an antiurban bias. Big cities are seen as haunts of iniquity and vice, corrupters of youth and health, and destroyers of family and community ties. Cities are despised as artificial creations that compare poorly with creations of nature. City dwellers are characterized as sophisticated but artificial; rural people are characterized as possessing homegrown goodness and warmth.

This general antiurban bias (which has been around at least since the time of ancient Rome), coupled with the very real problems of the industrial city, had a great deal of influence on early sociologists. For the most part, Durkheim, Weber, and others believed that the quality of human social life was significantly worse in the cities. Only recently has evidence emerged that rural life is not as idyllic and city life not as bleak as was supposed.

Gemeinschaft refers to society characterized by the personal and permanent ties associated with primary groups.

Gesellschaft refers to society characterized by the impersonal and instrumental ties associated with secondary groups.

Early Writers. Ferdinand Tönnies (1855–1930) offered one of the earliest sociological descriptions of the differences between urban and rural society. He argued that rural society was characterized by **gemeinschaft,** personal and permanent ties associated with primary groups. Urban society was characterized by **gesellschaft,** impersonal and instrumental ties associated with secondary groups. Durkheim saw the essence of urbanization as a shift from social cohesion built on similarity (mechanical solidarity) to a cohesion built on a complex division of labor and high interdependence (organic solidarity). Weber spoke of a shift from tradition to rationalism as a guide to social activities.

These early writers were not blind to the drawbacks of rural society. They recognized that rural society was static and confining, that tradition bound individuals to a station in life and to ways of thinking that left little room for innovation or individualism. Their preference for rural life was based on the security it provided—the security of knowing exactly what was expected of you, what your place in the social order was, and what your neighbor's place was. In addition, the long-lasting personal relationships characteristic of rural society were thought to be essential to informal social control. Many were concerned that when people did not have to worry about what the neighbors would think, deviance would become commonplace, and the social order would be threatened.

Wirth: Urban Determinism. The classic statement of the negative consequences of urban life for the individual and for social order was made by Louis Wirth in 1938. In his influential work "Urbanism As a Way of Life," Wirth suggested that the greater size, heterogeneity, and density of urban living necessarily led to a breakdown of the normative and moral fabric of everyday life.

Greater size means that many members of the community will be strangers to us. Greater density means that we will be forced into close and frequent contact with these strangers. Wirth postulated that individuals would try to protect themselves from this crowd by developing a cool personal style that would allow them to ignore some people (including people who were physically close, such as in a crowded elevator) and to interact with others, such as salesclerks, in an impersonal style so that their personality would not be engaged. The Kitty Genovese incident, described in Chapter 2, is rightly cited as the kind of thing that is more apt to happen among strangers than among lifelong neighbors. Wirth did not suggest that urbanites had no friends or primary ties, but he did think that the city bred a personal style that was cold and calculating (Flanagan 1993).

The heterogeneity of the city, in this view, leads to an awareness of alternative normative frameworks or subcultures. Wirth suggested that this awareness would lead to normative confusion for the individual and lack of integration for the community. Faced with a welter of differing norms, Wirth thought, the dweller in a heterogeneous city was apt to conclude that anything goes. Such an attitude, coupled with the lack of informal social control brought on by size, would lead to greater crime and deviance and a greater emphasis on formal controls.

In sum, Wirth argued that city living brought negative consequences for individuals and society. That is, he believed that if a well-integrated, warm, and conforming person from the farm moved to the city, that person would change and become calculating, indifferent, and nonconforming.

The Compositional Model. Later theorists have had a more benign view of the city. Compositional theorists suggest that individuals experience the city as a mosaic of small worlds that are manageable and knowable (Gans 1962). Thus, the person who lives in New York City does not have to cope with 9 million people and 500 square miles of city; rather, the individual's private world is made up of family, a small neighborhood, and an immediate work group. Compositional theorists argue that the primary group lives on in cities and that the quality of interpersonal ties is not affected even though the number of impersonal contacts is much greater than in rural areas.

The compositional model does recognize that deviance, loneliness, and other problems are greater in cities than in rural areas. It suggests, however, that

Concept Summary Comparing Three Theories of Urbanism

	Wirth's Urban Determinism	Compositional Theory	Subcultural Theory
Essential aspects of urban living	Size, heterogeneity, density	Neighborhood, mosaic of manageable worlds	Critical masss
Consequences for the individual	Withdrawal, normative confusion	No consequences	Opportunity to develop subcultures
Societal consequences	Indifference, deviance	No consequences	More diversity
Why is crime higher in urban places?	Normative confusion, low social control	Nonconformists attracted to urban places	Deviant subcultures can develop that encourage crime

deviants, singles, people without children, the lonely, and the alienated are attracted to the cities rather than created by them. Those with families and those willing to conform are attracted to the suburbs.

Thinking Critically

Campuses often bring large numbers of strangers together in crowded circumstances. Which theoretical view best describes the outcomes of this interaction? Can you find some examples to support all three perspectives?

The Subcultural View. In Wirth's view, the city has essentially negative effects; in the compositional view, the urban environment has few direct consequences. The subcultural view straddles the two positions and presents a more moderate picture of the city. The essential idea of the subcultural view is that of critical mass. Special subcultures—intellectuals, radicals, gays—cannot develop until there are a relatively large number of people sharing some relatively uncommon set of norms or values. For example, one homosexual in a small community will be under constant pressure to conform to general standards; only when there are many others will it be possible to sustain a gay community with its own set of norms and values. Similarly, a symphony orchestra, a football team, and a synagogue all await the development of a critical mass of people who share the same interest. Once they identify one another, they will have group support for their identities and standards. In this way, the greater diversity and size of the city leads to development of subcultures with different, perhaps even deviant, norms and values. Wirth might interpret these subcultures as evidence of a lack of moral integration of the community, but they can also be seen as private worlds within which individuals find cohesion and primary group support (Fischer 1995).

Empirical Consequences of Urban Living

One theory suggests that urban living has negative consequences, another that it has few consequences, and still another that it leads to the development of subcultures. This section reviews evidence about the effects of urban living on social networks, neighborhood integration, and a quality of life.

Social Networks. The effects of urban living on social networks are rather small. Surveys asking about strong ties show that urban people have as many intimate ties as rural people. There is a slight tendency for urban people to name fewer kin and more friends than rural people, but the kin omitted from the urban lists are not parents, children, and siblings but more distant relatives. Thus, urban living may narrow the kin group and expand the number of nonkin who are listed as intimates (Amato 1993; Fischer 1981). Overall, however, urban residents have the same number of intimate ties as do rural people, and they see their intimates as often. There is no evidence that urban people are disproportionately lonely, alienated, or estranged from family and friends.

The Neighborhood. Empirical research generally reveals the neighborhood to be a very weak group. Most city dwellers, whether central city or suburban, find that city living has freed them from the necessity of liking the people they live next to and has given them the opportunity to select intimates on a basis other than physical proximity; this freedom is something that people in rural areas do not have. There is growing consensus among urban researchers that physical proximity is no longer a primary basis of intimacy (Flanagan 1993). Rather, people form intimate networks on the basis of kin, friendship, and work groups; and they keep in touch by telephone rather than relying solely on face-to-face communication. In short, urban people do have intimates, but they are unlikely to live in the same neighborhood with them. When in trouble, they call on their good friends, parents, or adult children for help. In fact, one study of neighborhood interaction in Albany-Schenectady-Troy, New York, found that a substantial share—15 to 25 percent—of all interaction with neighbors was with *family* neighbors—parents or adult children who happen to live in the same neighborhood (Logan and Spitze 1994).

Neighbors are seldom strangers, however, and there are instances in which being nearby is more important than being emotionally close. When we are locked out of the house, we need a teaspoon of vanilla, or we want someone to accept a United Parcel Service package, we still rely on our neighbors (Wellman and Wortley 1990). Although we generally do not ask large favors of our neighbors and don't want them to rely heavily on us, most of us expect our neighbors to be good people who are willing to help in a pinch. This has much to do with the fact that neighborhoods are often segregated by social class and stage in the family life cycle. We know that our neighbors will be people pretty much like us.

Big cities are exciting places to live. For one thing, they are more ethnically and culturally diverse, a characteristic that many see as an advantage. Behaviors that would be considered inappropriate in many small towns, such as interracial dating, are more likely to be tolerated and even encouraged in big cities—another advantage according to some.

Quality of Life. Big cities are exciting places to live. People can choose from a wide variety of activities, 24 hours a day, seven days a week. The bigger the city, the more it offers in the way of entertainment, libraries, museums, zoos, parks, concerts, and galleries. The quality of medical services and police and fire protection also increases with city size. These advantages offer important incentives for big-city living.

On the other hand, there are also disadvantages: more noise, more crowds, more expensive housing, and more crime. The latter is a particularly important problem for many people. More than 50 percent of those living in cities over 1 million report that they would be afraid to walk alone at night in their neighborhood; only 29 percent of the rural population would be afraid. Data on crime rates suggest this fear might be justified: Crime rates are strongly correlated with city size. This is especially true of the kind of crime that people fear most—violence against the person (Knox 1995).

Because of these disadvantages, many people would rather live close to a big city than in it. For Americans, the ideal is a three-bedroom house on a spacious lot in the suburbs close enough to a big city that they can spend an evening or afternoon there. Some groups, however, prefer big-city living—in particular, childless people who work downtown. Many of these people are decidedly pro-urban and relish the entertainment and diversity that the city offers. Because of their affluence and childlessness, they can afford to dismiss many of the disadvantages of city living.

> **THINKING CRITICALLY**
>
> Where would *you* rather live—in a central city or in its suburbs? How does your answer reflect your various social statuses and roles?

Are City Folks Cold? From Tönnies's gemeinschaft/gesellschaft to Wirth's urban determinism, social theorists have assumed that urban dwellers tend to be cold and rational in their social relationships, whereas rural people are warm, open, and friendly. How much truth is there in these stereotypes? Some research evidence suggests that urban people do develop a cool indifference to nonintimates. Research on the bystander effect and on helping behavior has consistently demonstrated that people in big cities are less apt to help a stranger in trouble than are people in rural areas (Karp, Stone, and Yoels 1991; Knox 1995).

Sociological and media attention has been captured by cities such as Manhattan and San Francisco with their bright lights and ethnic diversity. Nevertheless, only about one third of the U.S. population actually live in these big-city centers. The rest live in suburbs and small towns. What is their experience?

Research suggests that urbanites do develop a cool indifference to nonintimates. At the same time, we must be careful not to stereotype central cities as only crime-ridden and inhumane. In many central cities, for example, strangers and friends come together for conversation or a leisurely game of checkers or chess.

SUBURBAN LIVING

The classic picture of a suburb is a middle-class development of very similar single-family detached homes on individual lots. Domesticity ("family values") and tranquility are assumed to prevail. Suburbs like this emerged and flourished after World War II.

The Emergence of American Suburbs. U.S. veterans returned in 1945 to an America embarking on two decades of economic growth and domestic values that are now recognized as unique in our history. The post-war baby boom fueled a need for more family housing, auto sales soared, and two-car nuclear families became common (Teaford 1993). Earlier in this chapter, we noted an antiurban bias that dates back to ancient Rome; antiurban bias has also been alive and well throughout the history of the United States (Groth 1994). After World War II, federal policies helped people put their money where their mouth was: The 1949 National Housing Act provided federally guaranteed, low-interest home mortgage loans, and the 1953 Interstate Highway Act began the system of metropolitan expressways that is so familiar today (Wood 1989). Now even a working-class family could commute to a single-family house and yard in the suburbs. This low-density housing pattern is still the lifestyle to which a majority of Americans aspire; it provides room for dogs, children, and barbecues. But this classic picture of suburbia is changing.

The Changing Suburbs. The suburbs are no longer bedroom communities that daily send their breadwinners to work in the central city. They are increasingly major manufacturing and retail trade centers in their own right. Most people who live in the suburbs work in the suburbs. While retaining the ability to go into the central city for a unique meal, foreign film, or concert, suburbanites hope to insulate themselves—both at home and at work—from the noise, crime, dirty streets, and bad schools associated with the inner city. Hence, many of the close-in suburban areas have become densely populated and substantially interlaced with junior colleges, retail trade centers, highways, and manufacturing plants. In some regions, *exurbs*, more like the bedroom communities of several decades ago, are developing outside this inner suburban ring.

These changes have altered the character of the inner suburbs. Suburban lots have become smaller, and neighborhoods of townhouses, duplexes, and apartment buildings have begun to appear (Knox 1995). Along with students and singles, couples without children and retired couples are seen in greater numbers. Suburbia has become more dense, more multicultural, and less dominated by the minivan set.

With expansion, suburbia as a whole has become more diverse. Ethnic minorities have found their ways to the suburbs; some wealthy suburbs are almost entirely African American, for example. Although each suburban neighborhood tends to have its own style, stemming in large part from the fact that each development includes houses of similar size and price, there is a wide variety of suburban styles. In addition to the neighborhoods of classic middle-class suburbia, there are working-class suburbs, exclusive mini-estate suburbs where people have horses and belong to the country club, and cosmopolitan suburban centers peopled with artists and writers (Knox 1995). Finally, some of the first suburbs are now 45 years old. Some older suburbs are becoming run-down (there is poverty in the suburbs); renting is more common than home owning, and deserted malls are appearing.

Suburban Problems. Many of the people who moved to suburbia did so to escape urban problems: They were looking for lower crime rates, less traffic, less crowding, and lower tax rates. The growth of the suburbs, however, has brought its own problems. Among the more important problems associated with suburban living are the following (Kelly 1989; Adler 1995b):

1. *Housing costs*. Generally, housing costs are lower in the suburbs than in central cities. Nevertheless, increased demand for suburban housing has driven housing costs in many areas up to a level that is beyond the reach of people who could have afforded a home 10 or 15 years ago.
2. *Higher density*. The increased density of the suburbs recreates the urban problems of crowding, traffic congestion, and crime.

3. *Fragmented governments*. Suburban governments are basically defensive organizations; they can protect their citizens' property from central-city taxes and their schools from central-city students. Beyond this, county governments and municipal governments of the small cities in the suburban ring are fragmented and relatively powerless. In many areas, they are at the mercy of decisions made in the central city—where they cannot vote. (These matters are discussed at greater length later in this chapter.)
4. *Transportation*. Living in suburbia depends on access to automobiles, as there are few adequate mass transit systems. On a macrosociological level, this situation causes pollution and traffic congestion. On a microsociological level, people who don't have cars find it nearly impossible to work or shop—and people who do have cars have to fight traffic to get there. Then, too, for central-city residents who don't own cars (about one-third of all minority residents of the central city do not), suburban jobs and opportunities are simply out of reach.
5. *Boredom*. For some critics (although probably not many actual residents), suburbia is boring. The architectural, social class, and ethnic homogeneity that characterizes each particular suburb makes for "banal places with the souls of shopping malls, affording nowhere to mingle except traffic jams, nowhere to walk except in the health club" (Adler 1995b, 43).

Ways to Improve the Suburbs. Architects, suburban planners, and others have begun in the last 10 years to suggest ways for improving suburban life. Among other ideas, they suggest the following (Adler 1995b):

Most of us are familiar with suburbs like the one on the left, in Walnut, California, where all the houses look alike, streets are wide, and driveways predominate. But some "new urbanists" are designing "neotraditional" suburbs that try to bring small-town charm to metropolitan living. The suburban neighborhood on the right, in Washington, D.C., features a more "pedestrian" design and front stoops where people can meet more easily.

1. Give up the large lawns that unnecessarily take time, cause fertilizer runoff, and waste fresh water.
2. Mix housing types for variety and design them with porches so that people are encouraged to be more neighborly.
3. Make serious plans to improve mass transit.
4. To facilitate walking, make the streets narrower and easier to cross, shrink parking lots, put in sidewalks, and bring back the corner store. In some communities, these things are beginning to happen (Pacelle 1996).
5. Rejuvenate deserted malls as town centers with activities for singles, parents, children, and older people.

The Other America: Small-Town and Rural Living

Approximately 25 percent of the nation's population lives in small towns (populations of less than 2,500) or rural areas. Some of these rural and small-town people are included in the metropolitan population count because they live within the orbit of a major metro area, but most live in nonmetropolitan areas—in South Dakota and Alabama but also in Vermont and Pennsylvania.

The nonmetropolitan population of the United States continues to grow. Although young people often leave to go to school or get jobs elsewhere, enough come back to keep populations growing. In addition, small-town growth is maintained by a small but steady stream of people seeking refuge from the problems of urban and suburban living. This development is made all the more possible by the recent burgeoning of communication technologies that allow for telecommuting (U.S. Congress 1995). With the Internet, you can work as a stockbroker from your remote cabin in the Rocky Mountains.

People find small-town living attractive for a number of reasons: It offers lots of open space, low property taxes, affordable housing, and relative freedom from worry about crime. In addition, an important attraction for many people is the perceived opportunity for more neighboring and community involvement. Studies show that this perception is correct: Small-town people do know more of their neighbors (Freudenburg 1986). This provides an important source of cohesion and social integration. It is not, however, an unalloyed blessing. Although the fact that everybody does indeed know everybody helps keep down the crime rate, some find that the lack of privacy and enforced conventionality are oppressive (Johansen and Fuguitt 1984). Indeed, several studies have found small-town and rural residents to be in somewhat poorer mental health than residents of large metropolitan areas (Beeson and Johnson 1987).

Rubes and Hicks? According to stereotype, rural people, especially farmers, are hicks, rednecks, and rubes. These portraits are very much exaggerated (Gahr 1993). On most social issues, from churchgoing to support for welfare, there are little or no size-of-place differentials. One study found no size-of-place or metropolitan/nonmetropolitan differences on the importance people attached to any of the following values: working hard, achievement, personal freedom, helping others, salvation, or leisure (Christenson 1984). All but the remotest cabin dwellers have access to national culture via satellite dishes, television, radio, movies, and news magazines. Nevertheless, although rural Americans watch the same television shows and shop from the same catalogs as their urban counterparts, the city continues to be the

Thinking Critically

We all hold stereotypes about what people are like if they're from California, or North Dakota, or Texas. Surveys of actual populations find few differences on many social issues. Does that mean these stereotypes are without foundation? On what kinds of matters do you expect that these groups really differ?

major source of innovation and change, and so the rural/urban difference seems unlikely to be totally eliminated. Because the speed of cultural diffusion is now much more rapid than before, however, rural/urban differences are far less profound than they were in the past (Flanagan 1993).

THE POLITICAL ECONOMY OF SPATIAL DISTRIBUTION

If you asked the average citizen why people leave central cities and move to suburbia, you would get answers such as high housing costs and high crime rates. Your respondent might also note that a lot of jobs have moved to suburbia. These answers are correct, but they don't go quite far enough. Why is housing cheaper in suburbia? Why have jobs left the central cities? Although some scholars have suggested that these changes are the result of neutral economic forces, others have suggested that they are the result of political decisions. In this section, we consider the political economy of spatial distribution: Why are housing costs, segregation, and poverty correlated with place?

THE FRAGMENTED CONTROL OF METROPOLITAN SPACE

The average metropolitan county contains dozens of different governments (see Figure 22.6). The central-city government is ringed by the governments of half a dozen incorporated suburbs; the balance of the county is under the jurisdiction of the county government. Although all of the people in the county are linked together in a common economic network, their taxes and their social services depend on which jurisdiction they live in. The suburbs cannot be taxed to support central-city services; the school district of suburb A does not have to take children from the central city or from suburb B; each suburban government can develop zoning ordinances to keep undesirable city growth from spilling over into its bound-

FIGURE 22.6
THE FRAGMENTED GOVERNMENT OF A METROPOLITAN COUNTY

The average metropolitan county is divided into half a dozen or more different governments. Despite the fact that they are all part of a common economic network, each jurisdiction controls its own taxes and expenditures. This system benefits affluent suburbs, which can withdraw their resources from the common pool yet share the amenities provided by other jurisdictions.

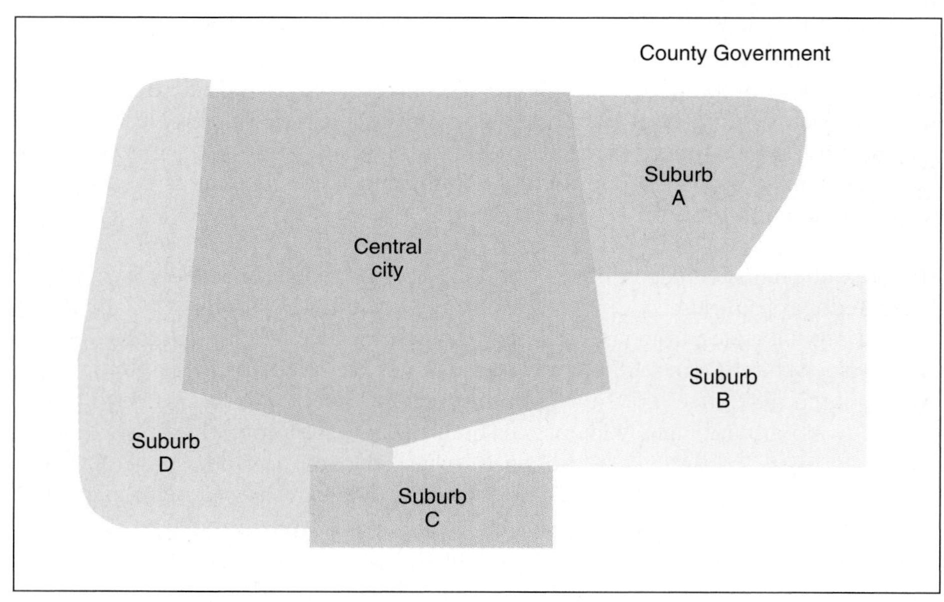

aries. As one scholar has phrased it, this fragmented political control of space has put city limits on equality (James 1989). City and suburban political boundaries limit the sharing of social resources and isolate the well-off from the poor.

Independent political control of space contributes to many of the problems associated with today's urban areas, especially to school segregation, poor funding of schools in the central cities, and central-city poverty in general. Central-city school districts may find that there are too few non-Hispanic white students in their districts to create integrated schools. The non-Hispanic white students are inaccessible because they live in another school district. Negative stereotypes (Farley, Steeh, and Krysan 1994) help propel the growth of African American and Hispanic suburbs, further increasing school segregation. The greater the proportion of African Americans and Hispanics in a particular suburban school district, the lower its capacity for providing racial balance.

Multiple government jurisdictions benefit people in affluent neighborhoods that have been able to protect their space and tax dollars. These people can drive into town and enjoy museums, parks, shopping, and entertainment and not have to help foot the bill. One solution that is often mentioned is to move major taxing and spending decisions to the county level. In this way, suburban home owners could be taxed to support urban services (many of which they enjoy). Not surprisingly, however, surveys indicate that suburban residents oppose such a change by a two-to-one margin (Baldassare 1989).

Space Is Money

For both Marxists and non-Marxists, land is a critical form of capital. Those who own land try to manipulate economic and political processes so as to maximize profit from their land or at least protect its current value (Savage and Warde 1993). Who are these profit maximizers? Although some are bankers and developers, most are home owners. In contemporary capitalism, home ownership may be the critical class distinction (Katznelson 1992; Paul 1989). For most of us, our home is our most valuable tangible asset. In protecting this investment, we act like capitalists.

One of the most important tools that owners use to protect land values is *zoning*—restricting the use of land to certain purposes. Zoning ordinances are political decisions that are made by city councils and county commissions. A typical zoning ordinance might forbid multifamily dwellings or inexpensive housing in middle-class suburbs or forbid construction of convenience stores or other businesses in residential neighborhoods. As exurbs push into rural America and modem-toting professionals invade small towns, new zoning battles emerge. In Butler County, Ohio, for instance, recently arrived home owners battle locals over whether the latter can hang freshly gutted deer carcasses in the front yard (Irwin 1995). In general, zoning ordinances are designed to keep out people or properties that will cause property values to go down or cause taxes to go up (Savage and Warde 1993).

The Politics of Housing

Owning one's own home is a nearly universal American Dream. It represents economic security and a modest kind of power—control over one's own space. It is a dream that has been realized by a larger proportion of Americans than 50 years ago. In 1940, 60 percent of Americans between ages 35 and 65 were renters. Members of the working class and the lower-middle class could never save up enough money to buy their own homes. Today things are different, despite the increase in housing costs over the past 15 years.

The dramatic increase in home ownership has been associated with suburban growth and central-city decay. The decline of central-city housing in favor of the suburbs, however, is not a foregone conclusion. There are many advantages to living downtown, and some of the most elegant neighborhoods in America are in central cities. Scholars suggest that two kinds of political decisions have helped to structure this systematic shift in housing investment: redlining and federal loan programs.

Redlining. The housing market rests on two commodities: loans and insurance. Both are controlled by the biggest commercial firms in the United States. Before a family can obtain a mortgage loan, it must have insurance; the same thing is true for remodeling loans. A substantial body of research demonstrates that both home insurance and mortgage loans are more difficult to obtain in some parts of the city than in others. The process whereby these financial investments are systematically denied to one area of the city and diverted to other, more favored areas is called *redlining* This practice gets its name from the literal drawing of a red line on a city map around sections where financial services are to be denied. Typically, the areas discriminated against are populated primarily by minorities and people with low incomes, and the favored areas are suburban. Insurance companies, for example, charge rates for central-city areas that are much higher than is justified by the increased risk of fire or vandalism; they may also terminate policies in redlined areas or simply define such areas as outside their territory. The same process occurs with home mortgages (Knox 1995; "Mortgages" 1991; "The Gap" 1992).

These discriminatory practices are part of a systematic process of disinvestment in low-income and minority—that is, central-city—neighborhoods. Rather than being a natural cycle of aging, urban decay is the result of deliberate action. The lack of investment in a neighborhood means no construction jobs, no repairs, and deteriorating housing. Ultimately, it leads to simple abandonment, a critical and rapidly growing problem in U.S. cities. Gaping windows and sagging doors provide targets for vandalism and havens for junkies, criminals, and rats; they also contribute to further decline.

Federal Loan Programs. Nearly half of all mortgage loans for home purchases are guaranteed by the federal government through either the Veteran's Administration (VA) or the Federal Housing Administration (FHA). The federal guarantees remove the risk for local lenders and encourage them to offer loans to people whose ability to buy is marginal, especially working-class and lower-middle-class people. These federal programs give preference to new housing and thus have been used almost exclusively to encourage suburban development rather than the purchase and upkeep of established central-city neighborhoods. Because loan guarantees are unavailable for older homes, renting becomes the rule, and the long decline begins. The lack of federal loan guarantees works in parallel with redlining practices virtually to exclude central-city home ownership.

The Consequences: Segregation and Poverty. Over the past 40 to 50 years, political decisions have been made that have resulted in systematic disinvestment

FOCUS ON ANOTHER CULTURE

Copenhagen—Why Does It Work?

"EMPHASIS IS ON MAINTAINING THE COMMUNITY FABRIC AND ARCHITECTURAL INTEGRITY OF URBAN NEIGHBORHOODS."

If you have ever traveled to Western Europe, you may have noticed that cities there are generally not in the same sad shape as many of those in the United States. The city of Copenhagen, Denmark, for example, is often described as a wonderful place by visitors and residents alike. Copenhagen is characterized by canals, clean and tidy parks, relaxed coffeehouses, well-preserved old buildings, safe streets, and cheerful people.

Like North American cities, Copenhagen in recent decades has seen its suburban fringes swell as residents migrated outward from the inner city. A largely agricultural nation until World War II, Denmark has strong pastoral traditions that many middle-class people strive to maintain symbolically by means of a single-family house with a lawn. This has left central Copenhagen, with its densely settled blocks of five- and six-story apartment buildings, home to a poorer population than the surrounding suburbs. Moreover, like cities in the Untied States, Copenhagen has become increasingly diverse ethnically as immigrants have arrived from less-developed and Eastern European countries.

Unlike the policy in the United States, however, Danish urban policy considers an entire metropolitan region, such as Copenhagen, a unified community. The lower income of central-city residents is not seen as resulting from personal characteristics, failure, or inability. In Denmark's view, the central city "incubates" many people as they start in their careers, giving them the means to move to the suburbs later. Instead of avoiding the problem of inner cities' lower tax base, as we do in the United States, the Danish government equalizes the economic burden among municipalities by taking tax revenues from wealthier suburbs and giving them directly to Copenhagen, where demand for government services is higher.

But policy efforts to maintain Copenhagen's vitality involve more than just transferring tax dollars. A nationally funded renewal campaign has been continuously in effect to make the city a more and more attractive place to live. Emphasis is on maintaining the community fabric and architectural integrity of urban neighborhoods. Buildings are restored, even if this is more expensive than constructing new ones would be. Playgrounds and green spaces are developed in what were once parking lots.

Copenhagen's renewal began in 1962, when cars were banned from a network of downtown streets. Since then, Copenhagen has expanded its pedestrian zone, public transit system, and bikeways. Fifty percent of downtown commuters now travel by bicycle. Downtown parking spaces and lots were gradually eliminated, to be replaced by walkways and parks.

Making Copenhagen's inner city a lively meeting place is a high priority. Today, the historical center of the city has many cafes, shops, and well-populated public squares; formerly rundown neighborhoods are now centers for young people and artists. Many offices that had moved out of the central city have moved back to Copenhagen. So have some people, particularly young professionals and parents whose children are grown. As a result, recreational and social use of the city center has tripled over the past 25 years, and central Copenhagen is as busy on Sundays and in the evenings as it is on workdays.

According to Jan Gehl, head of the urban design department at the University of Copenhagen, "A good city is like a good party. People don't want to leave early. They want to stay." He adds that a good city is also a safe city and points out that people on the streets keep Copenhagen's crime levels low (Walljasper 1994).

It is true that Denmark's urban problems are eased by the nation's social democratic policies, which place budgetary emphasis on citizens' economic and social needs. Indeed, urban problems in the United States will not be alleviated without greater attention to issues such as access to medical care, poverty, unemployment, substandard housing, inadequate public transportation, substandard education, and the proliferation of guns. Nevertheless, the case of Copenhagen illustrates that policies directed toward the development and renewal of central cities can work.

in central-city housing. The result is that the city is poorer than it was before and more racially differentiated from the suburbs.

Poverty exists in the suburbs, but it is found less often there than in either central cities or nonmetropolitan areas. The relatively low rate of poverty in the suburbs is the result of two trends: the exodus of jobs to the suburbs and the ability of suburban zoning regulations to exclude low-income housing (and thus low-income people), (Keating 1994).

URBAN REVITALIZATION

As cities continue to spread, some policy makers and even developers are beginning to be concerned that urban sprawl has become too much of what once seemed a good thing. For one thing, farmland necessary to feed a growing population is being turned into driveways and lawns while inner-city lots go empty. A 1995 Brookings Institute conference on urban sprawl, called "Alternatives to Sprawl," bemoaned its "enormous social, environmental and economic costs, which until now have been hidden, ignored, or quietly borne by society" (Adler 1995b, 43). Not only the environment but also commuting employees and businesses suffer, the latter from losses in worker productivity and underutilized investments in the central cities. Policy makers point out that to continue spreading out eventually will make the cost to build new roads and sewers prohibitive (Adler 1995b). Meanwhile, the problems of major central cities are interrelated: fewer working-class jobs, more poverty, more segregation, less money. Parts of our central cities look like bombed-out Sarajevo. A solution to all these problems is to revitalize the central city.

Some people, generally conservatives, treat these problems as if they were the outcome of neutral economic forces. They argue that people have voted with their feet. These critics see no point in trying to save big northern and midwestern cities. They urge migration as the answer to the poverty and joblessness of urban residents.

Nearly every major metropolitan area has neighborhoods that look like this. The obvious reason is lack of money: Industry, jobs, and, subsequently, working-class families have left the area. The public policy dilemma is whether to try to encourage redevelopment of such areas or simply bulldoze them.

Observers from the liberal side are more likely to point to the political and economic decisions that have left the urban poor increasingly isolated: tax breaks to subsidize suburban rather than urban housing, disproportionate spending on suburban and commuter transportation such as freeway and beltway systems, and zoning and taxation policies that have made the suburbs more attractive to investors than the central city. They believe that investment has been deliberately and disproportionately aimed away from central cities and that the solution is to reinvest in the central city (Savage and Warde 1993).

Among those who wish to salvage the central city, the major issue is urban revitalization, which involves the massive upgrading of central-city neighborhoods.

MUNICIPAL DEVELOPMENT AND GENTRIFICATION

In the United States, urban revitalization has generally occurred in two forms: municipal development and gentrification. Both are controversial.

Municipal Development. Government-sponsored revitalization has occurred in many big cities. The typical strategy is to replace low-income neighborhoods and decayed areas with green space, convention centers, and even amusement parks

(Adler 1995c) that bring in dollars and middle-class visitors. The city uses its right of eminent domain to acquire blocks of property and then uses tax breaks and other investment incentives to lure investors back to the downtown area. Under this planning, waterfronts and downtowns in many major cities have been transformed.

Gentrification. In the classic pattern of gentrification, a middle-class individual or couple buys a dilapidated older home at a bargain price and pours money and sweat into refurbishing it. After a second and a third house in the neighborhood is refurbished, the neighborhood begins to attract some attention from people with perhaps more capital and less daring. When a sufficient core of restored houses develops, boutiques, antique shops, gourmet shops, and other trendy stores begin to replace bars, barbershops, and pawnshops. Scruffy apartment houses are refurbished and turned into condominiums (Caulfield 1994).

Gentrification is to some extent a neutral economic process. The prices of suburban land and housing have become high enough and the commuting distances grown long enough that the city center once again appears to be a reasonable place to live. This is especially true for childless professionals who work and play downtown. Nevertheless, the impetus for gentrification is often the tax and loan breaks that are offered to encourage reinvestment in the downtown.

A question some ask is whether the gentrified neighborhood has been revitalized or taken over. Some argue that the long-time residents of a neighborhood benefit the most. Those "affected by decreasing property values in their neighborhood, deterioration, and increased crime—or the fear of increased crime—are the most likely beneficiaries, if they are able to remain in the neighborhood" (Schill and Nathan 1983). This is a big if. Evidence indicates that the previous residents can seldom afford to stay. The ones who aren't directly bought out find they cannot afford to shop in their own neighborhood, nor can they afford the rapidly rising property taxes (Savage and Warde 1993).

Criticisms of Municipal Development and Gentrification. Two primary charges can be made against both municipal development and gentrification and the resultant breaking up of neighborhoods. One relies on a somewhat romantic notion of urban villages; it argues that the invasion of yuppies is destroying strong and vital neighborhoods (Palen and London 1984). For the most part, however, urban revitalization is not aimed at strong ethnic or subcultural neighborhoods but at neighborhoods that have already disintegrated. The other charge has more substance: Municipal development and gentrification contribute to homelessness and reduce the stock of available housing for the working class and the poor (Wood 1989). Although empirical studies show that most of the displaced find other housing, two groups stand out as exceptions to this generalization: the unemployed and the transient homeless. The nightly and weekly rentals used by transients have almost disappeared from many of the nation's urban areas. The only alternatives are Salvation Army and city mission facilities, which have not expanded rapidly enough to take up the slack (Cravatts 1992).

The question has been posed by many observers: recovery for whom—for business or for the poor (Savage and Warde 1993)? The urban revitalization movement has created two cities out of one: a more prosperous city for yuppies and tourists and another for the poor, who have progressively fewer housing and work opportunities (Knox 1995). In the long run, the greater fiscal health of the central city brought about by urban revitalization may trickle down to the poor, but in the short term, urban investment decisions seem to have increased the disadvantages of central-city poor people.

Community Involvement

A more recent and hopeful development has been the movement toward greater community involvement among central-city residents themselves. Responding to shrinking government budgets and an apparent lack of interest in the suburbs, inner-city community associations have sprung up from Queens to D.C. Their goal is civic renewal. What do they do? Here are some examples:

- Austin, Texas: Local residents volunteer with a Parks Department health and nutrition program for children.
- Santa Barbara, California: A neighborhood organization responded to gang shootings by organizing a block-watching program.
- St. Louis, Missouri: A neighborhood association set up a skills bank in which people trade hours of, for example, baby-sitting for plumbing. Members also prune neighborhood trees and organize community clean-up days (Belluck 1996).
- Chattanooga, Tennessee: In 1969, this town was labelled the "dirtiest city in the country." Now it's one of the cleanest because more than 1,700 residents attended public meetings, decided on community goals, and rubbed elbows fixing things up (Alter 1995b).
- Houston, Texas: Artists got together with residents in a blighted inner-city neighborhood and decided to refurbish and display their works in a housing project that is also a home for single mothers (Kalb 1996).
- Across the country, citizens have formed voluntary associations such as Public Voice for Food and Health Policy, an advocacy group that conducted a study, for example, finding that supermarkets *can* make profits in the inner city and hence do not have to board their windows and flee to the suburbs ("Group Says" 1996).

More and more central-city residents are thinking like the NAACP's Oakland, California, chapter director, Shannon Reeves: "In the spirit of the Million Man March, we've got to be foot soldiers in our own neighborhoods. No one from the hills is going to come down to clean [our streets]. We've got to do that ourselves" (in Quellette 1996, 13). Meanwhile, in his 1995 presidential address to the American Sociological Association, Amitai Etzioni (1996) argued for the renewal of *authentic communities*—ones that are responsive to the true needs of all community members. He further pleaded for Americans to begin to see themselves as necessarily responsible participants in an overarching "community of communities" that ultimately embraces us all.

SOCIAL APPLICATIONS

WHY ARE METROPOLITAN AREAS RACIALLY SEGREGATED?

Central cities have become increasingly populated by minorities: One-third of the non-Hispanic white population live in cities of over 1 million, but two-thirds of the Hispanic and over half of the African American and Asian populations live in these largest urban areas. In several large American cities, such as Detroit, Atlanta, and Washington, D.C., racial and ethnic minorities comprise the numerical majority in a central city surrounded by largely nonminority suburbs.

Three trends have supported the development of racial segregation between cities and suburbs. From 1940 to 1980, there was a strong movement of rural African Americans and Hispanics to the largest urban centers. During the same period, there was a trend toward suburbanization by non-Hispanic white Americans. Most recently, large waves of Asian and Hispanic immigrants have settled largely in the biggest urban centers, thus contributing to the growth of the racial and ethnic minority population there (Gober 1993).

During the 1960s and 1970s, federal dollars were funneled to local areas to build public housing projects for the urban poor. The chief objective of these urban renewal projects was to replace unsafe, run-down tenement housing with higher-quality housing. The result, however, was to drive away the working class, decrease the quality of central-city housing, and increase racial segregation and crime. This is a remarkable record for a policy designed to improve housing.

Essentially, urban renewal bulldozed square miles of low-rise tenement buildings and replaced them with modern high-rise apartment buildings. The space saved was often used for freeways or public buildings. Despite the fact that the apartments were superior to the destroyed housing, the change had substantial negative consequences. First, unlike the destroyed units, the new housing was public housing. Thus, the working poor were displaced, and a dense aggregation of the poorest of the poor was created. Second, dense high-rises are poor places in which to raise children. Children who are playing 20 stories below their parents are effectively beyond parental supervision. Finally, by eliminating the front porch as a neighborhood meeting ground, the physical basis for neighborhood cohesion and integration was eliminated at the same time that increased density vastly increased the possibility of neighbors' annoying one another. Furthermore, all the new projects were located in areas where minority populations were high, thus contributing to the continuity of segregation.

Suburbinization was a disproportionately non-Hispanic white phenomenon because non-Hispanic whites were better able to afford new housing *and* because of racial discrimination. Studies during the 1970s and 1980s documented that race was more important than class in limiting African American suburbanization and that middle-class African Americans found it especially difficult to move into white suburbs (Farley 1977; Massey and Egger 1990). Thus, minority suburbanization frequently meant continued segregation. Today's African Americans who live in the suburbs are likely to live in suburbs largely populated by other African Americans (Massey and Denton 1988).

THINKING CRITICALLY

How does the racial segregation of metropolitan areas affect racial and ethnic issues, discussed in Chapter 11? How does this analysis of metropolitan racial segregation illustrate the sociological imagination, described in Chapter 1? Is the racial and ethnic segregation in metropolitan areas necessarily a negative development, do you think? Why or why not?

SOCIOLOGY ON THE NET

From the bible to the founders of our nation to the television depictions of today, our cities have gotten a lot of bad press. What is the state of our cities?

`http://www.hud.gov`

We are at the U.S. Department of Housing and Urban Development's **home page**. Click on the bottom part of the logo that is called **About HUD**. Click on the **Press Releases** section under HUD News and then scroll down to the **National Press Club Speech**. Open this selection and review the speech by Secretary Cisneros. What are some of the problems that the Secretary mentions? Where must the real leadership for urban rebirth be found? What values must guide this process? What programs are going to facilitate the process of urban renewal and change?

As Secretary Cisneros pointed out, our cities are divided by race and class. The Census Bureau has some good data on racial segregation in our cities.

`http://www.census.gov/pub/hhes/www/resseg.html`

This is a census report on residential segregation. Click on the **Definitions and References** section and briefly skim through the discussion of evenness and dissimilarity. We will use the measure of evenness called *dissimilarity*. Dissimilarity refers to the proportion of minority group members that would have to move to achieve an even distribution. In numerical terms, a dissimilarity score of 1.0 means that there is total segregation, and a dissimilarity score of 0 means that there is no segregation. Most scores fall in between these two numbers. Remember the higher the score, the greater the level of segregation. Go to the end of this document and click on the highlighted phrase **Residential Segregation**.

Now scroll down to the **Detailed Tables** and open the tables for **Blacks**. Scroll down the lists looking only at the dissimilarity scores. Which cities were the most segregated for blacks? What was the highest score that you found? What was the lowest? Now go back and do the same for the **Hispanics**. What was your high and low score? What region of the country had the highest levels of segregation? Were you surprised? Which of these two groups experiences the greatest level of segregation?

SUMMARY

1. The industrial city has three distinctive features: high density, a central business district, and a concentric spatial pattern.
2. The post-industrial city is characterized by low density and multiple nuclei. It is associated with the shift to tertiary production and the improvement of transportation and communication.
3. More than three-quarters of Americans live in metropolitan areas, but most of these live in the suburban ring rather than the central city. There have been three major changes in residence patterns: shrinking central cities, Sunbelt growth, and nonmetropolitan resurgence.
4. Urbanization is exploding in the less-developed world; many of its large cities will double in size in a decade. This urban growth is the result not of industrialization

but of high fertility and the high rural density and poverty that drive peasants toward the city.

5 Three major theories of the consequences of urban living are Wirth's urban determinism, compositional theory, and subcultural theory. Urban determinism suggests urban living has negative effects, compositional theory suggests it has no effects, and subcultural theory says it encourages the development of subcultures.

6 Urban living is associated with less reliance on neighbors and kin and more reliance on friends, with greater fear of crime and less warmth toward strangers, and with more diversity and entertainment.

7 Suburban living has become more diverse. Retail trade and manufacturing have moved to the suburbs, and the suburbs are now more densely populated, more congested, and less dominated by the minivan set.

8 Small-town and rural living is characterized by more emphasis on family and neighborliness, more social control, and less crowding. There are fewer cultural and lifestyle differences between rural and urban areas than there used to be.

9 The political economy of spatial distribution is concerned with political decisions that affect the allocation of people and dollars across space. This perspective suggests that home owners and elites both have a vested interest in growth and in increasing property values; they work together to keep lower-income people away from their neighborhoods and to segregate their tax dollars.

10 The decay of central-city housing and the growth of suburban housing reflect in part two processes: redlining and federal loan programs. The result is that central cities are poorer than they used to be and are racially segregated from their suburbs. There are city limits to equality.

11 Decaying central cities are being rebuilt through two processes of urban revitalization: municipal development and gentrification. Although these processes have improved the tax base of central cities, they raise questions about who benefits from revitalization. A recently emerging third option, community involvement, shows more promise.

12 Central cities have become increasingly populated by racial/ethnic minorities, partly due to unanticipated consequences of urban renewal programs in the 1960s and 1970s.

SUGGESTED READINGS

FLANAGAN, William G. 1993. *Contemporary Urban Sociology.* London and New York: Cambridge University Press. An up-to-date review of the major theories and debates in urban sociology. Includes a good overview of world systems theory and its application to the rapidly growing cities of the Third World, or periphery.

GOBER, Patricia. 1993. "Americans on the Move." *Population Bulletin* 48 (November): 1–39. A pamphlet that covers historical and contemporary residential mobility patterns, with a special emphasis on the economic factors that affect interstate migration.

GODDARD, Stephen B. 1994. *Getting There: The Epic Struggle between Road and Rail in the American Century.* New York: Basic Books. A fascinating account of the role of the automobile in fashioning modern cities, as well as of the political and economic struggle between the automobile industry and the rail industry, briefly described in Chapter 8 of this textbook.

GROTH, Paul. 1994. *Living Downtown: The History of Residential Hotels in the United States*. Berkeley: University of California Press. A fascinating social history, augmented with wonderful photographs, of what it meant and means to live in the residential hotels and boardinghouses of downtown American cities.

KELLY, Barbara M. (ed.). 1989. *Suburbia Re-examined*. New York: Greenwood Press. A collection of theory-based readings, empirical studies, and policy essays that document the development of and challenges to suburban quality of life created by increasing population pressure.

KNOX, Paul L. (ed.). 1994. *The Restless Urban Landscape*. Englewood Cliffs, N.J.: Prentice Hall. Readings in urban sociology from the conflict and symbolic interactionist perspectives, as well as discussions on topics such as the globalization of the city, Third World cities, urban aesthetics, and housing policies.

KNOX, Paul. 1995. *Urban Social Geography: An Introduction*, 3rd ed. New York: John Wiley & Sons. An up-to-date textbook for college students that provides a good introduction to and overview of urban sociology.

PARK, Robert Erza, Burgess, Ernest W., and McKenzie, Roderick D. 1984. *The City*. Chicago: University of Chicago Press. A classic; the first sociological analysis of urban life in the United States. (Originally published in 1925.)

RIIS, Jacob A. 1971. *How the Other Half Lives*. New York: Dover Publications. A liberally illustrated essay on conditions in U.S. urban slums at the turn of the century. Riis's early photographs provide ample documentation of the poverty and filth of the industrial city. (Originally published in 1901.)

SAVAGE, Mike, and Warde, Alan. 1993. *Urban Sociology, Capitalism and Modernity*. New York: Continuum Publishing Co. A readable but scholarly statement of the conflict, or political economy position. Savage and Warde discuss such topics as place and political identification, urban space and segregation, and urban participation and the social order.

TEAFORD, Jon C. 1993. *The Twentieth-Century American City*, 2nd ed. Baltimore: The Johns Hopkins University Press. An interesting and readable social history of the American city as it developed, blossomed, was challenged by its suburban ring, and now faces the possibility of regeneration.

U.S. Congress, Office of Technology Assessment. 1995. *The Technological Reshaping of Metropolitan America*. Washington, D.C.: U.S. Government Printing Office. A good book that describes in detail the impact of technology, from the automobile to the Internet, on metropolitan spatial distribution in the United States.

CHAPTER 23

Collective Behavior and Social Movements

OUTLINE

PROLOGUE

Have You Ever . . . Been in an audience—for example, at a rock concert or sporting event—and felt afraid that you might be crushed by the churning crowd? Written letters, handed out leaflets, or participated in mass mailings as part of a movement to change things? Run across a crowd or demonstration on campus?

Almost every campus has several demonstrations every term. These may range from five to six students carrying placards to hundreds of students demonstrating for or against abortion rights, affirmative action programs, gun control, gay rights, recycling, animal rights, or tuition hikes. Campuses are places where students can take part in a variety of social movements.

Most demonstrations and crowd gatherings come to a peaceful close. The TV cameras come and go, and the participants gradually fade away. Of course, not all demonstrations end peacefully. From New Jersey to Los Angeles to Beijing, the gathering of a crowd sometimes leads to violence. When a crowd grows from 100 to 1,000 or even 100,000, a peaceful demonstration may end up in police confrontations, property destruction, and even death. Every crowd has a volatile character that makes outcomes unpredictable.

This chapter is concerned with those occasions on which people step outside of their usual school/work/play routines to take part in collective behavior and social movements. Who are the people who step forward, what social processes govern the behavior of the groups they form, and what social factors influence the success (or failure) of various social movements?

- In April 1995, a bomb destroyed federal offices in Oklahoma City, killing 167 federal workers and others. A search for the terrorists led to men associated with the militia movement in the United States.
- In May 1992, Los Angeles erupted in flames as rioters protested the not-guilty verdict in the case concerning the police beating of Rodney King.
- In June 1990, a triumphant crowd of Detroit Pistons fans poured into the streets after the Pistons won the National Basketball Association championship. Jubilant (and drunk) fans got so carried away that seven people died in the ensuring melee.
- In June 1989, a month-long demonstration by 100,000 pro-democracy students in Tienanmen Square was violently quashed by the Chinese government. Several hundred students and soldiers died in the confrontation.
- Every day in the United States, people picket outside abortion clinics. In many places, these antiabortion activists have caused so much disruption that they are regularly hauled off to jail and saddled with large fines.

Sociology divides these kinds of activities into two related but distinct topics: collective behavior and social movements. **Collective behavior** is nonroutine action by an emotionally aroused gathering of people who face an ambiguous situation. It includes situations such as the impromptu celebration in Detroit. These are unplanned, relatively spontaneous actions, where individuals and groups improvise some joint response to an unusual or problematic situation.

Collective behavior is nonroutine action by an emotionally aroused gathering of people who face an ambiguous situation.

In contrast, a **social movement** is an ongoing, goal-directed effort to change social institutions from the outside. Examples include the antiabortion, gay rights, and civil rights movements. A social movement is extraordinarily complex. It may include sit-ins, demonstrations, and even riots, but it also includes meetings,

A **social movement** is an ongoing, goal-directed effort to change social institutions from the outside.

fund-raisers, legislative lobbying, and letter-writing campaigns (Johnston and Klandermans 1995).

Both collective behavior and social movements challenge the status quo. The primary distinction between them is that collective behavior is spontaneous and strictly confined to a particular place and time; a social movement is organized, broad based, and long term. Even a month-long demonstration in Beijing is an instance of collective behavior until and unless it develops into an organized attempt to change the political structure.

In this chapter, we examine the social structure of collective behavior and social movements; the circumstances under which people step outside the usual conventions; the processes through which some disorganized protests, riots, and outbreaks become organized, politicized social movements; and the responses of institutions and people who wish to maintain the status quo.

COLLECTIVE BEHAVIOR: CROWDS AND RIOTS

TYPES OF CROWDS

A **crowd** is a gathering of people who are reacting to a nonroutine event.

A **crowd** is a gathering of people who are reacting to a nonroutine event. This definition excludes most concert audiences, football spectators, and religious congregations, which are almost always pretty routine. In a small minority of cases, however, something happens to turn a passive audience into an aroused crowd. Winning the championship or clinching the division title can turn ordinary athletic spectators into an ecstatic crowd that revels in the streets. Similarly, people's behavior at rock concerts and revival meetings may change if the crowd becomes emotionally aroused.

The sociologist John Lofland (1981) has described six types of crowds, which result from the combination of three dominant emotions in two organizational forms. The three dominant emotions are fear, hostility, and joy. These may appear in two organizational forms: crowd (confined to one time and place) and mass (repeated in other times and places). Looking at these two dimensions in combination yields the six types of collective behavior illustrated in Figure 23.1.

You may wonder how a mass behavior that occurs over and over again can still fit the definition of collective behavior. The case of mass hostility (followed by mass joy and, later, mass disillusionment) can be illustrated by the waves of collective behavior that tumbled Communist governments across Eastern Europe in the fall of 1989. These mass uprisings were relatively spontaneous, unplanned events. Although repeated in nation after nation, they were not coordinated or the result of ongoing social movements. Similarly, the wave of race riots that swept U.S. cities in 1967 was not the result of a planned campaign but was the spontaneous response of aroused people to similar situations. It should be obvious, however, that there is a connection between collective behavior and social movements. Although one racial protest is an instance of collective behavior, a social movement is likely to emerge if the protests are repeated (Marx and McAdam 1994). Later in this chapter, we discuss the circumstances under which repeated but disorganized collective behavior is likely to turn into a social movement.

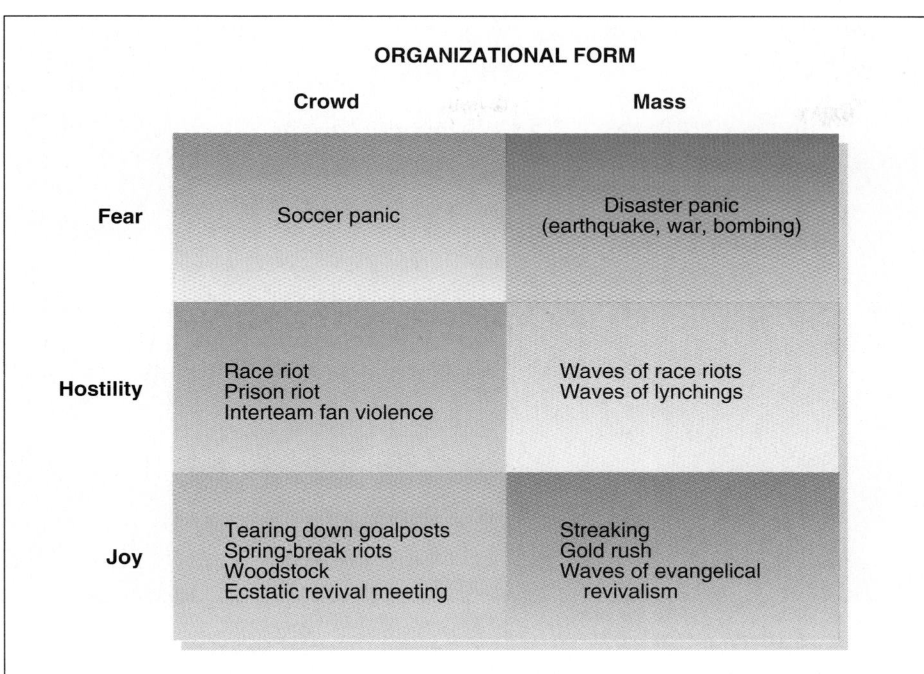

FIGURE 23.1
TYPES OF COLLECTIVE BEHAVIOR

All episodes of collective behavior are characterized by strong emotional arousal. In this typology, episodes of collective behavior are categorized by whether this dominant emotion is fear, hostility, or joy. Even joyful crowds are extremely volatile and may become violent and destructive. An isolated episode is a crowd behavior, but collective behavior takes on a mass form if it appears repeatedly.

SOURCE: Adapted from Lofland 1981.

THEORIES OF CROWD BEHAVIOR

There are many types of crowds—happy crowds and hostile crowds and panic-stricken crowds. All crowds, however, have a volatile quality that makes officials uneasy. Celebratory crowds can turn into violent rioters. Why does this happen?

In ongoing groups, norms, roles, and sanctions set goals and structure conformity. In the absence of social structure, what accounts for crowd behavior? Three general theories have been offered: contagion theory, convergence theory, and emergent norm theory.

Contagion Theory. According to **contagion theory,** the crowd situation leads to the development of unanimous and intense feelings and behaviors that are at odds with the usual predisposition of the individual participants (Turner and Killian 1987), This theory attempts to explain only one kind of crowd behavior: the escalating response. It suggests that crowds are moved to extreme and irrational behaviors—lynchings, prison riots, mass suicide, religious frenzy—through a vicious circle of exchange. One person yells an obscenity, another throws a rock, and a third shoots a gun. Finally, the crowd is fired up to an emotional level that its members would not have reached if they had coolly considered the matter on their own. Many contagion theorists believe that this circular stimulation heightens and reinforces antisocial behavior, stripping away the effects of socialization so that crowd responses become irrational and instinctual (Blumer 1969, LeBon 1896).

Contagion theory suggests that the crowd situation leads to the development of unanimous and intense feelings and behaviors that are at odds with the usual predispositions of the individual participants.

Convergence Theory. Whereas contagion theory argues that the crowd situation leads to escalating extremism among otherwise conforming individuals,

During the Spring of 1989, crowds of students and workers gathered in Beijing's Tienanmen Square and throughout China to demand greater democracy. After weeks of uncertainty, authorities crushed the protests on June 4. The month-long demonstrations are a classic case of mass crowds, with the dominant emotion vacillating between jubilation and terror.

Convergence theory contends that the cause, or triggering event, for crowd action selectively draws people who share a common set of predispositions.

convergence theory attempts to explain quiet as well as rowdy crowds. It contends that the cause, or triggering event, for crowd action selectively draws people who share a common set of predispositions. For example, street riots draw unattached, alienated, and angry young men; the convergence of many like-minded people provides the critical mass for their predispositions to be put into action. Crowds drawn by a religious revival will have another set of predispositions. According to convergence theory, there is no process within crowds; nothing new develops. Thus, the lynch mob is not a group of well-meaning citizens whipped up into a frenzy by circular stimulation; it is instead a collection of racist killers.

Emergent norm theory suggests that each crowd is governed by norms developed and validated by group processes within the crowd.

Emergent Norm Theory. **Emergent norm theory** suggests that each crowd is governed by norms developed and validated by group processes within the crowd. (Marx and McAdam 1994; Turner and Killian 1987). This theory views the crowd experience as an extension of the everyday processes by which we negotiate encounters (see Chapter 7). From this perspective, the major task of a crowd is to improvise a joint answer to the question, "What is going on here?" Once this answer is reached and the encounter framed, the crowd will be able to make sense of the encounter and decide what acts are appropriate. Is the police officer beating the defenseless woman, or is the police officer defending himself against a vicious and unprovoked assault? Whether right or wrong, the frame will evoke sets of norms about what the crowd *should* do.

Emergent norm theory does not assume that the crowd is unanimous in the definition it reaches. It assumes that the crowd is made up of leaders and followers, confused passersby, and curious spectators. Like the subject in Asch's experiment who didn't want to disagree publicly about which line was longest (see Chapter 5), many of these onlookers will keep silent despite disagreeing with views being expressed. They are not swept up by emotional contagion but merely doing what most of us do most of the time: maintaining an appearance of group conformity.

In 1930, these two black men were lynched by a mob in Marion, Indiana. Despite this clear photograph, official reports that the killers were "parties unknown." Between 1890 and 1930, there were over 1,000 lynching in the United States. Although lynching is often attributed to contagion that drives people to act against their better natures, the racial pattern of lynchings suggests that they were instead a product of shared values: racism.

Most modern scholars prefer emergent norm theory. It provides a broad framework that explains the behavior of the passive crowd as well as of the unruly mob. It suggests that the unruly crowd, far from representing a stripping away of normative inhibitions, actually develops new norms—for example, a shared conviction that looting is appropriate behavior in the situation—and internally validates them. Usually, such convictions are rationalized by reference to widely shared values and symbols.

In addition, emergent norm theory helps explain the cultural and historical differences in crowd behavior. The systematic variation in crowd targets and crowd

Concept Summary A Comparison of Theories About Crowd Behavior

	Contagion Theory	Convergence Theory	Emergent Norm Theory
Basic Assumptions	Through circular stimulation and reinforcement, irrational and extreme acts develop.	Crowds are characterized by like-minded people drawn together by common interest	New norms emerge during crowd interaction that validate group actions.
Evaluation	Explains only the escalating response	Ignores the heterogeneity of most crowds; assumes that crowds cause no change in individual behavior	Explains quiet crowds as well as the escalating response

THINKING CRITICALLY

From what you know now about crowd dynamics, how might you be able to help stop a crowd from panicking or from becoming a mob—or could you?

behavior over time and place suggests that crowd behavior has a clear normative component. Like other cultural responses, crowd behavior is patterned. Whether mob violence is directed at Jews, women, blacks, Catholics, or AIDS victims depends on cultural norms.

The form of crowd behavior also changes over time. The witch hunt and the lynch mob have almost disappeared as forms of collective actions; the demonstration, however, has gained in popularity. The fact that certain crowd behaviors remain characteristic of specific times and places suggests that each society has a repertoire of crowd behaviors from which to choose. This repertoire represents patterned responses to recurrent situations rather than any spontaneous or instinctive aspect of human nature (Marx and McAdam 1994).

Emergent norm theory is our best general-purpose theory of collective behavior, but it cannot stand entirely alone. Both contagion and convergence theories are also relevant in explaining crowd behavior. The roles of all three theories in explaining specific instances of collective behavior are examined in the next section.

TWO CASE STUDIES OF COLLECTIVE BEHAVIOR

Theory is useful to the extent that it helps us understand past events and predict future ones. One way to evaluate the theories of collective behavior is to test them against actual experience. In this section, we describe two very different types of crowds—a panic crowd and a race riot. Both represent crowd rather than mass behavior, but the first is dominated by fear and the second by hostility.

The British Soccer Tragedy. On April 16, 1989, over 180 people were seriously injured and 95 people were killed at a soccer match in Sheffield, England. The dead fans were accidentally crushed to death against a barrier fence by thousands of their own team's supporters.

Liverpool was scheduled to play Nottingham Forest in a stadium that could hold 54,000 fans. Because of inadequate guarding at the gates and perhaps the presence of broken barricades, more than a thousand unticketed Liverpool fans managed to overrun the entrances and get into the standing-room-only sections at the Liverpool end zone. Because of vast overcrowding and because illegal fans were pushing to get in quickly and then pushing to move to the front, the crowd panicked and pressed forward crushing the fans in the front.

British soccer (which Britons call football) has been described as a "slum sport played in slum stadiums" ("Disaster" 1989). It draws its fans heavily from the working class in the most depressed industrial areas of England. In the midst of a depressing environment, Liverpool's often victorious football team had been a source of great pride. "They took our industries away and our jobs away. But they can't take our football away from us" was the comment of one fan ("There's Comfort" 1989).

Because of the frequent violence associated with interteam rivalries, British stadiums are very different from American stadiums. The fans are surrounded by mounted police in full riot gear; prisonlike fences separate the fans from the playing field and from the opposing team's fans. Going to see a soccer game has all the drama of having a ringside ticket to a riot; it is not family entertainment but an activity that appeals to young people and especially young men.

A particular feature of British soccer stadiums is that the end zone is standing room only. There are broad steps or terraces in the end zones so that people stand-

Nearly 100 people died when panic stampeded a crowd of soccer fans in Sheffield, England, in 1989. They were crushed against heavy fences designed to keep the fans off the field. Almost a year later, over 1,400 Moslem pilgrims were crushed in a stampede in a Mecca tunnel. Such instances of short-lived panic are probably best explained by contagion theory

ing farther back can see, but there is no equivalent to reserved seating. This means that whenever the situation is tense or exciting, the crowd tends to press toward the front barriers. The absence of designated seating also means that it is relatively easy for a few extra fans to sneak in without being noticed. These standing-room-only tickets are cheaper than the seated tickets, and they are naturally most often sold to those with the least money—the youngest and the poorest fans.

ANALYSIS. The British soccer tragedy is a classic case of a panic crowd, and it is precisely the sort of event that contagion theory is designed to explain. People in the back pushed, and soon everyone was rushing forward in a blind panic. The whole thing took only a few minutes—too short a time for new norms to emerge or for any deliberate behavior.

At first glance, convergence theory appears to have merit for explaining this crowd: Violence resulted when crowd members of a particular sort were drawn together to watch rough play. A little reflection, however, suggests that convergence theory is not very plausible here. The killing of Liverpool fans by other Liverpool fans was an accident; although the fans were disproportionately young and male, they did not converge on the stadium to rough up other Liverpool fans. Under similar circumstances, a crowd of middle-aged, upper-class patrons of a sinking cruise ship could demonstrate the same panic reaction. This appears to be a simple instance of contagion.

The 1992 Los Angeles Race Riot. In early May 1992, South Central Los Angeles erupted in one of the most frightening race riots that America has seen. One year before, Rodney King, an African American male, had been viciously beaten by four white Los Angeles police officers after they stopped him for speeding. Caught on videotape by an onlooker, the beatings showed King being clubbed and kicked 56 times over 81 seconds. Television audiences around the world saw it, and many Americans watched it more than once. When the officers were brought to trial for beating King, more than three-quarters of both blacks and whites expected them to be found guilty (Church 1992). But on May 2, 1992, a mostly white jury found them not guilty—and parts of Los Angeles erupted in violent rioting that ultimately left 51 dead.

For several nights, fires broke out across the city. Wearing flat jackets to protect themselves from sniper attacks, fire crews stayed on the job for 48 hours straight, tracking arson activity as it moved through the city. In an event caught on video, several black males pulled a white truck driver, Reginald Denny, from his sand truck after he stopped for a red light. They bashed him with the vehicle's fire extinguisher, throttled him with beer bottles, karate-kicked him in the head, and stole his wallet. One fired a shotgun at him from close range. Denny was rescued by four other African Americans and taken to a hospital for four hours of brain surgery (Ellis 1992).

Meanwhile, looters broke into neighborhood stores and carried away everything from milk to TV sets. Parts of the city ceased to function. Downtown businesses and schools closed; professional sports events were called off (Ellis 1992). Los Angeles International airport closed because pilots could not see through the smoke from the fires. President George Bush federalized the area's National Guard. In televised messages, he condemned the disturbances and called the rioters' acts "murder." He also pronounced the tape of King's beating "revolting" and promised federal prosecution of the four police officers for violating King's civil rights.

ANALYSIS. We can see elements of all three theories in this example. On first glance, the rioting seems to present a classic case of contagion on the part of the rioters, who acted in ways that went far beyond their usual behaviors. Most of the violence and destruction took place in South Central Los Angeles, a 46-square-mile area characterized by gangs, poverty, and drug dealers. But even drug dealers and gang members do not ordinarily pull truck drivers to the pavement and gleefully beat them. Contagion certainly existed, but contagion theory is inadequate to describe fully the course of the riot. Frenzy and irrationality cannot explain the fact that many African American rioters apparently skipped over black-owned businesses to loot Korean-owned ones. Relations between blacks and Asian merchants had been tense for years, mainly because of a perception that Korean merchants had been exploiting African Americans by establishing shops in ghetto areas but refusing to hire blacks to work in them (Ellis 1992).

Convergence theory also helps us to understand the riot. According to a Time CNN poll, 42 percent of African Americans condemned the riot as completely unjustified and 46 percent said the riots were mostly caused by "people taking advantage of the situation to justify violence and looting" rather than "a genuine reaction to the verdict in the Rodney King case" (Ellis 1992). To many observers, the rioters were mostly young, angry ghetto black males who no longer listen to the established African American leadership. Remarked a Los Angeles attorney, Johnnie Cochran, when he was interviewed during the riot, "Nobody can talk to the people in the streets. Even their parents can't talk to them" (Church 1992).

Meanwhile, emergent norm theory points to how the rioters came to explain their behavior as an us-against-them confrontation with an apathetic and exploitative enemy. After the King verdict was announced, thousands of black residents of South Central Los Angeles gathered at the neighborhood African Methodist Episcopal (A.M.E.) Church to pray and protest the injustice. As they left the church, they were beset by rioting youth. "Nothing you're talking about is going to

This photograph shows a street scene during the Los Angeles riot in 1992. Like most recent riots in America, it is a race riot in the sense that the incident that provoked the mayhem was racially charged. Although the spark for the riot is black rage against the white community, most of the damage from the riot occurred within the black community. Such riots are more common when there are large numbers of unemployed young men. When the disaffected and angry are working- or middle-class adults, they are more likely to form a social movement to address their concerns.

do any good," the rioters shouted, "so come with us and let's burn." All three theories—contagion, convergence, and emergent norm—help to explain the 1992 Los Angeles race riot.

Social Movements

Collective behavior is by definition nonroutine and irregular. As such, it always challenges the established way of doing things. This challenge may be temporary or limited, such as a prison riot or a football melee, or it may be part of a repeated mass response to arousing conditions. In the latter case, collective behavior may be a prelude to a social movement—an organized attempt to change social structure or ideology that is carried on outside legitimate channels or that uses these channels in innovative ways (Marx and McAdam 1994). The Focus section of this chapter explores the birth-control movement as a challenge to many cherished 19th-century values.

Social movements such as the antinuclear movement, the environmental movement, the civil rights movement, and the antiabortion movement have stepped outside the usual legislative process in their attempt to challenge the status quo; they may use demonstrations, sit-ins, violence, and other tactics to affect public policy. In many cases, we might think of such behavior as deviance—the breaking of social norms. Recall from Chapter 8 that one of Robert Merton's classifications of deviants was the *rebel*, who not only spurns society's goals and the means to reach

This photograph shows a street scene during a race riot in Israel in 1996. The 10,000 Ethiopian Jewish immigrants in Israel protested the government's refusal to use their blood donations because of fear of AIDS. The protests turned to riots (Bartholet 1996).

those goals but also posits new and different goals and means. Merton's rebel would likely be a social movement activist.

Nevertheless, social movements can best be understood as political processes (Johnston and Klandermans 1995). Some social movements are very closely allied with traditional political groups such as parties; others seek to overthrow or radically change the state. Because all have the goal of affecting public policy decisions, however, they are a part of the political process. As a result, social movement members tend to be the same kinds of people who vote and write letters to their congressional representatives.

Stages of Social Movements

Social movements typically follow a four-stage pattern of development, emergence, coalescence, bureaucratization, and eventual decline. Not all social movements proceed through every stage. Some social movements are aborted before they become full-blown, and not every social movement declines. In this section, we use examples from the anti-smoking movement to describe the stages (Goldstein 1992).

Emergence. The first stage of a social movement is *emergence*, during which separate individuals, each believing that something is wrong and should be changed, gradually begin to define their concerns as a public issue. When persons with similar concerns come together or communicate with each other about those concerns, a social movement has begun to emerge. As early as 1938, a Johns Hopkins physician used life expectancy tables to show that smoking shortened people's lives. Subsequent laboratory studies also pointed to harmful health effects from smoking. But until 1954, when these findings were released to the public at a meeting of the American Medical Association, the separate research studies were just that—scattered and independent. It was at the 1954 meeting that people with similar concerns came together and began to see their research findings as a matter for public policy. Today's anti-smoking movement had begun to emerge.

Coalescence. Once a social movement has emerged, activists must define their grievances, the causes for those grievances, and their goals for change. We call this stage of coming to agreement on joint purposes *coalescence*. The anti-smoking movement defined the growing consumption of cigarettes in the United States as a serious social problem. It defined the problem's principal cause as advertising by the tobacco industry and sought to change things by agitating for health warning labels on cigarette packages and a ban on tobacco advertising on radio and television. In 1965, after a long battle with the tobacco industry, the anti-smoking movement gained some ground when Congress specified an official warning for ads and packages: "Caution: Cigarette Smoking May Be Hazardous to Your Health." In 1970, federal legislation banned smoking ads from radio and TV on the grounds of public interest, and Congress stepped up the warning: "Warning" The Surgeon General Has determined That Cigarette Smoking Is Dangerous to Your Health." Having coalesced, the anti-smoking movement had begun to win some victories.

Bureaucratization. As it gets established and grows powerful, a social movement becomes bureaucratized (Chapter 5). It depends less and less on specific individuals, noted for their zeal, and increasingly on hierarchical organization and a paid professional staff. The anti-smoking movement owes much of its early success to John Banzhaf, an attorney. Watching football on TV in 1967, Banzhaf was angered by the relentless smoking commercials and decided to change things. Eventually, Banzhaf quit his job and created the bureaucratic organization Action on Smoking and Health (ASH) to provide legal leadership to the movement (Goldstein 1992).

Eventual Decline. Once its goals are met and members feel they have no more to accomplish, a social movement is likely to decline. This is not necessarily the case, however; some social movements redefine their goals once their original intents have been realized (Lyman 1995). The anti-smoking movement has hardly declined, although it has had considerable success in getting Americans to give up smoking. In more and more regions, smoking has become redefined as deviant behavior. At this point, the anti-smoking movement has broadened its goals to encouraging constraints on smoking in public places and increasing the rights of nonsmokers (Goldstein 1992).

Social movements can decline for reasons other than having met their goals (Oegema and Klandermans 1994). Some decline because of poor leadership or depletion of resources. In some cases, a movement's leaders "sell out" or are co-opted by the other side. In some cases, a social movement is deliberately repressed by the established powers (Della Porta 1995; Miller 1983).

Theories of Social Movements

Most Americans have a relatively low interest in political processes. Chapter 15 documented that many Americans do not even bother to vote. What are the circumstances that prompt people to shake off this lethargy and try to change the system? Why do people step outside of their usual social roles and attempt to change the world or the community in which they live?

Two major theories explain the circumstances in which social movements arise: relative deprivation theory and resource mobilization theory. Both theories suggest that social movements arise out of inequalities and cleavages in society, but they offer somewhat different scenarios of how and why protests develop.

Relative Deprivation Theory. Proverty and justice are universal phenomena. Why is it that they so seldom lead to social movements? According to **relative deprivation theory,** social movements arise when people experience an intolerable gap between their rewards and what they believe they have a right to expect. They define their condition by comparing it with that of some better-off group or with expectations based on past experience. They may experience deprivation relative to other groups or other times rather than absolute deprivation—hence the label *relative* deprivation.

Relative deprivation theory argues that social movements arise when people experience an intolerable gap between their rewards and what they believe they have a right to expect; it is also known as *breakdown theory*.

Figure 23.2 diagrams three conditions for which relative deprivation theory would predict the development of a social movement. In condition A, disaster or taxation suddenly reduces the absolute level of living. If there is no parallel drop in what people expect, then they will feel that their deprivation is illegitimate. In condition B, both expectations and real standard of living are improving, but expectations continue to rise even after the standard of living has leveled off. Consequently, people feel deprived relative to what they had anticipated. Finally, in condition C, expectations rise faster than the standard of living, again creating a gap between reality and expectations.

FIGURE 23.2
THE GAP BETWEEN EXPECTATIONS AND REWARDS

Relative deprivation theory suggests that whenever there is a gap between expectations (E) and rewards (R) relative deprivation is created. It may occur when conditions are stable or improving as well as when the real standard of living is declining.

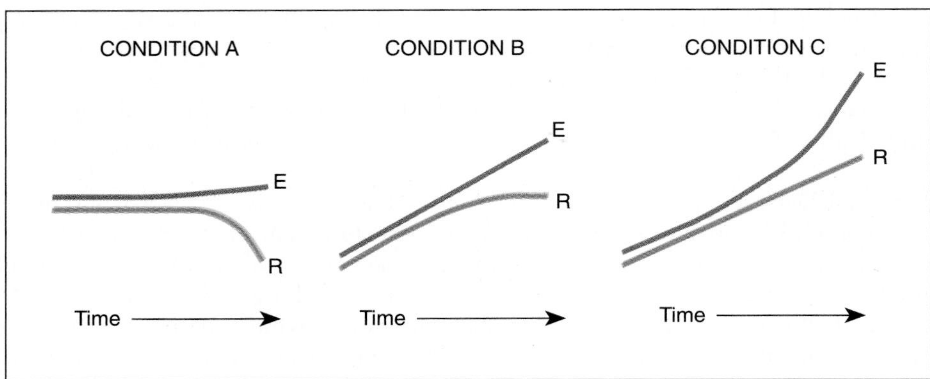

Relative deprivation theory has the merit of plausibly explaining the fact that many social movements occur in times when objective conditions either are improving (condition C) or at least represent a major improvement over the past (condition B). Because relative deprivation theory relies ultimately on the disorganizing effects of social change, it is often referred to as *breakdown theory*.

There are two major criticisms of relative deprivation theory. First, empirical evidence does not bear out of the prediction that those who are most deprived, absolutely or relatively, are the ones most likely to participate in a social movement. Often, participants are the best off in their groups rather than the worst off. In many other situations, individuals participate in and lead social movements on behalf of groups to which they do not belong. An example is the anti-apartheid movement on American campuses. Second, the theory fails to specify the conditions under which relative deprivation will lead to social movements. Why do some relatively deprived groups form social movements while others do not? In general, empirical studies suggest that relative deprivation by itself is not a good predictor of the development of social movements (Gurney and Tierney 1982; Johnston and Klandermans 1995).

Resource mobilization theory suggests that social movements develop when organized groups are competing for scarce resources; it is also known as solidarity theory.

Resource Mobilization Theory. According to **resource mobilization theory,** social movements develop when organized groups are competing for scarce resources. This theory differs from relative deprivation theory in two important ways. First, it argues that deprivation and competition are universal and thus relatively unimportant as predictors of social movements (Marx and McAdam 1994). Second, it assumes that the spark for turning deprivation into a movement is not anger and resentment but rather organization.

Research shows that the most effective social movements emerge from groups whose members have two characteristics: relative homogeneity and many overlapping ties. (Marx and McAdam 1994). This implies that a black civil rights group that admitted whites would be less effective than one consisting only of blacks. Furthermore, groups are stronger if, in addition to being homogenerous, their members share a strong network of ties—if they belong to the same clubs and organizations, if they work together, if they live in the same neighborhood. Research on the 1871 Paris Commune revolt shows, for instance, that neighborhood-based insurgent groups were much more cohesive, effective, and long-lived than units that drew volunteers from all parts of the city (Gould 1991).

Mobilization theory is often referred to as *solidarity theory* because it suggests that the building blocks of social movements are organized groups, not alienated, discontented individuals.

One major criticism of resource mobilization theory is that it underestimates the importance of grievance and spontaneity as triggers for social movements (Klandermans 1984; Zygmunt 1986). A second criticism is that it overlooks the importance of ideology in translating vague individual dissatisfactions into organized political agendas. Participants in the women's movement often say that "the personal is political." Derided for feminist ideology, this proposition illustrates a point that critics say resource mobilization theory generally seems to miss (Buechler 1993).

Integration. Recent research suggests that both theories have merit. Some social movements do develop out of a strongly felt sense of grievance; shared sentiment leads previously unacquainted people to join together to address their concern. Several of the protest groups that developed after the almost-disaster at the nuclear energy plant at Three Mile Island in 1980 were of this form (Cable, Walsh, and Warland 1988). But some social movements have more to do with the strength of previously existing social networks than with the strength of the grievance. The League of Women Voters, for example, is one of the many civic organizations that adopt a new cause each year.

Resource mobilization theory is clearly the dominant theoretical perspective in contemporary accounts of social movements. If it is broadened to take into account the important role that spontaneous outbursts, triggering events, and emotionality play in occasioning and sustaining social movements, it provides a useful model of why social movements develop. Figure 23.3 compares the two models.

Social Movement Organizations

Many social movements include a wide spectrum of different groups, all pursuing, in their own way, the same general goal. For example, there are probably 50 different social movement organizations (SMOs) within the environmental movement. These range from the relatively conventional Audubon Society to the radical Greenpeace movement to the self-styled "eco-terrorists" of Earth First! As

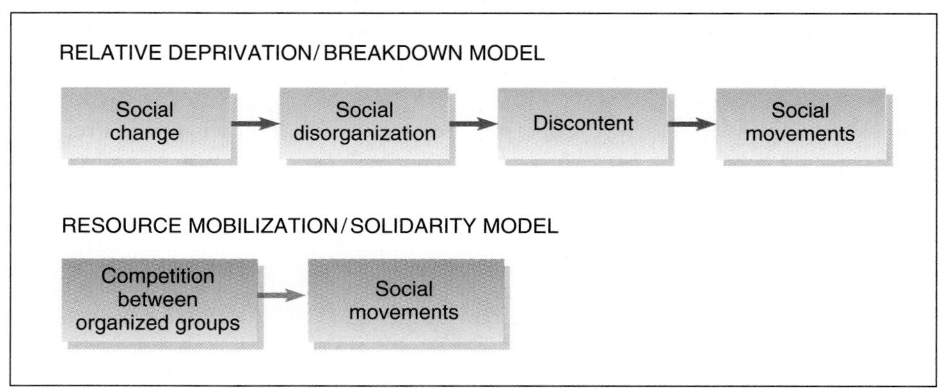

FIGURE 23.3
A Comparison of Relative Deprivation/Breakdown Models With Resource Mobilization/Solidarity Models

Source: Adapted from Useem 1980.

this example suggests, the tactics of SMOs within any given social movement may be highly divergent; some write letters and lobby their congressional representatives, while others disrupt nuclear power plants, chain themselves to trees, and blockade fishing grounds. The SMOs within a social movement usually reflect the racial, class, sex, age, and nationality schisms in the larger society (Benford 1989; Maheu 1995).

These divergent organizations are in some ways competitive: In the case of the environmental movement, for example, each is after the hearts and dollars of environmentally inclined citizens. Because this wide assortment of organizations provides avenues of participation for people with a variety of goals and styles, however, the existence of diverse SMOs is usually functional for the social movement. There is room for everybody (Cable and Cable 1995).

SMOS can be organized as professional or as volunteer, or *indigenous*, organizations. Professional SMOs, such as the Audubon Society and the Serria Club, may have offices in Washington, D.C., and relatively large paid staffs, which include fund-raisers and lobbyists who developed an interest in the organization's goals after being hired. Indigenous SMOs, in contrast, are staffed by volunteers who are personally involved—for example, neighbors who organize in the church basement to protest the building of a nuclear power plant in the neighborhood. Evidence suggests that the existence of both types of organizations within a movement contributes to the movement's success. This is especially true for social movements that seek to help the disadvantaged.

The Professional SMO. The professional SMO provides three clear benefits to a social movement (Staggenborg 1988). First, it is usually better at soliciting resources from groups outside the disadvantaged group itself. It appeals to what is called a *conscience constituency*, people who are ideologically committed to the group's cause. For example, Jewish supporters of antidiscrimination laws have given generous support to professional black SMOs such as the NAACP. Because this is a respectable organization with accountants and lawyers, outsiders are more comfortable investing in it. Second, the professional SMO is better at building coalitions with related interest groups. Third, the professional SMO provides continuity to the movement. While indigenous SMOs are likely to wax and wane with the urgency of the issues and the other demands on their leaders, professional SMOs provide long-term stability. The paid staff maintains the movement when the demonstrators from the indigenous SMOs have gone back to work. Anti-busing activity is the work of indigeneous SMOs. It has failed to become a real social movement largely because it lacks professional SMOs. Put another way, anti-busing activity has not become bureaucratized. (Olzak; Shonaham, and West 1994).

The Indigenous SMO. An effective social movement however also requires continuing indigenous organizations (Maheu, 1995). Indigenous organizations perform two vital functions. First, by keeping the aggrieved group actively supportive of the social movement, they help to maintain the sense of urgency necessary for sustained effort. Second, anger and grievance propel indigenous organizations to use innovative, direct-action tactics (sit-ins, demonstrations, eco-terrorism and the like)—tactics not likely to be endorsed by professional organizations. This provides publicity for the movement and helps keep it on the national agenda. It also has the ironic effect of increasing support for the professional (more conservative) organizations, which begin to seem quite reasonable compared with the extremists.

MOBILIZING THE MOVEMENT

Mobilization is the "process by which a unit gains significantly in the control of assets it previously did not control" (Etzioni 1968, 388). These assets may be weapons, technologies, goods, money, or members. The resources available to a social movement depend on two factors: the amount of resources controlled by group members and the proportion of their resources that the members are willing to contribute to the movement. Thus, mobilization can proceed by increasing the size of the membership, by increasing the proportion of assets that members are willing to give to the group, or by recruiting richer members.

The maximum state of mobilization, which Lofland (1979) has called white-hot mobilization, is reached when almost all members are full-time members who are totally dedicated to the movement and when the movement's resources and number of members are expanding dramatically. Most movements, of course, never achieve this state. As Lofland notes, in most social movements, only a few members are especially dedicated, funding is slim, the program is timid and unacted on, and recruitment is haphazard and sparse.

Mobilization proceeds through two tactics: the recruitment of individual adherents (micromobilization) and the recruitment of supportive organizations (bloc mobilization).

Micromobilization. The procedure through which SMOs attract individual new members has been called **frame alignment.** It is a process of convincing individuals that their interests, values, and beliefs and those of the social movement organization are complementary. According to Snow, Rockford, Worden, and Benford (1986), SMOs use four tactics for frame alignment:

Frame alignment is a process by which social movement organizations attract individual new recruits; it seeks to convince individuals that their interests, values, and beliefs and those of the SMO are complementary.

1. *Frame bridging* targets people who have interests similar, though perhaps not identical, with those of the SMO and attempts to convince them that the similarities are great enough that they should support the SMO. Thus, the Sierra Club may use computerized mailing lists to appeal to members of the National Wildflife Federation or the Audubon Society.
2. *Frame amplification* is equivalent to consciousness raising. This strategy gives structure to unfocused dissatisfaction by offering the SMO's frame as an explanation. It tries to convince people that their problems are caused by partiarchy or racism or whatever definition of the situation is used by the SMO.
3. *Frame extension* broadens the frame of the social movement so that more and more problems and concerns are included within its definition of the situation. For example, some peace movements have tried to attract more recruits by suggesting that the struggle for peace is also a struggle for social justice against racism, sexism, and proverty.
4. *Frame transformation* is equivalent to a religious conversion. It requires convincing individuals that the way they have seen things is entirely wrong. This is a strategy used by the Moonies, the Black Muslims, and radical feminists—groups that provide a radically different definition of a person's entire past and future and that frequently demand not just one evening a week but total, full-time dedication.

The environmental movement, like most social movements, contains a variety of SMOs—some professional, some amateur, some radical, and some relatively conservative. Although professional organizers provide many benefits, successful social movements also require the passion and commitment of those personally involved.

Who is most likely to be affected by these mobilization strategies? Studies of social movement activists show that, although ideology and grievances are important, the key factor is the strength of their personal ties with other movement activists. No matter how deeply committed they are ideologically to the movement, if they are not part of a network of others with similar convictions, they are unlikely to be more than token members (McAdam 1986; McAdam and Paulsen 1993).

Bloc Mobilization. In addition to converting or mobilizing adherents one at a time through frame alignment processes, social movement organizations can use a strategy called **bloc mobilization** to recruit other organizations to support their cause. For example, the anti-pornography movement has asked for and received support from PTAs, fundamentalist churches, and feminist organizations.

Bloc mobilization is a strategy whereby social movement organizations recruit other organizations to support their cause rather than trying to recruit single individuals.

Bloc mobilization is a very effective way to expand a movement's resources: It means access to other organizations' newsletters, members, and funds. It is, however, only suitable for social movements that make very low demands on their members. It would not be an effective means of recruiting members to a radical religious sect or an extremist political group.

The Free-Rider Problem. A serious problem that plagues all social movements is what is called the "free rider." The free rider is somebody who will benefit from the social movement but who declines to participate. The free rider sits back and lets others write the letters and do the demonstrating; he or she is glad that somebody is finally doing something but cannot be bothered to more than sound supportive. For example, there are likely to be more than 1 million abortions this year; few of these women will participate in the pro-choice movement. Similarly, only a tiny fraction of people who stand to benefit from a better environment participate in the environmental movement.

THINKING CRITICALLY

If you were going to start a social movement, how would you begin? What would you try to do about "free riders"?

How serious a problem are free riders? Studies of social movement success document that, with equal resources and organization, a social movement that represents a larger group will be more effective (Lyman 1995; Oliver and Marwell 1988). Policy makers are more likely to listen if you represent the views of 100 million people than if you represent the interests of 300 people. Free riders can contribute to a social movement's success if polls show that the number of passive supporters of a movement is very large. The most successful movements, of course, are consistently "working their margins"—trying to convert free riders into active participants (Lyman 1995).

Networks and Mobilization. According to resource mobilization theory, the likelihood that a grievance will be translated into an effective social movement is highly related to the existing linkages between aggrieved parties. This argument is illustrated in an example developed by Gerald Marwell and his associates (1988).

Assume there are two cities, Alpha and Beta, each of which has passed a law stating that all city employees must live within the city limits. The law provides a one-year period during which city employees who live in the suburbs can either move into the city or look for other employment. This year also provides time for the suburban employees to organize a social movement to change the law.

In each city, there are 400 suburban employees who will be affected by the law. These people form a public or constituency for a social movement. They can work with others to turn this constituency into an organized movement, or they can hope that somebody else will do it. What is the likelihood that an effective social movement will develop?

Resource mobilization theory suggests that the answer depends on the degree of organization. Organization, in turn, depends significantly on the size and density of the social networks in Alpha and Beta. In Marwell and associates' example,

> Alpha is fairly isolated, and most of its affected employees live in a single suburb, Centauri. They attend Centauri's churches; their children attend Centauri's public schools; they belong to Centauri chapters of social and service clubs; they are all served by the same local telephone exchange. In contrast, Beta is part of an ethnically diverse two-state megalopolis, and its affected employees are scattered across a dozen different suburbs in two states and four counties. Thus they rarely see one another after work. They go to different churches, send their children to different schools, read four or five different newspapers, and pay toll charges for telephone calls between many of the suburbs. (Marwell, Oliver, and Prahl 1988, 505)

It doesn't take a Ph.D in sociology to guess that the employees in Alpha are much more likely to form an effective social movement. The network already exists; the employees need only mobilize it for the purpose of protecting their jobs. They do not need to form new mailing lists or write new newsletters; they can probably put free notices of their meetings in church bulletins or announce them at softball games.

Research confirms that dense social networks (where everyone is linked to everyone else) are important in promoting effective social movements. This high density reduces the cost of mobilization because every person can be reached quickly. High density also increases arousal: Each person can be reached through many network links, and this multiple-channel contact increases the likelihood that the individual will become involved in the movement.

Factors Associated with Movement Success

Empirical analysis of social movements in the United States and around the world suggests that a number of factors are important to the success of a movement. First, in the face of resistance from the larger society, movements must be able to develop an ideology capable of sustaining the enthusiasm and continued participation of current members, while at the same time providing the motivation for new members to join (Oegema and Klandermans 1994). Research indicates that to succeed in this task, social movement organizations must create ideological frameworks that can convinced potential and current participants that a particular grievance is serious, that there is an urgent need to address the problem, that taking action is proper, and most importantly that such action will be effective (Benford 1993).

The relationship between the movement and third parties and the nature of movement demands also influence whether a movement will succeed or fail. Marx (1971) identified the following variables as important:

1. The demands of the movement are seen to be consistent with the broader values of society. For example, the movement seeks to increase freedom or reduce injustice.
2. The movement has the support of influential third parties or can demonstrate that its demands will benefit other groups as well. For example, the abolitionist movement gained the support of the early feminist movement because women believed that extending suffrage to blacks would help women gain suffrage.
3. The movement's demands are concrete and focused. A protest against a specific urban renewal project is more likely to succeed than is a general protest against poor housing.
4. The movement is able to exert pressure directly on the responsibly party without harming uninvolved third parties. For example, a fruit boycott that hurts truckers as well as fruit growers will generate ore opposition and less support.

THINKING CRITICALLY

Given what you know about the animal rights movement and about the factors associated with movement success, how likely do you think it is that this social movement will achieve its goals?

5. The movement adopts techniques with which the authorities have had little experience. The nonviolent sit-in had tremendous impact when it was first employed during the early civil rights movement; in 1980, however, hundreds of protesters sitting in at the Seabrook nuclear plant were hauled always with little publicity and the little effect. The police now know how to deal with the tactic, and the media no longer find it newsworthy.

6. Neutral third parties who have an interest in restoring harmony are present.

7. The movement's demands are negotiable rather than absolute.

8. The movement's demands involve a request for acceptance of social diversity, equal treatment, or inclusion, rather than a fundamental redistribution of income and power.

9. The movement seeks to veto proposed policies rather than implement new ones.

10. The movement is large enough to organize itself for conflict but not so large as to be perceived as a serious threat to the dominant group.

COUNTERMOVEMENTS

A **countermovement** seeks to reverse or resist change advocated by a social movement.

A major and growing category of social movements is the **countermovement,** which seeks to reverse or resist change advocated by a social movement (Lo 1982; Lyman 1995). Countermovements are almost always right wing in orientation; they seek to maintain traditional structures of status, power, and values. Resource mobilization theory is particularly appropriate for understanding countermovements. Because they defend the status quo, they are often closely tied to vested-interest groups (Lo 1982; Mottl 1980), and bloc mobilization is a chief means of recruiting members and resources.

The anti–affirmative action movement is an excellent example of a countermovement. Citizens in several states have pushed to repeal affirmative action policies and programs that resulted from the civil rights movement. As the anti–affirmative action movement emerged and coalesced in California, countermovement activists successfully lobbied the University of California Board of Regents to change its long-standing admissions policy so that race and gender preferences would no longer come into play. As the countermovement became bureaucratized and funded by the Republican Party ("GOP Gives" 1996), members created what they named the California Civil Rights Initiative. According to members of the countermovement, the initiative is meant to restore civil rights to *all* of California's citizens—and "fairness to California"—by knocking down race and gender preferences in any of the state's hiring or other programs (Burdman and Rojas 1996).

A CASE STUDY: TREES, OWLS, AND THE ENVIRONMENTAL MOVEMENT

Being in favor of protecting the environment sounds like an innocuous position to take. After all, who is in favor of dirty air, dirty water, and disappearing species? By default, nearly all of us.

Ruining our environment is part of the status quo; it is part of our accepted way of life, of manufacturing and packaging merchandise, and of dealing with garbage. The average American produces 35 pounds of garbage each week, only a tiny fraction of which is recycled. Environmental protectionism will entail costs: higher-priced goods, more bother over recycling, more regulation, and fewer consumer goods. It is also likely to result in the loss of some jobs.

The Battle for Trees and Owls. The battle over environmental policy is being fought on many fronts—over nuclear power, hazardous wastes, forests, and habitat. One of the most contentious in recent years has involved protecting old-growth forests. These forests provide a unique habitat, and some species—notably the spotted owl—do not live anywhere else. Over the last ten years, lumber companies won the right to clear-cut 130,000 acres of old-growth forests in the Pacific Northwest. To environmentalists, this is a tragic loss, but for loggers it creates much-needed jobs. A bumper sticker distributed during this highly acrimonious controversy said, "Save a logger. Kill an owl."

Radical environmentalists refer to lumber companies and developers as "eco-thugs." Environmentalists have not been much more complimentary about the government, which frequently finds itself caught in the middle. The U.S. Forest Service is a classic case. The service was set up to administer the logging and lumbering of U.S. forest land. Its major reason for being was to grow and protect forests to create and maintain logging roads *so that loggers could cut down the trees*. The forest service and the loggers were colleagues, not opponents.

In recent years, the environmental movement has challenged the U.S. Forest Service to protect the forests *from* the logger, not *for* the loggers. This effort to affect public policy has been joined on two fronts: in the courts and legislatures and literally in the trees. The professional SMOs of the environmental movement—the Sierra Club, the National Audubon Society, and the Wilderness Society—pursue the first strategy. They write letters to congressional representatives to urge support for clean-air laws or to lobby against dam projects; they throw a battery of lawyers into the effort to get court injunctions against development projects.

Dave Foreman, confounder of Earth First!, is arrested at a demonstration against logging old-growth forests in Oregon. Earth First! is one of the most radical of the SMOs within the environment movement. It performs a useful function for the movement of making all the other environmental organizations seem reasonable by comparison. Foreman himself declared that there were too many hippies and leftists in Earth First! and began developing an alternative SMO.

The militants despise the professionals for selling out, for being willing to negotiate and compromise. Among their tactics are sit-ins and demonstrations (mostly legal) and "monkey wrenching," or sabotage (mostly very illegal). For example, they have cut power lines, spiked trees to prevent their being logged, and damaged bulldozers. The forest service refers to these people as the "violent fringe," but supporters claim that their only crime is "to protect 4 billion years of evolution [and] I'm proud to be associated with that sort of criminal element" ("Trying" 1990, 25).

Although militants have done much to publicize and galvanize the environmental movement, they cannot succeed by themselves. Throwing one's body in front of the bulldozers will buy a few days or weeks, but permanent victory involves court orders and legal battles. Thus, both professional and indigenous, both conservative and radical SMOs are helpful in pushing forward the movement (Cable and Cable 1995).

Increasingly the movement has infiltrated government organizations. To the great dismay of its former allies, the forest service has expanded its mission to include providing recreation and protecting wildlife. This new mission puts the forest service in the middle of two angry groups, neither of which is willing to accept compromise. As a result, one forest service ranger jokes about being a "combat biologist" ("Oregon's" 1989). With the militants nipping at their heels, mainstream groups are likely to continue to take stronger positions on the environment than they did in the past.

The Environmental Movement Assessed. One reason that federal agencies have changed their policies on trees is the absolute size of the environmental constituency. The last decade has witnessed a strong growth in concern for the environment, with large majorities saying they are willing to pay more taxes to clean up the environment. Not all of today's activists are leftover hippies. Many of those involved in campaigns against hazardous waste and nuclear power, for example, are "just moms and dads who are willing to protect their children at any cost" ("Trying" 1990, 24).

The environmental movement has had some notable successes and is becoming partially institutionalized. Afraid of being buried in their own waste, many communities in the United States are experimenting with mandatory recycling. Nevertheless, there are many controversial issues left to be negotiated. It is estimated that 2 percent of the world's species will disappear every year. If every one of them produces battles the size of that now being fought over the spotted owl in the Pacific Northwest, we are in for a long war. As environmental protectionism starts to threaten the lifestyles and livelihoods of people other than isolated loggers, we are likely to see more controversy rather than less (Cable and Cable 1995).

The Media, Collective Behavior, and Social Movements

The Media and Collective Behavior

The mass media contribute to nonroutine collective behavior in three ways: (1) by publicizing the triggering event, (2) by demonstrating collective action techniques, and (3) by providing rationales for collective behavior.

Publicizing Events. Obviously, the media are an important means of quickly spreading the news. If a police officer shoots a minority youth, it will be on radio and television within minutes and in the newspapers within hours. The media reach the isolated as well as the integrated, the passive as well as the active. The mass media publicize triggering events faster and more thoroughly than rumor can.

Demonstrating Techniques. As already noted, each culture has a repertoire of possible collective actions. One of the ways people now learn this repertoire is by watching the evening news. Publicity surrounding one sit-in, riot, or crowd may stimulate a rash of similar events in other communities.

Providing Rationales. Nonroutine collective actions are typically spontaneous reactions to nonroutine events. Although norms may emerge to justify the actions, they are not well thought out. Many would not stand up under careful consideration at a later time. The media's attempt to explain events to the public may provide better-developed rationales. Following the Sheffield soccer disaster, for example, many commentators explained how unemployment and government policy had made the disaster inevitable. As one liberal member of Parliament put it, these fans were "treated like dirt inside and outside of the stadium" ("Disaster" 1989).

The Media and Social Movements

A social movement is a deliberate attempt to create change. To do so, it must reach the public and try to get public opinion on its side. The relationship between the media and social movements is one of mutual need. The movements need publicity, and the media need material. Sometimes both needs can be met satisfactorily. In this mutual exchange, however, most of the power belongs to the media. The media can affect a social movement's success by giving or withholding publicity and by slanting the story positively or negatively. What the media choose to cover "not only affects the success of the movement but also shapes its leadership and its meaning to the general public and to its own adherents—in short, what the movement actually is" (Molotch 1979, 81).

A particularly interesting example of the importance of the media can be seen in the Tienanmen Square uprising. Two major events in the spring of 1989 brought an usually large contingent of international journalists to Beijing—the historic visit of Mikhail Gorbachev and the Asian Development Bank's first meeting in the People's Republic of China. Aware that the whole world would be watching and that state authorities would feel somewhat forced to act repressively, student activists used these journalists to create a global stage. Thus, foreign media played a crucial role in the movement, not only by reporting events to their audiences back home but also by keeping Chinese citizens informed regarding movement developments (Zuo and Benford 1995).

> **Thinking Critically**
>
> Suppose you were interested in mobilizing public opinion against the death penalty. What kind of activity or event would you try to use to get the media's attention?

In both the West and East, then, media coverage appears to be a vital mechanism through which resource-poor organizations can generate public debate over their grievances. What does an organization have to do to get news coverage? Empirical studies show that four factors are critical (Kielbowicz and Scherer 1986):

FOCUS ON YESTERDAY

A Dirty Filthy Book

"THE ADVOCATES OF BIRTH CONTROL CREATED THEIR FIRST SMO IN 1860, WITH THE FORMATION OF THE MALTHUSIAN LEAGUE."

The practice of birth control became a trend in 18th-century France. Without the aid of any organized social movement, it spread from the urban bourgeoisie to the rural and poorer classes. It was in England and the United States that birth control became an organized social movement. A number of liberal reformers seized on excessive population as the chief cause of poverty and other social problems. These reformers suggested that the use of birth control by the poor would reduce welfare costs and, by decreasing the numbers of the poor, increase the demand for their labor and cause wages to rise.

In this period, a U.S. physician, Charles Knowlton, produced a book entitled *The Fruits of Philosophy: The Private Companion of Young Married People*. In it, he discussed coitus interruptus (withdrawal), but he favored postcoital douching; he stated that he was "quite confident that a liberal use of pretty cold water would be a never-failing preventative" (Himes 1936, 227). (In fact, douching is almost totally ineffective as a contraceptive.)

The advocates of birth control created their first SMO in 1860, with the formation of the Malthusian League. The movement did not take off, however, until 1877, when the British government prosecuted Annie Besant and Charles Bradlaugh for distributing Knowlton's book in England. The charge was distributing obscene material, and the resulting publicity was exactly what the new movement needed. The trial was widely reported in the only mass media of the day, the newspapers, which included the prosecutor's accusation that "this is a dirty, filthy book, and the test of it is that no human being would allow that book on his table, no decently educated English husband would allow even his wife to have it" (cited in Chandrasekhar 1981, 1). The methods and morals of birth control were given detailed discussion in the popular press, and sales of Knowlton's book went from only 1,000 a year to more than 200,000. In a groundswell of free publicity, Malthusian Leagues were formed in almost every Western nation. Among the reasons put forth for using birth control were that it would reduce both the misery and numbers of the poor, make early marriage possible and thus eliminate prostitution, and even lead to world peace. The birth control movement was an idealistic social movement that hoped to improve society by reforming individuals. (In succeeding generations, the Women's Christian Temperance Union—WCTU—sought to achieve the same goals by trying to get everyone to give up alcohol.)

The first birth-control clinic in the United States was opened by Margaret Sanger in 1916. Throughout New York City, she distributed 5,000 leaflets in Yiddish, Italian, and English. They began: "Mothers! Can you afford to have a large family? Do you want any more children? If not, why do you have them? DO NOT KILL, DO NOT TAKE LIFE, BUT PREVENT." After her clinic had been open 10 days, the police closed it and arrested her on a charge of "maintaining a public nuisance." She was held overnight and released on bail; she immediately reopened the clinic and was rearrested and sentenced to 30 days in jail. After several more convictions, she established the first permanent clinic in 1923.

The birth-control movement challenged many cherished values. It was opposed by physicians on the ground that the practice was injurious to health, by moralists on the ground that it encouraged pleasure seeking without concern for the consequences, by traditionalists on the ground that it altered women's natural functions, by nationalists on the ground that there would be too few soldiers, and by legal authorities on the ground that it was obscene. The birth-control movement was ultimately successful and is now a part of the institutional structure rather than an attacker of it. In fact, the government itself is now the chief provider of contraceptives to the poor.

1. *Dramatic, visible events*. This is particularly important for television. Sit-ins and demonstrations are more newsworthy than news conferences, and both are more newsworthy than pamphlets.
2. *Authoritative sources*. Journalists want to save time and gain credibility by going straight to the horse's mouth. This means they tend to rely on established leaders who have public recognition.
3. *Timing*. News is published or aired according to regular deadlines. If you want to be on the evening news, your action should be scheduled (so that the news cameras can be there) before three in the afternoon (so it can be edited before the news hour) on a day when not much else is going on.
4. *News nets*. Most reporters have a beat, a particular area of the news they cover. If your movement falls in the cracks, you are less likely to get coverage.

Because they rely on the media, social movements find themselves changing to maximize news coverage. The link between action and news-worthiness encourages direct action rather than more quiet forms of activity such as lobbying or letter writing. And since the public gets tired of watching demonstrators hauled off, the degree of extremism necessary to get news coverage may escalate. This may lead to inflamed rhetoric, greater conflict within the movement, and disproportionate attention to publicity rather than to other movement goals. Of course, if the alternative is no publicity at all, then it may be a price the movement has to pay. Without free publicity, the cost to a social movement of spreading its message is greatly increased.

The Sociologist's Contribution

Whether it originates with a social movement or a change in the global economy, any social change will have opponents. Every winner potentially produces loser. This means that change creates a situation of competition and conflict.

In Chapter 1, we discussed the appropriate role of sociologists in studying social issues. Should they be value-free, or should they take a stand? Issues of inequality, war, and peace bring this question into sharp focus. Although most sociologists go about their business as if sociology were unrelated to global conflict, an increasingly vocal minority argue that it is shortsighted to restrict our forces to divorce, educational equity, the state of U.S. race relations or the gay rights movement when people are destroying the environment and one another. These people believe that sociologists should be actively involved in issues of war and peace.

What can sociologists contribute to enhancing justice and protecting both the environment and world peace? A few of the areas that can be pursued include the following:

1. ***The study of conflict resolution.*** A growing number of universities have special courses or programs on conflict resolution. These courses are concerned with the development of techniques for handling disputes and negotiating peaceful settlements. Sociological research on topics such as small group decision making and organizational culture are relevant here.
2. ***Developing social justice perspectives.*** The Cold War didn't fizzle because the United States and the Soviet Union scared each other to death or because Gorbachev was nicer than his predecessors. The Cold War fizzled because the Soviet Union, and to a lesser extent the United States, couldn't afford it any more

(Bundy 1990), similarly, if East/West antagonisms should flare anew, money again will likely be at the root. Thus, the causes of both peace and war are largely economic. Sociological research can help us document the extent, causes, and role of inequality in the international arena.

3. ***Modeling practical development strategies.*** Sociological research may lead to the development of programs that are more effective in improving the well-being of Third World people. Studies of the consequences of transnational investment, foreign aid, and investment loans are examples of the kinds of research likely to be most useful.

The involvement of sociologists in issues of justice and conflict resolution is not likely to be the crucial factor that brings about peace. We can be sure, however, that scholarly neglect of these issues is both shortsighted and immoral. To the extent that knowledge of the principles of human behavior bears on issues of international conflict, we have an obligation—as scholars and citizens—to apply our knowledge to what is clearly one of the most critical policy issues of our century.

SOCIOLOGY ON THE NET

One of the more widespread and visible social movements is the "Woman's Rights" movement. One of the mainstream organizations is the Feminist Majority Foundation.

http://www.feminist.org/home.html

Check out the **Feminist Majority home page**. Click on the bar entitled **About the Feminist Majority Foundation**. Browse through the first four items: **The Feminist Majority**, **Why Are We Named the Feminist Majority?**, **What We're Doing For You** and **How to Contact Us**. What is this organization and who do they claim to represent? Now return to the **home page** and click on the **Take Action** bar. Is this an indigenous SMO or is it a professional SMO? Who is their conscience constituency? Is this organization best understood using relative deprivation theory or resource mobilization theory? Hint: Return to the Internet exercise in Chapter 3 and refresh your memory from the "Feminist Chronicles."

The environmental movement has taken many forms and can be found almost anywhere in the world. Earth First is a vocal part of this movement.

http://www.telalink.net/~zoomst/earthfirst/index.html

This is the **Earth First Home Page**. Is this a social movement or an organization according to your text? Is this a professional or an indigenous SMO? Go to the bottom of the page and click on the highlighted phrase **...the need for action!** Browse through the information and when you reach the bottom of the page, click on the highlighted **Earth First Journal**. Open a few of the selections and see what the organization is all about. You might even go to the **Gopher Archives**. How is this organization engaging in frame alignment? Review the factors for social movement success from the text. How well does Earth First measure up?

Countermovements seek to reverse or resist change. One such organization is the Family Research Council.

http://www.heritage.org/townhall/FRC

APPLICATIONS IN DIVERSITY

WHAT ARE THE GOALS OF THE GAY RIGHTS MOVEMENT?

Homosexual acts are illegal in 23 states (Gross 1994). Lesbians and gay men have been barred from service in the military; they are often barred from teaching in public schools; and they may be denied custody of their children and, in some cases, even visiting rights. Until a few years ago, they were barred from employment in the federal civil service and from immigration to the United States. In addition, they may be shunned by their families and co-workers, forced out of their jobs, and subjected to taunts and jeers.

As a result, most lesbians and gay men have concealed their sexual preference. As long as they did so, there could be no social movement. For a movement to exist, there must be a group of people who acknowledge to themselves and to one another that they are members of the same group and share a common interest.

The beginning of the gay rights movement came when sufficient numbers of prominent individuals were willing to step forward and define themselves as homosexuals. This development began in Germany at the end of the 19th century. It was abruptly halted by Hilter, who included homosexuals among the undesirables of the world and who sent known homosexuals to concentration camps. In the United States, the gay rights movement began in the 1920s, when the Society for Human Rights was established to "protect the rights of people who by reasons of mental and physical abnormalities are abused and hindered in the legal pursuit of the happiness which is guaranteed by the Declaration of Independence" (in Altman 1983, 133). The organizers were quickly driven back into the closet by a police raid, and it was not until after World War II that the two founding SMOs of the gay rights movement—the Mattachine Society for gay men and the Daughters of Bilitis for lesbians—were founded.

The early gay rights movement, as indicated in the preceding quote, seemed to accept society's view of its members as handicapped and abnormal. During the 1960s and 1970s, this view changed radically. Gay activists began to demand not just the absence of persecution, but acceptance. They wanted homosexuality to be recognized simply as a variation of sexual orientation—not viewed as sin or sickness.

The Current Movement

The gay rights movement is not unified. It is divided by sex, class, race, and political ideology. Broadly, however, the movement seeks to do five things (Altman 1983, 122):

1. *To define a gay community and a gay identity*. The movement seeks to help gay individuals realize they are not alone. As C. Wright Mills might have put it, movement members want homoxexuals to recognize that their problems are not merely personal troubles but are shared by others.
2. *To establish the legitimacy of a gay identity*. The movement seeks to reduce the shame and internalized self-hatred that some homosexuals, who were socialized to believe they were wicked and sick, experience.
3. *To achieve civil rights for lesbians and gay men*. The movement seeks to decriminalize homosexual acts and to establish antidiscrimination laws to protect homosexuals.
4. *To challenge the general ascription of gender roles in society*. The movement seeks to give people the right to choose roles rather than being forced to act out a role thrust on them by reason of their sex.
5. *To secure family rights*. The most recent goal of the movement is to allow gay couples to marry and have the same legal rights as other couples, such as health insurance and survivor's benefits for a partner. Not all lesbians and gay men favor legal marriage, but the movement is in agreement over equal rights for all couples.

Conflict within the Movement

There are several major schisms within the gay rights movement. The most important is that between men and women. Gay men and lesbians have some goals in common—in particular, civil rights goals. However, lesbians face a situation of double jeopardy. They may be discriminated against on the basis of sex as well as sexual preference. Lesbian women often believe that they will make more progress working with straight women than with gay men; they believe that improvements in the status of women (especially in economic terms) will be more beneficial than will general improvements for homosexuals. As a result, there is relatively little cooperation among male and female homosexual groups.

A second schism is of class and politics. On the one side are the middle-class professionals who wear gender-appropriate suits and insist that homosexuals are respectable, decent people—good parents, good credit risks, good neighbors. On the other side are people who insist that gay rights include the freedom to wear lavender and leather and who wish to dismantle the entire system of gender

APPLICATIONS IN DIVERSITY

Public demonstrations by the gay rights movement are designed to bring homosexuality out of the closet, to make it seem a less deviant and less dangerous practice. By publicly acknowledging their sexual preference, men such as the ones in this parade force society to acknowledge that there are relatively large numbers of people—many of them apparently normal and decent people—who are homosexuals. Thus, the public demonstration is a particularly important weapon in the social movement of homosexual rights.

roles and status politics. At times, this more radical faction has proposed and engaged in "outing"—publicly naming as gay or lesbian those who have remained "in the closet," or secretive about their sexual preferences. These two groups are, respectively, the people who want to tinker with the system—to extend the basic rights package just a little further—and the people who think that the whole system is a sham and want to overthrow it.

Successes, Failures, and Prospects

The gay rights movement has seen some notable successes. The American Psychological Association voted in 1974 to declare that homosexuality is not a sickness; Wisconsin and Massachusetts have passed laws making discrimination on the basis of sexual orientation illegal; and acknowledged homosexuals have been elected to public office, including that of U.S. senator. Public opinion polls show substantial increases in support for homosexual rights. In offices and families around the country, it is becoming possible to be open about one's homosexuality without losing the respect of others.

In many homes, offices, and neighborhoods, however, the position of an acknowledged lesbian or gay man would still be awkward at best. The military continues to discharge individuals who engage in homosexual activity, and in 23 states homosexual acts are still a crime. In addition to these assaults on their dignity, homosexuals also have a high risk of incurring physical assaults. "Gay bashing" is a relatively frequent recreational activity of young toughs, and homosexual activists claim that gays are seven times more likely than straights to be assaulted (Singer and Deschamps 1994).

For more than a decade, now, the male homosexual community has been galvanized by the specter of AIDS (acquired immunodeficiency syndrome). Many gays believe that proposals for mandatory AIDS testing are another basis for stigmatizing gays. Coupled with realistic health concerns, this fear has provided an impetus to organization. AIDS hotlines and information meetings have triggered gay men's networks that cut across class, race, and political cleavages. By increasing the solidarity of the group, these new networks may increase the effectiveness of the gay rights movement.

THINKING CRITICALLY

Based on what you know about the gay rights movement, what social structural conditions in the larger society helped to spark this social movement? What countermovements do you know of regarding gay rights? Of the five goals listed, which do you think are the most likely to be achieved, and why? Which least likely, and why?

Once you are at the **home page**, click on the highlighted phrase **Who is the *Family Research Council?*** Return to the **home page** and browse around a bit. Now open **Washington Watch** and scroll down to **Washington Watch, The Newsletter**. Open a newsletter in this section and skim through the articles. What is this countermovement against? What values do they believe should be restored? Return to the **home page** and click on the **Hot List of Links**. Scroll through the offerings. Can you find any other organizations that are part of this countermovement?

SUMMARY

❶ Collective behavior and social movements, although related, are distinct activities. Collective behavior is spontaneous and strictly confined to a particular place and time; a social movement is organized, broad based, and long term.

❷ Three theories explain crowd behavior: contagion theory, convergence theory, and emergent-norm theory. Emergent-norm theory is the dominant theoretical perspective today.

❸ Although sporadic, episodic, and often outside the law, crowd behavior is not random. Each society has a repertoire of collective actions from which to choose. In contemporary society, the mass media are an important source of information about this repertoire.

❹ Relative deprivation theory and resource mobilization theory offer two different scenarios for why inequalities and cleavages result in social movements. Relative deprivation theory stresses the eruption of anger over a sense of deprivation; resource mobilization theory stresses competition of organized groups over scarce resources.

❺ An integration of the two theories suggests that both a sense of grievance and organizational resources are important for an effective social movement to develop.

❻ Each social movement contains a variety of social movement organizations (SMOs), some professional and some indigenous. The variety of SMOs tends to enhance the movement's ability to mobilize resources.

❼ Mobilization occurs at two levels: the recruitment of individual adherents (micromobilization) and the recruitment of sympathetic organizations (bloc mobilization). Bloc mobilization is faster but is less likely to attract committed activists.

❽ Movements are more successful if their demands are consistent with the society's larger values, if they have an innovative and attention-getting strategy, and if they can gain the support of, or at least not harm, third-party organizations.

❾ When a social movement threatens to be at least partially successful, a countermovement often develops to defend the status quo. Countermovements depend highly on bloc mobilization.

❿ The environmental movement uses a variety of tactics in its effort to affect public policy, ranging from courtroom battles to eco-terrorism. Among the reasons for the movement's growing successes are the wide variety of SMOs within the movement and the size of its public constituency.

⓫ The media play an important and growing role in collective behavior and social movements. By publicizing incidents of collective behavior, the media increase the likelihood that these incidents will be known and repeated. Because resource-poor social movements depend on free publicity, they are often forced to become more extremist to continue attracting media coverage.

⑫ The gay rights movement is a current social movement with several goals, among them to achieve civil rights for lesbians and gay men.

SUGGESTED READINGS

CABLE, Sherry, and Cable, Charles. 1995. *Environmental Problems, Grassroots Solutions: The Politics of Grassroots Environmental Conflict*. New York: St. Martin's Press. A description of the environmental movement with details on how various regional, grassroots organizations address environmental issues and concerns.

GOLDSTEIN, Michael S. 1992. *The Health Movement: Promoting Fitness in America*. New York: Twayne Publishers. An interesting paperback that examines the origins of the health movement in the United States and speculates about its future. Specific chapters focus on the nutrition, exercise, and anti-smoking movements.

HAWES, Joseph M. 1991. *The Children's Rights Movement: A History of Advocacy and Protection*. Boston: Twayne Publishers. A readable and interesting account of the children's rights movement from its earliest days in Great Britain to the establishment of the Children's Defense Fund in the contemporary United States.

JASPER, James M., and Nelkin, Dorothy, 1992. *The Animal Rights Crusade: The Growth of a Moral Protest*. New York: Free Press. A rich description of the origins and development of the animal rights movement, including an analysis of the link between the animal rights movement, environmentalism, vegetarianism, and other New Age movements.

JOHNSTON, Hank, and Klandermans, Bert (eds.). 1995. *Social Movements and Culture*. Minneapolis; University of Minnesota Press. Theoretical essays, empirical studies, and case histories of social movements in the United States.

LYMAN, Stanford M. (ed.). 1995. *Social Movements: Critiques, Concepts, Case-Studies*. New York: New York University Press. A collection of essays and research reports that give a nice overview, as well as interesting examples, of the theories and concepts associated with social movements.

MARX, Gary T., and McAdam, Douglas. 1994. *Collective Behavior and Social Movements: Structure and Process*. Englewood Cliffs, N.J.: Prentice-Hall. A concise, well-written review of the major ideas and issues in the study of collective behavior and social movements. Written primarily from a resource mobilization perspective, the text pays close attention to the relationship between spontaneous and more sustained forms of collective action.

MORRIS, Aldon. 1984. *The Origins of the Civil Rights Movement*. New York: Free Press. A powerful account of the modern civil rights movement. Utilizing personal interviews and original documents, Morris draws particular attention to the importance of local African American community groups, in addition to the efforts of national leaders and organizations.

MORRISON, Peter A., and Lowry, Ira S. 1993. *A Riot of Color: The Demographic Setting of Civil Disturbances in Los Angeles*. Santa Monica, Calif.: Rand. A sociological analysis of race riots in Los Angeles.

WITTBERG, Patricia. 1994. *The Rise and Decline of Catholic Religious Orders: A Social Movement Perspective*. Albany: State University of New York Press. A book that offers a good way to combine an understanding of the institution of religion with knowledge about social movements.

GLOSSARY

Absolute poverty is the inability to provide the minimum requirements of life.

Accommodation occurs when two groups coexist as separate cultures in the same society.

Accounts are explanations of unexpected or untoward behavior. They are of two sorts: excuses and justifications.

Acculturation occurs when the minority group adopts the culture of the majority group.

An **achieved status** is optional, one that a person can obtain in a lifetime.

Achievement motivation is the continual drive to match oneself against standards of excellence.

Affirmative action refers to active efforts to recruit minority group members or women for jobs, promotions, and educational opportunities.

Ageism is the belief that chronological age determines the presence or absence of socially relevant characteristics and that age therefore legitimates unequal treatment.

Alienation occurs when workers have no control over the work process or the product of their labor; they are estranged from their work.

An **aggregate** is a collection of people who are temporarily clustered together in the same location.

An **ascribed status** is fixed by birth and inheritance and is unalterable in a person's lifetime.

An **authoritarian system** is a political system in which the leadership is not selected by the people and legally cannot be changed by them.

Anglo conformity is the process of acculturation in which new immigrant groups adopt the English language and English customs.

Anomie is a situation in which the norms of society are unclear or no longer applicable to current conditions.

Anticipatory socialization is role learning that prepares us for roles we are likely to assume in the future.

Antinatalism refers to social forces that discourage childbearing.

Assimilation is the full integration of the minority group into the institutions of society and the end of its identity as a subordinate group.

Authoritarianism is a tendency to be submissive to those in authority coupled with an aggressive and negative attitude toward those lower in status.

Authority is power supported by norms and values that legitimate its use.

Bloc mobilization is a strategy whereby social movement organizations recruit other organizations to support their cause rather than trying to recruit single individuals.

The **bourgeoisie** is the class whose members own the tools and materials for their work—the means of production.

Bureaucracy is a complex organization characterized by explicit rules and a hierarchical authority structure, all designed to maximize efficiency.

Capitalism is an economic system in which most wealth (land, capital, and labor) is private property, to be used by its owners to maximize their own gain; this economic system is based on competition.

Caste systems rely on ascribed statuses as the basis for distributing scarce resources.

A **category** is a collection of people who share a common characteristic.

Charisma refers to extraordinary personal qualities that set the individual apart from ordinary mortals.

Charismatic authority is a right to make decisions that is based on perceived extraordinary personal characteristics.

Churches are religious organizations that have become institutionalized. They have endured for generations, are supported by society's norms and values, and have become an active part of society.

Civil religion is a set of institutionalized rituals, beliefs, and symbols sacred to the nation.

Class, in Marx's Theory, refers to a person's relationship to the means of production.

Class consciousness occurs when one is aware of one's relationship to the means of production and recognizes one's true class identity.

Class systems rely largely on achieved statuses as the basis for distributing scarce resources.

Coercion is the exercise of power through force or the threat of force.

Cohabitation is living together without legal marriage.

Cohesion refers to the degree of attraction members feel to the group.

A **cohort** is a category of individuals who share a particular experience at the same point in time—for example, all of those who were born in 1930 or who married in 1990.

Collective behavior is nonroutine action by an emotionally aroused gathering of people who face an ambiguous situation.

Colonialism involves a foreign power's maintaining political, economic, and cultural domination over another people for an extended period of time.
Competition is a struggle over scarce resources that is regulated by shared rules.
Conflict is a struggle over scarce resources that is not regulated by shared rules; it may include attempts to destroy or neutralize one's rivals
Conflict theory addresses the points of stress and conflict in society and the ways in which they contribute to social change.
Contagion theory suggests that the crowd situation leads to the development of unanimous and intense feelings and behaviors that are at odds with the usual predispositions of the individual participants.
A **control group** is the group in an experiment that does not experience the independent variable.
Control variables are measures of background factors that may be confounding the true relationship between study variables.
Convergence theory contends that the cause, or triggering event, for crowd action selectively draws people who share a common set of predispositions.
Cooperation is interaction that occurs when people work together to achieve shared goals.
Core societies are rich, powerful nations that are economically diversified and relatively free of outside control.
Correlation occurs when there is an empirical relationship between two variables.
Countercultures are groups having values, interests, beliefs, and lifestyles that are opposed to those of the larger culture.
A **countermovement** seeks to reverse or resist change advocated by a social movement.
Credentialism is the use of educational credentials to measure social origins and social status.
Crimes are acts that are subject to legal penalties.
A **cross-sectional design** uses a sample (or cross section) of the population at a single point in time.
A **crowd** is a gathering of people who are reacting to a nonroutine event.
A **cult** is a sect that is independent of and often in conflict with the religious traditions of society.
Cultural capital refers to social assets, such as familiarity and identification with elite culture.
Cultural diversity refers to the social situation in which several fairly dissimilar peoples with distinct ways of life exist together in one society.
Cultural lag is the time interval between the arrival of a change in society and the completion of the adaptations that this change prompts.
Cultural relativity requires that each cultural trait be evaluated in the context of its own culture.
Culture is the total way of life shared by members of a society. It includes not only language, values, and symbolic meanings but also technology and material objects.
The **culture of poverty** is a set of values that emphasizes living for the moment rather than thrift, investment in the future, or hard work.

Deduction is the process of moving from theory to data by testing hypotheses drawn from theory.
Democracy is a political system that provides regular, constitutional opportunities for a change in leadership according to the will of the majority.
The **demographic transition** is the process of moving from the traditional balance of high birthrates, and death rates to a new balance of low birthrates and death rates.
Demography is the study of population—its size, growth, and composition.
Denominations are religious organizations that are separate from the larger society or state but have accommodated to society and to other religions.
The **dependency ratio** is the number of people under 15 and over 65 divided by the number of people aged 15 to 65.
The **dependent variable** is the effect in cause-and-effect relationships. It is dependent on the actions of the independent variable.
Deterrence theories suggest that deviance results when social sanctions, formal and informal, provide insufficient rewards for conformity.
Development refers to the process of increasing the productivity and standard of living of a society—longer life expectancies, more adequate diets, better education, better housing, and more consumer goods.
Deviance refers to norm violations that exceed the tolerance level of the community and result in negative sanctions.
Dialectic philosophy views change as a product of contradictions and conflict between the parts of society.
Differential association theory argues that people learn to be deviant when more of their associates favor deviance over conformity.
Differentials are differences in the incidence of a phenomenon across subcategories of the population.
Diffusion is the process by which cultural traits spread from group to group when one culture or subculture comes into contact with another.
Disclaimers are verbal devices employed in advance to ward off doubts and negative reactions that might result from one's conduct.

A **discovery** is the finding or uncovering of something that existed before but had remained unnoticed.

Discrimination is the unequal treatment of individuals on the basis of their membership in certain categories.

Disengagement theory, a functionalist theory of aging, argues that older people voluntarily disengage themselves from active social participation.

The **divorce rate** is calculated as the number of divorces each year per 1,000 married women.

A **dominant culture** is the culture seen as "best," the standard against which other cultures or subcultures are compared.

Double or triple jeopardy means having low status on two or three different dimensions of stratification.

Dramaturgy is a version of symbolic interaction theory that views social situations as scenes manipulated by the actors to convey the desired impression to the audience.

A **dual economy** consists of the complex giants of the industrial core and the small, competitive organizations that form the periphery.

Dysfunctions are consequences of social structures that have negative effects on the stability of society.

An **ecclesia** is a religious organization that automatically includes every member of a society.

Economic determinism means that economic relationships provide the foundation on which all other social and political arrangements are built.

Economic institutions are social structures concerned with the production and distribution of goods and services.

The **educational institution** is the social structure concerned with the transmission of knowledge, particularly to society's newcomers, children and immigrants.

Egalitarianism emphasizes equality in decision making, control of family resources, and child rearing.

Emergent norm theory suggests that each crowd is governed by norms developed and validated by group processes within the crowd.

An **established sect** is a sect that has adapted to its institutional environment, but not to the same degree as a church.

An **ethnic group** is a category whose members are thought to share a common origin and to share important elements of a common culture.

Ethnocentrism is the tendency to view the norms and values of our own culture as standards against which to judge the practices of other cultures.

Ethnomethodology is the study of the everyday strategies that individuals use to study and organize their worlds.

Exchange is voluntary interaction in which the parties trade tangible or intangible benefits with the expectation that all parties will benefit.

Excuses are explanations in which a person admits that the act in question was wrong or inappropriate but claims he or she couldn't help it.

Expectation states theory argues that status characteristics create expectation states in others about probable abilities and social status. When people act on the basis of these expectations, the expectations are confirmed.

The **experiment** is a method in which the researcher manipulates independent variables to test theories of cause and effect.

An **experimental group** is the group in an experiment that experiences the independent variable. Results for this group are compared with those for the control group.

Expressive activities or roles provide integration and emotional support.

An **extended family** exists when the wife-husband pair and their children live with other kin and share economic and child-rearing responsibilities with them.

Extrinsic rewards are tangible benefits such as income and security.

False consciousness is a lack of awareness of one's real position in the class structure.

The **family** is a relatively permanent group of persons, linked by ties of mutual consent, blood, marriage, or adoption, who live together and cooperate economically and in the rearing of children.

Fertility is the incidence of childbearing.

The **First World** consists of those rich nations that have relatively high degrees of economic and political autonomy: the United States, Western Europe, Japan, Canada, Australia, and New Zealand.

Folkways are norms that are the customary, normal, habitual ways a group does things.

Formal social controls are administrative sanctions such as fines, expulsion, and imprisonment.

A **frame** is an answer to the question, "What is going on here?" It is roughly equivalent to a *definition of the situation*.

Frame alignment is a process by which social movement organizations attract individual new recruits; it seeks to convince individuals that their interests, values, and beliefs and those of the SMO are complementary.

Functions are consequences of social structures that have positive effects on the stability of society.

Gemeinschaft refers to society characterized by the personal and permanent ties associated with primary groups.

Gender, or **gender role,** refers to the expected dispositions and behaviors, along with the rights and duties, that cultures assign to each sex.

The **generalized other** is the composite expectations of all the other role players with whom we interact; it is Mead's term for our awareness of social norms.
Gesellschaft refers to society characterized by the impersonal and instrumental ties associated with secondary groups.
A **group** is two or more people who interact on the basis of shared social structure and who recognize mutual dependency.
The **guinea-pig effect** occurs when subjects' knowledge that they are participating in an experiment affects their responses to the independent variable.

Hate crimes are motivated by bigotry based on race, religion, national origin, or sexual orientation.
The **hidden curriculum** of schools socializes young people into obedience and conformity.
Homogamy is the tendency to choose a mate similar to oneself.
Hypotheses are statements about relationships that we expect to find if our theory is correct.

The ***I*** is the spontaneous, creative part of the self.
Identity hierarchy is a ranking of an individual's various role identities in order of their importance to him or her.
An **ideology** is a set of norms and values that rationalizes the existing social structure.
In-groups are groups or social categories to which individuals feel they belong.
Incidence is the frequency with which a phenomenon occurs.
Income includes payments that people receive periodically from an occupation or investments.
The **independent variable** is the variable that does the causing in cause-and-effect relationships.
The **indirect inheritance model** argues that children have occupations in a social class similar to that of their parents because family's social class and income determine children's aspirations and opportunities.
Induction is the process of moving from data to theory by devising theories that account for empirically observed patterns.
Influence is the ability to affect others' decisions through persuasion and personal appeals.
The **informal economy** is that part of the economy that escapes the record keeping and regulation of the state.
Informal social control is self-restraint exercised because of fear of what others will think.
Information technology comprises computers and telecommunication tools for storing, using, and sending information.
Institutional racism occurs when the normal operation of apparently neutral processes systematically produces unequal results for majority and minority groups.
Institutions are enduring and complex social structures that meet basic human needs.
Instrumental activities or roles are task oriented.
The **interaction school of symbolic interaction** focuses on the active role of the individual in creating the self and self-concept.
An **interest group** is a group or organization that seeks to influence political decisions.
Intergenerational mobility is change in social class from one generation to the next.
Intragenerational mobility is change in social class within an individual's own career.
Internalization occurs when individuals accept the norms and values of their group and make conformity to these norms part of their self-concept.
Intrinsic rewards are rewards that arise from the process of work; they include enjoying the people you work with and taking pride in your creativity and accomplishments.
An **invention** is a new use of or a new combination of existing knowledge or technologies.

Justifications explain the good reasons the violator had for choosing to break the rule; often they are appeals to some alternative rule.

A **kin group** is a set of relatives who interact on the basis of shared social structure.

Labeling theory is concerned with the processes by which labels such as *deviant* come to be attached to specific people and specific behaviors.
Latent functions or dysfunctions are consequences of social structures that are neither intended nor recognized.
Laws are rules that are enforced and sanctioned by the authority of government. They may or may not be norms.
Life chances describe the probability that throughout the life course one will have (or not have) a wide range of opportunities, experiences, and achievements.
Life course refers to age-related transitions that are socially created, socially recognized, and shared.
Life expectancy is the average number of years that a group of infants can expect to live.
Lifetime divorce probability is the estimated probability that a marriage will ever end in divorce.
Linguistic relativity hypothesis argues that the grammar, structure, and categories embodied in a language affect how its speakers see reality.

The **looking-glass self** is the self-concept developed in the process of learning to view ourselves as we think others view us.

Macrosociology focuses on social structures and organizations and the relationships between them.
A **majority group** is a group that is culturally, economically, and politically dominant.
Manifest functions or dysfunctions are consequences of social structures that are intended and recognized.
Marriage is an institutionalized social structure that provides an enduring framework for regulating sexual behavior and childbearing.
The **mass media** are the carriers of impersonal communications directed toward a very large (mass) audience.
Matriarchal authority is normatively approved female dominance.
Matrilocal residence occurs when norms of residence require that a newly married couple take up residence with the wife's kin.
The ***me*** represents the self as social object.
A **metropolitan area** is a county that has a city of 50,000 or more in it plus any neighboring counties that are significantly linked, economically or socially, with the core county.
Microsociology focuses on interactions among individuals.
A **minority group** is a group that is culturally, economically, and politically subordinate.
Modernization theory sees development as the natural unfolding of an evolutionary process in which societies go from simple to complex institutional structures.
The **modernization theory of aging** argues that older people have low status in modern societies because the value of their traditional resources has eroded.
Monogamy is marriage in which there is only one wife and one husband.
Moral entrepreneurs are people who are in a position to create and enforce new definitions of morality.
Mores are norms associated with fairly strong feelings of right and wrong; they carry a moral connotation.
Mortality is the incidence of death.

Neocolonialism is the current economic domination of less developed and weaker nations by more developed and more powerful nations.
Neolocal residence occurs when norms of residence require that a newly married couple take up residence away from their relatives.
News coverage management involves ensuring that a candidate receives favorable media coverage.
A **nonmetropolitan area** is a county that has no major city in it and is not closely tied to a county that does have such a city.
The **norm of reciprocity** is the expectation that people will return favors and strive to maintain a balance of obligation in social relationships.
Norms are shared rules of conduct that specify how people ought to feel, think, and act.
A **nuclear family** consists of a husband, a wife, and their dependent children.

Oligarchy is the control of a bureaucratic organization by the few at the top.
Operational definitions describe the exact procedures by which a variable is measured.
Out-groups are groups or social categories to which individuals do not feel they belong.

Paid political announcements are media messages about a political candidate that are paid for by the candidate's campaign committee.
The **panel design** follows a sample over a period of time.
Participant observation includes a variety of research strategies—participating, interviewing, observing—that examine the contexts and meanings of human behavior.
Patriarchal authority is normatively approved male dominance.
Patrilocal residence occurs when norms of residence require that a newly married couple take up residence with the husband's kin.
Peripheral societies are poor and weak, with highly specialized economies over which they have relatively little control.
The **petit bourgeois** are those who use their own modest capital to establish small enterprises in which they and their families provide the primary labor.
The **petit bourgeoisie** includes those members of the bourgeoisie who use their modest capital to establish small enterprises in which they and their families provide primary labor.
Political alienation is a belief that voting is a useless exercise and individual citizens have no influence on decision making.
Political institutions are institutions concerned with the social structure of power; the most prominent political institution is the state.
A **political party** is an association specifically organized to win elections and secure power over the personnel and policies of the state.
Polyandry is a form of marriage in which one woman may have more than one husband at a time.

Polygamy is any form of marriage in which a person may have more than one spouse at a time.

Polygyny is a form of marriage in which one man may have more than one wife at a time.

Positivism is the belief that the social world can be studied with the same scientific accuracy and assurance as the natural world.

Power is the ability to direct others' behavior, even against their wishes.

The **power elite** consists of the people who occupy the top positions in three bureaucracies—the military, industry, and the executive branch of government—and who are thought to act together to run the United States in their own interests.

Prejudice is irrationally based negative attitudes toward categories of people.

The **preventive approach** to confronting crime involves addressing the social problems that give rise to it.

Primary groups are groups characterized by intimate, face-to-face interaction.

Primary production consists of extracting raw materials from the environment.

Primary socialization is personality development and role learning that occur during early childhood.

The **profane** represents all that is routine and taken for granted in the everyday world, things that are known and familiar and that we can control, understand, and manipulate.

A **profession** is an occupation that demands specialized skills and creative freedom.

Progress is change in a desirable direction.

The **proletariat** is the class whose members do not own the means of production. Members of this class must support themselves by selling their labor to those who own the means of production.

Pronatalism refers to the social forces that encourage childbearing.

The **prophetic function** of religion involves its ability to provide sacred standards that become a basis for social protest or criticism of existing social patterns.

Propinquity is spatial nearness.

A **public** is a category of citizens who are thought to share a common political agenda.

The **punitive approach** to confronting crime involves increasing penalties for convicted criminals, especially street criminals.

A **race** is a category of people treated as distinct on account of physical characteristics to which *social* importance has been assigned.

Racism is a belief that inherited physical characteristics determine the presence or absence of socially relevant abilities and characteristics and that such differences provide a legitimate basis for unequal treatment.

Rational-legal authority is a right to make decisions that is based on rationally established rules.

Reference groups are groups or categories to which individuals refer when making evaluations or judgments about themselves.

Relative deprivation theory argues that social movements arise when people experience an intolerable gap between their rewards and what they believe they have a right to expect; it is also known as *breakdown theory*.

Relative poverty is the inability to maintain what your society regards as a decent standard of living.

Religion is a system of beliefs and practices related to sacred things that unites believers into a moral community.

Replacement-level fertility is the level of fertility at which each woman bears approximately two children, one to replace herself and one to replace her partner. When this occurs, the next generation will be the same size as the current generation of parents.

Replication is the process of repeating an empirical study with another investigator or a different sample to see if the same results are obtained.

Resocialization occurs when a person abandons his or her self-concept and way of life for a radically different one.

Resource mobilization theory suggests that social movements develop when organized groups are competing for scarce resources; it is also known as solidarity theory.

Rites of passage are formal rituals that mark the end of one age status and the beginning of another.

A **role** is a set of norms specifying the rights and obligations associated with a status.

Role distancing is believing and explaining to others that one's current role is temporary and/or not a reflection of one's "real" self.

Role identity is the image one has of oneself in a specific social role.

Role making is the process whereby persons actively define or interpret their roles to suit their individual personalities.

Role prescriptions are the norms or requirements associated with the various roles individuals play.

Role taking involves imagining ourselves in the role of the other in order to determine the criteria the other will use to judge our behavior.

The **sacred** consists of events and things that we hold in awe and reverence—that we can neither understand nor control.

A **sample** is a systematic selection of representative cases from the larger population.

Sanctions are rewards for conformity and punishments for nonconformity.

Scapegoating occurs when people or groups who are blocked in their own goal attainment blame others for their failure.

Science is a way of knowing based on empirical evidence.

The **Second World,** mainly Russia and the former Communist bloc nations in Eastern Europe, comprises countries that hold an intermediate position in the international stratification system.

Secondary groups are groups that are formal, large, and impersonal.

Secondary production consists of the processing of raw materials.

Secondary socialization is personality development and role learning that occur after early childhood.

Sects are religious organizations that reject the social environment in which they exist.

Secularization is the process of transferring things, ideas, or events from the sacred realm to the profane.

The **segmented labor market** is a dual labor market in which hiring, advancement, and benefits vary systematically between the industrial core and the periphery.

The **segmented labor market** parallels the dual economy. There is one labor market for good jobs and another labor market for not-so-good jobs.

Segregation refers to the physical separation of minority and majority group members.

The **self** is a complex whole that includes unique attributes and normative responses. In sociology, these two parts are called the *I* and the *me*.

The **self-concept** is the self we are aware of. It is our thoughts about our personalities and social roles.

Self-esteem is the evaluative component of the self-concept; it is our judgment about our worth compared with that of others.

The **self-fulfilling prophecy** occurs when acting on the belief that a situation exists causes it to become real.

A **semicaste,** or **castelike, system** is a class system with some caste-system characteristics.

Semiperipheral societies are neither as wealthy and powerful as core nations nor as destitute and weak as peripheral countries.

Sex is a biological characteristic, male or female.

Sexism is a belief that men and women have biologically different capacities and that these form a legitimate basis for unequal treatment.

Sexual harassment consists of unwelcome sexual advances, requests for sexual favors, or other verbal or physical conduct of a sexual nature.

The **sick role** consists of the rights and obligations that accompany the social label sick.

Significant others are the role players with whom we have close personal relationships.

Situated identity is the role identity used in a particular situation. It implies that a person's identity depends on the situation.

Social change is any significant modification or transformation of social structures and sociocultural processes over time.

Social choice theory (or exchange theory) argues that individual decisions are based on cost/benefit calculations.

A **social class** is a category of people who share roughly the same class, status, and power and who have a sense of identification with each other.

Social control consists of the forces and processes that encourage conformity, including self-control, informal control, and formal control.

Social distance is the degree of intimacy in relationships between two groups.

Social epidemiology is the study of how social statuses relate to the distribution of illness and mortality.

Social mobility is the process of changing one's social class.

A **social movement** is an ongoing, goal-directed effort to change social institutions from the outside.

A **social network** is an individual's total set of relationships.

Social processes are the forms of interaction through which people relate to one another; they are the dynamic aspects of society.

A **social structure** is a recurrent pattern of relationships.

Social-desirability bias is the tendency of people to color the truth so that they sound nicer, richer, and more desirable than they really are.

Socialism is an economic system in which productive tools (land, labor, and capital) are owned and managed by the workers and used for the collective good.

Socialization is the process of learning the roles, statuses, and values necessary for participation in social institutions.

A **society** is a population that shares the same territory and is bound together by economic and political ties.

Sociobiology is the study of the biological basis of all forms of human behavior.

Socioeconomic status (SES) is a measure of social class that ranks individuals on income, education, occupation, or some combination.

The **sociological imagination** is the ability to see the intimate realities of our own lives in the context of common social structures; it is the ability to see personal troubles as public issues.

Sociology is the systematic study of human social interaction.

The **sociology of everyday life** focuses on the social processes that structure our experiences in ordinary face-to-face situations.

A **spin** is an interpretation of events that is favorable to the candidate. Campaign advisers who try to convince the media of a particular interpretation of events are called **spin doctors.**

The **state** is the social structure that successfully claims a monopoly on the legitimate use of coercion and physical force within a territory.

A **status** is a specialized position within a group.

In Weber's model of social class, **status** means social honor or prestige, expressed in lifestyle, and is one component of social class.

Status inconsistency results when one of an individual's statuses has considerably more (or less) prestige than the others or when an individual's various statuses are socially defined as inappropriately linked.

Stereotyping is a belief that people who belong to the same category share common characteristics.

Strain theory suggests that deviance occurs when culturally approved goals cannot be reached by culturally approved means.

Stratification is an institutionalized pattern of inequality in which social statuses are ranked on the basis of their access to scarce resources.

Street-level justice consists of the decisions the police make in the initial stages of an investigation.

Strong ties are relationships characterized by intimacy, emotional intensity, and sharing.

The **structural school of symbolic interaction** focuses on the self as a product of social roles.

Structural-functional theory addresses the question of how social organization is maintained; it is also known as *consensus theory*.

Subcultures are groups that share in the overall culture of society but also maintain a distinctive set of values, norms, lifestyles, and even language.

Survey research is a method that involves asking a relatively large number of people the same set of standardized questions.

Sustainable development meets the needs of the present without compromising the ability of future generations to meet their own needs.

Symbolic interaction theory addresses the subjective meaning of human acts and the processes through which people come to develop and communicate shared meanings.

The **technocratic idea of progress** is a belief in the sufficiency of scientific and technological innovation as the basis for general progress.

Technology involves the human application of knowledge to the making of tools and hence to humans' use of natural resources.

Tertiary production consists of the production of services.

A **theory** is an interrelated set of assumptions that explain observed patterns.

The **Third World** consists of the less developed nations that share a peripheral or marginal status in the world capitalist system.

Total institutions are facilities in which all aspects of life are strictly controlled for the purpose of radical resocialization.

Tracking (or homogenous grouping) is the practice of assigning students to instructional groups on the basis of ability or past achievement.

Traditional authority is a right to make decisions for others that is based on the sanctity of time-honored routines.

Transnationals are large corporations that operate internationally and have power that transcends the laws of any particular nation-state.

Trends are changes in phenomena over time.

The **underclass** is the group whose members are unemployed and unemployable, a substratum that is alienated from American institutions.

Urban elites are people native to peripheral countries who grow wealthy by collaborating with foreign investment and capital.

Urbanism is a distinctively urban mode of life that is developed in the cities but not confined there.

Urbanization is the process of population concentration in metropolitan areas.

Value-free sociology concerns itself with establishing what is, not what ought to be.

Values are shared ideas about desirable goals.

Variables are measured characteristics that vary from one individual or group to the next.

Vested interests are stakes in either maintaining or transforming the status quo.

Victimless crimes such as drug use, prostitution, gambling, and pornography are voluntary exchanges between persons who desire goods or services from each other.

Voluntary associations are nonprofit organizations designed to allow individuals an opportunity to pursue their shared interests collectively.

Weak ties are relationships with friends, acquaintances, and kin that are characterized by low intensity and intimacy.

Wealth includes all accumulated assets, such as savings, investments, homes, land, cars, and other possessions.

White-collar crime is committed by respectable people of high status in the course of their occupations.

World system theory is a conflict perspective of the economic relationships between developed and developing countries, the core and peripheral societies.

Zero population growth (ZPG) means that the number of births is the same as the number of deaths, so the population does not grow.

REFERENCES

Abate, Tom. 1995. "Beijing by Modem." San Francisco Chronicle, August 30: B-1.

Abelman, Robert, and Hoover, Stewart M. (eds.). 1990. Religious Television: Controversies and Conclusions. Norwood, N.J.: Ablex Publishing Corporation.

Abelman, Robert. 1990. "The Selling of Salvation in the Electronic Church." pp. 173–183 in Robert Abelman and Stewart M. Hoover (eds.). 1990. Religious Television: Controversies and Conclusions. Norwood, N.J.: Ablex Publishing Corporation.

Abrams, Bruce. 1990. "Why Televangelists Are Bad for Judaism and Why Judaism is Bad Televangelism." pp. 147–151 in Robert Abelman and Stewart M. Hoover (eds.). 1990. Religious Television: Controversies and Conclusions. Norwood, N.J.: Ablex Publishing Corporation.

"Absent Cigarette Sparks Debate over Stamp of a Blues Guitarist." 1994. The New York Times. September 18.

Achenbaum, W. Andrew. 1985. "Societal Perceptions of Aging and the Aged." In Robert Binstock and Ethel Shanas (eds.), Handbook of Aging and the Social Sciences. (2nd ed.) New York: Van Nostrand Reinhold.

Acock, Alan, and Kiecolt, Jill. 1989. "Is It Family Structure or Socioeconomic Status? Family Structure During Adolescence and Adult Adjustment." Social Forces 68:553–71.

Acton, Edward. 1986. Russia. New York: Longman.

Adams, Bert N. 1971. The American Family: A Sociological Interpretation. Chicago: Markham.

Adams, Bert N. 1979. "Mate Selection in the United States: A Theoretical Summarization." In W. R. Burr, Reuben Hill, F. Ivan Nye, and Ira L. Reiss (eds.), Contemporary Theories About the Family. Vol. 1. New York: Free Press.

Adams, Bert N. 1985. "The Family: Problems and Solutions." Journal of Marriage and the Family 47 (August): 525–29.

Adams, Carol J. 1994. "Down to Earth: Finding Spirituality in Everyday Acts." Ms. Magazine. May–June: 20–21.

Adams, Carolyn Teich. 1986. "Homelessness in the Postindustrial City: Views from London and Philadelphia." Urban Affairs Quarterly 21 (June): 527–49.

Adler, Jerry. 1994. "The Numbers Game." Newsweek, July 25: 56–57.

Adler, Jerry. 1995. "The Last Days of Auschwitz." Newsweek. January 16: 46–59.

Adler, Jerry. 1995b. "Bye-Bye, Suburban Dream." Newsweek. May 15: 40–53.

Adler, Jerry. 1995c. "Theme Cities." Newsweek. September 11: 68–69.

Affleck, Marilyn, Morgan, Carolyn, and Hayes, Maggie. 1989. "The Influence of Gender-Role Attitudes on Life Expectations of College Students." Youth and Society 20:307–19.

Agnew, Robert, and Petersen, David. 1989. "Leisure and Delinquency." Social Problems 36:322–50.

Ahlburg, Dennis. 1988. "An Analysis of the Population Crisis Committee's International Human Suffering Index." Unpublished manuscript. Minneapolis: University of Minnesota Center for Population Analysis and Policy.

Ahlburg, Dennis A. and DeVita, Carol J. 1992. "New Realities of the American Family." Population Bulletin 47 (2) (April). Washington, D.C.: Population Reference Bureau, Inc.

AID Horizons. February, 1983.

"The AIDS Front: Good News and Grim News." 1995. U.S. News & World Report. February 13: 7.

Aird, John S. 1972. Population Policy and Demographic Prospects in the People's Republic of China. U.S. Department of Health, Education and Welfare. Washington, D.C.: U.S. Government Printing Office.

Akers, Ronald. 1968. "Problems in the Sociology of Deviance: Social Definitions and Behavior." Social Forces 46:455–65.

"Alas, Slavery Lives." 1993. Time 141, 12 (March 22): 26.

Alba, Richard D. 1985. "The Twilight of Ethnicity Among Americans of European Ancestry: The Case of Italians." In Richard Alba (ed.), Ethnicity and Race in the U.S.A.: Toward the Twenty-First Century. Boston: Routledge & Kegan Paul.

Albas, Daniel, and Albas, Cheryl. 1988. "Aces and Bombers: The Postexam Impression Management Strategies of Students." Symbolic Interaction 11:289–302.

Alesci, Nina. 1993. "Can We Talk? Bertice Berry Begins National TV Talk Show." Footnotes 21 (9) (December): 5.

Alesci, Nina. 1994. "Environmental Newsletter Founded and Published by Sociologist." Footnotes 22 (4) (April): 10.

Alexander, Bobby C. 1994. Televangelism Reconsidered: Ritual in Search for Human Community. Atlanta, GA.: Scholars Press.

Alexander, Karl, Entwisle, Doris, Cadigan, Doris, and Pallas, Aaron. 1987. "Getting Ready for First Grade: Standards of Deportment in Home and School." Social Forces 66:57–84.

Alexander, Karl L., Entwisle, Doris, and Thompson, Maxine. 1987. "School Performance, Status Relations, and the Structure of Sentiment: Bringing the Teacher Back In." American Sociological Review 52:665–82.

Alexander, Karl L., Natriello, Gary, and Pallas, Aaron M. 1985. "For Whom the School Bell Tolls: The Impact of Dropping out on Cognitive Performance." American Sociological Review 50 (June): 409–20.

Allan, Emilie, and Steffensmeier, Darrell. 1989. "Youth Unemployment and Property Crime." American Sociological Review 54: 107–23.

Allen, James R., and Curran, James W. 1988. "Prevention of AIDS and HIV Infection: Needs and Priorities for Epidemiologic Research." American Journal of Public Health 78:380–86.

Allen, Katherine. 1989. Single Women/Family Ties. Newbury Park, Calif.: Sage.

Allen, Walter R., and Farley, Reynolds. 1986. "The Shifting Social and Economic Tides of Black America, 1950–1980." Annual Review of Sociology 12:277–306.

Alter, Jonathan. 1995. "Next: "The Revolt of the Revolted'." Newsweek. November 6: 46–47.

Alter, Jonathan. 1995b. "What Works." Newsweek. May 29: 18–26.

Altman, Dennis. 1983. The Homosexualization of America. Boston: Beacon Press. (Original published 1982.)

Amato, Paul R. 1993. "Urban-Rural Differences in Helping Friends and Family Members." Social Psychology Quarterly 56: 249–262.

Amato, Paul, and Keith, Bruce. 1991a. "Parental Divorce and Adult Well-Being: A Meta-Analysis." Journal of Marriage and the Family 53 (February): 43–58.

Amato, Paul, and Keith, Bruce. Forthcoming. "Parental Divorce and Adult Well-Being: A Meta-Analysis." Journal of Marriage and the Family 53 (February).

Ambrose, Thomas. 1989. "The Official Language Movement in the United States: Contexts, Issues, and Activities." Language Problems and Language Planning 13:264–79.

American Association of University Women. 1992. How Schools Shortchange Girls: A Study of Major Findings of Girls and Education. Washington, D.C.: American Association of University Women Foundation.

"American Black Male in Crisis." 1989. Lincoln Star, December 31,

American Council on Education. 1990. Personal Communication, April.

American Sociological Association. 1988. Proposed Code of Ethics, December 1988. Washington, D.C.: American Sociological Association.

Anderson, David C. 1994. "The Crime Funnel." The New York Times Magazine, June 12: 56–57.

Andersson, Bengt-Erik. 1989. "Effects of Public Day Care: A Longitudinal Study." Child Development 60:857–66.

Aneshensel, Carol S., Fielder, Eve, and Becerra, Rosina. 1989. "Fertility and Fertility-Related Behavior Among Mexican American and Non-Hispanic White Female Adolescents." Journal of Health and Social Behavior 30:56–76.

Ankrah, E. 1989. "AIDS: Methodological Problems in Studying Its Prevention and Spread." Social Science and Medicine 29:267–76.

"Another Winter for the Homeless." 1989. Population Today 17 (February): 3–4.

APA. 1993. Violence and Youth: Psychology's Response. Washington, DC: American Psychological Association.

Applebaum, , and Batt, . 1994. The New American Workplace. Ithaca: ILR Press.

Archer, Dane. 1985. "Social Deviance." In Gardner Lindzey and Elliot Aronson (eds.), The Handbook of Social Psychology Vol. 2. (3rd ed.) New York: Random House.

Aries, Philippe. 1962. Centuries of Childhood: A Social History of Family Life. New York: Knopf.

Arthur, Richard. 1992. Gangs and Schools. Holmes Beach, FL: Learning Publications, Inc.

Arum, Richard. 1966. "Do Private Schools Force Public Schools to Compete?" American Sociological Review 61 (February): 29–46.

Asch, Solomon E. 1955. "Opinions and Social Pressure." Scientific American 193 (November): 31–35.

Ash, Roberta. 1972. Social Movements in America. Chicago: Markham.

Ashford, Lori S. 1995. "New Perspectives on Population: Lessons from Cairo." Population Bulletin 50 (1) (March). Washington, D.C.: Population Reference Bureau.

Asimov, Nanette. 1995. "Out of Class." San Francisco Chronicle. December 10: 1, 7.

Association on American Indian Affairs. 1994. American Indian Religious Freedom Project. New York, NY: Association on American Indian Affairs.

Astin, Alexander, and Associates. 1989. The American Freshman: National Norms for Fall 1989. Los Angeles: Graduate School of Education, University of California.

Atchley, Robert C. 1982. "Retirement as a Social Institution." American Review of Sociology 8:263–287.

Atkin, David J., Moorman, Jay, and Lin, Carolyn A. 1991. "Ready for Prime Time: Network Series Devoted to Working Women in the 1980s." Journal of Marriage and the Family 54 (2) (May): 379–386.

Atkinson, Maxine P. and Blackwelder, Stephen P. 1993. "Fathering in the 20th Century." Journal of Marriage and the Family 55 (4) (November): 975–986.

Aufderheide, Patricia (ed). 1992. Beyond PC: Toward a Politics of Understanding. St. Paul: Graywolf. "Averting a Death Foretold." 1994. Newsweek. November 28: 72–73.

Austin, Regina, and Schill, Michael. 1994. "Black, Brown, Red, and Poisoned." The Humanist 54 (4) (July–August): 9–17.

Austrom, D., and Hanel, N. 1985. "Psychological Issues of Single Life in Canada: An Exploratory Study." International Journal of Women's Studies 8:12–23.

"Awarded." 1994. Newsweek. August 22: 45.

Babbie, Earl R. 1995. The Practice of Social Research. (7th ed.) Belmont, Calif.: Wadsworth.

Bader, Eleanor J. 1992. "A Qustion of Silence." The Humanist 52 (2) (March–April): 47–49.

"The Baha'i Faith: What Is It?" Publishing by Baha'i Booksource International, 5755 Rodeo Road, Los Angeles, CA, 90016.

Baldassare, Mark. 1986. Trouble in Paradise: The Suburban Transformation in America. New York: Columbia University Press.

Baldassare, Mark. 1989. "Citizen Support for Regional Government in the New Suburbia." Urban Affairs Quarterly 24:460–69.

Baldus, D. C., Pulaski, C. and Woodworth, G. 1986. "Arbitrariness and Discrimination in the Administration of the Death Penalty: A Challenge to State Supreme Courts." Stetson Law Review 15:133–261.

Ball, John, Lange, W. Robert, Myers, C. Patrick, and Friedman, Samuel. 1988. "Reducing the Risk of AIDS Through Methadone Maintenance Treatment." Journal of Health and Social Behavior 29: 299–314.

Barker, Eileen. 1986. "Religious Movements: Cult and Anticult Since Jonestown." Annual Review of Sociology 12:329–46.

Barnes, Edward. 1993. "Behind the Serbian Lines." Time. May 17: 32–35.

Barnet, Richard J. and Muller, Ronald E. 1974. Global Research: The Power of Multinational Corporations. NY: Simon and Schuster.

Barnet, Richard J., and Cavanaugh, John. 1996. "The Age of Globalization." pp. 388–395 in Susan J. Ferguson (ed.). Mapping the Social Landscape: Readings in Sociology. Mountain View, CA: Mayfield Press.

Baron, James. 1984. "Organizational Perspectives on Stratification." Annual Review of Sociology 10:37–69.

Baron, James N., and Bielby, William T. 1984. "The Organization of a Segmented Economy." American Sociological Review 49 (August): 454–73.

Baron, James N., and Reiss, Peter C. 1985a. "Same Time, Next Year: Aggregate Analysis of the Mass Media and Violent Behavior." American Sociological Review 50 (June): 347–63.

Baron, James N., and Reiss, Peter C. 1985b. "Reply to Phillips and Bollen." American Sociological Review 50 (June): 372–76.

Baron, Stephen. 1989. "Resistance and Its Consequences: The Street Culture of Punks." Youth and Society 21:207–37.

Barone, Michael, and Ujifusa, Grant. 1989. The Almanac of American Politics, 1990. Washington, D.C.: National Journal.

Bartholet, Jeffrey. 1996. "A New Kind of Blood Libel." Newsweek. February 12: 40.

Beamish, Rob. 1992. Marx, Method, and the Division of Labor. Urbana, Ill.: University of Illinois Press.

Bechhofer, F., and Elliott, B. 1985. "The Petite Bourgeoisie in Late Capitalism." Annual Review of Sociology 11:181–207.

Becker, Howard S. 1963. Outsiders: Studies in the Sociology of Deviance. New York: Free Press.

Becker, Marshall H. 1993. "A Medical Sociologist Looks at Health Promotion." Journal of Health and Social Behavior 34 (March): 1–6.

Becker, Marshall, and Joseph, Jill. 1988. "AIDS and Behavioral Change to Reduce Risk: A Review." American Journal of Public Health 78:394–411.

Beckwith, Carol. 1983. "Niger's Wodaabe: 'People of the Taboo.' " National Geographic 164 (October): 482–509.

Beegley, Leonard. 1989. The Structure of Stratification in the United States. Newton, Mass.: Allyn & Bacon.

Beeson, Peter G. and Johnson, David R. 1987. "A Panel Study of Change (1981–1986) in Rural Mental Health Status: Effects of the Rural Crisis." Paper presented at the National Conference on Mental Health Statistics, Denver, Colorado, May 19.

Beier, George J. 1976. "Can Third World Cities Cope?" Population Bulletin 31 (December): 1–34.

Belenky, Mary, Clinchy, Blythe, Goldberger, Nancy, and Tarule, Jill. 1986. Women's Ways of Knowing. New York: Basic Books.

Bell, Derrick. 1992. Race, Racism, and American Law. Boston: Little, Brown and Company.

Bell, Wendell, and Robinson, Robert V. 1978. "An Index of Evaluated Equality: Measuring Conceptions of Social Justice in England and the United States." In Richard F. Tomasson (ed), Comparative Studies in Sociology. Vol. 1. Greenwich, Conn.: JAI Press.

Bellah, Robert N. 1974. "Civil Religion in America." In Russel B. Richey and Donald G. Jones (eds.), American Civil Religion. New York: Harper & Row.

Bellah, Robert N., and Associates. 1985. Habits of the Heart: Individualism and Commitment in American Life. Berkeley: University of California Press.

Belloc, N. 1980. "Personal Behavior Affecting Mortality." In S. Preston (ed.), Biological and Social Aspects of Mortality and Length of Life. Liége, Belgium: International Union for the Scientific Study of Population.

Belluck, Pam. 1995. "Visiting A Room Upstairs to View the Man Upstairs." New York Times. September 15: 35, 40.

Belluck, Pam. 1996. "In Era of Shrinking Budgets, Community Groups Blossom." New York Times. February 25: 1, 16.

Benbow, C. P., and Stanley, J. C. 1983. "Sex Differences in Mathematical Reasoning: More Facts." Science 222:1029–31.

Benford, Robert D. 1989. "Review." American Journal of Sociology 94:1451–53.

Bengston, Vern L. and Achenbaum, W. Andrew. (Eds.) 1993. The Changing Contract Across Generations. New York: Aldine de Gruyter.

Bengston, Vern, Cutler, Neal, Mangen, David J., and Marshall, Victor W. 1985. "Generations, Cohorts, and Relations Between Age Groups." In Robert Binstock and Ethel Shanas (eds.), Handbook of Aging and the Social Sciences. (2nd ed.) New York: Van Nostrand Reinhold.

Benjamin, Lois. 1992. The Black Elite. Chicago: Nelson-Hall.

Bensman, Joseph, and Lilienfeld, Robert. 1979. Between Public and Private: The Lost Boundaries of Self. New York: Free Press.

Berger, Bennet M. 1981. The Survival of a Counterculture. Berkeley: University of California Press.

Berger, John, Rosenholtz, S. J., and Zelditch, M. 1980. "Status Organizing Process." Annual Review of Sociology 6:479–508.

Berger, Peter L. 1963. Invitation to Sociology: A Humanistic Perspective. New York: Doubleday.

Berk, Laura. 1989. Child Development. Newton, Mass: Allyn & Bacon.

Berry, Brian, and Kasarda, John. 1977. Contemporary Urban Ecology. New York: Macmillan.

Bertoli, Fernando, and Associates. 1984. "Infant Mortality by Socioeconomic Status for Blacks, Indians, and Whites: A Longitudinal Analysis of North Carolina, 1868–1977." Sociology and Social Research 68:364–77.

Biddle, B. J. 1986. "Recent Developments in Role Theory." Annual Review of Sociology 12:67–92.

Bielby, William T., and Baron, James N. 1986. "Men and Women at Work: Sex Segregation and Statistical Discrimination." American Journal of Sociology 91 (January): 759–98.

Bielby, William, and Bielby, Denise. 1989. "Family Ties: Balancing Commitments to Work and Family in Dual-Earner Households." American Sociological Review 54:776–89.

Billings, Dwight, B. 1990. "Religion as Opposition." American Journal of Sociology 96:1–31.

Billingsley, Andrew. 1989. "The Black Family." Address given at the 1989 meetings of the National Council on Family Relations, New Orleans, November.

Billson, Janet Mancini. 1992. "Sociologists Respond to Call for International Teaching Opportunity." Footnotes 20 (7) (September): 5.

Black, Cyril E. 1986. Understanding Soviet Politics. Boulder, Colo.: Westview Press.

Black, Donald. 1976. The Behavior of Law. New York: Academic Press.

"Black-White Gap Persisting." 1989. Population Today 17 (October): 4.

Blair, M. Elizabeth. 1993. "Commercialization of the Rap Music Subculture." Journal of Popular Culture 27 (3) (Winter): 21–34.

Blakely, Edward, and Shapira, Philip. 1984. "Industrial Restructuring: Public Policies for Investment in Advanced Industrial Societies." Annals of the American Academy of Political and Social Science 475:96–109.

Blau, F. D. 1977. Equal Pay in the Office. Lexington, Mass: Lexington Books.

Blau, Judith R. 1986. "The Elite Arts, More or Less de Rigueur: A Comparative Analysis of Metropolitan Culture." Social Forces 64 (June): 875–905.

Blau, Peter. (ed.) 1975. Approaches to the Study of Social Structure. New York: Free Press.

Blau, Peter M. 1987. "Contrasting Theoretical Perspectives." In J. Alexander, B. Giesen, R. Munch, and Smelser, N. (eds.). The Micro-Macro Link. Berkeley: University of California Press.

Blau, Peter M., and Meyer, Marshall W. 1971. Bureaucracy in Modern Society. (2nd ed.) New York: Random House.

Blau, Peter M., and Schwartz, Joseph E. 1984. Cross-Cutting Social Circles. Orlando, Fla.: Academic Press.

Blee, Kathleen M., and Billings, Dwight B. 1986. "Reconstructing Daily Life in the Past: An Hermeneutical Approach to Ethnographic Data." Sociological Quarterly 27 (Winter): 443–62.

Bloom, Samuel. 1988. "Structure and Ideology in Medical Education: An Analysis of Resistance to Change." Journal of Health and Social Behavior 29:294–306.

Blumberg, Rae Lesser. 1978. Stratification: Socioeconomic and Sexual Inequality. Dubuque, Iowa: Brown.

Blumer, H. 1934. "Collective Behavior." In A. M. Lee (ed.), New Outlines of the Principles of Sociology. New York: Barnes & Noble.

Blumer, H. 1969. Symbolic Interactionism: Perspective and Method. Englewood Cliffs, N.J.: Prentice-Hall.

Blumer, Herbert G. 1969. "Collective Behavior." pp. 65–121 in Alfred McClung Lee, ed. Principles of Sociology, 3rd ed. New York: Barnes & Noble Books.

Blumstein, Phillip, and Schwartz, Pepper. 1983. American Couples. New York: William Morrow.

Bobo, Lawrence, and Kluegel, James R. 1993. "Opposition to Race-Targeting: Self-Interest, Stratification Ideology, or Racial Attitudes?" American Sociological Review 58:443–464.

Bogert, Carroll. 1995. "'We Turned This Around.'" Newsweek. September 18: 50–51.

Bogert, Carroll, and Chubbuck, Katharine. 1995. "Making It Hard on Hillary." Newsweek. August 28: 45.

Bohland, James R. 1982. "Indian Residential Segregation in the Urban Southwest: 1970 and 1980." Social Science Quarterly 63 (December): 749–761.

Bohrnstedt, George W., and Fisher, Gene. 1986. "The Effects of Recalled Childhood and Adolescent Relationships Compared to Current Role Performances in Young Adults' Affective Functioning." Social Psychology Quarterly 49 (1): 19–32.

Boies, John. 1989. "Money, Business, and the State." American Sociological Review 54:821–33.

Bollier, David. 1982. Liberty and Justice for Some. New York: Frederick Ungar.

Bolton, R. 1994. "The Epidemiology of HIV Transmission: Trends, Structure, and Dynamics." American Review of Anthropology,

Bonacich, Edna. 1972. "A Theory of Ethnic Antagonism: The Split Labor Market." American Sociological Review 37 (October): 547–59.

Bonavia, David. 1984. "Reassessing Mao." In Molly Joel Coye, John Livingston and Jean Highland (eds.), China: Yesterday and Today. New York: Bantam Books.

Bonner, Florence. 1991. "Mission, Future of the Association of Black Sociologists." Footnotes 19 (4) (April): 5.

Booth, Alan, and Johnson, David. 1988. "Premarital Cohabitation and Marital Success." Journal of Family Issues 9:255–72.

Booth, Alan, Johnson, David, White, Lynn, and Edwards, John. 1984. Marital Instability and the Life Course: Methodology Report. Lincoln: Bureau of Sociological Research.

Bose, Christine E., and Rossi, Peter H. 1983. "Gender and Jobs: Prestige Standings of Occupations as Affected by Gender." American Sociological Review 48 (June): 316–330.

Bourdieu, P. 1973. "Cultural Reproduction and Social Reproduction." In R. Brown (ed.), Knowledge, Education, and Cultural Change. London: Tavistock.

Bouvier, Leon F. 1980. "America's Baby Boom Generation: The Fateful Bulge." Population Bulletin 35 (1): 1–45.

Bouvier, Leon, and Gardner, Robert W. 1986. "Immigration to the U.S.: The Unfinished Story." Population Bulletin 41 (November): 1–50.

Bowen, Howard R. 1977. Investment in Learning. San Francisco: Jossey-Bass.

Bowles, Samuel, and Gintis, Herbert. 1976. Schooling in Capitalist America: Educational Reform and the Contradictions of Economic Life. New York: Basic Books.

Bowles, Samuel, and Gintis, Herbert. 1986. Democracy and Capitalism: Property, Community, and the Contradictions of Modern Social Thought. New York: Basic.

Boyce, Joseph N. 1991. "Struggle Over Hospital in Los Angeles Pits Minority vs. Minority." The Wall Street Journal. April 1: A1, A4.

Bozett, Frederick (ed.). 1987. Gay and Lesbian Parents. New York: Praeger.

Bradshaw, York. 1988. "Reassessing Economic Dependency and Uneven Development: The Kenyan Experience." American Sociological Review 53:693–708.

Bradshaw, York, and Fraser, Elvis. 1989. "City Size, Economic Development, and Quality of Life in China." American Sociological Review 54:986–1003.

Braithwaite, John. 1981. "The Myth of Social Class and Criminality, Reconsidered." American Sociological Review 46 (February): 36–58.

Braithwaite, John. 1985. "White Collar Crime." Annual Review of Sociology 11:1–25.

Brake, Mike. 1980. The Sociology of Youth Culture and Youth Subcultures. Boston: Routledge & Kegan Paul.

Brake, Mike. 1985. Comparative Youth Culture: The Sociology of Youth Cultures and Youth Subcultures in America, Britain, and Canada. Boston: Routledge & Kegan Paul.

Braver, Sanford L., Fitzpatrick, Pamela J., and Bay, R. Curtis. 1991. "Noncustodial Parent's Report of Child Support Payments." Family Relations 40 (2) (April): 180–185.

Braverman, Harry. 1975. Labor and Monopoly Capital: The Degradation of Work in the Twentieth Century. New York: Monthly Review Press.

Breslow, Lester. 1987. "Setting Objectives for Public Health." Annual Review of Public Health 8:289–307.

Bridges, William. 1994. "The End of the Job." Fortune. September 19: 62–74.

Bright, Chris. 1990. "Shipping Unto Others." E: The Environmental Magazine 1:30–35.

Brody, Gene H., Stoneman, Zolinda, Flor, Douglas, and McCrary, Chris. 1994. "Religion's Role in Organizing Family Relationships: Family Process in Rural, Two-Parent African American Families." Journal of Marriage and the Family 56 (4) (November): 878–888.

Brooks, William C. 1994. "Black Males in the Work Force in the Twenty-First Century." pp. 263–270 in Richard G. Majors and Jacob U. Gordon, eds. The American Black Male: His Present Status and His Future. Chicago: Nelson-Hall.

Brossi, Kathleen B. 1979. A Cross-City Comparison of Felony Case Processing. Washington, D.C.: U.S. Government Printing Office.

Brown, Karen. 1996. "Marketplace." National Public Radio broadcast. February 2.

Brown, R. S., Moon, M., and Zoloth, B. S. 1980. "Incorporating Occupational Attainment in Studies of Male-Female Earnings Differentials." Journal of Human Resources 15:3–28.

Brownell, Arlene, and Shumaker, Sally A. 1984. "Social Support: An Introduction to a Complex Phenomenon." Journal of Social Issues 40 (4): 1–10.

Browning, Frank and Gerassi, John. 1980. The American Way of Crime. New York: G. P. Putnam's Sons.

Brubaker, Timothy H. 1991. "Families in Later Life: A Burgeoning Research Area." pp. 226–248 in Contemporary Families: Looking Forward, Looking Back, edited by Alan Booth. Minneapolis, MN: National Council on Family Relations.

Bruce, Steve. 1990. Pray TV: Televangelism in America. New York: Routledge.

Bryant, Howard. 1994. "Finding a Home for Orphaned Computers." The Alameda Newspaper Group, December 4: D-1, D-4.

Bryk, Anthony. 1988. "School Organization and Its Effects: Research Prepared for the Advisory Council on Education Statistics." Washington, D.C.: National Center for Education Statistics.

Buchsbaum, Herbert. 1993. "Islam in America." Scholastic Update, October 22: 15–18.

Buechler, Steven M. 1993. "Beyond Resource Mobilization? Emerging Trends in Social Movement Theory." The Sociological Quarterly 34:217–235.

Bumpass, Larry. 1984. "Children and Marital Disruption: A Replication and Update." Demography 21 (February): 71–82.

Bumpass, Larry, and Sweet, James. 1989. "National Estimates of Cohabitation." Demography 26:615–25.

Bumpass, Larry L., Raley, R. K. and Sweet, J. 1995. "The Changing Character of Stepfamilies: Implications of Cohabitation and Nonmarital Childbearing." Demography 32 (3) (August): 425–436.

Bumpass, Larry L. and Sweet, James A. 1995. "Cohabitation, Marriage, Nonmarital Childbearing, and Union Stability: Preliminary Findings from NSFH2." Population Association of America Annual Meeting, San Francisco, April.

Bundy, McGeorge. 1990. "From Cold War to Lasting Peace." Foreign Affairs 69 (1): 197–212.

Bunster, Ximena. 1977. "Talking Pictures: Field Method and Visual Mode." Signs: Journal of Women in Culture and Society 2 (1): 278–293.

Burby, Raymond, and Rohe, William. 1989. "Deconcentration of Public Housing." Urban Affairs Quarterly 25:117–41.

Burdman, Pamela. 1995. "Sexual Rights A Hot Issue in Beijing." San Francisco Chronicle, September 8: A1, A17.

Burdman, Pamela, and Rojas, Aurelio. 1996. "Anti-Affirmative Action Initiative Set for State Ballot." San Frnacisco Chronicle. February 22: A11, A16.

Burk, Martha and Shaw, Kirsten. 1995. "How the Entertainment Industry Demeans, Degrades, and Dehumanizes Women." pp. 436–438 in Sheila Ruth, ed. Issues in Feminism: An Introduction to Women's Studies, 3rd edition. Mountain View, CA: Mayfield Press.

Burke, Peter J. 1980. "The Self: Measurement Requirements from the Interactionist Perspective." Social Psychological Quarterly 43 (1): 18–29.

Burleigh, Nina. 1995. "Small Ants, Tall Tales." Time. September 18: 53.

Burnell, Barbara, and Burnell, James. 1989. "Community Interaction and Suburban Zoning Policies." Urban Affairs Quarterly 24:470–82.

Bush, Corlann Gee. 1993. "Women and the Assessment of Technology" pp. 192–264 in Albert H. Teich, editor. Technology and the Future, 6th edition. New York: St. Martin's Press.

Cable, Sherry, and Cable, Charles. 1995. Environmental Problems, Grassroots Solutions: The Politics of Grassroots Environmental Conflict. New York: St. Martin's Press.

Cable, Sherry, Walsh, Edward, and Warland, Rex. 1988. "Differential Paths to Political Activism: Comparisons of Four Mobilization Processes After the Three Mile Island Accident." Social Forces 66:951–69.

Cahill, Spencer E. 1983. "Reexamining the Acquisition of Sex Roles: A Social Interactionist Perspective." Sex Roles 9 (January): 1–15.

Call, Vaughn, Sprecher, Susan and Schwartz, Pepper. 1995. "The Incidence and Frequency of Marital Sex in a National Sample." Journal of Marriage and the Family 57 (3) (August): 639–652.

Callero, Peter L. 1985. "Role Identity Salience." Social Psychology Quarterly 48 (3): 203–15.

Camasso, Michael J., and Moore, Dan E. 1985. "Rurality and the Residualist Social Welfare Response." Rural Sociology 50 (Fall): 397–408.

Camp, Sharon L. and Barberis, Mary A. 1992. The International Human Suffering Index. Washington, D.C.: Population Crisis Committee.

Camp, Sharon L., and Speidel, J. Joseph. 1987. "The International Human Suffering Index." Washington, D.C.: Population Crisis Committee.

Campbell, Ernest Q. 1969. "Adolescent Socialization." In David A. Goslin (ed.), Handbook of Socialization Theory and Research. New York: Russell Sage Foundation.

Campbell, John L., and Allen, Michael Patrick. 1994. "The Political Economy of Revenue Extraction in the Modern State: A Time-Series Analysis of U.S. Income Taxes, 1916–1986." Social Forces 72:643–669.

Canada, Katherine and Pringle, Richard. 1995. "The Role of Gender in College Classroom Interactions: A Social Context Approach." Sociology of Education 68 (July): 161–186.

Caplow, Theodore. 1982. "Christmas Gifts and Kin Networks." American Sociological Review 47: 383–92.

Caplow, Theodore, and Chadwick, Bruce. 1979. "Inequality and Life-Style in Middletown, 1920–1978." Social Science Quarterly 60 (December): 367–386.

"Career Statistics." 1990. Husker Newsletter, March 1990, p. 1.

Carter, B. 1991. "Children's TV, Where Boys Are King." New York Times, May 1: A1, C18.

Catsambis, Sophia. 1994. "The Path to Math: Gender and Racial-Ethnic Differences in Mathematics Participation from Middle School to High School." Sociology of Education 67 (July): 199–215.

Caulfield, Jon. 1994. City Form and Everyday Life: Toronto's Gentrification and Critical Social Practice. Toronto: University of Toronto Press.

Centers for Disease Control. 1992. "HIV/AIDS Surveillance: First Quarter Edition." April. Atlanta, GA: U.S. Department of Health and Human Services Centers for Disease Control.

Centers for Disease Control. 1994. "Facts about Recent Trends in Reported U.S. AIDS Cases." August. Atlanta, GA: U.S. Department of Health and Human Services Centers for Disease Control.

"Central-City Populations Continue to Slip." 1990. Population Today 18 (1): 8.

Chafetz, Janet S. 1984. Sex and Advantage. Totawa, N. J.: Rowman and Allanheld.

Chambliss, William. 1978. "Toward a Political Economy of Crime." In Charles Reasons and Robert Rich (eds.), The Sociology of Law: A Conflict Perspective. Toronto: Butterworths.

Chandrasekhar, S. 1981. A Dirty, Filthy Book. Berkeley: University of California Press.

Chapman, Jane R., and Gates, Margaret (eds). 1978. The Victimization of Women. Sage.

Chapman, Nancy J., and Pancoast, Diane L. 1985. "Working with the Informal Helping Networks of the Elderly: The Experiences of Three Programs." Journal of Social Issues 41 (1): 47–64.

Chappell, Neena L., and Havens, Betty. 1980. "Old and Female: Testing the Double-Jeopardy Hypothesis." Sociological Quarterly 21 (Spring): 157–171.

Charny, M. C., Lewis, P. A., and Farrow, S. C. 1989. "Choosing Who Shall Not Be Treated." Social Science and Medicine 28:1331–38.

Chavira, Ricardo. 1991. "Browns vs. Blacks." Time. July 29: 12–16.

Cheal, David. 1988. The Gift Economy. Boston: Routledge & Kegan Paul.

Check, J. V. P. 1985. The Effects of Violent and Nonviolent Pornography, Report to the Department of Justice. Ottowa: Canada.

Chen, Kathy. 1995. "Women Pack Up After Fractious Meeting." The Wall Street Journal. September 15: B1.

Cherlin, Andrew. 1981. Marriage, Divorce, Remarriage. Cambridge, Mass.: Harvard University Press.

Cherlin, Andrew. 1990. "Message from the Chair." Family Forum (Winter): 1–2.

Cherlin, Andrew J., and Frank F. Furstenberg, Jr. 1994. "Stepfamilies in the United States: A Reconsideration." pp. 359–381 in John Hagan and Karen S. Cook, eds. Annual Review of Sociology, v 20.

Chevan, Albert. 1989. "The Growth of Home Ownership: 1940–1980." Demography 26:249–66.

"China's Demographic Disaster of 1958–1962." 1985. Population Today 13 (March): 7.

Chirot, Daniel. 1977. Social Change in the Twentieth Century. San Francisco, Calif.: Harcourt Brace Jovanovich.

Chirot, Daniel. 1986. Social Change in the Modern Era. San Diego, Calif.: Harcourt Brace Jovanovich.

Chodak, Symon. 1973. Societal Development: Five Approaches with Conclusions from Comparative Analysis. New York: Oxford University Press.

Christenson, James A. 1984. "Gemeinschaft and Gesell- schaft: Testing the Spatial and Communal Hypothesis." Social Forces 63 (September): 160–68.

Church, George J. 1992. "The Fire This Time." Time. May 11: 20–25.

Cicourel, Aaron V. 1985. "Text and Discourse." Annual Review of Anthropology 14:159–85.

Clarity, James F. 1994. "After Six Killings, the Old Sadness in Ulster." The New York Times. June 20: A3.

Clark, Nicola. 1993. "A Nannies' Advocate Argues Their Case." The Wall Street Journal. January 26: A14.

Clawson, Dan, and Neustadtl, Alan. 1989. "Interlocks, PACs, and Corporate Conservatism." American Journal of Sociology 94:749–73.

Clegg, Stewart, Boreham, Paul, and Dow, Geoff. 1986. Class, Politics, and the Economy. Boston: Routledge & Kegan Paul.

Clifford, Mark. 1994. "Levi's Law." Far Eastern Economic Review 157, 15 (April 14): 60.

Clinard, Marshall B. 1990. Corporate Corruption: The Abuse of Power. New York: Praeger.

Clinton, Hillary Rodham. 1990. "In France, Day Care is Every Child's Right." New York Times. April 7.

Coale, Ansley. 1973. Cited in M. Teitelbaum. 1975. "Relevance of Demographic Transition Theory to Developing Countries." Science 188 (May 2): 420–425.

Coates, Guy. 1996. "Louisiana Blacks Hold Rights Rally at Capitol." Associated Press. February 25.

Cobarrubias, Juan. 1983. "Ethical Issues in Status Planning." In Juan Cobarrubias and Joshua Fishman (eds.), Progress in Language Planning: International Perspectives. Berlin: Mouton.

Cobb, Charles, E., Jr. 1987. "Haiti Against All Odds." National Geographic 172: 654–671.

Cobb, S. 1979. "Social Support and Health Through the Life Course." In M. W. Riley (ed.), Aging from Birth to Death. Boulder, Colo.: Westview Press.

Cockerham, William C. 1989. Medical Sociology. (4th ed.) Englewood Cliffs, N.J.: Prentice-Hall.

Cockerham, William, Kunz, Gerhard, and Lueschen, Guenther. 1988. "Social Stratification and Health Life-Styles in Two Systems of Health Care Delivery: A Comparison of the United States and West Germany." Journal of Health and Social Behavior 29:113–26.

Cohn, Bob, and Turque, Bill. 1995. "Firing Up the Politics of Teen Smoking." Newsweek. August 21: 25.

Cohn, Richard M. 1982. "Economic Development and Status Change of the Aged." American Journal of Sociology 87 (5): 1150–61.

Cole, David. 1994. "Five Myths about Immigration." The Nation 259, 12 (October 17): 410–412.

Cole, Michael, and Cole, Sheila. 1989. The Development of Children. New York: Scientific American Books.

Coleman, James. 1988. "Competition and the Structure of Industrial Society: Reply to Braithwaite." American Journal of Sociology 94:632–36.

Coleman, James William. 1989. The Criminal Elite: The Sociology of White Collar Crime. New York: St. Martin's Press.

Coleman, James, and Associates. 1966. Equality of Educational Opportunity. Washington, D.C.: U.S. Government Printing Office.

Coleman, James, and Hoffer, Thomas. 1987. Public and Private High Schools, New York: Basic Books.

Coleman, James, Hoffer, Thomas, and Kilgore, Sally. 1982. High School Achievement: Public, Catholic, and Private Schools Compared. New York: Basic Books.

Collins, Randall. 1979. The Credential Society. Orlando, Fla.: Academic Press.

Comstock, Gary David. 1991. Violence against Lesbians and Gay Men. New York: Columbia University Press.

Comstock, George S. 1977. "Types of Portrayal and Aggressive Behavior." Journal of Communication 27 (Summer): 189–198.

Concar, David. 1993. "Examination Hell." New Scientist 140 (October 2): 51–54.

Conrad, John P. 1983. "Deterrence, the Death Penalty and the Data." In Ernest van den Haag and John P. Conrad (eds.), The Death Penalty: A Debate. New York: Plenum.

Conrad, Peter. 1992. "Medicalization and Social Control." pp. 209–232 in Judith Blake and John Hagen (eds.). Annual Review of Sociology, v. 18.

Cool, Linda, and McCabe, Justine. 1983. "The 'Scheming Hag' and the 'Dear Old Thing´: The Anthropology of Aging Women." In Jay Sokolvsky (ed.), Growing Old in Different Cultures. Belmont, Calif.: Wadsworth.

Cooley, Charles Horton. 1902. Human Nature and the Social Order. New York: Scribner's.

Cooley, Charles Horton. 1967. "Primary Groups." In A. Paul Hare, Edgar F. Borgotta, and Robert F. Bales (eds.), Small Groups: Studies in Social Interaction. (Rev. ed. New York: Knopf. (Originally published 1909.)

Cooper, Richard, and Associates. 1981. "Racism, Society, and Diseases: An Exploration of the Social and Biological Mechanisms of Differential Mortality." Journal of Health Services 11:389–414.

Corcoran, M. 1995. "Rags to Rags: Poverty and Mobility in the United States." pp. 237–267 in John Hagan and Karen S. Cook (eds.). Annual Review of Sociology, v. 21.

Cornell, Claire, and Gelles, Richard. 1982. "Adolescent to Parent Violence." Urban Social Change Review 15 (Winter): 8–14.

Cose, Ellis. 1994. "Truths about Spouse Abuse." Newsweek. August 8: 49.

Cose, Ellis. 1995. "Teaching Kids To Be Smart." Newsweek. August 21: 58–60.

Coser, Lewis A. 1956. The Functions of Social Conflict. New York: Free Press.

"Counting Trees as the Forest Burns." 1989. Newsweek, September 11, pp. 26, 28–29.

Cowan, Ruth Schwartz. 1993. "Less Work for Mother?" pp. 329–339 in Albert H. Teich, ed. Technology and the Future, 6th ed. New York: St. Martin's Press.

Cowgill, Donald O. 1974. "Aging and Modernization: A Revision of the Theory." In John Hendricks and C. Davis Hendricks (eds.), Dimensions of Aging: Readings. Cambridge, Mass.: Winthrop.

Cowley, Geofrey. 1994. "The Ever-Expanding Plague." Newsweek. August 22: 37.

Cowley, Geofrey. 1995. "A New Assault on Addiction." Newsweek. January 30: 51.

Cowley, Geofrey. 1996. "Living Longer with HIV." Newsweek. February 12: 60–62.

Cowley, Geofrey and Murr, Andrew. 1994. "Good Politics, Bad Medicine." Newsweek, December 5: 32–34.

Coye, Molly Joel, Livingston, John, and Highland, Jean (eds.). 1984. China: Yesterday and Today. (3rd ed.) New York: Bantam Books.

Craig, David. 1995. "Canadian Dollar Hits 9-Year Low." USA Today. January 12: 1B.

Craig, Stephen. 1992. "The Effect of Television Day Part on Gender Portrayals in Television Commercials: A Content Analysis." Sex Roles 26 (5/6): 197–211.

Cravatts, Richard L. 1992. "Loosen Codes and House the Homeless." The Wall Street Journal. February 6.

Crèvecoeur, J. Hector. 1974. "What Is an American?" In Richard J. Meister (ed.), Race and Ethnicity in Modern America. Lexington, Mass.: Heath. (Originally published 1782.)

Crimmins, Eileen M., Hayward, Mark D., and Saito, Yashuhiko. 1994. "Changing Mortality and Morbidity Rates and the Health Status and Life Expectancy of the Older Population." Demography 31 (1) (February): 168–169.

Crozier, Michael, and Friedberg, Erhard. 1980. Actors and Systems: The Politics of Collective Action. Chicago: University of Chicago Press.

Crutchfield, Robert D. 1989. "Labor Stratification and Violent Crime." Social Forces 68:489–512.

Cummings, Scott. 1987. "Vulnerability to the Effects of Recession: Minority and Female Workers." Social Forces 65 (March): 834–57.

Currie, Elliott. 1989. "Confronting Crime: Looking Toward the 21st Century." Justice Quarterly 6:5–25.

Curtis, Richard F. 1986. "Household and Family in Theory on Inequality." American Sociological Review 51 (April): 168–83.

Custred, Glynn and Wood, Tom. 1995. "Racial, Gender Preferences Hurt Everybody." San Francisco Chronicle. January 19: A21.

D'Souza, Dinesh. 1991. Illiberal Education: The Politics of Race and Sex on Campus. New York: The Free Press.

D'Souza, Dinesh and MacNeil, Robert. 1992. "The Big Chill? Interview with Dinesh D'Souza." pp. 29–39 in Paul Berman (ed.). Debating P. C.: The Controversy over Political Correctness on College Campuses. New York: Bantam Doubleday Dell Publishing Group, Inc.

Dahl, Jonathan. 1991. "Up to 20% of Homeless People Carry AIDS Virus, Says New Report by CDC." Wall Street Journal.

Dahl, Robert. 1961. Who Governs? New Haven, Conn.: Yale University Press.

Dahl, Robert. 1971. Polarchy. New Haven, Conn.: Yale University Press.

Dale, Roger, 1977. "Implications of the Rediscovery of the Hidden Curriculum of the Sociology of Teaching." In Denis Gleeson (ed.), Identity and Structure: Issues in the Sociology of Education. Driffield, England: Nafferton Books.

Daly, Martin, and Wilson, Margo. 1983. Sex, Evolution, and Behavior. (2nd ed.) Boston: Willard Grant.

Daly, Mary. 1990 [1978]. Gyn/Ecology: The Metaethics of Radical Feminism. Boston: Beacon Press.

"Danger: Children at Work." 1993. The Futurist 27 (Jan–Feb): 42–44.

Daniels, Roger, and Kitano, Harry H. L. 1970. American Racism: Exploration of the Nature of Prejudice. Englewood Cliffs, N.J.: Prentice–Hall.

Darby, John. 1976. Conflict in Northern Ireland: The Development of a Polarised Community. Dublin: Gill & Macmillan.

Darnton, John. 1994a. "'Lost Decade Drains Africa's Vitality." The New York Times. June 19: Y1, Y5.

Darnton, John. 1994b. "In Decolonized, Destitute Africa Bankers Are the New Overlords." The New York Times. June 20: A1, A6.

David, Henry. 1982. "Eastern Europe: Pronatalist Policies and Private Behavior." Population Bulletin 36 (6): 1–50.

Davies, Scott. 1995. "Leaps of Faith: Shifting Currents in Critical Sociology of Education." American Journal of Sociology 100 (6) (May): 1448–1478.

Davis, Bob, and Milbank, Dana. 1992. "If the U.S. Work Ethic Is Fading, Alienation May Be Main Reason." Wall Street Journal. February 7: A1, A5.

Davis, Cary. 1982. "The Future Racial Composition of the U.S." Intercom 8–10.

Davis, Cary, Haub, Carl, and Willette, JoAnne. 1983. "U.S. Hispanics: Changing the Face of America." Population Bulletin 33 (June): 1–43.

Davis, James Allan, and Smith, Tom W. 1986. General Social Surveys, 1972–1986. Chicago: National Opinion Research Center.

Davis, James, and Stasson, Mark. 1988. "Small-Group Performance: Past and Future Research Trends." Advances in Group Processes 5:245–77.

Davis, Kingsley. 1961. "Prostitution." In Robert K. Merton and Robert A. Nisbet (eds.), Contemporary Social Problems. San Francisco: Harcourt Brace Joranovich.

Davis, Kingsley. 1973. "Introduction." In Kingsley Davis (ed.), Cities. New York: W. H. Freeman.

Davis, Kingsley, and Moore, Wilbert E. 1945. "Some Principles of Stratification." American Sociological Review 10 (April): 242–249.

Davis, Mike. 1986. Prisoners of the American Dream: Politics and Economy in the History of the U.S. Working Class. London: Verso Books.

De Sherbinin, Alex, and Kalish, Susan. 1995. "First-Ever Social Summit Struggles with Toughest Issues." Population Today 23 (3) (March): 1–2.

Deaux, Kay. 1985. "Sex and Gender." Annual Review of Psychology 36:49–81.

Deegan, Mary Jo. 1987. Jane Addams and the Men of the Chicago School, 1892–1918. New Brunswick, N.J.: Transaction.

Delgado, Richard. 1983. "Limits to Proselytizing." In D. Bromley and J. T. Richardson (eds.), The Brainwashing/Deprogramming Controversy. New York: Mellen.

Della Porta, Donatella. 1995. Social Movements, Political Violence, and the State: A Comparative Analysis of Italy and Germany. New York: Cambridge University Press.

Dent, David J. 1992. "The New Black Suburbs." The New York Times Magazine. June 14: 18–23.

Denzin, Norman K. 1984. "Toward a Phenomenology of Domestic, Family Violence." American Journal of Sociology 90 (November) 483–513.

Derksen, Linda, and John Gartrell. 1993. "The Social Context of Recycling." American Sociological Review 58 (3) (June): 434–442.

Devine, Joel, Sheley, Joseph, and Smith, M. Dwayne. 1988. "Macroeconomic and Social Control Policy Influences in Crime

Rate Changes, 1948–85." American Sociological Review 53:407–20.

DeWitt, J. L. 1943. Japanese in the United States, Final Report: Japanese Evacuation from the West Coast, p. 34. Cited in Paul E. Horton and Gerald R. Leslie. Social Problems 1955. East Norwalk, Conn.: Appleton-Century-Crofts.

Diamond, Irene and Orenstein, Gloria Feman. 1990. Reweaving the World: The Emergence of Ecofeminism. San Francisco: Sierra Club Books.

"Different Votes." 1994. Time. May 23: 18.

DiMaggio, Paul, and Mohr, John. 1985. "Cultural Capital, Educational Attainment, and Marital Selection." American Journal of Sociology 90 (May): 1231–61.

DiMento, Joseph. 1989. "Can Social Science Explain Organizational Noncompliance with Environmental Law?" Journal of Social Issues 45:109–32.

"Disaster Throws the Spotlight." 1989. New York Times, April 17, p. 12.

DiTomaso, Nancy. 1987. "Symbolic Media and Social Solidarity: The Foundations of Corporate Culture." Sociology of Organizations 5:105–34.

Dobash, Russell, P., R. Dobash, R. Emerson, Wilson, Margo, and Daly, Martin. 1992. "The Myth of Sexual Symmetry in Marital Violence." Social Problems 39 (1) (February): 71–91.

Dobbelaere, Karel. 1981. "Secularization: A Multidimensional Concept." Current Sociology 29:1–21.

Dolnick, Edward. 1993. "Deafness As Culture." The Atlantic Monthly (September): 37–53.

Donato, Katharine M., Durand, Jorge, and Massey, Douglas S. 1992. "Stemming the Tide? Assessing the Deterrent Effects of the Immigration Reform and Control Act." Demography 29, 2 (May): 138–157.

Donnelley, Strachan, McCarthy, Charles R., and Singleton, Rivers, Jr. 1994. "The Brave New World of Animal Biotechnology." Special Supplement. Hastings Center Report 24 (1), January–February.

Dono, John E., et al. 1979. "Primary Groups in Old Age: Structure and Function." Research on Aging 1 (December): 403–433.

Dore, Ronald P. 1973. British Factory, Japanese Factory. Berkeley: University of California Press.

Dority, Barbara. 1994. "The Criminalization of Hatred." The Humanist 54 (3) (May–June): 38–39.

Dornbusch, Sanford. 1989. "The Sociology of Adolescence." Annual Review of Sociology 15:233–59.

Dougherty, Kevin. 1987. "The Effect of Community Colleges: Aid or Hindrance to Socioeconomic Attainment?" Sociology of Education 60:86–103.

Douglas, Jack D., and Waksler, Frances C. 1982. The Sociology of Deviance: An Introduction. Boston: Little, Brown.

Douglas, Susan. 1995. "Sitcom Women: We've Come a Long Way. Maybe." Mx. November/December: 76–80.

Douglas, Tom. 1983. Groups: Understanding People Gathered Together. London: Tavistock.

Dow, Peter B. 1991. Schoolhouse Politics: Lessons from the Sputnik Era. Cambridge, MA: Harvard University Press.

Downey, Douglas B. 1995. "When Bigger Is Not Better: Family Size, Parental Resources, and Children's Educational Performance." American Sociological Review 60 (5) (October): 746–761.

"Dramatic Fertility Declines in Two Countries?" 1989. Population Today 17 (9): 4.

Drum, Anthony M. 1995. City-building in America. Boulder, CO: Westview Press.

Dumaine, Brian. 1993. "Illegal Child Labor Comes Back." Fortune 127, 7 (April 5): 86–92.

Duncan, Greg. 1984. Years of Poverty, Years of Plenty. Ann Arbor: Institute for Social Research.

Duncan, Otis Dudley, Featherman, David L., and Duncan, Beverly. 1972. Socioeconomic Background and Achievement. New York: Seminar Books.

Durkheim, Emile. 1938. The Rules of Sociological Method. New York: Free Press. (Originally published 1895).

Durkheim, Emile. 1951. Suicide: A Study in Sociology. New York: Free Press. (Originally published 1897.)

Durkheim, Emile. 1961. The Elementary Forms of the Religious Life. London: Allen & Unwin. (Originally published 1915.)

Durning, Alan. 1989. "Poverty and the Environment: Reversing the Downward Spiral." Worldwatch Paper 92. Washington, D.C.: Worldwatch Institute.

Duster, Troy. 1995. "The Advantages of White Males." San Francisco Chronicle. January 19: A21.

Dworkin, Andrea. 1981. Pornography: Men Possessing Women. New York: Putnam.

Dwyer, Jeffrey W., and Seccombe, Karen . 1991. "Elder Care As Family Labor: The Influence of Gender and Family Position." Journal of Family Issues 12 (2) (June): 229–247.

Dye, Thomas R. 1983. Who's Running America? The Reagan Years. (3rd ed.) Englewood Cliffs, N.J.: Prentice-Hall.

Dye, Thomas R. 1986. Who's Running America: The Conservative Years. 4th ed. Englewood Cliffs, N.J.: Prentice-Hall.

Dye, Thomas, and Ziegler, Harmon. 1993. The Irony of Democracy, 9th ed. Duxbury, MA: Wadsworth.

Dyson, Michael Eric. 1993. Reflecting Black: African-American Cultural Criticism. Minneapolis: University of Minnesota Press.

Ebenstein, William. Today's Isms. Englewood Cliffs, N.J.: Prentice-Hall.

Eblen, Jack E. 1974. "New Estimates of the Vital Rates of the United States Black Population During the 19th Century." Demography 11 (2): 301–20.

Editors, The Harvard Law Review. 1989. "Family Law Issues Involving Children." Reprinted in Dolores Maggiore (ed.) Lesbians and Child Custody, pp. 157–194. New York: Garland.

Edwards, Bob. 1995. "No Laws Protect Women In Russia from Domestic Violence." Morning Edition, Segment #6, September 27. Washington, D.C.: National Public Radio.

Edwards, Richard. 1979. Contested Terrain. New York: Basic Books.

Eglit, Howard. 1985. "Age and the Law." In Robert Binstock and Ethel Shanas (eds.), Handbook of Aging and the Social Sciences. (2nd ed.) New York: Van Nostrand Reinhold.

Eisenhower, M. 1969. Commission Statement on Violence in Television Entertainment Programs. National Commission on the Causes and Prevention of Violence. Washington, D.C.: U.S. Government Printing Office.

Eisenstadt, S. N. 1985. "Macrosocietal Analysis—Background, Development, and Indications." In S. N. Eisenstadt and H. J. Helle (eds.), Macrosociological Theory: Perspectives on Sociological Theory. Newbury Park, Calif: Sage.

Elder, G. H., Jr. 1969. "Appearance and Education in Marriage Mobility." American Sociological Review 34 (August): 519–33.

Elder, G. H., Jr. 1974. Children of the Great Depression. Chicago: University of Chicago Press.

Elliott, Delbert S., and Ageton, Suzanne S. 1980. "Reconciling Race and Class Differences in Self-Reported Official Estimates of

Delinquency." American Sociological Review 45 (February): 95–110.

Elliott, Michael. 1994. "The Case for Kind Colonialism." Newsweek. July 18: 44.

Elliott, Michael. 1995. "The West At War." Newsweek. July 17: 24–27.

Ellis, David. 1992. "L.A. Lawless." Time. May 11: 26–29.

Ellison, Christopher. 1991. "Religious Involvement and Subjective Well-Being." Journal of Health and Social Behavior 32:80–99.

Ellison, Christopher. 1992. "Are Religious People Nice People? Evidence from the National Survey of Black Americans." Social Forces 71:411–430.

Ellison, Christopher G., and Sherkat, Darren E. 1993. "Conservative Protestantism and Support of Corporal Punishment." American Sociological Review 58:131–144.

Elmer-Dewitt, Philip. 1994. "A Royal Pain in the Wrist." Time. October 24: 60–61.

Elmer-Dewitt, Philip. 1995. "Snuff Porn on the Net." Time. February 20: 69.

Elshtain, Jean B. 1995. Democracy on Trial. New York: Basic Books.

Ember, Lois. 1994. "Minorities Still More Likely to Live Near Toxic Sites." Chemical & Engineering News 72 (36). September 5: 19.

Emerson, Richard M. 1962. "Power-Dependence Relations." American Sociological Review 27 (February): 31–41.

Engels, Friedrich. 1965. "Socialism: Utopian and Scientific." In Arthur P. Mendel (ed.), The Essential Works of Marxism. New York: Bantam Books. (Originally published 1880.)

Engels, Friedrich. 1972. The Origins of the Family, Private Property, and the State. (Eleanor Burke Leacock, trans.). New York: International Publishers. (Originally published 1884.)

England, Paula, and Dunn, Dana. 1988. "Evaluating Work and Comparative Worth." Annual Review of Sociology 14:227–48.

Ennis, James, and Schrauer, Richard. 1987. "Mobilizing Weak Support for Social Movements: The Role of Grievance, Efficacy, and Cost." Social Forces 62:390–409.

Entwisle, Doris R., Alexander, Karl L., and Olson, Linda Steffel. 1994. "The Gender Gap in Math: Its Possible Origins in Neighborhood Effects." American Sociological Review 59 (December): 822–838.

Erickson, Kai. 1986. "On Work and Alienation." American Sociological Review 51 (February): 1–8.

Eron, L. D. 1980. "Prescription for Reduction of Aggression." American Psychologist 35 (March): 244–52.

Espenshade, Thomas. 1990. "A Short History of U.S. Policy Toward Illegal Immigration." Population Today 18 (2): 6–8.

Esping-Andersen, Gosta, and von Kersbergen, Kees. 1992. "Contemporary Research on Social Democracy." pp. 187–208 in Judith Blake and John Hagen (eds.). Annual Review of Sociology, v. 18.

Etzioni, Amitai. 1968. The Active Society. New York: Free Press.

Etzioni, Amitai. 1996. "The Responsive Community: A Communitarian Perspective." American Sociological Review 61 (February): 1–11.

The Europa Yearbook. 1989. A World Survey. England: Europa Publications.

The Europa Yearbook. 1994. A World Survey: London: Europa Publications.

Exoo, Calvin F. 1994. The Politics of the Mass Media. St. Paul: West.

Faden, Ruth, and Kass, Nancy. 1988. "Health Insurance and AIDS." American Journal of Public Health 78: 437–39.

Falkenmark, Malin, and Widstrand, Carl. 1992. "Population and Water Resources: A Delicate Balance." Population Bulletin 47 (3) (November). Washington, D.C.: Population Reference Bureau, Inc.

Farkas, George, Grobe, Robert P., Sheehan, Daniel, and Shuan, Yuan. 1990. "Cultural Resources and School Success." American Sociological Review 55:127–142.

Farley, Reynolds. 1985. "Three Steps Forward and Two Back? Recent Changes in the Social and Economic Status of Blacks." In Richard Alba (ed.), Ethnicity and Race in the U.S.A.: Toward the Twenty-First Century. Boston: Routleldge & Kegan Paul.

Farley, Reynolds, Charlotte Steeh, and Maria Krysan. 1994. "Stereotypes and Segregation: Neighborhoods in the Detroit Area." American Journal of Sociology 100 (3) (November): 750–780.

Fee, Elizabeth, and Fox, Daniel M. eds. 1992. AIDS: The Making of a Chronic Disease. Berkeley: University of California Press.

Fejgin, Naomi. 1995. "Factors Contributing to the Academic Excellence of American Jewish and Asian Students." Sociology of Education 68 (January): 18–30.

Felson, Richard B. 1985. "Reflected Appraisal and the Development of Self." Social Psychology Quarterly 48 (1): 71–78.

Ferraro, Kenneth. 1989. "Reexamining the Double Jeopardy Health Thesis." Journal of Gerontology 44:514–17.

Ferree, Myra Marx. 1991. "The Gender Division of Labor in Two-Earner Marriages: Dimensions of Variability and Change." Journal of Family Issues 12 (2) (June): 158–180.

Festinger, Leon, Schachter, Stanley, and Back, Kurt. 1950. Social Pressure in Informal Groups. New York: Harper & Row.

Figueira-McDonough, Josefina. 1985. "Gender Differences in Informal Processing: A Look at Charge Bargaining and Sentence Reduction in Washington, D.C." Journal of Research in Crime and Delinquency 22 (May): 101–33.

Filipowski, Diane. 1992. "Acts of Hatred." Personnel Journal 71 (7) (July): 20.

Fine, Gary Alan. 1984. "Negotiated Orders and Organizational Cultures." Annual Review of Sociology 10:239–62.

Fine, Mark A. and Fine, David R. 1994. "An Examination and Evaluation of Recent Changes in Divorce Laws in Five Western Countries: The Critical Role of Values." Journal of Marriage and the Family 56 (2) (May): 249–264.

Fineman, Howard. 1995. "Race and Rage." Newsweek. April 3: 23–33.

Fineman, Howard. 1995. "Let the Party Begin." Newsweek. October 9: 37–40.

Fineman, Howard. 1995c. "The Rollback Begins." Newsweek. July

Fineman, Howard. 1995d. "Mediscare." Newsweek. September 18: 38–44.

Firebaugh, Glenn, and Davis, Kenneth. 1988. "Trends in Anti-Black Prejudice, 1972–84: Region and Cohort Effects." American Journal of Sociology 94:251–70.

Fischer, Claude S. 1976. The Urban Experience. San Diego, Calif.: Harcourt Brace Jovanovich.

Fischer, Claude S. 1979. "Urban-to-Rural Diffusion of Opinion in Contemporary America." American Journal of Sociology 84 (July): 151–59.

Fischer, Claude S. 1981. "The Public and Private Worlds of City Life." American Sociological Review 46 (June): 306–17.

Fischer, Claude S. 1982. To Dwell Among Friends: Personal Networks in Town and City. Chicago: University of Chicago Press.

Fischer, Claude S. 1995. "The Subcultural Theory of Urbanism: A Twentieth-Year Assessment." American Journal of Sociology 101 (3) (November): 543–577.

Fisher, A. D. 1987. "Alcoholism and Race: The Misapplication of Both Concepts to North American Indians. Canadian Sociological and Anthropological Review 24:80–95.

Fisher, Ian. 1994. "Prison Boot Camps Offer No Quick Fix." The New York Times. April 10: 11, 13.

Fishman, Joshua. 1985a. "Macrosociolinguistics and the Sociology of Language in the Early Eighties." Annual Review of Sociology 11:113–27.

Fishman, Joshua. 1985b. The Rise and Fall of the Ethnic Revival: Perspectives on Language and Ethnicity. Berlin: Mouton.

Fishman, Pamela M. 1978. "Interaction: The Work Women Do. Social Problems 25:397–406.

Fitzgerald, C. P. 1984. "Accomplishments of the Great Leap Forward." In Molly Joel Coye, John Livingston, and Jean Highland (eds.), China: Yesterday and Today. New York: Bantam Books.

Fitzpatrick, Kevin M., and Logan, John. 1985. "The Aging of the Suburbs, 1960–1980." American Sociological Review 50 (February): 106–17.

"Fixing Social Security." 1990. Newsweek, May 7, pp. 54ff.

Flanagan, William G. 1993. Contemporary Urban Sociology. London and New York: Cambridge University Press.

Flexner, Eleanor. 1972. Century of Struggle. New York: Atheneum.

Florman, Samuel. 1993. "Technology and the Tragic View." pp. 108–118 in Albert H. Teich, ed., Technology and the Future, 6th edition. New York: St. Martin's Press.

Forester, Tom. 1989. "The Myth of the Electronic Cottage." Computers and Society 19(2): 4–19.

Form, William. 1982. "Self-Employment Manual Workers: Petty Bourgeois or Working Class?" Social Forces 60 (June): 1050–70.

Form, William. 1985. Divided We Stand: Working Class Stratification in America. Urbana: University of Illinois Press.

Fox, Daniel M. 1995. "Revisiting the Politics of Art Museums." Society 32 (2) (January/February): 42–47.

Frankl, Razelle. 1984. "Television and Popular Religion: Changes in Church Offerings." In David Bromley and Anson Shupe (eds.), New Christian Politics. Macon, Ga.: Mercer University Press.

Fraser, Steven. 1995. The Bell Curve Wars: Race, Intelligence, and the Future of America. New York: Basic Books.

Freudenburg, William R. 1986. "The Density of Acquaintanceship: An Overlooked Variable in Community Research." American Journal of Sociology 92 (July): 27–63.

Freyka, Tomas. 1973. The Future of Population Growth: Alternative Paths to Equilibrium. New York: Wiley.

Friedan, Betty. 1995. "Beyond Gender." Newsweek. September 4: 30–32.

Friedman, Thomas L. 1996. "It's Tough to Get U.N. to Take a Stand Against Human Rights Abuses." New York Times. January 3.

Friedsam, H. J. 1965. "Competition." In Julius Gould and William L. Kolb (eds.), A Dictionary of the Social Sciences. New York: Free Press.

Frost, Jennifer J. and Forrest, Jacqueline Darroch. 1995. "Understanding the Impact of Effective Teenage Pregnancy Prevention Programs." Family Planning Perspectives 27 (5) (September/October): 188–195.

"Funds to Be Denied for Obscene Art." 1989. Lincoln Star.

Funk, Richard, and Willits, Fern. 1987. "College Attendance and Attitudinal Change: A Panel Study, 1970–81." Sociology of Education 60:224–31.

Furstenberg, Frank F., Jr., Brooks-Gunn, J., and Morgan, S. Philip. 1987. Adolescent Mothers in Later Life. Cambridge, England: Cambridge University Press.

"Future Organizational Trends of the ASA." 1989. Footnotes 17 (September): 1ff.

Gaes, Gerald G., and McGuire, William J. 1985. "Prison Violence: The Contribution of Crowding Versus Other Determinants of Prison Assault Rates." Journal of Research in Crime and Delinquency 22 (February): 41–65.

Gagnon, J. H. 1977. Human Sexualities. Glenview, Ill.: Scott, Foresman.

Gagnon, J. H., Roberts, E., and Greenblat, C. 1978. "Stability and Change in Rates of Marital Intercourse." Paper presented at the annual meetings of the International Academy of Sex Research, Toronto, Canada, August.

Gahr, William E. 1993. "Rural America: Blueprint for Tomorrow." The Annals of the American Academy of Political and Social Science 529 (September). Thousand Oaks, CA: Sage.

Gaines, Donna. 1991. Teenage Wasteland: Suburbia's Dead End Kids. New York: Pantheon Books.

Galen, Michele. 1994. "White, Male, and Worried." Business Week. January 31: 50–55.

Gallagher, James P. 1994. "Plans for Moscow Mosque Set Off Religious Turmoil." San Francisco Sunday Examiner and Chronicle. September 18: A9.

The Gallup Organization. 1995. "Major Gap in Priorities." The Gallup Organization Newsletter. April.

Gallup Poll. 1994. Public Opinion 1993. Wilmington, DE: Scholarly Resources Inc.

Gallup Poll Monthly. 1990. No. 297.

Gallup Poll Monthly. 1995, No. 353.

Gallup Report. 1984. Nos. 227/228.

Gallup Report. 1987. No. 259.

Gallup Report. 1989a. Nos. 282/283.

Gallup Report. 1989b. No. 285.

Gallup Report. 1989c. No. 286.

Gallup Report. 1989d. No. 288.

Gallup Report. 1989e. No. 289.

Gallup Report. 1992b.

Gamoran. Adam. 1992. "The Variable Effects of High School Tracking." American Sociological Review 57: 812–828.

Gamoran, Adam, and Mare, Robert. 1989. "Secondary School Tracking and Educational Inequality." American Journal of Sociology 94:1146–83.

Gamst, Frederick C. (ed.). 1995. Meanings of Work: Considerations for the Twenty-first Century. Albany, N.Y.: State University of New York Press.

Gans, Herbert J. 1962. The Urban Villagers. New York: Free Press.

Gans, Herbert. 1974. Popular Culture and High Culture. New York: Basic Books.

Gans, Herbert J. 1989. "Sociology in America: The Discipline and the Public." American Sociological Review 54:1–16.

Gans, Herbert J. 1992 [1971]. "The Uses of Poverty: The Poor Pay All." In Down To Earth Sociology, 6th Edition, James M. Henslin, editor. New York: Macmillan, Inc. The Free Press: 327–333.

Ganz, Alexander. 1985. "Where Has the Urban Crisis Gone? How Boston and Other Large Cities Have Stemmed Economic Decline." Urban Affairs Quarterly 20 (June): 449–68.

Garbarino, James. 1992. Toward A Sustainable Society: An Economic, Social and Environmental Agenda for Our Children's Future. Chicago: The Noble Press.

Gardner, Howard. 1983. Frames of Mind: The Theory of Multiple Intelligences. New York: Basic Books.
Gardner, L. I. 1972. "Deprivation Dwarfism." Scientific American 227 July: 76–82.
Gardner, LeGrande, and Shoemaker, Donald. 1989. "Social Bonds and Delinquency: A Comparative Analysis." Sociological Quarterly 30:481–500.
Gardner, Robert W., Robey, Bryant, and Smith, Peter C. 1985. "Asian Americans: Growth, Change, and Diversity." Population Bulletin 40 (October): 5–8.
Garfield, Richard M., and Taboada, Eugenio. 1986. "Health Services Reforms in Revolutionary Nicaragua." In Peter Rossett and John Vandermeer (eds.), Nicaragua: Unfinished Revolution. New York: Grove Press.
Garfinkel, H. 1963. "A Conception of, and Experiments with, 'Trust' as a Condition of Stable Concerted Actions." In O. J. Harvery (ed.), Motivation and Social Interaction. New York: Ronald Press.
Garfinkel, H. 1967. Studies in Ethnomethodology. Englewood Cliffs, N.J.: Prentice-Hall.
Garrett, William. 1987. "Religion, Law, and the Human Condition." Sociological Analysis 47 (Supplement): 1–34.
Gecas, Viktor. 1981. "Contents of Socialization." In Morris Rosenberg and Ralph H. Turner (eds.), Social Psychology: Sociological Perspectives. New York: Basic Books.
Gecas, Viktor. 1989. "The Social Psychology of Self-Efficiency." Annual Review of Sociology 15:291–316.
Gecas, Victor, and Schwalbe, Michael. 1983. "Beyond the Looking-Glass Self: Social Structure and Efficacy-Based Self-Esteem." Social Psychological Quarterly 46 (2): 77–88.
Geertz, Clifford. 1973. "Thick Description: Toward an Interpretive Theory of Culture." In Clifford Geertz, The Interpretation of Cultures: Selected Essays. New York: Basic Books.
Gelles, Richard J. 1994. "Ten Risk Factors." Newsweek. July 4: 29.
Gelles, Richard J., and Cornell, Claire. 1985. Intimate Violence in Families. Newbury Park, Calif.: Sage.
Gelles, Richard J., and Straus, Murray. 1988. Intimate Violence. New York: Simon & Schuster.
Genovese, Frank. 1988. "An Examination of Proposals for a U.S. Industrial Policy." American Journal of Economics and Sociology 47: 441–53.
"Geographic Polarization of Whites and Minorities in Large U.S. Cities: 1960–1980." 1986. Population Today 14 (March): 6–7.
Gerson, Kathleen. 1993. No Man's Land: Men's Changing Commitments to Family and Work. HarperCollins, Basic Books.
Gerth, H. H., and Mills, C. Wright (eds. and trans.). 1970. From Max Weber: Essays in Sociology. New York: Oxford University Press. (Originally published 1946.)
Gerzon, Mark. 1982. A Choice of Heroes: The Changing Faces of American Manhood. Boston: Houghton Mifflin.
Gibbs, Nancy. 1993. "Laying Down the Law." Time, August 23: 22–33.
Giddens, Anthony. 1984. The Constitution of Society. Cambridge, England: Polity Press.
Gill, Colen. 1985. Work, Unemployment, and the New Technology. Cambridge, England: Polity Press.
Gillespie, Ed. and Schellhas, Bob, eds. 1994. Contract with America: The Bold Plan by Rep. Newt Gingrich, Rep. Dick Army and the House Republicans to Change the Nation. Republican National Committee: Random House, Times Books.
Gingrich, Newt. 1995. "Cutting Cultural Funding: A Reply." Time. August 21: 70–71.
Ginsberg, Benjamin, and Weissburg, Robert. 1978. "Elections and the Mobilization of Popular Support." American Journal of Political Science 22: 31–55.
Girdner, Audrie, and Loftis, Anne. 1969. The Great Betrayal. London: Macmillan.
Glassner, Barry. 1989. "Fitness and the Postmodern Self." Journal of Health and Social Behavior 30:180–91.
Glenn, Norval. 1990. "Research on Marital Quality During the 1980s: A Critical Review." Journal of Marriage and the Family 52 (November).
Glenn, Norval D. 1994. "Television Watching, Newspaper Reading, and Cohort Differences in Verbal Ability." Sociology of Education 67 (July): 216–230.
Glenn, Norval D., and Supancic, Michael. 1984. "Social and Demographic Correlates of Divorce and Separation in the United States: An Updated Reconsideration." Journal of Marriage and the Family 46 (August): 563–75.
Glick, Paul C. 1984. "American Household Structure in Transition." Family Planning Perspectives 16 (5): 205–11.
Gober, Patricia. 1993. "Americans on the Move." Population Bulletin 48 (November): 1–39.
Goddard, Stephen B. 1994. Getting There: The Epic Struggle between Road and Rail in the American Century. New York: Basic Books.
Goffman, Erving. 1959. The Presentation of Self in Everyday Life. New York: Doubleday.
Goffman, Erving. 1961a. Asylums: Essays on the Social Situation of Mental Patients and Other Inmates. New York: Doubleday.
Goffman, Erving. 1961b. Encounters: Two Studies in the Sociology of Interaction. Indianapolis, Ind.: Bobbs-Merrill.
Goffman, Erving. 1963a. Behavior in Public Places: Notes on the Social Organization of Gatherings. New York: Free Press.
Goffman, Erving. 1963b. Stigmas: Notes on the Management of Spoiled Identity. Englewood Cliffs, N.J.: Prentice-Hall.
Goffman, Erving. 1967. Interaction Ritual: Essays on Face-to-Face Behavior. New York: Doubleday.
Goffman, Erving. 1971. "The Insanity of Place." In Erving Goffman, Relations in Public. New York: Harper & Row.
Goffman, Erving. 1974a. Gender Advertisements. New York: Harper & Row.
Goffman, Erving. 1974b. Frame Analysis: An Essay on the Organization of Experience. New York: Harper & Row.
Goffman, Erving. 1983. "The Interaction Order." American Sociological Review 48 (February): 1–17.
Golden, Tim. 1994. "Mexico's New Leader Calls for the Overhaul of the Justice System." The New York Times, December 7: A4.
Goldscheider, Frances and Goldscheider, Calvin. 1989. "Family Structure and Conflict: Nest-Leaving Expectations of Young Adults and Their Parents." Journal of Marriage and the Family 51:87–97.
Goldscheider, Frances and Goldscheider, Calvin. 1994. "Leaving and Returning Home in 20th Century America." Population Bulletin 48 (4) (March). Washington, D.C.: Population Reference Bureau, Inc.
Goldstein, Michael S. 1992. The Health Movement: Promoting Fitness in America. New York: Twayne Publishers.
Goliber, Thomas. 1989. "Africa's Expanding Population: Old Problems, New Policies." Population Bulletin 44 (3): 1–50.
Goode, Erich. 1989. Drugs in American Society. New York: Knopf.
Goode, William. 1959. "The Theoretical Importance of Love." American Sociological Review 24:37–48.
Goodgame, Dan. 1995. "This Time, Perot Wants a Party." Time. October 9: 52–54.

"GOP Sweepstakes." 1995. Associated Press, in the Bismarck Tribune. August 13 8A.

Gordon, Barnard K. 1993. "Japan's Universities: US Professor Recounts Surprising Experiences at Kobe." Far Eastern Economic Review 156 (2) (January 14): 34–36.

Gordon, Diana R. 1990. The Justice Juggernaut: Fighting Street Crime, Controlling Citizens. New Brunswick and London: Rutgers University Press.

Gordon, Myles. 1993. "Is There an Islamic Threat?" Scholastic Update, October 22, p. 11.

Gorman, Christine. 1996. "Are Animal Organs Safe for People?" Time. January 15: 58–59.

Gottdiener, Mark. 1985. "Whatever Happened to the Urban Crisis." Urban Affairs Quarterly 20 (June): 421–27.

Gottdiener, Mark, and Feagin, Joe. 1988. "The Paradigm Shift in Urban Sociology." Urban Affairs Quarterly 24:163–87.

Gottlieb, Benjamin H. 1981. "Social Networks and Social Support in Community Mental Health." In B. H. Gottlieb (ed.), Social Networks and Social Support. Vol. 4. Sage Series in Community Mental Health. Newbury Park, Calif.: Sage.

Goudy, Willis J., Powers, Edward A., Keith, Patricia, and Reger, Richard A. 1980. "Changes in Attitude Toward Retirement: Evidence from a Panel Study of Older Males." Journal of Gerontology 35:942–48.

Gould, Roger V. 1991. "Multiple Networks and Mobilization in the Paris Commune, 1871." American Sociological Review 56:716–729.

Gouldner, Alvin. 1960. "The Norm of Reciprocity." American Sociological Review 25 (February): 161–178.

Gove, Walter, Ortega, Suzanne, and Style, Carolyn. 1989. "The Maturational and Role Perspectives on Aging and Self Through the Adult Years: An Empirical Evaluation." American Journal of Sociology 94:1117–45.

Goya, Susan. 1993. "The Secret of Japanese Education." Phi Delta Kappan 75 (2) (October): 126–130.

Grady, William. 1993. "FCC Member: Electronic Highway to Bypass Poor." Chicago Tribune, November 6: 1.

Granovetter, Mark. 1973. "The Strength of Weak Ties." American Journal of Sociology 78 (May): 1360–80.

Greeley, Andrew M. 1979. "Ethnic Variations in Religious Commitment." In Robert Wuthnow (ed.), The Religious Dimension: New Directions in Quantitative Research. Orlando, Fla.: Academic Press.

Greenberg, David F. 1985. "Age, Crime, and Social Explanation." American Journal of Sociology, 91 (July): 1–21.

Greenberg, Michael R. 1989. "Black Male Cancer and American Urban Health Policy." Journal of Urban Affairs 11:113–30.

Greenblat, Cathy Stein. 1983. "The Salience of Sexuality in the Early Years of Marriage." Journal of Marriage and the Family 45 (May): 289–300.

Greenfield, Meg. 1995 "The Cultural Commissars." Newsweek. December 18: 76.

Greenfield, Meg. 1995b. "The Tyranny of 'the Spectrum'." Newsweek. September 25: 96.

Greenhalgh, Susan, Chuzhu, Zhu, and Nan, Li. 1994. "Restraining Population Growth in Three Chinese Villages, 1988–93." Population and Development Review 20 (2) (June): 365–395.

Griffith, Jeanne, Frase, Mary, and Ralph, John. 1989. "American Education: The Challenge of Change." Population Bulletin 44:1–50.

Grimes, Michael D. 1989. "Class and Attitudes Toward Structural Inequalities: An Empirical Comparison of Key Variables in Neo- and Post-Marxist Scholarship." Sociological Quarterly 30:441–63.

Gross, Edward. 1958. Work and Society. New York: Crowell.

Gross, Jane. 1994. "After a Ruling, Hawaii Weighs Gay Marriages." The New York Times. April 25: A1, C12.

Groth, Paul. 1994. Living Downtown: The History of Residential Hotels in the United States. Berkeley, CA: University of California Press.

"Group Says Supermarkets Can Make Profits in Inner City." 1996. Associated Press. March 5.

Guimond, Serge, Begin, Guy, and Palmer, Douglas. 1989. "Education and Causal Attributions: The Development of Person-Blame and System-Blame Ideology." Social Psychology Quarterly 52:126–40.

Gurney, Joan N., and Tierney, Kathleen J. 1982. "Relative Deprivation and Social Movements: A Critical Look at Twenty Years of Theory and Research." Sociological Quarterly 23 (Winter): 33–47.

Guterbock, Thomas M., and London, Bruce. 1983. "Race, Political Orientation, and Participation: An Empirical Test of Four Competing Theories. American Sociological Review 48 (August): 439–53.

Guy, Gregory. 1989. "International Perspectives on Linguistic Diversity and Language Rights." Language Problems and Language Planning 13:45–53.

Haas, Linda. 1990. "Gender Equality and Social Policy: Implications of a Study of Parental Leave in Sweden." Journal of Family Issues 11 (4) (December): 401–423.

Hadaway, C. Kirk, Marler, Penny Long, and Chaves, Mark. 1993. "What Polls Don't Show: A Closer Look at U.S. Church Attendance." American Sociological Review 58:741–752.

Hadden, Jeffrey K., and Shupe, Anson. 1988. Televangelism: Power and Politics on God's Frontier. New York: Henry Holt & Co.

Hagan, John, Gillis, A. R., and Simpson, John. 1985. "The Class Structure of Gender and Delinquency: Toward a Power-Control Theory of Common Delinquent Behavior." American Journal of Sociology 90 (May): 1151–78.

Hagestad, Gunhild O., and Neugarten, Bernice L. 1985. "Age and the Life Course." In Robert Binstock and Ethel Shanas (eds.), Handbook of Aging and the Social Sciences, (2nd ed.) New York: Van Nostrand Reinhold.

Hainsworth. Philip. 1986. Baha'i Focus on Peace. London: Baha'i Publishing Trust.

Halaby Charles N. 1986. "Worker Attachment and Workplace Authority." American Sociological Review 51 (October): 634–49.

Hall, E. 1969. The Hidden Dimension. New York: Doubleday.

Hall, John R. 1987. Gone from the Promised Land: Jonestown in American Cultural History. New Brunswick, N.J.: Transaction.

Halle, David. 1984. America's Working Man: Work, Home, and Politics Among Blue-Collar Property Owners. Chicago: University of Chicago Press.

Hallinan, M. 1988. "Equality of Educational Opportunity." Annual Review of Sociology 14:249–68.

Hallinan, Maureen T. 1994. "Tracking: From Theory To Practice." Sociology of Education 67 (2) (April): 79–84.

Hallinan, Maureen T., and Sorenson, Aage B. 1986. "Student Characteristics and Assignment to Ability Groups: Two Conceptual Formulations." Sociological Quarterly 27 (1): 1–13.

Hamilton, Malcolm B. 1995. The Sociology of Religion. London and New York: Routledge.

Hammer, Joshua. 1994. "Death Watch." Newsweek. August 8: 14–17.
Hammer, Joshua. 1995a. "A Voice Silenced." Newsweek. November 20: 64.
Hammer, Joshua. 1995b. "The Making of a Legend." Newsweek. December 18: 47.
Hammond, Ruth. 1994. "The Littlest Workers: Third World Economies Depend on Child Labor to Keep Wages Low." Utne Reader 63 (May–June): 20–22.
"Hand Scans." 1995. Newsweek. September 18: 14.
Hanks, Michael. 1981. "Youth, Voluntary Associations and Political Socialization." Social Forces 60 (September): 211–23.
Hapgood, Fred. 1994. "Notes From the Underground." Atlantic Monthly, August: 43–48.
Hardin, Clifford. 1968. "The Tragedy of the Commons." Science 162:1243–48.
Harlow, H. F., and Harlow, M. K. 1966. "Learning to Live." Scientific American pp. 244–72.
Harris Survey. 1989a. April 9.
Harris Survey. 1989b. October 29.
Harris, Chauncey D., and Ullman, Edward L. 1945. "The Nature of Cities." Annals of the American Association of Political and Social Science 242 (November): 7–17.
Harris, Louis, and Associates. 1975. The Myth and Reality of Aging in America. Washington, D.C.: National Council on Aging.
Harris, Othello. 1994. "Race, Sport, and Social Support." Sociology of Sport Journal 11 (1): 40–50.
Hartman, Heidi. 1981. "The Family as the Locus of Gender, Class and Political Struggles: The Example of Housework." Signs 6 (3): 366–94.
Hassin, Jeanette. 1994. "Living a Responsible Life: The Impact of AIDS on Social Identity of Intravenous Drug Users." Social Science and Medicine 38 (3): 391–400.
Hatcher, John. 1977. Plagues, Population, and the English Economy, 1348–1530. London: Macmillan.
Haub, Carl. 1991. "South Korea's Low Fertility Raises European-Style Issues." Population Today 19 (October): 3.
Haub, Carl. 1994a. "Russia's New Revolution: A Demographic Baby Bust." Population Today 22 (4) (April): 1–2.
Haub, Carl. 1994b. "Population Change in the Former Soviet Republics." Population Bulletin 48 (4) (December). Washington, D.C. Population Reference Bureau, Inc.
Haugen, Steven, and Mellor, Earl. 1990. "Estimating the Number of Minimum Wage Workers." Monthly Labor Review, January,
Hawes, Joseph M. 1991. The Children's Rights Movement: A history of Advocacy and Protection. Boston: Twayne Publishers.
Hayward, Mark, Grady, William, and McLaughlin, Steven. 1988. "Changes in the Retirement Process Among Older Men in the United States: 1972–1980." Demography 25:371–86.
Hayward, Mark, Grady, William, Hardy, Melissa, and Sommers, David. 1989. "Occupational Influences on Retirement, Disability, and Death." Demography 26:393–409.
Hechter, Michael. 1987. Principles of Group Solidarity. Berkeley: University of California Press.
Heclo, Hugh, and Madson, Henrik. 1987. Policy and Politics in Sweden: Principled Pragmatism. Philadelphia: Temple University Press.
Hedges, Larry V. and Nowell, Amy. 1995. "Sex Differences in Mental Test Scores, Variability, and Numbers of High-scoring Individuals." Science 269 (5220) (July 7): 41–46.
Heidensohn, Frances. 1985. Women and Crime: The Life of the Female Offender. New York: New York University Press.
Hendricks, Jon, and Hendricks, C. Davis. 1981. Aging in Mass Society: Myths and Realities. (2nd ed.) Cambridge. Mass.: Winthrop.
Hengesh, Donald J. 1991. "Think of Boot Camps as a Foundation for Change, Not an Instant Cure." Corrections Today 53 (October): 106.
Henley, Nancy M. 1977. Body Politics: Power, Sex and Nonverbal Communication. Englewood Cliffs. N.J.: Prentice-Hall.
Henley, Nancy M. 1985. "Psychology and Gender." Signs: Journal of Women in Culture and Society 11: 101–119.
Henslin, James M. 1994. "America's Homeless." Social Problems, Third Edition. Englewood Cliffs, New Jersey: Prentice Hall. Pg. 258.
Hentoff, Nat. 1993. "No: Equality among Victims." ABA Journal 79 (May): 45.
Herek, Gregory M. 1990. "The Context of Anti-Gay Violence." Journal of Interpersonal Violence 5 (3) (September): 316–333.
Herrnstein, Richard, and Murray, Charles. 1994. The Bell Curve: Intelligence and Class Structure in American Life. New York: Free Press.
Hess, Beth. 1985. "Aging Policies and Old Women: The Hidden Agenda." In Alice Rossi (ed.), Gender and the Life Course. Hawthorne, New York: Aldine.
Heyl, Barbara. 1979. The Madam as Entrepreneur: Career Management in House Prostitution. New Brunswick, N.J.: Transaction.
Heyns, Barbara. 1978. Summer Learning and the Effects of Schooling. Orlando, Fla.: Academic Press.
Hickok, Kathleen. 1981. "The Spinster in Victorian England: Changing Attitudes in Popular Poetry." Journal of Popular Culture 15 (3): 118–31.
Himes, Norman E. 1936. The Medical History of Contraception. Baltimore, Md.: Johns Hopkins University Press.
Hindelang, Michael J., Hirschi, Travis, and Weis, Joseph. 1981. Measuring Delinquency. Newbury Park, Calif.: Sage.
"Hiring Discrimination Blamed on Immigration Reform Law." 1990. Lincoln Star, p. 3.
Hirsch, Arnold R. 1983. Making the Second Ghetto: Race and Housing in Chicago, 1940–1960. New York: Cambridge University Press.
Hirschi, Travis. 1969. Causes of Delinquency. Berkeley and Los Angeles: University of California Press.
Hirschi, Travis, and Gottfredson, Michael. 1983. "Age and the Explanation of Crime." American Journal of Sociology 89 (November): 552–84.
Hochschild, Arlie R. 1985. The Managed Heart: The Commercialization of Human Feeling. Berkeley: University of California Press.
Hochschild, Jennifer. 1981. What's Fair? American Beliefs About Distributive Justice. Cambridge, Mass.: Harvard University Press.
Hodge, Robert W., Siegel, Paul, and Rossi, Peter. 1964. "Occupational Prestige in the United States, 1925–63." American Journal of Sociology 70 (November): 286–302.
Hodge, Robert W., Treiman, Donald J., and Rossi, Peter. 1966. "A Comparative Study of Occupational Prestige." In Reinhard Bendix and Seymour Martin Lipset (eds.), Class, Status, and Power. (2nd ed.) New York: Free Press.
Hoess, Rudolf. 1960. Commandant of Auschwitz, translated by Constantine Fitzgibbon. Cleveland, Ohio: The World Publishing Company.
Hoffman, Saul, and Duncan, Greg. 1988. "What Are the Economic Consequences of Divorce?" Demography 25:641–45.

Hogan, D. P. 1981. Transitions and Social Change: The Early Lives of American Men. Orlando, Fla.: Academic Press.

Hogan, Dennis P., and Astone, Nan Marie. 1986. "The Transition to Adulthood." Annual Review of Sociology 12:109–30.

Hogan, Dennis P., Eggebeen, David J., and Clogg, Clifford C. 1993. "The Structure of Intergenerational Exchanges in American Families." American Journal of Sociology 98:1428–1458.

Hoge, Dean R. and DeZulueta, Ernesto. 1985. "Salience as a Condition for Various Social Consequences of Religious Commitment." Journal for the Scientific Study of Religion 24:21–38.

Holden, Karen, Burkhauser, Richard, and Feaster, Daniel. 1988. "The Timing of Falls into Poverty After Retirement and Widowhood." Demography 25:405–14.

Hollander, Paul. 1982. "Research on Marxist Societies: The Relationship Between Theory and Practice." Annual Review of Sociology 8:319–51.

Holloway, Marguerite. 1993. "Hard Times: Occupational Injuries among Children Are Increasing." Scientific American 269, 4 (October): 14–16.

Holloway, Marguerite. 1994. "Trends in Women's Health: A Global View." Scientific American. August: 76–83.

Homans, George. 1950. The Human Group. San Diego, Calif.: Harcourt Brace Jovanovich.

Hooks, Gregory. 1984. "The Policy Response to Factory Closings: A Comparison of the United States, Sweden, and France." Annals of the American Academy of Political and Social Science 475:110–24.

Hooks, Gregory. 1990. "The Rise of the Pentagon and U.S. State Building: The Defense Program as Industry Policy." American Journal of Sociology 96:358–404.

Hoover, Stewart M. 1990. "Ten Myths about Religious Broadcasting." pp. 23–39 in Robert Abelman and Stewart M. Hoover (eds.). Religious Television: Controversies and Conclusions. Norwood, N.J.: Ablex Publishing Corporation.

Hornblower, Margot. 1995. "Putting Tongues in Check." Time. October 9: 40–50.

Horton, Michael. 1990. "The TV Gospel." pp. 123–150 in Michael Horton (ed.). Agony of Deceit: What Some TV Preachers Are Really Teaching. Chicago: Moody Press.

Horwitz, Allan V. 1984. "The Economy and Social Pathology." Annual Review of Sociology 10:95–119.

Hostetler, John. 1963. Amish Society. Baltimore, Md.: Johns Hopkins University Press.

Houston, Jeanne Wakatsuke, and Houston, James D. 1973. Farewell to Manzanar. Boston: Houghton Mifflin.

"How Many People Can the World Feed?" 1985. Population Today 13 (January): 1, 8.

"How We're Changing: Demographic State of the Nation 1995." 1994. Current Population Reports, Series P-23, No. 188. Washington, D.C.: U.S. Government Printing Office.

Howery, Carla. 1983. "Sociologists Shaping Public Policy: Two Profiles." Footnotes 11 (August): 12.

Hoyt, Danny, and Babchuk, Nicholas. 1983. "Adult Kinship Networks: The Selective Formation of Intimate Ties." Social Forces 62 (September): 84–101.

Huber, Joan, and Form, William H. 1973. Income and Ideology: An Analysis of the American Political Formula. New York: Free Press.

Huber, Joan, and Spitze, Glenna. 1983. Sex Stratification: Children, Housework, and Jobs. Orlando, Fla.: Academic Press.

Hudson, Robert B., and Strate, John. 1985. "Aging and Political Systems." In Robert H. Binstock and Ethel Shanas (eds.). Handbook of Aging and the Social Sciences (2nd ed.) New York: Van Nostrand Reinhold.

Huff-Corzine, Lin, Corzine, Jay, and Moore, David. 1986. "Southern Exposure: Deciphering the South's Influence on Homicide Rates." Social Forces 64:906–24.

Hughes, Robert. 1993. Culture of Complaint: The Fraying of America. New York: Oxford University Press.

Hull, John D. 1994. "A Daughter's Last Gift," Time. September 5: 45.

Humpreys, Laud. 1970. Tearoom Trade: Impersonal Sex in Public Places. Hawthorne, N.Y.: Aldine.

Hurlbert, Jeanne S. 1989. "The Southern Region: A Test of the Hypothesis of Cultural Distinctiveness." Sociological Quarterly 30:245–66.

Hyde, Janet S., Fennema, Elizabeth, and Lamon, Susan. 1990. "Gender Differences in Mathematics Performance: A Meta-analysis." Psychological Bulletin 106: 139–155.

Iannaccone, Laurence R. 1994. "Why Strict Churches Are Strong." American Journal of Sociology 99 (5) (March): 1180–1211.

Idelson, Holly. 1993. "House Hate Crimes Measure Would Increase Sentences." Congressional Quarterly Weekly Report 51 (38) (September 25): 2563.

"Income Gap Fast Becoming a Gulf, Census Reports." 1996. New York Times. June 20.

Ingoldsby, Bron B. and Smith, Suzanna. 1995. Families in Multicultural Perspective. New York: The Guilford Press.

Inkeles, Alex, and Smith, David H. 1974. Becoming Modern: Individual Change in Six Developing Countries. Cambridge, Mass.: Harvard University Press.

Invararity, James, and McCarthy, Daniel. 1988. "Punishment and Social Structure Revisited: Unemployment and Imprisonment in the United States." Sociological Quarterly 29:263–79.

Irwin, Julie. 1995. "Zoning Law Battles Reflect Culture Clashes." The Cincinnati Enquirer. June 8: C12.

Isikoff, Michael. 1995. "To Be or Not To Be: In Newt's Congress, the Culture Wars May Be a Fight to the Finish." Newsweek. January 23: 64–67.

Jacobs, David. 1988. "Corporate Economic Power and the State: A Longitudinal Assessment of Two Explanations." American Journal of Sociology 93:852–881.

Jacobs, James B. 1993. "Should Hate Be a Crime?" The Public Interest 113 (Fall): 113–125.

Jacobs, Jerry. 1989. "Long-Term Trends in Occupational Segregation." American Journal of Sociology 95:160–73.

Jacoby, Russell, and Glaubeiman, Naomi (eds.). 1995. The Bell Curve Debate: History, Documents, Opinions. New York: Random House/Time Books.

James, David R. 1989. "City Limits on Racial Equality." American Sociological Review 54:963–85.

Janis, Irving. 1982. Groupthink: Psychological Studies of Policy Decisions and Fiascoes. Boston: Houghton Mifflin.

Jasper, James M. and Nelkin, Dorothy. 1992. The Animal Rights Crusade: The Growth of a Moral Protest. New York: Free Press.

Jeffe, Douglas, and Jeffe, Sherry. 1989. "Gun Control: A Silent Majority Raises Its Voice." Public Opinion, May/June, p. 9ff.

Jencks, Christopher, Smith, M., Acland, H., Bane, J. J., Cohen D., Gintis, H., Heyns, B., and Michelson, S. 1972. Inequality: A Reassessment of the Effect of Family and Schooling in America. New York: Basic Books.

Jenkins, J. Craig, and Brent, Barbara. 1989. "Social Protest, Hegemonic Competition, and Social Reform." American Sociological Review 54:891–909.

Jenkins, J. Craig, and Eckert, Craig M. 1986. "Channeling Black Insurgency: Elite Patronage and Professional Social Movement Organizations in the Development of the Black Movement." American Sociological Review 51 (December): 812–29.

Jessor, R., and Jessor, S. 1977. Problem Behavior and Psychosocial Development: A Longitudinal Study of Youth. Orlando, Fla.: Academic Press.

Jindra, Michael. 1994. "Star Trek Fandom as a Religious Phenomenon." Sociology of Religion 55 (1): 27–51.

Jiobu, Robert. 1988. "Ethnic Hegemony and the Japanese of California." American Sociological Review 53:353–67.

Johansen, Harley, and Fuguitt, Glenn. 1984. The Changing Rural Village in America: Demographic and Economic Trends Since 1950. Cambridge, Mass.: Ballinger.

Johnson, Benton. 1957. "A Critical Appraisal of the Church Sect Typology." American Sociological Review 22 (1): 88–92.

Johnson, Dirk. 1994. "Economies Come to Life on Indian Reservations." The New York Times. July 3: 1Y, 10Y–11Y.

Johnson, Kenneth. 1989. "Recent Population Redistribution Trends in Nonmetropolitan America." Rural Sociology 54:301–26.

Johnson, Richard E. 1980. "Social Class and Delinquent Behavior: A New Test." Criminology 18 (1): 86–93.

Johnson, Robert C. 1993. "Science, Technology, and Black Community Development." pp. 265–282 in Albert H. Teich, ed. Technology and the Future, 6th edition. New York: St. Martin's Press.

Johnston, Hank, and Klandermans, Bert (eds.). 1995. Social Movements and Culture. Minneapolis, MN: University of Minnesota Press.

Jones Jr., Malcolm. 1994. "Doctor to the Hopeless." Newsweek. August 22: 60.

Jones, Elaine R. 1995. "The Great Debate over Affirmative Action." San Francisco Chronicle. January 19: A21.

Jones, James H. 1981. Bad Blood: The Tuskegee Syphilis Experiment. New York: Free Press.

Kaa, Dirk. 1987. "Europe's Second Demographic Transition." Population Bulletin 42 (March): 1–50.

Kahl, Anne, and Clark, Donald. 1986. "Employment in Health Services." Monthly Labor Review 109 (8): 17–37.

Kalab, Kathleen. 1987. "Student Vocabularies of Motive: Accounts for Absence." Symbolic Interaction 10:71–83.

Kalb, Loretta. 1996. "Beautifying Blight." Sacramento Bee. February 4: H1.

Kalish, Susan. 1994. "Rising Costs of Raising Children." Population Today 22 (7) (July/August): 4–5.

Kalish, Susan. 1994a. "Culturally Sensitive Family Planning: Bangladesh Story Suggests It Can Reduce Family Size." Population Today 22 (February): 5.

Kalish, Susan, 1994b. "International Migration: New Findings on Magnitude, Importance." Population Today 22 (March): 1–2.

Kalish, Susan. 1995. "Multiracial Births Increase as U.S. Ponders Racial Definitions." Population Today 23 (4) (April): 1–2.

Kanet, Roger. 1989. "New Thinking and New Foreign Policy Under Gorbachev." Political Science and Politics 22:215–24.

Kanter, Rosabeth Moss. 1977. Men and Women of the Corporation. New York: Basic Books.

Kantrowitz, Barbara and Rosenberg, Debra. 1994. "Redy, Teddy? You're Online." Newsweek. September 12: 60–61.

Kaplan, Howard. 1989. "Methodological Problems in the Study of Psychosocial Influences on the AIDS Process." Social Science and Medicine 29:277–92.

Kaplan, Howard B., Martin, Steven S., and Johnson, Robert J. 1986. "Self-Rejection and the Explanation of Deviance: Specification of the Structure Among Latent Constructs." American Journal of Sociology 92 (September): 384–411.

Karliner, Joshua, Faber, Daniel, and Rice, Robert. 1986. "An Environmental Perspective." In Peter Rosset and John Vandermeer (eds.), Nicaragua: Unfinished Revolution. New York: Grove Press.

Karp, David A., Stone, Gregory P., and Yoels, William C. 1991. Being Urban: A Sociology of City Life, 2nd ed. New York: Praeger.

Katel, Peter. 1994. "The Bust in Boot Camps." Newsweek 123 (February 21): 26.

Katz, Michael. 1987. Reconstructing American Education. Cambridge, Mass.: Harvard University Press.

Katz, Neil. 1989. "Conflict Resolution and Peace Studies." The Annals 504 (July): 14–21.

Katznelson, Ira. 1992. Marxism and the City. Oxford: Clarendon Press.

Kay, Jane. 1994. "Still Trying to Repair Nature." San Francisco Examiner. September 18: A-4.

Kazancigil, Ali. 1993. "UNESCO's International Governmental Social Science Program." Footnotes 21 (1) (January): 9.

Keating, William Dennis. 1994. The Suburban Racial Dilemma: Housing and Neighborhoods. Philadelphia: Temple University Press.

Kelly, Barbara M. (ed.). 1989. Suburbia Re-examined. New York: Greenwood Press.

Kempton, Murray. 1992. "A New Colonialism." Newsday, July 7: 36.

Kendall, Patricia, and Reader, George. 1988. "Innovations in Medical Education of the 1950s Contrasted with Those of the 1970s and 1980s." Journal of Health and Social Behavior 29:279–93.

Kennan, George. 1989. "After the Cold War." New York Times Magazine, February 5, 1989, pp. 32ff.

Kent, Debra. 1990. "Offense Intended." Seventeen. April: 90, 92.

"Kenya." 1989. Population Today 17 (10): 5.

Kephart, William M. 1983 and 1987. Extraordinary Groups: The Sociology of Unconventional Life-Styles. (2nd and 3rd ed.) New York: St. Martin's Press.

Keppeler, Victor E., Blumberg, Mark, and Potter, Gary W. 1993. The Mythology of Crime and Criminal Justice. Prospect Heights, IL: Waveland Press.

Kerbo, Harold R. 1991. Social Stratification and Inequality: Class Conflict in Historical and Comparative Perspective, 2nd edition. New York: McGraw-Hill.

Kerckhoff, Alan C., and Davis, Keith E. 1962. "Value Consensus and Need Complementarity in Mate Selection." American Sociological Review 27 (June): 295–303.

Kerr, Sarah. 1994. "The Mystery of Mexican Politics." The New York Review of Books. November 17: 29.

Kessler, Ronald C., and McLeod, Jane. 1984. "Sex Differences in Vulnerability to Undesirable Life Events." American Sociological Review 49 (October): 620–31.

Kessler, Ronald C., Turner, J. Blake, and House, James. 1989. "Unemployment, Reemployment, and Emotional Functioning in a Community Sample." American Sociological Review 54:648–57.

Keyfitz, Nathan. 1987. "The Family that Does not Reproduce Itself." In Kingsley Davis, Mikhail Bernstam, and Rita Ricardo-Campbell, (eds.), Below Replacement Fertility in Industrial Societies: Causes, Consequences, Policies. Cambridge, England: Cambridge University Press.

Kielbowicz, Richard B., and Scherer, Clifford. 1986. "The Role of the Press in the Dynamics of Social Movements." Research in Social Movements, Conflicts, and Change 9:71–96.

Kilborn, Peter T. 1994. "New York Police Force Lagging in Recruitment of Black Officers." The New York Times, July 17:

Kilbourne, Jean. 1994. "'Gender Bender' Ads: Same Old Sexism." The New York Times, May 15: F-13.

Kilner, John. 1988. "Selecting Patients When Resources Are Limited: A Study of U.S. Medical Directors of Kidney Dialysis and Transplantation Facilities." American Journal of Public Health 78 (2): 144–47.

Kimball, Roger. 1992. "The Periphery V. the Center: The MLA in Chicago." pp. 61–84 in Paul Berman (ed.). Debating P.C.: The Controversy over Political Correctness on College Campuses. New York: Bantam Doubleday Dell Publishing Group, Inc.

Kindel, Sharen. 1995. "Keeping Economic Priorities Straight: An Interview with Alice Tepper Marlin." Hemispheres. November: 25–28.

Kinsella, Kevin, and Taeuber, Cynthia M. 1993. An Aging World II. International Population Reports P95/92-3. U.S. Department of Commerce. Washington, D.C.: U.S. Government Printing Office.

Kinsey, A. C. 1948. Sexual Behavior in the Human Male. Philadelphia: Saunders.

Kinsey, A. C. 1953. Sexual Behavior in the Human Female. Philadelphia: Saunders.

Kinzer, Stephen. 1993. "In Retreat, Europe's Neo-Nazis May Be More Perilous." The New York Times, December 12: A5.

Kitson, Gay, and Sussman, Marvin. 1982. "Marital Complaints, Demographic Characteristics, and Symptoms of Mental Distress in Divorce." Journal of Marriage and the Family 44:87–101.

Klandermas, Bert. 1984. "Mobilization and Participation: Social-Pyschological Expansion of Resource Mobilization Theory." American Sociological Review 49 (October): 583–600.

Kleck, Gary. 1981. "Racial Discrimination in Criminal Sentencing: A Critical Evaluation of the Evidence with Additional Evidence on the Death Penalty." American Sociological Review 46 (December): 783–805.

Kleck, Gary. 1982. "On the Use of Self-Report Data to Determine the Class Distribution of Criminal and Delinquent Behavior." American Sociological Review 47 (June): 427–33.

Klein, Joe. 1994. "The Legacy of Summerton." Newsweek (May 16): 26–30.

Klepper, Steven, and Nagin, Daniel. 1989. "The Deterrent Effect of Perceived Certainty and Severity of Punishment Revisited." Criminology 27:721–46.

Kluegel, James R., and Smith, Eliot R. 1983. "Affirmative Action Attitudes: Effects of Self-Interest, Racial Affect, and Stratification Beliefs on Whites' Views." Social Forces 61 (March): 170–81.

Knoke, David. 1981. "Commitment and Detachment in Voluntary Associations." American Sociological Review 46 (2): 141–58.

Knox, Paul L. (Ed.). 1994. The Restless Urban Landscape. Englewood Cliffs, N.J.: Prentice Hall.

Knox, Paul. 1995. Urban Social Geography: An Introduction, 3rd edition. New York: John Wiley & Sons, Inc.

Koblik, Steven. 1975. Sweden's Development from Poverty to Affluence 1750–1970. Minneapolis, MN: University of Minnesota Press.

Kochanek, Kenneth D., and Hudson, Bettie L. 1995. "Advance Report of Final Mortality Statistics, 1992." Monthly Vital Statistics Report 43 (6) (March 22). U.S. Department of Health and Human Services, National Center for Health Statistics.

Kogamawa, Joy. 1981. Obason. Toronto: Lester and Orpen Dennys.

Kohn, Melvin, and Schooler, Carmi, and Associates. 1983. Work and Personality: An Inquiry into the Impact of Social Stratification. Norwood, N.J.: Ablex.

Kohn, Robert L. 1972. "The Meaning of Work: Interpretation and Proposals for Measurement." In A. Campbell and P. Converse (eds.), The Human Meaning of Social Change. New York: Basic Books.

Kolbert, Elizabeth. 1995. "Americans Despair of Popular Culture." The New York Times. August 20: H1, H23.

Kollock, Peter, Blumstein, Philip, and Schwartz, Pepper. 1985. "Sex and Power in Interaction: Conversational Privileges and Duties." American Sociological Review 50 (February): 34–46.

Konig, René. 1968. "Auguste Comte." In David J. Sills (ed.), International Encyclopedia of the Social Sciences. Vol. 3. New York: Macmillan and Free Press.

Korpi, Walter. 1989. "Power, Politics, and State Autonomy in the Development of Social Citizenship." American Sociological Review 54: 309–28.

Korte, C. 1980. "Urban-Nonurban Differences in Social Behavior: Social Psychological Models of Urban Impact." Journal of Social Issues 36 (1): 29–51.

Kozol, Jonathan. 1991. Savage Inequalities: Children in America's Schools. New York: Crown Publishers.

Krieger, Lisa M. 1995. "AIDS Loses Urgency in Nation's List of Worries." San Francisco Examiner, January 29: A-1, A-9.

Krohn, Marvin D., Akers, Ronald L., Radosevich, Marcia J., and Lanza-Kaduce, Lonn. 1980. "Social Status and Deviance." Criminology 18:303–18.

Kunen, James S. 1996. "The End of Integration." Time. April 29: 39–45.

Kutner, Nancy. 1987. "Issues in the Application of High-Cost Medical Technology: The Case of Organ Transplantation." Journal of Health and Social Behavior 28:23–36.

Lacayo, Richard. 1994. "Checking Out." Time. September 5: 40–41.

Ladjali, Malika. 1991. "Conception, Contraception: Do Algerian Women Really Have a Choice?" pp. 125–141 in Meredeth Turshen (ed.). Women and Health in Africa. Trenton, NJ: Africa World Press, Inc.

Langton, John. 1984. "The Ecological Theory of Bureaucracy: The Case of Josiah Wedgwood and the British Pottery Industry." Administrative Science Quarterly 29: 330–54.

Lareau, Annette, 1987. "Social Class Differences in Family-School Relationships: The Impact of Cultural Capital." Sociology of Education 60:73–85.

LaRossa, Ralph. 1988. "Fatherhood and Social Change." Family Relations 37:451–57.

Larson, Reed. 1978. "Thirty Years of Research on the Subjective Well-Being of Older Americans." Journal of Gerontology 33 (January): 109–25.

Laumann, Edward O., John H. Gagnon, Robert T. Michael and Stuart Michaels. 1994. The Social Organization of Sexuality: Sexual Practices in the United States. Chicago: The University of Chicago Press.

Lavee, Yoar, McCubbin, Hamilton I., and Patterson, Joan M. 1985. "The Double ABCX Model of Family Stress and Adaptation: An

Empirical Test by Analysis of Structural Equations with Latent Variables." Journal of Marriage and the Family 47 (November): 811–25.

Layton, Dennis. 1993. "Sociologists Teaching in Eastern Europe: 'Frustration with Inspiration.'" Footnotes 21 (5) (May): 8.

Leach, Penelope. 1994. Children First. New York: Alfred Knopf.

Lebergott, Stanley. 1975. Wealth and Want. Princeton, N.J.: Princeton University Press.

LeBon, Gustav. 1896. The Crowd: A Study of the Popular Mind. London: Ernest Benn.

Lee, Gary R., and Stone, Loren Hemphill. 1980. "Mate-Selection Systems and Criteria: Variation According to Family Structure." Journal of Marriage and the Family 42 (May): 319–26.

Lee, Valerie E., Marks, Helen M., and Byrd, Tina. 1994. "Sexism in Single-Sex and Coeducational Independent Secondary School Classrooms." Sociology of Education 67 (April): 92–120.

Lee, Valerie, and Bryk, Anthony. 1989. "A Multilevel Model of the Social Distribution of High School Achievement." Sociology of Education 62:172–92.

Lehman, Edward. 1988. "The Theory of the State Versus the State of Theory." American Sociological Review 53:807–23.

Lemert, Edwin. 1981. "Issues in the Study of Deviance." Sociological Quarterly 22 (Spring): 285–305.

Lenski, Gerhard. 1966. Power and Privilege: A Theory of Social Stratification. New York: McGraw-Hill.

Lenski, Gerhard, Lenski, Jean, and Nolan, Patrick. 1991. Human Societies: An Introduction to Macrosociology. 6th ed. New York: McGraw-Hill.

Leo, John. 1993. "Radical Feminism in the Senate." U.S. News & World Report, July 19: 19.

Lerner, Robert, Rothman, Stanley, and Lichter, S. Robert. 1989. "Christian Religious Elites." Public Opinion 11 (March/April): 54–59.

Leslie, Connie. 1994. "This Isn't PS 123." Newsweek (September 26): 70.

Leslie, Connie. 1995. "You Can't High-Jump If the Bar Is Set Low." Newsweek (November 6): 81, 83.

"Lessons from Bigotry 101." 1989. Newsweek, September 25, pp. 48–50.

Levin, William. 1988. "Age Stereotyping: College Student Evaluations." Research on Aging 10:134–48.

Levinger, George. 1986. "The Editor's Page." Journal of Social Issues 43 (3): x.

Lewis, Oscar. 1969. "The Culture of Poverty." In Daniel P. Moynihan (ed.), On Understanding Poverty. New York: Basic Books.

Lichter, Daniel T. 1989. "Race, Employment Hardship, and Inequality in the American Nonmetropolitan South." American Sociological Review 54:436–46.

Lichter, Daniel T. and Eggebeen, David J. 1993. "Rich Kids, Poor Kids: Changing Income Inequality among American Children." Social Forces 71:761–780.

Lieberson, Stanley. 1980. A Piece of the Pie: Blacks and White Immigrants Since 1880. Berkeley: University of California Press.

Lieberson, Stanley. 1985. "Unhyphenated Whites in the United States." In Richard Alba (ed.), Ethnicity and Race in the U.S.A.: Toward the Twenty-First Century. Boston: Routledge & Kegan Paul.

Lieberson, Stanley, and Waters, Mary. 1988. From Many Strands: Ethnic and Racial Groups in Contemporary America. New York: Russell Sage Foundation.

Lieberson, Stanley, and Waters, Mary C. 1993. "The Ethnic Responses of Whites: What Causes Their Instability, Simplification, and Inconsistency?" Social Forces 72:421–450.

Liebow, Elliot. 1967. Tally's Corner. Boston: Little, Brown.

Light, Donald W. 1988. "Toward a New Sociology of Medical Education." Journal of Health and Social Behavior 29:307–22.

Lin, Chien and Liu, William T. 1993. "Intergenerational Relationships Among Chinese Immigrant Families from Taiwan." pp. 271–286 in Harriette Pipes McAdoo, Ed. Family Ethnicity: Strength in Diversity. Newbury Park, CA: Sage.

Lin, Nan, and Ensel, Walter. 1989. "Life Stress and Health Stressors and Resources." American Sociological Review 54:382–99.

Lincoln, James R., and McBride, Kerry. 1987. "Japanese Industrial Organization in Comparative Perspective." Annual Review of Sociology 13:289–312.

Lincoln, Yvonna, and Guba, Egan. 1985. Naturalistic Inquiry. Newbury Park, Calif.: Sage.

Link, Bruce. 1987. "Understanding Labeling Effects in the Area of Mental Disorders: An Assessment of the Effects of Expectations of Rejection." American Sociological Review 52 (February): 96–112.

Linz, D., Penrod, S., and Donnerstein, E. 1986. "Media Violence and Antisocial Behavior: Alternative Legal Policies." Journal of Social Issues 42 (3).

Lipman, Joanne. 1993. "The Nanny Trap." The Wall Street Journal. April 14: A1, A8.

Lipset, Seymour. 1990. "Politics and Society in the U.S.S.R." Political Science and Politics 23 (March): 20–8.

Liska, Allen E., Chamlin, Mitchell B., and Reed, Mark. 1985. "Testing the Economic Production and Conflict Models of Crime Control." Social Forces 64 (September): 119–38.

Litwak, Eugene. 1961. "Voluntary Association and Neighborhood Cohesion." American Sociological Review 26 (April): 266–71.

Lo, Clarence Y. H. 1982. "Countermovements and Conservative Movements in the Contemporary U.S." Annual Review of Sociology 8:10–34.

Lofland, John. 1979. "White-Hot Mobilization." In M. Zald and J. McCarthy (eds.), the Dynamics of Social Movements. Boston: Little, Brown.

Lofland, John. 1981. "Collective Behavior: The Elementary Forms." In M. Rosenberg and Ralph Turner (eds.), Social Psychology: Sociological Perspectives. New York: Basic Books.

Lofland, John. 1985. Protest: Studies of Collective Behavior and Social Movements. New Brunswick, N.J.: Transaction.

Lofland, Lyn H. 1978. The Craft of Dying: The Modern Face of Death. Newbury Park, Calif.: Sage.

Logan, John, and Zhou, Min. 1989. "Do Suburban Growth Controls Control Growth?" American Sociological Review 54:461–71.

Logan, John R. and Spitze, Glenna D. 1994. "Family Neighbors." American Journal of Sociology 100 (2) (September): 453–476.

London, Bruce, and Robinson, Thomas. 1989. "The Effect of International Dependence on Income Inequality and Political Violence." American Sociological Review 54:305–08.

Love, Douglas, and Torrence, William. 1989. "The Impact of Worker Age on Unemployment and Earnings After Plant Closings." Journal of Gerontology 44:S190–5.

Lurigio, Arthur. 1990. "Introduction." Crime and Delinquency 36:3–5.

Lutz, Wolfgang. 1994. "The Future of World Population." Population Bulletin 49 (1) (June). Washington, D.C.: Population Reference Bureau, Inc.

Lyman, Stanford M., ed. 1995. Social Movements: Critiques, Concepts, Case Studies. New York: New York University Press.

Lynch, J. J. 1979. The Broken Heart: The Medical Consequences of Loneliness. New York: Basic Books.

MacKinnon, Ian and Kelsey, Tim. 1989. "Turks Leave Their Kidneys in London." The Canberra Times. January 19.

MacLeod, Jay. 1987. Ain't No Making It: Leveled Aspiratons in a Low-Income Neighborhood. Boulder, Colo.: Westview.

Maher, Timothy, Haas, Ain, Levine, Betty, and Liell, John. 1985. "Whose Neighborhood? The Role of Established Residents in Historical Preservation Areas." Urban Affairs Quarterly 21 (December): 267–81.

Maheu, Louis, ed. 1995. Social Movements and Social Classes: The Future of Collective Action. Newbury Park, CA.: Sage.

Malamuth, Neil, and Donnerstein, Edward (eds.). 1984. Pornography and Sexual Aggression. Orlando, Fla.: Academic Press.

Malthus, Thomas Robert. 1982 [1798]. Essay on the Principle of Population As It Affects the Future Improvement of Society with Remarks on the Speculation of Mr. Goodwin, M. Condorcet, and Other Writers. New York: Penguin Classics.

Mannheim, Karl. 1929. Ideology and Utopia: An Introduction to the Sociology of Knowledge. San Diego, Calif.: Harcourt Brace Jovanovich.

"Man Get 10 Years for Amish Barn Fires." 1994. The New York Times, June 9: A16.

Manski, Charles, and Wise, David. (eds.) 1983. College Choice in America. Cambridge: Harvard University Press.

Marecek, Jeanne. 1995. "Gender, Politics, and Psychology's Ways of Knowing." The American Psychologist 50 (3) (March): 162–164.

Marger, Martin N. 1994. Race and Ethnic Relations. Belmont, CA: Wadsworth.

Marini, Margaret. 1989. "Sex Differences in Earnings in the United States." Annual Review of Sociology 15:343–80.

Marini, Margaret Mooney. 1984. "Age and Sequencing Norms in the Transition to Adulthood." Social Forces 63 (September): 229–44.

Marmot, M. G., Kogevinas, M., and Elston, M. 1987. "Social/Economic Status and Disease." Annual Review of Public Health 8:111–35.

Marsden, Peter V. 1987. "Core Discussion Networks of Americans." American Sociological Review 52 (February): 122–131.

Marsh, Herbert W. 1993. "The Effects of Participation in Sport During the Last Two Years of High School." Sociology of Sport Journal 10 (1): 18–43.

Marsh, Robert M., and Mannari, Hiroshi. 1976. Modernization and the Japanese Factory. Princeton, N.J.: Princeton University Press.

Marshall, Susan E. 1985. "Ladies Against Women: Mobilization Dilemmas of Antifeminist Movements." Social Problems 32 (April): 348–62.

Martin, Philip, and Midgley, Elizabeth. 1994. "Immigration to the United States. Journey to an Uncertain Destination." Population Bulletin 49 (2) (September). Population Reference Bureau, Inc.

Martin, Teresa, and Bumpass, Larry. 1989. "Recent Trends in Marital Disruption." Demography 26:37–51.

Martz, Larry. 1987. "God and Money." Newsweek, April 6, 16–22.

Marwell, Gerald, and Oliver, Pamela. 1984. "Collective Action Theory and Social Movement Research." Research in Social Movements, Conflicts, and Change 7:1–27.

Marwell, Gerald, Oliver, Pamela, and Prahl, Ralph. 1988. "Social Networks and Collective Action: A Theory of the Critical Mass III." American Journal of Sociology 94:502–34.

Marx, Gary T. (ed.). 1971. Racial Conflict. Boston: Little, Brown.

Marx, Gary T. and McAdam, Douglas. 1994. Collective Behavior and Social Movements: Structure and Process. Englewood Cliffs, N.J.: Prentice-Hall.

Marx, Karl, and Engels, Friedrich. 1965. "The Communist Manifesto." In Arthur Mendel (ed.), Essential Works of Marxism. New York: Bantam Books. (Originally published 1848.)

Masatsugu, Mitsuyuki. 1982. The Modern Samurai Society: Duty and Dependence in Contemporary Japan. New York: American Management Association.

Massey, Douglas S., and Bitterman, Brooks. 1985. "Explaining the Paradox of Puerto Rican Segregation." Social Forces 64 (December): 306–31.

Massey, Douglas, and Denton, Nancy. 1988. "Suburbanization and Segregation in U.S. Metropolitan Areas." American Journal of Sociology 94:592–626.

Massey, Douglas S., and Mullan, Brendan P. 1984. "Processes of Hispanic and Black Spatial Assimilation." American Journal of Sociology 89 (January): 836–73.

Matsueda, Ross, and Heimer, Karen. 1987. "Race, Family Structure, and Delinquency: A Test of Differential Association and Social Control Theories." American Sociological Review 52:826–40.

Mauro, Tony. 1995. "Debate Widens Over Religion in Public Life." USA TODAY. June 30: 8A.

McAdam, Doug. 1986. "Recruitment to High-Risk Activism." American Journal of Sociology 92 (July): 64–90.

McAdam, Doug, and Paulsen, Ronnelle. 1993. "Specifying the Relationship between Social Ties and Activism." American Journal of Sociology 99: 640–667.

McAllister, Ian. 1977. The Northern Ireland Social Democratic and Labour Party. London: Macmillan.

McConnell, Harvey. 1977. "The Indian War on Alcohol." Social Resources Series, Alcohol I 76:72–81.

McDill, Edward L., Natriello, Gary, and Pallas, Aaron. 1986. "A Population at Risk: Potential Consequences of Tougher School Standards for School Dropouts." American Journal of Education 94 (February): 135–81.

McDonald, Hamish. 1992. "Boys of Bondage: Child Labour, Though Banned, is Rampant." Far Eastern Economic Review 155, 27 (July 9): 18.

McFarlane, S. Neil. 1985. Superpower Rivalry and Third World Radicalism: The Idea of National Liberation. London: Croom Helm.

McGhee, Jerrie L. 1985. "The Effect of Siblings on the Life Satisfaction of the Rural Elderly." Journal of Marriage and the Family 47 (February): 85–90.

McGinn, Robert E. 1991. Science, Technology, and Society. Englewood Cliffs, NJ: Prentice Hall.

McGuigan, Patrick. 1989. "Loose Cannons: Self-Inflicted Wounds at the National Rifle Association." Policy Review 49 (Summer): 54–6.

McKeown, T., and Record, R. G. 1962. "Reasons for the Decline of Mortality in England and Wales During the Nineteenth Century." Population Studies 16 (March): 94–122.

McKeown, T., Record, R. G., and Turner, R. D. 1975. "An Interpretation of the Decline of Mortality in England and Wales During the Twentieth Century." Population Studies 29 (November): 390–421.

McLanahan, Sara. 1985. "Family Structure and the Reproduction of Poverty." American Journal of Sociology 90 (January): 873–901.

McLanahan, Sara. 1988. "Family Structure and Dependency: Early Transitions to Female Household Headship." Demography 25:1–16.

McLanahan, Sara, and Booth, Karen. 1989. "Mother-Only Families: Problems, Prospects, and Policies." Journal of Marriage and the Family 51:557–80.

McLanahan, Sara, Garfinkel, Irwin, and Watson, Dorothy. 1986. "Family Structure, Poverty, and the Underclass." Paper presented at the Workshop on Contemporary Urban Conditions sponsored by the Committee on National Urban Policy of the National Research Council, July.

McLaughlin, Steven, and Associates. 1988. The Changing Lives of American Women. Chapel Hill: University of North Carolina Press.

McNeil, William H. 1976. Peoples and Plagues. Garden City, New York: Anchor Press.

McPherson, J. Miller, and Smith-Lovin, Lynn. 1986. "Sex Segregation in Voluntary Associations." American Sociological Review 51 (February): 61–79.

McPherson, Miller. 1983. "The Size of Voluntary Organizations." Social Forces 61:1044–64.

McQueen, 1982. Gone Tomorrow. Melbourne, Australia: Angus & Robertson.

Mead, George Herbert. 1934. Mind, Self, and Society: From the Standpoint of a Social Behaviorist. (Charles W. Morris, ed.) Chicago: University of Chicago Press.

Medley, Morris. 1976. "Satisfaction with Life Among Persons Sixty-Five Years and Older." Journal of Gerontology 32 (July): 448–55.

Mellon, Margaret. 1993. "Altered Traits." Nucleus. Fall: 4–6, 12.

Menard, Scott. 1986. "A Research Note on International Comparisons of Inequality of Income." Social Forces 64: 778–793.

Merino, Garreton. 1994. Social Movements and the Process of Democratization: A Conceptual Framework. Santiago: FLASCO, Program Chile.

Merton, Robert. 1949. "Discrimination and the American Creed." In Robert MacIver (ed.), Discrimination and National Welfare. New York: Harper & Row.

Merton, Robert. 1957. Social Theory and Social Structure. (2nd ed.) New York: Free Press.

Mesler, Bill. 1995. "Arms Welfare, Washington Style." San Francisco Bay Guardian. February 15: 19.

Messenger, John C. 1969. Inis Beag: Isle of Ireland. New York: Holt, Rinehart & Winston.

Messner, Michael A. 1992. Power at Play: Sports and the Problem of Masculinity. Boston, Mass: Beason Press.

Messner, Steven F. 1989. "Economic Discrimination and Societal Homicide Rates: Further Evidence on the Cost of Inequality." American Sociological Review 54:597–611.

Messner, Steven F. and Krohn, Marvin D. 1990. "Class, Compliance Structures, and Delinquency: Assessing Integrated Structural-Marxist Theory." American Journal of Sociology 96:300–328.

Messner, Steven F. and Rosenfeld, Richard. 1994. Crime and the American Dream. Belmont, CA: Wadsworth.

"Mexico's Population: A Profile." 1987. Population Education Interchange 16 (May): 1–4.

Michaels, Marguerite. 1993. "Rio's Dead End Kids." Time. August 9: 35, 37.

Michalowski, Raymond J. and Kramer, Ronald C. 1987. "The Space Between Laws: The Problem of Corporate Crime in a Transnational Context." Social Problems 34:34–53.

Michels, R. 1962. Political Parties. New York: Free Press.

Michels, Robert. 1949 [originally published 1911]. Political Parties: A Sociological Study of the Oligarchial Tendencies in Modern Democracy. Translated by Eden and Cedar Paul. Glencoe, Ill: The Free Press.

Michener, H. Andrew, DeLamater, John D., and Schwartz, Shalom H. 1986. Social Psychology. San Diego, Calif.: Harcourt Brace Jovanovich.

Miles, Ian, Rush, Howard, Turner, Kevin, and Bessant, John. 1988. Information Horizons: The Long-Term Social Implications of New Information Technologies. Aldershot, England: Elgar.

Milgram, Stanley. 1970. "The Experience of Living in Cities." Science 167 (March): 461–68.

Miller, Frederick D. 1983. "The End of SDS and the Emergence of Weathermen: Demise through Success." pp. 279–297 in Jo Freeman, ed. Social Movements of the Sixties and Seventies. New York: Longman.

Miller, Karen A., Kohn, Melvin L., and Schooler, Carmi. 1985. "Educational Self-Direction and the Cognitive Functioning of Students." Social Forces 63 (June): 923–44.

Miller, Karen, Kohn, Melvin, and Schooler, Carmi. 1986. "Educational Self-direction and Personality." American Sociological Review 51:372–90.

Mills, C. Wright. 1940. "Situated Actions and Vocabularies of Motives." American Sociological Review 5:904–13.

Mills, C. Wright. 1956. The Power Elite. New York: Oxford University Press.

Mills, C. Wright. 1959. The Sociological Imagination. Oxford, England: Oxford University Press.

Mire, Soraya. 1993. "A Wrongful Rite." Self-published xerox.

Mirsky, Mark. 1993. "False Gods." Partisan Review 60 (4) (Fall): 662–671.

Mizrahi, Terry. 1986. Getting Rid of Patients: Contradictions in the Socialization of Physicians. New Brunswick, N.J.: Rutgers University Press.

Mizruchi, Mark. 1989. "Similarity of Political Behavior Among Large American Corporations." American Journal of Sociology 95:401–24.

Mizruchi, Mark S. 1990. "Determinants of Political Opposition Among Large American Corporations." Social Forces 68: 1065–1088.

Moen, Phyllis, Dempster-McClain, Donna, and Williams, Robin. 1989. "Social Integration and Longevity: An Event-History Analysis of Women's Roles and Resilience." American Sociological Review 54:635–47.

Mokhiber, Russell. 1988. Corporate Crime and Violence: Big Business Power and the Abuse of the Public Trust. San Francisco: Sierra Club Books.

Molotch, Harvy. 1979. "Media and Movements." In M. Zald and J. McCarthy (eds.), The Dynamics of Social Movements. Cambridge, Mass.: Winthrop.

Monroe, Charles R. 1995. World Religions: An Introduction. Amherst, NY: Prometheus.

Moore, Charles, and Hoban-Moore, Patricia. 1990. "Some Lessons from Reagan's HUD: Housing Policy and Public Service." Political Science and Politics 23 (March): 13–17.

Moore, David W. 1995. "Americans' Most Important Source of Information: Local TV News." Gallup Poll Monthly 360 (September): 2–5.

Moore, Helen A., and Whitt, Hugh P. 1986. "Multiple Dimensions of the Moral Majority Platform: Shifting Interest Group Coalitions." The Sociological Quarterly 27 (3): 423–39.

Moore, Stephen. 1990. "Who Should America Welcome?" Society 25, 5 (July/August): 55–62.

Moorman, Jeanne, and Hernandez, Donald. 1989. "Married-Couple Families with Step-, Adopted, and Biological Children." Demography 26:267–77.

Morganthau, Tom. 1993. "America: Still a Melting Pot?" Newsweek. August 9: 16–23.

Morganthau, Tom. 1994. "IQ: Is It Destiny?" Newsweek. October 24: 53–62.

Morganthau, Tom. 1995. "What Color Is Black?" Newsweek. February 13: 63–70.

Morris, Aldon. 1984. The Origins of the Civil Rights Movement. New York: Free Press.

Morrison, Scott. 1994. "Read All About It! Local News Media Show a Propaganda Bias." Maclean's. August 15: 22.

"Mortgages: The Color Bias in Lending." 1991. Time. November 4: 65.

Mortimer, Jeyland T. 1979. Changing Attitudes Toward Work. Scarsdale, N.Y.: Work in America Institute.

Mortimer, Jeyland T., and Simmons, R. G. 1978. "Adult Socialization." Annual Review of Sociology 4:421–54.

Mott, Frank, and Mott, Susan. 1980. "Kenya's Record Population Growth: A Dilemma of Development." Population Bulletin 35 (3): 1–45.

Mottl, Tahi L. 1980. "The Analysis of Countermovements." Social Problems 27 (June): 620–35.

Mufson, Steven. 1995. "China's New Problem—It's Getting Older." The San Francisco Chronicle. August 12.

Mukerji, Chandra, and Schudson, Michael. 1986. "Popular Culture." Annual Review of Sociology 12:47–66.

Muller, Edward. 1988. "Democracy, Economic Development, and Income Inequality." American Sociological Review 53:50–68.

Munch, Richard, and Smelser, Neil J. 1987. "Relating the Micro and Macro." In J. Alexander, B. Giesen, R. Munch, and N. Smelser (eds.), The Micro-Macro Link. Berkeley: University of California Press.

Mura, David. 1988. "Strangers in the Village." pp. 135–160 in Rick Simonson and Scott Walker, editors. The Graywolf Annual Five: Multicultural Literacy. Saint Paul: Graywolf Press.

Murdock, George Peter. 1949. Social Structure. New York: Free Press.

Murdock, George Peter. 1957. "World Ethnographic Sample." American Anthropologist 59 (August): 664–97.

Murr, Andrew, and Adam Rogers. 1995. "Violence, Reel to Real." Newsweek. December 11: 46–48.

Mushane, Michael, Palumbo, Dennis, Maynard-Moody, Steven, and Levine, James. 1989. "Community Correctional Innovation: What Works and Why?" Journal of Research on Crime and Delinquency 26: 136–67.

Musick, Judith S. 1993. Young, Poor, and Pregnant: The Psychology of Teenage Motherhood. New Haven: Yale University Press.

Mutran, Elizabeth, and Reitzes, Donald C. 1984. "Intergenerational Support Activities and Well-Being Among the Elderly: A Convergence of Exchange and Symbolic Interaction Perspectives." American Sociological Review 49 (February): 117–30.

Myrdal, Gunnar. 1962. Challenge to Affluence. New York: Random House.

Nagorski, Andrew. 1995. "Back to the Gulag." Newsweek. September 25: 46–47.

Nakanishi, Don. 1989. "A Quota on Excellence?" Change, November–December. pp. 38–47.

Naoi, Atsushi, and Schooler, Carmi. 1986. "Occupational Conditions and Psychological Functioning in Japan." American Journal of Sociology 90 (4): 729–52.

Nardi, Peter M. 1992. Men's Friendships: Research on Men and Masculinities. Newbury Park, CA: Sage.

Nasaw, David. 1985. Children of the City: At Work and At Play. New York: Oxford University Press.

Nathanson, C. A. 1984. "Sex Differences in Mortality." Annual Review of Sociology 10:191–213.

National Advisory Commission on Civil Disorder. 1968. Report of the National Advisory Commission on Civil Disorders. New York: Bantam Books.

National Association of Scholars. 1992. "The Wrong Way to Reduce Campus Tensions." pp. 7–10 in Patricia Aufderheide (ed.). Beyond PC: Toward a Politics of Understanding. St. Paul, MN: Graywolf Press.

Navarro, Vicente. 1992. Why the United States Does Not Have a National Health Program. Amityville, N.Y.: Baytwood Publishing Co.

Navarro, Vicente. 1993. Dangerous to Your Health: Capitalism in Health Care. New York: Monthly Review Press.

Navarro, Vicente. 1994. The Politics of Health Policy: The U.S. Reforms, 1980–1984. Cambridge: Blackwell.

Nee, Viktor. 1989. "A Theory of Market Transition: From Redistribution to Markets in State Socialism." American Sociological Review 54:663–81.

Neidert, Lisa. J., and Farley, Reynolds. 1985. "Assimilation in the United States: An Analysis of Ethnic and Generation Differences in Status and Achievement." American Sociological Review 50 (December): 840–50.

Nelan, Bruce W. 1993. "Is Haiti Worth It?" Time 142 (November 1): 26–29.

Nemeth, Charlan J. 1985. "Dissent, Group Process, and Creativity: The Contribution of Minority Influence." Advances in Group Processes 2:57–75.

"Netwatch." 1994. Time. September 5: 20.

Neugarten, Bernice. 1968. "The Awareness of Middle Age." In Bernice Neugarten (ed.), Middle Age and Aging. Chicago: University of Chicago Press.

Neugarten, Bernice L., and Neugarten, Dail A. 1986. "Changing Meanings of Age in the Aging Society." In Alan Pifer and Lydia Bronte (eds.), Our Aging Society: Paradox and Promise. New York: Norton.

Neuhauser, Kevin. 1989. "The Radicalization of the Brazilian Catholic Church in Comparative Perspective." American Sociological Review 54:233–44.

Neustadtl, Alan, and Clawson, Dan. 1988. "Corporate Political Groupings: Does Ideology Unify Business Political Behavior?" American Sociological Review 53:172–90.

Nichols, Martha, Jacobi, Peter A., Dunlop, John T., Lindauer, David L., Talcott, Greg, Grayson, David, and Reimers, Fernando. 1993. "Third-world Families at Work: Child Labor or Child Care?" Harvard Business Review 71, 1 (Jan–Feb): 12–22.

Niebuhr, H. Richard. 1957. The Social Sources of Denominationalism. New York: Holt, Rinehart & Winston. (Originally published 1929.)

Nielsen, Frances. 1985. "Toward a Theory of Ethnic Solidarity in Modern Societies." American Sociological Review 50 (April): 133–49.

"Nigeria: 4 Political Prisoners Freed." 1996. Associated Press, World Digest. January 3.

Nilsson, Goran B. 1975. "Swedish Liberalism at Mid-Nineteenth Century." pp. 141–166 in Steven Koblik (ed.). Sweden's Development from Poverty to Affluence 1750–1970. Minneapolis: University of Minnesota Press.

"1989 AIDS." 1989. Newsweek, July 3, p. 57.

"1995 Report on the Participation of Women and Minorities in the American Sociological Association." 1995. Washington, D.C.: American Sociological Association.

Nisbet, Robert A. 1969. Social Change and History. New York: Oxford University Press.

NORC. 1993. General Social Surveys, 1972–1991: Cumulative Codebook. University of Chicago: National Opinion Research Center.

Norman, Jane, and Harris, Myron. 1981. The Private Life of the American Teenager. New York: Rawson, Wade.

Nothof, Anne. 1994. "Cowboy Poetry in Pincher Creek: The Gathering of '91." Journal of Popular Culture 27 (4) (Spring): 153–167.

"Now It's Bush's War." 1989. Newsweek, September 18, p. 22.

"Now, Legal Immigration Reform?" 1988. Population Today 6 (September): 3.

Noyes, John Humphrey. 1961. History of American Socialism. New York: Hillary House. (Originally published 1869.)

O'Dea, Thomas F. 1966. The Sociology of Religion. Englewood Cliffs, N.J.: Prentice-Hall.

O'Hare, William P. 1992. America's Minorities—The Demographics of Diversity. Population Reference Bureau: Population Bulletin 47 (4).

O'Hare, William. 1989. "Hispanic Americans in the 1980s." Population Today 17 (July–August): 6–8.

Oakes, Jeannie. 1985. Keeping Track: How Schools Structure Inequality. New Haven: Yale University Press.

Oakes, Jeannie. 1992. Educational Matchmaking: Academic and Vocational Tracking in Comprehensive High Schools. Santa Monica, CA: Rand.

Oakes, Jeannie. 1994. "More than Misapplied Technology: A Normative and Poliical Response to Hallinan on Tracking." Sociology of Education 67 (2) (April): 84–89.

Oakes, Jeannie and Quartz, Karen Hunter (eds.) 1995. Creating New Educational Communities. Chicago: University of Chicago Press.

Oberschall, A. 1973. Social Conflict and Social Movements. Englewood Cliffs, N.J.: Prentice-Hall.

Oberschall, Anthony, and Leifer, Eric J. 1986. "Efficiency and Social Institutions: Uses and Misuses of Economic Reasoning in Sociology." Annual Review of Sociology 12:233–53.

"Observing." 1990. Footnotes 18 (January): 1 ff.

Odim, Onuoha O. 1992. "Letters to the Editor: The Reality of Racial Fear." Wall Street Journal. May 28: B2.

Oegema, Dirk, and Klandermans, Bert. 1994. "Why Social Movement Sympathizers Don't Participate: Erosion and Nonconversion of Support." American Sociological Review 59 (October): 703–722.

Ogburn, William F. 1922. Social Change with Respect to Culture and Original Nature. New York: Huebsch. Reprinted 1966 by Dell,

Olesen, Virginia, Schatzman, Nellie, Hatton, Diane, and Chico, Nan. 1990. "The Mundane Ailment and the Physical Self." Social Science and Medicine 30:449–55.

Oliver, Pamela, and Marwell, Gerald. 1988. "The Paradox of Group Size in Collective Action: A Theory of the Critical Mass II." American Sociological Review 53:1–8.

Olsen, Gregg M. 1992. The Struggle for Economic Democracy in Sweden. Aldershot, Great Britain: Avebury.

Olsen, Gregg M. 1996. "Re-modeling Sweden: The Rise and Demise of the Compromise in a Global Economy." Social Problems 43 (1) (February): 1–20.

Olzak, Susan. 1989. "Analysis of Events in the Study of Collective Action." Annual Review of Sociology 15:119–41.

Olzak, Susan, Shanahan, Suzanne, and West, Elizabeth. 1994. "School Desegregation, Interracial Exposure, and Antibusing Activity in Contemporary Urban America." American Journal of Sociology 100 (1) (July): 196–241.

Omram, Abdul. 1977. "Epidemiological Transition in the U.S." Population Bulletin 32 (2): 1–45.

"On Sociology in Japan and Japanese Sociological Society." 1994. Footnotes 22 (3) (March): 6.

Oppenheimer, Martin. 1985. White-Collar Politics. New York: Monthly Review Press.

Oppenheimer, Valerie Kincade. 1994. "Women's Rising Employment and the Future of the Family in Industrial Societies." Population and Development Review 20 (2) (June): 293–342.

"Oregon's Not-So-Sweet Home." 1989. Newsweek, December 12, p. 55.

Orenstein, Peggy. 1994. School Girls: Young Women, Self-Esteem, and the Confidence Gap. New York: Doubleday.

O'Rourke, Lawrence M. 1996. "Clinton to Sign Welfare Reform Bill." The Sacramento Bee. August 1.

Orum, Anthony. 1987. "In Defense of Domhoff: A Comment on Manning's Review of Who Rules America Now." American Journal of Sociology 92 (January): 975–77.

Osborne, Robert and Cormack, Robert. 1991. "Religion and the Labour Market: Patterns and Profiles." pp. 49–71 in Robert Cormack and Robert Osborne (eds.). Discrimination and Public Policy in Northern Ireland. Oxford: Clarendon Press.

Osgood, D. Wayne, and Wilson, Janet. 1989. "Role Transitions and Mundane Activities in Late Adolescence and Early Adulthood." Paper read at the 1989 meetings of the Midwest Sociological Society, St. Louis.

Ost, John, and Antweiler, Phillip. 1986. "The Social Impact of High-Cost Medical Technology: Issues and Conflicts Surrounding the Decision to Adopt CAT Scanners." Research in the Sociology of Health Care 4:33–92.

Ostrowidzki, Vic. 1995. "Perot Undecided on Presidential Bid." Seattle Post-Intelligencer. August 14: A3.

Otten, Alan L. 1990. "Who Cares for Kids Depends on Their Status." The Wall Street Journal. November 29, p. B1.

Ouchi, William G., and Wilkins, Alan L. 1985. "Organizational Culture." Annual Review of Sociology 11:457–83.

Ouellette, Dan. 1996. "NAACP: The Next Generation." The Bay Area Express. March 18: 1, 12–19.

Pacelle, Mitchell. 1996. "More Stores Spurn Malls for the Village Square." The Wall Street Journal. February 16: B1.

Painter, Nell Irvin. 1994. "It's Time to Acknowledge the Damage Inflicted by Intolerance." The Chronicle of Higher Education 40 (29) (March 23): A64.

Palen, J. John, and London, Bruce (eds.). 1984. Gentrification, Displacement, and Neighborhood Revitalization. Albany: State University of New York Press.

Pampel, Fred C., and Williamson, John B. 1985. "Age Structure, Politics, and Cross-National Patterns of Public Pension Expenditures." American Sociological Review 50 (December): 782–99.

Parelius, Robert, and Parelius, Ann. 1987. The Sociology of Education. (2nd ed.) Englewood Cliffs: Prentice-Hall.

Parenti, Michael. 1993. Democracy of the Few, 6th ed. New York: St. Martin's Press.

Park, Robert Erza, Burgess, Ernest W., and McKenzie, Roderick D. 1984 [1925]. The City. Chicago: University of Chicago Press.
Parsons, Talcott. 1951. The Social System. New York: Free Press.
Parsons, Talcott. 1964. "The School Class as a Social System: Some of Its Functions in American Society." In Talcott Parsons (ed.), Social Structure and Personality. New York: Free Press.
Parsons, Talcott. 1966. Societies: Evolutionary and Comparative Perspectives. Englewood Cliffs, N.J.: Prentice-Hall.
Paternoster, Raymond. 1989. "Absolute and Restrictive Deterrence in a Panel of Youth: Explaining the Onset, Persistence/Desistance, and Frequency of Delinquent Offending." Social Problems 36:289–309.
Patterson, Thomas E. 1993. Out of Order. New York: Knopf.
Patterson, Thomas, Clifford, J. G., and Hagan, Kenneth. 1983. American Foreign Policy. Lexington MA:D.C. Heath.
Paul, R. E. 1989. "Is the Emperor Naked? Some Questions on the Adequacy of Sociological Theory in Urban and Regional Research." International Journal of Urban and Regional Research 13:709–20.
Paz, Juan J. 1993. "Support of Hispanic Elderly." pp. 177–183 in Harriette Pipes McAdoo, Ed. Family Ethnicity: Strength in Diversity. Newbury Park, CA: Sage.
Peach, Mark. 1994. "The Nonacademic Curriculum of the Japanese Preschool." Childhood Education 71 (1) (Fall): 9–14.
Pear, Robert. 1992. "New Look at the U.S. in 2050: Bigger, Older and Less White." New York Times. December 14: A1, A10.
Pearlin, Lenard I. 1982. "Discontinuities in the Study of Aging." In Tamara K. Hareven and Kathleen J. Adams (eds.), Aging and Life Course Transition: An Interdisciplinary Perspective. New York: Guilford Press.
Pearson, John. 1994. "Special Report: Rethinking Work." Business Week. October 17: 74–93.
Pebley, Anne R., and Westoff, Charles F. 1982. "Women's Sex Preferences in the United States: 1970 to 1975." Demography 19 (2): 177–90.
Pedersen, Daniel. 1994. "An End to 'The Troubles'?" Newsweek, September 12: 30.
Pelto, Perti. 1973. The Snowmobile Revolution: Technology and Social Changes in the Arctic. Menlo Park, CA: Cummings Press.
Perrow, Charles. 1986. Complex Organizations: A Critical Essay. (3rd ed.) New York: Random House.
Perry-Jenkins, Maureen and Folk, Karen. 1994. "Class, Couples, and Conflict: Effects of the Division of Labor on Assessments of Marriage in Dual-Earner Families." Journal of Marriage and the Family 56 (1) (February): 165–180.
Peters, et al. 1993. "Enforcing Divorce Settlements." Demography 30: 719–729.
Petersen, William. 1988. "Politics and the Measurement of Ethnicity." In William Alonso and Paul Starr (eds.), The Politics of Numbers. New York: Russell Sage Foundation.
Peterson, Karen S. 1996. "Some Worse Off When Parent Marries Again." USA Today. January 4: 1D, 2D.
Peterson, Nicolas. 1993. "Demand Sharing: Reciprocity and the Pressure for Generosity among Foragers." American Anthropologist 95, 4 (December): 860–874.
Peterson, Richard. 1989. "Firm Size, Occupational Segregation, and the Effects of Family Status on Women's Wages." Social Forces 68:397–414.
Peterson, Ruth. 1988. "Youthful Offender Designations and Sentencing in the New York Criminal Courts." Social Problems 35:111–30.
Peterson, William. 1978. "Chinese Americans and Japanese Americans." In Thomas Sowell (ed.), American Ethnic Groups. Washington, D.C.: Urban Institute.
Pettersen, Larry. 1993. "Japan's 'Cram Schools.'" Educational Leadership 50 (5) (February): 56–59.
Pettigrew, Thomas F. 1982. "Prejudice." In Thomas F. Pettigrew, George M. Fredrickson, Dale T. Knobel, Nathan Glazer, and Reed Ueda (eds.), Prejudice: Dimensions of Ethnicity. Cambridge, Mass.: Harvard University Press.
Pettigrew, Thomas F. 1985. "New Black-White Patterns: How Best to Conceptualize Them?" Annual Review of Sociology 11:329–46.
Peyser, Marc. 1994a. "Between a Wing and a Prayer." Newsweek, September 19: 58.
Peyser, Marc. 1994b. "Strike Three, You're Not Out." Newsweek, August 29: 53.
Phares, Ross. 1964. Bible in Pocket, Gun in Hand. Lincoln: University of Nebraska Press.
Phillips, David P. 1983. "The Impact of Mass Media Violence on U.S. Homocides." American Sociological Review 48 (August): 560–68.
Phillips, David P., and Bollen, Kenneth A. 1985. "Same Time, Last Year: Selective Data Dredging for Negative Findings." American Sociological Review 50 (June): 364–71.
Piliavin, Irving, Gartner, Rosemary, Thornton, Craig, and Matsueda, Ross. 1986. "Crime, Deterrence, and Rational Choice." American Sociological Review 51:101–19.
Pina, Darlene L. and Vern L. Bengston. 1993. "The Division of Household Labor and Wives' Happiness: Ideology, Employment, and Perceptions of Support." Journal of Marriage and the Family 55 (4) (November): 901–912.
Pitts, Jesse R. 1964. "The Structural-Functional Approach." In Harold T. Christensen (ed.), Handbook of Marriage and the Family. Skokie, Ill.: Rand McNally.
Plummer, Gayle, 1985. "Haitian Migrants and Backyard Imperialism." Race and Class 26:35–43.
Podolsky, Doug. 1986–1987. "NIAAA Minority Research Activities." Alcohol Health and Research World 11 (2): 4–7.
Pollock, Philip H., III. 1982. "Organizations and Alienation: The Mediation Hypothesis Revisited." The Sociological Quarterly 23 (Spring): 143–55.
Pontell, Henry N. and Calavita, Kitty. 1993. "White-Collar Crime in the Savings and Loan Scandal." The Annals of the American Academy of Political and Social Sciences 525 (January): 31–45.
"Population Growth to Create New Array of LDC Mega-Cities." 1985. Population Today 13 (June): 3.
Population Reference Bureau. 1990. World Population Data Sheet. Washington, D.C.: Population Reference Bureau.
Population Reference Bureau. 1991. World Environment Data Sheet. Washington, D.C.: Population Reference Bureau.
Population Reference Bureau. 1994. 1994 World Population Data Sheet. Washington, D.C.: Population Reference Bureau.
Population Reference Bureau. 1995. 1995 World Population Data Sheet. Washington, D.C.: Population Reference Bureau.
Porter, Paul, and Sweet, David. 1984. Rebuilding American's Cities: Roads to Recovery. New Brunswick, N.J.: Center for Urban Policy Research.
Portes, Alejandro, and Sassen-Koob, Saskia. 1987. "Making It Underground: Comparative Material on the Informal Sector in Western Market Economies." American Journal of Sociology 93:30–61.

Portes, Alejandro, and Truelove, Cynthia. 1987. "Making Sense of Diversity: Recent Research on Hispanic Minorities in the United States." Annual Review of Sociology 13:359–85.

Post, Tom. 1993. "Sailing into Big Trouble." Newsweek 122 (November 1): 34–35.

Post, Tom. 1994. "Quality Not Quantity." Newsweek. November 28: 36–37.

Poston, Dudley, and Gu, Baochang. 1987. "Socioeconomic Development, Family Planning, and Fertility in China." Demography 24:531–51.

Potuchek, Jean L. 1992. "Employed Wives' Orientation to Breadwinning: A Gender Theory Analysis." Journal of Marriage and the Family 54 (3) (August): 548–558.

Power, Carla. 1995. "Battling for Souls." Newsweek. October 30: 46–47.

Powers, Richard H. 1984. The Dilemma of Education in a Democracy. Chicago: Regnery Gateway.

Pratt, William. 1984. "Understanding U.S. Fertility: Findings from the National Survey of Family Growth Cycle III." Population Bulletin 39 (1): 1–50.

Presser, Harriet. 1988. "Shift Work and Child Care Among Young Dual-Earner American Parents." Journal of Marriage and the Family 50:133–48.

Presser, Harriet. 1989. "Can We Make Time for Children?" Demography 26:523–43.

Preston, Samuel H. 1976. Mortality Patterns in National Populations with Special Reference to Recorded Causes of Death. Orlando, Fla.: Academic Press.

Preston, Samuel H. 1984. "Children and the Elderly: Divergent Paths for America's Dependents." Demography 21 (November): 435–58.

Provence. Sally, and Lipton, Rose. 1962. Infants in Institutions: A Comparison of Their Development with Family-Reared Infants During the First Year of Life. New York: International Universities Press.

Przeworski, Adam. 1985. Capitalism and Social Democracy. Cambridge, England: Cambridge University Press.

Public Opinion. 1986a. Vol. 9, no. 1.

Public Opinion. 1986b. Vol. 9, no. 6.

Public Opinion. 1989a. March–April, p. 21.

Public Opinion. 1989b. May–June, p. 33.

Quadagno, Jill. 1990. "Race, Class, and Gender in the U.S. Welfare State: Nixon's Failed Family Assistance Plan." American Sociological Review 55:11–28.

"Quebec Encouraging Births with New Baby Bonuses." 1988. Population Today 16 (July–August): 8.

Quinn, Naomi. 1977. "Anthropological Studies of Women's Status." Annual Review of Anthropology 6:181–225.

Quinney, Richard. 1980. Class, State, and Crime. (2nd ed.) New York: Longman.

Radelet, Michael L. 1981. "Racial Characteristics and the Imposition of the Death Penalty." American Sociological Review 46:918–927.

Radelet, Michael L. 1989. "Executions of Whites for Crimes Against Blacks" Exceptions to the Rule?" The Sociological Quarterly 30:529–544.

Rapport, Shirl. 1994. "Hush: It's Epilepsy." Newsweek. August 1: 12.

Rawlings, Stephen. 1978. "Perspectives on American Husbands and Wives." Current Population Reports, Special Studies Series P-23 No. 77. U.S. Department of Commerce, Bureau of the Census. Washington, D.C.: U.S. Government Printing Office.

Razzell, P. 1974. "An Interpretation of the Modern Rise of Population in Europe: A Critique." Population Studies 28 (March): 5–15.

Reichman, Nancy. 1989. "Breaking Confidences: Organizational Influences on Insider Trading." Sociological Quarterly 30:185–204.

Reid, Robert. 1986. Land of Lost Content: The Luddite Revolt, 1812. London: Heinemann.

Reinharz, Shulamit. 1992. Feminist Methods in Social Research. New York: Oxford University Press.

Reiss, I. L., and Lee, G. L. 1988. The Family System in America,4th

Reiss, Ira L. 1980. Family Systems in America. (3rd ed.) New York: Holt, Rinehart & Winston.

Reiss, Spencer and Katel, Peter. 1994. "The Return of Terror." Newsweek. August 8: 24–25.

Reiterman, Tim. 1982. Raven: The Untold Story of the Rev. Jim Jones and His People. New York: Dutton.

Renner, Craig, and Navarto, Vicente. 1989. "Why Is Our Population of Uninsured and Underinsured Persons Growing? The Consequences of the Deindustrialization of America." Annual Review of Public Health 10:85–94.

Repetto, Robert. 1987. "Population, Resources, Environment: An Uncertain Future." Population Bulletin 42 (2): 1–50.

"Report: Chinese Orphanages Kill Babies." 1996. Associated Press, in The DesMoines Register. January 7.

Reskin, Barbara, and Hartmann, Heidi (eds.). 1986. Women's Work, Men's Work: Sex Segregation on the Job. Washington, D.C.: National Academy Press.

Reskin, Barbara. 1989. "Women Taking 'Male" Jobs Because Men Leave Them." IlliniWeek, July 20, p. 7.

Retherford, R. D. 1975. The Changing Sex Differential in Mortality. Westport/London: Greenwood.

Rich, Robert. 1977. The Sociology of Law. Washington, D.C.: University Press of America.

Richardson, James T. 1988. "Changing Times: Religion, Economics, and the Law in Contemporary America." Sociological Analysis 49 (S): 1–14.

Richardson, John G. 1980. "Variation in Date of Enactment of Compulsory School Attendance Laws." Sociology of Education 53:153–63.

Ridgeway, Cecilia L., Berger, Joseph, and Smith, LeRoy. 1985. "Nonverbal Cues and Status: An Expectation States Approach." American Journal of Sociology 90 (March): 955–78.

Riding, Alan. 1985. Distant Neighbors: A Portrait of the Mexicans. New York: Alfred A. Knopf.

Riedmann, Agnes. 1987. "Ex-Wife at the Funeral: Keyed Antistructure." Free Inquiry in Sociology 16: 123–29.

Rimer, Sara. 1988. "Child Care at Home: 2 Women, Complex Roles." New York Times, December 26.

Risman, Barbara J., and Ferree, Myra Marx. 1995. "Making Gender Visible." American Sociological Review 60 (October): 775–782.

Robertson, Roland. 1970. The Sociological Interpretation of Religion. Oxford, England: Blackwell.

Robinson, J. Gregg, and McIlwee, Judith. 1989. "Women in Engineering: A Promise Unfulfilled." Social Problems 36:455–72.

Rockett, Ian R. H. 1994. Population and Health: An Introduction to Epidemiology. Population Bulletin 49 (3) (November). Washington, D.C.: Population Reference Bureau.

Rogers, Everett M. 1960. Social Change in Rural Society: A Textbook in Rural Sociology. East Norwalk, Conn.: Appleton-Century-Crofts.

Rogers, Patrick. 1994. "Surviving the Second Wave." Newsweek, September 19: 50–51.

Ronan, Laura, and Reichman, Walter. 1987. "Back to Work." Alcohol Health and Research World 11:34.

Roof, Wade Clark, and Hoge, Dean R. 1980. "Church Involvement in America: Social Factors Affecting Membership and Participation." Review of Religious Research 21 (4): 405–26.

Roof, Wade Clark. 1989. "Multiple Religious Switching: A Research Note." Journal for the Scientific Study of Religion 28:530–35.

Rook, Karen S., and Dooley, David. 1985. "Applying Social Support Research: Theoretical Problems and Future Directions." Journal of Social Issues 41 (1): 5–28.

Rosario, Louise. 1992. "Race for Kindergartens." Far Eastern Economic Review 155 (10) (March 12): 23–25.

Roscow, Irving. 1974. Socialization to Old Age. Berkeley: University of California Press.

Rose, Peter. 1981. They and We: Racial and Ethnic Relations in the United States. (3rd ed.) New York: Random House.

Rosecrance, John. 1985. "Compulsive Gambling and the Medicalization of Deviance." Social Problems 32 (February): 273–84.

Rosenbaum, James, and Kariya, Takehiko. 1989. "From High School to Work: Market and Institutional Mechanisms in Japan." American Journal of Sociology 94:1334–65.

Rosenbaum, Walter A., and Button, James W. 1993. "The Unquiet Future of Intergenerational Politics." The Gerontologist 33 (4):481–490.

Rosenberg, Debra. 1994. "Men, Women, Computers." Newsweek. May 16: 48–55.

Rosenberg, Morris. 1965. Society and the Adolescent Self-Image: Princeton, N.J.: Princeton University Press.

Rosenberg, Morris, 1979. Conceiving the Self. New York: Basic Books.

Rosenberg, Morris, Schooler, Carmi, and Schoenbach, Carrie. 1989. "Self-Esteem and Adolescent Problems: Modeling Reciprocal Effects." American Sociological Review 54:1004–18.

Rosenstiel, Thomas. 1995. "Buying Off the Elderly." Newsweek. October 2: 40–41.

Rosenstiel, Thomas. 1995b. "Newt's Show and Tell." Newsweek. January 1: 16–19.

Rosenthal, A. M. 1964. Thirty-Eight Witnesses. New York: McGraw-Hill.

Rosenthal, Carolyn J. 1985. "Kinkeeping in the Familial Division of Labor." Journal of Marriage and the Family 47 (Nov.): 965–74.

Ross, Catherine E., and Wu, Chia-ling. 1995. "The Links Between Education and Health." American Sociological Review 60 (October): 719–745.

Rosset, Peter, and Vandermeer, John (eds.). 1986. Nicaragua: Unfinished Revolution. New York: Grove Press.

Rossi, Alice. 1984. "Gender and Parenthood." American Sociological Review 49 (February): 1–19.

Rothschild, Joyce. 1986. "Alternatives to Bureaucracy: Democratic Participation in the Economy." Annual Review of Sociology 12:307–28.

Rothschild-Whitt, Joyce. 1979. "The Collectivistic Organization: An Alternative to Rational Bureaucratic Models." American Sociological Review 44 (4): 509–27.

Roy, William G. 1984. "Class Conflict and Social Change in Historical Perspective." Annual Review of Sociology 10:483–506.

Roy, William, and Bonacich, Philip. 1988. "Interlocking Directorates and Communities of Interest Among American Railroad Companies, 1905." American Sociological Review 53:368–79.

Rubel, Maxmilien. 1968. "Karl Marx." In David Sills (ed.), International Encyclopedia of the Social Sciences. Vol. 10. New York: Macmillan and Free Press.

Rubin, Lillian B. 1992. Worlds of Pain: Life in the Working-Class Family. New York: Basic Books.

Rubin, Rita. 1995. "Can't Reach Your Doctor? Try E-mail." U.S. News & World Report. February 13: 82–84.

Ruggles, Steven. 1994. "The Origins of African-American Family Structure." American Sociological Review 59 (Feburary): 136–151.

Rule, James, and Attewell, Paul. 1989. "What Do Computers Do?" Social Problems 36:225–41.

Rutter, D. R., and Quine, Lyn. 1990. "Inequalities in Pregnancy Outcome: A Review of Psychosocial and Behavioral Mediators." Social Science and Medicine 30:553–68.

Ryan, T. Timothy. 1993. "Indian Crusader Seeks to Halt Child Slavery." Far Eastern Economic Review 156, 27 (July 8): 62–63.

Ryan, William. 1981. Equality. New York: Pantheon Books.

Ryden, Bengt, and Bergstrom, Villy (eds.). 1982. Sweden: Choices for Economic and Social Policy in the 1980s. London: George Allen & Unwin.

Saad, Lydia. 1996. "Issues Referendum Reveals Populist Leanings But Traditional, Conservative Views also Evident." The Gallup Organization Newsletter 61 (4), May 24.

Sack, Kevin. 1995. "Public Hospitals Around Country Cut Basic Service." New York Times. August 20: A1.

Said, Edward W. 1981. Covering Islam: How the Media and the Experts Determine How We See the Rest of the World. New York: Pantheon Books.

Saigo, Roy. 1989. "The Barriers of Racism." Change, November–December, pp. 8, 10, 69.

Saks, Michael J. and Krupat, Edward. 1988. Social Psychology and Its Applications. New York: Harper & Row.

Sallot, Jeff and Fraser, Damian. 1994. "The Politics of Fear." World Press Review 41 (6) (June): 8–11.

Saltman, Juliet. 1991. "Maintaining Racially Diverse Neighborhoods." Urban Affairs Quarterly 26 (3) (March): 416–441.

Sameulsson, Kurt. 1975. "The Philosophy of Swedish Welfare Policies." pp. 332–356 in Steven Koblik (ed.). Sweden's Development from Poverty to Affluence 1750–1970. Minneapolis: University of Minnesota Press.

Sampson, Robert. 1987. "Urban Black Violence: The Effect of Male Joblessness and Family Disruption." American Journal of Sociology 93:348–82.

Sampson, Robert. 1988. "Local Friendship Ties and Community Attachment in Mass Society: A Multilevel Systemic Model." American Sociological Review 53:766–79.

Sampson, Robert, and Groves, W. Byron. 1989. "Community Structure and Crime: Testing Social-Disorganization Theory." American Journal of Sociology 94:774–802.

San Miguel, Guadalupe, Jr. 1987. Let Them All Take Heed. Austin: University of Texas Press.

Sandefur, Gary D., and Sakamoto, Arthur. 1988. "American Indian Household Structure and Income." Demography 25:71–80.

Santelli, John S., Davis, Mary, Celentano, David D., Crump, Aria Davis, and Burwell, LaWanda G. 1995. "Combined Use of Condoms with Other Contraceptive Methods among Inner-City Baltimore Woman." Family Planning Perspectives 27 (2) (March/April): 74–78.

Sapiro, Virginia. 1986. Women in American Society. Palo Alto, Calif.: Mayfield.

Saraceno, Chiara. 1984. "The Social Construction of Childhood: Child Care and Education Policies in Italy and the United States." Social Problems 3 (February): 351–63.

Sarkitov, Nikolay. 1987. "From 'Hard Rock' to 'Heavy Metal": The Stupefaction Effect." Sotsiologicheskie-Issledovaniya. 14 (July–August): 93–4.

Sassen, Saskia. 1988. The Mobility of Capital and Labor: A Study in International Investment and Labor Flow. Cambridge, England: Cambridge University Press.

Sassen, Saskia. 1990. "Economic Restructuring and the American City." Annual Review of Sociology 16: 465–300.

"Saudi Arabia Power Change Appears Permanent." 1996. Los Angeles Times. January 3.

Savage, Mike, and Warde, Alan. 1993. Urban Sociology, Capitalism and Modernity. New York: Continuum Publishing Co.

Scanzoni, John. 1989. "Alternative Images for Public Policy: Family Structure Versus Families Struggling." Policy Studies Review 8:610–21.

Schaefer, Richard R. 1990. Racial and Ethnic Groups, 4th ed. HarperCollins.

Schapiro, Mark. 1994. "The Fine Art of Sexual Harassment." Harper's Magazine. July: 62–63.

Scheff, Thomas J. 1988. "Shame and Conformity: The Deference-Emotion System." American Sociological Review 53:395–406.

Schervish, Paul. 1983. The Structural Determinants of Unemployment: Vulnerability and Power in Market Relations. Orlando, Fla.: Academic Press.

Schill, Michael H., and Nathan, Richard P. 1983. Revitalizing America's Cities: Neighborhood Reinvestment and Displacement. Albany: State University of New York Press.

Schlafly, Phyllis. 1977. The Power of the Positive Woman. New Rochelle, N.Y.: Arlington House.

Schlesinger, Arthur, Jr. 1965. A Thousand Days. Boston: Houghton Mifflin.

Schmidt, Hans. 1971. The U.S. Occupation of Haiti, 1915–1934. New Brunswick, N.J.: Rutgers University Press.

Schmidt, Steffen W., Shelley, Mack C. II, and Bardes, Barbbara A. 1995. American Government and Politics Today, 1995–96 edition. Saint Paul/Minneapolis: West Publishing Co.

Schneider, David J. 1981. "Tactical Self-Presentations: Toward a Broader Conceptualization." In J. T. Tedeschi (ed.), Impression Management Theory and Social Psychological Research. Orlando, Fla.: Academic Press.

Schoen, Robert, and Kluegel, James. 1988. "The Widening Gap in Black and White Marriage Rates." American Sociological Review 53:895–907.

Schultz, T. Paul. 1993. "Investments in the Schooling and Health of Men and Women." The Journal of Human Resources 28:694–734.

Schuman, Howard, and Scott, Jacqueline. 1989. "Generations and Collective Memories." American Sociological Review 54:359–81.

Schur, Edwin M. 1979. Interpreting Deviance: A Sociological Introduction. New York: Harper & Row.

Schwartz, Barry. 1983. "George Washington and the Whig Conception of Heroic Leadership." American Sociological Review 48 (February): 18–33.

Schwartz, Shalom H., and Gottlieb, Avi. 1980. "Bystander Anonymity and Reaction to Emergencies." Journal of Personality and Social Psychology 39 (3): 418–40.

Scott, Marvin B., and Lyman, Stanford M. 1968. "Accounts." American Sociological Review 33 (December): 46–62.

Seagraves, Anne. 1990. Women of the Sierra. Lakeport, CA: WESANNE Publications.

Seaman, Barbara. 1972. Free and Female. New York: Fawcett.

Searle, John. 1992. "The Storm over the University." pp. 85–123 in Paul Berman (ed.). Debating P.C.: The Controversy over Political Correctness on College Campuses. New York: Bantam Doubleday Dell Publishing Group, Inc.

Segal, Howard P. 1985. Technological Utopianism in American Culture 1830–1940. Chicago: University of Chicago Press.

Seligman, Clive. 1989. "Environmental Ethics." Journal of Social Issues 45: 169–84.

Selik, Richard, Castro, Kenneth, and Pappaioanou, Marguerite. 1988. "Distribution of AIDS Cases by Racial/Ethnic Group and Exposure Category, United States, June 1, 1981–July 4, 1988." Morbidity and Mortality Weekly Report 37 (July): 1–10.

Seltzer, Judith. 1994. "Marital Dissolution and Children." Annual Review of Sociology: 235–266.

Selznick, Philip. 1995. "Thinking About Community: Ten Theses." Society 32 (5) (July/August): 33–37.

Sen, Gita, and Grown, Caren. 1987. Development, Crises, and Alternative Visions. NY: Monthly Review Press.

"Senate Delivers on Crime." 1994. The Oakland Tribune, August 26: 1.

Senser, Robert A. 1994. "The Crime of Child Slavery: Child Labor in South Asia." Current 361 (March–April): 29–34.

"'Separate But Equal' Again?" 1994. Newsweek. May 16: 32.

Serpe, Richard. 1987. "Stability and Change in Self: A Structural Symbolic Interactionist Explanation." Social Psychology Quarterly 50 (1): 44–55.

Serrill, Michael S. 1993. "Selling the Children." Time. June 21: 53–55.

Shafer, John. 1989. "Theories of Alcohol Abuse: What Do Native Americans Think?" Unpublished manuscript, Department of Sociology, University of Nebraska–Lincoln.

Shaheen, Jack G. 1994. "Arab Images in American Comic Books." Journal of Popular Culture 28 (1) (Summer): 123–133.

Shalin, Dmitri, 1986. "Pragmatism and Social Interaction." American Sociological Review 51 (February): 9–29.

Shapiro, Laura. 1994. "A Tomato with a Body that Just Won't Quit." Newsweek. June 6: 80–82.

Shamir, Boas. 1986. "Self-Esteem and the Psychological Impact of Unemployment." Social Psychology Quarterly 49 (1): 61–72.

Shavit, Yossi. 1984. "Tracking and Ethnicity in Israeli Secondary Education." American Sociological Review 49 (April): 210–20.

Sheler, Jeffery L. 1995. "Keeping Faith in His Time." U.S. News & World Report. October 9: 72–77.

Shelton, Beth Anne. 1992. Women, Men and Time. New York: Greenwood Press.

Shepard, William. 1985. To Secure the Blessings of Liberty. Chico, Calif.: Scholars Press and Crossroads.

Sherif, Muzafer. 1936. The Psychology of Social Norms. New York: Harper & Row.

Shiomi, Toshiyuki. 1993. "One Saturday Off in the Schools." Japan Quarterly 40 (2) (April–June): 36–42.

Shkilnyk, Anastasia M. 1985. A Poison Stronger Than Love: The Destruction of an Ojibwa Community. New Haven: Yale University Press.

Shupe, Anson, and Stacy, William A. 1982. Born-Again Politics and the Moral Majority: What Social Surveys Really Show. New York: Mellen Press.

Sidel, Ruth, and Sidel, Victor. 1984. "Health Care from Liberation to the Cultural Revolution." In Molly Joel Coye, John Livingston, and Jean Highland (eds.), China: Yesterday and Today. New York: Bantam Books.

Sidey, Hugh. 1994. "War and Remembrance." Time. May 23: 64.

Sidorsky, David. 1993. "Multiculturalism and the University." Partisan Review 30 (4) (Fall): 709–723.

Signorielli, Nancy. 1993. Mass Media Images and Impact on Health, Westport, CT: Greenwood Press.

Silvestri, George, and Lukosiewicz, John. 1989. "Projections of Occupational Employment 1988–2000." Monthly Labor Review 122 (November): 42–66.

Simmel, Georg. 1950. The Sociology of Georg Simmel. (Kurt Wolff, ed. and trans.) New York: Free Press. (Originally published 1908.)

Simmel, Georg. 1955. Conflict. (Kurt H. Wolf, trans.) New York: Free Press.

Simon, Julian L. 1981. The Ultimate Resource. Princeton, N.J.: Princeton University Press.

Simon, Julian L. 1986. Theory of Population and Economic Growth. New York: Basil Blackwell.

Simmons, Roberta, Bureson, R., Carlton-Ford, S., and Blyth, D. 1987. "The Impact of Cumulative Change in Early Adolescence." Child Development 58:1220–34.

Simon, Rita, and Landis, Jean. 1989. "Poll Report: A Woman's Place and Role." Public Opinion Quarterly 53:265–76.

Simons, Ronald, and Gray, Phyllis. 1989. "Perceived Blocked Opportunity as an Explanation of Delinquency Among Lower-Class Black Males." Journal of Research on Crime and Delinquency 26:90–101.

Simpson, Miles. 1990. "Political Rights and Income Inequality: A Cross-National Test." American Sociological Review 55:682–693.

Simpson, Richard L. 1985. "Social Control of Occupations and Work." Annual Review of Sociology 11:415–36.

Singer, Bennett L. and Deschamps, David. 1994. Gay & Lesbian Stats: A Pocket Guide of Facts and Figures. New York: The New Press.

Sjoberg, Gideon. 1960. The Preindustrial City. New York: Free Press.

Sloan, Irving. 1981. Youth and the Law. Dobbs Ferry, N.Y.: Oceana.

Small, Stephen A. and Luster, Tom. 1994. "Adolescent Sexual Activity: An Ecological, Risk-Factor Approach." Journal of Marriage and the Family 56 (1) (February): 181–192.

Smith, Douglas A., and Visher, Christy A. 1981. "Street-Level Justice: Situational Determinants of Police Arrest Decisions." Social Problems 29 (2): 167–77.

Smith, Douglas. 1987. "Police Response to Interpersonal Violence: Defining the Parameters of Legal Control." Social Forces 65 (March): 767–82.

Smith, Geri. 1994. "Zedillo Will Need More Muscle to Take Charge in Mexico." Business Week, December 12: 63.

Smith, H. Lovell and Winje, Carolyn. 1992. "August Biennial Report on the Participation of Women and Minorities in ASA for 1990 and 1991." Washington, DC: American Sociological Association photocopy.

Smith, Kevin, and Stone, Lorence. 1989. "Rags, Riches, and Bootstraps." Sociological Quarterly 30: 93–107.

Smith, Tom W. 1992. "The International Social Survey Program." Footnotes 20 (5) (May): 10.

Smith-Lovin, Lynn, and Brady, Charles. 1989. "Interruptions in Group Discussions: The Effect of Gender and Group Composition." American Sociological Review 54:424–35.

Smock, Pamela J. 1993. "The Economic Costs of Marital Disruption for Young Women over the Past Two Decades." Demography 30 (3) (August): 353–371.

"Sociology Grad Student Jailed: Scholars' Privilege under Attack." 1993. Footnotes 21 (6) (August): 2.

Sohoni, Neera Kuckreja. 1994. "Where Are the Girls?" Ms. July/August: 96.

Sommer, John W. (ed.). 1995. The Academy in Crisis: The Political Economy of Higher Education. New Brunswick: Transaction.

Snow, David A., and Anderson, Leon. 1987. "Identity Work Among the Homeless: The Verbal Construction and Avowal of Personal Identities." American Journal of Sociology 92 (May): 1336–71.

Snow, David A., Rochford, E. Burke, Jr., Worden, Steven K., and Benford, Robert D. 1986. "Frame Alignment Processes, Micromobilization, and Movement Participation." American Sociological Review 51 (August): 464–81.

Snow, David, Baker, Susan, and Anderson, Leon. 1988. "On the Precariousness of Measuring Insanity in Insane Contexts." Social Problems 35: 192–96.

Snow, David, Baker, Susan, Anderson, Leon, and Martin, Michael. 1986. "The Myth of Pervasive Mental Illness Among the Homeless." Social Problems 33: 407–23.

Sokolovsky, Jay, and Cohen, Carl. 1981. "Being Old in the Inner City: Support Systems of the SRO Aged." In Christine Fry (ed.), Dimensions: Aging, Culture, and Health. New York: Praeger.

Soldo, Beth. 1981. "The Living Arrangements of the Elderly in the Near Future." In Sara B. Kiesler, James N. Morgan, and Valerie Kincade Oppenheimer (eds.), Aging, Social Change. Orlando, Fla.: Academic Press.

Sombart, Werner. 1974. "Why Is There No Socialism in the U.S.?" Excerpted in John Laslett and S. M. Lipset (eds.), Failure of a Dream: Essays in the History of American Socialism. New York: Doubleday Anchor Books. (Originally published 1906.)

Sone, Monica. 1953. Nisei Daughter. Boston: Little, Brown.

Sorokin, Pitirim, and Lundin, Walter. 1959. Power and Morality. Boston: Sargent.

Souryal, Claire and MacKenzie, Doris Layton. 1994. "'Shock Therapy': Can Boot Camps Provide Effective Drug Treatment?" Corrections Today 56 (February): 48.

Sowell, Thomas. 1981. Ethnic America: A History. New York: Basic Books.

Spalding, Rose J. (ed.). 1987. The Political Economy of Revolutionary Nicaragua. London: Allen & Unwin.

Specter, Michael. 1994. "The Great Russia Will Live Again." The New York Times Magazine. June 19: 26–52.

Spilka, Bernard, Shaver, Phillip, and Kirkpatrick, Lee A. 1985. "A General Attribution Theory for the Psychology of Religion." The Journal for the Scientific Study of Religion 24 (1): 1–20.

Spiro, Melford E. 1956. Kibbutz: Venture in Utopia. Cambridge, Mass.: Harvard University Press.

Spitz, René. 1945. "Hospitalism: An Inquiry into the Genesis of Psychiatric Conditions in Early Childhood." In Anna Freud, Heinz Hartman, and Ernst Kris (eds.), The Psychoanalytic Study of the Child. Vol 1. New York: International Universities Press.

Spitze, Glenna. 1986. "The Division of Task Responsibility in U.S. Households: Longitudinal Adjustments to Change." Social Forces 64 (March): 689–701.

Spring, Joel H. 1995. "In Service to the State: The Political Context of Higher Education in the United States." pp. 45–68 in Sommer, John W. (ed.). 1995. The Academy in Crisis: The Political Economy of Higher Education. New Brunswick: Transaction.

Squires, Gregory, DeWolfe, Ruthanne, and DeWolfe, Alan. 1979. "Urban Decline or Disinvestment." Social Problems 27: 79–95.

Stacey, Judith. 1993. "Good Riddance to 'The Family': A Response to

David Popenoe." Journal of Marriage and the Family 55 (3) (August): 545–547.

Stack, Steven, and Wasserman, Ira. 1995. "The Effect of Marriage, Family, and Religious Tied on African American Suicide Ideology." Journal of Marriage and the Family 57 (1) (February): 215–222.

Staggenborg, Susan. 1988. "The Consequences of Professionalization and Formalization in the Pro-Choice Movement." American Sociological Review 53:585–606.

Stark, Rodney, and Bainbridge, William S. 1985. The Future of Religion. Berkeley: University of California Press.

Stark, Rodney, and Bainbridge, William Sims. 1979. "Of Churches, Sects, and Cults: Preliminary Concepts for a Theory of Religious Movements." Journal for the Scientific Study of Religion 18 (2): 117–33.

Stark, Rodney, and Bainbridge, William Sims. 1981. "American-Born Sects: Initial Findings." Journal for the Scientific Study of Religion 20 (2): 130–49.

Stark, Rodney, and Finke, Roger. 1988. "American Religion in 1976: A Statistical Portrait." Sociological Analysis 49 (1): 39–51.

Starr, Paul. 1982. The Social Transformation of American Medicine. New York: Basic Books.

State of World Population. 1992. NY: United Nations Population Fund.

Stearn, Peter N. 1976 "The Evolution of Traditional Culture Toward Aging." In Jon Hendricks and C. Davis Hendricks (eds.), Dimensions of Aging: Readings. Cambridge, Mass.: Winthrop.

Stearns, Linda B., and Allan, Kenneth, D. 1996. "Economic Behavior in Institutional Environments." American Sociological Review 61 (August): 699–718.

Steffensmeier, Darrel J., Allan, Emilie, Harer, Miles, and Streifel, Cathy. 1989. "Age and the Distribution of Crime." American Journal of Sociology 94:803–31.

Steinberg, L., Blinde, P. L., and Chan, K. S. 1984. "Dropping Out Among Language Minority Youth." Review of Educational Research 54:113–32.

Steinmetz, George, and Wright, Erik. 1989. "The Fall and Rise of the Petty Bourgeoisie." American Journal of Sociology 94:973–1018.

Stephens, John D. 1980. The Transition from Capitalism to Socialism. Atlantic Highlands. N.J.: Humanities Press.

Stevenson, David Lee and Baker, David P.. 1992. "Shadow Education and Allocation in Formal Schooling: Transition to University in Japan." American Journal of Sociology 97 (6) (May): 1639–1658.

Stimpson, Catherine R. 1992. "On Differences: Modern Language Association Presidential Address 1990." pp. 40–60 in Paul Berman (ed.). Debating P.C.: The Controversy over Political Correctness on College Campuses. New York: Bantam Doubleday Dell Publishing Group, Inc.

Stokes, Randall, and Anderson, Andy. 1990. "Disarticulation and Human Welfare in Less Developed Countries." American Sociological Review 55:63–74.

Stokes, Randall, and Hewitt, John. P. 1976. "Aligning Actions." American Sociological Review 41:839–49.

Stolte, John F. 1983. "The Legitimation of Structural Inequality." American Sociological Review 48 (June): 331–42.

Stone, John. 1985. Racial Conflict in Contemporary Society. Cambridge, Mass.: Harvard University Press.

Strain, Charles R., and Goldberg, Steven. 1987. "Introduction: Modern Technology and the Humanities." In Steven Goldberg and Charles Strain (eds.), Technological Change and the Transformation of America. Carbondale: Southern Illinois University Press.

Straus, Murray A. and Gelles, Richard. 1988. "How Violent Are American Families? Estimates from the National Family Violence Resurvey and Other Studies." pp. 14–36 in Family Abuse and Its Consequences: New Directions in Research. edited by Gerald T. Hotaling, David Finkelhor, John T. Kirkpatrick, and Murray A. Straus. Newbury Park, CA: Sage.

Straus, Murray, and Gelles, Richard. 1986. "Societal Change and Change in Family Violence from 1975 to 1985 as Revealed by Two National Surveys." Journal of Marriage and the Family 48:465–79.

Straus, Scott. 1996. "Too Many Children Make Them Poor." San Francisco Chronicle. March 7: A-1, A-13.

Streib, Gordon. 1985. "Social Stratification and Aging." In Robert Binstock and Ethel Shanas (eds.), Handbook of Aging and the Social Sciences. (2nd ed.) New York: Van Nostrand Reinhold.

Stroebe, Margaret S., and Stroebe, Wolfgang. 1983. "Who Suffers More? Sex Differences in Health Risks of the Widowed." Psychological Bulletin 93:279–301.

Strossen, Nadine. 1993. "Yes: Discriminatory Crimes." ABA Journal 79 (May): 44.

Stryker, Sheldon. 1981. "Symbolic Interactionism: Themes and Variations." In Morris Rosenberg and Ralph H. Turner (eds.), Social Psychology: Sociological Perspectives. New York: Basic Books.

Sudo, Phil. 1993. "The Faith and the Followers." Scholastic Update, October 22, pp. 2–5.

Summers, Gene. 1984. "Preface." Annals of the American Academy of Political and Social Science 475:9–14.

Suomi, S. J., Harlow, H. H., and McKinney, W. T. 1972. "Monkey Psychiatrists." American Journal of Psychiatry 128 (February): 927–32.

"Survey Report, Kenya." 1986. Population Today 14 (June): 5.

"Survey Report, Mexico." 1990. Population Today 18 (February): 5.

"Surveys Find More Doctors for Euthanasia." 1996. San Francisco Chronicle. February 12.

Sutherland, Anne, and Nash, Jeffrey E. 1994. "Animal Rights as a New Environmental Cosmology." Qualitative Sociology 17 (2): 171–185.

Sutherland, Edwin, H. 1983. White Collar Crime: The Uncut Version. New Haven and London: Yale University Press.

Sutherland, Edwin H. 1961. White-Collar Crime. New York: Holt, Rinehart & Winston.

Suzuki, Bob. 1989. "Asian Americans as the Model Minority." Change, November–December, pp. 12–20.

Swidler, Ann. 1986. "Culture in Action: Symbols and Strategies." American Sociological Review 51 (April): 273–86.

Switzer, Arlene. 1989. "Interview." Human Resources Management 188 (February 8): 20.

Taeuber, Cynthia M. 1992. "Sixty-five Plus in America." Current Population Reports. Series P-23, No. 178. Washington, D.C.: U.S. Government Printing Office.

Tamir, Lois M. 1982. Men in Their Forties: The Transition to Middle Age. New York: Springer.

Tannen, Deborah. 1990. You Just Don't Understand. New York: William Morrow and Co., Inc.

Tannen, Deborah. 1994. Talking from 9 to 5: How Women's and Men's Conversational Styles Affect Who Gets Heard, Who Gets Credit, and What Gets Done At Work. New York: William Morrow and Co., Inc.

Tannenbaum, Frank. 1979. "The Survival of the Fittest." In George

Modelski (ed.), Transnational Corporations and the World Order. New York: W. H. Freeman. (Originally published 1968.)

Tarrow, Sidney. 1988. "National Politics and Collective Action: Recent Theory and Research in Western Europe and the United States." Annual Review of Sociology 14:421–40.

Taylor, Robert. 1986. "Receipt of Support from Family Among Black Americans: Demographic and Familial Differences." Journal of Marriage and the Family 48:67–77.

Teachman, Jay. 1987. "Family Background, Educational Resources, and Educational Attainment." American Sociological Review 52:548–57.

Teachman, Jay D. 1991. "Who Pays? Receipt of Child Support in the United States." Journal of Marriage and the Family 53 (3) (August): 759–772.

Teaford, Jon C. 1993. The Twentieth-Century American City, 2nd edition. Baltimore, MD: The Johns Hopkins University Press.

Tedeschi, James T., and Riess, Marc. 1981. "Identities, the Phenomenal Self, and Laboratory Research." In J. T. Tedeschi (ed.), Impression Management Theory and Social Psychological Research. Orlando, Fla.: Academic Press.

"The Forbes Four Hundred." 1989. Forbes 144 (October 23): 145–290.

"The Future of Gay America." 1990. Newsweek, March 12, pp. 20ff.

Teitelbaum, Michael S. 1987. "The Fear of Population Decline." Population Today 15 (March) 6–8.

Terry, Don. 1994. "Chicago's Gangs: Machiavelli's Descendants." The New York Times. September 16: 14y.

"The Gap Between Black and White Mortgage Approval Rates." 1992. The Wall Street Journal. March 31: A10.

"The Rise of Black Mayors." 1989. Parade Magazine, December, Robbins, Thomas. 1986. "Review." Sociological Analysis 47:83–4.

"The Triumph of the Alkali Lake Indian Band." 1987. Alcohol Health and Research World 12 (1): 57.

"The War at Home: Arab-Americans Torn, Worried." 1991. Daily Nebraskan, January 12, pg. 1.

"The World's Poorest 370 Million People." 1989. Population Today 17 (April): 4.

Thelin, John R. 1992. "The Curriculum Crusades and the Conservative Backlash." Change 24 (1) (Jan–Feb): 17–24.

"There's Comfort in Loving." 1989. New York Times, April 22, p. 4.

Thoits, Peggy. 1986a. "Multiple Identities: Examining Gender and Marital Status Differences in Distress." American Sociological Review 51:259–72.

Thoits, Peggy. 1986b. "Self-Labeling Processes in Mental Illness: The Role of Emotional Deviance." American Journal of Sociology 91:221–49.

Thoits, Peggy. 1987. "Gender and Marital Status Differences in Control and Distress: Common Stress Versus Unique Stress Explanations." Journal of Health and Social Behavior 28:7–22.

Thomas, Darwin L., and Cornwall, Marie. 1990. "Religion and Family in the 1980's." pp. 265–274 in Alan Booth (ed.), Contemporary Families. Minneapolis: National Council on Family Relations.

Thomas, Evan, and Cohn, Bob. 1995. "Rethinking the Dream." Newsweek. June 26: 18–21.

Thomas, Melvin E. 1993. "Race, Class, and Personal Income: An Empirical Test of the Declining Significance of Race Thesis, 1968–1988." Social Problems 40, 3 (August): 328–342.

Thomas, Melvin E. 1993. "Race, Class, and Personal Income: An Empirical Test of the Declining Significance of Race Thesis, 1968–1988." Social Problems 40 (3) (August): 328–342.

Thomas, Paulette. 1994. "Widening Rich-Poor Gap Is a Threat to the 'Social Fabric,' White House Says." The Wall Street Journal, February 15: A10, A18.

Thomas, W. I., and Thomas, Dorothy. 1928. The Child in America: Behavior Problems and Programs. New York: Knopf.

Thomis, Malcolm I. 1970. The Luddites: Machine-Breaking in Regency England. Hamden, Conn.: Archon Books.

Thomlinson, Ralph. 1976. Population Dynamics: Causes and Consequences of World Demographic Change. (2nd ed.) New York: Random House.

Thompson, Anthony P. 1983. "Extramarital Sex: A Review of the Research Literature." Journal of Sex Research, February 1–21.

Thompson, Kevin. 1989. "Gender and Adolescent Drinking Problems: The Effects of Occupational Structure." Social Problems 36:30–47.

Thompson, Linda, and Walker, Alexis. 1989. "Gender in Families." Journal of Marriage and the Family 51:845–71.

Thomson, Elizabeth, and Ugo Colella. 1992. "Cohabitation and Marital Stability: Quality or Commitment?" Journal of Marriage and the Family 54 (2) (May): 259–267.

Thornberry, Terence P., and Farnworth, Margaret. 1982. "Social Correlates of Criminal Involvement: Further Evidence on the Relationship Between Social Status and Criminal Behavior." American Sociological Review 47 (August): 505–18.

Thornton, Arland, Alwin, Duane, and Camburn, Donald. 1983. "Causes and Consequences of Sex-Role Attitudes and Attitude Change." American Sociological Review 48 (April): 211–27.

Thorson, James A. 1995. Aging in a Changing Society. Belmont, CA: Wadsworth Publishing Co.

Thurow, Lester C. 1980. The Zero-Sum Society. NY: Basic Books.

Tien, H. Yuan. 1989. "Second Thoughts on the Second Child." Population Today 17 (4): 6–8.

Tien, Chang-Lin. 1994. "America's Scapegoats." Newsweek. October 31: 19.

Tilly, Charles. 1978. From Mobilization to Revolution. Reading, Mass.: Addison-Wesley.

Tilly, Charles. 1979. "Repertoires of Contention in America and Britain, 1750–1830." In M. Zald and J. McCarthy (eds.), The Dynamics of Social Movements. Cambridge, Mass.: Winthrop.

Tittle, Charles R., Villemez, Wayne, and Smith, Douglas. 1978. "The Myth of Social Class and Criminality: An Empirical Assessment of the Empirical Evidence." American Sociological Review 43 (October): 643–56.

Tomeh, Aida K. 1973. "Formal Voluntary Organizations: Participation, Correlates, and Interrelationships." Sociological Inquiry 43 (3–4): 89–122.

Torres-Gil, Fernando. 1986. "Hispanics: A Special Challenge." In Alan Pifer and Lydia Bronte (eds.), Our Aging Society: Paradox and Promise. New York: Norton.

Traks, Huanani-Kay. 1993. From A Negative Daughter: Colonialism and Sovereignty in Hawaii. Monroe, ME: Common Courage Press.

Traub, James. 1993. "Back to Basics: P.C. vs. English." The New Republic 208 (6) (February 8): 18–20.

Traub, James. 1994. "Can Separate Be Equal?" Harper's Magazine (June): 35–47.

Treas, Judith. 1995. Older Americans in the 1990s and Beyond. Population Bulletin 50 (2) (May). Washington, DC: Population Reference Bureau, Inc.

Treaster, Joseph B. 1994. "Drug Study Puts Emphasis on Treatment." New York Times, June 19: Y-9.

Treverton, Gregory. 1990. "The Defense Debate." Foreign Affairs 69 (1): 183–96.

Troeltsch, Ernst. 1931. The Social Teaching of the Christian Churches. New York: Macmillan.

Troiden, Richard R. 1988. Gay and Lesbian Identity: A Sociological Analysis. New York: General Hall, Inc.

Troost, Kay Michael and Filsinger, Erik. 1993. "Emerging Biosocial Perspectives on the Family." pp. 677–710 in Boss, Pauline G., William J. Doherty, Ralph LaRossa, Walter R. Schumm, and Suzanne K. Steinmetz, eds. Sourcebook of Family Theories and Methods: A Contextual Approach. New York: Plenum Press.

"Trying to Take Back the Planet." 1990. Newsweek, February 5, pp. 24ff.

Tuchman, Barbara. 1978. A Distant Mirror: The Calamitous Fourteenth Century. New York: Knopf.

Tucker, M. Belinda, and Taylor, Robert. 1989. "Demographic Correlates of Relationship Status Among Black Americans." Journal of Marriage and the Family 51:655–65.

Turner, Jonathan H. 1972. Patterns of Social Organization. New York: McGraw-Hill.

Turner, Jonathan H. 1982. The Structure of Sociological Theory. (3rd ed.) Homewood, Ill.: Dorsey Press.

Turner, Jonathan, and Musick, David. 1985. American Dilemmas. New York: Columbia University Press.

Turner, Ralph. 1962. "Role Taking: Process Versus Conformity." pp. 20–39 in A. Rose, ed. Human Behavior and Social Processes. London: Routledge and Kegan Paul.

Turner, Ralph H. 1964. "Collective Behavior." In R. E. L. Faris (ed.), Handbook of Modern Sociology. Skokie, Ill.: Rand-McNally.

Turner, Ralph H. 1985. "Unanswered Questions in the Convergence Between Structuralist and Interactionist Role Theories." In S. N. Eisenstadt and H. J. Helle (eds.), Microsociological Theory: Perspectives on Sociological Theory. Vol. 2. Newbury Park,

Turner, Ralph, and Killian, Lewis. 1972. Collective Behavior. (2nd ed.) Englewood Cliffs, N.J.: Prentice-Hall.

Turner, Ralph H. and Killian, Lewis M. 1987. Collective Behavior, 3rd ed. Englewood Cliffs, N.J.: Prentice-Hall.

"22 Percent of Mexico Moving North?" 1989. Population Today 17 (November): 4.

Udry, J. Richard. 1988. "Biological Predispositions and Social Control in Adolescent Sexual Behavior." American Sociological Review 53:709–22.

Udry, J. Richard. 1994. "The Nature of Gender." Demography 31 (4) (November): 561–573.

Uhlenberg, Peter. 1980. "Death and the Family." Journal of Family History 5:313–20.

Ulbrich, Patricia, Warheit, George, and Zimmerman, Rick. 1989. "Race, Socioeconomic Status, and Psychological Distress: An Examination of Differential Vulnerability." Journal of Health and Social Behavior 30:131–46.

Unger, Donald G., and Wandersman, Lois P. 1985. "Social Support and Adolescent Mothers: Action Research Contributions to Theory and Applications." Journal of Social Issues. 41 (1): 29–46.

United Nations. 1984. "Mortality and Health Policy." Population Studies, no. 91. New York: United Nations.

United Nations. 1988. 1986 Demographic Yearbook. New York: United Nations.

United Nations. 1989. 1987 Demographic Yearbook. New York: United Nations.

United Nations. 1994. "World Contraceptive Use 1994." New York, NY: United Nations Department for Economic and Social Information and Policy Analysis, Population Division.

United Nations. 1994b. "Urban Agglomerations 1994." New York, NY: United Nations Department for Economic and Social Information and Policy Analysis, Population Division.

United Nations Population Fund. 1991. Population and the Environment: The Challenges Ahead. New York: United Nations Population Fund.

U.S. Bureau of the Census. 1992a. "Money Income of Households, Families, and Persons in the United States: 1991." Current Population Reports, Series P-60, No. 180. Washington D.C.: U.S. Government Printing Office.

U.S. Bureau of the Census, 1992b. "Population Projections of the United States by Age, Sex, Race, and Hispanic Origin." Current Population Reports, Series P-25, No. 1092. Washington D.C.: U.S. Government Printing Office.

U.S. Bureau of the Census. 1993a. Statistical Abstract of the United States: 1993. Washington, D.C.: U.S. Government Printing Office.

U.S. Bureau of the Census. 1993b. "Money Income of Households, Families and Persons in the United States: 1992." Current Population Reports, Series P-60, No. 184. Washington D.C.: U.S. Government Printing Office.

U.S. Bureau of the Census. 1993c. "Poverty in the United States: 1992." Current Population Reports, Series P-60, No. 185. Washington D.C.: U.S. Government Printing Office.

U.S. Bureau of the Census. 1993d. "The Hispanic Population in the U.S.: March 1992." Current Population Reports, Series P-20, No. 465RV. Washington D.C.: U.S. Government Printing Office.

U.S. Bureau of the Census. 1986. "Fertility of American Women: June 1985." Current Population Reports, Series P-20, no. 406. Washington, D.C.: U.S. Government Printing Office.

U.S. Bureau of the Census. 1988. "Projections of the Population of the United States by Age, Sex, and Race: 1988 to 2080." Current Population Reports, Series P-25, no. 1018. Washington, D.C.: U.S. Government Printing Office.

U.S. Bureau of the Census. 1989a. Statistical Abstract of the United States: 1989. Washington, D.C.: U.S. Government Printing Office.

U.S. Bureau of the Census. 1989b. "The Black Population of the United States: March 1988." Current Population Reports, Series P-20, no. 442. Washington, D.C.: U.S. Government Printing Office.

U.S. Bureau of the Census. 1989c. "The Hispanic Population of the United States: March 1988." Current Population Reports, Series P-60, no. 166. Washington, D.C.: U.S. Government Printing Office.

U.S. Bureau of the Census. 1989d. "Household and Family Characteristics: March 1988." Current Population Reports, Series P-20, no. 437. Washington, D.C.: U.S. Government Printing Office.

U.S. Bureau of the Census. 1989e. "Marital Status and Living Arrangements: March 1988." Current Population Reports, Series P-20, no. 433. Washington, D.C.: U.S. Government Printing Office.

U.S. Bureau of the Census. 1989f. "Money Income of Households, Families, and Persons in the United States: 1987." Current Population Reports, Series P-60, no. 162. Washington, D.C.: U.S. Government Printing Office.

U.S. Bureau of the Census. 1989g. "Money Income and Poverty Status in the United States: 1988." Current Population Reports, Series P-60, no. 166. Washington, D.C.: U.S. Government Printing Office.

U.S. Bureau of the Census. 1989h. "Patterns of Metropolitan Area and County Population Growth: 1980 to 1987." Current Population Reports, Series P-25, no. 1039. Washington, D.C.: U.S. Government Printing Office.

U.S. Bureau of the Census. 1989i. "Population Profile of the United States: 1989." Current Population Reports, Series P-23, no. 159. Washington, D.C.: U.S. Government Printing Office.

U.S. Bureau of the Census. 1989j. "Fertility of American Women: June 1988." Current Population Reports, Series P-20, no. 436. Washington, D.C.: U.S. Government Printing Office.

U.S. Bureau of the Census. 1989k. "Voting and Registration in the Election of November 1988 (Advance Report)." Current Population Reports, Series P-20, no. 435. Washington, D.C.: U.S. Government Printing Office.

U.S. Bureau of the Census. 1993. Statistical Abstract of the United States: 1993. Washington, D.C.: U.S. Government Printing Office.

U.S. Bureau of the Census. 1994. Statistical Abstract of the United States: 1994. Washington, D.C.: U.S. Government Printing Office.

U.S. Bureau of the Census. 1994b. "How We're Changing: Demographic State of the Nation 1995." Current Population Reports, Special Studies Series P-23, No. 188.

U.S. Bureau of the Census. 1994c. "Statistical Brief: The World at a Glance 1994." SB/94-4. Washington, D.C.: U.S. Government Printing Office.

U.S. Bureau of the Census. 1995. Statistical Abstract of the United States. Washington, D.C.: Government Printing Office.

U.S. Bureau of Labor Statistics. 1994. Employment in Perspective: Women in the Labor Force. Report 872. Washington, DC: U.S. Department of Labor.

U.S. Bureau of Labor Statistics. 1995. The Employment Situation: December 1994. Washington, DC: U.S. Department of Labor.

U.S. Centers for Disease Control. 1988. Morbidity and Mortality Weekly Report 37 (May 13).

U.S. Congress. 1995. The Technological Reshaping of Metropolitan America. U.S. Congress, Office of Technology Assessment. Washington, D.C.: U.S. Government Printing Office.

U.S. Department of Commerce. 1994. "Housing of American Indians on Reservations—An Overview." Washington, DC: U.S. Bureau of the Census document SB/94-32. Issued December.

U.S. Department of Education. 1985. The Condition of Education, 1985. Washington, D.C.: Government Printing Office.

U.S. Department of Education. 1989. "Projections of Education Statistics to 2000." Washington, D.C.: U.S. Government Printing Office.

U.S. Department of Health and Human Services. 1988. Vital Statistics of the United States 1986, Volume II—Mortality, Part A. Public Health Service, Washington, D.C.: U.S. Government Printing Office.

U.S. Department of Health and Human Services. 1995. "Excess Deaths and Other Mortality Measures for the Black Population." National Centers for Disease Control and Prevention.

U.S. Department of Housing and Urban Development. 1977. Redlining and Disinvestment as Discriminatory Practices in Residential Mortgage Loans. Washington, D.C.: U.S. Government Printing Office.

U.S. Department of Justice. 1993a. Uniform Crime Reports, 1992. Bureau of Justice Statistics. Washington D.C.: U.S. Government Printing Office.

U.S. Department of Justice. 1993b. Sourcebook of Criminal Justice Statistics, 1992. Washington D.C.: U.S. Government Printing Office.

U.S. Department of Justice. 1989a. Uniform Crime Reports, 1988. Bureau of Justice Statistics. Washington, D.C.: U.S. Government Printing Office.

U.S. Department of Justice. 1989b. "Prisoners in 1988." Bureau of Justice Statistics Bulletin. Washington, D.C.: Bureau of Justice Statistics.

U.S. Department of Justice. 1989c. Sourcebook of Criminal Justice Statistics: 1988. Bureau of Justice Statistics. Washington, D.C.: U.S. Government Printing Office.

U.S. Department of Justice. 1994. "Violence Between Intimates." Bureau of Justice Statistics: Selected Findings. Publication # NCJ-149259. November. U.S. Department of Justice, Publisher.

U.S. Department of Labor. 1993. Employment and Earnings: October 1993. Washington D.C.: U.S. Government Printing Office.

U.S. Department of Labor. 1985. The Impact of Technology on Labor in Four Industries. Bulletin 2263. Washington, D.C.: U.S. Government Printing Office.

U.S. Department of Labor. 1986a. Employment Projections for 1995: Data and Methods. Bureau of Labor Statistics Bulletin 2253. Washington, D.C.: U.S. Government Printing Office.

U.S. Department of Labor. 1986b. The Impact of Technology on Labor in Four Industries. Bulletin 2263. Washington, D.C.: U.S. Government Printing Office.

U.S. Department of Labor. 1990. Employment and Earnings: March 1990. Washington, D.C.: U.S. Government Printing Office.

"U.S. Had More Than 7000 Hate Crimes in '93, F.B.I. Head Says." 1994. The New York Times, June 29: A9.

U.S. Immigration and Naturalization Service. 1994. 1993 Statistical Yearbook of the Immigration and Naturalization Service. Washington, D.C.: U.S. Government Printing Office.

"U.S. Metro Areas on the March Again." 1986. Population Today 14 (January): 12.

U.S. National Center for Health Statistics. 1987. "Health Care Coverage by Sociodemographic and Health Characteristics, U.S.: 1984." Series 10, no. 162. Washington D.C.: U.S. Government Printing Office.

U.S. National Center for Health Statistics. 1988. "Current Estimates from the National Health Interview Survey, United States: 1987." Series 10, no. 166. Washington, D.C.: U.S. Government Printing Office.

"U.S. to Face Population Decline?" 1989. Population Today 17 (March): 3.

University of Pennsylvania Rescinds Its Politically Correct Speech Code." 1993. Time (November 29): 67.

Unks, Gerald. 1992. "Three Nations' Curricula: What Can We Learn from Them?" NASSP Bulletin 76 (548) (December): 30–47.

Unnever, James D., Frazier, Charles E., and Henretta, John C. 1980. "Race Differences in Criminal Sentencing." Sociological Quarterly 21 (Spring): 197–205.

Useem, Bert. 1980. "Solidarity Model, Breakdown Model, and the Boston Anti-Busing Movement." American Sociological Review 45 (June): 357–69.

Vago, Steven. 1989. Law and Society. (2nd ed.) Englewood Cliffs, N.J.: Prentice-Hall.

Valdivieso, Rafael, and Davis, Cary. 1988. "U.S. Hispanics: Challenging Issues for the 1990s." Population Reference Bureau, Population Trends and Public Policy no. 17, December, pp. 1–16.

Vallas, Steven P., and Yarrow, Michael. 1987. "Advanced Technology and Worker Alienation." Working and Occupations 14 (February): 126–42.

Van Biema, David, and David B. Jackson. 1993. "When White Makes Right." Time, August 9: 40–43.

"Vandals Don't Deter Blacks in Move to a White L.I. Area." 1991. New York Times, October 2.

van de Walle, Etienne, and Knodel, John. 1980. "Europe's Fertility Transition." Population Bulletin 34 (6): 1–43.

van den Berghe, Pierre L. 1978. Man in Society. New York: Elsevier North-Holland.

van der Tak, Jean, Haub, Carl, and Murphy, Elaine. 1979. "Our Population Predicament: A New Look." Population Bulletin 34 (5): 1–49.

Vanfossen, Beth, Jones, James, and Spade, Joan. 1987. "Curriculum Tracking and Status Maintenance." Sociology of Education 60:104–22.

Varner, Gary E. 1994. "The Prospects for Consensus and Convergence in the Animal Rights Debate." Hastings Center Report 24 (1): 24–28.

Vaughn, Brian, Gove, Frederick, and Egeland, Byron. 1980. "The Relationship Between Out-of-Home Care and the Quality of Infant-Mother Attachment in an Economically Disadvantaged Population." Child Development 51:1203–14.

Veblen, Thorstein. 1919. The Vested Interests and the State of the Industrial Arts. New York: Huebsch.

Vedlitz, Arnold, and Johnson, Charles A. 1982. "Community Racial Segregation, Electoral Structure, and Minority Representation." Social Science Quarterly 63 (December): 729–36.

Vega, W. A., and Amero, H. 1994. "Latino Outlook: Good Health, Uncertain Prognosis." American Review of Public Health, v. 15.

Ventura, Stephanie J., Martin, Joyce A., Taffel, Selma M., Mathews, T. J., and Clarke, Sally Cl. 1995. Advance Report of Final Natality Statistics, 1993. National Center for Health Statistics, Monthly Vital Statistics Report 44 (3). U.S. Department of Health and Human Services. September 21.

Verbrugge, Lois. 1989a. "Recent, Present, and Future Health of American Adults." Annual Review of Public Health 10:333–61.

Verbrugge, Lois. 1989b. "The Twain Meet: Empirical Explanations of Sex Differences in Health and Mortality. Journal of Health and Social Behavior 30:282–304.

Villemez, Wayne, and Bridges, William. 1988. "When Bigger Is Better: Differences in the Individual-Level Effect of Firm and Establishment Size." American Sociological Review 53:237–55.

Vogel, Ronald, and Swanson, Bert. 1989. "The Growth Machine Versus the Antigrowth Coalition: The Battle for Our Communities." Urban Affairs Quarterly 25:63–85.

Volti, Rudi. 1992. Society & Technological Change, 2nd edition. New York: St. Martin's Press.

"Voting Registration in the Election of November '92." 1993. Current Population Reports. Series P-20, no. 466. Washington, DC: U.S. Government Printing Office.

Wagner, David G., Ford, Rebecca S., and Ford, Thomas W. 1986. "Can Gender Inequalities Be Reduced." American Sociological Review 51 (February): 47–61.

Waitzkin, Howard. 1983. The Second Sickness. New York: Free Press.

Waitzkin, Howard. 1989. "A Critical Theory of Medical Discourse: Ideology, Social Control, and the Processing of Social Context in Medical Encounters." Journal of Health and Social Behavior 30:220–39.

Wald, Kenneth D. 1987. Religion and Politics in the United States. New York: St. Martin's Press.

Walder, Andrew. 1989. "Social Change in Post-Revolution China." Annual Review of Sociology 15:405–24.

Waldholz, Michael. 1991. "Uninsured Infants Taken to Hospital Get Fewer Services." Wall Street Journal. December 18: B3.

Waldinger, Roger. 1989. "Immigration and Urban Change." Annual Review of Sociology 15:211–32.

Waldman, Steven. 1994. "Winners and Losers." Newsweek. July 25: 19–22.

Waldman, Steven. 1992. "Benefits 'R' Us." Newsweek, August 10, pp. 56–58.

Waldron, Ingrid. 1983. "Sex Differences in Human Mortality: The Role of Genetic Factors." Social Science and Medicine 17 (6): 321–33.

Wallace, Walter. 1969. Sociological Theory. Hawthorne, N.Y.: Aldine.

Wallerstein, J., and Kelly, J. 1980. Surviving the Breakup. New York: Basic.

Walljasper, Jay. 1994. "Something Urban in Denmark: The Revitalization of Copenhagen and Aalborg Offer Hope for American Cities." Utne Reader 65 (September/October): 158–159.

Walsh, James. 1995. "Spirit of sisterhood." Time. September 18: 79.

Walshok, Mary Lindenstein. 1993. "Blue Collar Women." pp. 256–264 in Albert H. Teich, ed. Technology and the Future, 6th edition. New York: St. Martin's Press.

Walster, Elaine, Arenson, V., Abrahams, D., and Rottman, L. 1966. "Importance of Physical Attractiveness in Dating Behavior." Journal of Personality and Social Psychology 4 (November): 508–16.

Walte, Juan J. and Hasson, Judi. 1995. "Republicans: Many Voices on Foreign Policy." USA Today. January 12: 4A.

Warr, Mark. 1985. "Fear of Rape Among Urban Women." Social Problems 32 (February): 238–50.

Watson, Russell. 1995. "When Words Are the Best Weapon." Newsweek, February 27: 35–40.

Watson, Traci. 1994. "Hyping Gene Therapy." U.S. News & World Report. November 14: 122.

Weber, Max. 1954. Law in Economy and Society. (Max Rheinstein, ed.; Edward Shils and Max Reinstein, trans.) Cambridge, Mass.: Harvard University Press.

Weber, Max. 1958. The Protestant Ethic and the Spirit of Capitalism. (Talcott Parsons, trans.) New York: Scribner's. (Originally published 1904–5.)

Weber, Max. 1970a. "Bureaucracy." In H. H. Gerth and C. Wright Mills (trans.), From Max Weber: Essays in Sociology. New York: Oxford University Press. (Originally published 1910.)

Weber, Max. 1970b. "Class, Status, and Party." In H. H. Gerth and

Weber, Max. 1970c. "Religion." In H. H. Gerth and C. Wright Mills (trans.), From Max Weber: Essays in Sociology. New York: Oxford University Press. (Originally published 1922.)

Weber, Max. 1970e. "The Sociology of Charismatic Authority." In

Wechsler, David. 1958. The Measurement and Appraisal of Adult Intelligence. (4th ed.) Baltimore, Md.: Williams & Wilkins.

Wehrfritz, George. 1995. "Nightmare Cities." Newsweek. December 26: 106–108.

Weibel-Orlando, Joan. 1986–1987. "Drinking Patterns of Urban and Rural American Indians." Alcohol Health and Research World 11 (2): 8–12,54.

Weil, Frederick. 1985. "The Variable Effects of Education on Liberal Attitudes." American Sociological Review 50:458–74.

Weil, Frederick. 1989. "The Sources and Structure of Legitimation in Western Democracies." American Sociological Review 54:682–706.

Weinberg, Alvin M. 1993. "Can Technology Replace Social Engineering?" pp. 30–39 in Albert H. Teich, ed. Technology and the Future, 6th edition. New York: St. Martin's Press.

Weiss, Steganie. 1992. "Kids at Work." NEA Today 10, 9 (May): 3.

Weitz, Rose. 1989. "Uncertainty and the Lives of Persons with AIDS." Journal of Health and Social Behavior 30:270–81.

Weitzman, Lenore. 1985. The Divorce Revolution: The Unexpected Social and Economic Consequences for Women and Children in America. New York: Free Press.

"Weitzman's Research Plays Key Role in New Legislation." 1985. Footnotes 13 (8): 1, 9.

Welch, Charles, E., III, and Glick, Paul C. 1981. "The Incidence of Polygamy in Contemporary Africa: A Research Note." Journal of Marriage and the Family 43 (February): 191–4.

Welch, Susan, Gruhl, John, Steinman. Michael, and Comer, John. 1990. American Government. (3rd ed.) St. Paul, Minn.: West.

Wellman, Barry, and Berkowitz, S. D. (eds.). 1988. Social Structures: A Network Approach. New York: Cambridge University Press.

Wellman, Barry. 1979. "The Community Question: The Intimate Networks of East Yorkers." American Journal of Sociology 84 (March): 1201–31.

Wessells, Michael G. 1990. Computer, Self, and Society. Englewood Cliffs, NJ: Prentice Hall.

West, Candace. 1984. Routine Complications: Troubles with Talk Between Doctors and Patients. Bloomington: Indiana University Press.

Westoff, Charles. 1987. "Perspective on Nuptiality and Fertility." In Kingsley Davis, Mikhail Bernstam, and Rita Ricardo-Campbell (eds.), Below Replacement Fertility in Industrial Societies: Causes, Consequences, Policies. Cambridge, England: Cambridge University Press.

"What the States Are Doing." 1995. The Washington Post. July 30: A4.

Wheeler, Stanton and Rothman, Mitchell Lewis. 1982. "The Organization as Weapon in White Collar Crime," Michigan Law Review 80 (7) (June): 1403–1439.

Wheelock, Jaime. 1986. "A Strategy for Development: The Agroindustrial Axis." In Peter Rosset and John Vandermeer (eds.), Nicaragua: Unfinished Revolution. New York: Grove Press.

"When Taxes Pay for Art." 1989. Newsweek, July 3, p. 68.

Whitaker, Mark. 1995. "Whites v. Blacks." Newsweek. October 16: 28–35.

Whitaker, Mark. 1995a. "And Now What?" Newsweek. October 30: 29–44.

Whitburn, Julie. 1994. "Race for a Place on the Escalator." New York Times Educational Supplement (February 25): A20.

White, Lynn K., and Booth, Alan. 1985. "The Quality and Stability of Remarriage: The Role of Stepchildren." American Sociological Review 50 (October): 689–98.

White, Lynn, and Edwards, John. 1990. "Emptying the Nest and Parental Well-Being." American Sociological Review 55:235–42.

White, Lynn. 1990. "Determinants of Divorce: A Review of Research in the Eighties." Journal of Marriage and the Family 52 (November).

Whitman, David and Friedman, Dorian. 1994. "The White Underclass." U.S. News & World Report, October 17: 40–53.

Whitt, J. Allen. 1979. "Toward a Class-Dialectical Model of Power." American Sociological Review 44 (February): 81–99.

Whitworth, John M. 1975. God's Blueprints: A Sociological Study of Three Utopian Sects. Boston: Routledge & Kegan Paul.

Whorf, Benjamin L. 1956. Language, Thought, and Reality. Cambridge, Mass.: MIT Press.

Wiesenfeld, A. R., and Weiss, H. M. 1979. "Hairdressers and Helping: Influencing the Behavior of Informal Caregivers." Professional Psychology 7:786–92.

Wilentz, Amy. 1993. "Love and Haiti." The New Republic 209:18–19.

Wilkie, Jane Riblett. 1988. "Marriage, Family Life, and Women's Employment." pp. 149–166 in Women Working, 2nd ed., edited by Ann Helton Stromberg and Shirley Harkess. Mountain View, CA: Mayfield Press.

Wilkins, Beth M., and Ritter, Beth R.. 1994. "Will the House Win: Does Sovereignty Rule in Indian Casinos?" Great Plains Research 4 (August): 305–324.

Williams, Kirk, and Drake, Susan. 1980. "Social Structure, Crime, and Criminalization: An Empirical Examination of the Conflict Perspective." Sociological Quarterly 21 (Autumn): 563–75.

Williams, David R., and Chiquita Collins. 1995. "U.S. Socioeconomic and Racial Differences in Health: Patterns and Explanations." pp. 349–369 in John Hagan and Karen S. Cook, eds. American Review of Sociology, v. 21.

Williams, Kirk, and Flewelling, Robert. 1988. "The Social Production of Criminal Homicide: A Comparative Study of Disaggregated Rates in American Cities." American Sociological Review 53:421–31.

Williams, Robin M., Jr. 1970. American Society: A Sociological Interpretation. (3rd ed.) New York: Knopf.

William, Robin M., Jr. 1994. "The Sociology of Ethnic Conflicts." pp. 49–124 in John Hagan and Karen S. Cook, eds. Annual Review of Sociology, v 20.

Wilson, Edward O. 1978. "Introduction: What Is Sociobiology?" In Michael S. Gregory, Anita Silvers, and Diane Sutch (eds.), Sociobiology and Human Nature. San Francisco: Jossey-Bass.

Wilson, James D. 1995. "What Works." Newsweek. May 29: 18–24.

Wilson, James Q. 1992. "Crime, Race, and Values." Society 30 (1) (November): 90–93.

Wilson, Thomas C. 1986. "Interregional Migration and Racial Attitudes." Social Forces 65 (September): 177–86.

Wilson, William J. 1978. The Declining Significance of Race. Chicago: University of Chicago Press.

Wilson, William J. 1987. The Truly Disadvantaged. Chicago: University of Chicago Press.

Wilson, William J. (ed.). 1988. The Ghetto Underclass. Annals 501.

Wimberly, Dale. 1990. "Investment Dependence and Alternative Explanations of Third World Mortality: A Cross-National Study." American Sociological Review 55:75–91.

Wines, Michael. 1994. "Taxpayers Are Angry. They're Expensive Too." The New York Times, November 20: E5.

Wingert, Pat and Kantrowitz, Barbara. 1990. "The Day Care Generation." Newsweek Special Issue (Winter/Spring): 86–92.

Winkelstein, Warren, and Associates. 1988. "The San Francisco Men's Health Study: Continued Decline in HIV Sero- conversion Rates Among Homosexual/Bisexual Men." American Journal of Public Health 78:1472–4.

Winslow, Ron. 1992. "Infant Health Problems Cost Business Billions." Wall Street Journal. May 1: B1, B5.

Wirth, Louis. 1938. "Urbanism as a Way of Life." American Journal of Sociology 44 (1): 1–24.

Wittberg, Patricia. 1994. The Rise and Decline of Catholic Religious Orders: A Social Movement Perspective. Albany: State University of New York Press.

Wojthiewicz, Roger, McLanahan, Sara, and Garfinkel, Irwin. 1990. "The Growth of Families Headed by Women: 1950–1980."

Demography 27:19–30.

Wolfgang, Marvin E., and Reidel, Marc. 1973. "Race, Judicial Discretion, and the Death Penalty." Annals of the American Academy of Political and Social Science 407:119–133.

"Woman Loses Custody of Kids Because of Punishment, Cultism." 1990. Lincoln Star, February 1, pp. 1ff.

Wood, Robert C. 1989. "Rethinking the Suburbs." pp. 223–228 in Barbara M. Kelly, ed. Suburbia Re-examined. New York: Greenwood Press.

Woodrum, Eric, and Bell, Arnold. 1989. "Race, Politics, and Civil Religion Among Blacks." Sociological Analysis 49:353–67. Lerner, Robert, Rothman, Stanely, and Lichter, S. Robert. 1989.

Woods, Kathryn and Clouse, Meghan. 1994. Facts about Female Genital Mutilation. Santa Cruz, CA: Body Image Task Force.

Woodward, Kenneth L. 1995. "The Giggles Are for God." Newsweek. February 20: 54.

Woodward, Kenneth L., and Johnson, Patrice. 1995. "The Advent of Kwanzaa." Newsweek. December 11: 88.

"World Bank's Conable Voices Concern over Population Growth Effects." 1988. Population Today 16 (11): 4.

Wright, Erik O. 1985. Classes. London: Verso.

Wright, Gavin. 1978. The Political Economy of the Cotton South. New York: Norton.

Wright, James. 1988a. "The Mentally Ill Homeless: What Is Myth and What Is Fact?" Social Problems 35:182–91.

Wright, James D. 1988b. "Second Thoughts About Gun Control." Public Interest 91 (Spring): 23–39.

Wright, James, and Lam, Julie. 1987. "Homelessness and the Low-Income Housing Supply." Social Policy 17:48–53.

Wright, Robert. 1994. The Moral Animal: Evolutionary Psychology and Everyday Life. New York: Pantheon Books.

Wright, Robert. 1995. "HyperDemocracy." Newsweek. January 26: 15–25.

Wright, Robin. 1995a. "For Women Around the World, Survival Is Problem No. 1." Los Angeles Times, September 3: M2.

Wright, Robin. 1995b. "The Martin Luther of Islam." San Francisco Examiner, January 29: A-7.

Wrigley, E. A. 1969. Population in History. New York: McGraw-Hill.

Wrong, Dennis. 1961. "The Oversocialized Conception of Man in Modern Sociology." American Sociological Review 26 (April): 183–93.

Wrong, Dennis. 1979. Power. New York: Harper & Row.

Wu, Lawrence L. 1996. "Effects of Family Instability Income, and Income Instability on the Risk of a Premarital Birth." American Sociological Review 61 (June): 386–406.

Wulf, Steve. 1995. "Generation Excluded." Newsweek. October 23: 86.

Wuthnow, Robert, and Witten, Marsha. 1988. "New Directions in the Sociology of Culture." Annual Review of Sociology 8:49–67.

Wuthnow, Robert. 1988. "Government Activity and Civil Privatism." Journal for the Scientific Study of Religion 27: 157–74.

Wylie, Ruth. 1979. The Self-Concept: Theory and Research on Selected Topics. Vol. 2. (Rev. ed.) Lincoln: University of Nebraska Press.

Yamane, David. 1994. "Professional Socialization for What?" Footnotes 22 (3) (March): 7.

Yanagashita, Machiko. 1993. "Slow Growth Will turn to Decline of the Japanese Population." Population Today 21 (5) (May): 4–5.

Yankauer, Alfred. 1988. "AIDS and Public Health." American Journal of Public Health 78:364–5.

Yared, Roberta. 1989. "U.S. Black Life Expectancy Falls for Second Straight Year." Population Today 17 (1): 3–4.

Yinger, J. Milton. 1957. Religion, Society, and the Individual. New York: Macmillan.

Yinger, J. Milton. 1985. "Ethnicity." Annual Review of Sociology 11:151–80.

"York Woman Appeals Custody Ruling." 1990. Lincoln Star, February 1, p. 1, 4.

Young, Morley. 1993. "The Dark Underside of Japanese Education." Phi Delta Kappan 75 (2) (October): 130–133.

Young, Kimball. 1954. Isn't One Wife Enough? New York: Holt, Rinhart & Winston.

Yount, Kristin R. 1991. "Ladies, Flirts, and Tomboys: Strategies for Managing Sexual Harassment in an Underground Coal Mine." Journal of Contemporary Ethnography 19:396–422.

Yu, Elaine. 1993. "NACSA Hold Conference on 'Gender Issues in Chinese Societies.'" Footnotes 21 (9) (December): 5.

Yuenger, James. 1994. "At Lagos Airport, Extortion Becomes Business As Usual." The Chicago Tribune. September 6.

Zillman, D., and Bryant, J. 1982. "Pornography, Sexual Callousness and the Trivialization of Rape." Journal of Communication 32 (4): 10–21.

Zillman, Dolf. (ed.). 1994. Media, Children and the Family: Social Scientific, Psychodynamic, and Clinical Perspectives. Hillsdale, N.J.: L. Erlbaum Associates.

Zipp, John F., Landerman, Richard, and Luebke, Paul. 1982. "Political Parties and Political Participation: A Reexamination of the Standard Socioeconomic Model." Social Forces 60 (June): 1140–53.

Zuo, JiPing, and Benford, Robert. 1995. "Mobilization Processes and the 1989 Chinese Democracy Movement." The Sociological Quarterly 36:

Zurcher, Louis. 1983. Social Roles: Conformity, Conflict, and Creativity. Newbury Park, Calif.: Sage.

Zygmunt, Joseph E. 1986. "Collective Behavior as a Phase of Societal Life: Blumer's Emergent Views and Their Implications." Research in Social Movements, Conflicts, and Change 9:25–46.

Name Index

Subject Index

Photo Credits

Applications Logo Images: Chuck Savage, Alan Schein, David Woods, Harvey Lloyd, William Taufic, Charles Gupton, Pete Saloutos, Ariel Skelley, Randy Ury, Tom & DeeAnn McCarthy, Pete Saloutos, ©95 Mugshots, ©93 Mugshots, Don Mason, B. O'Shaughnessy, C/B Productions, ©96 Mugshots, Michael K. Daly, ©96 Mugshots, David Pollack, Bryan F. Peterson, Clark J. Mishler, Tom & DeeAnn McCarthy, Tom & DeeAnn McCarthy - The Stock Market; **2** James Lemass, Gamma Liaison; **4** Bruce Esbin, Omni Photo Communications; **6** Brown Brothers; **7** Brown Brothers; **8** The Bettmann Archive; **9** top Brown Brothers; **9** bottom Jeff Greenberg, Omni Photo Communications; **10** top The Bettmann Archive; **10** bottom The Granger Collection; **11** Bob Daemmrich, Stock-Boston; **16** Donald Dietz, Stock-Boston; **20** Jeff Greenberg, Omni Photo Communications; **28** Esbin/Anderson, Omni Photo Communications; **31** Douglas Burrows, Gamma Liaison; **33** Jeff Greenberg, Omni Photo Communications; **36** Tom Tracy, The Stock Market; **39** Ed Kashi; **41** Neal Graham, Omni Photo Communications; **45** Ed Kashi; **48** A/P Worldwide Photos; **58** Jonathan Elderfield, Gamma Liaison; **60** left Charles D. Winters, Stock-Boston; **60** right Martin Rogers, Stock-Boston; **64** Victor Englebert, Black Star; **66** left Joe Sohm/Chromosohm; **66** right Brad Markel, Gamma Liaison; **67** Ed Kashi; **71** ©Mugshots by Gabe Palmer; **75** left Bob Daemmrich, Stock-Boston; **75** right Fredrick D. Bodin, Stock-Boston; **78** Pete Souza, Liaison International; **86** Stan Shoneman, Omni Photo Communications; **90** Frank Siteman, Omni Photo Communications; **92** Gamma Liaison; **93** Rick Browne, Stock-Boston; **95** left Joel Sohm/Chromosohm, Stock-Boston; **95** right Martin Rogers, Stock-Boston; **96** Cynthia Johnson, Gamma Liaison; **99** Vince Stream, The Stock Market; **102** Frank Bigbear, Bockley Gallery; **108** Robert A. Isaacs, Photo Researchers; **111** Bill Binzen, The Stock Market; **113** From "Opinions and Social Pressure, Solomon E. Asch, 1955, *Scientific American*, 193, p. 33. Copyright 1955 by *Scientific American* and William Vandivert; **115** Jeff Greenberg, Omni Photo Communications; **118** David Burnett/Contact, The Stock Market; **122** David Brinkerhoff; **123** Comstock; **129** Ed Kashi; **130** Ed Kashi; **136** Terry Towery, Omni Photo Communications; **138** John Coletti, Stock-Boston; **139** Martin Rogers, Stock-Boston; **143** David Woods, The Stock Market; **145** Bob Daemmrich, Stock-Boston; **148** Ed Kashi; **149** Yvonne Hemsey, Liaison International; **150** Addison Geary, Stock-Boston; **153** Sygma; **162** ©Mugshots, The Stock Market; **167** Farrell Grehah, Photo Researchers; **170** Bill Gallery, Stock-Boston; **171** Evan Agoshni, Gamma Liaison; **172** Bob Daemmrich, Stock-Boston; **175** Bob Daemmrich, Stock-Boston; **178** Bob Daemmrich, Stock-Boston; **186** Eric Kroll, Omni Photo Communications; **188** Ed Kashi; **192** David Brinkerhoff; **205** Gamma Liaison; **207** Pierre Perin, Gamma Liaison Network; **208** Ed Kashi; **216** John Lei, Omni Photo Communications; **230** left Rhoda Sidney, Stock-Boston; **230** right Ann McQueen, Stock-Boston; **233** Frank Clarkson, Liaison International; **236** Tim Davis, Photo Researchers; **238** Stock-Boston; **243** Tim Carlson, Stock-Boston; **246** left Ed Kashi; **246** right Larry Mulvihill, Photo Researchers; **252** Bulcao/Liaison; **258** Larry Mulvihill, Photo Researchers; **259** Jim Balog, Black Star; **266** Philip John Bailey, Stock Boston;

269 left ©Sotographs, Liaison International; **269** right Cesar Paredes, The Stock Market; **272** Jean-Michel Turpin, Gamma Liaison; **277** ©Daher, Gamma Liaison; **282** J. L. Bulcao, Gamma Liaison; **288** Gamma Liaison; **289** top J. Pat Carter, Gamma Liaison; **289** bottom, Gamma Liaison; **290** Stock-Boston; **292** Historical Picture Service, Chicago; **296** Stock-Boston; **298** The Bettmann Archive; **299** ©Gifford/ Liaison, Gamma Liaison; **300** left Bill Grimes, Black Star; **300** right John Launois, Black Star; **301** J. P. Laffont, Sygma; **305** C. Niklas Hill, Gamma Liaison; **307** left Pete Souza, Liaison International; **307** right Gerard Kosicki, Gamma Liaison; **309** ©Jean Marc Bigoux, Gamma Liaison; **318** ©RB/Studio 95, The Stock Market; **324** Stock-Boston; **325** James Sugar, Black Star; **328** Charlie Westerman, Liaison International; **332** Tannenbaum, Sygma; **334** Robert A. Isaacs, Photo Researchers; **340** top Evan Agostini, Gamma Liaison; **340** bottom The Bettmann Archive; **346** Oscar Williams; **350** left Brown Brothers; **350** right David Young-Wolff, PhotoEdit; **351** Barrie Fanton, Omni Photo Communications; **352** Chuck Savage, The Stock Market; **357** Jon Levy, Gamma Liaison; **358** Richard Hutchings, Photo Researchers; **359** left Mark Gamba, The Stock Market; **359** right Chuck Savage, The Stock Market; **360** Stock-Boston; **361** Jeffrey Muir Hamilton, Stock-Boston; **363** John Lei, Stock Boston; **368** Richard Pasley, Stock-Boston; **372** Tony O'Brien, Stock-Boston; **378** Ariel Skelley, The Stock Market; **381** Stuart Cohen, Stock-Boston; **383** Jerry Irman; **387** Oneida Community collection, George Arents Research Library at Syracuse University; **388** Michael A. Keller, The Stock Market; **393** Ellis Herwig, Stock-Boston; **394** Ed Kashi; **406** Wil & Deni McIntyre; **414** Palmer/Kane, Inc., The Stock Market; **417** Robert Houser, Comstock; **420** Eric Kroll, Omni Photo Communications; **423** Jeffrey W. Myers, Stock-Boston; **430** left Ed Bock, The Stock Market; **430** right Zigy Kaluzny, Gamma Liaison; **434** Bob Daemmrich, Stock-Boston; **439** Jerry Cook, Photo Researchers; **446** ©92SOHM, The Stock Market; **449** John Coletti, Stock-Boston; **452** David Crosse; **453** Michael Fernandez, Gamma Liaison; **458** Dirck Halstead, Gamma Liaison; **464** Gary Gold, Gamma Liaison; **471** Rod Rolle, Gamma Liaison; **475** Michael Dwyer, Stock-Boston; **480** Lenore Weber, Omni Photo Communications; **482** Cary Wolinsky, Stock-Boston; **487** Joan Lebold Cohen, Photo Researchers; **491** Allen Green, Photo Researchers; **493** Blair Seitz, Photo Researchers; **495** Ed Kashi; **497** Shelley Katz, Black Star; **498** Charles Gupton, Stock Boston; **500** Jose Luis Pelaez, The Stock Market; **508** John Barr, Gamma Liaison; **511** top Heidi Brodner, Gamma Liaison; **511** bottom Michael Swarz, Gamma Liaison; **513** David Austen, Stock-Boston; **517** Rhoda Sidney, PhotoEdit; **519** Jerry Irwin; **520** Sipa; **525** John Pinderhughes, The Stock Market; **528** top Gamma Presse Images; **528** bottom Lester Sloan, Gamma Liaison; **531** Raphael Gaillarde, Gamma Liaison; **538** Dick Spahr, Gamma Liaison; **542** Bonnie Kamin, Comstock; **549** Wil and Deni McIntyre, Photo Researchers; **550** Detroit News/GP, Gamma Liaison; **554** J & M Studios, Liaison International; **555** Terry Ashe, Gamma Liaison; **558** David Nichols, Liaison International; **560** ©Forsyth, Omni Photo Communications; **563** Hank Morgan, Photo Researchers; **572** Jose Pelaez, The Stock Market; **574** left Don Fitcher, Stock-Boston; **574** right David R. Austen, Stock-Boston; **577** Peter Turnley, Black Star; **578** Sally Wiener Grotta, The Stock Market; **584** Stock-Boston; **585** Ed Kashi; **587** top Stock-Boston; **587** bottom Stock-Boston; **589** Andy Uzzle, Gamma Liaison; **596** Stephen Ferry, Gamma Liaison; **604** David Austen, Stock-Boston; **606** Owen Franken, Stock-Boston; **608** Owen Franken, Stock-Boston; **613** Forrest Anderson, Gamma Liaison; **614** Anthony Suau, Gamma Liaison; **615** Robin Moyer, Gamma Liaison; **616** Yoram Lehman, Peter Arnold, Inc.; **628** Alan Schein, The Stock Market; **630** Joseph Nettis, Stock-Boston; **632** Angelina Lax, Photo Researchers; **638** Nedra Westwater, Black Star; **639** Lawrence Migdale, Stock-Boston; **641** Greg Weiner, Liaison International; **642** J. L. Bulcao, Gamma Liaison; **644** left John Lei, Omni Photo Communications; **644** right David Sailors, The Stock Market; **650** Dagmar Fabricius, Stock-Boston; **658** Filipiacchi, Liaison; **662** A. Clopet, Sipa; **663** The Bettmann Archive; **665** Tony White, Sipa; **667** John T. Barr, Gamma Liaison; **668** W. Yurman, Gamma Liaison; **673** N. Utsumi, Gamma Liaison; **677** David Cross; **684** Renato Rotolo, Gamma Liaison